COMMENTARY

ON

THE EPISTLES OF PAUL THE APOSTLE

TO

THE CORINTHIANS

VOL. I

THE CALVIN TRANSLATION SOCIETY,

INSTITUTED IN MAY M.DCCC.XLIII.

JOHANNES CALVINUS. NATUS. X. JUL. MDIX. OBIIT. XXVII. MAI. MDLXIV. PROMPTE ET SINCERE IN OPERE DOMINI

FOR THE PUBLICATION OF TRANSLATIONS OF THE WORKS OF
JOHN CALVIN.

COMMENTARY

ON THE

EPISTLES OF PAUL THE APOSTLE

TO

THE CORINTHIANS

BY JOHN CALVIN

TRANSLATED FROM THE ORIGINAL LATIN, AND COLLATED WITH
THE AUTHOR'S FRENCH VERSION,

BY THE REV. JOHN PRINGLE

VOLUME FIRST

Baker Books

A Division of Baker Book House Co.
Grand Rapids, Michigan 49516

Calvin's Commentaries
22-Volume Set
ISBN: 0-8010-2440-4

Originally printed for the
Calvin Translation Society
Edinburgh, Scotland

Reprinted 2003 by Baker Books
a division of Baker Book House Company
P.O. Box 6287, Grand Rapids, MI 49516-6287

Printed in the United States of America

For information about academic books, resources for Christian
leaders, and all new releases available from Baker Book
House, visit our web site:
http://www.bakerbooks.com/

TRANSLATOR'S PREFACE.

THE SIXTEENTH CENTURY was distinguished by a large and valuable accession of Expositors of the Sacred Volume. Mosheim reckons up not fewer than fifty-five writers, who, in the course of that century, devoted their labours, to a greater or less extent, to the interpretation or illustration of the inspired writings—a circumstance which at once indicated the progress of the principles of the Reformation, and contributed most materially to their diffusion. Nor were expository treatises, in illustration of the Sacred Scriptures, simply increased in number; they were marked by a decided improvement in point of intrinsic value. It is to the honour of a large proportion of the Interpreters of that age, that, rejecting the practice so well exposed by BISHOP HORSLEY, of " drawing I know not what mystical meanings, by a certain cabalistic alchymy, from the simplest expressions of holy writ," they made it their endeavour, in every case, to ascertain the true meaning of the Spirit of God, by a careful examination of the text and context.

In unbending integrity of purpose in the investigation of the Inspired Oracles—which must be regarded as one of the primary excellences of an Expositor—JOHN CALVIN is surpassed by none in his own, or indeed in any age. His readers, even where they may not be prepared to adopt his interpretation of a passage, cannot fail to perceive that it is his sincere desire and honest endeavour to ascertain its true meaning. His uprightness of design is more especially observable in connection with passages bearing on controverted points. In such cases the candid reader will discover no disposition to wrest a single expression for the purpose of enlisting it on the side of a particular system of opinion ; but, on the contrary, the utmost fairness of interpretation is uniformly apparent.

Every one that is acquainted with CALVIN's history, and considers the trying scenes through which he was called to pass, must feel astonished that he should have found leisure to prepare, in addition to all his other writings, Commentaries on nearly the whole of the Sacred Scriptures. That he wrote so much, and more especially as an Expositor, appears to have been chiefly owing to the frequent and urgent solicitations of his intimate and beloved friend FAREL, who "not merely entreated CALVIN, but frequently urged him with great vehemence to write one Commentary after another, from a conviction that he possessed the gifts requisite for exposition in a very extraordinary manner, and that, with the blessing of God, his works of this kind would be extensively useful. 'Being an inconsiderable man myself,' said he, 'I am wont to require very much from those that possess the greatest excellence, and often press them hard to labour beyond their strength.' It was his conviction that every one who had received superior talents was bound to devote them to the advancement of the kingdom of God."[1]

THE EPISTLES OF PAUL TO THE CORINTHIANS form a most important part of the Sacred Writings. Though not so systematic as the Epistle to the ROMANS, they contain many passages, bearing directly on the fundamentally important doctrines of the Christian system, while they are of the highest utility in connection with Practical Theology. The disorders that had unhappily crept into the Church at Corinth, gave occasion for the Apostle's handling at greater length than in any of his other Epistles various important points as to doctrine and worship ; while the relaxed state of discipline that had begun to prevail among them rendered it necessary to exhibit more fully the principles which ought to regulate the administration of the Christian Church. In

[1] Kirch-hoffer's Life of Farel, pp. 281, 282.

this the overruling hand of Him who brings good out of evil is strikingly apparent.

While in the selection of the particular places into which the Gospel was first introduced, and in which Christian Churches were first planted, there is a display of Divine sovereignty which it is beyond our power to fathom, this at least is abundantly manifest, that the places selected were not those in which the triumphs of the Gospel were likely to be most easily effected, but quite the reverse. As the skill of the workman appears so much the more strikingly, when the tools employed by him are few and simple, and the materials to be wrought upon are hard and unyielding; so the wonders achieved in the first ages of the Church, through *the foolishness of preaching*, (1 Cor. i. 21,) excite so much the more our astonishment, when we take into view the peculiarly formidable obstacles that opposed its progress in the places that were selected as the scenes of its triumphs. Of this the inspired narrative furnished in the Acts of the Apostles presents numerous and striking illustrations; and when we observe the particular Churches to which Paul's Epistles are addressed—in the order in which they are presented to our view in the New Testament—it might almost seem as if the order of arrangement had been designed for the very purpose of calling our particular attention to the fact that the triumphs of the Gospel had been most signal in those places in which its success might have appeared most unlikely. It is a remarkable circumstance, and, assuredly, it is not to be looked upon as merely accidental, that the Christian Church to which the *first* of Paul's Epistles—in the order in which they stand—is addressed, is one that had been planted, not in some obscure village, or inconsiderable town, or even in some city of secondary importance, but in ROME itself, the metropolis of the then known world; while the *second* of the Churches to whom Paul's Epistles are addressed is that of CORINTH, a city that was proverbial among Heathens themselves for its extraordinary profligacy, and consequently the most unlikely place of all to be the scene of the triumphs of a religion that will allow of no compromise with iniquity.

When PAUL first visited CORINTH, appearances were most unpromising; but, having received special encouragement from his Divine Master, he continued to labour at Corinth for *a year and six months,* (Acts xviii. 11;) and such was the success of his labours in that profligate city, that after enumerating some of the worst descriptions of character, he says to the Corinthian converts,—"*And such were some of you,*" (1 Cor. vi. 11.) While, however, the notorious wickedness that prevailed at Corinth was the occasion of illustrating so much the more clearly the power of Christianity in subduing human depravity, that extreme dissoluteness of manners to which the Corinthian Christians had been addicted previously to their conversion, and which was daily witnessed by them in the unconverted around them, was fitted to exert a most injurious influence; and while the disorders that prevailed in the Corinthian Church after Paul left them, were in part attributable to the insidious efforts of false teachers, there seems every reason to believe that they were, in a very considerable degree, owing to the contagion of corrupt manners around them. It is to this that we must trace their preference of the ornaments of speech to the plain unadorned doctrine of the cross—their party jealousies—their vexatious law-suits—their unseemly fellowship with heathens in their idol-feasts; and their philosophical speculations, leading them to question the possibility of a resurrection from the dead: while the flagrant case of incest, fallen into by one of their number, and connived at by the others, must still more manifestly be ascribed, in part, to the contagion of evil example. Yet even in this we have occasion still farther to mark the overruling hand of God in making evil subservient to good— the disordered state of the Corinthian Church having given occasion for exhortations and reproofs that are fraught with invaluable instruction to the Church of Christ in every successive age.

CALVIN's Commentary on the FIRST EPISTLE to the Corinthians was *first published* in the year 1546, and his Commentary on the SECOND EPISTLE was published in the course of the same year. It was a year that was greatly "unfavourable to Calvin's repose. He was obliged to cheer the drooping spirits of the Genevese, whom the designs of CHARLES V. against THE REFORMED RELIGION had alarmed. But, besides the cares which the fear of all these evils occasioned him, he was deeply afflicted at the state of GENEVA, and the general and daring profligacy of its inhabitants."[1]

In the course of the same year (as is stated by BEZA) one of the members of the senate, "instigated, it is supposed, by two ministers of the Consistory, both of them given to drunkenness, and not less afraid than others of the rigour of the law, accused CALVIN of preaching false doctrine." It may well appear surprising that in such circumstances he should have found leisure for preparing this valuable portion of his Expository Works. This, however, is not peculiar to this portion of his Commentaries ; for the greater part of them were prepared amidst numerous engagements and harassing occurrences. Yet they do not bear the marks of haste, but might seem to have been prepared in quiet retirement.

The reader will observe that THE DEDICATION, which is prefixed to the Commentary on the First Epistle to the Corinthians in all the ordinary editions of CALVIN'S works, bears date in 1556. It is however stated, at the same time, by CALVIN in the close of the Dedication, that the Commentary to which it is prefixed had been originally published by him ten years previously. It will farther be observed that in the commencement of the Dedication, CALVIN alludes to an individual to whom he had originally dedicated the Commentary, but whose name he had been under the painful necessity—contrary to his usual manner —of erasing from his writings. The individual alluded to is JAMES OF BURGUNDY. The original Dedication, which is exceedingly rare, is contained in " Lettres de Calvin à Jaque de Bourgogne," kindly allowed to the Translator by Mr. Laing, Edinburgh, from the Library of Writers to the

---

[1] Mackenzie's Life of Calvin, p. 63.

Signet.   A translation of *that* Dedication, as well as of the
one that was subsequently prefixed by Calvin to this part
of his Commentaries, will be found below.

The circumstances connected with the case of James of
Burgundy, are briefly stated by BAYLE in his Dictionary,
(Art. *Philip of Burgundy*,) in the following terms:—"James
of Burgundy, Lord of Fallaix, grandson, I suppose, of Baldwin, another natural son of Duke Philip, professed the
Protestant religion, but being scandalized at the disputes
which arose at Geneva between BOLSEC and CALVIN in the
year 1551, he and his wife turned aside from the doctrine
of the Reformed.   He had carried it fair in the Church
several years.   CALVIN dedicated to him his Commentary on
the First Epistle of St. Paul to the Corinthians, but afterwards he suppressed that Dedication, and prefixed another
to THE MARQUIS OF VIC."

Farther, Bayle, in the Art. *Calvin*, remarks, when speaking of Beza's Life of CALVIN—"We do not find in the edition
of 1564, in 12mo, what I have transcribed from the folio
edition of 1565, when I said that the grandson of a bastard
of Philip, the good Duke of Burgundy, forsook the Church
of Rome."

The editor of "Lettres de Calvin," states that, after much
fruitless search in many quarters for two documents referred
to in CALVIN's Letters, viz. the Dedication of Calvin's Commentary on the First Epistle to the Corinthians, and an
Apology for the Master of Falais, presented to the Emperor
Charles the Fifth, and composed by CALVIN, he had at length
obtained them from one of the librarians of Geneva.   The
Dedication, he states, had been "transcribed from a copy
that is at present at Strasburg."   "These pieces," he adds,
"arrived just in time for being printed in the last sheet of
the Letters, to which I have not failed to append them, as
being absolutely necessary to render them intelligible.   I
flatter myself that the public will receive them with delight,
as an authentic document,[1] hitherto wanting in the ecclesiastical history of this country.   Even those who have neither

---

[1] "Un monument authentique;"—"An authentic monument."

interest nor inclination for knowing this history to the
bottom, will admire the beauty of CALVIN's genius, the insinuating turns of the Dedication, and the liberty and
modesty that reign equally in the Apology; and they will
agree with me in thinking, that CALVIN was no less expert
in the art of pleading, than he had been in the art of
preaching."

JAMES OF BURGUNDY was the grandson of Baldwin, a
natural son of Philip, Duke of Burgundy, whom the Emperor Maximilian, in 1501, put in possession of Falais, a
"Manor of Brabant, situated on the borders of the county
of Namur, upon the river Mohaine, between the towns of
Huy and Henneguy." He was "elevated to the court of
the Emperor Charles the Fifth. He embraced the views of
the Protestants at the age of fifteen. He afterwards married Jolande of Brederode, a descendant of the ancient
Counts of Holland, and aunt to Henry of Brederode." . . .
" This marriage increased the suspicions that he had conceived as to the religion in which he was brought up, so
that he adopted the resolution of leaving his native country,
where he reckoned his life no longer safe. His withdraw-
ment led to a law-suit, before the court of Malines, for the
confiscation of his lands. During his exile, the Master of
Falais changed his abode from time to time, having taken
refuge first at Cologne, afterwards at Strasburg, and at
Basle, and, last of all, at Geneva. There is ground to believe that he was a person of merit, upon the testimony
of CALVIN himself, who, after pronouncing upon him the
highest eulogiums in his Dedication to the First Epistle
to the Corinthians, carried on a familiar correspondence
with him for nearly ten years, and takes pleasure in sub-
scribing himself very frequently his friend unreservedly
for ever.[1]

" It is true that this friendship did not always continue,
but, on the contrary, changed into irreconcilable aversion.
It may at first view be thought, that the fault was altogether on the side of the Master of Falais, and that CALVIN

---

[1] " Entier amy à jamais ;"—" Thorough friend for ever."

must have had sufficient reasons for carrying matters so far. We must, however, beware of forming a rash judgment. We often see the greatest animosities between the best friends arise out of nothing. Frequently the two parties are equally in the wrong; and in many cases the fault is found to have been on the side of the one that had been least suspected." . . . The reader who peruses superficially the statement of Beza, quoted by Bayle, might imagine not merely that the Master of Falais had approved of all that Bolsec had done or said, but also that he entirely abandoned the side of the Protestants, and entered again the communion of the Romish Church. He might, therefore, fall into a mistake on all these points.

" I do not believe that the Master of Falais ever thought of approving of the conduct of Bolsec, who ventured in a full church to contradict a minister, when preaching the doctrine of predestination. Neither CALVIN nor Beza say so. Besides, the Master of Falais protests in his Apology, that he has no sympathy with those that support their religion in a turbulent and seditious manner. Assuredly he must have been a fanatic, to do what Bolsec did on that occasion; but to say that he had done well, he must have been a downright madman.

" Nor is there any better proof that the Master of Falais was of Bolsec's opinion on the subject of predestination. CALVIN, Beza, and Castalio himself, (who would not have failed to mention it,) say no such thing. Besides this, the Confession of the Master of Falais, such as he had published in his Apology, is quite in unison with CALVIN's sentiments; and it may be presumed that he had not renounced these views in three years afterwards, while experience tells us, that persons do not readily change the speculative opinions that they have once imbibed. What was then, properly, the ground of quarrel between CALVIN and the Master of Falais? In my opinion it was this: After Bolsec had been put in prison, on the 16th October 1551, for having contradicted the doctrine of CALVIN, and given occasion of offence in the Church, CALVIN was disposed to punish him with all possible severity. To accomplish his purpose in accordance with forms, he asked the opinion of the Churches of Switzerland, hinting to them at the same time what he desired from them."

" ' We are desirous,' says he, 'to clear our Church from this pestilence in such a way that it will not, on being expelled from it, do injury to the neighbouring Churches,' meaning, plainly enough, that he must either be put to death, or suffered to remain in prison during his whole life."

The Master of Falais was of another mind ; whether it was that he was influenced by a regard to his own interest, and that, being sickly, he imagined that his life depended on that of his physician ; or whether it was that, from a principle of humanity and Christian forbearance, he reckoned that Bolsec's imprudence did not merit so severe a punishment, he wrote to the clergy of the Cantons, or to his friends in that quarter, and thereby defeated the design of CALVIN, who received replies less full and distinct, and much more moderate, than he had expected and desired. CALVIN finding himself thwarted by the Master of Falais, got into a passion, broke entirely with him, and roused up against him so many enemies at Geneva, that he was obliged to retire into the district of Vaud.

" Judge, now, which of the two was in the right—CALVIN or the Master of Falais." . . . " I do not know what became of the Master of Falais after this time, nor *when* he died, nor *where*, nor *in what communion.* I cannot, however, subscribe to the views of Mr. Bayle, who says that the Master of Falais turned aside from the doctrine of the Reformed, and that he renounced the Reformed Church. I am of opinion that Beza, on whose authority Mr. Bayle proceeds, means nothing more than this, that the Master of Falais left the Church of Geneva on quarrelling with CALVIN. This does not mean that he renounced the Reformed Church, or abandoned the Protestant party. For it was possible to quarrel with Calvin, to reject his views on predestination and on persecution, and spurn the discipline of the Church of Geneva, and yet, after all, be as good a Protestant, and member of the Reformed Church, as CALVIN himself."

From the extracts furnished above from an introductory notice by the editor[1] of the work already referred to, ("Lettres de Calvin à Jaque de Bourgogne,") it will abundantly appear that the writer is desirous to present as favourable a view of James of Burgundy as the circumstances of the case will at all admit of. His attempt to shew that James of Burgundy may have, after all, remained in connection with the Reformed Church, appears to be more ingenious than solid, and seems directly at variance with a statement by CALVIN in his *second* Dedication to this part of his Commentaries, to this effect, that the individual to whom the former Dedication was addressed "has intentionally made it his object, not merely to withdraw as much as possible from me personally, but also *to have no connection with our Church.*"[2] This expression naturally conveys the idea that he had not simply left the Church of Geneva, but had withdrawn entirely from the Reformed Church. But however matters may have been as to this, the case, as a whole, was of such a nature as could not fail to be painful in the extreme to the mind of CALVIN. In proportion, however, to the pain excited in his mind by this distressing case, must have been the happiness afforded him by an occurrence of an opposite nature, which took place about the same time.

THE CHURCH OF GENEVA, which had suffered from the defection of James of Burgundy, was strengthened by the accession of an Italian nobleman, GALEAZUS CARACCIOLUS, who, having been led to espouse the Protestant faith, took up his residence at Geneva in the year 1551, with a view to enjoy the society of Calvin, and have opportunity of attending upon his ministry. The particulars of his history, and more especially of his conversion from Popery, are interestingly narrated in a work entitled—"THE ITALIAN CONVERT—NEWES FROM ITALY OF A SECOND MOSES—THE LIFE OF GALEACIUS CARACCIOLUS, THE NOBLE MARQUESSE OF VICO," &c. London, 1635.

[1] " Avertissement de l'Editeur."
[2] " Nihil haberet cum Ecclesià nostrà commune;"—" De n'avoir rien de commun avec nostre Eglise ;"—Might have nothing in common with our Church.

This work was written originally in Italian, "by Nicola Balbani, minister of the Italian Church in Geneva. It was translated into Latin by Beza; into French by Minutoli and by Sieur de Lestan; and into English by William Crashaw."[1]

The writer of the work referred to presents, in the dedicatory epistle, the following brief summary of the leading facts of this interesting case :—

"I present you with as strange a story as, out of the holy stories, was ever heard. Will your Honours have the whole in briefe, afore it bee laid down at large? Thus it is :— Galeacius Caracciolus, son and heir-apparent to Calantonius, Marquesse of Vicum in Naples, bred, borne and brought up in Popery—a courtier to the Emperor Charles the Fifth, nephew to the Pope, Paul the Fourth, being married to the Duke of Nucerne's daughter, and having by her six goodly children, at a sermon of Peter Martyr's was first touched,— after by reading Scripture, and other good means, was fully converted—laboured with his lady, but could not persuade her; therefore, that he might enjoy Christ and serve Him with a good conscience, he left the lands, livings, and honours of a Marquesdome, the comforts of his lady and children, the pleasures of Italy, his credit with the Emperor, his kindred with the Pope, and forsaking all for the love of Jesus Christ, came to Geneva, and there lived a poore and meane, yet an honourable and a holy life for fortie years; and though his father, his lady, his kinsmen, yea, the Emperor and Pope did all they could to reclaim him, yet continued he constant to the end, and lived and died the blessed servant of God, leaving behind him a rare example to all ages."[2]

Caracciolus was born at Naples in January 1517. His

[1] M'Crie's History of the Reformation in Spain, p. 352.—*Note.*

[2] *Baxter*, in his "Treatise of Conversion," makes the following interesting allusion to the case of Caracciolus :—"As it was with Caracciolus, the Marquis of Vicum, when his conscience bid him leave his land, and friends, and all for Christ, to forsake Popery, and betake himself to these countries where he might enjoy the gospel, his house and lands then came in his eyes : 'What! must I leave all these for mere conscience, and live I know not how.' His wife hangs upon him, his children with tears do cry after him, ' O father! leave us not.' And many a sob and sigh it costs his heart before he could resolve to get away."—*Baxter's Works*, vol. vii. p. 69.—*Ed.*

father's name was Calantonius, who was descended from the
ancient and noble family of the Caracciolies in the district
of Capua, and was elevated by Charles the Fifth to the rank
of Vico.   His mother was descended from the noble family
of the Caraffi, and was sister to Pope Paul the Fourth.   His
wife, Victoria, was daughter to the Duke of Nuceria, one of
the principal noblemen of Italy.   She brought him a large
fortune.   He had by her six children—four sons and two
daughters.   His mind was first influenced in favour of the
Protestant religion by repeated conversations held by him
with a nobleman nearly related to him, who had, along with
various persons of distinction in Italy, been induced to renounce Popery, chiefly through the instrumentality of a
Spanish nobleman, who at that time resided at Naples—
Joannes Waldesius.   The more immediate instrument, however, of his conversion, was the celebrated Peter Martyr
Vermilius.   Caracciolus having from curiosity gone to hear
him, was savingly impressed by what he heard; and it is
to be noticed as an interesting coincidence, that the means
of his conversion was a discourse on a passage in the *First
Epistle to the Corinthians.*

   " At that time PETER MARTYR was in hand with Paul's
First Epistle to the Corinthians, and as hee was showing the
weakness and deceitfulnesse of the judgment of man's reason in spiritual things, as likewise the power and efficacy of
the Word of God in those men in whom the Lord worketh
by His Spirit—amongst other things hee used this simily
or comparison: If a man, walking in a large place, see
afarre off men and women dancing together, and heare no
sound of instrument, hee will judge them mad, or at least
foolish; but if he come neerer them, and perceive their
order and heare their musicke, and mark their measures
and their courses, he will then bee of another minde, and
not only take delight in seeing them, but feele a desire in
himselfe to beare them company and dance with them.
Even the same (said Martyr) betides many men, who, when
they behold in others a suddaine and great change of their
lookes, apparell, behaviour, and whole course of life, at the
first sight they impute it to melancholy, or some other fool-

ish humour; but if they look more narrowly into the matter, and begin to heare and perceive the harmony and sweet
consent of God's Spirit, and His word in them, by the joint
power of which two this change was made and wrought,
(which afore they counted folly,) then they change their
opinion of them, and first of all begin to like them, and that
change in them, and afterwards feele in themselves a motion and desire to imitate them, and to bee of the number
of such men, who, forsaking the world and his vanities, doe
think that they ought to reform their lives by the rule of
the gospel, that so they may come to true and sound holiness. This comparison, by the grace of God's Spirit, wrought
so wonderfully with Galeacius, as himself hath often told
his friends, that from that hour he resolved with himself
more carefully to restraine his affections from following the
world and his pleasures, as before they did, and to set his
mind about seeking out the truths of religion and the way
to true happinesse. . . . . And thus farre, in this short
time, had the Lord wrought with him by that sermon :—as
first, to consider with himself seriously whether he were
right or no : *secondly*, to take up an exercise continuall of
reading Scripture : *thirdly*, to change his former company
and make choice of better. And this was done in the year
1541, and in the foure and twentieth year of his age."

Caracciolus having thus had his eyes opened to the errors
of Popery, and being fully satisfied that it was his duty to
embrace the Protestant faith, found himself placed in peculiarly trying circumstances. Even those of his countrymen
who were personally inclined towards the Protestant cause
could not be persuaded to hold meetings in private for their
mutual edification, but were prepared not merely to conceal
their real sentiments, but even to practise occasional conformity to the rites of Popery. In these circumstances he was
called to consider whether he would be prepared to spend
the remainder of his life in daily violation of the dictates of
conscience, or forsake all for Christ.

" The sacrifice of his secular dignities and possessions did
not cost him a sigh, but as often as he reflected on the distress which his departure would inflict on his aged father,

who, with parental pride, regarded him as the heir of his titles and the stay of his family,—or his wife whom he loved, and by whom he was loved tenderly, and on the dear pledges of their union, he was thrown into a state of unutterable anguish, and started back with horror from the resolution to which conscience had brought him. At length, by an heroic effort of zeal, which few can imitate and many will condemn, he came to the determination of bursting the tenderest ties which perhaps ever bound man to country and kindred."[1]

The reader will observe that the author of the work already referred to—"The Life of Galeacius Caracciolus," &c., entitles it—"The Italian Convert—Newes from Italy of a Second Moses "—and in accordance with this title the writer, in the dedicatory epistle prefixed to the work, institutes a comparison between Moses and the subject of his narrative in a variety of interesting particulars.

" I may say much rather than Jacob—Few and evil have my dayes been ; yet in these few daies of mine something have I seene, more have I read, more have I heard ; yet never saw I, heard I, or read I any example (all things laid together) more nearly seconding the example of Moses than this of the most renowned Marquesse Galeacius. Moses was the adopted son of a king's daughter ; Galeacius the natural sonne and heire apparent to a Marquesse ; Moses a courtier in the court of Pharaoh, Galeacius in the court of the emperor Charles the Fifth ; Moses by adoption a kinne to a Queene, Galeacius by marriage to a Duke, by blood son to a Marquesse, nephew to a Pope ; Moses in possibility of a kingdom, he in possession of a Marquesdome ; Moses in his youth brought up in the heathenisme of Egypt, Galeacius noozeled in the superstition of Popery ; Moses at last saw the truth and embraced it, so did Galeacius ; Moses openly fell from the heathenisme of Egypt, so did Galeacius from the superstition of Popery. But all this is nothing to that which they both suffered for their conscience. What Moses suffered

---

[1] M'Crie's History of the Reformation in Spain, p. 354.

Saint Paul tells us—'Moses, when he was come to years, refused to be called the sonne of Pharaoh's daughter, and chose rather to suffer adversitie with the people of God, than to enjoy the pleasures of sinne for a season; esteeming the rebuke of Christ greater riches than the treasures of Egypt.' Nay, Moses had rather be a base bricke maker amongst the oppressed Israelites, being true Christians, than to be the sonne of a king's daughter in the court of Pharaoh amongst idolaters. In like case noble Galeacius, when he was come to years and knowledge of Christ, refused to be called sonne and heir to a Marquesse, cup-bearer to an Emperour, nephew to a Pope, and chose rather to suffer affliction, persecution, banishment, losse of lands, livings, wife, children, honours and preferments, than to enjoy the sinfull pleasures of Italy for a season, esteeming the rebuke of Christ greater riches than the honours of a Marquesdome without Christ, and therefore, seeing hee must either want Christ or want them, hee dispoyled himself of all these to gaine Christ. . . . . . So excellent was the fact of Moses, and so heroical, that the Holy Ghost vouchsafes it remembrance both in the Old and New Testament, that so the Church in all ages might know it and admire it, and doth chronicle it in the epistle to the Hebrewes almost two thousand years after it was done. If God himself did so to Moses, shall not God's Church be careful to commend to posterity this second Moses, whose love to Christ Jesus was so zealous, and so inflamed by the heavenly fire of God's Spirit, that no earthly temptations could either quench or abate it; but to winne Christ, and to enjoy Him in the liberty of His Word and Sacraments, he delicately contemned the honours and pleasures of the Marquesdome of Vicum—Vicum, one of the paradises of Naples, Naples, the paradise of Italy—Italy of Europe—Europe of the earth; yet all these paradises were nothing to him in comparison of attaining the celestial paradise, there to live with Jesus Christ."

" And for my part I freely and truly professe, I have bin oft ravisht with admiration of this noble example—to see an Italian so excellent a Christian—one so neere the Pope so neere to Jesus Christ, and such blessed fruit to blossome in

the Pope's own garden ; and to see a nobleman of Italy forsake that for Christ, for which I feare many amongst us
would forsake Christ Himselfe. And surely (I confesse
truth) the serious consideration of this so late, so true, so
strange an example hath bin a spur to my slownes, and
whetted my dull spirits, and made me to esteeme more
highly of religion than I did before. I know it is an accu-
sation of myself, and a disclosing of my own shame to confesse thus much ; but it is a glory to God, an honour to religion, a credit to the truth, and a praise to this noble Marquesse, and therefore I will not hide it. And why should I
shame to confess it, when that famous and renowned man of
God, holy Calvine, freely confesseth,[1] as in the sequel of this
story you shall heare, that this nobleman's example did
greatly confirme him in his religion, and did revive and
strengthen his faith, and cheere up all the holy graces of
God in him."

Caracciolus had no sooner left Naples, forsaking country
and kindred for the sake of Christ and his gospel, than every
possible effort was employed by his family and relatives, and
all that were concerned for the credit of the religion that he
had abandoned, to induce him to return.

On his refusing to do so, " sentence was passed against
him, and he was deprived of all the property which he in-
herited from his mother." " In the following year . . .
an offer was made to him in the name of his uncle now
POPE PAUL IV.,[2] that he should have a protection against

[1] The reader will find the statement referred to in the *second* dedication
prefixed by CALVIN to his commentary on 1st Corinthians—" Cæterum quia
et ego, quantum ad fidei meæ pietatisque confirmationem valeat tuum
exemplum experior," &c. ;—"As however I, for my part, know by experience
the tendencies of your example to strengthen my faith and piety," &c.—*Ed.*

[2] It is remarked by David Dundas Scott, Esq., Translator of Ranke's
History of the Popes of Rome, in connexion with the case of certain relatives of Pope Paul IV. who had incurred his severe displeasure, that
" although Paul seems to have relaxed the stern severity of the arch-
inquisitor in regard to his Protestant nephew, [Galeacius Caracciolus,] by
permitting him to be dealt with in the way of remonstrance and bribery,
when another would have been arrested and put to death, still the com-
pulsory retirement of the latter, after literally leaving ' brethren and sisters,
and father and mother, and wife and children, and lands for Christ's sake
and the gospel' to Geneva, where he spent the evening of his days as a

the Inquisition, provided he would take up his residence within the Venetian States ; a proposal to which neither his safety nor the dictates of his conscience would permit him to accede." He went repeatedly to Italy, and had interviews with his aged father, but was refused the privilege of seeing his wife and family, until about six years after he had quitted Naples. His wife, VICTORIA, then wrote to him, earnestly requesting an interview with him, and fixing the place of meeting. This she did on two different occasions, but in both instances, on his arrival at the appointed place, after a fatiguing and dangerous journey, he had the disappointment of finding that she did not make her appearance. At length, impatient of delay, he went once more to Italy, and at his father's house had an interview with Victoria, when he entreated her to accompany him to Geneva, " promising that no restraint should be laid on her conscience, and that she should be at liberty to practise her religion under his roof. After many protestations of affection, she finally replied, that she could not reside out of Italy, nor in a place where any other religion than that of the Church of Rome was professed, and farther, that she could not live with him as her husband so long as he was infected with heresy." The scene at their final parting was peculiarly tender. " Bursting into tears, and embracing her husband, Vittoria besought him not to leave her a widow, and her babes fatherless. The children joined in the entreaties of their mother, and the eldest daughter, a fine girl of thirteen, grasping his knees, refused to part with him. How he disengaged himself, he knew not ; for the first thing which brought him to recollection was the noise made by the sailors on reaching the opposite shore of the Gulf." (of Venice.) " He used often to relate to his intimate friends, that the parting scene continued

ruling elder in the Italian Reformed Church, presented a striking contrast to the brilliant fortunes of his cousins the Caraffas, during their enjoyment of the Papal favour. But when the Pope found these ungrateful, and when that favour was lost, the Genevan exile [Caracciolus] must have felt peculiarly thankful for the deliverance he had had from such temptations and reverses, and one can hardly suppose but that the Pope himself must have been affected by the contrast at all points between his many Roman Catholic and one Reformed relative."—Ranke's History of the Romish Popes, p. 223. *Note.*

long to haunt his mind ; and that not only in dreams, but
also in reveries into which he fell during the day ; he thought
he heard the angry voice of his father, saw Vittoria in tears,
and felt his daughter dragging at his heels."[1]

Caracciolus spent the remainder of his days at Geneva,
with the exception of five years spent by him at Nion and
Lausanne, for the sake of economy in his living, and continued steadfast in his attachment to the Protestant faith.
He was on terms of intimate friendship with CALVIN, which
continued unbroken until the death of the Reformer in 1564
—thirteen years subsequent to the time when Caracciolus
went to reside at Geneva. *One* step taken by him during
his exile must be regarded as (to say the least) of greatly
questionable propriety—that of contracting a second marriage, about nine years after he went to reside at Geneva.
CALVIN, on being consulted by him as to the propriety of
such a step, "felt great scruples as to the expediency" of it,
but "ultimately gave his approbation to it, after he had consulted the divines of Switzerland and the Grisons."[2] Accordingly, the courts of Geneva having legally pronounced
a sentence of divorce against Vittoria, on the ground of her
obstinate refusal to live with her husband, he married Anne
Fremejere, the widow of a French refugee from Rouen, with
whom he continued to live happily in a state of dignified
frugality.[3] He was held, deservedly, by the Church of
Geneva, and wherever he was known, in the greatest esteem,

---

[1] M'Crie's History of the Reformation in Spain, p. 357.

[2] The part which CALVIN acted as to this matter will be found to be in
exact accordance with the views expressed by him, when commenting on
1 Cor. vii. 15—a passage on which opposite opinions have been entertained
by eminent interpreters. It may be noticed in connexion with this case,
that the United Brethren, when labouring in the West India Islands, near
the close of the last century, felt greatly at a loss as to the course proper
to be pursued in the case of converted negroes, whose husbands or wives
had (as very frequently happened) been purchased by proprietors from
other islands, and were, in consequence of this, parted from them for ever.
" For some time" they " prohibited the converts from contracting another
marriage, apprehending this to be inconsistent with the principles of
Christianity." Afterwards, however, in particular cases, they judged it
better " not to hinder," though they " did not advise, a regular marriage
with another person."—Brown's History of Missions, vol. i. p. 367.

[3] M'Crie's History of the Reformation in Spain, p. 358.

as one whose piety was of a very high order. Matthew Henry, in one part of his Writings,[1] makes mention of " a noble saying of the Marquis of Vico, ' Let their money perish with them, who esteem all the wealth of this world worth one hour's communion with God in Jesus Christ,' " and assuredly the devotedness manifested by him to the cause of Christ affords ample evidence that the sentiment was deeply inwrought into his mind. He died at Geneva in 1586, in the sixty-eighth year of his age.

CALVIN's Commentary on Paul's Epistles to the CORINTHIANS having, (in common with a large portion of his Commentaries on other parts of the Scriptures) been translated by himself into French for the benefit of his countrymen, the Latin original and French version have been carefully collated, and any additional terms or clauses that occur in the latter, tending to bring out more fully the Author's meaning, will be found given at the bottom of the page. " CALVIN," says Pasquier (Biographia Evangelica) " was a good writer, both in Latin and French, and our French tongue is highly obliged to him for enriching it with so great a number of fine expressions." D'AUBIGNÉ, when speaking of CALVIN's early education, states that " he made great progress in Latin literature. He became familiar with Cicero, and learned from this great master to employ the language of the Romans with a facility, purity, and ease that excite the admiration even of his enemies. But at the same time, he found riches in this language which he afterwards transferred to his own." . . . . " CALVIN when called upon to discuss and to prove, enriched his mother-tongue with modes of connexion and dependence, with shadows, transitions, and dialectic forms, that it did not as yet possess."[2]

The OLD ENGLISH TRANSLATION of this part of CALVIN's

[1] Communicant's Companion.
[2] D'Aubigné's History of the Reformation, (Oliver and Boyd's Edition,) vol. iii. pp. 482-3.

Commentaries having been published in black letter in 1573, about thirty years after the Commentary itself was first published by CALVIN, it is not to be wondered that it abounds with obsolete terms and phrases, fitted to render it unpalatable to modern taste. In addition to this, the Author's meaning has, in not a few instances, been manifestly misapprehended, and in almost all cases CALVIN's critical observations are entirely omitted. The Translator, Mr. Thomas Timme, was the author of various works, one of which more particularly—quaintly entitled " A Silver Bell," appears to have gained much celebrity. It has been thought proper to subjoin to this Preface a *fac-simile* of the title-page to this old English version, with a copy of "The Epistle Dedicatorie" to the ARCHBISHOP OF CANTERBURY.

In preparing the present Translation of this part of CALVIN's COMMENTARIES, care has been taken to bring out as fully as possible the Author's meaning, while the reader will find in a variety of instances in the *Notes* some additional light thrown on some important but difficult passages —derived chiefly from the labours of interpreters that have appeared subsequently to the times of CALVIN. The Translator is fully persuaded that CALVIN's Commentaries on *both* of Paul's Epistles to the Corinthians will be found, in so far at least as the Author's meaning is properly brought out in the Translation, to justify most amply the confident expectation of the Author himself, (as expressed in his *first* Dedication to the Commentary on the *First* Epistle)—that it would "furnish no ordinary assistance for thoroughly understanding PAUL's mind."

J. P.

ELGIN, *October* 1848.

A
COMMEN-
tarie vpon S. Paules
Epistles to the Co-
rinthians.

𝔚𝔯𝔦𝔱𝔱𝔢𝔫 𝔟𝔶 M. Iohn Caluin:
and translated out of La-
tine into Englishe, by
Thomas Tymme
Minister.

❡ Imprinted at London, for
Iohn Harison and George
Byshop.
1573.

HONVI SED VIRIVTE

❡ TO THE MOST REVE-
rend Father in God, and his sin-
guler good Lord, Edmond, *by the*
grace of God, Archebiſhop of Can-
terburie, Primate and Metropoli-
tane of all England, Thomas Timme
wisheth the plentifull riches of the
Spirite, in Christ Iesu.

AFter long exercise *in translating such Latine Commentaries vppon*
the holy Scriptures, as I thought most like to further my country
men, *which vnderstand not that tongue, to the soūd knowledg of true*
Religion : at last I tooke in hand M. Caluins *exposition vpon Saint*
Pauls Epistles to the Corinthiās. *And, as in my poore iudgment, the*
writer is a most excellent instrument of God, for the simple setting
foorth of his trueth, so in making my choyse (most reuerend Father)
I could not deuise with my selfe, a more fyt personage, to whom
I might dedicate his trauayle, by my willing paynes translated, than
to your Grace : So much the rather, for that as your selfe can skil-
fully iudge, so they, for whom I haue taken this labour vppon me,
by your allowance (whereon they may and will rest) shalbe the more
encouraged to lyke, and with greater diligence to reade, and to take the
profite ment them thereby. And although my part herein be the least,
and in respect thereof, vnwoorthye to be presented to your hands, your
woorthines in eche condition considered : yet calling to mynde the benefites,
which long ago in Cambridge, *and els where since, I haue receyued by*
your Graces preferment : I thought it better nowe at the last, to aduen-
ture the offer of this simple gift, being such as I haue, than vtterly to
shewe my self vnthankeful for that I haue receyued. Most humbly ther-
fore beseeching your Grace, that as heretofore it hath pleased you to
incourage me in this excercise, by licensing the first booke which I trans-
lated to passe the Englishe presse, so now you will vouchsafe to take in
good part M. Caluins *present, offered you by me. I ceasse to trouble*
you further, recommending your Grace, and all your godly affayres to
almighty God, whom I hartely beseeche to direct in all heauenly wisdome,
grace, and knowledge, now and euer.

Your Graces most humble at all tymes
to commaunde, *Thomas Tymme.*

THE

COMMENTARIES OF JOHN CALVIN

ON

THE FIRST EPISTLE OF PAUL THE APOSTLE

TO THE

CORINTHIANS.

THE AUTHOR'S
FIRST EPISTLE DEDICATORY.

TO THAT ILLUSTRIOUS MAN, JAMES OF BURGUNDY,

MASTER OF FALAIS AND BREDA.

WOULD that this my Commentary, in which I have attempted to expound an Epistle not less obscure than useful, published, as it now is, in accordance with the earnest solicitations of many for a long time past, and even reiterated demands, may be correspondingly answerable to the hopes and wishes of all! I say this, not with the view of earning from this work any meed of praise—an ambition that ought to be quite away from the minds of Christ's servants—but from a desire that it may do good to all, which it cannot do, if it does not meet with acceptance. I have, for my part, laboured with the utmost faithfulness, and with no less diligence, that it may, without any show, be of the greatest service to the Church of God. How far I have succeeded, my readers will judge for themselves.

This much at least I am confident that I have secured—that it will furnish no ordinary assistance for thoroughly understanding Paul's mind. That it will to you, most illustrious Sir, prove exceedingly acceptable, is so far from appearing to me doubtful, that I find it necessary even to warn you against allowing yourself to be carried beyond due bounds by an undue attachment to me, though, if it should so happen, I shall nevertheless regard your judgment as of so much importance, that I shall reckon myself to have succeeded admirably in my labours, if they have secured your unqualified approbation.

In dedicating my Work to you,[1] however, I have not been influenced solely by the hope of its being acceptable to you, but by various other considerations; and more especially this, that your personal character corresponded admirably with the argument of Paul's Epistle. For while too many in the present day convert the Gospel into a cold and shadowy philosophy, imagining that they have sufficiently discharged their duty, if they simply give a nod of assent to what they hear, you, on the other hand, are an illustrious pattern of that living efficacy,[2] which Paul so much insists upon. When, I say, we behold you, we perceive what is that vigour of spirit which, as Paul testifies, ought to breathe in the Gospel. This, assuredly, I do not mention on your account, but because I consider it to be of great importance by way of example.

It would have been an important point gained, though there had been nothing more than this, that, in the first

---

[1] In the interesting volume already referred to—" Lettres de Calvin à Jaque de Bourgogne"—there is preserved the original letter of CALVIN to James of Burgundy, (received on the 6th February 1546,) requesting permission to dedicate to him the Commentary on the First Epistle to the Corinthians. The following translation of such parts of said letter as bear upon this point, will be interesting to the reader:—

" Since my letter was written, I have taken another thought as to the Dedicatory Epistle to my Commentary; for as there is much trouble and difficulty in binding one's self to fill up a certain number of pages, and no more, I send it quite complete. At the same time it is with the understanding, that it is not to be printed, except by your order. Accordingly I enclose it in this, in order that Vendelin may not have it otherwise than through your hands. If it does not appear to you expedient that I should address it to you, I shall, on receiving notice to that effect, prepare a new one.

" Be not surprised, however, if I speak of you briefly; for I was afraid of coming upon some thorny points by going more into detail. But, according as matters shall turn out, we shall be able, God willing, in the second impression, to present fully in detail everything that will be necessary."

In a subsequent letter to James of Burgundy, (received on the 2d April 1546,) CALVIN expresses in the following terms his high satisfaction on receiving permission to dedicate the Commentary to him:—" I give praise to our Lord, because the present of my Commentary is agreeable to you." (Lettres de Calvin, &c., pp. 39, 40, 46.)—*Ed.*

[2] Among other passages in the First Epistle to the Corinthians, which CALVIN may be supposed to have had more particularly in his eye, there are the following,—i. 24; ii. 4; and iv. 20. In commenting on the last of these passages, he complains, as above, of the very general lack in his times of " *spiritualis efficacia*," (spiritual efficacy.)—*Ed.*

order of nobility, in the elevated station of honour which you had obtained, and amidst a large abundance of fortune and wealth, (situations in life that are all of them at the present day overrun with so many corruptions,) you have yourself lived moderately and temperately, and have regulated your household in a chaste and honourable discipline. You have done both admirably. For you have conducted yourself in such a manner, as to lead all to perceive, by clear tokens, that you are altogether free from ambition. While retaining your splendour, as was necessary, it has been in such a manner, that, moderate as has been your style of living, no symptom of meanness was to be seen; while, at the same time, it was abundantly apparent that you avoided magnificence rather than courted it. You have shown yourself affable and kind to all, so that all were constrained to commend your moderation, while there was not even the slightest token of haughtiness or insolence to give offence to any one. As to your household, suffice it to say, in one word, that it has been regulated in such a manner, as to reflect the mind and manners of the Lord, as a mirror does the person. Even this would have been an illustrious and rare pattern of virtue for imitation.

I reckon it, however, of much greater importance, that while you have been groundlessly charged before the Emperor, through the calumnies of wicked men, and that, too, simply because Christ's kingdom, whenever it begins to flourish in any quarter, drives them to madness and fury, you bear up with unconquerable magnanimity, and are now in exile from your native country, with no less credit than you had when adorning it previously with your presence. Other things I pass over, because it were tedious to enlarge. It ought indeed to be more than simply common and customary among Christians, not merely to leave contentedly behind them estates, castles, and princely domains, for Christ's sake, but even cheerfully and willingly to despise in comparison with Him every thing that is most valued under heaven. In consequence, however, of the backwardness and indifference, too, of almost all of us, as the virtue itself is worthy of special admiration, so when it is seen in you so conspicuously, I do most earnestly desire that it may stir up many to a desire of emulation, that they may not in future be always lurking idly in their nests, but may at length discover openly some spark, if they have any, of Christian spirit.

As to your being assaulted from time to time with fresh accusations by those who are manifestly the infuriated enemies of piety, they will gain nothing by this, except to make themselves more and more odious by their gross indulgence in falsehood. At least every man in his senses, perceives that they are mad dogs, that would fain tear you in pieces, and when they cannot bite, take revenge upon themselves by barking. It is well that they do so at a distance, so as to be perfectly harmless. From the injuries of the wicked, however, much as they have diminished your pecuniary resources, there has accrued to you no less glory among the pious. You, however, as becomes a Christian, look beyond this. For you rest satisfied with nothing short of the heavenly glory, which is laid up for us with God, and will be manifested, so soon as " our outward man perishes."—(2 Cor. iv. 16.)

Farewell, most illustrious Sir, with your noble partner. The Lord Jesus long preserve you both in safety for the spread of His kingdom, and always triumph in you over Satan, and the whole band of his troops !

GENEVA, 24*th January* 1546.

THE AUTHOR'S

SECOND EPISTLE DEDICATORY,

TO LORD GALLIAZUS CARACCIOLUS:

A NOBLEMAN, DISTINGUISHED STILL MORE BY EMINENT VIRTUES THAN BY
ILLUSTRIOUS DESCENT, ONLY SON AND RIGHTFUL HEIR OF THE
MARQUIS OF VICO, HEALTH :—

WOULD that when this Commentary first saw the light, I
had either not known at all, or else had known thoroughly
the individual whose name, hitherto inscribed upon this page,
I am now under the necessity of erasing! I have, it is true,
no fear of his upbraiding me with fickleness, or complaining
that I have taken from him what I had previously given,
for having intentionally made it his object, not merely to
withdraw as much as possible from me personally, but also
to have no connection with our Church, he has left himself
no just ground of complaint. It is, however, with reluctance
that I deviate from my custom, so as to erase any one's name
from my writings, and it grieves me that that individual
should have quitted the lofty eminence that I had assigned
him,[1] so as not to hold out a light to others, as it was my
desire that he should.[2] As, however, it is not in my power
to remedy this evil, let him, so far as I am concerned, remain
buried, as I am desirous even now of sparing his credit by
not mentioning his name.

To you, however, most illustrious Sir, I should have had
to look out for some apology, for now putting you in his

---

[1] " Par mon Epistre ;"—" By my Epistle."
[2] " Par bon exemple ;"—" By a good example."

place, did I not freely take this liberty, from the confidence
that I have in your incredible kindness of disposition, and
your affection towards me personally, which is well known
to all our friends.   To return again to wishes, would that I
had known you ten years sooner, for I should not have had
occasion at present for making any change.   So far as an
example to the Church generally is concerned, it is a fortunate circumstance ; because there will not only be no loss
incurred by burying in oblivion the individual who has withdrawn from us, but in place of him we shall have in you a
compensation[1] much more abundant and every way superior.
For although you do not court public applause—satisfied to
have God alone as your witness—and though it is not my
design to herald your praises, yet it were not proper to conceal altogether from my readers what is useful and profitable
to be known :—that a man, sprung from a family of the first
rank,[2] prosperous in honours and wealth, blest with a spouse
of the noblest descent and strictest virtue, a numerous offspring, domestic quiet and harmony, and happy in his entire
condition in life, has, of his own accord, with the view of
joining the camp of Christ, quitted his native country, has
left behind him a fertile and lovely domain, a splendid pat-
rimony, and a residence not less commodious than delightful, has stript himself of domestic splendour, has left father,
wife, children, relatives, and connections, and after bidding
farewell to so many worldly allurements, satisfied with our
mean style, adopts our frugal and homely way of living, just
as if he were one of ourselves.[3]   I make mention, however,
of these things to others, in such a way as not to overlook
at the same time my own individual advantage ; for if I hold
up here, as in a mirror, your virtues before the eyes of my
readers, in order that they may set themselves to imitate

---

[1] " On aura en vous pour recompense vn exemple ;"—" We shall have
in you, by way of compensation, an example."
[2] " Vn homme de maison anciene et grand parentage ;"—" A man of an
ancient house and great parentage."
[3] " Vit frugalement et selon la façon du commun peuple, ne plus ne
moins qu'un autre d'entre nous le premier qu'on scache prendre ;"—" He
lives frugally, and after the manner of the common people, neither more
nor less than one of ourselves, the first that might be fixed upon."

them, it were a shame if I, who have a nearer view of them, were not more keenly affected by a daily and distinct contemplation of them. As, however, I for my part know by experience the tendency of your example to strengthen my faith and piety, and all the children of God that live here acknowledge, as I do, that they have derived from this source no ordinary advantage, I have thought that it might be of importance, that, by my publishing it, the like benefit were made to flow out to a still greater distance. But for this,[1] it were utter folly to expatiate in the praises of a man, whose nature and disposition are at the farthest distance possible from ostentation, and that, too, before persons who are in foreign and far distant regions. Hence, if any considerable number to whom, in consequence of distance, you have been hitherto unknown, shall, on this admirable example being presented to them, prepare to imitate it, by leaving the nests to which they too fondly cling, I shall have obtained an ample reward for what I have written.

It ought, indeed, to have been more than simply common and customary among Christians, not simply to leave contentedly behind them estates, castles, and princely domains, where Christ cannot be followed otherwise, but even cheerfully and willingly to despise, in comparison with Him, everything that is most valued under heaven.[2] Such, however, is the backwardness or rather indifference that pervades all of us, that, while many give a cold assent[3] to the doctrine of the gospel, scarcely one in a hundred will, for the sake of it, if he possesses the most insignificant little farm, allow himself to be torn from it. Scarcely one is induced, without the greatest difficulty, to renounce the smallest conveniences : so very far are they from being prepared to abandon, as were

[1] " Autrement, si je n'auoye cest esgard ;"—" Otherwise, if I had not this in view."

[2] The reader will observe that CALVIN here repeats, in precisely the same words, a statement which had been made by him in his previous dedication to James of Burgundy, and unquestionably the conduct of Caracciolus still more strikingly exemplified the spirit of self-denial which CALVIN here recommends.—*Ed.*

[3] "Consentent à la doctrine de l'Evangile tellement quellement, et comme faisans signe de la teste ;"—" They consent to the doctrine of the gospel in some sort of way, and as giving a nod of assent with the head."

befitting, life itself.[1]   Above all things, I should wish that
all resembled you in that first of all excellences—self-denial.
For you are well prepared to bear witness to me, and I in
like manner to you, how little pleasure we feel in cultivating
the society of those, who, after leaving their native country,
come at length to manifest, that they have not left their old
dispositions behind them.

As, however, it were better that my readers should revolve
in their minds, more than I can express in words, I now
turn to entreat, that God, who has encouraged you hitherto
by the wonderful efficacy of His Spirit, may furnish you
with an unconquerable perseverance unto the end.   For I am
well aware with what arduous conflicts God has exercised
you, and from which, in accordance with your singular prudence, you conclude, that a hard and laborious warfare is
still awaiting you.   Well knowing, however, from ample experience, how necessary it is for us to have a hand held out
to us from heaven, you will, of your own accord, unite with
me in imploring from that source the gift of perseverance.
As for myself, I will entreat Christ our King, to whom
supreme power has been given by the Father, and in whose
hands all the treasures of spiritual blessings have been deposited, that He may long preserve you safely to us for the
spread of His kingdom ; and that He may in you accomplish
farther triumphs over Satan and his bands.

24th January 1556, ten years after this Commentary was
first published.

---

[1] "Pour ceste querelle ;"—" In that contest."

THE ARGUMENT

FIRST EPISTLE TO THE CORINTHIANS.

THE advantages of this Epistle are various and manifold; for it contains many special topics,[1] the handling of which successively in their order, will show how necessary they are to be known. Nay, it will appear in part from the argument itself, in the recital of which I shall study to be brief, yet in such a way as to take in the whole, without omitting any of the leading points.

Corinth, as every one knows, was a wealthy and celebrated city of Achaia. While it was destroyed by L. Mummius for no other reason than that the advantageousness of its situation excited his suspicions, posterity afterwards rebuilt it for the same reason that Mummius had for destroying it.[2] The convenience of the situation, too, occasioned its being restored again in a short time. For as it had the Ægean Sea contiguous on the one side, and the Ionian on the other, and as it was a thoroughfare between Attica and the Peloponnesus, it was very conveniently situated for imports and exports. Paul, after teaching there for a year and a half, as Luke mentions in the Acts, constrained at length by the wickedness of the Jews, sailed thence into Syria (Acts xviii. 11, 18.) During Paul's absence false apostles had crept in, not, in my opinion, to disturb the Church openly with wicked doctrines, or designedly to undermine sound doctrine; but, priding themselves in the splendour and magnificence of

---

[1] " Bonnes matieres, et points de doctrine ;"—" Good subjects and points of doctrine."

[2] Strabo describes Mummius as " μεγαλαφρων μαλλον ἠ φιλοτεχνος,"—" a man of magnanimity rather than a lover of the arts."—Ed.

their address, or rather, being puffed up with an empty loftiness of speech, they looked upon Paul's simplicity, and even the Gospel itself, with contempt. They afterwards, by their ambition, gave occasion for the Church being split into various parties ; and, last of all, reckless as to every thing, provided only they were themselves held in estimation, made it their aim to promote their own honour, rather than Christ's kingdom and the people's welfare.

On the other hand, as those vices prevailed at Corinth with which mercantile cities are wont to be particularly infested,—luxury, pride, vanity, effeminacy, insatiable covetousness, and ambition ; so they had found their way even into the Church itself, so that discipline was greatly relaxed. Nay more, purity of doctrine had already begun to decline, so that the main article of religion—the resurrection of the dead—was called in question. Yet amidst this great corruption in every department, they were satisfied with themselves, equally as though every thing had been on the best possible footing. Such are Satan's usual artifices. If he cannot prevent the progress of doctrine, he creeps forward secretly to make an attack upon it : if he cannot by direct falsehoods suppress it, so as to prevent it from coming forth to light, he digs secret mines for its overthrow ; and in fine, if he cannot alienate men's minds from it, he leads them by little and little to deviate from it.

As to those worthless persons, however, who had disturbed the Corinthian Church, it is not without good ground that I conclude that they were not open enemies of the truth. We see that Paul nowhere else spares false doctrines. The Epistles to the Galatians, to the Colossians, to the Philippians, and to Timothy, are short ; yet in all of them he does not merely censure the false apostles, but also points out at the same time in what respects they injured the Church. Nor is it without good reason ; for believers must not merely be admonished as to the persons whom they ought to shun, they must also be shown the evil against which they should be on their guard. I cannot therefore believe that, in this comparatively long Epistle, he was prepared to pass over in silence what he carefully insists upon in others that are much shorter.   In addition to this, he makes mention of many faults of the Corinthians, and even some that are apparently trivial, so that he appears to have had no intention of passing over any thing in them that was deserving of reproof.   Besides, he must, in any other view, be regarded as wasting many words in disputing against those absurd teachers and prating orators.[1]   He censures their ambition ; he reproves them for transforming the gospel into human philosophy ; he shows that they are destitute of the efficacy of the Spirit, inasmuch as they are taken up with mere ornaments of speech, and seek after a mere dead letter ; but not a word is there as to a single false doctrine.   Hence I conclude that they were persons who did not openly take away any thing from the substance of the gospel, but, as they burned with a misdirected eagerness for distinction, I am of opinion that, with the view of making themselves admired, they contrived a new method of teaching, at variance with the simplicity of Christ.   This must necessarily be the case with all that have not as yet thrown off self, that they may engage unreservedly in the Lord's work.   The first step towards serving Christ is to lose sight of ourselves, and think only of the Lord's glory and the salvation of men.   Farther, no one will ever be qualified for teaching that has not first himself tasted the influence of the gospel, so as to speak not so much with the mouth, as with the dispositions of the heart.   Hence, those that are not regenerated by the Spirit of God—not having felt inwardly the influence of the gospel, and know not what is meant when it is said that we must become new creatures, (John iii. 7) have a dead preaching, whereas it ought to be lively and efficacious ; and, with the view of playing off their part, they disfigure the gospel by painting it over, so as to make it a sort of worldly philosophy.

Nor was it difficult for those of whom we are now speaking to accomplish this at Corinth.   For merchants are usually led away with outward disguises, and they do not merely allow themselves to be imposed upon by the empty

---

[1] " Ces habiles docteurs, et plaisans harangueurs ;"—" Those expert teachers and pleasant orators."

40 THE ARGUMENT ON THE

show with which they deceive others, but in a manner take
delight in this. Besides, as they have delicate ears, so that
they cannot bear to be rudely taken to task, so if they meet
with teachers of the milder sort, that will handle them
gently, they give them, as it were, a reward in turn by
caressing them.[1] It is so, I grant, everywhere ; but it is
more especially common in wealthy and mercantile cities.
Paul, who was in other respects a god-like man, and distinguished by admirable virtues, was, nevertheless, not
adorned with outward elegance, and was not puffed up with
show, with the view of setting himself off to advantage. In
fine, as he was inwardly replenished with the genuine excellence of the Spirit, so he had nothing of outward show.
He knew not to flatter, and was not concerned to please
men. (Gal. i. 10.) The one object that he had in view
was, that Christ might reign, himself and all others being
brought under subjection to him. As the Corinthians were
desirous of doctrine that was ingenious, rather than useful,
the gospel had no relish for them. As they were eager for
new things, Christ had now become stale. Or if they had
not as yet fallen into these vices, they were, nevertheless,
already of their own accord predisposed to corruptions of
that nature. Such were the facilities afforded to the false
apostles for adulterating the doctrine of Christ among them ;
for *adulterated* it is, when its native simplicity is stained,
and in a manner painted over, so as to differ nothing from
worldly philosophy. Hence, to suit the taste of the Corinthians, they seasoned their preaching in such a way that
the true savour of the gospel was destroyed. We are now
in possession of the design that Paul had in view in writing
this Epistle. I shall now take in the sum of the argument,
by noting down briefly the particular heads of discourse.

He begins with an ascription of praise,[2] that is in effect
an exhortation, that they should go on as they have begun,
and in this way he soothes them beforehand, that he may

---

[1] " En flattant et mignardant ces bons maistres ;"—" By flattering and
caressing these good masters."
[2] " En s'esiouïssant de leur avancement en l'Evangile ;"—" While exult-
ing in their proficiency in the gospel."

make them the more docile. Immediately afterwards, however, he proceeds to chide them, making mention of the dissensions with which their Church was infested. Being desirous to cure this evil, he calls upon them to exchange haughtiness for humility. For he overthrows all the wisdom of the world, that the preaching of the Cross may alone be exalted. He also at the same time abases them as individuals, in exhorting them to look around and see what class of persons chiefly the Lord has adopted as members of his flock.

In the *second chapter* he brings forward, by way of example, his own preaching, which, in the account of men, was base and contemptible, but had nevertheless been signalized by the influence of the Spirit. And in the meantime he unfolds at greater length the sentiment, that there is a heavenly and secret wisdom that is contained in the gospel, which cannot be apprehended by any acuteness or perspicacity of intellect, or by any perception of sense, and is not influenced by human reasonings, and needs no meretricious ornament of words or embellishment, but simply by the revelation of the Spirit comes to be known by the understandings of men, and is sealed upon their hearts. He at length comes to this conclusion, that the preaching of the gospel does not merely differ widely from the wisdom of the flesh, and consists in the abasement of the Cross, but cannot be estimated as to its true nature by the judgment of the flesh ; and this he does, with the view of drawing them off from a mistaken confidence in their own judgment, by which they measured every thing amiss.

The beginning of the *third chapter* contains the application of this last department of the subject to their case. For Paul complains, that, being carnal, they were scarcely capable of learning the first rudiments of the gospel. He intimates in this way, that the distaste which they had contracted for the word, arose from no fault in the word itself, but from their ignorance ; and at the same time he indirectly admonishes them, that they need to have their minds renewed, before they will begin to judge aright. He afterwards shows in what estimation the ministers of the gospel

ought to be held—that it ought to be in such a way, that
the honour given to them does not in any degree detract
from the glory that is due to God—as there is one Lord, and
all are his servants : all are mere instruments ; he alone imparts efficacy, and from him proceeds the entire result. He
shows them, at the same time, what they ought to have as
their aim—to build up the Church. He takes occasion from
this to point out the true and proper method of building
aright.   It is to have Christ alone as the foundation, and the
entire structure harmonizing with the foundation. And
here, having stated in passing that he is a wise master-
builder, he admonishes those that come after him to make
the end[1] correspond with the beginning. He exhorts also
the Corinthians not to allow their souls to be desecrated by
corrupt doctrines, inasmuch as they are temples of God.
Here he again brings to nought proud fleshly wisdom, that
the knowledge of Christ may alone be in estimation among
believers.

In the beginning of the *fourth chapter* he points out what
is the office of a true apostle.   And as it was their corrupt
judgment that prevented them from recognising him as such,
putting it aside, he appeals to the day of the Lord.   Farther,
as he was contemptible in their view from an appearance of
abasement, he teaches them that this ought to be regarded
as an honour to him rather than a disgrace.   He afterwards
brings forward tokens, from which it might in reality appear
that he had not consulted his own glory, or his own belly
(Rom. xvi. 18), but had with faithfulness devoted himself
exclusively to Christ's work.   He comes at length to infer
what honour is due to him from the Corinthians.   In the
close of the chapter he recommends Timothy to them, until
he shall come to them himself ; and at the same time he forewarns them that, on his coming, he will openly discover how
little account he makes of those empty boastings by which
the false apostles endeavoured to recommend themselves.

In the *fifth chapter* he takes them to task, for silently
tolerating an incestuous connection between a son-in-law and

---

[1] " De leur besongne ;"—" Of their work."

a mother-in-law, and instructs them that in connexion with a crime of such enormity, there was good reason why they should be covered with shame, instead of being elated with pride. From this he passes on to lay down a general doctrine to this effect, that crimes of that nature ought to be punished with excommunication, that indulgence in sin may be repressed, and that the infection may not spread from one individual to the others.

The *sixth chapter* consists chiefly of two parts. In the *first* he inveighs against law-suits, with which they harassed one another, before unbelievers, to the great dishonour of the gospel. In the *second* he reproves indulgence in fornication, which had come to such a pitch, that it was almost looked upon as a lawful thing. He sets out with a heavy threatening, and afterwards enforces that threatening with arguments.

The *seventh chapter* contains a discussion in reference to virginity, marriage, and celibacy. So far as we may conjecture from Paul's words, a superstitious notion had become prevalent among the Corinthians of this nature—that virginity was a distinguished, and in a manner angelic virtue, so that marriage was held by them in contempt, as though it had been a profane thing. With the view of removing this error, he teaches that every one must consider what his gift is, and not strive in this matter beyond his ability, inasmuch as all have not the same calling. Accordingly he shows who they are that may abstain from marriage, and what ought to be the design of abstaining from it ; and on the other hand, who they are that ought to enter into the married state, and what is the true principle of Christian marriage.

In the *eighth chapter* he prohibits them from having fellowship with idolaters in their impure sacrifices, or giving countenance to anything of such a nature as might injure weak consciences. And as they excused themselves on this pretext, that they did not by any means connect themselves with idolaters in any corrupt sentiment, inasmuch as they acknowledged in their heart *one* God, and regarded idols as empty contrivances, he sets aside this excuse, on this principle that every one ought to have a regard to his brethren, and that there are many weak persons whose faith might be staggered by such dissimulation.

In the *ninth chapter* he shows that he requires from them nothing more than he himself practised, that he may not be reckoned so unreasonable as to impose upon others a law that he did not himself observe. For he puts them in mind how he had voluntarily refrained from availing himself of the liberty granted him by the Lord, lest he should give occasion of offence to any one, and how he had, in things indifferent, put on as it were various appearances, with the view of accommodating himself to all, that they may learn from his example that no one should be so devoted to self as not to endeavour to accommodate himself to his brethren for their edification.

Now as the Corinthians were highly satisfied with themselves, as we said in the outset, in the beginning of the *tenth chapter* he admonishes them, from the example of the Jews, not to deceive themselves by a mistaken confidence; for if they are puffed up on account of outward things and gifts of God, he shows that the Jews were not without similar ground of glorying, and yet all this availed them nothing, because they abused their privileges. After alarming them by this threatening he returns immediately to the subject on which he had previously entered, and shows how unseemly it is for those who partake of the Lord's Supper to be participants in the "table of devils," that being a shameful and insufferable pollution. He at length draws this conclusion, that all our actions should be regulated in such a manner as not to be an occasion of offence to any one.

In the *eleventh chapter* he clears the public assemblies from certain corrupt observances, which were at variance with Christian decorum and propriety, and shows what gravity and modesty ought to be exercised when we stand in the view of God and angels. He takes them to task, however, chiefly for their corrupt administration of the Supper. He subjoins the method of correcting the abuse that had crept in, which is by calling them back to our Lord's original institution, as the only sure rule and permanent law of right acting.

As, however, many abused spiritual gifts for purposes of ambition, he enters into a discussion, in the *twelfth chapter*, as to the purpose for which they are conferred by God, and also as to what is the proper and genuine use of them, which is, that by contributing mutually to each other's advantage, we may be united together in one body, that of Christ. This doctrine he illustrates by drawing a similitude from the human body, in which, although there are different members and various faculties, there is nevertheless such a symmetry and fellow-feeling, that what has been conferred on the members severally contributes to the advantage of the whole body—and hence love is the best directress in this matter.[1]

The subject he follows out at greater length, and illustrates it more fully in the *thirteenth chapter*. The sum is this—that all things must be viewed in relation to love. He takes occasion from this to make a digression for the purpose of commending that virtue, that he may the more strongly recommend the pursuit of it, and may encourage the Corinthians the more to cultivate it.

In the *fourteenth chapter* he begins to point out more particularly in what respect the Corinthians had erred in the use of spiritual gifts; and as mere show bulked so much in their estimation, he teaches them that in all things edification alone should be looked to. For this reason he prefers prophecy to all other gifts, as being more useful, while the Corinthians set a higher value on tongues, purely from empty show. In addition to this, he lays down the right order of procedure, and at the same time reproves the fault of sounding forth in unknown tongues without any advantage, while in the meantime the doctrine and exhortations, which ought ever to hold the foremost place, were left in the background. He afterwards forbids women to teach publicly, as being a thing unseemly.

In the *fifteenth chapter* he inveighs against a very pernicious error, which, although we can scarcely suppose it to

---

[1] " Ainsi, il conclud, que charité nous seruira d'vne bonne regle pour nous bien gouuerner en cest endroit;"—" Thus, he concludes, that charity will furnish us with a good rule for directing us aright in this matter."

have spread generally among the Corinthians, had nevertheless taken possession of the minds of some of them to such a degree, that it was necessary that a remedy should be openly administered. He appears, however, to have intentionally delayed mentioning this matter until the close of the Epistle, for this reason—that if he had set out with this, or had entered upon it immediately after commencing, they might have thought that they were all reckoned to be in fault. The hope of a resurrection, accordingly, he shows to be so necessary, that, if it is taken away, the whole gospel falls to pieces. Having established the doctrine itself by powerful arguments, he subjoins also the principle and manner of it. In fine, he carefully draws out a full discussion of this point.

The *sixteenth chapter* consists of two parts. In the first of these he exhorts them to relieve the necessity of the brethren at Jerusalem. They were at that time pinched with famine, and they were cruelly treated by the wicked. The apostles had assigned to Paul the charge of stirring up the Churches of the Gentiles to afford them help. He accordingly exhorts them to lay up in store whatever they were inclined to contribute, that it might be transmitted to Jerusalem without delay. He at length concludes the Epistle with a friendly exhortation and congratulations.

Hence we may gather, as I stated in the outset, that the Epistle is replete with most profitable doctrine, containing, as it does, a variety of discussions on many important topics.

COMMENTARY

ON THE

FIRST EPISTLE TO THE CORINTHIANS.

CHAPTER I.

1. Paul, called *to be* an apostle of Jesus Christ through the will of God, and Sosthenes *our* brother,

2. Unto the church of God which is at Corinth, to them that are sanctified in Christ Jesus, called *to be* saints, with all that in every place call upon the name of Jesus Christ our Lord, both theirs and ours :

3. Grace *be* unto you, and peace, from God our Father, and *from* the Lord Jesus Christ.

1. Paulus, vocatus apostolus Jesu Christi per voluntatem Dei, et Sosthenes frater,

2. Ecclesiæ Dei quæ est Corinthi, sanctificatis in Christo Jesu, vocatis sanctis, una cum omnibus qui invocant nomen Domini nostri Jesu Christi in quovis loco tam sui quam nostri :[1]

3. Gratia vobis et pax a Deo Patre nostro, et Domino Jesu Christi.

1. *Paul, called to be an Apostle.* In this manner does Paul proceed, in almost all the introductions to his Epistles, with the view of procuring for his doctrine authority and favour. The former he secures to himself from the station that had been assigned to him by God, as being an Apostle of Christ sent by God ; the latter by testifying his affection towards those to whom he writes. We believe much more readily the man whom we look upon as regarding us with affection, and as faithfully endeavouring to promote our welfare. In this salutation, therefore, he claims for himself authority, when he speaks of himself as *an Apostle of Christ,* and that, too, as *called by God,* that is, set apart *by*

[1] "Le leur et le nostre," ou, "le Seigneur (di-ie) et de eux et de nous ;" —"Both theirs and ours," or, "the Lord (I say) both of them and of us."

the will of God. Now, two things are requisite in any one that would be listened to in the Church, and would occupy the place of a teacher ; for he must be *called* by God to that office, and he must faithfully employ himself in the discharge of its duties. Paul here lays claim to both. For the name, *Apostle,* implies that the individual conscientiously acts the part of an ambassador for Christ (2 Cor. v. 19), and proclaims the pure doctrine of the gospel. But as no one ought to assume this honour to himself, unless he be *called* to it, he adds, that he had not rashly intruded into it, but had been appointed[1] to it by God.

Let us learn, therefore, to take these two things together when we wish to ascertain what kind of persons we ought to esteem as ministers of Christ,—a call to the office, and faithfulness in the discharge of its duties. For as no man can lawfully assume the designation and rank of a minister, unless he be called, so it were not enough for any one to be called, if he does not also fulfil the duties of his office. For the Lord does not choose ministers that they may be dumb idols, or exercise tyranny under pretext of their calling, or make their own caprice their law ; but at the same time marks out what kind of persons they ought to be, and binds them by his laws, and in fine chooses them for the ministry, or, in other words, that in the first place they may not be idle, and, secondly, that they may confine themselves within the limits of their office. Hence, as the apostleship depends on the *calling,* so the man who would be reckoned an apostle, must show himself to be really such : nay more, so must every one who demands that credit be given him, or that his doctrine be listened to. For since Paul rests on these arguments for establishing his authority, worse than impudent were the conduct of that man who would think to have any standing without such proofs.

It ought, however, to be observed, that it is not enough for any one to hold out to view the title to a call to the office, along with faithfulness in discharging its duties, if he does not in reality give proof of both. For it often happens

---

[1] " Constitué, ordonné, et établi ;"—" Appointed, ordained, and established."

that none boast more haughtily of their titles than those that are destitute of the reality ; as of old the false prophets, with lofty disdain, boasted that they had been sent by the Lord.   Nay, at the present day, what else do the Romanists make a noise about, but " ordination from God, and an inviolably sacred succession even from the Apostles themselves,"[1] while, after all, it appears that they are destitute of those things of which they vaunt ?   Here, therefore, it is not boasting that is required, but reality.   Now, as the name is assumed by good and bad alike, we must come to the test, that we may ascertain who has a right to the name of Apostle, and who has not.   As to Paul, God attested his *calling* by many revelations, and afterwards confirmed it by miracles.   The *faithfulness* must be estimated by this,— whether or not he proclaimed the pure doctrine of Christ. As to the twofold call—that of God and that of the Church —see my Institutes.[2]

An Apostle.   Though this name, agreeably to its etymology, has a general signification, and is sometimes employed in a general sense, to denote any kind of ministers,[3] yet, as a peculiar designation, it is applicable to those that were set apart by the Lord's appointment to publish the Gospel throughout the whole world.   Now, it was of importance that Paul should be reckoned in that number, for two reasons, — *first,* because much more deference was paid to them than to other ministers of the gospel ; and, *secondly,*

---

[1] " Et aujour d'huy, qu'est ce qu'entonnent à plene bouche les Romanisques, sinon ces gros mots, Ordination de Dieu, La sainte et sacrée succession depuis le temps mesme des Apostres ;"—" And at the present day, what do the Romanists sound forth with open mouth, but those grand terms, Ordination from God,—The holy and sacred succession from the very times of the Apostles."

[2] *Institutes,* vol. iii. p. 67.

[3] Αποστολος, (an apostle,) derived from αποστελλειν, (to send forth,) signifies literally *a messenger.*   The term is employed by classical writers to denote *the commander of an expedition,* or a *delegate,* or *ambassador.* (See Herodotus, v. 38.)   In the New Testament it is in various instances employed in a general sense to denote a *messenger.* (See Luke xi. 49 ; John xiii. 16 ; Phil. ii. 25.)   In one instance it is applied to Christ himself, (Heb. iii. 1.)   Most frequently, however, it is applied to those extraordinary *messengers* who were (to use the words of Leigh in his Critica Sacra) Christ's " legates *a latere*," from his side.—*Ed.*

because they alone, properly speaking, had authority to instruct all the Churches.

By the will of God. While the Apostle is accustomed cheerfully to acknowledge himself indebted to God for whatever he has of good, he does so more especially in reference to his apostleship, that he may free himself from all appearance of presumption. And assuredly as a call to salvation is of grace, so also a call to the office of apostle is of grace, as Christ teaches in these words: " Ye have not chosen me, but I have chosen you," (John xv. 16.) Paul, however, at the same time indirectly intimates, that all who attempt to undermine his apostleship, or in any way oppose it, contend against an appointment of God. For Paul here makes no useless boast of honorary titles, but designedly vindicates his apostleship from malicious aspersions. For as his authority must have been sufficiently established in the view of the Corinthians, it would have been superfluous to make particular mention of " the will of God," had not wicked men attempted by indirect means to undermine that honourable rank which had been divinely assigned him.

And Sosthenes our brother. This is that Sosthenes who was ruler of the Jewish synagogue that was at Corinth, of whom Luke makes mention in Acts xviii. 17. His name is added for this reason, that the Corinthians, knowing his ardour and steadfastness in the gospel, could not but hold him in deserved esteem, and hence it is still more to his honour to be made mention of now as Paul's *brother*, than formerly as *ruler of the synagogue.*

2. *To the Church of God which is at Corinth.* It may perhaps appear strange that he should give the name of a Church of God to a multitude of persons that were infested with so many distempers, that Satan might be said to reign among them rather than God. Certain it is, that he did not mean to flatter the Corinthians, for he speaks under the direction of the Spirit of God, who is not accustomed to flatter. But[1] among so many pollutions, what appearance

---

[1] " Mais (dira quelqu'un ;)"—" But (some one will say.)"

of a Church is any longer presented ?   I answer, the Lord
having said to him, " Fear not : I have much people in this
place" (Acts xviii. 9, 10 ;) keeping this promise in mind,
he conferred upon a godly few so much honour as to recognise them as a Church amidst a vast multitude of ungodly
persons.   Farther, notwithstanding that many vices had
crept in, and various corruptions both of doctrine and manners, there were, nevertheless, certain tokens still remaining
of a true Church.   This is a passage that ought to be carefully observed, that we may not require that the Church,
while in this world, should be free from every wrinkle and
stain, or forthwith pronounce unworthy of such a title every
society in which everything is not as we would wish it.   For
it is a dangerous temptation to think that there is no Church
at all where perfect purity is not to be seen.   For the man
that is prepossessed with this notion, must necessarily in the
end withdraw from all others, and look upon himself as the
only saint in the world, or set up a peculiar sect in company
with a few hypocrites.

What ground, then, had Paul for recognising a Church at
Corinth ?   It was this : that he saw among them the doctrine of the gospel, baptism, the Lord's Supper—tokens by
which a Church ought to be judged of.   For although some
had begun to have doubts as to the resurrection, the error
not having spread over the entire body, the name of the
Church and its reality are not thereby affected.   Some
faults had crept in among them in the administration of the
Supper, discipline and propriety of conduct had very much
declined : despising the simplicity of the gospel, they had
given themselves up to show and pomp; and in consequence
of the ambition of their ministers, they were split into
various parties.   Notwithstanding of this, however, inasmuch
as they retained fundamental doctrine : as the one God was
adored among them, and was invoked in the name of Christ :
as they placed their dependence for salvation upon Christ,
and, had a ministry not altogether corrupted :   there was,
on these accounts, a Church still existing among them.
Accordingly, wherever the worship of God is preserved un-
infringed, and that fundamental doctrine, of which I have

spoken, remains, we must without hesitation conclude that
in that case a Church exists.

Sanctified in Christ Jesus, called to be saints. He makes
mention of the blessings with which God had adorned them,
as if by way of upbraiding them, at least in the event of
their showing no gratitude in return. For what could be
more base than to reject an Apostle through whose instrumentality they had been set apart as God's peculiar portion.
Meanwhile, by these two epithets, he points out what sort
of persons ought to be reckoned among the true members of
the Church, and who they are that belong of right to her
communion. For if you do not by holiness of life show
yourself to be a Christian, you may indeed be *in* the Church,
and pass undetected,[1] but *of* it you cannot be. Hence all
must be *sanctified in Christ* who would be reckoned among
the people of God. Now the term *sanctification* denotes
separation. This takes place in us when we are regenerated
by the Spirit to newness of life, that we may serve God and
not the world. For while by nature we are unholy, the
Spirit consecrates us to God. As, however, this is effected
when we are ingrafted into the body of Christ, apart from
whom there is nothing but pollution, and as it is also by
Christ, and not from any other source that the Spirit is conferred, it is with good reason that he says that we are
sanctified in Christ, inasmuch as it is by Him that we cleave
to God, and in Him become new creatures.

What immediately follows—*called to be saints*—I understand to mean: As ye have been called unto holiness. It
may, however, be taken in two senses. Either we may
understand Paul to say, that the ground of sanctification is
the call of God, inasmuch as God has chosen them ; meaning, that this depends on his grace, not on the excellence of
men ; or we may understand him to mean, that it accords
with our profession that we be holy, this being the design
of the doctrine of the gospel. The former interpretation
appears to suit better with the context, but it is of no great

---

[1] "Tu te pourras bien entretenir en l'Eglise tellement quellement,
estant meslé parmi les autres ;"—" You may quite well have a standing
in the Church in some sort of way, being mixed up among others."

consequence in which way you understand it, as there is an entire agreement between the two following positions—that our holiness flows from the fountain of divine election, and that it is the end of our calling.

We must, therefore, carefully maintain, that it is not through our own efforts that we are holy, but by the call of God, because He alone sanctifies those who were by nature unclean. And certainly it appears to me probable, that, when Paul has pointed out as it were with his finger the fountain of holiness thrown wide open, he mounts up a step higher, to the good pleasure of God, in which also Christ's mission to us originated. As, however, we are called by the gospel to harmlessness of life (Phil. ii. 15,) it is necessary that this be accomplished in us in reality, in order that our calling may be effectual. It will, however, be objected, that there were not many such among the Corinthians. I answer, that the weak are not excluded from this number; for here God only begins his work in us, and by little and little carries it forward gradually and by successive steps. I answer farther, that Paul designedly looks rather to the grace of God in them than to their own defects, that he may put them to shame for their negligence, if they do not act a suitable part.

With all that call. This, too, is an epithet common to all the pious; for as it is one chief exercise of faith to *call upon the name* of God, so it is also by this duty chiefly that believers are to be estimated. Observe, also, that he says that Christ is called upon by believers, and this affords a proof of his divinity—invocation being one of the first expressions of Divine homage. Hence invocation here by synecdoche[1] (κατὰ συνεκδοχήν) denotes the entire profession of faith in Christ, as in many passages of Scripture it is taken generally for the whole of Divine worship. Some explain it as denoting mere profession, but this appears to be meagre, and at variance with its usual acceptation in Scripture. The little words *nostri* (*ours*) and *sui* (*theirs*) I have put in the genitive, understanding them as referring to Christ,

---

[1] *Synecdoche*, a figure of speech, by which part is taken for the whole.— *Ed.*

while others, understanding them as referring to place, render them in the ablative. In doing so I have followed Chrysostom. This will, perhaps, appear harsh, as the expression *in every place* is introduced in the middle, but in Paul's Greek style there is nothing of harshness in this construction. My reason for preferring this rendering to that of the Vulgate is, that if you understand it as referring to place, the additional clause will be not merely superfluous, but inappropriate. For what place would Paul call his own? *Judea* they understand him to mean; but on what ground? And then, what place could he refer to as inhabited by others? " All other places of the world" (say they;) but this, too, does not suit well. On the other hand, the meaning that I have given it suits most admirably; for, after making mention of *all that in every place call upon the name of Christ our Lord*, he adds, *both theirs and ours*, manifestly for the purpose of showing that Christ is the one common Lord, without distinction, of all that call upon him, whether they be Jews or Gentiles.

In every place. This Paul has added, contrary to his usual manner; for in his other Epistles he makes mention in the salutation of those only for whom they are designed. He seems, however, to have had it in view to anticipate the slanders of wicked men, that they might not have it to allege that, in addressing the Corinthians, he assumed a confident air, and claimed for himself an authority that he would not venture to assert in writing to other Churches. For we shall see by and by, that he was unjustly loaded with this reproach, too, as though he were preparing little nests[1] for himself, with the view of shunning the light, or were withdrawing himself in a clandestine way from the rest of the Apostles. It appears, then, that expressly for the purpose of refuting this falsehood, he places himself in a commanding position, from which he may be heard afar off.

3. *Grace be to you and peace.* For an exposition of this prayer, let my readers consult the beginning of my Commentary on the Epistle to the Romans (Rom. i. 7;) for I do not willingly burden my readers with repetitions.

---

[1] " Nids et cachettes;"—" Nests and lurking-holes."

4. I thank my God always on your behalf, for the grace of God which is given you by Jesus Christ;

5. That in every thing ye are enriched by him, in all utterance, and *in* all knowledge;

6. Even as the testimony of Christ was confirmed in you:

7. So that ye come behind in no gift; waiting for the coming of our Lord Jesus Christ:

8. Who shall also confirm you unto the end, *that ye may be* blameless in the day of our Lord Jesus Christ.

9. God *is* faithful, by whom ye were called unto the fellowship of his Son Jesus Christ our Lord.

4. Gratias ago Deo meo semper de vobis propter gratiam Dei, quæ data vobis est in Christo Jesu.

5. Quia in omnibus ditati estis in ipso, in omni sermone,[1] et in omni cognitione.

6. Quemadmodum testimonium Christi confirmatum fuit in vobis.

7. Ut nullo in dono destituamini, exspectantes revelationem Domini nostri Jesu Christi.

8. Qui etiam confirmabit vos usque in finem inculpatos, in diem Domini nostri Jesu Christi.

9. Fidelis Deus, per quem vocati estis in communionem Filii ipsius Jesu Christi Domini nostri.

4. *I give thanks to my God.* Having in the salutation secured for himself authority from the station assigned him, he now endeavours to procure favour for his doctrine, by expressing his affection for them. In this way he soothes their minds beforehand, that they may listen patiently to his reproofs.[2] He persuades them of his affection for them by the following tokens—his discovering as much joy in the benefits bestowed upon them, as if they had been conferred upon himself; and his declaring that he entertains a favourable opinion of them, and has good hopes of them as to the future. Farther, he qualifies his congratulations in such a way as to give them no occasion to be puffed up, as he traces up to God all the benefits that they possessed, that the entire praise may redound to him, inasmuch as they are the fruits of his grace. It is as though he had said—"I congratulate you indeed, but it is in such a way as to ascribe the praise to God." His meaning, when he calls God *his* God, I have explained in my Commentary upon the Epistle to the Romans (Rom. i. 8.) As Paul was not prepared to flatter the Corinthians, so neither has he commended them on false grounds. For although all were not worthy of such

[1] " Parole," ou " éloquence;"—" Utterance," or " eloquence."
[2] The same view of Paul's design here is given by Theodoret: " Μέλλων κατηγορεῖν, προθεραπεύει την ἀκοὴν ὥστε δεκτὴν γενέσθαι την ἰατρείαν;"—" As he is about to censure them, he soothes beforehand the organ of hearing, that the remedy to be applied may be the more favourably received."—*Ed.*

commendations, and though they corrupted many excellent
gifts of God by ambition, yet the gifts themselves it became
him not to despise, because they were, in themselves, deserving of commendation. Farther, as the gifts of the Spirit
are conferred for the edification of all, it is with good reason
that he enumerates them as gifts common to the whole
Church.[1] But let us see what he commends in them.

For the grace, &c. This is a general term, for it comprehends blessings of every kind that they had obtained through
means of the gospel. For the term *grace* denotes here not
the favour of God, but by metonymy[2] ($\mu\epsilon\tau\omega\nu\nu\mu\iota\kappa\hat{\omega}\varsigma$), the
gifts that he bestows upon men gratuitously. He imme-
diately proceeds to specify particular instances, when he
says that *they are enriched in all things*, and specifies what
those *all things* are—the doctrine and word of God. For in
these riches it becomes Christians to abound; and they
ought also to be esteemed by us the more, and regarded by
us as so much the more valuable, in proportion as they are
ordinarily slighted. The phrase *in ipso* (*in him*) I have
preferred to retain, rather than render it *per ipsum* (*by him,*)
because it has in my opinion more expressiveness and force.
For we are *enriched in Christ*, inasmuch as we are members
of his body, and are engrafted into him : nay more, being
made one with him, he makes us share with him in every
thing that he has received from the Father.

6. *Even as the testimony*, &c. Erasmus gives a different
rendering, to this effect, " that by these things the testimony of Christ was confirmed in them ;" that is, by knowledge and by the word. The words, however, convey another
meaning, and if they are not wrested, the meaning is easy
—that God has sealed the truth of his gospel among the
Corinthians, for the purpose of confirming it. Now, this
might be done in two ways, either by miracles, or by the
inward testimony of the Holy Spirit. Chrysostom seems to
understand it of miracles, but I take it in a larger sense ;
and, first of all, it is certain, that the gospel is properly

[1] " Que chacun ha en son endroit ;"—"Which every one has severally."
[2] A figure of speech, by which one term is put for another—the cause
for the effect, the effect for the cause, &c.—*Ed.*

confirmed in our experience by faith, because it is only when we receive it by faith that we "set to our seal that God is true" (John iii. 33.) And though I admit that miracles ought to have weight for the confirmation of it, yet we must go higher in search of the origin, namely this, that the Spirit of God is the earnest and seal. Accordingly, I explain these words in this manner—that the Corinthians excelled in knowledge, inasmuch as God had from the beginning given efficacy to his gospel among them, and that not in one way merely, but had done so both by the internal influence of the Spirit, and by excellence and variety of gifts, by miracles, and by all other helps. He calls the gospel *the testimony of Christ*, or *respecting* Christ, because the entire sum of it tends to discover Christ to us, "in whom all the treasures of knowledge are hid" (Col. ii. 3.) If any one prefers to take it in an active sense, on the ground that Christ is the primary author of the gospel, so that the Apostles were nothing but secondary or inferior witnesses, I shall not much oppose it. I feel better satisfied, however, with the former exposition. It is true that a little afterwards (chap. ii. 1) *the testimony of God* must, beyond all controversy, be taken in an active sense, as a passive signification would not be at all suitable. Here, however, the case is different, and, what is more, that passage strengthens my view, as he immediately subjoins what it is[1]—*to know nothing but Christ.* (Chap. ii. 2.)

7. *So that ye come behind in no gift.* Ὑστερεῖσθαι means to be in want of what you would otherwise stand in need of.[2] He means, therefore, that the Corinthians abound in all the gifts of God, so as not to be in want of anything, as if he had said, "The Lord has not merely honoured you with the light of the gospel, but has eminently endowed you with all those graces that may be of service to the saints for helping them forward in the way of salvation." For he

---

[1] " Quel est ce tesmoignage ;"—" What this testimony is."

[2] The word is used in this sense in the following passages : Luke xv. 15; 2 Cor. xi. 8; Phil. iv. 12; and Heb. xi. 37. The proper meaning is—to come too late for a thing, and so miss of it. Xenophon uses it in this sense. Αβροκόμας ὑστέρησε τῆς μάχης:—" Abrocomas came too late for the battle." The word occurs in the same sense in Heb. iv. i. and xii. 15.—*Ed.*

gives the name of gifts (χαρίσματα) to those spiritual graces
that are, as it were, means of salvation to the saints. But
it is objected, on the other hand, that the saints are never
in such abundance as not to feel in want of graces to some
extent, so that they must always of necessity be "*hungering
and thirsting*" (Matt. v. 6.) For where is the man that does
not come far short of perfection? I answer, "As they are
sufficiently endowed with needful gifts, and are never in
such destitution but that the Lord seasonably relieves their
need; Paul on this ground ascribes to them such wealth."
For the same reason he adds: *waiting for the manifestation*,
meaning, that he does not ascribe to them such abundance
as to leave nothing to be desired; but merely as much as
will suffice, until they shall have arrived at perfection. The
participle *waiting* I understand in this sense, "In the meantime while you are waiting." Thus the meaning will be,
"So that ye are in want of no gift in the meantime while
you are waiting for the day of perfected revelation, by which
Christ our wisdom (verse 30th) will be fully manifested."

8. *Who will also confirm you.* The relative here refers not
to Christ, but to God, though the word *God* is the remoter
antecedent. For the Apostle is going on with his congratulation, and as he has told them previously what he thought
of them, so he now lets them know what hope he has of them
as to the future, and this partly for the purpose of assuring
them still farther of his affection for them, and partly that
he may exhort them by his own example to cherish the
same hope. It is as if he had said—Though the expectation of a salvation to come keeps you still in suspense, you
ought nevertheless to feel assured that the Lord will never
forsake you, but will on the contrary increase what he has
begun in you, that when that day comes on which "we must
all appear before the judgment-seat of Christ," (2 Cor. v. 10,)
we may be found there blameless.

Blameless. In his Epistles to the Ephesians and Colossians
(Eph. i. 4, and Col. i. 22) he teaches that this is the end of
our calling—that we may appear pure and unreproachable
in the presence of Christ. It is, however, to be observed,
that this glorious purity is not in the first instance perfected

in us ; nay, rather, it goes well with us if we are every day making progress in penitence, and are being *purged from the sins* (2 Peter i. 9) that expose us to the displeasure of God, until at length we put off, along with the mortal body, all the offscourings of sin.   Of the *day of the Lord* we shall have occasion to speak when we come to the fourth chapter.

9. *God is faithful.*   When the Scripture speaks of God as faithful the meaning in many cases is, that in God there is steadfastness and evenness of tenor, so that what he begins he prosecutes to the end,[1] as Paul himself says elsewhere, that *the calling of God is without repentance* (Rom. xi. 29.) Hence, in my opinion, the meaning of this passage is, that God is steadfast in what he purposes.   This being the case, he consequently does not make sport as to his calling, but will unceasingly take care of his work.[2]   From God's past benefits we ought always to hope well as to the future. Paul, however, has something higher in view, for he argues that the Corinthians cannot be cast off, having been once, called by the Lord into Christ's fellowship.   To apprehend fully, however, the force of this argument, let us observe first of all, that every one ought to regard his calling as a token of his election.   Farther, although one cannot judge with the same certainty as to another's election, yet we must always in the judgment of charity conclude that all that are called are called to salvation ; I mean efficaciously and fruitfully.   Paul, however, directed his discourse to those in whom the word of the Lord had taken root, and in whom some fruits of it had been produced.

Should any one object that many who have once received the word afterwards fall away, I answer that the Spirit alone is to every one a faithful and sure witness of his election, upon which perseverance depends.   This, however, did not stand in the way of Paul's being persuaded, in the judgment

---

[1] CALVIN probably refers to the following (among other) passages:— 1 Thess. v. 24 ; 2 Thess iii. 3 ; Heb. x. 23.

[2] " La vocation donc qu'il fait d'un chacun des siens, n'est point un jeu, et en les appellant il ne se mocque point, ainsi il entretiendra et pour suyura son œuvre perpetuellement ;"—" The calling, therefore, that he makes of each of his own, is not mere play; and in calling them he does not make sport, but will unceasingly maintain and prosecute his work."

of charity, that the calling of the Corinthians would prove firm and immoveable, as being persons in whom he saw the tokens of God's fatherly benevolence. These things, however, do not by any means tend to beget carnal security, to divest us of which the Scriptures frequently remind us of our weakness, but simply to confirm our confidence in the Lord. Now this was needful, in order that their minds might not be disheartened on discovering so many faults, as he comes afterwards to present before their view. The sum of all this may be stated thus,—that it is the part of Christian candour to hope well of all who have entered on the right way of salvation, and are still persevering in that course, notwithstanding that they are at the same time still beset with many distempers. Every one of us, too, from the time of his being *illuminated* (Heb. x. 32) by the Spirit of God in the knowledge of Christ, ought to conclude with certainty from this that he has been adopted by the Lord to an inheritance of eternal life. For effectual calling ought to be to believers an evidence of divine adoption ; yet in the meantime we must all walk *with fear and trembling* (Phil. ii. 12.) On this point I shall touch again to some extent when we come to the tenth chapter.

Into the fellowship. Instead of this rendering Erasmus translates it *into partnership.* The old interpreter renders it *society.* I have preferred, however, to render it *fellowship,* as bringing out better the force of the Greek word κοινωνιας.[1] For this is the design of the gospel, that Christ may become ours, and that we may be ingrafted into his body. Now when the Father gives him to us in possession, he also communicates himself to us in him ; and hence arises a participation in every benefit. Paul's argument, then, is this—" Since you have, by means of the gospel which you have received by faith, been called into the fellowship of

---

[1] CALVIN in his *Institutes,* (vol ii. p. 24,) after speaking of Christ's being represented by Paul as " offered to us in the gospel with all the abundance of heavenly blessings, with all his merits, all his righteousness, wisdom, and grace, without exception," remarks—" And what is meant by the *fellowship* (κοινωνια) of Christ, which, according to the same apostle (1 Cor. i. 9) is offered to us in the gospel, all believers know."—*Ed.*

Christ, you have no reason to dread the danger of death,[1] having been made *partakers* of him (Heb. iii. 14) who rose a conqueror over death." In fine, when the Christian looks to himself he finds only occasion for trembling, or rather for despair; but having been called into the fellowship of Christ, he ought, in so far as assurance of salvation is concerned, to think of himself no otherwise than as a member of Christ, so as to reckon all Christ's benefits his own. Thus he will obtain an unwavering hope of final perseverance, (as it is called,) if he reckons himself a member of him who is beyond all hazard of falling away.

10. Now I beseech you, brethren, by the name of our Lord Jesus Christ, that ye all speak the same thing, and *that* there be no divisions among you; but *that* ye be perfectly joined together in the same mind and in the same judgment.

11. For it hath been declared unto me of you, my brethren, by them *which are of the house* of Chloe, that there are contentions among you.

12. Now this I say, that every one of you saith, I am of Paul; and I of Apollos; and I of Cephas; and I of Christ.

13. Is Christ divided? was Paul crucified for you? or were ye baptized in the name of Paul?

10. Observo autem vos, fratres, per nomen Domini nostri Jesu Christi, ut idem loquamini omnes, et non sint inter vos dissidia: sed apte cohæreatis in una mente et in una sententia.[2]

11. Significatum enim mihi de vobis fuit, fratres mei, ab iis qui sunt Chloes, quod contentiones sint inter vos.

12. Dico autem illud,[3] quod unusquisque vestrum dicat, Ego quidem sum Pauli, ego autem Apollo, ego autem Cephæ, ego autem Christi.

13. Divisusne est Christus? numquid pro vobis crucifixus est Paulus? aut vos in nomen Pauli baptizati estis?

10. *Now I beseech you, brethren.* Hitherto he has handled the Corinthians mildly, because he knew that they were much too sensitive. Now, however, after preparing their minds for receiving correction, acting the part of a good and skilful surgeon, who soothes the wound when about to apply a painful remedy, he begins to handle them with more severity. Even here, however, as we shall still farther see, he uses great moderation. The sum is this: " It is my

[1] " La mort et perdition;"—" Death and perdition."
[2] " Et en une mesme volonte," ou " et mesme avis;"—" And in the same disposition," or " and the same judgment."
[3] " Et ie di ceci," ou " Or ce que ie di *c'est* qu'un chacun;"—" And this I say," or, " Now what I say *is this*, that every one."

hope that the Lord has not in vain conferred upon you so many gifts, so as not to have it in view to bring you to salvation, but you ought at the same time to take heed lest graces so distinguished be polluted by your vices. See, then, that you be agreed among yourselves ; and it is not without good reason that I call for agreement among yourselves, for I have been informed that you are in a state of disagreement, amounting even to hostility, and that there are parties and contentions raging among you, by which true unity of faith is torn asunder." As, however, they might not perhaps be sufficiently aroused by mere exhortation, he uses earnest entreaty, for he adjures them, *by the name of Christ*, that, as they loved him, they should aim at promoting harmony.

That ye all speak the same thing. In exhorting them to harmony, he employs three different forms of expression : for, *in the first place*, he requires such agreement among them that all shall have one voice ; *secondly*, he takes away the evil by which unity is broken and torn asunder ; and, *thirdly*, he unfolds the nature of true harmony, which is, that they be agreed among themselves in mind and will. What he has placed *second* is *first in order*,—that we beware of strifes. For from this a *second* thing will naturally follow,—that we be in harmony ; and then at length a *third* thing will follow, which is here mentioned *first*,—that we all speak, as it were, with one mouth ; a thing exceedingly desirable as a fruit of Christian harmony. Let us then observe, that nothing is more inconsistent on the part of Christians than to be at variance among themselves, for it is the main article of our religion that we be in harmony among ourselves ; and farther, on such agreement the safety of the Church rests and is dependent.

But let us see what he requires as to Christian unity. If any one is desirous of nice distinctions—he would have them *first of all* joined together in one mind ; *secondly*, in one judgment ; and, *thirdly*, he would have them declare in words that agreement. As, however, my rendering differs somewhat from that of Erasmus, I would, in passing, call my readers to observe, that Paul here makes use of a participle, which denotes things that are *fitly and suitably joined together.*[1] For the verb καταρτιζεσθαι itself (from which the participle κατηρτισμένος comes) properly signifies, to be *fitted* and *adjusted*, just as the members of the human body are connected together by a most admirable symmetry.[2]

For *sententia* (judgment) Paul has γνώμην : but I understand it here as denoting the will, so that there is a complete division of the soul, and the *first* clause refers to faith, the *second* to love.   Then only will there be Christian unity among us, when there is not merely a good agreement as to doctrine, but we are also in harmony in our affections and dispositions, and are thus in all respects of one mind.   Thus Luke bears witness to believers in the primitive Church, (Acts ii. 46,) that they had "one heart and one soul."   And without doubt this will be found wherever the Spirit of Christ reigns.   When, however, he exhorts them to speak the same thing, he intimates still more fully from the effect, how complete the agreement ought to be—so that no diversity may appear even in words.   It is difficult, indeed, of attainment, but still it is necessary among Christians, from whom there is required not merely one faith, but also one confession.

11. *It has been declared.*   As general observations have usually little effect, he intimates, that what he had said was more particularly applicable to them.   The application, therefore, is designed with the view of leading the Corinthians to perceive, that it was not without good reason that

---

[1] " Et assemblés l'une à l'autre ;"—" And associated with each other."

[2] The verb καταρτιζω properly signifies, *to repair*, or *refit*, or *restore* to its original condition what has been disarranged or broken ; and in this sense it is applied to the repairing of nets, ships, walls, &c. (See Matt. iv. 21 ; Mark i. 19.)   We might with perfect propriety understand the Apostle as alluding here to the *repairing* of a ship that has been broken or damaged, and as intimating that a Church, when shattered by divisions, is (so to speak) not sea-worthy, and must be carefully *repaired*, before she can be fit for purposes of commerce, by conveying to the nations of the earth the " true riches."   The allusion, however, most probably is, as CALVIN thinks, to the members of the human body, which are so admirably *adjusted* to each other.   It deserves to be noticed, that Paul makes use of a derivative from the same verb (κατάρτισις) in 2 Cor. xiii. 9, on which Beza observes, " that the Apostle's meaning is, that whereas the members of the Church were all (as it were) dislocated and out of joint, they should now again be joined together in love, and they should endeavour to make perfect what was amiss amongst them either in faith or manners."—*Ed*

Paul had made mention of harmony. For he shows that they had not merely turned aside from a holy unity,[1] but had even fallen into contentions, which are worse[2] than jarrings of sentiment. And that he may not be charged with believing too readily what was said,[3] as though he lightly lent his ear to false accusations, he speaks with commendation of his informants, who must have been in the highest esteem, as he did not hesitate to adduce them as competent witnesses against an entire Church. It is not indeed altogether certain, whether *Chloe* is the name of a place or of a woman, but to me it appears more probable that it is the name of a woman.[4] I am of opinion, therefore, that it was a well-regulated household that acquainted Paul with the distempered condition of the Corinthian Church, being desirous that it might be remedied by him. The idea entertained by many, in accordance with Chrysostom's view, that he refrained from mentioning names, lest he should bring odium upon them, appears to me to be absurd. For he does not say that some of the household had reported this to him, but, on the contrary, makes mention of them all, and there is no doubt that they would willingly have allowed

---

[1] " La sancte union qui doit estre entre les Chrestiens ;"—" That holy unity which ought to be among Christians."

[2] " Bien plus dangereuses ;"—" Much more dangerous."

[3] It is remarked by Beza that the verb here employed, δηλοω, (to *declare*,) has a stronger signification than σημαινω, (to *intimate*,) just as there is a difference of meaning between the Latin words *declarare* (to *declare*) and *significare* (to *intimate*,) an example of which is furnished in a letter of Cicero to Lucretius, " tibi non *significandum* solum, sed etiam *declarandum* arbitror, nihil mihi esse potuisse tuis literis gratius ;" " I think it ought to be not merely *intimated* to you but *declared*, that nothing could be more agreeable to me than your letters." The emphatic word εδηλωθη, (it has been *declared*,) appears to have been made use of by the Apostle to convey more fully to the mind of the Corinthians, that he had not hastily given heed to a mere *report.—Ed.*

[4] Some have thought that by τῶν Χλόης, (those of Chloe,) the Apostle means persons who were in a *flourishing* condition in religion ; from χλόη, green herbage, (Herodotus, iv. 34, Euripides, Hipp. 1124.) One writer supposes Paul to mean *seniores*, (elders,) deriving the word χλόη from כלה, old age. These conjectures, however, are manifestly more ingenious than solid. It is certain that the name Χλόη, (Chloe,) was frequent among the Greeks as the name of a female. It is most natural to understand by των Χλόης, those of Chloe, as equivalent to των Χλόης οικτιων—*those of the household of Chloe.—Ed.*

their names to be made use of.   Farther, that he might not
exasperate their minds by undue severity, he has modified
the reproof by an engaging form of address ; not as though
he would make light of the distemper, but with the view of
bringing them to a more teachable spirit, for perceiving the
severity of the malady.

12. *I say then*, &c.   Some think there is here an instance
of μιμησις, *imitation*, as if Paul were here repeating their
expressions.   Now, although the manuscripts differ as to the
particle ὅτι, I am of opinion that it is the conjunction (*because*) rather than the relative (*which*), so that there is simply
an explanation of the preceding statement in this sense :
" My reason for saying that there are contentions among you
is, because every one of you glories in the name of some individual."   It will, however, be objected, that in these words
there is no appearance as yet of contention.   My answer is,
that where there are jarrings in religion, it cannot but be
that men's minds will soon afterwards burst forth in open
strife.   For as nothing is more effectual for uniting us, and
there is nothing that tends more to draw our minds together,
and keep them in a state of peace, than agreement in religion, so, on the other hand, if any disagreement has arisen
as to matters of this nature, the effect necessarily is, that
men's minds are straightway stirred up for combat, and in
no other department are there more fierce contendings.[1]
Hence it is with good reason that Paul brings it forward as
a sufficient evidence of contention, that the Corinthians were
infested with sects and parties.

I am of Paul.   He makes mention here of Christ's faithful servants—Apollos, who had been his successor at Corinth,
and Peter himself too, and then adds himself to their number, that he may appear to plead not so much his own cause
as that of Christ.   In any other point of view it is not likely
that there were any parties that espoused the separate interests of ministers joined together by a sacred agreement.[2]

---

[1] " Et n'y a en chose quelconque debats si grans ni tant à craindre que
sont ceux-là ;"—" And in no department are there disputes so great, or so
much to be dreaded as those."

[2] " Autrement veu que ces trois estoyent d'un sainct accord ensemble en

He has, however, as he afterwards mentions, transferred to himself and Apollos what was applicable to others ; and this he has done, in order that they might more candidly consider the thing itself, viewing it apart from respect of persons. It will, however, be replied, that he makes mention here even of those who professed that they were *of Christ.* Was this, too, worthy of blame? I answer, that in this way he shows more fully what unseemly consequences result from those depraved affections, when we give ourselves up to men, as in that case Christ must be acknowledged merely in part, and the pious have no alternative left them, but to separate themselves from others, if they would not renounce Christ.

As, however, this passage is wrested in various ways, we must endeavour to ascertain more minutely what Paul intends here. His object is, to maintain Christ's exclusive authority in the Church, so that we may all exercise dependence upon him, that he alone may be recognised among us as Lord and Master, and that the name of no individual be set in opposition to his. Those, therefore, that draw away disciples after them (Acts xx. 30,) with the view of splitting the Church into parties, he condemns as most destructive enemies of our faith. Thus then he does not suffer men to have such pre-eminence in the Church as to usurp Christ's supremacy. He does not allow them to be held in such honour as to derogate even in the slightest degree from Christ's dignity. There is, it is true, a certain degree of honour that is due to Christ's ministers, and they are also themselves masters in their own place, but this exception must always be kept in view, that Christ must have without any infringement what belongs to him—that he shall nevertheless be the sole Master, and looked upon as such. Hence the aim of good ministers is this, that they may all in common serve Christ, and claim for him exclusively power,

leur ministere, il n'est point vray-semblable, qu'il y eust aucunes partialitéz entre les Corinthiens pour se glorifier en l'un plustost qu'en l'autre ;"— " Otherwise, seeing that those three were united in their ministry by a sacred agreement, it is not likely that there were any parties among the Corinthians that were prepared to glory in one of them rather than in another."

authority, and glory—fight under his banner—obey him alone, and bring others in subjection to his sway. If any one is influenced by ambition, that man gathers disciples, not to Christ, but to himself. This then is the fountain of all evils—this the most hurtful of all plagues—this the deadly poison of all Churches, when ministers seek their own interests rather than those of Christ. In short, the unity of the Church consists more especially in this one thing—that we all depend upon Christ alone, and that men thus occupy an inferior place, so as not to detract in any degree from his pre-eminence.

13. *Is Christ divided?* This intolerable evil was consequent upon the divisions that prevailed among the Corinthians : for Christ alone must reign in the Church. And as the object of the gospel is, that we be reconciled to God through him, it is necessary, in the first place, that we should all be bound together in him. As, however, only a very few of the Corinthians, who were in a sounder condition than the others,[1] retained Christ as their Master, (while all made it their boast that they were Christians,) Christ was by this means torn asunder. For we must be one body, if we would be kept together under him as our head. If, on the other hand, we are split asunder into different bodies, we start aside from him also. Hence to glory in his name amidst strifes and parties is to tear him in pieces : which indeed is impossible, for never will he depart from unity and concord, because " He cannot deny himself " (2 Tim. ii. 13.)   Paul, therefore, by setting before them this absurdity, designs to lead the Corinthians to perceive that they are estranged from Christ, inasmuch as they are divided, for *then* only does he reign in us, when we have him as the bond of an inviolably sacred unity.

Was Paul crucified for you? By two powerful considerations, he shows how base a thing[2] it is to rob Christ of the honour of being the sole Head of the Church—the sole Teacher —the sole Master ; or to draw away from him any part of that

---

[1] " Mieux avisez que les autres ;"—" Better advised than the others."
[2] " Combien c'est vne chose insupportable ;"—" How insufferable a thing it is."

honour, with the view of transferring it to men. The *first* is, that we have been redeemed by Christ on this footing, that we are not our own masters. This very argument Paul makes use of in his Epistle to the Romans (xiv. 9,) when he says, " For this end Christ died and rose again, that he might be Lord both of the living and the dead." To him, therefore, let us live and die, because we are always his. Also in this same Epistle (vii. 23,) " Ye are bought with a price : be not ye the servants of men." As the Corinthians, therefore, had been purchased with the blood of Christ, they in a manner renounced the benefit of redemption, when they attached themselves to other leaders. Here is a doctrine that is deserving of special notice—that we are not at liberty to put ourselves under bondage to men,[1] because we are the Lord's heritage. Here, therefore, he accuses the Corinthians of the basest ingratitude, in estranging themselves from that Leader, by whose blood they had been redeemed, however they might have done so unwitingly.

Farther, this passage militates against the wicked contrivance of Papists, by which they attempt to bolster up their system of indulgences. For it is from the blood of Christ and the martyrs[2] that they make up that imaginary treasure of the Church, which they tell us is dealt out by means of indulgences. Thus they pretend that the martyrs by their death merited something for us in the sight of God, that we may seek help from this source for obtaining the pardon of our sins. They will deny, indeed, that they are on that account our redeemers ; but nothing is more manifest than that the one thing follows from the other. The question is as to the reconciling of sinners to God ; the question is as to the obtaining of forgiveness ; the question is as to the appeasing of the Lord's anger ; the question is as to redemp-

---

[1] *Addicere* nos hominibus in servitutem"—" de nous assuiettir aux hommes en seruitude;"—" To give ourselves up to men, so as to be in bondage to them." CALVIN very probably had in his eye the celebrated sentiment of Horace, (Epist. i. 1. 14,) " Nullius *addictus* jurare in verba magistri;"—" Bound to swear allegiance to no master," while enforcing the sentiment by a powerful consideration, to which the heathen poet was an entire stranger.—*Ed.*

[2] " Du sang de Christ, et des martyrs tous ensemble:"—" From the blood of Christ, and of all the martyrs together."

tion from our iniquities. This they boast is accomplished partly by the blood of Christ, and partly by that of the martyrs. They make, therefore, the martyrs partners with Christ in procuring our salvation. Here, however, Paul in strong terms denies that any one but Christ has been crucified for us. The martyrs, it is true, died for our benefit, but (as Leo[1] observes) it was to furnish an example of perseverance, not to procure for us the gift of righteousness.

Or were ye baptized in the name of Paul ? Here we have a *second* argument, which is taken from the profession of baptism ; for we enlist ourselves under the banners of him in whose name we are baptized. We are, accordingly, bound[2] to Christ, in whose name our baptism is celebrated. Hence it follows that the Corinthians are chargeable with perfidy and apostacy, if they place themselves under subjection to men. Observe here that the nature of baptism resembles a contract[3] of mutual obligation ; for as the Lord by that symbol receives us into his household, and introduces us among his people, so we pledge our fidelity to him, that we will never afterwards have any other spiritual Lord. Hence as it is on God's part a covenant of grace that he contracts with us, in which he promises forgiveness of sins and a new life, so on our part it is an oath of spiritual warfare, in which we promise perpetual subjection to him. The former department Paul does not here touch upon, because the sub-

[1] *Leo,* ad Palæstinos, Ep. 81. The passage alluded to above is quoted at large in the *Institutes.* (Vol. ii. p. 238.) " Although the death of many saints was precious in the sight of the Lord, (Ps. cxvi. 15,) yet no innocent man's slaughter was the propitiation of the world. The just *received* crowns, did not *give* them ; and the fortitude of believers produced *examples of patience, not gifts of righteousness ;* for their deaths were for themselves ; and none by his final end paid the debt of another, except Christ our Lord, in whom alone all are crucified, all dead, buried, and raised up." *Leo,* from whose writings this admirable passage is extracted, was a Roman bishop, who flourished in the fifth century, and was one of the most distinguished men of his age. He was a most zealous defender of the doctrines of grace, in opposition to Pelagianism and other heresies. —*Ed.*

[2] " Obligez par serment ;"—" Bound by oath."

[3] " *Syngrapha* (the term employed by CALVIN) was a contract or bond, formally entered into between two parties, signed and sealed by both, and a copy given to each." Cic. Verr. i. 36. Dio. xlviii. 37. It is derived from a Greek term συγγραφὴ (a legal instrument or obligation.) Herodot. i. 48; and Demosth. cclxviii. 13.   π. στιφ.—*Ed.*

ject did not admit of it; but in treating of baptism it ought not to be omitted. Nor does Paul charge the Corinthians with apostacy simply on the ground of their forsaking Christ and betaking themselves to men; but he declares that if they do not adhere to Christ alone—that very thing would make them covenant-breakers.

It is asked, what it is to be *baptized in the name of Christ?* I answer that by this expression it is not simply intimated that baptism is founded on the authority of Christ, but depends also on his influence, and does in a manner consist in it; and, in fine, that the whole effect of it depends on this—that the name of Christ is therein invoked. It is asked farther, why it is that Paul says that the Corinthians were *baptized in the name of Christ*, while Christ himself commanded (Matt. xxviii. 19) the Apostles to baptize in the name of the Father, and of the Son, and of the Holy Spirit. I answer, that in baptism the *first* thing to be considered is, that God the Father, by planting us in his Church in unmerited goodness, receives us by adoption into the number of his sons. *Secondly,* as we cannot have any connection with him except by means of reconciliation, we have need of Christ to restore us to the Father's favour by his blood. *Thirdly,* as we are by baptism consecrated to God, we need also the interposition of the Holy Spirit, whose office it is to make us new creatures. Nay farther, our being washed in the blood of Christ is peculiarly his work; but as we do not obtain the mercy of the Father, or the grace of the Spirit, otherwise than through Christ alone, it is on good grounds that we speak of him as the peculiar object in view in baptism, and more particularly inscribe his name upon baptism. At the same time this does not by any means exclude the name of the Father and of the Spirit; for when we wish to sum up in short compass the efficacy of baptism, we make mention of Christ alone; but when we are disposed to speak with greater minuteness, the name of the Father and that of the Spirit require to be expressly introduced.

14. I thank God that I baptized none of you, but Crispus and Gaius;

14. Gratias ago Deo meo, quod neminem baptizaverim vestrûm, nisi Crispum et Gaium:

15. Lest any should say that I had baptized in mine own name.

16. And I baptized also the household of Stephanas: besides, I know not whether I baptized any other.

17. For Christ sent me not to baptize, but to preach the gospel: not with wisdom of words, lest the cross of Christ should be made of none effect.

18. For the preaching of the cross is to them that perish foolishness; but unto us which are saved it is the power of God.

19. For it is written, I will destroy the wisdom of the wise, and will bring to nothing the understanding of the prudent.

20. Where *is* the wise? where *is* the scribe? where *is* the disputer of this world? hath not God made foolish the wisdom of this world?

15. Ne quis dicat, quod in meum nomen baptizaverim.

16. Baptizavi autem et Stephanæ familiam ; præterea nescio, num quem alium baptizaverim.

17. Non enim misit me Christus ut baptizarem, sed ut evangelizarem : non in sapientia sermonis, ne inanis reddatur crux Christi.

18. Nam sermo crucis iis, qui pereunt, stultitia est; at nobis qui salutem consequimur, potentia Dei est.

19. Scriptum est enim; (Ies. xxix. 14 :) perdam sapientiam sapientum, et intelligentiam intelligentum auferam e medio.

20. Ubi sapiens? ubi scriba? ubi disputator hujus saeculi? nonne infatuavit Deus sapientiam mundi hujus?

14. *I thank my God.* In these words he reproves very sharply the perversity of the Corinthians, which made it necessary for him to avoid, in a manner, a thing so sacred and honourable as that of the administration of baptism. Paul, indeed, would have acted with propriety, and in accordance with the nature of his office, though he had baptized ever so many. He rejoices, however, that it had happened otherwise, and acknowledges it as having been so ordered, in the providence of God, that they might not take occasion from that to glory in him, or that he might not bear any resemblance to those ambitious men who endeavoured in this way to catch followers. But what if he had baptized many? There would have been no harm in it, but (as I have said) there is couched under this a heavy reproach against the Corinthians and their false apostles, inasmuch as a servant of the Lord found occasion to rejoice that he had refrained from a work, otherwise good and commendable, lest it should become an occasion of harm to them.

17. *For Christ sent me not.* He anticipates an objection that might, perhaps, be brought against him—that he had not discharged his duty, inasmuch as Christ commands his Apostles to baptize as well as teach. Accordingly he re-

plies, that this was not the principal department of his office, for the duty of teaching had been principally enjoined upon him as that to which he should apply himself. For when Christ says to the Apostles, (Matt. xxviii. 19, Mark xvi. 15,) *Go, preach and baptize,* he connects baptism with teaching simply as an addition or appendage, so that teaching always holds the first place.

Two things, however, must be noticed here. The *first* is, that the Apostle does not here absolutely deny that he had a command to baptize, for this is applicable to all the Apostles : *Go and baptize ;* and he would have acted rashly in baptizing even *one,* had he not been furnished with authority, but simply points out what was the chief thing in his calling. The *second* thing is, that he does not by any means detract here, as some think, from the dignity or utility of the sacrament. For the question here is, not as to the efficacy of baptism, and Paul does not institute this comparison with the view of detracting in any degree from *that ;* but because it was given to few to teach, while many could baptize ; and farther, as many could be taught at the same time, while baptism could only be administered to individuals successively, one by one, Paul, who excelled in the gift of teaching, applied himself to the work that was more especially needful for him, and left to others what they could more conveniently accomplish. Nay farther, if the reader considers minutely all the circumstances of the case, he will see that there is *irony*[1] tacitly conveyed here, dexterously contrived for making those feel acutely, who, under colour of administering a ceremony, endeavour to catch a little glory at the expense of another's labour. Paul's labours in building up that Church had been incredible. There had come after him certain effeminate masters, who had drawn over followers to their party by the sprinkling of water ;[2] Paul, then, giving up to them the title of honour, declares himself contented with having had the burden.[3]

[1] " Ironie, c'est à dire, mocquerie ;"—" Irony, that is to say, mockery."
[2] " Seulement en les arrousant d'eau : c'est à dire, baptizant ;"—" Simply by sprinkling them with water, that is to say, baptizing."
[3] " Toute la charge et la pesanteur du fardeau ;"—" The whole charge and weight of the burden."

Not with wisdom of words.   There is here an instance of *anticipation,* by which a twofold objection is refuted.   For these pretended teachers might reply that it was ludicrous to hear Paul, who was not endowed with eloquence, making it his boast that the department of teaching had been assigned to him.   Hence he says, by way of concession, that he had not been formed to be an orator,[1] to set himself off by elegance of speech, but a minister of the Spirit, that he might, by plain and homely speech, bring to nothing the wisdom of the world.   Now, lest any one should object that he hunted after glory by his preaching, as much as others did by baptism, he briefly replies, that as the method of teaching that he pursued was the farthest removed from show, and breathed nothing of ambition, it could give no ground of suspicion on that head.   Hence, too, if I mistake not, it may readily be inferred what was the chief ground of the controversy that Paul had with the wicked and unfaithful ministers of the Corinthians.   It was that, being puffed up with ambition, that they might secure for themselves the admiration of the people, they recommended themselves to them by a show of words and mask of human wisdom.

From this main evil two others necessarily followed—that by these disguises (so to speak) the simplicity of the gospel was disfigured, and Christ was, as it were, clothed in a new and foreign garb, so that the pure and unadulterated knowledge of him was not to be found.   Farther, as men's minds were turned aside to neatness and elegance of expression, to ingenious speculations, and to an empty show of superior sublimity of doctrine, the efficacy of the Spirit vanished, and nothing remained but the dead letter.   The majesty of God, as it shines forth in the gospel, was not to be seen, but mere disguise and useless show.   Paul, accordingly, with the view of exposing these corruptions of the gospel, makes a transition here to the manner of his preaching.   This he declares to be right and proper, while at the same time it was diametrically opposed to the ambitious ostentation of those men.[2]   It is as though he had said—" I am well aware

[1] " Vn Rhetoricien ou harangueur ;"—" A Rhetorician, or declaimer."
[2] " Ces vaillans docteurs;"—" Those valiant teachers."

how much your fastidious teachers delight themselves in their high-sounding phrases. As for myself, I do not simply *confess* that my preaching has been conducted in a rude, coarse, and unpolished style, but I even *glory* in it. For it was right that it should be so, and this was the method that was divinely prescribed to me." By the *wisdom of words*, he does not mean λογοδαιδαλία,[1] which is mere empty talk, but true eloquence, which consists in skilful contrivance of subjects, ingenious arrangement, and elegance of expression. He declares that he had nothing of this: nay more, that it was neither suitable to his preaching nor advantageous.

Lest the cross of Christ should be made of none effect. As he had so often previously presented the name of Christ in contrast with the arrogant wisdom of the flesh, so now, with the view of bringing down thereby all its pride and loftiness, he brings forward to view the cross of Christ. For all the wisdom of believers is comprehended in the cross of Christ, and what more contemptible than a cross? Whoever, therefore, would desire to be truly wise in God's account, must of necessity stoop to this abasement of the cross, and this will not be accomplished otherwise than by his first of all renouncing his own judgment and all the wisdom of the world. Paul, however, shows here not merely what sort of persons Christ's disciples ought to be, and what path of learning they ought to pursue, but also what is the method of teaching in Christ's school. " *The cross of Christ* (says he) would have been *made of none effect*, if my preaching had been adorned with eloquence and show." *The cross of Christ* he has put here for the benefit of redemption, which must be sought from Christ crucified. Now the doctrine of the gospel which calls us to this, should savour of the nature of the Cross, so as to be despised and contemptible, rather than glorious, in the eyes of the world. The meaning, therefore, is, that if Paul had made use of philosophical acuteness and studied address in the presence of the

---

[1] The term λογοδαιδαλία properly denotes speech ingeniously contrived. It is compounded of λογος (speech) and Δαιδαλος (Dædalus,) an ingenious artist of Athens, celebrated for his skill in statuary and architecture. Hence everything that was skilfully contrived was called Dædalean. See Lucr. iv. 555, and v. 235 ; Virg. G. iv. 179; and Aen. vii. 282.—*Ed.*

Corinthians, the efficacy of the cross of Christ, in which the salvation of men consists, would have been buried, because it cannot come to us in that way.

Here two questions are proposed : *first*, whether Paul here condemns in every respect *the wisdom of words*, as opposed to Christ ; and *secondly*, whether he means that eloquence and the doctrine of the gospel are invariably opposed, so they cannot agree together, and that the preaching of the gospel is vitiated, if the slightest tincture of eloquence[1] is made use of for adorning it.   To the *first* of these I answer—that it were quite unreasonable to suppose, that Paul would utterly condemn those arts which, it is manifest, are excellent gifts of God, and which serve as instruments, as it were, to assist men in the accomplishment of important purposes.   As for those arts, then, that have nothing of superstition, but contain solid learning,[2] and are founded on just principles, as they are useful and suited to the common transactions of human life, so there can be no doubt that they have come forth from the Holy Spirit ; and the advantage which is derived and experienced from them, ought to be ascribed exclusively to God.   What Paul says here, therefore, ought not to be taken as throwing any disparagement upon the arts, as if they were unfavourable to piety.

The *second* question is somewhat more difficult, for he says, that *the cross of Christ* is *made of none effect* if there be any admixture of *the wisdom of words*.   I answer, that we must consider who they are that Paul here addresses.   The ears of the Corinthians were tickled with a silly fondness for high sounding style.[3]   Hence they needed more than others to be brought back to the abasement of the cross, that they might learn to embrace Christ as he is, unadorned, and the gospel in its simplicity, without any false ornament.   I ac-

---

[1] " Eloquence et rhetorique ;"—" Eloquence and rhetoric."

[2] " Vne bonne erudition, et sçauoir solide ;"—" Good learning, and solid wisdom."

[3] " Les Corinthiens auoyent les oreilles chatouilleuses, et estoyent transportez d'vn fol appetit d'auoir des gens qui eussent vn beau parler ;"— " The Corinthians had *itching ears*, (2 Tim. iv. 3,) and were carried away with a silly eagerness to have persons that had a good manner of address."

knowledge, at the same time, that this sentiment in some respects holds invariably, that *the cross of Christ* is *made of none effect,* not merely by the wisdom of the world, but also by elegance of address.   For the preaching of Christ crucified is simple and unadorned, and hence it ought not to be obscured by false ornaments of speech.   It is the prerogative of the gospel to bring down the wisdom of the world in such a way that, stript of our own understanding, we show ourselves to be simply docile, and do not think or even desire to know anything, but what the Lord himself teaches.   As to the wisdom of the flesh, we shall have occasion to consider more at large ere long, in what respects it is opposed to Christ.   As to eloquence, I shall advert to it here in a few words, in so far as the passage calls for.

We see that God from the beginning ordered matters so, that the gospel should be administered in simplicity, without any aid from eloquence.   Could not he who fashions the tongues of men for eloquence, be himself eloquent if he chose to be so?   While he *could* be so, he did not *choose* to be so. *Why* it was that he did not choose this, I find two reasons more particularly.   The *first* is, that in a plain and unpolished manner of address, the majesty of the truth might shine forth more conspicuously, and the simple efficacy of his Spirit, without external aids, might make its way into the hearts of men.   The *second* is, that he might more effectually try our obedience and docility, and train us at the same time to true humility.   For the Lord admits none into his school but little children.[1]   Hence those alone are capable of heavenly wisdom who, contenting themselves with the preaching of the cross, however contemptible it may be in appearance, feel no desire whatever to have Christ under a mask.   Hence the doctrine of the gospel required to be regulated with this view, that believers should be drawn off from all pride and haughtiness.

But what if any one should at the present day, by discoursing with some degree of elegance, adorn the doctrine of the gospel by eloquence ?   Would he deserve to be on that

---

[1] " Les humbles ;"—" The humble."

account rejected, as though he either polluted it or obscured Christ's glory. I answer in the *first* place, that eloquence is not at all at variance with the simplicity of the gospel, when it does not merely not disdain to give way to it, and be in subjection to it, but also yields service to it, as a handmaid to her mistress. For as Augustine says, " He who gave Peter a fisherman, gave also Cyprian an orator." By this he means, that both are from God, notwithstanding that the one, who is much the superior of the other as to dignity, is utterly devoid of gracefulness of speech ; while the other, who sits at his feet, is distinguished by the fame of his eloquence. That eloquence, therefore, is neither to be condemned nor despised, which has no tendency to lead Christians to be taken up with an outward glitter of words, or intoxicate them with empty delight, or tickle their ears with its tinkling sound, or cover over the cross of Christ with its empty show as with a veil ;[1] but, on the contrary, tends to call us back to the native simplicity of the gospel, tends to exalt the simple preaching of the cross by voluntarily abasing itself, and, in fine, acts the part of a herald[2] to procure a hearing for those fishermen and illiterate persons, who have nothing to recommend them but the energy of the Spirit.

I answer *secondly*, that the Spirit of God, also, has an eloquence of his own, but of such a nature as to shine forth with a native lustre peculiar to itself, or rather (as they say) intrinsic, more than with any adventitious ornaments. Such is the eloquence that the Prophets have, more particularly Isaiah, David, and Solomon. Moses, too, has a sprinkling of it. Nay farther, even in the writings of the Apostles, though they are more unpolished, there are notwithstanding some sparks of it occasionally emitted. Hence the eloquence that is suited to the Spirit of God is of such a nature that it does not swell with empty show, or spend itself in empty sound,

[1] " Ni à offusquer de sa pompe la croix de Christ, comme qui mettroit vne nuée au deuant ;"—" Nor to darken the cross of Christ with its empty show, as if one were drawing a cloud over it."
[2] " Brief, à seruir comme de trompette ;"—" In short, to serve as a trumpet."

but is solid and efficacious, and has more of substance than elegance.

18. *For the preaching of the cross,* &c. In this first clause a concession is made. For as it might very readily be objected, that the gospel is commonly held in contempt, if it be presented in so bare and abject a form, Paul of his own accord concedes this, but when he adds, that it is so in the estimation of *them that perish,* he intimates that no regard must be paid to their judgment. For who would choose to despise the gospel at the expense of *perishing?* This statement, therefore, must be understood in this way: "However the preaching of the cross, as having nothing of human wisdom to recommend it to esteem, is reckoned *foolishness* by *them that perish;* in *our* view, notwithstanding, the wisdom of God clearly shines forth in it." He indirectly reproves, however, the perverted judgment of the Corinthians, who, while they were, through seduction of words, too easily allured by ambitious teachers, regarded with disdain an Apostle who was endowed with *the power of God* for their *salvation,* and that simply because he devoted himself to the preaching of Christ. In what way the preaching of the cross is the power of God unto salvation, we have explained in commenting upon Rom. i. 16.

19. *For it is written,* &c. He shows still farther, from the testimony of Isaiah, how unreasonable a thing it is that the truth of the gospel should be regarded with prejudice on the ground that the wise of this world hold it in contempt, not to say derision. For it is evident from the words of the Prophet, that their opinion is regarded as nothing in the account of God. The passage is taken from Isaiah xxix. 14, where the Lord threatens that he will avenge himself upon the hypocrisy of the people by this kind of punishment, that *wisdom will perish from the wise,* &c. Now the application of this to the subject in hand is this: "It is nothing new or unusual for men to form utterly absurd judgments, who appear in other respects to be distinguished for wisdom. For in this manner the Lord has been wont to punish the arrogance of those who, depending on their own judgment, think to be leaders to themselves and others. In this manner did He,

among the Israelitish people of old, destroy the wisdom of those who were the leaders of the people.   If this happened among a people, whose wisdom the other nations had occasion to admire, what will become of others ?"

It is proper, however, to compare the words of the Prophet with those of Paul, and to examine the whole matter still more closely. The Prophet, indeed, makes use of neuter verbs when he says, *Wisdom will perish and prudence will vanish*, while Paul turns them into the active form, by making them have a reference to God.   They are, however, perfectly the same in meaning.   For this is a great prodigy which God declares he will exhibit, so that all will be filled with astonishment.   *Wisdom*, therefore, *perishes*, but it is by the Lord's destroying it : *wisdom vanishes*, but it is by the Lord's covering it over and effacing it. As to the second term *αθετεῖν*, (which Erasmus renders *reject*,) as it is ambiguous, and is sometimes taken to mean *efface*, or *expunge*, or *obliterate*, I prefer to understand it in this sense here, so as to correspond with the Prophet's word *vanish*, or *be hid*. At the same time, there is another reason that has weighed more with me,[1]—that the word *reject* was not in accordance with the subject, as will appear ere long.   Let us see, then, as to the meaning.

The Prophet's meaning, without doubt, is precisely this, that they would no longer have governors that would rule well, because the Lord will deprive them of sound judgment and intelligence.   For as he elsewhere threatens to send blindness upon the whole nation (Isaiah vi. 10,) so here, upon the leaders ; which is just as though he were plucking the eyes out of the body.   However this may be, a great difficulty arises from the circumstance, that the term *wisdom* or *prudence* was taken by Isaiah in a good sense, while Paul quotes it for an opposite purpose, as though the wisdom of men were condemned by God, as being perverted, and their prudence set aside as being mere vanity.   I confess that it is commonly expounded in this way ; but as it is certain

---

[1] " Combien que j'aye vne raison encore plus valable, qui m'a induit à changer ceste translation ;"—" At the same time, I have a still more forcible reason, which has induced me to alter this translation."

that the oracles of the Holy Spirit are not perverted by the
Apostles to meanings foreign to their real design, I choose
rather to depart from the common opinion of interpreters
than to charge Paul with falsehood. In other respects, too,
the natural meaning of the Prophet's words accords not ill
with Paul's intention ; for if even the wisest become fools,
when the Lord takes away a right spirit, what confidence is
to be placed in the wisdom of men ? Farther, as it is God's
usual way of punishing, to strike blind those who, following
implicitly their own judgment, are wise in their own esteem,
it is not to be wondered if carnal men, when they rise up
against God, with the view of subjecting His eternal truth
to their rashness, are turned into fools, and become vain in
their imaginations. We now see with what appropriateness
Paul makes use of this testimony. Isaiah declares that the
vengeance of God upon all those that served God with their
own inventions would be, that *wisdom would vanish from
their wise men.* Paul, with the view of proving that the
wisdom of this world is vain and worthless, when it exalts
itself against God, adduces this testimony from Isaiah.

20. *Where is the wise ? where is the scribe ?* This expression of triumph is added for the purpose of illustrating the
Prophet's testimony. Paul has not taken this sentiment
from Isaiah, as is commonly thought, but speaks in his own
person. For the passage which they point to (Isaiah xxxiii.
18) has nothing corresponding to the subject in hand, or
nearly approaching to it. For in that passage, while he
promises to the Jews deliverance from the yoke of Senna-
cherib, that he may magnify the more this great blessing
from God, he shows how miserable is the condition of those
that are oppressed by the tyranny of foreigners. He says,
that they are in a constant fever of anxiety, from thinking
themselves beset with scribes or questors, treasurers, and
counters of towers. Nay more, he says, that the Jews were
involved in such difficulties, that they were stirred up to
gratitude by the very remembrance of them.[1] It is a mis-

[1] The passage referred to in Isaiah is happily rendered by Lowth :—
*Thine heart shall reflect on the past terror : Where is now the accomptant ?
where the weigher of tribute ? where is he that numbered the towers ?* The

take, therefore, to suppose that this sentence is taken from the Prophet.[1] The term *world*, ought not to be taken in connection with the last term merely, but also with the other two. Now, by the *wise of this world*, he means those who do not derive their wisdom from illumination by the Spirit through means of the word of God, but, endowed with mere worldly sagacity, rest on the assurance which it affords.

It is generally agreed, that by the term *scribes* is meant teachers. For as סָפַר, *saphar*, among the Hebrews, means to relate or recount, and the noun derived from it, סֵפֶר, *sepher*, is used by them to signify a book or volume, they employ the term סוֹפְרִים, *sopherim*, to denote learned men, and those that are conversant with books ; and, for the same reason, too, *sopher regis* is often used to denote a chancellor or secretary. The Greeks, following the etymology of the Hebrew term, have translated it γραμματεις, *scribes*.[2] He appropriately gives the name of investigators[3] to those that show off their acuteness by starting difficult points and involved questions. Thus in a general way he brings to nothing man's entire intellect, so as to give it no standing in the kingdom of God. Nor is it without good reason that he inveighs so vehemently against the wisdom of men, for it is impossible to express how difficult a thing

last of these expressions Lowth explains to mean, " the commander of the enemy's forces, who surveyed the fortifications of the city, and took an account of the height, strength, and situation of the walls and towers, that he might know where to make the assault with the greatest advantage."—*Ed.*

[1] " The words of Paul, 1 Cor. i. 20, τοῦ σοφός; τοῦ γραμματεύς ; τοῦ συζητητής, κ.τ.λ., are not, as some have imagined, a quotation of the words of this verse," (Isaiah xxxiii. 18 ;) " the only points of agreement between them being merely the occurrence of γραμματεύς, and the repetition of the interrogative τοῦ. It is not impossible, however, that the structure of the one passage may have suggested the other."—*Henderson on Isaiah.*—*Ed.*

[2] The Hebrew phrase referred to occurs in 2 Kings xii. 10. ספר המלך (the king's scribe.) It is rendered by the Septuagint, ὁ γραμματεύς τοῦ βασιλέως. The corresponding Greek term, γραμματεύς, is employed by the classical writers to denote a clerk or secretary, (Demosth. 269. 19.) The γραμματεῖς (notaries) " had the custody of the laws and the public records, which it was their business to write, and to repeat to the people and senate when so required."—*Potter's Grecian Antiquities*, vol. i. p. 10?.—*Ed.*

[3] CALVIN here has manifestly in his eye the original meaning of συζητητης, which is derived from συν and ζητεω (*to inquire together*,) and comes very naturally to mean one that indulges in arguments or disputes. The term was applied to the subtle Sophists, or disputants in the Greek academies.—*Ed.*

it is to eradicate from men's minds a misdirected confidence
in the flesh, that they may not claim for themselves more
than is reasonable.   Now there is more than ought to be, if,
depending even in the slightest degree upon their own wisdom, they venture of themselves to form a judgment.

   Hath not God made foolish, &c.   By *wisdom* here he
means everything that man can comprehend either by the
natural powers of his understanding, or as deriving aid from
practice, from learning, or from a knowledge of the arts.
For he contrasts the wisdom of the world with the wisdom
of the Spirit.   Hence, whatever knowledge a man may come
to have without the illumination of the Holy Spirit, is included in the expression, *the wisdom of this world.*   This
he says God has utterly *made foolish,* that is, He has convicted it of folly.   This you may understand to be effected in
two ways ; for whatever a man knows and understands, is
mere vanity, if it is not grounded in true wisdom ; and it is
in no degree better fitted for the apprehension of spiritual
doctrine than the eye of a blind man is for discriminating
colours.   We must carefully notice these two things—that
a knowledge of all the sciences is mere smoke, where the
heavenly science of Christ is wanting ; and man, with all
his acuteness, is as stupid for obtaining of himself a knowledge of the mysteries of God, as an ass is unqualified for
understanding musical harmonies.   For in this way he
reproves the destructive pride of those who glory in the
wisdom of the world so as to despise Christ, and the entire
doctrine of salvation, thinking themselves happy when they
are taken up with creatures ; and he beats down the arrogance of those who, trusting to their own understanding,
attempt to scale heaven itself.

   There is also a solution furnished at the same time to the
question, how it happens that Paul in this way throws down
upon the ground every kind of knowledge that is apart from
Christ, and tramples, as it were, under foot what is manifestly one of the chief gifts of God in this world.   For what
is more noble than man's reason, in which man excels the
other animals ?   How richly deserving of honour are the
liberal sciences, which polish man, so as to give him the

dignity of true humanity! Besides this, what distinguished and choice fruits they produce! Who would not extol with the highest commendations civil prudence[1] (not to speak of other things,) by which governments, principalities, and kingdoms are maintained? A solution of this question, I say, is opened up to view from the circumstance, that Paul does not expressly condemn either man's natural perspicacity, or wisdom acquired from practice and experience, or cultivation of mind attained by learning; but declares that all this is of no avail for acquiring spiritual wisdom. And, certainly, it is madness for any one, confiding either in his own acuteness, or the assistance of learning, to attempt to fly up to heaven, or, in other words, to judge of the secret mysteries of the kingdom of God,[2] or to break through (Exod. xix. 21) to a discovery of them, for they are hid from human view. Let us, then, take notice, that we must restrict to the specialities of the case in hand what Paul here teaches respecting the vanity of the wisdom of this world—that it rests in the mere elements of the world, and does not reach to heaven. In other respects, too, it holds true, that without Christ sciences in every department are vain, and that the man who knows not God is vain, though he should be conversant with every branch of learning. Nay more, we may affirm this, too, with truth, that these choice gifts of God—expertness of mind, acuteness of judgment, liberal sciences, and acquaintance with languages, are in a manner profaned in every instance in which they fall to the lot of wicked men.

21. For after that in the wisdom of God the world by wisdom knew not God, it pleased God by the foolishness of preaching to save them that believe.

22. For the Jews require a sign, and the Greeks seek after wisdom:

23. But we preach Christ crucified, unto the Jews a stumblingblock, and unto the Greeks foolishness;

21. Quoniam enim in sapientia Dei non cognovit mundus per sapientiam Deum, placuit Deo per stultitiam prædicationis salvos facere credentes.

22. Siquidem et Judaei signum petunt et Graeci sapientiam quærunt.

23. Nos autem prædicamus Christum crucifixum, Judaeis quidem scandalum, Graecis autem stultitiam:

[1] "La prudence civile, c'est à dire la science des lois;"—" Civil prudence, that is to say, the science of laws."

[2] See *Institutes*, vol. i. pp. 323, 324.—*Ed.*

24. But unto them which are called, both Jews and Greeks, Christ the power of God, and the wisdom of God.	24. Ipsis autem vocatis, tam Judaeis, quam Graecis, Christum Dei potentiam, et Dei sapientiam.
25. Because the foolishness of God is wiser than men; and the weakness of God is stronger than men.	25. Nam stultitia Dei sapientior est hominibus, et infirmitas Dei robustior est hominibus.

21. *For since the world knew not.* The right order of things was assuredly this, that man, contemplating the wisdom of God in his works, by the light of the understanding furnished him by nature, might arrive at an acquaintance with him. As, however, this order of things has been reversed through man's depravity, God designs in the first place to make us see ourselves to be fools, before *he makes us wise unto salvation*, (2 Tim. iii. 15;) and secondly, as a token of his wisdom, he presents to us what has some appearance of folly. This inversion of the order of things the ingratitude of mankind deserved. By *the wisdom of God* he means the workmanship of the whole world, which is an illustrious token and clear manifestation of his wisdom: God therefore presents before us in his creatures a bright mirror of his admirable wisdom, so that every one that looks upon the world, and the other works of God, must of necessity break forth in admiration of him, if he has a single spark of sound judgment. If men were guided to a right knowledge of God by the contemplation of his works, they would know God in the exercise of wisdom, or by a natural and proper method of acquiring wisdom; but as the whole world gained nothing in point of instruction from the circumstance, that God had exhibited his wisdom in his creatures, he then resorted to another method for instructing men.[1] Thus it must be reckoned as our own fault, that we do not attain a saving acquaintance with God, before we have been emptied of our own understanding.

He makes a concession when he calls the gospel *the foolishness of preaching*, having that appearance in the view of those foolish sages (μωροσόφοις) who, intoxicated with false

---

[1] The reader will find the same train of thought as above in the *Institutes*, vol. i. p. 396.—*Ed.*

confidence,[1] fear not to subject God's sacred truth to their senseless criticism.   And indeed in another point of view nothing is more absurd in the view of human reason than to hear that God has become mortal—that life has been sub- jected to death—that righteousness has been veiled under the appearance of sin—and that the source of blessing has been made subject to the curse, that by this means men might be redeemed from death, and become partakers of a blessed immortality—that they might obtain life—that, sin being destroyed, righteousness might reign—and that death and the curse might be swallowed up.   We know, neverthe- less, in the meantime, that the gospel is *the hidden wisdom*, (1 Cor. ii. 7,) which in its height surmounts the heavens, and at which angels themselves stand amazed.   Here we have a most beautiful passage, from which we may see how great is the blindness of the human mind, which in the midst of light discerns nothing.   For it is true, that this world is like a theatre, in which the Lord presents to us a clear manifes- tation of his glory, and yet, notwithstanding that we have such a spectacle placed before our eyes, we are stone-blind, not because the manifestation is furnished obscurely, but because we are *alienated in mind*, (Col. i. 21,) and for this matter we lack not merely inclination but ability.   For notwithstanding that God shows himself openly, it is only with the eye of faith that we can behold him, save only that we receive a slight perception of his divinity, sufficient to render us inexcusable.

Accordingly, when Paul here declares that God is not known through means of his creatures, you must understand him to mean that a pure knowledge of him is not attained. For that none may have any pretext for ignorance, mankind make proficiency in the universal school of nature, so far as to be affected with some perception of deity, but what God is, they know not, nay more, they straightway become vain in their imaginations, (Rom. i. 21.)   Thus the light shineth in darkness, (John i. 5.)   It follows, then, that mankind do not err thus far through mere ignorance, so as not to be

---

" Et outrecuidance ;"—" And presumption."

chargeable with contempt, negligence, and ingratitude. Thus it holds good, that all *have known God, and yet have not glorified him*, (Rom. i. 21,) and that, on the other hand, no one under the guidance of mere nature ever made such proficiency as to know God. Should any one bring forward the philosophers as exceptions, I answer, that in them more especially there is presented a signal token of this our weakness. For there will not be found one of them, that has not from that first principle of knowledge, which I have mentioned, straightway turned aside into wandering[1] and erroneous speculations, and for the most part they betray a silliness worse than that of old wives. When he says, that *those are saved that believe*, this corresponds with the foregoing statement—that the gospel is *the power of God unto salvation.* Farther, by contrasting believers, whose number is small, with a blind and senseless world, he teaches us that we err if we stumble at the smallness of their number, inasmuch as they have been divinely set apart to salvation.

22. *For the Jews require a sign.* This is explanatory of the preceding statement—showing in what respects the preaching of the gospel *is accounted foolishness.* At the same time he does not simply explain, but even goes a step farther, by saying that the Jews do not merely despise the gospel, but even abhor it. "The Jews," says he, "desire through means of miracles to have before their eyes an evidence of divine power: the Greeks are fond of what tends to gratify human intellect by the applause of acuteness. We, on the other hand, *preach Christ crucified*, wherein there appears at first view nothing but weakness and folly. He is, therefore, *a stumblingblock to the Jews*, when they see him as it were forsaken by God. To the Greeks it appears like a fable, to be told of such a method of redemption." By the term *Greeks* here, in my opinion, he does not mean simply Gentiles, but has in view those who had the polish of the liberal sciences, or were distinguished by superior intelligence. At the same time by *synecdoche*, all the others come in like manner to be included. Between Jews and

---

[1] "Extrauagantes ;"—"Extravagant."

Greeks, however, he draws this distinction, that the former, striking against Christ by an unreasonable zeal for the law, raged against the gospel with unbounded fury, as hypocrites are wont to do, when contending for their superstitions; while the Greeks, on the other hand, puffed up with pride, regarded him with contempt as insipid.

When he ascribes it to the Jews as a fault, that they are eagerly desirous of signs, it is not on the ground of its being wrong in itself to demand signs, but he exposes their baseness in the following respects :—that by an incessant demand for miracles, they in a manner sought to bind God to their laws —that, in accordance with the dulness of their apprehension, they sought as it were to *feel him out*[1] in manifest miracles —that they were taken up with the miracles themselves, and looked upon them with amazement—and, in fine, that no miracles satisfied them, but instead of this, they every day gaped incessantly for new ones.   Hezekiah is not reproved for having of his own accord allowed himself to be confirmed by a sign, (2 Kings xix. 29, and xx. 8,) nor even Gideon for asking a two-fold sign, (Judges vi. 37, 39.)   Nay, instead of this, Ahaz is condemned for refusing a sign that the Prophet had offered him, (Isaiah vii. 12.)   What fault, then, was there on the part of the Jews in asking miracles?   It lay in this, that they did not ask them for a good end, set no bounds to their desire, and did not make a right use of them.   For while faith ought to be helped by miracles, their only concern was, how long they might persevere in their unbelief.   While it is unlawful to prescribe laws to God, they wantoned with inordinate desire.   While miracles should conduct us to an acquaintance with Christ, and the spiritual grace of God, they served as a hindrance in their way.   On this account, too, Christ upbraids them, (Mark viii. 12.)   *A perverse generation seeketh after a sign.*   For there were no

---

[1] There can be no doubt that CALVIN refers here to an expression made use of by Paul in his discourse to the Athenians, Acts xvii. 27. εἰ ἄρα γε ψηλαφήσειαν αὐτὸν καὶ εὕροιεν, (if haply they may *feel him out* and find him.) The allusion is to a blind man *feeling his way.*   The same word is employed by Plato, (Phœd. § 47, edit. Forster.)   Ὁ δὲ μοι φαίνονται ψηλαφῶντες οἱ πολλοὶ ὥσπερ ἐν σκότει, (In this respect the many seem to me to be *feeling their way* as it were in the dark.)—*Ed.*

bounds to their curiosity and inordinate desire, and for all that they had so often obtained miracles, no advantage appeared to arise from them.

24. *Both Greeks and Jews.* He shows by this contrast, that the fact that Christ was so unfavourably received, was not owing to any fault on his part, nor to the natural disposition of mankind generally, but arose from the depravity of those who were not enlightened by God, inasmuch as the elect of God, whether Jews or Gentiles, are not hindered by any *stumblingblock* from coming to Christ, that they may find in him a sure salvation. He contrasts *power* with the *stumblingblock*, that was occasioned by abasement, and *wisdom* he contrasts with *folly.* The sum, then, is this :—" I am aware that nothing except signs has effect upon the obstinacy of the Jews, and that nothing soothes down the haughtiness of the Greeks, except an empty show of wisdom. We ought, however, to make no account of this ; because, however our Christ in connection with the abasement of his cross is a *stumblingblock* to the Jews, and is derided by the Greeks, he is, notwithstanding, to all the elect, of whatever nation they may be, at once *the power of God unto salvation* for surmounting these *stumblingblocks*, and the *wisdom of God* for throwing off that mask."[1]

25. *For the foolishness of God.* While the Lord deals with us in such a way as to seem to act foolishly, because he does not exhibit his wisdom, what appears *foolishness* surpasses in *wisdom* all the ingenuity of men. Farther, while God appears to act with weakness, in consequence of his concealing his power, that *weakness,* as it is reckoned, is *stronger* than any power of men. We must, however, always keep it in view, that there is a concession, as I have noticed a little ago.[2] For no one can but perceive, that in strict propriety neither foolishness nor weakness can be ascribed to God, but it was necessary, by such ironical expressions, to beat down the mad presumption of the flesh, which does not scruple to rob God of all his glory.

---

[1] " Pour oster et faire esvanoir ceste vaine apparence, et masque de sagesse ;"—" For taking away and causing to vanish, that empty show and mask of wisdom."   [2] See p. 84.

26. For ye see your calling, brethren, how that not many wise men
after the flesh, not many mighty,
not many noble, *are called:*

27. But God hath chosen the
foolish things of the world, to confound the wise : and God hath chosen
the weak things of the world to confound the things which are mighty ;

28. And base things of the world,
and things which are despised, hath
God chosen, *yea*, and things which
are not, to bring to nought things
that are :

29. That no flesh should glory in
his presence.

30. But of him are ye in Christ
Jesus, who of God is made unto us
wisdom, and righteousness, and sanctification, and redemption :

31. That, according as it is written, He that glorieth, let him glory
in the Lord.

26. Videte (*vel, videtis*) vocationem
vestram, fratres, quod non multi[1]
sapientes secundum carnem, non
multi potentes, non multi nobiles :

27. Sed stulta mundi elegit Deus,
ut sapientes pudefaciat: et infirma
mundi elegit Deus, ut patefaciat
fortia :

28. Et ignobilia mundi et con-
tempta elegit Deus, et ea quæ non
erant, ut quæ erant aboleret ;

29. Ne glorietur ulla caro coram
Deo.

30. Ex ipso vos estis[2] in Christo
Jesu, qui factus est nobis sapientia
a Deo, et justitia, et sanctificatio, et
redemptio.[3]

31. Ut (quemadmodum scriptum
est) Qui gloriatur, in Domino glorietur (Jer. ix. 24.)

26. *Behold your calling.* As the mood of the Greek verb
(βλέπετε) is doubtful, and the indicative suits the context
equally as well as the imperative, I leave it to the reader's
choice which of them he may prefer. The meaning is manifestly the same in either case, for supposing it to be the indicative (*ye see,*) he would in that case summon them as
witnesses—as of a thing that is manifest, and call them forward as it were to a thing that is present. On the other
hand, understanding it in the imperative, he stirs them up,
as it were, from their drowsiness to a consideration of the
matter itself. The term *calling* may be taken in a collective
sense to mean the multitude of those that are called—in this
sense : " Ye see what description of persons they are among
you that the Lord has called." I am, however, rather inclined
to think, that he points out the manner of their calling, and
it is a most forcible argument, because it follows from this,
that, if they despise the abasement of the cross, they in a
manner make void their calling, in which God had acted in
such a manner, as to take away all merit from human wis-

[1] " Que vous n'estes point beaucoup ;"—" That you are not many."
[2] " Or c'est de luy que vous estes ;"—" Now it is of him that ye are."
" Redemption, *ou rançon ;*"—" Redemption, *or ransom.*"

dom, and power, and glory. Hence he tacitly accuses them of ingratitude, because, forgetful alike of God's grace and of themselves, they regard the gospel of Christ with disdain.

Two things, however, must be observed here—that he was desirous from the example of the Corinthians to confirm the truth of what he had said : and farther, that he designed to admonish them, that they must be entirely divested of pride, if they duly considered the order of things that the Lord had observed in their calling. *To put to shame*, says he, *the wise and noble*, and *to bring to nought things that are*. Both expressions are appropriate, for fortitude and wisdom vanish when they are *put to shame*, but what has an existence requires to be *brought to nought*. By the choosing of the poor, and the foolish, and the ignoble, he means, that God has preferred them before the great, and the wise, and the noble. For it would not have sufficed, for beating down the arrogance of the flesh, if God had placed them all upon a level. Hence, those who appeared to excel he put in the background, in order that he might thoroughly abase them. That man, however, were an arrant fool, who would infer from this, that God has in this manner abased the glory of the flesh, in order that the great and noble might be shut out from the hope of salvation. There are some foolish persons that make this a pretext for not merely triumphing over the great, as if God had cast them off, but even despising them as far beneath them. Let us, however, bear in mind, that this is said to the Corinthians, who, though they had no great distinction in the world, were nevertheless, even without any occasion, puffed up. God, therefore, by confounding the mighty, and the wise, and the great, does not design to elate with pride the weak, the illiterate, and the abject, but brings down all of them together to one level. Let those, therefore, that are contemptible in the eyes of the world, think thus with themselves : " What modesty is called for on our part, when even those that have high honour in the view of the world have nothing left them ?[1] If the effulgence of the sun is obscured, what must become of the

---

[1] " Dieu ne permet de presumer d'eux mesmes ; "—" God does not allow them to have confidence in themselves."

stars ?   If the light of the stars is extinguished, what must become of opaque objects ?" The design of these observations is, that those who have been called by the Lord, while of no estimation in the view of the world, may not abuse these words of Paul by pluming their crests, but, on the contrary, keeping in mind the exhortation—*Thou standest by faith, be not high-minded, but fear*, (Rom. xi. 20,) may walk thoughtfully in the sight of God with fear and humility.

Paul, however, does not say here, that there are *none* of the noble and mighty that have been called by God, but that there are *few*. He states the design of this—that the Lord might bring down the glory of the flesh, by preferring the contemptible before the great.   God himself, however, by the mouth of David, exhorts kings to embrace Christ,[1] (Ps. ii. 12,) and by the mouth of Paul, too, he declares, that *he will have all men to be saved*, and that his Christ is offered alike to small and great, alike to kings and their subjects, (1 Tim. ii. 1-4.)   He has himself furnished a token of this. Shepherds, in the first place, are called to Christ : then afterwards come philosophers : illiterate and despised fishermen hold the highest rank of honour ; yet into their school there are received in process of time kings and their counsellors, senators and orators.

28. *Things that are not.*   He makes use of similar terms in Rom. iv. 17, but in a different sense.   For in that passage, when describing the universal call of the pious, he says, that we are nothing previously to our being called, which must be understood as referring to reality in the sight of God, however we may appear to be something in the eyes of men.   Here, the *nothingness* (οὐδένεια) of which he speaks must be viewed as referring to the opinion of men, as is manifest from the corresponding clause, in which he says that this is done in order *that the things that are may be brought to nought.*   For there is nothing except in appearance, because in reality we are all nothing.   *Things that are*, therefore, you must explain to mean *things that appear*, so that this passage corresponds with such statements as these :—*He raiseth up the poor out of the dunghill*, (Ps. cxiii. 7.)

---

[1] " A faire hommage à Christ ;"—" To do homage to Christ."

He raiseth up them that are cast down, (Ps. cxlvi. 8,) and the like. Hence we may clearly see how great is the folly of those who imagine that there is in mankind some degree of merit or worthiness, which would hold a place antecedent to God's choice.

29. *That no flesh should glory.* Though the term *flesh* here, and in many passages of Scripture, denotes all mankind, yet in this passage it carries with it a particular idea ; for the Spirit, by speaking of mankind in terms of contempt, beats down their pride, as in Isaiah xxxi. 3—*The Egyptian is flesh and not spirit.* It is a sentiment that is worthy to be kept in remembrance—that there is nothing left us in which we may justly glory. With this view he adds the expression *in God's presence.* For *in the presence of the world* many delight themselves for the moment in a false glorying, which, however, quickly vanishes like smoke. At the same time, by this expression all mankind are put to silence when they come into the presence of God ; as Habakkuk says— *Let all flesh keep silence before God*, (Hab. ii. 20.) Let every thing, therefore, that is at all deserving of praise, be recognised as proceeding from God.

30. *Of him are ye.* Lest they should think that any of those things that he had said were inapplicable to them, he now shows the application of those things to them, inasmuch as *they are* not otherwise than *of God.* For the words *ye are* are emphatic, as though he had said—" You have your beginning from God, who *calleth those things which are not*," (Rom. iv. 17,) passing by those things that appear to be ; and your subsistence is founded upon Christ, and thus you have no occasion to be proud. Nor is it of creation merely that he speaks, but of that spiritual existence, into which we are born again by the grace of God.

Who of God is made unto us. As there are many to be found who, while not avowedly inclined to draw back from God, do nevertheless seek something apart from Christ, as if he alone did not contain all things[1] in himself, he reckons up in passing what and how great are the treasures with

---

[1] " Toute plenitude ;"—" All fulness." (Col. i. 19.)

which Christ is furnished, and in such a way as to intimate at the same time what is the manner of subsistence in Christ. For when he calls Christ our *righteousness*, a corresponding idea must be understood—that *in us* there is nothing but *sin;* and so as to the other terms.   Now he ascribes here to Christ four commendatory titles, that include his entire excellence, and every benefit that we receive from him.

In the *first* place, he says that *he is made unto us wisdom*, by which he means, that we obtain in him an absolute perfection of wisdom, inasmuch as the Father has fully revealed himself to us in him, that we may not desire to know any thing besides him.   There is a similar passage in Col. ii. 3 —*In whom are hid all the treasures of wisdom and know-ledge.*   Of this we shall have occasion to speak afterwards when we come to the next chapter.

Secondly, he says that he is *made unto us righteousness,* by which he means that we are on his account acceptable to God, inasmuch as he expiated our sins by his death, and his obedience is imputed to us for righteousness.   For as the righteousness of faith consists in remission of sins and a gracious acceptance, we obtain both through Christ.

Thirdly, he calls him our *sanctification,* by which he means, that we who are otherwise unholy by nature, are by his Spirit renewed unto holiness, that we may serve God.   From this, also, we infer, that we cannot be justified freely through faith alone without at the same time living holily.   For these fruits of grace are connected together, as it were, by an indissoluble tie,[1] so that he who attempts to sever them does in a manner tear Christ in pieces.   Let therefore the man who seeks to be justified through Christ, by God's un-merited goodness, consider that this cannot be attained without his taking him at the same time for *sanctification,* or, in other words, being renewed to innocence and purity of life.   Those, however, that slander us, as if by preaching a free justification through faith we called men off from good works, are amply refuted from this passage, which intimates

---

[1] The reader will find the same train of thought as above in the *Insti-tutes,* vol. ii. p. 386.—*Ed.*

that faith apprehends in Christ regeneration equally with forgiveness of sins.

Observe, on the other hand, that these two offices of Christ are conjoined in such a manner as to be, notwithstanding, distinguished from each other. What, therefore, Paul here expressly distinguishes, it is not allowable mistakingly to confound.

Fourthly, he teaches us that he is given to us for *redemption,* by which he means, that through his goodness we are delivered at once from all bondage to sin, and from all the misery that flows from it. Thus *redemption* is the first gift of Christ that is begun in us, and the last that is completed. For the commencement of salvation consists in our being drawn out of the labyrinth of sin and death; yet in the meantime, until the final day of the resurrection, *we groan* with desire for *redemption,* (as we read in Rom. viii. 23.) If it is asked in what way Christ is given to us *for redemption,* I answer—" Because he made himself a ransom."

In fine, of all the blessings that are here enumerated we must seek in Christ not the half, or merely a part, but the entire completion. For Paul does not say that he has been given to us by way of filling up, or eking out righteousness, holiness, wisdom, and redemption, but assigns to him exclusively the entire accomplishment of the whole. Now as you will scarcely meet with another passage of Scripture that more distinctly marks out all the offices of Christ, you may also understand from it very clearly the nature and efficacy of faith. For as Christ is the proper object of faith, every one that knows what are the benefits that Christ confers upon us is at the same time taught to understand what faith is.

31. *He that glorieth let him glory in the Lord.* Mark the end that God has in view in bestowing all things upon us in Christ—that we may not claim any merit to ourselves, but may give him all the praise. For God does not despoil with the view of leaving us bare, but forthwith clothes us with his glory—yet on this condition, that whenever we would glory we must go out of ourselves. In short, man, brought to nothing in his own estimation, and acknow-

ledging that there is nothing good anywhere but in God alone, must renounce all desire for his own glory, and with all his might aspire and aim at the glory of God exclusively. This is also more clearly apparent from the context in the writings of the Prophet, from whom Paul has borrowed this testimony ; for in that passage the Lord, after stripping all mankind of glory in respect of strength, wisdom, and riches, commands us to glory only *in knowing him*, (Jer. ix. 23, 24.) Now he would have us know him in such a way as to *know* that it is *he that exercises judgment, righteousness, and mercy.* For this knowledge produces in us at once confidence in him and fear of him. If therefore a man has his mind regulated in such a manner that, claiming no merit to himself, he desires that God alone be exalted ; if he rests with satisfaction on his grace, and places his entire happiness in his fatherly love, and, in fine, is satisfied with God alone, that man *truly* " glories in the Lord." I say *truly*, for even hypocrites on false grounds glory in him, as Paul declares, (Rom. ii. 17,) when being either puffed up with his gifts, or elated with a base confidence in the flesh, or abusing his word, they nevertheless take his name upon them.

CHAPTER II.

1. And I, brethren, when I came to you, came not with excellency of speech or of wisdom, declaring unto you the testimony of God.

2. For I determined not to know any thing among you save Jesus Christ and him crucified.

1. Et ego, quum venissem ad vos, fratres, veni non in excellentia sermonis vel sapientiæ, annuntians vobis testimonium Dei.

2. Non enim eximium duxi, (*vel, duxi pro scientia*,) scire quicquam inter vos,[1] nisi Iesum Christum, et hunc crucifixum.

1. *And I, when I came.* Paul having begun to speak of his own method of teaching, had straightway fallen into a discussion as to the nature of gospel preaching generally.

---

[1] " Car je n'ay point eu en estime de sçauoir aucune chose *ou* rien deliberé de sçauoir entre vous ;"—" I had nothing in esteem as knowledge ; *or*, I determined to know nothing among you."

Now again he returns to speak of himself, to show that nothing in him was despised but what belonged to the nature of the gospel itself, and did in a manner adhere to it. He allows therefore that he had not had any of the aids of human eloquence or wisdom to qualify him for producing any effect, but while he acknowledges himself to be destitute of such resources, he hints at the inference to be drawn from this—that the power of God shone the more illustriously in his ministry, from its standing in no need of such helps. This latter idea, however, he will be found bringing forward shortly afterwards. For the present he simply grants that he has nothing of human wisdom, and in the meantime reserves to himself this much—that he *published the testimony of God.* Some interpreters, indeed, explain the *testimony of God* in a passive sense; but as for myself, I have no doubt that another interpretation is more in accordance with the Apostle's design, so that *the testimony of God* is that which has come forth from God—the doctrine of the gospel, of which he is the author and witness. He now distinguishes between *speech* and *wisdom* (λόγον ἀπὸ τῆς σοφίας.) Hence what I noticed before[1] is here confirmed —that hitherto he has not been speaking of mere empty prattling, but has included the entire training of human learning.

2. *For I did not reckon it desirable.* As κρίνειν, in Greek, has often the same meaning as ἐκλέγειν, that is to choose out anything as precious,[2] there is, I think, no person of sound judgment but will allow that the rendering that I have given is a probable one, provided only the construction admits of it. At the same time, if we render it thus—" No kind of knowledge did I hold in esteem," there will be nothing harsh in this rendering. If you understand something to be supplied, the sentence will run smoothly enough in this way—" No-

[1] CALVIN refers to what he had said when commenting on an expression which occurs in chap. i. 17—*not with wisdom of words.* See p. 73.—*Ed*
[2] Xenophon uses κρινω in the sense of *choosing out,* or *preferring :* in Mem. iv. 4, sec. 16, ουχ ὁπως τους αυτους χορους κρινωσιν οἱ πολιται—" not that the citizens should *prefer* the same dances." See also Menander, p. 230, line 245, edit. Cleric. In the New Testament we find κρινω used in the sense of *esteeming,* in Rom. xiv. 5.—*Ed.*

thing did I value myself upon, as worth my knowing, or on the ground of knowledge." At the same time I do not altogether reject a different interpretation—viewing Paul as declaring that he esteemed nothing as knowledge, or as entitled to be called knowledge, except Christ alone. Thus the Greek preposition αντι, would, as often happens, require to be supplied. But whether the former interpretation is not disapproved of, or whether this latter pleases better, the substance of the passage amounts to this: " As to my wanting the ornaments of speech, and wanting, too, the more elegant refinements of discourse, the reason of this was, that I did not aspire at them, nay rather, I despised them, because there was one thing only that my heart was set upon—that I might preach Christ with simplicity."

In adding the word *crucified,* he does not mean that he preached nothing respecting Christ except the cross; but that, with all the abasement of the cross, he nevertheless preached Christ. It is as though he had said: " The ignominy of the cross will not prevent me from looking up to him[1] from whom salvation comes, or make me ashamed to regard all my wisdom as comprehended in him—in him, I say, whom proud men despise and reject on account of the reproach of the cross." Hence the statement must be explained in this way: " No kind of knowledge was in my view of so much importance as to lead me to desire anything but Christ, *crucified though he was.*" This little clause is added by way of enlargement (αὔξησιν,) with the view of galling so much the more those arrogant masters, by whom Christ was next to despised, as they were eager to gain applause by being renowned for a higher kind of wisdom. Here we have a beautiful passage, from which we learn what it is that faithful ministers ought to teach, what it is that we must, during our whole life, be learning, and in comparison with which everything else must be "counted as dung." (Phil. iii. 8.)

3. And I was with you in weakness, and in fear, and in much trembling.

3. Et ego in infirmitate,[2] et in timore, et in tremore multo fui apud vos:

[1] " Ne fera point que ie n'aye en reuerence et admiration;"—" Will not prevent me from holding in reverence and admiration."
[2] " En infirmité ou foiblesse;"—" In weakness or feebleness."

4. And my speech and my preaching *was* not with enticing words of man's wisdom, but in demonstration of the Spirit and of power:

5. That your faith should not stand in the wisdom of men, but in the power of God.

4. Et sermo meus, et prædicatio mea, non in persuasoriis humanæ sapientiæ sermonibus, sed in demonstratione Spiritus et potentiæ:

5. Ut fides vestra non sit in sapientia hominum, sed in potentia Dei.

3. *And I was with you in weakness.* He explains at greater length what he had previously touched upon—that he had nothing shining or excellent in him in the eyes of men, to raise him to distinction. He concedes, however, to his adversaries what they desired in such a way as to make those very things which, in their opinion, tended to detract from the credit of his ministry, redound to its highest commendation. If he appeared less worthy of esteem from his being so mean and abject according to the flesh, he shows that the power of God shone out the more conspicuously in this, that he could effect so much, while sustained by no human helps. He has in his eye not merely those foolish boasters[1] who aimed at mere show, with the view of obtaining for themselves a name, but the Corinthians, too, who gazed with astonishment on their empty shows. Accordingly a recital of this kind was fitted to have great weight with them. They were aware that Paul had brought nothing with him in respect of the flesh that was fitted to help him forward, or that might enable him to insinuate himself into the favour of men, and yet they had seen the amazing success which the Lord had vouchsafed to his preaching. Nay more, they had in a manner beheld with their own eyes the Spirit of God present in his doctrine. When, therefore, despising his simplicity, they were tickled with a desire for a kind of wisdom, I know not of what sort, more puffed up and more polished, and were captivated with outward appearance, nay, even with adventitious ornament, rather than with the living efficacy of the Spirit, did they not sufficiently discover their ambitious spirit? It is with good reason, therefore, that Paul puts them in mind of his first *entering in among them,* (1 Thess. ii. 1,) that they may not draw back from that divine efficacy, which they once knew by experience.

[1] "Thrasones." The appellation is borrowed from Thraso, a foolish captain in Terence (Eun. iii. 1.)—*Ed.*

The term *weakness* he employs here, and in several instances afterwards, (2 Cor. xi. 30 ; xii. 5, 9, 10,) as including everything that can detract from a person's favour and dignity in the opinion of others. *Fear and trembling* are the effects of that *weakness*. There are, however, two ways in which these two terms may be explained by us. Either we may understand him to mean, that when he pondered the magnitude of the office that he sustained, it was tremblingly, and not without great anxiety, that he occupied himself in it ; or that, being encompassed with many dangers, he was in constant alarm and incessant anxiety. Either meaning suits the context sufficiently well. The second, however, is, in my opinion, the more simple. Such a spirit of modesty, indeed, becomes the servants of the Lord, that, conscious of their own weakness, and looking, on the other hand, at once to the difficulty and the excellence of so arduous an office, they should enter on the discharge of it with reverence and *fear*. For those that intrude themselves confidently, and in a spirit much elated, or who discharge the ministry of the word with an easy mind, as though they were fully equal to the task, are ignorant at once of themselves and of the task.[1]

As, however, Paul here connects *fear* with *weakness*, and as the term *weakness* denotes everything that was fitted to render him contemptible, it follows necessarily that this *fear* must relate to dangers and difficulties. It is certain, however, that this *fear* was of such a nature as did not prevent Paul from engaging in the Lord's work, as facts bear witness. The Lord's servants are neither so senseless as not to perceive impending dangers, nor so devoid of feeling as not to be moved by them. Nay more, it is necessary for them to be seriously afraid on two accounts chiefly— *first*, that, abased in their own eyes, they may learn wholly to lean and rest upon God alone, and *secondly*, that they may be trained to a thorough renunciation of self. Paul, therefore, was not devoid of the influence of *fear*, but that *fear* he controlled in such a manner as to go forward, not-

[1] " Ne cognoissent ni eux ni la chose qu'ils ont entre mains;"—" They know not either themselves or the thing that they have in hand."

withstanding, with intrepidity through the midst of dangers, so as to encounter with undaunted firmness and fortitude all the assaults of Satan and of the world; and, in fine, so as to struggle through every impediment.

4. *And my preaching was not in the persuasive words.* By the *persuasive words of man's wisdom* he means that exquisite oratory which aims and strives rather by artifice than by truth, and also an appearance of refinement, that allures the minds of men. It is not without good reason, too, that he ascribes persuasiveness (το πιθανον)[1] to human wisdom. For the word of the Lord constrains us by its majesty, as if by a violent impulse, to yield obedience to it. Human wisdom, on the other hand, has her allurements, by which she insinuates herself[2] and her blandishments, as it were, by which she may conciliate for herself the affections of her hearers. With this he contrasts the *demonstration of the Spirit and of power,* which most interpreters consider as restricted to miracles; but I take it in a more general sense, as meaning the hand of God powerfully exercised in every way through the instrumentality of the Apostle. *Spirit and power* he seems to have made use of by hypallage,[3] (καθ᾽ ὑπαλλαγὴν,) to denote *spiritual power,* or at least with the view of showing by signs and effects in what manner the presence of the Spirit had shown itself in his ministry. He appropriately, too, makes use of the term ἀποδείξεως, *(demonstration;)* for such is our dulness in contemplating the works of God, that when he makes use of inferior instruments, they serve as so many veils to hide

---

[1] This passage has largely exercised the ingenuity of critics, from the circumstance that the adjective πειθοῖς, occurring nowhere else in the New Testament, or in any of the writings of classical authors, it is supposed that there has been some corruption of the reading. Some suppose it to be a contraction or corruption of πειθανοις or πιθανοις, and Chrysostom, in one or two instances, when quoting the passage, uses the adjective πιθανοις, while in other cases he has πειθοῖς. It is perhaps in allusion to those instances in which Chrysostom makes use of the adjective πιθανοις, that CALVIN employs the phrase το πιθανον (persuasiveness.) Semler, after adducing various authorities, suggests the following reading:—ἐν πειθοῖ σοφιας, taking πειθοῖ as the dative of ἡ πειθω, (persuasion.) Bloomfield considers πειθοῖ to be a highly probable reading, but prefers to retain πειθοῖς.—*Ed.*

[2] " Secrettement et doucement;"—" Secretly and softly."

[3] A figure of speech by which words change their cases with each other. —*Ed.*

from us his influence, so that we do not clearly perceive it. On the other hand, as in the furtherance given to Paul's ministry, there was no aid furnished from the flesh or the world, and as the hand of God was as it were made bare, (Isaiah lii. 10,) his influence was assuredly the more apparent.

5. *That your faith should not be in the wisdom of men.* *To be* is used here as meaning *to consist.* His meaning, then, is, that the Corinthians derived this advantage from his having preached Christ among them without dependence on human wisdom, and relying solely on the Spirit's influence, that their faith was founded not on men but on God. If the Apostle's preaching had rested exclusively on the power of eloquence, it might have been overthrown by superior eloquence, and besides, no one would pronounce that to be solid truth which rests on mere elegance of speech. It may indeed be *helped by it,* but it ought not *to rest upon it.* On the other hand, *that* must have been most powerful which could stand of itself without any foreign aid. Hence it forms a choice commendation of Paul's preaching, that heavenly influence shone forth in it so clearly, that it surmounted so many hindrances, while deriving no assistance from the world. It follows, therefore, that they must not allow themselves to be moved away from his doctrine, which they acknowledge to rest on the authority of God. Paul, however, speaks here of the faith of the Corinthians in such a way as to bring forward this, as a general statement. Let it then be known by us that it is the property of faith to rest upon *God* alone, without depending on *men;* for it requires to have so much certainty to go upon, that it will not fail, even when assailed by all the machinations of hell, but will perseveringly endure and sustain every assault. This cannot be accomplished unless we are fully persuaded that God has spoken to us, and that what we have believed is no mere contrivance of men. While faith ought properly to be founded on the word of God alone, there is at the same time no impropriety in adding this second prop,—that believers recognise the word which they hear as having come forth from God, from the effect of its influence.

6. Howbeit we speak wisdom among them that are perfect: yet not the wisdom of this world, nor of the princes of this world, that come to nought:

7. But we speak the wisdom of God in a mystery, *even* the hidden *wisdom,* which God ordained before the world unto our glory:

8. Which none of the princes of this world knew: for had they known *it,* they would not have crucified the Lord of glory.

9. But, as it is written, Eye hath not seen, nor ear heard, neither have entered into the heart of man, the things which God hath prepared for them that love him.

6. Porro sapientiam loquimur inter perfectos : sapientiam quidem non sæculi hujus, neque principum sæculi hujus, qui abolentur :

7. Sed loquimur sapientiam Dei in mysterio, quæ est recondita : quam præfinivit Deus ante sæcula in gloriam nostram,

8. Quam nemo principum sæculi hujus cognovit : si enim cognovissent, nequaquam Dominum gloriæ crucifixissent.

9. Sed quemadmodum Scriptum est (Ies. lxiv. 4.) " Quæ oculus non vidit, nec auris audivit, nec in cor hominis ascenderunt, quæ præparavit Deus iis, qui ipsum diligunt."

6. *We speak wisdom.* Lest he should appear to despise wisdom, as *unlearned and ignorant men* (Acts iv. 13) contemn learning with a sort of barbarian ferocity, he adds, that he is not devoid of *that* wisdom, which was worthy of the name, but was esteemed as such by none but competent judges. By those that were *perfect,* he means not those that had attained a wisdom that was full and complete, but those who possess a sound and unbiassed judgment. For םת, which is always rendered in the Septuagint by τελειος, means *complete.*[1] He twits, however, in passing, those that had no relish for his preaching, and gives them to understand that it was owing to their own fault : " If my doctrine is disrelished by any of you, those persons give sufficient evidence from that very token, that they possess a depraved and vitiated understanding, inasmuch as it will invariably be acknowledged to be the highest wisdom among men of sound intellect and correct judgment." While Paul's preaching was open to the view of all, it was, nevertheless, not always estimated according to its value, and this is the reason why he appeals to sound and unbiassed judges,[2] who

---

[1] Thus we read, (Gen. xxv. 27,) that Jacob was איש תם, " a *perfect* man," *i. e.* without any manifest blemish. See also Job i. 1, 8. The corresponding word תמים, is frequently applied to the sacrificial victims, to denote their being *without blemish.* Ex. xii. 5 ; Lev. i. 3.—*Ed.*

[2] " Il ne s'en rapporte pas a vn chacvn, mais requiert des iuges entiers ;" —" He does not submit the case to every one, but appeals to competent judges."

would declare that doctrine, which the world accounted insipid, to be true wisdom.   Meanwhile, by the words *we
speak*, he intimates that he set before them an elegant
specimen of admirable wisdom, lest any one should allege
that he boasted of a thing unknown.

Yet not the wisdom of this world.   He again repeats by
way of anticipation what he had already conceded—that the
gospel was not human wisdom, lest any one should object
that there were few supporters of that doctrine ; nay more,
that it was contemned by all that were most distinguished
for intellect.   Hence he acknowledges of his own accord what
might be brought forward by way of objection, but in such
a way as not at all to give up his point.

The princes of this world.   By the *princes of this world*
he means those that have distinction in the world through
means of any endowment, for sometimes there are persons,
who, though they are by no means distinguished by acuteness of intellect, are nevertheless held in admiration from
the dignity of the station which they hold.   That, however,
we may not be alarmed by these imposing appearances, the
Apostle adds, that they *come to nought*, or perish.   For it
were unbefitting, that a thing that is eternal should depend
upon the authority of those who are frail, and fading, and
cannot give perpetuity even to themselves :   " When the
kingdom of God is revealed, let the wisdom of this world
retire, and what is transient give place to what is eternal ;
for the princes of this world have their distinction, but it is
of such a nature as is in one moment extinguished.   What
is this in comparison with the heavenly and incorruptible
kingdom of God ?"

7. *The wisdom of God in a mystery.*   He assigns the
reason why the doctrine of the gospel is not held in high
esteem by the *princes of this world*—because it is involved
in mysteries, and is consequently *hidden*.   For the gospel
so far transcends the perspicacity of human intellect, that
to whatever height those who are accounted men of superior
intellect may raise their view, they never can reach its elevated height, while in the meantime they despise its meanness, as if it were prostrate at their feet.   The consequence is,

that the more proudly they contemn it, they are the farther
from acquaintance with it—nay more, they are removed to
so great a distance as to be prevented from even seeing it.

Which God hath ordained. Paul having said that the
gospel was a *hidden* thing, there was a danger lest believers
should, on hearing this, be appalled by the difficulty, and
retire in despair. Accordingly he meets this danger, and
declares that it had notwithstanding been appointed to us,
that we might enjoy it. Lest any one, I say, should reckon
that he has nothing to do with the *hidden wisdom,* or should
imagine it to be unlawful to direct his eyes towards it, as not
being within the reach of human capacity, he teaches that
it has been communicated to us in accordance with the
eternal counsel of God. At the same time he has something
still farther in view, for by an implied comparison he extols
that grace which has been opened up by Christ's advent, and
distinguishes us above our fathers, who lived under the law.
On this point I have spoken more at large in the end of the
last chapter of the Romans. *First* of all then he argues from
what God had *ordained,* for if God has appointed nothing in
vain, it follows, that we will be no losers by listening to the
gospel which he has appointed for us, for he accommodates
himself to our capacity in addressing us. In accordance with
this Isaiah (xlv. 19) says—" I have not spoken in a lurking
place, or in a dark corner.[1] I have not in vain said to the
seed of Jacob, Seek ye me." *Secondly,* with the view of
rendering the gospel attractive, and alluring us to a desire
of acquaintance with it, he draws an argument still farther
from the design that God had in view in giving it to us—
" *for our glory.*" In this expression, too, he seems to draw
a comparison between us and the fathers, our heavenly
Father not having vouchsafed to them that honour which he
reserved for the advent of his Son.[2]

[1] In allusion, it is generally thought, to the deep and dark caverns from
which the heathen oracles gave forth their responses. Such was the cave
(antrum) of the Cumean Sibyl, described by Virgil, Æn. vi. 42-44, and
also the cavern in the temple of Apollo at Delphi, described by Strabo
(lib. ix.) "φασι δ᾽ ειναι το μαντειον αντρον κοιλον μετα βαθους, ου μαλα ευροστομον;"
—" They say that the oracle is a hollow cavern of considerable depth, but
not at all wide in the opening."—*Ed.*

[2] Locke, in accordance with CALVIN's view, understands Paul as if he

8. *None of the princes of this world knew.*   If you supply
the words *by their own discernment,* the statement would not
be more applicable to them than to the generality of mankind, and the very lowest of the people ; for what are the
attainments of all of us as to this matter, from the greatest
to the least ?   Only we may perhaps say, that *princes,* rather
than others, are charged with blindness and ignorance—for
this reason, that they alone appear in the view of the word
clear-sighted and wise.   At the same time I should prefer to
understand the expression in a more simple way, agreeably
to the common usage of Scripture, which is wont to speak
in terms of universality of those things that happen $\epsilon\pi\iota$ τo
$\pi o\lambda v$, that is *commonly,* and also to make a negative statement in terms of universality, as to those things that happen
only $\epsilon\pi\iota$ $\overset{\text{"}}{\epsilon}\lambda\alpha\tau\tau o\nu$, that is *very seldom.*   In this sense there
were nothing inconsistent with this statement, though there
were found a few men of distinction, and elevated above
others in point of dignity, who were at the same time endowed with the pure knowledge of God.

For had they known.   The wisdom of God shone forth
clearly *in Christ,* and yet *there* the *princes* did not perceive
it ; for those who took the lead in the crucifixion of Christ
were on the one hand the chief men of the Jews, high in
credit for holiness and wisdom ; and on the other hand
Pilate and the Roman empire.   In this we have a most distinct proof of the utter blindness of all that are wise only
according to the flesh.   This argument of the Apostle, however, might appear to be weak.   " What ! do we not every
day see persons who, with deliberate malice, fight against
the truth of God, as to which they are not ignorant ; nay,
even if a rebellion so manifest were not to be seen by us with
our eyes, what else is the sin against the Holy Ghost than a
wilful obstinacy against God, when a man knowingly and
willingly does not merely oppose his word, but even fights
against it.   It is on this account, too, that Christ declares

had said: " Why do you make divisions, by glorying, as you do, in your
distinct teachers ? The glory that God has ordained us (Christian teachers
and professors) to, is to be expounders, preachers, and believers of those
revealed truths and purposes of God, which, though contained in the sacred
Scriptures of the Old Testament, were not understood in former ages."—*Ed.*

that the Pharisees, and others of that description, *knew him*, (John vii. 28,) while he deprives them of all pretext of ignorance, and accuses them of impious cruelty in persecuting him, the faithful servant of the Father, for no other reason but that they hated the truth."

I answer that there are two kinds of ignorance. The *one* arises from inconsiderate zeal, not expressly rejecting what is good, but from having an impression that it is evil. No one, it is true, sins in ignorance in such a way as not to be chargeable meanwhile in the sight of God with an evil conscience, there being always a mixture of hypocrisy, or pride, or contempt; but at the same time judgment, and all intelligence in the mind of man, are sometimes so effectually choked, that nothing but bare ignorance is to be seen by others, or even by the individual himself. Such was Paul before he was enlightened; for the reason why he hated Christ and was hostile to his doctrine was, that he was through ignorance hurried away with a preposterous zeal for the law.[1] Yet he was not devoid of hypocrisy, nor exempt from pride, so as to be free from blame in the sight of God, but those vices were so completely covered over with ignorance and blindness as not to be perceived or felt even by himself.

The *other* kind of ignorance has more of the appearance of insanity and derangement, than of mere ignorance; for those that of their own accord rise up against God, are like persons in a phrensy, who, seeing, see not. (Matth. xiii. 13.) It must be looked upon, indeed, as a settled point, that infidelity is always blind; but the difference lies here, that in some cases malice is covered over with blindness to such a degree that the individual, through a kind of stupidity, is without any perception of his own wickedness. This is the case with those who, with a good intention, as they speak, or in other words, a foolish imagination, impose upon themselves. In some cases malice has the ascendency in such a manner, that in spite of the checks of conscience, the individual rushes forward into wickedness of this sort

[1] " Vne zele de la loy desordonné et mal reglé;"—" An inordinate and ill regulated zeal for the law."

with a kind of madness.[1] Hence it is not to be wondered,
if Paul declares that *the princes of this world would not have
crucified Christ, had they known* the wisdom of God. For
the Pharisees and Scribes did not know Christ's doctrine to
be true, so as not to be bewildered in their mind, and wander on in their own darkness.

9. *As it is written, "What eye hath not seen."* All are
agreed that this passage is taken from Isaiah lxiv. 4, and as
the meaning is at first view plain and easy, interpreters do
not give themselves much trouble in expounding it. On
looking, however, more narrowly into it, two very great difficulties present themselves. The *first* is, that the words that
are here quoted by Paul do not correspond with the words
of the Prophet. The *second* is, that it seems as though Paul
had perverted the Prophet's declaration to a purpose quite
foreign to his design.

First then as to the words ; and as they may be taken in
different senses, they are explained variously by interpreters.
Some render the passage thus : " From the beginning of the
world men have not heard, nor perceived with their ears,
and eye hath not seen any god beside Thee, who doth act in
such a manner towards him that waiteth for him." Others
understand the discourse as addressed to God, in this manner : " Eye hath not seen, nor hath ear heard, O God, besides
thee, the things which thou dost for those that wait for
thee." Literally, however, the Prophet's meaning is : "From
the beginning of the world men have not heard, nor have
they perceived with the ears, hath not seen a god, (or O
God,) besides thee, will do (or will prepare) for him that
waiteth for him." If we understand אלהים (God) to be
in the accusative, the relative *who* must be supplied. This
exposition, too, appears, at first view, to suit better with the
Prophet's context in respect of the verb that follows being
used in the third person ;[2] but it is farther removed from

---

[1] The distinction drawn by CALVIN is illustrated by a statement of Solomon in Prov. xxi. 27. " The sacrifice of the wicked is abomination: how
much more when he bringeth it *with a wicked mind.*" בזמה—" with a
wicked design."—*Ed.*

[2] " Assauoir, Fera, or Preparera ;"—" Namely—*He* will do, or *He* will
prepare."

Paul's meaning, on which we ought to place more dependence than on any other consideration.   For where shall we find a surer or more faithful interpreter than the Spirit of God of this authoritative declaration, which He himself dictated to Isaiah—in the exposition which He has furnished by the mouth of Paul.   With the view of obviating, however, the calumnies of the wicked, I observe that the Hebrew idiom admits of our understanding the Prophet's true meaning to be this : " O God, neither hath eye seen, nor hath ear heard : but thou alone knowest the things which thou art wont to do to those that wait for thee."   The sudden change of person forms no objection, as we know that it is so common in the writings of the Prophets, that it needs not be any hindrance in our way.   If any one, however, prefers the former interpretation, he will have no occasion for charging either us or the Apostle with departing from the simple meaning of the words, for we supply less than they do, as they are under the necessity of adding a mark of comparison to the verb, rendering it thus : " *who* doth act *in such a manner.*"

As to what follows respecting the *entering* of these things *into the heart of man,* though the expression is not made use of by the Prophet, it does not differ materially from the clause *besides thee.*   For in ascribing this knowledge to God alone, he excludes from it not merely the bodily senses of men, but also the entire faculty of the understanding.   While, therefore, the Prophet makes mention only of sight and hearing, he includes at the same time by implication all the faculties of the soul.   And without doubt these are the two instruments by which we attain the knowledge of those things that find their way into the understanding.   In using the expression *them that love him,* he has followed the Greek interpreters, who have translated it in this way from having been misled by the resemblance between one letter and another ;[1] but as that did not affect the point in hand, he did

[1] The word made use of by Isaiah is מחכה, which is a part of the verb חכה, to *wait for,* and CALVIN's meaning most probably is, that the "Greek interpreters" had (from the resemblance between ב and כ) been led into the mistake of supposing it to be a part of the verb חבב, to *love,* while the corresponding part of the latter verb—מחובב, manifestly differs very widely from the word made use of by the Prophet.   There appears, how-

not choose to depart from the common reading, as we frequently have occasion to observe how closely he follows the received version. Though the words, therefore, are not the same, there is no real difference of meaning.

I come now to the subject-matter. The Prophet in that passage, when mentioning how signally God had on all occasions befriended his people in their emergencies, exclaims, that his acts of kindness to the pious surpass the comprehension of human intellect. "But what has this to do," some one will say, "with spiritual doctrine, and the promises of eternal life, as to which Paul is here arguing?" There are three ways in which this question may be answered. There were no inconsistency in affirming that the Prophet, having made mention of earthly blessings, was in consequence of this led on to make a general statement, and even to extol that spiritual blessedness which is laid up in heaven for believers. I prefer, however, to understand him simply as referring to those gifts of God's grace that are daily conferred upon believers. In these it becomes us always to observe their source, and not to confine our views to their present aspect. Now their source is that unmerited goodness of God, by which he has adopted us into the number of his sons. He, therefore, who would estimate these things aright, will not contemplate them in their naked aspect, but will clothe them with God's fatherly love, as with a robe, and will thus be led forward from temporal favours to

ever, to have been an oversight, in this instance, on the part of Calvin, as the word in the Septuagint version is *not* the word made use of by the *Apostle*—ἀγαπῶσιν, "them that love" (him,) but (corresponding to the word made use of by the *Prophet*) ὑπομένουσιν, "them that wait for" (him.) It is not a little singular, that Clemens Romanus (Ep. ad Cor. Sect. xxxiv.) quotes the words of Isaiah precisely as Paul quotes them, with the exception of the last clause, which he gives as follows: ὅσα ἡτοίμασε τοῖς ὑπομένουσιν αὐτὸν—"which he hath prepared for them that *wait for* him." Some have supposed the citation to have been taken from one or other of the two Apocryphal books, entitled, "The Ascension of Esaiah," and "The Apocalyps of Elias," in both of which this passage was found, but, as is justly observed by *Horne* in his *Introduction* (vol. ii. pp. 381, 427,) "it is so near to the Hebrew here both in sense and words, that we cannot suppose it to be taken from any other source, nor in this case would the Apostle have introduced it with the formula of quotation—*as it is written.*" In accordance with Calvin's remark, that "though the words are not the same, there is no real difference of meaning," it is well observed by *Poole* in his *Annotations*, that "*waiting for*" God is "the certain product and effect of *love* to him."—*Ed.*

eternal life. It might also be maintained that the argument is from the less to the greater; for if man's intellect is not competent to measure God's earthly gifts, how much less will it reach the height of heaven? (John iii. 12.) I have, however, already intimated which interpretation I prefer.

10. But God hath revealed *them* unto us by his Spirit: for the Spirit searcheth all things, yea, the deep things of God.

11. For what man knoweth the things of a man, save the spirit of man which is in him? even so the things of God knoweth no man, but the Spirit of God.

12. Now we have received, not the spirit of the world, but the Spirit which is of God; that we might know the things that are freely given to us of God.

13. Which things also we speak, not in the words which man's wisdom teacheth, but which the Holy Ghost teacheth; comparing spiritual things with spiritual.

10. Nobis autem Deus revelavit per Spiritum suum: Spiritus enim omnia scrutatur, etiam profunditates Dei.

11. Quis enim hominum novit, quæ ad eum pertinent, nisi spiritus hominis, qui est in ipso? Ita et quæ Dei sunt, nemo novit, nisi Spiritus Dei.

12. Nos autem non spiritum mundi accepimus, sed Spiritum qui est ex Deo: ut sciamus quæ a Christo donata sunt nobis:

13. Quæ et loquimur, non in eruditis humanæ sapientiæ sermonibus, sed Spiritus sancti, spiritualibus spiritualia coaptantes.

10. *But God hath revealed them to us.* Having shut up all mankind in blindness, and having taken away from the human intellect the power of attaining to a knowledge of God by its own resources, he now shows in what way believers are exempted from this blindness,—by the Lord's honouring them with a special illumination of the Spirit. Hence the greater the bluntness of the human intellect for understanding the mysteries of God, and the greater the uncertainty under which it labours, so much the surer is our faith, which rests for its support on the revelation of God's Spirit. In this, too, we recognise the unbounded goodness of God, who makes our defect contribute to our advantage.

For the Spirit searcheth all things. This is added for the consolation of the pious, that they may rest more securely in the revelation which they have from the Spirit of God, as though he had said: "Let it suffice us to have the Spirit of God as a witness, for there is nothing in God that is too profound for him to reach." For such is the import here of the word *searcheth.* By the *deep things* you must understand—not secret judgments, which we are forbidden to *search into,* but the entire doctrine of salvation, which would have been to no purpose set before us in the Scriptures, were it not that God elevates our minds to it by his Spirit.

11. *For what man knoweth?* Two different things he intends to teach here : *first*, that the doctrine of the Gospel cannot be understood otherwise than by the testimony of the Holy Spirit ; and *secondly*, that those who have a testimony of this nature from the Holy Spirit, have an assurance as firm and solid, as if they felt with their hands what they believe, for the Spirit is a faithful and indubitable witness. This he proves by a similitude drawn from our own *spirit:* for every one is conscious of his own thoughts, and on the other hand what lies hid in any man's heart, is unknown to another. In the same way what is the counsel of God, and what his will, is hid from all mankind, for " who hath been his counsellor ?" (Rom. xi. 34.) It is, therefore, a secret recess, inaccessible to mankind ; but, if the Spirit of God himself introduces us into it, or in other words, makes us acquainted with those things that are otherwise hid from our view, there will then be no more ground for hesitation, for nothing that is in God escapes the notice of the Spirit of God.

This similitude, however, may seem to be not altogether very appropriate, for as the tongue bears an impress of the mind, mankind communicate their dispositions to each other, so that they become acquainted with each other's thoughts. Why then may we not understand from the word of God what is his will? For while mankind by pretences and falsehoods in many cases conceal their thoughts rather than discover them, this cannot happen with God, whose word is undoubted truth, and his genuine and lively image. We must, however, carefully observe how far Paul designed to extend this comparison. A man's innermost thought, of which others are ignorant, is perceived by himself alone : if he afterwards makes it known to others, this does not hinder but that his spirit alone knows what is in him. For it may happen that he does not persuade : it may even happen that he does not properly express his own meaning ; but even if he attains both objects, this statement is not at variance with the other—that his own spirit alone has the true knowledge of it. There is this difference, however, between God's thoughts and those of men, that men mutually understand each other; but the word of God is a kind of *hidden wisdom,* the loftiness of which is not reached by the weakness of the human intellect. Thus the light shineth in darkness, (John i. 5,) aye and until the Spirit opens the eyes of the blind.

The spirit of a man. Observe, that the *spirit of a man* is taken here for the soul, in which the intellectual faculty, as it is called, resides. For Paul would have expressed himself inaccurately if he had ascribed this knowledge to man's intellect, or in other words, the faculty itself, and not to the soul, which is endued with the power of understanding.

12. *Now we have received, not the spirit of the world.* He heightens by contrast the certainty of which he had made mention. "The Spirit of revelation," says he, "which we have received, is not of the world, so as to be merely creeping upon the ground, so as to be subject to vanity, or be in suspense, or vary or fluctuate, or hold us in doubt and perplexity. On the contrary, it is from God, and hence it is above all heavens, of solid and unvarying truth, and placed above all risk of doubt."

It is a passage that is most abundantly clear, for refuting that diabolical doctrine of the Sophists as to a constant hesitancy on the part of believers. For they require all believers to be in doubt, whether they are in the grace of God or not, and allow of no assurance of salvation, but what hangs on moral or probable conjecture. In this, however, they overthrow faith in two respects: for *first* they would have us be in doubt, whether we are in a state of grace, and then afterwards they suggest a *second* occasion of doubt —as to final perseverance.[1] Here, however, the Apostle declares in general terms, that the elect have the Spirit given them, by whose testimony they are assured that they have been adopted to the hope of eternal salvation. Undoubtedly, if they would maintain their doctrine, they must of necessity either take away the Spirit of God from the

---

[1] The reader will find this subject treated of at greater length in the *Institutes,* vol. ii. p. 143.—*Ed.*

elect, or make even the Spirit himself subject to uncertainty. Both of these things are openly at variance with Paul's doctrine. Hence we may know the nature of faith to be this, that conscience has from the Holy Spirit a sure testimony of the good-will of God towards it, so that, resting upon this, it does not hesitate to invoke God as a Father. Thus Paul lifts up our faith above the world, that it may look down with lofty disdain upon all the pride of the flesh ; for otherwise it will be always timid and wavering, because we see how boldly human ingenuity exalts itself, the haughtiness of which requires to be trodden under foot by the sons of God through means of an opposing haughtiness of heroical magnanimity.[1]

That we may know the things that are given us by Christ. The word *know* is made use of to express more fully the assurance of confidence. Let us observe, however, that it is not acquired in a natural way, and is not attained by the mental capacity, but depends entirely on the revelation of the Spirit. The things that he makes mention of as *given by Christ* are the blessings that we obtain through his death and resurrection—that being reconciled to God, and having obtained remission of sins, we know that we have been adopted to the hope of eternal life, and that, being sanctified by the Spirit of regeneration, we are made new creatures, that we may live to God. In Ephes. i. 18, he says what amounts to the same thing—" *That ye may know what is the hope of your calling.*"

13. *Which things also we speak, not in the learned words,* &c. He speaks of himself, for he is still employed in commending his ministry. Now it is a high commendation that he pronounces upon his preaching, when he says of it that it contains a secret revelation of the most important matters —the doctrine of the Holy Spirit, the sum of our salvation, and the inestimable treasures of Christ, that the Corinthians may know how highly it ought to be prized. In the meantime he returns to the concession that he had made before—that his preaching had not been adorned with any

[1] " Fondée en vne magnanimité heroique ;"—" Founded upon a heroical magnanimity."

glitter of words, and had no lustre of elegance, but was contented with the simple doctrine of the Holy Spirit. By *the learned words of human wisdom*[1] he means those that savour of human learning, and are polished according to the rules of the rhetoricians, or blown up with philosophical loftiness, with a view to excite the admiration of the hearers. *The words taught by the Spirit,* on the other hand, are such as are adapted to a pure and simple style, corresponding to the dignity of the Spirit, rather than to an empty ostentation. For in order that eloquence may not be wanting, we must always take care that the wisdom of God be not polluted with any borrowed and profane lustre. Paul's manner of teaching was of such a kind, that the power of the Spirit shone forth in it single and unattired, without any foreign aid.

Spiritual things with spiritual. Συγκρινεσθαι is used here, I have no doubt, in the sense of *adapt.* This is sometimes the meaning of the word,[2] (as Budæus shows by a quotation from Aristotle,) and hence συγκριμα is used to mean what is knit together or glued together, and certainly it suits much better with Paul's context than *compare* or *liken,* as others have rendered it. He says then that he *adapts spiritual things to spiritual,* in accommodating the words to the subject ;[3] that is, he tempers that heavenly wisdom of the Spirit with a simple style of speech, and of such a nature as carries in its front the native energy of the Spirit. In the meantime he reproves others, who, by an affected elegance of expression and show of refinement, endeavour to obtain the applause of men, as persons who are either devoid of

---

[1] " A similar rendering is given in some of the old English versions of the Scriptures. Thus, Wiclif's version, (1380,) it is rendered " not in wise wordis of mannes wisdom :" in Tyndale's version (1534)—" not in the connynge wordes of mannes wysdome :" and in Rheims version (1582)— " not in learned wordes of humane wisedom."—*Ed.*

[2] " Es bons autheurs ;"—" In good authors."

[3] Beza's view is substantially the same—" Verba rei accommodantes, ut, sicut spiritualia sunt quæ docemus, neque sinceritas doctrinæ cælestis ullis humanis commentis est depravata, ita spirituale sit nostrum illius docendæ genus ;"—" Accommodating the words to the subject, so that as the things that we teach are spiritual, and the purity of heavenly doctrine is not corrupted by human contrivances, our mode of teaching it may in like manner be spiritual."—*Ed.*

solid truth, or, by unbecoming ornaments, corrupt the spiritual doctrine of God.

14. But the natural man receiveth not the things of the Spirit of God: for they are foolishness unto him: neither can he know *them*, because they are spiritually discerned.

15. But he that is spiritual judgeth all things, yet himself is judged of no man.

16. For who hath known the mind of the Lord, that he may instruct him? But we have the mind of Christ.

14. Animalis autem homo non comprehendit quæ sunt Spiritus Dei. Sunt enim illi stultitia; nec potest intelligere, quia spiritualiter diiudicantur.

15. Spiritualis autem diiudicat omnia, ipse vero a nemine (*vel, nullo*) diiudicatur.

16. Quis enim cognovit mentem Domini, qui adjuvet ipsum? nos autem mentem Christi habemus.

14. *But the animal man.*[1]   By the *animal man* he does not mean (as is commonly thought) the man that is given up to gross lusts, or, as they say, to his own sensuality, but any man that is endowed with nothing more than the faculties[2] of nature.[3] This appears from the corresponding term, for he draws a comparison between the *animal* man and the *spiritual.* As *the latter* denotes the man whose understanding is regulated by the illumination of the Spirit of God, there can be no doubt that *the former* denotes the man that is left in a purely natural condition, as they speak. For the soul[4] belongs to nature, but the Spirit is of supernatural communication.

He returns to what he had previously touched upon, for his object is to remove a stumblingblock which might stand in the way of the weak—that there were so many that de-

[1] " *Or l'homme naturel.*   A le traduire du Grec mot a mot, il y auroit l'homme animal;"—" *But the natural man.* Rendering the Greek literally it means the animal man."

[2] " Les facultés et graces;"—" The faculties and gifts."

[3] Beza's definition of the term is much similar—" Homo non aliâ quam naturali animi luce præditus;"—"A man that is not endowed with anything more than the natural light of the mind."—*Ed.*

[4] " Anima" " the soul" corresponds to the Greek term ψυχη, and the Hebrew term נפש, while *spiritus* (spirit) corresponds to πνευμα and רוח; but CALVIN employs the epithet *animalis* (*animal*) as a derivative from *anima*, (*the soul*,) and as designating the man whose *soul* is in a purely natural state—without supernatural illumination—in other words, the man of mere *mind.*—*Ed.*

spised the gospel. He shows that we ought to make no account of a contempt of such a nature as proceeds from ignorance, and that it ought, consequently, to be no hindrance in the way of our going forward in the race of faith, unless perhaps we choose to shut our eyes upon the brightness of the sun, because it is not seen by the blind. It would, however, argue great ingratitude in any individual, when God bestows upon him a special favour, to reject it, on the ground of its not being common to all, whereas, on the contrary, its very rareness ought to enhance its value.[1]

For they are foolishness to him, neither can he know them. " The doctrine of the gospel," says he, "is insipid[2] in the view of all that are wise merely in the view of man. But whence comes this ? It is from their own blindness. In what respect, then, does this detract from the majesty of the gospel ?" In short, while ignorant persons depreciate the gospel, because they measure its value by the estimation in which it is held by men, Paul derives an argument from this for extolling more highly its dignity. For he teaches that the reason why it is contemned is that it is unknown, and that the reason why it is unknown is that it is too profound and sublime to be apprehended by the understanding of man. What a superior wisdom[3] this is, which so far transcends all human understanding, that man cannot have so much as a taste of it![4] While, however, Paul here tacitly imputes it to the pride of the flesh, that mankind dare to condemn as foolish what they do not comprehend, he at the same time shows how great is the weakness or rather bluntness of the human understanding, when he declares it to be incapable of spiritual apprehension. For he teaches, that it is not owing simply to the obstinacy of the human will, but to the impotency, also, of the understanding, that man does not attain to the *things of the Spirit.* Had he said that men are not *willing* to be wise, *that* indeed would have been true, but

[1] " D'autant qu'il est fait à peu de gens, d'autant doit-il estre trouué plus excellent ;"—" The fewer it is conferred upon, it ought to be accounted so much the more valuable."

[2] " Et n'auoir point de goust ;"—" And has no relish."

[3] " O quelle sagesse !"—" O what wisdom !"

[4] " Vn petit goust ;"—" A slight taste."

he states farther that they are not *able*.   Hence we infer, that faith is not in one's own power, but is divinely conferred.

Because they are spiritually discerned.   That is, the Spirit of God, from whom the doctrine of the gospel comes, is its only true interpreter, to open it up to us.   Hence in judging of it, men's minds must of necessity be in blindness until they are enlightened by the Spirit of God.[1]   Hence infer, that all mankind are by nature destitute of the Spirit of God : otherwise the argument would be inconclusive.   It is from the Spirit of God, it is true, that we have that feeble spark of reason which we all enjoy ; but at present we are speaking of that special discovery of heavenly wisdom which God vouchsafes to his sons alone.   Hence the more insufferable the ignorance of those who imagine that the gospel is offered to mankind in common in such a way that all indiscriminately are free[2] to embrace salvation by faith.

15. *But the spiritual man judgeth all things.*   Having stript of all authority man's carnal judgment, he now teaches, that *the spiritual* alone are fit judges as to this matter, inasmuch as God is known only by his Spirit, and it is his peculiar province to distinguish between his own things and those of others, to approve of what is his own, and to make void all things else.   The meaning, then, is this : " Away with all the discernment of the flesh as to this matter !   It is *the spiritual man* alone that has such a firm and solid acquaintance with the mysteries of God, as to distinguish without fail between truth and falsehood—between the doctrine of God and the contrivances of man, so as not to fall into mistake.[3]   *He*, on the other hand, *is judged by no man*, because the assurance of faith is not subject to men, as

---

[1] The reader will find the Apostle's statement respecting the "natural man" commented upon at some length in the *Institutes*, vol. i. 323-4.—*Ed*.

[2] CALVIN obviously does not mean to deny that "all indiscriminately" are *invited* and *warranted* to "embrace salvation by faith."   He says in the *Harmony*, vol. iii. p. 109, " For since by his word he [God] *calls all men indiscriminately to* salvation, and since the end of preaching is, that all should betake themselves to his guardianship and protection, it may justly be said that he *wills* to gather all to himself."   His meaning is, that the will requires to be set *free* by the Spirit of God.—*Ed*.

[3] " En cest endroit ;"—" In this matter."

though they could make it totter at their nod,[1] it being superior even to angels themselves." Observe, that this prerogative is not ascribed to the man as an individual, but to the word of God, which *the spiritual* follow in judging, and which is truly dictated to them by God with true discernment. Where *that* is afforded, a man's persuasion[2] is placed beyond the range of human judgment. Observe, farther, the word rendered *judged :* by which the Apostle intimates, that we are not merely enlightened by the Lord to perceive the truth, but are also endowed with a spirit of discrimination, so as not to hang in doubt between truth and falsehood, but are able to determine what we ought to shun and what to follow.

But here it may be asked, who is *the spiritual man,* and where we may find one that is endowed with so much light as to be prepared to *judge of all things,* feeling as we do, that we are at all times encompassed with much ignorance, and are in danger of erring : nay more, even those who come nearest to perfection from time to time fall and bruise themselves. The answer is easy : Paul does not extend this faculty to everything, so as to represent all that are renewed by the Spirit of God as exempt from every kind of error, but simply designs to teach, that the wisdom of the flesh is of no avail for judging of the doctrine of piety, and that this right of judgment and authority belong exclusively to the Spirit of God. In so far, therefore, as any one is regenerated, and according to the measure of grace conferred upon him, does he judge with accuracy and certainty, and no farther.

He himself is judged by no man. I have already explained on what ground he says that *the spiritual man* is not subject to the judgment of any man—because the truth of faith, which depends on God alone, and is grounded on his word, does not stand or fall according to the pleasure of men.[3] What he says afterwards, that *the spirit of one Pro-*

---

[1] " Pour estre ou n'estre point selon qu'il leur plaira ;"—" So as to be or not to be, according as it shall please them."

[2] " Et foy ;"—" And faith."

[3] " N'est point suiete au plaisir des hommes, pour estre ou n'estre point, selon qu'ils voudront ;"—" It is not subject to the pleasure of men, so as to be, or not to be, according as they shall choose."

phet is subject to the other Prophets, (1 Cor. xiv. 32,) is not at all inconsistent with this statement. For what is the design of that subjection, but that each of the Prophets listens to the others, and does not despise or reject their revelations, in order that what is discovered to be the truth of God,[1] may at length remain firm, and be received by all? Here, however, he places the science of faith, which has been received from God,[2] above the height of heaven and earth, in order that it may not be estimated by the judgment of men. At the same time, ὑπ' οὐδενός may be taken in the neuter gender as meaning—*by nothing,* understanding it as referring to a thing, and not to a man. In this way the contrast will be more complete,[3] as intimating that *the spiritual man,* in so far as he is endowed with the Spirit of God, *judgeth all things,* but *is judged by nothing,* because he is not subject to any human wisdom or reason. In this way, too, Paul would exempt the consciences of the pious from all decrees, laws, and censures of men.

16. *For who hath known?* It is probable that Paul had an eye to what we read in the 40th chapter of Isaiah. The Prophet there asks, *Who hath been God's counsellor? Who hath weighed his Spirit,*[4] (Isaiah xl. 13,) or hath aided him both in the creation of the world and in his other works? and, in fine, who hath comprehended the reason of his works? Now, in like manner Paul, by this interrogation, designs to teach, that his secret counsel which is contained in the gospel is far removed from the understanding of men. This then is a confirmation of the preceding statement.

But we have the mind of Christ. It is uncertain whether he speaks of believers universally, or of ministers exclusively. Either of these meanings will suit sufficiently well with the context, though I prefer to view it as referring more parti-

[1] " La pure verité du Seigneur ;"—" The pure truth of the Lord."
[2] " Mais yci il establit et conferme la science de foy, laquelle les eleus recoyuent de Dieu ;"—" But here he establishes and confirms the science of faith, which the elect have received from God."
[3] " Et expresse ;"—" And exact."
[4] The expression made use of by Isaiah is, Who hath *directed* the Spirit of the LORD? Our author, quoting from memory, seems to have had in his eye an expression that occurs in a preceding part of the same passage, " and *weighed* the mountains in scales."—*Ed.*

cularly to himself and other faithful ministers.[1] He says,
then, that the servants of the Lord are taught by the par-
amount authority of the Spirit, what is farthest removed
from the judgment of the flesh, that they may speak fearlessly as from the mouth of the Lord,—which gift flows out
afterwards by degrees to the whole Church.

CHAPTER III.

1. And I, brethren, could not speak unto you as unto spiritual, but as unto carnal, *even* as unto babes in Christ.
2. I have fed you with milk, and not with meat : for hitherto ye were not able *to bear it,* neither yet now are ye able.
3. For ye are yet carnal : for whereas *there is* among you envying, and strife, and divisions, are ye not carnal, and walk as men?

4. For while one saith, I am of Paul; and another, I *am* of Apollos : are ye not carnal ?

1. Et ego, fratres, non potui vobis loqui tanquam spiritualibus, sed tanquam carnalibus, tanquam pueris in Christo.[2]
2. Lactis potu vos alui, non solido cibo. Nondum enim eratis capaces, ac ne nunc quidem estis :

3. Siquidem estis adhuc carnales. Postquam enim sunt inter vos æmulatio et contentio, et factiones; nonne carnales estis, et secundum hominem ambulatis?
4. Quum enim dicat unus, Ego sum Pauli : alter vero, Ego Apollo : nonne carnales estis?

1. *And I, brethren.* He begins to apply to the Corinthians themselves, that he had said respecting carnal persons, that they may understand that the fault was their
own—that the doctrine of the Cross had not more charms
for them. It is probable, that in mercantile minds like

---

[1] CALVIN, when alluding to this passage, as he evidently does in his Commentary on Romans xi. 34, views the expression, *We have the mind of Christ,* as applicable to believers universally—" Nam et Paulus ipse alibi, postquam testatus erat omnia Dei mysteria ingenii nostri captum longe excedere, mox tamen subjicit, fideles tenere mentem Domini : quia non spiritum hujus mundi acceperint, sed a Deo sibi datum, per quem de incomprehensibili alioqui ejus bonitate edocentur;"—" For even Paul himself, in another place, after testifying that all the mysteries of God far exceed the capacity of our understanding, does nevertheless immediately add, that believers are in possession of the Lord's mind, because they have received not the spirit of this world, but that which has been given them by God, whereby they are instructed as to his otherwise incomprehensible goodness."—*Ed.*
[2] " C'est à dire comme à enfans en Christ;"—" That is to say, as to babes in Christ."

theirs there was too much confidence and arrogance still lingering, so that it was not without much ado and great difficulty that they could bring themselves to embrace the simplicity of the gospel.   Hence it was, that undervaluing the Apostle, and the divine efficacy of his preaching, they were more prepared to listen to those teachers that were subtle and showy, while destitute of the Spirit.[1]   Hence, with the view of beating down so much the better their insolence, he declares, that they belong to the company of those who, stupified by carnal sense, are not prepared to receive the spiritual wisdom of God.   He softens down, it is true, the harshness of his reproach by calling them *brethren*, but at the same time he brings it forward expressly as a matter of reproach against them, that their minds were suffocated with the darkness of the flesh to such a degree that it formed a hindrance to his preaching among them. What sort of sound judgment then must they have, when they are not fit and prepared as yet even for hearing ! He does not mean, however, that they were altogether *carnal*, so as to have not one spark of the Spirit of God—but that they had still greatly too much of carnal sense, so that the flesh prevailed over the Spirit, and did as it were drown out his light. Hence, although they were not altogether destitute of grace, yet, as they had more of the flesh than of the Spirit, they are on that account termed *carnal*.   This sufficiently appears from what he immediately adds—that they were *babes in Christ ;* for they would not have been *babes* had they not been begotten, and that begetting is from the Spirit of God.

Babes in Christ.   This term is sometimes taken in a good sense, as it is by Peter, who exhorts us to be like *new-born babes,* (1 Peter ii. 2,) and in that saying of Christ, *Unless ye become as these little children, ye shall not enter into the kingdom of God,* (Luke xviii. 17.)   Here, however, it is taken in a bad sense, as referring to the understanding.   For we must be *children in malice, but not in understanding,* as he says

---

[1] " Combien qu'il n'y eust en eux aucune efficace de l'Esprit;"—"Though there was in them no efficacy of the Spirit."

afterwards in chapter xiv. 20,—a distinction which removes all occasion of doubt as to the meaning. To this also there is a corresponding passage in Ephes. iv. 14. *That we be no longer children tossed to and fro with every wind of doctrine, and made the sport[1] of human fallacies, but may day by day grow up,* &c.

2. *I have fed you with milk.* Here it is asked, whether Paul transformed Christ to suit the diversity of his hearers. I answer, that this refers to the manner and form of his instructions, rather than to the substance of the doctrine. For Christ is at once *milk to babes,* and *strong meat to those that are of full age,* (Heb. v. 13, 14,) the same truth of the gospel is administered to both, but so as to suit their capacity. Hence it is the part of a wise teacher to accommodate himself to the capacity of those whom he has undertaken to instruct, so that in dealing with the weak and ignorant, he begins with first principles, and does not go higher than *they are able to follow,* (Mark iv. 33,) and so that, in short, he drops in his instructions by little and little,[2] lest it should run over, if poured in more abundantly. At the same time, those first principles will contain everything necessary to be known, no less than the farther advanced lessons that are communicated to those that are stronger. On this point read Augustine's 98th homily on John. This tends to refute the specious pretext of some, who, while they do but mutter out, from fear of danger, something of the gospel in an indistinct manner,[3] pretend to have Paul's example here.

---

[1] Our author gives in this, as in many other instances, the substance of the passage quoted rather than the *express words.* In the expression " *made the sport of* human fallacies," he seems to have had in his eye the term κυβμια—rendered by our translators *sleight* (of men,) which, as CALVIN himself remarks when commenting upon the passage, is " translatum ab *aleatoribus,* quod inter eos multæ sint *fallendi* artes ;" borrowed from *players at dice,* there being many arts of *deception* practised among them.— *Ed.*

[2] " Il leur propose la doctrine petit à petit, et par maniere de dire, la face distiller en eux ;"—" He presents instruction to them by little and little, and, so to speak, makes it drop upon them."

[3] " Ne parlans de l'Euangile que quelques mots bien obscurement, et comme entre les dents, pour la crainte qu'ils ont de tomber en quelque danger de leurs personnes ;"—" Speaking merely some words of the gospel very indistinctly, and, as it were, through their teeth, from the fear that they have of incurring some personal danger."

Meanwhile, they present Christ at such a distance, and covered over, besides, with so many disguises, that they constantly keep their followers in destructive ignorance. I shall say nothing of their mixing up many corruptions, their presenting Christ not simply in half, but torn to fragments,[1] their not merely concealing such gross idolatry, but confirming it also by their own example, and, if they have said anything that is good, straightway polluting it with numerous falsehoods.   How unlike they are to Paul is sufficiently manifest; for *milk* is nourishment and not poison, and nourishment that is suitable and useful for bringing up children until they are farther advanced.

For ye were not yet able to bear it.   That they may not flatter themselves too much on their own discernment, he first of all tells them what he had found among them at the beginning, and then adds, what is still more severe, that the same faults remain among them to this day.   For they ought at least, in putting on Christ, to have put off the flesh ; and thus we see that Paul complains that the success which his doctrine ought to have had was impeded.   For if the hearer does not occasion delay by his slowness, it is the part of a good teacher to be always going up higher,[2] till perfection has been attained.

3. *For ye are as yet carnal.*   So long as the flesh, that is to say, natural corruption, prevails in a man, it has so completely possession of the man's mind, that the wisdom of God finds no admittance.   Hence, if we would make proficiency in the Lord's school, we must first of all renounce our own judgment and our own will.   Now, although among the Corinthians some sparks of piety were emitted, they were kept under by being choked.[3]

For since there are among you.   The proof is derived from the effects ; for as *envying, and strifes, and divisions,* are the fruits of the flesh, wherever they are seen, it is certain

---

[1] " Par pieces et morceaux;"—" Into pieces and morsels."

[2] " D'avancer tousiours ses escholiers, et monter plus haut;"—" To be always carrying forward his pupils, and going up higher."

[3] " L'estouffement toutesfois venant de leurs affections perverses, surmontoit;"—" The suffocation, nevertheless, proceeding from their perverse affections, prevailed."

that the root is there in its vigour. Those evils prevailed among the Corinthians; and accordingly he proves from this that they are *carnal*. He makes use of the same argument, too, in Gal. v. 25. *If ye live in the Spirit, walk also in the Spirit.* For while they were desirous to be regarded as spiritual, he calls them to look at their *works*, by which *they denied* what with their mouth they *professed*. (Titus i. 16.) Observe, however, the elegant arrangement that Paul here pursues: for from *envying* spring up *contentions*, and these, when they have once been enkindled, break out into deadly sects: but the mother of all these evils is ambition.

Walk as men. From this it is manifest that the term *flesh* is not restricted to the lower appetites merely, as the Sophists pretend, the seat of which they call sensuality, but is employed to describe man's whole nature. For those that follow the guidance of nature, are not governed by the Spirit of God. These, according to the Apostle's definition, are *carnal*, so that the flesh and man's natural disposition are quite synonymous, and hence it is not without good reason that he elsewhere requires that we be *new creatures in Christ*. (2 Cor. v. 17.)

4. *For while one saith.* He now specifies the particular kind of contentions,[1] and he does this by personating the Corinthians, that his description may have more force—that each one gloried in his particular master, as though *Christ* were not *the one Master of all*. (Matt. xxiii. 8.) Now, where such ambition still prevails, the gospel has little or no success. You are not, however, to understand that they declared this openly in express words, but the Apostle reproves those depraved dispositions to which they were given up. At the same time it is likely, that, as a predilection arising from ambition is usually accompanied with an empty talkativeness,[2] they openly discovered by their words the absurd bias of their mind, by extolling their teachers to the skies in magnificent terms, accompanying

[1] " Qui estoyent entr'eux;"—" Which were among them."
[2] " Cette façon de jetter son cœur sur un homme par ambition, est accompagnée d'un sot babil;"—" This way of setting one's heart upon an individual through ambition, is accompanied with a foolish talkativeness."

this at the same time with contempt of Paul and those like him.

5. Who then is Paul, and who *is* Apollos, but ministers by whom ye believed, even as the Lord gave to every man?

6. I have planted, Apollos watered; but God gave the increase.

7. So then neither is he that planteth any thing, neither he that watereth; but God that giveth the increase.

8. Now he that planteth and he that watereth are one; and every man shall receive his own reward according to his own labour.

9. For we are labourers together with God; ye are God's husbandry, *ye are* God's building.

5. Quis ergo est Paulus, aut quis Apollos, nisi ministri, per quos credidistis, et sicut unicuique Dominus dedit?

6. Ego plantavi, Apollos rigavit; at Deus incrementum dedit.

7. Ergo neque qui plantat aliquid est, neque qui rigat; sed Deus qui dat incrementum.

8. Qui autem plantat, et qui rigat, unum[1] sunt. Porro quisque propriam mercedem secundum laborem suum recipiet.

9. Dei enim cooperarii sumus,[2] Dei agricultura, Dei ædificatio estis.

5. *Who then is Paul?* Here he begins to treat of the estimation in which ministers ought to be held, and the purpose for which they have been set apart by the Lord. He names himself and Apollos rather than others, that he may avoid any appearance of envy.[3] "What else," says he, "are all ministers appointed for, but to bring you to faith through means of their preaching?" From this Paul infers, that no man ought to be gloried in, for faith allows of no glorying except in Christ alone. Hence those that extol men above measure, strip them of their true dignity. For the grand distinction of them all is, that they are ministers of faith, or, in other words, that they gain disciples to Christ, not to themselves. Now, though he appears in this way to depreciate the dignity of ministers, yet he does not assign it a lower place than it ought to hold. For he says much when he says, that we receive faith through their ministry. Nay farther, the efficacy of external doctrine receives here extra-

---

[1] " Sont *vn,* ou *vne chose;*"—" Are *one,* or *one thing.*"

[2] " Car nous sommes ouuriers avec Dieu, ou, nous ensemble sommes ouuriers de Dieu;"—" For we are workers with God, or we are together God's workmen."

[3] " Afin que le propos soit moins odieux, et qu'on ne dise qu'il porte enuie aux autres;"—" That the discourse may be less offensive, and that none may say that he bears envy towards others."

ordinary commendation, when it is spoken of as the instrument of the Holy Spirit; and pastors are honoured with no common title of distinction, when God is said to make use of them as his ministers, for dispensing the inestimable treasure of faith.

As the Lord hath given to every man. In the Greek words used by Paul the particle of comparison ὡς, *as,* is placed after ἑκάστῳ—*to every man;* but the order is inverted.[1] Hence to make the meaning more apparent, I have rendered it "Sicut unicuique,"—"as to every man," rather than "Unicuique sicut,"—"to every man as." In some manuscripts, however, the particle καὶ, *and,* is wanting, and it is all in one connection, thus: *Ministers by whom ye believed as the Lord gave to every man.* If we read it in this way, the latter clause will be added to explain the former,—so that Paul explains what he meant by the term *minister:* "Those are *ministers* whose services God makes use of, not as though they could do anything by their own efforts, but in so far as they are guided by his hand, as instruments." The rendering that I have given, however, is, in my opinion, the more correct one. If we adopt it, the statement will be more complete, for it will consist of two clauses, in this way: In the first place, those are *ministers* who have devoted their services to Christ, that you might believe in him: farther, they have nothing of their own to pride themselves upon, inasmuch as they do nothing of themselves, and have no power to do anything otherwise than by the gift of God, and every man according to his own measure—which shows, that whatever each individual has, is derived from another. In fine, he unites them all together as by a mutual bond, inasmuch as they require each other's assistance.

6. *I have planted, Apollos watered.* He unfolds more clearly the nature of that ministry by a similitude, in which the nature of the word and the use of preaching are most

---

[1] An instance of the same kind occurs in Rom. xii. 3. ἑκάστῳ ὡς ὁ Θεὸς ἐμέρισε μέτρον πίστεως—"as God hath distributed to every one the measure of faith." CALVIN, when commenting on the passage, observes, that it is an instance of "anastrophe, seu vocum inversio, pro *Quemadmodum unicuique;*"—"anastrophe, or inversion of words for *As to every one.*"—*Ed.*

appropriately depicted.   That the earth may bring forth
fruit, there is need of ploughing and sowing, and other means
of culture ; but after all this has been carefully done, the
husbandman's labour would be of no avail, did not the Lord
from heaven *give the increase*, by the breaking forth of the
sun, and still more by his wonderful and secret influence.
Hence, although the diligence of the husbandman is not in
vain, nor the seed that he throws in useless, yet it is only
by the blessing of God that they are made to prosper, for
what is more wonderful than that the seed, after it has
rotted, springs up again !   In like manner, the word of the
Lord is seed that is in its own nature fruitful : ministers are
as it were husbandmen, that plough and sow.   Then follow
other helps, as for example, irrigation.   Ministers, too, act a
corresponding part when, after casting the seed into the
ground, they give help to the earth as much as is in their
power, until it bring forth what it has conceived : but as for
making their labour actually productive, *that* is a miracle of
divine grace—not a work of human industry.

Observe, however, in this passage, how necessary the
preaching of the word is, and how necessary the continuance
of it.[1]   It were, undoubtedly, as easy a thing for God to bless
the earth without diligence on the part of men, so as to
make it bring forth fruit of its own accord, as to draw out,
or rather press out[2] its increase, at the expense of much
assiduity on the part of men, and much sweat and sorrow ;
but as *the Lord hath so ordained* (1 Cor. ix. 14) that man
should labour, and that the earth, on its part, yield a return
to his culture, let us take care to act accordingly.   In like
manner, it were perfectly in the power of God, without the
aid of men, if it so pleased him, to produce faith in persons
while asleep ; but he has appointed it otherwise, so that
faith is produced *by hearing*. (Rom. x. 17.)   That man,
then, who, in the neglect of this means, expects to attain
faith, acts just as if the husbandman, throwing aside the

---

[1] " Combien aussi il est necessaire qu'elle continue et soit tousiours
entretenue ;"—" How necessary it is also, that it continue and be always
kept up."
[2] " Tous les ans ;"—" Every year."

plough, taking no care to sow, and leaving off all the labour of husbandry, were to open his mouth, expecting food to drop into it from heaven.

As to *continuance*[1] we see what Paul says here—that it is not enough that the seed be sown, if it is not brought forward from time to time by new helps. He, then, who has already received the seed, has still need of *watering*, nor must endeavours be left off, until full maturity has been attained, or in other words, till life is ended. Apollos, then, who succeeded Paul in the ministry of the word at Corinth, is said to have *watered* what he had sown.

7. *Neither is he that planteth anything.* It appears, nevertheless, from what has been already said, that their labour is of some importance. We must observe, therefore, why it is that Paul thus depreciates it; and first of all, it is proper to notice that he is accustomed to speak in two different ways of ministers,[2] as well as of sacraments. For in some cases he views a minister as one that has been set apart by the Lord for, in the first instance, regenerating souls, and, afterwards, nourishing them up unto eternal life, for *remitting sins*, (John xx. 23,) for renewing the minds of men, for raising up the kingdom of Christ, and destroying that of Satan. Viewed in that aspect he does not merely assign to him the duty of *planting* and *watering*, but furnishes him, besides, with the efficacy of the Holy Spirit, that his labour may not be in vain. Thus[3] in another passage he calls himself a *minister of the Spirit*, and *not of the letter*, inasmuch as he writes the word of the Lord on men's hearts. (2 Cor. iii. 6.)

In other cases he views a minister as one that is a servant, not a master—an instrument, not the hand; and in short as man, not God. Viewed in that aspect, he leaves him nothing but his labour, and that, too, dead and powerless, if the Lord does not make it efficacious by his Spirit. The

---

[1] Our author refers to what he had, a little before, adverted to, (p. 127,) as to the necessity for the word of God *continuing* to be dispensed.—*Ed.*

[2] CALVIN will be found adverting to the same subject at considerable length, when commenting on 1 Cor. ix. 1.—*Ed.*

[3] " Suyuant ceste consideration ;"—" In accordance with this view."

reason is, that when it is simply the ministry that is treated of, we must have an eye not merely to man, but also to God, working in him by the grace of the Spirit—not as though the grace of the Spirit were invariably tied to the word of man, but because Christ puts forth his power in the ministry which he has instituted, in such a manner that it is made evident, that it was not instituted in vain.   In this manner he does not take away or diminish anything that belongs to Him, with the view of transferring it to man.   For He is not separated from the minister,[1] but on the contrary His power is declared to be efficacious in the minister.   But as we sometimes, in so far as our judgment is depraved, take occasion improperly from this to extol men too highly, we require to distinguish for the purpose of correcting this fault, and we must set the Lord on the one side, and the minister on the other, and then it becomes manifest, how indigent man is in himself, and how utterly devoid of efficacy.

Let it be known by us, therefore, that in this passage ministers are brought into comparison with the Lord, and the reason of this comparison is—that mankind, while estimating grudgingly the grace of God, are too lavish in their commendations of ministers, and in this manner they snatch away what is God's, with the view of transferring it to themselves.   At the same time he always observes a most becoming medium, for when he says, that *God giveth the increase*, he intimates by this, that the efforts of men themselves are not without success.   The case is the same as to the sacraments, as we shall see elsewhere.[2]   Hence, al-

---

[1] " Car en ces façons de parler Christ n'est point separé du ministre;"— " In these modes of expression Christ is not separated (or viewed apart) from the minister."

[2] CALVIN most probably refers here to the statements afterwards made by him, when commenting on Gal. iii. 27, to the following effect : " Respondeo, Paulum de Sacramentis bifariam solere loqui.   Dum negotium est cum hypocritis, qui nudis signis superbiunt, tum concionatur, quam inanis ac nihili res sit externum signum: et in præposteram fiduciam fortiter invehitur.   Quare? non respicit Dei institutionem, sed impiorum corruptelam.   Quum autem fideles alloquitur, qui rite utuntur signis, illa tunc conjungit cum sua veritate, quam figurant.   Quare? neque enim fallacem pompam ostentat in Sacramentis, sed quæ externa ceremonia figurat, exhibet simul re ipsa.   Hinc fit, ut veritas, secundum Dei institutum,

though our heavenly Father does not reject our labour in cultivating his field, and does not allow it to be unproductive, yet he will have its success depend exclusively upon his blessing, that he may have the entire praise. Accordingly, if we are desirous to make any progress in labouring, in striving, in pressing forward, let it be known by us, that we will make no progress, unless he prospers our labours, our strivings, and our assiduity, in order that we may commend ourselves, and everything we do to his grace.

8. *He that planteth, and he that watereth are one.* He shows farther, from another consideration, that the Corinthians are greatly to blame in abusing, with a view to maintain their own sects and parties, the names of their teachers, who in the meantime are, with united efforts, aiming at one and the same thing, and can by no means be separated, or torn asunder, without at the same time leaving off the duties of their office. *They are one,* says he ; in other words, they are so linked together, that their connection does not allow of any separation, because all ought to have one end in view, and they serve one Lord, and are engaged in the same work. Hence, if they employ themselves faithfully in cultivating the Lord's field, they will maintain unity ; and, by mutual communication, will help each other—so far from their names serving as standards to stir up contendings. Here we have a beautiful passage for exhorting ministers to concord. Meanwhile, however, he indirectly reproves those ambitious teachers, who, by giving occasion for contentions, discovered thereby that they were not the servants of Christ,

conjuncta sit cum signis ;"—" I answer, it is customary with Paul to speak of the Sacraments in two different ways. When he has to do with hypocrites, who glory in mere symbols, he in that case proclaims aloud the emptiness and worthlessness of the outward symbol, and denounces in strong terms their absurd confidence. Why so ? It is because he has in view, not the ordinance of God, but the corruption of it by wicked men. When, on the other hand, he addresses believers, who make a proper use of the symbols, he in that case views them in connection with the reality which they represent. Why so ? It is because he does not make a show of any false splendour as belonging to the Sacraments, but presents before our view in reality what the outward ceremony represents. Hence it comes that, agreeably to the divine appointment, the reality is associated with the symbols." The same subject is touched upon in the *Institutes,* vol. iii. p. 305.—*Ed.*

but the slaves of vain-glory—that they did not employ themselves in *planting* and *watering,* but in rooting up and burning.

Every man will receive his own reward.   Here he shows what is the end that all ministers should have in view—not to catch the applause of the multitude, but to please the Lord.   This, too, he does with the view of calling to the judgment-seat of God those ambitious teachers, who were intoxicated with the glory of the world, and thought of nothing else ; and at the same time admonishing the Corinthians, as to the worthlessness of that empty applause which is drawn forth by elegance of expression and vain ostentation.   He at the same time discovers in these words the fearlessness of his conscience, inasmuch as he ventures to look forward to the judgment of God without dismay.   For the reason why ambitious men recommend themselves to the esteem of the world is, that they have not learned to devote themselves to God, and that they do not set before their eyes Christ's heavenly kingdom.   Accordingly, as soon as God comes to be seen, that foolish desire of gaining man's favour disappears.

9. *For we are fellow-labourers with God.*   Here is the best argument.   It is the Lord's work that we are employed in, and it is to him that we have devoted our labours : hence, as he is faithful and just, he will not disappoint us of our reward.   That man, accordingly, is mistaken who looks to men, or depends merely on their remuneration.   Here we have an admirable commendation of the ministry—that while God could accomplish the work entirely himself, he calls us, puny mortals,[1] to be as it were his coadjutors, and makes use of us as instruments.   As to the perversion of this statement by the Papists, for supporting their system of free-will, it is beyond measure silly, for Paul shows here, not what men can effect by their natural powers, but what the Lord accomplishes through means of them by his grace.   As to the exposition given by some—that Paul, being God's workman, was a fellow-workman with his colleagues, that is, with the other teachers—it appears to me harsh and forced, and

---

[1] " Poures vers de terre ;"—" Mere worms of the dust."

there is nothing whatever in the case that shuts us up to have recourse to that refinement. For it corresponds admirably with the Apostle's design to understand him to mean, that, while it is peculiarly the work of God to build his temple, or cultivate his vineyard, he calls forth ministers to be *fellow-labourers*, by means of whom He alone works; but, at the same time, in such a way, that they in their turn labour in common with him. As to the reward of works, consult my *Institutes*.[1]

God's husbandry, God's building. These expressions may be explained in two ways. They may be taken *actively* in this sense: " You have been planted in the Lord's field by the labour of men in such a way, that our heavenly Father himself is the true Husbandman, and the Author of this plantation. You have been built up by men in such a way, that he himself is the true Master-builder.[2] Or, it may be taken in a passive sense, thus: " In labouring to *till* you, and to *sow* the word of God among you and *water* it, we have not done this on our own account, or with a view to advantage to accrue to us, but have devoted our service to the Lord. In our endeavours to *build you up*, we have not been influenced by a view to our own advantage, but with a view to your being God's *planting* and *building*. This latter interpretation I rather prefer, for I am of opinion, that Paul meant here to express the idea, that true ministers labour not for themselves, but for the Lord. Hence it follows, that the Corinthians were greatly to blame in devoting themselves to men,[3] while of right they belonged exclusively to God. And, in the first place, he calls them his *husbandry*, following out the metaphor previously taken up, and then afterwards, with the view of introducing himself to a larger discussion, he makes use of another metaphor, derived from architecture.[4]

---

[1] The subject of *Rewards* is largely treated of in the *Institutes*, vol. ii. pp. 413-427. The reader will find the expression " labourers together with God" commented upon in the *Institutes*, vol. i. p. 392.—*Ed.*

[2] " Et conducteur de l'œuvre ;"—" And conductor of the work."

[3] " De se rendre suiets aux hommes, et attacher là leurs affections ;"— " In making themselves subject to men, and placing their affections there."

[4] " De la massonerie, ou charpenterie ;"—" From masonry, or carpentry."

10. According to the grace of God which is given unto me, as a wise master-builder, I have laid the foundation, and another buildeth thereon. But let every man take heed how he buildeth thereupon.

11. For other foundation can no man lay than that is laid. which is Jesus Christ.

12. Now if any man build upon this foundation gold, silver, precious stones. wood, hay, stubble;

13. Every man's work shall be made manifest: for the day shall declare it, because it shall be revealed by fire; and the fire shall try every man's work of what sort it is.

14. If any man's work abide which he hath built thereupon, he shall receive a reward.

15. If any man's work shall be burnt. he shall suffer loss: but he himself shall be saved; yet so as by fire.

10. Ut sapiens architectus, secundum gratiam Dei mihi datam, fundamentum posui, alius autem superædificat: porro unusquisque videat, quomodo superædificet.

11. Fundamentum enim aliud nemo potest ponere, præter id quod positum est, quod est Iesus Christus.

12. Si quis autem superstruat super fundamentum hoc aurum, argentum, lapides pretiosos, ligna, fœnum, stipulam,

13. Cuiuscunque opus manifestum fiet: dies enim manifestabit, quia in igne revelabitur, et cuiuscunque opus quale sit, ignis probabit.

14. Si cuius opus maneat quod superædificaverit, mercedem accipiet.

15. Si cuius opus arserit, jacturam faciet: ipse autem salvus fiet, sic tamen tanquam per ignem.[1]

10. *As a wise master-builder.* It is a most apt similitude, and accordingly it is frequently met with in the Scriptures, as we shall see ere long. Here, however, the Apostle declares his fidelity with great confidence and fearlessness, as it required to be asserted in opposition not merely to the calumnies of the wicked, but also to the pride of the Corinthians, who had already begun to despise his doctrine. The more, therefore, they lowered him, so much the higher does he raise himself up, and speaking as it were from a pulpit of vast height, he declares[2] that he had been the first *master-builder* of God among them in laying the foundation, and that he had with *wisdom* executed that department of duty, and that it remained that others should go forward in the same manner, regulating the superstructure in conformity with the rule of the foundation. Let us observe that these things are said by Paul *first* of all for the purpose of commending his doctrine, which he saw was despised by the Corinthians ; and, *secondly,* for the purpose of repressing the

[1] " Par feu. ou parmi le feu;"—" By fire, or amidst the fire."

[2] " Il leur fait assavoir, et declare fort et ferme :"—" He gives them to know. and declares strongly and firmly."

insolence of others, who from a desire for distinction, affected a new method of teaching. These he accordingly admonishes to attempt nothing rashly in God's building. Two things he prohibits them from doing: they must not venture to lay another foundation, and they must not raise a superstructure that will not be answerable to the foundation.

According to the grace. He always takes diligent heed not to usurp to himself a single particle of the glory that belongs to God, for he refers all things to God, and leaves nothing to himself, except his having been an instrument. While, however, he thus submits himself humbly to God, he indirectly reproves the arrogance of those who thought nothing of throwing *the grace of God* into the shade,[1] provided only they were themselves held in estimation. He hints, too, that there was nothing of the *grace* of the Spirit in that empty show, for which they were held in esteem, while on the other hand he clears himself from contempt, on the ground of his having been under divine influence.[2]

11. *For other foundation can no man lay.* This statement consists of two parts; *first,* that Christ is the only foundation of the Church; and *secondly,* that the Corinthians had been rightly founded upon Christ through Paul's preaching. For it was necessary that they should be brought back to Christ alone, inasmuch as their ears were tickled with a fondness for novelty. It was, too, of no small importance that Paul should be recognised as the principal, and, so to speak, fundamental *master-builder,* from whose doctrine they could not draw back, without forsaking Christ himself. The sum is this—that the Church must by all means be founded upon Christ alone, and that Paul had executed this department of duty so faithfully that nothing could be found to be wanting in his ministry. Hence, whoever may come after him, can in no other way serve the Lord with a good conscience, or

---

[1] " Ne faisoyent point de conscience d'amoindrir ou offusquer la grace de Dieu;"—" Made no scruple of disparaging or obscuring the grace of God."

[2] " Monstrant, quant à luy qu'il a esté poussé et conduit de Dieu, il se defend et maintient contre tout mepris;"—" Showing, as to himself, that he had been led on and conducted by God, he guards and defends himself against all contempt."

be listened to as ministers of Christ, than by studying to make their doctrine correspond with his, and retain the *foundation* which he has laid. Hence we infer, that those are not faithful workmen for building up the Church, but on the contrary are *scatterers* of it, (Matt. xii. 30,) who succeed faithful ministers, but do not make it their aim to conform themselves to their doctrine, and carry forward what has been well commenced, so as to make it quite manifest[1] that they are attempting no new work. For what can be more pernicious than by a new manner of teaching to harass believers, who have been well instructed in pure doctrine, so that they stagger in uncertainty as to the true foundation. Now the fundamental doctrine, which it were unlawful to undermine, is, that we learn Christ, for Christ is the only *foundation* of the Church; but there are many who, while they make use of Christ's name in pretence, tear up the whole truth of God by the roots.[2]

Let us observe, then, in what way the Church is rightly built upon Christ. It is when he alone is set forth for righteousness, redemption, sanctification, wisdom, satisfaction and cleansing; in short, for life and glory; or if you would have it stated more briefly, when he is proclaimed in such a manner that his office and influence are understood in accordance with what we found stated in the close of the first chapter. (1 Cor. i. 30.) If, on the other hand, Christ is only in some degree acknowledged, and is called a Redeemer only in name, while in the meantime recourse is had to some other quarter for righteousness, sanctification and salvation, he is driven off from the *foundation*, and spurious[3] stones are substituted in his room. It is in this manner that Papists act, who rob him of almost all his ornaments, leaving him scarcely anything but the bare name. Such persons, then, are far from being founded on Christ. For as Christ is the *foundation* of the Church, because he is

[1] " En sorte qu'on puisse voir a l'œil;"—" So that one may see with the eye."

[2] "Arrachent et renversent entierement;"—" They tear up and entirely overthrow "

[3] " Et non convenantes;"—" And not suitable."

the only source of salvation and eternal life—because in him we come to know God the Father—because in him we have the source of every blessing ; if he is not acknowledged as such he is no longer regarded as the *foundation*.

But it is asked—" Is Christ only a part, or simply the commencement of the doctrine of salvation, as the foundation is merely a part of the building ; for if it were so, believers would have only their commencement in Christ, and would be perfected without him. Now this Paul might seem to intimate." I answer that this is not the meaning of the words ; otherwise he would contradict himself when he says elsewhere, that " in him are hid all the treasures of wisdom and knowledge." (Col. ii. 3.) He, then, who has learned Christ, (Eph. iv. 20,) is already complete in the whole system of heavenly doctrine. But as Paul's ministry had contemplated rather the founding of the Corinthians than the raising up among them of the top-stone of the building, he merely shows here what he had done in respect of his having preached Christ in purity. With respect to himself therefore, he calls him the *foundation*, while at the same time he does not thereby exclude him from the rest of the building. In fine, Paul does not put any kind of doctrine in opposition to the knowledge of Christ, but on the contrary there is a comparison between himself and the ministers.

12. *Now if any man build upon this foundation.* He pursues still farther the metaphor. It would not have been enough to have laid the foundation if the entire superstructure did not correspond ; for as it were an absurd thing to raise a structure of vile materials on a foundation of gold, so it were greatly criminal to bury Christ under a mass of strange doctrines.[1] By *gold*, then, and *silver*, and *precious stones*, he means doctrine worthy of Christ, and of such a nature as to be a superstructure corresponding to such a foundation. Let us not imagine, however, that this doctrine is apart from Christ, but on the contrary let us understand that we must continue to preach Christ until the very completion of

[1] " Ce seroit vne chose mal seante que Christ fust suffoqué en mettant et meslant auec luy quelques doctrines estranges ; "—" It were an unseemly thing that Christ should be choked by placing upon him and mixing up with him some strange doctrines."

the building. Only we must observe order, so as to begin with general doctrine, and more essential articles, as the foundations, and then go on to admonitions, exhortations, and everything that is requisite for perseverance, confirmation, and advancement.

As there is an agreement thus far as to Paul's meaning, without any controversy, it follows on the other hand, that by *wood, stubble* and *hay,* is meant doctrine not answering to the foundation, such as is forged in men's brain, and is thrust in upon us as though it were the oracles of God.[1] For God will have his Church trained up by the pure preaching of his own word, not by the contrivances of men, of which sort also is that which has no tendency to edification, as for example curious *questions,* (1 Tim. i. 4,) which commonly contribute more to ostentation, or some foolish appetite, than to the salvation of men.

He forewarns them that *every man's work* will one day *be made manifest of what sort it is,* however it may be for a time concealed, as though he had said: "It may indeed happen, that unprincipled workmen may for a time deceive, so that the world does not perceive how far each one has laboured faithfully or fraudulently, but what is now as it were buried in darkness must of necessity come to light, and what is now glorious in the eyes of men, must before the face of God fall down, and be regarded as worthless."

13. *For the day will declare it.* In the old translation it is *the day of the Lord,*[2] but it is probable that the words *of the Lord* were added by some one by way of explanation. The meaning unquestionably is complete without that addition. For with propriety we give the name of *day* to the time when darkness and obscurity are dispelled, and the truth is brought to light. Hence the Apostle forewarns us, that it cannot always remain a secret who have acted fraudu-

---

[1] " On veut à force faire receuoir pour oracles et reuelations procédées de Dieu;"—" They would force us to receive it as if it were oracles and revelations that have come forth from God."

[2] It is so in two of the old English versions. In Wiclif's version (1380) the rendering is as follows: *For the dai of the Lord schal declare.* The Rheims version (1582) reads thus: *For the day of our Lord will declare.* —*Ed.*

lently in the work of the Lord, or who have conducted themselves with fidelity, as though he had said : "The darkness
will not always remain : the light will one day break forth ;
which will make all things manifest." That day, I own, is
God's—not man's, but the metaphor is more elegant if you
read simply—*the day*, because Paul in this way conveys the
idea, that the Lord's true servants cannot always be accurately distinguished from false workmen, inasmuch as virtues
and vices are concealed by the darkness of the night. That
night, however, will not always continue. For ambition is
blind—man's favour is blind—the world's applause is blind,
but this darkness God afterwards dispels in his own time.
Take notice, that he always discovers the assurance of a good
conscience, and with an unconquerable magnanimity despises
perverse judgments ; *first*, in order that he may call back the
Corinthians from popular applause to a right rule of judgment ; and *secondly*, for the purpose of confirming the
authority of his ministry.

Because it will be revealed by fire. Paul having spoken of
doctrine metaphorically, now also applies metaphorically the
name of *fire* to the very touchstone of doctrine, that the corresponding parts of the comparison may harmonize with each
other. The *fire*, then, here meant is the Spirit of the Lord,
who tries by his touchstone what doctrine resembles *gold*
and what resembles *stubble*. The nearer the doctrine of God
is brought to this fire, so much the brighter will be its lustre.
On the other hand, what has had its origin in man's head
will quickly vanish,[1] as stubble is consumed in the fire.
There seems also to be an allusion to *the day* of which he
makes mention : "Not only will those things which vain
ambition, like a dark night, concealed among the Corinthians, be brought to light by the brightness of the sun, but
there will also be a strength of heat, not merely for drying
up and cleansing away the refuse, but also for burning up
everything wrong." For however men may look upon themselves, as forming acute judgments, their discernment, not-

---

[1] "Celle, qui aura esté forgée au cerveau des hommes s'esuanouira tout
incontinent, et s'en ira en fumée ;"—"That which has been forged in man's
brain, will quickly vanish, and go off in smoke."

withstanding, reaches no farther than appearance, which,
for the most part, has no solidity.   There is nothing but that
day to which the Apostle appeals, that tests everything to
the quick, not merely by its brightness, but also by its fiery
flame.

14. *If any man's work remains, he will receive a reward.*
His meaning is, that those are fools who depend on man's
estimation, so as to reckon it enough to be approved by men,
for *then only* will the work have praise and recompense—
when it has stood the test of the *day of the Lord.*   Hence
he exhorts His true ministers to have an eye to *that day.*
For by the word *remains,* he intimates that doctrines fly
about as it were in an unsettled state, nay more, like empty
bubbles, they glitter for the moment, until they have come
to be thoroughly tested.   Hence it follows, that we must
reckon as nothing all the applauses of the world, the emptiness of which will in a very little be exposed by heaven's
judgment.

15. *If any man's work shall be burned.*   It is as though
he had said : Let no man flatter himself on the ground that,
in the opinion of men, he is reckoned among the most eminent *master-builders,* for as soon as the day breaks in, his
whole work must go utterly to nothing, if it is not approved of
by the Lord.   This, then, is the rule to which every one's
ministry requires to be conformed.   Some explain this of
doctrine, so that $\zeta\eta\mu\iota o\hat{\upsilon}\sigma\theta\alpha\iota$[1] means simply *to perish,* and then
what immediately follows they view as referring to the foun-
dation, because in the Greek $\theta\epsilon\mu\epsilon\lambda\iota o\varsigma$ (foundation) is in the
masculine gender.   They do not, however, sufficiently attend
to the entire context.   For Paul in this passage subjects to
trial, not his own doctrine, but that of others.[2]   Hence it
were out of place to make mention at present of the foundation.   He has stated a little before, that *every man's work
will be tried by fire.*   He comes afterwards to state an alter-

---

[1] " Le mot Grec suyuant, qui signifie souffrir perte ou dommage ;"—
" The Greek word following, which signifies to suffer loss or damage."

[2] " Car ce n'est pas sa doctrine, mais celle des autres que Sainct Paul
dit, qui viendra a l'examen ;"—" For it is not his own doctrine, but that of
others, that St. Paul says will come to be tested."

native, which ought not to be extended beyond that general observation. Now it is certain that Paul spoke there simply of the structure which had been erected upon the foundation. He has already in the first clause promised a reward to good master-builders,[1] whose labour shall have been approved of. Hence the contrast in the second clause suits admirably well—that those who have mixed *stubble*, or *wood*, or *straw*, will be disappointed of the commendation which they had expected.

He himself will be saved, &c. It is certain that Paul speaks of those who, while always retaining the *foundation*, mix *hay* with *gold*, *stubble* with *silver*, and *wood* with *precious stones*—that is, those who build upon Christ, but in consequence of the weakness of the flesh, admit something that is man's, or through ignorance turn aside to some extent from the strict purity of God's word. Such were many of the saints, Cyprian, Ambrose, Augustine, and the like. Add to these, if you choose, from those of later times, Gregory and Bernard, and others of that stamp, who, while they had it as their object to build upon Christ, did nevertheless often deviate from the right system of building. Such persons, Paul says, could be saved, but on this condition—if the Lord wiped away their ignorance, and purged them from all dross.

This is the meaning of the clause *so as by fire*. He means, therefore, to intimate, that he does not take away from them the hope of salvation, provided they willingly submit to the *loss* of their labour, and are purged by the mercy of God, as gold is refined in the furnace. Farther, although God sometimes purges his own people by afflictions, yet here by the name of *fire*, I understand the touchstone of the Spirit, by which the Lord corrects and removes the ignorance of his people, by which they were for a time held captive. I am aware, indeed, that many refer this to the cross,[2] but I am confident that my interpretation will please all that are of sound judgment.

---

[1] " Et fideles ouuriers ;"—" And faithful workmen."
[2] " Et affliction ;"—" And affliction."

It remains, that we give an answer in passing to the Papists, who endeavour from this passage to prop up Purgatory. " The sinners[1] whom God forgives, pass through the fire, that they may be saved." Hence they in this way suffer punishment in the presence of God, so as to afford satisfaction to his justice. I pass over their endless fictions in reference to the measure of punishment, and the means of redemption from them, but I ask, who they are that pass through *the fire ?* Paul assuredly speaks of ministers alone. " There is the same reason," they say, " as to all." It is not for us[2] but for God to judge as to this matter. But even granting them this, how childishly they stumble at the term *fire.* For to what purpose is this *fire,*[3] but for burning up the *hay* and *straw,* and on the other hand, for proving the *gold* and *silver.* Do they mean to say that doctrines are discerned by the *fire* of their purgatory? Who has ever learned from *that,* what difference there is between truth and falsehood ? Farther, when will that day come that will shine forth so as to discover every one's work ? Did it begin at the beginning of the world, and will it continue without interruption to the end ? If the terms *stubble, hay, gold,* and *silver* are figurative, as they must necessarily allow, what correspondence will there be between the different clauses, if there is nothing figurative in the term *fire ?* Away, then, with such silly trifles, which carry their absurdity in their forehead, for the Apostle's true meaning is, I think, sufficiently manifest.

16. Know ye not that ye are the temple of God, and *that* the Spirit of God dwelleth in you?

17. If any man defile the temple of God, him shall God destroy; for the temple of God is holy, which *temple* ye are.

16. An nescitis, quod templum Dei estis et Spiritus Dei habitat in vobis?

17. Si quis templum Dei corrumpit,[4] hunc perdet Deus. Templum enim Dei sanctum est, quod estis vos.

[1] " Les pecheurs, (disent-ils) ;"—" The sinners, (say they)."
[2] " Je respon, que ce n'est pas à nous;"—" I answer, that it is not for us."
[3] " Car à quel propos est-il yci parlé du feu ?"—" For to what purpose does he speak here of fire ?"
[4] " Viole, ou destruit;"—" Violates, or destroys."

18. Let no man deceive himself. If any man among you seemeth to be wise in this world, let him become a fool, that he may be wise.

19. For the wisdom of this world is foolishness with God. For it is written, He taketh the wise in their own craftiness.

20. And again, The Lord knoweth the thoughts of the wise, that they are vain.

21. Therefore let no man glory in men. For all things are yours;

22. Whether Paul, or Apollos, or Cephas, or the world, or life, or death, or things present, or things to come; all are yours;

23. And ye are Christ's; and Christ *is* God's.

18. Nemo se decipiat, si quis videtur sapiens esse inter vos: in sæculo hoc stultus fiat,[1] ut fiat sapiens.

19. Sapientia enim mundi huius stultitia est apud Deum. Scriptum est enim (Job v. 13) Deprehendens sapientes in astutia sua.

20. Et rursum (Ps. xciv. 11) Dominus novit cogitationes sapientum vanas esse.

21. Proinde nemo glorietur in hominibus, omnia enim vestra sunt;

22. Sive Paulus, sive Apollos, sive Cephas, sive mundus, sive vita, sive mors, sive præsentia, sive futura: omnia vestra sunt,

23. Vos autem Christi; Christus autem Dei.

16. *Know ye not,* &c. Having admonished the teachers as to their duty, he now addresses himself to the pupils— that they, too, may take heed to themselves. To the teachers he had said, " You are the master-builders of the house of God." He now says to the people, " You are *the temples of God.* It is your part, therefore, to take care that you be not in any way defiled." Now, the design[2] is, that they may not prostitute themselves to the service of men. He confers upon them distinguished honour in speaking thus, but it is in order that they may be made the more reprehensible ; for, as God has set them apart as a *temple* to himself, he has at the same time appointed them to be guardians of his *temple.* It is sacrilege, then, if they give themselves up to the service of men. He speaks of all of them collectively as being one *temple of God ;* for every believer is a *living stone,* (1 Peter ii. 5,) for the rearing up of the building of God. At the same time they also, in some cases, individually receive the name of *temples.* We shall find him a little afterwards (chap. vi. 19) repeating the same sentiment, but for another purpose. For in that passage he

---

[1] " Si auevn entre vous cuide estre sage, qu'il soit fait fol en ce monde, afin qu'il soit sage—ou, sage en ce monde, qu'il soit fait fol, afin, &c. ;"— " If any one among you seemeth to be wise, let him become a fool in this world, that he may be wise—or, wise in this world, let him become a fool, that," &c.

[2] " De cest aduertissement ;"—" Of this caution."

treats of chastity; but here, on the other hand, he exhorts them to have their faith resting on the obedience of Christ alone. The interrogation gives additional emphasis; for he indirectly intimates, that he speaks to them of a thing that they knew, while he appeals to them as witnesses.

And the Spirit of God. Here we have the reason why they are *the temple of God.* Hence *and* must be understood as meaning *because.* This is customary, as in the words of the poet—"Thou hadst heard it, *and* it had been reported."[1] "For this reason," says he, "are ye the *temples of God,* because He dwells in you by his Spirit; for no unclean place can be the habitation of God." In this passage we have an explicit testimony for maintaining the divinity of the Holy Spirit. For if he were a creature, or merely a gift, he would not make us *temples of* GOD, by dwelling in us. At the same time we learn, in what manner God communicates himself to us, and by what tie we are bound to him—when he pours down upon us the influence of his Spirit.

17. *If any man corrupts the temple of God.* He subjoins a dreadful threatening—that, as the *temple of God* ought to be inviolably sacred, that man, whoever he may be, that corrupts it, will not pass with impunity. The kind of profanation of which he now speaks, is, when men intrude themselves, so as to bear rule in the Church in the place of God. For as that faith, which is devoted to the pure doctrine of Christ, is called elsewhere spiritual *chastity,* (2 Cor. xi. 2,) so it also sanctifies our souls for the right and pure worship of God. For as soon as we are tinctured with the contrivances of men, the temple of God is polluted, as it were, with filth, because the sacrifice of faith, which he claims for himself alone, is in that case offered to creatures.

18. *Let no man deceive himself.* Here he puts his finger upon the true sore, as the whole mischief originated in this—that they were wise in their own conceit. Hence he exhorts them not to deceive themselves with a false impression, by arrogating any wisdom to themselves—by which he means, that all are under a mistake, who depend upon their own judgment. Now, he addresses himself, in my opinion,

---

[1] Audieras, *et* fama fuit. Virg. Eclog. ix. 11.

to hearers as well as teachers. For the former discovered a partiality for those ambitious men, and lent an ear to them,[1] because they had too fastidious a taste, so that the simplicity of the gospel was insipid to their taste ; while the latter aimed at nothing but show, that they might be in some estimation. He accordingly admonishes both to this effect —" Let no one rest satisfied with his own wisdom, but let him *who thinketh himself to be wise, become a fool in this world,*" or, " Let him who is distinguished in this world by reputation for wisdom, of his own accord empty himself,[2] and *become a fool* in his own estimation."

Farther, in these words the Apostle does not require, that we should altogether renounce the wisdom that is implanted in us by nature, or acquired by long practice ; but simply, that we subject it to the service of God, so as to have no wisdom but through his word. For this is what is meant by *becoming a fool in this world,* or in our own estimation— when we are prepared to give way to God, and embrace with fear and reverence everything that he teaches us, rather than follow what may appear to us plausible.[3]

The meaning of the clause *in this world,* is as though he had said—" According to the judgment or opinion of the world." For the wisdom of the world is this—if we reckon ourselves sufficient of ourselves for *taking counsel* as to all matters (Psalms xiii. 2) for governing ourselves, and for managing whatever we have to do—if we have no dependence on any other[4]—if we feel no need of the guidance of another, but are competent to govern ourselves.[5] He, therefore, on the other hand, is *a fool in this world,* who, renouncing his own understanding, allows himself to be directed by the Lord, as if with his eyes shut—who, distrusting himself, leans wholly upon the Lord, places his

---

[1] " Trop facilement;"—" Too readily."
[2] " Soit fait fol en soy de son bon gré s'abbaissant, et s'aneantissant soy-mesme;"—" Let him become, of his own accord, a fool in his own estimation, abasing and emptying himself."
[3] " Bon et raisonnable;"—" Good and reasonable."
[4] " Que de nous-mesmes;"—" Than ourselves."
[5] " Nous semble que nous sommes assez suffisans de nous conduire, et gouuerner nous-mesmes;"—" It appears to us, that we are quite competent to conduct and govern ourselves."

whole wisdom in him, and yields himself up to God in docility and submission.   It is necessary that our wisdom should
in this way vanish, in order that the will of God may have
authority over us, and that we be emptied of our own understanding, that we may be filled with the wisdom of God.
At the same time, the clause[1] may either be taken in connection with the first part of the verse, or joined with the
last, but as the meaning is not much different, I leave every
one to choose for himself.

19. *For the wisdom of this world.* This is an argument
taken from things opposite.   To maintain the one is to
overturn the other.   As, therefore, *the wisdom of this world
is foolishness with God,* it follows that we cannot be wise in
the sight of God, unless we are fools in the view of the
world.   We have already explained (chap. i. 20) what he
means by the *wisdom of this world;* for natural perspicacity is a gift of God, and the liberal arts, and all the
sciences by which wisdom is acquired, are gifts of God.
They are confined, however, within their own limits ; for
into God's heavenly kingdom they cannot penetrate.   Hence
they must occupy the place of handmaid, not of mistress :
nay more, they must be looked upon as empty and worthless, until they have become entirely subject to the word
and Spirit of God.   If, on the other hand, they set themselves in opposition to Christ, they must be looked upon as
dangerous pests, and, if they strive to accomplish anything
of themselves, as the worst of all hindrances.[2]   Hence *the
wisdom of the world,* in Paul's acceptation, is that which
assumes to itself authority, and does not allow itself to be
regulated by the word of God, or to be subdued, so as to
yield itself up in entire subjection to him.   Until, therefore,
matters have come to this, that the individual acknowledges
that he knows nothing but what he has learned from God,
and, giving up his own understanding, resigns himself unreservedly to Christ's guidance, he is wise in the world's
account, but he is foolish in the estimation of God.

---

[1] " *En ce monde;*"—" *In this world.*"
[2] " Ce sont de grans empeschemens, et bien à craindre;"—" They are
great hindrances, and much to be dreaded."

For it is written, He taketh the wise. He confirms this from *two* Scripture proofs, the *first* of which is taken from Job v. 13, where the wisdom of God is extolled on this ground, that no wisdom of the world can stand before it. Now it is certain, that the Prophet speaks there of those that are cunning and crafty; but as the wisdom of man is invariably such without God,[1] it is with good reason that Paul applies it in this sense,—that whatever wisdom men have of themselves is reckoned of no account in the sight of God. The *second* is from Psalm xciv. 11, where David, after claiming for God alone the office and authority of the Instructor of all, adds, that *He knows the thoughts of all to be vain.* Hence, in whatever estimation they are held by us, they are, in the judgment of God, *vain.* Here we have an admirable passage for bringing down the confidence of the flesh, while God from on high declares that everything that the mind of man conceives and contrives is mere *vanity.*[2]

21. *Therefore let no man glory in men.* As there is nothing that is more *vain* than man, how little security there is in leaning upon an evanescent shadow! Hence he infers with propriety from the preceding statement, that we must not *glory in men,* inasmuch as the Lord thus takes away from mankind universally every ground of glorying. At the same time this inference depends on the whole of the foregoing doctrine, as will appear ere long. For as we belong to Christ alone, it is with good reason that he teaches us, that any supremacy of man, by which the glory of Christ is impaired, involves sacrilege.

22. *All things are yours.* He proceeds to show what place and station teachers should occupy[3]—such as not to detract in any degree from the authority of Christ, the one Master. As therefore Christ is the Church's sole master, and as he alone without exception is worthy to be listened to, it is necessary to distinguish between him and others, as even

---

[1] " Quand la sagesse de Dieu n'y est point;"—" When the wisdom of God is not in it."

[2] The humbling tendency of the statement referred to is well brought out by Fuller of Kettering. (*Fuller's Works,* vol. iv. p. 389.)

[3] " C'est à dire, quelle estime on en doit auoir;"—" That is to say, in what esteem they ought to be held "

Christ himself has testified respecting himself, (Matt. xxiii. 8,) and no other is recommended to us by the Father with this honourable declaration,[1] "Hear ye him." (Matt. xvii. 5.)   As, therefore, he alone is endowed with authority to rule us by his word, Paul says that others *are ours*—meaning, that they are appointed to us by God with the view of our making use of them—not that they should exercise dominion over our consciences.   Thus on the one hand, he shows that they are not useless, and, on the other hand, he keeps them in their own place, that they may not exalt themselves in opposition to Christ.   What he adds, as to *death, life*, and the rest, is hyperbolical, so far as concerns the passage before us.   He had it in view, however, to reason, as it were, from the greater to the less, in this manner: "Christ having put in subjection to us *life* and *death*, and everything, can we doubt, whether he has not also made men subject to us, to help us by their ministrations—not to oppress us by tyranny."

Now if any one takes occasion from this to allege, that the writings both of Paul and of Peter are subject to our scrutiny, inasmuch as they were men, and are not exempted from the common lot of others, I answer, that Paul, while he does not by any means spare himself or Peter, admonishes the Corinthians to distinguish between the person of the individual, and the dignity or distinction of office.   "As for myself, viewed as a man, I wish to be judged of simply as a man, that Christ alone may have distinction in our ministry."   This, however, in a general way, we must hold,[2] that all who discharge the office of the ministry, are *ours*, from the highest to the lowest, so that we are at liberty to withhold our assent to their doctrine, until they show that it is from Christ.   For they must all be *tried*, (1 John iv. 1,) and we must yield obedience to them, only when they have satisfactorily shown themselves to be faithful servants of Christ. Now as to Peter and Paul, this point being beyond all con-

---

[1] "Nul autre ne nous a esté donné du Pere authorizé de ce titre et commandement;"—"No other has been given to us by the Father, authorized by this distinction and injunction."

[2] "Pour vne maxime;"—"As a maxim."

148 COMMENTARY ON THE CHAP. III. 23.

troversy, and the Lord having furnished us with amply sufficient evidence, that their doctrine has come forth from Him, when we receive as an oracle from heaven, and venerate everything that they have delivered to us, we hear not so much *them,* as Christ speaking in them.

23. *Christ is God's.* This subjection relates to Christ's humanity, for by taking upon him our flesh, he assumed "the form" and condition "of a servant," that he might make himself obedient to his Father in all things. (Phil. ii. 7, 8.) And assuredly, that we may cleave to God through him, it is necessary that he have God as his *head.* (1 Cor. xi. 3.) We must observe, however, with what intention Paul has added this. For he admonishes us, that the sum of our felicity consists in this,[1] that we are united to God who is the chief good, and this is accomplished when we are gathered together under the *head* that our heavenly Father has set over us. In the same sense Christ said to his disciples, "Ye ought to rejoice, because I go to the Father, for the Father is greater than I," (John xiv. 28,) for there he set himself forth as the medium, through which believers come to the original source of every blessing. It is certain, that those are left destitute of that signal blessing, who depart from the unity of the Head.[2] Hence this order of things suits the connection of the passage—that those subject themselves to Christ alone, who desire to remain under God's jurisdiction.

CHAPTER IV.

1. Let a man so account of us, as of the ministers of Christ, and stewards of the mysteries of God.

2. Moreover it is required in stewards, that a man be found faithful.

1. Sic nos æstimet homo ut ministros Christi, et dispensatores arcanorum Dei.

2. Cæterum in ministris hoc quæritur, ut fidelis aliquis reperiatur.

[1] "Car il nous donne à entendre, et remonstre, que le comble et la perfection de nostre felicité consiste là;"—"For he gives us to understand, and shows, that the summit and perfection of our felicity consists in this."
[2] "Qui ne retienent ce seul Chef;"—"Who do not retain that sole Head."

3. But with me it is a very small thing that I should be judged of you, or of man's judgment : yea, I judge not mine own self.

4. For I know nothing by myself; yet am I not hereby justified : but he that judgeth me is the Lord.

5. Therefore judge nothing before the time, until the Lord come, who both will bring to light the hidden things of darkness, and will make manifest the counsels of the hearts ; and then shall every man have praise of God.

3. Mihi viro pro minimo est, a vobis diiudicari, aut ab humano die :[1] imo nec me ipsum diiudico.

4. Nullius enim rei mihi sum conscius : sed non in hoc sum justificatus. Porro qui me diiudicat, Dominus est.

5. Itaque ne ante tempus quicquam iudicetis, donec venerit Dominus, qui et illustrabit abscondita tenebrarum, et manifestabit consilia cordium ; et tunc laus erit cuique a Deo.

1. *Let a man so account of us.* As it was a matter of no little importance to see the Church in this manner torn by corrupt factions, from the likings or dislikings that were entertained towards individuals, he enters into a still more lengthened discussion as to the ministry of the word. Here there are *three* things to be considered in their order. In the *first* place, Paul describes the office of a pastor of the Church. *Secondly,* he shows, that it is not enough for any one to produce a title, or even to undertake the duty—a faithful administration of the office being requisite. *Thirdly,* as the judgment formed of him by the Corinthians was preposterous,[2] he calls both himself and them to the judgment-seat of Christ. In the first place, then, he teaches in what estimation every teacher in the Church ought to be held. In this department he modifies his discourse in such a manner as neither, on the one hand, to lower the credit of the ministry, nor, on the other, to assign to man more than is expedient. For both of these things are exceedingly dangerous, because, when ministers are lowered, contempt of the word arises,[3] while, on the other hand, if they are extolled beyond measure, they abuse liberty, and become " wanton against the Lord." (1 Tim. v. 11.) Now the medium observed by Paul

---

[1] " De iour humain—c'est à dire, de iugement d'homme ;"—" Of man's day—that is to say, of man's judgment."

[2] " Pource que les Corinthiens iugeoyent de luy d'vne mauuaise sorte, et bien inconsidereement ;"—" As the Corinthians judged of him in an unfavourable way, and very rashly."

[3] " Facilement on viendra à mespriser la parole de Dieu ;"—" They will readily come to despise the word of God."

consists in this, that he calls them *ministers of Christ;* by which he intimates, that they ought to apply themselves not to their own work but to that of the Lord, who has hired them as his servants, and that they are not appointed to bear rule in an authoritative manner in the Church, but are subject to Christ's authority[1]—in short, that they are servants, not masters.

As to what he adds—*stewards of the mysteries of God,* he expresses hereby the kind of service. By this he intimates, that their office extends no farther than this, that they are *stewards of the mysteries of God.* In other words, what the Lord has committed to their charge they deliver over to men from hand to hand—as the expression is[2]—not what they themselves might choose. "For this purpose has God chosen them as ministers of his Son, that he might through them communicate to men his heavenly wisdom, and hence they ought not to move a step beyond this." He appears, at the same time, to give a stroke indirectly to the Corinthians, who, leaving in the back-ground the heavenly mysteries, had begun to hunt with excessive eagerness after strange inventions, and hence they valued their teachers for nothing but profane learning. It is an honourable distinction that he confers upon the gospel when he terms its contents *the mysteries of God.* But as the sacraments are connected with these mysteries as appendages, it follows, that those who have the charge of administering the word are the authorized *stewards* of them also.

2. *But it is required in ministers.*[3] It is as though he had said, it is not enough to be a *steward* if there be not an upright stewardship. Now the rule of an upright stewardship, is to conduct one's self in it with fidelity. It is a passage that ought to be carefully observed, for we see how haughtily[4] Papists require that everything that they do

---

[1] " Ils sont eux-mesmes comme les autres sous la domination de Christ;" —" They are themselves, in common with others, under the dominion of Christ."

[2] Our Author makes use of the same expression when commenting on 1 Cor. xi. 23, and xv. 3.—*Ed.*

[3] " Entre les dispensateurs ;"—" Among stewards."

[4] " Et d'une façon magistrale ;"—" And with a magisterial air."

and teach should have the authority of law, simply on the ground of their being called pastors. On the other hand, Paul is so far from being satisfied with the mere title, that, in his view, it is not even enough that there is a legitimate call, unless the person who is called conducts himself in the office with fidelity. On every occasion, therefore, on which Papists hold up before us the mask of a name, for the purpose of maintaining the tyranny of their idol, let our answer be, that Paul requires more than this from the *ministers of Christ*, though, at the same time, the Pope and his attendant train are wanting not merely in fidelity in the discharge of the office, but also in the ministry itself, if everything is duly considered.

This passage, however, militates, not merely against wicked teachers, but also against all that have any other object in view than the glory of Christ and the edification of the Church. For every one that teaches the truth is not necessarily faithful, but only he who desires from the heart to serve the Lord and advance Christ's kingdom. Nor is it without good reason that Augustine assigns to *hirelings*, (John x. 12,) a middle place between the *wolves* and the good teachers. As to Christ's requiring *wisdom* also on the part of the good *steward*, (Luke xii. 42,) he speaks, it is true, in that passage with greater clearness than Paul, but the meaning is the same. For the *faithfulness* of which Christ speaks is uprightness of conscience, which must be accompanied with sound and prudent counsel. By a faithful minister Paul means one who, with knowledge as well as uprightness,[1] discharges the office of a good and faithful minister.

3. *But with me it is a very small thing.* It remained that he should bring before their view his *faithfulness*, that the Corinthians might judge of him from this, but, as their judgment was corrupted, he throws it aside and appeals to the judgment-seat of Christ. The Corinthians erred in this, that they looked with amazement at foreign masks, and gave no heed to the true and proper marks of distinction.[2]

[1] " Auec science et bonne discretion, et d'vn cœur droit;"—" With knowledge and good discretion, as well as with an upright heart."

[2] " Ils estoyent rauis en admiration de ces masques externes, comme gens tout transportez, et ne regardoyent point a discerner vrayement ne

He, accordingly, declares with great confidence, that he despises a perverted and blind judgment of this sort. In this way, too, he, on the one hand, admirably exposes the vanity of the false Apostles who made the mere applause of men their aim, and reckoned themselves happy if they were held in admiration ; and, on the other hand, he severely chastises the arrogance[1] of the Corinthians, which was the reason why they were so much blinded in their judgment.

But, it is asked, on what ground it was allowable for Paul, not merely to set aside the censure of one Church, but to set himself above the judgment of men? for this is a condition common to all pastors—to be judged of by the Church. I answer, that it is the part of a good pastor to submit both his doctrine and his life for examination to the judgment of the Church, and that it is the sign of a good conscience not to shun the light of careful inspection. In this respect Paul, without doubt, was prepared for submitting himself to the judgment of the Corinthian Church, and for being called to render an account both of his life and of his doctrine, had there been among them a proper scrutiny,[2] as he often assigns them this power, and of his own accord entreats them to be prepared to judge aright. But when a faithful pastor sees that he is borne down by unreasonable and perverse affections, and that justice and truth have no place, he ought to appeal to God, and betake himself to his judgment-seat, regardless of human opinion, especially when he cannot secure that a true and proper knowledge of matters shall be arrived at.

If, then, the Lord's servants would bear in mind that they must act in this manner, let them allow their doctrine and life to be brought to the test, nay more, let them voluntarily present themselves for this purpose ; and if anything is objected against them, let them not decline to answer. But if they see that they are condemned without being heard in

proprement ;"—" They were ravished with admiration of those foreign masks, as persons quite transported, and were not careful to distinguish truly or properly."

[1] " Et orgueil ;"—" And pride."

[2] " Si entr'eux il y eust eu vne legitime et droite façon de iuger ;"—" If there had been among them a lawful and right method of judging."

their own defence, and that judgment is passed upon them
without their being allowed a hearing, let them raise up
their minds to such a pitch of magnanimity, as that, despising the opinions of men, they will fearlessly wait for God as
their judge.   In this manner the Prophets of old, having to
do with refractory persons,[1] and such as had the audacity to
despise the word of God in their administration of it, required
to raise themselves aloft, in order to tread under foot that
diabolical obstinacy, which manifestly tended to overthrow
at once the authority of God and the light of truth.   Should
any one, however, when opportunity is given for defending
himself, or at least when he has need to clear himself, appeal to God by way of subterfuge, he will not thereby make
good his innocence, but will rather discover his consummate
impudence.[2]

Or of man's day.   While others explain it in another
manner, the simpler way, in my opinion, is to understand
the word *day* as used metaphorically to mean *judgment,* because there are stated *days* for administering justice, and
the accused are summoned to appear on a certain *day.*   He
calls it *man's day*[3] when judgment is pronounced, not according to truth, or in accordance with the word of the Lord,
but according to the humour or rashness of men,[4] and in
short, when God does not preside.   " Let men," says he,
" sit for judgment as they please : it is enough for me that
God will annul whatever they have pronounced."

Nay, I judge not mine own self.   The meaning is : " I do
not venture to judge myself, though I know myself best ;
how then will you judge me, to whom I am less intimately
known ?"   Now he proves that he does not venture to judge

---

[1] " Ils auoyent affaire à des gens opiniastres et pleins de rebellion ;"—
" They had to do with persons that were obstinate, and full of rebellion."
[2] " Se demonstrera estre merueilleusement impudent ;"—" He will show
himself to be marvellously impudent."
[3] The word *day,* which is the literal rendering of the original word
(ἡμέρας) is made use of in some of the old English versions.   Thus in
Wiclif's version, (1380,) the rendering is : " of mannes daie ;" in Tyndale's, (1534,) " of man's daye ;" and in the Rheims version, (1582,) " of
man's day."—*Ed.*
[4] " Selon les sottes affections, ou les mouuemens temeraires des hommes ;"
—" According to the foolish affections, or rash impulses of men."

himself by this, that though he is not conscious to himself of anything wrong, he is not thereby acquitted in the sight of God. Hence he concludes, that what the Corinthians assume to themselves, belongs exclusively to God. " As for me," says he, " when I have carefully examined myself, I perceive that I am not so clear-sighted as to discern thoroughly my true character ; and hence I leave this to the judgment of God, who alone can judge, and to whom this authority exclusively belongs. As for you, then, on what ground will you make pretensions to something more ?"

As, however, it were very absurd to reject all kinds of judgment, whether of individuals respecting themselves, or of one individual respecting his brother, or of all together respecting their pastor, let it be understood that Paul speaks here not of the actions of men, which may be reckoned good or bad according to the word of the Lord, but of the eminence of each individual, which ought not to be estimated according to men's humours. It belongs to God alone to determine what distinction every one holds, and what honour he deserves. The Corinthians, however, despising Paul, groundlessly extolled others to the skies, as though they had at their command that knowledge which belonged exclusively to God. This is what he previously made mention of as *man's day*—when men mount the throne of judgment, and, as if they were gods, anticipate the day of Christ, who alone is appointed by the Father as judge, allot to every one his station of honour, assign to some a high place, and degrade others to the lowest seats. But what rule of distinction do they observe ? They look merely to what appears openly ; and thus what in their view is high and honourable, is in many instances *an abomination in the sight of God.* (Luke xvi. 15.) If any one farther objects, that the ministers of the word may in this world be distinguished by their works, as trees *by their fruits,* (Matt. vii. 16,) I admit that this is true, but we must consider with whom Paul had to deal. It was with persons who, in judging, looked to nothing but show and pomp, and arrogated to themselves a power which Christ, while in this world, refrained from using—that of assigning to every one his *seat in the kingdom*

of God. (Matt. xx. 23.) He does not, therefore, prohibit us
from esteeming those whom we have found to be faithful
workmen, and pronouncing them to be such ; nor, on the
other hand, from judging persons to be bad workmen according to the word of God, but he condemns that rashness
which is practised, when some are preferred above others in
a spirit of ambition—not according to their merits, but
without examination of the case.[1]

4. *I am not conscious to myself of anything faulty.* Let
us observe that Paul speaks here not of his whole life,
but simply of the office of apostleship. For if he had been
altogether unconscious to himself of anything wrong,[2] that
would have been a groundless complaint which he makes in
Rom. vii. 15, where he laments that *the evil which he would
not, that he does,* and that he is by sin kept back from giving
himself up entirely to God. Paul, therefore, felt *sin dwelling in him,* and confessed it ; but as to his apostleship,
(which is the subject that is here treated of,) he had conducted himself with so much integrity and fidelity, that his
conscience did not accuse him as to anything. This is a
protestation of no common character, and of such a nature
as clearly shows the piety and sanctity of his breast ;[3] and
yet he says that *he is not thereby justified :* that is, pure,
and altogether free from guilt in the sight of God. Why ?
Assuredly, because God sees much more distinctly than we ;
and hence, what appears to us cleanest, is filthy in his eyes.
Here we have a beautiful and singularly profitable admonition, not to measure the strictness of God's judgment by our
own opinion ; for we are dim-sighted, but God is pre-
eminently discerning. We think of ourselves too indulgently, but God is a judge of the utmost strictness. Hence
the truth of what Solomon says—" *Every man's ways appear
right in his own eyes, but the Lord pondereth the hearts.*"
(Prov. xxi. 2.)

---

[1] " Comme on dit ;"—" As they say."

[2] " Si nihil prorsus sibi consciret ;"—our author most probably had in his
eye a well-known passage in Horace, (Ep. J. i. 61,) " Nil conscire sibi ;"
—" To be conscious to one's self of nothing wrong."—*Ed.*

[3] " Combien sa conscience estoit pure et nette ;"—"How pure and clean
his conscience was."

Papists abuse this passage for the purpose of shaking the assurance of faith, and truly, I confess, that if their doctrine were admitted, we could do nothing but tremble in wretchedness during our whole life. For what tranquillity could our minds enjoy if it were to be determined from our works whether we are well-pleasing to God? I confess, therefore, that from the main foundation of Papists there follows nothing but continual disquietude for consciences; and, accordingly, we teach that we must have recourse to the free promise of mercy, which is offered to us in Christ, that we may be fully assured that we are accounted righteous by God.

5. *Therefore judge nothing before the time.* From this conclusion it is manifest, that Paul did not mean to reprove every kind of judgment without exception, but only what is hasty and rash, without examination of the case. For the Corinthians did not mark with unjaundiced eye the character of each individual, but, blinded by ambition, groundlessly extolled one and depreciated another, and took upon themselves to mark out the dignity of each individual beyond what is lawful for men. Let us know, then, how much is allowed us, what is now within the sphere of our knowledge, and what is deferred until the day of Christ, and let us not attempt to go beyond these limits. For there are some things that are now seen openly, while there are others that lie buried in obscurity until the day of Christ.

Who will bring to light. If this is affirmed truly and properly respecting the day of Christ, it follows that matters are never so well regulated in this world but that many things are involved in darkness, and that there is never so much light, but that many things remain in obscurity. I speak of the life of men, and their actions. He explains in the second clause, what is the cause of the obscurity and confusion, so that all things are not now manifest. It is because there are wonderful recesses and deepest lurking-places in the hearts of men. Hence, until the thoughts of the hearts are brought to light, there will always be darkness.

And then shall every one have praise. It is as though

he had said, " You now, O Corinthians, as if you had the adjudging of the prizes,[1] crown some, and send away others with disgrace, but this right and office belong exclusively to Christ.   You do that *before the time*—before it has become manifest who is worthy to be crowned, but the Lord has appointed a day on which he will make it manifest." This statement takes its rise from the assurance of a good conscience, which brings us also this advantage, that committing our *praises* into the hands of God, we disregard the empty breath of human applause.

6. And these things, brethren, I have in a figure transferred to myself and *to* Apollos for your sakes; that ye might learn in us not to think *of men* above that which is written, that no one of you be puffed up for one against another.

7. For who maketh thee to differ *from another?* and what hast thou that thou didst not receive? now if thou didst receive *it*, why dost thou glory, as if thou hadst not received *it?*

8. Now ye are full, now ye are rich, ye have reigned as kings without us: and I would to God ye did reign, that we also might reign with you.

6. Hæc autem, fratres, transfiguravi in me ipsum et Apollo propter vos, ut in nobis disceretis, ne quis supra id quod scriptum est, de se sentiat : ut ne quis pro hoc vel illo infletur adversus alterum.

7. Quis enim te discernit? quid autem habes, quod non acceperis? si vero etiam acceperis, quid gloriaris tanquam non acceperis?

8. Jam saturati estis, jam ditati estis, absque nobis regnum adepti estis; atque utinam sitis adepti ut et nos vobiscum regnemus.

6. *I have in a figure transferred.*   Hence we may infer, that it was not those who were attached to Paul that gave rise to parties, as *they*, assuredly, had not been so instructed, but those who had through ambition given themselves up to vain teachers.[2]   But as he could more freely and less invidiously bring forward his own name, and that of his brethren, he preferred to point out in his own person the fault that existed in others.   At the same time, he strikes a severe blow at the originators of the parties, and points his finger to the sources from which this deadly divorce took its rise.   For he shows them, that if they had been satisfied

---

[1] Tanquam *agonothetæ.*   The allusion is to the presiding officers or umpires (αγωνοθέται) who adjudged the prizes in the Grecian games.   (See Herod. vi. 127.)—*Ed.*

[2] " A ces docteurs pleins d'ostentation ;"—" To those teachers, full of ostentation."

with good teachers, they would have been exempted from this evil.[1]

That in us. Some manuscripts have it "that in *you.*" Both readings suit well, and there is no difference of meaning; for what Paul intends is this—"I have, for the sake of example, transferred these things to myself and Apollos, in order that you may transfer this example to yourselves." "*Learn* then *in us,*" that is, "in that example which I have placed before you in our person as in a mirror;" or, "*Learn in you,*" that is, "apply this example to yourselves." But what does he wish them to *learn? That no one be puffed up for his own teacher against another,* that is, that they be not lifted up with pride on account of their teachers, and do not abuse their names for the purpose of forming parties, and rending the Church asunder. Observe, too, that pride or haughtiness is the cause and commencement of all contentions, when every one, assuming to himself more than he is entitled to do, is eager to have others in subjection to him.

The clause *above what is written* may be explained in two ways—either as referring to Paul's writings, or to the proofs from Scripture which he has brought forward. As this, however, is a matter of small moment, my readers may be left at liberty to take whichever they may prefer.

7. *For who distinguisheth thee ?* The meaning is—"Let that man come forward, whosoever he be, that is desirous of distinction, and troubles the Church by his ambition. I will demand of him who it is that makes him superior to others ? that is, who it is that has conferred upon him the privilege of being taken out of the rank of the others, and made superior to others ?" Now this whole reasoning depends on the order which the Lord has appointed in his Church—that the members of Christ's body may be united together, and that every one of them may rest satisfied with his own place, his own rank, his own office, and his own honour. If one member is desirous to quit his place, that he may leap

---

[1] " S'ils se contentent de bons et fideles docteurs, ils seront hors de danger d'vn tel mal;"—" If they had contented themselves with good and faithful teachers, they would have been beyond the risk of such an evil."

over into the place of another, and invade his office, what will become of the entire body ? Let us know, then, that the Lord has so placed us in the Church, and has in such a manner assigned to every one his own station, that, being under one head, we may be mutually helpful to each other. Let us know, besides, that we have been endowed with a diversity of gifts, in order that we may serve the Lord with modesty and humility, and may endeavour to promote the glory of him who has conferred upon us everything that we have. This, then, was the best remedy for correcting the ambition of those who were desirous of distinction—to call them back to God, in order that they might acknowledge that it was not according to any one's pleasure that he was placed in a high or a low station, but that this belonged to God alone ; and farther, that God does not confer so much upon any one as to elevate him to the place of the Head, but distributes his gifts in such a manner, that He alone is glorified in all things.

To distinguish here means to render eminent.[1] Augustine, however, does not inaptly make frequent use of this declaration for maintaining, in opposition to the Pelagians,[2] that whatever there is of excellence in mankind, is not implanted in him by nature, so that it could be ascribed either to nature or to descent ; and farther, that it is not acquired by free will, so as to bring God under obligation, but flows from his pure and undeserved mercy. For there can be no doubt that Paul here contrasts the grace of God with the merit or worthiness of men.[3]

And what hast thou ? This is a confirmation of the preceding statement, for that man cannot on good ground extol himself, who has no superiority above others. For what greater vanity is there than that of boasting without any ground for it ? Now, there is no man that has anything of excellency from himself ; therefore the man that extols him-

---

[1] " Rendre excellent, ou mettre en reputation ;"—" To render eminent, or exalt to fame."

[2] The reader will find a variety of passages of this tenor quoted from Augustine in the *Institutes,* vol. i. pp. 370-1.—*Ed.*

[3] " Comme estans choses contraires ;"—" As being things opposite."

self is a fool and an idiot. The true foundation of Christian modesty is this—not to be self-complacent, as knowing that we are empty and void of everything good—that, if God has implanted in us anything that is good, we are so much the more debtors to his grace ; and in fine, that, as Cyprian says, we must glory in nothing, because there is nothing that is our own.

Why dost thou glory as if thou hadst not received it ? Observe, that there remains no ground for our glorying, inasmuch as it is by *the grace of God that we are what we are,* (1 Cor. xv. 10.) And this is what we had in the first chapter, that Christ is the source of all blessings to us, that we may learn to *glory in the Lord,* (1 Cor. i. 30, 31,) and this we do, only when we renounce our own glory. For God does not obtain his due otherwise than by our being emptied, so that it may be seen that everything in us that is worthy of praise is derived.

8. *Now ye are full.* Having in good earnest, and without the use of any figure, beat down their vain confidence, he now also ridicules it by way of irony,[1] because they are so self-complacent, as if they were the happiest persons in the world. He proceeds, too, step by step, in exposing their insolence. In the *first* place, he says, that they were *full :* this refers to the past. He then adds, *Ye are rich :* this applies to the future. *Lastly,* he says, that they had *reigned as kings :* this is much more than either of those two. It is as though he had said, " What will you attain to, when you appear to be not merely *full* for the present, but are also *rich* for the future—nay more, are *kings ?*" At the same time, he tacitly upbraids them with ingratitude, because they had the audacity to despise *him,* or rather *those,* through means of whom they had obtained everything.

Without us, says he. " For Apollos and I are now esteemed nothing by you, though it is by our instrumentality that the Lord has conferred everything upon you. What inhumanity there is in resting with self-complacency

---

[1] " Vsant d'ironie, c'est à dire, d'vne façon de parler qui sonne en mocquerie ;"—" Making use of irony, that is to say, a form of speech that has a tone of mockery."

in the gifts of God, while in the meantime you despise those
through whose instrumentality you obtained them !"

And I would to God that ye did reign.[1] Here he declares
that he does not envy their felicity, (if indeed they have
any,) and that from the beginning he has not sought to
reign among them, but only to bring them to the kingdom
of God. He intimates, however, on the other hand, that
the kingdom in which they gloried was merely imaginary,
and that their glorying was groundless and pernicious,[2] there
being no true glorying but that which is enjoyed by all the
sons of God in common, under Christ their Head, and every
one of them according to the measure of the grace that has
been given him.

For by these words : *that ye also may reign with us,* he
means this—" You are so renowned in your own opinion
that you do not hesitate to despise me, and those like me,
but mark, how vain is your glorying. For you can have no
glorying before God, in which we have not a share—for if
honour redounds to you from having the gospel of God, how
much more to us, by whose ministry it was conveyed to you!
And assuredly, this is a madness[3] that is common to all the
proud, that by drawing everything to themselves, they strip
themselves of every blessing—nay more, they renounce the
hope of everlasting salvation."

9. For I think that God hath set
forth us the apostles last, as it were
appointed to death: for we are made
a spectacle unto the world, and to
angels, and to men.

10. We *are* fools for Christ's sake,

9. Existimo enim, quod Deus
nos postremos Apostolos demonstra-
verit tanquam morti destinatos :
nam theatrum facti sumus mundo,
et angelis, et hominibus.

10. Nos stulti propter Christum,

[1] " A bitter taunt," says *Lightfoot,* "chastising the boasting of the Corinthians, who had forgot from whom they had first received those evange-
lical privileges, concerning which they now prided themselves. They were
enriched with spiritual gifts ; they reigned, themselves being judges, in the
very top of the dignity and happiness of the gospel ; and that, ' *without
us,*' saith the Apostle, ' as though ye owed nothing to us for these privileges,' and, ' *O would to God ye did reign,* and that it went so happily
and well with you indeed, that we also might reign with you, and that we
might partake of some happiness in this your promotion, and might be of
some account among you!' "—*Ed.*
[2] " Fausse et dangereuse :"—" Groundless and dangerous."
[3] " C'est vne folie, et bestise :"—" This is a folly and stupidity."

but ye *are* wise in Christ; we *are* weak, but ye *are* strong; ye *are* honourable, but we *are* despised.

11. Even unto this present hour we both hunger, and thirst, and are naked, and are buffeted, and have no certain dwelling-place:

12. And labour, working with our own hands: being reviled, we bless: being persecuted, we suffer it:

13. Being defamed, we entreat: we are made as the filth of the world, *and are* the offscouring of all things unto this day.

14. I write not these things to shame you, but as my beloved sons I warn *you*.

15. For though ye have ten thousand instructors in Christ, yet *have ye* not many fathers: for in Christ Jesus I have begotten you through the gospel.

vos autem prudentes in Christo: nos infirmi, vos autem robusti: vos gloriosi, nos autem ignobiles.

11. Ad hanc enim horam usque et sitimus, et esurimus, et nudi sumus, et colaphis cædimur.

12. Et circumagimur, et laboramus operantes manibus propriis: maledictis lacessiti benedicimus: persequutionem patientes sustinemus:

13. Conviciis affecti obsecramus: quasi exsecrationes mundi facti sumus, omnium reiectamentum usque ad hunc diem.

14. Non quo pudorem vobis incutiam, hæc scribo: sed ut filios meos dilectos admoneo.

15. Nam etsi decem millia pædagogorum habueritis in Christo, non tamen multos patres; in Christo enim Iesu par Evangelium ego vos genui.

9. *For I think*, &c.   It is uncertain whether he speaks of himself exclusively, or takes in at the same time Apollos and Silvanus, for he sometimes calls such persons apostles. I prefer, however, to understand it of himself exclusively. Should any one be inclined to extend it farther, I shall have no particular objection, provided only he does not understand it as Chrysostom does, to mean that the apostles were as if for the sake of ignominy reserved to the last place.[1]   For there can be no doubt that by the term *last*, he means those who were admitted to the rank of apostles subsequently to the resurrection of Christ.   Now, he admits that he is like those who are exhibited to the people when on the eve of being led forth to death.   For such is the meaning of the word *exhibited*—as those who on occasion of a triumph were led round[2] for the sake of show, and were afterwards hurried away to prison to be strangled.

This he expresses more distinctly by adding, that they *were made a spectacle.*   " This," says he, " is my condition,

[1] " Et bien peu estimez ;"—" And very little esteemed."
[2] " On pourmenoit par toute la ville les poures prisonniers ;"—" They led the poor prisoners round the whole town."

that I exhibit to the world a spectacle of my miseries, like
those who having been condemned to fight with wild
beasts,[1] or to the games of the gladiators, or to some other
mode of punishment, are brought forth to the view of the
people, and that not before a few spectators, but before the
whole *world.*"   Observe here the admirable steadfastness of
Paul, who, while he saw himself to be dealt with by God in
this manner, was nevertheless not broken or dispirited. For
he does not impute it to the wantonness of the wicked, that
he was, as it were, led forth with ignominy to the sport of the
arena, but ascribes it wholly to the providence of God.

The second clause—*to angels and to men,* I take to be
expository in this sense—" I am made a sport and spectacle,
not merely to earth, but also to heaven." This passage has
been commonly explained as referring to devils, from its
seeming to be absurd to refer it to good angels. Paul, however, does not mean, that all who are witnesses of this calamity are gratified with such a spectacle. He simply means,
that the Lord has so ordered his lot that he seems as though
he had been appointed to furnish sport to the whole world.

10. *We are fools for Christ's sake.* This contrast is throughout ironical, and exceedingly pointed, it being unseemly and
absurd that the Corinthians should be in every respect happy
and honourable, according to the flesh, while in the meantime they beheld their master and father afflicted with the
lowest ignominy, and with miseries of every kind. For
those who are of opinion that Paul abases himself in this
manner, in order that he may in earnestness ascribe to the
Corinthians those things which he acknowledges himself to
be in want of, may without any difficulty be refuted from
the little clause that he afterwards subjoins. In speaking,
therefore, of the Corinthians as *wise in Christ,* and *strong,*
and *honourable,* he makes a concession ironically, as though
he had said[2]—" You desire, along with the gospel, to retain

---

[1] " Condamnez à seruir de passe-temps en combattant contre des
bestes ;"—" Condemned to serve as a pastime in fighting against wild
beasts."

[2] " C'est une concession ironique, c'est à dire, qu'il accorde ce dont ils
se vantoyent, mais c'est par mocquerie, comme s'il disoit ;"—" It is an

commendation for *wisdom*,[1] whereas I have not been able to
preach Christ otherwise than by becoming *a fool* in this
world. Now when I have willingly, on your account, submitted to be *a fool,* or to be reckoned such, consider
whether it be reasonable that you should wish to be
esteemed *wise.* How ill these things consort—that I who
have been your master, am *a fool for Christ's sake,* and you,
on the other hand, remain *wise !"* In this way, *being wise in
Christ* is not taken here in a good sense, for he derides the
Corinthians for wishing to mix up together Christ and the
wisdom of the flesh, inasmuch as this were to endeavour to
unite things directly contrary.

The case is the same as to the subsequent clauses—" You
are *strong,* says he, and *honourable,* that is, you glory in the
riches and resources of the world, you cannot endure the
ignominy of the cross. In the meantime, is it reasonable
that I should be on your account[2] mean and contemptible,
and exposed to many infirmities ? Now the complaint carries
with it so much the more reproach[3] on this account, that
even among themselves he was *weak and contemptible.*
(2 Cor. x. 10.) In fine, he derides their vanity in this respect, that, reversing the order of things, those who were
sons and followers were desirous to be esteemed *honourable*
and noble, while their father was in obscurity, and was exposed also to all the reproaches of the world.

11. *For to this hour.* The Apostle here describes his condition, as if in a picture, that the Corinthians may learn,
from his example, to lay aside that loftiness of spirit, and
embrace, as he did, the cross of Christ with meekness of
spirit. He discovers the utmost dexterity in this respect,
that in making mention of those things which had rendered
him contemptible, he affords clear proof of his singular fidel-

ironical concession ; that is to say—he grants what they boast of, but it is
in mockery, as though he had said."
[1] " En faisant profession de l'Euangile, vous voulez auec cela estre estimez prudens ;"—" In making a profession of the gospel, you wish, along
with that, to be esteemed wise."
[2] " Pour l'amour de vous ;"—" From love to you."
[3] " Est d'autant plus picquante, et aigre ;"—" Is so much the more
cutting and severe."

ity and indefatigable zeal for the advancement of the gospel ;
and, on the other hand, he tacitly reproves his rivals, who,
while they had furnished no such proof, were desirous, nevertheless, to be held in the highest esteem.   In the words
themselves there is no obscurity, except that we must take
notice of the distinction between those two participles—
λοιδορουμενοι και βλασφημουμενοι (*reviled* and *defamed*.)   As
λοιδορια means—that harsher sort of raillery, which does not
merely give a person a slight touch, but a sharp bite, and
blackens his character by open contumely, there can be no
doubt that λοιδορειν means—wounding a person with reproach
as with a sting.[1]   I have accordingly rendered it—*harassed
with revilings*.   Βλασφημια signifies a more open reproach,
when any one is severely and atrociously slandered.[2]

12. When he says that *while persecuted he suffers it*, and
that he *prays* for his *revilers*, he intimates that he is not
merely afflicted and abased by God, by means of the cross, but
is also endowed with a disposition to abase himself willingly.
In this, perhaps, he gives a stroke to the false apostles, who
were so effeminate and tender, that they could not bear to be
touched even with your little finger.   In speaking of their
labouring he adds—*with our own hands*, to express more
fully the meanness of his employment[3]—" I do not merely
gain a livelihood for myself by my own labour, but by mean
labour, *working with my own hands*."

13. *As the execrations of the world.*   He makes use of
two terms, the former of which denotes a man who, by public *execrations*, is devoted, with the view to the cleansing of

---

[1] λοιδορια is supposed by Eustathius to be derived from λογος, a *word*, and
δορυ, a *spear*.   A similar figure is employed by the Psalmist, when he speaks
of words that are *drawn swords*.   (Ps. lv. 21.)—*Ed.*

[2] " Or *le premier* signifie non seulement se gaudir d'vn homme, mais aussi
toucher son honneur comme en le blasonnant, et le naurer en termes pic-
quans : ce que nous disons communement, Mordre en riant.   *Le second*
signifie quand on detracte apertement de quelqu'vn sans vser de couuerture de paroles ;"—" Now *the first* means not simply to make one's self
merry at another's expense, but also to touch his reputation, as if with the
view of blackening it, and wounding it by cutting expressions, as we commonly say—to give a good humoured bite.   *The second* means when persons slander any one openly, without using any disguise of words."

[3] " Que c'estoit vn mestier ville, et mechanique ;"—" That it was a
mean and mechanical occupation."

a city,[1] for such persons, on the ground of their cleansing the rest of the people, by receiving in themselves whatever there is in the city of crimes, and heinous offence, are called by the Greeks sometimes καθαρμοι, but more frequently καθάρματα.[2] Paul, in adding the preposition περὶ (around) seems to have had an eye to the expiatory rite itself, inasmuch as those unhappy men who were devoted to execrations were *led round* through the streets, that they might carry away with them whatever there was of evil[3] in any corner, that the cleansing might be the more complete. The plural number might seem to imply that he speaks not of himself exclusively, but also of the others who were his associates, and who were not less held in contempt by the Corinthians. There is, however, no urgent reason for regarding what he says as extending to more than himself. The other term—περίψημα, (offscouring,) denotes filings or scrapings of any kind, and also the sweepings that are cleared away with a brush.[4] As to both terms consult the annotations of Budæus.[5]

In so far as concerns the meaning of the passage before us, Paul, with the view of expressing his extreme degradation, says that he is held in abomination by the whole world,

---

[1] " Comme c'estoit vne chose qui se faisoit anciennement entre les payens;"—" As this was a thing that was practised anciently among the heathens."

[2] The Scholiast on Aristophanes, Plut. 454, gives the following explanation of the term κάθαρμα: Καθάρματα ἐλέγοντο οἱ ἐπὶ τῆ, καθάρσει λοιμοῦ τινος ἤ τινος ἑτέρας νόσου θυόμενοι τοις Θεοῖς. Τοῦτο δὲ τὸ ἔθος καὶ παρὰ 'Ρωμαίοις ἐπικράτησε. Those were called *cleansings* who were sacrificed to the gods for the *cleansing out* of some famine, or some other calamity. This custom prevailed also among the Romans.—*Ed.*

[3] " De malediction ;"—" Of curse."

[4] " Les ballieures d'vne maison ;"—" The sweepings of a house."

[5] The view given by Budæus of the *former* term (περικαθάρματα) is stated by Leigh in his Critica Sacra to be the following: That " the Apostle had allusion unto the expiations in use among the heathens, in time of any pestilence or contagious infection; for the removal of such diseases they then sacrificed certain men unto their gods, which men they termed καθάρματα. As if the Apostle had said—We are as despicable and as odious in the sight of the people, as much loaded with the revilings and cursings of the multitude, as those condemned persons who were offered up by way of public expiation." The *latter* term (περίψημα) Budæus renders as follows: " Scobem aut ramentum et quicquid limando deteritur ;"—" Filings or scrapings, or whatever is cleared off by filing."—*Ed.*

like a man set apart for expiation,[1] and that, like offscourings, he is nauseous to all.   At the same time he does not
mean to say by the former comparison that he is an expiatory victim for sins, but simply means, that in respect of disgrace and reproaches he differs nothing from the man on
whom the execrations of all are heaped up.

14. *I write not these things to shame you.*   As the foregoing instances of irony were very pointed, so that they
might exasperate the minds of the Corinthians, he now obviates that dissatisfaction by declaring, that he had not said
these things with a view to cover them with shame, but
rather to admonish them with paternal affection.   It is indeed certain that this is the nature and tendency of a father's
chastisement, to make his son feel ashamed ; for the first
token of return to a right state of mind is the shame which
the son begins to feel on being reproached for his fault.
The object, then, which the father has in view when he
chastises his son with reproofs, is that he may bring him to
be displeased with himself.   And we see that the tendency
of what Paul has said hitherto, is to make the Corinthians
ashamed of themselves.   Nay more, we shall find him a little
afterwards (1 Cor. vi. 5) declaring that he made mention of
their faults in order that they may begin to be ashamed.
Here, however, he simply means to intimate, that it was not
his design to heap disgrace upon them, or to expose their
sins publicly and openly with a view to their reproach.   For
he who admonishes in a friendly spirit, makes it his particular care that whatever there is of shame, may remain with
the individual whom he admonishes,[2] and may in this manner be buried.   On the other hand, the man who reproaches
with a malignant disposition, inflicts disgrace upon the man
whom he reproves for his fault, in such a manner as to hold
him up to the reproach of all.   Paul then simply affirms that
what he had said, had been said by him, with no disposition

---

[1] " Destiné à porter toutes les execrations et maudissons du monde ;"—
" Set apart to bear all the execrations and curses of the world."

[2] " Tasche sur toutes choses que toute la honte demeure entre lui et
celui lequel il admoneste ;"—" Endeavours above all things that the shame
may remain between him and the person whom he admonishes."

to upbraid, or with any view to hurt their reputation, but, on the contrary, with paternal affection he admonished them as to what he saw to be defective in them.

But what was the design of this admonition? It was that the Corinthians, who were puffed up with mere empty notions, might learn to glory, as he did, in the abasement of the cross, and might no longer despise him on those grounds on which he was deservedly honourable in the sight of God and angels—in fine, that, laying aside their accustomed haughtiness, they might set a higher value on those *marks*[1] *of Christ* (Gal. vi. 17) that were upon him, than on the empty and counterfeit show of the false apostles. Let teachers[2] infer from this, that in reproofs they must always use such moderation as not to wound men's minds with excessive severity, and that, agreeably to the common proverb, they must mix honey or oil with vinegar—that they must above all things take care not to appear to triumph over those whom they reprove, or to take delight in their disgrace—nay more, that they must endeavour to make it understood that they seek nothing but that their welfare may be promoted. For what good will the teacher[3] do by mere bawling, if he does not season the sharpness of his reproof by that moderation of which I have spoken? Hence if we are desirous to do any good by correcting men's faults, we must distinctly give them to know, that our reproofs proceed from a friendly disposition.

15. *For though you had ten thousand.* He had called himself *father,* and now he shows that this title belongs to him peculiarly and specially, inasmuch as he alone has *begotten them in Christ.* In this comparison, however, he has an eye to the false apostles to whom the Corinthians showed all deference, so that Paul was now almost as nothing among

---

[1] " Les marques et fletrisseurs de Christ en luy ;"—" The marks and brands of Christ in him." The allusion, as our Author himself remarks, when commenting upon Gal. vi. 17, is to "the marks with which barbarian slaves, or fugitives, or malefactors were *branded.*" Hence the expression of Juvenal: *stigmate* dignum credere—" to reckon one worthy of being *branded* as a slave." (Juv. x. 183.)— *Ed.*

[2] " Les docteurs et ministres ;"—" Teachers and ministers."

[3] " Le ministre :"—" The minister."

them. Accordingly he admonishes them to consider what
honour ought to be rendered to a *father*, and what to a *pedagogue*.[1] "You entertain respect for those new teachers.
To this I have no objection, provided you bear in mind that
I am your *father*, while they are merely *pedagogues.*" Now
by claiming for himself authority, he intimates that he is
actuated by a different kind of affection from that of those
whom they so highly esteemed. "They take pains in instructing you. Be it so. Very different is the love of a *father*,
very different his anxiety, very different his attachment from
those of a *pedagogue*. What if he should also make an allusion to that imperfection of faith[2] which he had previously
found fault with ? For while the Corinthians were giants
in pride, they were children in faith, and are, therefore, with
propriety, sent to *pedagogues*.[3] He also reproves the absurd
and base system of those teachers in keeping their followers
in the mere first rudiments, with the view of keeping them
always in bonds under their authority.[4]

[1] " The Greek word *pedagogue*," says *Calmet*, " now carries with it an
idea approaching to contempt. With no other word to qualify it, it excites
the idea of a pedant, who assumes an air of authority over others, which
does not belong to him. But among the ancients a pedagogue was a person to whom they committed the care of their children, to lead them, to
observe them, and to instruct them in their first rudiments. Thus the
office of a pedagogue nearly answered to that of a governor or tutor, who
constantly attends his pupil, teaches him, and forms his manners. Paul
(1 Cor. iv. 13) says : ' For though you have ten thousand instructors
(*pedagogues*) in Christ, yet have ye not many fathers'—representing himself as their father in the faith, since he had *begotten them in the gospel.*
The *pedagogue*, indeed, may have some power and interest in his pupil,
but he can never have the natural tenderness of a *father* for him."—*Ed.*

[2] " Quel mal y auroit-il, quand nous dirions, qu'il fait aussi vne allusion
à ceste petitesse et enfance en la foy ? "—" What harm were there, though
we should say that he also makes an allusion to that littleness and childhood in the faith ? "

[3] Our Author evidently alludes to the etymology of the original term
παιδαγωγοὺς, as being derived from παῖς, a *boy*, and ἄγω, to *lead*. Such instructors were generally slaves, whose business it was to attend upon their
youthful charge, to observe their behaviour, and to *lead* them to and from
school. (Herod. viii. 75, Eur. Ion, 725.)—*Ed.*

[4] " La mauuaise procedure et façon d'enseigner des docteurs, d'autant
qu'ils amusoyent leurs disciples aux premiers rudimens et petis commencemens, et les tenoyent tousiours là ;"—" The base procedure and method of
instruction of the teachers, inasmuch as they amused their followers with
the first rudiments and little beginnings, and kept them constantly there."

For in Christ. Here we have the reason why he alone ought to be esteemed as the *father* of the Corinthian Church —because he had *begotten* it. And truly it is in most appropriate terms that he here describes spiritual generation, when he says that he has *begotten them in Christ,* who alone is the life of the soul, and makes the gospel the formal cause.[1] Let us observe, then, that we are *then* in the sight of God truly *begotten,* when we are ingrafted into Christ, out of whom there will be found nothing but death, and that this is effected by means of *the gospel,* because, while we are by nature flesh and hay, the word of God, as Peter (1 Peter i. 24, 25) teaches from Isaiah, (xl. 6, 7, 8,) is *the incorruptible seed* by which we are renewed to eternal life. Take away the gospel, and we will all remain accursed and dead in the sight of God. That same word by which we are *begotten* is afterwards *milk* to us for nourishing us, and it is also *solid food* to sustain us for ever.[2]

Should any one bring forward this objection, "As new sons are *begotten* to God in the Church every day, why does Paul say that those who succeeded him were not *fathers?*" the answer is easy—that he is here speaking of the *commencement* of the Church. For although many had been *begotten* by the ministry of others, this honour remained to Paul untouched—that he had founded the Corinthian Church. Should any one, again, ask, "Ought not all pastors to be reckoned *fathers,* and if so, why does Paul deprive all others of this title, so as to claim it for himself exclusively?" I answer—"He speaks here comparatively." Hence, however the title of *fathers* might be applicable to them in other respects, yet in respect of Paul, they were merely *instructors.* We must also keep in mind what I touched upon a little ago,[3] that he is not speaking of all, (for as to those who were like himself, as, for example, Apollos, Silvanus, and Timotheus, who aimed at nothing but the advancement of Christ's kingdom, he would have had no objection to their being so

----

[1] " Qu'on appelle ;"—" As they call it."

[2] Our Author probably refers to what he had said when commenting on 1 Cor. iii. 2. See p. 122.—*Ed.*

[3] See p. 166.

named, and having the highest honour assigned to them,) but is reproving those who, by a misdirected ambition, transferred to themselves the glory that belonged to another. Of this sort were those who robbed Paul of the honour that was due to him, that they might set themselves off in his spoils.

And, truly, the condition of the Church universal at this day is the same as that of the Corinthian Church was at that time. For how few are there that love the Churches with a *fatherly*, that is to say, a disinterested affection, and lay themselves out to promote their welfare ! Meanwhile, there are very many *pedagogues*, who give out their services as hirelings, in such a manner as to discharge as it were a mere temporary office, and in the meantime hold the people in subjection and admiration.[1] At the same time, even in that case it is well when there are many *pedagogues*, who do good, at least, to some extent by teaching, and do not destroy the Church by the corruptions of false doctrine. For my part, when I complain of the multitude of *pedagogues*, I do not refer to Popish priests, (for I would not do them the honour of reckoning them in that number,) but those who, while agreeing with us in doctrine, employ themselves in taking care of their own affairs, rather than those of Christ. We all, it is true, wish to be reckoned *fathers*, and require from others the obedience of sons, but where is the man to be found who acts in such a manner as to show that he is a *father ?*[2]

There remains another question of greater difficulty : As Christ forbids us to *call any one father upon earth, because we have one Father in heaven,* (Matt. xxiii. 9,) how does

[1] " Qui se loent, comme ouuriers à la iournée, pour exercer l'office à leur profit, ainsi qu'on feroit vne chose qu'on aura prise pour vn temps certain, et cependant tenir le peuple en obeissance, et acquerir bruit, ou estre en admiration enuers iceluy:"—" Who hire themselves out, as workmen for the day, in order to exercise the office to their own advantage, as if one were doing a thing that he had taken up for a certain time, and in the meantime to hold the people in subjection, and acquire fame, or be in admiration among them."

[2] " Combien y en a-t-il qui facent office de père, et qui demonstrent par effet ce qu'ils veulent estre appelez ?"—" How many are there of them that discharge the office of a father, and show in deeds what they wish to be called ?"

Paul dare to take to himself the name of *father?* I answer, that, properly speaking, God alone is the Father, not merely of our soul, but also of our flesh. As, however, in so far as concerns the body, he communicates the honour of his paternal name to those to whom he gives offspring, while, as to souls, he reserves to himself exclusively the right and title of Father, I confess that, on this account, he is called in a peculiar sense *the Father of spirits,* and is distinguished from earthly *fathers,* as the Apostle speaks in Hebrews xii. 9. As, however, notwithstanding that it is he alone who, by his own influence, begets souls, and regenerates and quickens them, he makes use of the ministry of his servants for this purpose, there is no harm in their being called *fathers,* in respect of this ministry, as this does not in any degree detract from the honour of God. The word, as I have said,[1] is the spiritual seed. God alone by means of it regenerates our souls by his influence, but, at the same time, he does not exclude the efforts of ministers. If, therefore, you attentively consider, what God accomplishes by himself, and what he designs to be accomplished by ministers, you will easily understand in what sense he alone is worthy of the name of *Father,* and how far this name is applicable to his ministers, without any infringement upon his rights.

16. Wherefore I beseech you, be ye followers of me.

17. For this cause have I sent unto you Timotheus, who is my beloved son, and faithful in the Lord, who shall bring you into remembrance of my ways which be in Christ, as I teach every where in every church.

18. Now some are puffed up, as though I would not come to you.

19. But I will come to you shortly, if the Lord will, and will know, not the speech of them which are puffed up, but the power.

20. For the kingdom of God *is* not in word, but in power.

21. What will ye? shall I come unto you with a rod, or in love, and *in* the spirit of meekness?

16. Adhortor ergo vos, imitatores mei estote.

17. Hac de causa misi ad vos Timotheum, qui est filius meus dilectus et fidelis in Domino: qui vobis in memoriam reducat vias meas, quæ sunt in Christo, quemadmodum ubique in omnibus Ecclesiis doceam.

18. Perinde quasi non sum ad vos venturus, inflati sunt quidam:

19. Veniam autem brevi ad vos, si Dominus voluerit, et cognoscam non sermonem eorum qui sunt inflati, sed virtutem.

20. Neque enim in sermone regnum Dei est, sed in virtute.

21. Quid vultis? in virga veniam ad vos, an in dilectione spirituque mansuetudinis?

[1] See p. 170.

16. *I exhort you.* He now expresses also, in his own words, what he requires from them in his fatherly admonition—that, being his sons, they do not degenerate from their father. For what is more reasonable than that sons endeavour to be as like as possible to their father.[1] At the same time he gives up something in respect of his own right, when he *exhorts* them to this, by way of entreaty rather than of command. But to what extent he wishes them to be *imitators of him,* he shows elsewhere, when he adds, *as he was of Christ.* (1 Cor. xi. 1.) This limitation must always be observed, so as not to follow any man, except in so far as he leads us to Christ. We know what he is here treating of. The Corinthians did not merely shun the abasement of the cross, but they also regarded their *father* with contempt, on this account, that, forgetting earthly glory, he gloried rather in reproaches for Christ ; and they reckoned themselves and others fortunate in having nothing contemptible according to the flesh. He accordingly admonishes them to devote themselves, after his example, to the service of Christ, so as to endure all things patiently.

17. *For this cause.* The meaning is: "That you may know what my manner of life is, and whether I am worthy to be imitated, listen to what Timothy has to say, who will be prepared to be a faithful witness of these things. Now as there are two things that secure credit to a man's testimony —a knowledge of the things which he relates, and fidelity— he lets them know that Timothy possesses both of these things. For in calling him his *dearly beloved son,* he intimates that he knew him intimately, and was acquainted with all his affairs ; and farther, he speaks of him as *faithful in the Lord.* He gives also two things in charge to Timothy —*first,* to recall to the recollection of the Corinthians those things which they should of themselves have had in remembrance, and in this he tacitly reproves them ; and *secondly,* to testify to them, how uniform and steady his manner of teaching was in every place. Now it is probable that he had been assailed by the calumnies of the false apostles, as

---

[1] " Taschent à suyure les bonnes mœurs de leurs peres;"—" Endeavour to follow the good manners of their fathers."

though he assumed more authority over the Corinthians than he did over others, or as though he conducted himself in a very different way in other places ; for it is not without good reason that he wishes this to be testified to them. It is then the part of a prudent minister so to regulate his procedure, and to observe such a method of instruction, that no such objection may be brought against him, but he shall be prepared to answer on the same ground as Paul does.

18. *As though I would not come to you.* This is the custom of the false apostles—to take advantage of the absence of the good, that they may triumph and vaunt without any hindrance. Paul, accordingly, with the view of reproving their ill-regulated conscience, and repressing their insolence, tells them, that they cannot endure his presence. It happens sometimes, it is true, that wicked men, on finding opportunity of insulting, rise up openly with an iron front against the servants of Christ, but never do they come forward ingenuously to an equal combat,[1] but on the contrary, by sinister artifices they discover their want of confidence.

19. *But I will come shortly.* "They are in a mistake," says he, " in raising their crests during my absence, as though this were to be of long duration, for they shall in a short time perceive how vain their confidence has been." He has it not, however, so much in view to terrify them, as though he would on his arrival thunder forth against them, but rather presses and bears down upon their consciences, for, however they might disguise it, they were aware that he was furnished with divine influence.

The clause, *if the Lord will,* intimates, that we ought not to promise anything to others as to the future, or to determine with ourselves, without adding this limitation : in so far as *the Lord will permit.* Hence James with good reason

---

[1] " Si est-ce que jamais ils ne vienent à combatre franchement, et s' ils ne voyent leur auantage : mais plustot en vsant de ruses et circuits obliques, ils monstrent leur deffiance, et comment ils sont mal asseurez ;"— " So it is, that they never come forward frankly to a combat, and unless they have a view to their own advantage ; but on the contrary, by making use of tricks and indirect windings, they show their want of confidence, and how distrustful they are."

derides the rashness of mankind (James iv. 15) in planning what they are to do ten years afterwards, while they have not security for living even a single hour. We are not, it is true, bound by a constant necessity to the use of such forms of expression, but it is the better way to accustom ourselves carefully to them, that we may exercise our minds from time to time in this consideration—that all our plans must be in subjection to the will of God.

And I will know not the speech. By *speech* you must understand that prating in which the false apostles delighted themselves, for they excelled in a kind of dexterity and gracefulness of speech, while they were destitute of the zeal and efficacy of the Spirit. By the term *power*, he means that spiritual efficacy, with which those are endowed who dispense the word of the Lord with earnestness.[1] The meaning, therefore, is : " I shall see whether they have so much occasion for being puffed up ; and I shall not judge of them by their mere outward talkativeness, in which they place the sum-total[2] of their glory, and on the ground of which they claim for themselves every honour. If they wish to have any honour from me, they must bring forward that *power* which distinguishes the true servants of Christ from the merely pretended : otherwise I shall despise them, with all their show. It is to no purpose, therefore, that they confide in their eloquence, for I shall reckon it nothing better than smoke."

20. *For the kingdom of God is not in word.* As the Lord governs the Church by his word, as with a sceptre, the administration of the gospel is often called *the kingdom of God*. Here, then, we are to understand by *the kingdom of God* whatever tends in this direction, and is appointed for this purpose—that God may reign among us. He says that this kingdom does not consist in *word*, for how small an affair is it for any one to have skill to prate eloquently, while he has nothing but empty tinkling.[3] Let us know, then, a

[1] " D'vn bon zele, et pure affection ;"—" With a right zeal and a pure affection."

[2] " Proram et puppim ;"—" Prow and stern."

[3] " Sçaura bien babiller et parler eloquemment, et cependant il n'aura

mere outward gracefulness and dexterity in teaching is like a body that is elegant and of a beautiful colour, while the *power* of which Paul here speaks is like the soul. We have already seen[1] that the preaching of the gospel is of such a nature, that it is inwardly replete with a kind of solid majesty. This majesty shows itself, when a minister strives by means of *power* rather than of *speech*—that is, when he does not place confidence in his own intellect, or eloquence, but, furnished with spiritual armour, consisting of zeal for maintaining the Lord's honour—eagerness for the raising up of Christ's kingdom—a desire to edify—the fear of the Lord— an invincible constancy—purity of conscience, and other necessary endowments, he applies himself diligently to the Lord's work. Without this, preaching is dead, and has no strength, with whatever beauty it may be adorned. Hence in his second epistle, he says, that in Christ nothing avails but *a new creature* (2 Cor. v. 17)—a statement which is to the same purpose. For he would have us not rest in outward masks, but depend solely on the internal *power* of the Holy Spirit.

But while in these words he represses the ambition of the false apostles, he at the same time reproves the Corinthians for their perverted judgment, in measuring the servants of Christ by what holds the lowest place among their excellences. Here we have a remarkable statement, and one that is not less applicable to us than to them. As to our gospel, of which we are proud,[2] where is it in most persons except in the tongue? Where is newness of life? Where is spiritual efficacy? Nor is it so among the people merely.[3] On the contrary, how many there are, who, while endeavouring to procure favour and applause from the gospel, as though it were some profane science, aim at nothing else

rien qu'vn son retentissant en l'air;"—" Has skill to prate well, and speak eloquently, and in the meantime has nothing but a sound tinkling in the air."

[1] See pp. 73, 76.

[2] " Duquel nous nous vantons et glorifions tant;"—" Of which we boast and glory so much."

[3] " Et ce n'est point au peuple seulement qu'est ce defaut;"—" And it is not among the people merely that this defect exists."

than to speak with elegance and refinement! I do not
approve of restricting the term *power* to miracles, for from
the contrast we may readily gather that it has a more extensive import.

21. *What will ye?* The person who divided the Epistles
into chapters ought to have made this the beginning of the
fifth chapter. For having hitherto reproved the foolish
pride of the Corinthians, their vain confidence, and their
judgment as perverted and corrupted by ambition, he now
makes mention of the vices with which they were infected,
and on account of which they ought to be ashamed—" You
are puffed up, as though everything were on the best possible footing among you, but it were better if you did with
shame and sighing acknowledge the unhappiness of your
condition, for if you persist, I shall be under the necessity of
laying aside mildness, and exercising towards you a paternal
severity." There is, however, still more of emphasis in this
threatening in which he gives them liberty to choose, for
he declares that it does not depend upon himself whether he
shall show himself agreeable and mild, but that it is their
own fault that he is necessitated to use severity. " It is
for you," says he, " to choose in what temper you would
have me. As for me, I am prepared to be mild, but if you
go on as you have done hitherto, I shall be under the necessity of taking up the *rod.*" He thus takes higher ground,
after having laid claim to *fatherly* authority over them, for
it would have been absurd to set out with this threatening,
without first opening up the way by what he said, and preparing them for entertaining fears.

By the term *rod*, he means that severity with which a
pastor ought to correct his people's faults. He places in contrast with this, *love, and the spirit of meekness*—not as though
the father hated the sons whom he chastises, for on the contrary the chastisement proceeds from love, but because by
sadness of countenance and harshness of words, he appears as
though he were angry with his son. To express myself more
plainly—in one word, a father always, whatever kind of look
he may put on, regards his son with affection, but that affection he manifests when he teaches him pleasantly and

lovingly ; but when, on the other hand, being displeased with his faults, he chastises him in rather sharp terms, or even with the *rod*, he puts on the appearance of a person in a passion. As then love does not appear when severity of discipline is exercised, it is not without good reason, that Paul here conjoins *love* with a *spirit of meekness.* There are some that understand the term *rod* to mean excommunication—but, for my part, though I grant them that excommunication is a part of that severity with which Paul threatens the Corinthians, I at the same time extend it farther, so as to include all reproofs that are of a harsher kind.

Observe here what system a good pastor ought to observe ; for he ought of his own accord to be inclined to mildness, with the view of drawing to Christ, rather than driving. This mildness, so far as in him lies, he ought to maintain, and never have recourse to bitterness, unless he be compelled to do so. On the other hand, he must not *spare the rod,* (Prov. xiii. 24,) when there is need for it, for while those that are teachable and agreeable should be dealt with mildly, sharpness requires to be used in dealing with the refractory and contumacious. We see, too, that the Word of God does not contain mere doctrine, but contains an intermixture of bitter reproofs, so as to supply pastors with a *rod.* For it often happens, through the obstinacy of the people, that those pastors who are naturally the mildest[1] are constrained to put on, as it were, the countenance of another, and act with rigour and severity.

CHAPTER V.

1. It is reported commonly *that there is* fornication among you, and such fornication as is not so much as named among the Gentiles, that one should have his father's wife.

2. And ye are puffed up, and have not rather mourned, that he that hath done this deed might be taken away from among you.

1. Omnino auditur in vobus scortatio, et talis scortatio, quæ ne inter Gentes quidem nominatur, ut quis uxorem patris habeat.

2. Et vos inflati estis, ac non magis luxistis, ut e medio vestri removeretur, qui facinus hoc admisit.

[1] " Qu'on pourra trouuer ;"—" That one could find."

3. For I verily, as absent in body, but present in spirit, have judged already, as though I were present, *concerning* him that hath so done this deed,

4. In the name of our Lord Jesus Christ, when ye are gathered together, and my spirit, with the power of our Lord Jesus Christ,

5. To deliver such an one unto Satan for the destruction of the flesh, that the spirit may be saved in the day of the Lord Jesus.

3. Ego quidem certe tanquam absens corpore, præsens autem spiritu, jam iudicavi tanquam præsens, qui hoc ita designavit,

4. In nomine Domini nostri Iesu Christi, congregatis vobis et spiritu meo, cum potentia Domini nostri Iesu Christi, eiusmodi inquam hominem.

5. Tradere Satanæ in exitium carnis, ut spiritus salvus fiat in die Domini Iesu.

1. *It is generally reported that there is among you.* Those contentions having originated, as has been observed,[1] in presumption and excessive confidence, he most appropriately proceeds to make mention of their diseases, the knowledge of which should have the effect of humbling them. First of all, he shows them what enormous wickedness it is to allow one of their society to have an illicit connection with his mother-in-law. It is not certain, whether he had seduced her from his father as a prostitute, or whether he kept her under pretence of marriage. This, however, does not much affect the subject in hand; for, as in the former case, there would have been an abominable and execrable whoredom, so the latter would have involved an incestuous connection, abhorrent to all propriety and natural decency. Now, that he may not seem to charge them on doubtful suspicions, he says, that the case which he brings forward is well known and in general circulation. For it is in this sense that I take the particle ὅλως (generally) as intimating that it was no vague rumour, but a matter well known, and published everywhere so as to cause great scandal.

From his saying that such a kind of whoredom was *not named even among the Gentiles,* some are of opinion, that he refers to the incest of Reuben, (Gen. xxxv. 22,) who, in like manner, had an incestuous connection with his mother-in-law. They are accordingly of opinion, that Paul did not make mention of Israel, because a disgraceful instance of this kind had occurred among them, as if the annals of the

---

[1] See p. 121.

Gentiles did not record many incestuous connections of that kind! This, then, is an idea that is quite foreign to Paul's intention; for in making mention of the Gentiles rather than of the Jews, he designed rather to heighten the aggravation of the crime. " You," says he, " permit, as though it were a lawful thing, an enormity, which would not be tolerated even among the Gentiles—nay more, has always been regarded by them with horror, and looked upon as a prodigy of crime." When, therefore, he affirms that it was *not named among the Gentiles*, he does not mean by this, that no such thing had ever existed among them, or was not recorded in their annals, for even tragedies have been founded upon it ;[1] but that it was held in detestation by the Gentiles, as a shameful and abominable monstrosity, for it is a beastly lust, which destroys even natural modesty. Should any one ask, " Is it just to reproach all with the sin of one individual ?" I answer, that the Corinthians are accused, not because one of their number has sinned, but because, as is stated afterwards, they encouraged by connivance a crime that was deserving of the severest punishment.

2. *And ye are puffed up.* " Are ye not ashamed," says he, " to glory in what affords so much occasion for humiliation ?" He had observed previously, that even the highest excellence gives no just ground of glorying, inasmuch as mankind have nothing of their own, and it is only through the grace of God that they possess any excellence. (1 Cor. iv. 7.) Now, however, he attacks them from another quarter. " You are," says he, " covered with disgrace : what ground have you, then, for pride or haughtiness ? For there is an amazing blindness in glorying in the midst of disgrace, in spite, as it were of angels and men."

When he says, *and have not rather mourned,* he argues by way of contrast ; for where there is grief there is no more glorying. It may be asked : " Why ought they to have *mourned* over another man's sin ?" I answer, for two reasons : *first*, in consequence of the communion that exists among the members of the Church, it was becoming that all

---

[1] CALVIN probably had in his eye, among other instances, the Œdipus Tyrannus of Sophocles.—*Ed.*

should feel hurt at so deadly a fall on the part of one of their number; and *secondly*, when such an enormity is perpetrated in a particular Church, the perpetrator of it is an offender in such a way, that the whole society is in a manner polluted. For as God humbles the father of a family in the disgrace of his wife, or of his children, and a whole kindred in the disgrace of one of their number, so every Church ought to consider, that it contracts a stain of disgrace whenever any base crime is perpetrated in it. Nay, farther, we see how the anger of God was kindled against the whole nation of Israel on account of the sacrilege of one individual —Achan. (Joshua vii. 1.) It was not as though God had been so cruel as to take vengeance on the innocent for another man's crime; but, as in every instance in which anything of this nature has occurred among a people, there is already some token of his anger, so by correcting a community for the fault of one individual, he distinctly intimates that the whole body is infected and polluted with the contagion of the offence. Hence we readily infer, that it is the duty of every Church to *mourn* over the faults of individual members, as domestic calamities belonging to the entire body. And assuredly a pious and dutiful correction takes its rise in our being inflamed with holy zeal through displeasure at the offence; for otherwise severity will be felt to be bitter.[1]

That he might be taken away from among you. He now brings out more distinctly what he finds fault with in the Corinthians—remissness, inasmuch as they connived at such an abomination. Hence, too, it appears that Churches are furnished with this power[2]—that, whatever fault there is within them, they can correct or remove it by strictness of discipline, and that those are inexcusable that are not on the alert to have filth cleared away. For Paul here condemns the Corinthians. Why? Because they had been remiss in the punishment of one individual. Now he would have accused them unjustly, if they had not had this power. Hence the power of excommunication is established from

---

[1] " Et ne profitera pas;"—" And will do no good '
[2] " Et authorité;"—" And authority."

this passage.   On the other hand, as Churches have this mode of punishment put into their hands, those commit sin,[1] as Paul shows here, that do not make use of it, when it is required ; for otherwise he would act unfairly to the Corinthians in charging them with this fault.

3. *I truly*, &c.   As the Corinthians were wanting in their duty, having condemned their negligence, he now shows what ought to be done.   In order that this stain may be removed, they must cast out this incestuous person from the society of the faithful.   He prescribes, then, as a remedy for the disease, excommunication, which they had sinfully delayed so long.   When he says, that he had, *while absent in body*, already determined this, he severely reproves in this way the remissness of the Corinthians, for there is here an implied contrast.   It is as though he had said : " You who are *present* ought before this time to have applied a remedy to this disease, having it every day before your eyes, and yet you do nothing ;[2] while for my part I cannot, even though *absent*, endure it."   Lest any one should allege that he acted rashly in forming a judgment when at so great a distance, he declares himself to be *present in spirit*, meaning by this, that the line of duty was as plain to him as if he were present, and saw the thing with his eyes.   Now it is of importance to observe what he teaches as to the mode of excommunication.

4. *When you are gathered together and my spirit*—that is, when ye are *gathered together* with me, but *in spirit*, for they could not meet together as to bodily presence.   He declares, however, that it would be all one as though he were personally present.   It is to be carefully observed, that Paul, though an Apostle, does not himself, as an individual, excommunicate according to his own pleasure, but consults with the Church, that the matter may be transacted by common authority.   He, it is true, takes the lead, and shows the way, but, in taking others as his associates, he intimates with sufficient plainness, that this authority does not belong

---

[1] " Offensent Dieu ;"—" Offend God."
[2] " Vous dissimulez ;"—" You connive."

to any one individual.   As, however, a multitude never accomplishes anything with moderation or seriousness, if not governed by counsel, there was appointed in the ancient Church a Presbytery,[1] that is, an assembly of elders, who, by the consent of all, had the power of first judging in the case.   From them the matter was brought before the people, but it was as a thing already judged of.[2]   Whatever the matter may be, it is quite contrary to the appointment of Christ and his Apostles—to the order of the Church, and even to equity itself, that this right should be put into the hands of any one man, of excommunicating at his pleasure any that he may choose.   Let us take notice, then, that in excommunicating this limitation be observed—that this part of discipline be exercised by the common counsel of the elders, and with the consent of the people, and that this is a remedy in opposition to tyranny.   For nothing is more at variance with the discipline of Christ than tyranny, for which you open a wide door, if you give one man the entire power.

In the name of our Lord.   For it is not enough that we assemble, if it be not *in the name of Christ;* for even the wicked assemble together for impious and nefarious conspiracies.   Now in order that an assembly may be held in Christ's name, two things are requisite : *first,* that we begin by calling upon his name ; and *secondly,* that nothing is attempted but in conformity with his word.   *Then* only do men make an auspicious commencement of anything that they take in hand to do, when they with their heart call upon the Lord that they may be governed by his Spirit, and that their plans may, by his grace, be directed to a happy issue ; and farther, when they *ask at his mouth,* as the Prophet speaks, (Isaiah xxx. 2,) that is to say, when, after consulting his oracles, they surrender themselves and all their designs to his will in unreserved obedience.   If this is

---

[1] "Qu'on appeloit le Presbytère ;"—"What they called a Presbytery."

[2] "Puis apres la chose estoit renuoyee au peuple par eux, avec un advertissement touteffois de ce qui leur en sembloit ;"—"The matter was afterwards brought by them before the people, with an intimation, however, of their views respecting it."   See CALVIN's *Institutes,* vol. iii. pp. 233-5.—*Ed.*

becoming even in the least of our actions, how much less ought it to be omitted in important and serious matters, and least of all, when we have to do with God's business rather than our own?   For example, excommunication is an ordinance of God, and not of men; on any occasion, therefore, on which we are to make use of it, where shall we begin, if not with God.[1]   In short, when Paul exhorts the Corinthians to assemble *in the name of Christ,* he does not simply require them to make use of Christ's name, or to confess him with the mouth, (for the wicked themselves can do that,) but to seek him truly and with the heart, and farther, he intimates by this the seriousness and importance of the action.

He adds, *with the power of our Lord,* for if the promise is true, *As often as two or three are gathered together in my name, I am in the midst of them,* (Matt. xviii. 20,) it follows, that whatever is done in such an assembly is a work of Christ.   Hence we infer, of what importance excommunication, rightly administered, is in the sight of God, inasmuch as it rests upon the power of God.   For that saying, too, must be accomplished, *Whatsoever ye shall bind on earth shall be bound in heaven.*   (Matt. xviii. 18.)   As, however, this statement ought to fill despisers[2] with no ordinary alarm, so faithful pastors, as well as the Churches generally, are by this admonished in what a devout spirit[3] they should go to work in a matter of such importance.   For it is certain that the power of Christ is not tied to the inclination or opinions of mankind, but is associated with his eternal truth.

5. *To deliver to Satan for the destruction of the flesh.*   As the Apostles had been furnished with this power among others, that they could *deliver over to Satan* wicked and obstinate persons, and made use of him as a scourge to correct them, Chrysostom, and those that follow him, view these words of Paul as referring to a chastisement of that kind, agreeably to the exposition that is usually given of another passage, in reference to Alexander and Hymeneus, (1 Tim

---

[1] " Le nom de Dieu ;"—" The name of God."
[2] " Contempteurs de Dieu ;"—" Despisers of God."
[3] " En quelle crainte et obeissance :"—" With what fear and obed.ence "

i. 20.) *To deliver over to Satan,* they think, means nothing but the infliction of a severe punishment upon the body. But when I examine the whole context more narrowly, and at the same time compare it with what is stated in the Second Epistle, I give up that interpretation, as forced and at variance with Paul's meaning, and understand it simply of excommunication.   For *delivering over to Satan* is an appropriate expression for denoting excommunication ; for as Christ reigns *in* the Church, so Satan reigns *out of* the Church, as Augustine, too, has remarked,[1] in his sixty-eighth sermon on the words of the Apostle, where he explains this passage.[2]   As, then, we are received into the communion of the Church, and remain in it on this condition, that we are under the protection and guardianship of Christ, I say, that he who is cast out of the Church is in a manner delivered over to the power of Satan, for he becomes an alien, and is cast out of Christ's kingdom.

The clause that follows, *for the destruction of the flesh,* is made use of for the purpose of softening ; for Paul's meaning is not that the person who is chastised is given over to Satan to be utterly ruined, or so as to be given up to the devil in perpetual bondage, but that it is a temporary condemnation, and not only so, but of such a nature as will be salutary.   For as the salvation equally with the condemnation of the spirit is eternal, he takes the *condemnation of the flesh* as meaning *temporal* condemnation.   " We will condemn him in this world for a time, that the Lord may preserve him in his kingdom."   This furnishes an answer to the objection, by which some endeavour to set aside this exposition, for as the sentence of excommunication is directed rather against the soul than against the outward man, they inquire how it can be called *the destruction of the flesh.* My answer, then, is, (as I have already in part stated,) that the *destruction of the flesh* is opposed to *the salvation of the spirit,* simply because the former is temporal and the latter is eternal.   In this sense the Apostle in Heb. v. 7, uses the

---

[1] " L'a tres-bien noté ;"—" Has very well remarked."
[2] The reader will find the same sentiment quoted in the *Institutes,* vol iii. p. 252.— *Ed.*

expression *the days of Christ's flesh,* to mean the course of his mortal life.   Now the Church in chastising offenders with severity, spares them not in this world, in order that God may spare them.[1]   Should any one wish to have anything farther in reference to the rite of excommunication, its causes, necessity, purposes, and limitation, let him consult my Institutes.[2]

6. Your glorying *is* not good. Know ye not that a little leaven leaveneth the whole lump? 7. Purge out therefore the old leaven, that ye may be a new lump, as ye are unleavened. For even Christ our passover is sacrificed for us: 8. Therefore let us keep the feast, not with old leaven, neither with the leaven of malice and wickedness; but with the unleavened *bread* of sincerity and truth.

6. Non est bona gloriatio vestra: an nescitis, quod exiguum fermentum totam massam fermentat? 7. Expurgate ergo vetus fermentum, ut sitis nova conspersio, sicut estis azymi: nam Pascha nostrum pro nobis immolatum est, Christus.[3] 8. Proinde epulemur non in fermento veteri, neque in fermento malitiae et pravitatis, sed in azymis sinceritatis veritatis.[4]

6. *Your glorying is not good.*   He condemns their glorying, not simply because they extolled themselves beyond what is lawful for man, but because they delighted themselves in their faults.   He had previously stripped mankind of all glory ; for he had shown that, as they have nothing of their own, whatever excellence they may have, they owe the entire praise of it to God alone.   (1 Cor. iv. 7.)   What he treats of here, however, is not that God is defrauded of his right, when mortals arrogate to themselves the praise of their excellences, but that the Corinthians are guilty of arrant folly in extolling themselves without any just ground. For they proudly gloried as if everything had been in a golden style among them, while in the meantime there was so much among them that was wicked and disgraceful.

Know ye not.   That they might not think that it was a matter of little or no importance that they gave encourage-

[1] " Mais c'est afin que Dieu leur espargne ;"—" But it is in order that God may spare them."
[2] See *Institutes,* vol. iii. pp. 249-256.
[3] " Nostre Pasque, assavoir Christ ;"— " Our passover, namely, Christ."
[4] " Avec pains sans leuain, c'est a dire, de syncerité et de verité ;"— " With unleavened bread, that is to say, of sincerity and truth."

ment to so great an evil, he shows the destructive tendency
of indulgence and dissimulation in such a case.   He makes
use of a proverbial saying, by which he intimates that a
whole multitude is infected by the contagion of a single individual.   For this proverb has in this passage[1] the same
meaning as in those expressions of Juvenal : " A whole herd
of swine falls down in the fields through disease in one of
their number, and one discoloured grape infects another."[2]
I have said *in this passage*, because Paul, as we shall see,
makes use of it elsewhere (Gal. v. 9) in another sense.

7. *Purge out therefore.*   Having borrowed a similitude from
leaven, he pursues it farther, though he makes a transition
from a particular point to a general doctrine.   For he is no
longer speaking of the case of incest, but exhorts them
generally to purity of life, on the ground that we cannot
remain in Christ if we are not cleansed.   He is accustomed
to do this not unfrequently.   When he has made a particular
statement, he takes occasion to pass on to general exhortations.   He had made mention of *leaven* on another account,
as we have seen.   As this same metaphor suited the general
doctrine which he now subjoins, he extends it farther.

Our Passover.[3]   Before coming to the subject-matter, I

[1] " Ha en ce passage un mesme sens comme ce qu'on dit communee-
ment, Qu'il ne faut qu'vne brebis rongneuse pour gaster tout le troupeau;"
—" Has in this passage the same meaning as what is commonly said :—
There needs but one diseased sheep to infect a whole flock."

[2] ———————— grex totus in agris
Unius scabie cadit, et porrigine porci:
Uvaque conspecta livorem ducit ab uva.
JUV. II. 79-81.

[3] " Would any one," asks *Hervey*, (in his *Theron and Aspasio*, vol. i.
p. 64, *note*,) " venture to say—' Paul our passover is sacrificed for us ?'
Yet this, I think, may be, or rather is in effect said, by the account which
some persons give of Christ's satisfaction.   The very thought of such a
blasphemous absurdity is too painful and offensive for the serious Christian
to dwell upon.   I would therefore direct his attention to a more pleasing
object.   Let him observe the exquisite skill which here and everywhere
conducts the zeal of our inspired writer.   The odes of Pindar are celebrated for their fine transitions, which, though bold and surprising, are
perfectly natural.   We have in this place" (1 Cor. v. 7) " a very masterly
stroke of the same beautiful kind.   The Apostle, speaking of the incestuous criminal, passes, by a most artful digression, to his darling topic—a
crucified Saviour.   Who would have expected it on such an occasion ?
Yet, when thus admitted, who does not see and admire both the propriety
of the subject and the delicacy of its introduction ?"—*Ed.*

shall say a few words in reference to the words. *Old leaven* receives that name on the same principle as the *old man*, (Rom. vi. 6,) for the corruption of nature takes the precedence in us, previously to our being renewed in Christ. *That,* therefore, is said to be *old* which we bring with us from the womb, and must perish when we are renewed by the grace of the Spirit.[1] The verb ἐτύθη, which occurs between the name *Christ* and the term which denotes a sacrifice,[2] may refer to either. I have taken it as referring to the sacrifice, though this is of no great importance, as the meaning is not affected. The verb ἑορτάζωμεν, which Erasmus rendered " Let us celebrate the feast," signifies also to partake of the solemn feast which was observed after the sacrifice had been offered up. This interpretation appeared to suit better with the passage before us. I have, accordingly, followed the Vulgate in preference to Erasmus, as this rendering is more in accordance with the mystery of which Paul treats.

We come now to the subject-matter. Paul, having it in view to exhort the Corinthians to holiness, shows that what was of old figuratively represented in the passover, ought to be at this day accomplished in us, and explains the correspondence which exists between the figure and the reality. In the first place, as the passover consisted of two parts— a sacrifice and a sacred feast—he makes mention of both. For although some do not reckon the paschal lamb to have been a sacrifice, yet reason shows that it was properly a sacrifice, for in that rite the people were reconciled to God by the sprinkling of blood. Now there is no reconciliation without a sacrifice ; and, besides, the Apostle now expressly confirms it, for he makes use of the word θύεσθαι, which is applicable to sacrifices, and in other respects, too, the context would not correspond. The lamb, then, was sacrificed yearly ; then followed a feast, the celebration of which

---

[1] Our Author gives a similar definition of the expression *the old man*, when commenting on Rom. vi. 6. " Totam autem naturam significat, quam afferimus ex utero, quæ adeo regni Dei capax non est, ut interire eatenus oporteat, quatenus in veram vitam instauramur ;"—" It denotes the whole of that nature which we bring with us from the womb, and is so far from being fit for the kingdom of God, that it must perish, in so far as we are renewed to a true life."—*Ed.*

[2] " Assauoir, *Pasque;*"—" Namely, *passover.*"

lasted for seven successive days. *Christ*, says Paul, is *our Passover*.[1] He was sacrificed once, and on this condition, that the efficacy of that one oblation should be everlasting. What remains now is, that we eat,[2] not once a-year, but continually.

8. Now, in the solemnity of this sacred feast we must abstain from *leaven*, as God commanded the fathers to abstain. But from what leaven? As the outward passover was to them a figure of the true *passover*, so its appendages were figures of the reality which we at this day possess. If, therefore, we would wish to feed on Christ's flesh and blood, let us bring to this feast *sincerity and truth*. Let these be our loaves of *unleavened bread*. Away with all *malice and wickedness*, for it is unlawful to mix up *leaven* with the *passover*. In fine, he declares that we shall be members of Christ only when we shall have renounced *malice* and deceit. In the meantime we must carefully observe this passage, as showing that the ancient passover was not merely μνημοσυνον,[3] a memorial of a past benefit, but also a sacrament, representing Christ who was to come, from whom we have this privilege, that we pass from death to life. Otherwise, it would not hold good, that in *Christ* is the *body* of the legal shadows. (Col. ii. 17.) This passage will also be

---

[1] *Charnock* makes the following pointed observations on the form of expression here employed:—" *Christ the Passover—i.e.* the paschal lamb. The lamb was called the passover. The sign for the thing signified by it. 2 Chron. xxxv. 11. And they killed the passover, *i.e.* the lamb; for the passover was properly the angel's passing over *Israel*, when he was sent as an executioner of God's wrath upon the *Egyptians*. So Matt. xxvi. 17. Where shall we prepare for thee to eat the passover? *i.e.* the paschal lamb. *Our passover, i.e.* our paschal lamb. He is called God's lamb, John i. 29. *God's* in regard of the *author, ours* in regard of the *end: God's* lamb in regard of *designation, ours* in regard of *acceptation. Our passover, i.e.* not only of the Jews, but of the Gentiles. *That* was restrained to the Israelitish nation, *this* extends, in the offers of it, to all, and belongs to all that are under the new administration of the covenant of grace. *For us,* (ὑπὲρ ἡμῶν,) *i.e.* not only for our good, but *in our stead*, to free us from eternal death—to purchase for us eternal life."—*Charnock's* Works, vol. ii. p. 847.—*Ed.*

[2] " Il ne reste plus sinon que nous en soyons nourris;"—"Nothing remains, but that we be nourished by it."

[3] Our author most probably alludes to Exodus xii. 14, " And this day shall be unto you for a *memorial*," &c. The term used in the Septuagint is μνημοσυνον, answering to the Hebrew term זכרון.—*Ed.*

of service for setting aside the sacrilege of the Papal mass. For Paul does not teach that Christ is offered daily, but that the sacrifice having been offered up once for all, it remains that the spiritual feast be celebrated during our whole life.

9. I wrote unto you in an epistle not to company with fornicators:

10. Yet not altogether with the fornicators of this world, or with the covetous, or extortioners, or with idolaters; for then must ye needs go out of the world.

11. But now I have written unto you not to keep company, if any man that is called a brother be a fornicator, or covetous, or an idolater, or a railer, or a drunkard, or an extortioner; with such an one no not to eat.

12. For what have I to do to judge them also that are without? do not ye judge them that are within?

13. But them that are without God judgeth. Therefore put away from among yourselves that wicked person.

9. Scripsi vobis in Epistola, Ne commisceamini scortatoribus:

10. Neque in universum scortatoribus mundi hujus, vel avaris, vel rapacibus, vel idololatris: quandoquidem debuissetis ex hoc mundo exire.

11. Nunc autem scripsi vobis, Ne commisceamini : si is qui frater nominatur, vel scortator sit, vel avarus, vel idololatra, vel maledicus, vel ebriosus, vel rapax: cum tali ne cibum quidem sumatis.

12. Quid enim mea refert extraneos iudicare ? an non eos qui intus sunt iudicatis ?

13. Extraneos vero Deus iudicat: eiicite scelestum ex vobis ipsis.

9. *I wrote to you in an epistle.* The epistle of which he speaks is not at this day extant. Nor is there any doubt that many others are lost. It is enough, however, that those have been preserved to us which the Lord foresaw would suffice. But this passage, in consequence of its obscurity, has been twisted to a variety of interpretations, which I do not think it necessary for me to take up time in setting aside, but will simply bring forward what appears to me to be its true meaning. He reminds the Corinthians of what he had already enjoined upon them—that they should refrain from intercourse with the wicked. For the word rendered *to keep company with*, means to be on terms of familiarity with any one, and to be in habits of close intimacy with him.[1] Now, his reminding them of this tends

---

[1] The original word, συναναμίγνυσθαι, literally means *to be mixed up together with.* It is the rendering of the Septuagint for the Hebrew word יתבולל, in Hosea vii. 8. *Ephraim hath mixed himself among the people.* —*Ed.*

to expose their remissness, inasmuch as they had been admonished, and yet had remained inactive.

He adds an exception, that they may the better understand that this refers particularly to those that belong to the Church, as they did not require to be admonished[1] to avoid the society of the world.   In short, then, he prohibits the Corinthians from holding intercourse with those who, while professing to be believers, do, nevertheless, live wickedly and to the dishonour of God.   "Let all that wish to be reckoned brethren, either live holily and becomingly, or be excommunicated from the society of the pious, and let all the good refrain from intercourse and familiarity with them.   It were superfluous to speak as to the openly wicked, for you ought of your own accord to shun them, without any admonition from me."   This exception, however, increases the criminality of remissness, inasmuch as they cherished in the bosom of the Church an openly wicked person ; for it is more disgraceful to neglect those of your own household than to neglect strangers.

10. *Since you would have required.*   It is as to this clause especially that interpreters are not agreed.   For some say, "You must sooner quit Greece."   Ambrose, on the other hand, says, "You must rather die."   Erasmus turns it into the optative, as if Paul said, "Would that it were allowable for you to leave the world altogether;[2] but as you cannot do this, you must at least quit the society of those who falsely assume the name of Christians, and in the meantime exhibit in their lives the worst example."   Chrysostom's exposition has more appearance of truth.   According to him, the meaning is this : "When I command you to shun fornicators, I do not mean all such ; otherwise you would require to go in quest of another world ; for we must live among thorns so long as we sojourn on earth.   This only do I require, that you do not keep company with fornicators, who wish to be regarded as brethren, lest you should seem by your suffer-

---

[1] "Ce seroit vne chose superflue de les admonester," &c. ;—"It were a superfluous thing to admonish them," &c.

[2] The rendering of Erasmus is as follows: "Alioqui utinam videlicet e mundo exissetis ;"—"Otherwise I would, truly, that you had departed out of the world."

ance to approve of their wickedness." Thus the term *world*
here, must be taken to mean the present life, as in John
xvii. 15. *I pray not, Father, that thou shouldest take them
out of the world, but that thou shouldest deliver them from
the evil.*

Against this exposition a question might be proposed by
way of objection : " As Paul said this at a time when Christians were as yet mingled with heathens, and dispersed
among them, what ought to be done now, when all have
given themselves to Christ in name? For even in the present day we must go out of the world, if we would avoid the
society of the wicked; and there are none that are strangers,
when all take upon themselves Christ's name, and are consecrated to him by baptism." Should any one feel inclined
to follow Chrysostom, he will find no difficulty in replying,
to this effect : that Paul here took for granted what was
true—that, where there is the power of excommunication,
there is an easy remedy for effecting a separation between
the good and the bad, if Churches do their duty. As to
strangers, the Christians at Corinth had no jurisdiction, and
they could not restrain their dissolute manner of life. Hence
they must of necessity have quitted the world, if they wished
to avoid the society of the wicked, whose vices they could
not cure.

For my own part, as I do not willingly adopt interpretations which cannot be made to suit the words, otherwise than
by twisting the words so as to suit them, I prefer one that
is different from all these, taking the word rendered *to go
out* as meaning *to be separated,* and the term *world* as meaning *the pollutions of the world.* " What need have you of
an injunction as to *the children of this world,* (Luke xvi. 8,)
for having once for all renounced the world, it becomes you
to stand aloof from their society ; for *the whole world lieth
in the wicked one.*"[1] (1 John v. 19.) If any one is not
satisfied with this interpretation, here is still another that is
probable : " I do not write to you in general terms, that you
should shun the society of *the fornicators of this world,*

---

[1] " Car tout le monde est mis a mal;"—" For the whole world is addicted to evil."

though *that* you ought to do, without any admonition from me." I prefer, however, the former; and I am not the first contriver of it, but, while it has been brought forward previously by others, I have adapted it more fully, if I mistake not, to Paul's thread of discourse. There is, then,[1] a sort of intentional omission, when he says that he makes no mention of those that are *without,* inasmuch as the Corinthians ought to be already separated from them, that they may know that even at home[2] they required to maintain this discipline of avoiding the wicked.

11. *If he who is called a brother.* In the Greek there is a participle[3] without a verb.[4] Those that view this as referring to what follows, bring out here a forced meaning, and at variance with Paul's intention. I confess, indeed, that that is a just sentiment,[5] and worthy of being particularly noticed—that no one can be punished by the decision of the Church, but one whose sin has become matter of notoriety; but these words of Paul cannot be made to bear that meaning. What he means, then, is this : " If any one is reckoned a brother among you, and at the same time leads a wicked life, and such as is unbecoming a Christian, keep aloof from his society." In short, being *called* a brother, means here a false profession, which has no corresponding reality. Farther, he does not make a complete enumeration of crimes, but merely mentions five or six by way of example, and then afterwards, under the expression *such an one,* he sums up the whole ; and he does not mention any but what fall under the knowledge of men. For inward impiety, and anything that is secret, does not fall within the judgment of the Church.

[1] " En ceste sentence;"—" In this sentence."

[2] " C'est à dire, entr'eux;"—" That is to say, among themselves."

[3] " Au texte Grec il y a de mot à mot, Si aucun frere nommé," &c.;—" In the Greek text it is literally, If any one, called a brother," &c.

[4] It is so according to the common reading, which is as follows:—ἰάν τις, ἀδελφὸς ὀνομαζόμενος, ἢ πόρνος, ἢ πλεονέκτης, κ.τ.λ.—"If any one, called a brother —either a fornicator, or covetous," &c.; but, as stated by Bloomfield, " seven MSS., and many versions, and Fathers, the Ed. Princ., and those of Beza, Schmid., and Beng., have ἢ, (before πόρνος,) which is approved by Wets., and Matth., and edited by Griesb., Knapp., Vat., and Tittm. ;" and, in Bloomfield's opinion, " rightly."—*Ed.*

[5] " Qu'ils en tirent;"—" Which they draw from it."

It is uncertain, however, what he means by an *idolater.*
For how can he be devoted to idolatry who has made a profession of Christ ? Some are of opinion that there were
among the Corinthians at that time some who received
Christ but in half, and in the mean time were involved,
nevertheless, in corrupt superstition, as the Israelites of old,
and afterwards the Samaritans maintained a kind of worship
of God, but at the same time polluted it with wicked superstitions. For my part, I rather understand it of those who,
while they held idols in contempt, gave, nevertheless, a pretended homage to the idols, with the view of gratifying the
wicked. Paul declares that such persons ought not to be
tolerated in the society of Christians ; and not without
good reason, inasmuch as they made so little account of
trampling God's glory under foot. We must, however, observe the circumstances of the case—that, while they had a
Church there, in which they might worship God in purity,
and have the lawful use of the sacraments, they came into
the Church in such a way as not to renounce the profane
fellowship of the wicked. I make this observation, in order
that no one may think that we ought to employ equally
severe measures against those who, while at this day dispersed under the tyranny of the Pope, pollute themselves
with many corrupt rites. These indeed, I maintain, sin
generally in this respect, and they ought, I acknowledge,
to be sharply dealt with, and diligently urged,[1] that they
may learn at length to consecrate themselves wholly to
Christ ; but I dare not go so far as to reckon them worthy
of excommunication, for their case is different.[2]

With such an one not even to take food. In the first place,
we must ascertain whether he addresses here the whole
Church, or merely individuals. I answer, that this is said,
indeed, to individuals, but, at the same time, it is connected
with their discipline in common ; for the power of excommunicating is not allowed to any individual member, but to

---

[1] " Il les faut redarguer auec seuerite, et les soliciter continuellement
par admonitions;"—" They ought to be reproved with severity, and plied
perseveringly with admonitions."

[2] " Car leur condition n'est pas telle comme estoit celle des Corinthiens;"
—" For their condition is not like that of the Corinthians."

CHAP. V. 12.   FIRST EPISTLE TO THE CORINTHIANS.   195

the entire body. When, therefore, the Church has excommunicated any one, no believer ought to receive him into terms of intimacy with him; otherwise the authority of the Church would be brought into contempt, if each individual were at liberty to admit to his table those who have been excluded from the table of the Lord. By *partaking of food* here, is meant either living together, or familiar association in meals. For if, on going into an inn, I see one who has been excommunicated sitting at table, there is nothing to hinder me from dining with him; for I have not authority to exclude him. What Paul means is, that, in so far as it is in our power, we are to shun the society of those whom the Church has cut off from her communion.

The Roman antichrist, not content with this severity, has burst forth into interdicts, prohibiting any one from helping one that has been excommunicated to food, or fuel, or drink, or any other of the supports of life.[1] Now, *that* is not strictness of discipline, but tyrannical and barbarous cruelty, that is altogether at variance with Paul's intention. For he means not that he should be *counted as an enemy, but as a brother*, (2 Thes. iii. 15;) for in putting this public mark of disgrace upon him, the intention is, that he may be filled with shame, and brought to repentance. And with this dreadful cruelty, if God is pleased to permit, do they rage even against the innocent.[2] Now, granting that there are sometimes those who are not undeserving of this punishment, I affirm, on the other hand, that this kind of interdict[3] is altogether unsuitable to an ecclesiastical court.

12. *For what have I to do to judge them that are without?* There is nothing to hinder us from judging these also—nay

[1] " Est venu furieusement jusques aux defenses et menaces, Que nul ne fust si hardi de donner à boire ou à manger, ou de feu à celuy qui seroit excommunier, ou de luy aider aucunement des choses necessaires à la vie presente;"—" Has in his fury gone so far as to issue forth prohibitions and threatenings—'Let no one be so daring as to give meat, or drink, or fuel, to the man who has been excommunicated, or to help him in any way with the things necessary for the present life.'"

[2] " Et ces bourreaux encore exercent ceste cruaute extreme, mesme contre les innocens;"—" And these hangmen do, besides, exercise this extreme cruelty even against the innocent."

[3] " Telle façon d'excommunier;"—" Such a method of excommunication."

more, even devils themselves are not exempt from the judgment of the word which is committed to us.   But Paul is
speaking here of the jurisdiction that belongs peculiarly to
the Church.   "The Lord has furnished us with this power,
that we may exercise it upon those who belong to his
household.   For this chastisement is a part of discipline
which is confined to the Church, and does not extend to
strangers.   We do not therefore pronounce upon them their
condemnation, because the Lord has not subjected them to
our cognizance and jurisdiction, in so far as that chastisement and censure are concerned.   We are, therefore, constrained to leave them to the judgment of God."   It is in
this sense that Paul says, that *God will judge them,* because
he allows them to wander about[1] unbridled like wild beasts,
because there is no one that can restrain their wantonness.

13. *Put away that wicked person.*   This is commonly explained as referring to the person who was guilty of an illicit connection with his mother-in-law.   For as to those who
understand the expression to mean—" Put away *evil* or
wickedness," they are refuted by the Greek words made
use of by Paul, the article (τὸν) being in the masculine
gender.   But what if you should view it as referring to the
devil, who, undoubtedly in the person of a wicked and unprincipled man,[2] is encouraged to establish his throne among
us?   For ὁ πονηρος (the wicked one) taken simply and without any addition, denotes the prince of all crimes,[3] rather
than some wicked man.   If this meaning is approved of,
Paul shows how important it is[4] not to tolerate wicked
persons, as by this means Satan is expelled from his kingdom which he keeps up among us, when indulgence is given

---

[1] " Et courir à trauers champs ;"—" And run across the fields."

[2] " Quand on supporte un homme meschant et mal-vivant ;"—" When
a wicked and unprincipled man is allowed to continue."—*Ed.*

[3] It is well observed by Witsius in his Dissertations on the Lord's
Prayer, (Biblical Cabinet, No. xxiv. pp. 361, 362,) that the appellation of *the
evil One* is properly applied to Satan, " because he does nothing but what is
evil—because all the evil that exists in the universe originated with him—
because in doing evil, and in persuading others to do evil, he finds his only
delight, the wicked and malignant solace of his desperate misery."—*Ed.*

[4] " Combien il est utile et necessaire ;"—" How useful it is and necessary."

to the wicked.[1] If any one, however, prefers to understand it as referring to a *man,* I do not oppose it.   Chrysostom compares the rigour of the law with the mildness of the gospel, inasmuch as Paul was satisfied with excommunication in case of an offence for which the law required the punishment of death, but for this there is no just ground. For Paul is not here addressing judges that are armed with the sword, but an unarmed multitude[2] that was allowed merely to make use of brotherly correction.

CHAPTER VI.

1. Dare any of you, having a matter against another, go to law before the unjust, and not before the saints?

2. Do ye not know that the saints shall judge the world? and if the world shall be judged by you, are ye unworthy to judge the smallest matters?

3. Know ye not that we shall judge angels? how much more things that pertain to this life?

4. If then ye have judgments of things pertaining to this life, set them to judge who are least esteemed in the church.

5. I speak to your shame. Is it so, that there is not a wise man among you? no, not one that shall be able to judge between his brethren?

6. But brother goeth to law with brother, and that before the unbelievers.

7. Now therefore there is utterly a fault among you, because ye go to law one with another. Why do ye not rather take wrong? Why do ye not rather *suffer yourselves to* be defrauded?

1. Audet aliquis vestrum, negotium habens cum altero, litigare sub iniustis, et non sub sanctis?

2. An nescitis, quod sancti mundum iudicabunt? quodsi in vobis iudicatur mundus, indigni estis minimis iudiciis?

3. An nescitis, quod angelos iudicabimus, nedum ad victum pertinentia?

4. Iudicia ergo de rebus ad victum pertinentibus si habueritis, qui contemptibiles sunt in Ecclesia,[3] eos constituite.

5. Ad erubescentiam vestram dico: adeo non est inter vos sapiens, ne unus quidem, qui possit iudicare inter fratres?

6. Sed frater cum fratre litigat, idque sub infidelibus.

7. Jam quidem omnino delictum in vobis est, quod iudicia habetis inter vos: cur non potius iniuriam sustinetis?[4]

---

[1] " Quand il y a vne license de malfaire, et les meschans sont soufferts ;" —" When there is a license to do evil, and the wicked are tolerated."

[2] " Desnuée de puissance externe ;"—" Destitute of external power."

[3] " De moindre estime en l'Eglise, ou, de nulle estime, assauoir au pris des autres ;"—" Of least esteem in the Church, or of no esteem; that is, in comparison with others."

[4] " Pourquoy plustost n'endurez-vous l'injure? Pourquoy plustost ne

8. Nay, ye do wrong, and defraud, and that *your* brethren.

8. Sed vos infertis iniuriam, et fraudatis, et quidem fratres.

HERE he begins to reprove another fault among the Corinthians—an excessive fondness for litigation, which took its rise from avarice. Now, this reproof consists of two parts. The *first* is, that by bringing their disputes before the tribunals of the wicked, they by this means made the gospel contemptible, and exposed it to derision. The *second* is, that while Christians ought to endure injuries with patience, they inflicted injury on others, rather than allow themselves to be subjected to any inconvenience. Thus, the first part is particular : the other is general.

1. *Dare any of you.* This is the first statement—that, if any one has a controversy with a brother, it ought to be decided before godly judges, and that it ought not to be before those that are ungodly. If the reason is asked, I have already said, that it is because disgrace is brought upon the gospel, and the name of Christ is held up as it were to the scoffings of the ungodly. For the ungodly, at the instigation of Satan, are always eagerly on the watch[1] for opportunities of finding occasion of calumny against the doctrine of godliness. Now believers, when they make them parties in their disputes, seem as though they did on set purpose furnish them with a handle for reviling. A *second* reason may be added—that we treat our brethren disdainfully, when we of our own accord subject them to the decisions of unbelievers.

But here it may be objected : " As it belongs to the office of the magistrate, and as it is peculiarly his province to administer justice to all, and to decide upon matters in dispute, why should not even unbelievers, who are in the office of magistrate, have this authority, and, if they have it, why are we prevented from maintaining our rights before their tribunals ?" I answer, that Paul does not here condemn those who from necessity have a cause before unbelieving judges,[2]

receuez-vous dommage ?"—" Why do you not rather suffer injury ? Why do you not rather submit to loss ? "

[1] " Espient incessamment et d'vne affection ardente ;"—" Watch incessantly and with eager desire."

[2] " Qui sont necessairement contraints de maintenir et plaider leurs

as when a person is summoned to a court ; but those who, of their own accord, bring their brethren into this situation, and harass them, as it were, through means of unbelievers, while it is in their power to employ another remedy. It is wrong, therefore, to institute of one's own accord a law-suit against *brethren* before *unbelieving* judges. If, on the other hand, you are summoned to a court, there is no harm in appearing there and maintaining your cause.

2. *Know ye not that the saints.* Here we have an argument from the less to the greater ; for Paul, being desirous to show that injury is done to the Church of God when judgments on matters of dispute connected with earthly things are carried before unbelievers, as if there were no one in the society of the godly that was qualified to judge, reasons in this strain : " Since God has reckoned the saints worthy of such honour, as to have appointed them to be judges of the whole world, it is unreasonable that they should be shut out from judging as to small matters, as persons not qualified for it." Hence it follows, that the Corinthians inflict injury upon themselves, in resigning into the hands of unbelievers the honour[1] that has been conferred upon them by God.

What is said here as to *judging the world* ought to be viewed as referring to that declaration of Christ : *When the Son of Man shall come, ye shall sit,* &c. (Matt. xix. 28.) *For all power of judgment has been committed to the Son,* (John v. 22,) in such a manner that he will receive his *saints* into a participation with him in this honour, as assessors. Apart from this, they *will judge the world,* as indeed they begin already to do, because their piety, faith, fear of the Lord, good conscience, and integrity of life, will make unbelievers altogether inexcusable, as it is said of Noah, that *by his faith he condemned* all the men of his age. (Heb. xi. 7.) But the former signification accords better with the Apostle's design, for unless you take the *judging* here spoken of in its proper acceptation, the reasoning will not hold.

causes sous iuges infideles ;"—" Who are from necessity shut up to maintain and defend their law-suits before unbelieving judges."
    [1] " L'honneur et la prerogatiue ;"—" The honour and the prerogative."

But even in this sense[1] it may seem not to have much weight, for it is as if one should say: "The saints are endowed with heavenly wisdom, which immeasurably transcends all human doctrines: therefore they can judge better as to the stars than astrologers." Now this no one will allow, and the ground of objection is obvious—because piety and spiritual doctrine do not confer a knowledge of human arts. My answer here is this, that between expertness in judging and other arts there is this difference, that while the latter are acquired by acuteness of intellect and by study, and are learned from masters,[2] the former depends rather on equity and conscientiousness.

But[3] "lawyers will judge better and more confidently than an illiterate Christian: otherwise the knowledge of law is of no advantage." I answer, that their advice is not here excluded, for if the determination of any obscure question is to be sought from a knowledge of the laws, the Apostle does not hinder Christians from applying to lawyers.[4] What he finds fault with in the Corinthians is simply this, that they carry their disputes before unbelieving judges, as if they had none in the Church that were qualified to pass judgment, and farther, he shows how much superior is the judgment that God has assigned to his believing people.

The words rendered *in you* mean here, in my opinion, *among you.* For whenever believers meet in one place, under the auspices of Christ,[5] there is already in their assembly a sort of image of the future judgment, which will be perfectly brought to light on the last day. Accordingly Paul says, that the world is judged in the Church, because *there* Christ's tribunal is erected, from which he exercises his authority.[6]

---

[1] "Mais, dira quelqu'vn, encore à le prendre ainsi;"—"But, some one will say, even taking it in this way."

[2] "Sous precepteurs et maistres;"—"Under preceptors and masters."

[3] "Mais, dira quelqu'vn:"—"But, some one will say."

[4] "Ne defend point aux Chrestiens d'aller demander conseil aux Legistes;"—"Does not hinder Christians from going to ask the advice of lawyers."

[5] "Au nom de Christ;"—"In the name of Christ."

[6] "Auquel estant comme assis, il exerce sa iurisdiction;"—"On which being as it were seated, he exercises his authority."

3. *Know ye not that we shall judge angels?* This passage
is taken in different ways.   Chrysostom states that some
understood it as referring to priests,[1] but this is exceedingly
far-fetched.   Others understand it of the angels in heaven,
in this sense—that the angels are subject to the judgment
of God's word, and may be judged by us, if need be, by
means of that word, as it is said in the Epistle to the Galatians—*If an angel from heaven bring any other gospel, let
him be accursed.* (Gal. i. 8.) Nor does this exposition appear at first view unsuitable to the thread of Paul's discourse ; for if all whom God has enlightened by his word
are endowed with such authority, that through means of
that word they judge not only men but angels too, how much
more will they be prepared to judge of small and trivial
matters ?   As, however, Paul speaks here in the future tense,
as referring to the last day, and as his words convey the idea
of an actual judgment, (as the common expression is,) it were
preferable, in my opinion, to understand him as speaking of
apostate[2] angels.   For the argument will be not less conclusive in this way : " Devils, who sprang from so illustrious
an origin, and even now, when they have fallen from their
high estate, are immortal creatures, and superior to this
corruptible world, shall be judged by us. What then ?
Shall those things that are subservient to the belly be exempted from our judgment ?

4. *If you have judgments then as to things pertaining to this
life.* We must always keep in view what causes he is treating of ; for public trials are beyond our province, and ought
not to be transferred to our disposal ; but as to private matters it is allowable to determine without the cognizance of
the magistrate.   As, then, we do not detract in any degree
from the authority of the magistrate by having recourse to
arbitration, it is not without good reason that the Apostle
enjoins it upon Christians to refrain from resorting to profane, that is, unbelieving judges.   And lest they should
allege that they were deprived of a better remedy, he directs
them to choose out of the Church arbiters, who may settle

[1] " Des prestres et ministres ;"—" Of priests and ministers."
[2] " Apostats et rebelles ;"—" Apostate and rebellious."

causes agreeably and equitably. Farther, lest they should
allege that they have not a sufficient number of qualified
persons, he says that the meanest is competent to discharge
this office.   There is, therefore, no detracting here from the
dignity of the office of magistrates, when he gives orders that
their office be committed to contemptible persons, for this
(as I have already said) is stated by anticipation, as though
he had said : " Even the lowest and meanest among you will
discharge this office better than those unbelieving judges to
whom you have recourse.   So far are you from necessity in
this way."

Chrysostom comes near this interpretation, though he ap-
pends to it something additional ; for he is of opinion, that
the Apostle meant to say, that, even though the Corinthians
should find no one among themselves who had sufficient
wisdom for judging, they must nevertheless make choice of
some, of whatever stamp they were.   Ambrose touches
neither heaven nor earth.[1] I think I have faithfully brought
out the Apostle's intention—that the lowest among believers
was preferred by him to unbelievers, as to capacity of judging.
There are some that strike out a quite different meaning, for
they understand the word $\kappa\alpha\theta\iota\zeta\epsilon\tau\epsilon$ to be in the present tense
—*You set them to judge*, and by *those that are least esteemed
in the Church* they understand profane persons.[2] This, however, is more ingenious than solid, for that were a poor designation of unbelievers.[3] Besides, the form of expression, *if
you have*, would not suit so well with a reproof, for the expression would have required rather to be *while you have*,
for that *condition* takes away from the force of it.   Hence I
am the more inclined to think, that a remedy for the evil is
here prescribed.

---

[1] " Sainct Ambrose ne touche ne ciel ne terre (comme on dit) en l'exposition de ces mots ;"—" St. Ambrose touches neither heaven nor earth
(as the expression is) in the exposition of these words."—Our Author's
meaning seems to be that Ambrose *hangs in suspense*, or *gives no decided
opinion.—Ed.*
[2] " Les gens profanes et infideles ;"—" Profane and unbelieving persons."
[3] "Car ce seroit vne façon de parler bien maigre et de peu de grace,
d'appeler ainsi les infideles ;"—" For it were a very meagre and awkward
way of speaking, to describe unbelievers in this manner."

That this statement, however, was taken up wrong by the ancients, appears from a certain passage in Augustine. For in his book—" On the Work of Monks," where he makes mention of his employments, he declares that among his numerous engagements, the most disagreeable of all was, that he was under the necessity of devoting a part of the day to secular affairs, but that he at the same time endured it patiently, because the Apostle[1] had imposed upon him this necessity. From this passage, and from a certain epistle, it appears that the bishops were accustomed to sit at certain hours to settle disputes, as if the Apostle had been referring to them here. As, however, matters always become worse, there sprang from this error, in process of time, that jurisdiction which the officials of the bishops assume to themselves in money matters. In that ancient custom there are two things that are deserving of reproof—that the bishops were involved in matters that were foreign to their office; and that they wronged God in making his authority and command a pretext for turning aside from their proper calling. The evil, however, was in some degree excusable, but as for the profane custom, which has come to prevail in the Papacy, it were the height of baseness to excuse or defend it.

5. *I speak to your shame.* The meaning is—" If other considerations do not influence you, let it at least be considered by you, how disgraceful it is to you that *there is not so much as one among you* who is qualified to settle an affair amicably among *brethren*—an honour which you assign to *unbelievers.* Now this passage is not inconsistent with the declaration which we met with above, when he stated that he did not make mention of their faults with the view of *shaming them,* (1 Cor. iv. 14,) for instead of this, by putting them to *shame* in this manner, he calls them back from disgrace,[2] and shows that he is desirous to promote their honour. He does not wish them, then, to form so unfavourable an opinion of their society, as to take away from all their *brethren* an honour which they allow to *unbelievers.*

---

[1] " Sainct Paul;"—" Saint Paul."
[2] " Il les garde de tomber en reproche;"—" He guards them against falling into reproach."

7. *Now indeed there is utterly a fault.* Here we have the *second* part of the reproof, which contains a general doctrine ; for he now reproves them, not on the ground of their expos- ing the gospel to derision and disgrace, but on the ground of their going to law with each other. This, he says, is a *fault.* We must, however, observe the propriety of the term which he employs. For ἥττημα in Greek signifies weakness of mind, as when one is easily broken down[1] by injuries, and cannot bear anything : it comes afterward to be applied to vices of any kind, as they all arise from weakness and defi- ciency in fortitude.[2] What Paul, then, condemns in the Corinthians is this—that they harassed one another with law-suits. He states the reason of it—that they were not prepared to bear injuries patiently. And, assuredly, as the Lord commands us (Matt. v. 44 ; Rom. xii. 21) not to be over- come by evils, but on the contrary to overcome injuries by acts of kindness, it is certain, that those who cannot control themselves so as to suffer injuries patiently, commit sin by their impatience. If contention in law-suits among believers is a token of that impatience, it follows that it is *faulty.*

In this way, however, he seems to discard entirely judg- ments as to the affairs of individuals. "Those are altogether in the wrong who go to law. Hence it will not be allowable in any one to maintain his rights by having recourse to a magistrate." There are some that answer this objection in this way—-that the Apostle declares that where there are law-suits *there is utterly a fault,* because, of necessity, the one or the other has a bad cause. They do not, however, escape by this sophistry, because he says that they are *in fault,* not merely when they inflict injury, but also when

---

[1] " Aiseement abbatu et irrité ;"—" Easily hurt and irritated."

[2] The Greek term ἥττημα is supposed by some to be derived originally from the Hebrew verb חתת, to be *broken,* (which is rendered by ἡττάομαι in various instances in the Septuagint.) Our author had probably an eye to this when stating the original meaning of the term to be " weakness of mind, as when one is easily *broken down* by injuries." The term properly denotes *defect.* It is instructive to observe, that a disposition to " go to law with brethren," rather than " suffer wrong," is represented by the Apostle as indicative of a *defect,* that is, in Christian meekness or brotherly love ; while the opposite disposition, recommended by the Apostle, would, according to the standard of the world's morality, discover *defect,* in respect of *want of spirit.*—Ed.

they do not patiently endure it.   For my own part, my answer is simply this—having a little before given permission
to have recourse to arbiters, he has in this shown, with sufficient clearness, that Christians are not prohibited from
prosecuting their rights moderately, and without any breach
of love.   Hence we may very readily infer, that his being
so severe was owing to his taking particularly into view the
circumstances of the case.   And, undoubtedly, wherever
there is frequent recourse to law-suits, or where the parties
contend with each other pertinaciously with rigour of law,[1]
it is in that case abundantly plain, that their minds are
immoderately inflamed with wrong dispositions, and are not
prepared for equity and endurance of wrongs, according to
the commandment of Christ.   To speak more plainly, the
reason why Paul condemns law-suits is, that we ought to
suffer injuries with patience.   Let us now see whether any
one can carry on a law-suit without impatience ; for if it is
so, to go to law will not be wrong in all cases, but only ἐπὶ
τὸ πολύ—*for the most part*.   I confess, however, that as
men's manners are corrupt, impatience, or lack of patience
(as they speak) is an almost inseparable attendant on law-
suits.   This, however, does not hinder your distinguishing
between the thing itself and the improper accompaniment.
Let us therefore bear in mind, that Paul does not condemn
law-suits on the ground of its being a wrong thing in itself
to maintain a good cause by having recourse to a magistrate,
but because it is almost invariably accompanied with corrupt
dispositions ; as, for example, violence, desire of revenge,
enmities, obstinacy, and the like.

It is surprising that this question has not been more carefully handled by ecclesiastical writers.   Augustine has bestowed more pains upon it than the others, and has come
nearer the mark ;[2] but even he is somewhat obscure, though
there is truth in what he states.   Those who aim at greater
clearness in their statements tell us that we must distinguish

---

[1] " Et qu'ils veulent veoir le bout du proces ; (comme on dit ;)"—" And
are desirous to see the issue of the case, (as the expression is.)"

[2] Our Author, when treating at some length of the same subject in the
Institutes, (vol. iii. p. 543,) makes a particular reference to Augustine.
(Ep. v. ad Marcell.)—*Ed*.

between public and private revenge; for while the magistrate's vengeance is appointed by God, those who have recourse to it do not rashly take vengeance at their own hand, but have recourse to God as an Avenger.[1] This, it is true, is said judiciously and appropriately; but we must go a step farther; for if it be not allowable even to desire vengeance from God, then, on the same principle, it were not allowable to have recourse to the magistrate for vengeance.

I acknowledge, then, that a Christian man is altogether prohibited from revenge, so that he must not exercise it, either by himself, or by means of the magistrate, nor even desire it. If, therefore, a Christian man wishes to prosecute his rights at law, so as not to offend God, he must, above all things, take heed that he does not bring into court any desire of revenge, any corrupt affection of the mind, or anger, or, in fine, any other poison. In this matter love will be the best regulator.[2]

If it is objected, that it very rarely happens that any one carries on a law-suit entirely free and exempt from every corrupt affection, I acknowledge that it is so, and I say farther, that it is rare to find a single instance of an upright litigant; but it is useful for many reasons to show that the thing is not evil in itself, but is rendered corrupt by abuse: *First,* that it may not seem as if God had to no purpose appointed courts of justice; *Secondly,* that the pious may know how far their liberties extend, that they may not take anything in hand against the dictates of conscience. For it is owing to this that many rush on to open contempt of God, when they have once begun to transgress those limits;[3] *Thirdly,* that they may be admonished, that they must always keep within bounds, so as not to pollute by their own misconduct the remedy which the Lord has per-

[1] " Se retirent à Dieu comme à celuy *à qui appartient la vengeance;*" —" They have recourse to God, as *to him to whom vengeance belongeth.*" (Ps. xciv. 1.)

[2] " Pour estre bien gouuerné en ceci, il faut estre gaeni d'vne vraye charité;" —" To be properly regulated in this, we must be adorned with true love."

[3] " Plusieurs tombent en ceste malediction, de *mepriser Dieu* ouuertement;"—" Many fall into that curse of openly *contemning God.*" (Ps. x. 13.)

mitted them to employ; *Lastly,* that the audacity of the wicked may be repressed by a pure and uncorrupted zeal, which could not be effected, if we were not allowed to subject them to legal punishments.

8. *But ye do injury.* Hence we see for what reason he has inveighed against them with so much bitterness—because there prevailed among them such a base desire of gain, that they did not even refrain from *injuring* one another. He premised a little before, with the view of exposing the magnitude of the evil, that those are not Christians who know not to endure injuries. There is, then, an amplification here, founded on a comparison : for if it is wrong not to *bear* injuries patiently, how much worse is it to *inflict* them ?

And that your brethren. Here is another aggravation of the evil; for if those are doubly culpable who defraud strangers, it is monstrous for *brother* to be cheated or despoiled by *brother.* Now all of us are brethren that call upon *one Father in heaven.* (Matt. xxiii. 9.) At the same time, if any one acts an unprincipled part towards strangers, Paul does not palliate the crime; but he teaches that the Corinthians were utterly blinded in making sacred brotherhood a matter of no moment.

9. Know ye not that the unrighteous shall not inherit the kingdom of God? Be not deceived: neither fornicators, nor idolaters, nor adulterers, nor effeminate, nor abusers of themselves with mankind,

10. Nor thieves, nor covetous, nor drunkards, nor revilers, nor extortioners, shall inherit the kingdom of God.

11. And such were some of you: but ye are washed, but ye are sanctified, but ye are justified in the name of the Lord Jesus, and by the Spirit of our God.

9. An nescitis, quod iniusti regnum Dei hereditate non obtinebunt? Ne erretis, neque scortatores, neque idololatræ, neque mœchi, neque molles, neque pæderastæ.

10. Neque fures, neque avari, neque ebriosi, neque maledici, neque rapaces regnum Dei hereditate obtinebunt.

11. Et hæc fuistis,[1] sed abluti estis, sed sanctificati estis, sed iustificati estis in nomine Domini Jesu, et in Spiritu Dei nostri.

9. *Know ye not,* &c. By *unrighteousness* here you may

---

[1] " Et telles choses auez-vous este," ou " este aucuns;"—" And such things were you," or " were some of you."

understand what is opposed to strict integrity. The *un-righteous*, then, that is, those who inflict injury on their brethren, who defraud or circumvent others, who, in short, are intent upon their own advantage at the expense of injuring others, *will not inherit the kingdom of God.* That by the *unrighteous* here, as for example *adulterers,* and *thieves* and *covetous,* and *revilers,* he means those who do not repent of their sins, but obstinately persist in them, is too manifest to require that it should be stated. The Apostle himself, too, afterwards expresses this in the words employed by him, when he says that the Corinthians formerly *were such.* The wicked, then, do *inherit the kingdom of God,* but it is only in the event of their having been first converted to the Lord in true repentance, and having in this way ceased to be wicked. For although conversion is not the ground of pardon, yet we know that none are reconciled to God but those who repent. The interrogation, however, is emphatic, for it intimates that he states nothing but what they themselves know, and is matter of common remark among all pious persons.

Be not deceived. He takes occasion from one vice to speak of many. I am of opinion, however, that he has pointed out those vices chiefly which prevailed among the Corinthians. He makes use of three terms for reproving those lascivious passions which, as all historical accounts testify, reigned, nay raged, to an extraordinary height in that city. For it was a city that abounded in wealth, (as has been stated elsewhere.)[1] It was a celebrated mart, which was frequented by merchants from many nations. Wealth has luxury as its attendant—the mother of unchastity and all kinds of lasciviousness. In addition to this, a nation which was of itself prone to wantonness, was prompted to it by many other corruptions.

The difference between *fornicators* and *adulterers* is sufficiently well known. By *effeminate* persons I understand those who, although they do not openly abandon themselves to impurity, discover, nevertheless, their unchastity by blandishments of speech, by lightness of gesture and apparel, and

[1] See page 37.

other allurements.   The fourth description of crime is the most abominable of all—that monstrous pollution which was but too prevalent in Greece.

He employs three terms in reproving injustice and injuries.   He gives the name of *thieves* to those who take the advantage of their brethren by any kind of fraud or secret artifice.   By *extortioners*, he means those that violently seize on another's wealth, or like harpies[1] draw to themselves from every quarter, and devour.   With the view of giving his discourse a wider range, he afterwards adds all *covetous* persons too.   Under the term *drunkards* you are to understand him as including those who go to excess in eating. He more particularly reproves *revilers*, because, in all probability, that city was full of gossip and slanders.   In short, he makes mention chiefly of those vices to which, he saw, that city was addicted.

Farther, that his threatening may have more weight, he says, *be not deceived;* by which expression he admonishes them not to flatter themselves with a vain hope, as persons are accustomed, by extenuating their offences, to inure themselves to contempt of God.   No poison, therefore, is more dangerous than those allurements which encourage us in our sins.   Let us, therefore, shun, not as the songs of the Sirens,[2] but as the deadly bites of Satan, the talk of profane persons, when turning the judgment of God and reproofs of sins into matter of jest.   Lastly, we must also notice here the propriety of the word κληρονομειν—*to inherit;* which shows that *the kingdom of heaven* is the *inheritance of sons,*

---

[1] " Comme bestes rauissantes;"—." Like ravenous beasts."   The harpies, it is well known, were fabulous monsters, proverbial for rapacity.   It deserves to be noticed that their name ἁρπυίαι, and the term made use of by Paul to denote *extortioners,* (ἅρπαγες,) are both of them derived from ἁρπάζω, to seize upon, or take by violence.—*Ed.*

[2] The Sirens were a kind of marine monsters, which were supposed to inhabit certain rocky islands on the south-west coast of Italy, and decoyed, it was alleged, by their enchanting music, mariners to their destruction. Homer in his Odyssey (viii. 45) speaks of their *melodious song.* (λιγυρῆ ἀοιδῆ.)   Our Author, it will be observed, in the connexion in which he alludes to " the songs of the Sirens," strongly expresses his belief of the *reality* of Satanic influence, as contrasted with what is *merely fabulous.*— *Ed.*

and therefore comes to us through the privilege of adoption.

11. *And such were ye.* Some add a term of speciality : *Such were some of you,* as in Greek the word τινὲς is added ; but I am rather of opinion that the Apostle speaks in a general way. I consider that term to be redundant, in accordance with the practice of the Greeks, who frequently make use of it for the sake of ornament, not by way of restriction. We must not, however, understand him as putting all in one bundle, so as to attribute all these vices to each of them, but he simply means to intimate, that no one is altogether free from these vices, until he has been renewed by the Spirit. For we must hold this, that man's nature universally contains the seed of all evils, but that some vices prevail and discover themselves more in some than in others, according as the Lord brings out to view the depravity of the flesh by its fruits.

Thus Paul, in the first chapter of his Epistle to the Romans, piles up many different kinds of vices and crimes, which flow from ignorance of God, and that ingratitude, of which he had shown all unbelievers to be guilty, (Rom. i. 21-32)—not that every unbeliever is infected with all these vices, but that all are liable to them, and no one is exempt from them all. For he who is not an adulterer, sins in some other way. So also in the third chapter he brings forward as applicable to the sons of Adam universally those declarations—*their throat is an open sepulchre : their feet are swift to shed blood : their tongue is deceitful or poisonous,* (Rom. iii. 13-15)—not that all are sanguinary and cruel, or that all are treacherous or revilers ; but that, previously to our being formed anew by God, one is inclined to cruelty, another to treachery, another to impurity, another to deceit ; so that there is no one in whom there does not exist some trace of the corruption common to all ; and we are all of us, to a man, by an internal and secret affection of the mind, liable to all diseases, unless in so far as the Lord inwardly restrains them from breaking forth openly.[1] The simple meaning, there-

---

[1] " Suiets a toutes sortes de vices, sinon entant que le Seigneur les reprime au dedans, afin qu'ils ne sortent dehors, et vienent à estre mis en

fore, is this, that prior to their being regenerated by grace, some of the Corinthians were *covetous*, others *adulterers*, others *extortioners*, others *effeminate*, others *revilers*, but now, being made free by Christ, they were such no longer.

The design of the Apostle, however, is to humble them, by calling to their remembrance their former condition; and, farther, to stir them up to acknowledge the grace of God towards them. For the greater the misery is acknowledged to be, from which we have escaped through the Lord's kindness, so much the more does the magnitude of his grace shine forth. Now the commendation of grace is a fountain[1] of exhortations, because we ought to take diligent heed, that we may not make void the kindness of God, which ought to be so highly esteemed. It is as though he had said: " It is enough that God has drawn you out of that mire in which you were formerly sunk ;" as Peter also says, " *The time past is sufficient to have fulfilled the lusts of the Gentiles.*"   (1 Pet. iv. 3.)

But ye are washed. He makes use of three terms to express one and the same thing, that he may the more effectually deter them from rolling back into the condition from which they had escaped. Hence, though these three terms have the same general meaning, there is, nevertheless, great force in their very variety. For there is an implied contrast between *washing* and defilement—*sanctification* and pollution—*justification* and guilt. His meaning is, that having been once *justified*, they must not draw down upon themslves a new condemnation—that, having been *sanctified*, they must not pollute themselves anew—that, having been *washed*, they must not disgrace themselves with new defilements, but, on the contrary, aim at purity, persevere in true holiness, and abominate their former pollutions. And hence we infer what is the purpose for which God reconciles us to himself by the free pardon of our sins. While I have said that one thing is expressed by three

effet ;"—" Liable to all kinds of vices, unless in so far as the Lord inwardly restrains them, that they may not break forth outwardly, and come to be put in practice."
    [1] " Vne fontaine abondante ;"—" An abundant fountain."

terms, I do not mean that there is no difference whatever in their import, for, properly speaking, God justifies us when he frees us from condemnation, by not imputing to us our sins; he cleanses us, when he blots out the remembrance of our sins. Thus these two terms differ only in this respect, that the one is simple, while the other is figurative; for the term *washing* is metaphorical, Christ's blood being likened to water. On the other hand, he sanctifies by renewing our depraved nature by his Spirit. Thus sanctification is connected with regeneration. In this passage, however, the Apostle had simply in view to extol, with many commendations, the grace of God, which has delivered us from the bondage of sin, that we may learn from this how much it becomes us to hold in abhorrence everything that stirs up against us God's anger and vengeance.

In the name of the Lord Jesus, &c. With propriety and elegance he distinguishes between different offices. For the blood of Christ is the procuring cause of our cleansing: righteousness and sanctification come to us through his death and resurrection. But, as the cleansing effected by Christ, and the attainment of righteousness, are of no avail except to those who have been made partakers of those blessings by the influence of the Holy Spirit, it is with propriety that he makes mention of the Spirit in connection with Christ. Christ, then, is the source of all blessings to us: from him we obtain all things; but Christ himself, with all his blessings, is communicated to us by the Spirit. For it is by faith that we receive Christ, and have his graces applied to us. The Author of faith is the Spirit.

12. All things are lawful unto me, but all things are not expedient: all things are lawful for me, but I will not be brought under the power of any.

13. Meats for the belly, and the belly for meats: but God shall destroy both it and them. Now the body *is* not for fornication, but for the Lord; and the Lord for the body.

12. Omnium mihi est potestas, at non omnia conducunt: omnium mihi est potestas, sed ego sub nullius[1] redigar potestatem.

13. Escæ ventri, et venter escis: Deus vero et has et illum destruet. Corpus autem non scortationi, sed Domino, et Dominus corpori.

[1] "D'aucune chose, ou d'aucun;"—"Of anything, or of any one."

14. And God hath both raised up the Lord, and will also raise up us by his own power.

15. Know ye not that your bodies are the members of Christ? shall I then take the members of Christ, and make *them* the members of an harlot? God forbid.

16. What? know ye not that he which is joined to an harlot is one body? for two, saith he, shall be one flesh.

17. But he that is joined unto the Lord is one spirit.

18. Flee fornication. Every sin that a man doeth is without the body; but he that committeth fornication sinneth against his own body.

19. What? know ye not that your body is the temple of the Holy Ghost *which is* in you, which ye have of God, and ye are not your own.

20. For ye are bought with a price: therefore glorify God in your body, and in your spirit, which are God's.

14. Porro Deus et Dominum suscitavit, et nos suscitabit per potentiam suam.

15. An nescitis, quod corpora vestra membra sunt Christi? tollens igitur membra Christi, faciam membra meretricis? Absit.

16. An nescitis, quod qui adhæret meretrici, unum corpus est? erunt enim, inquit, duo in carnem unam.

17. Qui autem Domino adhæret, unus spiritus est.

18. Fugite scortationem. Omne peccatum quod commiserit homo, extra corpus est: qui autem scortatur, in proprium corpus peccat.

19. An nescitis, quod corpus vestrum templum est Spiritus sancti, qui in vobis est, quem habetis a Deo, et non estis vestri?

20. Empti enim estis pretio: glorificate iam Deum in corpore vestro et in spiritu vestro, quæ Dei sunt.

12. *All things are lawful for me.* Interpreters labour hard to make out the connection of these things,[1] as they appear to be somewhat foreign to the Apostle's design. For my own part, without mentioning the different interpretations, I shall state what, in my opinion, is the most satisfactory. It is probable, that the Corinthians even up to that time retained much of their former licentiousness, and had still a savour of the morals of their city. Now when vices stalk abroad with impunity,[2] custom is regarded as law, and then afterwards vain pretexts are sought for by way of excuse; an instance of which we have in their resorting to the pretext of Christian liberty, so as to make almost everything allowable for themselves to do. They revelled in excess of luxury. With this there was, as usual, much pride mixed up. As it was an outward thing, they did not think that

[1] " A le conioindre avec ce qui a este dit auparauant;"—" To connect it with what has been said before."

[2] " Or où on peche à bride auallée, et là où les vices ne sont point corrigez;"—" Where persons sin with a loose bridle, and where vices are not punished."

there was any sin involved in it : nay more, it appears from
Paul's words that they abused liberty so much as to extend
it even to fornication.   Now therefore, most appropriately,
after having spoken of their vices, he discusses those base
pretexts by which they flattered themselves in outward
sins.

It is, indeed, certain, that he treats here of outward things,
which God has left to the free choice of believers, but by
making use of a term expressive of universality, he either
indirectly reproves their unbridled licentiousness, or extols
God's boundless liberality, which is the best directress to us
of moderation.   For it is a token of excessive licentiousness,
when persons do not, of their own accord, restrict themselves,
and set bounds to themselves, amidst such manifold abundance.   And in the *first* place, he limits liberty[1] by two
exceptions ; and *secondly*, he warns them, that it does not by
any means extend to fornication.   These words, *All things
are lawful for me,* must be understood as spoken in name of
the Corinthians, κατ᾽ ἀνϑυποφορὰν, (by anticipation,) as
though he had said, I am aware of the reply which you are
accustomed to make, when desirous to avoid reproof for outward vices.   You pretend that *all things are lawful* for you,
without any reserve or limitation.

But all things are not expedient.   Here we have the *first*
exception, by which he restricts the use of liberty—that
they must not abandon themselves to licentiousness, because
respect must be had to edification.[2]   The meaning is, " It is
not enough that this or that is allowed us, to be made use of
indiscriminately ; for we must consider what is profitable to
our brethren, whose edification it becomes us to study.   For
as he will afterwards point out at greater length, (1 Cor. x.
23, 24,) and as he has already shown in Romans xiv. 13, &c.,
every one has liberty inwardly[3] in the sight of God on this
condition, that all must restrict the use of their liberty with
a view to mutual edification.

I will not be brought under the power of anything.   Here

---

[1] " La liberte Chrestienne ;"—" Christian liberty."
[2] " L'edification du prochain ;"—" The edification of their neighbour."
[3] " En sa conscience ;"—" In his conscience."

we have a *second* restriction—that we are constituted lords of all things, in such a way, that we ought not to bring ourselves under bondage to anything; as those do who cannot control their appetites.   For I understand the word τινος (any) to be in the neuter gender, and I take it as referring, not to persons, but to things, so that the meaning is this: "We are lords of all things; only we must not abuse that lordship in such a way as to drag out a most miserable bondage, being, through intemperance and inordinate lusts, under subjection to outward things, which ought to be under subjection to us."   And certainly, the excessive moroseness of those who grudge to yield up anything for the sake of their brethren, has this effect, that they unadvisedly put halters of necessity around their own necks.

13. *Meats for the belly, and the belly for meats.*   Here he shows what use ought to be made of outward things—for the necessity of the present life, which passes away quickly as a shadow, agreeably to what he says afterwards. (1 Cor. vii. 29.)   *We must use this world so as not to abuse it.*   And hence, too, we infer, how improper it is for a Christian man to contend for outward things.[1]   When a dispute, therefore, arises respecting corruptible things, a pious mind will not anxiously dwell upon these things; for liberty is one thing —the use of it is another.   This statement accords with another—that *the kingdom of God is not meat and drink.* (Rom. xiv. 17.)

Now the body is not for fornication.   Having mentioned the exceptions, he now states still farther, that our liberty ought not by any means to be extended to *fornication.*   For it was an evil that was so prevalent at that time, that it seemed in a manner as though it had been permitted; as we may see also from the decree of the Apostles, (Acts xv. 20,) where, in prohibiting the Gentiles from fornication, they place it among things indifferent; for there can be no doubt that this was done, because it was very generally looked

---

[1] " Il s'en faut que l'homme Chrestien se doyue soucier ne debatre pour les choses externes;"—" A Christian man ought not to be solicitous, or to contend for outward things."

upon as a lawful thing. Hence Paul says now, There is a difference between *fornication* and *meats*, for the Lord has not ordained *the body for fornication*, as he has *the belly for meats*. And this he confirms from things contrary or opposite, inasmuch as it is consecrated to Christ, and it is impossible that Christ should be conjoined with fornication. What he adds—*and the Lord for the body*, is not without weight, for while God the Father has united us to his Son, what wickedness there would be in tearing away our body from that sacred connection, and giving it over to things unworthy of Christ![1]

14. *And God hath also raised up the Lord.* He shows from Christ's condition how unseemly fornication is for a Christian man; for Christ having been received into the heavenly glory, what has he in common with the pollutions of this world? *Two* things, however, are contained in these words. The *first* is, that it is unseemly and unlawful, that our body, which is consecrated to Christ, should be profaned by fornication, inasmuch as Christ himself has been raised up from the dead, that he might enter on the possession of the heavenly glory. The *second* is, that it is a base thing to prostitute our body[2] to earthly pollutions, while it is destined to be a partaker[3] along with Christ of a blessed immortality and of the heavenly glory. There is a similar statement in Col. iii. 1, *If we have risen with Christ*, &c., with this difference, that he speaks here of the *last* resurrection only, while in that passage he speaks of the *first* also, or in other words, of the grace of the Holy Spirit, by which we are fashioned again to a new life. As, however, the resurrection is a thing almost *incredible* (Acts xxvi. 8) to the human mind, when the Scripture makes mention of it, it reminds us of *the power of God*, with the view of confirming our faith in it. (Matt. xxii. 29.)

15. *Know ye not that our bodies are the members*, &c.

---

[1] " Choses du tout indignes de Christ ;"—" Things altogether unworthy of Christ."

[2] " C'est vne meschancete d'abandonner nostre corps, et le prostituer ;" —" It is wickedness to surrender our body, and prostitute it."

[3] " Estre vn iour participant ;"—" To be one day a participant."

Here we have an explanation, or, if you prefer it, an amplification of the foregoing statement. For that expression, *the body is for the Lord,* might, owing to its brevity, be somewhat obscure. Hence he says, as if with the view of explaining it, that Christ is joined with us and we with him in such a way, that we become one body with him. Accordingly, if I have connection with an harlot, I tear Christ in pieces, so far as it is in my power to do so; for it is impossible for me to draw Him into fellowship with such pollution.[1] Now as that must be held in abhorrence,[2] he makes use of the expression which he is accustomed to employ in reference to things that are absurd—*God forbid.*[3] Observe, that the spiritual connection which we have with Christ belongs not merely to the soul, but also to the body, so that we are *flesh of his flesh,* &c. (Eph. v. 30.) Otherwise the hope of a resurrection were weak, if our connection were not of that nature—full and complete.

16. *Know ye not that he that is joined to an harlot.* He brings out more fully the greatness of the injury that is done to Christ by the man that has intercourse with an harlot; for he becomes *one body,* and hence he tears away a member from Christ's body. It is not certain in what sense he accommodates to his design the quotation which he subjoins from Gen. ii. 24. For if he quotes it to prove that two persons who commit fornication together become *one flesh,* he turns it aside from its true meaning to what is quite foreign to it. For Moses speaks there not of a base and prohibited cohabitation of a man and a woman, but of the marriage connection which God blesses. For he shows that that bond is so close and indissoluble, that it surpasses the relationship which subsists between a father and a son, which, assuredly,

---

[1] "Vne pollution si fade et infame;"—"A pollution so filthy and infamous."

[2] "Pour ce que ceci est vne chose abominable, et que nous deuons auoir en horreur;"—"As that is an abominable thing, and we must hold it in abhorrence."

[3] The original expression, Μὴ γένοιτο! *Away with it!* corresponds to the Hebrew term חללה, *far be it!* Thus in Gen. xviii. 25, מעשת כדבר הזה חללה לך, *Far be it from thee to act in this manner!* Homer makes use of a similar expression—μὴ τοῦτο θεὸς τελέσειεν, *forbid that heaven should accomplish that!* (Od. xx. 234.)—*Ed.*

can have no reference to fornication. This consideration has led me sometimes to think, that this quotation is not brought forward to confirm the immediately preceding statement, but one that is more remote, in this way—" Moses says, that by the marriage connection husband and wife become *one flesh,* but *he that is joined to the Lord* becomes not merely one flesh, but *one spirit* with him."[1] And in this way the whole of this passage would tend to magnify the efficacy and dignity of the spiritual marriage which subsists between us and Christ.

If, however, any one does not altogether approve of this exposition, as being rather forced, I shall bring forward another. For as fornication is the corruption of a divine institution, it has some resemblance to it ; and what is affirmed respecting the former, may to some extent be applied to the latter ; not that it may be honoured with the praises due to the former,[2] but for the purpose of expressing the more fully the heinousness of the sin. The expression, therefore, that *they two become one flesh,* is applicable in the true and proper sense to married persons only ; but it is applied to fornicators, who are joined in a polluted and impure fellowship, meaning that contagion passes from the one to the other.[3] For there is no absurdity in saying that fornication bears some resemblance to the sacred connection of marriage, as being a corruption of it, as I have said ; but the former has a curse upon it, and the other a blessing. Such is the correspondence between things that are contrasted in an antithesis. At the same time, I would prefer to understand it, in the first instance, of marriage, and then, in an improper sense,[4] of fornication, in this way—" God pro-

---

[1] " Mais nous sommes faits non seulement vne mesme chair auec le Seigneur, auquel nous adherons, mais aussi vn mesme esprit ; "—" But we have become not merely one flesh with the Lord, to whom we are joined, but also one spirit."

[2] " Non que la paillardise soit digne de estre ornee des louanges qui appartienent a l'ordonnance du marriage ; "—" Not that fornication is worthy to be honoured with the praises that belong to the ordinance of marriage."

[3] " Pour monstrer que la contagion et vilenie passe de l'vn a l'autre ; " " To show that contagion and pollution pass from the one to the other."

[4] Our Author makes use of the adverb—*abusive,* (improperly,) referring,

nounces husband and wife to be *one flesh*, in order that neither of them may have connection with another flesh ; so that the adulterer and adulteress do, also, become *one flesh*, and involve themselves in an accursed connection. And certainly this is more simple, and agrees better with the context.

17. *He that is joined to the Lord.* He has added this to show that our connection with Christ is closer than that of a husband and wife, and that the former, accordingly, must be greatly preferred before the latter, so that it must be maintained with the utmost chastity and fidelity. For if he who is joined to a woman in marriage ought not to have illicit connection with an harlot, much more heinous were this crime in believers, who are not merely *one flesh* with Christ, but also *one spirit*. Thus there is a comparison between greater and less.

18. *Flee fornication. Every sin*, &c. Having set before us honourable conduct, he now shows how much we ought to abhor *fornication*, setting before us the enormity of its wickedness and baseness. Now he shows its greatness by comparison—that this sin alone, of all sins, puts a brand of disgrace upon the body. The body, it is true, is defiled also by theft, and murder, and drunkenness, in accordance with those statements—*Your hands are defiled with blood.* (Isaiah i. 15.) *You have yielded your members instruments of iniquity unto sin*, (Rom. vi. 19,) and the like. Hence some, in order to avoid this inconsistency, understand the words rendered *against his own body*, as meaning *against us, as being connected with Christ ;* but this appears to me to be more ingenious than solid. Besides, they do not escape even in this way, because that same thing, too, might be affirmed of idolatry equally with fornication. For he who prostrates himself before an idol, sins against connection with Christ. Hence I explain it in this way, that he does not altogether deny that there are other vices, in like manner, by which our body is dishonoured and disgraced, but that his meaning is simply this—that defilement does not attach itself to

it is probable, to the figure of speech called by Quinctilian (viii. 6) *abusio* —the same as *catachresis* (perversion.)—*Ed.*

our body from other vices in the same way[1] as it does from *fornication*. My hand, it is true, is defiled by theft or murder, my tongue by evil speaking, or perjury,[2] and the whole body by drunkenness ; but *fornication* leaves a stain impressed upon the body, such as is not impressed upon it from other sins. According to this comparison, or, in other words, in the sense of less and more, other sins are said to be *without the body*—not, however, as though they do not at all affect the body, viewing each one by itself.

19. *Know ye not that your body.* He makes use of two additional arguments, in order to deter us from this filthiness. *First,* That *our bodies are temples of the Spirit ;* and, *secondly,* that *the Lord has bought us to himself as his property.* There is an emphasis implied in the term *temple ;* for as the Spirit of God cannot take up his abode in a place that is profane, we do not give him a habitation otherwise than by consecrating ourselves to him as *temples.* It is a great honour that God confers upon us when he *desires to dwell* in us. (Psalm cxxxii. 14.) Hence we ought so much the more to fear, lest he should depart from us, offended by our sacrilegious actings.[3]

And ye are not your own. Here we have a *second* argument—that we are not at our own disposal, that we should live according to our own pleasure. He proves this from the fact that the Lord has purchased us for himself, by paying the price of our redemption. There is a similar statement in Rom. xiv. 9. *To this end Christ died and rose again, that he might be Lord of the living and the dead.* Now the word rendered *price* may be taken in two ways ; either simply, as we commonly say of anything that it has cost a price,[4] when we mean that it has not been got for nothing ; or, as used instead of the adverb τιμίως, *at a dear rate,* as we are

---

[1] " N'en demeure point tellement imprimee en nostre corps ; "—" Does not remain impressed upon our body in the same way."

[2] " Par mesdisance, detraction, et periure ; "—" By evil-speaking, detraction, and perjury."

[3] " Par nos vilenies plenes de sacrilege ; "—" By our defilements, full of sacrilege."

[4] Thus, ἐξευρίσκειν τιμῆς τι is employed by classical writers to mean—getting a thing *at a price,* that is, at a high price. See Herod. vii. 119.—*Ed.*

accustomed to say of things that have cost us much.   This latter view pleases me better.   In the same way Peter says, *Ye are redeemed, not with gold and silver, but with the pre-cious*[1] *blood of the Lamb, without spot.* (1 Peter i. 18, 19.)   The sum is this,[2] that redemption must hold us bound, and with a bridle of obedience restrain the lasciviousness of our flesh.

20. *Glorify God.*   From this conclusion, it appears that the Corinthians took a liberty to themselves in outward things, that it was necessary to restrain and bridle.   The re-proof therefore is this: he shows that the body is subject to God no less than the soul, and that accordingly it is reason-able that both be devoted to his glory.   " As it is befitting that the mind of a believer should be pure, so there must be a corresponding outward profession also before men, inas-much as the power of both is in the hands of God, who has redeemed both."   With the same view he declared a little ago, that not only our souls but our bodies also are *temples of the Holy Spirit,* that we may not think that we discharge our duty to him aright, if we do not devote our-selves wholly and entirely to his service, that he may by his word regulate even the outward actions of our life.

CHAPTER VII.

1. Now concerning the things whereof ye wrote unto me: *It is* good for a man not to touch a woman.

2. Nevertheless, *to avoid* fornica-tion, let every man have his own wife, and let every woman have her own husband.

1. Porro, de quibus scripsistis mihi, bonum est viro mulierem non tangere.

2. Propter fornicationes autem unusquisque uxorem suam habeat, et unaquæque proprium maritum.

As he had spoken of fornication, he now appropriately pro-ceeds to speak of marriage, which is the remedy for avoiding

---

[1] Our Author has very manifestly in his eye the epithet τιμίος, (precious,) as made use of by the Apostle Peter, in reference to the blood of Christ— τιμίῳ αἵματι, ὡς ἀμνοῦ ἀμώμου κ. τ. λ.—"precious blood, as of a Lamb without blemish," &c.—*Ed.*

[2] " Le sommaire et la substance du propos revient là;"—" The sum and substance of the discourse amount to this."

fornication. Now it appears, that, notwithstanding the greatly scattered state of the Corinthian Church, they still retained some respect for Paul, inasmuch as they consulted him on doubtful points. What their questions had been is uncertain, except in so far as we may gather them from his reply. This, however, is perfectly well known, that immediately after the first rise of the Church, there crept into it, through Satan's artifice, a superstition of such a kind, that a large proportion of them, through a foolish admiration of celibacy,[1] despised the sacred connection of marriage; nay more, many regarded it with abhorrence, as a profane thing. This contagion had perhaps spread itself among the Corinthians also; or at least there were idly-disposed spirits, who, by immoderately extolling celibacy, endeavoured to alienate the minds of the pious from marriage. At the same time, as the Apostle treats of many other subjects, he intimates that he had been consulted on a variety of points. What is chiefly of importance is, that we listen to his doctrine as to each of them.

1. *It is good for a man.* The answer consists of two parts. In the *first*, he teaches that it were *good* for every one to abstain from connection with a woman, provided it was in his power to do so. In the *second*, he subjoins a correction to this effect, that as many cannot do this, in consequence of the weakness of their flesh, these persons must not neglect the remedy which they have in their power, as appointed for them by the Lord. Now we must observe what he means by the word *good*, when he declares that it is *good* to abstain from marriage, that we may not conclude, on the other hand, that the marriage connection is therefore *evil*—a mistake which Jerome has fallen into, not so much from ignorance, in my opinion, as from the heat of controversy. For though that great man was endowed with distinguished excellences, he laboured, at the same time, under one serious defect, that when disputing he allowed himself to be hurried away into great extravagancies, so that he did not keep within the bounds of truth. The inference

---

[1] " C'est à dire, l'abstinence du mariage;"—" That is to say, abstinence from marriage."

then which he draws is this : " It is *good not to touch a woman :* it is therefore *wrong* to do so."[1]   Paul, however, does not make use of the word *good* here in such a signification as to be opposed to what is evil or vicious, but simply points out what is expedient on account of there being so many troubles, vexations, and anxieties that are incident to married persons.   Besides, we must always keep in view the limitation which he subjoins.   Nothing farther, therefore, can be elicited from Paul's words than this—that it is indeed expedient and profitable for a man not to be bound to a wife, provided he can do otherwise.   Let us explain this by a comparison.   Should any one speak in this way : " It were *good* for a man not to eat, or to drink, or to sleep"—he would not thereby condemn eating, or drinking, or sleeping, as things that were wrong—but as the time that is devoted to these things is just so[2] much taken from the soul, his meaning would be, that we would be happier if we could be free from these hindrances, and devote ourselves wholly[3] to meditation on heavenly things.   Hence, as there are in married life many impediments which keep a man entangled, it were on that account *good* not to be connected in marriage.

But here another question presents itself, for these words of Paul have some appearance of inconsistency with the words of the Lord, in Gen. ii. 18, where he declares, that *it is not good for a man* to be without a wife.   What the Lord there pronounces to be *evil* Paul here declares to be *good*. I answer, that in so far as a wife is *a help* to her husband, so as to make his life happy, that is in accordance with God's institution ; for in the beginning God appointed it so, that the man without the woman was, as it were, but half a man, and felt himself destitute of special and necessary assistance, and the wife is, as it were, the completing of the

---

[1] Our Author, when commenting on Matt. xix. 10, animadverts in strong terms on Jerome's manner of handling the subject of marriage, as discovering "a malicious and wicked disposition." *Harmony*, vol. ii. p. 386.—*Ed.*

[2] " C'est autant de perdu quant aux choses spirituelles ;"—" It is so much of loss as to spiritual things."

[3] " Nous employer entierement et incessamment ;"—" Employ ourselves entirely and unceasingly."

man. Sin afterwards came in to corrupt that institution of God ; for in place of so great a blessing there has been substituted a grievous punishment, so that marriage is the source and occasion of many miseries. Hence, whatever evil or inconvenience there is in marriage, that arises from the corruption of the divine institution. Now, although there are in the meantime some remains still existing of the original blessing, so that a single life is often much more unhappy than the married life ; yet, as married persons are involved in many inconveniences, it is with good reason that Paul teaches that it would be *good for a man* to abstain. In this way, there is no concealment of the troubles that are attendant upon marriage ; and yet, in the meantime, there is no countenance given to those profane jests which are commonly in vogue with a view to bring it into discredit, such as the following : that a wife is a necessary evil, and that a wife is one of the greatest evils. For such sayings as these have come from Satan's workshop, and have a direct tendency to brand with disgrace God's holy institution ; and farther, to lead men to regard marriage with abhorrence, as though it were a deadly evil and pest.

The sum is this, that we must remember to distinguish between the pure ordinance of God and the punishment of sin, which came in subsequently. According to this distinction, it was in the beginning *good for a man*, without any exception, to be joined to a wife, and even yet, it is *good* in such a way, that there is in the meantime a mixture of bitter and sweet, in consequence of the curse of God. To those, however, who have not the gift of continency, it is a necessary and salutary remedy in accordance with what follows.

2. *But to avoid fornication.* He now commands, that those who are liable to the vice of incontinency should have recourse to the remedy. For though it may seem that the statement is universal, it ought, nevertheless, to be restricted to those who feel themselves urged by necessity. As to this, every one must judge for himself. Whatever difficulty, therefore, is perceived to be in marriage, let all that cannot resist the promptings of their flesh, know that this com-

mandment has been enjoined upon them by the Lord.   But
it is asked—" Is this the only reason for entering into
matrimony, that we may cure incontinency?" I answer, that
this is not Paul's meaning; for as for those that have the
gift of abstinence from marriage, he leaves *them* at liberty,[1]
while he commands others to provide against their infirmity
by marrying.   The sum is this—that the question is not as
to the reasons for which marriage has been instituted, but
as to the persons for whom it is necessary.   For if we look
to the first institution, it could not be a remedy for a disease
which had as yet no existence, but was appointed for begetting offspring ; but after the fall, this second purpose was
added.

This passage is also opposed to (πολυγαμία) *polygamy*.
For the Apostle desires that *every woman have her own husband*, intimating that the obligation is mutual.   The man,
therefore, who has once pledged his fidelity to a woman as
his wife, must not separate from her, as is manifestly done
in case of a second connection.

3. Let the husband render unto
the wife due benevolence : and likewise also the wife unto the husband.

4. The wife hath not power of her
own body, but the husband : and
likewise also the husband hath not
power of his own body, but the wife.

5. Defraud ye not one the other,
except *it be* with consent for a time,
that ye may give yourselves to fasting and prayer ; and come together
again, that Satan tempt you not for
your incontinency.

3. Uxori vir debitam benevolen-
tiam vicissim præstet, similiter et
uxor marito.

4. Mulier corporis sui potestatem
non habet, sed maritus : similiter et
maritus corporis sui potestatem non
habet, sed uxor.

5. Ne fraudetis alter alterum, nisi
ex mutuo consensu ad tempus, ut
vacetis ieiunio et orationi : et rursum in unum redite, ne tentet vos
Satanas propter incontinentiam vestram.

3. *The husband to the wife.*   He now prescribes the rules
to be observed in the marriage connection, or he teaches
what is the duty of husband and wife.   And in the first
place he lays down a general doctrine as to mutual benevolence—that the husband love his wife, and the wife her
husband ; for as to the interpretation which others give to

---

[1] " Il laisse la liberté de se marier ou ne se marier point ;"— ' He gives
liberty to marry or not marry "

the expression *due benevolence*—duty of marriage—I do not
know how far it is suitable. The reason that inclines them
to this view is, that it is immediately added, *The husband
has not power of his own body,* &c.; but it will suit better
to regard that as an inference drawn from the preceding
statement. Husband and wife, therefore, are bound to mutual
benevolence: hence it follows, that they have, neither the
one nor the other, *the power of their own body.* But it may
be asked, why the Apostle here puts them upon a level,
instead of requiring from the wife obedience and subjection.
I answer, that it was not his intention to treat of all their
duties, but simply of the mutual obligation as to the marriage bed. In other things, therefore, husband and wife
differ, both as to duty and as to authority: in this respect
the condition of both is alike—as to the maintaining of conjugal fidelity. For this reason, also, polygamy (πολυγαμία)
is again condemned; for if this is an invariable condition of
marriage, that the husband surrenders *the power of his own
body,* and gives it up to his wife, how could he afterwards
connect himself with another, as if he were free?

5. *Defraud ye not one the other.* Profane persons might
think that Paul does not act with sufficient modesty in discoursing in this manner as to the intercourse of a husband
with his wife; or at least that it was unbecoming the dignity
of an Apostle. If, however, we consider the reasons that
influenced him, we shall find that he was under the necessity
of speaking of these things. In the first place, he knew how
much influence a false appearance of sanctity has in beguil-
ing devout minds, as we ourselves know by experience. For
Satan dazzles us with an appearance of what is right, that
we may be led to imagine that we are polluted by intercourse
with our wives, and leaving off our calling, may think of pursuing another kind of life. Farther, he knew how prone every
one is to self-love, and devoted to his own gratification. From
this it comes, that a husband, having had his desire gratified,
treats his wife not merely with neglect, but even with disdain; and there are few that do not sometimes feel this
disdain of their wives creep in upon them. It is for these
reasons that he treats so carefully of the mutual obligations

of the married life. " If at any time it comes into the minds
of married persons to desire an unmarried life, as though it
were holier, or if they are tempted by irregular desires,[1] let
them bear in mind that they are bound by a mutual connection." The husband is but the one half of his body, and
so is it, also, as to the wife.   Hence they have not liberty of
choice, but must on the contrary restrain themselves with
such thoughts as these : " Because the one needed help from
the other, the Lord has connected us together, that we may
assist each other."   Let each then be helpful to each other's
necessity, and neither of them act as if at his or her own
disposal.

Unless by mutual consent.   He requires *mutual consent*, in
the first place, because the question is not as to the continency of one merely, but of two ; and besides, he immediately adds two other exceptions.   The *first* is, that it be
done only *for a time,* as perpetual continency is not in their
power, lest if they should venture to make an attempt beyond
their power, they might fall before Satan's stratagems.   The
second is, that they do not abstain from conjugal intercourse,
on the ground of that abstinence being in itself a good and
holy work, or as if it were the worship of God,[2] but that they
may be at leisure for better employments.   Now though
Paul had taken such pains in guarding this, yet Satan
prevailed so far as to drive[3] many to unlawful divorce, from
a corrupt desire for an unmarried life.   The husband, leaving
his wife, fled to the desert, that he might please God better
by living as a monk.   The wife, against her husband's will,
put on the veil—the badge of celibacy.   Meanwhile they did
not consider that by violating their marriage engagement
they broke the Lord's covenant, and by loosing the marriage
tie, they cast off the Lord's yoke.

This vice, it is true, was corrected in some measure by the
ancient canons ; for they prohibited a husband from leaving
his wife against her will, on pretence of continency ; and in

---

[1] "Ou qu'ils soyent tentez de se debaucher en paillardises ;"—"Or are
tempted to defile themselves with whoredoms."

[2] " Un seruice agreable à Dieu ;"—" A service agreeable to God."

[3] " Solicité et induit plusieurs ;"—" Enticed and induced many."

like manner a wife from refusing to her husband the use of her body. In this, however, they erred—that they permitted both together to live in perpetual celibacy, as if it were lawful for men to decree anything that is contrary to the Spirit of God. Paul expressly commands, that married persons do not *defraud each other, except for a time.* The bishops give permission to leave off the use of marriage for ever. Who does not see the manifest contrariety? Let no one, therefore, be surprised, that we make free to dissent on this point from the ancients, who, it is evident, deviated from the clear statements of the word of God.

That ye may have leisure for fasting and prayer. We must take notice, that Paul does not speak here of every kind of *fasting,* or every kind of *prayer.* That sobriety and temperance, which ought to be habitual on the part of Christians, is a kind of *fasting.* *Prayer,* too, ought to be not merely daily, but even continual. He speaks, however, of that kind of *fasting* which is a solemn expression of penitence, with the view of deprecating God's anger, or by which believers prepare themselves for *prayer,* when they are undertaking some important business. In like manner, the kind of *prayer* that he speaks of is such as requires a more intense affection of the mind.[1] For it sometimes happens, that we require (leaving off everything else) to *fast* and *pray;* as when any calamity is impending, if it appears to be a visitation of God's wrath ; or when we are involved in any difficult matter, or when we have something of great importance to do, as, for example, the ordaining of pastors.[2] Now it is with propriety that the Apostle connects these two things, because *fasting* is a preparation for *prayer,* as Christ also connects them, when he says, *This kind of devils goeth not out but by fasting and prayer.* (Matth. xvii. 21.)

When, therefore, Paul says, *that ye may be at leisure,* the meaning is, that having freed ourselves from all impediments, we may apply ourselves to this one thing. Now if any one

---

[1] " L'affection du cœur plus ardente et extraordinaire ;"—" A more ardent and extraordinary affection of the mind." See *Institutes* (vol. iii. p. 261.)

[2] " Comme quand on veut elire ou ordonner des pasteurs et ministres ;" —" As when persons wish to elect or ordain pastors and ministers."

objects, that the use of the marriage bed is an evil thing, inasmuch as it hinders *prayer*, the answer is easy—that it is not on that account worse than meat and drink, by which *fasting* is hindered.   But it is the part of believers to consider wisely *when* it is time to eat and drink, and *when* to fast.   It is also the part of the same wisdom to have intercourse with their wives when it is seasonable, and to refrain from that intercourse when they are called to be engaged otherwise.

And come together again, that Satan tempt you not.   Here he brings forward the reason, from ignorance of which the ancients have fallen into error, in rashly and inconsiderately approving of a vow of perpetual continency.   For they reasoned in this manner : " If it is good for married persons sometimes to impose upon themselves *for a time* a voluntary continency with *mutual consent*, then, if they impose this upon themselves for ever, it will be so much the better." But then, they did not consider how much danger was involved in this, for we give Satan an occasion for oppressing us, when we attempt anything beyond the measure of our weakness.[1]   " But we must resist Satan."[2]   What if arms and shield be wanting?   " They must be sought from the Lord," say they.   But in vain shall we beseech the Lord to assist us in a rash attempt.   We must, therefore, carefully observe the clause—*for your incontinency:* for we are exposed to Satan's temptations in consequence of the infirmity of our flesh.   If we wish to shut them out, and keep them back, it becomes us to oppose them by the remedy, with which the Lord has furnished us.   Those, therefore, act a rash part, who give up the use of the marriage bed.   It is as if they had made an agreement with God as to perpetual strength.[3]

6. But I speak this by permission, *and* not of commandment.

6. Hoc autem dico secundum veniam, non secundum præceptum.

[1] " Par dessus nos forces, et la mesure de nostre imbecilité ;"—" Beyond our strength, and the measure of our weakness."
[2] " Mais (dira quelqu'vn) il faut resister à Satan ;"—" But (some will say) we must resist Satan."
[3] " Qu'il leur donnera tousiours la puissance de s'en passer ;"—" That he would give them always the power to do without it."

7. For I would that all men were even as I myself. But every man hath his proper gift of God, one after this manner, and another after that.

8. I say therefore to the unmarried and widows, It is good for them if they abide even as I.

9. But if they cannot contain, let them marry: for it is better to marry than to burn.

7. Optarim enim, omnes homines esse sicut me: sed unusquisque proprium donum habet ex Deo, alius sic, alius autem sic.

8. Dico autem inconiugatis et viduis: bonum ipsis est, si maneant ut ego.

9. Si autem non continent, matrimonium contrahant: melius enim est matrimonium contrahere quam uri.

6. *By permission.* That they might not, by taking their stand upon a precept of the kind that he had prescribed, loosen unduly the restraints of lust,[1] he adds a limitation—that he had written these things on account of their infirmity—that they may bear in mind that marriage is a remedy for unchastity, lest they should inordinately abuse the advantage of it, so as to gratify their desire by every means; nay more, without measure or modesty. He has it also in view to meet the cavils of the wicked, that no one might have it in his power to object in this way: "What! are you afraid that husbands and wives will not of their own accord be sufficiently inclined to carnal delight that you prompt them to it?" For even the Papists, those little saints,[2] are offended with this doctrine, and would gladly have a contest with Paul, on the ground of his keeping married persons in mutual cohabitation, and not allowing them to turn aside to a life of celibacy. He assigns, then, a reason for his doctrine, and declares, that he had not recommended connubial intercourse to married persons with the view of alluring them to delight, or as though he took pleasure in commanding it, but had considered what was required by the infirmity of those that he is addressing.

Foolish zealots[3] for celibacy make a wrong use of both clauses of this verse; for as Paul says that he speaks *by permission,* they infer from this, that there is therefore something wrong in conjugal intercourse, for where there is

---

[1] "Leurs affections desordonnees;"—"Their inordinate affections."

[2] "Les hypocrites qui veulent estre estimez de petis saincts;"—"Hypocrites, who wish to be regarded as little saints."

[3] "Les sots et indiscrets zelateurs;"—"Foolish and inconsiderate zealots."

need of pardon,[1] there must be sin.   Farther, from his saying
that he speaks *not by commandment,* they infer, that it is,
therefore, a holier thing to leave off the use of marriage and
turn to celibacy.   To *the former,* I answer, that as there is,
I acknowledge, an inordinate excess in all human affections,
I do not deny that there is as to this matter an irregularity,
($\dot{a}\tau a\xi ia,$)[2] which, I allow, is vicious.[3]   Nay more, this affection, I allow, is beyond others violent, and next to brutish.
But, on the other hand, I also maintain, that whatever there
is of vice or baseness, is so covered over by the honourable-
ness of marriage, that it ceases to be a vice, or at least is
not reckoned a fault by God, as Augustine elegantly discourses in his book " On the advantage of Marriage," and
frequently in other places.   You may then take it briefly
thus :[4] conjugal intercourse is a thing that is pure, honourable and holy, because it is a pure institution of God : the
immoderate desire with which persons burn is a fault arising
from the corruption of nature ; but in the case of believers
marriage is a veil, by which that fault is covered over, so
that it no longer appears in the sight of God.   To the *second*
I answer : as the term *commandment* is properly applied to
those things which relate to the duties of righteousness,
and things in themselves pleasing to God, Paul on this
account says that he does not speak *by commandment.*
He has, however, sufficiently shewn previously, that the
remedy, which he had enjoined, must necessarily be made
use of.

7. *For I should wish, that all.*   This is connected with the
exposition of the foregoing statement ; for he does not fail

---

[1] " Où permission et pardon ha lieu ;"—" Where permission and pardon
have place."

[2] The term $\dot{a}\tau a\xi ia$ is used by our author in the Harmony (vol. i. p. 320)
to mean *disorder,* as contrasted with the *orderly* condition of the *kingdom
of God.*   It contains an allusion to the *disorderly conduct of soldiers,
who quit their ranks.*   It is used in this sense by Thucydides (vii. 43.)—
Ed.

[3] " Vn appetit desmesuré, lequel ie concede estre vicieux ;"—" An immoderate desire, which, I allow, is vicious."

[4] " Pour resolution donc de ce poinct en peu de paroles, disons en ceste
sorte ;"—" For a solution, then, of this point in a few words, let us express
it in this way."

to intimate, what is the more convenient way, but he wishes every one to consider what has been given him.[1] Why, then, has he, a little before, spoken *not by way of commandment?* It is for this reason, that he does not willingly constrain them to marry, but rather desires that they may be free from that necessity. As this, however, is not free to all, he has respect to infirmity. If this passage had been duly weighed, that perverse superstition connected with the desire of celibacy, which is the root and cause of great evils, would never have gained a footing in the world. Paul here expressly declares, that every one has not a free choice in this matter, because virginity is a special gift, that is not conferred upon all indiscriminately. Nor does he teach any other doctrine than what Christ himself does, when he says, that *all men are not capable of receiving this saying.* (Matth. xix. 11.) Paul, therefore, is here an interpreter of our Lord's words, when he says that this power has not been given to all—that of living without marriage.

What, in the meantime, has been done? Every one, without having any regard to his *power*, has, according to his *liking*, vowed perpetual continency. Nor has the error as to this matter been confined to the common people and illiterate persons; for even the most eminent doctors, devoting themselves unreservedly to the commendation of virginity, and forgetting human infirmity, have overlooked this admonition of Paul—nay rather, of Christ himself. Jerome, blinded by a zeal, I know not of what sort, does not simply fall, but rushes headlong, into false views. Virginity, I acknowledge, is an excellent gift; but keep it in view, that it is a *gift*. Learn, besides, from the mouth of Christ and of Paul, that it is not common to all, but is given only to a few. Guard, accordingly, against rashly devoting what is not in your own power, and what you will not obtain as a gift, if forgetful of your calling you aspire beyond your limits.

At the same time the ancients erred even in their estimate of virginity, for they extol it as if it were the most excellent of all virtues, and wish it to be regarded as the worship of

---

[1] " Donné de Dieu;"—"Given by God."

God.[1] Even in this there is a dangerous error ; and now
follows another—that, after celibacy had begun to be so
much esteemed, many, vying with each other, rashly vowed
perpetual continency, while scarcely the hundredth part of
them were endowed with the power and gift.   Hence, too,
a *third* sprung up—that the ministers of the Church were
forbidden to enter into marriage, as a kind of life unbecoming
the holiness of their order.[2]   As for those who, despising
marriage, rashly vowed perpetual continency, God punished their presumption, first, by the secret flames of lust ;[3]
and then afterwards, by horrible acts of filthiness.   The
ministers of the Churches being prohibited from lawful
marriage, the consequence of this tyranny was, that the
Church was robbed of very many good and faithful ministers ; for pious and prudent men would not insnare themselves in this way.   At length, after a long course of time,
lusts, which had been previously kept under, gave forth their
abominable odour.   It was reckoned a small matter for those,
in whom it would have been a capital crime to have a wife,
to· maintain with impunity concubines, that is, prostitutes ;
but no house was safe from the impurities of the priests.
Even that was reckoned a small matter ; for there sprung
up monstrous enormities, which it were better to bury in
eternal oblivion than to make mention of them by way of
example.[4]

8. *I say, then, to the unmarried.* This depends on what
goes before, and is a sort of inference from it. He had said
that the gifts of God are variously distributed—that continency is not in the power of all, and that those who have it
not ought to have recourse to the remedy. He now directs
his discourse to *virgins,* to all that are *unmarried,* and to
widows, and he allows that an unmarried life ought to be

---

[1] " Comme vn service agreable à Dieu ;"—" As a service agreeable to
God."

[2] " Comme vn estat indigne et non conuenable à la sanctete de l'ordre ;"
—" As a condition unbefitting, and unsuitable to the holiness of their
order."

[3] " De passions et cupiditez desordonnees ;"—" Of inordinate passions
and lusts."

[4] The reader will find the same subject largely treated of by our author
in the *Institutes,* vol. iii. pp. 268-272.—*Ed.*

desired by them, provided they have the power ; but that regard must always be had by each individual to the power that he possesses. The sum is this, that an unmarried life has many advantages, and that these are not to be despised, provided every one measures himself according to his own size and measure.[1] Hence, though virginity should be extolled even to the third heavens, this, at the same time, always remains true—that it does not suit all, but only those who have a special *gift* from God. For as to the objection that is brought forward by Papists—that in baptism, also, we promise to God purity of life, which it is not in our power to perform, the answer is easy—that in that we promise nothing but what God requires from all his people, but that continency is a special gift, which God has withheld from many. Hence those who make a vow of continency, act precisely as if any unlearned and illiterate person were to set himself off as a prophet, or teacher, or interpreter of languages.

We must also notice carefully the word *continue ;* for it is possible for a person to live chastely in a state of celibacy for a time, but there must be in this matter no determination made for to-morrow. Isaac was unmarried until he was thirty years of age, and passed in chastity those years in which the heats of irregular desire are most violent ; yet afterwards he is called to enter into the married life. In Jacob we have a still more remarkable instance. Hence the Apostle would wish those who are at present practising chastity, to continue in it and persevere ; but as they have no security for the continuance of the gift, he exhorts all to consider carefully what has been *given* them. This passage, however, shows that the Apostle was at that time unmarried ; for as to the inference drawn by Erasmus, that he was married, because he makes mention of himself in connection with married persons, it is frivolous and silly ; for we might, on the same principle, infer that he was a widower,[2]

---

[1] " Se mesure a son aulne (comme on dit) c'est à dire, selon sa faculté ;" —" Measures himself by his own ell, (as they say,) that is to say, according to his ability."

[2] " Qu'il estoit sans femme ;"—" That he was unmarried."

because he speaks of himself in connection with widows.[1]
Now the words intimate, that at that time he was unmarried ; for I do not give any countenance to the conjecture,
that he had put away his wife somewhere, and had of his
own accord abandoned the use of the marriage bed.   For
where, in that case, had been the injunction,[2] *Come together
again without delay ?* (1 Cor. vii. 5.)   It would certainly be
an absurdity to say, that he did not obey his own precepts,
and did not observe the law which he imposed upon others.
It is, however, a singular token of modesty, that, while he
is himself endowed with the gift of continency, he does not
require others to bind themselves to his rule, but allows them
that remedy for infirmity which he dispenses with.   Let us,
then, imitate his example, so that if we excel in any particular gift, we do not rigorously insist upon it on the part of
others, who have not as yet reached that height.

9. *But if they cannot contain.*   While he advises to abstain from marriage, he always speaks conditionally—*if it
can be done, if there is ability ;* but where the infirmity of
the flesh does not allow of that liberty, he expressly enjoins
marriage as a thing that is not in the least doubtful.   For
this is said *by way of commandment,* that no one may look
upon it as mere advice.   Nor is it merely fornicators that
he restrains, but those also who are defiled in the sight of
God by inward lust ; and assuredly he that *cannot contain*
tempts God, if he neglects the remedy of marriage.   This
matter requires—not advice, but strict prohibition.

For it is better.   There is not strictly a comparison here,
inasmuch as lawful *marriage is honourable in all things,* (Heb.
xiii. 4,) but, on the other hand, *to burn* is a thing that is exceedingly wrong.   The Apostle, however, has made use of
a customary form of expression, though not strictly accurate,
as we commonly say : " It is better to renounce this world,
that we may, along with Christ, enjoy the inheritance of the
heavenly kingdom, than to perish miserably in carnal de-

---

[1] " Entre ceux qui n'estoyent point mariez ;"—"Among those that were
unmarried."

[2] " Car comment se fust-il donc acquitté de ce qu'il commande yci aux
gens mariez ?"—"For how, in that case, would he have discharged the
duty that he enjoins upon married persons ?"

lights." I mention this, because Jerome constructs upon this passage a childish sophism[1]—that marriage is good, inasmuch as it is not so great an evil as *to burn*. I would say, if it were a matter of sport, that he foolishly amuses himself, but in a matter so weighty and serious, it is an impious scoff, unworthy of a man of judgment. Let it then be understood, that marriage is a good and salutary remedy, because *to burn* is a most base abomination in the sight of God. We must, however, define what is meant by *burning ;* for many are stung with fleshly desires, who, nevertheless, do not require forthwith to have recourse to marriage. And to retain Paul's metaphor, it is one thing *to burn* and another to feel heat. Hence what Paul here calls *burning*, is not a mere slight feeling, but a boiling with lust, so that you cannot resist. As, however, some flatter themselves in vain, by imagining that they are entirely free from blame, if they do not yield assent to impure desire, observe that there are three successive steps of temptation. For in some cases the assaults of impure desire have so much power that the will is overcome : *that* is the worst kind of *burning*, when the heart is inflamed with lust. In some instances, while we are stung with the darts of the flesh, it is in such a manner that we make a stout resistance, and do not allow ourselves to be divested of the true love of chastity, but on the contrary, abhor all base and filthy affections.

Hence all must be admonished, but especially the young, that whenever they are assailed by their fleshly inclinations, they should place the fear of God in opposition to a temptation of this sort, cut off all inlets to unchaste thoughts, entreat the Lord to give them strength to resist, and set themselves with all their might to extinguish the flames of lust. If they succeed in this struggle, let them render thanks unto the Lord, for where shall we find the man who does not experience some molestation from his flesh ? but if we bridle its violence, before it has acquired the mastery, it is well. For we do not *burn*, though we should feel a disagreeable heat—not that there is nothing wrong in that feeling of heat, but acknowledging before the Lord, with humility and

[1] " Vn sophisme plus que puerile ;"—" A worse than childish sophism."

sighing,[1] our weakness, we are meanwhile, nevertheless, of good courage.   To sum up all, so long as we come off victorious in the conflict, through the Lord's grace, and Satan's darts do not make their way within, but are valiantly repelled by us, let us not become weary of the conflict.

There is an intermediate kind of temptation[2]—when a man does not indeed admit impure desire with the full assent of his mind, but at the same time is inflamed with a blind impetuosity, and is harassed in such a manner that he cannot with peace of conscience call upon God.   A temptation, then, of such a kind as hinders one from calling upon God in purity, and disturbs peace of conscience, is *burning*, such as cannot be extinguished except by marriage.   We now see, that in deliberating as to this, one must not merely consider whether he can preserve his body free from pollution : the mind also must be looked to, as we shall see in a little.

10. And unto the married I command, *yet* not I, but the Lord, Let not the wife depart from *her* husband :

11. But and if she depart, let her remain unmarried, or be reconciled to *her* husband : and let not the husband put away *his* wife.

12. But to the rest speak I, not the Lord : If any brother hath a wife that believeth not, and she be pleased to dwell with him, let him not put her away.

13. And the woman which hath an husband that believeth not, and if he be pleased to dwell with her, let her not leave him.

14. For the unbelieving husband is sanctified by the wife, and the unbelieving wife is sanctified by the husband : else were your children unclean ; but now are they holy.

15. But if the unbelieving depart, let him depart.   A brother or a sister is not under bondage in such *cases :* but God hath called us to peace.

10. Coniugibus denuntio, non ego, sed Dominus : Uxor a marito ne discedat.

11. Quodsi discesserit, maneat innupta, aut viro reconcilietur : et vir uxorem ne dimittat.

12. Reliquis ego dico, non Dominus : Si quis frater uxorem habet infidelem, et ipsa consentit cum eo habitare, ne dimittat eam :

13. Et mulier si maritum habet infidelem, et ipse consentit cum ea habitare, ne relinquat eum.

14. Sanctificatus est enim vir infidelis in uxore : et sanctificata est uxor incredula in viro : alioque liberi vestri immundi essent : nunc autem sancti sunt.

15. Quod si infidelis discedit, discedat : non enim subiectus est servituti frater aut soror in talibus, in pace autem vocavit nos Deus.

[1] " Auec pleurs et humilité ;"—" With tears and humility."
[2] " Il y a vne autre espece de tentation moyenne entre les deux que i'ay dites ;"—" There is another kind of temptation, intermediate between the two that I have mentioned."

16. For what knowest thou, O wife, whether thou shalt save *thy* husband? or how knowest thou, O man, whether thou shalt save *thy* wife?	16. Quid enim scis, mulier, an maritum servatura sis? aut quid scis, O vir, an uxorem sis servaturus?
17. But as God hath distributed to every man, as the Lord hath called every one, so let him walk. And so ordain I in all churches.	17. Nisi unusquisque ut ei gratiam divisit Dominus, sic ambulet: et sic in Ecclesiis omnibus praecipio.

10. *To the married I command.* He now treats of another condition of marriage—its being an indissoluble tie. Accordingly, he condemns all those divorces that were of daily occurrence among the heathens, and were not punished among the Jews by the law of Moses. *Let not,* says he, *the husband put away his wife, and let not the wife depart from her husband.* Why? Because they are joined together by an indissoluble bond. It is surprising, however, that he does not make an exception, at least in case of adultery; for it is not likely that he designed to curtail in anything the doctrine of Christ. To me it appears clear, that the reason why he has made no mention of this[1] is, that as he is discoursing of these things only in passing, he chose rather to send back the Corinthians to the Lord's permission or prohibition, than to go over everything in detail. For when persons intend to teach anything in short compass, they content themselves with a general statement. Exceptions are reserved for a minuter and more extended and particular discussion.

But as to what he subjoins—*not I, but the Lord*—he intimates by this correction, that what he teaches here is taken from the law of God. For other things that he taught he had also from the revelation of the Spirit; but he declares that God is the author of this, in respect of its being expressly taken from the law of God. If you inquire as to the particular passage, you will nowhere find it in so many words; but as Moses in the beginning testifies, that the connection between a husband and wife is so sacred, that for the sake of it *a man ought to leave his father and mother.* (Gen. ii. 24.) It is easy to gather from this, how inviolable a con-

---

[1] "Il n'a pas voulu toucher ce poinct;"—"He has not chosen to touch upon this point."

nection it is. For by right of nature a son is bound to his father and mother, and cannot shake off that yoke. As the connection of marriage is preferred to that bond, much less ought *it* to be dissolved.

11. *But if she depart.* That this is not to be understood of those who have been put away for adultery, is evident from the punishment that followed in that case ; for it was a capital crime even by the Roman laws, and almost by the common law of nations. But as husbands frequently divorced their wives, either because their manners were not congenial, or because their personal appearance did not please them, or because of some offence ;[1] and as wives, too, sometimes deserted their husbands on account of their cruelty, or excessively harsh and dishonourable treatment, he says that marriage is not dissolved by divorces or dissensions of that nature. For it is an agreement that is consecrated by the name of God, which does not stand or fall according to the inclination of men, so as to be made void whenever we may choose. The sum is this : other contracts, as they depend on the mere inclination of men, are in like manner dissolved by that same inclination ; but those who are connected by marriage are no longer free, so as to be at liberty, if they change their mind, to *break in pieces the pledge,*[2] (as the expression is,) and go each of them elsewhere in quest of a new connection. For if the rights of nature cannot be dissolved, much less can this, which, as we have said already, is preferred before the principal tie of nature.

But as to his commanding the wife, who is separated from her husband, to *remain unmarried,* he does not mean by this that separation is allowable, nor does he give permission to the wife to live apart from her husband ; but if she has been expelled from the house, or has been put away,

---

[1] " Pource qu'elles n'estoyent assez belles, ou pour quelque autre despit ou desplaisir ;"—" Because they were not handsome enough, or on the ground of some other offence or dislike."

[2] The phrase used by our Author—*frangant tesseram*—(*break the pledge*) contains an allusion to the custom among the Romans of having, on occasion of a league of hospitality being formed, a tally (*tessera*) or piece of wood cut into two parts, of which each party kept one. If either of the parties acted inconsistently with the engagement, he was said—*confregisse tesseram*—*to have broken the pledge.* See Plaut. Cist. II. i. 27.—*Ed.*

she must not think that even in that case she is set free from his power; for it is not in the power of a husband to dissolve marriage. He does not therefore give permission here to wives to withdraw, of their own accord, from their husbands, or to live away from their husband's establishment, as if they were in a state of widowhood; but declares, that even those who are not received by their husbands, continue to be bound, so that they cannot take other husbands.

But what if a wife is wanton, or otherwise incontinent? Would it not be inhuman to refuse her the remedy, when constantly burning with desire? I answer, that when we are prompted by the infirmity of our flesh, we must have recourse to the remedy; after which it is the Lord's part to bridle and restrain our affections by his Spirit, though matters should not succeed according to our desire. For if a wife should fall into a protracted illness, the husband would, nevertheless, not be justified in going to seek another wife. In like manner, if a husband should, after marriage, begin to labour under some distemper, it would not be allowable for his wife to change her condition of life. The sum is this —God having prescribed lawful marriage as a remedy for our incontinency, let us make use of it, that we may not, by tempting him, pay the penalty of our rashness. Having discharged this duty, let us hope that he will give us aid should matters go contrary to our expectations.

12. *To the rest I say.* By *the rest* he means those who are exceptions, so that the law, common to others, is not applicable to them; for an unequal marriage is on a different footing, when married persons differ among themselves in respect of religion. Now this question he solves in two clauses. The *first* is, that the believing party ought not to withdraw from the unbelieving party, and ought not to seek divorce, unless she is put away. The *second* is, that if an unbeliever put away his wife on account of religion, a *brother* or a *sister* is, by such rejection, freed from the bond of marriage. But why is it that Paul speaks of himself as the author of these regulations, while they appear to be somewhat at variance with what he had, a little before, brought forward, as from the Lord? He does not mean that they are

from himself in such a way as not to be derived from the Spirit of God ; but, as there was nowhere in the law or in the Prophets any definite or explicit statement on this subject, he anticipates in this way the calumnies of the wicked, in claiming as his own what he was about to state. At the same time, lest all this should be despised as the offspring of man's brain, we shall find him afterwards declaring, that his statements are not the contrivances of his own understanding. There is, however, nothing inconsistent with what goes before ; for as the obligation and sanctity of the marriage engagement depend upon God, what connection can a pious woman any longer maintain with an unbelieving husband, after she has been driven away through hatred of God ?

14. *For the unbelieving husband is sanctified.* He obviates an objection, which might occasion anxiety to believers. The relationship of marriage is singularly close, so that the wife is the half of the man—so that *they two are one flesh*— (1 Cor. vi. 16)—so that *the husband is the head of the wife ;* (Eph. v. 23;) and she is her husband's partner in everything; hence it seems impossible that a believing husband should live with an ungodly wife, or the converse of this, without being polluted by so close a connection. Paul therefore declares here, that marriage is, nevertheless, sacred and pure, and that we must not be apprehensive of contagion, as if the wife would contaminate the husband. Let us, however, bear in mind, that he speaks here not of contracting marriages, but of maintaining those that have been already contracted ; for where the matter under consideration is, whether one should marry an unbelieving wife, or whether one should marry an unbelieving husband, then that exhortation is in point—*Be not yoked with unbelievers, for there is no agreement between Christ and Belial.* (2 Cor. vi. 14.) But he that is already bound has no longer liberty of choice ; hence the advice given is different.

While this *sanctification* is taken in various senses, I refer it simply to marriage, in this sense—It might seem (judging from appearance) as if a believing wife contracted infection from an unbelieving husband, so as to make the

connection unlawful; but it is otherwise, for the piety of
the one has more effect in sanctifying marriage than the
impiety of the other in polluting it.   Hence a believer may,
with a pure conscience, live with an unbeliever, for in respect
of the use and intercourse of the marriage bed, and of
life generally, he is sanctified, so as not to infect the believing party with his impurity.   Meanwhile this *sanctification* is of no benefit to the unbelieving party; it only serves
thus far, that the believing party is not contaminated by
intercourse with him, and marriage itself is not profaned.

But from this a question arises—" If the faith of a husband or wife who is a Christian *sanctifies* marriage, it follows
that all marriages of ungodly persons are impure, and differ
nothing from fornication."   I answer, that *to the ungodly all
things are impure,* (Tit. i. 15,) because they pollute by their
impurity even the best and choicest of God's creatures.   Hence
it is that they pollute marriage itself, because they do not
acknowledge God as its Author, and therefore they are not
capable of true sanctification, and by an evil conscience abuse
marriage.   It is a mistake, however, to conclude from this
that it differs nothing from fornication; for, however impure
it is to them, it is nevertheless pure in itself, inasmuch as it
is appointed by God, serves to maintain decency among men,
and restrains irregular desires; and hence it is for these
purposes approved by God, like other parts of political order.
We must always, therefore, distinguish between the nature
of a thing and the abuse of it.

Else were your children.   It is an argument taken from
the effect—" If your marriage were impure, then the children that are the fruit of it would be impure; but *they are
holy;* hence the marriage also is holy.   As, then, the ungodliness of one of the parents does not hinder the children
that are born from being holy, so neither does it hinder the
marriage from being pure."   Some grammarians explain
this passage as referring to a civil sanctity, in respect of the
children being reckoned legitimate, but in this respect the
condition of unbelievers is in no degree worse.   That exposition, therefore, cannot stand.   Besides, it is certain that
Paul designed here to remove scruples of conscience, lest

any one should think (as I have said) that he had contracted defilement. The passage, then, is a remarkable one, and drawn from the depths of theology ; for it teaches, that the children of the pious are set apart from others by a sort of exclusive privilege, so as to be reckoned *holy* in the Church.

But how will this statement correspond with what he teaches elsewhere—that *we are all by nature children of wrath ;* (Eph. ii. 3 ;) or with the statement of David—*Behold I was conceived in sin,* &c. (Ps. li. 7.) I answer, that there is a universal propagation of sin and damnation throughout the seed of Adam, and all, therefore, to a man, are included in this curse, whether they are the offspring of believers or of the ungodly ; for it is not as regenerated by the Spirit, that believers beget children after the flesh. The natural condition, therefore, of all is alike, so that they are liable equally to sin and to eternal death. As to the Apostle's assigning here a peculiar privilege to the children of believers, this flows from the blessing of the covenant, by the intervention of which the curse of nature is removed ; and those who were by nature unholy are consecrated to God by grace. Hence Paul argues, in his Epistle to the Romans, (xi. 16,) that the whole of Abraham's posterity are holy, because God had made a covenant of life with him—*If the root be holy,* says he, *then the branches are holy also.* And God calls all that were descended from Israel his sons : now that the partition is broken down, the same covenant of salvation that was entered into with the seed of Abraham[1] is communicated to us. But if the children of believers are exempted from the common lot of mankind, so as to be set apart to the Lord, why should we keep them back from the sign ? If the Lord admits them into the Church by his word, why should we refuse them the sign ? In what respects the offspring of the pious are holy, while many of them become degenerate, you will find explained in the tenth and eleventh chapters of the Epistle to the Romans ; and I have handled this point there.

[1] " Auec Abraham, et auec la semence ;"—" With Abraham and with his seed."

15. *But if an unbeliever depart.* This is the second department of his statement, in which he sets at liberty a believing husband, who is prepared to dwell with an unbelieving wife, but is rejected by her, and in like manner a woman who is, without any fault on her part, repudiated by her husband; for in that case the unbelieving party makes a divorce with God rather than with his or her partner. There is, therefore, in this case a special reason, inasmuch as the first and chief bond is not merely loosed, but even utterly broken through. While some are of opinion that we are at this day situated in a much similar way with Papists,[1] we ought to consider wisely what difference there is between the two cases, that we may not attempt anything rashly.[2]

In peace. Here, too, interpreters differ; for some take it in this way—" We are called *in peace:* let us therefore avoid all ground and occasion of quarrels." I take it in a more simple way: " Let us, so far as we can, cultivate peace with all, to which we have been called. We must not, therefore, rashly separate from unbelievers, unless they first make a divorce. God, therefore, has *called us in peace* to this end, that we might cultivate peace with all, by acting properly towards every one." This, then, belongs to the former department of his statement—that *believers ought to remain with unbelievers, if they are pleased,* &c., (verses 12 and 13,) because a desire for divorce is at variance with our profession.

16. *For what knowest thou, O woman?* Those who are of opinion that this observation is a confirmation of the *second* department of his statement, expound it thus: " An uncertain hope ought not to detain thee," &c. But, in my opinion, the exhortation is taken from the advantage to be derived; for it is a great and distinguished blessing if a wife *gain* (1 Cor. ix. 19) her husband. Now, unbelievers are not in so hopeless a condition but that they may be brought to believe. They are dead, it is true, but God can even raise the dead. So long, therefore, as there remains any hope of

---

[1] " Que nous auons auiourd'huy semblable cause de nous departir d'avec les Papistes;"—" That we have at this day similar ground of separation from Papists."

[2] See p. xxii. *n.* 2.

doing good, and the pious wife knows not but that she may by her *holy conversation* (1 Pet. iii. 1) bring back her husband into the way,[1] she ought to try every means before leaving him ; for so long as a man's salvation is doubtful, it becomes us to be prepared rather to hope the best.

As to his saying, however, that *a husband may be saved by his wife*, the expression, it is true, is not strictly accurate, as he ascribes to man what belongs to God ; but there is no absurdity in it. For as God acts efficaciously by his instruments which he makes use of, he does, in a manner, communicate his power to them, or, at least, he connects it with their service in such a manner, that what he does he speaks of as being done by them, and hence, too, he sometimes ascribes to them the honour which is due to himself alone. Let us, however, bear in mind, that we have nothing in our power, except in so far as we are directed by him as instruments.

17. *Unless every one, according as God has dispensed his grace*, &c. Such is the literal meaning : only I have in my rendering made use of the nominative,[2] in order that the connection may be more easy and natural. The meaning is : " What, then, is to be done, *unless*[3] that every one walk according to the grace given to him, and according to his calling ? Let every one, therefore, labour for this, and use his endeavour, that he may do good to his neighbours, and, more especially, when he ought to be excited to it by the particular duty of his calling." He mentions two things—the *calling*, and *the measure of grace*. These he desires us to look to in deliberating as to this matter ; as it ought to be no small stimulus to us to duty, that God condescends to make us ministers of his grace for the salvation of our brethren ; while the *calling*, on the other hand, should hold us, as it

---

[1] " Au bon chemin ;"—" Into the good way."

[2] Our Author refers to the word ἕκαστος, (every one,) which occurs in the first clause of the verse in the dative case, and in the second clause in the accusative, and in both instances rendered by him in the nominative—*unusquisque* (every one.)—*Ed.*

[3] The particles which occur in the original, εἰ μὴ, (unless,) might in this passage, and in several other instances in the New Testament, (as well as in classical writers,) be rendered *only*. They correspond to the Hebrew particles אִם־לֹא. See Genesis xxiv. 38.—*Ed.*

were, under God's yoke, even where an individual feels his situation to be an unpleasant one.

And so in all the Churches. I am of opinion that he added this, with the view of obviating the calumnies of some who boasted that he assumed more authority over the Corinthians than he ventured to do over others. At the same time he might have also another end in view—that this doctrine might have the more weight, when the Corinthians understood that it was already published *in all the Churches.* For we embrace the more readily what we understand that we have in common with all the pious. The Corinthians, on the other hand, would have felt it hateful to be bound more closely than others.

18. Is any man called being circumcised? let him not become uncircumcised. Is any called in uncircumcision? let him not be circumcised.

19. Circumcision is nothing, and uncircumcision is nothing, but the keeping of the commandments of God.

20. Let every man abide in the same calling wherein he was called.

21. Art thou called *being* a servant? care not for it: but if thou mayest be made free, use *it* rather.

22. For he that is called in the Lord, *being* a servant, is the Lord's freeman: likewise also he that is called, *being* free, is Christ's servant.

23. Ye are bought with a price; be not ye the servants of men.

24. Brethren, let every man, wherein he is called, therein abide with God.

18. Circumcisus aliquis vocatus est? ne arcessat præputium: in præputio aliquis vocatus est? ne circumcidatur.

19. Circumcisio nihil est, et præputium nihil est, sed observatio mandatorum Dei.

20. Unusquisque in qua vocatione fuit vocatus, maneat.

21. Servus vocatus es? ne sit tibi curæ: at si etiam possis liber fieri, magis utere.

22. Etenim qui in Domino vocatus est servus, libertus Domini est: similiter et qui liber vocatus est, servus est Christi.

23. Pretio empti estis: nolite fieri servi hominum.

24. Unusquisque in eo, in quo vocatus est, fratres, maneat apud Deum.

18. *Circumcised,* &c. As he had made mention of the *calling,* he takes occasion, from a particular instance, to make a digression for a little into a general exhortation, as he is wont to do in many instances; and, at the same time, he confirms, by different examples, what he had said respecting marriage. The sum is this, that in external things you must not rashly abandon the *calling* on which you have once entered by the will of God. And he begins with *circumcision,* respecting which many at that time disputed.

Now, he says that with God it makes no difference whether you are a Gentile or a Jew.   Hence he exhorts every one to be contented with his condition.   It must always be kept in view, that he treats only of lawful modes of life, which have God as their approver and author.

19. *Circumcision is nothing.*   While this similitude was suited to the subject in hand, it appears to have been designedly made use of with the view of reproving, in passing, the superstition and haughtiness of the Jews.   For, as the Jews gloried in circumcision, it was possible that many might feel dissatisfied with the want of it, as if their condition were the worse on that account.   Paul, therefore, places both conditions upon a level, lest, through hatred of the one, the other should be foolishly desired.   These things, however, must be understood as referring to the time when circumcision was at length abolished ; for, if he had had an eye to the covenant of God, and his commandment, he would, without doubt, have estimated it higher.   In another passage, it is true, he makes light of *the letter of circumcision,* (Rom. ii. 27,) and declares that it is of no account in the sight of God ; but here, as he simply contrasts circumcision with uncircumcision, and makes both alike, it is certain that he speaks of it as a matter of indifference and of no moment.   For the abolishing of it has this effect—that the mystery which had been previously conveyed under it, does not now any longer belong to it : nay more, it is now no longer a sign, but a thing of no use. For baptism has come in the place of the symbol used under the law on this footing, that it is enough that we be circumcised by the Spirit of Christ, while our old man is buried with Christ.

But the keeping of the commandments.   As this was one of the *commandments,* so long as the Church was bound to legal ceremonies, we see that it is taken for granted, that circumcision had been abolished by the advent of Christ, so that the *use* of it, indeed, was allowed among the ignorant and weak, but *advantage* in it—there was none.   For Paul speaks of it here as a thing of no moment : " As these are outward things, let them not take up your attention, but devote yourself rather to piety and the duties which God requires, and which are alone precious in his sight." As to the circumstance that Papists bring forward this passage for the purpose of overthrowing justification by faith, it is utterly childish ; for Paul is not disputing here as to the ground of justification, or the way in which we obtain it, but simply as to the object to which the aim of believers ought to be directed. " Do not occupy yourselves to no purpose in things of no profit, but, on the contrary, exercise yourselves in duties that are well pleasing to God."

20. *Every man in the calling in which.* This is the source from which other things are derived,—that every one should be contented with his *calling*, and pursue it, instead of seeking to betake himself to anything else. A *calling* in Scripture means a lawful mode of life, for it has a relation to God as *calling* us,[1]—lest any one should abuse this statement[2] to justify modes of life that are evidently wicked or vicious. But here it is asked, whether Paul means to establish any obligation,[3] for it might seem as though the words conveyed this idea, that every one is bound to his *calling*, so that he must not abandon it. Now it were a very hard thing if a tailor[4] were not at liberty to learn another trade, or if a merchant were not at liberty to betake himself to farming. I answer, that this is not what the Apostle intends, for he has it simply in view to correct that inconsiderate eagerness, which prompts some to change their condition without any proper reason, whether they do it from superstition, or from any other motive. Farther, he calls every one to this rule also—that they bear in mind what is suitable to their *calling*. He does not, therefore, impose upon any one the necessity of continuing in the kind of life which he has once taken up, but rather condemns that

---

[1] " Car d'autant que ce nom vient d'vn mot qui signifie *Appeler*, il ha vne correspondance mutuelle à Dieu, qui nous *appelle* a ceci ou à cela ;" —" For as this term comes from a word which signifies *to call*, it has a mutual relationship to God, who *calls* us to this or that."

[2] " Ceque ie di, afinque nul n'abuse ceste sentence ;"—" Which thing I say, in order that no one may abuse this statement."

[3] " Vne obligation et necessite ;"—" An obligation and necessity."

[4] " Vn cordonnier ;"—" A shoemaker."

restlessness, which prevents an individual from remaining in his condition with a peaceable mind,[1] and he exhorts, that every one stick by his trade, as the old proverb goes.

21. *Art thou called being a servant?* We see here that Paul's object[2] is to satisfy their consciences ; for he exhorts servants to be of good cheer, and not be cast down, as if servitude were a hinderance in the way of their serving God. *Care not for it then,* that is to say, be not concerned how you may throw off the yoke, as if it were a condition unbecoming a Christian, but be contented in mind.   And hence we infer, not merely that it is owing to the providence of God that there are different ranks and stations in the world, but also, that a regard to them is enjoined by his word.

But if thou mayest even be made free. The particle *even* (in my opinion) has simply this force,—" If, in place of servitude, you could attain *even* to liberty, it would be more advantageous for you."   It is uncertain, however, whether he continues his discourse to servants, or turns to address those that are free.   In the latter case, γενέσθαι would here mean simply *to be.*   Either meaning suits sufficiently well, and they amount to the same thing.   He means to intimate, that liberty is not merely good, but also more advantageous than servitude.   If he is speaking to *servants,* his meaning will be this—While I exhort you to be free from anxiety, I do not hinder you from *even* availing yourselves of liberty, if an opportunity presents itself to you.   If he is addressing himself to those that are *free,* it will be a kind of concession, as though he had said—I exhort servants to be of good courage, though a state of freedom is preferable,[3] and more to be desired, if one has it in his choice.

22. *For he that is called in the Lord, being a servant.* To be *called in the Lord, being a servant,* is to be chosen out of the rank of servants, and made a partaker of the grace of Christ. Now this statement is designed to furnish consolation to servants, and, at the same time, to beat down the haughtiness

---

[1] " Paisiblement, et en repos de conscience ;"—" Peaceably, and with quiet of conscience."

[2] " Tout le but a quoy tend Sainct Paul;"—" The whole object at which St. Paul aims."

[3] " Soit beaucoup meilleur ;"—" Is much better."

of those that are free-born.   As servants feel their situation irksome, in respect of their being mean and despicable, it is of importance that the bitterness of servitude be alleviated by some consolation.   Those, on the other hand, that are free, need to be restrained, in order that they may not be unduly elated on account of their more honourable condition, and be lifted up with pride.   The Apostle does both ; for he teaches, that as the liberty of the spirit is greatly preferable to the liberty of the flesh, servants ought to feel the unpleasantness of their condition the more tolerable, when they take into view that inestimable gift with which they have been endowed ; and, on the other hand, that those who are free ought not to be puffed up, inasmuch as their condition in the principal respect is not superior to that of servants. We must not, however, infer from this, that those that are free are made inferior to servants, or that political order is subverted.   The Apostle saw what suited both.   Those that were free required (as I have said) to be restrained, that they might not in a wanton manner triumph over servants. To servants, on the other hand, some consolation required to be administered, that they might not be disheartened. Now these things tend rather to confirm political order, while he teaches that the inconvenience of the flesh is compensated by a spiritual benefit.

23. *Ye are bought with a price.*   We had these words in the preceding chapter, (1 Cor. vi. 20,) but for a different purpose.   As to the word *price*, I have stated there, what is my view of it.[1]   The sum is this, that he exhorts servants, indeed, not to be anxious as to their condition, but wishes them rather to take heed not to subject themselves to the wicked or depraved inclinations of their masters.   " We are holy to the Lord, because he has redeemed us : let us, therefore, not defile ourselves for the sake of men, as we do when we are subject to their corrupt desires."   This admonition was very necessary at that time, when servants were driven by threats and stripes, and even fear of death, to obey every kind of command without selection or exception, so that they reckoned the procuring of prostitutes, and other crimes

[1] See p. 220.

of that nature, to be duties belonging to servants, equally
with honourable employments. It is, therefore, not without
reason that Paul makes this exception—that they are not
to yield obedience in things base and wicked. Would that
this were thoroughly and entirely impressed upon the minds
of all ! There would not, in that case, be so many that prostitute themselves to the lusts of men, as if exposed for sale.
As for us, let us bear in mind, that we belong to him who
has redeemed us.

24. *Let him abide with God.* I have already noticed
above,[1] that men are not here bound by a perpetual necessity,
so as never to have it in their power to change their condition, if at any time there should be a fit occasion for it ; but
that he simply represses those thoughtless humours, which
hurry men hither and thither, so that they are harassed by
a continual restlessness. Hence Paul says, that it is all
one in the sight of God what a person's manner of life is in
this world, inasmuch as this diversity does not hinder agreement in piety.

25. Now concerning virgins I have
no commandment of the Lord: yet
I give my judgment, as one that
hath obtained mercy of the Lord to
be faithful.

26. I suppose therefore that this
is good for the present distress, *I say,*
that *it is* good for a man so to be.

27. Art thou bound unto a wife ?
seek not to be loosed. Art thou
loosed from a wife ? seek not a wife.

28. But and if thou marry, thou
hast not sinned; and if a virgin
marry, she hath not sinned. Nevertheless such shall have trouble in
the flesh: but I spare you.

25. De virginibus autem praecep-
tum Domini non habeo : sed consilium do, tanquam misericordiam
consequutus a Domino, ut sim fidelis.

26. Arbitror igitur hoc bonum
esse propter instantem necessitatem,
quod bonum sit homini sic esse.

27. Alligatus es uxori ? ne quaeras solutionem.   Solutus es ab uxore ? ne quaeras uxorem

28. Quodsi etiam duxeris uxorem,
non peccasti : et si nupserit virgo,
non peccavit : attamen afflictionem
in carne habebunt eiusmodi. Ego
autem vobis parco.

25. *Concerning virgins.* He now returns to treat of marriage, of which he had begun to speak in the commencement
of the chapter. What he is now about to state he had
previously touched upon, but briefly and somewhat obscurely.
He accordingly intimates more explicitly what his views are
respecting *virginity;* but as it is a matter that is liable to

[1] See p. 248.

be misapprehended, and is full of difficulties, he always speaks, as we shall see, conditionally. *Virgins* here I understand as meaning virginity. As to this, he says *he has no commandment of the Lord;* because the Lord does not in any part of the Scriptures declare what persons ought to remain unmarried. Nay, on the contrary, inasmuch as the Scripture says, that *male and female were created together,* (Gen. ii. 21,) it seems as if it called every one equally and without exception to marriage :[1] at least celibacy is nowhere enjoined upon any one, or commended.

He says that *he gives advice,* not as if there were anything doubtful in it, and had little or no stability, but as being certain, and deserving to be maintained without any controversy. The word, too, that he employs, γνώμη, signifies not merely advice, but a decisive judgment.[2] Papists, however, rashly infer from this, that it is allowable to go beyond the limits of God's word, since nothing was farther from Paul's intention than to go beyond the limits of God's word : for if any one attends more closely, he will see, that Paul here advances nothing but what is included in what Christ says in Matt v. 32, and xix. 5 ; but in the way of anticipating an objection, he acknowledges that he has no express precept in the law, pointing out *who* ought to marry, and *who not.*

Having obtained mercy to be faithful. He secures authority for his decision, that no one may think himself at liberty to reject it, if he chooses. For he declares that he does not speak simply as a man, but as a faithful teacher of the Church, and an Apostle of Christ. According to his custom, he declares himself to be indebted for this to *the mercy of God,*[3] as it was no common honour, nay superior to all

---

[1] " Appelle indifferemment et sans exception tous hommes et femmes à se marier ;"—" Calls all men and women indiscriminately and without exception to marry."

[2] Such is the view that Beza takes of the meaning of the term here— " Sententiam in hac re meam dico ;"—" I give you my authoritative decision as to this matter."—*Ed.*

[3] The original word, ἠλεημένος, which has occasioned no inconsiderable difficulty to interpreters, is ingeniously supposed by *Granville Penn,* in his *Supplemental Annotations,* to be a dialectic variation of πλημένος, for εἰλημένος, *bound,* (from εἰλέω, *to bind,*) in which case the meaning would be this : " as one *bound* by the Lord to be faithful." Taking the word in this light, the expression is much similar to what we find employed by

human merits. Hence it appears, that whatever things have
been introduced into the Church by human authority,[1] have
nothing in common with this advice of Paul. But *faithful*
here means *truthful*—one who does not do what he does
merely from pious zeal, but is also endowed with knowledge,
so as to teach with purity and *faithfulness*. For it is not
enough for a teacher to be conscientious, if he has not also
prudence and acquaintance with the truth.

26. *I think therefore that this is good.* While I translate
this passage of Paul's writings differently from Erasmus or
the Vulgate, I at the same time do not differ from them as
to its meaning. They divide Paul's words in such a way,
that the same thing is repeated twice. I, on the other hand,
make it simply one proposition, and not without authority,
for I follow ancient and approved manuscripts, which make
it all one sentence, with merely a *colon* between. The meaning is this : " I think it expedient on account of the necessity, with which the saints are always harassed in this life,
that all should enjoy the liberty and advantage of celibacy,
as this would be of advantage to them." There are some,
however, that view the term *necessity* as referring to the age
of the Apostle, which was, undoubtedly, full of trouble to the
pious : but he appears to me to have had it rather in view
to express the disquietude with which the saints are incessantly harassed in the present life. I view it, therefore, as
extending to all ages, and I understand it in this way, that
the saints are often, in this world, driven hither and thither,
and are exposed to many and various tempests,[2] so that their
condition appears to be unsuitable for marriage. The phrase
so to be, signifies to remain unmarried, or to abstain from
marriage.

27. *Art thou bound to a wife ?* Having stated what would
be most advantageous, he adds at the same time, that we
ought not to be so much influenced by the advantages of
celibacy, that one that is bound by the tie of marriage

---

the Apostle in a subsequent chapter of this Epistle—ἀνάγκη γάρ μοι ἐπί-
κειται, *necessity is laid upon me.* (1 Cor. ix. 16.)— *Ed.*

[1] " Du cerueau des hommes ;"—" From man's brain."
[2] " Diuerses afflictions et orages ;"—" Various afflictions and tempests."

should shake off the connection. It is therefore a restriction upon the preceding statement, lest any one, influenced by his commendation of celibacy, should turn his thoughts to it, and despise marriage, forgetful of his necessity or of his *calling.* Now in these words he does not merely forbid the breaking up of the connection of marriage, but also represses the dislikes that are wont to creep in, that every one may continue to live with his wife willingly and cheerfully.

Art thou loosed from a wife? This second clause must be taken with a reservation, as is manifest from the entire context. He does not, then, allow to all the choice of perpetual celibacy, but only to those to whom it is given. Let no one, therefore, who is not constrained by any necessity, rashly insnare himself, for liberty ought not to be lightly thrown away.[1]

28. *But if thou shouldest even marry.* As there was a danger of one's thinking from the preceding statement, that he tempted God, if he knowingly and willingly bound himself to marriage, (as that would be to renounce his liberty,) he removes this scruple; for he gives liberty to widows to marry, and says, that those that marry do not sin. The word *even* also seems to be emphatic—to intimate, that even though there be no positive necessity urging to it, the unmarried are not prohibited from marrying whenever they may see fit.

And if a virgin marry. Whether this is an amplification, or simply an illustration, this, in the first place, is beyond all controversy, that Paul designed to extend the liberty of marriage to all. Those who think that it is an amplification, are led to think so by this, that it seems to approach nearer to a fault, and is more open to reprehension, or at least has more occasion of shame, to loose the virgin girdle (as the ancients express themselves) than, upon the death of a husband, to enter into a second marriage. The argument then would be this : " If it is lawful for a virgin to marry,

[1] " Car il ne faut pas quitter legerement sa liberté sans y bien penser ;' —" For he ought not to abandon his liberty lightly, without thinking much as to it."

much more may widows." I am rather of opinion, that he makes both equal in this way : " As it is allowable for a virgin, so is it for widows also." For second marriages among the ancients were not without some mark of reproach, as they adorned those matrons, who had contented themselves with one marriage during their whole life, with a chaplet of chastity[1]—an honour that tended to reflect reproach upon those that had married repeatedly. And it is a well known saying of Valerius,[2] that " it betokens a legitimate excess [3] when a second marriage is desired." The Apostle, therefore, makes virgins and widows alike as to liberty of marriage.

Nevertheless such shall have trouble in the flesh. He frequently repeats the reason why he leans more to the side of celibacy in his exhortations, lest he should seem to prefer the one condition to the other on its own account, rather than on account of its consequences. He says, that there are many troubles that are connected with the married life, and that on that account he wishes all to be free from marriage, who desire to be exempt from troubles. When he says, that they will have *trouble of the flesh*, or *in the flesh*, he means, that the anxieties and distresses in which married persons are involved arise from the affairs of the world. The *flesh*, therefore, is taken here to mean the outward man. To *spare* means to *indulge*, or to wish them to be exempted from the troubles that are connected with marriage. " I am desirous to make provision for your infirmity, that you may not have trouble : now marriage brings with it many troubles. This is the reason why I should wish you not to require to marry—that you may be exempt from all its evils." Do not, however, infer from this that Paul reckons marriage to be a necessary evil : for those troubles of which he speaks do not arise so much from the nature of marriage, as from the corruption of it, for they are the fruits of original sin.

---

[1] In accordance with this, *Univira*, (the wife of *one* husband,) is often found in ancient inscriptions as an epithet of honour.—*Ed.*

[2] " Autheur ancien;"—" An ancient author."

[3] " C'est à dire, colorée et reglée par les lois;"—" That is to say, coloured over and regulated by the laws."

29. But this I say, brethren, the time *is* short: it remaineth, that both they that have wives be as though they had none :

30. And they that weep, as though they wept not; and they that rejoice, as though they rejoiced not ; and they that buy, as though they possessed not ;

31. And they that use this world, as not abusing *it ;* for the fashion of this world passeth away.

32. But I would have you without carefulness. He that is unmarried careth for the things that belong to the Lord, how he may please the Lord :

33. But he that is married careth for the things that are of the world, how he may please *his* wife.

34. There is difference *also* between a wife and a virgin. The unmarried woman careth for the things of the Lord, that she may be holy both in body and in spirit : but she that is married careth for the things of the world, how she may please *her* husband.

35. And this I speak for your own profit ; not that I may cast a snare upon you, but for that which is comely, and that ye may attend upon the Lord without distraction.

29. Hoc autem dico, fratres, quia[1] tempus contractum est : reliquum est, ut qui uxores habent, sint tanquam non habentes :

30. Et qui flent, tanquam non flentes : et qui gaudent, tanquam non gaudentes : et qui emunt, tanquam non possidentes :

31. Et qui utuntur hoc mundo, tanquam non utentes : praeterit enim figura mundi hujus.

32. Velim autem vos absque solicitudine esse. Qui cœlebs est, curat ea quae sunt Domini, quomodo placiturus sit Domino :

33. Coniugatus curat ea quae sunt mundi, qualiter uxori placiturus sit, et divisus est.

34. Et mulier caelebs, et virgo curat ea quae sunt Domini, ut sancta sit corpore et spiritu : at quae maritum habet, curat ea quae sunt mundi, quomodo placitura sit marito.

35. Hoc autem ad utilitatem vestram dico, non ut laqueum vobis iniiciam, sed ad honestatem ac decorum, ut Domino adhaereatis absque ulla distractione.

29. *Because the time is short,* &c. Again he discourses respecting the holy use of marriage, for the purpose of repressing the wantonness of those who, when they have married, think of nothing but the delights of the flesh. They have no remembrance of God. Hence he exhorts believers not to give way to unbridled desire in such a way, that marriage should have the effect of plunging them into the world. Marriage is a remedy for incontinency. It has really the effect, if it be used with moderation. He therefore exhorts married persons to live together chastely in the fear of the Lord. This will be effected, if marriage is made use of by them, like other helps of this earthly life, having their hearts directed

---

[1] " Ou, Mais ie vous di ceci, mes freres, que le temps ;"—" Or, But I say this to you, my brethren, that the time."

upwards to meditation on the heavenly life. Now, he draws his argument from the shortness of human life : " This life," says he, " which we are now spending is frail, and of short duration. Let us not therefore be held entangled by it. Let *those* accordingly *who have wives, be as though they had none.*" Every one, it is true, has this philosophy in his mouth, but few have it truly and in good earnest impressed upon their minds. In my first translation, I had followed a manuscript, to which (as I afterwards discovered) not one of the many others gave any countenance. I have accordingly deemed it proper to insert the particle *because,* to make the meaning more apparent, and in accordance also with the reading in some ancient copies. For as in those cases in which we are deliberating as to anything, we look to the future rather than to the past, he admonishes us as to the shortness of the time that is to come.

As though they had none. All things that are connected with the enjoyment of the present life are sacred gifts of God, but we pollute them when we abuse them. If the reason is asked, we shall find it to be this, that we always dream of continuance in the world, for it is owing to this that those things which ought to be helps in passing through it become hinderances to hold us fast. Hence, it is not without good reason, that the Apostle, with the view of arousing us from this stupidity, calls us to consider the shortness of this life, and infers from this, that we ought to *use* all the things of this world, *as if we did not use* them. For the man who considers that he is a stranger in the world uses the things of this world as if they were another's—that is, as things that are lent us for a single day. The sum is this, that the mind of a Christian ought not to be taken up with earthly things, or to repose in them ; for we ought to live as if we were every moment about to depart from this life. By *weeping* and *rejoicing,* he means adversity and prosperity ; for it is customary to denote causes by their effects.[1] The Apostle, however, does not here command Christians to part

---

[1] " Or de prosperite s'ensuit ioye, comme d'aduersitez pleurs ;"—" Now joy is attendant on prosperity, as tears are on adversities."

with their possessions, but simply requires that their minds be not engrossed in their possessions.[1]

31. *And they that use this world.* In the *first* clause there is the participle χρώμενοι (*using,*) in the *second,* there is a compound of it—καταχρώμενοι (*abusing.*) Now the preposition κατα in a compound state is generally taken in a bad sense, or at least denotes intensity.[2] Paul, therefore, directs us to a sober and frugal use of things, such as may not impede or retard our course, but may allow of our always hastening forward toward the goal.

For the fashion of this world passeth away. By the term here used, the Apostle has elegantly expressed the vanity of the world. "There is nothing," says he, "that is firm or solid;[3] for it is a mere show or outward appearance, as they speak." He seems, however, to have had an allusion to theatrical representations, in which, on the curtain being drawn up in a single moment, a new appearance is presented, and those things that held the eyes of the spectators in astonishment, are immediately withdrawn from their view. I do not see why it is that Erasmus has preferred the term *habitus* (form.) He certainly, in my opinion, obscures Paul's doctrine; for the term *fashion* is tacitly opposed to substance.[4]

32. *But I would wish you.* He returns to the *advice* which he had spoken of, (verse 25,) but had not as yet fully explained, and in the outset he pronounces, as he is wont, a commendation upon celibacy, and then afterwards allows every one the liberty of choosing what he may consider to suit him best. It is not, however, without good reason that he returns so frequently to proclaim the advantages of celibacy, for he saw that the burdens of matrimony were far from light. The

---

[1] " Enterrez en icelles;"—" Buried in them."

[2] " Tellement que le mot signifie yci, Abusans, ou Vsans trop;"—" So that the word means here abusing, or using too much." The verb καταχϱάομαι is frequently made use of by classical writers to mean *using to the uttermost, using up,* or *misusing.* See *Dem.* 430, 10, and *Lys.* 153, 46. —*Ed.*

[3] " En ce monde;"—" In this world."

[4] " Comme s'il disoit, que ce monde n'ha point vn estre, mais seulement vne monstre et vaine apparence;"—" As if he had said, that this world has not an existence, but only a show and mere appearance."

man who can exempt himself from them, ought not to refuse such a benefit, and it is of advantage for those who resolve to marry, to be forewarned of those inconveniences, that they may not afterwards, on meeting with them unexpectedly, give way to despondency. This we see happens to many, for having promised themselves unmixed honey, on being disappointed in that expectation, they are very readily cast down by the slightest mishap.[1] Let them know, therefore, in good time, what they have to expect, that they may be prepared to endure everything patiently. The meaning is this: "Marriage brings along with it hinderances, from which I should wish you to be free and exempt."

As, however, he has previously made use of the term *trouble*, (verse 28,) and now makes mention of *cares* or *anxieties*, it may admit of doubt whether they have a different signification, or not. I am of opinion that the *trouble* referred to is what arises from things of a distressing nature, such as loss of children, widowhood, quarrels, and little differences, (as lawyers speak,)[2] many occasions of dislike, faults of children, difficulty in bringing up a family, and the like. The *anxieties*, on the other hand, are, in my opinion, connected with things that are joyful, as for example marriage fooleries, jests, and other things with which married persons are taken up.[3]

He that is unmarried careth for the things of the Lord. Mark the kind of exemption from anxieties that he desires in behalf of Christians—that they may devote to the Lord all their thoughts and aims. This, he says, belongs to celibacy; and therefore he desires all to enjoy this liberty. He does not mean, however, that it is invariably so in unmarried life, as experience shows it to be quite otherwise in priests, monks, and nuns, than whose celibacy nothing can be conceived to be farther from God. Add to this the many base fornicators who abstain from marriage for the very

---

[1] " Qu'ils puissent rencontrer ;"—" That they may meet with."

[2] " Qui sourdent entre le mari et la femme ;"—" That arise between a husband and wife."

[3] Our Author's meaning is, that while $\vartheta\lambda\iota\psi\iota\varsigma$ (trouble) invariably relates to what is of a distressing nature, $\mu\epsilon\rho\iota\mu\nu\alpha$ (care) is applied to anything that *takes up* the attention of the mind.—*Ed.*

purpose of having greater liberty for the indulgence of lust, and that their vice may not appear. Where there is *burning*, (verse 9,) no love of God can exist. But Paul's meaning is this—that an unmarried person is free, and is not hindered from thinking of the things of God. The pious make use of this liberty. Others turn everything to their own destruction.

33. *He that is married careth for the things of the world.* By *the things of the world* you must understand the things that belong to the present life; for the world is taken here to mean the condition of this earthly life. But from this some one will infer, that all, therefore, who are married are strangers to the kingdom of God,[1] as thinking of nothing but this earth. I answer, that the Apostle speaks only of a portion of the thoughts, as though he had said: " They have one eye directed to the Lord, but in such a way as to have the other directed to their wife; for marriage is like a burden, by which the mind of a pious man is weighed down, so that he does not move God-ward with so much alacrity." Let us always, however, bear in mind, that these evils do not belong to marriage, but proceed from the depravity of men. Hence the calumnies of Jerome,[2] who scrapes together all these things for the purpose of bringing marriages into disrepute, fall. For, were any one to condemn agriculture, merchandise, and other modes of life, on this ground, that amidst so many corruptions of the world, there is not one of them that is exempt from certain evils, who is there that would not smile at his folly ? Observe, then, that whatever evil there is in marriage, has its origin somewhere else ; for at this day a man would not have been turned away from the Lord by the society of his wife, if he had remained in a state of innocence, and had not corrupted the holy institution of God ; but a wife would have been a *help-meet* to him in everything good, as she was created for that end. (Gen. ii. 18.)

But some one will say : " If anxieties that are faulty and

---

[1] " Forclos du royaume de Dieu ;"—" Shut out from the kingdom of God."

[2] See *Harmony*, vol. ii. p. 386.

blameworthy are invariably connected with marriage, how is
it possible for married persons to call upon God, and serve
him, with a pure conscience ?"   I answer, that there are *three*
kinds of anxieties.   There are some that are evil and wicked
in themselves, because they spring from distrust.   Of these
Christ speaks in Matt. vi. 25.   There are others that are
necessary, and are not displeasing to God ; as, for example,
it becomes the father of a family to be concerned for his
wife and children, and God does not mean that we should be
mere stumps, so as to have no concern as to ourselves.   The
third class are a mixture of the two former; when we are
anxious respecting those things as to which we ought to
feel anxiety, but feel too keenly excited, in consequence of
that excess which is natural to us.   Such anxieties, therefore, are not by any means wrong in themselves, but they
are corrupt, in consequence of αταξια, that is to say, undue
excess.[1]   And the Apostle did not intend merely to condemn
here those vices by which we contract guilt in the sight of
God, but he desires in a general way, that we may be freed
from all impediments, so as to be wholly at leisure for the
service of God.

And is divided.   It is surprising how there has come to
be so much diversity upon this passage.   For the common
Greek version is so widely different from the old Latin
translation, that the diversity cannot be ascribed to mistake
or inadvertence, in the way in which a mistake often happens in a single letter or a single word.   Now the Greeks
commonly read it literally, " He that is married thinks of
the things of the world, how he may please his wife: a
married woman and a virgin are divided: She that is
unmarried, thinketh of the things of the Lord," &c.   And
being divided they understand as meaning *to differ*, as if
it had been said: "There is a great difference between a
married woman and a virgin ; for the one is at leisure to
attend to the things of God exclusively, while the other is
taken up with various matters."   But as this interpretation
is somewhat at variance with the simple meaning of the
word, I do not approve of it, especially as the meaning of

[1] See p. 231.

the other reading (which is found also in some Greek manuscripts) is more suitable and less forced. We may, accordingly, understand it in this manner—that a man who is married is *divided*,[1] inasmuch as he devotes himself partly to God and partly to his wife, and is not wholly and exclusively God's.

34. *The unmarried woman and the virgin.* What he had laid down as to men he now declares in like manner as to women—that virgins and widows are not prevented by earthly things from devoting their whole cares and their whole affections to God. Not that all act this part, but that there is opportunity for it, if the mind is so disposed. When he says, *that she may be holy in body and in spirit*, he shows what kind of chastity is true and acceptable to God—when the mind is kept unpolluted in the sight of God. Would to God that this were more carefully attended to! As to *the body*, we see what kind of devotement to the Lord there commonly is on the part of monks, nuns, and the whole scum of the Papistical clergy, than whose celibacy nothing can be imagined that is more obscene.[2] But not to speak at present of chastity of *body*, where is there one to be found among those that are held in admiration in consequence of their reputation for continency, that does not burn with base lusts? We may, however, infer from this statement of Paul, that no chastity is well pleasing to God that does not extend to the *soul* as well as to the *body*. Would to God that those who prate in such haughty terms as to continency, did but understand that they have to do with God! They would not be so confident in their contendings with us. At the

---

[1] Kypke (in his *Observationes Sacrae*) renders the original word μεμέρισται, as CALVIN does—*divided* or *perplexed*, and brings forward a passage from *Achilles Tatius*, in which εμεμέριστο is used in a similar sense. In the Syriac version, on the other hand, the rendering is as follows: *Discrimen autem est inter mulierem et virginem—There is a difference between a wife and a virgin.* The Greek commentators interpret the clause thus :— Μεμέρισται, τουτ᾽ εστιν, διαφερουσιν αλληλων, και ου την αυτην εχουσι φροντιδα— *They differ from one another and have not the same care.* Bloomfield considers *divided* or *distracted* to be a harsh interpretation, and not agreeable to the context, and renders the clause—" There is a difference between." —*Ed.*

[2] " Plus infame et puante ;"—" More infamous and abominable."

same time, there are none in the present day who dispute on the subject of continency in more magnificent style than those who are openly and in the most shameless manner guilty of fornication. But though they should conduct themselves ever so honourably in the sight of men, that is nothing, if they do not keep their minds pure and exempt from all uncleanness.

35. *And this for your benefit.* Observe the Apostle's moderation.[1] Though he knew the vexations, troubles, and difficulties of the married life, and, on the other hand, the advantages of celibacy, yet he does not venture to prescribe. On the contrary, having commended celibacy, and being afraid that some of his readers might be led away by such commendations, and might straightway say within themselves what the Apostles said in reply to Christ—*It is good, therefore, so to be,* (Matt. xix. 10)[2]—not in the meantime taking into view their ability, he here declares in express terms, that he points out, indeed, what is most advantageous, but does not wish to impose a necessity upon any one.

And here you have two things worthy of observation. The *first* is, for what purpose celibacy is to be desired—not on its own account, nor on the ground of its being a state that is nearer to perfection, but that we may cleave to God without distraction—*that* being the one thing that a Christian man ought exclusively to look to during his whole life. The *second* thing is, that no snare must be put upon men's consciences, so as to keep back any one from marriage, but that every one must have liberty allowed him. It is well known what grievous errors have been fallen into on both these points. As to the *second* point, those assuredly have been bolder than Paul, who have not shrunk from passing a law respecting celibacy, with the view of prohibiting the whole of the clergy from matrimony. The same may be said of those who have made vows of perpetual continency,

---

[1] " La prudence et moderation de l'Apostre ;"—" The prudence and moderation of the Apostle."

[2] Our author, quoting from memory, gives the substance of the passage referred to, while the words which he employs correspond with what we find in the 26th verse of this chapter.—*Ed.*

which are snares by which not a few myriads of souls have been drawn into endless ruin. Hence, if the Holy Spirit has spoken by the mouth of Paul, Papists cannot clear themselves from the crime of *fighting against God*, (Acts v. 39,) while binding men's consciences in a matter in which He designed that they should remain free ; unless, perhaps, He[1] has since that time adopted a new plan, so as to construct a snare, which he had previously disapproved of.

36. But if any man think that he behaveth himself uncomely toward his virgin, if she pass the flower of *her* age, and need so require, let him do what he will, he sinneth not: let them marry.

37. Nevertheless he that standeth stedfast in his heart, having no necessity, but hath power over his own will, and hath so decreed in his heart that he will keep his virgin, doeth well.

38. So then he that giveth *her* in marriage doeth well; but he that giveth *her* not in marriage doeth better.

36. Si quis autem virgini suae indecorum iudicat, si excedat florem aetatis, et ita fieri debet: quod voluerit faciat, non peccat: nubant.

37. Qui autem stat firmus in corde, necessitatem non habens, potestatem vero habens supra sua voluntate, et hoc decrevit in corde suo, servare suam virginem, bene facit.

38. Itaque et qui nuptum collocat, bene facit; et qui non collocat, melius facit.

36. *But if any one thinketh that it were unseemly for his virgin.* He now directs his discourse to parents, who had children under their authority. For having heard the praises of celibacy, and having heard also of the inconveniences of matrimony, they might be in doubt, whether it were at all a kind thing to involve their children in so many miseries, lest it should seem as if *they* were to blame for the troubles that might befall them. For the greater their attachment to their children, so much the more anxiously do they exercise fear and caution on their account.[2] Paul, then, with the view of relieving them from this difficulty, teaches that it is their duty to consult their advantage, exactly as

---

[1] " Le Sainct Esprit ;"—" The Holy Spirit."

[2] " Tant plus ils craignent qu'il ne leur adviene quelque inconvenient, et tant plus sont ils diligens à se donner garde pour eux ;"—" So much the more do they fear lest they should meet with any inconvenience, and so much the more careful are they to use precautions on their account."

one would do for himself when at his own disposal.[1] Now
he still keeps up the distinction, which he has made use of
all along, so as to commend celibacy, but, at the same time,
to leave marriage as a matter of choice ; and not simply a
matter of choice, but a needful remedy for incontinency,
which ought not to be denied to any one.   In the *first* part of
the statement he speaks as to the giving of daughters in
marriage, and he declares that those do not sin in giving
away their daughters in marriage, who are of opinion that
an unmarried life is not suitable for them.

The word ἀσχημονεῖν (to be *unseemly*) must be taken as referring to a special propriety, which depends on what is natural
to the individual; for there is a *general* propriety, which philosophers make to be a part of temperance. *That* belongs equally to all. There is another, that is *special*, because one thing
becomes one individual that would not be *seemly* in another.
Every one therefore should consider (as Cicero observes) what
is the part that nature has assigned to him.[2]   Celibacy will be
seemly for one, but he must not measure all by his own foot ;[3]
and others should not attempt to imitate him without taking
into view their ability ; for it is the imitation of the ape—
which is at variance with nature. If, therefore, a father,
having duly considered his daughter's disposition, is of opinion that she is not prepared for celibacy, let him give her
away in marriage.[4]

By *the flower of her age* he means the marriageable age.
This lawyers define to be from twelve to twenty years of
age. Paul points out, in passing, what equity and humanity
ought to be exercised by parents, in applying a remedy in

---

[1] " Quand il n'est point sous la puissance d'autruy ;"—" When he is not
under the power of another."

[2] " La condition et propriete que nature luy a donnee ;"—" The condition
and propriety that nature has assigned to him."   See Cic. de Off. I. 28.
—*Ed.*

[3] " Comme on dit ;"—" As they say."

[4] CALVIN seems to have understood the verb ἀσχημονεῖν here as meaning
to be unseemly. The ordinary meaning of the word is, *to act in an unseemly manner.* It occurs in this sense in 1 Cor. xiii. 5, and in various
instances in the Classics, (see Eur. Hec. 407,) and the construction of the
passage seems to require that it be understood as meaning, that the father
thinks that he *acts improperly towards* his virgin daughter, or *incurs
somewhat of disgrace with respect to her.*—*Ed.*

that tender and slippery age, when the force of the disease requires it. *And it requires to be so.* In this clause I understand him as referring to the girl's infirmity—in the event of her not having the gift of continency; for in that case, necessity constrains her to marry. As to Jerome's making a handle of the expression *sinneth not,* for reviling marriage, with a view to its disparagement, as if it were not a praiseworthy action to dispose of a daughter in marriage, it is quite childish.[1] For Paul reckoned it enough to exempt fathers from blame, that they might not reckon it a cruel thing to subject their daughters to the vexations connected with marriage.

37. *But he who standeth firm in his heart.* Here we have the *second* part of the statement, in which he treats of young women who have the gift of abstaining from marriage. He commends therefore those fathers who make provision for their tranquillity; but let us observe what he requires. In the *first* place, he makes mention of a steadfast purpose—*If any one has fully resolved with himself.* You must not, however, understand by this the resolution formed by monks— that is, a voluntary binding over to perpetual servitude—for such is the kind of vow that they make; but he expressly makes mention of this *firmness* of purpose, because mankind often contrive schemes which they next day regret. As it is a matter of importance, he requires a thoroughly matured purpose.

In the *second* place he speaks of the person as *having no necessity;* for many, when about to deliberate, bring obstinacy with them rather than reason. And in the present case[2] they do not consider, when they renounce marriage, what is in their *power,* but reckon it enough to say—"such is my *choice.*" Paul requires them to have *power,* that they may not decide rashly, but according to the measure of the grace that has been *given* them. The absence of *necessity* in the case he appropriately expresses in the following clause, when

---

[1] " C'est vne cauillation puerile ;"—" It is a childish cavil."
[2] " Et mesme quand il est question du propos dont il est yci fait mention ;"—" And even when there is a doubt on the subject, of which he has here made mention."

he says that *they have power over their own will.* For it is as though he had said—" I would not have them resolve before knowing that they have power to fulfil, for it is rash and ruinous[1] to struggle against an appointment of God." But, " according to this system," some one will say, " vows are not to be condemned, provided these conditions were annexed." I answer that, as to the gift of continency, as we are uncertain respecting the will of God as to the future, we ought not to form any determination for our whole life. Let us make use of the gift as long as it is allowed us. In the meantime, let us commit ourselves to the Lord, prepared to *follow whithersoever he may call us.* (Rev. xiv. 4.)

Hath decreed in his heart. Paul seems to have added this to express the idea more fully, that fathers ought to look carefully on all sides, before giving up anxiety and intention as to giving away their daughters in marriage. For they often decline marriage, either from shame or from ignorance of themselves, while, in the meantime, they are not the less wanton, or prone to be led astray.[2] Parents must here consider well what is for the interests of their daughters, that by their prudence they may correct their ignorance, or unreasonable desire.

Now this passage serves to establish the authority of parents, which ought to be held sacred, as having its origin in the common rights of nature. Now if in other actions of inferior moment no liberty is allowed to children, without the authority of their parents, much less is it reasonable that they should have liberty given them in the contracting of marriage. And that has been carefully enacted by civil law, but more especially by the law of God. So much the more detestable, then, is the wickedness of the Pope, who, laying aside all respect, either for Divine or human laws, has been so daring as to free children from the yoke of subjection to their parents. It is of importance, however, to mark the reason. This, says he, is on account of the dig-

---

[1] " Vne arrogance pernicieuse ; "—" A pernicious arrogance."
[2] " Elles ne sont de rien moins suiettes à affections desordonnees, ou à estre seduites et abusees ;"—" They are not at all the less liable to inordinate affections, or to be seduced and deceived."

nity of the sacrament. Not to speak of the ignorance of making marriage a sacrament, what honour is there, I beseech you, or what dignity, when, contrary to the general feeling of propriety in all nations, and contrary to God's eternal appointment, they take off all restraints from the lusts of young persons, that they may, without any feeling of shame, sport themselves,[1] under pretence of its being a sacrament? Let us know, therefore, that in disposing of children in marriage, the authority of parents is of first-rate importance, provided they do not tyrannically abuse it, as even the civil laws restrict it.[2] The Apostle, too, in requiring exemption from *necessity*,[3] intimated that the deliberations of parents ought to be regulated with a view to the advantage of their children. Let us bear in mind, therefore, that this limitation is the proper rule—that children allow themselves to be governed by their parents, and that they, on the other hand, do not drag their children by force to what is against their inclination, and that they have no other object in view, in the exercise of their authority, than the advantage of their children.

38. *Therefore he that giveth in marriage.* Here we have the conclusion from both parts of the statement, in which he states, in a few words, that parents are free from blame if they give away their daughters in marriage, while he at the same time declares that *they do better* if they keep them at home unmarried. You are not, however, to understand that celibacy is here preferred to marriage, otherwise than under the exception which was a little before expressed. For if power be wanting on the part of the daughter,[4] the father acts an exceedingly bad part if he endeavours to keep her back from marriage, and would be no longer a father to her, but a cruel tyrant. The sum of the whole discussion

---

[1] " S'esgayent et desbauchent;"—" Sport and debauch themselves."

[2] " Comme aussi à ceste fin les loix ciuiles restraignent l'authorite d'iceux;"—" As also for this end civil laws restrict their authority."

[3] " En requirant yci que les enfans   sentent   en eux ceste liberte et exemption de la necessite du mariage;"—" In requiring here that children feel in themselves this freedom and exemption from the necessity of marriage."

[4] " Car quand la puissance defaudra à la fille de s'abstenir de mariage;" —" For when the daughter has not power to abstain from marriage."

amounts to this—that celibacy is better than marriage, because it has more liberty, so that persons can serve God with greater freedom; but at the same time, that no necessity ought to be imposed, so as to make it unlawful for individuals to marry, if they think proper; and farther, that marriage itself is a remedy appointed by God for our infirmity,[1] which all ought to use that are not endowed with the gift of continency. Every person of sound judgment will join with me in acknowledging and confessing, that the whole of Paul's doctrine on this point is comprehended in these *three* articles.

39. The wife is bound by the law as long as her husband liveth; but if her husband be dead, she is at liberty to be married to whom she will; only in the Lord.
40. But she is happier if she so abide, after my judgment: and I think also that I have the Spirit of God.

39. Mulier alligata est Legi, quamdiu maritus ejus vivit: si autem dormierit maritus ejus, libera est, ut cui vult nubat, modo in Domino.
40. Beatior vero est, si sic maneat, secundum meam sententiam: existimo autem, me quoque Spiritum Dei habere.

39. *The wife is bound.* He had previously spoken indiscriminately of husbands and wives, but as wives, on account of the modesty of their sex, might seem to have less liberty, he has thought it necessary to give in addition some special directions in reference to them. He now, therefore, teaches that women are not less at liberty than men to marry a second time, on their becoming widows.[2] We have already mentioned above,[3] that those who desired a second marriage were branded with the reproach of intemperance, and that, with the view of putting some kind of slight upon them, those who had been contented with being once married, were wont to be presented with the "chaplet of chastity." Nay more, this first opinion had, in course of time, become prevalent among Christians; for second marriages had no blessing pronounced upon them, and some Councils prohibited the clergy from being present on such occasions. The

[1] " Pour subuenir à nostre infirmite;"—" To help our infirmity."
[2] " Apres auoir perdu leurs premiers maris;"—" After having lost their first husbands."
[3] See p. 255.

Apostle here condemns tyranny of that sort, and declares, that no hinderance ought to be thrown in the way of widows' marrying, if they think proper.

It is of little consequence, and so far as the sense is concerned it matters nothing, whether we say that the wife is bound *legi*, (*to* the law,) in the dative, or *lege*, (*by* the law,) in the ablative. For it is the law that declares the connection between husband and wife to be indissoluble. If, however, you read it in the dative, the term will convey the idea of authority or obligation.[1] Now he reasons from contraries; for if a woman is bound to her husband for life, she is, then, set at liberty by his death. After she has been set at liberty, *let her be married to whom she will.*

When the verb *to sleep* means *to die*,[2] it refers not to the soul, but to the body, as is manifest from its constant use in Scripture.[3] It is a foolish part, therefore, that is acted by certain fanatics, who, from this little word, make it their endeavour to prove that the souls of men, after being separated from their bodies, are destitute of thought and intelligence, or, in other words, of their life.

Only in the Lord. This is thought to be added for the purpose of admonishing them in passing, that they ought not to yoke themselves with the irreligious, or to covet their society. This, I acknowledge, is true, but I am of opinion that more is meant—that they should do this in a religious way, and in the fear of the Lord,[4] for it is in this manner that marriages are formed auspiciously.

40. *But she is happier if she so abide.* Why? Is it because widowhood is of itself a virtue? No; but because it will have less to distract, and is more exempt from earthly

---

[1] " Authorite ou puissance et suiection ;"—" Authority or power and subjection."

[2] " Comme en ce passage ;"—" As in this passage."

[3] The original expression is ἐὰν δὲ κοιμηθῇ ὁ ἀνὴρ αὐτῆς—"If her husband has *fallen asleep.*" The metaphor is not peculiar to the Scriptures, but is made use of also by heathen writers, of which we have a beautiful instance in Callimachus—

$$\text{———}ἱερὸν ὕπνον$$
$$\text{Κοιμαται}\cdot \text{Θνησκειν μη λεγε τους αγαθους}\cdot$$

He sleeps a sacred sleep—say not that good men die.—Ed.

[4] "Auec reuerence, sagement, et en la crainte du Seigneur ;"—"With reverence, wisely, and in the fear of the Lord."

cares. As to what he adds—*according to my judgment,* he does not mean by this expression that his opinion was doubtful; but it is as if he had said that such was his *decision* as to this question; for he immediately adds that *he has the Spirit of God,* which is sufficient to give full and perfect authority. There appears, at the same time, to be somewhat of irony when he says *I think.* For as the false apostles were ever and anon boasting in high-sounding terms of their having the Spirit of God, for the purpose of arrogating to themselves authority, and in the meantime endeavoured to derogate from that of Paul, he says that he thinks that *he* is not less a partaker of the Spirit than *they.*

CHAPTER VIII.

1. Now as touching things offered unto idols, we know that we all have knowledge. Knowledge puffeth up, but charity edifieth.
2. And if any man think that he knoweth any thing, he knoweth nothing yet as he ought to know.
3. But if any man love God, the same is known of him.
4. As concerning therefore the eating of those things that are offered in sacrifice unto idols, we know that an idol *is* nothing in the world, and that *there is* none other God but one.
5. For though there be that are called gods, whether in heaven or in earth, (as there be gods many, and lords many,)
6. But to us *there is but* one God, the Father, of whom *are* all things, and we in him; and one Lord Jesus Christ, by whom *are* all things, and we by him.
7. Howbeit *there is* not in every man that knowledge: for some with conscience of the idol unto this hour eat *it* as a thing offered unto an idol; and their conscience being weak is defiled.

1. De iis porro quæ idolis immolantur, scimus, quod omnes scientiam habemus: scientia inflat, caritas autem ædificat.
2. Si quis autem videtur sibi aliquid scire, nondum quicquam scit, qualiter scire oportet.
3. At si quis diligit Deum, hic cognitus est ab illo.
4. De esu ergo eorum quæ idolis immolantur, novimus, quod idolum nihil est in mundo, et quod non est alius Deus nisi unus.
5. Nam etsi sunt qui vocentur dii, sive in cœlo sive super terram, quemadmodum sunt dii multi et domini multi:
6. Nobis tamen unus Deus Pater, ex quo omnia, et nos in ipso: et unus Dominus Iesus Christus, per quem omnia, et nos per ipsum.
7. At non est in omnibus scientia: quidam autem cum idoli conscientia nunc quoque tanquam idolo immolatum edunt, et conscientia eorum, infirma quum sit, polluitur.

He now passes on to another question, which he had

merely touched upon in the sixth chapter, without fully discussing. For when he had spoken of the avarice of the Corinthians, and had drawn that discussion to a close with this statement—*Neither covetous, nor extortioners, nor fornicators, &c., shall inherit the kingdom of God,* he passed on to speak of the liberty of Christians—*All things are lawful for me.* He had taken occasion from this to speak of *fornication,* and from that, of *marriage.* Now, therefore, he at length follows out what he had touched upon as to things intermediate—how we ought to restrain our liberty in intermediate things. By intermediate things, I mean those that are neither good nor bad in themselves, but indifferent, which God has put in our power, but in the use of which we ought to observe moderation, that there may be a difference between liberty and licentiousness. In the outset, he selects one instance, distinguished above all the others, as to which the Corinthians grievously offended—their having been present on occasion of the sacred banquets, which were held by idolaters in honour of their gods, and eating indiscriminately of the meats that were offered to them. As this gave much occasion of offence, the Apostle teaches them that they rashly perverted the liberty granted them by the Lord.

1. *Concerning things offered unto idols.* He begins with a concession, in which he voluntarily grants and allows to them everything that they were prepared to demand or object. "I see what your pretext is: you make Christian liberty your pretext. You hold out that *you have knowledge,* and that there is not one of you that is so ignorant as not to know that *there is but one God.* I grant all this to be true, but of what avail is that knowledge which is ruinous to the brethren?" Thus, then, he grants them what they demand, but it is in such a way as to show that their excuses are empty and of no avail.

Knowledge puffeth up. He shows, from the effects, how frivolous a thing it is to boast of *knowledge,* when *love* is wanting. "Of what avail is *knowledge,* that is of such a kind as *puffs us up* and elates us, while it is the part of *love* to *edify?*" This passage, which otherwise is somewhat obscure, in consequence of its brevity, may easily be understood in this way—"Whatever is devoid of *love* is of no account in the sight of God; nay more, it is displeasing to him, and much more so what is openly at variance with *love*.   Now that *knowledge* of which you boast, O ye Corinthians, is altogether opposed to *love*, for it *puffs up* men with pride, and leads to contempt of the brethren, while *love* is concerned for the welfare of brethren, and exhorts us to *edify* them. Accursed, then, be that *knowledge* which makes men proud, and is not regulated by a desire of *edifying*."

Paul, however, did not mean, that this is to be reckoned as a fault attributable to *learning*—that those who are learned are often self-complacent, and have admiration of themselves, accompanied with contempt of others.   Nor did he understand this to be the natural tendency of learning—to produce arrogance, but simply meant to show what effect *knowledge* has in an individual, that has not the fear of God, and love of the brethren; for the wicked abuse all the gifts of God, so as to exalt themselves.   Thus riches, honours, dignities, nobility, beauty, and other things of that nature, *puff up;* because men, elated through a mistaken confidence in these things, very frequently become insolent.[1]   Nor is it always so; for we see that many who are rich and beautiful, and abounding in honours, and distinguished for dignity and nobility, are, nevertheless, of a modest disposition, and not at all tainted with pride.   And even when it does happen to be so, it is, nevertheless, not proper that we should put the blame upon what we know to be gifts of God; for in the *first* place that were unfair and unreasonable; and farther, by putting the blame upon things that are not blameworthy, we would exempt the persons themselves from blame, who alone are in fault.   My meaning is this—"If riches *naturally tend* to make men proud, then a rich man, if proud, is free from blame, for the evil arises from riches."

We must, therefore, lay it down as a settled principle, that knowledge is good in itself; but as piety is its only foundation,[2] it becomes empty and useless in wicked men: as love

---

[1] " Et intraittables;"—" And insufferable."

[2] " La crainte de Dieu est le seul et vray fondement d'icelle;"—" The fear of God is its only true foundation."

is its true seasoning, where *that* is wanting it is tasteless.
And truly, where there is not that thorough knowledge of
God which humbles us, and teaches us to do good to the
brethren, it is not so much *knowledge,* as an empty notion
of it, even in those that are reckoned the most learned. At
the same time, knowledge is not by any means to be blamed
for this, any more than a sword, if it falls into the hands of
a madman. Let this be considered as said[1] with a view to
certain fanatics, who furiously declaim against all the liberal
arts and sciences, as if their only use were to *puff* men *up,*
and were not of the greatest advantage as helps in common
life.[2] Now those very persons, who defame them in this style,
are ready to burst with pride, to such an extent as to verify
the old proverb—" Nothing is so arrogant as ignorance."

2. *And if any man thinketh.* That man *thinketh that he
knoweth something,* who is delighted with the opinion that
he entertains of his own knowledge, and despises others, as
if he were far above them. For Paul does not here condemn
knowledge, but that ambition and haughtiness which ungodly men contract in consequence of it. Otherwise he
does not exhort us to be sceptical, so as to be always hesi-
tating and hanging in doubt, and he does not approve of a
false and counterfeit modesty, as if it were a good thing to
think that we are ignorant of what we do know. That man,
therefore, who *thinketh that he knoweth something,* or, in
other words, who is insolent from an empty notion of his
own knowledge, so that he prefers himself before others,
and is self-conceited, *he knoweth nothing yet as he ought to
know.* For the beginning of all true knowledge is acquaintance with God, which produces in us humility and submission ; nay more, it prostrates us entirely instead of elating
us. But where pride is, *there* is ignorance of God[3]—a beautiful passage ! Would to God that all knew it aright, so as
properly to understand the rule of right knowledge !

[1] " J'ai bien voulu dire ceci ;"—" I have felt prepared to say this."
[2] " Moyens et instrumens tres-vtiles, tant à la cognoissance de Dieu,
qu'à la conduite de la vie commune ;"—" Most useful means and instruments, both for the knowledge of God, and for the conduct of common
life."
[3] " Là regne ignorance et faute de cognoissance de Dieu ;"—" There
ignorance reigns, and deficiency in acquaintance with God."

3. *But if any man loves God.* Here we have the conclusion, in which he shows what is especially commendable in Christians, and even renders knowledge, and all other endowments worthy of commendation, if we *love God;* for if it is so, we will also love our neighbours in him. By this means all our actions will be properly regulated, and consequently approved by God. He shows, therefore, from consequences, that no learning is commendable that is not dipped in the *love of God;* because that alone secures, that whatever endowments we have are approved by him, as it is said in the second Epistle—*If any man be in Christ he is a new creature.* (2 Cor. v. 17.) By this he intimates, that without the Spirit of regeneration, all things else, whatever they may have of show, are of no value. To be *known by God* means to be held in any estimation, or to be reckoned among his sons. Thus he erases all proud persons from the *book of life,* (Phil. iv. 3,) and from the roll of the pious.

4. *Concerning, therefore, the eating of those things.* He now returns to the statement with which he had set out, and speaks more plainly in reference to the pretext made use of by the Corinthians. For as the whole of the evil took its rise from this root—that they were pleased with themselves, and despised others, he condemns, in general, that contemptuous knowledge which is not seasoned with love. Now, however, he explains particularly, what is the kind of knowledge on which they valued themselves—that *an idol* is an empty figment of the human brain, and must therefore be reckoned as *nothing;* and accordingly, that the consecration, that is gone through in name of the idol, is a foolish imagination, and of no importance, and that a Christian man, therefore, is not polluted, who, without reverence for the idol, eats of things offered to idols. This is the sum of the excuse, and it is not set aside by Paul as false, (for it contains excellent doctrine,) but because they abused it, in opposition to *love.*

As to the words, Erasmus reads thus—" An idol has no existence." I prefer the rendering of the old translation— *An idol is nothing.* For the argument is this—that *an idol is nothing,* inasmuch as there is but one God; for it follows admirably—" If there is no other God besides our God, then an idol is an empty dream, and mere vanity." When he says —*and there is none other God but one,* I understand the conjunction *and* as meaning *because.* For the reason why *an idol is nothing* is, that it must be estimated according to the thing that it represents. Now it is appointed for the purpose of representing God: nay more, for the purpose of representing false gods, inasmuch as there is but one God, who is invisible and incomprehensible. The reason, too, must be carefully observed—*An idol is nothing because there is no God but one;* for he is the invisible God, and cannot be represented by a visible sign, so as to be worshipped through means of it. Whether, therefore, idols are erected to represent the true God, or false gods, it is in all cases a perverse contrivance. Hence Habakkuk calls idols *teachers of lies,* (Hab. ii. 18,) because they deal falsely in pretending to give a figure or image of God, and deceive men under a false title. Hence οὐδεν (*nothing*) refers not to essence, but to quality—for an idol is made of some substance—either silver, or wood, or stone; but as God does not choose to be represented in this way, it is vanity and *nothing* as to meaning and use.

5. *For though there be that are called.* " They have," says he, " the name, but the reality is wanting." He uses the word *called* here, to mean—*renowned in the estimation of men.* He has also made use of a general division, when he says *in heaven or on earth.* The gods that are made mention of as being *in heaven,* are the heavenly hosts, as the Scripture terms the sun, moon, and the other stars. How very far they are, however, from being entitled to divine honours, Moses shows from this, that they were created for our use. The sun is our servant; the moon is our handmaid. How absurd, therefore, it is to render to them divine honours! By the gods that are *on earth,* are properly meant, in my opinion, men and women for whom religious worship has been appointed.[1] For, as Pliny observes, those who had deserved

---

[1] "Ausquels on a attribue diuinite, et en leur honneur dressé quelque seruice diuin;"—" To whom they have ascribed divinity, and have appointed some divine service in honour of them."

well of mankind had their memory consecrated by religion,
so as to be worshipped as deities—Jupiter, Mars, Saturn,
Mercury, and Apollo, who were mortal men, but were, after
death, exalted to the rank of deities ; and, more recently,
Hercules, Romulus, and at length the Cæsars—as if it were
in the power of mankind to make deities at their pleasure,
while they cannot give to themselves either life or immortality.   There are also other gods that are terrestrial, taken
either from cattle or from brute creatures, as, for example,
among the Egyptians, the ox, the serpent, the cat, the onion,
the garlic ; and, among the Romans, the boundary-stone,[1]
and the stone Vesta.   They are gods, then, only in name ;
but Paul says that he does not stop to notice deifications of
this sort.[2]

6. *But to us there is but one God, the Father.*   Though Paul
says these things by anticipation, he repeats the excuse made
by the Corinthians, in such a way as at the same time to convey instruction.   For, from what is more especially peculiar
to God, he proves that there is but one God : " Whatever has
its origin from what is foreign to itself, is not eternal, and,
consequently, is not God.   All things have their origin from
one Being : he alone, therefore, is God."   Again—"*He* is
assuredly God who gives existence to all, and from whom
all things flow, as from the supreme source ; but there is
only *One,* from whom all things flow, and hence *there is but
one God.*"   When he adds—*and we in him,* (εἰς αὐτόν,) he
means, that we subsist in God, as it was by him that we were
once created.   For this clause might, indeed, seem to have
another signification—that as we have our beginning from
him, so we ought to devote our life to him as its end ; and
it is used in this sense in Rom. xi. 39.   Here, however, it
is taken for ἐν αὐτῷ, which is commonly made use of by the
Apostles.   His meaning, therefore, is, that as we were once
created by God, so it is by his power that we are preserved
in our present condition.   That this is its meaning, is

---

[1] The allusion is to Terminus, the god of boundaries, of whom mention
is made by Livy (i. 10, and v. 54.)—*Ed.*

[2] " Telles consecrations faites à l'appetit des hommes;"—" Such consecrations made according to the humour of men."

evident from what he affirms respecting Christ immediately afterwards—that we are *by him*. For he designed to ascribe the same operation to the Father and to the Son, adding, however, the distinction which was suitable to the Persons. He says, then, that we subsist *in* the Father, and that it is *by* the Son, because the Father is indeed the foundation of all existence; but, as it is by the Son that we are united to him, so he communicates to us through him the reality of existence.

One Lord. These things are affirmed respecting Christ relatively, that is, in relationship to the Father. For all things that are God's are assuredly applicable to Christ, when no mention is made of persons; but as the person of the Father is here brought into comparison with the person of the Son, it is with good reason that the Apostle distinguishes what is peculiar to them.

Now the Son of God, after having been manifested in the flesh, received from the Father dominion and power over all things, that he might reign alone in heaven and on earth, and that the Father might exercise his authority through his hands. For this reason our Lord is spoken of as *one*.[1] But in respect of dominion being ascribed to him alone, this is not to be taken as meaning that worldly distinctions[2] are abolished. For Paul speaks here of spiritual dominion, while the governments of the world are political; as when he said a little before—*there are many that are called lords* —(verse 5)—he meant that, not of kings, or of others who excel in rank and dignity, but of idols or demons, to whom foolish men ascribe superiority and rule. While, therefore, our religion acknowledges but one Lord, this is no hindrance in the way of civil governments having many lords, to whom honour and respect are due in that *one Lord*.

7. *But there is not in all that knowledge.* He refutes, in a single word, all that he had previously brought forward in their name, showing that it is not enough that they know

[1] " Pour ceste raison quand il est parlé de nostre Seigneur, il est dit que nous n'en auons qu'vn, assauoir Christ;"—" For this reason, when mention is made of our Lord, it is declared that we have only one, namely, Christ."

[2] " Les degrez, estats, et gouuernemens du monde;"—"Ranks, conditions, and governments of the world."

that what they do is right, if they have not at the same time a regard to their brethren.   When he said above—*We know that we all have knowledge*, (verse 1,) he referred to those whom he reproved for abusing their liberty.   Now, on the other hand, he calls them to consider, that there are many weak and ignorant persons associated with them, to whom they ought to accommodate themselves.   " You have, it is true, a correct judgment in the sight of God, and if you were alone in the world, it would be as lawful for you to eat of things offered to idols, as of any other kinds of food. But consider your brethren, to whom you are debtors.   You have knowledge ; they are ignorant.   Your actions ought to be regulated not merely according to your knowledge, but also according to their ignorance."   This reply is particularly deserving of notice ; for there is nothing to which we are more prone[1] than this, that every one follows his own advantage, to the neglect of that of others.   Hence we feel prepared to rest in our own judgment, and do not consider, that the propriety of those works that we do in the sight of men depends not merely on our own conscience, but also on that of our brethren.

Some with conscience of the idol.   This is their ignorance, that they were still under the influence of some superstitious notion, as if there were some virtue in the idol, or some virtue in a wicked and idolatrous consecration.   Paul, however, does not speak of idolaters, who were entire strangers to pure religion, but of ignorant persons who had not been sufficiently instructed, to understand that *an idol is nothing*, and therefore that the consecration, which was gone through in name of the idol, is of no importance.   Their idea, therefore, was this : " As an idol is something, the consecration which is gone through in its name is not altogether vain, and hence those meats are not pure, that have been once dedicated to idols."   Hence they thought, that, if they ate of them, they contracted some degree of pollution, and were, in a manner, partakers with the idol.   This is the kind of *offence* that Paul reproves in the Corinthians—when we in-

---

[1] " Il n'y a rien plus commun et ordinaire que ce vice;"— " There is nothing that is more common and ordinary than this fault."

duce weak brethren, by our example, to venture upon anything against their conscience.

And their conscience. God would have us try or attempt nothing but what we know for certain is agreeable to him. Whatever, therefore, is done with a doubting conscience, is, in consequence of doubts of that kind, faulty in the sight of God. And this is what he says, (Rom. xiv. 23,) *Whatsoever is not of faith is sin.* Hence the truth of the common saying, that "those build for hell, who build against their conscience." For as the excellence of actions depends on the fear of God and integrity of conscience, so, on the other hand, there is no action, that is so good in appearance, as not to be polluted by a corrupt affection of the mind. For the man, who ventures upon anything in opposition to conscience, does thereby discover some contempt of God; for it is a token that we fear God, when we have respect to his will in all things. Hence you are not without contempt of God, if you so much as move a finger while uncertain, whether it may not be displeasing to him. As to *meats*, there is another thing to be considered, for they are not *sanctified* to us otherwise than *by the word.* (1 Tim. iv. 5.) If that word is wanting, there remains nothing but pollution—not that the creatures of God are polluted, but because man's use of them is impure. In fine, as men's hearts are purified by faith, so without faith there is nothing that is pure in the sight of God.

8. But meat commendeth us not to God: for neither, if we eat, are we the better; neither, if we eat not, are we the worse.

9. But take heed, lest by any means this liberty of yours become a stumblingblock to them that are weak.

10. For if any man see thee which hast knowledge sit at meat in the idol's temple, shall not the conscience of him which is weak be emboldened to eat those things which are offered to idols;

11. And through thy knowledge shall the weak brother perish, for whom Christ died?

8. Atqui esca nos non commendat Deo: neque si comedamus, abundamus, neque si non comedamus, deficimur aliquo.

9. Sed videte, ne quo modo facultas haec vestra offendiculo sit infirmis.

10. Si quis enim videat te, utcunque scientiam habeas, in epulo simulacrorum accumbentem; nonne conscientia eius, quum tamen infirmus sit, aedificabitur ad edendum quæ sunt idolis immolata?

11. Et peribit frater, qui infirmus est, in tua scientia, propter quem Christus mortuus est?

12. But when ye sin so against the brethren, and wound their weak conscience, ye sin against Christ.	12. Sic autem peccantes in fratres, et vuluerantes conscientiam illorum infirmam, in Christum peccatis.
13. Wherefore, if meat make my brother to offend, I will eat no flesh while the world standeth, lest I make my brother to offend.	13. Quapropter si esca offendit fratrem meum, nequaquam vescar carnibus in aeternum, ne fratri meo sim offendiculo.

8. *Meat recommendeth us not to God.* This was, or may have been, another pretext made use of by the Corinthians —that the worship of God does not consist in meats, as Paul himself teaches in his Epistle to the Romans, (xiv. 17,) that *the kingdom of God is not meat or drink.* Paul answers : " We must at the same time take care that our liberty does not do injury to our neighbours." In this he tacitly acknowledges, that in the sight of God it matters not what kinds of food we partake of, because he allows us the free use of them, so far as conscience is concerned ; but that this liberty, as to the external use of it, is made subject to love. The argument of the Corinthians, therefore, was defective, inasmuch as they inferred the whole from a part, for in the use of them a regard to the claims of love is included. It is, therefore, certain, that *meat recommendeth us not to God ;* and Paul acknowledges this, but he states this exception, that love is recommended to us by God, which it were criminal to overlook.

Neither if we eat, are we the better. He does not speak of improvement as to the stomach ; for the man who has dined has a better filled stomach than the man who goes fasting ; but he means, that we have neither more nor less of righteousness from eating or from abstaining. Besides, he does not speak of every kind of abstinence, or of every kind of eating. For excess and luxury are in themselves displeasing to God, while sobriety and moderation are well-pleasing to him. But let it be understood by us, that *the kingdom of God,* which is spiritual, does not consist in these outward observances, and therefore, that things indifferent are in themselves of no importance in the sight of God. While he brings this forward in the person of others by *anthypophora,*[1]

---

[1] " Par une maniere d'anticipation ;"—" By way of anticipation." *An-*

he at the same time admits that it is true, for it is taken from his own doctrine, which we touched upon a little ago.

9. *Take heed that your liberty.* He leaves their liberty untouched, but moderates the use of it thus far—that it may not give occasion of stumbling to the weak. And he expressly desires that regard be had to the weak, that is, to those who are not yet thoroughly confirmed in the doctrine of piety, for as they are wont to be regarded with contempt, it is the will and command of the Lord, that regard should be had to them. In the meantime, he hints that strong giants, who may be desirous tyrannically to subject our liberty to their humour, may safely be let alone,[1] because we need not fear giving offence to those who are not drawn into sin through infirmity, but eagerly catch at something to find fault with. What he means by *an occasion of stumbling* we shall see erelong.

10. *If any one see thee.* From this it appears more clearly, how much liberty the Corinthians allowed themselves; for when the wicked made a kind of sacred banquet for their idols, they did not hesitate[2] to go to it, to eat of the sacrifice along with them. Paul now shows what evil resulted from this. In the *first* clause, instead of the words *who hast knowledge,* I have rendered the expression thus—*though thou shouldest have;* and in the *second* clause, in the expression *who is weak,* I have introduced the word *notwithstanding.* This I found it necessary to do for the clearing up of Paul's meaning. For he makes a concession, as if he had said: "Be it so, that thou hast knowledge; he who seeth thee, though he is not endowed with knowledge, is *notwithstanding* confirmed by thine example to venture upon the same thing, while he would never have taken such a step if he had not had one to take the lead. Now when he has one to imitate, he thinks that he has a sufficient excuse in the

thypophora is a figure of speech which derives its name from the Greek term ἀνϑυποφορά, *a reply to an objection.* (See p. 214.) It is used in this sense by Dionysius Halicarnassensis.—*Ed.*

[1] "Nous ne nous en devons point soucier, mais les laisser là;"—"We should not concern ourselves as to them, but leave them there."

[2] "Les Corinthiens n'auoyent point de honte;"—"The Corinthians were not ashamed."

circumstance that he is imitating another, while in the meantime he is acting from an evil conscience." For *weakness*
here means ignorance, or scruple of conscience. I am aware,
at the same time, in what way others explain it ; for they
understand *the occasion of stumbling* to be this—when ignorant persons, induced by example, imagine that in this
way they perform some kind of religious service to God, but
this idea is quite foreign to Paul's meaning. For he reproves them, as I have said,[1] because they emboldened the
ignorant to hurry on, contrary to conscience, to attempt what
they did not think it lawful for them to do. To be *built up*
means here—to be *confirmed*.[2] Now that is a ruinous kind
of *building*, that is not founded on sound doctrine.

11. *And thy brother perish.* Mark how serious an evil it
is, that mankind commonly think so little of—that of ven-
turing upon anything with a doubtful or opposing conscience.
For the object to which our whole life ought to be directed,
is the will of the Lord. This, therefore, is the one thing
that vitiates all our actions, when we disregard *it*.[3] This
we do, not merely by an outward action, but even by a
thought of the mind, when we allow ourselves in anything
in opposition to conscience, even though the thing be not
evil in itself. Let us bear in mind, therefore, that whenever
we take a step in opposition to conscience, we are on the
high road to ruin.

I read, however, the sentence interrogatively, thus: *Shall
he perish through thy knowledge ?* as though he had said :
" Is it reasonable that thy knowledge should give occasion
of ruin to thy brother ? Is it for this reason that thou
knowest what is right, that thou mayest cause another's

---

[1] See pp. 279, 280.

[2] The original word οἰκοδομηθήσεται, *shall be built up*, is used here, in the
opinion of some learned critics, to mean *encouraged* or *emboldened,* and a
parallel passage is pointed to in Mal. iii. 15, where the Hebrew word
נבנו is rendered in the Septuagint ἀνοικοδομοῦνται, *built up* or *emboldened.*
It deserves notice, however, that the Apostle had in the commencement of
the chapter spoken of love as *edifying*, while *knowledge puffeth up*, and it
is not improbable that he made use of the same word here *ironically*, as
we would say—" Will not this be *edifying* the wrong way ?"—*Ed.*

[3] " Quand nous entreprenons quelque chose contre ceste saincte volonte;"
—" When we attempt anything in opposition to that holy will."

ruin!"   He makes use of the term *brother*, in order to expose their pride as unfeeling, in this way : " It is true that
the person whom you despise is *weak*, but still he is your
brother, for God has adopted him.   You act a cruel part,
therefore, in having no concern for your brother."   There
is, however, still greater force in what follows—that even
those that are ignorant or weak have been *redeemed with
the blood of Christ ;* for nothing were more unseemly than
this, that while Christ did not hesitate to die, in order that
the weak might not perish, we, on the other hand, reckon
as nothing the salvation of those who have been redeemed
with so great a price.   A memorable saying, by which we
are taught how precious the salvation of our brethren ought
to be in our esteem, and not merely that of all, but of each
individual in particular, inasmuch as the blood of Christ was
poured out for each individual !

12. *When ye sin so against the brethren,* &c.   For if the
soul of every one that is weak is the price of Christ's blood,
that man who, for the sake of a very small portion of meat,
hurries back again to death the brother who has been redeemed by Christ, shows how contemptible the blood of
Christ is in his view.   Hence contempt of this kind is an
open insult to Christ.   In what way a weak conscience may
be wounded has been already explained—when it is *built up*
in what is evil (verse 10) so as daringly and rashly to rush
on farther than the individual thinks to be lawful for him.

13. *Wherefore if meat make my brother to offend.*   With
the view of reproving more severely their disdainful liberty,
he declares, that we ought not merely to refrain from a single
banquet rather than injure a *brother*, but ought to give up
the eating of meats during our whole life.   Nor does he
merely prescribe what ought to be done, but declares that
he would himself act in this way.   The expression, it is true,
is hyperbolical, as it is scarcely possible that one should refrain from eating flesh during his whole life, if he remain in
common life ;[1] but his meaning is, that he would rather
make no use of his liberty in any instance, than be an *occa-*

[1] " S'il demeure en la conuersation et communication auec les autres ?"
—" If he remains in converse and fellowship with others."

sion of offence to the weak. For participation is in no case lawful, unless it be regulated by the rule of love. Would that this were duly pondered by those who make everything subservient to their own advantage, so that they cannot endure to give up so much as a hair's-breadth of their own right for the sake of their brethren ; and that they would attend not merely to what Paul teaches, but also to what he marks out by his own example! How greatly superior he is to us! When *he,* then, makes no hesitation in subjecting himself thus far to his brethren, which of us would not submit to the same condition ?

But, however difficult it is to act up to this doctrine, so far as the meaning is concerned, it is easy, were it not that some have corrupted it by foolish glosses, and others by wicked calumnies. Both classes err as to the meaning of the word *offend.* For they understand the word *offend* to mean, *incurring the hatred or displeasure of men,* or what is nearly the same thing, *doing what displeases them, or is not altogether agreeable to them.* But it appears very manifestly from the context, that it means simply to hinder a brother by bad example (as an obstacle thrown in his way) from the right course, or to give him occasion of falling. Paul, therefore, is not here treating of the retaining of the favour of men, but of the assisting of the weak, so as to prevent their falling, and prudently directing them, that they may not turn aside from the right path. But (as I have said) the former class are *foolish,* while the latter are also *wicked* and impudent.

Those are *foolish,* who allow Christians scarcely any use of things indifferent, lest they should *offend* superstitious persons. " Paul," say they, " prohibits here everything that may give occasion of *offence.* Now to eat flesh on Friday will not fail to give *offence,* and hence we must abstain from it, not merely when there are some weak persons present, but in every case without exception, for it is possible that they may come to know of it." Not to speak of their misinterpretation of the word rendered *occasion of offence,* they fall into a grievous blunder in not considering that Paul here inveighs against those who impudently abuse their knowledge in the presence of the weak, whom they take no pains to instruct.

Hence there will be no occasion for reproof, if instruction has been previously given. Farther, Paul does not command us to calculate, whether there may be an occasion of offence in what we do, except when the danger is present to our view.

I come now to the other class. These are pretended followers of Nicodemus,[1] who under this pretext conform themselves to the wicked by participating in their idolatry, and not contented with justifying what they do amiss, are desirous also to bind others to the same necessity. Nothing could be said with greater plainness to condemn their perverse dissimulation than what Paul here teaches—that all who by their example allure the weak to idolatry, commit a grievous outrage against God as well as men. Yet they eagerly shield themselves from this by endeavouring to show that superstitions ought to be cherished in the hearts of the ignorant, and that we ought to lead the way before them to idolatry, lest a free condemnation of idolatry should *offend* them. Hence I will not do them the honour of dwelling upon a refutation of their impudence. I simply admonish my readers to compare Paul's times with ours, and judge from this whether it is allowable to be present at mass, and other abominations, giving so much *occasion of offence* to the weak.

CHAPTER IX.

1. Am I not an apostle? am I not free? have I not seen Jesus Christ our Lord? are not ye my work in the Lord?

2. If I be not an apostle unto others, yet doubtless I am to you: for the seal of mine apostleship are ye in the Lord.

3. Mine answer to them that do examine me is this,

1. Non sum liber? non sum Apostolus?[2] nonne Iesum Christum Dominum nostrum vidi? nonne opus meum vos estis in Domino?

2. Si aliis non sum Apostolus, vobis tamen sum: sigillum enim Apostolatus mei vos estis in Domino.

3. Haec mea defensio est apud eos, qui in me inquirunt.

[1] Our author speaks of the same class of persons when commenting on John vii. 50. See CALVIN's *Commentary on John,* vol. i. p. 317.—*Ed.*

[2] " Ne suis-ie point Apostre? ne suis-ie point en liberte;"—" Am I not an Apostle? Am I not free?" " The order of the words in CALVIN's *Latin* version is the order in which they are read in the VAT., *Alex.,* and some other MSS. and ancient versions, and in which they are quoted by Origen, Tertullian and Augustine. . . . The Latin retains the primitive order; we read, therefore, in Wiclif's version—' Whether I am not free? am I not Apostle?'"—*Penn. Ed.*

4. Have we not power to eat and to drink?

5. Have we not power to lead about a sister, a wife, as well as other apostles, and *as* the brethren of the Lord, and Cephas?

6. Or I only and Barnabas, have not we power to forbear working?

7. Who goeth a warfare any time at his own charges? who planteth a vineyard, and eateth not of the fruit thereof? or who feedeth a flock, and eateth not of the milk of the flock?

8. Say I these things as a man? or saith not the law the same also?

9. For it is written in the law of Moses, Thou shalt not muzzle the mouth of the ox that treadeth out the corn. Doth God take care for oxen?

10. Or saith he *it* altogether for our sakes? For our sakes, no doubt, *this* is written: that he that ploweth should plow in hope: and that he that thrasheth in hope should be partaker of his hope.

11. If we have sown unto you spiritual things, *is it* a great thing if we shall reap your carnal things?

12. If others be partakers of *this* power over you, *are* not we rather? Nevertheless we have not used this power; but suffer all things, lest we should hinder the gospel of Christ.

4. Numquid non habemus potestatem edendi et bibendi?

5. Numquid potestatem non habemus circumducendae uxoris sororis, quemadmodum et reliqui Apostoli, et fratres Domini, et Cephas?

6. An ego solus et Barnabas non habemus potestatem hoc agendi?[1]

7. Quis militavit suo sumptu unquam? quis plantat vitem, et ex fructu ejus non comedit? quis pascit gregem, et lacte gregis non vescitur?

8. Num secundum hominem haec dico?

9. Numquid lex quoque eadem non dicit? in lege enim Mosis (*Deut.* xxv. 4) scriptum est: non obligabis os bovi trituranti: numquid boves curae sunt Deo,

10. Vel propter nos omnino dicit? Et sane propter nos scriptum est: quoniam debet sub spe, qui arat, arare, et qui triturat, sub spe participandi. (*Alias: quia debeat sub spe qui arat, arare, et qui triturat sub spe, spei suae particeps esse debeat.*)

11. Si nos vobis spiritualia seminavimus, magnum, si carnalia vestra metamus?

12. Si alii hanc in vos sumunt potestatem, an non magis nos? atqui non usi sumus facultate hac: sed omnia sufferimus, ut ne quam offensionem demus Evangelio Christi.

1. *Am I not free?* He confirms by facts what he had stated immediately before,—that he would rather never taste of flesh during his whole life, than give occasion of stumbling to a brother, and, at the same time, he shows that he requires nothing more from them than what he had himself practised. And, assuredly, natural equity requires that whatever law is imposed by any one upon others, should be submitted to by himself. More especially a Christian teacher should impose upon himself this necessity, that he may have it always in his power to confirm his doctrine by an exemplary life. We know by experience, that it is a very

---

[1] " De ne trauailler point ;"—" To refrain from working."

unpleasant thing that Paul required from the Corinthians—
to refrain, for the sake of their brethren, from making use
of the liberty that was allowed them. He could scarcely
have demanded this, if he had not taken the lead and shown
them the way. And he had, it is true, promised that he
would do this, but, as he might not be believed by all on
his simply promising for the future, he makes mention of
what he had already done. He brings forward a remarkable
instance, in respect of his having denied himself the liberty
which he might otherwise have used, purely in order that
he might give the false Apostles no occasion for calumniating. He had preferred to earn his food with his own
hands, rather than be supported at the expense of the Corinthians, to whom he administered the Gospel.

He treats, however, at great length of the right of the
Apostles to receive food and clothing. This he does, partly
for the purpose of stirring them up the more to forego many
things for the sake of their brethren after his example, because they were unduly tenacious in the retaining of their
own rights, and partly for the purpose of exposing more
fully in view the unreasonableness of calumniators, who took
occasion for reviling from what was anything but blameworthy. He speaks, also, interrogatively, in order to press
the matter home more closely. The question—*Am I not
free?* is of a general nature. When he adds—*Am I not an
Apostle?* he specifies a particular kind of liberty. " If I
am an Apostle of Christ, why should my condition be worse
than that of others ?" Hence he proves his liberty on the
ground of his being an Apostle.

Have I not seen Jesus Christ? He expressly adds this,
in order that he may not be reckoned inferior in any respect
to the other Apostles, for this one thing the malevolent and
envious bawled out on all occasions—that he had received
from the hands of men whatever he had of the gospel, inasmuch as he had never seen Christ. And, certainly, he had
not had converse with Christ while he was in the world, but
Christ had appeared to him after his resurrection. It was
not a smaller privilege, however, to have seen Christ in his
immortal glory, than to have seen him in the abasement of

mortal flesh. He makes mention, also, afterwards of this vision, (1 Cor. xv. 8,) and mention is made of it twice in the Acts, (ix. 3, and xxii. 6.) Hence this passage tends to establish his call, because, although he had not been set apart as one of the twelve, there was no less authority in the appointment which Christ published from heaven.

Are not ye my work? He now, in the *second* place, establishes his Apostleship from the effect of it, because he had gained over the Corinthians to the Lord by the gospel. Now this is a great thing that Paul claims for himself, when he calls their conversion *his work*, for it is in a manner a new creation of the soul. But how will this correspond with what we had above—that *he that planteth is nothing, and he that watereth is nothing?* (1 Cor. iii. 7.) I answer, that as God is the efficient cause, while man, with his preaching, is an instrument that can do nothing of itself, we must always speak of the efficacy of the ministry in such a manner that the entire praise of the work may be reserved for God alone. But in some cases, when the ministry is spoken of, man is compared with God, and then that statement holds good— *He that planteth is nothing, and he that watereth is nothing;* for what can be left to a man if he is brought into competition with God? Hence Scripture represents ministers as nothing in comparison with God; but when the ministry is simply treated of without any comparison with God, then, as in this passage, its efficacy is honourably made mention of, with signal encomiums. For, in that case, the question is not, what man can do of himself without God, but, on the contrary, God himself, who is the author, is conjoined with the instrument, and the Spirit's influence with man's labour. In other words, the question is not, what man himself accomplishes by his own power, but what God effects through his hands.[1]

2. *If I am not an Apostle to others.* The sum of this tends to the establishing of his authority among the Corinthians, so as to place it beyond all dispute. "If there are those," says he, "who have doubts as to my Apostleship, to you, at least, it ought to be beyond all doubt, for, as I planted your

[1] See pp. 128-130.

Church by my ministry, you are either not believers, or you must necessarily recognise me as an Apostle. And that he may not seem to rest in mere words, he states that the reality itself was to be seen,[1] because God had sealed his Apostleship by the faith of the Corinthians. Should any one, however, object, that this suits the false Apostles too, who gather disciples to themselves, I answer, that pure doctrine is above all things required, in order that any one may have a confirmation of his ministry in the sight of God from its effect. There is nothing, therefore, here to furnish impostors with matter of congratulation, if they have deceived any of the populace, nay, even nations and kingdoms, by their falsehoods. Although in some cases persons are the occasion of spreading the kingdom of Christ, who, nevertheless, *do not preach the gospel sincerely,* as is said in Phil. i. 16, it is not without good reason that Paul infers from the fruit of his labour, that he is divinely commissioned : for the structure of the Corinthian Church was such, that the blessing of God could easily be seen shining forth in it, which ought to have served as a confirmation of Paul's office.

3. *My defence.* Apart from the principal matter that he has at present in hand, it appears also to have been his intention to beat down, in passing, the calumnies of those who clamoured against his call, as if he had been one of the ordinary class of ministers. " I am accustomed," says he, " to put you forward as my shield, in the event of any one detracting from the honour of my Apostleship." Hence it follows, that the Corinthians are injurious and inimical to themselves, if they do not acknowledge him as such, for if their faith was a solemn attestation of Paul's Apostleship, and his *defence,* against slanderers, the one could not be invalidated without the other falling along with it.

Where others read—*those who interrogate me,* I have rendered it—*those that examine me*—for he refers to those who raised a dispute as to his Apostleship.[2] Latin writers,

---

[1] " La verite et l'effet le demonstre ;"—" Truth and reality demonstrate it."

[2] " Ceux qui vouloyent mettre en debat son Apostolat, et le controller, comme on dit ;"—" Those who were desirous to bring his Apostleship into dispute, and overhale it, as they say."

I confess, speak of a criminal being *interrogated*[1] according
to the laws, but the meaning of the word ἀνακρίνειν which
Paul makes use of, seemed to me to be brought out better
in this way.

4. *Have we not power?*   He concludes from what has been
already said, that he had a right to receive food and clothing from them,[2] for Paul ate and drank, but not at the expense of the Church.   This, then, was one liberty that he dispensed with.   The other was, that he had not a wife—to be
maintained, also, at the public expense.   Eusebius infers from
these words that Paul was married, but had left his wife
somewhere, that she might not be a burden to the Churches,
but there is no foundation for this, for he might bring forward this, even though unmarried.   In honouring a Christian
wife with the name of *sister*, he intimates, first of all, by
this, how firm and lovely ought to be the connection between
a pious pair, being held by a double tie.   Farther, he hints
at the same time what modesty and honourable conduct
ought to subsist between them.   Hence, too, we may infer,
how very far marriage is from being unsuitable to the ministers of the Church.   I pass over the fact, that the Apostles
made use of it, as to whose example we shall have occasion
to speak ere long, but Paul here teaches, in general terms,
what is allowable for all.

5. *Even as the other Apostles.*   In addition to the Lord's
permission, he mentions the common practice of others.
And with the view of bringing out more fully the waiving
of his right, he proceeds step by step.   In the first place, he
brings forward the *Apostles.*   He then adds, " Nay, even
the brethren of the Lord themselves also make use of it without hesitation—nay more, Peter himself, to whom the first
place is assigned by consent of all, allows himself the same
liberty."   By *the brethren of the Lord*, he means John and
James, who *were accounted pillars*, as he states elsewhere.
(Gal. ii. 9.)   And, agreeably to what is customary in Scrip-

---

[1] The expression is made use of by Suetonius.   (Aug. 33.)   Reum
ita fertur *interrogásse*.   (He is said to have *interrogated* the criminal in
such a manner.)—*Ed.*

[2] " Combien qu'il n'en ait pas usé ;"—" Though he had not made use
of it."

ture, he gives the name of *brethren* to those who were connected with Him by relationship.

Now, if any one should think to establish Popery from
this, he would act a ridiculous part. We confess that Peter
was acknowledged as first among the Apostles, as it is necessary that in every society there should always be some one
to preside over the others, and they were of their own accord
prepared to respect Peter for the eminent endowments by
which he was distinguished, as it is proper to esteem and
honour all that excel in the gifts of God's grace. That pre-
eminence, however, was not lordship—nay more, it had nothing resembling lordship. For while he was eminent among
the others, still he was subject to them as his colleagues.
Farther, it is one thing to have pre-eminence in one Church,
and quite another, to claim for one's self a kingdom or dominion over the whole world. But indeed, even though we
should concede everything as to Peter, what has this to do
with the Pope? For as Matthias succeeded Judas, (Acts i.
26,) so some Judas might succeed Peter. Nay more, we see
that during a period of more than nine hundred years among
his successors, or at least among those who boast that they
are his successors, there has not been one who was one whit
better than Judas. This, however, is not the place to treat
of these points. Consult my Institutes. (vol. iii. pp. 108-124.)

One thing farther must here be noticed, that the Apostles
had no horror of marriage, which the Papal clergy so much
abominate, as unbecoming the sanctity of their order. But
it was after their time that that admirable discovery was
made, that the priests of the Lord are polluted if they have
intercourse with their lawful wives; and, at length matters
came to such a pitch, that Pope Syricius did not hesitate to
call marriage "*a pollution of the flesh*, in which no one can
please God." What then must become of the poor Apostles,
who continued in that pollution until death? Here, however,
they have contrived a refined subtilty to effect their escape;
for they say that the Apostles gave up the use of the marriage bed, but *led about* their wives with them, that they
might receive the fruits of the gospel, or, in other words,
support at the public expense. As if they could not have

been maintained by the Churches, unless they wandered about from place to place; and farther, as if it were a likely thing that they would run hither and thither of their own accord, and without any necessity, in order that they might live in idleness at the public expense! For as to the explanation given by Ambrose, as referring to other persons' wives, who followed the Apostles for the purpose of hearing their doctrine, it is exceedingly forced.

7. *Who hath gone a warfare at his own charges?* It is the present tense that is used[1] as meaning—is *accustomed to go* a warfare. I have, however, with the view of taking off somewhat of the harshness, rendered it in the preterite. Now, by *three* comparisons, and these, too, taken from common life, he makes it out that it was allowable for him to live, if he chose, at the public expense of the Church, to show that he assumes nothing to himself but what human nature itself teaches us is reasonable. The *first* is taken from military law, for soldiers are wont to have their provisions furnished to them at the public expense. The *second* is taken from vine-dressers, for the husbandman plants a vine—not to throw away his pains, but to gather the fruit. The *third* is taken from keepers of cattle, for the shepherd does not lay out his labour for nothing, but *eats of the milk of the flock*—that is, he is supported from the produce. As natural equity points out this as reasonable, who will be so unjust as to refuse sustenance to the pastors of the Church? While it may happen, that some serve as soldiers at their own expense, as, for example, the Romans in ancient times, when no tribute was as yet paid, and there were no taxes,[2] this does not militate against Paul's statement, for he simply takes his argument from common and everywhere received practice.

8. *Say I these things as a man?* Lest any one should cavil, and say that in the things of the Lord the case is different, and therefore that he had to no purpose brought forward so many comparisons, he now adds, that the very same

---

[1] The verb is στρατεύεται, *goeth* a warfare, or *serves* as a soldier. —*Ed.*

[2] The Roman soldiers received no pay (*stipendium*) from the public expense until 347 years after the founding of Rome. (See Liv. iv. 59 and v. 7.)—*Ed.*

thing is commanded by the Lord. To speak *as a man* sometimes means—speaking according to the perverse judgment of the flesh, (as in Rom. iii. 5.) Here, however, it means—bringing forward only those things that are in common use among men, and are merely current (as they speak) in a human court. Now, that God himself designed that the labours of men should be remunerated by wages, he proves from this, that he prohibits the *muzzling of the mouth of the ox that treadeth out the corn;* and with the view of applying it to the subject in hand, he says, that God was not concerned as to oxen, but rather had regard to men.

In the first place, it may be asked, Why has he more particularly selected this proof, while he had in the law passages that were much clearer? as for example, Deut. xxiv. 15, *The wages of the hireling shall not remain with thee over night.* If any one, however, will take a nearer view, he will acknowledge that there is more force in this quotation, in which the Lord requires cattle to be taken care of, for from this it is inferred, from the less to the greater, how much equity he requires among men, when he wishes that it should be shown to brute animals. When he says, that *God does not take care for oxen,* you are not to understand him as meaning to exclude oxen from the care of God's Providence, inasmuch as he does not overlook even the least sparrow. (Matt. vi. 26, and x. 29.) Nor is it as if he meant to expound that precept allegorically, as some hair-brained spirits take occasion from this to turn everything into allegories. Thus they turn dogs into men, trees into angels, and turn all scripture into a laughing-stock.

Paul's meaning is simple—that, when the Lord enjoins humanity to oxen, he does not do it for the sake of oxen, but rather from a regard to men, on whose account, too, the very oxen were created. That compassion, therefore, towards oxen should be a stimulus to us to stir up to the exercise of humanity among us, as Solomon says, (Prov. xii. 10,) *The righteous man hath a care over his beast, but the bowels of the wicked are cruel.* Let it then be understood by you, that God is not *so* concerned for oxen, as to have had merely a regard to oxen in making that law, for he had mankind in view, and wished to accustom them to equity, that they might not defraud the workman of his hire. For it is not the ox that has the principal part in plowing or treading out the corn, but man, by whose industry the ox himself is set to work. Hence, what he immediately adds—*He that ploweth, should plow in hope*, &c. is an exposition of the precept, as if he had said, that it extends generally to any kind of recompense for labour.

10. *Because he that ploweth ought to plow in hope.* There is a twofold reading in this passage, even in the Greek manuscripts, but the one that is more generally received is—*He that thrasheth, in hope of partaking of his hope.* At the same time, the one that does not repeat the term *hope* twice in the second clause appears simpler, and more natural.[1] Hence, if I were at liberty to choose, I would prefer to read it thus : *He that ploweth should plow in hope, and he that thrasheth in hope of participating.* As, however, the most of the Greek manuscripts agree in the former reading, and as the meaning remains the same, I have not ventured to make a change upon it. Now he expounds the preceding injunction, and hence he says, that it is an unjust thing that the husbandman should lay out his pains to no purpose in plowing and thrashing, but that the end of his labour is the hope of receiving the fruits. As it is so, we may infer, that this belongs to oxen also, but Paul's intention was to extend it farther, and apply it principally to men. Now, the husbandman is said to be *a partaker of his hope*, when he enjoys the produce which he has obtained when reaping, but hoped for when plowing.

11. *If we have sown unto you spiritual things.* There was one cavil remaining—for it might be objected, that labours connected with this life should without doubt have food and clothing as their reward ; and that plowing and thrashing yield fruit, of which those that labour in these things are

---

[1] The common reading is—καὶ ὁ ἀλοῶν τῆς ἐλπίδος αὐτοῦ μετέχειν ἐπ᾽ ἐλπίδι, *and he that thrasheth in hope should be a partaker of his hope.* In the other reading, the ἐπ᾽ ἐλπίδι (*in hope*) are omitted. The latter is the reading in five ancient and three later MSS. The common reading is construed by Bloomfield as follows :—καὶ ὁ ἀλοῶν (ὀφείλει ἀλοᾷν) ἐπ᾽ ἐλπίδι (τοῦ) μετέχειν τῆς ἐλπίδος αὐτοῦ. " And he that thrasheth ought to thrash in hope to partake of (the fruits of) his hope."—*Ed.*

partakers; but that it is otherwise with the gospel, because its fruit is spiritual; and hence the minister of the word, if he would receive fruit corresponding to his labour, ought to demand nothing that is carnal. Lest any one, therefore, should cavil in this manner, he argues from the greater to the less. "Though food and clothing are not of the same nature with a minister's labours, what injury do you sustain, if you recompense what is inestimable with a thing that is small and contemptible? For in proportion to the superiority of the soul above the body, does the word of the Lord excel outward sustenance,[1] inasmuch as it is the food of the soul."

12. *If others assume this power over you.* Again he establishes his own right from the example of others. For why should he alone be denied what others assumed as their due? For as no one laboured more than he among the Corinthians, no one was more deserving of a reward. He does not, however, make mention of what he has done, but of what he would have done in accordance with his right, if he had not of his own accord refrained from using it.

But we have not used this power. He returns now to the point on which the matter hinges—that he had of his own accord given up that power which no one could refuse him, and that he was prepared rather *to suffer all things*, than by the use of his liberty throw any impediment in the way of the progress of the gospel. He wishes, therefore, that the Corinthians should, after his example, keep this end in view —to do nothing that would hinder or retard the progress of the gospel; for what he declares respecting himself it was their duty to perform according to their station; and he confirms here what he had said previously—that we must consider what is *expedient.* (1 Cor. vi. 12.)

13. Do ye not know that they which minister about holy things live *of the things* of the temple? and they which wait at the altar are partakers with the altar?

13. Nescitis, quod qui sacris operantur, ex sacrario[2] edunt? et qui altari ministrant (*ad verbum: adstant*) altaris sunt participes?

---

[1] " Et le vestement;"—" And clothing."
[2] " Des choses qui sont sacrifiees;"—" Of the things that are sacrificed."

14. Even so hath the Lord ordained that they which preach the gospel should live of the gospel.

15. But I have used none of these things: neither have I written these things, that it should be so done unto me: for *it were* better for me to die, than that any man should make my glorying void.

16. For though I preach the gospel, I have nothing to glory of: for necessity is laid upon me; yea, woe is unto me, if I preach not the gospel!

17. For if I do this thing willingly, I have a reward: but if against my will, a dispensation *of the gospel* is committed unto me.

18. What is my reward then? *Verily* that, when I preach the gospel, I may make the gospel of Christ without charge, that I abuse not my power in the gospel.

19. For though I be free from all *men*, yet have I made myself servant unto all, that I might gain the more.

20. And unto the Jews I became as a Jew, that I might gain the Jews; to them that are under the law, as under the law, that I might gain them that are under the law;

21. To them that are without law, as without law, (being not without law to God, but under the law to Christ,) that I might gain them that are without law.

22. To the weak became I as weak, that I might gain the weak: I am made all things to all *men*, that I might by all means save some.

14. Sic et Dominus ordinavit, ut qui Evangelium annuntiant, vivant ex Evangelio.

15. Ego autem nullo horum usus sum: neque vero haec scripsi, ut ita mihi fiat: mihi enim satius est mori, quam ut gloriam meam quis exinaniat.

16. Nam si evangelizavero, non est quod glorier: quandoquidem necessitas mihi incumbit, ut vae sit mihi, si non evangelizem.

17. Si enim volens hoc facio, mercedem habeo: si autem invitus, dispensatio mihi est credita.

18. Quae igitur mihi merces? ut quum evangelizo, gratuitum impendam Evangelium Christi, ut non abutar potestate mea in Evangelio.

19. Liber enim quum essem ab omnibus, servum me omnibus feci, ut plures lucrifaciam.

20. Itaque factus sum Iudaeis tanquam Iudaeus, ut Iudaeos lucrifaciam: iis qui sub Lege erant, tanquam Legi subiectus, ut eos qui erant sub Lege lucrifaciam;

21. Iis qui sine Lege erant, tanquam exlex, (tametsi non absque Lege, Deo, sed subiectus Legi Christi,) ut eos qui sine Lege erant lucrifaciam.

22. Factus sum infirmis tanquam infirmus, ut infirmos lucrifaciam: omnibus omnia factus sum, ut omnino aliquos servem.

13. *Know ye not.* Apart from the question that he discusses, he appears to have dwelt the longer in taking notice of this point, with the view of reproaching the Corinthians indirectly for their malignity in allowing the ministers of Christ to be reviled in a matter that was so justifiable. For if Paul had not of his own accord refrained from using his liberty, there was a risk of the progress of the gospel being obstructed. Never would the false Apostles have gained that point, had not ingratitude, to which the Corinthians were already prone, opened up the way for their calumnies.

For they ought to have repelled them sharply; but instead of this they showed themselves excessively credulous, so that they would have been prepared to reject the gospel, if Paul had used his right. Such contempt of the gospel, and such cruelty towards their Apostle, deserved to be more severely reproved; but Paul, having found another occasion, touches upon it indirectly and mildly, with his usual modesty, that he may admonish them without affronting them.

Again he makes use of a new comparison, to prove that he had not used the power that he had from the Lord. Nor does he any longer borrow examples from any other source, but shows that this has been appointed by the Lord—that the Churches should provide for the support of their ministers. There are some that think that there are *two* comparisons in this passage, and they refer the *former* to the Lord's priests, and the *latter* to those that acted as priests to the heathen gods. I am, however, rather of opinion that Paul expresses, as he is accustomed, the same thing by different terms. And, truly, it would have been a weak argument that was derived from the practice of the heathens, among whom the revenues of the priesthood were not devoted to food and clothing, but to magnificent dresses, royal splendour, and profuse luxury. These would, therefore, have been things too remote. I do not call it in question, however, that he has pointed out different kinds of ministerial offices; for there were priests of a higher order, and there were afterwards Levites, who were inferior to them, as is well known; but that is not much to the point.

The sum is this—" The Levitical priests were ministers of the Israelitish Church; the Lord appointed *them* sustenance from their ministry; hence in ministers of the Christian Church the same equity must be observed at the present day. Now the ministers of the Christian Church are those that preach the gospel." This passage is quoted by Canonists, when they wish to prove that idle bellies must be fattened up, in order that they may perform their masses;[1] but how absurdly, I leave it to children themselves to judge. Whatever is stated in the Scriptures as to the support to

---

[1] " Et autres brimborions ;"—" And other baubles."

be given to ministers, or the honour that is to be put upon
them, they immediately seize hold of it, and twist it to their
own advantage.   For my part, however, I simply admonish
my readers to consider attentively Paul's words.   He argues
that pastors, who labour in the preaching of the gospel, ought
to be supported, because the Lord in ancient times appointed
sustenance for the priests, on the ground of their serving the
Church.   Hence a distinction must be made between the
ancient priesthood and that of the present day.   Priests
under the law were set apart to preside over the sacrifices, to
serve the altar, and to take care of the tabernacle and temple.   Those at the present day are set apart to preach the
word and to dispense the sacraments.   The Lord has appointed no sacrifices for his sacred ministers to be engaged in ;[1]
there are no altars for them to stand at to offer sacrifices.

Hence appears the absurdity of those who apply this comparison, taken from sacrifices, to anything else than to the
preaching of the gospel.   Nay farther, it may be readily
inferred from this passage, that all Popish priests, from the
head himself to the lowest member, are guilty of sacrilege,
who devour the revenues appointed for true ministers, while
they do not in any way discharge their duty.   For what
ministers does the Apostle order to be maintained ?   Those
that apply themselves to the preaching of the gospel.   What
right then have *they* to claim for themselves the revenues of
the priesthood ?[2]   " Because they hum a tune and perform
mass."[3]   But God has enjoined upon them nothing of that
sort.   Hence it is evident that they seize upon the reward
due to others.   When, however, he says that the Levitical
priests were *partakers with the altar,* and that they ate of
the things of *the Temple,* he marks out ($\mu\epsilon\tau\omega\nu\nu\mu\iota\kappa\hat{\omega}\varsigma$) by
metonymy, the offerings that were presented to God.   For
they claimed to themselves the sacred victims entire, and
of smaller animals they took the right shoulder, and kid-

---

[1] " Auiourd'huy ;"— " At the present day."

[2] " De quel droict s'usurpent ces ventres paresseux le reuenu des benefices, qu'ils appelent ?"—" By what right do these lazy bellies claim to
themselves the revenue of the benefices, as they call it ?"

[3] " Pource qu'ils gringotent des messes et anniuersaires ;"—" Because
they hum a tune at masses and anniversaries."

neys and tail, and, besides this, tithes, oblations, and first-
fruits. The word ἱερόν, therefore, in the *second* instance,[1] is
taken to mean *the Temple.*

15. *Nor have I written these things.* As he might seem
to be making it his aim, that in future a remuneration should
be given him by the Corinthians, he removes that suspicion,
and declares that, so far from this being his desire, *he would
rather die* than give occasion for his being deprived of this
ground of glorying—that he bestowed labour upon the
Corinthians without any reward. Nor is it to be wondered
that he set so high a value upon this glorying, inasmuch as
he saw that the authority of the gospel in some degree
depended upon it. For he would in this way have given a
handle to the false apostles to triumph over him. Hence
there was a danger, lest the Corinthians, despising him, should
receive them with great applause. So much did he prefer,
even before his own life, the power of advancing the gospel.

16. *For if I preach the gospel.* To show how very important it was not to deprive himself of that ground of
glorying, he intimates what would have happened, if he had
simply discharged his ministry—that he would in this way
have done nothing else than what the Lord had enjoined
upon him by a strict necessity. By doing *that,* he says, he
would have had no occasion for glorying, as it was not in his
power to avoid doing it.[2] It is asked, however, what *glorying*
he here refers to, for he glories elsewhere in his exercising
himself in the office of teaching *with a pure conscience.*
(2 Tim. i. 3.) I answer, that he speaks of a glorying that he
could bring forward in opposition to the false apostles, when
they endeavoured to find a pretext for reviling, as will appear more fully from what follows.

This is a remarkable statement, from which we learn, in
the first place, what, as to ministers, is the nature, and
what the closeness of the tie that is involved in their call-

---

[1] In the original, the words τὰ ἱερὰ and τοῦ ἱεροῦ, occur in the same clause,
and our Author's meaning is, that in the *second* instance the noun ἱερον,
denotes *the temple.*—*Ed.*

[2] " Veu qu'il y estoit contraint, et ne pouuoit euiter telle necessite ;"—
" Inasmuch as he was constrained to it, and could not avoid such a necessity."

ing, and farther, what the pastoral office imports and includes.
Let not the man, then, who has been once *called* to it,
imagine that he is any longer at liberty to withdraw when he
chooses, if, perhaps, he is harassed with vexatious occurrences, or weighed down with misfortunes, for he is devoted
to the Lord and to the Church, and bound by a sacred tie,
which it were criminal to break asunder. As to the *second*
point,[1] he says that a curse was ready to fall upon him, *if he
did not preach the gospel.* Why? Because he has been
called to it, and therefore is constrained by *necessity.* How,
therefore, will any one who succeeds to his office avoid this
necessity ? What sort of successors, then, have the Apostles
in the Pope and the other mitred bishops, who think that
there is nothing that is more unbecoming their station, than
the duty of teaching!

17. *For if I do this thing willingly.* By *reward* here is
meant what the Latins term *operæ pretium,* recompense for
labour,[2] and what he had previously termed *glorying.* Others,
however, interpret it otherwise—as meaning that a *reward*
is set before all who discharge their duty faithfully and
heartily. But, for my part, I understand the man who *does
this thing willingly,* to be the man who acts with such cheerfulness, that, being intent upon edifying, as his one object
of desire, he declines nothing that he knows will be profitable to the Church ; as, on the other hand, he terms those
unwilling, who in their actings submit, indeed, to necessity,
but act grudgingly, because it is not from inclination. For
it always happens that the man who undertakes any busi-

---

[1] That is, the duty which the pastoral office involves.—*Ed.*

[2] "Ce que nous appelons chef-d'œuvre ;"—"What we call a masterpiece."
The idiomatic phrase, *operae pretium,* is ordinarily employed by the classical writers to mean—something *of importance,* or *worth while.* Thus *Livy,*
in his Preface, says : "facturusne operae pretium sim ;"—"whether I am
about to do a work of importance," and *Cicero* (Cat. iv. 8) says : "Operae
pretium est ;"—"It is *worth while.*" CALVIN, however, seems to make
use of the phrase here in a sense more nearly akin to its original and
literal signification—*recompense for labour*—what amply rewarded the
self-denial that he had exercised—consisting in the peculiar satisfaction
afforded to his mind in reflecting on the part that he had acted. The term
made use of by him in his French Translation—*chef-d'œuure* (*masterpiece*)
corresponds with the Latin phrase *operae pretium* in this respect, that
a *masterpiece* is a work, which the successful artist, or workman, sets a
value upon, and in which he feels *satisfaction,* as *amply recompensing* the
pains bestowed.—*Ed.*

ness with zeal, is also prepared of his own accord to submit to everything, which, if left undone, would hinder the accomplishment of the work. Thus Paul, being one that acted *willingly*, did not teach in a mere perfunctory manner, but left nothing undone that he knew to be fitted to promote and further his doctrine. *This* then was his *recompense for labour*,[1] and *this* his ground of *glorying*—that he did with readiness of mind forego his right in respect of his applying himself to the discharge of his office willingly and with fervent zeal.

But if unwillingly, a dispensation is committed to me. In whatever way others explain these words, the natural meaning, in my opinion, is this—that God does not by any means approve of the service done by the man who performs it grudgingly, and, as it were, with a reluctant mind. Whenever, therefore, God has enjoined anything upon us, we are mistaken, if we think that we have discharged it aright, when we perform it *grudgingly ;* for the Lord requires that his servants be *cheerful*, (2 Cor. ix. 7,) so as to delight in obeying him, and manifest their cheerfulness by the promptitude with which they act. In short, Paul means, that he would act in accordance with his calling, only in the event of his performing his duty willingly and cheerfully.

18. *What then is my reward ?* He infers from what goes before, that he has a ground of glorying in this, that he laboured gratuitously in behalf of the Corinthians, because it appears from this, that he applied himself willingly to the office of teaching, inasmuch as he vigorously set himself to obviate all the hinderances in the way of the gospel; and not satisfied with merely teaching, endeavoured to further the doctrine of it by every method. This then is the sum : " I am under the necessity of preaching the gospel : if I do it not, wo is unto me, for I resist God's calling. But it is not enough to preach, unless I do it willingly ; for he who fulfils the commandment of God unwillingly, does not act, as becomes him, suitably to his office. But if I obey God willingly, it will in that case be allowable for me to glory. Hence it was necessary for me to make the gospel *without charge*, that I might glory on good ground."

---

[1] " Son chef-d'œuure ;"—" His masterpiece."

Papists endeavour from this passage to establish their contrivance as to works of *supererogation.*[1] "Paul," they say, "would have fulfilled the duties of his office by preaching the gospel, but he adds something farther over and above.   Hence he does something beyond what he is bound to do, for he distinguishes between what is done willingly and what is done from necessity."   I answer, that Paul, it is true, went a greater length than the ordinary calling of pastors required, because he refrained from taking pay, which the Lord allows pastors to take.   But as it was a part of his duty to provide against every occasion of offence that he foresaw, and as he saw, that the course of the gospel would be impeded, if he made use of his liberty, though that was out of the ordinary course, yet I maintain that even in that case he rendered to God nothing more than was due.   For I ask : " Is it not the part of a good pastor to remove occasions of offence, so far as it is in his power to do so ?"   I ask again, "Did Paul do anything else than this ?"   There is no ground, therefore, for imagining that he rendered to God anything that he did not owe to him, inasmuch as he did nothing but what the necessity of his office (though it was an extraordinary necessity) demanded.   Away, then, with that wicked imagination,[2] that we compensate for our faults in the sight of God by works of *supererogation !*[3] Nay more, away with the very term, which is replete with diabolical pride.[4]   This passage, assuredly, is mistakingly perverted to bear that meaning.

The error of Papists is refuted in a general way in this manner : Whatever works are comprehended under the law, are falsely termed works of *supererogation,* as is manifest from the words of Christ. (Luke xvii. 10.)   *When ye have done all things that are commanded you, say, We are unprofitable servants : we have done what we were bound to*

---

[1] " C'est à dire, d'abondant ;"—" That is to say, over and above."

[2] " Ceste perverse et mal-heureuse imagination;"—" That perverse and miserable fancy."

[3] " C'est à dire, lesquelles nous faisons de superabondant ;"—" That is to say, what we do over and above."

[4] Our Author expresses himself in similar terms elsewhere as to the word *merit.* See *Harmony,* vol. ii. p. 197.—*Ed.*

do. Now we acknowledge that no work is good and acceptable to God, that is not included in God's law. This *second*
statement I prove in this way : There are two classes of
good works ; for they are all reducible either to the service of
God or to love. Now nothing belongs to *the service of God*
that is not included in this summary : *Thou shalt love the
Lord with all thy heart, with all thy soul, with all thy strength.*
There is also no duty of *love* that is not required in that precept—*Love thy neighbour as thyself.* (Mark xii. 30, 31.) But as
to the objection that is brought forward by Papists, that it is
possible for one to be acceptable, if he devotes the *tenth* part
of his income, and infer from this, that if he goes so far as
to devote the *fifth* part, he does a work of *supererogation,*
it is easy to remove away this subtilty. For that the deeds
of the pious are approved, is not by any means owing to their
perfection, but it is because the imperfection and deficiency
are not reckoned to their account. Hence even if they were
doing an hundred-fold more than they do, they would not,
even in that case, exceed the limits of the duty that they owe.

That I may not abuse my power. From this it appears,
that such a use of our liberty as gives occasion of offence, is
an uncontrolled liberty and abuse. We must keep, therefore,
within bounds, that we may not give occasion of offence.
This passage also confirms more fully what I just now
touched upon, that Paul did nothing beyond what the duty
of his office required, because it was not proper that the
liberty, that was allowed him by God, should be in any way
abused.

19. *Though I was free from all.* Εκ πάντων, that is, *from
all,* may be taken either in the neuter gender or in the masculine. If in the neuter, it will refer to *things ;* if in the
masculine, to *persons.* I prefer the *second.* He has as yet
shown only by one particular instance how carefully he had
accommodated himself to the weak. Now he subjoins a
general statement, and afterwards enumerates several instances. The *general* observation is this—that while he was
not under the power of any one, he lived as if he had been
subject to the inclination of all, and of his own accord subjected himself to *the weak,* to whom he was under no sub-

jection. The *particular* instances are these—that among
the Gentiles he lived as if he were a Gentile, and among the
Jews he acted as a Jew: that is, while among Jews he carefully observed the ceremonies of the law, he was no less careful not to give occasion of offence to the Gentiles by the
observance of them.

He adds the particle *as*, to intimate that his liberty was
not at all impaired on that account, for, however he might
accommodate himself to men, he nevertheless remained always like himself inwardly in the sight of God. To *become
all things* is to assume all appearances, as the case may require, or to put on different characters, according to the
diversity among individuals. As to what he says respecting
his *being without law* and *under the law*, you must understand it simply in reference to the ceremonial department ;
for the department connected with morals was common to
Jews and Gentiles alike, and it would not have been allowable for Paul to gratify men to that extent. For this doctrine holds good only as to things indifferent, as has been
previously remarked.

21. *Though not without law to God.* He wished by this
parenthesis to soften the harshness of the expression, for it
might have seemed harsh at first view to have it said, that
he *had come to be without law.* Hence in order that this
might not be taken in a wrong sense, he had added, by way
of correction, that he had always kept in view one law—that
of subjection to Christ. By this too he hints that odium
was excited against him groundlessly and unreasonably, as
if he called men to an unbridled licentiousness, while he
taught exemption from the bondage of the Mosaic law. Now
he calls it expressly *the law of Christ*, in order to wipe away
the groundless reproach, with which the false apostles
branded the gospel, for he means, that in the doctrine of
Christ nothing is omitted, that might serve to give us a perfect rule of upright living.

22. *To the weak I became as weak.* Now again he employs a general statement, in which he shows to what sort
of persons he accommodated himself, and with what design.
He judaized in the presence of the Jews, but not before

them all, for there were many headstrong persons, who, under the influence of Pharisaical pride or malice, would have wished that Christian liberty were altogether taken away. To those persons he would never have been so accommodating, for Christ would not have us care for persons of that sort. *Let them alone,* (says he,) *they are blind, and leaders of the blind.* (Matt. xv. 14.) Hence we must accommodate ourselves to the weak, not to the obstinate.[1]

Now his *design* was, that he might bring them to Christ—not that he might promote his own advantage, or retain their good will. To these things a *third* must be added—that it was only in things indifferent, that are otherwise in our choice, that he accommodated himself to the weak. Now, if we consider how great a man Paul was, who stooped thus far, ought we not to feel ashamed—we who are next to nothing in comparison with him—if, bound up in self, we look with disdain upon the weak, and do not deign to yield up a single point to them? But while it is proper that we should accommodate ourselves to the weak, according to the Apostle's injunction, and that, in things indifferent, and with a view to their edification, those act an improper part, who, with the view of consulting their own ease, avoid those things that would offend men, and the wicked, too, rather than the weak. Those, however, commit a two-fold error, who do not distinguish between things indifferent and things unlawful, and accordingly do not hesitate, for the sake of pleasing men, to engage in things that the Lord has prohibited. The crowning point, however, of the evil is this—that they abuse this statement of Paul to excuse their wicked dissimulation. But if any one will keep in view these three things that I have briefly pointed out, he will have it easily in his power to refute those persons.

We must observe, also, the word that he makes use of in the concluding clause;[2] for he shows for what purpose he endeavours to *gain* all—with a view to their salvation. At

[1] The reader will find this sentiment more fully brought out in the *Harmony*, vol. ii. p. 258.—*Ed.*

[2] " *Afin que totalement i'en sauue quelques uns ;*"—" *That I may by all means save some.*"

the same time, he here at length modifies the general statement, unless perhaps you prefer the rendering of the old
translation, which is found even at this day in some Greek
manuscripts.[1] For in this place, too, he repeats it—*that I
may by all means save some.*[2] But as the indulgent temper,
that Paul speaks of, has sometimes no good effect, this limitation is very suitable—that, although he might not do good
to all, he, nevertheless, had never left off consulting the
advantage of at least a few.[3]

23. And this I do for the gospel's sake, that I might be partaker thereof with *you*.	23. Hoc autem facio propter Evangelium, ut particeps eius fiam.
24. Know ye not that they which run in a race run all, but one receiveth the prize? So run, that ye may obtain.	24. An nescitis, quod qui in stadium currunt, omnes quidem currunt, sed unus accipit praemium? Sic currite, ut comprehendatis.
25. And every man that striveth for the mastery is temperate in all things. Now they *do it* to obtain a corruptible crown; but we an incorruptible.	25. Porro quicunque certat, per omnia temperans est:[4] illi quidem igitur, ut perituram coronam accipiant, nos autem, ut aeternam.
26. I therefore so run, not as uncertainly; so fight I, not as one that beateth the air:	26. Ego itaque sic curro, ut non in incertum: sic pugilem ago, non velut aërem feriens:
27. But I keep under my body, and bring *it* into subjection: lest that by any means, when I have preached to others, I myself should be a castaway.	27. Verum subigo corpus meum, et in servitutem redigo, ne quo modo fiat, ut, quum aliis praedicaverim, ipse reprobus[5] efficiar.

23. *That I may become a partaker of it.* As the Corinthians might think with themselves, that this was a peculiarity in Paul's case on the ground of his office, he argues,

[1] The rendering of the Vulgate, referred to by CALVIN, is—*Ut omnes servarem,* (*That I might save all.*) Four ancient Greek MSS. have *ἵνα πάντας σώσω, that I might save all.* The same rendering is given in the Syriac version, and is embraced by Mill, Benzelius, and Bp. Pearce. In Wiclif's version, (1380,) the rendering is—"To alle men I am made alle things to make alle saaf." In the Rheims version, (1582,) it is rendered—"That I might saue al."—*Ed.*

[2] "Afin que ie sauue tous;"—"That I may save all."

[3] "Le profit et salut pour le moins de quelques uns;"—"The profit and welfare of at least some individuals."

[4] "Il s'abstient en toutes choses, ou—vit entierement par regime;"—"He abstains in all things, or—he lives entirely according to prescribed rule."

[5] "Reprouué, ou, trouué non receuable;"—"Reprobate, or, found not admissible."

from the very design of it, that this is common to all Christians. For when he declares, that his aim had been, that he *might become a partaker of the gospel,* he indirectly intimates, that all who do not act the same part with him are unworthy of the fellowship of the gospel. To *become a partaker of the gospel* is to receive the fruit of it.

24. *Know ye not, that they who run in a race.* He has laid down the doctrine, and now, with the view of impressing it upon the minds of the Corinthians, he adds an exhortation. He states briefly, that what they had hitherto attained was nothing, unless they steadfastly persevered, inasmuch as it is not enough to have once entered on the Lord's way, if they do not strive until they reach the goal, agreeably to that declaration of Christ—*He that shall endure unto the end,* &c. (Matt. x. 22.) Now he borrows a similitude from the race-course.[1] For as in that case many descend into the arena, but he alone is crowned who has first reached the goal, so there is no reason why any one should feel satisfied with himself on the ground of his having once entered upon the race prescribed in the gospel, unless he persevere in it until death. There is, however, this difference between our contest and theirs, that among them only *one* is victorious, and obtains the palm—the man who has got before all the others;[2] but our condition is superior in this respect, that there may be *many* at the same time.[3] For God requires from us nothing more than that we press on vigorously until we reach the goal.[4] Thus one does not hinder another: nay more, those who run in the Christian race are mutually helpful to each other. He expresses the same sentiment in another form in 2 Tim. ii. 5, *If any one striveth, he is not crowned, unless he strives lawfully.*

So run. Here we have the application of the similitude

---

[1] " De ceux qui courent à la lice pour quelque pris ;"—" From those who run in the race-course for some prize."

[2] " Qui a mieux couru que les autres, et est le premier venu au but ;"— " Who has run better than the others, and has come first to the goal."

[3] " Il y en peut auoir plusieurs de nous qui soyent couronnez ;"—" There may be many of us that are crowned."

[4] " Que nous ne perdions point courage, mais que perseuerions constamment jusques à la fin ;"—" That we do not lose heart, but persevere steadfastly unto the end."

—that it is not enough to have set out, if we do not continue to run during our whole life. For our life is like a race-course. We must not therefore become wearied after a short time, like one that stops short in the middle of the race-course, but instead of this, death alone must put a period to our running. The particle ὅυτω, (*so,*) may be taken in two ways. Chrysostom connects it with what goes before, in this manner: as those who run do not stop running until they have reached the goal, so do ye also persevere, and do not stop running so long as you live. It will, however, correspond not inaptly with what follows: "You must not run *so* as to stop short in the middle of the race-course, but *so* as to obtain the prize." As to the term *stadium,* (*race-course,*) and the different kinds of races,[1] I say nothing, as these things may be obtained from grammarians, and it is generally known that there were some races on horseback, and others on foot. Nor are these things particularly needed for understanding Paul's meaning.

25. *Now every one that striveth.* As he had exhorted to perseverance, it remained to state in what way they must persevere. This *second* thing he now sets before them by a comparison taken from pugilists; not indeed in every particular,[2] but in so far as was required by the subject in hand, within which he confines himself—how far they ought to yield to the weakness of the brethren. Now he argues from the less to the greater, that it is an unseemly thing if we grudge to give up our right, inasmuch as the pugilists eating their coliphium,[3] and that sparingly and not to the

---

[1] " Qui estoyent anciennement en vsage ;"—"Which were anciently in use."

[2] " Non pas qu'il vueille appliquer la similitude en tout et par tout ;"— "Not that he meant to apply the similitude out and out."

[3] " C'estoit vne sorte de pain propre pour entretenir et augmenter la force, duquel vsoyent ordinairement les lutteurs et telles gens. Les Grecs le nommoyent coliphium ;"—"This was a kind of bread that was fitted to maintain and increase strength, which was commonly made use of by wrestlers, and persons of that sort. The Greeks call it coliphium." The term coliphium is supposed to be compounded of κῶλον, a limb, and ιφι, strongly—*a means of strengthening the limbs.* It is defined by Tymme, in his Translation of CALVIN on the Corinthians, to be " a kinde of breade whereof the Wrastelers did use in tyme past to eate, to be *more strong.*" It is made mention of by *Juvenal.* (ii. 53.)—*Ed.*

full, voluntarily deny themselves every delicacy, in order that they may have more agility for the combat, and they do this, too, for the sake of *a corruptible crown.*　But if they value so highly a crown of leaves that quickly fades, what value ought we to set upon a crown of immortality ?　Let us not, therefore, think it hard to give up a little of our right. It is well known that wrestlers were contented with the most frugal diet, so that their simple fare has become proverbial.

26. *I therefore so run.*　He returns to speak of himself, that his doctrine may have the more weight, on his setting himself forward by way of pattern.　What he says here some refer to *assurance of hope*—(Heb. vi. 11)—" I do not run in vain, nor do I run the risk of losing my labour, for I have the Lord's promise, which never deceives."　It rather appears to me, however, that his object is to direct the course of believers straight forward toward the goal, that it may not be wavering and devious.　" The Lord exercises us here in the way of running and wrestling, but he sets before us the object at which we ought to aim, and prescribes a sure rule for our wrestling, that we may not weary ourselves in vain."　Now he takes in both the similitudes that he had employed.　" I know," says he, "*whither* I am running, and, like a skilful wrestler, I am anxious that I may not miss my aim."　Those things ought to kindle up and confirm the Christian breast, so as to devote itself with greater alacrity to all the duties of piety ;[1] for it is a great matter not to wander in ignorance through uncertain windings.

27. *But I keep under my body.*[2]　Budaeus reads *Observo ;* (*I keep a watch over ;*) but in my opinion the Apostle has employed the word ὑπωπιάζειν[3] here, to mean *treating in a servile manner.*[4]　For he declares that he does not indulge self, but restrains his inclinations—which cannot be accom-

---

[1] " Toutes choses concernantes la piete et crainte de Dieu;"—" All things that relate to piety and the fear of God."

[2] " Mais ie matte et reduy en seruitude mon corps ;"—" But I mortify my body, and bring it into servitude."

[3] Its original meaning is to strike *under the eye*, being compounded of ὑπό, (*under*,) and ὤψ, (*the eye*,) to beat black and blue, as the wrestlers were accustomed to do with the *cestus*.　(See Arist. Pac. 541.)—*Ed.*

[4] " Manier rudement et d'une façon seruile ;"—" To handle roughly, and in a servile manner."

plished unless the body is tamed, and, by being held back from its inclinations, is habituated to subjection, like a wild and refractory steed.   The ancient monks, with a view to yield obedience to this precept, contrived many exercises of discipline, for they slept on benches, they forced themselves to long watchings, and shunned delicacies.   The main thing, however, was wanting in them, for they did not apprehend why it was that the Apostle enjoins this, because they lost sight of another injunction—*to take no concern for our flesh to fulfil the lusts thereof.* (Rom. xiii. 14.) For what he says elsewhere (1 Tim. iv. 8) always holds good—that *bodily exercise profiteth little.*   Let us, however, treat the body so as to make a slave of it,[1] that it may not, by its wantonness, keep us back from the duties of piety; and farther, that we may not indulge it, so as to occasion injury, or offence, to others.

That, when I have preached to others. Some explain these words in this way—"Lest, after having taught others with propriety and faithfulness, I should incur the judgment of condemnation in the sight of God by a wicked life." But it will suit better to view this expression as referring to men, in this way—"My life ought to be a kind of rule to others. Accordingly, I strive to conduct myself in such a manner, that my character and conduct may not be inconsistent with my doctrine, and that thus I may not, with great disgrace to myself, and a grievous occasion of offence to my brethren, neglect those things which I require from others." It may also be taken in connection with a preceding statement, (verse 23,) in this way—"Lest I should be defrauded of the gospel, of which others are partakers through means of my labours."

CHAPTER X.

1. Moreover, brethren, I would not that ye should be ignorant, how that all our fathers were under the cloud, and all passed through the sea;

1. Nolo autem vos ignorare, fratres, quod patres nostri omnes sub nube fuerunt, et omnes mare transierunt.

---

[1] Our author has evidently in view the literal meaning of the original word here used δουλαγωγῶ, *I reduce to slavery.* It is used in this sense by Diodorus Siculus. (12. 24.)—*Ed.*

2. And were all baptized unto Moses in the cloud and in the sea;

3. And did all eat the same spiritual meat;

4. And did all drink the same spiritual drink: for they drank of that spiritual Rock that followed them: and that Rock was Christ.

5. But with many of them God was not well pleased: for they were overthrown in the wilderness.

2. Et omnes in Mose fuerunt baptizati in nube et in mari,

3. Et omnes eandem escam spiritualem manducarunt,

4. Et omnes eundem biberunt spiritualem potum: bibebant autem e spirituali, quae eos consequebatur, petra. Petra, autem, erat Christus.

5. Verum complures eorum grati non fuerunt Deo: prostrati enim fuerunt in deserto.

What he had previously taught by two similitudes, he now confirms by examples. The Corinthians grew wanton, and gloried, as if they had served out their time,[1] or at least had finished their course, when they had scarcely left the starting-point. This vain exultation and confidence he represses in this manner—" As I see that you are quietly taking your ease at the very outset of your course, *I would not have you ignorant* of what befell the people of Israel in consequence of this, that their example may arouse you." As, however, on examples being adduced, any point of difference destroys the force of the comparison, Paul premises, that there is no such dissimilarity between us and the Israelites, as to make our condition different from theirs. Having it, therefore, in view to threaten the Corinthians with the same vengeance as had overtaken them, he begins in this manner —" Beware of glorying in any peculiar privilege, as if you were in higher esteem than they were in the sight of God." For they were favoured with the same benefits as we at this day enjoy; there was a Church of God among them, as there is at this day among us; they had the same sacraments, to be tokens to them of the grace of God;[2] but, on their abusing their privileges, they did not escape the judgment of God.[3] Be afraid, therefore; for the same thing is impending

---

[1] " Comme feroyent des gendarmes, qui ont desia fidelement serui si long temps, que pour leur faire honneur on les enuoye se reposer le reste de leur vie:"—" After the manner of soldiers, who have already served with fidelity for so long a time, that with the view of putting honour upon them, they were discharged, so as to be exempted from labour during the remainder of their life."

[2] " Aussi bien qu'à nous;"—" As well as to us."

[3] " Ils ont senti le jugement de Dieu, et ne l'ont peu euiter;"—" They have felt the judgment of God, and have not been able to escape it."

over *you*. Jude makes use of the same argument in his Epistle. (Jude, verse 5.)

1. *All were under the cloud.* The Apostle's object is to show, that the Israelites were no less the people of God than we are, that we may know, that we will not escape with impunity the hand of God, which punished them[1] with so much severity. For the sum is this—"If God spared not them, neither will he spare you, for your condition is similar." That similarity he proves from this—that they had been honoured with the same tokens of God's grace, for the sacraments are badges by which the Church of God is distinguished. He treats first of baptism, and teaches that the cloud, which protected the Israelites in the desert from the heat of the sun, and directed their course, and also their passage through the sea, was to them as a baptism. He says, also, that in the manna, and the water flowing from the rock, there was a sacrament which corresponded with the sacred Supper.

They were, says he, *baptized in Moses,* that is, under the ministry or guidance of Moses. For I take the particle εἰς to be used here instead of ἐν, agreeably to the common usage of Scripture, because we are assuredly baptized in the name of Christ, and not of any mere man, as he has stated in 1 Cor. i. 13, and that for two reasons. These are, *first,* because we are by baptism initiated[2] into the doctrine of Christ alone ; and, *secondly,* because his name alone is invoked, inasmuch as baptism is founded on his influence alone. They were, therefore, *baptized in Moses,* that is, under his guidance or ministry, as has been already stated. How ? *In the cloud and in the sea.* "They were, then, baptized twice," some one will say. I answer, that there are *two* signs made mention of, making, however, but *one* baptism, corresponding to ours.

Here, however, a more difficult question presents itself. For it is certain, that the advantage of those gifts, which

---

[1] " Eux, qui estoyent son peuple ;"—" Those who were his people."

[2] " Nous nous assuietissons et faisons serment ;"—" We submit ourselves, and make oath."

Paul makes mention of, was temporal.[1] The *cloud* protected them from the heat of the sun, and showed them the way: these are outward advantages of the present life. In like manner, their passage through the *sea* was attended with this effect, that they got clear off from Pharaoh's cruelty, and escaped from imminent hazard of death. The advantage of *our* baptism, on the other hand, is spiritual. Why then does Paul turn earthly benefits into sacraments, and seek to find some spiritual mystery[2] in them? I answer, that it was not without good reason that Paul sought in miracles of this nature something more than the mere outward advantage of the flesh. For, though God designed to promote his people's advantage in respect of the present life, what he had mainly in view was, to declare and manifest himself to be their God, and under *that*, eternal salvation is comprehended.

The *cloud*, in various instances,[3] is called the symbol of his presence. As, therefore, he declared by means of it, that he was present with them, as his peculiar and chosen people, there can be no doubt that, in addition to an earthly advantage, they had in it, besides, a token of spiritual life. Thus its use was twofold, as was also that of the passage through the sea, for a way was opened up for them through the midst of the sea, that they might escape from the hand of Pharaoh; but to what was this owing, but to the circumstance, that the Lord, having taken them under his guardianship and protection, determined by every means to defend them? Hence, they concluded from this, that they were the objects of God's care, and that he had their salvation in charge. Hence, too, the Passover, which was instituted to celebrate the remembrance of their deliverance, was nevertheless, at the same time, a sacrament of Christ. How so? Because God had, under a temporal benefit, manifested himself as a Saviour. Any one that will attentively consider these things, will find that there is no absurdity in

---

[1] " Et terrien ;"—" And earthly."
[2] " Mystere et secret ;"—" Mystery and secret."
[3] " Par toute l'Escriture ;"—" Throughout the whole of Scripture."

Paul's words. Nay more, he will perceive both in the spiritual substance and in the visible sign a most striking correspondence between the baptism of the Jews, and ours.

It is however objected again, that we do not find a word of all this.[1] This I admit, but there is no doubt, that God by his Spirit supplied the want of outward preaching, as we may see in the instance of the brazen serpent, which was, as Christ himself testifies, a spiritual sacrament, (John iii. 14,) and yet not a word has come down to us as to this thing,[2] but the Lord revealed to believers of that age, in the manner he thought fit, the secret, which would otherwise have remained hid.

3. *The same spiritual meat.* He now makes mention of the other sacrament, which corresponds to the Holy Supper of the Lord. " The manna," says he, " and the water that flowed forth from the rock, served not merely for the food of the body, but also for the spiritual nourishment of souls." It is true, that both were means of sustenance for the body, but this does not hinder their serving also another purpose. While, therefore, the Lord relieved the necessities of the body, he, at the same time, provided for the everlasting welfare of souls. These two things would be easily reconciled, were there not a difficulty presented in Christ's words, (John vi. 31,) where he makes the manna the corruptible food of the belly, which he contrasts with the true food of the soul. That statement appears to differ widely from what Paul says here. This knot, too, is easily solved. It is the manner of scripture, when treating of the sacraments, or other things, to speak in some cases according to the capacity of the hearers, and in that case it has respect not to the nature of the thing, but to the mistaken idea of the hearers. Thus, Paul does not always speak of circumcision in the same way, for when he has a view to the appointment of God in it, he says, that it was *a seal of the righteousness of the faith*, (Rom. iv. 11,) but when he is disputing with those who gloried in an outward and bare sign, and reposed in it a mis-

---

[1] " Es Escritures ;"—" In the Scriptures."
[2] " Nous n'en auons maintenant pas un seul mot en toute l'Escriture ;"— " We have not a single word of it in the whole of Scripture."

taken confidence of salvation, he says, that it is a token of condemnation, because men bind themselves by it *to keep the whole law.* (Gal. v. 2, 3.) For he takes merely the opinion that the false apostles had of it, because he contends, not against the pure institution of God, but against their mistaken view. In this way, as the carnal multitude preferred Moses to Christ, because he had fed the people in the desert for forty years, and looked to nothing in the manna but the food of the belly, (as indeed they sought nothing else,) Christ in his reply does not explain what was meant by the manna, but, passing over everything else, suits his discourse to the idea entertained by his hearers. " Moses is held by you in the highest esteem, and even in admiration, as a most eminent Prophet, because he filled the bellies of your fathers in the desert. For this one thing you object against me: I am accounted nothing by you, because I do not supply you with food for the belly. But if you reckon corruptible food of so much importance, what ought you to think of the life-giving bread, with which souls are nourished up unto eternal life?" We see then that the Lord speaks there—not according to the nature of the thing, but rather according to the apprehension of his hearers.[1] Paul, on the other hand, looks here—not to the ordinance of God, but to the abuse of it by the wicked.

Farther, when he says that the fathers ate *the same spiritual meat,* he shows, *first,* what is the virtue and efficacy of the Sacraments, and, *secondly,* he declares, that the ancient Sacraments of the Law had the same virtue as ours have at this day. For, if the manna was spiritual food, it follows, that it is not bare emblems that are presented to us in the Sacraments, but that the thing represented is at the same time truly imparted, for God is not a deceiver to feed us with empty fancies.[2] A sign, it is true, *is* a sign, and retains its essence, but, as Papists act a ridiculous part, who dream of transformations, (I know not of what sort,) so it is not for us to separate between the reality and the emblem

---

[1] See CALVIN on John, vol. i. p. 247.—*Ed.*

[2] " Choses qui ayent apparence sans effet ;"—" Things that have an appearance, without reality."

which God has conjoined.   Papists confound the reality and
the sign : profane men, as, for example, Suenckfeldius, and
the like, separate the signs from the realities.   Let us maintain a middle course,[1] or, in other words, let us observe
the connection appointed by the Lord, but still keep them
distinct, that we may not mistakingly transfer to the one
what belongs to the other.

It remains that we speak of the *second* point—the resemblance between the ancient signs and ours.   It is a well-
known dogma of the schoolmen—that the Sacraments of the
ancient law were emblems of grace, but ours confer it.   This
passage is admirably suited for refuting that error, for it
shows that the reality of the Sacrament was presented to
the ancient people of God no less than to us.   It is therefore
a base fancy of the Sorbonists, that the holy fathers under the
law had the signs without the reality.   I grant, indeed, that
the efficacy of the signs is furnished to us at once more
clearly and more abundantly from the time of Christ's manifestation in the flesh than it was possessed by the fathers.
Thus there is a difference between us and them only in degree, or, (as they commonly say,) of " more and less," for we
receive more fully what they received in a smaller measure.
It is not as if they had had bare emblems, while we enjoy
the reality.[2]

Some explain it to mean, that they[3] *ate the same meat*
together among themselves, and do not wish us to understand that there is a comparison between us and them ; but
these do not consider Paul's object.   For what does he
mean to say here, but that the ancient people of God were
honoured with the same benefits with us, and were partakers of the same sacraments, that we might not, from confiding in any peculiar privilege, imagine that we would be
exempted from the punishment which they endured ?   At

---

[1] " Entre ces deux extremitez ;"—" Between these two extremes."

[2] Our author, having occasion to refer to the same " Scholastic dogma"
as to the Sacraments of the Old and New Testaments, (when commenting
on Rom. iv. 12,) says, "Illis enim vim justificandi adimunt, his attribuunt;"
—" They deny to the former the power of justifying, while they assign it
to the latter."—*Ed.*

[3] " Les Israelites ;"—" The Israelites."

the same time, I should not be prepared to contest the point with any one; I merely state my own opinion. In the meantime, I am well aware, what show of reason is advanced by those who adopt the opposite interpretation—that it suits best with the similitude made use of immediately before—that all the Israelites had the same race-ground marked out for them, and all started from the same point: all entered upon the same course : all were partakers of the same hope, but many were shut out from the reward. When, however, I take everything attentively into consideration, I am not induced by these considerations to give up my opinion; for it is not without good reason that the Apostle makes mention of two sacraments merely, and, more particularly, baptism. For what purpose was this, but to contrast them with us ? Unquestionably, if he had restricted his comparison to the body of that people, he would rather have brought forward circumcision, and other sacraments that were better known and more distinguished, but, instead of this, he chose rather those that were more obscure, because they served more as a contrast between us and them. Nor would the application that he subjoins be otherwise so suitable—" All things that happened to them are ensamples to us, inasmuch as we there see the judgments of God that are impending over us, if we involve ourselves in the same crimes."

4. *That rock was Christ.* Some absurdly pervert these words of Paul, as if he had said, that Christ was the spiritual rock, and as if he were not speaking of that rock which was a visible sign, for we see that he is expressly treating of outward signs. The objection that they make—that the rock is spoken of as *spiritual,* is a frivolous one, inasmuch as that epithet is applied to it simply that we may know that it was a token of a spiritual mystery. In the mean time, there is no doubt, that he compares our sacraments with the ancient ones. Their *second* objection is more foolish and more childish—" How could a rock," say they, " that stood firm in its place, *follow* the Israelites ?"—as if it were not abundantly manifest, that by the word *rock* is meant the stream of water, which never ceased to accompany the

people. For Paul extols[1] the grace of God, on this account, that he commanded the water that was drawn out
from the rock to flow forth wherever the people journeyed,
as if the rock itself had followed them. Now if Paul's
meaning were, that Christ is the spiritual foundation of the
Church, what occasion were there for his using the past
tense ?[2] It is abundantly manifest, that something is here
expressed that was peculiar to the fathers. Away, then,
with that foolish fancy by which contentious men choose
rather to show their impudence, than admit that they are
sacramental forms of expression ![3]

I have, however, already stated,[4] that the reality of the
things signified was exhibited in connection with the ancient
sacraments. As, therefore, they were emblems of Christ, it
follows, that Christ was connected with them, not locally, nor
by a natural or substantial union, but sacramentally. On
this principle the Apostle says, that *the rock was Christ*, for
nothing is more common than metonymy in speaking of
sacraments. The name of the thing, therefore, is transferred
here to the sign—not as if it were strictly applicable, but
figuratively, on the ground of that connection which I have
mentioned. I touch upon this, however, the more slightly,
because it will be more largely treated of when we come to
the 11th Chapter.

There remains another question. "Seeing that we now in
the Supper eat the body of Christ, and drink his blood, how
could the Jews be partakers of *the same spiritual meat and
drink*, when there was as yet no flesh of Christ that they
could eat ? " I answer, that though his flesh did not as yet
exist, it was, nevertheless, food for them. Nor is this an
empty or sophistical subtilty, for their salvation depended
on the benefit of his death and resurrection. Hence, they
required to receive the flesh and the blood of Christ, that

---

[1] " Celebre et magnifie ;"—" Celebrates and extols."

[2] " Estoit ;"—" Was."

[3] " C'est à dire, lesquelles il ne faut prendre cruëment, et à la lettre,
comme on dit ;"—".That is to say—which must not be taken strictly or
according to the letter, as they say." The reader will find this subject
handled at some length in the *Harmony*, vol. iii. pp. 207, 208.—*Ed.*

[4] See p. 317.

they might participate in the benefit of redemption. This reception of it was the secret work of the Holy Spirit, who wrought in them in such a manner, that Christ's flesh, though not yet created, was made efficacious in them. He means, however, that they ate in their own way, which was different from ours,[1] and this is what I have previously stated,[2] that Christ is now presented to us more fully, according to the measure of the revelation. For, in the present day, the eating is substantial, which it could not have been then—that is, Christ feeds us with his flesh, which has been sacrificed for us, and appointed as our food, and from this we derive life.

5. *But many of them.* We have now the reason why the Apostle has premised these things—that we might not claim for ourselves any dignity or excellence above them, but might walk in humility and fear, for thus only shall we secure, that we have not been favoured in vain with the light of truth, and with such an abundance of gracious benefits. " God," says he, " had chosen them all as his people, but many of them fell from grace. Let us, therefore, take heed, lest the same thing should happen to us, being admonished by so many examples, for God will not suffer *that* to go unpunished in *us,* which he punished so severely in *them.*"

Here again it is objected: " If it is true, that hypocrites and wicked persons in that age ate *spiritual meat,* do unbelievers in the present day partake of the reality in the sacraments?" Some, afraid lest the unbelief of men should seem to detract from the truth of God, teach that the reality is received by the wicked along with the sign. This fear, however, is needless, for the Lord offers, it is true, to the worthy and to the unworthy what he represents, but all are not capable of receiving it. In the meantime, the sacrament does not change its nature, nor does it lose anything of its efficacy. Hence the manna, in relation to God, was *spiritual meat* even to unbelievers, but because the mouth of unbelievers was but carnal, they did not eat what was given them. The fuller discussion, however, of this question I reserve for the 11th Chapter.

---

[1] " D'vne autre façon et mesure que nous ne faisons pas ;"—" In another way and measure than we do."   [2] See p. 317.

For they were overthrown. Proof is here furnished, by adducing a token, that they did not *please God*—inasmuch as he exercised his wrath upon them with severity,[1] and took vengeance on their ingratitude. Some understand this as referring to the whole of the people that died in the desert, with the exception of only two—Caleb and Joshua. (Numbers xiv. 29.) I understand him, however, as referring merely to those, whom he immediately afterwards makes mention of in different classes.

6. Now these things were our examples, to the intent we should not lust after evil things, as they also lusted.

6. Haec autem typi nobis fuerunt, ne simus concupiscentes malorum, sicut illi concupiverunt.

7. Neither be ye idolaters, as *were* some of them; as it is written, The people sat down to eat and drink, and rose up to play.

7. Neque idololatræ sitis, quemadmodum quidam eorum : sicut scriptum est. (*Exod.* xxxii. 6.) Sedit populus ad edendum et bibendum, et surrexerunt ad ludendum.

8. Neither let us commit fornication, as some of them committed, and fell in one day three and twenty thousand.

8. Neque scortemur, quemadmodum et quidam eorum scortati sunt, et ceciderunt uno die viginti tria millia.

9. Neither let us tempt Christ, as some of them also tempted, and were destroyed of serpents.

9. Neque tentemus Christum, quemadmodum et quidam eorum tentarunt, et exstincti sunt a serpentibus.

10. Neither murmur ye, as some of them also murmured, and were destroyed of the destroyer.

10. Neque murmuretis, quemadmodum et quidam eorum murmurarant, et perditi fuerunt a vastatore.

11. Now all these things happened unto them for ensamples : and they are written for our admonition, upon whom the ends of the world are come.

11. Haec autem omnia typi contigerunt illis : scripta autem sunt ad nostri admonitionem, in quos fines saeculorum inciderunt.

12. Wherefore let him that thinketh he standeth take heed lest he fall.

12. Proinde qui se putat stare, videat ne cadat.

6. *Now these things were types to us.* He warns us in still more explicit terms, that we have to do with the punishment that was inflicted upon them, so that they are a lesson to us, that we may not provoke the anger of God as they did. "God," says he, "in punishing them has set before us, as in a picture, his severity, that, instructed by their example, we may learn to fear." Of the term *type* I shall speak presently. Only for the present I should wish my readers to

---

[1] " Il a fait vne horrible vengence sur eux;"—" He inflicted dreadful vengeance upon them."

know, that it is not without consideration that I have given a different rendering from that of the old translation,[1] and of Erasmus. For they obscure Paul's meaning, or at least they do not bring out with sufficient clearness this idea—that God has in that people presented a picture for our instruction.

That we might not lust after evil things. He now enumerates particular instances, or certain examples, that he may take occasion from this to reprove some vices, as to which it was proper that the Corinthians should be admonished. I am of opinion, that the history that is here referred to is what is recorded in Numbers xi. 4, &c., though others refer it to what is recorded in Numbers xxvi. 64. The people, after having been for some time fed with manna, at length took a dislike to it, and began to desire other kinds of food, which they had been accustomed to partake of in Egypt. Now they sinned in two ways, for they despised the peculiar gift of God, and they eagerly longed after a variety of meats and delicacies, contrary to the will of God. The Lord, provoked by this lawless appetite, inflicted upon the people a grievous blow. Hence the place was called the *graves of lust*,[2] *because there they buried those whom the Lord had smitten.* (Numbers xi. 34.) The Lord by this example testified how much he hates those lusts that arise from dislike of his gifts, and from our lawless appetite, for whatever goes beyond the measure that God has prescribed is justly reckoned evil and unlawful.

7. *Neither be ye idolaters.* He touches upon the history that is recorded in Exod. xxxii. 7, &c. For when Moses made a longer stay upon the mountain than the unseemly fickleness of the people could endure, Aaron was constrained to make a calf, and set it up as an object of worship. Not that the people wished to change their God, but rather to have some visible token of God's presence, in accordance with their carnal apprehension. God, in punishing at that time this idolatry with the greatest severity, showed by that example how much he abhors idolatry.

---

[1] The rendering of the Vulgate is—*in figura, (in figure.)* Wiclif (1380) eads the clause thus: " But these thingis ben don in figure of us."—*Ed.*

[2] Our Author gives here the literal meaning of *Kibroth-hatta-avah.*—*Ed.*

As it is written, The people sat down. This passage is rightly interpreted by few, for they understand intemperance among the people to have been the occasion of wantonness,[1] in accordance with the common proverb, " Dancing comes after a full diet."[2]   But Moses speaks of a sacred feast, or in other words, what they celebrated in honour of the idol. Hence *feasting* and *play* were two appendages of idolatry. For it was customary, both among the people of Israel and among the votaries of superstition, to have a feast in connection with a sacrifice, as a part of divine worship, at which no profane or unclean persons were allowed to be present.   The Gentiles, in addition to this, appointed sacred games in honour of their idols, in conformity with which the Israelites doubtless on that occasion worshipped their calf,[3] for such is the presumption of the human mind, that it ascribes to God whatever pleases itself.   Hence the Gentiles have fallen into such a depth of infatuation as to believe, that their gods are delighted with the basest spectacles, immodest dances, impurity of speech, and every kind of obscenity.   Hence in imitation of them the Israelitish people, having observed their sacred banquet, rose up to celebrate the games, that nothing might be wanting in honour of the idol.   This is the true and simple meaning.

But here it is asked, why the Apostle makes mention of the feast and the games, rather than of adoration, for this is the chief thing in idolatry, while the other two things were merely appendages.   The reason is, that he has selected what best suited the case of the Corinthians.   For it is not likely, that they frequented the assemblies of the wicked, for the purpose of prostrating themselves before the idols, but partook of their feasts, held in honour of their deities, and did not keep at a distance from those base ceremonies, which were tokens of idolatry.   It is not therefore without good reason that the Apostle declares, that their particular

---

[1] " Et esgayement desbordé ;"—" And unbridled excess."

[2] " Apres la panse vient la danse ;"—" After dinner comes the dance."

[3] " Et ne faut point douter que les Israelites n'ayent pour lors adoré leur veau auec telle ceremonie et obseruation que les Gentils faisoyent leurs idoles ;"—" And we cannot doubt, that the Israelites on that occasion adored their calf with the same ceremony and care as the Gentiles did their idols."

form of offence is expressly condemned by God. He intimates, in short, that no part of idolatry[1] can be touched
without contracting pollution, and that those will not escape
punishment from the hand of God, who defile themselves
with the outward tokens of idolatry.

8. *Neither let us commit fornication.* Now he speaks of
fornication, in respect of which, as appears from historical
accounts, great licentiousness prevailed among the Corinthians, and we may readily infer from what goes before, that
those who had professed themselves to be Christ's were not
yet altogether free from this vice. The punishment of this
vice, also, ought to alarm us, and lead us to bear in mind,
how loathsome impure lusts are to God, for there perished
in one day twenty-three thousand, or as Moses says, twenty-
four. Though they differ as to number, it is easy to reconcile them, as it is no unusual thing, when it is not intended
to number exactly and minutely each head,[2] to put down
a number that comes near it, as among the Romans there
were those that received the name of *Centumviri,*[3] (The
Hundred,) while in reality there were two above the hundred. As there were, therefore, about twenty-four thousand
that were overthrown by the Lord's hand—that is, above
twenty-three, Moses has set down the number *above* the
mark, and Paul, the number *below* it, and in this way there
is in reality no difference. This history is recorded in Numbers xxv. 9.

There remains, however, one difficulty here—why it is that
Paul attributes this punishment to fornication, while Moses
relates that the anger of God was aroused against the people
on this account—that they had initiated themselves in the
sacred rites of Baalpeor.[4] But as the defection began with

---

[1] " Tant petite soit elle ;"—" Be it ever so little."

[2] " De faire vn denombrement entier des personnes par testes, comme
on dit ;"—" To make a complete enumeration of persons by heads, as
they say."

[3] " Les juges qui estoyent deputez pour cognoistre des matieres ciuiles,
estoyent nommez les cent, et toutes fois il y en auoit deux par dessus ;"—
" The judges who were deputed to take cognizance of civil matters were
called The Hundred, and yet there were two above the hundred." As the
Centumviri were chosen out of the thirty-five tribes, into which the Roman people were divided, three from each tribe, they consisted properly
of 105 persons.—*Ed.*

[4] " Auoit sacrifié à Baalpheor ;"—" Had sacrificed to Baalpeor."

fornication, and the children of Israel fell into that impiety, not so much from being influenced by religious considerations,[1] as from being allured by the enticements of harlots, everything evil that followed from it ought to be attributed to fornication. For Balaam had given this counsel, that the Midianites should prostitute their daughters to the Israelites, with the view of estranging them from the true worship of God. Nay more, their excessive blindness, in allowing themselves to be drawn into impiety[2] by the enticements of harlots, was the punishment of lust. Let us learn, accordingly, that fornication is no light offence, which was punished on that occasion by God so severely and indeed in a variety of ways.

9. *Neither let us tempt Christ.* This part of the exhortation refers to the history that is recorded in Numb. xxi. 6. For the people, having become weary of the length of time, began to complain of their condition, and to expostulate with God—" Why has God deceived us," &c. This murmuring of the people Paul speaks of as a *tempting;* and not without good reason, for *tempting* is opposed to patience. What reason was there at that time why the people should rise up against God, except this—that, under the influence of base desire,[3] they could not wait in patience the arrival of the time appointed by the Lord? Let us, therefore, take notice, that the fountain of that evil against which Paul here warns us is impatience, when we wish to go before God, and do not give ourselves up to be ruled by Him, but rather wish to bind him to our inclination and laws. This evil God severely punished in the Israelitish people. Now he remains always like himself—a just Judge. Let us therefore not *tempt* him, if we would not have experience of the same punishment.

This is a remarkable passage in proof of the eternity of Christ; for the cavil of Erasmus has no force—" Let us not tempt Christ, as some of them tempted *God;*" for to supply

---

[1] " Non pas tant pour affection qu'ils eussent à la fausse religion ;"— " Not so much from any attachment that they had to a false religion."

[2] " Vne impiete si vileine ;"—" An impiety so base."

[3] " Vn desir importun et desordonné ;"—" An importunate and inordinate desire."

the word *God* is extremely forced.[1] Nor is it to be wondered that Christ is called the Leader of the Israelitish people. For as God was never propitious to his people except through that Mediator, so he conferred no benefit except through his hand. Farther, the angel who appeared at first to Moses, and was always present with the people during their journeying, is frequently called יהוה, Jehovah.[2] Let us then regard it as a settled point, that that angel was the Son of God, and was even then the guide of the Church of which he was the Head. As to the term *Christ*, from its having a signification that corresponds with his human nature, it was not as yet applicable to the Son of God, but it is assigned to him by the communication of properties, as we read elsewhere, that *the Son of Man came down from heaven.* (John iii. 13.)

10. *Neither murmur ye.* Others understand this to be the murmuring that arose, when the twelve, who had been sent to spy out the land, disheartened, on their return, the minds of the people. But as that murmuring was not punished suddenly by any special chastisement from the Lord, but was simply followed by the infliction of this punishment— that all were excluded from the possession of the land, it is necessary to explain this passage otherwise. It was a most severe punishment, it is true, to be shut out from entering the land,[3] but the words of Paul, when he says that they were *destroyed by* the *destroyer*, express another kind of chastisement. I refer it, accordingly, to the history, which is recorded in the sixteenth chapter of Numbers. For when God had punished the pride of Korah and Abiram, the people raised a tumult against Moses and Aaron, as if they had been to blame for the punishment which the Lord had inflicted. This madness of the people God punished by sending down fire from heaven, which swallowed up many

[1] Billroth, in his Commentary on the Epistles to the Corinthians, alleges, that the view that is here taken by CALVIN " could have been suggested only by reasons of a dogmatical character." The objection thus brought forward, however, is satisfactorily set aside in a valuable note by Dr. Alexander, in his translation of Billroth. See Biblical Cabinet, No. xxi. pp. 246, 247. See also *Henderson* on Inspiration, pp. 553, 554.—*Ed.*

[2] " C'est à dire, l'Eternel;"—" That is to say, the Eternal."

[3] " De n'entrer point en la iouïssance de la terre promise;"—" Not to enter on the enjoyment of the promised land."

of them—upwards of fourteen thousand.   It is, therefore, a striking and memorable token of God's wrath against rebels and seditious persons, that murmur against him.

Those persons, it is true, *murmured* against Moses; but as they had no ground for insulting him, and had no occasion for being incensed against him, unless it was that he had faithfully discharged the duty which had been enjoined upon him by God, God himself was assailed by that murmuring.   Let us, accordingly, bear in mind that we have to do with God, and not with men, if we rise up against the faithful ministers of God, and let us know that this audacity[1] will not go unpunished.

By the *destroyer* you may understand the Angel, who executed the judgment of God.   Now he sometimes employs the ministry of bad angels, sometimes of good, in punishing men, as appears from various passages of Scripture.   As Paul here does not make a distinction between the one and the other, you may understand it of either.

11. *Now all these things happened as types.*   He again repeats it—that all these things happened to the Israelites, that they might be types to us—that is, ensamples, in which God places his judgments before our eyes.   I am well aware, that others philosophize on these words with great refinement, but I think that I have fully expressed the Apostle's meaning, when I say, that by these examples, like so many pictures, we are instructed what judgments of God are impending over idolaters, fornicators, and other contemners of God. For they are lively pictures, representing God as angry on account of such sins.   This exposition, besides being simple and accurate, has this additional advantage, that it blocks up the path of certain madmen,[2] who wrest this passage for the purpose of proving, that among that ancient people there was nothing done but what was shadowy.   First of all, they assume that that people is a figure of the Church.   From this they infer, that everything that God promised to them, or accomplished for them—all benefits, all punishments,[3]

1 " Ceste temerite outrecuidee;"—" This presumptuous rashness."
2 " Elle ferme la bouche à vn tas d'enragez;"—" It shuts the mouth of a troop of madmen."
3 " Qui leur sont aduenues;"—" Which happened to them."

only prefigured what required to be accomplished in reality after Christ's advent. This is a most pestilential frenzy, which does great injury to the holy fathers, and much greater still to God. For that people was a figure of the Christian Church, in such a manner as to be at the same time a true Church. Their condition represented ours in such a manner that there was at the same time, even then, a proper condition of a Church. The promises given to them shadowed forth the gospel in such a way, that they had it included in them. Their sacraments served to prefigure ours in such a way, that they were nevertheless, even for that period, true sacraments, having a present efficacy. In fine, those who at that time made a right use, both of doctrine, and of signs, were endowed with the same spirit of faith as we are. These madmen, therefore, derive no support from these words of Paul, which do not mean that the things that were done in that age were types, in such a way as to have at that time no reality, but a mere empty show. Nay more, they expressly teach us, (as we have explained,) that those things which may be of use *for our admonition,* are there set forth before us, as in a picture.

They are written for our admonition. This second clause is explanatory of the former ; for it was of no importance to the Israelites, but to us exclusively, that these things should be committed to record.[1] It does not, however, follow from this, that these inflictions were not true chastisements from God, suited for their correction at that time, but as God then inflicted his judgments, so he designed that they should be kept everlastingly in remembrance for our instruction. For of what advantage were the history of them to the dead ; and as to the living, how would it be of advantage to them, unless they repented, admonished by the examples of others? Now he takes for granted the principle, as to which all pious persons ought to be agreed—that there is nothing revealed in the Scriptures, that is not profitable to be known.

Upon whom the ends of the world are come. The word

[1] " Car quant aux Israelites qui viuoyent lors, il n'estoit point requis que ces choses fussent enregistrees et mises par escrit, mais seulement pour nous ;"—" For in so far as concerned the Israelites who lived at that time, it was not requisite that these things should be recorded and committed to writing, but solely on our account."

τέλη (ends) sometimes means *mysteries;*[1] and that signification would not suit ill with this passage. I follow, however, the common rendering, as being more simple. He says then, that the ends of all ages have come upon us, inasmuch as the fulness of all things is suitable to this age, because it is now the last times. For the kingdom of Christ is the main object of the Law and of all the Prophets. But this statement of Paul is at variance with the common opinion —that God, while more severe under the Old Testament, and always ready and armed for the punishment of crimes, has now begun to be exorable, and more ready to forgive. They explain, also, our being under the law of grace, in this sense—that we have God more placable than the ancients had. But what says Paul? If God inflicted punishment upon them, he will not the more spare you. Away, then, with the error, that God is now more remiss in exacting the punishment of crimes! It must, indeed, be acknowledged, that, by the advent of Christ, God's goodness has been more openly and more abundantly poured forth towards men; but what has this to do with impunity for the abandoned, who abuse his grace?[2]

This one thing only must be noticed, that in the present day the mode of punishment is different; for as God of old was more prepared to reward the pious with outward tokens of his blessing, that he might testify to them his fatherly love, so he showed his wrath more by corporal punishments. *Now,* on the other hand, in that fuller revelation which we enjoy, he does not so frequently inflict visible punishments, and does not so frequently inflict corporal punishment even upon the wicked. You will find more on this subject in my Institutes.[3]

12. *Wherefore let him that thinketh he standeth.* The

[1] The term is applied in this sense, more especially to the Eleusinian mysteries, which were called τὰ μεγάλα τέλη—*the great mysteries.* Plat. Rep. 560 E. See also Eurip. Med. 1379.—*Ed.*

[2] " Dequoy sert cela pour prouuer que les meschans, et ceux qui abusent de la grace de Dieu demeureront impunis?"—" Of what use is this for proving that the wicked, and those that abuse the grace of God, will go unpunished?"

[3] Our Author probably refers more particularly to that part of the *Institutes* in which he states the points of difference between the Old and the New Testaments. See *Institutes,* vol. i. pp. 525-529.—*Ed.*

Apostle concludes from what goes before, that we must not glory in our beginnings or progress, so as to resign ourselves to carelessness and inactivity.[1]   For the Corinthians gloried in their condition in such a way, that, forgetting their weakness, they fell into many crimes.   This was a false confidence of such a kind as the Prophets frequently reprove in the Israelitish people.   As, however, Papists wrest this passage for the purpose of maintaining their impious doctrine respecting faith, as having constantly doubt connected with it,[2] let us observe that there are two kinds of assurance.

The *one* is that which rests on the promises of God, because a pious conscience feels assured that God will never be wanting to it ; and, relying on this unconquerable persuasion, triumphs boldly and intrepidly over Satan and sin, and yet, nevertheless, keeping in mind its own infirmity, casts itself[3] upon God, and with carefulness and anxiety commits itself to him.   This kind of assurance is sacred, and is inseparable from faith, as appears from many passages of Scripture, and especially Romans viii. 33.

The *other* arises from negligence, when men, puffed up with the gifts that they have, give themselves no concern, as if they were beyond the reach of danger, but rest satisfied with their condition.   Hence it is that they are exposed to all the assaults of Satan.   This is the kind of assurance which Paul would have the Corinthians to abandon, because he saw that they were satisfied with themselves under the influence of a silly conceit.   He does not, however, exhort them to be always anxiously in doubt as to the will of God, or to tremble from uncertainty as to their salvation, as Papists dream.[4]   In short, let us bear in mind, that Paul is here addressing persons who were puffed up with a base confidence in the flesh, and represses that assurance which is grounded upon men—not upon God.   For after commending

---

[1] " Que nous-nous endormions comme gens asseurez, et sans grand soin ;"—" That we should resign ourselves to sleep, as persons who are confident, and without much care."

[2] " Par laquelle ils disent qu'il nous faut tousiours douter de la foy ;"— " By which they say that we must always doubt as to faith."

[3] " Se remet du tout ;"—" Commits itself wholly."

[4] The reader will observe that our Author has already touched upon this subject at some length, when commenting on chapter ii. 12.   See pp. 112, 113.—*Ed.*

the Colossians for the solidity or *steadfastness of their faith,* (Col. ii. 5,) he exhorts them to be *rooted in Christ,* to *remain firm,* and *to be built up* and *confirmed in the faith.* (Col. ii. 7.)

13. There hath no temptation taken you but such as is common to man: but God *is* faithful, who will not suffer you to be tempted above that ye are able; but will with the temptation also make a way to escape, that ye may be able to bear *it*.	13. Tentatio vos non apprehendit nisi humana. Fidelis autem Deus, qui non sinet vos tentari supra quam potestis: sed dabit una cum tentatione etiam exitum, ut possitis sustinere.
14. Wherefore, my dearly beloved, flee from idolatry.	14. Quapropter, dilecti mei, fugite ab idololatria.
15. I speak as to wise men; judge ye what I say.	15. Tanquam prudentibus loquor: iudicate ipsi quod dico.
16. The cup of blessing, which we bless, is it not the communion of the blood of Christ? The bread which we break, is it not the communion of the body of Christ?	16. Calix benedictionis, cui benedicimus, nonne communicatio est sanguinis Christi? panis, quem frangimus, nonne communicatio est corporis Christi?
17. For we *being* many are one bread, *and* one body: for we are all partakers of that one bread.	17. Quoniam unus panis, unum corpus multi sumus: omnes enim de uno pane participamus.
18. Behold Israel after the flesh: are not they which eat of the sacrifices partakers of the altar?	18. Videte Israel secundum carnem: nonne qui edunt hostias, altari communicant?

13. *No temptation has taken you.*[1] Let others take their own way of interpreting this. For my part, I am of opinion that it was intended for their consolation, lest on hearing of such appalling instances of the wrath of God, as he had previously related, they should feel discouraged, being overpowered with alarm. Hence, in order that his exhortation might be of advantage, he adds, that there is room for repentance. "There is no reason why you should despond; for I have not had it in view to give you occasion for despair, nor has anything happened to you but what is common to men." Others are of opinion that he rather chides their cowardice in giving way, on being so slightly tried;[2] and unquestionably the word rendered *human* is sometimes taken to mean moderate.[3] The meaning, then, according to

---

[1] " Tentation ne vous a point *saisis,* ou *surprins*;"—" No temptation has *taken,* or *overtaken* you."

[2] " Pour si petites et legeres tentations;"—" On so small and light trials."

[3] The word ανθρωπινος (*human*) may be understood here to mean—*proportioned to man's strength,* or *suited to man's weakness.* It is rendered in Tyndale's version, and also in Cranmer's: " Soche as followeth the

them would be this : " Did it become you thus to give way under a slight trial ?" But as it agrees better with the context, if we consider it as consolation, I am on this account rather inclined to that view.

But God is faithful. As he exhorted them to be of good courage as to the past, in order that he might stir them up to repentance, so he also comforts them as to the future with a sure hope, on the ground that *God would not suffer them to be tempted beyond their strength.* He exhorts them, however, to look to the Lord, because a temptation, however slight it may be, will straightway overcome us, and all will be over with us, if we rely upon our own strength. He speaks of the Lord as *faithful,* not merely as being true to his promises, but as though he had said : The Lord is the sure guardian of his people, under whose protection you are safe, for he never leaves his people destitute. Accordingly, when he has received you under his protection, you have no cause to fear, provided you depend entirely upon him. For certainly this were a species of deception, if he were to withdraw his aid in the time of need, or if he were, on seeing us weak and ready to sink under the load, to lengthen out our trials still farther.[1]

Now God helps us in two ways, that we may not be overcome by the temptation ; for he supplies us with strength, and he sets limits to the temptation. It is of the *second* of these ways that the Apostle here chiefly speaks. At the same time, he does not exclude the former—that God alleviates temptations, that they may not overpower us by their weight. For he knows the measure of our power, which he has himself conferred. According to that, he regulates our

---

nature of man." Most interpreters understand in a similar sense an expression which occurs in 2 Sam. vii. 14—*the rod of men, and stripes of the children of men.—Ed.*

[1] Mr. Fuller of Kettering, when comparing 1 Cor. x. 13, with 2 Cor. i. 8, justly observes : " The *ability* in the former of these passages, and the *strength* in the latter, are far from being the same. The one is expressive of that divine support which the Lord has promised to give to his servants under all their trials : the other, of the power which we possess naturally as creatures. We may be tried beyond this, as all the martyrs have been, and yet not beyond the other. The outward man may perish, while the inward man is renewed day by day."—Fuller's Works, vol. iii. p. 609.—*Ed.*

temptations.   The term *temptation* I take here as denoting, in a general way, everything that allures us.

14. *Wherefore, my beloved, flee,* &c.   The Apostle now returns to the particular question, from which he had for a little digressed, for, lest bare doctrine should have little effect among them, he has introduced those general exhortations that we have read, but now he pursues the discussion on which he had entered—that it is not allowable for a Christian man to connect himself with the superstitions of the wicked, so as to take part in them.   *Flee,* says he, *from idolatry.*   In the first place, let us observe what meaning he attaches to the term *Idolatry.*   He certainly did not suspect the Corinthians of such a degree of ignorance or carelessness[1] as to think, that they worshipped idols in their heart. But as they made no scruple of frequenting the assemblies of the wicked, and observing along with them certain rites instituted in honour of idols, he condemns this liberty taken by them, as being a very bad example.   It is certain, then, that when he here makes mention of *idolatry,* he speaks of what is outward, or, if you prefer it, of the profession[2] of idolatry.   For as God is said to be worshipped by the bending of the knee, and other tokens of reverence, while the principal and genuine worship of him is inward, so is it also as to idols, for the case holds the same in things opposite. It is to no purpose that very many in the present day endeavour to excuse outward actions[3] on this pretext, that the heart is not in them, while Paul convicts of idolatry those very acts, and assuredly with good reason.   For, as we owe to God not merely the secret affection of the heart, but also outward adoration, the man who offers to an idol an appearance of adoration takes away so much of the honour due to God.   Let him allege as he may that his heart is quite away from it.   The action itself is to be seen, in which the honour that is due to God is transferred to an idol.

15. *I speak as to wise men.*   As he was about to take his argument from the mystery of the Supper, he arouses them

---

[1] " Tant despourueus de sens et cognoissance de Dieu ;"—" So devoid of judgment and knowledge of God."

[2] " La profession et demonstrance ;"—" The profession and display."

[3] " Les actes ou gestes externes d'idolatrie ;"—" The outward acts or gestures of idolatry."

by this little preface, that they may consider more attentively the magnitude of the thing.[1]　" I do not address mere novices.　You understand the efficacy of the sacred Supper : in it we are ingrafted into the Lord's body.　How unseemly a thing is it then, that you should enter into fellowship with the wicked, so as to be united in one body?"　At the same time, he tacitly reproves their want of consideration in this respect, that, while accurately instructed in the school of Christ, they allowed themselves in gross vice, as to which there was no difficulty in forming an opinion.

16. *The cup of blessing.*　While the sacred Supper of Christ has two elements—bread and wine—he begins with the second.　He calls it, *the cup of blessing,* as having been set apart for a mystical benediction.[2]　For I do not agree with those who understand *blessing* to mean *thanksgiving,* and interpret the verb *to bless,* as meaning to *give thanks.* I acknowledge, indeed, that it is sometimes employed in this sense, but never in the construction that Paul has here made use of, for the idea of Erasmus, as to supplying a preposition,[3] is exceedingly forced.　On the other hand, the meaning that I adopt is easy, and has nothing of intricacy.

To *bless the cup,* then, is to set it apart for this purpose, that it may be to us an emblem of the blood of Christ.　This is done by the word of promise, when believers meet together according to Christ's appointment to celebrate the remembrance of his death in this Sacrament.　The consecration, however, which the Papists make use of, is a kind of sorcery derived from heathens,[4] which has nothing in common with the pure rite observed by Christians.　Everything, it is true, that we eat *is sanctified by the word of God,* as Paul himself elsewhere bears witness, (1 Tim. iv. 5;) but that *blessing* is for a different purpose—that our use of the gifts of God may be pure, and may tend to the glory of their Author, and to our advantage.　On the other hand, the design of the

---

[1] " L'excellence de ce mystere ;"—" The excellence of this mystery."

[2] " A la consecration mystique ;"—" For a mystical consecration."

[3] " Qu'on supplee *Pour ;*"—" That *for* should be supplied."　The original words ὃ εὐλογοῦμεν, are supposed by many eminent interpreters to be instead of καθ' ὃ εὐλογοῦμεν τὸν Θεόν—*for which we give thanks to God.*—Ed.

[4] The reader will find this subject more largely dwelt upon in the *Harmony,* vol. p. iii. 206.—*Ed.*

mystical *blessing* in the Supper is, that the wine may be no longer a common beverage, but set apart for the spiritual nourishment of the soul, while it is an emblem of the blood of Christ.

Paul says, that the *cup* which has been in this manner *blessed* is κοινωνίαν—the *communion* of the blood of the Lord.   It is asked, in what sense? Let contention be avoided, and there will be nothing of obscurity.   It is true, that believers are united together by Christ's blood, so as to become one body. It is also true, that a unity of this kind is with propriety termed κοινωνία. (*communion.*)   I make the same acknowledgment as to *the bread.*   Farther, I observe what Paul immediately adds, as it were, by way of explanation—that we *all become one body, because we are together partakers of the same bread.*   But whence, I pray you, comes that κοινωνία (*communion*) between us, but from this, that we are united to Christ in such a way, that *we are flesh of his flesh, and bone of his bones?* (Eph. v. 30.)   For we must first of all be incorporated (so to speak) into Christ, that we may be united to each other.   In addition to this, Paul is not disputing at present merely in reference to a mutual fellowship among men, but as to the spiritual union between Christ and believers, with the view of drawing from this, that it is an intolerable sacrilege for them to be polluted by fellowship with idols.   From the connection of the passage, therefore, we may conclude, that (κοινωνίαν) the *communion of the blood* is that connection which we have with the blood of Christ, when he ingrafts all of us together into his body, that he may live in us, and we in him.

Now, when the cup is called a *participation*, the expression, I acknowledge, is figurative, provided that the truth held forth in the figure is not taken away, or, in other words, provided that the reality itself is also present, and that the soul has as truly *communion in the blood*, as we drink wine with the mouth.   But Papists could not say this, that *the cup of blessing is a participation in the blood of Christ*, for the Supper that they observe is mutilated and torn : if indeed we can give the name of the Supper to that strange ceremony which is a patchwork of various human contrivances, and scarcely retains the slightest vestige of the institution of our Lord. But, supposing that everything else were as it ought to be, this one thing is at variance with the right use of the Supper—the keeping back of the whole of the people from partaking of the cup, which is the half of the Sacrament.

The bread which we break. From this it appears, that it was the custom of the ancient Church to break one loaf, and distribute to every one his own morsel, in order that there might be presented more clearly to the view of all believers their union to the one body of Christ. And that this custom was long kept up appears from the testimony of those who flourished in the three centuries that succeeded the age of the Apostles. Hence arose the superstition, that no one dared to touch the bread with his hand, but each one had it put into his mouth by the priest.

17. *For we are one bread.* I have already stated above,[1] that it was not Paul's particular design here to exhort us to love, but he mentions this by the way, that the Corinthians may understand that we must, even by external profession, maintain that unity which subsists between us and Christ, inasmuch as we all assemble together to receive the symbol of that sacred unity. In this second part of the statement, he makes mention only of the one part of the Sacrament, and it is the manner of Scripture to describe by Synecdoche[2] the entire Supper by *the breaking of bread.* It is necessary to warn my readers, in passing, as to this, lest any less experienced person should be put off his guard by the foolish cavil that is brought forward by certain sycophants—as if Paul, by mentioning merely the bread, had it in view to deprive the people of the one half of the Sacrament.

18. *Behold Israel after the flesh.* He establishes it by another example, that such is the nature of all sacred observances, that they bind us in a kind of fellowship with God. For the law of Moses admits no one to a feast upon a sacrifice, but the man who has duly prepared himself. I speak not of priests merely, but of those among the common people who eat of the remains of the sacrifice. Hence it follows, that all who eat of the flesh of the sacrificed victim, are *partakers with the altar,* that is, of the sanctification,

---

[1] See p. 335.
[2] A figure of speech in which a part is put for the whole.—*Ed.*

with which God has set apart his Temple, and the sacred rites that are performed in it.

This expression *after the flesh*, may seem to be added in order that the Corinthians, on comparing the two, might set a higher value on the efficacy of our Supper. " If there was so much virtue in the ancient figures and in those rudiments of youthful education, how much more must we reckon that there is in our mysteries, in which God shines forth much more fully upon us !" At the same time, it is more simple, in my opinion, to say that Paul intended merely by this mark to distinguish the Jews that were still under the law from those that had been converted to Christ. Now there was a contrast that remained to be made—that if the sacred rites appointed by God sanctify those who observe them, pollution, on the other hand, is contracted from the sacred rites rendered to idols.[1] For it is God alone that sanctifies, and hence all strange gods pollute.[2] Again, if mysteries[3] unite and connect believers with God, it follows, that the wicked are in like manner introduced by their superstitious rites into fellowship[4] with idols. But the Apostle, before proceeding to this, answers by an *anthypophora*[5] (anticipation) a question that might be proposed by way of objection.

19. What say I then ? that the idol is any thing, or that which is offered in sacrifice to idols is any thing ?

20. But I *say*, that the things which the Gentiles sacrifice, they sacrifice to devils, and not to God : and I would not that ye should have fellowship with devils.

21. Ye cannot drink the cup of the Lord, and the cup of devils : ye cannot be partakers of the Lord's table, and of the table of devils.

22. Do we provoke the Lord to jealousy ? are we stronger than he ?

19. Quid ergo dico ? idolum, aliquid esse ? aut idolo immolatum, aliquid esse ?

20. Sed quæ immolant Gentes, dæmoniis immolant, non Deo : nolo autem vos participes fieri dæmoniorum.

21. Non potestis calicem Domini bibere, et calicem dæmoniorum : non potestis mensæ Domini communicare, et mensæ dæmoniorum.

22. An provocamus Dominum ? numquid fortiores illo sumus ?

[1] " Des sacrifices et autres ceremonies des idoles ;"—" Sacrifices and other ceremonies rendered to idols."

[2] " Rendent profanes ceux qui les seruent ;"—"Render profane those who serve them."

[3] " Les sacremens ;"—" The sacraments."

[4] " Vne conionction et union auec leurs idoles ;"—" A connection and union with their idols."

[5] Anthypophora (ἀνθυποφορα) is a figure of speech, by which a speaker *anticipates* the objections of his opponent, and answers them. See p. 281, note.—*Ed.*

23. All things are lawful for me, but all things are not expedient: all things are lawful for me, but all things edify not.	23. Omnia mihi licent, sed non omnia conducunt: omnia mihi licent, at non omnia ædificant.
24. Let no man seek his own, but every man another's *wealth*.	24. Nemo quod suum est quærat, sed quisque quod alterius est.

19. *What do I say then ?* It might seem at first view as if the Apostle either argued inconclusively, or ascribed to idols something of existence and of power. Now it might readily be objected—"What comparison is there between the living God and idols ? God connects us with himself by the sacraments. Be it so. How comes it that idols, which are *nothing*, (1 Cor. viii. 4,) have so much power, as to be able to do the like ? Do you think that *idols are anything*, or can do anything ?" He answers, that he does not look to the idols themselves,[1] but rather has in view the intention of those who sacrifice to idols. For that was the source of the pollution that he had indirectly pointed out. He confesses, therefore, that an idol is nothing. He confesses that it is a mere delusion when the Gentiles take it upon them to go through solemn rites of dedication,[2] and that the creatures of God are not polluted by such fooleries. But as the design of them is superstitious and condemnable, and as the work is base, he infers, that all who connect themselves with them as associates, are involved in pollution.

20. *But the things[3] that the Gentiles sacrifice.* To complete the answer, a negative must be understood in this way : "I do not say that *an idol is anything*, nor do I imagine it to be endued with any virtue, but I say that *the Gentiles sacrifice to the devil and not to gods* those things which they do sacrifice, and hence I estimate the work by their wicked and impious superstition. For we must always look to the intention with which a thing is done. He, then, who connects himself with them, declares that he has fellowship with them in the same impiety." He proceeds accordingly

[1] " Simplement, et en soy ;"—" Simply, and in themselves."
[2] "Les ceremonies des dedicaces et consecrations solennelles desquelles les Gentils vsent, ne sont que vent, et n'emportent rien ;"—" The ceremonies of solemn dedications and consecrations, which the Gentiles make use of, are mere wind, and signify nothing."
[3] " Mais ie di, que les choses ;"—" But I say, that the things."

with what he had commenced : " If we had to do with God only, those things would be nothing, but, in relation to men, they become faulty ; because no one sits down to an idol feast, who does not declare himself to be a worshipper of the idol."

Some, however, understand the term *demons* here as meaning the imaginary deities of the Gentiles, agreeably to their common way of speaking of them ; for when they speak of *demons* they meant inferior deities, as, for example, heroes,[1] and thus the term was taken in a good sense.   Plato, in a variety of instances, employs the term to denote *genii*, or angels.[2]   That meaning, however, would be quite foreign to Paul's design, for his object is to show that it is no light offence to have to do with actions that have any appearance of putting honour upon idols.   Hence it suited his purpose, not to extenuate, but rather to magnify the impiety that is involved in it.   How absurd, then, it would have been to select an honourable term to denote the most heinous wickedness !   It is certain from the Prophet Baruch, (iv. 7,) that *those things that are sacrificed to idols are sacrificed to devils.* (Deut. xxxii. 17 ; Ps. xcvi. 5.)   In that passage in the writings of the Prophet, the Greek translation, which was at that time in common use, has δαιμόνια—*demons*, and this is its common use in Scripture.   How much more likely is it then, that Paul borrowed what he says from the Prophet, to express the enormity of the evil, than that, speaking after the manner of the heathen, he extenuated what he was desirous to hold up to utter execration !

It may seem, however, as if these things were somewhat

[1] " Ils entendoyent ceux qui estans hommes de grand renom, auoyent este faits dieux;"—" They meant those, who, being men of great renown, had been made gods."

[2] The following instances may be adduced from Plato (in Sympos.) :—Παν το δαιμονιον μεταξυ εστι θεου τε και θνητου—Every *demon* holds a middle place between God and mortal man ; Θεος ανθρωπω ου μιγνυται, αλλα δια δαιμονιων πασα εστιν η ομιλια και η διαλεκτος θεοις προς ανθρωπους—God does not hold direct converse with man, but all intercourse and communication is carried on between gods and men by means of *demons ;* Το Δαιμονιον εστιν ερμηνευον και διαπορθμενον θεοις τα παρ ανθρωπων, και ανθρωποις τα παρα θεων, των μεν τας δεησεις και θυσιας, των δε τας επιταξεις και αμοιβας των θυσιων— A *demon* is an interpreter and reporter from men to the gods, and from the gods to men —of the prayers and the sacrifices of the one, and the injunctions and rewards of devotion on the part of the other.—*Ed.*

at variance with what I stated a little ago[1]—that Paul had an eye to the intention of idolaters, for it is not their intention to worship devils, but imaginary deities of their own framing. I answer, that the two things are quite in harmony, for when men become so *vain in their imaginations* (Rom. i. 21) as to render divine honour to creatures, rather than to the one God, this punishment is in readiness for them—that they serve Satan. For they do not find that "middle place"[2] that they are in search of, but Satan straightway presents himself to them, as an object of adoration, whenever they have turned their back upon the true God.

I would not that ye. If the term *demon* were used in an indifferent sense, how spiritless were Paul's statement here, while, instead of this, it has the greatest weight and severity against idolaters! He subjoins the reason—because no one can have fellowship at the same time with God and with idols. Now, in all sacred observances, there is a profession of fellowship. Let us know, therefore, that we are then, and then only, admitted by Christ to the sacred feast of his body and blood, when we have first of all bid farewell to every thing sacrilegious.[3] For the man who would enjoy the one, must renounce the other. O thrice miserable the condition of those[4] who, from fear of displeasing men, do not hesitate to pollute themselves with unlawful superstitions! For, by acting in this way, they voluntarily renounce fellowship with Christ, and obstruct their approach to his health-giving table.

22. *Do we provoke the Lord?* Having laid down the doctrine, he assumes a more vehement tone, from observing, that what was a most atrocious offence against God was regarded as nothing, or, at least, was looked upon as a very trivial error. The Corinthians wished the liberty that they took to be reckoned excusable, as there is not one of us

---

[1] See p. 338.

[2] CALVIN has very probably in his eye here the sentiment of Plato already quoted—that "every *demon* holds a *middle place* between God and mortal man." See p. 339, *n.* 2.—*Ed.*

[3] " Quand auant que nous y presenter, nous auons renoncé à tous sacrileges, c'est a dire à toute impiete et idolatrie;"—" When, before approaching it, we have renounced everything sacrilegious, that is to say, all impiety and idolatry."

[4] " O plus que miserable la condition de ceux;"—" O more than miserable the condition of those."

that willingly allows himself to be found fault with, but, on the contrary, we seek one subterfuge after another, under which to shelter ourselves.   Now Paul says, and not without reason, that in this way we wage war against God ; for nothing does God more require from us than this—that we adhere strictly to everything that he declares in his word. Do not those, then, who use subterfuges,[1] in order that they may be at liberty to transgress the commandment of God, arm themselves openly against God ? Hence that curse which the Prophet denounces against all those who call *evil, good, and darkness, light.*   (Isaiah v. 20.)

Are we stronger ?   He warns them how dangerous a thing it is to *provoke God*—because no one can do this but to his own ruin.[2]   Among men the chance of war, as they speak, is doubtful, but to contend with God is nothing short of voluntarily courting destruction.   Accordingly, if we fear to have God as an enemy, let us shudder at the thought of framing excuses for manifest sins, that is, whatever stand opposed to his word.   Let us, also, shudder at the thought of calling in question those things that he has himself pronounced upon—for this is nothing less than to rise up against heaven after the manner of the giants.[3]   (Gen. xi. 4.)

23. *All things are lawful for me.*   Again he returns to the right of Christian liberty, by which the Corinthians defended themselves, and sets aside their objection by giving the same explanation as before.   " To eat of meats that were sacrificed, and be present at the banquet, was an outward thing, and therefore was in itself lawful."   Paul declares that he does not by any means call this in question, but he replies, that we must have a regard to edification. *All things are lawful for me,* says he, *but all things are not profitable,* that is, for our neighbours, for no one, as he immediately adds, ought to seek his own advantage exclusively, and if anything is not profitable to the brethren, it must be abstained from.   He, in the next place, expresses

---

[1] " Qui ne veulent point venir au poinct ;"—" Who are not willing to come to the point."

[2] " Ruine et condemnation ;"—" Ruin and condemnation."

[3] The reader will find the same incident in Sacred History referred to by our Author, and dwelt upon at considerable length, in the *Harmony,* vol. i. p. 58.   See also CALVIN on Genesis, vol. i. p. 328.—*Ed.*

the kind of advantage—when it *edifies,* for we must not have respect merely to the advantage of the flesh. " What then?[1] Does a thing that is in other respects permitted by God, come on this account to be unlawful—if it is not expedient for our neighbour. Then in that case our liberty would be placed under subjection to men." Consider attentively Paul's words, and you will perceive that liberty, nevertheless, remains unimpaired, when you accommodate yourself to your neighbours, and that it is only the use of it that is restricted, for he acknowledges that it is *lawful,* but says that it ought not to be made use of, if it does not *edify.*

24. *Let no one seek his own.* He handles the same subject in the 14th Chapter of the Romans. *Let no one please himself, but endeavour to please his brethren for their edification.* This is a precept that is very necessary, for we are so corrupted by nature, that every one consults his own interests, regardless of those of his brethren. Now, as the law of love calls upon us to *love our neighbours as ourselves,* (Matth. xxii. 39,) so it requires us to consult their welfare. The Apostle, however, does not expressly forbid individuals to consult their own advantage, but he requires that they should not be so devoted to their own interests, as not to be prepared to forego part of their right, as often as the welfare of their brethren requires this.

25. Whatsoever is sold in the shambles, *that* eat, asking no question for conscience sake:

26. For the earth *is* the Lord's, and the fulness thereof.

27. If any of them that believe not bid you *to a feast,* and ye be disposed to go; whatsoever is set before you, eat, asking no question for conscience sake.

28. But if any man say unto you, This is offered in sacrifice unto idols, eat not for his sake that shewed it, and for conscience sake: for the earth *is* the Lord's, and the fulness thereof:

29. Conscience, I say, not thine own, but of the other: for why is my liberty judged of another *man's* conscience?

25. Quicquid in macello venditur, edite, nihil disceptantes propter conscientiam.

26. Domini enim est terra, et plenitudo eius. (*Ps.* xxiv. 1.)

27. Si quis autem infidelium vos vocat, et vultis ire, quicquid vobis apponitur edite, nihil disceptantes propter conscientiam.

28. Quodsi quis vobis dixerit, Hoc est idolo immolatum: ne edatis propter eum qui indicavit, et propter conscientiam.

29. Conscientiam autem dico, non tuam, sed alterius: utquid enim libertas mea iudicatur ab alia conscientia?

[1] " Dira quelqu' vn;"—" Some one will say."

30. For if I by grace be a partaker, why am I evil spoken of for
that for which I give thanks?

31. Whether therefore ye eat, or
drink, or whatsoever ye do, do all to
the glory of God.

32. Give none offence, neither to
the Jews, nor to the Gentiles, nor
to the church of God:

33. Even as I please all *men* in
all *things*, not seeking mine own
profit, but the *profit* of many, that
they may be saved.

30. Si ergo per gratiam sum particeps, quid in eo blasphemor, in
quo gratias ago?

31. Sive ergo editis, sive bibitis,
sive quid aliud facitis, omnia in
gloriam Dei facite.

32. Nullis satis offendiculo, sive
Iudæis, sive Græcis, et Ecclesiæ
Dei:

33. Quemadmodum ego quoque
per omnia omnibus placeo, non
quærens quod mihi est utile, sed
quod multis, ut salvi fiant.

25. *Whatsoever is sold in the shambles.* He has spoken
above of dissembling in connection with idolatry, or, at least,
as to those actions which the Corinthians could not engage
in, without professing themselves to be the associates of the
wicked in their superstitions. He now requires them, not
merely to abstain from all professions of idolatry, but also
to avoid carefully all occasions of offence, which are wont to
arise from the indiscriminate use of things indifferent. For,
although there was but one kind of offence on the part of
the Corinthians,[1] there were, at the same time different degrees of it. Now, as to the eating of food, he makes, in the
first place, this general statement—that it is lawful to eat,
with a safe conscience, any kind of food, because the Lord
permits it. In the *second* place, he restricts this liberty as
to the use of it—lest weak consciences should be injured.
Thus this conclusion is divided into two parts: the *first* relates to liberty and power as to things indifferent: the *second*
to a limitation of it—that the use of it may be regulated in
accordance with the rule of love.

Debating nothing.[2] 'Ανακρίνεσθαι, the word that Paul
makes use of, means to reason on both sides,[3] in such a way,
that the person's mind vacillates, inclining now to this side,
and then to that.[4] Accordingly, in so far as concerns a

---

[1] " Car combien que les Corinthiens faissent en cela plusieurs fautes
qui estoyent toutes comprises sous vne generalite ;"—" For although the
Corinthians in this case committed many faults which were all comprehended under one general description."

[2] " Sans en enquerir rien ;"—" Without asking any question as to it."

[3] " Debatre en son entendement *pour* et *contre*, comme on dit ;"—" To
debate in one's mind *for* and *against*, as they say."

[4] 'Ανακρίνω, properly means to *examine narrowly.* It is stated by
Bloomfield, that " the best recent Commentators consider the expression

distinction of meats, he frees our consciences from all scruple and hesitation ; because it is proper that, when we are certain from the word of the Lord that he approves of what we do, we should have ease and tranquillity in our minds.

For conscience sake—that is to say, Before the judgment-seat of God—" In so far as you have to do with God, there is no occasion for your disputing with yourself, whether it be lawful or not.   For I allow you to eat freely of all kinds of meat, because the Lord allows you everything without exception."

26. *The earth is the Lord's.* He establishes, from the testimony of David, the liberty which he had allowed. (Psalms xxiv. 1, and l. 12.) But it will be asked by some one, " What has this to do with the point ?"   I answer, If *the fulness of the earth*[1] *is the Lord's,* there is nothing in the world that is not sacred and pure.   We must always keep in view, what the question is of which the Apostle treats.   It might be doubted, whether the creatures of God were polluted by the sacrifices of the wicked. Paul says they are not, inasmuch as the rule and possession of the whole earth remain always in the hands of God.   Now, what things the Lord has in his hands, he preserves by his power, and consequently sanctifies them.   The sons of God, therefore, have the pure use of everything, because they receive them no otherwise than from the hand of God.

The *fulness of the earth,*[2] is an expression which is made use of by the Prophet to denote the abundance of blessings, with which the earth is furnished and adorned by the Lord. For if the earth were stripped of trees, herbs, animals, and other things, it would be like a house devoid of furniture and every kind of utensil : nay more, it would be mutilated and disfigured. Should any one object, that the earth is cursed on account of sin, the answer is easy—that he has an eye to its pure and perfect nature, because Paul is speaking of believers, to whom all things are sanctified through Christ.

μηδὲν ἀνακρίνοντες, as put for μηδὲν κρέας (that is, κρέατος γένος) ἀνακρίνοντες, examining no kind of meat, to see whether it be idol-meat or not." This interpretation is natural, and agrees particularly well with the expression, as repeated in the 27th verse.—*Ed.*

[1] " C'est à dire, le contenu d'icelle ;"—" That is to say, what it contains."
[2] " Lequel mot nous auons traduit, Le contenu de la terre ;"—" Which expression we have rendered—What the earth contains."

27. *If any one of them that believe not invites you.* Here follows an exception, to this effect, that if a believer has been warned, that what is set before him has been offered to an idol, and sees that there is a danger of offence being given, he sins against the brethren if he does not abstain. He shows then, in short, that care must be taken not to hurt weak consciences.

When he says—*and you are willing to go,* he intimates indirectly, that he does not altogether approve of it, and that it would be better if they declined, but as it is a thing indifferent, he does not choose to forbid it absolutely. And, certainly, there could be nothing better than to keep at a distance from such snares—not that those are expressly to be condemned, who accommodate themselves to men only in so far as conscience permits,[1] but because it becomes us to proceed with caution,[2] where we see that we are in danger of falling.

29. *Conscience, I say, not thine own.* He always carefully takes heed not to diminish liberty, or to appear to take from it in any degree. "Thou oughtest to bear with the weak conscience of thy brother, that thou mayest not abuse thy right, so as to give occasion of offence to him ; but in the meantime thy conscience remains, nevertheless, free, because it is exempted from that subjection. Let not, therefore, the restraint which I impose upon thee as to outward use, become by any means a snare to entangle thy conscience."

It must be observed here, that the term *conscience* is taken here in its strict acceptation ; for in Rom. xiii. 5, and 1 Tim. i. 5, it is taken in a larger sense. "We ought, says Paul, to obey princes, *not merely for the sake of wrath, but also for that of conscience*"—that is, not merely from fear of punishment, but because the Lord orders it so, and it is our duty. Is it not reasonable, too, that we should for the same reason accommodate ourselves to weak brethren—that is, because we are to this extent subject to them in the sight of God ? Farther, *the end of the commandment is love out of a good conscience.* Is not the affection of *love* included in a

---

[1] "Seulement autant que faire se peut sans offenser Dieu ;"—"Only so far as they can do so without offending God."

[2] "Auec grand auis et prudence ;"—"With great care and prudence."

good conscience? Hence its meaning here is, as I have already stated, more restricted, inasmuch as the soul of a pious man looks exclusively to the tribunal of God, has no regard to men, is satisfied with the blessing of liberty procured for it by Christ, and is bound to no individuals, and to no circumstances of time or place.

Some manuscripts repeat the statement—*The earth is the Lord's.* But the probability is, that some reader having put it on the margin, it had crept into the text.[1] It is not, however, a matter of great importance.

For why is my liberty. It is doubtful, whether Paul speaks in this way of himself, or whether he makes this objection in the name of the Corinthians. If we take it as spoken in his own name, it will be a confirmation of the preceding statement. " In restricting yourself, for the sake of another man's conscience, your liberty is not thereby made subject to him." If in the name of the Corinthians, the meaning will be this: "You impose upon us an unjust law, in requiring that our liberty should stand or fall at the caprice of others." I am of opinion, that Paul says this of himself, but explains it in another way, for hitherto I have been stating the views of others. To be *judged,* then, I explain here as meaning—to be *condemned,* agreeably to the common acceptation of the word in Scripture. Paul warns us of the danger that must ensue, if we make use of our liberty unreservedly, so as to give occasion of offence to our neighbours—that they will *condemn* it. Thus, through our fault, and our unreasonableness, the consequence will be, that this special benefit from God will be *condemned.* If we do not guard against this danger, we corrupt our liberty by our abuse of it. This consideration, then, tends very much to confirm Paul's exhortation.

30. *If therefore by grace.* This argument is similar to the preceding one, or nearly so. " As it is owing to the kindness of God that *all things are lawful for me,* why should I act in such a manner, that it should be reckoned to my account as a vice?" We cannot, it is true, prevent the wicked from reviling us, nor even the weak from being

---

[1] It is omitted in the Alex., Clermont, and in all of the more ancient MSS.; and in the Syriac, Arabic, and Vulgate versions.—*Ed.*

sometimes displeased with us; but Paul here reproves the forwardness of those, who of their own accord give occasion of offence, and hurt weak consciences, when neither necessity or expediency calls for it. He would have us, then, make a good use of our benefits,[1] that the weak may not have occasion of reviling from our inconsiderate use of liberty.

31. *Whether, therefore, ye eat, or drink.* Lest they should think, that in so small a matter they should not be so careful to avoid blame, he teaches that there is no part of our life, and no action so minute,[2] that it ought not to be directed to the glory of God, and that we must take care that, even in eating and drinking, we may aim at the advancement of it. This statement is connected with what goes before; for if we are eagerly desirous of the glory of God, as it becomes us to be, we will never allow, so far as we can prevent it, his benefits to lie under reproach. It was well expressed anciently in a common proverb, that we must not *live to eat; but eat to live.*[3] Provided the end of living be at the same time kept in view, the consequence will thus be, that our food will be in a manner sacred to God, inasmuch as it will be set apart for his service.

32. *Be not occasions of stumbling to any.* This is the *second* point, which it becomes us to have an eye to—the rule of love. A desire, then, for the glory of God, holds the *first* place; a regard to our neighbour holds the *second.* He makes mention of *Jews and Gentiles*, not merely because the Church of God consisted of those two classes, but to teach us that we are debtors to all, even to strangers, that we may, if possible, *gain* them.   (1 Cor. ix. 20, 21.)

33. *Even as I please all men in all things.* As he speaks in a general way, and without exception, some extend it by mistake to things that are unlawful, and at variance with the word of the Lord—as if it were allowable, for the sake of our neighbour, to venture farther than the Lord permits us. It is, however, more than certain, that Paul accommo-

---

[1] " C'est a dire, de nostre liberte;"—" That is to say, of our liberty."

[2] " Qu'il n'y a rien en toute nostre vie, tant petit soit-il;"—" That there is nothing in our whole life, be it ever so small."

[3] The proverbial expression referred to occurs in Auctor. ad Herenn. 4. 28:—" *Esse* oportet ut *vivas*, non *vivere* ut *edas*;"—" You should *eat* to *live*—not *live* to *eat*."—*Ed.*

dated himself to men only in things indifferent, and in things lawful in themselves. Farther, the end must be carefully observed—*that they may be saved.* Hence what is opposed to their salvation ought not to be conceded to them,[1] but we must use prudence, and that of a spiritual kind.[2]

CHAPTER XI.

1. Be ye followers of me, even as I also *am* of Christ.

2. Now I praise you, brethren, that ye remember me in all things, and keep the ordinances, as I delivered *them* to you.

3. But I would have you know, that the head of every man is Christ; and the head of the woman *is* the man; and the head of Christ *is* God.

1. Imitatores mei estote, sicut et ego Christi.

2. Laudo autem vos, fratres, quod omnia mea meministis et traditiones[3] tenetis, quemadmodum vobis tradidi.

3. Volo autem vos scire, quod omnis viri caput est Christus, caput autem mulieris, vir: caput autem Christi, Deus.

[1] " Il ne leur faut pas accorder, et s'accommoder à eux en cela;"—"It is not proper to concede to them, and to accommodate ourselves to them in that."

[2] The view here given by CALVIN of the spirit by which Paul was actuated in this part of his conduct, is most successfully brought out, at greater length, by the Rev. Andrew Fuller, when comparing 1 Cor. x. 33, with Gal. i. 10.—"Though both these kinds of action are expressed by one term—to *please*—yet they are exceedingly diverse; no less so than a conduct which has the glory of God and the good of mankind for its object, and one that originates and terminates in self. The former of these passages should be read in connection with what precedes and follows it, (verses 31-33.) Hence it appears plain, that the *things* in which the Apostle *pleased all men*, require to be restricted to such things as tend to their ' profit, that they may be saved.' Whereas the things in which, according to the latter passage, he could *not* please men, and yet be the servant of Christ, were of a contrary tendency. Such were the objects pursued by the false teachers whom he opposed, and who desired to 'make a fair show in the flesh, lest they should suffer persecution for the cross of Christ.' (Ch. vi. 12.) The *former* is that sweet inoffensiveness of spirit which teaches us to lay aside all self-will and self-importance, that charity which ' seeketh not her own,' and ' is not easily provoked;' it is that spirit, in short, which the same writer elsewhere recommends from the example of Christ himself: 'We, then, who are strong, ought to bear the infirmities of the weak, and not to please ourselves. Let every one of us please his neighbour, for his good to edification: for even Christ pleased not himself; but, as it is written, The reproaches of them that reproached thee fell on me.' But the *latter* spirit referred to is that sordid compliance with the corruptions of human nature, of which flatterers and deceivers have always availed themselves, not for the glory of God or the good of men, but for the promotion of their own selfish designs."—*Fuller's Works*, vol. iii. pp. 595, 596.—*Ed.*

[3] " Mes ordonnances;"—"My ordinances."

4. Every man praying or prophesying, having *his* head covered, dishonoureth his head.

5. But every woman that prayeth or prophesieth with *her* head uncovered dishonoureth her head: for that is even all one as if she were shaven.

6. For if the woman be not covered, let her also be shorn: but if it be a shame for a woman to be shorn or shaven, let her be covered.

7. For a man indeed ought not to cover *his* head, forasmuch as he is the image and glory of God: but the woman is the glory of the man.

8. For the man is not of the woman; but the woman of the man.

9. Neither was the man created for the woman; but the woman for the man.

10. For this cause ought the woman to have power on *her* head because of the angels.

11. Nevertheless neither is the man without the woman, neither the woman without the man, in the Lord.

12. For as the woman *is* of the man, even so *is* the man also by the woman; but all things of God.

13. Judge in yourselves: is it comely that a woman pray unto God uncovered?

14. Doth not even nature itself teach you, that, if a man have long hair, it is a shame unto him?

15. But if a woman have long hair, it is a glory to her: for *her* hair is given her for a covering.

16. But if any man seem to be contentious, we have no such custom, neither the Churches of God.

4. Omnis vir orans aut prophetans velato capite, dedecore afficit caput suum.

5. Omnis mulier orans aut prophetans aperto capite, dedecore afficit caput suum: perinde enim acsi radatur.

6. Si enim non velatur mulier, etiam tondeatur: si autem mulieri turpe est tonderi aut radi, veletur.

7. Vir quidem velato esse capite non debet, quum sit imago et gloria Dei: mulier autem gloria viri est.

8. Non enim est vir ex muliere, sed mulier ex viro.

9. Etenim non est creatus vir mulieris causa, sed mulier causa viri.

10. Propterea debet mulier potestatem habere super caput suum, propter angelos.

11. Cæterum neque vir absque muliere, neque mulier absque viro in Domino.

12. Quemadmodum enim mulier ex viro, sic et vir per mulierem: omnia autem ex Deo.

13. In vobis ipsis iudicate, deceatne mulierem retecto capite Deum precari.

14. An ne ipsa quidem natura vos docet, quod si vir comam alat, dedecus illi sit?

15. Si vero mulier comam alat, gloria sit illi? quoniam illi coma instar velamenti data est.

16. Quodsi quis videtur contentiosus esse, nos talem consuetudinem non habemus, neque Ecclesiæ Dei.

1. *Imitators of me.* From this it appears, how absurdly chapters are divided, inasmuch as this sentence is disjoined from what goes before, with which it ought to have been connected, and is joined to what follows, with which it has no connection. Let us view this, then, as the close of the preceding chapter. Paul had there brought forward his own example in confirmation of his doctrine. Now, in order that the Corinthians may understand that this would be becom-

ing in them, he exhorts them to *imitate* what he had done, *even as he had imitated Christ.*

Here there are two things to be observed—*first,* that he prescribes nothing to others that he had not first practised himself; and, *secondly,* that he directs himself and others to Christ as the only pattern of right acting. For while it is the part of a good teacher to enjoin nothing in words but what he is prepared to practise in action, he must not, at the same time, be so austere, as straightway to require from others everything that he does himself, as is the manner of the superstitious. For everything that they contract a liking for they impose also upon others, and would have their own example to be held absolutely as a rule. The world is also, of its own accord, inclined to a misdirected imitation, ($\kappa\alpha\kappa o\zeta\eta\lambda\acute{\iota}\alpha\nu$)[1] and, after the manner of apes, strive to copy whatever they see done by persons of great influence. We see, however, how many evils have been introduced into the Church by this absurd desire of imitating all the actions of the saints, without exception. Let us, therefore, maintain so much the more carefully this doctrine of Paul—that we are to follow men, provided they take Christ as their grand model, ($\pi\rho\omega\tau\acute{o}\tau\upsilon\pi o\nu$,) that the examples of the saints may not tend to lead us away from Christ, but rather to direct us to him.

2. *Now I praise you.* He passes on now to another subject—to instruct the Corinthians, what decorum ought to be observed in the sacred assemblies. For as a man's dress or gesture has in some cases the effect of disfiguring, and in others of adorning him, so all actions are set off to advantage by decorum, and are vitiated by the want of it. Much, therefore, depends upon decorum ($\tau\grave{o}$ $\pi\rho\epsilon\pi o\nu$,)[2] and that not merely for securing for our actions gracefulness and beauty, but also to accustom our minds to propriety. While this is true in a general way as to everything, it holds especially

---

[1] " $K\alpha\kappa o\zeta\eta\lambda\acute{\iota}\alpha,$ *an absurd imitation.* The term is used in this sense by Lucian. (V. 70.) Our author makes use of the same term in the *Harmony,* vol. i. p. 209, *n.* 2.—*Ed.*

[2] $T\grave{o}$ $\pi\rho\acute{\epsilon}\pi o\nu$ may be defined to be the union of propriety and grace. $\pi\rho\acute{\epsilon}\pi o\nu$ and $\kappa\alpha\lambda\grave{o}\nu$ being used among the Greeks and among the Romans, *pulchrum* and *decorum,* as synonymous terms. See Cic. de Off. i. 27.—*Ed.*

as to sacred things;[1] for what contempt, and, eventually,
what barbarism will be incurred, if we do not preserve dignity in the Church, by conducting ourselves honourably and
becomingly?   Hence he prescribes some things that are
connected with public order, by which sacred assemblies are
rendered honourable.   But in order to prepare them the
more for obedience, he commends, in the outset, their obedience in the past, inasmuch as they observed his ordinances; for inasmuch as he *had begotten* that Church to the
Lord, (1 Cor. iv. 15,) he had delivered to them a certain system, by which it was to be governed.   By retaining this,
the Corinthians gave reason to hope, that they would also in
future be docile.

It is surprising, however, that, while he now bestows upon
them this commendation, he had previously blamed them
for many things.   Nay more, if we consider the state of the
Church, such as has been previously described, they were
far from deserving this praise.   I answer, that there were
some that were infected with those vices which he had previously reproved, and indeed, some with one, others with
another; but, in the meantime, the form which he had prescribed to them had been retained by the entire body.   For
there is nothing of inconsistency in saying, that very many
sins, and of various kinds, prevail among a particular people
—some cheating, others plundering—some envying, others
quarrelling, and another class guilty of fornication—while,
at the same time, in respect of the public form of the Church,
the institutions of Christ and his Apostles are maintained.

This will appear more clearly when we come to see what
Paul means by παραδόσεις; (traditions;)[2] and independently
of this, it is necessary to speak of this word, for the purpose
of replying to Papists, who arm themselves with this passage for the purpose of defending their traditions.   It is a
common maxim among them, that the doctrine of the Apostles
consists partly of writings and partly of traditions.   Under
this *second* department they include not merely certain
foolish superstitions, and puerile ceremonies, with which

---

[1] " Es choses qui concernent le seruice de Dieu;"—" In things that concern the service of God."

[2] " Traditions ou ordonnances;"—" Traditions or ordinances."

they are stuffed, but also all kinds of gross abomination, directly contrary to the plain word of God, and their tyrannical laws, which are mere torments to men's consciences. In this way there is nothing that is so foolish, nothing so absurd—in fine, nothing so monstrous, as not to have shelter under this pretext, and to be painted over with this varnish. As Paul, therefore, makes mention here of *traditions,* they seize, as they are accustomed to do, upon this little word, with the view of making Paul the author of all those abominations, which we set aside by plain declaration of Scripture.

I do not deny, that there were certain traditions[1] of the Apostles that were not committed to writing, but I do not admit that they were parts of doctrine, or related to things necessary for salvation. What then? They were connected with order and government. For we know that every Church has liberty to frame for itself a form of government that is suitable and profitable for it, because the Lord has not prescribed anything definite. Thus Paul, the first founder of the Corinthian Church, had also framed for its regulation pious and seemly enactments—that *all things might be done decently and in order,* as he afterwards enjoins. (1 Cor. xiv. 40.) But what has this to do with those silly trifles of ceremonies, which are to be seen in Popery?[2] What has it to do with a worse than Jewish superstition? What has it to do with a tyranny worthy of Phalaris,[3] by which they torture miserable consciences? What has it to do with so many monstrous rites of idolatry? For the foundation of all right enactment was this : to observe the moderation that Paul made use of—not to compel persons to follow their enactments,[4] while, in the meantime, contriving everything that might strike their fancy, but to require that they

---

[1] " Quelques ordonnances ;"—" Certain enactments."

[2] " Les sottes ceremonies et badinages, qu'on voit auiourd'huy en la Papaute ;"—" The silly ceremonies and fooleries that are to be seen in Popery at this day."

[3] " Ceste tyrannie plus que barbare ;"—" That worse than barbarous cruelty." Phalaris, the tyrant of Agrigentum in Sicily, was infamous for his cruelty. Cicero on more than one occasion employs the term *Phalarismus* to denote excessive cruelty. See Cic. Att. vii. 12, and Fam. vii. 11.—*Ed.*

[4] " Leurs arrests et determinations ;"—" Their decrees and determinations."

should be *imitated, in so far as they are imitators of Christ.*
But now, after having had the audacity to criticise everything agreeably to their own humour, to demand obedience
from all is exceedingly absurd.   Farther, we must know
that Paul commends their obedience in the past, in order
that he may render them docile also for the time to come.

3. *But I would have you know.*   It is an old proverb :
" Evil manners beget good laws."[1]   As the rite here treated
of had not been previously called in question, Paul had given
no enactment respecting it.[2]   The error of the Corinthians
was the occasion of his showing, what part it was becoming
to act in this matter.   With the view of proving, that it is an
unseemly thing for women to appear in a public assembly with
their heads uncovered, and, on the other hand, for men to
pray or prophesy with their heads covered, he sets out with
noticing the arrangements that are divinely established.

He says, that *as Christ is subject to God as his head, so is
the man subject to Christ, and the woman to the man.*   We
shall afterwards see, how he comes to infer from this, that
women ought to have their heads covered.   Let us, for the
present, take notice of those four gradations which he points
out.   God, then, occupies the *first* place : Christ holds the
second place.   How so ?   Inasmuch as he has in our flesh
made himself subject to the Father, for, apart from this,
being of one essence with the Father, he is his equal.   Let
us, therefore, bear it in mind, that this is spoken of Christ
as mediator.   He is, I say, inferior to the Father, inasmuch
as he assumed our nature, *that he might be the first-born
among many brethren.*

There is somewhat more of difficulty in what follows.
Here the man is placed in an intermediate position between
Christ and the woman, so that Christ is not the head of the
woman.   Yet the same Apostle teaches us elsewhere, (Gal.
iii. 28,) that *in Christ there is neither male nor female.*   Why
then does he make a distinction here, which in that passage

---

[1] Matthew Henry makes use of this proverb in his Commentary, when
summing up the contents of Luke xv.—*Ed.*

[2] " N'en auoit rien touché es enseignemens qu'il auoit donnez ;"—" Had
not touched upon it at all in the instructions which he had given."

he does away with? I answer, that the solution of this depends on the connection in which the passages occur. When he says that there is no difference between the man and the woman, he is treating of Christ's spiritual kingdom, in which individual distinctions[1] are not regarded, or made any account of; for it has nothing to do with the body, and has nothing to do with the outward relationships of mankind, but has to do solely with the mind—on which account he declares that there is no difference, even between *bond* and *free.* In the meantime, however, he does not disturb civil order or honorary distinctions, which cannot be dispensed with in ordinary life. Here, on the other hand, he reasons respecting outward propriety and decorum—which is a part of ecclesiastical polity. Hence, as regards spiritual connection in the sight of God, and inwardly in the conscience, Christ is the head of the man and of the woman without any distinction, because, as to that, there is no regard paid to male or female; but as regards external arrangement and political decorum, the man follows Christ and the woman the man, so that they are not upon the same footing, but, on the contrary, this inequality exists. Should any one ask, what connection marriage has with Christ, I answer, that Paul speaks here of that sacred union of pious persons, of which Christ is the officiating priest,[2] and He in whose name it is consecrated.

4. *Every man praying.* Here there are two propositions. The first relates to the *man,* the other to the *woman.* He says that the *man* commits an offence against Christ his head, if he *prays or prophesies with his head covered.* Why so? Because he is subject to Christ, with this understanding, that he is to hold the first place in the government of the house—for the father of the family is like a king in his own house. Hence the glory of God shines forth in him, in consequence of the authority with which he is invested. If he covers his head, he lets himself down from that preeminence which God had assigned to him, so as to be in subjection. Thus the honour of Christ is infringed upon.

---

[1] " Les qualites externes :"—" External qualities."
[2] " Autheur et conducteur ;"—" Author and conductor."

For example,[1] If the person whom the prince has appointed as his lieutenant, does not know how to maintain his proper station,[2] and instead of this, exposes his dignity to contempt on the part of persons in the lowest station, does he not bring dishonour upon his prince? In like manner, if the *man* does not keep his own station—if he is not subject to Christ in such a way as to preside over his own family with authority, he obscures, to that extent, the glory of Christ, which shines forth in the well regulated order of marriage The *covering*, as we shall see ere long, is an emblem of authority intermediate and interposed.

Prophesying I take here to mean—declaring the mysteries of God for the edification of the hearers, (as afterwards in chapter xiv.) as *praying* means preparing a form of prayer, and taking the lead, as it were, of all the people—which is the part of the public teacher,[3] for Paul is not arguing here as to every kind of prayer, but as to solemn prayer in public. Let us, however, bear in mind, that in this matter the error is merely in so far as decorum is violated, and the distinction of rank which God has established, is broken in upon. For we must not be so scrupulous as to look upon it as a criminal thing for a teacher to have a cap on his head, when addressing the people from the pulpit. Paul means nothing more than this—that it should appear that the man has authority, and that the woman is under subjection, and this is secured when the man uncovers his head in the view of the Church, though he should afterwards put on his cap again from fear of catching cold. In fine, the *one* rule to be observed here is το πρέπον—*decorum.* If *that* is secured, Paul requires nothing farther.

5. *Every woman praying or prophesying.* Here we have the *second* proposition—that women ought *to have their heads covered* when they *pray* or *prophesy;* otherwise they *dishonour their head.* For as the *man* honours his head by

---

[1] " Mais afin de mieux entendre ceci, prenons vn exemple ;"—" But, that we may understand this better, let us take an example."

[2] " Se maintenir, et vser de son authorite ;"—" To keep his place, and maintain his authority."

[3] " Du ministre et docteur de l'Eglise ;"—" Of the minister and teacher of the Church."

showing his liberty, so the *woman*, by showing her subjection. Hence, on the other hand, if the woman uncovers her head, she shakes off subjection—involving contempt of her husband. It may seem, however, to be superfluous for Paul to forbid the woman to prophesy with her head uncovered, while elsewhere he wholly *prohibits women from speaking in the Church.* (1 Tim. ii. 12.) It would not, therefore, be allowable for them to prophesy even with a covering upon their head, and hence it follows that it is to no purpose that he argues here as to a covering. It may be replied, that the Apostle, by here condemning the one, does not commend the other. For when he reproves them for prophesying with their head uncovered, he at the same time does not give them permission to prophesy in some other way, but rather delays his condemnation of that vice to another passage, namely in chapter xiv. In this reply there is nothing amiss, though at the same time it might suit sufficiently well to say, that the Apostle requires women to show their modesty—not merely in a place in which the whole Church is assembled, but also in any more dignified assembly, either of matrons or of men, such as are sometimes convened in private houses.

For it is all one as if she were shaven. He now maintains from other considerations, that it is unseemly for women to have their heads bare. *Nature itself,* says he, abhors it. To see a woman shaven is a spectacle that is disgusting and monstrous. Hence we infer that the woman *has her hair given her for a covering.* Should any one now object, that her hair is enough, as being a natural covering, Paul says that it is *not,* for it is such a covering as requires another thing to be made use of for covering *it.* And hence a conjecture is drawn, with some appearance of probability—that women who had beautiful hair were accustomed to uncover their heads for the purpose of showing off their beauty. It is not, therefore, without good reason that Paul, as a remedy for this vice, sets before them the opposite idea—that they be regarded as remarkable for unseemliness, rather than for what is an incentive to lust.[1]

[1] " Sainct Paul pour remedier à ce vice, propose tout le contraire de ce

7. *The man ought not to cover his head, because he is the image.* The same question may now be proposed respecting the *image,* as formerly respecting the *head.* For both sexes were created in the image of God, and Paul exhorts women no less than men to be formed anew, according to that image. The *image,* however, of which he is now speaking, relates to the order of marriage, and hence it belongs to the present life, and is not connected with conscience. The simple solution is this—that he does not treat here of innocence and holiness, which are equally becoming in men and women, but of the distinction, which God has conferred upon the man, so as to have superiority over the woman. In this superior order of dignity the glory of God is seen, as it shines forth in every kind of superiority.

The woman is the glory of the man. There is no doubt that the woman is a distinguished ornament of the man ; for it is a great honour that God has appointed her to the man as the partner of his life, and a helper to him,[1] and has made her subject to him as the body is to the head. For what Solomon affirms as to a careful wife—that *she is a crown to her husband,* (Prov. xii. 4,) is true of the whole sex, if we look to the appointment of God, which Paul here commends, showing that the woman was created for this purpose—that she might be a distinguished ornament of the man.

8. *For the man is not from the woman.* He establishes by *two* arguments the pre-eminence, which he had assigned to men above women. The *first* is, that as the woman derives her origin from the man, she is therefore inferior in rank. The *second* is, that as the woman was created for the sake of the man, she is therefore subject to him, as the work ultimately produced is to its cause.[2] That the man is the beginning

qui leur sembloit ; disant, que tant s'en faut qu'en cela il y ait vne beaute pour attirer les hommes à connoitise, que plustot c'est vne chose laide et deshonneste ;"—" St. Paul, with the view of remedying this vice, sets forward quite the reverse of what appeared to them—saying, that so far from there being a beauty in this to allure men to lust, it is rather a thing that is ugly and unseemly."

[1] " Pour estre compagne à l'homme, pour viure auec luy, et pour luy aider ;"—" To be a companion to the man, to live with him, and to aid him."

[2] " Ainsi que l'œuure tendant à quelque fin est au dessous de sa cause

of the woman and the end for which she was made, is evident from the law. (Gen. ii. 18.) *It is not good for a man to be alone. Let us make for him,* &c. Farther, God *took one of Adam's ribs and formed Eve.* (Gen. ii. 21, 22.)

10. *For this cause ought the woman to have power.*[1] From that authority he draws an argument[2] in favour of outward decorum. "She is subject," says he, "let her then wear a token of subjection." In the term *power,* there is an instance of metonymy,[3] for he means a token by which she declares herself to be under the power of her husband; and it is a covering, whether it be a robe, or a veil,[4] or any other kind of covering.[5]

It is asked, whether he speaks of *married* women exclusively, for there are some that restrict to *them* what Paul here teaches, on the ground that it does not belong to virgins to be under the authority of a husband. It is however a mistake, for Paul looks beyond this—to God's eternal law, which has made the female sex subject to the authority of men. On this account all women are born, that they may acknowledge themselves inferior in consequence of the superiority of the male sex. Otherwise it were an inconclusive argument that Paul has drawn from *nature,* in saying that it were not one whit more seemly for a woman to *have*

---

et fin pour laquelle on le fait;"—"As a work fitted for some design is inferior to its cause and the design for which it is made."

[1] " Doit auoir sur la teste vne enseigne qu'elle est sous puissance;"—" She ought to have upon her head a token that she is under authority."

[2] " Vn argument et consequence;"—" An argument and inference."

[3] " Il y a de mot à mot au Grec, La femme doit auoir puissance sur la teste. Mais au mot de *puissance* il y a une figure appellee metonymie;"—" It is literally in the Greek, The woman ought to have power upon her head. But in the word *power* there is a figure called metonymy."

[4] " C'est la couuerture de teste, soit un chapperon, ou couurechef, ou coiffe, ou chose semblable;"—"It is a covering of the head, whether it be a hood, or a kerchief, or a coif, or anything of that kind."

[5] The term ἰξουσία (*exousia*) is considered by Bloomfield to be the *name* of an article of dress of which mention is made in Ruth iii. 15, and Isaiah iii. 23, and consisted of " a piece of cloth of a square form thrown over the head and tied under the chin." Granville Penn, on the other hand, considers it as nothing more than the (τι) κατα κιφαλης in the third verse of the chapter—*something on the head,* or a *covering on the head,* and notices it as remarkable, that in Wiclif's version (1380) the rendering is—" the woman schal have an *hilying* on hir heed," which the glossary explains by *covering.—Ed.*

her head uncovered than to be *shaven*—this being applicable
to virgins also.

Because of the angels. This passage is explained in various ways. As the Prophet Malachi (in the seventh verse
of the second chapter) calls priests *angels of God,* some are
of opinion that Paul speaks of *them;* but the ministers
of the word have nowhere that term applied to them by
itself—that is, without something being added ; and the
meaning would be too forced. I understand it, therefore,
in its proper signification. But it is asked, why it is that
he would have women have their heads covered *because
of the angels*—for what has this to do with them ? Some
answer : " Because they are present on occasion of the
prayers of believers, and on this account are spectators of
unseemliness, should there be any on such occasions." But
what need is there for philosophizing with such refinement ?
We know that angels are in attendance, also, upon Christ as
their head, and minister to him.[1] When, therefore, women
venture upon such liberties, as to usurp for themselves the
token of authority, they make their baseness manifest to
the angels. This, therefore, was said by way of amplifying,
as if he had said, " If women uncover their heads, not only
Christ, but all the angels too, will be witnesses of the outrage." And this interpretation suits well with the Apostle's
design. He is treating here of different ranks. Now he
says that, when women assume a higher place than becomes
them, they gain this by it—that they discover their impudence in the view of the angels of heaven.

11. *But neither is the man without the woman.* This is
added partly as a check upon men, that they may not insult
over women ;[2] and partly as a consolation to women, that
they may not feel dissatisfied with being under subjection.
" The male sex (says he) has a distinction over the female
sex, with this understanding, that they ought to be connected together by mutual benevolence, for the one cannot

---

[1] " Et sont tousiours à son commandement et seruice;"—" And are
always at his commandment and service."
[2] " Qu'ils n'ayent les femmes en desdain et mocquerie;"—" That they
may not hold women in disdain and derision."

do without the other. If they be separated, they are like the mutilated members of a mangled body. Let them, therefore, be connected with each other by the bond of mutual duty."[1]

When he says, *in the Lord,* he by this expression calls the attention of believers to the appointment of the Lord, while the wicked look to nothing beyond pressing necessity.[2] For profane men, if they can conveniently live unmarried, despise the whole sex, and do not consider that they are under obligations to it by the appointment and decree of God. The pious, on the other hand, acknowledge that the male sex is but the half of the human race. They ponder the meaning of that statement—*God created man : male and female created he them.* (Gen. i. 27, and v. 2.) Thus they, of their own accord, acknowledge themselves to be debtors to the weaker sex. Pious women, in like manner, reflect upon their obligation.[3] Thus the man has no standing without the woman, for that would be the head severed from the body ; nor has the woman without the man, for that were a body without a head. "Let, therefore, the man perform to the woman the office of the head in respect of ruling her, and let the woman perform to the man the office of the body in respect of assisting him, and that not merely in the married state, but also in celibacy ; for I do not speak of cohabitation merely, but also of civil offices, for which there is occasion even in the unmarried state." If you are inclined rather to refer this to the whole sex in general, I do not object to this, though, as Paul directs his discourse to individuals, he appears to point out the particular duty of each.

12. *As the woman is of the man.* If this is one of the reasons, why the man has superiority—that the woman was taken out of him, there will be, in like manner, this motive to friendly connection—that the male sex cannot maintain

[1] " Par ce lien d'aide et amitie mutuelle;"—" By this tie of mutual assistance and amity."
[2] " La necessite qui les presse et contraint;"—" The necessity that presses and constrains them."
[3] " Pensent à leur deuoir, et que de leur costé elles sont obligees aux hommes;"—" Think of their duty, and of their being under obligation, on their part, to men."

and preserve itself without the aid of women.   For this remains a settled point—that *it is not good for man to be alone*.
(Gen. ii. 18.)   This statement of Paul may, it is true, be
viewed as referring to propagation, because human beings
are propagated not by men alone, but by men and women ;
but I understand it as meaning this also—that the woman
is a needful help to the man, inasmuch as a solitary life is
not expedient for man.   This decree of God exhorts us to
cultivate mutual intercourse.

But all things of God.   God is the Source of both sexes,
and hence both of them ought with humility to accept and
maintain the condition which the Lord has assigned to them.
Let the *man* exercise his authority with moderation, and
not insult over the woman who has been given him as his
partner.   Let the *woman* be satisfied with her state of subjection, and not take it amiss that she is made inferior to
the more distinguished sex.   Otherwise they will both of
them throw off the yoke of God, who has not without good
reason appointed this distinction of ranks.   Farther, when
it is said that the man and the woman, when they are
wanting in their duty to each other, are rebels against the
authority of God, the statement is a more serious one than
if Paul had said, that they do injury to one another.

Doth not even nature itself.   He again sets forth *nature* as
the mistress of decorum, and what was at that time in
common use by universal consent and custom—even among
the Greeks—he speaks of as being *natural*, for it was not
always reckoned a disgrace for men to have long hair.[1]   Historical records bear, that in all countries in ancient times,
that is, in the first ages, men wore long hair.   Hence also

[1] It is remarked by President Edwards, that "the emphasis used, *αὐτὴ
ἡ φύσις, nature itself,* shows that the Apostle does not mean custom, but
nature in the proper sense.   It is true it was long custom that made
having the head covered a token of subjection, and a feminine habit or appearance, as it is custom that makes any outward action or word a sign or
signification of anything ; but nature itself, nature in its proper sense,
teaches that it is a shame for a man to appear with the established signs
of the female sex.   Nature itself shows it to be a shame for a father to
bow down or kneel to his own child or servant, because bowing down is,
by custom, an established token of subjection and submission."   Edwards
on Original Sin, part ii., chap. iii., sec. 3.—*Ed.*

the poets, in speaking of the ancients, are accustomed to apply to them the common epithet of *unshorn*.[1] It was not until a late period that barbers began to be employed at Rome—about the time of Africanus the elder. And at the time when Paul wrote these things, the practice of having the hair shorn had not yet come into use in the provinces of Gaul or in Germany. Nay more, it would have been reckoned an unseemly thing for men, no less than for women, to be shorn or shaven ; but as in Greece it was reckoned an unbecoming thing for a man to allow his hair to grow long, so that those who did so were remarked as effeminate, he reckons as *nature* a custom that had come to be confirmed.[2]

16. *But if any man seem.* A *contentious* person is one whose humour inclines him to stir up disputes, and does not care what becomes of the truth. Of this description are all who, without any necessity, abolish good and useful customs —raise disputes respecting matters that are not doubtful— who do not yield to reasonings—who cannot endure that any one should be above them. Of this description, also, are those (ἀκοινώνητοι) would-be-singular persons[3] who, from a foolish affectation,[4] aim at some new and unusual way of acting. Such persons Paul does not reckon worthy of being replied to, inasmuch as contention is a pernicious thing, and ought, therefore, to be banished from the Churches. By this he teaches us, that those that are obstinate and fond of quarrelling, should rather be restrained by authority than confuted by lengthened disputations. For you will never have an end of contentions, if you are disposed to contend with a combative person until you have vanquished him ;

[1] Instances of this occur in Ovid, Fast. ii. 30, and in Hor., Od. 2, 15, 11. Gaul, to the north of the Alps, was called Gallia *comata*, from the inhabitants *wearing their hair long.* Homer applies to the Greeks in his time the epithet of καρηκομόωντες—*long-haired.* Hom. Il., ii. 11.—*Ed.*

[2] " Il appelle Nature ceste coustume desia confermee par vn long temps et vsage commun ;"—" He gives the appellation of Nature to this custom, already confirmed by length of time and common use."

[3] " Qui ne se veulent en rien accommoder aux autres ;"—" Who are not disposed to accommodate themselves to others in anything."—The Greek word made use of by CALVIN here (ακοινωνητος) is employed by classical writers to mean—having no intercourse, or not caring to have intercourse with others. See Arist., Top. iii. 2, 8. ; Plat. Legg., 774 A.—*Ed.*

[4] " Et appetit sans raison ;"—" And unreasonable desire."

for though vanquished a hundred times, he would argue still.   Let us therefore carefully mark this passage, that we may not allow ourselves to be carried away with needless disputations, provided at the same time we know how to distinguish *contentious* persons.   For we must not always reckon as *contentious* the man who does not acquiesce in our decisions, or who ventures to contradict us ; but when temper and obstinacy show themselves, let us then say with Paul, that *contentions are at variance with the custom of the Church.*[1]

17. Now in this that I declare *unto you* I praise *you* not, that ye come together not for the better, but for the worse.

18. For first of all, when ye come together in the church, I hear that there be divisions among you; and I partly believe it.

19. For there must be also heresies among you, that they which are approved may be made manifest among you.

20. When ye come together therefore into one place, *this* is not to eat the Lord's supper.

21. For in eating every one taketh before *other* his own supper: and one is hungry, and another is drunken.

22. What? have ye not houses to eat and to drink in? or despise ye the church of God, and shame them that have not? What shall I say to you? shall I praise you in this? I praise *you* not.

17. Hoc autem denuntians non laudo, quod non melius, sed in peius convenitis.

18. Primum enim, convenientibus vobis in Ecclesiam, audio dissidia inter vos esse : et ex parte credo.

19. Oportet enim haereses quoque esse in vobis, ut qui probe sunt, manifesti fiant inter vos.

20. Convenientibus ergo vobis in unum, non est Dominicam coenam edere.

21. Unusquisque enim propriam coenam praesumit edendo : atque hic quidem esurit, ille autem ebrius est.

22. Numquid domos non habetis, ad edendum et bibendum, aut Ecclesiam Dei contemnitis, et pudore afficitis eos qui non habent? Quid vobis dicam? Laudabo vos in hoc? Non laudo,

His reproof of the fault previously noticed was but a mild and gentle admonition, because the Corinthians sinned in ignorance, so that it was proper that they should readily be forgiven.   Paul, too, had praised them in the outset, because they had faithfully *kept his enactments.* (1 Cor. xi. 2.)   Now he begins to reprove them more sharply, because they

---

[1] " Que ce n'est point la coustume de l'Eglise d'entrer en debats et contentions ;"—" That it is not the custom of the Church to enter into strifes and contentions."

offended more grievously in some things, and not through ignorance.

17. *But, in warning you as to this, I do not praise.*[1] For I translate it in this way, because Paul appears to have made the participle and the verb change places.[2] I am also not satisfied with the interpretation of Erasmus, who takes παραγγέλλειν as meaning to *command.* The verb to *warn* would suit better, but as to this I do not contend. There is an antithesis between this clause and the beginning of this chapter. " While I have praised you, do not think that it is unqualified commendation; for I have something to find fault with, as it is worthy of severe reproof." This, however, in my opinion, does not refer exclusively to the Lord's Supper, but also to other faults of which he makes mention. Let this then be taken as a general statement, that the Corinthians are reproved, because they *came together not for the better but for the worse.* Particular effects of this evil will be brought forward afterwards.

He finds fault with them, then, in the *first* place, because they *come not together for the better,*—and *secondly,* that they *come together for the worse.* The *second,* it is true, is the more serious, but even the *first* is not to be endured, for if we consider what is transacted in the Church, there ought never to be a *coming together* without some fruit. *There* the doctrine of God is listened to, prayers are offered up, the Sacraments are administered. The fruit of the Word is, when confidence in God and fear of him are increased in us—when progress is made in holiness of life—when we put off more and more the *old man,* (Col. iii. 9)—when we advance in *newness of life,* &c. (Rom. vi. 4.) The Sacraments have a tendency to exercise us in piety and love. The prayers, too, ought to be

---

[1] " *Or ie vous rememore ceci, non point eu louant.* Il y a au Grec mot à mot. Or rememorant ie ne loue point ;"—" *But I put you in mind of this, not praising you for it.* It is literally in the Greek : But putting you in mind I do not praise."

[2] In explanation of this remark, let it be observed that the reading in the Alexandrine MS. is as follows : Τοῦτο δὲ παραγγέλλω οὐκ ἐπαινῶν—But I warn you as to this, not praising. This reading is followed in the Latin and Syrian versions. In Wiclif (1380) the rendering is : " But this thing I comaunde, not preisynge." In Rheims (1582)—" And this I commaund ; not praising it."—*Ed.*

of use for promoting all these purposes. In addition to this, the Lord works efficaciously by his Spirit, because he wills not that his ordinances should be vain. Hence if the sacred assemblies are of no benefit to us, and we are not made better by them, it is our ingratitude that is to blame, and therefore we deserve to be reproved. For the effect of our conduct is, that those things, which, from their own nature, and from God's appointment, ought to have been salutary, become unprofitable.

Then follows the *second* fault—that they *come together for the worse.* This is much more criminal, and yet it almost always follows the other, for if we derive no advantage from God's benefits, he employs this method of punishing our carelessness—that we are *made worse* by them. It usually happens, too, that negligence gives birth to many corruptions, especially on this account, that those who do not observe the natural use of things usually fall erelong into hurtful inventions.[1]

18. *When ye come together in the Church, I hear there are divisions.* Some take the words *divisions* and *heresies,* as referring to that disorder (ἀταξίαν)[2] of which he speaks soon afterwards. I consider them as having a more extensive signification, and certainly it is not likely that he would employ terms so improper and unsuitable for the purpose of exposing that abuse.[3] For as to their alleging that he has expressed himself in more severe terms, with the view of exposing more fully the heinousness of the offence, I would readily grant this, if the meaning corresponded. It is, then, a reproof of a general kind—that they were not of one accord as becomes Christians, but every one was so much taken up with his own interests, that he was not prepared to accommodate himself to others. Hence arose that abuse, as to which we shall see in a little—hence sprung ambition and

---

[1] " Principalement pource que ceux qui ne regardeut pas à tenir le droit et naturel usage des choses, sont suiets à tomber incontinent en beaucoup d'inuentions peruerses et dangereuses;"—" Chiefly because those who do not take care to observe the right and natural use of things, are liable to fall straightway into many perverse and dangerous inventions."

[2] See p. 231, *n.* 2.

[3] " Qu'il leur remonstrera qu'ils fout en la Cene;"—" Which he will show that they have fallen into as to the Supper. '

pride, so that every one exalted himself and despised others —hence sprung carelessness as to edification—hence sprung profanation of the gifts of God.

He says that he *partly believes it,* that they might not think that he charged them all with this heinous crime, and might accordingly complain, that they were groundlessly accused. In the meantime, however, he intimates that this had been brought to him not by mere vague rumour, but by credible information, such as he could not altogether discredit.

19. *For there must be also heresies.* He had previously spoken of *divisions.* (verse 18.) Now he uses the term *heresies,* with the view of amplifying the more, as we may infer, too, from the word *also,* for it is added for the sake of amplification. (πρὸς αὔξησιν.) It is well known in what sense the ancients used those two terms,[1] and what distinction they made between Heretics and Schismatics.[2] *Heresy* they made to consist in disagreement as to doctrine, and *schism,* on the contrary, in alienation of affection, as when any one withdrew from the Church from envy, or from dislike of the pastors, or from ill nature. It is true, that the Church cannot but be torn asunder by false doctrine, and thus heresy is the root and origin of schism, and it is also true that envy or pride is the mother of almost all heresies, but at the same time it is of advantage to distinguish in this way between these two terms.

But let us see in what sense Paul employs them. I have already expressed my disapprobation of those who explain heresy as meaning the setting up of a separate table, inasmuch as the rich did not partake of their Supper along with the poor ; for he had it in view to point out something more hateful. But without mentioning the opinions of others, I take *schism* and *heresy* here in the way of less and greater. Schisms, then, are either secret grudges—when we do not see that agreement which ought to subsist among the pious —when inclinations at variance with each other are at work—when every one is mightily pleased with his own way,

---

[1] " Schisme et Heresie ;"—" Schism and Heresy."

[2] " Voyez l'Institution ;"—" See my Institutes," (vol. iii. p. 48.)

and finds fault with everything that is done by others. *Heresies* are when the evil proceeds to such a pitch that open hostility is discovered, and persons deliberately divide themselves into opposite parties.   Hence, in order that believers might not feel discouraged on seeing the Corinthians torn with *divisions*, the Apostle turns round this occasion of offence in an opposite direction, intimating that the Lord does rather by such trials make proof of his people's constancy. A lovely consolation ! " So far, says he, should we be from being troubled, or cast down, when we do not see complete unity in the Church, but on the contrary some threatenings of separation from want of proper agreement, that even if sects should start up,[1] we ought to remain firm and constant. For in this way hypocrites are detected—in this way, on the other hand, the sincerity of believers is tried.   For as this gives occasion for discovering the fickleness of those who were not rooted in the Lord's Word, and the wickedness of those who had assumed the appearance of good men, so the good afford a more signal manifestation of their constancy and sincerity."

But observe what Paul says—*there must be*, for he intimates by this expression, that this state of matters does not happen by chance, but by the sure providence of God, because he has it in view to try his people, as gold in the furnace, and if it is agreeable to the mind of God, it is, consequently, expedient.   At the same time, however, we must not enter into thorny disputes, or rather into labyrinths as to a fatal necessity.   We know that there never will be a time when there will not be many reprobates.   We know that they are governed by the spirit of Satan, and are effectually drawn away to what is evil.   We know that Satan, in his activity, leaves no stone unturned with the view of breaking up the unity of the Church.   From this—not from fate—comes that necessity of which Paul makes mention.[2] We know, also, that the Lord, by his admirable wisdom,

---

[1] " De tous costez ;"—" On all sides."

[2] " De là vient ceste necessite de laquelle S. Paul fait mention, et non pas de ce Fatum que les Stoiques ont imaginé, que l'on nomme communeement Destinee.   Voyez l' Institution ;"—" From this comes that necessity of which St. Paul makes mention, and not from that Fate of

turns Satan's deadly machinations so as to promote the salvation of believers.[1] Hence comes that design of which he speaks—*that the good may shine forth more conspicuously ;* for we ought not to ascribe this advantage to *heresies*, which, being evil, can produce nothing but what is evil, but to God, who, by his infinite goodness, changes the nature of things, so that those things are salutary to the elect, which Satan had contrived for their ruin. As to Chrysostom's contending that the particle *that* (ἵνα) denotes not the cause, but the event, it is of no great moment. For the cause is the secret counsel of God,[2] by which things that are evil are overruled in such a manner, as to have a good issue. We know, in fine, that the wicked are impelled by Satan in such a manner, that they both act and are acted upon with the consent of their wills.[3] Hence they are without excuse.

20. *This is not to eat the Lord's supper.* He now reproves the abuse that had crept in among the Corinthians as to the Lord's Supper, in respect of their mixing up profane banquets with the sacred and spiritual feast, and that too with contempt of the poor. Paul says, that in this way it is not *the Lord's supper* that is partaken of—not that a single abuse altogether set aside the sacred institution of Christ, and reduced it to nothing, but that they polluted the sacrament by observing it in a wrong way. For we are accustomed to say, in common conversation, that a thing is not done at all, if it is not done aright. Now this was no trivial abuse, as we shall afterwards see. If you understand the words *is not* as meaning, *is not allowable*,[4] the meaning

which the Stoics have dreamed, and which is commonly called destiny. See the Institutes." (Vol. i. p. 241.)

[1] " Conuertit au profit et salut des fideles les machinations de Satan horribles et pernicieuses ;"—" Turns the horrible and pernicious machinations of Satan to the advantage and salvation of believers."

[2] " Car à parler proprement, la cause de ceci depend du secret conseil de Dieu ;"—" For, properly speaking, the cause of this depends on the secret counsel of God."

[3] " Ce qu'ils font, et ce que Satan leur fait faire, ils le font volontairement, et non point par force ;"—" What they do, and what Satan makes them do, they do voluntarily, and not from force."

[4] Paraeus and some others take the words οὐκ ἔστι, *is not*, as used for οὐκ ἔξεστι, *is not allowable.*—*Ed.*

will amount to the same thing—that the Corinthians were not in a state of preparation for partaking of *the Lord's supper*, as being in so divided a state. What I stated a little ago, however, is more simple—that he condemns that profane admixture, which had nothing in it akin to the Lord's Supper.

21. *For every one of you taketh before others his own supper.* It is truly wonderful, and next to a miracle,[1] that Satan could have accomplished so much in so short a time. We are, however, admonished by this instance, how much antiquity, without reason on its side, can effect, or, in other words, how much influence a long continued custom has, while not sanctioned by a single declaration of the word of God. This, having become customary, was looked upon as lawful. Paul was then at hand to interfere. What then must have been the state of matters after the death of the Apostles? With what liberty Satan must have sported himself.[2] Yet here is the great strength of Papists: "The thing is ancient—it was done long ago—let it, therefore, have the weight of a revelation from heaven."

It is uncertain, however, what was the origin of this abuse, or what was the occasion of its springing up so soon. Chrysostom is of opinion, that it originated in the love-feasts,[3] ($\dot{a}\pi\dot{o}\ \tau\hat{\omega}\nu\ \dot{a}\gamma a\pi\hat{\omega}\nu$) and that, while the rich had been accustomed[4] to bring with them from their houses the means of feasting with the poor indiscriminately and in common, they afterwards began to exclude the poor, and to guzzle over their delicacies by themselves. And, certainly, it appears from Tertullian, that that custom was a very ancient one.[5] Now they gave the name of *Agapae*[6] to those com-

---

[1] " Quasi incroyable;"—" As it were incredible."

[2] " A ioué ses tours;"—" Have played off his tricks."

[3] " Vne sorte de banquets qui se faisoyent par charite;"—" A kind of banquets that were held, by way of love."

[4] " Premierement;"—" At first."

[5] PLINY is supposed to refer to the $A\gamma a\pi a\iota$ (*love-feasts*) in his 97th letter to Trajan, where he says of the Christians in Bithynia, of which he was governor, that, upon examination, they affirmed, that after having taken their *sacramentum*—" morem sibi discedendi fuisse, rursusque coëundi ad capiendum cibum, promiscuum tamen et innoxium;"—" it was customary for them to depart, and come together again for the purpose of taking an innocent repast in common."—*Ed.*

[6] " *Agapas*, c'est à dire Charitez;"—" *Agapae*, that is to say—Loves."

mon entertainments, which they contrived among themselves, as being tokens of fraternal affection, and consisted
of alms. Nor have I any doubt, that it took its rise from
sacrificial rites commonly observed both by Jews and Gentiles. For I observe that Christians, for the most part,
corrected the faults connected with those rites, in such a
manner, as to retain at the same time some resemblance.
Hence it is probable, that, on observing that both Jews and
Gentiles added a feast to their sacrifice, as an appendage
to it, but that both of them sinned in respect of ambition,
luxury, and intemperance, they instituted[1] a kind of banquet, which might accustom them rather to sobriety and
frugality,[2] and might, at the same time, be in accordance
with a spiritual entertainment in respect of mutual fellowship. For in it the poor were entertained at the expense
of the rich, and the table was open to all. But, whether
they had from the very first fallen into this profane abuse,
or whether an institution, otherwise not so objectionable,
had in this way degenerated in process of time, Paul would
have them in no way mix up this spiritual banquet with
common feasts. "This, indeed, looks well—that the poor
along with the rich partake in common of the provisions
that have been brought, and that the rich share of their
abundance along with the needy, but nothing ought to have
such weight with us as to lead us to profane the holy
sacrament."[3]

And one is hungry. This was one evil in the case, that
while the rich indulged themselves sumptuously, they appeared, in a manner, to reproach the poor for their poverty.
The inequality he describes hyperbolically, when he says,
that some are *drunken* and others are *hungry,* for some had
the means of stuffing themselves well, while others had
slender fare. Thus the poor were exposed to the derision
of the rich, or at least they were exposed to shame. It was,

---

[1] " Par succession de temps ;"—" In process of time."
[2] " Qu'autrement ;"—" Than otherwise."
[3] " Mais il n'y a consideration aucune qui nous doyue tant esmouuoir,
que pour cela nous venions à profaner ce sainct mystere ;"—" But there is
no consideration that should have so much influence over us, that we
should come, on that account, to profane this holy sacrament."

therefore, an unseemly spectacle, and not in accordance with the *Lord's supper.*

22. *Have ye not houses?* From this we see that the Apostle was utterly dissatisfied with this custom of feasting, even though the abuse formerly mentioned had not existed. For, though it seems allowable for the whole Church to partake at one common table, yet this, on the other hand, is wrong—to convert a sacred assembly to purposes foreign to its nature. We know for what exercises a Church should assemble—to hear doctrine, to pour forth prayers, and sing hymns to God, to observe the sacraments,[1] to make confession of their faith, and to engage in pious observances, and other exercises of piety. If anything else is done there, it is out of place. Every one has his own house appointed him for eating and drinking, and hence that is an unseemly thing in a sacred assembly.

What shall I say to you? Having fully stated the case, he now calls them to consider, whether they are *worthy to be praised,* for they could not defend an abuse that was so manifest. He presses them still further, by asking—" What else could I do? Will you say that you are unjustly reproved?" Some manuscripts connect the words *in this* with the verb that follows—in this way: *Shall I praise you? In this I do not praise you.*[2] The other reading, however, is the more generally received among the Greeks, and it suits better.

23. For I have received of the Lord that which also I delivered unto you, That the Lord Jesus the *same* night in which he was betrayed took bread:

24. And when he had given thanks, he brake *it*, and said, Take, eat: this is my body, which is broken for you: this do in remembrance of me.

23. Ego enim accepi a Domino, quod etiam tradidi vobis: quod Dominus Iesus nocte qua traditus est, accepit panem:

24. Et gratiis actis, fregit, et dixit, Accipite, edite: hoc est corpus meum quod pro vobis frangitur: hoc facite in mei memoriam.

[1] " Pour receuoir et administrer les sacrements;"—" To receive and administer the sacraments."

[2] The earlier English versions follow this reading. Thus Wiclif, (1380) —*What schal I seie to zou? I preise zou: but hereynne I preise zou not;* Tyndale, (1534)—*What shall I saye unto you? Shall I prayse you: In this prayse I you not;* Cranmer, (1539)—*What shall I saye unto you? Shall I prayse you? In this prayse I you not.—Ed.*

25. After the same manner also *he took* the cup, when he had supped, saying, This cup is the new testament in my blood : this do ye, as oft as ye drink *it*, in remembrance of me.

26. For as often as ye eat this bread, and drink this cup, ye do shew the Lord's death till he come.

27. Wherefore, whosoever shall eat this bread, and drink *this* cup of the Lord, unworthily, shall be guilty of the body and blood of the Lord.

28. But let a man examine himself, and so let him eat of *that* bread, and drink of *that* cup.

29. For he that eateth and drinketh unworthily, eateth and drinketh damnation to himself, not discerning the Lord's body.

25. Similiter et calicem, postquam coenaverant, dicens, Hic calix Novum testamentum est in sanguine meo : hoc facite, quotiescunque biberitis, in mei memoriam.

26. Quotiescunque enim ederitis panem hunc, et biberitis hunc calicem, mortem Domini annuntiabitis, donec veniat.

27. Itaque quisquis ederit panem hunc, aut biberit calicem Domini indigne, reus erit corporis et sanguinis Domini.

28. Probet autem homo se ipsum, et sic de pane illo edat, et de calice bibat.

29. Qui enim ederit aut biberit indigne, iudicium sibi edit ac bibit, non discernens corpus Domini.

Hitherto he has been exposing the abuse ;[1] now he proceeds to show what is the proper method of rectifying it. For the institution of Christ is a sure rule, so that if you turn aside from it but a very little, you are out of the right course. Hence, as the Corinthians had deviated from this rule, he calls them back to it. It is a passage that ought to be carefully observed, as showing that there is no remedy for correcting and purging out abuses, short of a return to God's pure institution. Thus the Lord himself—when he was discoursing respecting marriage, (Matt. xix. 3,) and the Scribes brought forward custom, and also the permission given by Moses—simply brings forward his Father's institution, as being an inviolable law. When we do this at the present day, the Papists cry out, that we are leaving nothing untouched.[2] We openly demonstrate, that it is not in one point merely that they have degenerated from our Lord's first institution, but that they have corrupted it in a thousand ways. Nothing is more manifest than that their Mass is diametrically opposed to the sacred Supper of our Lord. I

[1] " Qu'ils commettoyent en la Cene ;"—" Which they had fallen into as to the Supper."

[2] " Que nous gastons tout, et ne laissons rien en son entièr ;"—" That we are destroying everything, and are leaving nothing entire."

go farther—we show in the plainest manner, that it is full of wicked abominations : hence there is need of reformation. We demand—what it appears Paul had recourse to—that our Lord's institution be the common rule, to which we agree on both sides to make our appeal. This they oppose with all their might. Mark then the nature of the controversy at this day in reference to the Lord's Supper.

23. *I received from the Lord.* In these words he intimates, that there is no authority that is of any avail in the Church, but that of the Lord alone. "I have not delivered to you an invention of my own : I had not, when I came to you, contrived a new kind of *Supper*, according to my own humour, but have Christ as my authority, *from whom I received what I have delivered unto you,* in the way of handing it over."[1] Return, then, to the original source. Thus, bidding adieu to human laws, the authority of Christ will be maintained in its stability.

That night in which he was betrayed.   This circumstance as to time instructs us as to the design of the sacrament— that the benefit of Christ's death may be ratified in us. For the Lord might have some time previously committed to the Apostles this covenant-seal,[2] but he waited until the time of his oblation, that the Apostles might see soon after accomplished in reality in his body, what he had represented to them in the *bread* and the *wine*. Should any one infer from this, that the Supper ought, therefore, to be celebrated at night and after a bodily repast, I answer, that, in what our Lord did, we must consider what there is that he would have to be done by us. It is certain, that he did not mean to institute a kind of nightly festival, like that in honour of Ceres,[3] and farther, that it was not his design to invite his

---

[1] Our Author seems to allude here to what he had said previously, when commenting on 1 Cor. iv. 1, as to the duty devolving on *stewards of the mysteries of God.*   See p. 150.—*Ed.*

[2] " Car le Seigneur pouuoit bien quelque temps deuant ordonner à ses Apostres l'obseruation de ce Sacrement ;"—" For the Lord might have on some previous occasion appointed to his Apostles the observance of this Sacrament."

[3] " Vne ceremonie, qui ne peust faire que de nuit, comme les Payens auoyent la feste de Ceres ;"—" A ceremony which could only be observed at night, as the heathens held the festival of Ceres."   The *time* when the

people to come to this spiritual banquet with a well-filled stomach. Such actions of Christ as are not intended for our imitation, should not be reckoned as belonging to his institution.[1] In this way, there is no difficulty in setting aside that subtilty of Papists, by which they shift off[2] what I have already stated as to the duty of maintaining and preserving Christ's institution in its simplicity. "We will, therefore," say they, "not receive the Lord's Supper except at night, and we will therefore take it—not when fasting, but after having dined." All this, I say, is mere trifling; for it is easy to distinguish what our Lord did, in order that we might imitate it, or rather what he did with the view of commanding us to do the like.

24. *Having given thanks.* Paul observes elsewhere, that every gift that we receive from the hand of God *is sanctified to us by the word and prayer.* (1 Tim. iv. 5.) Accordingly, we nowhere read that the Lord tasted bread along with his disciples, but there is mention made of his *giving thanks,* (John vi. 23,) by which example he has assuredly instructed us to do the like. This *giving of thanks,* however, has a reference to something higher, for Christ *gives thanks* to the Father for his mercy[3] towards the human race, and the inestimable benefit of redemption; and he invites us, by his example, to raise up our minds as often as we approach the sacred table, to an acknowledgment of the boundless love of God towards us, and to have our minds kindled up to true gratitude.[4]

Take, eat, this is my body. As Paul designed here to instruct us in a few words as to the right use of the sacrament, it is our duty to consider attentively[5] what he sets before us, and allow nothing to pass unobserved, inasmuch

festival was held, was in accordance with the peculiar secrecy with which its rites were observed.—*Ed.*

[1] " Pour partie, ou de la substance de son institution ;"—" As a part of his institution, or of the essence of it."

[2] " Ils se mocquent ;"—" They deride."

[3] " Sa misericorde infinie ;"—" His infinite mercy."

[4] " Et n'en soyons enuers luy ingrats, mais soyons enflambez à vne vraye recognoissance ;"—" And may not be ungrateful towards him, but may be kindled up to a true acknowledgment."

[5] " Et bien poiser ;"—" And ponder well."

as he says nothing but what is exceedingly necessary to be known, and worthy of the closest attention.   In the first place, we must take notice, that Christ here distributes the bread among the Apostles, that all may partake of it in common, and thus every one may receive his portion, that there may be an equal participation among all.   Accordingly, when there is not a table in common prepared for all the pious—where they are not invited to the *breaking of bread* in common, and where, in fine, believers do not mutually participate, it is to no purpose that the name of the *Lord's Supper* is laid claim to.

But for what purpose[1] are the people called to mass, unless it be that they may come away empty from an unmeaning show?[2]   It has, therefore, nothing in unison with the supper.   Hence, too, we infer that Christ's promise is no more applicable to the mass than to the feast of the Salii;[3] for when Christ promises that he will give us *his body*, he at the same time commands us to *take and eat of the bread*. Hence, unless we obey this command, it is to no purpose that we glory in his promise.   To explain this more familiarly in other words—the promise is annexed to the commandment in a conditional way, as it were: hence it has its accomplishment only if the condition also is accomplished.   For example, it is written, *Call upon me; I will answer thee.*   (Ps. l. 15.)   It is our part to obey the command of God, that he may accomplish for us what he promises; otherwise we shut ourselves out from the accomplishment of it.[4]

What do Papists do?   They neglect participation, and

---

[1] "Mais ie vous prie, à quel propos;"—"But for what purpose, I pray you."

[2] "Comme s'il retournoit de voir vne bastelerie inutile et sotte;"—"As if they were returning from seeing a useless and foolish mountebank scene."

[3] "Vn banquet de la confrairie des Sacrificateurs de Mars, lesquels les Romains nommoyent Salii;"—"To the banquet of the fraternity of the priests of Mars, whom the Romans called Salii."   They received this name from their going through the city *leaping* and *dancing*.   The feast which they partook of, after finishing their procession, was exceedingly sumptuous.   Hence the expression—"Epulari Saliarem in modum"—"to feast sumptuously."   Cic. Att. v. 9.—*Ed.*

[4] "Nous reiettons l'effet, et luy fermons la porte;"—"We reject its accomplishment, and shut the door against it."

consecrate the bread for a totally different purpose, and in the meantime they boast that they have the Lord's body. While, by a wicked divorce, they *put asunder those things which Christ has joined together*, (Matt. xix. 6,) it is manifest that their boasting is vain. Hence, whenever they bring forward the clause—*This is my body*, we must retort upon them the one that immediately precedes it—*Take and eat*. For the meaning of the words is: "By participating in the breaking of bread, according to the order and observance which I have prescribed, you shall be participants also in my body." Hence, when an individual eats of it by himself, the promise in that case goes for nothing. Besides, we are taught in these words what the Lord would have us do. *Take,* says he. Hence those that offer a sacrifice to God have some other than Christ as their authority, for we are not instructed in these words to perform a sacrifice.

But what do Papists say as to their mass? At first they were so impudent as to maintain, that it was truly and properly called a sacrifice. Now, however, they admit that it is indeed a commemorative sacrifice, but in such a way, that the benefit of redemption is, through means of their daily oblation,[1] applied to the living and the dead. However that may be, they present the appearance of a sacrifice.[2] In the first place, there is rashness in this, as being without any command from Christ; but there is a still more serious error involved in it—that, while Christ appointed the Supper for this purpose, that we might *take and eat*, they pervert it to a totally different use.

This is my body. I shall not recount the unhappy contests that have tried the Church in our times as to the meaning of these words. Nay rather, would to God that we could bury the remembrance of them in perpetual oblivion! I shall state, first of all, *sincerely* and *without disguise*, and then farther, I shall state *freely* (as I am wont to do) what my views are. Christ calls the bread *his body;* for I set aside,

[1] "Par leur belle oblation qu'ils font tous les iours;"—"By their admirable oblation, which they make every day."
[2] "Vne apparence et representation de sacrifice;"—"An appearance and representation of a sacrifice."

without any disputation, that absurd contrivance, that our
Lord did not exhibit the bread to the Apostles, but his
body, which they beheld with their eyes, for it immediately
follows—*This cup is the New Testament in my blood.* Let
us regard it then as beyond all controversy that Christ is
here speaking of the bread. Now the question is—" In
what sense?" That we may elicit the true meaning, we
must hold that the expression is figurative; for, assuredly,
to deny this is exceedingly dishonest.[1] Why then is the
term *body* applied to the bread? All, I think, will allow
that it is for the same reason that John calls the Holy
Spirit a *dove*. (John i. 32.) Thus far we are agreed. Now
the reason why the Spirit was so called was this—that he had
appeared in the form of a dove. Hence the name of the Spirit
is transferred to the visible sign. Why should we not maintain that there is here a similar instance of metonymy, and
that the term *body* is applied to the bread, as being the sign
and symbol of it? If any are of a different opinion they
will forgive me; but it appears to me to be an evidence of
a contentious spirit, to dispute pertinaciously on this point.
I lay it down, then, as a settled point, that there is here a
sacramental form of expression,[2] in which the Lord gives to
the sign the name of the thing signified.

We must now proceed farther, and inquire as to the reason
of the metonymy. Here I reply, that the name of the thing
signified is not applied to the sign simply as being a representation of it, but rather as being a symbol of it,[3] by which
the reality is presented to us. For I do not allow the force
of those comparisons which some borrow from profane or
earthly things; for there is a material difference between
them and the sacraments of our Lord. The statue of Hercules is called Hercules, but what have we there but a bare,
empty representation? On the other hand the Spirit is
called a *dove*, as being a sure pledge of the invisible presence

---

[1] " Ce seroit vne impudence et opinionastrete trop grande;"—" This
were excessive impudence and obstinacy."

[2] " C'est à dire, qui est ordinaire en matiere des Sacremens;"—" That
is to say, what is usual in connection with Sacraments."

[3] " Vn gage et tesmoignage externe;"—" An outward token and evidence."

of the Spirit. Hence the *bread* is *Christ's body*, because it assuredly testifies, that the body which it represents is held forth to us, or because the Lord, by holding out to us that symbol, gives us at the same time his own body; for Christ is not a deceiver, to mock us with empty representations.[1] Hence it is regarded by me as beyond all controversy, that the reality is here conjoined with the sign; or, in other words, that we do not less truly become participants in Christ's body in respect of spiritual efficacy, than we partake of the bread.

We must now discuss the manner. Papists hold forth to us their system of transubstantiation: they allege that, when the act of consecration has been gone through, the substance of the bread no longer exists, and that nothing remains but the accidents.[2] To this contrivance we oppose— not merely the plain words of Scripture, but the very nature of the sacraments. For what is the meaning of the *supper*, if there is no correspondence between the visible sign and the spiritual reality? They would have the sign to be a false and delusive appearance of bread. What then will the thing signified be, but a mere imagination? Hence, if there must be a correspondence between the sign and its reality, it is necessary that the bread be real—not imaginary—to represent Christ's real body. Besides, Christ's body is here given us not simply, but *as food*. Now it is not by any means the colour of the bread that nourishes us, but the substance. In fine, if we would have reality in the thing itself, there must be no deception in the sign.

Rejecting then the dream of Papists, let us see in what manner Christ's body is given to us. Some explain, that it is given to us, when we are made partakers of all the blessings which Christ has procured for us in his body—when, I say, we by faith embrace Christ as crucified for us, and raised up from the dead, and in this way are effectually made partakers of all his benefits. As for those who are

---

[1] "Pour penser qu'il nous repaisse d'ombres et vaines figures;"—"To think that he would feed us with shadows and empty representations."

[2] By the *accidents* of the bread are meant its colour, taste, smell, and shape.—*Ed.*

of this opinion, I have no objection to their holding such a view.   As for myself, I acknowledge, that it is only when we obtain Christ himself, that we come to partake of Christ's benefits.   He is, however, *obtained,* I affirm, not only when we believe that he was made an offering for us, but when he dwells in us—when he is one with us—when we are *members of his flesh,* (Eph. v. 30,)—when, in fine, we are incorporated with him (so to speak) into one life and substance.   Besides, I attend to the import of the words, for Christ does not simply present to us the benefit of his death and resurrection, but the very body in which he suffered and rose again.   I conclude, that Christ's body is *really,* (as the common expression is,)—that is, *truly* given to us in the Supper, to be wholesome food for our souls.   I use the common form of expression, but my meaning is, that our souls are nourished by the substance of the body, that we may truly be made one with him, or, what amounts to the same thing, that a life-giving virtue from Christ's flesh is poured into us by the Spirit, though it is at a great distance from us, and is not mixed with us.[1]

There now remains but one difficulty—how is it possible that his body, which is in heaven, is given to us here upon earth ?   Some imagine that Christ's body is infinite, and is not confined to any one space, but *fills heaven and earth,* (Jer. xxiii. 24,) like his Divine essence.   This fancy is too absurd to require refutation.   The Schoolmen dispute with more refinement as to his glorious body.   Their whole doctrine, however, reduces itself to this—that Christ is to be sought after in the bread, as if he were included in it. Hence it comes, that the minds of men behold the bread

---

[1] In this passage, as, also, in some other parts of his writings, CALVIN seems to affirm the real presence of Christ in the Lord's Supper, in some mysterious manner, while he was, as is well known, opposed to *consubstantiation,* as well as to *transubstantiation.*   The late venerable Dr. Dick of Glasgow, while treating of the Lord's Supper— while he makes mention of CALVIN in terms of the highest respect, as " one of the brightest ornaments of the Reformation," who, " in learning, genius, and zeal, had few equals, and no superior,"—animadverts on some expressions made use of in the *Institutes,* which seem not altogether in harmony with his general system of views in reference to the presence of Christ in the sacrament of the Supper.   Dick's Lectures on Theology, vol. iv. pp. 225, 226.—*Ed.*

with wonderment, and adore it in place of Christ. Should any one ask them whether they adore the bread, or the appearance of it, they will confidently affirm that they do *not*, but, in the mean time, when about to adore Christ, they turn to the bread. They turn, I say, not merely with their eyes, and their whole body, but even with the thoughts of the heart. Now what is this but unmixed idolatry? But that participation in the body of Christ, which, I affirm, is presented to us in the Supper, does not require a local presence, nor the descent of Christ, nor infinite extension,[1] nor anything of that nature, for the Supper being a heavenly action, there is no absurdity in saying, that Christ, while remaining in heaven, is received by us. For as to his communicating himself to us, *that* is effected through the secret virtue of his Holy Spirit, which can not merely bring together, but join in one, things that are separated by distance of place, and far remote.

But, in order that we may be capable of this participation, we must rise heavenward. Here, therefore, faith must be our resource, when all the bodily senses have failed. When I speak of *faith*, I do not mean any sort of opinion, resting on human contrivances, as many, boasting of faith on all occasions, run grievously wild on this point. What then? You see bread—nothing more—but you learn that it is a symbol[2] of Christ's body. Do not doubt that the Lord accomplishes what his words intimate—that the body, which thou dost not at all behold, is given to thee, as a spiritual repast. It seems incredible, that we should be nourished by Christ's flesh, which is at so great a distance from us. Let us bear in mind, that it is a secret and wonderful work of the Holy Spirit, which it were criminal to measure by the standard of our understanding. "In the meantime, however, drive away gross imaginations, which would keep thee from looking beyond the bread. Leave to Christ the true nature of flesh, and do not, by a mistaken apprehension, extend his body over heaven and earth: do not divide him

---

[1] " Vne estendue de son corps infinie ;"—" An infinite extension of his body."

[2] " Vn signe et tesmoignage ;"—" A sign and evidence."

into different parts by thy fancies, and do not adore him in this place and that, according to thy carnal apprehension. Allow him to remain in his heavenly glory, and aspire thou thither,[1] that he may thence communicate himself to thee." These few things will satisfy those that are sound and modest. As for the curious, I would have them look somewhere else for the means of satisfying their appetite.

Which is broken for you. Some explain this as referring to the distribution of the bread, because it was necessary that Christ's body should remain entire, as it had been predicted, (Exod. xii. 46,) *A bone of him shall not be broken.* As for myself — while I acknowledge that Paul makes an allusion to the breaking of bread, yet I understand the word *broken* as used here for *sacrificed*—not, indeed, with strict propriety, but at the same time without any absurdity. For although *no bone was broken,* yet the body itself having been subjected, first of all, to so many tortures and inflictions, and afterwards to the punishment of death in the most cruel form, cannot be said to have been uninjured. This is what Paul means by its being *broken.* This, however, is the *second* clause of the promise, which ought not to be passed over slightly. For the Lord does not present his body to us simply, and without any additional consideration, but as having been *sacrificed* for us. The *first* clause, then, intimates, that the body is presented to us : this *second* clause teaches us, what advantage we derive from it—that we are partakers of redemption, and the benefit of his sacrifice is applied to us. Hence the Supper is a mirror which represents to us Christ crucified, so that no one can profitably and advantageously receive the supper, but the man who embraces Christ crucified.

Do this in remembrance of me. Hence the Supper is a memorial (μνημόσυνον[2]) appointed as a help to our weakness;

---

[1] "Esleve ton esprit et ton cœur jusques là;"—" Raise thy mind and heart thither."

[2] It is worthy of notice, that our Author has made use of the same Greek term (when commenting on 1 Cor. v. 8) in reference to the Passover, which was intended partly as a *memorial* (μνημόσυνον.) See p. 189. The term is of frequent occurrence in the same sense in Herod .us, and occasionally in other Classical authors.—*Ed.*

for if we were sufficiently mindful of the death of Christ, this help would be unnecessary. This is common to all sacraments, for they are helps to our weakness. What is the nature of that remembrance which Christ would have us cherish with regard to him, we shall hear presently. As to the inference, however, which some draw from this—that Christ is not present in the Supper, because a *remembrance* applies to something that is absent; the answer is easy—that Christ is absent from it in the sense in which the Supper is a commemoration. For Christ is not visibly present, and is not beheld with our eyes, as the symbols are which excite our remembrance by representing him. In short, in order that he may be present with us, he does not change his place, but communicates to us from heaven the virtue of his flesh, as though it were present.[1]

25. *The cup, when he had supped.* The Apostle seems to intimate, that there was some interval of time between the distribution of the *bread* and that of the *cup*, and it does not quite appear from the Evangelists whether the whole of the transaction was continuous.[2] This, however, is of no great moment, for it may be that the Lord delivered in the meantime some address, after distributing the bread, and before giving the cup. As, however, he did or said nothing that was not in harmony with the sacrament, we need not say that the administration of it was disturbed or interrupted. I would not, however, render it as Erasmus does— *supper being ended,* for, in a matter of so great importance, ambiguity ought to be avoided.

This cup is the New Testament. What is affirmed as to the *cup,* is applicable also to the *bread;* and thus, by this form of expression, he intimates what he had before stated more briefly—that *the bread is the body.* For it is so to us, that it may be a *testament in his body,* that is, a covenant, which has been once confirmed by the offering up of his body, and is now confirmed by eating, when believers feast upon

---

[1] " Du ciel il fait descouler sur nous la vertu de sa chair presentement, et vrayement ;"—" He makes the virtue of his flesh pour down upon us from heaven presently and truly."

[2] " Continuel et sans interualle ;"—" Continuous, and without an interval."

that sacrifice.   Accordingly, while Paul and Luke use the words—*testament in the blood*, Matthew and Mark employ the expression—*blood of the testament*, which amounts to the same thing.   For the blood was poured out to reconcile us to God, and now we drink of it in a spiritual sense, that we may be partakers of reconciliation.   Hence, in the Supper, we have both a covenant, and a confirmatory pledge of the covenant.

I shall speak in the Epistle to the Hebrews, if the Lord shall allow me opportunity, as to the word *testament*.   It is well known, however, that sacraments receive that name, from being *testimonies* to us of the divine will, to confirm[1] it in our minds.   For as a covenant is entered into among men with solemn rites, so it is in the same manner that the Lord deals with us.   Nor is it without strict propriety that this term is employed ; for in consequence of the connection between the word and the sign, the covenant of the Lord is really included in the sacraments, and the term *covenant* has a reference or relation to us.   This will be of no small importance for understanding the nature of the sacraments; for if they are *covenants*, then they contain promises, by which consciences may be roused up to an assurance of salvation. Hence it follows, that they are not merely outward signs of profession before men, but are inwardly, too, helps to faith.

This do, as often as ye drink.   Christ, then, has appointed a two-fold sign in the Supper.   *What God hath joined together let not man put asunder.*   (Matt. xix. 6.)   To distribute, therefore, the *bread* without the *cup*, is to maim Christ's institution.[2]   For we hear Christ's words.   As he commands us to eat of the *bread*, so he commands us to drink of the *cup*.   To obey the one half of the command and neglect the other half—what is this but to make sport of his commandment ?   And to keep back the people from that *cup*, which Christ sets before all, after first drinking of it, as is done under the tyranny of the Pope—who can deny that this is diabolical presumption ?   As to the cavil that they bring

---

[1] " Confermer et seeller ;"—" Confirm and seal."
[2] " L'institution du Fils de Dieu ;"—" The institution of the Son of God."

forward—that Christ spoke merely to the Apostles, and not to the common people—it is exceedingly childish, and is easily refuted from this passage—for Paul here addresses himself to men and women indiscriminately, and to the whole body of the Church. He declares that he *had delivered this to them agreeably to the commandment of the Lord.* (verse 23.) By what spirit will those pretend to be actuated, who have dared to set aside this ordinance? Yet even at this day this gross abuse is obstinately defended; and what occasion is there for wonder, if they endeavour impudently to excuse, by words and writings, what they so cruelly maintain by fire and sword?

26. *For as often as ye shall eat.* Paul now adds what kind of remembrance ought to be cherished—that is, with thanksgiving: not that the remembrance consists wholly in confession with the mouth; for the chief thing is, that the efficacy of Christ's death be sealed in our consciences; but this knowledge should stir us up to a confession in respect of praise, so as to declare before men what we feel inwardly before God. The Supper then is (so to speak) a kind of memorial, which must always remain in the Church, until the last coming of Christ; and it has been appointed for this purpose, that Christ may put us in mind of the benefit of his death, and that we may recognise it[1] before men. Hence it has the name of the Eucharist.[2] If, therefore, you would celebrate the Supper aright, you must bear in mind, that a profession of your faith is required from you. Hence we see how shamelessly those mock God, who boast that they have in the mass something of the nature of the Supper. For what is the mass? They confess (for I am not speaking of Papists, but of the pretended followers of Nicodemus) that it is full of abominable superstitions. By outward gesture they give a pretended approval of them.

---

[1] " Que de nostre part le recognoissions;"—"That we, on our part, may recognise it."

[2] From εὐχαριστήσας, (*having given thanks,*) which is made use of by Paul, and also by the Evangelists, (see *Harmony*, vol. iii. p. 205, *n.* 1,) in their account of the original appointment of the Supper. The term is at the same time expressive of the spirit of the institution, in respect of *thanksgiving.—Ed.*

What kind of *showing forth of the death of Christ* is this? Do they not rather renounce it?

Until he come.   As we always need a help of this kind, so long as we are in this world, Paul intimates that this commemoration has been given us in charge, until Christ come to judgment.   For as he is not present with us in a visible form, it is necessary for us to have some symbol of his presence, by which our minds may exercise themselves.

27. *Therefore he who shall eat this bread unworthily.*   If the Lord requires gratitude from us in the receiving of this sacrament—if he would have us acknowledge his grace with the heart, and publish it with the mouth—that man will not go unpunished, who has put insult upon him rather than honour; for the Lord will not allow his commandment to be despised.   Now, if we would catch the meaning of this declaration, we must know what it is to *eat unworthily*.   Some restrict it to the Corinthians, and the abuse that had crept in among them, but I am of opinion that Paul here, according to his usual manner, passed on from the particular case to a general statement, or from one instance to an entire class.   There was one fault that prevailed among the Corinthians.   He takes occasion from this to speak of every kind of faulty administration or reception of the Supper. "God," says he, "will not allow this sacrament to be profaned without punishing it severely."

To *eat unworthily*, then, is to pervert the pure and right *use* of it by our *abuse* of it.   Hence there are various degrees of this *unworthiness*, so to speak; and some offend more grievously, others less so.   Some *fornicator*, perhaps, or *perjurer*, or *drunkard*, or *cheat*, (1 Cor. v. 11,) intrudes himself without repentance.   As such downright contempt is a token of wanton insult against Christ, there can be no doubt that such a person, whoever he is, receives the Supper to his own destruction.   Another, perhaps, will come forward, who is not addicted to any open or flagrant vice, but at the same time not so prepared in heart as became him.   As this carelessness or negligence is a sign of irreverence, it is also deserving of punishment from God.   As, then, there are various degrees of *unworthy participation*, so the Lord punishes some more slightly; on others he inflicts severer punishment.

Now this passage gave rise to a question, which some afterwards agitated with too much keenness—whether the *unworthy* really partake of the Lord's body? For some were led, by the heat of controversy, so far as to say, that it was received indiscriminately by the good and the bad; and many at this day maintain pertinaciously, and most clamorously, that in the first Supper Peter received no more than Judas. It is, indeed, with reluctance, that I dispute keenly with any one on this point, which is (in my opinion) not an essential one; but as others allow themselves, without reason, to pronounce, with a magisterial air, whatever may seem good to them, and to launch out thunderbolts upon every one that mutters anything to the contrary, we will be excused, if we calmly adduce reasons in support of what we reckon to be true.

I hold it, then, as a settled point, and will not allow myself to be driven from it, that Christ cannot be disjoined from his Spirit. Hence I maintain, that his body is not received as dead, or even inactive, disjoined from the grace and power of his Spirit. I shall not occupy much time in proving this statement. Now in what way could the man who is altogether destitute of a living faith and repentance, having nothing of the Spirit of Christ,[1] receive Christ himself? Nay more, as he is entirely under the influence of Satan and sin, how will he be capable of receiving Christ? While, therefore, I acknowledge that there are some who receive Christ truly in the Supper, and yet at the same time *unworthily,* as is the case with many weak persons, yet I do not admit, that those who bring with them a mere historical faith,[2] without a lively feeling of repentance and faith, receive anything but the sign. For I cannot endure to maim Christ,[3] and I shudder at the absurdity of affirming that he

---

[1] " Veu que par consequent il n'ha rien de l'Esprit de Christ;"— " Since he has, consequently, nothing of the Spirit of Christ."

[2] " Vne foy historique qu'on appelle; (c'est à dire pour consentir simplement à l'histoire de l'Euangile;")—" An historical faith, as they call it; (that is to say, to give a simple assent to the gospel history.")

[3] " Car ie n'ose proposer et imaginer Christ à demi;"—" For I dare not present and imagine Christ in half."

gives himself to be eaten by the wicked in a lifeless state, as it were.   Nor does Augustine mean anything else when he says, that the wicked receive Christ merely in the sacrament, which he expresses more clearly elsewhere, when he says that the other Apostles ate *the bread—the Lord;* but Judas only the *bread of the Lord.*[1]

But here it is objected, that the efficacy of the sacraments does not depend upon the worthiness of men, and that nothing is taken away from the promises of God, or falls to the ground, through the wickedness of men. This I acknowledge, and accordingly I add in express terms, that Christ's body is presented to the wicked no less than to the good, and this is enough so far as concerns the efficacy of the sacrament and the faithfulness of God. For God does not there represent in a delusive manner, to the wicked, the body of his Son, but presents it in reality; nor is the bread a bare sign to them, but a faithful pledge. As to their rejection of it, that does not impair or alter anything as to the nature of the sacrament.

It remains, that we give a reply to the statement of Paul in this passage. " Paul represents the unworthy as guilty, inasmuch as *they do not discern the Lord's body :* it follows, that they receive his body." I deny the inference; for though they reject it, yet as they profane it and treat it with dishonour when it is presented to them, they are deservedly held guilty ; for they do, as it were, cast it upon the ground, and trample it under their feet. Is such sacrilege trivial ? Thus I see no difficulty in Paul's words, provided you keep in view what God presents and holds out to the wicked— not what they receive.

28. *But let a man examine himself.*   An exhortation drawn from the foregoing threatening. " If those that *eat unworthily* are *guilty of the body and blood of the Lord,* then let no man approach who is not properly and duly prepared. Let every one, therefore, take heed to himself, that he may not fall into this sacrilege through idleness or carelessness."

---

[1] This celebrated saying of Augustine (which occurs in Hom. in Joann. 62) is quoted also in the *Institutes,* (vol. iii. p. 436,) where our author handles at great length the subject here adverted to.—*Ed.*

But now it is asked, what sort of *examination* that ought to be to which Paul exhorts us.   Papists make it consist in auricular confession.   They order all that are to receive the Supper, to examine their life carefully and anxiously, that they may unburthen all their sins in the ear of the priest. Such is *their* preparation![1]   I maintain, however, that this holy *examination* of which Paul speaks, is widely different from torture.   Those persons,[2] after having *tortured* themselves with reflection for a few hours, and making the priest —such as he is—privy to their vileness,[3] imagine that they have done their duty.   It is an *examination* of another sort that Paul here requires—one of such a kind as may accord with the legitimate use of the sacred Supper.

You see here a method that is most easily apprehended. If you would wish to use aright the benefit afforded by Christ, bring faith and repentance.   As to these two things, therefore, the trial must be made, if you would come duly prepared.   Under repentance I include love ; for the man who has learned to renounce himself, that he may give himself up wholly to Christ and his service, will also, without doubt, carefully maintain that unity which Christ has enjoined.   At the same time, it is not a perfect faith or repentance that is required, as some, by urging beyond due bounds, a perfection that can nowhere be found, would shut out for ever from the Supper every individual of mankind. If, however, thou aspirest after the righteousness of God with the earnest desire of thy mind, and, humbled under a view of thy misery, dost wholly lean upon Christ's grace, and rest upon it, know that thou art a worthy guest to approach that table—*worthy* I mean in this respect, that the Lord does not exclude thee, though in another point of view there is something in thee that is not as it ought to be.   For faith, when it is but begun, makes those *worthy* who were *unworthy.*

29. *He who shall eat unworthily, eateth judgment to him-*

---

[1] " Voyla leur belle preparation ;"—" See their admirable preparation ! "
[2] " Ces miserables ;"—" Those miserable creatures."
[3] " Et qu'ils on debagoulé leur turpitude à monsieur le prestre ;"— " And when they have blabbed out their baseness to Mr. Priest "

self. He had previously pointed out in express terms the heinousness of the crime, when he said that those who should *eat unworthily* would be *guilty of the body and blood of the Lord.* Now he alarms them, by denouncing punishment;[1] for there are many that are not affected with the sin itself, unless they are struck down by the judgment of God. This, then, he does, when he declares that this food, otherwise health-giving, will turn out to their destruction, and will be converted into poison to those that *eat unworthily.*

He adds the reason—because *they distinguish not the Lord's body,* that is, as a sacred thing from a profane. "They handle the sacred body of Christ *with unwashen hands,* (Mark vii. 2,)[2] nay more, as if it were a thing of nought, they consider not how great is the value of it.[3] They will therefore pay the penalty of so dreadful a profanation." Let my readers keep in mind what I stated a little ago,[4] that the body[5] is presented to them, though their *unworthiness* deprives them of a participation in it.

30. For this cause many *are* weak and sickly among you, and many sleep.	30. Propterea inter vos infirmi sunt multi, et aegroti, et dormiunt multi.
31. For if we would judge ourselves, we should not be judged.	31. Si enim ipsi nos iudicassemus, non iudicaremur.
32. But when we are judged, we are chastened of the Lord, that we should not be condemned with the world.	32. Porro quum iudicamur, a Domino corripimur, ne cum hoc mundo damnemur.
33. Wherefore, my brethren, when ye come together to eat, tarry one for another.	33. Itaque, fratres mei, dum convenitis àd edendum, alii alios exspectate.
34. And if any man hunger, let	34. Si autem quispiam esurit,

---

[1] "La punition que Dieu en fera;"—"The punishment that God will inflict upon it."

[2] "Ils manient le corps precieux de Christ irreueremment, c'est à dire, sans nettoyer leur conscience;"—"They handle the precious body of Christ irreverently, that is to say, without washing their conscience."

[3] In the *Vat.* and *Alex.* MSS. and the *Copt.* version, the reading is simply μη διακρίνων τὸ σῶμα—*not distinguishing the body;* while later copies have τὸ σῶμα τοῦ Κυρίου—*the body of the Lord.* The verb διακρίνω is employed by Herodotus in the sense of distinguishing, in the following expression: διακρίνων οὐδενα—*without any distinction of persons.* (Herod. iii. 39.) It is supposed by some that the word, as employed here, contains an allusion to the *distinguishing* of meats under the Mosaic law.—*Ed.*

[4] See p. 387.

[5] "Le corps de Christ;"—"The body of Christ."

him eat at home; that ye come not together unto condemnation. And the rest will I set in order when I come.

domi edat, ne in iudicium edatis; cætera autem, quum venero, disponam.

30. *For this cause*, &c. After having treated in a general way of *unworthy eating*, and of the kind of punishment that awaits those who pollute this sacrament, he now instructs the Corinthians as to the chastisement which they were at that time enduring. It is not known whether a pestilence was raging there at that time, or whether they were labouring under other kinds of disease. However it may have been as to this, we infer from Paul's words, that the Lord had sent some scourge upon them for their correction. Nor does Paul merely conjecture, that it is on that account that they are punished, but he affirms it as a thing that was perfectly well known by him. He says, then, that many lay *sick*— that many were kept long in a languishing condition, and that many had died, in consequence of that abuse of the Supper, because they had offended God. By this he intimates, that by diseases and other chastisements from God, we are admonished to think of our sins ; for God does not afflict us without good reason, for he takes no pleasure in our afflictions.

The subject is a copious and ample one ; but let it suffice to advert to it here in a single word. If in Paul's times an ordinary abuse of the Supper[1] could kindle the wrath of God against the Corinthians, so that he punished them thus severely, what ought we to think as to the state of matters at the present day ? We see, throughout the whole extent of Popery, not merely horrid profanations of the Supper, but even a sacrilegious abomination set up in its room. In the *first* place, it is prostituted to *filthy lucre* (1 Tim. iii. 8) and merchandise. *Secondly*, it is maimed, by taking away the use of the cup. *Thirdly*, it is changed into another aspect,[2] by its having become customary for one to partake of his own feast separately, participation being done away.[3]

[1] " Vn tel abus de la Cene qui n'estoit pas des plus grans;"—" Such an abuse of the Supper, as was not one of the greatest."
[2] " Vne forme estrange et du tout autre;"—"A strange and quite different form."
[3] " Sans en distribuer ne communiquer aux autres;"—" Without distributing or communicating of it to others."

Fourthly, there is *there* no explanation of the meaning of the sacrament, but a mumbling that would accord better with a magical incantation, or the detestable sacrifices of the Gentiles, than with our Lord's institution. *Fifthly*, there is an endless number of ceremonies, abounding partly with trifles, partly with superstition, and consequently manifest pollutions. *Sixthly*, there is the diabolical invention of sacrifice, which contains an impious blasphemy against the death of Christ. *Seventhly*, it is fitted to intoxicate miserable men with carnal confidence, while they present it to God as if it were an expiation, and think that by this charm they drive off everything hurtful, and that without faith and repentance. Nay more, while they trust that they are armed against the devil and death, and are fortified against God by a sure defence, they venture to sin with much more freedom,[1] and become more obstinate. *Eighthly*, an idol is *there* adored in the room of Christ. In short, it is filled with all kinds of abomination.[2]

Nay even among ourselves, who have the pure administration of the Supper restored to us,[3] in virtue of a return, as it were, from captivity,[4] how much irreverence! How much hypocrisy on the part of many! What a disgraceful mixture, while, without any discrimination, wicked and openly abandoned persons intrude themselves, such as no man of character and decency would admit to common intercourse![5] And

---

[1] " Ils pechent plus audacieusement, et à bride auallee ;"—" They sin more daringly, and with a loose bridle."

[2] The above paragraph is aptly designated in the old English translation by Thomas Tymme, (1573) "a lyuely description of the Popishe Masse."—*Ed.*

[3] "Le pur vsage de la Cene en son entier, qui nous a este finalement rendu par la grace de Dieu ;"—" The pure use of the Supper in its completeness, which has been at last restored to us by the grace of God."

[4] CALVIN here employs the term *postliminum*, (*restoration from captivity*,) and most felicitously compares the restoration of the pure observance of religious ordinances, consequent upon the Reformation from Popery, to the recovery, by a Roman citizen, of his superior privileges, on his return from a state of captivity, during which they had been—not forfeited—but merely suspended.—*Ed.*

[5] "Lesquels vn homme de bien, et qui auroit honnestete en quelque recommendation, ne receuroit iamais à sa table ;"—" Whom a man of principle—that had any regard to decency—would never admit to his table."

yet after all, we wonder how it comes that there are so many wars, so many pestilences, so many failures of the crop, so many disasters and calamities—as if the cause were not manifest! And assuredly, we must not expect a termination to our calamities, until we have removed the occasion of them, by correcting our faults.

31. *For if we would judge ourselves.* Here we have another remarkable statement—that God does not all of a sudden become enraged against us, so as to inflict punishment immediately upon our sinning, but that, for the most part, it is owing to our carelessness, that he is in a manner constrained to punish us, when he sees that we are in a careless and drowsy state, and are flattering ourselves in our sins.[1] Hence we either avert, or mitigate impending punishment, if we first call ourselves to account, and, actuated by a spirit of repentance, deprecate the anger of God by inflicting punishment voluntarily upon ourselves.[2] In short, believers anticipate, by repentance, the judgment of God, and there is no other remedy, by which they may obtain absolution in the sight of God, but by voluntarily *condemning themselves.*

You must not, however, apprehend, as Papists are accustomed to do, that there is here a kind of transaction between us and God, as if, by inflicting punishment upon ourselves of our own accord, we rendered satisfaction to him, and did, in a manner, redeem ourselves from his hand. We do not, therefore, anticipate the judgment of God, on the ground of our bringing any compensation to appease him. The reason is this—because God, when he chastises us, has it in view to shake us out of our drowsiness, and arouse us to repentance. If we do this of our own accord, there is no longer any reason, why he should proceed to inflict his judgment upon us. If, however, any one, after having begun to feel

---

[1] " Quand il voit que nous ne nous soucions de rien, et que nous-nous endormons en nos pechez, et nous flattons en nos ordures et vilenies;"— " When he sees that we are quite careless, and are asleep in our sins, and are flattering ourselves in our filthinesses and pollutions."

[2] "Prions nostre bon Dieu d'addoucir la rigueur de sa iustice ; par manier de dire nous punissans nous-mesmes sans attendre qu'il y mette la main;"—" We beseech our good God to mitigate the rigour of his justice—punishing ourselves (so to speak) instead of waiting till he put forth his hand to do it."

displeased with himself, and meditate repentance, is, nevertheless, still visited with God's chastisements, let us know
that his repentance is not so valid or sure, as not to require
some chastisement to be sent upon him, by which it may be
helped forward to a fuller development.   Mark how repentance wards off the judgment of God by a suitable remedy—
not, however, by way of compensation.

32. *But when we are judged.*   Here we have a consolation
that is exceedingly necessary ; for if any one in affliction
thinks that God is angry with him, he will rather be discouraged than excited to repentance.   Paul, accordingly,
says, that God is angry with believers in such a way as not
in the meantime to be forgetful of his mercy : nay more,
that it is on this account particularly that he punishes them
—that he may consult their welfare.   It is an inestimable
consolation[1]—that the punishments by which our sins are
chastened are evidences, not of God's anger for our destruction, but rather of his paternal love, and are at the same
time of assistance towards our salvation, for God is angry
with us as his sons, whom he will not leave to perish.

When he says—*that we may not be condemned with the
world,* he intimates two things.   The *first* is, that the children
of this world, while they sleep on quietly and securely in
their delights,[2] are fattened up, like hogs, for *the day of
slaughter.*   (Jer. xii. 3.)   For though the Lord sometimes
invites the wicked, also, to repentance by his chastisements,
yet he often passes them over as strangers,[3] and allows them
to rush on with impunity, until they *have filled up the
measure* of their final condemnation.   (Gen. xv. 16.)   This
privilege, therefore, belongs to believers exclusively—that
by punishments they are called back from destruction.   The
second thing is this—that chastisements are necessary reme-

---

[1] " Y a-il plus grande consolation pour le Chrestien que ceste-ci ? "—" Is
there a greater consolation for the Christian than this ? "

[2] " Sont tout asseurez, et ne se soucians du iugement de Dieu s'endor-
ment en leurs plaisirs et voluptez ; "—" Are quite confident, and not concerning themselves as to the judgment of God, sleep on in their pleasures
and delights."

[3] " Il aduient souuent qu'il les met en oubli comme estrangers ; "—" It
often happens that he overlooks them as strangers."

dies for believers, for otherwise they, too, would rush on to everlasting destruction,[1] were they not restrained by temporal punishment.

These considerations should lead us not merely to patience, so as to endure with equanimity the troubles that are assigned to us by God, but also to gratitude, that, giving thanks to God our Father, we may resign ourselves[2] to his discipline by a willing subjection. They are also useful to us in various ways; for they cause our afflictions to be salutary to us, while they train us up for mortification of the flesh, and a pious abasement—they accustom us to obedience to God—they convince us of our own weakness—they kindle up in our minds fervency in prayer—they exercise hope, so that at length whatever there is of bitterness in them is all swallowed up in spiritual joy.

33. *Wherefore, my brethren.* From the discussion of a general doctrine, he returns to the particular subject with which he had set out, and comes to this conclusion, that equality must be observed in the Lord's Supper, that there may be a real participation, as there ought to be, and that they may not celebrate every one his own supper; and farther, that this sacrament ought not to be mixed up with common feasts.

34. *The rest I will set in order when I come.* It is probable, that there were some things in addition, which it would be of advantage to put into better order, but as they were of less importance, the Apostle delays the correction of them until his coming among them. It may be, at the same time, that there was nothing of this nature; but as one knows better what is necessary when he is present to see, Paul reserves to himself the liberty of arranging matters when present, according as occasion may require. Papists arm themselves against us with this buckler, too, for defending their *mass.* For they interpret *this* to be the *setting in order* which Paul here promises—as if he would

---

[1] " Ils tomberoyent aussi bien que les autres en ruine eternelle;"— " They would fall, as well as others, into everlasting destruction."

[2] "Voluntairement, à soustenir tel chastisement qu'il luy plaira nous enuoyer;"—" Willingly to bear such chastisement as he may be pleased to send upon us."

have taken the liberty[1] of overturning that eternal appointment of Christ, which he here so distinctly approves of!
For what resemblance does the mass bear to Christ's institution? But away with such trifles, as it is certain that
Paul speaks only of outward decorum. As this is put in the
power of the Church, so it ought to be arranged according
to the condition of times, places, and persons.

CHAPTER XII.

1. Now concerning spiritual *gifts*, brethren, I would not have you ignorant.

2. Ye know that ye were Gentiles, carried away unto these dumb idols, even as ye were led.

3. Wherefore I give you to understand, that no man speaking by the Spirit of God calleth Jesus accursed; and *that* no man can say that Jesus is the Lord, but by the Holy Ghost.

4. Now there are diversities of gifts, but the same Spirit.

5. And there are differences of administrations, but the same Lord.

6. And there are diversities of operations, but it is the same God which worketh all in all.

7. But the manifestation of the Spirit is given to every man to profit withal.

1. Porro de spiritualibus, fratres, nolo vos ignorare.

2. Scitis, quum Gentes eratis, qualiter simulacra muta, prout ducebamini, sequuti sitis.

3. Quamobrem notum vobis facio, quod nemo in Spiritu Dei loquens, dicit anathema Iesum: et nemo potest dicere Dominum Iesum, nisi per Spiritum sanctum.

4. Divisiones autem donorum sunt, sed unus Spiritus.

5. Et divisiones ministeriorum sunt, sed unus Dominus.

6. Et divisiones facultatum sunt, sed Deus unus, qui operatur omnia in omnibus.

7. Unicuique autem datur manifestatio Spiritus ad utilitatem.

1. *Now concerning spiritual things.* He goes on to correct another fault. As the Corinthians abused the gifts of God for ostentation and show, and love was little, if at all, regarded, he shows them for what purpose believers are adorned by God with spiritual gifts—for the edification of their brethren. This proposition, however, he divides into two parts; for, in the *first* place, he teaches, that God is the author of those gifts, and, *secondly*, having established this, he reasons as to their design. He proves from their own

[1] " Mais c'est bien à propos, comme si ce sainct personnage se fust donne ceste license ;"—" But this is a likely thing truly! As if that holy personage would have allowed himself this liberty ! "

experience, that those things in which they gloried, are bestowed upon men through the exercise of God's favour; for
he reminds them how ignorant they were, and stupid, and
destitute of all spiritual light, previously to God's calling
them.   Hence it appears, that they had been furnished with
them—not by nature, but through God's unmerited benignity.

As to the words ; when he says—*I would not that ye
should be ignorant,* we must supply the expression—*as to
what is right,* or *as to what is your duty,* or some similar expression ; and by *spiritual things* he means *spiritual gifts,*
as to which we shall have occasion to see afterwards.   In
what follows there is a twofold reading ; for some manuscripts have simply ὅτι : others add ὅτε.   The former means
because—assigning a reason : the latter means *when ;* and
this latter reading suits much better.   But besides this
diversity, the construction is in other respects confused ; but
still, the meaning is evident.   Literally, it is this : *Ye know,
that when ye were Gentiles, after dumb idols, according as ye
were led, following.*   I have, however, faithfully given Paul's
meaning.   By *dumb idols* he means—having neither feeling
nor motion.

Let us learn from this passage how great is the blindness
of the human mind, when it is without the illumination of
the Holy Spirit, inasmuch as it stands in amazement at
dumb idols,[1] and cannot rise higher in searching after God ;
nay more, it is *led* by Satan as if it were a brute.[2]   He
makes use of the term *Gentiles* here, in the same sense as
in Eph. ii. 12.   *Ye were at one time Gentiles,* says he, *without
God, strangers to the hope of salvation,* &c.   Perhaps, too, he
reasons by way of contrast.   What if[3] they should now show

---

[1] " Il demeure là abbruti apres les idoles;"—"It remains there, in a
brutish attachment to idols."

[2] This idea is brought out more fully by *Bloomfield,* who observes that
ἀπάγεσθαι (to be carried away) is " a strong term, denoting being hurried
away by a force which cannot be resisted ; and here refers to the blind infatuation by which the heathens were led away into idolatry and vice, like
brute beasts that have no understanding.   This," he adds, " is especially
alluded to in ὡς ἂν ἤγεσθε—*as ye might be led,* viz. by custom, example, or
inclination, just as it might happen."—*Ed.*

[3] " Que ce sera une vilenie à eux s'ils," &c. ;—" It will be a disgrace to
them if they," &c.

themselves to be less submissive to God, after his having taken them under his care, to be governed by his word and Spirit, than they formerly discovered themselves to be forward and compliant, in following the suggestions of Satan!

3. *Wherefore I give you to know.* Having admonished them from their own experience, he sets before them a general doctrine, which he deduces from it; for what the Corinthians had experienced in themselves is common to all mankind—to wander on in error,[1] previously to their being brought back, through the kindness of God, into the way of truth. Hence it is necessary that we should be directed by the Spirit of God, or we shall wander on for ever. From this, too, it follows, that all things that pertain to the true knowledge of God, are the gifts of the Holy Spirit. He at the same time derives an argument from opposite causes to opposite effects. *No one, speaking by the Spirit of God, can revile Christ;* so, on the other hand, *no one can speak well of Christ, but by the Spirit of Christ.* To *say that Jesus is accursed* is utter blasphemy against him. To *say that Jesus is the Lord,* is to speak of him in honourable terms and with reverence, and to extol his majesty.

Here it is asked—"As the wicked sometimes speak of Christ in honourable and magnificent terms, is this an indication that they have the Spirit of God?" I answer—"They undoubtedly have, so far as that effect is concerned; but the gift of regeneration is one thing, and the gift of bare intelligence, with which Judas himself was endowed, when he preached the gospel, is quite another." Hence, too, we perceive how great our weakness is, as we cannot so much as move our tongue for the celebration of God's praise, unless it be governed by his Spirit. Of this the Scripture, also, frequently reminds us, and the saints everywhere acknowledge—that unless the Lord open their mouths, they are not fit to be the heralds of his praise. Among others, Isaiah says—I am a man of unclean lips, &c. (Isaiah vi. 5.)

4. *Now there are diversities of gifts.* The symmetry of

---

[1] "D'estre errans et abusez en diuerses sortes;"—"To be wandering and deluded in various ways."

the Church[1] consists, so to speak, of a manifold unity,[2] that is, when the variety of gifts is directed to the same object, as in music there are different sounds, but suited to each other with such an adaptation, as to produce concord.   Hence it is befitting that there should be a distinction of gifts as well as of offices, and yet all harmonize in one.   Paul, accordingly, in the 12th chapter of Romans, commends this variety, that no one may, by rashly intruding himself into another's place, confound the distinction which the Lord has established.   Hence he orders every one to be contented with his own gifts, and cultivate the particular department that has been assigned to him.[3]   He prohibits them from going beyond their own limits by a foolish ambition.   In fine, he exhorts that every one should consider how much has been given him, what measure has been allotted to him, and to what he has been called.   Here, on the other hand, he orders every one to bring what he has to the common heap, and not keep back the gifts of God in the way of enjoying every one his own, apart from the others,[4] but aim unitedly at the edification of all in common.   In both passages, he brings forward the similitude of the human body, but, as may be observed, on different accounts.   The sum of what he states amounts to this—that gifts are not distributed thus variously among believers, in order that they may be used apart, but that in the division there is a unity, inasmuch as one Spirit is the source of all those gifts, one God is the Lord of all administrations, and the author of all exercises of power.   Now God, who is the beginning, ought also to be the end.

One Spirit.   This passage ought to be carefully observed

---

[1] " La proportion et ordre bien compassé qui est en l'Eglise ;"—" The proportion and well regulated order that is in the Church."

[2] " Consiste en vne vnite faite de plusieurs parties assemblees ;"—" Consists of a unity made up of many parts put together."

[3] " Il veut donc qu'un chacun se contentant du don qu'il a receu, s'employe a le faire valoir, et s'acquitter de son deuoir ;"—" He would, therefore, have every one, contenting himself with the gift that he has received, to employ himself in improving it, and carefully discharge his duty."

[4] " Pour en iouyr à part, sans en communiquer à ses freres ;"—" So as to enjoy them apart, without imparting of them to his brethren."

in opposition to fanatics,[1] who think that the name Spirit means nothing essential, but merely the gifts or actions of divine power.   Here, however, Paul plainly testifies, that there is *one* essential power of God, whence all his works proceed.   The term *Spirit*, it is true, is sometimes transferred by metonymy to the gifts themselves.   Hence we read of the Spirit of knowledge—of judgment—of fortitude —of modesty.[2]   Paul, however, here plainly testifies that judgment, and knowledge, and gentleness, and all other gifts, proceed from *one* source.   For it is the office of the Holy Spirit to put forth and exercise the power of God by conferring these gifts upon men, and distributing them among them.

One Lord.   The ancients made use of this testimony in opposition to the Arians, for the purpose of maintaining a Trinity of persons.   For there is mention made here of *the Spirit, secondly* of *the Lord*, and *lastly* of God, and to these Three, one and the same operation is ascribed.   Thus, by the name *Lord*, they understood Christ.   But for my part, though I have no objection to its being understood in this way, I perceive, at the same time, that it is a weak argument for stopping the mouths of Arians ; for there is a correspondence between the word *administrations* and the word *Lord*.   *The administrations*, says Paul, *are different*, but there is only one God whom we must serve, whatever *administration* we discharge.   This antithesis, then, shows what is the simple meaning, so that to confine it to Christ is rather forced.

6. *One God that worketh.*   Where we use the word *powers* the Greek term is ἐνεργήματα, a term which contains an allusion to the verb *worketh*, as in Latin *effectus* (an effect) corresponds with the verb *efficere* (to effect.)   Paul's meaning is, that although believers may be endowed with different powers, they all take their rise from one and the same power on the part of God.   Hence the expression employed here—*worketh all things in all*—does not refer to the general providence of God, but to the liberality that he exercises

---

[1] " Vn tas d'esprits enragez;"—" A troop of furious spirits."
[2] " De discretion ;"—" Of discretion."

towards us, in bestowing upon every one some gift. The
sum is this—that there is nothing in mankind that is good
or praiseworthy but what comes from God alone. Hence it
is out of place here to agitate the question—in what manner
God acts in Satan and in reprobates.

7. *But the manifestation of the Spirit is given to every
man.* He now points out the purpose for which God has
appointed his gifts, for he does not confer them upon us in
vain, nor does he intend that they shall serve the purpose
of ostentation. Hence we must inquire as to the purpose
for which they are conferred. As to this Paul answers—
(*with a view to utility*)—πρὸς τὸ συμφερον ; that is, that the
Church may receive advantage thereby. *The manifestation
of the Spirit* may be taken in a passive as well as in an active
sense—in a *passive* sense, because wherever there is prophecy, or knowledge, or any other gift, the Spirit of God
does there *manifest* himself—in an *active* sense, because the
Spirit of God, when he enriches us with any gift, unlocks
his treasures, for the purpose of *manifesting* to us those
things that would otherwise have been concealed and shut
up. The second interpretation suits better. The view taken
by Chrysostom is rather harsh and forced—that this term is
used,[1] because unbelievers do not recognise God, except by
visible miracles.

8. For to one is given by the
Spirit the word of wisdom; to another the word of knowledge by the
same Spirit ;

9. To another faith by the same
Spirit ; to another the gifts of healing by the same Spirit;

10. To another the working of
miracles ; to another prophecy; to
another discerning of spirits ; to another *divers* kinds of tongues; to another the interpretation of tongues :

11. But all these worketh that
one and the selfsame Spirit, dividing
to every man severally as he will.

8. Huic quidem per Spiritum
datur sermo sapientiae, alteri datur
sermo cognitionis, secundum eundem
Spiritum.

9. Alii fides in eodem Spiritu,
alii dona sanationum in eodem
Spritu.

10. Alii facultates potentiarum,
alii autem prophetia, alii autem dis-
cretiones spirituum, alii genera linguarum, alii interpretatio linguarum.

11. Porro omnia haec efficit unus
et idem Spiritus, distribuens seor-
sum cuique prout vult.

[1] " Que ceci est appelé *Manifestation :*"—" That this is termed a *Manifestation.*"

12. For as the body is one, and hath many members, and all the members of that one body, being many, are one body; so also *is* Christ.	12. Quemadmodum enim corpus unum est, et membra habet multa : omnia autem membra corporis unius quum multa sint, corpus autem est unum: ita et Christus.
13. For by one Spirit are we all baptized into one body, whether *we be* Jews or Gentiles, whether *we be* bond or free; and have been all made to drink into one Spirit.	13. Etenim per unum Spiritum nos omnes in unum corpus baptizati sumus, sive Iudaei, sive Graeci : sive servi, sive liberi : et omnes in uno Spiritu potum hausimus.

8. *To one is given.* He now subjoins an enumeration, or, in other words, specifies particular kinds—not indeed all of them, but such as are sufficient for his present purpose. " Believers," says he, " are endowed with different gifts, but let every one acknowledge, that he is indebted for whatever he has to the Spirit of God, for he pours forth his gifts as the sun scatters his rays in every direction. As to the difference between these gifts, *knowledge* (or understanding) and *wisdom* are taken in different senses in the Scriptures, but here I take them in the way of less and greater, as in Colossians ii. 3, where they are also joined together, when Paul says, that *in Christ are hid all the treasures of wisdom and knowledge. Knowledge*, therefore, in my opinion, means *acquaintance with sacred things—wisdom*, on the other hand, means the perfection of it. Sometimes *prudence* is put, as it were, in the middle place between these two, and in that case it denotes skill[1] in applying knowledge to some useful purpose. They are, it is true, very nearly allied ; but still you observe a difference when they are put together. Let us then take *knowledge* as meaning *ordinary information*, and *wisdom*, as including revelations that are of a more secret and sublime order.[2]

The term *faith* is employed here to mean a special faith,

---

[1] " Le sçauoir et la dexterite ;"—" Skill and dexterity." As to this use of the term *prudentia*, (*prudence*,) see Cicero dė Officiis, i. 43.—*Ed.*

[2] One of the most satisfactory views of this subject is that of Dr. Henderson in his Lecture on " Divine Inspiration," (pp. 193, 196,) who understands by σοφία, (*wisdom*,) in this passage, " the sublime truths of the gospel, directly revealed to the Apostles, of which the λογος (*word*) was the supernatural ability rightly to communicate them to others ;" and by λόγος γνώσεως, (*word of knowledge*,) the faculty of "infallibly explaining truths and doctrines which had been previously divulged."—*Ed.*

as we shall afterwards see from the context. A special faith is of such a kind as does not apprehend Christ wholly, for redemption, righteousness, and sanctification, but only in so far as miracles are performed in his name. Judas had a faith of this kind, and he wrought miracles too by means of it. Chrysostom distinguishes it in a somewhat different manner, calling it the faith of miracles, not of doctrines.[1] This, however, does not differ much from the interpretation previously mentioned. By the *gift of healings*[2] every one knows what is meant.

As to the *workings of powers*, or, as some render it, the *operations of influences*, there is more occasion for doubt. I am inclined, however, to think, that what is meant is the influence which is exercised against devils, and also against hypocrites. When, therefore, Christ and his Apostles by authority restrained devils, or put them to flight, that was ἐνέργημα, (*powerful working*,) and, in like manner, when Paul smote the sorcerer with blindness, (Acts xiii. 11,) and when Peter struck Ananias and Sapphira dead upon the spot with a single word. The gifts of *healing* and of miracles, therefore, serve to manifest the goodness of God, but this last, his severity for the destruction of Satan.[3]

By *prophecy*, I understand the singular and choice endowment of unfolding the secret will of God, so that a Pro-

---

[1] Chrysostom's words are: Πίστιν οὐ ταύτην λέγει τὴν τῶν δογμάτων ἀλλὰ τὴν τῶν σημείων. "By this faith he means not that of doctrines, but that of miracles."—It was called by the schoolmen *fides miraculorum* (*faith of miracles*.)—*Ed.*

[2] The plural is made use of, it is manifest, to intimate the number and variety of the diseases that were healed—the Apostles having been invested with power to *heal all manner of sickness, and all manner of disease.* (Matt. x. 1.)—*Ed.*

[3] There does not appear to be sufficient ground for understanding the *miracles* here referred to as necessarily *deeds of terror*, while the connection in which the expression occurs seems to intimate, that the *miracles* here meant were more than ordinarily stupendous manifestations of Divine power, such as would powerfully constrain the beholder to exclaim, *This is the finger of God!* Thus, "the resuscitation of the dead, the innocuous handling of serpents, or drinking of empoisoned liquor, the dispossession of demons, and the infliction of blindness," as in the case of Elymas, the sorcerer, and of death itself, as in the case of Ananias and Sapphira, were *mighty deeds*—to which "no mere created power could possibly pretend, under any circumstances, or by the application of any means whatever." See *Henderson on Inspiration*, pp. 203-206.—*Ed.*

phet is a messenger, as it were, between God and man.[1] My reason for taking this view will be explained more fully afterwards.

The *discerning of spirits*, was a clearness of perception in forming a judgment as to those who professed to be *something*. (Acts v. 36.) I speak not of that natural wisdom, by which we are regulated in judging. It was a special illumination, with which some were endowed by the gift of God. The use of it was this—that they might not be imposed upon by masks, or mere pretences,[2] but might by that spiritual judgment distinguish, as by a particular mark, the true ministers of Christ from the false.

There was a difference between the *knowledge of tongues*, and the *interpretation* of them, for those who were endowed with the former were, in many cases, not acquainted with the language of the nation with which they had to deal. The *interpreters*[3] rendered foreign tongues into the native language. These endowments they did not at that time acquire by labour or study, but were put in possession of them by a wonderful revelation of the Spirit.[4]

[1] " Apportant la volonte de Dieu aux hommes;"—" Communicating the will of God to men."

[2] " Par la montre et belle apparence que les gens ont aucunesfois;"— " By the show and fair appearance which persons sometimes have."

[3] " Et en tel cas ceux que auoyent le don d'interpretation des langues;" —" And in such a case, those who had the gift of interpreting languages."

[4] The following classification of the *gifts*, (χαρίσματα,) here enumerated by the Apostle, is suggested by Dr. Henderson, as tending to show the " beautiful symmetry " of the passage:—

I. 'Ω μὲν—λόγος σοφίας	(I. *To one, the word of wisdom*,)
2. ἄλλῳ δὲ λόγος γνώσεως . .	(2. *to another, the word of knowledge*.)
II. 'ΕΤΕΡΩ δὲ πίστις	(II. *To another, faith*,)
1. ἄλλῳ δὲ χαρίσματα ἰαμάτων	(1. *to another, gifts of healing*,)
2. ἄλλῳ δὲ ἐνεργήματα δυνάμεων	(2. *to another, working of miracles*,)
3. ἄλλῳ δὲ προφητεία	(3. *to another, prophecy*,)
4. ἄλλῳ δὲ διακρίσεις πνευμάτων	(4. *to another, discerning of spirits*.)
III. 'ΕΤΕΡΩ δὲ γένη γλωσσῶν . .	(III. *To another, divers kinds of tongues*,)
2. ἄλλῳ δὲ ἑρμηνεία γλωσσῶν .	(2. *to another, interpretation of tongues*.)

Thus the *first* class includes " the word of wisdom," and " the word of knowledge." Under the head of *faith*, that is, the faith of miracles, four kinds of gifts are enumerated—" gifts of healing,"—" working of miracles,"

11. *One and the same spirit distributing.* Hence it follows that those act amiss who, having no concern as to
participation, break asunder that holy harmony, that is fitly
adjusted in all its parts, only when under the guidance of
the same Spirit, all conspire toward one and the same object. He again calls the Corinthians to unity, by reminding
them that all have derived from one fountain whatever they
possess, while he instructs them, at the same time, that no
one has so much as to have enough within himself, so as not
to require help from others. For this is what he means by
these words—*distributing to every one severally as he willeth.*
The Spirit of God, therefore, distributes them among us, in
order that we may make all contribute to the common advantage. To no one does he give all, lest any one, satisfied
with his particular portion, should separate himself from
others, and live solely for himself. The same idea is intended in the adverb *severally,* as it is of great importance
to understand accurately that diversity by which God unites
us mutually to one another.[1] Now, when *will* is ascribed to
the Spirit, and that, too, in connection with power, we may
conclude from this, that the Spirit is truly and properly God.

12. *For as the body is one.* He now derives a similitude
from the human body, which he makes use of also in Rom.
xii. 4; but it is for a different purpose, as I have already
stated above.[2] In that passage, he exhorts every one to be
satisfied with his own calling, and not to invade another's
territory; as ambition, curiosity, or some other disposition,
induces many to take in hand more than is expedient.
Here, however, he exhorts believers to cleave to each other
in a mutual distribution of gifts, as they were not conferred upon them by God that every one should enjoy his
own separately, but that one should help another. It is
usual, however, for any society of men, or congregation, to
be called a *body,* as one city constitutes a *body,* and so,

—" prophecy," and " discerning of spirits;" while the *third* class includes
" divers kinds of tongues," and " the interpretation of tongues." See
Henderson on Inspiration, pp. 185-187.—*Ed.*
    [1] " Par laquelle Dieu nou conioint et oblige mutuellement les uns aux
autres;"—" By which God connects and binds us mutually to one another."
    [2] See p. 398.

in like manner, one senate, and one people. Menenius
Agrippa,[1] too, in ancient times, when desirous to conciliate
the Roman people, when at variance with the senate, made
use of an apologue, not very unlike the doctrine of Paul
here.[2] Among Christians, however, the case is very different; for they do not constitute a mere political body, but
are the spiritual and mystical body of Christ, as Paul himself afterwards adds. (ver. 27.) The meaning therefore
is—" Though the members of the body are various, and
have different functions, they are, nevertheless, linked together in such a manner that they coalesce in one.[3] We,
accordingly, who are members of Christ, although we are
endowed with various gifts, ought, notwithstanding, to have
an eye to that connection which we have in Christ."

So also is Christ. The name of Christ is used here instead
of the Church, because the similitude was intended to apply—not to God's only-begotten Son, but to us. It is a passage that is full of choice consolation, inasmuch as he calls
the Church *Christ;* for Christ[4] confers upon us this honour
—that he is willing to be esteemed and recognised, not in
himself merely, but also in his members. Hence the same
Apostle says elsewhere, (Eph. i. 23,) that the Church is his
completion,[5] as though he would, if separated from his members, be incomplete. And certainly, as Augustine elegantly

[1] Menenius Agrippa, a Roman consul, on occasion of a rebellion breaking out among the common people against the nobles and senators, whom
they represented as useless and cumbersome to the state, was successful in
quelling the insurrection, by a happy use of the apologue referred to, founded
on the intimate connection and mutual dependence of the different parts
of the body. The reader will find this interesting incident related by *Livy,*
Book ii. chap. 32.— *Ed.*

[2] " En remonstrant que les membres du corps ayans conspiré contre le
ventre, et se voulans separer d'auec luy s'en trouuerent mal les premiers;"
—" By showing that the members of the body, having conspired against
the belly, and wishing to separate from it, were the first to experience the
bad effects of this."

[3] " Ils prenent nourriture et accroissement l'un auec l'autre;"—" They
take nourishment and increase, one with another."

[4] " Ce bon Seigneur Iesus;"—" This good Lord Jesus."

[5] CALVIN, along with some other interpreters, understands the term
πλήρωμα, (*fulness,*) in the passage referred to, in an *active* sense. *Theo-
phylact* observes that the Church is the Πλήρωμα—*completion* of Christ, as
the body and limbs are of the head. The term may, however, be taken
in a *passive* sense, as meaning *a thing to be filled or completed.—Ed.*

expresses himself in one part of his writings—"Since we are *in* Christ a fruit-bearing vine, what are we *out of* him but dry twigs?" (John xv. 4.) In this, then, our consolation lies —that, as he and the Father are one, so we are one with him. Hence it is that his name is applied to us.

13. *For we are all baptized by one Spirit.* Here there is a proof brought forward from the effect of baptism. "We are," says he, "engrafted by baptism into Christ's body, so that we are by a mutual link bound together as members, and live one and the same life. Hence every one, that would remain in the Church of Christ, must necessarily cultivate this fellowship." He speaks, however, of the baptism of believers, which is efficacious through the grace of the Spirit, for, in the case of many, baptism is merely in the letter—the symbol without the reality; but believers, along with the sacrament, receive the reality. Hence, with respect to God, this invariably holds good—that baptism is an engrafting into the body of Christ, for God in that ordinance does not represent anything but what he is prepared to accomplish, provided we are on our part capable of it. The Apostle, also, observes here a most admirable medium, in teaching that the nature of baptism is—to connect us with Christ's body. Lest any one, however, should imagine, that this is effected by the outward symbol, he adds that it is the work of the Holy Spirit.

Whether Jews or Greeks. He specifies these instances, to intimate, that no diversity of condition obstructs that holy unity which he recommends. This clause, too, is added suitably and appropriately, for envy might at that time arise from two sources—because the Jews were not willing that the Gentiles should be put upon a level with them ; and, where one had some excellence above others, with the view of maintaining his superiority, he withdrew himself to a distance from his brethren.

We have all drunk in one Spirit. It is literally, "*We* have drunk *into* one Spirit," but it would seem that, in order that the two words ἐν (*in*) and ἐν (*one*) might not immediately follow each other, Paul intentionally changed ἐν (*in*) into εἰς (*into*,) as he is accustomed frequently to do. Hence his meaning seems rather to be, that we are made to drink through the influence, as he had said before, of the Spirit of Christ, than that we have drunk into the same Spirit. It is uncertain, however, whether he speaks here of Baptism or of the Supper. I am rather inclined, however, to understand him as referring to the Supper, as he makes mention of *drinking*, for I have no doubt that he intended to make an allusion to the similitude of the sign. There is, however, no correspondence between *drinking* and baptism. Now, though the cup forms but the half of the Supper, there is no difficulty arising from that, for it is a common thing in Scripture to speak of the sacraments by synecdoche.[1] Thus he mentioned above in the tenth chapter (verse 17) simply the *bread*, making no mention of the cup. The meaning, therefore, will be this—that participation in the cup has an eye to this—that we drink, all of us, of the same cup. For in that ordinance we drink of the life-giving blood of Christ, that we may have life in common with him—which we truly have, when he lives in us by his Spirit. He teaches, therefore, that believers, so soon as they are initiated by the baptism of Christ, are already imbued with a desire of cultivating mutual unity,[2] and then afterwards, when they receive the sacred Supper, they are again conducted by degrees to the same unity, as they are all refreshed at the same time with the same drink.

14. For the body is not one member, but many.

15. If the foot shall say, Because I am not the hand, I am not of the body; is it therefore not of the body?

16. And if the ear shall say, Because I am not the eye, I am not of the body; is it therefore not of the body?

17. If the whole body *were* an

14. Etenim corpus non est unum membrum, sed multa.

15. Si dixerit pes: Quoniam non sum manus, non sum ex corpore: an propterea non est ex corpore?

16. Et si dixerit auris: Quia non sum oculus, non sum ex corpore: an propterea non est ex corpore?

17. Si totum corpus oculus, ubi

---

[1] A figure of speech, by which a part is put for the whole. (See p. 53, *n.* 1.)   See *Quinctilian*. (*Inst.* viii. 6, 19.)

[2] " Si tost qu'ils sont amenez à Christ par le baptesme, desia leur est donné un goust de l'affection qu'ils doyuent auoir d'entretenir entr'eux unite et conionction naturelle ;"—" So soon as they are brought to Christ by baptism, there is already given to them some taste of the disposition which they ought to have, to maintain among themselves a natural unity and connection."

eye, where *were* the hearing? If the whole *were* hearing, where *were* the smelling?

18. But now hath God set the members every one of them in the body, as it hath pleased him.

19. And if they were all one member, where *were* the body?

20. But now *are they* many members, yet but one body.

21. And the eye cannot say unto the hand, I have no need of thee: nor again the head to the feet, I have no need of you.

22. Nay, much more those members of the body, which seem to be more feeble, are necessary :

23. And those *members* of the body, which we think to be less honourable, upon these we bestow more abundant honour ; and our uncomely *parts* have more abundant comeliness.

24. For our comely *parts* have no need : but God hath tempered the body together, having given more abundant honour to that *part* which lacked :

25. That there should be no schism in the body ; but *that* the members should have the same care one for another.

26. And whether one member suffer, all the members suffer with it ; or one member be honoured, all the members rejoice with it.

27. Now ye are the body of Christ, and members in particular.

auditus? si totum auditus, ubi olfactus?

18. Nunc vero Deus posuit membra, unumquodque ipsorum in corpore prout voluit.

19. Quodsi essent omnia unum membrum, ubi corpus?

20. At nunc multa quidem membra, unum autem corpus.

21. Nec potest oculus dicere manui : Ego te opus non habeo. Nec rursum caput pedibus : Vobis opus non habeo.

22. Quin potius, quae infirmiora corporis membra videntur esse, necessaria sunt :

23. Et quae iudicamus viliora esse in corpore, his abundantiorem honorem circumdamus : et quae minus honesta sunt in nobis, plus decoris habent.

24. Quae autem decora sunt in nobis, non habent opus, sed Deus contemperavit corpus, tribuens honorem abundantiorem opus habenti,

25. Ut ne dissidium esset in corpore, sed ut membra alia pro aliis invicem eandem sollicitudinem habeant.

26. Et sive patitur unum membrum, compatiuntur omnia membra : sive glorificatur unum membrum, congaudent omnia membra.

27. Vos autem estis corpus Christi, et membra ex parte.

15. This is a bringing out still farther (ἐπεξεργασία) of the preceding statement, or in other words, an exposition of it, with some amplification, with the view of placing in a clearer light, what he had previously stated in a few words. Now all this accords with the apologue of Menenius Agrippa.[1] "Should a dissension break out in the body, so that the feet would refuse to discharge their office to the rest of the body, and the belly in like manner, and the eyes, and the hands, what would be the effect? Would not the result be —the destruction of the whole body?" At the same time

[1] See p. 405.

Paul here insist smore particularly on this one point—that
each member ought to rest satisfied with its own place and
station, and not envy the others, for he institutes a comparison between the more distinguished members, and those
that have less dignity.   For the *eye* has a more honourable
place in the body than the *hand*, and the *hand* than the
foot.   But if our hands were, from a feeling of envy, to
refuse to discharge their office, would nature endure this ?
Would the hand be listened to, when wishing to be separated
from the body ?

To be not of the body, means here—to have no communication with the other members, but to live for itself, and to
seek only its own advantage.   " Would it then," says Paul,
" be allowable for the hand to refuse to do its office to the
other members, on the ground of its bearing envy to the
eyes ?"   These things are said of the natural body, but they
must be applied to the members of the Church, lest ambition
or misdirected emulation and envy should be the occasion of
bad feeling among us,[1] so as to lead one that occupies an
inferior station to grudge to afford his services to those
above him.

17. *If the whole body were an eye.*   He sets aside a foolish
aiming at equality, by showing the impossibility of it.   " If
all the members," says he, " desire the honour that belongs
to the *eye*, the consequence will be, that the whole body will
perish ; for it is impossible that the body should remain safe
and sound, if the members have not different functions, and
a mutual correspondence between them.   Hence equality
interferes with the welfare of the body, because it produces
a confusion that entails present ruin.   What madness, then,
would it be, should one member, instead of giving way to
another,[2] conspire for its own ruin and that of the body !"

18. *But now God hath placed.*   Here we have another
argument, taken from the appointment of God.   " It has
pleased God, that the body should consist of various members, and that the members should be endowed with various

---

[1] " Nous face restraindre et espargner les vns enuers les autres ;"—
" Make us restrict and spare ourselves—one towards another."

[2] " De s'accommoder et soumettre à l'un des autres membres ;"—" To
accommodate itself, and submit to one of the other members."

offices and gifts. That member, therefore, which will not rest satisfied with its own station, will wage war with God after the manner of the giants.[1] Let us, therefore, be subject to the arrangement which God has appointed, that we may not, to no purpose, resist his will."[2]

19. *If all were one member.* He means, that God has not acted at random, or without good reason, in assigning different gifts to the members of the body; but because it was necessary that it should be so, for the preservation of the body; for if this symmetry were taken away, there would be utter confusion and derangement. Hence we ought to submit ourselves the more carefully to the providence of God, which has so suitably arranged everything for our common advantage. *One member* is taken here to mean a mass, that is all of one shape, and not distinguished by any variety; for if God were to fashion our body into a mass of this kind, it would be a useless heap.[3]

20. *Many members—one body.* He repeats this the oftener, because the stress of the whole question lies here— that the unity of the body is of such a nature as cannot be maintained but by a diversity of members; and that, while the members differ from each other in offices and functions, it is in such a way as to have a mutual connection with each other for the preservation of the one body. Hence no body can retain its standing without a diversified symmetry of the members, that we may know to consult public as well as private advantage, by discharging, every one, the duty of his own station.

21. *And the eye cannot say to the hand.* Hitherto he has been showing, what is the office of the less honourable members—to discharge their duty to the body, and not envy the more distinguished members. *Now,* on the other hand, he enjoins it upon the more honourable members, not to despise the inferior members, which they cannot dispense with.

---

[1] " Comme les poetes ont dit anciennement des geans;"—" As the poets have told of the giants in ancient times." The fabled war of the giants with the gods is referred to in Homer's Odyssey, 7, 59, 206; 10, 120. —*Ed.*

[2] " De peur de perdre temps, and nous gaster en resistant à la volonté;"— " Lest we should lose time, and do hurt to ourselves by resisting his will."

[3] " Un amas de chair inutile;"—" A heap of useless flesh."

The *eye* excels the *hand,* and yet cannot despise it, or insult over it, as though it were useless ; and he draws an argument from utility, to show that it ought to be thus—" Those members, that are less esteemed, are the more necessary : hence, with a view to the safety of the body, they must not be despised." He makes use of the term *weaker* here, to mean *despised,* as in another passage, when he says that he *glories in his infirmities,* (2 Cor. xii. 9,) he expresses, under this term, those things which rendered him contemptible and abject.

23. *Which are less honourable.* Here we have a *second* argument—that the dishonour of one member turns out to the common disgrace of the whole body, as appears from the care that we take to cover the parts that are *less honourable.* "Those parts that are *comely,"* says he, "do not require adventitious ornament ; but the parts that involve shame, or are less comely, are cared for by us with greater concern. Why so? but because their shame would be the common disgrace of the whole body." *To invest with honour* is to put on a covering for the sake of ornament, in order that those members may be honourably concealed, which would involve shame if uncovered.[1]

24. *But God hath tempered the body together.* He again repeats, what he had stated once before, (ver. 18,) but more explicitly,—that God has appointed this symmetry, and that with a view to the advantage of the whole body, because it cannot otherwise maintain its standing. "For whence comes it, that all the members are of their own accord concerned for the honour of a less comely member, and agree together to conceal its shame? This inclination has been implanted in them by God, because without this adjustment *a schism in the body* would quickly break out. Hence it appears that the body is not merely shattered, and the order of nature perverted, but the authority of God is openly set at nought, whenever any one assumes more than belongs to him."[2]

---

[1] It is observed by *Raphelius,* that τιμὴν περιτιθέναι " signifies, in general, (*honorem exhibere,*) *to give honour;* but in this passage, by a metonymy, to *cover over with a garment* those members of the body which, if seen, would have a disagreeable and unseemly appearance ; and this is a kind of honour put upon them."—*Ed.*

[2] " Et que ne porte sa vocation ;"—"And does not keep within his calling."

26. *Whether one member suffers.* "Such a measure of *fel-low-feeling,*" (συμπάθεια,)[1] says he, "is to be seen in the human body, that, if any inconvenience is felt by any member, all the others grieve along with it, and, on the other hand, rejoice along with it, in its prosperity. Hence there is no room there for envy or contempt." To be *honoured,* here, is taken in a large sense, as meaning, to be *in prosperity and happiness.* Nothing, however, is better fitted to promote harmony than this community of interest, when every one feels that, by the prosperity of others, he is proportionally enriched, and, by their penury, impoverished.

27. *But ye are the body of Christ.* Hence what has been said respecting the nature and condition of the human body must be applied to us; for we are not a mere civil society, but, being ingrafted into Christ's body, are truly members one of another. Whatever, therefore, any one of us has, let him know that it has been given him for the edification of his brethren in common; and let him, accordingly, bring it forward, and not keep it back—buried, as it were, within himself, or make use of it as his own. Let not the man, who is endowed with superior gifts, be puffed up with pride, and despise others; but let him consider that there is nothing so diminutive as to be of no use—as, in truth, even the least among the pious brings forth fruit, according to his slender capacity, so that there is no useless member in the Church. Let not those who are not endowed with so much honour, envy those above them, or refuse to do their duty to them, but let them maintain the station in which they have been placed. Let there be mutual affection, mutual *fellow-feeling,* (συμπάθεια,) mutual concern. Let us have a regard to the common advantage, in order that we may not destroy the Church by malignity, or envy, or pride, or any disagreement; but may, on the contrary, every one of us, strive to the utmost of his power to preserve it. Here is a large subject, and a magnificent one;[2] but I content

[1] The term is made use of in this sense by classical authors. Polyb. 22, 11, 12. See CALVIN'S *Harmony,* vol. ii. p. 232.—*Ed.*

[2] " Voyci vne belle matiere riche et abondante;"— " Here is a fine subject, rich and copious."

myself with having pointed out the way in which the above similitude must be applied to the Church.

Members severally. Chrysostom is of opinion, that this clause is added, because the Corinthians were not the universal Church ; but this appears to me rather forced.[1] I have sometimes thought that it was expressive of impropriety, as the Latins say—*Quodammodo,*[2] (*in a manner.*)[3] When, however, I view the whole matter more narrowly, I am rather disposed to refer it to that division of members of which he had made mention. They are then *members severally,* according as each one has had his portion and definite work assigned him. The context itself leads us to this meaning. In this way *severally,* and *as a whole,* will be opposite terms.

28. And God hath set some in the Church, first apostles, secondarily prophets, thirdly teachers, after that miracles, then gifts of healings, helps, governments, diversities of tongues.

28. Et alios quidem posuit Deus in Ecclesia, primum apostolos, deinde Prophetas, tertio Doctores, postea Potestates, deinde dona sanationum, opitulationes, gubernationes, genera linguarum.

29. *Are* all apostles? *are* all prophets? *are* all teachers? *are* all workers of miracles?

29. Numquid omnes Apostoli? numquid omnes Prophetæ? numquid omnes Doctores? numquid omnes Potestates?

30. Have all the gifts of healing? do all speak with tongues? do all interpret?

30. Numquid omnes dona habent sanationum? numquid omnes linguis loquuntur? numquid omnes interpretantur?

31. But covet earnestly the best gifts: and yet shew I unto you a more excellent way.

31. Sectamini autem dona potiora.[4]

He has in the beginning of the chapter spoken of *gifts :* now he begins to treat of *offices,* and this order it is proper that we should carefully observe. For the Lord did not appoint ministers, without first endowing them with the requisite gifts, and qualifying them for discharging their duty.

[1] It is remarked by *Billroth,* that " the view of Chrysostom is out of place; for such a notion does not pertain to the argumentation of the Apostle." Biblical Cabinet, No. xxii., p. 39.—*Ed.*

[2] An instance of this will be found in *Cicero de Amicitia,* 8.—*Ed.*

[3] " Comme nous disons en Langue vulgaire, Aucunement;"—" As we say in common language—In a manner."

[4] " Ou, Soyez couuoiteux des plus excellens dons, ou, estes-vous enuieux des plus excellens dons?"—" Or, Be ambitious of the most excellent gifts, or, are you envious of the most excellent gifts?"

Hence we must infer, that those are fanatics, and actuated by an evil spirit, who intrude themselves into the Church, while destitute of the necessary qualifications, as many boast that they are under the influence of the Spirit, and glory in a secret call from God, while in the meantime they are unlearned and utterly ignorant. The natural order, on the other hand, is this—that gifts come before the office to be discharged. As, then, he has taught above, that everything that an individual has received from God, should be made subservient to the common good, so now he declares that offices are distributed in such a manner, that all may together, by united efforts, edify the Church, and each individual according to his measure.[1]

28. *First, Apostles.* He does not enumerate all the particular kinds, and there was no need of this, for he merely intended to bring forward some examples. In the fourth Chapter of the Epistle to the Ephesians, (verse 11,) there is a fuller enumeration of the offices, that are required for the continued government of the Church. The reason of this I shall assign there, if the Lord shall permit me to advance so far, though even there he does not make mention of them all. As to the passage before us, we must observe, that of the offices which Paul makes mention of, some are perpetual, others temporary. Those that are perpetual, are such as are necessary for the government of the Church; those that are temporary, are such as were appointed at the beginning for the founding of the Church, and the raising up of Christ's kingdom; and these, in a short time afterwards, ceased.

To the *first* class belongs the office of *Teacher*, to the *second* the office of *Apostle ;* for the Lord created the Apostles, that they might spread the gospel throughout the whole world, and he did not assign to each of them certain limits or parishes, but would have them, wherever they went, to discharge the office of ambassadors among all nations and languages. In this respect there is a difference between them and *Pastors,* who are, in a manner, tied to their parti-

---

[1] " Selon sa portion et mesure ;"—" According to his portion and measure."

cular churches. For the *Pastor* has not a commission to preach the gospel over the whole world, but to take care of the Church that has been committed to his charge. In his Epistle to the Ephesians he places *Evangelists* after the *Apostles*, but here he passes them over; for from the highest order, he passes immediately to *Prophets*.

By this term he means, (in my opinion,) not those who were endowed with the gift of prophesying, but those who were endowed with a peculiar gift, not merely for interpreting Scripture, but also for applying it wisely for present use.[1] My reason for thinking so is this, that he prefers prophecy to all other gifts, on the ground of its yielding more edification—a commendation that would not be applicable to the predicting of future events. Farther, when he describes the office of *Prophet*, or at least treats of what he ought principally to do, he says that he must devote himself to consolation, exhortation, and doctrine. Now these are things that are distinct from prophesyings.[2] Let us, then, by *Prophets* in this passage understand, *first* of all, eminent interpreters of Scripture, and farther, persons who are endowed with no common wisdom and dexterity in taking a right view of the present necessity of the Church, that they may speak suitably to it, and in this way be, in a manner, ambassadors to communicate the divine will.

Between them and *Teachers* this difference may be pointed out, that the office of *Teacher* consists in taking care that sound doctrines be maintained and propagated, in order that the purity of religion may be kept up in the Church. At the same time, even this term is taken in different senses, and here perhaps it is used rather in the sense of *Pastor*, unless you prefer, it may be, to take it in a general way for all that are endowed with the gift of teaching, as in Acts xiii. 1, where also Luke conjoins them with Prophets. My reason for not agreeing with those who make the whole of the office of *Prophet* consist in the interpretation of Scrip-

---

[1] " De l'accommoder prudemment, et l'appliquer en vsage selon les personnes et le temps;"—" To make use of it wisely, and apply it to use according to persons and time."

[2] " Et advertissemens des choses à venir;"—" And intimations or things to come."

ture, is this—that Paul restricts the number of those who ought to speak, to *two or three;* (1 Cor. xiv. 29,) which would not accord with a bare interpretation of Scripture. In fine, my opinion is this—that the Prophets here spoken of are those who make known the will of God, by applying with dexterity and skill prophecies, threatenings, promises, and the whole doctrine of Scripture, to the present use of the Church. If any one is of a different opinion, I have no objection to his being so, and will not raise any quarrel on that account. For it is difficult to form a judgment as to gifts and offices of which the Church has been so long deprived, excepting only that there are some traces, or shadows of them still to be seen.

As to *powers* and *gift of healings*, I have spoken when commenting on the 12th Chapter of the Romans. Only it must be observed that here he makes mention, not so much of the gifts themselves, as of the administration of them. As the Apostle is here enumerating offices, I do not approve of what Chrysostom says, that ἀντιλήψεις, that is, *helps* or *aids*, consist in supporting the weak. What is it then? Undoubtedly, it is either an office, as well as gift, that was exercised in ancient times, but of which we have at this day no knowledge whatever; or it is connected with the office of Deacon, or in other words, the care of the poor; and this latter idea pleases me better.[1] In Romans xii. 7, he makes mention of two kinds of deacons. Of these I have treated when commenting upon that passage.

By *Governments* I understand *Elders*, who had the charge of discipline. For the primitive Church had its Senate,[2] for the purpose of keeping the people in propriety of deport-

[1] This view of the import of the term ἀντιλήψεις, (*helps*,) is generally acquiesced in by modern interpreters. It is remarked by Dr. Dick, (in his *Theology*, vol. iv. p. 390,) that "there are no persons who may be so reasonably supposed to be meant by *helps*, as *deacons*;" who "were instituted for the express purpose of *helping* the Apostles, for the purpose of relieving them from the care of the poor, that they might devote themselves exclusively to the ministry of the word." He observes also, (p. 389,) that "it does not follow, because *some* of the offices and ministrations enumerated in this place were miraculous and extraordinary, that they were *all* of that description."—*Ed.*

[2] "Auoit comme son Senate, ou Consistoire;"—"Had its Senate, as it were, or Consistory."

ment, as Paul shows elsewhere, when he makes mention of two kinds of Presbyters.[1] (1 Tim. v. 17.) Hence *government* consisted of those Presbyters who excelled others in gravity, experience, and authority.

Under *different kinds of tongues* he comprehends both the knowledge of languages, and the gift of interpretation. They were, however, two distinct gifts ; because in some cases an individual spoke in different languages, and yet did not understand the language of the Church with which he had to do. This defect was supplied by interpreters.[2]

29. *Are all Apostles?* It may indeed have happened, that one individual was endowed with many gifts, and sustained two of the offices which he has enumerated ; nor was there in this any inconsistency. Paul's object, however, is to show in the *first* place, that no one has such a fulness in everything as to have a sufficiency within himself, and not require the aid of others ; and *secondly,* that offices as well as gifts are distributed in such a manner that no one member constitutes the whole body, but each contributing his portion to the common advantage, they then altogether constitute an entire and perfect body. For Paul means here to take away every occasion of proud boasting, base envyings, haughtiness, and contempt of the brethren, malignity, ambition, and everything of that nature.

31. *Seek after the more excellent gifts.* It might also be rendered—*Value highly ;* and it would not suit ill with the passage, though it makes little difference as to the meaning ; for Paul exhorts the Corinthians to esteem and desire those gifts especially, which are most conducive to edification. For this fault prevailed among them—that they aimed at show, rather than usefulness. Hence *prophecy* was neglected, while *languages* sounded forth among them, with great show, indeed, but with little profit. He does not, however, address individuals, as though he wished that every one should aspire at prophecy, or the office of teacher ; but

---

[1] " Deux ordres de Prestres : c'est à dire d'Anciens ;"—" Two kinds of Presbyters : that is to say, Elders."

[2] Our Author repeats here what he had stated when commenting on verse 10th. (See p. 403.)—*Ed.*

simply recommends to them a desire to promote edification, that they may apply themselves the more diligently to those things that are most conducive to edification.

CHAPTER XIII.

1. Though I speak with the tongues of men and of angels, and have not charity, I am become *as* sounding brass, or a tinkling cymbal.

2. And though I have *the gift of* prophecy, and understand all mysteries and all knowledge; and though I have all faith, so that I could remove mountains, and have not charity, I am nothing.

3. And though I bestow all my goods to feed *the poor*, and though I give my body to be burned, and have not charity, it profiteth me nothing.

1. Et adhuc excellentiorem viam vobis demonstro. Si linguis hominum loquar et Angelorum, caritatem autem non habeam, factus sum tympanum sonans, aut cymbalum tinniens.

2. Et si habeam prophetiam, et noverim mysteria omnia omnemque scientiam, et si habeam omnem fidem, adeo ut montes loco dimoveam, caritatem autem non habeam, nihil sum.

3. Et si insumam in alimoniam omnes facultates meas, et si tradam corpus meum ut comburar, caritatem autem non habeam, nihil mihi prodest.

THE division of the Chapter being so absurd, I could not refrain from changing it, especially as I could not conveniently interpret it otherwise. For what purpose did it serve to connect with what goes before a detached sentence, which agrees so well with what comes after—nay more, is thereby rendered complete? It is likely, that it happened through a mistake on the part of the transcribers. However it may be as to this, after having commanded that regard should be had chiefly to edification, he now declares that he will show them something of greater importance—that everything be regulated according to the rule of *love*. This, then, is *the most excellent way*, when *love* is the regulating principle of all our actions. And, in the outset, he proceeds upon this—that all excellencies[1] are of no value without *love;* for nothing is so excellent or estimable as not to be vitiated in the sight of God, if *love*[2] is wanting. Nor

---

[1] " Quelles qu'elles soyent ;"—" Whatever they are."
[2] *Penn*, in his *Annotations*, gives the following account of the term *charity*, as made use of in our English translation—" If the Latin version

does he teach anything here but what he does elsewhere, when he declares, that it is the *end of the law*, and the *bond of perfection*, (1 Tim. i. 5,) and also when he makes the holiness of the godly consist entirely in this, (Col. iii. 14,)— for what else does God require from us in the second Table of the Law? It is not then to be wondered, if all our deeds are estimated by this test—their appearing to proceed from love. It is also not to be wondered, if gifts, otherwise excellent, come to have their true value only when they are made subservient to *love*.

1. *If I should speak with the tongues of men.* He begins with eloquence, which is, it is true, an admirable gift, considered in itself, but, when apart from *love*, does not recommend a man in the estimation of God. When he speaks of the *tongue of angels*, he uses a hyperbolical expression to denote what is singular, or distinguished. At the same time, I explain it rather as referring to the diversity of languages, which the Corinthians held in much esteem, measuring everything by ambition—not by fruit.[1] "Make yourself master," says he, "of all the languages, not of men merely, but even of Angels. You have, in that case, no reason to think, that you are of higher estimation in the sight of God than a mere cymbal, if you have not *love*."

2. *And if I should have the gift of prophecy.* He brings down to nothing the dignity of even this endowment,[2] which, nevertheless, he had preferred to all others. *To know all*

---

had not rendered αγαπη, in this place, by ' *charitas*,' instead of ' *amor—love*,' we should not have found the word ' *charity*' in our English version. But Wiclif, who only knew the Latin Scripture, adopted from it that word, and rendered, ' and I have not *charite*.' When the knowledge of the Greek was acquired by our learned Reformers, the first revisers of Wiclif were sensible of the unsuitableness of this translation, and rendered this clause—'and yet had no *love*,' as it is printed in the ' *Newe Testament in Englishe and Latin, of* 1548;' and they rendered αγαπη—' *love*,' throughout this chapter. Our last revisers abandoned this sound correction of their immediate predecessors, and brought back the Latinising ' charity' of Wiclif, who was only excusable for employing that word, because he translated from a Latin text, in ignorance of its Greek original."—*Ed.*

[1] " Par le fruit qui s'en pouuoit ensuyure;"—"By the fruit that might result from it."

[2] " La dignite mesme de la prophetie;"—"The dignity even of prophecy."

mysteries, might seem to be added to the term *prophecy*, by way of explanation, but as the term *knowledge* is immediately added, of which he had previously made mention by itself, (1 Cor. xiv. 8,) it will deserve your consideration, whether the *knowledge of mysteries* may not be used here to mean *wisdom*. As for myself, while I would not venture to affirm that it is so, I am much inclined to that opinion.

That *faith*, of which he speaks, is special, as is evident from the clause that is immediately added—*so that I remove mountains*. Hence the Sophists accomplish nothing, when they pervert this passage for the purpose of detracting from the excellence of faith. As, therefore, the term *faith* is (πολύσημον) *used in a variety of senses*, it is the part of the prudent reader to observe in what signification it is taken. Paul, however, as I have already stated, is his own interpreter, by restricting *faith*, here, to miracles. It is what Chrysostom calls the " faith of miracles," and what we term a " special faith," because it does not apprehend a whole Christ, but simply his power in working miracles; and hence it may sometimes exist in a man without the Spirit of sanctification, as it did in Judas.[1]

3. *And if I should expend all my possessions.*[2] This, it is true, is worthy of the highest praise, if considered in itself; but as liberality in many cases proceeds from ambition—not from true generosity, or even the man that is liberal is destitute of the other departments of love, (for even liberality, that is inwardly felt, is only one department of *love*,) it may happen that a work, otherwise so commendable, has, indeed, a fair show in the sight of men, and is applauded by them, and yet is regarded as nothing in the sight of God.

And if I should give up my body. He speaks, undoubtedly, of martyrdom, which is an act that is the most lovely and excellent of all; for what is more admirable than that invincible fortitude of mind, which makes a man not hesitate to pour out his life for the testimony of the gospel ?

---

[1] The reader will observe, that this is, in substance, what has been stated by Calvin previously, when commenting on 1 Cor. xii. 10. (See p. 403.) —*Ed.*

[2] " Et si ie distribue tous mes biens ;"—" And if I should distribute all my goods."

Yet even this, too, God regards as nothing, if the mind is destitute of *love*. The kind of punishment that he makes mention of was not then so common among Christians; for we read that tyrants, at that time, set themselves to destroy the Church, rather by swords than by flames,[1] except that Nero, in his rage, had recourse, also, to burning. The Spirit appears, however, to have predicted here, by Paul's mouth, the persecutions that were coming. But this is a digression. The main truth in the passage is this—that as *love* is the only rule of our actions, and the only means of regulating the right use of the gifts of God, nothing, in the absence of it, is approved of by God, however magnificent it may be in the estimation of men. For where it is wanting, the beauty of all virtues is mere tinsel—is empty sound —is not worth a straw—nay more, is offensive and disgusting. As for the inference which Papists draw from this— that *love* is therefore of more avail for our justification than faith, we shall refute it afterwards. At present, we must proceed to notice what follows.

4. Charity suffereth long, *and* is kind: charity envieth not: charity vaunteth not itself, is not puffed up,

5. Doth not behave itself unseemly, seeketh not her own, is not easily provoked, thinketh no evil;

6. Rejoiceth not in iniquity, but rejoiceth in the truth;

7. Beareth all things, believeth all things, hopeth all things, endureth all things.

8. Charity never faileth: but whether *there be* prophecies, they shall fail; whether *there be* tongues, they shall cease; whether *there be* knowledge, it shall vanish away.

4. Caritas patiens est, benigne agit, caritas non aemulatur, caritas non agit insolenter, non inflatur:

5. Non agit indecenter, non quaerit sua ipsius, non provocatur, non cogitat malum:

6. Non gaudet ob iniustitiam, congaudet autem veritati.

7. Omnia fert, omnia credit, omnia sperat, omnia sustinet.

8. Caritas nunquam excidit: sive prophetiae abolebuntur, sive linguae cessabunt, sive scientia destruetur.

4. *Love is patient.* He now commends *love* from its effects or fruits, though at the same time these eulogiums

---

[1] " Les tyrans faisoyent plustot trancher la teste aux Chrestiens et vsoyent plustot du glaiue que du feu pour destruire l'Eglise;"—" Tyrants practised rather the beheading of Christians, and made use of the sword, rather than of fire, for the destruction of the Church."

are not intended merely for its commendation, but to make the Corinthians understand what are its offices, and what is its nature. The object, however, mainly in view, is to show how necessary it is for preserving the unity of the Church. I have also no doubt that he designed indirectly to reprove the Corinthians, by setting before them a contrast, in which they might recognise, by way of contraries, their own vices.

The *first* commendation of love is this—that, by patient endurance of many things, it promotes peace and harmony in the Church. Near akin to this is the *second* excellence—gentleness and lenity, for such is the meaning of the verb χρηστεύεσθαι.[1] A *third* excellence is—that it counteracts *emulation,* the seed of all contentions. Under *emulation* he comprehends envy, which is a vice near akin to it, or rather, he means that emulation, which is connected with envy, and frequently springs from it. Hence where envy reigns—where every one is desirous to be the first, or appear so, love *there* has no place.

What I have rendered—*does not act insolently*—is in the Greek οὐ περπερεύεται. Erasmus has rendered it, *is not froward.*[2] It is certain that the word has different significations; but, as it is sometimes taken to mean—being *fierce, or insolent, through presumption,* this meaning seemed to be more suitable to the passage before us.[3] Paul, therefore, ascribes to *love* moderation, and declares that it is a bridle to restrain men, that they may not break forth into ferocity, but may

---

[1] The distinction between the *first* and *second* of the commendations here bestowed upon *love* is stated by *Bloomfield* as follows: Μακροθυμεῖ, " denotes *lenity,* as opposed to passion and revenge : and χρηστεύεται, *gentleness,* as opposed to severity and misanthropy."—*Ed.*

[2] This rendering is followed in two of the old English translations, viz. Tyndale (1534) and Cranmer (1539.) " Love doth not frowardly."—*Ed.*

[3] Interpreters are by no means agreed as to the precise import of the original term περπερεύεται. Most ancient and many modern commentators explain it as meaning—" to act precipitately and rashly"—and in accordance with this, is the rendering given by our Translators in the *Margin*—*is not rash.* No *single* expression, however, appears to bring out more satisfactorily the import of the original word than that which our Translators have inserted in the *text*—*vaunteth not itself.* *Beausobre* makes use of *two* epithets. " N'est point *vaine* et *insolente ;*"—" Is not *vain* and *insolent.*"—*Ed.*

live together in a peaceable and orderly manner. He adds, farther, that it has nothing of the nature of pride.[1] That man, then, who is governed by *love, is not puffed up* with pride, so as to despise others and feel satisfied with himself.[2]

5. *Doth not behave itself unseemly.* Erasmus renders it— *" Is not disdainful;"* but as he quotes no author in support of this interpretation, I have preferred to retain its proper and usual signification. I explain it, however, in this way— that *love* does not exult in a foolish ostentation, or does not bluster, but observes moderation and propriety. And in this manner, he again reproves the Corinthians indirectly, because they shamefully set at nought all propriety by an unseemly haughtiness.[3]

Seeketh not its own. From this we may infer, how very far we are from having *love* implanted in us by nature; for we are naturally prone to have love and care for ourselves, and aim at our own advantage. Nay, to speak more correctly, we rush headlong into it.[4] For so perverse an inclination the remedy[5] is *love,* which leads us to leave off caring for ourselves, and feel concerned for our neighbours, so as to love them and be concerned for their welfare. Farther, *to seek one's own things,*[6] is to be devoted to self, and to be wholly taken up with concern for one's own advantage. This definition solves the question, whether it is lawful for a Christian to be concerned for his own advantage? for Paul does not

[1] " Il dit consequemment que charite *ne s'enfle point;"*—" He says consequently, that love *is not puffed up."*

[2] *Bloomfield* considers the distinction between this clause and the preceding one to be this, that the former " refers to *pride as shown in words,"* and the latter to " the *carriage* and *bearing,* to denote pride and haughtiness on account of certain external advantages." A similar view is taken by *Barnes,* who considers the *former* clause as referring to " the *expression* of the feelings of pride, vanity," &c. ; and the *latter,* to " the feeling itself."—*Ed.*

[3] The proper meaning of the verb ασχημονειν, is to *offend against decorum.* See Eurip. Hec. 407.—*Ed.*

[4] " Nous sommes transportez-là, et nous-nous y iettons sans moderation aucune :"—" We are hurried into it, and rush into it without any restraint."

[5] " Le remede unique ;"—" The only remedy."

[6] " Car il y a ainsi à le traduire mot à mot ;"—" For that is the literal meaning."

here reprove every kind of care or concern for ourselves, but the excess of it, which proceeds from an immoderate and blind attachment to ourselves. Now the excess lies in this —if we think of ourselves so as to neglect others, or if the desire of our own advantage calls us off from that concern, which God commands us to have as to our neighbours.[1] He adds, that *love* is also a bridle to repress quarrels, and this follows from the first two statements. For where there is gentleness and forbearance, persons in that case do not, on a sudden, become angry, and are not easily stirred up to disputes and contests.[2]

7. *Beareth all things*, &c. By all these statements he intimates, that love is neither impatient nor spiteful. For to *bear* and *endure all things* is the part of forbearance: to *believe* and *hope all things* is the part of candour and kindness. As we are naturally too much devoted to self, this vice renders us morose and peevish. The effect is, that every one wishes that others should carry him upon their shoulders, but refuses for his part to assist others. The remedy for this disease is *love*, which makes us subject to our brethren, and teaches us to apply our shoulders to *their burdens*. (Gal. vi. 2.) Farther, as we are naturally *spiteful*, we are, consequently, suspicious too, and take almost everything amiss. *Love*, on the other hand, calls us back to *kindness*, so that we think favourably and candidly of our neighbours.

When he says *all things*, you must understand him as referring to the things that *ought* to be *endured*, and in such a manner as is befitting. For we are not to bear with vices, so as to give our sanction to them by flattery, or, by winking at them, encourage them through our supineness. Farther, this *endurance* does not exclude corrections and just

---

[1] *Granville Penn* translates the clause as follows: " Seeketh not *what is not its own*,"—in accordance with the reading of the Vat. MS. οὐ ζητεῖ τὰ μὴ ἑαυτῆς. (*Seeketh not the things that are not its own*.) He supposes the μὴ (*not*) to have " lapsed, or been erroneously rejected from all the later copies."—*Ed.*

[2] The last clause of the verse, which is in our translation, *thinketh no evil*, is rendered by Bishop Pearce, " *meditateth no mischief*"—a sense in which the expression λογίζεσθαι κακον occurs in the Septuagint, in Ps. xxxv. 4, and xli. 7. It is beautifully rendered by *Bloomfield*, " does not enter it into a note-book, for future revenge."—*Ed.*

punishments.   The case is the same as to kindness in judging of things.

Love *believeth all things*—not that the Christian knowingly and willingly allows himself to be imposed upon—not that he divests himself of prudence and judgment, that he may be the more easily taken advantage of—not that he unlearns the way of distinguishing black from white.   What then? He requires here, as I have already said, *simplicity* and *kindness* in judging of things; and he declares that these[1] are the invariable accompaniments of *love*.   The consequence will be, that a Christian man will reckon it better to be imposed upon by his own kindness and easy temper, than to wrong his brother by an unfriendly suspicion.

8. *Love never faileth.*   Here we have another excellence of *love*—that it endures for ever.   There is good reason why we should eagerly desire an excellence that will never come to an end.   Hence *love* must be preferred before temporary and perishable gifts.   *Prophesyings have an end, tongues fail, knowledge ceases.*   Hence *love* is more excellent than they on this ground—that, while they fail, it survives.

Papists pervert this passage, for the purpose of establishing the doctrine which they have contrived, without any authority from Scripture—that the souls of the deceased pray to God on our behalf.   For they reason in this manner: "Prayer is a perpetual office of love—love endures in the souls of departed saints—therefore they pray for us." For my part, although I should not wish to contend too keenly on this point, yet, in order that they may not think that they have gained much by having this conceded to them, I reply to their objection in a few words.

In the *first* place, though love *endures for ever*, it does not necessarily follow that it is (as the expression is) in constant exercise.   For what is there to hinder our maintaining that the saints, being now in the enjoyment of calm repose, do not exercise *love* in present offices?[2]   What absurdity, I pray you, would there be in this?   In the *second* place, were I

---

[1] " Ceux deux vertus ;"—" These two virtues."

[2] " En secourant et aidant presentement à ceux qui sont en ce monde ;" —" In presently succouring and aiding those that are in this world."

to maintain, that it is *not* a perpetual office of *love* to intercede for the brethren, how would they prove the contrary ?
That a person may intercede for another, it is necessary that
he be acquainted with his necessity.   If we may conjecture
as to the state of the dead, it is a more probable supposition,
that departed saints are ignorant of what is doing here, than
that they are aware of our necessities. Papists, it is true, imagine, that they see the whole world in the reflection of light
which they enjoy in the vision of God ; but it is a profane
and altogether heathenish contrivance, which has more of the
savour of Egyptian theology,[1] than it has of accordance with
Christian philosophy. What, then, if I should maintain that
the saints, being ignorant of our condition, are *not* concerned
in reference to us ? With what argument will Papists press
me, so as to constrain me to hold their opinion ? What if I
should affirm, that they are so occupied and swallowed up,
as it were, in the vision of God, that they think of nothing
besides ? How will they prove that this is not agreeable to
reason ? What if I should reply, that the perpetuity of *love*,
here mentioned by the Apostle, will be after the last day,
and has nothing to do with the time that is intermediate ?
What if I should say that the office of mutual intercession
has been enjoined only upon the living, and those that are
sojourning in this world, and consequently does not at all
extend to the departed ?

But I have already said more than enough ; for the very
point for which they contend I leave undetermined, that I
may not raise any contention upon a matter that does not call
for it. It was, however, of importance to notice, in passing,
how little support is given them from this passage, in which
they think they have so strong a bulwark. Let us reckon
it enough, that it has no support from any declaration of
scripture, and that, consequently, it is maintained by them
rashly and inconsiderately.[2]

Whether knowledge, it will be destroyed. We have already
seen the meaning of these words ; but from this arises a

---

[1] See *Institutes*, vol. i. p. 190.—*Ed.*
[2] " C'est folie et presomption grande à eux de l'affermer ;"—" It is great
folly and presumption in them to affirm it."

question of no small importance—whether those who in this world excel either in learning, or in other gifts, will be on a level with idiots in the kingdom of God? In the *first* place, I should wish to admonish[1] pious readers, not to harass themselves more than is meet in the investigation of these things. Let them rather seek the way by which the kingdom of God is arrived at, than curiously inquire, what is to be our condition there; for the Lord himself has, by his silence, called us back from such curiosity. I now return to the question. So far as I can conjecture, and am able even to gather in part from this passage—inasmuch as learning, knowledge of languages, and similar gifts are subservient to the necessity of this life, I do not think that there will be any of them then remaining. The learned, however, will sustain no loss from the want of them, inasmuch as they will receive the fruit of them, which is greatly to be preferred.[2]

9. For we know in part, and we prophesy in part:

10. But when that which is perfect is come, then that which is in part shall be done away.

11. When I was a child, I spake as a child, I understood as a child, I thought as a child: but when I became a man, I put away childish things.

12. For now we see through a glass, darkly; but then face to face: now I know in part; but then shall I know even as also I am known.

13. And now abideth faith, hope, charity, these three; but the greatest of these *is* charity.

9. Ex parte enim cognoscimus, et ex parte prophetamus:

10. At ubi venerit quod perfectum est, tunc, quod ex parte est, abolebitur.

11. Quum essem puer, ut puer loquebar, ut puer sentiebam, ut puer cogitabam: at postquam factus sum vir, abolevi puerilia.

12. Cernimus enim nunc per speculum in aenigmate: tunc autem facie ad faciem: nunc cognosco ex parte: tunc vero cognoscam, quemadmodum et cognitus sum.

13. Nunc autem manet fides, spes, caritas, tria haec: sed maxima ex his est caritas.

He now proves that *prophecy*, and other gifts of that nature, are done away,[3] because they are conferred upon us to help our infirmity. Now our imperfection will one day

[1] " En premier lieu, i'admoneste et prie ;"—" In the first place, I admonish and beseech."
[2] " Qui est plus excellent sans comparaison ;"—" Which is, beyond comparison, more excellent."
[3] " Seront un iour abolis ;"—" Will one day be done away."

have an end. Hence the use, even of those gifts, will, at the same time, be discontinued, for it were absurd that they should remain and be of no use. They will, therefore, perish. This subject he pursues to the end of the chapter.

9. *We know in part.* This passage is misinterpreted by most persons, as if it meant that our knowledge, and in like manner our prophecy, is not yet perfect, but that we are daily making progress in them. Paul's meaning, however, is—that it is owing to our imperfection that we at present have knowledge and prophecy. Hence the phrase *in part* means —" Because we are not yet perfect.". Knowledge and prophecy, therefore, have place among us so long as that imperfection cleaves to us, to which they are helps. It is true, indeed, that we ought to make progress during our whole life, and that everything that we have is merely begun. Let us observe, however, what Paul designs to prove—that the gifts in question are but temporary. Now he proves this from the circumstance, that the advantage of them is only for a time—so long as we aim at the mark by making progress every day.

10. *When that which is perfect is come.* " When the goal has been reached, then the helps in the race will be done away." He retains, however, the form of expression that he had already made use of, when he contrasts *perfection* with what is *in part.* " Perfection," says he, " when it will arrive, will put an end to everything that aids imperfection." But when will that perfection come ? It begins, indeed, at death, for then we put off, along with the body, many infirmities ; but it will not be completely manifested until the day of judgment, as we shall hear presently. Hence we infer, that the whole of this discussion is ignorantly applied to the time that is intermediate.

11. *When I was a child.* He illustrates what he had said, by a similitude. For there are many things that are suitable to children, which are afterwards done away on arriving at maturity. For example, education is necessary for childhood ; it does not comport with mature age.[1] So long

---

[1] " Elle ne conuient point à ceux qui sont en aage de discretion ;"—" It does not become those who are at the age of discretion."

as we live in this world, we require, in some sense, education. We are far from having attained, as yet, the perfection
of wisdom. That perfection, therefore, which will be in a
manner a maturity of spiritual age, will put an end to education and its accompaniments. In his Epistle to the Ephesians, (iv. 14,) he exhorts us to be *no longer children ;* but he
has there another consideration in view, of which we shall
speak when we come to that passage.

12. *We now see through a glass.*   Here we have the application of the similitude. "The measure of knowledge, that
we now have, is suitable to imperfection and childhood, as it
were ; for we do not as yet see clearly the mysteries of the
heavenly kingdom, and we do not as yet enjoy a distinct
view of them."   To express this, he makes use of another
similitude—that *we now see only as in a glass,* and therefore
but obscurely.   This obscurity he expresses by the term
enigma.[1]

In the first place, there can be no doubt that it is the
ministry of the word, and the means that are required for
the exercise of it, that he compares to a *looking-glass.* For
God, who is otherwise invisible, has appointed these means
for discovering himself to us. At the same time, this may
also be viewed as extending to the entire structure of the
world, in which the glory of God shines forth to our view,
in accordance with what is stated in Rom. i. 16 ; and 2 Cor.
iii. 18.   In Rom. i. 20 the Apostle speaks of the creatures
as *mirrors,*[2] in which God's invisible majesty is to be seen ;
but as he treats here particularly of spiritual gifts, which
are subservient to the ministry of the Church, and are its
accompaniments, we shall not wander away from our present subject.

[1] The original term αἴνιγμα, (*enigma,*) properly means, a *dark saying.*
It is employed by classical writers in this sense. See Pind. Fr. 165.
Aesch. Pr. 610. The Apostle is generally supposed to have had in his
eye Numbers xii. 8, which is rendered in the Septuagint as follows : Στόμα
κατὰ στόμα λαλήσω αὐτῶ ἐν ἴδει, καὶ οὐ δι' αἰνίγματων ;—"I will speak to him
mouth to mouth in a vision, and not by *dark sayings.*"—*Ed.*

[2] " Et l'Apostre, en l'onzieme aux Heb., d. 13, nomme les creatures,
miroirs ;"—" And the Apostle, in Heb. xi. 13, speaks of the creatures as
mirrors."   There is obviously a mistake here in the quotation. Most
probably CALVIN had in his eye Heb. xi. 3, as a passage similar *in substance* to Rom. i. 20, quoted by him in his Latin Commentary.—*Ed.*

The ministry of the word, I say, is like a *looking-glass*. For the angels have no need of preaching, or other inferior helps, nor of sacraments, for they enjoy a vision of God of another kind;[1] and God does not give them a view of his face merely in a mirror, but openly manifests himself as present with them. We, who have not as yet reached that great height, behold the image of God as it is presented before us in the word, in the sacraments, and, in fine, in the whole of the service of the Church. This vision Paul here speaks of as partaking of obscurity—not as though it were doubtful or delusive, but because it is not so distinct as that which will be at last afforded on the final day. He teaches the same thing in other words, in the *second* Epistle—(2 Cor. v. 7) —that, *so long as we dwell in the body we are absent from the Lord; for we walk by faith, not by sight.* Our faith, therefore, at present beholds God as absent. How so? Because it sees not his face, but rests satisfied with the image in the *mirror;* but when we shall have left the world, and gone to him, it will behold him as near and before its eyes.

Hence we must understand it in this manner—that the knowledge of God, which we now have from his word, is indeed certain and true, and has nothing in it that is confused, or perplexed, or dark, but is spoken of as comparatively *obscure,* because it comes far short of that clear manifestation to which we look forward; for then *we shall see face to face.*[2] Thus this passage is not at all at variance with other passages, which speak of the clearness, at one time, of the law,

---

[1] " Ils ont vn autre iouissance de la presence de Dieu;"—" They have another enjoyment of the presence of God."

[2] " The blessed God's manifestation of himself," says Mr. Howe, " is emphatically expressed in 1 Cor. xiii. 12—of *seeing face to face,* which signifies on *his* part, gracious vouchsafement,—his offering his blessed face to view,—that he hides it not, nor turns it away, as here sometimes he doth, in just displeasure. And his face means, even his most conspicuous glory, such as, in this state of mortality, it would be mortal to us to behold; for 'no man,' not so divine a man as Moses himself, ' could see his face and live.' And it signifies, on *their* part who are thus made perfect, their applying and turning their face towards his, viz., that they see not casually, or by fortuitous glances, but eye to eye, by direct and most voluntary intuition; which, therefore, on their part, implies moral perfection, the will directing and commanding the eye, and upon inexpressible relishes of joy and pleasure, forbidding its diversion, holds it steady and intent." Howe's Works, (Lond. 1834,) p. 1016.— *Ed.*

at another time, of the entire Scripture, but more especially of the gospel. For we have in the word (in so far as is expedient for us) a naked and open revelation of God, and it has nothing intricate in it, to hold us in suspense, as wicked persons imagine ;[1] but how small a proportion does this bear to *that* vision, which we have in our eye! Hence it is only in a comparative sense, that it is termed *obscure*.

The adverb *then* denotes the last day, rather than the time that is immediately subsequent to death. At the same time, although full vision will be deferred until the day of Christ, a nearer view of God will begin to be enjoyed immediately after death, when our souls, set free from the body, will have no more need of the outward ministry, or other inferior helps. Paul, however, as I noticed a little ago, does not enter into any close discussion as to the state of the dead, because the knowledge of that is not particularly serviceable to piety.

Now I know in part. That is, the measure of our present knowledge is imperfect, as John says in his Epistle, (1 John iii. 1, 2,) that *we know, indeed, that we are the sons of God, but* that *it doth not yet appear, until we shall see God as he is. Then* we shall see God—not in his image, but in himself, so that there will be, in a manner, a mutual view.

13. *But now remaineth faith, hope, love.* This is a conclusion from what goes before—that love is more excellent than other gifts ; but in place of the enumeration of gifts that he had previously made, he now puts *faith* and *hope* along with *love*, as all those gifts are comprehended under this summary. For what is the object of the entire ministry, but that we may be instructed as to these things ?[2] Hence the term *faith* has a larger acceptation here, than in previous instances ; for it is as though he had said—"There are, it is true, many and various gifts, but they all point to this object, and have an eye to it."

To *remain*, then, conveys the idea, that, as in the reckoning up of an account, when everything has been deducted,

[1] " Comme imaginent les moqueurs et gens profanes ;"—" As scoffers and profane persons imagine."
[2] " En ces trois choses ;"—" In these three things."

this is the sum that *remains*. For faith does not *remain* after death, inasmuch as the Apostle elsewhere contrasts it with *sight*, (2 Cor. v. 7,) and declares that it remains only so long as we are *absent from the Lord*. We are now in possession of what is meant by *faith* in this passage—that knowledge of God and of the divine will, which we obtain by the ministry of the Church ; or, if you prefer it, faith universal, and taken in its proper acceptation. *Hope* is nothing else than perseverance in *faith*. For when we have once believed the word of God, it remains that we persevere until the accomplishment of these things. Hence, as *faith* is the mother of *hope*, so it is kept up by it, so as not to give way.

The greatest of these is love. It is so, if we estimate its excellence by the effects which he has previously enumerated ; and farther, if we take into view its perpetuity. For every one derives advantage from his own *faith* and *hope*, but *love* extends its benefits to others. *Faith* and *hope* belong to a state of imperfection : *love* will remain even in a state of perfection. For if we single out the particular effects of *faith*, and compare them, *faith* will be found to be in many respects superior. Nay, even *love* itself, according to the testimony of the same Apostle, (1 Thes. i. 3,) is an effect of *faith*. Now the effect is, undoubtedly, inferior to its cause. Besides, there is bestowed upon *faith* a signal commendation, which does not apply to *love*, when John declares that it is *our victory, which overcometh the world*.   (1 John v. 4.) In fine, it is by faith that we are born again—that we become the sons of God—that we obtain eternal life, and that *Christ dwells in us.* (Eph. iii. 17.) Innumerable other things I pass over ; but these few are sufficient to prove what I have in view—that faith is, in many of its effects, superior to love. Hence it is evident, that it is declared here to be superior—not in every respect, but inasmuch as it will be perpetual, and holds at present the first place in the preservation of the Church.

It is, however, surprising how much pleasure Papists take in thundering forth these words. "If *faith* justifies," say they, "then much more does *love*, which is declared to be *greater*." A solution of this objection is already furnished from what I have stated, but let us grant that *love* is in every respect superior; what sort of reasoning is that—that because it is greater, therefore it is of more avail for justifying men! Then a king will plow the ground better than a husbandman, and he will make a shoe better than a shoe-maker, because he is more noble than either! Then a man will run faster than a horse, and will carry a heavier burden than an elephant, because he is superior in dignity! Then angels will give light to the earth better than the sun and moon, beause they are more excellent! If the power of justifying depended on the dignity or merit of faith, they might perhaps be listened to; but we do not teach that faith justifies, on the ground of its having more worthiness, or occupying a higher station of honour, but because it receives the righteousness which is freely offered in the gospel. Greatness or dignity has nothing to do with this. Hence this passage gives Papists no more help, than if the Apostle had given the preference to *faith* above everything else.

CHAPTER XIV.

1. Follow after charity, and desire spiritual *gifts*, but rather that ye may prophesy.

2. For he that speaketh in an *unknown* tongue speaketh not unto men, but unto God: for no man understandeth *him;* howbeit in the spirit he speaketh mysteries.

3. But he that prophesieth speaketh unto men *to* edification, and exhortation, and comfort.

4. He that speaketh in an *unknown* tongue edifieth himself; but he that prophesieth edifieth the church.

5. I would that ye all spake with tongues, but rather that ye prophesied: for greater *is* he that prophesieth than he that speaketh with tongues, except he interpret, that the church may receive edifying.

6. Now brethren, if I come unto you speaking with tongues, what shall I profit you, except I shall speak

1. Sectamini caritatem: aemulamini spiritualia, magis autem ut prophetetis.

2. Nam qui loquitur lingua, non hominibus loquitur sed Deo: nullus enim audit; Spiritu vero loquitur mysteria.

3. Caeterum qui prophetat, hominibus loquitur ad aedificationem, exhortationem, et consolationem.

4. Qui loquitur lingua, se ipsum aedificat; at qui prophetat, Ecclesiam aedificat.

5. Volo autem omnes vos loqui linguis, magis tamen ut prophetetis; maior enim qui prophetat, quam qui linguis loquitur: nisi interpretetur, ut Ecclesia aedificationem accipiat.

6. Nunc autem, fratres, si venero ad vos linguis loquens, quid vobis prodero, nisi vobis loquar aut per

to you either by revelation, or by	revelationem, aut per scientiam,
knowledge, or by prophesying, or by	aut per prophetiam, aut per doctri-
doctrine?	nam?

As he had previously exhorted them to *follow after the more excellent gifts*, (1 Cor. xii. 31,) so he exhorts them now to *follow after love*,[1] for that was the distinguished excellence,[2] which he had promised that he would show them. They will, therefore, regulate themselves with propriety in the use of gifts, if *love* prevails among them. For he tacitly reproves the want of *love*, as appearing in this—that they had hitherto abused their gifts, and, inferring from what goes before, that where they do not assign to *love* the chief place, they do not take the right road to the attainment of true excellence, he shows them how foolish their ambition is, which frustrates their hopes and desires.

1. *Covet spiritual gifts.* Lest the Corinthians should object that they wronged God, if they despised his gifts, the Apostle anticipates this objection by declaring, that it was not his design to draw them away even from those gifts that they had abused—nay rather he commends the pursuit of them, and wishes them to have a place in the Church. And assuredly, as they had been conferred for the advantage of the Church, man's abuse of them ought not to give occasion for their being thrown away as useless or injurious, but in the meantime he commends *prophecy* above all other gifts, as it was the most useful of them all. He observes, therefore, an admirable medium, by disapproving of nothing that was useful, while at the same time he exhorts them not to prefer, by an absurd zeal, things of less consequence to what was of primary importance. Now he assigns the first place to *prophecy*. *Covet*, therefore, *spiritual gifts*—that is, " Ne-

---

[1] " The word διώκετε," says Doddridge, " properly signifies—to *pursue with an eagerness like that with which hunters follow their game.* And it may be intended to intimate, how hard it is to obtain and preserve such a truly benevolent spirit in the main series of life; considering, on the one hand, how many provocations we are like to meet with, and on the other, the force of self-love, which will in so many instances be ready to break in upon it."—*Ed.*

[2] " C'estoit ceste voye et vertu excellente;"—" This was that distinguished way and excellence."

glect no gift, for I exhort you to seek after them all, provided only *prophecy* holds the first place."

2. *For he that speaketh in another[1] tongue, speaketh,* &c. He now shows from the effect, why it was that he preferred *prophecy* to other gifts, and he compares it with the gift of *tongues,* in which it is probable the Corinthians exercised themselves the more, because it had more of show connected with it, for when persons hear a man speaking in a foreign tongue, their admiration is commonly excited. He accordingly shows, from principles already assumed, how perverse a thing this is, inasmuch as it does not at all contribute to the edifying of the Church. He says in the outset—*He that speaketh in another tongue, speaketh not unto men, but unto God:* that is, according to the proverb, "He sings to himself and to the Muses."[2] In the use of the word *tongue,* there is not a *pleonasm,*[3] as in those expressions—"She spake thus *with her mouth,*" and "I caught the sound *with these ears.*" The term denotes a *foreign language.* The reason why he does not speak to men is—because *no one heareth,* that is, *as an articulate voice.* For all hear a sound, but they do not understand what is said.

He *speaketh in the Spirit*—that is, "by a spiritual gift, (for in this way I interpret it along with Chrysostom.)" He

---

[1] It is remarked by *Granville Penn,* that "the context shows that the Apostle means, a language *foreign* to that of the auditors, and, therefore, *not known* to them"—as "we learn from verse 21 that we are to supply ἑτέρᾳ —'*other,*' not αγνωστη—'unknown.' We have," he adds, "had lamentable proof of the abuse to which the latter injudicious rendering can be perverted in the hands of ignorant or insidious enthusiasm, by assuming the term to mean, 'a tongue *unknown to all mankind;*' and from thence, by an impious inference, *supernatural and divine;* instead of relatively, '*unknown to another people.*' And yet, after all, '*unknown*' is not the Apostle's word, but only an *Italic supplement* suggested by the English revisers of the seventeenth century."—*Ed.*

[2] "Comme on dit en prouerbe—Il presche à soy-mesme et aux murailles;"—"As they say proverbially—He preaches to himself and the bare walls." The proverb, "Sibi canit et Musis"—("He sings to himself and the Muses,") is believed to have originated in a saying of *Antigenides,* a celebrated musician of Thebes, who, when his scholar Ismenias sung with good taste, but not so as to gain the applause of the people, exclaimed—"Mihi cane et Musis;"—("Sing to me and the Muses")—meaning that it was enough, if he pleased good judges.—*Ed.*

[3] A *pleonasm* is a figure of speech—involving a *redundancy of expression.*—*Ed.*

speaketh *mysteries* and hidden things, and things, therefore, that are of no profit." Chrysostom understands *mysteries* here in a good sense, as meaning—special revelations from God. I understand the term, however, in a bad sense, as meaning—dark sayings, that are obscure and involved, as if he had said, " He speaks what no one understands."

3. *He that prophesieth, speaketh unto men.* " Prophecy," says he, " is profitable to all, while a foreign language is a treasure hid in the earth. What great folly, then, it is to spend all one's time in what is useless, and, on the other hand, to neglect what appears to be most useful !" To *speak to edification,* is to speak what contains doctrine fitted to edify. For I understand this term to mean doctrine, by which we are trained to piety, to faith, to the worship and fear of God, and the duties of holiness and righteousness. As, however, we have for the most part need of goads, while others are pressed down by afflictions, or labour under weakness, he adds to doctrine, *exhortation and consolation.* It appears from this passage, and from what goes before, that *prophecy* does not mean the gift of foretelling future events : but as I have said this once before,[1] I do not repeat it.

4. *He that speaketh in another tongue, edifieth himself.* In place of what he had said before—that he *speaketh unto God,* he now says—he *speaketh to himself.* But whatever is done in the Church, ought to be for the common benefit. Away, then, with that misdirected ambition, which gives occasion for the advantage of the people generally being hindered ! Besides, Paul speaks by way of concession : for when ambition makes use of such empty vauntings,[2] there is inwardly no desire of doing good ; but Paul does, in effect, order away from the common society of believers those men of mere show, who look only to themselves.

5. *I would that ye all spake with tongues.* Again he declares that he does not give such a preference to prophecy,

---

[1] See p. 415.

[2] " Iettent ainsi de grandes bouffées et se brauent en leur parler :"— " Make use in this way of great puffings, and boast themselves in their talk."

as not to leave some place for foreign tongues. This must be carefully observed. For God has conferred nothing upon his Church in vain, and languages were of some benefit.[1] Hence, although the Corinthians, by a misdirected eagerness for show, had rendered that gift partly useless and worthless, and partly even injurious, yet Paul, nevertheless, commends the use of tongues. So far is he from wishing them abolished or thrown away. At the present day, while a knowledge of languages is more than simply necessary, and while God has at this time, in his wonderful kindness, brought them forward from darkness into light, there are at present great theologians, who declaim against them with furious zeal. As it is certain, that the Holy Spirit has here honoured the use of tongues with never-dying praise, we may very readily gather, what is the kind of spirit that actuates those reformers,[2] who level as many reproaches as they can against the pursuit of them. At the same time the cases are very different. For Paul takes in languages of any sort—such as served merely for the publication of the gospel among all nations. They, on the other hand, condemn those languages, from which, as fountains, the pure truth of scripture is to be drawn. An exception is added—that we must not be so taken up with the use of languages, as to treat with neglect *prophecy*, which ought to have the first place.

Unless he interpret. For if interpretation is added, there will then be prophecy. You must not, however, understand Paul to give liberty here to any one to take up the time of the Church to no profit by muttering words in a foreign tongue. For how ridiculous it were, to repeat the same thing in a variety of languages without any necessity! But it often happens, that the use of a foreign tongue is seasonable. In short, let us simply have an eye to this as our end —that edification may redound to the Church.

6. *Now, brethren, if I should come.* He proposes himself as an example, because in his person the case was exhibited

---

[1] " Les langues aidoyent lors aucunement à l'auancement des Eglises ;" —" Languages, at that time, were of some help for the advancement of the Churches."
[2] " Ces gentils reformateurs ;"—" Those pretty reformers."

more strikingly.[1] The Corinthians experienced in themselves abundant fruit from his doctrine. He asks them,
then, of what advantage it would be to them, if he were to
make use of foreign languages among them. He shows
them by this instance, how much better it were to apply
their minds to prophesyings. Besides, it was less invidious
to reprove this vice in his own person, than in that of another.

He mentions, however, four different kinds of edification
—*revelation, knowledge, prophesying*, and *doctrine*. As
there are a variety of opinions among interpreters respecting
them, let me be permitted, also, to bring forward my conjecture. As, however, it is but a conjecture, I leave my
readers to judge of it. *Revelation* and *prophesying* I put in
one class, and I am of opinion that the latter is the administration of the former. I am of the same opinion as to
knowledge and *doctrine*. What, therefore, any one has obtained by *revelation*, he dispenses by *prophesying*. *Doctrine*
is the way of communicating knowledge. Thus a *Prophet*
will be—one who interprets and administers *revelation*. This
is rather in favour of the definition that I have given above,
than at variance with it. For we have said that *prophesying* does not consist of a simple and bare interpretation of
Scripture, but includes also *knowledge* for applying it to
present use—which is obtained only by *revelation*, and the
special inspiration of God.

7. And even things without life giving sound, whether pipe or harp, except they give a distinction in the sounds, how shall it be known what is piped or harped?

8. For if the trumpet give an uncertain sound, who shall prepare himself to the battle?

9. So likewise ye, except ye utter by the tongue words easy to be understood, how shall it be known what is spoken? for ye shall speak into the air.

10. There are, it may be, so many

7. Quin et inanimia vocem reddentia, sive tibia, sive cithara, nisi distinctionem sonis dederint : quomodo cognoscetur, quod tibia canitur aut cithara?

8. Etenim si incertam vocem tuba dederit, quis apparabitur ad bellum?

9. Sic et vos per linguam, nisi significantem sermonem dederitis : quomodo intelligetur quod dicitur? eritis enim in aërem loquentes.

10. Tam multa, verbi gratia, ge-

[1] "Estoit plus propre pour leur imprimer ce qu'il dit ;"—"Was the more calculated to impress upon them what he says."

kinds of voices in the world, and none of them *is* without signification.

11. Therefore if I know not the meaning of the voice, I shall be unto him that speaketh a barbarian, and he that speaketh *shall be* a barbarian unto me.

12. Even so ye, forasmuch as ye are zealous of spiritual *gifts*, seek that ye may excel to the edifying of the church.

13. Wherefore let him that speaketh in an *unknown* tongue pray that he may interpret.

14. For if I pray in an *unknown* tongue, my spirit prayeth, but my understanding is unfruitful.

15. What is it then? I will pray with the spirit, and I will pray with the understanding also: I will sing with the spirit, and I will sing with the understanding also.

16. Else when thou shalt bless with the spirit, how shall he that occupieth the room of the unlearned say Amen at thy giving of thanks, seeing he understandeth not what thou sayest?

17. For thou verily givest thanks well, but the other is not edified.

---

nera vocum sunt in mundo, et nihil horum mutum.

11. Itaque si nesciero vim vocis, ero ei qui loquitur, barbarus: et qui loquitur, apud me barbarus.

12. Itaque et vos, quandoquidem sectatores estis spirituum, ad ædificationem Ecclesiæ quærite, ut excellatis.

13. Quapropter qui loquitur lingua, oret ut interpretetur.

14. Nam si orem lingua, spiritus meus orat, mens autem mea fructu caret.

15. Quid igitur est? orabo spiritu, sed orabo et mente: canam spiritu, sed canam et mente.

16. Alioqui si benedixeris spiritu, is qui implet locum idiotæ, quomodo dicturus est Amen ad tuam gratiarum actionem? quandoquidem quid dicas, nescit.

17. Nam tu quidem bene gratias agis, sed alius non ædificatur.

---

7. *Nay even things without life.* He brings forward similitudes, first from musical instruments, and then afterwards from the nature of things generally, there being no voice that has not some peculiarity, suitable for distinction.[1] "Even *things without life*," says he, "instruct us." There are, it is true, many random sounds or crashes, without any modulation,[2] but Paul speaks here of voices in which there is something of art, as though he had said—"A man cannot give life to a harp or flute, but he makes it give forth a sound that is regulated in such a manner, that it can be distinguished. How absurd then it is, that even men, endowed with intelligence, should utter a confused, indistinguishable sound!"

---

[1] "C'est à dire, pour signifier quelque chose;"—"That is to say, for signifying something."

[2] "Sans mesure ou distinction;"—"Without measure or distinction."

We must not, however, enter here upon any minute discussion as to musical harmonies, inasmuch as Paul has
merely taken what is commonly understood ; as, for example,
the sound of the trumpet,[1] of which he speaks shortly afterwards ; for it is so much calculated to raise the spirits, that
it rouses up—not only men, but even horses.   Hence it is
related in historical records, that the Lacedemonians, when
joining battle, preferred the use of the flute,[2] lest the army
should, at the first charge, rush forward upon the enemy
with too keen an onset.[3]   In fine, we all know by experience
what power music has in exciting men's feelings, so that
Plato affirms, and not without good reason, that music has
very much effect in influencing, in one way or another, the
manners of a state.   To *speak into the air* is to *beat the air*
(1 Cor. ix. 26) to no purpose.   "Thy voice will not reach
either God or man, but will vanish into air."

  10. *None of them dumb.*[4]   He now speaks in a more

---

[1] " It is well known that trumpets were exclusively employed in almost all
ancient armies, for the purpose of directing the movements of the soldiers,
and of informing them what they were to do—as when to attack, advance,
or retreat.   This was the custom in even the most early Jewish armies, as
the Law directed two silver trumpets to be made for the purpose.   (Num.
x. 1, 2, 9.)   Of course, a distinction of tones was necessary, to express the
various intimations which were in this manner conveyed ; and if the trumpeter did not give the proper intonation, the soldiers could not tell how to
act, or were in danger, from misconception, of acting wrongly." *Illustrated
Commentary.—Ed.*

[2] " Ils vsoyent plustost de fluste, que de trompette ;"—" They used the
flute, rather than the trumpet."

[3] The use of the flute on such occasions by the Lacedemonians, is supposed by Valerius Maximus to have " been intended to raise the courage
of the soldiers, that they might begin the onset with greater violence and
fury ;" but the reason stated by CALVIN accords with the account given of
it by Thucydides (with whom the rest of the ancient historians agree)—
that it was designed to " render them cool and sedate—trumpets and other
instruments being more proper to inspire with heat and rage ;" which passions they thought were " fitted rather to beget disorder and confusion,
than to produce any noble and memorable actions—valour not being the
effect of a sudden and vanishing transport, but proceeding from a settled
and habitual firmness and constancy of mind."   Potter's Gr. Ant. vol. ii.
p. 84.—*Ed.*

[4] " That in this passage," says Dr. Henderson, " φωνὴ, which properly
signifies *sound*, then *voice*, must be taken in the sense of *language* or dialect, is evident : for it would not be true, that there are no *sounds* or *voices*
in the world (ἄφωνων) *without signification*, according as these terms are
usually understood.   The meaning is—every language is intelligible to

general way, for he now takes in the natural voices of
animals. He uses the term *dumb* here, to mean *confused*—
as opposed to an articulate voice; for the barking of dogs
differs from the neighing of horses, and the roaring of lions
from the braying of asses. Every kind of bird, too, has its
own particular way of singing and chirping. The whole
order of nature, therefore, as appointed by God, invites us
to observe a distinction.[1]

11. *I shall be to him that speaketh a barbarian.*[2] The
tongue ought to be an index of the mind—not merely in the
sense of the proverb, but in the sense that is explained by
Aristotle in the commencement of his book—" On Interpretation."[3] How foolish then it is and preposterous in a
man, to utter in an assembly a voice of which the hearer understands nothing—in which he perceives no token from
which he may learn what the person means ! It is not
without good reason, therefore, that Paul views it as the

some nation or other; and it is only to persons who are ignorant of it, that
its words are destitute of signification.   This the Apostle illustrates in a
very forcible manner: ' Therefore, if I know not the meaning of the voice,
(τῆς φωνῆς, *of the language*,) I shall be to him that speaketh a barbarian,
and he that speaketh shall be a barbarian unto me.' We shall be like
two foreigners, who do not understand each other's tongue. The very use
of the term *interpret* and *interpretation*, as applied to this subject, also proves
that he could only have intelligent language in view : it being a contradiction in terms to speak of interpreting that which has no meaning." Henderson on Inspiration, pp. 219, 220.—*Ed.*

[1] " C'est à dire, nous monstre aucunement qu'il faut parler en sorte que
nous soyons entendus;"—" That is to say, it shows us, in a manner, that
we must speak so as to be understood."

[2] " The Greeks, after the custom of the Egyptians, mentioned by Herodotus, (lib. 2,) called all those *barbarians* who did not speak their language. In process of time, however, the Romans having subdued the
Greeks, delivered themselves by the force of arms from that opprobrious
appellation; and joined the Greeks in calling all barbarians who did not
speak either the Greek or the Latin language. Afterwards, *barbarian*
signified any one who spoke a language which another did not understand.
Thus the Scythian philosopher, Anacharsis, said, that among the Athenians
the Scythians were *barbarians;* and among the Scythians the Athenians
were *barbarians.* In like manner Ovid. Trist. v. 10, ' *Barbarus* hic ego
sum, quia *non intelligor* ulli;'—' I am a *barbarian* here, because *I am
not understood* by any one.' This is the sense which the Apostle affixes to
the word *barbarian*, in the present passage." *M'Knight.—Ed.*

[3] " La langue doit estre comme vn image, pour exprimer et representer
ce qui est en l'entendement;"—" The tongue should be like an image, to
express and represent what is in the understanding."

height of absurdity, that a man should be a *barbarian* to the hearers, by chattering in an unknown tongue, and at the same time he elegantly treats with derision the foolish ambition of the Corinthians, who were eager to obtain praise and fame by this means. "This reward," says he, "you will earn—that you will be a *barbarian.*" For the term *barbarian*, whether it be an artificial one, (as Strabo thinks,[1]) or derived from some other origin, is taken in a bad sense. Hence the Greeks, who looked upon themselves as the only persons who were good speakers, and had a polished language, gave to all others the name of *barbarians*, from their rude and rustic dialect. No language, however, is so cultivated as not to be reckoned barbarous, when it is not understood. "*He that heareth,*" says Paul, "will be unto me a *barbarian*, and I will be so to him in return." By these words he intimates, that to speak in an unknown tongue, is not to hold fellowship with the Church, but rather to keep aloof from it, and that he who will act this part, will be deservedly despised by others, because *he* first despises *them.*

12. *Since you are in pursuit of spiritual gifts.* Paul concludes that the gift of tongues has not been conferred with the view of giving occasion of boasting to a few, without yielding advantage to the Church. "If spiritual gifts," says he, "delight you, let the end be edification. *Then* only may you reckon, that you have attained an excellence that is true and praiseworthy—when the Church receives advantage from you. Paul, however, does not hereby give permission to any one to cherish an ambition to excel, even to the benefit of the Church, but by correcting the fault, he shows how far short they come of what they are in pursuit of, and at the same time lets them know who they are that should be most highly esteemed. He would have a man to be held

---

[1] He considers the term βάρβαρος, (barbarian,) to be a term constructed in imitation of the sense—to convey the idea of one that speaks with difficulty and harshness. See *Strabo*, Book xiv. p. 662. *Bloomfield* considers the term *barbarian* to be derived—" not" as some think, "from the Arabic *berber*, to murmur, but from the Punic *berber*, a *shepherd*—having been originally appropriated to the indigenous and pastoral inhabitants of Africa; who, to their more civilised fellow-men on the other side of the Mediterranean, appeared *rustics* and barbarians. Hence the term βάρβαρος came at length to mean a *rustic* or *clown.*"—*Ed.*

in higher estimation, in proportion as he devotes himself with eagerness to promote edification.   In the meantime, it is our part to have this one object in view—that the Lord may be exalted, and that his kingdom may be, from day to day, enlarged.

The term *spirits,*[1] he employs here, by metonymy, to denote *spiritual gifts,* as the *spirit* of doctrine, or of understanding, or of judgment, is employed to denote spiritual doctrine, or understanding, or judgment.   Otherwise we must keep in view what he stated previously, that it is one and the same Spirit, who *distributeth to every man* various gifts *according to his will.*   (1 Cor. xii. 11.)

13. *Wherefore let him that speaketh in another tongue.* This is an anticipation, by way of reply to a question which might very readily be proposed to him.   " If any one, therefore, is able to speak a foreign language, will the gift be useless?   Why should that be kept back, which might be brought out to light, to the glory of God?"   He shows the remedy.   "Let him," says he, "ask from God the gift of interpretation also.   If he is without this, let him abstain in the meantime from ostentation."[2]

14. *For if I pray in another tongue.*[3]   While this ex-

---

[1] *"Les dons spirituels,* il y a mot à mot, *les esprits ;"*—" *Spiritual gifts*— it is literally, *spirits.*"

[2] " De parler à ostentation ;"—" From speaking for ostentation's sake."

[3] " What is it," says *Witsius,* (in his " Sacred Dissertations,") "to pray with the *tongue ?* with the *spirit ?* with the *mind ?*   (1 Cor. xiv. 14, 15.) The *tongue* means here a language unknown to others, and employed by one who is endowed with a supernatural gift of the Holy Spirit.   .   .   . To *pray with the tongue,* is to pray in a language unknown to others ; as, for instance, to pray in the Hebrew language in presence of Greeks.   In that sense he had said, (ver. 2,) ' He that speaketh with the tongue, speaketh not unto men, but unto God ; for no man understandeth him ;' that is, he who speaks in a foreign tongue, the knowledge of which he has acquired by an extraordinary gift of the Spirit, has God only for a witness.   He cannot reckon as his witnesses, or as persons aware of what he is doing, those who are ignorant of the language, and to whose edification he has contributed little or nothing.   The *spirit* means here that extraordinary gift, by which a man is led to act in a certain way, accompanied by almost ecstatic emotions, so that sometimes he is neither aware what he says, nor do others understand what he means.   To *pray with the Spirit,* is to pray in such a manner as to show that you feel the presence of an extraordinary gift of the Spirit, which moves and hurries you along, in a powerful manner, to those actions which excite astonishment.   Νους, *intelligence, mind,* seems here to be chiefly used in a transitive sense, to mean what we give

ample, too, serves to confirm what he has previously maintained, it forms, at the same time, in my opinion, an additional particular. For it is probable that the Corinthians had been in fault in this respect also, that, as they discoursed, so they also prayed in foreign tongues. At the same time, both abuses took their rise from the same source, as indeed they were comprehended under one class. What is meant by *praying in a tongue*,[1] appears from what goes before—to frame a prayer in a foreign language.

The meaning of the term *spirit*, however, is not so easily explained. The idea of Ambrose, who refers it to the Spirit that we receive in baptism, has not only no foundation, but has not even the appearance of it. Augustine takes it in a more refined way, as denoting that apprehension, which conceives ideas and signs of things, so that it is a faculty of the soul that is inferior to the understanding. There is more plausibility in the opinion of those who interpret it as meaning the breathing of the throat—that is, the breath. This interpretation, however, does not accord with the meaning which the term invariably bears in Paul's discussion in this place: nay more, it appears to have been

another to understand. Such is the meaning of תבונה, to which νοῦς corresponds. חט אזנך לתבונתי, *incline thine ear to my understanding*, that is, to those things which I shall give thee to understand. (Prov. v. 1.) To *pray with the mind*, is to pray in such a manner that the prayers which you deliberately *conceive*, may be conceived and understood by others. Paul, accordingly, proposes himself as an example of the proper manner of conducting prayers. *If I pray in a tongue* unknown to the assembly in whose presence I pray, but which I have learned by Divine inspiration, *my spirit prayeth*, I am acting under the influence of that gift, which impels and arouses me to unusual and remarkable proceedings; but *my understanding is unfruitful*, I do not enable another to understand with advantage the conceptions of my mind. *What then? I will pray with the Spirit;* when the vehement emotion of the Spirit comes upon me, I will not struggle against it, *but I will pray with the understanding also;* I will show that I am not mad, but possessed of a sound understanding; and I will endeavour that others, as well as myself, be edified by my prayer." Biblical Cabinet, vol. xxiv. pp. 36-38.—*Ed.*

[1] " Que c'est que *prier de langue*, (car il y a ainsi mot à mot, là où nous traduisons *Prier en langage incognu*) ;"—" What it is to *pray in a tongue*, for such is the literal meaning, where we render it—*to pray in an unknown language.*" Wiclif (1380) gives the literal rendering—*For if I preie in tunge.* Tyndale, (1534,) *If I pray with tonges.* Cranmer, (1539,) *For if I praye with tongue.* Rheims, (1582,) *For if I pray with the tongue.*—*Ed.*

repeated the oftener by way of concession. For they gloried
in that honorary distinction, which Paul, it is true, allows
them, while, on the other hand, he shows how preposterous
it is to abuse[1] a thing that is good and excellent.   It is as
though he had said—" Thou makest thy boast to me of
spirit, but to what purpose, if it is useless?"   From this consideration, I am led to agree with Chrysostom, as to the
meaning of this term, who explains it, as in the previous instance, (verse 12,) to mean a spiritual gift.   Thus *my spirit*
will mean—*the gift conferred upon me.*[2]

But here a new question arises ; for it is not credible (at
least we nowhere read of it) that any spoke under the influence of the Spirit in a language that was to themselves
unknown.   For the gift of tongues was conferred—not for the
mere purpose of uttering a sound, but, on the contrary, with
the view of making a communication.   For how ridiculous
a thing it would be, that the tongue of a Roman should be
framed by the Spirit of God to pronounce Greek words,
which were altogether unknown to the speaker, as parrots,
magpies, and crows, are taught to mimic human voices ! If,
on the other hand, the man who was endowed with the gift
of tongues, did not speak without sense and understanding,

---

[1] " Quel danger il y a, quand on abuse ;"—" What danger there is, when
one abuses."

[2] " What the Apostle means by τὸ πνεῦμα μου, (*my spirit*,) is, neither the
Holy Spirit moving him to speak, nor any spiritual endowment with which
he was gifted, but, as the phrase signifies in other passages in which it
occurs, (Rom. i. 9 ; 1 Cor. v. 3 ; 2 Tim. iv. 22 ; Philem. 25,) *his own
mind*, with which he engaged in the service.   By νοῦς, as contrasted with
this, it is manifest he cannot mean his faculty of understanding—for it is
comprehended under the former.   The word must, therefore, signify the
meaning or *sense* which he attached to the language he employed—an acceptation in which he uses the term, ver. 19.   So far as he himself was
concerned, he derived benefit—connecting, as he did, intelligent ideas with
the words to which he gave utterance ; but the meaning of what he uttered (ἄκαρπος) produced *no fruit* in the hearers, inasmuch as they did not
understand him.   It must be observed, however, that the Apostle is here
only supposing a case, such as that which frequently presented itself in the
Church at Corinth ; not that he would have it to be believed that it ever occurred in his own experience.   On the contrary, he avers that, whenever he
engaged either in prayer or praise, it was in a way that was intelligible, and
consequently profitable both to himself and others, τῷ πνεύματι—τῷ νοΐ, *with
the spirit—with the understanding.*"   Henderson on Inspiration, pp. 231,
232.—*Ed.*

Paul would have had no occasion to say, that *the spirit prays, but the understanding is unfruitful,* for the *understanding* must have been conjoined with the *spirit.*

I answer, that Paul here, for the sake of illustration, makes a supposition, that had no reality, in this way : " If the gift of tongues be disjoined from the understanding, so that he who speaks is a *barbarian* to himself, as well as to others, what good would he do by babbling in this manner?" For it does not appear that the mind is here said to be *unfruitful,* (ἄκαρπον,) on the ground of no advantage accruing to the Church, inasmuch as Paul is here speaking of the private prayers of an individual. Let us therefore keep it in view, that things that are connected with each other are here disjoined for the sake of illustration—not on the ground that it either can, or usually does, so happen. The meaning is now obvious. " If, therefore, I frame prayers in a language that is not understood by me, and the *spirit* supplies me with words, the *spirit* indeed itself, which regulates my tongue, will in that case *pray,* but my mind will either be wandering somewhere else, or at least will have no part in the prayer."

Let us take notice, that Paul reckons it a great fault if the mind is not occupied in prayer. And no wonder ; for what else do we in prayer, but pour out our thoughts and desires before God ? Farther, as prayer is the spiritual worship of God, what is more at variance with the nature of it, than that it should proceed merely from the lips, and not from the inmost soul ? And these things must have been perfectly familiar to every mind, had not the devil besotted the world to such a degree, as to make men believe that they pray aright, when they merely make their lips move. So obstinate, too, are Papists in their madness, that they do not merely justify the making of prayers without understanding, but even prefer that the unlearned should mutter in unknown mumblings.[1] Meanwhile they mock God by an

[1] " Mais qui plus est, aiment mieux que les idiots et ignorans barbotent des patinostres en langage qui leur est incognu ;"—" But, what is more, they like better that unlearned and ignorant persons should mutter over paternosters in a language which they do not understand."

acute sophism[1]—that the *final intention* is enough, or, in other words, that it is an acceptable service to God, if a Spaniard curses God in the German language, while in his mind he is tossed with various profane cares, provided only he shall, by setting himself to his form of prayer, make up matters with God by means of a thought that quickly vanishes.[2]

15. *I will pray with the spirit.* Lest any one should ask, by way of objection, " Will the spirit then be useless in prayer?" he teaches, that it is lawful, indeed, to *pray with the spirit*, provided the mind be at the same time employed, that is, the *understanding*. He allows, therefore, and sanctions the use of a spiritual gift in prayer, but requires, what is the main thing, that the mind be not unemployed.[3]

When he says, *I will sing Psalms*, or, *I will sing*, he makes use of a particular instance, instead of a general statement. For, as the praises of God were the subject-matter of the Psalms, he means by *the singing of Psalms*[4]—*blessing God*, or *rendering thanks* to him, for in our supplications, we either ask something from God, or we acknowledge some blessing that has been conferred upon us. From this passage, however, we at the same time infer, that the custom of singing was, even at that time, in use among believers, as appears, also, from Pliny, who, writing at least forty years, or thereabouts, after the death of Paul, mentions, that the Christians were accustomed to sing Psalms to Christ before day-break.[5] I have also no doubt, that, from the very first, they followed the custom of the Jewish Church in singing Psalms.

16. *Else, if thou wilt bless with the spirit.* Hitherto he

[1] " Ils ont vne solution bien aigue et peremptoire;"—" They have a very acute and peremptory solution."

[2] " Vne pensee esuanouissante en l'air, qu'ils appellent Intention finale;" —" A thought vanishing into air, which they call final Intention."

[3] " Que ne soit point sans intelligence;"—" That it be not without understanding."

[4] The original word is ψαλῶ—*I will sing Psalms*. It is the same verb that is made use of by *James*, (v. 13,) εὐθυμεῖ τίς; ψαλλέτω—*Is any one cheerful: let him sing Psalms.—Ed.*

[5] Pliny's letter, referred to by CALVIN, (written A.D. 107,) is given at full length (as translated by Dr. Lardner) in Horne's Introduction, vol. i. pp. 205, 206.—*Ed.*

has been showing, that the prayers of every one of us will be vain and unfruitful, if the understanding does not go along with the voice. He now comes to speak of public prayers also. "If he that frames or utters forth prayers in the name of the people is not understood by the assembly, how will the common people add an expression of their desires in the close, so as to take part in them? For there is no fellowship in prayer, unless when all with one mind unite in the same desires. The same remark applies to *blessing*, or giving thanks to God."

Paul's expression, however, intimates,[1] that some one of the ministers uttered or pronounced prayers in a distinct voice, and that the whole assembly followed in their minds the words of that one person, until he had come to a close, and then they all said *Amen*—to intimate, that the prayer offered up by that one person was that of all of them in common.[2] It is known, that *Amen* is a Hebrew word, derived from the same term from which comes the word that signifies *faithfulness* or *truth*.[3] It is, accordingly, a token of confirmation,[4] both in affirming, and in desiring.[5] Farther, as the word was, from long use, familiar among the Jews, it made its way from them to the Gentiles, and the Greeks made use of it as if it had belonged originally to their own language. Hence it came to be a term in common use among all na-

---

[1] " Signifie et presuppose ;"—" Intimates and presupposes."

[2] "'*Amen*,' or ' So be it,' was, among the Jews, used by the congregation at the end of a *prayer* or *blessing*, to denote their assent to, or appropriation of, that which one person had pronounced. Many instances of this practice occur in the Old Testament. From the Jewish Synagogue this, with many other customs of worship, passed to the Christian Church, in which it is still generally retained. Justin Martyr particularly notices the unanimous and loud 'Amen' at the conclusion of the Lord's Supper, observing, that when the minister had finished the prayer and the thanksgiving, all the people present, with a joyful exclamation, said 'Amen.'— ('Apol.' vol. ii. p. 97.)"—*Illustrated Commentary.—Ed.*

[3] The word to which CALVIN, refers is אָמֵן, (*Amen*,) *truth*. The term occurs in Isaiah lxv. 16, אֱלֹהֵי אָמֵן, (*Elohe Amen*,) *the God of truth*.

[4] " Confirmation et approbation ;"—" Confirmation and approbation."

[5] " AMEN," says *Witsius*, in his Dissertations on the Lord's Prayer, " is a Hebrew particle, expressive both of strong affection and of ardent desire. . . . *Luther*, with his wonted liveliness of manner, wrote to *Melancthon* in the following terms:—' I pray for you, I have prayed, and I will pray, and I have no doubt I shall be heard, for I feel the AMEN in my heart.'"—*Biblical Cabinet*, vol. xxiv. p. 382.—*Ed.*

tions.   Now Paul says—" If in public prayer thou makest
use of a foreign tongue, that is not understood by the *unlearned* and the common people among whom thou speakest,
there will be no fellowship, and thy *prayer* or *blessing* will
be no longer a public one."   " Why ?"   " No one," says he,
" can add his *Amen* to thy prayer or psalm, if he does not
understand it."

Papists, on the other hand, reckon that to be a sacred
and legitimate observance, which Paul so decidedly rejects.
In this they discover an amazing impudence.   Nay more,
this is a clear token from which we learn how grievously,
and with what unbridled liberty, Satan rages in the dogmas
of Popery.[1]   For what can be clearer than those words of
Paul—that an *unlearned* person cannot take any part in
public prayer if he does not understand what is said ?   What
can be plainer than this prohibition—" let not prayers or
thanksgivings be offered up in public, except in the vernacular tongue."   In doing every day, what Paul says should
not, or even cannot, be done, do they not reckon *him* to be
illiterate ?   In observing with the utmost strictness what he
forbids, do they not deliberately contemn God ?   We see,
then, how Satan sports among them with impunity.   Their
diabolical obstinacy shows itself in this—that, when admonished, they are so far from repenting, that they defend this
gross abuse by fire and sword.

18. I thank my God, I speak with
tongues more than ye all :

19. Yet in the church I had rather
speak five words with my understanding, that *by my voice* I might teach
others also, than ten thousand words
in an *unknown* tongue.

20. Brethren, be not children in
understanding: howbeit in malice be
ye children, but in understanding be
men.

21. In the law it is written, With

18. Gratias ago Deo meo, quod
magis quam vos omnes linguis
loquor :

19. Sed in Ecclesia volo quinque
verba mente mea loqui, ut et alios
instituam, potius quam decem millia
verborum, lingua.

20. Fratres, ne sitis pueri sensibus, sed malitia pueri sitis: sensibus
vero sitis perfecti.

21. In lege scriptum est : (*Ies.*

[1] " Par lequel nous voyons comment Satan a tenu ses rangs, et dominé
en la Papaute furieusement, et d'une license merueilleusement desbordee;"
—" From which we see how Satan has maintained his place, and has ruled
in Popery with fury, and with a liberty amazingly reckless."

men of other tongues and other lips will I speak unto this people; and yet for all that will they not hear me, saith the Lord.

22. Wherefore tongues are for a sign, not to them that believe, but to them that believe not : but prophesying *serveth* not for them that believe not, but for them which believe.

23. If therefore the whole church be come together into one place, and all speak with tongues, and there come in *those that are* unlearned, or unbelievers, will they not say that ye are mad ?

24. But if all prophesy, and there come in one that believeth not, or *one* unlearned, he is convinced of all, he is judged of all :

25. And thus are the secrets of his heart made manifest ; and so falling down on *his* face he will worship God, and report that God is in you of a truth.

xxviii. 11, 12 :) Alienis linguis et labiis alienis loquar populo huic : et ne sic quidem audient me, dicit Dominus.

22. Itaque linguæ signi vice sunt, non iis qui credunt, sed incredulis : contra prophetia non incredulis, sed credentibus.

23. Ergo si convenerit Ecclesia tota simul, et omnes linguis loquantur, ingrediantur autem indocti aut increduli, nonne dicent vos insanire ?

24. Quodsi omnes prophetent, ingrediatur autem incredulus aut indoctus, coarguitur ab omnibus, diiudicatur ab omnibus,

25. Et sic occulta cordis eius manifesta fiunt ; atque ita procidens in faciem, adorabit Deum, renuntians, quod Deus revera in vobis sit.

18. *I thank*, &c. As there are many that detract from another's excellencies, in which they cannot themselves have distinction, Paul, that he might not seem to depreciate, through malignity or envy, the gift of tongues, anticipates that suspicion, by showing that he is, in this respect, superior to them all. " See," says he, " how little occasion you have to suspect the design of my discourse, as if I depreciated what I myself lacked ; for if we were to contend as to tongues, there is not one of you that could bear comparison with me. While, however, I might display myself to advantage in this department, I am more concerned for edification." Paul's doctrine derives no small weight from the circumstance, that he has not an eye to himself. Lest, however, he should appear excessively arrogant, in preferring himself before all others, he ascribes it all to God. Thus he tempers his boasting with modesty.

19. *I would rather speak five words.* This is spoken *hyperbolically,* unless you understand *five words,* as meaning *five sentences.* Now as Paul, who might otherwise have exulted loftily in his power of speaking with tongues, voluntarily abstains from it, and, without any show, aims at *edi-*

fication exclusively, he reproves, by this means, the empty
ambition of those, that are eagerly desirous to show themselves off with empty *tinkling.* (1 Cor. xiii. 1.) The authority of the Apostle ought, also, to have no little weight in
drawing them off from vanity of this kind.

20. *Brethren, be not children in understanding.* He proceeds a step farther; for he shows that the Corinthians are
so infatuated, that they, of their own accord, draw down
upon themselves, and eagerly desire, as though it were a
singular benefit, what the Lord threatens that he will send,
when he designs to inflict upon his people the severest punishment. What dreadful madness is this—to pursue eagerly
with their whole desire, what, in the sight of God, is regarded as a curse! That we may, however, understand
more accurately Paul's meaning, we must observe, that this
statement is grounded on the testimony of Isaiah, which he
immediately afterwards subjoins. (Isaiah xxviii. 11, 12.) And
as interpreters have been misled, from not observing the
connection to be of this nature, to prevent all mistake, we
shall first explain the passage in Isaiah, and then we shall
come to Paul's words.

In that chapter the Prophet inveighs with severity against
the ten tribes, which had abandoned themselves to every
kind of wickedness. The only consolation is, that God had
still a people uncorrupted in the tribe of Judah; but straightway he deplores the corruption of that tribe also; and he
does so the more sharply, because there was no hope of
amendment. For thus he speaks in the name of God—
*Whom shall I teach knowledge ? those that are weaned from
their mother ? those that are drawn from the breasts.* By
this he means, that they are no more capable of instruction
than little children but lately weaned.

It is added—*Precept upon precept, instruction upon instruction, charge upon charge, direction upon direction, here
a little, and there a little.* In these words he expresses, in
the style of a mimic,[1] the slowness and carelessness by which
they were kept back. "In teaching them, I lose my labour,

---

[1] *Mimetice.* Our author has here evidently in his eye the Greek adverb
μιμητικῶς—*imitatively.* See Plut. 2. 18. B.—*Ed.*

for they make no progress, because they are beyond measure uncultivated, and what they had been taught by means of long-continued labour, they in a single moment forget."

It is added still farther—*He that speaketh to that people is like one that maketh use of stammering lips, and a foreign language.* This is the passage that Paul quotes. Now the meaning is,[1] that the people have been visited with such blindness and madness, that they no more understand God when speaking to them, than they would some barbarian or foreigner, stammering in an unknown tongue—which is a dreadful curse. He has not, however, quoted the Prophet's words with exactness, because he reckoned it enough to make a pointed reference to the passage, that the Corinthians, on being admonished, might attentively consider it. As to his saying that it was *written in the law,*[2] this is not at variance with common usage; for the Prophets had not a ministry distinct from the law, but were the interpreters of the law, and their doctrine is, as it were, a sort of appendage to it; hence the law included the whole body of Scripture, up to the advent of Christ. Now Paul from this infers as follows—" Brethren, it is necessary to guard against that childishness, which is so severely reproved by the Prophet—that the word of God sounds in your ears without any fruit. Now, when you reject prophecy, which is placed within your reach, and prefer to stand amazed at empty sound, is not this voluntarily to incur the curse of God?[3]

---

[1] " Or le Prophete signifie;"—" Now the Prophet means."

[2] " *It is written in the law.* ' In the law,' that is, in the Scripture, in opposition to *the words of the Scribes;* for that distinction was very usual in the schools. ' *This* we learn out of *the law,* and *this* from *the words of the Scribes.* The words of *the law* (that is, of the Scripture) have no need of confirmation, but *the words of the Scribes* have need of confirmation.' The former Prophets, and the latter, and the Hagiographa, are each styled by the name of *the law.*" *Lightfoot.—Ed.*

[3] *Henderson* on *Isaiah,* when commenting on the passage here quoted by the Apostle, (Isaiah xxviii. 9-11,) observes, that it " contains the taunting language of the drunken priests and judges of the Jews, who repel with scorn the idea that they should require the plain and reiterated lessons which Jehovah taught by his messengers. Such elementary instruction was fit" (in their view) " only for babes: it was an insult to their understanding to suppose that they stood in need of it. . . . . The language of verse 10 " (*precept upon precept,* &c.) " more resembles that of inebriated persons, than any used by persons in a state of sobriety. The words are

Farther, lest the Corinthians should say in reply, that to be spiritually *children* is elsewhere commended, (Matt. xviii. 4,) Paul anticipates this objection, and exhorts them, indeed, to be *children in malice,* but to beware of being *children in understanding.* Hence we infer how shameless a part those act, who make Christian simplicity consist in ignorance. Paul would have all believers to be, as far as possible, in full maturity as to *understanding.* The Pope, inasmuch as it is easier to govern asses than men, gives orders, under pretext of simplicity, that all under him shall remain uninstructed.[1] Let us from this draw a comparison between the dominion of Popery, and the institution of Christ, and see how far they agree.[2]

22. *Therefore tongues are for a sign.* This passage may be explained in two ways, by considering the word *therefore* as referring merely to the preceding sentence, or as having a bearing generally on the whole of the foregoing discussion. If it is a particular inference, the meaning will be—" You see, brethren, that what you so eagerly desire is not a blessing bestowed by God upon believers, but a punishment, by

---

obviously selected to suit the character of those supposed to employ them; and, by their monosyllabic and repetitious forms, admirably express the initiatory process of tuition which they indignantly despised. . . . The language they employed in cavilling at the Prophetic warnings was all but barbarous; it consisted of barely intelligible sounds: they should, by way of condign punishment, hear the foreign, and to them apparently mocking accents of the Chaldeans, whom God would employ as the interpreters of his severe but righteous will. . . . The passage is employed by Paul (1 Cor. xiv. 20, 21) quite in the spirit of the connection in which it here stands. He tacitly compares the Corinthian faction, which boasted of the faculty of speaking in unknown tongues, to the puerile characters adverted to, verse 9, (παιδία, νηπιάζετε, &c.,) and then reminds them, that speaking in such languages had been represented in the Jewish Scriptures—ἐν τῷ νόμῳ (*in the law*) as a punishment, or a mark of the Divine displeasure, and not as a matter of desire or envy."—*Ed.*

[1] " En ignorance et bestise;"—" In ignorance and stupidity."

[2] CALVIN makes a similar observation when commenting on Eph. iv. 14. " Nam postquam Christo nati sumus, debemus adolescere, ita ut non simus intelligentia pueri. Hinc apparet, qualis sub Papatu sit Christianismus, ubi, quam diligentissime possunt, in hoc laborant pastores, ut plebem in prima infantia detineant;"—" For after being born to Christ, we ought to grow, and not to be *children in understanding.* (1 Cor. xiv. 20.) Hence it appears what sort of Christianity there is in connection with Popery, in which the pastors labour as strenuously as they can to keep the people in infancy."—*Ed.*

which he inflicts vengeance upon unbelievers." In this way, Paul would not be viewed as taking in the use of tongues under all circumstances, but simply as touching upon what had in *one* instance occurred. Should any one, however, prefer to extend it to the whole discussion, I have no objection, though I do not dislike the former interpretation.

Taking it in a general way, the meaning will be— " *Tongues*, in so far as they are given *for a sign*—that is, for a miracle—are appointed not properly for *believers*, but for *unbelievers*." The advantages derived from *tongues* were various. They provided against necessity—that diversity of tongues might not prevent the Apostles from disseminating the gospel over the whole world : there was, consequently, no nation with which they could not hold fellowship. They served also to move or terrify *unbelievers* by the sight of a miracle—for the design of this miracle, equally with others, was to prepare those who were as yet at a distance from Christ for rendering obedience to him. Believers, who had already devoted themselves to his doctrine, did not stand so much in need of such preparation. Hence, the Corinthians brought forward that gift improperly and out of its right place, allowing prophecy in the meantime to be neglected, which was peculiarly and specially set apart for *believers*, and ought, therefore, to be familiar to them, for in *tongues* they looked to nothing farther than the miracle.

23. *If therefore the whole Church come together.* As they did not see their fault, in consequence of having their minds pre-occupied with a foolish and depraved desire, he tells them that they will be exposed to the scorn of the wicked or the unlearned, if any, on coming into their assembly, should hear them uttering a sound, but not speaking. For what unlearned person will not reckon those to be out of their right mind, who, in place of speech, utter empty sound, and are taken up with that vanity, while they were gathered together for the purpose of hearing the doctrine of God ? This statement has much that is cutting : " You applaud yourselves in your own sleeve ; but the wicked and the unlearned laugh at your fooleries. You do not, therefore, see

what to the unlearned and unbelieving is perfectly manifest."

Here Chrysostom starts a question : " If *tongues* were given to unbelievers *for a sign*, why does the Apostle say now, that they will be derided by them ?" He answers, that they are *for a sign* to fill them with astonishment—not to instruct them, or to reform them. At the same time he adds, that it is owing to their wickedness, that they look upon the sign as madness. This explanation does not satisfy me ; for however an unbeliever or unlearned person may be affected by a miracle, and may regard with reverence the gift of God, he does not cease on that account to deride and condemn an unseasonable abuse of the gift,[1] and think thus with himself : " What do these men mean, by wearying out themselves and others to no purpose ? Of what avail is their speaking, if nothing is to be learned from it ?" Paul's meaning, therefore, is—that the Corinthians would be justly convicted of madness by the unbelieving and unlearned, however much they might please themselves.[2]

24. *But if all prophesy.* As he had previously showed them, how much more advantageous prophecy is to *those that are of the household of faith* (Gal. vi. 10) than the gift of tongues, so he now shows that it would be useful also to *those that are without.* (1 Cor. v. 13.) This is a most powerful consideration for showing the Corinthians their error. For what a base part it is to depreciate a gift that is most useful both within and without, and to be wholly taken up with another gift which is useless to those that are *within* the house; and, in addition to this, gives occasion of offence to those that are *without !* He sets before them this advantage of prophecy, that it summons the consciences of the wicked to the tribunal of God, and strikes them with a lively apprehension of divine judgment in such a manner, that he who before in utter regardlessness despised sound doctrine, is constrained to give glory to God.

---

[1] " Le sot abus de ce don, quand on le met en auant sans raison et consideration ;"—" The foolish abuse of this gift, when they bring it forward without reason and consideration."

[2] " En ceste façon de faire ;"—" In this manner of acting."

We shall find it, however, much easier to understand this passage, if we compare it with another that occurs in the Epistle to the Hebrews (iv. 12.) *The Word of God is quick and powerful, and sharper than any two-edged sword; piercing to the dividing asunder of soul and spirit, and of the joints and marrow—a discerner of the thoughts of the heart.*[1] For in both passages, it is the same kind of efficacy of the Word of God that is spoken of: only in that other passage it is spoken of more fully and distinctly. So far as the passage before us is concerned, it is not difficult to understand now, what is meant by being *convinced* and *judged.* The consciences of men are in a torpid state,[2] and are not touched with any feeling of dissatisfaction on account of their sins, so long as they are enveloped in the darkness of ignorance. In short, unbelief is like a lethargy that takes away feeling. But the Word of God penetrates even to the farthest recesses of the mind, and by introducing, as it were, a light, dispels darkness, and drives away that deadly torpor. Thus, then, unbelievers are *convinced,* inasmuch as they are seriously affected and alarmed, on coming to know that they have to do with God ; and, in like manner, they are *judged* in this respect, that whereas they were previously involved in darkness, and did not perceive their own wretchedness and baseness, they are now brought into the light of day, and are constrained to bear witness against themselves.

When he says, that they are judged and convinced *by all,* you must understand him as meaning *all that prophesy;* for he had said a little before, *If ye all prophesy,* (verse 24.) He has expressly made use of a general term, with the view of removing the dislike that they felt for prophecy.[3] The unbeliever, I say, is *convinced*—not as if the Prophet pronounced a judgment upon him either silently in the mind, or openly with the mouth, but because the conscience of the

[1] " Des pensees et intentions du cœur ;"—" Of the thoughts and intents of the heart."

[2] " Elles sont comme endormies et stupides :"—" They are, as it were, drowsy and stupid."

[3] "Afin de monstrer qu'il ne se faut point lasser de la prophetie ;"—" In order to show that they ought not to entertain a feeling of dislike for prophecy."

hearer apprehends from the doctrine his own judgment. He is *judged*, inasmuch as he descends into himself, and, after thorough examination, comes to know himself, while previously he was unmindful of himself.   To the same purpose, too, is that saying of Christ : *The Spirit, when he is come, will convince the world of sin,* (John xvi. 8 ;) and this is what he immediately adds—that *the secrets of his heart are made manifest.*   For he does not mean, in my opinion, that it becomes manifest to others what sort of person he is, but rather that his own conscience is aroused, so that he perceives his sins, which previously lay hid from his view.

Here again Chrysostom asks, how it comes to pass that prophecy is so effectual for arousing *unbelievers,* while Paul had said a little before that it was not given to them.   He answers, that it was not given to them as a useless sign, but for the purpose of instructing them.   For my part, however, I think that it will be simpler, and therefore more suitable, to say that it was not given to unbelievers, who perish, whose hearts *Satan has blinded, that they may not see the light which shines forth from it.* (2 Cor. iv. 3, 4.)   It will also suit better to connect this statement with the prophecy[1] of Isaiah (xxviii. 11, 12,) because the Prophet speaks of unbelievers, among whom prophecy is of no profit or advantage.

25. *Falling down on his face, he will worship.*   For it is only the knowledge of God that can bring down the pride of the flesh.   To that, prophecy brings us.   Hence, it is its proper effect and nature to bring down men from their loftiness, that they may, with prostrate homage, render worship to God.   To many, however, prophecy also is of no benefit—nay more, they are made worse by what they hear.   Nor was it even Paul's intention to ascribe this effect to prophecy, as if it were always the result of it.   He simply designed to show how much advantage is derived from it, and what is its office.   It is therefore a singular commendation, that it extorts from unbelievers this confession—that God is present with his people, and that his majesty shines forth in the midst of their assembly.

---

[1] The reader will observe that this is the prophecy to which the Apostle refers in the 21st verse.—*Ed.*

26. How is it then, brethren? when ye come together, every one of you hath a psalm, hath a doctrine, hath a tongue, hath a revelation, hath an interpretation. Let all things be done unto edifying.

27. If any man speak in an *unknown* tongue, *let it be* by two, or at the most *by* three, and *that* by course; and let one interpret.

28. But if there be no interpreter, let him keep silence in the church; and let him speak to himself, and to God.

29. Let the prophets speak two or three, and let the other judge.

30. If *any thing* be revealed to another that sitteth by, let the first hold his peace.

31. For ye may all prophesy one by one, that all may learn, and all may be comforted.

32. And the spirits of the prophets are subject to the prophets.

33. For God is not *the author* of confusion, but of peace, as in all churches of the saints.

26. Quid igitur est, fratres? Quoties convenitis, unusquisque vestrum canticum habet, doctrinam habet, linguam habet, revelationem habet, interpretationem habet: omnia ad aedificationem fiant.

27. Sive lingua quis loquitur, fiat per duos, aut ad summum tres, idque vicissim, et unus interpretetur.

28. Quodsi non sit interpres, taceat in Ecclesia: caeterum sibi ipsi loquatur et Deo.

29. Prophetae autem duo aut tres loquantur, et caeteri diiudicent.

30. Quodsi alii fuerit revelatum assidenti, prior taceat:

31. Potestis enim singulatim omnes prophetare, ut omnes discant, et omnes consolationem accipiant.[1]

32. Et spiritus prophetarum prophetis sunt subiecti:

33. Non enim seditionis est Deus, sed pacis, quemadmodum in omnibus Ecclesiis sanctorum.[2]

26. *What is it then?* He now shows the way in which they may remedy those evils. In the first place, each gift must have its place, but in order and in measure. Farther, the Church must not be taken up to no purpose with unprofitable exercises, but must, in whatever is done, have an eye to edification. He speaks, however, in the first place of edification in this way: " Let every one, according as he has been endowed with some particular gift, make it his aim to lay it out for the advantage of all." For it is in this way that we must understand the word rendered *every one*—that no one may take it as implying universality, as though all to a man were endowed with some such gift.

27. *If any one speak in another tongue.* He now describes the order and limits the measure. " If you have a mind to speak with other tongues, *let only two speak, or, at most, not*

---

[1] " Que tous soyent consolez, ou, exhortez;"—" That all may be comforted, or, exhorted."

[2] "Comme en toutes les Eglises des saincts, ou, comme *on voit* en toutes;"—"As in all the Churches of the saints, or, as *one sees* in all."

more than three, and let there be at the same time an inter-
preter sitting by. Without an interpreter, *tongues* are of no
advantage : let them, therefore be dispensed with." It is
to be observed, however, that he does not *command,* but
merely *permits;* for the Church can, without any inconvenience, dispense with *tongues,* except in so far as they are
helps to prophecy, as the Hebrew and Greek languages are
at this day.   Paul, however, makes this concession, that he
may not seem to deprive the assembly of believers of any
gift of the Spirit.

At the same time, it might seem as if even this were not
agreeable to reason, inasmuch as he said before, (verse 22,)
that *tongues,* in so far as they are for a *sign,* are suited to
unbelievers.   I answer, that, while a miracle may be performed more particularly with a view to unbelievers, it,
nevertheless, does not follow, that it may not be of some
advantage to believers also.   If you understand, that an
unknown tongue is a sign to unbelievers in the sense that
Isaiah's words[1] bear, the method of procedure, which Paul
here prescribes, is different.   For he allows of other tongues
in such a way that, interpretation being joined with them,
nothing is left obscure.   He observes, therefore, a most admirable medium in correcting the fault of the Corinthians.
On the one hand, he does not at all set aside any gift of God
whatever,[2] in order that all his benefits may be seen among
believers.   On the other hand he makes a limitation—that
ambition do not usurp the place that is due to the glory of
God, and that no gift of inferior importance stand in the
way of those that are of chief moment ; and he adds the
sauce[3]—that there be no mere ostentation, devoid of advantage.

28. *Let him speak to himself and to God.* "Let him enjoy," says he, "his gift in his own conscience, and let him
give thanks to God."   For in this way I explain the expression—to *speak to himself and to God,* as meaning—to recog-

---

[1] The words referred to are those which Paul had quoted above in ver.
21.—*Ed.*

[2] " Tant petit soit-il ;"—" Be it ever so small."

[3] " Ascauoir l'interpretation ;"—" Namely, the interpretation."

nise in his own mind with thanksgiving the favour conferred upon him,[1] and to enjoy it as his own, when there is not an opportunity for bringing it forward in a public manner. For he draws a contrast between this *secret* way of speaking, and speaking *publicly* in the Church—which he forbids.[2]

29. *Prophets, two or three.* As to *prophecy*, too, he prescribes limits, because "multitude," as they commonly say, "breeds confusion." This is true, for we know it by every day's experience. He does not, however, restrict the number so definitely, as when he was treating of tongues, for there is less danger, in the event of their applying themselves for a longer time to prophesyings, nay more, continued application would be the most desirable thing of all; but Paul considered what the weakness of men could bear.

There still remains, however, a question—why it is that he assigns the like number to prophesyings and to tongues, except that, as to the latter, he adds particularly—*at the most*, for if *tongues* are less useful, there ought assuredly to be a more sparing use of them? I answer, that even in *tongues*, as he takes the term, prophecy is included; for *tongues* were made use of either for discourses,[3] or for prayers. In the former department, the interpreter was in the place of the prophet: thus it was the principal and more frequent exercise of it. Only he limits the measure of it, lest it should fall into contempt through a feeling of disgust, and lest those who were less skilful should prevent those that were better qualified from having time and opportunity of speaking; for he would, undoubtedly, have those to whom he assigns the duty of speaking, to be of the more select class, and appointed by their common suffrages.[4] None, however, are more inclined to push themselves forward, than those who have but a slight smattering of learning, so that the proverb holds good, "Ignorance is pert."[5] Paul had it in view to

---

[1] "Le benefice et don de Dieu ;"—" The kindness and gift of God."

[2] "En ce cas;"—" In this case."

[3] "Pour traiter de quelques matieres de la religion ;"—" For treating of some matters of religion."

[4] "Par l'approbation commune de l'Eglise ;"—" By the common approbation of the Church."

[5] The Latins have a similar proverb—" Stater in lagena bis bis clamat ;"

remedy this evil, by assigning the office of speaking to *two or three.*

Let the others judge.   Lest he should give any occasion to *the others* to complain—as though he were desirous that the gift of God[1] should be suppressed among them and buried, he shows in what way they may lawfully make use of it for the benefit of the Church, even by *keeping silence*—if they set themselves to *judge* of what is said by others.   For it is of no small advantage, that there should be some that are skilful in judging, who will not allow sound doctrine to be perverted by the impostures of Satan, or to be otherwise corrupted by silly trifles.   Paul, accordingly, teaches that the other prophets will be useful to the Church, even by *keeping silence.*

It may seem, however, to be absurd that men should have liberty given them to judge of the doctrine of God, which ought to be placed beyond all controversy.   I answer, that the doctrine of God is not subjected to the scrutiny of men, but there is simply permission given them to judge by the Spirit of God, whether it is his word that is set before them, or whether human inventions are, without any authority, set off under this pretext, as we shall have occasion to notice again ere long.

30. *But if anything be revealed to another.*   Here is another advantage—that whenever there will be occasion, the way will also be open to them.[2]   Hence they have no longer any occasion to complain, that the Spirit is bound, or that his mouth is shut.   For all have opportunity and liberty allowed them of speaking, when there is occasion for it, provided only no one unseasonably intrudes—having it in view to please himself, rather than to serve some useful purpose.   Now he requires this modesty on the part of all— that every one in his place shall give way to another that

---

—" A penny in an earthen pot is constantly tinkling."   The Germans say—"The higher the head, the humbler the heart."—*Ed.*

[1] " Le don de Dieu qu'ils ont receu ;"—" The gift of God which they have received."

[2] " Que toutes fois et quantes qu'il sera besoin, eux aussi auront lieu de parler ;"—" That as often, and in as far as there will be occasion, they will also have opportunity of speaking."

has something better to bring forward.[1]   For this only is the
true liberty of the Spirit—not that every one be allowed to
blab out rashly whatever he pleases, but that all, from the
highest to the lowest, voluntarily allow themselves to be
under control, and that the one Spirit be listened to, by
whatever mouth he speaks.   As to the certainty of the revelation, we shall see ere long.

31. *You can all, one by one.*   In the *first* place, when he
says *all*, he does not include believers universally, but only
those that were endowed with this gift.   Farther, he does
not mean that all ought to have equally their turn, but that,
according as it might be for the advantage of the people,
each one should come forward to speak either more frequently or more seldom.[2]   "No one will remain always unemployed ; but an opportunity of speaking will present itself,
sometimes to one and at other times to another."

He adds, *that all may learn.*   This is applicable, it is
true, to the whole of the people, but it is particularly suited
to the Prophets, and Paul more especially refers to them.
For no one will ever be a good teacher, who does not show
himself to be teachable, as no one will ever be found who
has, in himself alone, such an overflowing in respect of perfection of doctrine, as not to derive benefit from listening to
others.   Let all, therefore, undertake the office of teaching
on this principle, that they do not refuse or grudge, to be
scholars to each other in their turn, whenever there shall
be afforded to others the means of edifying the Church.

He says, in the *second* place, *that all may receive consolation.*   Hence we may infer, that the ministers of Christ,

---

[1] "*But if anything be revealed to another that sitteth by.*   That is very
frequently said of the Jewish doctors, היה יושב.   *He sat*—which means
not barely *he was sitting*, but *he taught out of the seat of the teacher*, or
he sat teaching, or *ready to teach*.   So that, indeed, *he sat* and *he taught*
are all one.   Examples among the Talmudists are infinite.   In the same
sense the Apostle : 'If something be revealed to some minister, who *hath
a seat* among those that teach, &c., not revealed in that very instant : but
if he saith that he hath received some revelation from God, then ὁ πρῶτος
σιγάτω—let the first be silent : let *him* be silent who ψαλμὸν ἔχει—*hath a
psalm*—and give way to him.' "   *Lightfoot.—Ed.*

[2] "Ainsi qu'il sera auisé pour le mieux ;"—"As it shall be judged for
the better."

so far from envying, should rather rejoice with all their
heart, that they are not the only persons that excel, but
have fellow-partakers of the same gift—a disposition which
Moses discovered, as is related in sacred history. (Numbers
xi. 28.) For when his servant, inflamed with a foolish
jealousy, was greatly displeased, because the gift of prophecy
was conferred upon others also, he reproves him : "Nay,"
says he, "would that all the people of God were sharers with
me in this superior gift !" And, undoubtedly, it is a special
consolation for pious ministers, to see the Spirit of God,
whose instruments they are, working in others also, and
they derive also from this no small confirmation. It is a
consolation, too, that it contributes to the spread of the
word of God, the more it has of ministers and witnesses.

As, however, the word παρακαλεῖσθαι, which Paul here
employs, is of doubtful signification,[1] it might also be rendered *may receive exhortation.*[2] Nor would this be unsuitable, for it is sometimes of advantage to listen to others, that
we may be more powerfully stirred up to duty.

32. *And the spirits of the Prophets.* This, too, is one of
the reasons, why it is necessary for them to take turns—because it will sometimes happen that, in the doctrine of one
Prophet, the others may find something to reprove. "It is
not reasonable," says he, "that any one should be beyond
the sphere of scrutiny. In this way it will sometimes come
to a person's turn to speak, who was among the audience
and was sitting silent."

This passage has been misunderstood by some, as if Paul
had said, that the Lord's Prophets were not like persons
taken with a sudden frenzy, who, when a divine impulse
(ἐνθουσιασμὸς) had once seized them,[3] were no longer masters of themselves.[4] It is indeed true that God's Prophets

---

[1] " Ha double signification;"—" Has a double signification."

[2] Thus in Acts xv. 32, παρεκάλεσαν means *exhorted,* while the noun
παρακλήσις is used in the immediately preceding verse in the sense of *consolation.—Ed.*

[3] " Depuis que leur folie les prenoit, laquelle ils appeloyent vn mouue-
ment Diuin;"—" Whenever their folly seized them, which they called a
Divine impulse."

[4] The reference here is manifestly to those who practised *divination,*

are not disordered in mind ; but this has nothing to do with this passage of Paul's writings. For it means, as I have already stated, that no one is exempted from the scrutiny of others, but that all must be listened to, with this understanding, that their doctrine is, nevertheless, to be subjected to examination. It is not, however, without difficulty, for the Apostle declares that their *spirits are subject.* Though it is of gifts that he speaks, how can prophecy, which is given by the Holy Spirit, be judged of by men, so that the Spirit himself is not judged by them ? In this manner, even the word of God, which is revealed by the Spirit, will be subjected to examination. The unseemliness of this needs not be pointed out, for it is of itself abundantly evident. I maintain, however, that neither the Spirit of God nor his word is restrained by a scrutiny of this kind. The Holy Spirit, I say, retains his majesty unimpaired, so as to *judge all things, while he is judged by no one.* (1 Cor. ii. 15.) The sacred word of God, too, retains the respect due to it, so that it is received without any disputation, as soon as it is presented.

" What is it then," you will say, " that is subjected to examination ?" I answer—If any one were furnished with a full revelation, that man would undoubtedly, along with his gift, be above all scrutiny. There is, I say, no subjection, where there is a plenitude of revelation ; but as God has distributed

(Θεομαντεία,) of whom there were three sorts among the Grecians, distinguished by three distinct ways of receiving the *divine afflatus,* (ἐνθουσιασμὸς.) See POTTER's Grecian Antiquities, vol. i. pp. 349-354. Virgil describes in the following terms the frantic state of the Sibyl, when pretending to be under divine impulse :—

> " Non comtæ mansere comæ ; sed pectus anhelum,
> Et rabie fera corda tument : majorque videri,
> Nec mortale sonans, afflata est numine quando
> Jam propiore dei."

> " But when the headstrong god, not yet appeased,
> With holy frenzy had the Sibyl seized,
> Terror froze up her grisly hair ; her breast
> Throbbing with holy fury, still expressed
> A greater horror, and she bigger seems,
> Swoln with the afflatus, whilst in holy screams
> She unfolds the hidden mysteries of fate."
> VIRG. AEN. VI. 48-51.—*Ed.*

his spirit to every one in a certain measure, in such a way that, even amidst the greatest abundance, there is always something wanting, it is not to be wondered, if no one is elevated to such a height, as to look down from aloft upon all others, and have no one to pass judgment upon him. We may now see how it is, that, without any dishonour to the Holy Spirit, his gifts admit of being examined. Nay more, where, after full examination, nothing is found that is worthy of reproof, there will still be something, that stands in need of polishing. The sum of all, therefore, is this—that the gift is subjected to examination in such a way, that whatever is set forth, the Prophets consider as to it—whether it has proceeded from the Spirit of God; for if it shall appear that the Spirit is the author of it, there is no room left for hesitation.

It is, however still farther asked—"What rule is to be made use of in examining?" This question is answered in part by the mouth of Paul, who, in Romans xii. 6, requires that prophecy be regulated according to the *proportion of faith.* As to the passing of judgment, however, there is no doubt, that it ought to be regulated by the word and Spirit of God —that nothing may be approved of, but what is discovered to be from God—that nothing may be found fault with but in accordance with his word—in fine, that God alone may preside in this judgment, and that men may be merely his heralds.

From this passage of Paul's writings, we may conjecture how very illustrious that Church was, in respect of an extraordinary abundance and variety of spiritual gifts. There were colleges of Prophets, so that pains had to be taken, that they might have their respective turns. There was so great a diversity of gifts, that there was a superabundance. We now see our leanness, nay, our poverty; but in this we have a just punishment, sent to requite our ingratitude. For neither are the riches of God exhausted, nor is his benignity lessened; but we are neither deserving of his bounty, nor capable of receiving his liberality. Still we have an ample sufficiency of light and doctrine, provided there were no deficiency in respect of the cultivation of piety, and the fruits that spring from it.

33. *For God is not of confusion.*[1] We must understand the word Author, or some term of that kind.[2] Here we have a most valuable statement, by which we are taught, that we do not serve God unless in the event of our being lovers of *peace,* and eager to promote it. Whenever, therefore, there is a disposition to quarrel, *there,* it is certain, God does not reign. And how easy it is to say this! How very generally all have it in their mouths! Yet, in the meantime, the most of persons fly into a rage about nothing, or they trouble the Church, from a desire that they may, by some means, rise into view, and may *seem to be somewhat.* (Gal. ii. 6.)

Let us, therefore, bear in mind, that, in judging as to the servants of Christ, this mark must be kept in view —whether or not they aim at *peace* and concord, and, by conducting themselves peaceably, avoid contentions to the utmost of their power, provided, however, we understand by this a *peace* of which the truth of God is the bond. For if we are called to contend against wicked doctrines, even though heaven and earth should come together, we must, nevertheless, persevere in the contest. We must, indeed, in the first place, make it our aim, that the truth of God may, without contention, maintain its ground ; but if the wicked resist, we must set our face against them, and have no fear, lest the blame of the disturbances should be laid to our charge. For accursed is that *peace* of which revolt from God is the bond, and blessed are those contentions by which it is necessary to maintain the kingdom of Christ.

[1] " Car Dieu n'est point *Dieu* de confusion ;"—" For God is not *a God* of confusion."

[2] *Granville Penn* reads the verse as follows : *For they are not spirits of disorder, but of peace.* He thinks it probable, that " the *singular,* ἐστι, has caused a vitiation of this passage, by suggesting the introduction of a *singular* nominative to agree with it, namely ὁ Θεός—' God ;' whereas in the reading of Tertullian, as early as the second or third century, ἐστι referred to the neuter plural, πνεύματα : ' Et spiritus prophetarum prophetis subditi sunt—non enim eversionis *sunt,* sed pacis.' (And the spirits of the Prophets are subject to the Prophets—for *they are* not of disorder but of peace.) The Greek, therefore, stood thus : οὐ γάρ ἐστιν ἀκαταστασίας (πνεύματα) ἀλλ' εἰρήνης. This early external testimony, combined with the internal testimony of the context, is sufficient evidence, that Θεός has been unskilfully inserted by philoponists here, as Θεός, Κύριος, Χριστός, have been intruded into many other passages of the Sacred Text."—*Ed.*

As in all the Churches. The comparison[1] does not refer merely to what was said immediately before, but to the whole of the foregoing representation. " I have hitherto enjoined upon you nothing that is not observed in *all the Churches,* and, in this manner, they are maintained in *peace.* Let it be your care, therefore, to borrow, what other Churches have found by experience to be salutary, and most profitable for maintaining *peace.*" His explicit mention of the term *saints* is emphatic—as if with the view of exempting rightly constituted Churches from a mark of disgrace.[2]

34. Let your women keep silence in the churches: for it is not permitted unto them to speak ; but *they are commanded* to be under obedience, as also saith the law.

35. And if they will learn anything, let them ask their husbands at home: for it is a shame for women to speak in the church.

36. What! came the word of God out from you? or came it unto you only?

37. If any man think himself to be a prophet, or spiritual, let him acknowledge that the things that I write unto you are the commandments of the Lord.

38. But if any man be ignorant, let him be ignorant.

39. Wherefore, brethren, covet to prophesy, and forbid not to speak with tongues.

40. Let all things be done decently and in order.

34. Mulieres vestrae in Ecclesiis taceant ; non enim permissum est ipsis loqui, sed subiectae sint, quemadmodum et Lex dicit.

35. Si quid autem velint discere, domi maritos suos interrogent : turpe enim est mulieribus in Ecclesia loqui.

36. An a vobis sermo Dei profectus est, aut ad vos solos pervenit ?

37. Si quis videtur sibi propheta esse aut spiritualis, agnoscat, quae scribo vobis, Domini esse mandata.

38. Si quis autem ignorat, ignoret.

39. Itaque, fratres, aemulamini prophetiam, et linguis loqui ne prohibeatis.

40. Porro omnia decenter et ordine fiant.

It appears that the Church of the Corinthians was infected with this fault too, that the talkativeness of women was allowed a place in the sacred assembly, or rather that the fullest liberty was given to it. Hence he forbids them to speak in public, either for the purpose of teaching or of prophesying. This, however, we must understand as referring

---

[1] " Ce mot, *Comme ;*"—" This word, *As.*"

[2] " Comme s'il vouloit dire qu'il n'y auroit point de propos d'auoir quelque souspeçon sur les Eglises bien reformees ;"—" As if he meant to say, that there was no occasion for having any suspicion as to Churches thoroughly reformed."

to ordinary service, or where there is a Church in a regularly constituted state ; for a necessity may occur of such a nature as to require that a woman should speak in public ; but Paul has merely in view what is becoming in a duly regulated assembly.

34. *Let them be in subjection, as also saith the law.* What connection has the object that he has in view with the subjection under which the law places women ? "For what is there," some one will say, "to hinder their being in subjection, and yet at the same time teaching ?" I answer, that the office of teaching[1] is a superiority in the Church, and is, consequently, inconsistent with *subjection*. For how unseemly a thing it were, that one who is under subjection to one of the members, should preside[2] over the entire body ! It is therefore an argument from things inconsistent—If the woman is under subjection, she is, consequently, prohibited from authority to teach in public.[3] And unquestionably,[4] wherever even natural propriety has been maintained, women have in all ages been excluded from the public management of affairs. It is the dictate of common sense, that female government is improper and unseemly. Nay more, while originally they had permission given to them at Rome to plead before a court,[5] the effrontery of Caia Afrania[6] led to their being interdicted, even from this. Paul's reasoning, however, is simple—that authority to teach is not suitable to the station that a woman occupies, because, if she teaches, she presides over all the *men*, while it becomes her to be *under subjection*.

---

[1] " D'enseigner ou de prescher ;"—" Of teaching or of preaching."

[2] " Eust preeminence et authorite ;"—" Should have pre-eminence and authority."

[3] " Elle ne peut donc auoir authorite publique de prescher ou enseigner ;"—" She cannot, therefore, have public authority to preach or teach."

[4] " Entre toutes les nations et peuples ;"—" Among all nations and peoples."

[5] " On les souffroit proposer deuant les iuges, et plaider publiquement ;" —" They were allowed to make an appearance before the judges, and plead publicly."

[6] *Caia Afrania* was the wife of a senator, Licinius Buccio. The circumstance referred to by CALVIN is related by Valerius Maximus, (lib. 8. c. 3. n. 2,) in the following terms:—" Muliebris verecundiae oblita, suas

35. *If they wish to learn any thing.* That he may not
seem, by this means, to shut out women from opportunities
of learning, he desires them, if they are in doubt as to anything, to inquire in private, that they may not stir up any
disputation in public. When he says, *husbands,* he does not
prohibit them from consulting the Prophets themselves, if
necessary. For all husbands are not competent to give an
answer in such a case ; but, as he is reasoning here as to external polity, he reckons it sufficient to point out what is
unseemly, that the Corinthians may guard against it. In
the meantime, it is the part of the prudent reader to consider, that the things of which he here treats are intermediate
and indifferent, in which there is nothing unlawful, but what
is at variance with propriety and edification.

36. *Did the word of God come out from you?* This is a
somewhat sharper reproof, but nothing more than was needful for beating down the haughtiness of the Corinthians.
They were, beyond measure, self-complacent. They could
not endure that either themselves, or what belonged to them,
should be found fault with in anything. He asks, accordingly, whether they are the only Christians in the world ;
nay, farther, whether they are the first, or are to be the last ?
" *Did the word of God,*" says he, " *come out from you ?*" that is,
" Did it originate with you ?" " Has it ended with you ?" that
is, " Will it spread no farther ?" The design of the admonition
is this—that they may not, without having any regard to
others, please themselves in their own contrivances or customs. And this is a doctrine of general application ; for no
Church should be taken up with itself exclusively, to the
neglect of others ; but on the contrary, they ought all, in
their turn, to hold out the right hand to each other, in the
way of cherishing mutual fellowship, and accommodating

per se causas agebat, et importunis clamoribus judicibus obstrepebat ; non
quod advocati ei deessent, sed quia impudentia abundabat. Hinc factum
est, ut mulieres perfrictae frontis et matronalis pudoris oblitae, *Afraniæ*
per contumeliam dicerentur ;"—" Forgetful of the modesty that becomes
a female, she pleaded her own cause in person, and annoyed the judges
with a senseless clamouring—not from any want of advocates to take her
case in hand, but from excessive impudence. In consequence of this, women that were of bold front, and were forgetful of the modesty that becomes a matron, were, by way of reproach, called *Afranias.*"—*Ed.*

themselves to each other, in so far as a regard to harmony requires.[1]

But here it is asked, whether every Church, according as it has had the precedence of another in the order of time,[2] has it also in its power to bind it to observe its institutions?[3] For Paul seems to intimate this in what he says. For example, Jerusalem was the mother of all the Churches, inasmuch as *the word of the Lord had come out from it.* Was she then at liberty to assume to herself a superior right, so as to bind all others to follow her? I answer, that Paul here does not employ an argument of universal application, but one that was specially applicable to the Corinthians, as is frequently the case. He had, therefore, an eye to individuals, rather than to the thing itself. Hence it does not necessarily follow, that Churches that are of later origin must be bound to observe, in every point, the institutions of the earlier ones, inasmuch as even Paul himself did not bind himself by this rule, so as to obtrude upon other Churches the customs that were in use at Jerusalem. Let there be nothing of ambition—let there be nothing of obstinacy—let there be nothing of pride and contempt for other Churches —let there be, on the other hand, a desire to edify—let there be moderation and prudence; and in that case, amidst a diversity of observances, there will be nothing that is worthy of reproof.

Let us, therefore, bear in mind, that the haughtiness of the Corinthians is here reproved, who, concerned for themselves exclusively,[4] showed no respect to the Churches of earlier origin, from which they had received the gospel, and did not endeavour to accommodate themselves to other Churches, to which the gospel had flowed out from them. Would to God that there were no Corinth in our times, in respect of this fault, as well as of others! But we see how

---

[1] " Autant qu'il est requis pour nourrir paix et concorde;"—" In so far as it is requisite for maintaining peace and harmony."

[2] " Et est plus ancienne;"—" And is more ancient."

[3] " A ses ordonnances et manieres de faire;"—" To its ordinances and methods of acting."

[4] " Ne regardans qu'a eux mesmes, et se plaisans en leur façons de faire;"—" Looking only to themselves, and pleasing themselves in their modes of acting."

savage men, who have never *tasted* the gospel, (Heb. vi. 5,) trouble the Churches of the saints by a tyrannical enforcement of their own laws.[1]

37. *If any one thinks himself.* Mark here the judgment, which he had previously assigned to the Prophets—that they should receive what they recognised as being from God. He does not, however, desire them to inquire as to his doctrine, as though it were a doubtful matter, but to receive it as the sure word of God, inasmuch as they will recognise it as the word of God, if they judge rightly. Farther, it is in virtue of apostolical authority, that he takes it upon himself to prescribe to them the sentence which they ought to pronounce.[2]

There is still greater confidence in what he immediately adds—*He that is ignorant, let him be ignorant.* This, it is true, was allowable for Paul, who was fully assured as to the revelation that he had received from God, and he ought also to have been well known to the Corinthians, so that they should have looked upon him in no other light, than as an Apostle of the Lord. It is not, however, for every one to advance such a claim for himself, or if he does, he will, by his boasting, throw himself open to merited derision, for *then* only is there ground for such confidence, when what is affirmed with the mouth shows itself in reality. It was with truth that Paul affirmed, that his precepts were those of the Lord. Many will be prepared to pretend the same thing on false grounds. His great object is this—that it may be clearly perceived, that he who does not allow himself to be under control, speaks as from the Holy Spirit, not from his own brain. That man, therefore, who is no other than a pure organ of the Holy Spirit, will have the courage to declare fearlessly with Paul, that those who shall reject his doctrine, are not *Prophets* or *spiritual* persons ; and this he will do in virtue of a right that belongs to him, in accordance with what we had in the beginning of the Epistle—*he that is spiritual, judgeth all things.* (1 Cor. ii. 15.)

---

[1] " En voulant d'vne façon tyrannique contraindre tout le monde à receuoir leurs loix ;"—" By endeavouring, in a tyrannical way, to constrain every one to receive their laws."

[2] " En cest endroit ;"—" In this case."

But it may be asked here, how it is that Paul declares those things to be *commandments of the Lord,* as to which no statement is to be found in the Scriptures ? Besides this, there is also another difficulty that presents itself—that if they are the *commandments of the Lord,* they are necessary to be observed, and they bind the conscience, and yet they are rites connected with polity, as to the observance of which no such necessity exists. Paul, however, merely says, that he enjoins nothing, but what is in accordance with the will of God. Now God endowed him with wisdom, that he might recommend this order in external things at Corinth, and in other places—not that it might be an inviolable law, like those that relate to the spiritual worship of God, but that it might be a useful directory to all the sons of God, and not by any means to be despised.

38. *But if any man be ignorant.* The old translation reads thus : *He that knows not this, will be unknown ;*[1] but this is a mistake. For Paul had it in view to cut off every handle from contentious persons, who make no end of disputing, and that, under the pretence of inquiring—as if the matter were not yet clear ; or at least he intimates in general terms, that he regarded as of no account any one that would call in question what he said. " If any one is ignorant, I do not stop to take notice of his doubts, for the certainty of my doctrine is not at all impaired thereby. Let him go then, whoever he may be. As for you, do not the less on that account give credit to Christ, as speaking by me." In fine, he intimates, that sceptics, contentious persons, and subtile disputants,[2] do not by the questions they raise diminish, in

[1] *Beausobre,* when adverting to this reading, says : " La Vulgate porte, *il sera ignoré,* Dieu *le méconnoîtra ;* ce qui veut dire, *le punira.* Ce sens est fort bon ;"—" The Vulgate renders it : *he will be unknown*—God *will disown him*—meaning to say : *He will punish him.* This is a very good meaning." In *one* Greek MS. the reading is ἀγνοεῖται—*is unknown.* Wiclif, (1380) renders it—*And if ony man unknowith : he schal be unknowen.* The view taken by CALVIN, however, is the more generally approved, and seems to accord better with the general strain of the passage. —*Ed.*

[2] " Les sophistes qui ne font iamais que disputer, sans rien resoudre ou accorder, ne les contentieux, et subtils iaseurs ;"—" Sophists who are never but disputing, without coming to any solution or agreement, nor contentious persons, and subtile prattlers."

any degree, the authority of sound doctrine, and of that
truth as to which believers ought to feel assured, and at the
same time he admonishes us, not to allow their doubts to be
any hinderance in our way. That elevation of mind, however, which despises all human judgments, ought to be
founded on ascertained truth. Hence, as it would be the
part of perverse rashness, either to maintain pertinaciously,
in opposition to the views of all others, an opinion that has
once been taken up, or audaciously to cling to it, while others
are in doubt, so, on the other hand, when we have felt assured
that it is God that speaks, let us fearlessly break through
all human impediments and all difficulties.[1]

39. *Wherefore, brethren.* This is the conclusion in connection with the principal question—that *prophecy* is to be
preferred to other gifts, because it is the most useful gift of
all, while at the same time other gifts ought not to be despised. We must observe, however, his manner of speaking.
For he intimates, that *prophecy* is worthy of being eagerly
and ardently aspired at by all. In the meantime, he exhorts
them not to envy others the rarer gift,[2] which is not so much
to be desired ; nay more, to allow them the praise that is
due to them, divesting themselves of all envy.

40. *All things decently and in order.* Here we have a
more general conclusion, which does not merely include, in
short compass, the entire case, but also the different parts.
Nay farther, it is a rule by which we must regulate[3] every-

---

[1] " Sans nous en soucier aucunement ;"—" Without giving ourselves
any concern as to them."

[2] " Autres, qui ont le don des langues, qui est vn don plus rare ;"—
" Others, who have the gift of tongues, which is a rarer gift."

[3] " This precept is sometimes applied to support the use of rites and
ceremonies in the worship of God, not commanded in Scripture. But any
one who considers the place which it holds in this discourse, will be sensible that it hath no relation to rites and ceremonies, but to the *decent*
and *orderly* exercise of the spiritual gifts. Yet by parity of reasoning, it
may be extended even to the rites of worship, provided they are left free
to be used by every one as he sees them expedient."—*M'Knight.* " To
adduce this text, as a direct argument about any particular external ceremonies used in divine worship, (which always appear *decent* and *orderly*
to those who invent, impose, or are attached to them, and the contrary to
those who dissent from them,) is doubtless wresting it from its proper
meaning."—*Scott.—Ed.*

thing, that has to do with external polity.   As he had discoursed, in various instances, as to rites, he wished to sum
up everything here in a brief summary—that decorum should
be observed—that confusion should be avoided.   This statement shows, that he did not wish to bind consciences by the
foregoing precepts, as if they were in themselves necessary,
but only in so far as they were subservient to propriety and
peace.   Hence we gather (as I have said)[1] a doctrine that is
always in force, as to the purpose to which the polity of the
Church ought to be directed.   The Lord has left external
rites in our choice with this view—that we may not think
that his worship consists wholly in these things.

In the meantime, he has not allowed us a rambling and
unbridled liberty, but has inclosed it (so to speak) with
railings,[2] or at least has laid a restriction upon the liberty
granted by him in such a manner, that it is after all only
from his word that we can judge as to what is right.   This
passage, therefore, when duly considered, will show the difference between the tyrannical edicts of the Pope, which
oppress men's consciences with a dreadful bondage, and the
godly regulations of the Church, by which discipline and
order are maintained.   Nay farther, we may readily infer
from this, that the latter are not to be looked upon as human
traditions, inasmuch as they are founded upon this general
injunction, and have a manifest approval, as it were, from
the mouth of Christ himself.

[1] See p. 469.
[2] Cancellos (ut ita loquar) circumdedit. CALVIN has here very probably in his eye an expression made use of by Cicero, " Si extra hos cancellos egredi conabor, quos mihi circumdedi ;"—" If I shall attempt to go
beyond those limits, which I have marked out for myself."—(Cic. Quint.
10.)—Ed.

COMMENTARY

ON

THE EPISTLES OF PAUL THE APOSTLE

TO

THE CORINTHIANS

VOL. II

COMMENTARY

ON THE

EPISTLES OF PAUL THE APOSTLE

TO

THE CORINTHIANS.

BY JOHN CALVIN.

TRANSLATED FROM THE ORIGINAL LATIN, AND COLLATED WITH
THE AUTHOR'S FRENCH VERSION,

BY THE REV. JOHN PRINGLE.

VOLUME SECOND.

BAKER BOOK HOUSE
Grand Rapids, Michigan

COMMENTARY

ON THE

FIRST EPISTLE TO THE CORINTHIANS.

CHAPTER XV.

1. Moreover, brethren, I declare unto you the gospel which I preached unto you, which also ye have received, and wherein ye stand;

2. By which also ye are saved, if ye keep in memory what I preached unto you, unless ye have believed in vain:

3. For I delivered unto you first of all that which I also received, how that Christ died for our sins according to the Scriptures;

4. And that he was buried, and that he rose again the third day according to the Scriptures:

5. And that he was seen of Cephas, then of the twelve:

6. After that he was seen of above five hundred brethren at once; of whom the greater part remain unto this present, but some are fallen asleep.

7. After that he was seen of James; then of all the apostles.

8. And last of all he was seen of me also, as of one born out of due time.

9. For I am the least of the apostles, that am not meet to be

1. Notum autem vobis facio, fratres, evangelium quod evangelizavi vobis, quod et recepistis, in quo etiam stetistis.

2. Per quod etiam salutem habetis: quo pacto annuntiarim vobis, si tenetis, nisi frustra credidistis.

3. Tradidi enim vobis imprimis quod et acceperam, quod Christus mortuus fuerit, pro peccatis nostris secundum Scripturas,

4. Et quod sepultus sit, et quod resurrexit tertio die, secundum Scripturas.

5. Et quod visus fuit Cephæ, deinde ipsis duodecim:

6. Postea visus fuit plus quam quingentis fratribus simul, ex quibus plures manent[1] adhuc ad hunc usque diem: quidam autem obdormierunt.

7. Deinde visus fuit Iacobo: post apostolis omnibus:

8. Postremo vero omnium, velut abortivo, visus fuit et mihi.

9. Ego enim sum minimus apostolorum, qui non sum idoneus ut

---

[1] " Sont viuans;"—" Are alive."

called an apostle, because I persecuted the church of God.

10. But by the grace of God I
am what I am : and his grace which
was bestowed upon me was not in
vain ; but I laboured more abundantly than they all : yet not I, but
the grace of God which was with
me.

dicar apostolus : quandoquidem per-
sequutus sum ecclesiam Dei.

10. Sed gratia Dei sum id quod
sum : et gratia ejus, quæ mihi collata
est, non fuit inanis, sed copiosius
quam illi omnes laboravi : non ego
tamen, sed gratia Dei quæ mihi ad-
erat.

1. *Now I make known to you.* He now enters on another subject—the resurrection—the belief of which among
the Corinthians had been shaken by some wicked persons. It .is uncertain, however, whether they doubted
merely as to the ultimate resurrection of the body, or as to
the immortality of the soul also. It is abundantly well
known, that there were a variety of errors as to this point.
Some philosophers contended that souls are immortal. As
to the resurrection of the body, it never entered into the
mind of any one of them. The Sadducees, however, had
grosser views ; for they thought of nothing but the present
life ; nay more, they thought that the soul of man was a
breath of wind without substance. It is not, therefore, altogether certain (as I have already said) whether the Corinthians had at this time gone to such a height of madness, as
to cast off all expectation of a future life, or whether they
merely denied the resurrection of the body ; for the arguments which Paul makes use of seem to imply, that they
were altogether bewitched with the mad dream of the Sadducees.

For example, when he says, *Of what advantage is it to be
baptized for the dead ?* (verse 29.) *Were it not better to eat
and to drink ?* (verse 32.) *Why are we in peril every hour ?*
(verse 30,) and the like, it might very readily be replied, in
accordance with the views of the philosophers, " Because
after death the soul survives the body." Hence some apply
the whole of Paul's reasoning contained in this chapter to
the immortality of the soul. For my part, while I leave
undetermined what the error of the Corinthians was, yet I
cannot bring myself to view Paul's words as referring to anything else than the resurrection of the body. Let it, therefore be regarded as a settled point, that it is of this exclu-

sively that he treats in this chapter.   And what if the impiety of Hymeneus and Philetus had extended thus far,[1] who said that *the resurrection was already past*, (2 Tim. ii. 18,) and that there would be nothing more of it ? Similar to these, there are at the present day some madmen, or rather devils,[2] who call themselves Libertines.[3]   To me, however, the following conjecture appears more probable— that they were carried away by some delusion,[4] which took away from them the hope of a future resurrection, just as those in the present day, by imagining an allegorical resurrection,[5] take away from us the true resurrection that is promised to us.

However this may be, it is truly a dreadful case, and next to a prodigy, that those who had been instructed by so distinguished a master, should have been capable of falling so quickly[6] into errors of so gross a nature.   But what is there that is surprising in this, when in the Israelitish Church the Sadducees had the audacity to declare openly that man differs nothing from a brute, in so far as concerns the essence of the soul, and has no enjoyment but what is common to him with the beasts ? Let us observe, however, that blindness of this kind is a just judgment from God, so that those who do not rest satisfied with the truth of God, are tossed hither and thither by the delusions of Satan.

It is asked, however, why it is that he has left off or deferred to the close of the Epistle, what should properly have had the precedence of everything else ? Some reply, that this was done for the purpose of impressing it more deeply upon the memory.   I am rather of opinion that Paul did

---

[1] " Iusques a Corinthe ;"—" As far as Corinth."

[2] Possedez d'autres diables ;"—" Possessed by other devils."

[3] " The *Libertines* of Geneva were rather a cabal of rakes than a set of fanatics ; for they made no pretence to any religious system, but only pleaded for the liberty of leading voluptuous and immoral lives.   This cabal was composed of a certain number of licentious citizens, who could not bear the severe discipline of CALVIN, who punished with rigour, not only dissolute manners, but also whatever carried the aspect of irreligion and impiety."—*Paterson's History of the Church*, vol. ii. p. 383.—*Ed.*

[4] " Par quelque opinion fantastique ;"—" By some fantastic notion."

[5] " Vne ie ne scay quelle resurrection allegorique ;"—" An allegorical resurrection, I know not of what sort."

[6] " Si soudainement seduits ;"—" So suddenly seduced."

not wish to introduce a subject of such importance, until he had asserted his authority, which had been considerably lessened among the Corinthians, and until he had, by repressing their pride, prepared them for listening to him with docility.

I make known to you. To *make known* here does not mean to teach what was previously unknown to them, but to recall to their recollection what they had heard previously. " Call to your recollection, along with me, that gospel which you had learned, before you were led aside from the right course." He calls the doctrine of the resurrection the *gospel,* that they may not imagine that any one is at liberty to form any opinion that he chooses on this point, as on other questions, which bring with them no injury to salvation.

When he adds, *which I preached to you,* he amplifies what he had said : " If you acknowledge me as an apostle, I have assuredly taught you so." There is another amplification in the words—*which also ye have received,* for if they now allow themselves to be persuaded of the contrary, they will be chargeable with fickleness. A *third* amplification is to this effect, that they had hitherto continued in that belief with a firm and steady resolution, which is somewhat more than that they had once believed. But the most important thing of all is, that he declares that their salvation is involved in this, for it follows from this, that, if the resurrection is taken away, they have no religion left them, no assurance of faith, and in short, have no faith remaining. Others understand in another sense the word *stand,* as meaning that they are *upheld ;* but the interpretation that I have given is a more correct one.[1]

2. *If you keep in memory—unless in vain.*[2] These two

---

[1] It is remarked by Bloomfield, that " in ἱστήκατε (which means ' ye have persevered, and do persevere,') there is an *agonistic* metaphor, (as in Eph. vi. 13,) or an *architectural* one, like ἱδραῖοι γίνεσθε, (be steadfast,) in 1 Cor. xv. 58."—*Ed.*

[2] " Our version does not express intelligibly the sense of ἐκτὸς εἰ μὴ εἰκῆ ἐπιστεύσατε, by rendering it so literally—*unless ye have believed in vain. To believe in vain,* according to the use of ancient languages, is to believe *without just reason and authority,* giving credit to idle reports as true and authentic. Thus *Plutarch,* speaking of some story which passed current,

expressions are very cutting.   In the *first*, he reproves their carelessness or fickleness, because such a sudden fall was an evidence that they had never understood what had been delivered to them, or that their knowledge of it had been loose and floating, inasmuch as it had so quickly vanished. By the *second*, he warns them that they had needlessly and uselessly professed allegiance to Christ, if they did not hold fast this main doctrine.[1]

3. *For I delivered to you first of all.* He now confirms what he had previously stated, by explaining that the resurrection had been preached by him, and that too as a fundamental doctrine of the gospel. *First of all*, says he, as it is wont to be with a foundation in the erecting of a house. At the same time he adds to the authority of his preaching, when he subjoins, that he *delivered* nothing but *what he had received*, for he does not simply mean that he related what he had from the report of others, but that it was what had been enjoined upon him by the Lord.[2] For the word[3] must be explained in accordance with the connection of the passage. Now it is the duty of an apostle to bring forward nothing but what he *has received from the Lord,* so as from hand to hand[4] (as they say) to administer to the Church the pure word of God.

That Christ died, &c. See now more clearly whence he received it, for he quotes *the Scriptures* in proof. In the first place, he makes mention of the death of Christ, nay also of his burial, that we may infer, that, as he was like us in

says, τοῦτο ἡμεῖς εἴπομεν ἐν τί τῶν εἰκῆ πεπιστευμένων—"this I said was one of those tales which are believed without any good authority." (Sympos. lib. i. quæst. 6.) The Latins used *credere frustra—to believe in vain,* or *temere—(rashly.)* .... *Kypke* .... takes notice that ἐκτὸς εἰ μὴ, for *except* or *unless*, which has long been a suspected phrase, is used more than ten times by *Lucian.* It is also used by *Plutarch* in the Life of Demosthenes, vol. iv. p. 416, l. 9."—*Alexander's Paraphrase on* 1 Cor. xv. (London, 1766,) pp. 63, 64.—*Ed.*

[1] " Ce principal poinct de la foy ;"—" This main article of faith."

[2] " Que le Seigneur mesme luy auoit enseignee et commandee ;"— " What the Lord himself had taught and commanded him."

[3] " Le mot de *recevoir* ;"—" The word *receive.*"

[4] The Reader will find our Author making use of the same proverbial expression when commenting on 1 Cor. iv. 1, and xi. 23. See vol. i. pp. 150, 373.—*Ed.*

these things, he is so also in his resurrection. He has, therefore, died with us that we may rise with him. In his burial, too, the reality of the death in which he has taken part with us, is made more clearly apparent. Now there are many passages of Scripture in which Christ's death and resurrection are predicted, but nowhere more plainly[1] than in Isaiah liii., in Daniel ix. 26, and in Psalm xxii.

For our sins. That is, that by taking our curse upon him he might redeem us from it. For what else was Christ's death, but a sacrifice for expiating our sins—what but a satisfactory penalty, by which we might be reconciled to God—what but the condemnation of one, for the purpose of obtaining forgiveness for us ? He speaks also in the same manner in Rom. iv. 25, but in that passage, on the other hand, he ascribes it also to the resurrection as its effect— that it confers righteousness upon us ; for as sin was done away through the death of Christ, so righteousness is procured through his resurrection. This distinction must be carefully observed, that we may know what we must look for from the death of Christ, and what from his resurrection. When, however, the Scripture in other places makes mention only of his death, let us understand that in those cases his resurrection is included in his death, but when they are mentioned separately, the commencement of our salvation is (as we see) in the one, and the consummation of it in the other.

5. *That he was seen by Cephas.* He now brings forward *eye witnesses,* (αὐτόπτας,) as they are called by Luke, (i. 2,) who saw the accomplishment of what the Scriptures had foretold would take place. He does not, however, adduce them all, for he makes no mention of women. When, therefore, he says that he appeared first to Peter, you are to understand by this that he is put before all the *men,* so that there is nothing inconsistent with this in the statement of Mark (xvi. 9) that *he appeared to Mary.*

But how is it that he says, that *he appeared to the twelve,* when, after the death of Judas, there were only eleven re-

---

[1] " Il n'y en a point de plus expres, et où il en soit traitté plus apertement ;"—" There are none of them that are more explicit, or where it is treated of more plainly "

maining? Chrysostom is of opinion that this took place after Matthias had been chosen in his room. Others have chosen rather to correct the expression, looking upon it as a mistake.[1] But as we know, that there were *twelve* in number that were set apart by Christ's appointment, though one of them had been expunged from the roll, there is no absurdity in supposing that the name was retained. On this principle, there was a body of men at Rome that were called Centumviri,[2] while they were in number 102.[3] By *the twelve*, therefore, you are simply to understand the chosen Apostles.

It does not quite appear *when* it was that this *appearing to more than five hundred* took place. Only it is possible that this large multitude assembled at Jerusalem, when he manifested himself to them. For Luke (xxiv. 33) makes mention in a general way of the disciples who had assembled with the eleven; but how many there were he does not say. Chrysostom refers it to the ascension, and explains the word ἐπάνω to mean, *from on high*.[4] Unquestionably, as to what he says in reference to his having appeared to James apart, this may have been subsequently to the ascension.

By *all the Apostles* I understand not merely the *twelve*,

[1] *Granville Penn* supposes that the common reading εἶτα τοῖς δώδεκα— *then to the twelve*, is a corruption for εἶτα τοῖς δὲ δέκα—*and then to the ten*, understanding the Apostle as meaning, that Christ appeared first to Cephas, and then to the other *ten*. Dr. Adam Clarke, after stating that " instead of δώδεκα, *twelve*, ἔνδεκα, *eleven*, is the reading of D* E F G, *Syriac* in the margin, some of the *Slavonic, Armenian, Vulgate, Itala*, and several of the *Fathers*," and that " this reading is supported by Mark xvi. 14," remarks : " Perhaps the term *twelve* is used here *merely* to point out the *society of the Apostles*, who, though at this time they were only *eleven*, were still called the *twelve*, because this was their *original number*, and a number which was afterwards *filled up*." " The *twelve* was a name, not of number, but of office."—*M'Knight.—Ed.*

[2] C'est a dire, les Cents;"—" That is to say, the Hundred."

[3] The reader will find the same term referred to by CALVIN when commenting on 1 Cor. x. 8. (See CALVIN on the Corinthians, vol. i. p. 324, n. 3.)—*Ed.*

[4] " This peculiar use of ἐπάνω for πλεῖον, (which seems to have been popular or provincial, not being found in the Classical writers,) occurs also in Mark xiv. 5, but with a genitive. Perhaps, however, it has properly no regimen, but is used parenthetically, like the Latin *plus trecentos*, 300 and more."—*Bloomfield.* The word ἐπάνω is used in a similar way in the Septuagint. Thus in Exodus xxx. 14, ἀπὸ εἰκοσαετοῦς καὶ ἐπάνω—*from twenty years old and above*, and in Lev. xxvii. 7, ἀπὸ ἑξήκοντα ἐτῶν καὶ ἐπάνω—*from sixty years old and above.—Ed.*

but also those disciples to whom Christ had assigned the office of preaching the gospel.[1] In proportion as our Lord was desirous that there should be many witnesses of his resurrection, and that it should be frequently testified of, let us know that it should be so much the more *surely believed among us.* (Luke i. 1.) Farther, inasmuch as the Apostle proves the resurrection of Christ from the fact that he appeared to many, he intimates by this, that it was not figurative but true and natural, for the eyes of the body cannot be witnesses of a spiritual resurrection.

8. *Last of all to me, as to one born prematurely.* He now introduces himself along with the others, for Christ had manifested himself to him as alive, and invested with glory.[2] As it was no deceptive vision, it was calculated to be of use[3] for establishing a belief in the resurrection, as he also makes use of this argument in Acts xxvi. 8. But as it was of no small importance that his authority should have the greatest weight and influence among the Corinthians, he introduces, by the way, a commendation of himself personally, but at the same time qualified in such a manner that, while he claims much for himself, he is at the same time exceedingly modest. Lest any one, therefore, should meet him with the objection: " Who art thou that we should give credit to thee?" he, of his own accord, confesses his unworthiness, and, in the first place, indeed he compares himself to one that is *born prematurely*, and that, in my opinion, with reference to his sudden conversion. For as infants do not come forth from the womb, until they have been there formed and matured during a regular course of time, so the Lord observed a regular period of time in creating, nourishing, and forming his Apostles. Paul, on the other hand, had been cast forth from the womb when he had scarcely received the vital spark.[4] There are some that understand the term

---

[1] CALVIN's view accords with that of Chrysostom, who says, ἦσαν γὰρ καὶ ἄλλοι ἀπόστολοι, ὡς οἱ ἑβδομήκοντα—" for there were also other Apostles, such as the seventy."—*Ed.*

[2] " En sa vie et gloire immortelle ;"—" In his life and immortal glory."

[3] " Elle estoit suffisante et receuable ;"—" It was sufficient and admissible."

[4] In accordance with the view taken by CALVIN, *Bloomfield* considers

rendered *abortive* as employed to mean *posthumous ;*[1] but the former term is much more suitable, inasmuch as he was in one moment begotten, and born, and a man of full age. Now this premature birth renders the grace of God more illustrious in Paul than if he had by little and little, and by successive steps, grown up to maturity in Christ.

9. *For I am the least.* It is not certain whether his enemies threw out this for the purpose of detracting from his credit, or whether it was entirely of his own accord, that he made the acknowledgment. For my part, while I have no doubt that he was at all times voluntarily, and even cheerfully, disposed to abase himself, that he might magnify the grace of God, yet I suspect that in this instance he wished to obviate calumnies. For that there were some at Corinth that made it their aim to detract from his dignity by malicious slander, may be inferred not only from many foregoing passages, but also from his adding a little afterwards a comparison, which he would assuredly never have touched upon if he had not been constrained to it by the wickedness of some. " Detract from me as much as you please—I shall suffer myself to be cast down below the ground—I shall

---

the original term ἔκτρωμα to mean, *a child born before the due time,* (in which sense the term *abortivus,* is employed by Horace, Sat. i. 3. 46,) the Apostle " calling himself so as being an Apostle not formed and matured by previous preparation and instruction." *Penn,* after quoting the definition given by Eustathius of the term ἔκτρωμα—τὸ μήπω τετυπώμενον—*an unformed foetus,* remarks: " To all the other Apostles our Lord appeared after his resurrection, when they had attained their *adult form* in his ministry; but to St. Paul he appeared at the first moment of his spiritual conception, and *before he was formed or moulded.*" The same view, in substance, is given by *M'Knight.* " Although he" (Paul) " calls himself *an abortive Apostle,* it was not on account of his being sensible of any imperfection in his commission, or of any weakness in his qualifications as an Apostle; for he affirms, 2 Cor. xi. 5, that he was *in nothing behind the very greatest of the Apostles ;* but he called himself an *abortive Apostle,* because, as he tells us (verse 9,) he had *persecuted the Church of God,* and because he was made an Apostle without that previous course of instruction and preparation, which the other Apostles enjoyed who had attended Jesus Christ during his ministry on earth ; so that, in the proper sense of the word, he was ἔκτρωμα—one born before he was brought to maturity. That want, however, was abundantly supplied by the many revelations which his master gave him after he made him an Apostle."—*Ed.*

[1] " C'est a dire qui est nay apres la mort de son pere ;"—" That is to say, one that is born after the death of his father."

suffer myself to be of no account whatever,[1] that the goodness of God towards me may shine forth the more.   Let me,
therefore, be reckoned the *least of the Apostles :* nay more,
I acknowledge myself to be unworthy of this distinction.
For by what merits could I have attained to that honour ?
When *I persecuted the Church of God,* what did I merit ?
But there is no reason why you should judge of me according to my own worth,[2] for the Lord did not look to what I
was, but made me by his grace quite another man." The
sum is this, that Paul does not refuse to be the most worthless of all, and next to nothing, provided this contempt does
not impede him in any degree in his ministry, and does not
at all detract from his doctrine.   He is contented that, as to
himself, he shall be reckoned unworthy of any honour, provided only he commends his apostleship in respect of the
grace conferred upon him.   And assuredly God had not
adorned him with such distinguished endowments in order
that his grace might lie buried or neglected, but he had designed thereby to render his apostleship illustrious and distinguished.

10. *And his grace was not vain.*   Those that set free-will
in opposition to the grace of God, that whatever good we
do may not be ascribed wholly to Him, wrest these words
to suit their own interpretation—as if Paul boasted, that he
had by his own industry taken care that God's grace toward
him had not been misdirected.   Hence they infer, that God,
indeed, offers his grace, but that the right use of it is in man's
own power, and that it is in his own power to prevent its
being ineffectual.   I maintain, however, that these words of
Paul give no support to their error, for he does not here
claim anything as his own, as if he had himself, independently of God, done anything praiseworthy.   What then ?
That he might not seem to glory to no purpose in mere
words, while devoid of reality, he says, that he affirms nothing
that is not openly apparent.   Farther, even admitting that
these words intimate, that Paul did not abuse the grace of

---

[1] " Estre estimé moins que rien ;"—" To be esteemed less than nothing."
[2] " Par ma petite et basse condition ;"—" By my little and low condition."

God, and did not render it ineffectual by his negligence, I maintain, nevertheless, that there is no reason on that account, why we should divide between him and God the praise, that ought to be ascribed wholly to God, inasmuch as he confers upon us not merely the power of doing well, but also the inclination and the accomplishment.

But more abundantly. Some refer this to vain-glorious boasters,[1] who, by detracting from Paul, endeavoured to set off themselves and their goods to advantage, as, in their opinion at least, it is not likely that he wished to enter upon a contest with the Apostles. When he compares himself, however, with the Apostles, he does so merely for the sake of those wicked persons, who were accustomed to bring them forward for the purpose of detracting from his reputation, as we see in the Epistle to the Galatians. (i. 11.) Hence the probability is, that it is of the Apostles that he speaks, when he represents his own labours as superior to theirs, and it is quite true, that he was superior to others, not merely in respect of his enduring many hardships, encountering many dangers, abstaining from things lawful, and perseveringly despising all *perils;* (2 Cor. xi. 26;) but also because the Lord gave to his labours a much larger measure of success.[2] For I take *labour* here to mean the fruit of his labour that appeared.

Not I, but the grace. The old translator, by leaving out the article, has given occasion of mistake to those that are not acquainted with the Greek language, for in consequence of his having rendered the words thus—*not I, but the grace of God with me,*[3] they thought that only the half of the praise is ascribed to God, and that the other half is reserved for man. They, accordingly, understand the meaning to be that Paul laboured not alone, inasmuch as he could

---

[1] " Thrasones."   See CALVIN on the Corinthians, vol. i. p. 98, *n.* 1.

[2] " Dieu donnoit plus heureuse issue à ses labeurs, et les faisoit proufiter plus amplement ;"—" God gave to his labours a more prosperous issue, and made them much more successful."

[3] In the Alexandrine MS. the reading is: Οὐκ ἐγὼ δὲ, ἀλλ᾽ ἡ χάρις τοῦ Θεοῦ σὺν ἐμοί.   *But not I, but the grace of God with me.*—Corresponding to this is the rendering of Wiclif, (1380,)—*But not I, but the grace of God with me.*—*Ed.*

do nothing without co-operating grace,[1] but at the same time it was under the influence of his own free-will, and by means of his own strength.　His words, however, have quite a different meaning, for what he had said was his own, he afterwards, correcting himself, ascribes wholly to the grace of God—*wholly*, I say, not in part, for whatever he might have seemed to do, was *wholly*, he declares, the work of grace.　A remarkable passage certainly, both for laying low the pride of man, and for magnifying the operation of Divine grace in us.　For Paul, as though he had improperly made himself the author of anything good, corrects what he had said, and declares the *grace of God* to have been the efficient cause of the whole.　Let us not think that there is here a mere pretence of humility.[2]　It is in good earnest that he speaks thus, and from knowing that it is so in truth. Let us learn, therefore, that we have nothing that is good, but what the Lord has graciously given us, that we do nothing good but what he *worketh in us*, (Phil. ii. 13)—not that we do nothing ourselves, but that we do nothing without being influenced—that is, under the guidance and impulse of the Holy Spirit.

11. Therefore whether *it were* I or they, so we preach, and so ye believed.

12. Now, if Christ be preached that

11. Sive ego igitur, sive illi, ita prædicamus, et ita credidistis.

12. Si autem Christus prædica-

---

[1] See *Institutes*, vol. i. pp. 307, 354.

[2] *Heideggerus* seems to have had CALVIN'S exposition here in his view in the following observations on the expression made use of by the Apostle: "Non *Gratia Dei mecum*, uti vetus Itala vertit, quasi effectus inter Gratiam Dei, et Pauli arbitrium distribueretur; nihil enim habuit ipse, quod non acceperit; sed ἡ σὺν ἐμοί *quæ mecum*, ut totum et in solidum omne gratiæ soli acceptum feratur.　Neque ita loquitur solius humilitatis et modestiæ explicandæ ergo, quanquam et hanc testari voluit; sed quia potens illa gratia demonstratio et testimonium irrefragabile erat resurrectionis Domini."—" Not the *grace of God with me*, as the old Italic version renders it, as though the effect were divided between God's grace and Paul's free-will; for he has nothing that he has not received, but ἡ σὺν ἐμοί, *which with me*, that every thing may be wholly and entirely ascribed to grace alone.　Nor does he speak thus, merely for the purpose of showing humility and modesty, though he had it also in view to testify this, but because that grace was a powerful demonstration and irrefragable testimony of our Lord's resurrection."—Heideggeri Labores Exegetici in Cor. (Tiguri. 1700) p.154.— *Ed.*

he rose from the dead, how say some among you that there is no resurrection of the dead?

13. But if there be no resurrection of the dead, then is Christ not risen:

14. And if Christ be not risen, then *is* our preaching vain, and your faith *is* also vain.

15. Yea, and we are found false witnesses of God; because we have testified of God that he raised up Christ: whom he raised not up, if so be that the dead rise not.

16. For if the dead rise not, then is not Christ raised:

17. And if Christ be not raised, your faith *is* vain; ye are yet in your sins.

18. Then they also which are fallen asleep in Christ are perished.

19. If in this life only we have hope in Christ, we are of all men most miserable.

tur excitatus a mortuis, quomodo dicunt quidam, mortuorum resurrectionem non esse?

13. Si autem mortuorum resurrectio non est, neque Christus resurrexit.

14. Quodsi Christus non resurrexit, inanis igitur est prædicatio nostra, inanis et fides vestra.

15. Invenimur etiam falsi testes Dei, quia testati sumus a Deo, quod suscitaverit Christum; quem non suscitavit, siquidem mortui non resurgunt.

16. Si enim mortui non resurgunt, neque Christus resurrexit.

17. Si autem Christus non resurrexit, vana est fides vestra: adhuc estis in peccatis vestris.

18. Ergo et qui obdormierunt in Christo perierunt.

19. Quodsi in hac vita solum speramus in Christo, miserrimi sumus omnium hominum.

11. *Whether I or they.* Having compared himself with the other Apostles, he now associates himself with them, and them with him, in agreement as to their preaching. " I do not now speak of myself, but we have all taught so with one mouth, and still continue to teach so." For the verb κηρύσσομεν (*we preach*) is in the present tense—intimating a continued act, or perseverance in teaching.[1] " If, then, it is otherwise, our apostleship is void: nay more—*so ye believed:* your religion, therefore, goes for nothing."

12. *But of Christ.* He now begins to prove the resurrection of all of us from that of Christ. For a mutual and reciprocal inference holds good on the one side and on the other, both affirmatively and negatively—from Christ to us in this way: *If Christ is risen, then we will rise—If Christ is not risen, then we will not rise*—from us to Christ on the other hand: *If we rise, then Christ is risen—If we do not rise, then neither is Christ risen.* The ground-work of the argument to be drawn from Christ to us in the former inference is this: " Christ did not die, or rise again for himself,

[1] " Perseuerance à enseigner ceste mesme chose;"—" Perseverance in teaching this same thing."

but for us : hence his resurrection is the foundation[1] of ours,
and what was accomplished in him, must be fulfilled in us
also." In the negative form, on the other hand, it is thus :
" Otherwise he would have risen again needlessly and to no
purpose, because the fruit of it is to be sought, not in his
own person, but in his members."

Observe the ground-work, on the other hand, of the former
inference to be deduced from us to him ; for the resurrection
is not from nature, and comes from no other quarter than
from Christ alone. For in Adam we die, and we recover life
only in Christ ; hence it follows that his resurrection is the
foundation of ours, so that if *that* is taken away, it cannot
stand.[2] The ground-work of the negative inference has been
already stated ; for as he could not have risen again but on
our account, his resurrection would be null and void,[3] if it
were of no advantage to us.

14. *Then is our preaching vain*—not simply as having
some mixture of falsehood, but as being altogether an empty
fallacy. For what remains if Christ has been swallowed up
by death—if he has become extinct—if he has been overwhelmed by the curse of sin—if, in fine, he has been overcome by Satan? In short, if that fundamental article is
subverted, all that remains will be of no moment. For the
same reason he adds, that their *faith will be vain*, for what
solidity of faith will there be, where no hope of life is to be
seen ? But in the death of Christ, considered in itself,[4] there

---

[1] " La substance et le fondement de la nostre ;"—" The substance and
foundation of ours."

[2] " Si ce fondement est osté, nostre resurrection ne pourra consister ;"
—" If this foundation is taken away, our resurrection cannot possibly
stand."

[3] Billroth, when quoting the above statement of CALVIN, remarks, that
" CALVIN seems to have deceived himself with the double meaning of the
words which he uses—' nulla ejus resurrectio foret ;'—these may mean
either ' ejus resurrectio non est,' or ' ejus resurrectio non est vera resurrectio,' *his resurrection is no real resurrection*, and indeed only the latter suits
his view of Paul's argument." It is justly observed, however, by Dr.
Alexander, in his translation of Billroth, that CALVIN may be considered
to have "used the word *nulla* here in the sense of our *null, void, useless*,"
his assertion being to this effect—that "if we rise not, then Christ's resurrection becomes *null*." See Biblical Cabinet, vol. xxiii. p. 86.—*Ed.*

[4] " C'est à dire, sans la resurrection ;"—" That is to say, apart from his
resurrection."

is seen nothing but ground of despair, for *he* cannot be the
author of salvation to others, who has been altogether vanquished by death. Let us therefore bear in mind, that the
entire gospel consists mainly in the death and resurrection
of Christ, so that we must direct our chief attention to this,
if we would desire, in a right and orderly manner, to make
progress in the gospel—nay more, if we would not remain
barren and unfruitful. (2 Peter i. 8.)

15. *We are also found to be false witnesses.* The other
disadvantages, it is true, which he has just now recounted,
were more serious, as regards us—that *faith was made vain*
—that the whole doctrine of the gospel was useless and
worthless, and that we were bereft of all hope of salvation. Yet this also was no trivial absurdity—that the
Apostles, who were ordained by God to be the heralds of
his eternal truth, were detected as persons who had deceived
the world with falsehoods; for this tends to God's highest
dishonour.

The expression, *false witnesses of God,* we may understand
in two ways—either that by *lying* they used the name of
God under a false pretext, or that they were detected as
liars, in testifying what they had received from God. The
second of these I rather prefer, because it involves a crime
that is much more heinous, and he had spoken previously as
to men.[1] Now, therefore, he teaches that, if the resurrection of Christ is denied, God is made guilty of falsehood in
the witnesses that have been brought forward and hired by
him.[2] The reason, too, that is added, corresponds well—
because they had declared what was false, not as from themselves, but from God.

I am at the same time well aware that there are some that
give another rendering to the particle κατα. The old interpreter renders it *against;*[3] Erasmus, on the other hand—*con-*

---

[1] " Et aussi il auoit desia parlé du deshonneur qui en reuindroit aux
hommes, c'est à dire aux Apostres et autres prescheurs;"—" And besides,
he had spoken previously of the dishonour that resulted from it to men—
that is to say, to the Apostles and other preachers."

[2] " Comme subornez;"—" As it were hired."

[3] In accordance with this Wiclif (1380) renders the words thus—" We
haw seide witnessynge agens God."—*Ed.*

cerning.[1] But, as it has also among the Greeks the force of ἀπό, (*from,*) this signification appeared to me to be more in accordance with the Apostle's design. For he is not speaking here of the reputation of men, (as I have already stated,[2]) but he declares that God will be exposed to the charge of falsehood, inasmuch as what they publish has come forth from him.

17. *Ye are yet in your sins.* For although Christ by his death atoned for our sins, that they might no more be imputed to us in the judgment of God, and has *crucified our old man,* that *its lusts might no longer reign in us,* (Rom. vi. 6, 12 ;) and, in fine, has *by death destroyed the power of death, and the devil himself,* (Heb. ii. 14 ;) yet there would have been none of all these things, if he had not, by rising again, come off victorious. Hence, if the resurrection is overthrown, the dominion of sin is set up anew.

18. *Then they who are fallen asleep.* Having it in view to prove, that if the resurrection of Christ is taken away, faith is useless, and Christianity[3] is a mere deception, he had said that the *living* remain in their sins ; but as there is a clearer illustration of this matter to be seen in the *dead,* he adduces them as an example. " Of what advantage were it to the dead that they once were Christians ? Hence our brethren who are now dead, did to no purpose live in the faith of Christ." But if it is granted that the essence of the soul is immortal, this argument appears, at first sight, conclusive ; for it will very readily be replied, that the dead have not *perished,* inasmuch as their souls live in a state of separation from their bodies. Hence some fanatics conclude that there is no life in the period intermediate between death

---

[1] *Raphelius* adduces two instances of κατα being employed by classical writers in the sense of *concerning.* Ταῦτα μὲν δὴ κατα πάντων Περσῶν ἔχομεν λέγειν—" And these are things that we may affirm *concerning* all the Persians."—(Xen. Cyrop., Book i. p. 6, line 33.) 'Ο κατα τῶν τεχνῶν καὶ ἐπιστημῶν λέγειν εἰώθαμεν ταυτὸν καὶ κατα τῆς ἀρετῆς φατέον ἐστίν—" What we are accustomed to say *in reference to* the arts and sciences, may also be said *in reference to* virtue."—(Plutarch, chap. 4.) *Bloomfield* suggests that the Apostle probably employed κατα in the " very rare " sense of *concerning,* " as wishing to include the sense—*to the prejudice of*—which *falsification* would occasion, inasmuch as it would almost imply a want of *power* in God to raise the dead, for the Gentile philosophers *denied* it."—*Ed.*

[2] See p. 19.

[3] " La profession de Chrestiente ;"—" The profession of Christianity."

and the resurrection ; but this frenzy is easily refuted.[1] For although the souls of the dead are now living, and enjoy quiet repose, yet the whole of their felicity and consolation depends exclusively on the resurrection ; because it is well with them on this account, and no other, that they wait for that day, on which they shall be called to the possession of the kingdom of God. Hence as to the hope of the dead, all is over, unless that day shall sooner or later arrive.

19. *But if in this life.* Here is another absurdity—that we do not merely by believing lose our time and pains, in-asmuch as the fruit of it perishes at our death, but it were better for us not to believe ; for the condition of unbelievers were preferable, and more to be desired. To *believe in this life* means here to limit the fruit of our faith to this life, so that our faith looks no farther, and does not extend beyond the confines of the present life. This statement shows more clearly that the Corinthians had been imposed upon by some mistaken fancy of a figurative resurrection, such as Hymen-eus and Philetus, as though the last fruit of our faith were set before us in this life. (2 Tim. ii. 17, 18.) For as the resurrection is the completion of our salvation, and as to all blessings is, as it were, the farthest goal,[2] the man who says that our resurrection is already past, leaves us nothing better to hope for after death. However this may be, this passage gives at all events no countenance to the frenzy of those who imagine that the soul sleeps as well as the body, until the day of the resurrection.[3] They bring forward, it is

---

[1] It is mentioned by Beza in his life of CALVIN, that before leaving France in 1534, he " published his admirable treatise, entitled Psychopannychia, against the error of those who, reviving a doctrine which had been held in the earliest ages, taught that the soul, when separated from the body, falls asleep."—CALVIN's *Tracts*, vol. i. p. xxvi.—*Ed.*

[2] This statement as to the *resurrection* is strikingly in contrast with the celebrated sentiment of Horace. (Epist. i. 16, 79.) " Mors est ultima linea rerum ;"—" Death is the ultimate limit of things." Heathen philosophers denied the possibility of a *resurrection*. Thus *Pliny*, Hist. Nat. L. ii. c. 7, says—" Revocare defunctos ne Deus quidem potest ;"—" To call back the dead is what God himself cannot do."

[3] *Pareus*, in commenting on this passage, adverts in the following terms to the tenet above referred to—" Nequaquam vero hinc sequitur, quod Psychopannychitae finxerunt : animas post mortem dormire, aut in nihilum cum corporibus redigi. *Perire* enim dicuntur infideles quoad animas, non physicè, quod corruptae intereant ; sed theologicè, quod viventes felicita-

true, this objection—that if the soul continued to live when separated from the body, Paul would not have said that, if the resurrection were taken away, we would *have hope only in this life,* inasmuch as there would still be some felicity remaining for the soul.   To this, however, I reply, that Paul did not dream of Elysian fields,[1] and foolish fables of that sort, but takes it for granted, that the entire hope of Christians looks forward to the final day of judgment—that pious souls do even at this day rest in the same expectation, and that, consequently, we are bereft of everything, if a confidence of this nature deceives us.

But why does he say that *we would be the most miserable of all men,* as if the lot of the Christian were worse than that of the wicked?   For *all things,* says Solomon, *happen alike to the good and to the bad.*   (Eccles. ix. 2.)   I answer, that all men, it is true, whether good or bad, are liable to distresses in common, and they feel in common the same inconveniences, and the same miseries ; but there are two reasons why Christians have in all ages fared worse, in addition to which, there was one that was peculiar to the times of Paul.   The *first* is, that while the Lord frequently chastises the wicked, too, with his lashes, and begins to inflict his judgments upon them, he at the same time peculiarly afflicts his own in various ways ;—in the *first* place, because he *chastises those whom he loves,* (Heb. xii. 6 ;) and *secondly,* in order that he may train them to patience, that he may try their obedience, and that he may gradually prepare them by the cross for a true renovation.   However it may be as to this, that statement always holds good in the case of believers—*It is time, that judgment should begin at the house of God.* (Jer. xxv. 29 ; 1 Pet. iv. 17.[2])   Again, *we are reck-*

tem cœlestem non consequantur ; sed in tartara ad pœnas solæ vel cum corporibus tandem detrudantur :"—" By no means, however, does it follow from this, according to the contrivance of the soul-sleepers, that souls sleep after death, or are reduced to nothing along with the body.   For unbelievers are said to *perish* as to their souls, not physically, as though they corrupted and died, but theologically, because, while living, they do not attain heavenly felicity, but are at length thrust down to hell for punishment, alone, or along with the body."—*Ed.*

[1] Described at great length by *Virgil.*   (Æn. 6, 637-703.)—*Ed.*
[2] CALVIN, in commenting on 1 Peter iv. 17, when speaking of *judgment*

oned as sheep appointed for slaughter. (Ps. xliv. 23.) Again, *ye are dead, and your life is hid with Christ in God.* (Col. iii. 3.) Meanwhile, the condition of the wicked is for the most part the more desirable, because the Lord feeds them up, as hogs for the day of slaughter.

The *second* reason is, that believers, even though they should abound in riches and in blessings of every kind, they nevertheless do not go to excess, and do not gormandize at their ease; in fine, they do not enjoy the world, as unbelievers do, but go forward with anxiety, constantly *groaning*, (2 Cor. v. 2,) partly from a consciousness of their weakness, and partly from an eager longing for the future life. Unbelievers, on the other hand, are wholly intent on intoxicating themselves with present delights.[1]

The *third* reason, which was peculiar, as I have said,[2] to the age of the Apostle, is—that at that time the name of *Christians* was so odious and abominable, that no one could then take upon himself the name of Christ without exposing his life to imminent peril. It is, therefore, not without good reason that he says that Christians would be *the most miserable of all men,* if their confidence were confined to this world

20. But now is Christ risen from the dead, *and* become the first-fruits of them that slept.

21. For since by man *came* death, by man *came* also the resurrection of the dead.

22. For as in Adam all die, even so in Christ shall all be made alive.

20. Nunc autem Christus resurrexit a mortuis, primitiæ eorum qui domierunt, fuit.

21. Quandoquidem enim per hominem mors, etiam per hominem resurrectio mortuorum.

22. Quemadmodum enim in Adam omnes moriuntur, ita et in Christo omnes vivificabuntur.

beginning at the house of God, says: " Ideo dicit Paulus, (1 Cor. xv. 19,) Christianos sublata fide resurrectionis, omnium hominum miserrimos fore: et merito, quia dum alii absque metu sibi indulgent, assidue ingemiscunt fideles: dum aliorum peccata dissimulat Deus, et alios torpore sinit, suos sub crucis disciplina multo rigidius exercet;"—" Hence Paul says, and justly, (1 Cor. xv. 19,) that Christians, if the hope of a resurrection were taken away, would be *of all men the most miserable,* because, while others indulge themselves without fear, believers incessantly groan: while God seems to let the sins of others pass unnoticed, and allows others to be in a torpid state, he exercises his own people more strictly under the discipline of the cross."—*Ed.*

1 " Es voluptez et delices de ce monde;"—" With the pleasures and delights of this world."

2 See p. 22.

23. But every man in his own order: Christ the first-fruits; afterward they that are Christ's at his coming.

24. Then *cometh* the end, when he shall have delivered up the kingdom to God, even the Father; when he shall have put down all rule, and all authority and power.

25. For he must reign, till he hath put all enemies under his feet.

26. The last enemy *that* shall be destroyed *is* death.

27. For he hath put all things under his feet. But when he saith, All things are put under *him, it is* manifest that he is excepted which did put all things under him.

28. And when all things shall be subdued unto him, then shall the Son also himself be subject unto him that put all things under him, that God may be all in all.

23. Unusquisque autem in proprio ordine. Primitiæ Christus, deinde, qui Christi erunt in adventu ipsius.

24. Postea finis, quum tradiderit regnum Deo et Patri, quum aboleverit omnem principatum, et omnem potestatem, et virtutem.

25. Oportet enim ipsum regnare, donec posuerit omnes inimicos sub pedes suos.

26. Novissimus destruetur hostis mors.

27. Omnia enim subjecit sub pedes eius: quum omnia dixerit, clarum est, quod omnia sunt subjecta praeter eum, qui omnia illi subjecit.

28. Quum autem subjecerit illi omnia, tunc et ipse Filius subjicietur ei, qui omnia illi subjecit, ut sit Deus omnia in omnibus.

20. *But now hath Christ risen.* Having shown what dreadful confusion as to everything would follow, if we were to deny that the dead rise again, he now again assumes as certain, what he had sufficiently established previously—that *Christ has risen;* and he adds that he is the *first-fruits,*[1] by a similitude taken, as it appears, from the ancient ritual of the law. For as in the *first-fruits* the produce of the entire year was consecrated, so the power of Christ's resurrection is extended to all of us—unless you prefer to take it in a more simple way—that in him the first fruit of the resurrection was gathered. I rather prefer, however, to understand the statement in this sense—that the rest of the dead

[1] "Although the resurrection of Christ, compared with *first-fruits* of any kind, has very good harmony with them, yet it more especially agrees with the offering of the *sheaf,* commonly called עוֹמֶר, *omer*, not only as the thing itself, but also as to the circumstances of the *time.* For first there was the *passover,* and the day following was a *sabbatic* day, and on the day *following* that, the first-fruits were offered. So Christ, our *passover,* was crucified: the day following his crucifixion was the *Sabbath,* and the day following *that,* he, the *first-fruits of them that slept,* rose again. All who died before Christ, and were raised again to life, died afterwards; but Christ is the *first-fruits* of all who shall be raised from the dead to die no more."—*Lightfoot.—Ed.*

will follow him, as the entire harvest does the *first-fruits*;[1] and this is confirmed by the succeeding statement.

21. *Since by man came death.* The point to be proved is, that Christ is the *first-fruits*, and that it was not merely as an individual that he was raised up from the dead. He proves it from contraries, because death is not from nature, but from man's sin. As, therefore, Adam did not die for himself alone, but for us all, it follows, that Christ in like manner, who is the antitype,[2] did not rise for himself alone; for he came, that he might restore everything that had been ruined in Adam.

We must observe, however, the force of the argument; for he does not contend by similitude, or by example, but has recourse to opposite causes for the purpose of proving opposite effects. The cause of death is Adam, and we die in him : hence Christ, whose office it is to restore to us what we lost in Adam, is the cause of life to us ; and his resurrection is the ground-work and pledge of ours. And as the former was the beginning of death, so the latter is of life. In the fifth chapter of the Romans he follows out the same comparison ; but there is this difference, that in that passage he reasons respecting a spiritual life and death, while he treats here of the resurrection of the body, which is the fruit of spiritual life.

23. *Every one in his own order.* Here we have an antici-

[1] " The *first-fruits* were by the command of God presented to him at a stated season, not only as a token of the gratitude of the Israelites for his bounty, but as an earnest of the approaching harvest. In this sense he is called the *first-fruits* of the dead. He was the first in order of time, for although some were restored to life by the Prophets, and by himself during his personal ministry, none came out of their graves to return to them no more till after his resurrection; and as he was the first in respect of time, so he was the first in order of succession; all the saints following him as the harvest followed the presentation of the *first-fruits* of the temple. The interval is long, and the dreary sterility of the grave might justify the thought, that the seed committed to it has perished for ever. But our hope rests upon his power, which can make the wilderness blossom as the rose ; and we wait till heavenly influences descend as the dew of herbs, when the barren soil shall display all the luxuriance of vegetation, and death itself shall teem with life."—*Dick's Theology*, vol. iv. pp. 50, 51.—*Ed.*

[2] " Le premier patron de la resurrection pour opposer à la mort d'Adam ;"—" The first pattern of the resurrection, in opposition to the death of Adam."

pation of a question that might be proposed: "If Christ's life," some one might say, "draws ours along with it, why does not this appear? Instead of this, while Christ has risen from the grave, we lie rotting there." Paul's answer is, that God has appointed another order of things. Let us therefore reckon it enough, that we now have in Christ the *first-fruits*,[1] and that his coming[2] will be the time of our resurrection. For *our life* must still be *hid with him*, because he has not yet *appeared*. (Col. iii. 3, 4.) It would therefore be preposterous to wish to anticipate that day of the revelation of Christ.

24. *Then cometh the end, when he shall have delivered.* He put a bridle upon the impatience of men, when he forewarned them, that the fit time for the new life[3] would not be before Christ's coming. But as this world is like a stormy sea, in which we are continually tossed, and our condition is so uncertain, or rather is so full of troubles, and there are in all things such sudden changes, this might be apt to trouble weak minds. Hence he now leads them forward to that day, saying that all things will be set in order. *Then,* therefore, shall come *the end*—that is, the goal of our course—a quiet harbour—a condition that will no longer be exposed to changes; and he at the same time admonishes us, that that *end* must be waited for, because it is not befitting that we should be crowned in the middle of the course. In what respect Christ will *deliver up the kingdom to the Father,* will be explained in a little. When he says, *God and the Father,* this may be taken in two senses—either that God the Father is called the God and Father of Christ, or that the name of *Father* is added by way of explanation. The conjunction *et* (*and*) will in the *latter* case mean *namely*. As to the *former* signification, there is nothing either absurd, or unusual, in the saying, that Christ is inferior to God, in respect of his human nature.

---

[1] " Les premices de la resurrection ;"—" The first-fruits of the resurrection."

[2] " Quand il viendra en jugement ;"—" When he will come to judgment."

[3] " C'est à dire, de la resurrection ;"—" That is to say, of the resurrection."

When he shall have abolished all rule. Some understand this as referring to the powers that are opposed to Christ himself; for they have an eye to what immediately follows, *until he shall have put all his enemies,* &c. This clause, however, corresponds with what goes before, when he said, that Christ would not sooner *deliver up the kingdom.* Hence there is no reason why we should restrict in such a manner the statement before us. I explain it, accordingly, in a general way, and understand by it—all powers that are lawful and *ordained by God.* (Rom. xiii. 1.) In the *first* place, what we find in the Prophets (Is. xiii. 10 ; Ezek. xxxii. 7) as to the darkening of the sun and moon, that God alone may shine forth, while it has begun to be fulfilled under the reign of Christ, will, nevertheless, not be fully accomplished until the last day ; but then *every height shall be brought low,* (Luke iii. 5,) that the glory of God may alone shine forth. Farther, we know that all earthly principalities and honours are connected exclusively with the keeping up of the present life, and, consequently, are a part of the world. Hence it follows that they are temporary.

Hence as the world will have an end, so also will government, and magistracy, and laws, and distinctions of ranks, and different orders of dignities, and everything of that nature. There will be no more any distinction between servant and master, between king and peasant, between magistrate and private citizen. Nay more, there will be then an end put to angelic principalities in heaven, and to ministries and superiorities in the Church, that God may exercise his power and dominion by himself alone, and not by the hands of men or angels. The angels, it is true, will continue to exist, and they will also retain their distinction. The righteous, too, will shine forth, every one according to the measure of his grace ; but the angels will have to resign the dominion, which they now exercise in the name and by the commandment of God. Bishops, teachers, and Prophets will cease to hold these distinctions, and will resign the office which they now discharge. *Rule,* and *authority,* and *power* have much the same meaning in this passage; but these three terms are conjoined to bring out the meaning more fully.

25. *For he must reign.*   He proves that the time is not yet
come when Christ will *deliver up the kingdom to the Father,*
with the view of showing at the same time that the *end* has
not yet come, when all things will be put into a right and
tranquil state, because Christ has not yet subdued all his
enemies.   Now that *must* be brought about, because the
Father has placed him at his right hand with this understanding, that he is not to resign the authority that he has
received, until they have been subdued under his power.
And this is said for the consolation of the pious, that they
may not be impatient on account of the long delay of the
resurrection.   This statement occurs in Ps. cx. 1.

Paul, however, may seem to refine upon the word *until*
beyond what the simple and natural meaning of the word
requires ; for the Spirit does not in that passage give intimation of what shall be afterwards, but simply of what must
be previously.   I answer, that Paul does not conclude that
Christ will *deliver up the kingdom to the Father,* on the
ground of its having been so predicted in the Psalm, but he
has made use of this quotation from the Psalm, for the purpose of proving that the day of *delivering up the kingdom*
had not yet arrived, because Christ has still to do with his
enemies.   Paul, however, explains in passing what is meant
by Christ's sitting at the right hand of the Father, when in
place of that figurative expression he makes use of the simple
word *reign.*

The last enemy—death.   We see that there are still many
enemies that resist Christ, and obstinately oppose his reign.
But *death* will be *the last enemy*[1] *that will be destroyed.*
Hence Christ must still be the administrator of his Father's

---

[1] " It may not be improper to remark that there is an inaccuracy in
our common version, which so vitiates its application that it does not seem
to sustain the conclusion to which the Apostle had arrived.   It was his
purpose to establish the perfection of our Saviour's conquest, the advancement of his triumphs, and the prostration of all enemies whatever beneath
his power.   Now to say that ' the last enemy that shall be destroyed is
death,' by no means affords a proof of this position.   Though death
might be destroyed, and be the last enemy that shall be destroyed, it
would not thence appear but that other enemies might remain not destroyed.   But the proper rendering is, ' Death, the last enemy, should be
destroyed.' "—*R. Hall's Works,* (Lond. 1846.) vol. vi. pp. 140, 141.—*Ed.*

kingdom.   Let believers, therefore, be of good courage, and
not give up hope, until everything that must precede the
resurrection be accomplished.   It is asked, however, in what
sense he affirms that death shall be the *last enemy*[1] *that will
be destroyed*, when it has been already destroyed by Christ's
death, or at least by his resurrection, which is the victory
over death, and the attainment of life ? I answer, that it was
destroyed in such a way as to be no longer deadly to believers, but not in such a way as to occasion them no un-
easiness.   The Spirit of God, it is true, dwelling in us is
life ; but we still carry about with us a mortal body. (1
Peter i. 24.)   The substance of death in us will one day be
drained off, but it has not been so as yet.   We are *born
again of incorruptible seed*, (1 Peter i. 23,) but we have not
yet arrived at perfection.   Or to sum up the matter briefly in
a similitude, the sword of death which could penetrate into
our very hearts has been blunted.   It wounds nevertheless
still, but without any danger ;[2] for we die, but by dying we
enter into life.   In fine, as Paul teaches elsewhere as to
sin, (Rom. vi. 12,) such must be our view as to death—that
it *dwells* indeed in us, but it does not *reign.*

27. *He hath put all things under his feet.* Some think
that this quotation is taken from Psalm viii. 7, and I have
no objection to this, though there would be nothing out of
place in reckoning this statement to be an inference that is

[1] " *Ultimum* vero seu *novissimum hostem* cur vocat ? *Chrysostomus* putat,
quia ultimo accessit. *Primus* fuit Satan, solicitans hominem ad peccatum. *Alter* voluntas hominis, sponte se a Deo avertens. *Tertius* peccatum. *Quartus* denique mors, superveniens peccato. Sed haud dubie
Apostolus novissimum vocat duratione, respectu aliorum externorum hos-
tium Ecclesiæ, quos Christus in fine abolebit omnes. Postremo et mortem corporalem pellet, suscitando omnes ex morte: ut hoc mortale induat
immortalitatem ;"—" But why does he call it (death), the *latest* or *last
enemy ? Chrysostom* thinks, because it came last. The *first* was Satan
tempting man to sin. The *second*—man's will, voluntarily turning aside
from God. The *third*—sin. Then at length the *fourth*—death, following in the train of sin. There can be no doubt, however, that the Apostle
calls it the *last* in respect of duration, in relation to the other external
enemies of the Church, all of which Christ will in the end abolish. Last
of all, he will drive away the death of the body, by raising up all from
death, that this mortal may put on immortality." *Pareus* in loc.—*Ed.*

[2] " Mais c'est sans danger de mort ;"—" But it is without danger of
death."

drawn by Paul from the nature of Christ's kingdom. Let us follow, however, the more generally received opinion. Paul shows from that Psalm, that God the Father has conferred upon Christ the power of all things, because it is said, *Thou hast put all things under his feet.* The words are in themselves plain, were it not that there are two difficulties that present themselves — *first*, that the Prophet speaks here not of Christ alone, but of the whole human race ; and *secondly*, that by *all things* he means only those things that have to do with the convenience of the life of the body, as we find in Gen. ii. 19. The solution of the former difficulty is easy ; for as Christ is the *first-born of every creature*, (Col. i. 15,) and the *heir of all things*, (Heb. i. 2,) God, the Father, has not conferred upon the human race the use of all creatures in such a way as to hinder that in the mean time the chief power, and, so to speak, the rightful dominion, remain in Christ's hands. Farther, we know, that Adam lost the right that had been conferred upon him, so that we can no longer call anything our own. For the *earth was cursed*, (Gen. iii. 17,) and everything that it contains ; and it is through Christ alone that we recover what has been taken from us.[1] It is with propriety, therefore, that this commendation belongs to Christ personally—that the Father has *put all things under his feet*, inasmuch as we rightfully possess nothing except in him. For how shall we become heirs of God, if we are not his sons, and by whom are we made his sons but by Christ ?

The solution of the *second* difficulty is as follows—that the Prophet, it is true, especially mentions *fowls of heaven, fishes of the sea,* and *beasts of the field*, because this kind of dominion is visible, and is more apparent to the eye ; but at the same time the general statement reaches much farther—to the heavens and the earth, and everything that they contain. Now the subjection must have a corrrespondence with the character of him who rules—that is, it has a suitableness to his condition, so as to correspond with it. Now

---

[1] The reader will find the same difficulties solved by CALVIN in his Commentary on the Psalms, vol. i. pp. 106, 108.—*Ed.*

Christ does not need animals for food, or other creatures for any necessity. He rules, therefore, that all things may be subservient to his glory, inasmuch as he adopts us as participants in his dominion. The fruit of this openly appears in visible creatures ; but believers feel in their consciences an inward fruit, which, as I have said, extends farther.

All things put under him, except him who put all things under him. He insists upon two things—*first*, that all things must be brought under subjection to Christ before he restores to the Father the dominion of the world, and *secondly*, that the Father has given all things into the hands of his Son in such a way as to retain the principal right in his own hands. From the *former* of these it follows, that the hour of the last judgment is not yet come—from the *second*, that Christ is now the medium between us and the Father in such a way as to bring us at length to him. Hence he immediately infers as follows : *After he shall have subjected all things to him, then shall the Son subject himself to the Father.* " Let us wait patiently until Christ shall vanquish all his enemies, and shall bring us, along with himself, under the dominion of God, that the kingdom of God may in every respect be accomplished in us."

This statement, however, is at first view at variance with what we read in various passages of Scripture respecting the eternity of Christ's kingdom. For how will these things correspond—*Of his kingdom there will be no end,* (Dan. vii. 14, 27; Luke i. 33 ; 2 Peter i. 11,) and *He himself shall be subjected ?* The solution of this question will open up Paul's meaning more clearly. In the *first* place, it must be observed, that all power was delivered over to Christ, inasmuch as he was manifested in the flesh. It is true that such distinguished majesty would not correspond with a mere man, but, notwithstanding, *the Father has exalted him* in the same nature in which he was abased, and has *given him a name, before which every knee must bow,* &c. (Phil. ii. 9, 10.) Farther, it must be observed, that he has been appointed Lord and highest King, so as to be as it were the Father's Vicegerent in the government of the world—not that he is employed and the Father unemployed, (for how could that be, inasmuch as he is the wisdom and counsel of the Father, is of one essence with him, and is therefore himself God?) But the reason why the Scripture testifies, that Christ now holds dominion over the heaven and the earth in the room of the Father is—that we may not think that there is any other governor, lord, protector, or judge of the dead and living, but may fix our contemplation on him alone.[1] We acknowledge, it is true, God as the ruler, but it is in the face of the man Christ. But Christ will then restore the kingdom which he has received, that we may cleave wholly to God.[2] Nor will he in this way resign the kingdom, but will transfer it in a manner from his humanity to his glorious divinity, because a way of approach will then be opened up, from which our infirmity now keeps us back. Thus then Christ will be *subjected to the Father*, because the vail being then removed, we shall openly behold God reigning in his

---

[1] " Mais que nous fichions les yeux de nostre entendement en luy seul;"
—" But that we may fix the eyes of our understanding on him alone."

[2] " The mediatorial kingdom of Christ . . . . will end when its design is accomplished ; he will cease to exercise an authority which has no longer an object. When all the elect are converted by the truth, and, being collected into one body, are presented to the Father ' a glorious Church, not having spot, or wrinkle, or any such thing ;' when idolatry, superstition, and heresy are overthrown, and all evil is expelled from the kingdom of God ; when the plans and efforts of wicked spirits are defeated, and they are shut up in their prison, from which there is no escape ; when death has yielded up his spoils, and laid his sceptre at the feet of his Conqueror ; when the grand assize has been held, his impartial sentence has pronounced the doom of the human race, and their everlasting abodes are allotted to the righteous and the ungodly, nothing will remain to be done by the power with which our Saviour was invested at his ascension; and his work being finished, his commission will expire. On this subject we cannot speak with certainty, and are in great danger of error, because the event is future, and our information is imperfect. Here analogy fails, and the utmost caution is necessary in borrowing an illustration from human affairs ; but without insinuating that the two cases are exactly similar, may we not say, that as a regent or vicegerent of a King to whom the royal authority has been intrusted for a time, resigns it at the close, and the sovereign himself resumes the reins of government; so our Redeemer, who now sways the sceptre of the universe, will return his delegated power to him from whom he received it, and a new order of things will commence under which the dependence of men upon the Godhead will be immediate; and Father, Son, and Holy Ghost, one in essence, counsel, and operation, will reign for ever over the inhabitants of heaven. This is the probable meaning of the words, *Then shall the Son himself be subject unto him that put all things under him.*"—*Dick's Theology*, vol. iii. pp. 250, 251.—*Ed.*

majesty,[1] and Christ's humanity will then no longer be interposed to keep us back from a closer view of God.[2]

28. *That God may be all in all.* Will it be so in the Devil and wicked men also? By no means—unless perhaps we choose to take the verb *to be* as meaning, *to be known and openly beheld.* In that case the meaning will be: " For the present, as the Devil resists God, as wicked men confound and disturb the order which he has established, and as endless occasions of offence present themselves to our view, it does not distinctly appear that *God is all in all;* but when Christ will have executed the judgment which has been committed to him by the Father, and will have cast down Satan and all the wicked, the glory of God will be conspicuous in their destruction. The same thing may be said also respecting powers that are sacred and lawful in their kind, for they in a manner hinder God's being seen aright by us in himself. *Then,* on the other hand, God, holding the government of the heaven and the earth by himself, and without any medium, will in that respect be *all,* and will consequently at last be so, not only in all persons, but also in all creatures."

This is a pious interpretation,[3] and, as it corresponds sufficiently well with the Apostle's design, I willingly embrace it. There would, however, be nothing out of place in understanding it as referring exclusively to believers, in whom God has now begun his kingdom, and will then perfect it, and in such a way that they shall cleave to him wholly. Both meanings sufficiently refute of themselves the wicked frenzies of some who bring forward this passage in proof of them. Some imagine, that God will be *all in all* in this respect, that all things will vanish and dissolve into nothing. Paul's words, however, mean nothing but this, that all things will be brought back to God, as their alone beginning and end, that they may be closely bound to him. Others infer from this that the Devil and all the wicked will be saved—

[1] " Nous contemplerons nostre Dieu face à face, regnant en sa maieste;" —" We shall behold our God face to face, reigning in his majesty."

[2] " Pour nous empescher de veoir de pres la maieste de Dieu;"—" To keep us back from a near view of the majesty of God."

[3] " Ce sens contient doctrine saincte;"—" This view contains sacred doctrine."

as if God would not altogether be better known in the
Devil's destruction, than if he were to associate the Devil
with himself, and make him one with himself. We see then,
how impudently madmen of this sort wrest this statement
of Paul for maintaining their blasphemies.

29. Else what shall they do which
are baptized for the dead, if the
dead rise not at all? why are they
then baptized for the dead?

30. And why stand we in jeopardy
every hour?

31. I protest by your rejoicing
which I have in Christ Jesus our
Lord, I die daily.

32. If after the manner of men I
have fought with beasts at Ephesus,
what advantageth it me, if the dead
rise not? let us eat and drink; for
to-morrow we die.

33. Be not deceived: evil communications corrupt good manners.

34. Awake to righteousness, and
sin not; for some have not the
knowledge of God: I speak this to
your shame.

29. Quid alioqui facient qui baptizantur pro mortuis, si omnino
mortui non resurgunt? quid etiam
baptizantur pro mortuis?

30. Quid etiam nos periclitamur
omni hora?

31. Quotidie morior per nostram
gloriam, fratres, quam habeo in
Christo Iesu Domino nostro.

32. Si secundum hominem pug-
navi ad bestias Ephesi, quid mihi
prodest? edamus et bibamus: cras
enim moriemur.

33. Ne erretis: Mores honestos
corrumpunt mala colloquia.

34. Evigilate juste, et ne pec-
cetis: ignorantiam enim Dei quidam
habent: ad pudorem vobis incuti-
endum dico.

29. *Else what shall they do.* He resumes his enumeration of the absurdities, which follow from the error under
which the Corinthians laboured. He had set himself in the
outset to do this, but he introduced instruction and consolation, by means of which he interrupted in some degree the
thread of his discourse. To this he now returns. In the
first place he brings forward this objection—that the baptism which those received who are already regarded as dead,
will be of no avail if there is no resurrection. Before expounding this passage, it is of importance to set aside the
common exposition, which rests upon the authority of the
ancients, and is received with almost universal consent.
Chrysostom, therefore, and Ambrose, who are followed by
others, are of opinion[1] that the Corinthians were accustomed,
when any one had been deprived of baptism by sudden
death, to substitute some living person in the place of the

[1] " This," it is stated by *Barnes,* " was the opinion of Grotius, Michaelis,
Tertullian, and Ambrose."—*Ed.*

deceased—to be baptized at his grave.   They at the same
time do not deny that this custom was corrupt, and full of
superstition, but they say that Paul, for the purpose of con-
futing the Corinthians, was contented with this single fact,[1]
that while they denied that there was a resurrection, they in
the mean time declared in this way that they believed in it.
For my part, however, I cannot by any means be persuaded
to believe this,[2] for it is not to be credited, that those who
denied that there was a resurrection had, along with others,
made use of a custom of this sort.   Paul then would have
had immediately this reply made to him: " Why do you
trouble us with that old wives' superstition, which you do
not yourself approve of ?"   Farther, if they had made use of
it, they might very readily have replied: " If this has been
hitherto practised by us through mistake, rather let the mistake be corrected, than that it should have weight attached
to it for proving a point of such importance.

Granting, however, that the argument was conclusive, can
we suppose that, if such a corruption as this had prevailed
among the Corinthians, the Apostle, after reproving almost
all their faults, would have been silent as to this one ?   He
has censured above some practices that are not of so great
moment.   He has not scrupled to give directions as to
women's having the head covered, and other things of that
nature.   Their corrupt administration of the Supper he has
not merely reproved, but has inveighed against it with the
greatest keenness.   Would he in the meantime have uttered
not a single word in reference to such a base profanation of
baptism, which was a much more grievous fault?   He has
inveighed with great vehemence against those who, by
frequenting the banquets of the Gentiles, silently countenanced their superstitions.   Would he have suffered this
horrible superstition of the Gentiles to be openly carried on
in the Church itself under the name of sacred baptism ?   But
granting that he might have been silent, what shall we say
when he expressly makes mention of it ?   Is it, I pray you,

---

[1] " De ce seul argument ;"—" With this single argument."
[2] " Mais ie ne voy rien qui me puisse amener à suyure ceste coniecture ;"
—" But I see nothing that could induce me to follow that conjecture."

a likely thing that the Apostle would bring forward in the shape of an argument a sacrilege[1] by which baptism was polluted, and converted into a mere magical abuse, and yet not say even one word in condemnation of the fault? When he is treating of matters that are not of the highest importance, he introduces nevertheless this parenthesis, that he *speaks as a man.* (Rom. iii. 5 ; vi. 19 ; Gal. iii. 15.) Would not this have been a more befitting and suitable place for such a parenthesis? Now from his making mention of such a thing without any word of reproof, who would not understand it to be a thing that was allowed? For my part, I assuredly understand him to speak here of the right use of baptism, and not of an abuse of it of that nature.

Let us now inquire as to the meaning. At one time I was of opinion, that Paul here pointed out the universal design of baptism, for the advantage of baptism is not confined to this life ; but on considering the words afterwards with greater care, I perceived that Paul here points out something peculiar. For he does not speak of all when he says, *What shall they do, who are baptized?* &c. Besides, I am not fond of interpretations, that are more ingenious than solid. What then? I say, that those are *baptized for dead,* who are looked upon as already dead, and who have altogether despaired of life ; and in this way the particle ὑπέρ will have the force of the Latin *pro,* as when we say, *habere pro derelicto ;—to reckon as abandoned.*[2] This signification is not a forced one. Or if you would prefer another signification, to be *baptized for the dead* will mean—to be baptized so as to profit the dead—not the living.[3] Now it is well known, that from the very commencement of the Church, those who had, while yet catechumens,[4] fallen into disease,[5] if their life was manifestly in danger, were accustomed to ask baptism, that they might not leave this world before they

---

[1] " Ce sacrilege horrible ;"—" This horrible sacrilege."

[2] The form of expression referred to is made use of by Cicero. (Att. 8. 1.) —*Ed.*

[3] " Proufite apres la mort, et non pas la vie durant ;"—" Profits after death, and not during life."

[4] " Estans encore sur la premiere instruction de la doctrine Chrestienne ;"—" Being as yet in the first rudiments of Christian doctrine."

[5] " Quelque maladie dangereuse ;"—" Some dangerous malady."

had made a profession of Christianity; and this, in order that they might carry with them the seal of their salvation. It appears from the writings of the Fathers, that as to this matter, also, there crept in afterwards a superstition, for they inveigh against those who delayed baptism till the time of their death, that, being once for all purged from all their sins, they might in this state meet the judgment of God.[1] A gross error truly, which proceeded partly from great ignorance, and partly from hypocrisy! Paul, however, here simply mentions a custom that was sacred, and in accordance with the Divine institution—that if a catechumen, who had already in his heart embraced the Christian faith,[2] saw that death was impending over him, he asked baptism, partly for his own consolation, and partly with a view to the edification of his brethren. For it is no small *consolation* to carry the token of his salvation sealed in his body. There is also an *edification,* not to be lost sight of—that of making a confession of his faith. They were, then, *baptized for the dead,* inasmuch as it could not be of any service to them in this world, and the very occasion of their asking baptism was that they despaired of life. We now see that it is not without good reason that Paul asks, *what they would do* if there remained no hope after death?[3]

[1] Cornelius à Lapide, in his Commentary on the Canonical Epistles, (Paris, 1631,) p. 423, adverts in the following terms to the custom referred to by CALVIN: "Inter conversos olim multi erant qui Baptismum diu differebant, etiam usque ad mortem, adeoque ægri in lecto baptizabantur, ut per Baptismum expiati ab omni culpa et pœna illico puri evolarent in cœlum;"—"Among the converted there were anciently many who deferred baptism for a long time, even up to the time of their death, and were accordingly baptized when sick in bed, that cleared by baptism from all fault and punishment, they might fly up to heaven pure." Milner, in his Church History, (vol. ii. 276,) when treating of Gregory Nazianzen, says, "In another discourse, he protests against the too common practice of delaying baptism, which, from the example of Constantine, had grown very fashionable, for reasons equally corrupt and superstitious. Men lived in sin as long as they thought they could safely, and deferred baptism till their near approach to death, under a groundless hope of washing away all their guilt at once." See also Turretine's Theology, (Geneva, 1690,) vol. iii. p. 435.—*Ed.*

[2] "Si celuy qui n' estoit pas encore parfaitement instruit en la doctrine Chrestienne, et toutesfois auoit desia de vraye affection embrassé la foy;"—"If one, that had not as yet been fully instructed in Christian doctrine, but yet had already embraced the faith with true affection."

[3] "Baptism," says Dr. Dick, in his Lectures on Theology, (vol. iv. pp.

This passage shows us, too, that those impostors who had disturbed the faith of the Corinthians, had contrived a figurative resurrection, making the farthest goal of believers to be in this world. His repeating it a second time, *Why are they also baptized for the dead?* gives it greater emphasis: "Not only are those baptized who think that they are to live longer, but those too who have death before their eyes; and that, in order that they may in death reap the fruit of their baptism."

30. *Why are we also?* "If our resurrection and ultimate felicity are in this world, why do we of our own accord abandon it, and voluntarily encounter death?" The argument might also be unfolded in this manner: "To no purpose would we *stand in peril every hour,* if we did not look for a better life, after death has been passed through." He speaks, however, of voluntary dangers, to which believers expose their lives for the purpose of confessing Christ. "This magnanimity of soul, I say, in despising death, would be ascribed to rashness rather than firmness, if the saints perished at death, for it is a diabolical madness to purchase by death an immortal fame."[1]

31. *I die daily.* Such a contempt of death he declares to be in himself, that he may not seem to talk bravely when beyond the reach of danger. "I am every day," says he,

183, 184,) "imports our interest in the resurrection of Christ and its consequences. It was called by the ancients 'the earnest of good things to come,' and 'the type of the future resurrection.' May not this be the meaning of that passage in the fifteenth chapter of the first Epistle to the Corinthians, concerning which there has been such a diversity of opinion? 'Else what shall they do which are baptized for the dead, if the dead rise not? why are they then baptized for the dead?' (1 Cor. xv. 29.) Some of the Fathers understood the expression, ὑπὲρ τῶν νεκρῶν, to mean to be baptized *into the hope of the resurrection of the dead;* or, what amounts to the same thing, to submit to baptism that they might fill up the places of those who had died, thus declaring their belief that they had not perished, but were alive in a better world, and their hope that, through Jesus Christ, to whom they dedicated themselves in baptism, they also should be raised again to enjoy the same glorious recompense. According to this view of the passage, a resurrection to life is one of the blessings signified and sealed by this institution. It assures us of a triumph over death and the grave, through the redeeming blood of Christ, with which we are sprinkled; and of admission into heaven, for which we are qualified by the washing of regeneration."—*Ed.*

[1] "Quand quelques fois les mondaines s'exposent à la mort seulement pour acquerir vn bruit immortel;"—"When worldly persons in some cases expose themselves to death, merely to acquire an immortal fame."

" incessantly beset with death.   What madness were it in
me to undergo so much misery, if there were no reward in
reserve for me in heaven ?   Nay more, if my glory and bliss
lie in this world, why do I not rather *enjoy* them, than of
my own accord *resign* them ?"   He says that he *dies daily*,
because he was constantly beset with dangers so formidable
and so imminent, that death in a manner was impending
over him.   A similar expression occurs in Psalm xliv. 22,
and we shall, also, find one of the same kind occurring in
the second Epistle.   (2 Cor. xi. 23.)

By our glory.   The old translation reads *propter, (because
of,)*[1] but it has manifestly arisen from the ignorance of transcribers ; for in the Greek particle[2] there is no ambiguity.
It is then an oath, by which he wished to arouse the Corinthians, to be more attentive in listening to him, when reasoning as to the matter in hand.[3]   " Brethren, I am not some
philosopher prattling in the shade.[4]   As I expose myself
every day to death, it is necessary that I should think in
good earnest of the heavenly life.   Believe, therefore, a man
who is thoroughly experienced."

It is also a form of oath that is not common, but is suited
to the subject in hand.   Corresponding to this was that celebrated oath of Demosthenes, which is quoted by Fabius,[5]
when he swore by the Shades of those who had met death
in the field of Marathon, while his object was to exhort them
to defend the Republic.[6]   So in like manner Paul here swears

---

[1] The rendering in Wiclif (1380) is—*for youre glorie.—Ed.*
[2] The particle *ἦ*, made use of in solemn protestation.—*Ed.*
[3] " Veu qu'il parloit à bon escient, ayant luy-mesme les mains à la besongne, ainsi qu' on dit ;"—" Inasmuch as he spoke in good earnest, having
himself his hands in the work, as they say."
[4] " Quelque Philosophe qui triomphe de dire, estant loin de la prat-
tique ;"—" Some Philosopher, that talks loftily, while far from the scene
of action."
[5] " Lequel Quintilian allegue ;"—" Which Quintilian quotes."
[6] " Quid denique Demosthenes ? . . . . non illud jusjurandum per
cæsos in Marathone ac Salamine propugnatores reipublicæ, satis manifesto
docet, præceptorem ejus Platonem fuisse ?"—" What in fine as to Demosthenes ? . . . . Does not that celebrated oath by these defenders of the
Republic who were slain at Marathon and Salamis, afford ample evidence,
that Plato was his preceptor ?"   *Quinctilian,* (Edin. 1810,) vol. ii. p. 455.
The celebrated oath of the Grecian orator referred to, was in these terms—
νὴ τοὺς ἐν Μαραθῶνι πεπτωκότας.—" By those who fell at Marathon."—*Ed.*

by *the glory which Christians have in Christ.* Now that glory is in heaven. He shows, then, that what they called in question was a matter of which he was so well assured, that he was prepared to make use of a sacred oath—a display of skill which must be carefully noticed.

32. *If according to the manner of men.* He brings forward a notable instance of death, from which it might be clearly seen that he would have been worse than a fool, if there were not a better life in reserve for us beyond death; for it was an ignominious kind of death to which he was exposed. " To what purpose were it," says he, " for me to incur infamy in connection with a most cruel death, if all my hopes were confined to this world?" *According to the manner of men,* means in this passage, *in respect of human life, so that we obtain a reward in this world.*

Now by those that *fought with beasts,* are meant, not those that were thrown to wild beasts, as Erasmus mistakingly imagined, but those that were condemned to be set to fight with wild beasts—to furnish an amusement to the people. There were, then, two kinds of punishment, that were totally different—to be thrown to wild beasts, and to fight with wild beasts. For those that were thrown to wild beasts were straightway torn in pieces; but those that fought with wild beasts went forth armed into the arena, that if they were endued with strength, courage, and agility, they might effect their escape by dispatching the wild beasts. Nay more, there was a game in which those who fought with wild beasts were trained, like the gladiators.[1] Usually, however, very few escaped, because the man who had dispatched one wild beast, was required to fight with a second,[2] until the cruelty of the spectators was satiated, or rather was melted into pity; and yet there were found men so abandoned and

---

[1] " Et mesme comme il y auoit le ieu de l'escrime pour duire des gens à combatre les vns contre les autres, pour donner passetemps au peuple, aussi il y auoit vn ieu auquel on façonnoit des gens à combatre contre les bestes es spectacles publiques ;"—" Nay more, as there was a game of fencing for training persons for fighting with each other, to afford amusement to the people, so there was a game in which they made persons fight with wild beasts in the public shows."

[2] " N' estoit pas quitte, mais il luy faloit retourner au combat contre la seconde."—" He was not let go, but had to return to fight with a second."

desperate, as to hire themselves out for this![1]   And this, I
may remark by the way, is that kind of *hunting* that is
punished so severely by the ancient canons, as even civil
laws brand it with a mark of infamy.[2]

I return to Paul.[3] We see what an extremity God allowed his servant to come to, and how wonderfully, too, he
rescued him. Luke,[4] however, makes no mention of this
fight. Hence we may infer that he endured many things
that have not been committed to writing.

Let us eat and drink.   This is a saying of the Epicureans,
who reckon man's highest good as consisting in present enjoyment. Isaiah also testifies that it is a saying made use
of by profligate persons, (Is. xxii. 13,) who, when the Prophets of God threaten them with ruin,[5] with the view of
calling them to repentance, making sport of those threatenings, encourage themselves in wantonness and unbridled
mirth, and in order to show more openly their obstinacy,
say, " Since die we must, let us meanwhile enjoy the time,
and not torment ourselves before the time with empty fears."
As to what a certain General said to his army,[6] " My fellow-

---

[1] " Sometimes freemen, of desperate circumstances, sought a precarious
subsistence by hazarding their lives in this profession; but it was chiefly
exercised by slaves, and prisoners of war, whom their masters or conquerors devoted to it; or by condemned persons, to whom was thus afforded an
uncertain prolongation of existence, dependent upon their own prowess,
activity, or skill."—*Illustrated Commentary.*—*Ed.*

[2] " What was called *venatio*," (*hunting*,) " or the fighting of wild beasts
with one another, or with men called *bestiarii*, (*fighters with wild beasts*,)
who were either forced to this by way of punishment, as the primitive
Christians often were; or fought voluntarily, either from a natural ferocity
of disposition, or induced by hire, (*auctoramento*,) Cic. Tusc. Quæst. ii. 17.
Fam. vii. 1., Off. ii. 16., Vat. 17.   An incredible number of animals of
various kinds were brought from all quarters, for the entertainment of the
people, and at an immense expense.   Cic. Fam. viii. 2, 4, 6.   They were
kept in inclosures, called *vivaria*, till the day of exhibition.   Pompey in
his second consulship exhibited at once 500 lions, who were all dispatched
in five days; also 18 elephants.   Dio. 39. 38.   Plin. 8. 7.   *Adam's Roman Antiquities*, (Edin. 1792,) pp. 343, 344.—*Ed.*

[3] " Ie retourne maintenant à parler de Sainct Paul;"—" I now return
to speak of St. Paul."

[4] " Sainct Luc aux Actes;"—" St. Luke in the Acts."

[5] " De ruine et perdition;"—" With ruin and perdition."

[6] " Car quant a ce qui on trouue entre les histoires anciennes que
quelqu'vn disoit aux soldats;"—" For as to its being recorded in ancient
histories, that one said to his soldiers."

soldiers, let us dine heartily, for we shall sup to-day in the regions below,"[1] that was an exhortation to meet death with intrepidity, and has nothing to do with this subject. I am of opinion, that Paul made use of a jest in common use among abandoned and desperately wicked persons, or (to express it shortly) a common proverb among the Epicureans to the following purpose : " If death is the end of man, there is nothing better than that he should indulge in pleasure, free from care, so long as life lasts." Sentiments of this kind are to be met with frequently in Horace.[2]

33. *Be not deceived. Evil communications corrupt good manners.* As nothing is easier than to glide into profane speculation, under the pretext of inquiring,[3] he meets this danger, by warning them that *evil communications* have more effect than we might suppose, in polluting our minds and corrupting our morals.[4] To show this, he makes use of a quotation from the poet Menander,[5] as we are at liberty to borrow

---

[1] The allusion is to Leonidas, king of Sparta, when addressing 300 Spartans, at the Pass of Thermopylæ, who " by an act of intrepidity, rarely paralleled in history, set themselves to defend that Pass, in opposition to 20,000 Persian troops, and during the night spread dreadful havoc and consternation among the Persians, but the morning light at length discovering their small number, they were immediately surrounded and slaughtered."—*Robertson's History of Greece*, p. 151.—*Ed.*

[2] The following instances may be quoted as a specimen :—

" O beate Sesti !
Vitæ summa brevis nos vetat inchoare longam,
Jam te premet nox, fabulæque Manes
Et domus exilis Plutonia :

O happy Sestius ! the brief span of human life forbids us to indulge a distant hope. Soon will night descend upon thee, and the fabulous Manes, and the shadowy mansion of Pluto."—*Hor. Carm.* I. 4, 13-17.

" Sapias, vina liques, et spatio brevi
Spem longam reseces. Dum loquimur, fugerit invida
Aetas. Carpe diem, quam minimum credula postero.

Be wise ; rack off your wines ; and abridge your distant hopes in adaptation to the brevity of life. While we speak, envious age has been flying. Seize the present day, depending as little as possible on any future one."—*Hor. Carm.* I. 11. 6-8.

[3] " De douter et s'enquerir ;"—" Of doubting and inquiring."

[4] " Les bonnes mœurs ;"—" Good manners."

[5] " *Menander* was a celebrated comic poet of Athens, educated under Theophrastus. His writings were replete with elegance, refined wit, and judicious observations. Of one hundred and eight comedies which he wrote, nothing remains but a few fragments. He is said to have drowned himself in the fifty-second year of his age, B. C. 293, because the compositions of his rival Philemon obtained more applause than his own."—*Barnes.*—*Ed.*

from every quarter everything that has come forth from God. And as all truth is from God, there is no doubt that the Lord has put into the mouth of the wicked themselves, whatever contains true and salutary doctrine. I prefer, however, that, for the handling of this subject, recourse should be had to Basil's Oration to the Young. Paul, then, being aware that this proverb was in common use among the Greeks, chose rather to make use of it, that it might make its way into their minds more readily, than to express the same thing in his own words. For they would more readily receive what they had been accustomed to—as we have experience of in proverbs with which we are familiar.

Now it is a sentiment that is particularly worthy of attention, for Satan, when he cannot make a direct assault upon us,[1] deludes us under this pretext, that there is nothing wrong in our raising any kind of disputation with a view to the investigation of truth. Here, therefore, Paul in opposition to this, warns us that we must guard against *evil communications*, as we would against the most deadly poison, because, insinuating themselves secretly into our minds, they straightway corrupt our whole life. Let us, then, take notice, that nothing is more pestilential than corrupt doctrine and profane disputations, which draw us off, even in the smallest degree, from a right and simple faith ;[2] for it is not without good reason that Paul exhorts us not to be *deceived.*[3]

---

[1] " Pour nous seduire ;"—" To draw us aside."

[2] " De la simplicite de la foy ;"—" From the simplicity of the faith."

[3] " The connection is not that in which we should have expected such a maxim to be inserted. It is in the midst of a very affecting and instructive view of the resurrection of the dead and the life everlasting ; but the occasion of it was this: the Corinthians had received, from the intrusion of false teachers, principles which militated against that great doctrine. They had been taught to explain it away, and to resolve it merely into a moral process which takes place in the present world; interpreting what is said of the resurrection of the dead in a mystical and figurative manner. The apostle insinuates, that it was by a mixture of the corrupt communications of these men with the Christian Church, and the intimate contact into which they had permitted themselves to come with them, that they had been led off from the fundamental doctrine of the gospel, and rejected a primary part of the apostolic testimony. ' For if there be no resurrection of the dead, then,' as he observed, ' is Christ not risen, and if Christ be not risen, then is our preaching vain, and your faith is also vain ; ye are

34. *Awake righteously.* As he saw that the Corinthians were in a manner intoxicated,[1] through excessive carelessness, he arouses them from their torpor. By adding, however, the adverb *righteously*, he intimates in what way he would have them *wake up.* For they were sufficiently attentive and clear-sighted as to their own affairs : nay more, there can be no doubt that they congratulated themselves on their acuteness ; but in the mean time they were drowsy, where they ought most of all to have been on the watch. He says accordingly, *awake righteously*—that is, " Direct your mind and aim to things that are good and holy."

He adds at the same time the reason, *For some*, says he, *among you are in ignorance of God.* This required to be stated : otherwise they might have thought that the admonition was unnecessary ; for they looked upon themselves as marvellously wise. Now he convicts them of *ignorance of God,* that they may know that the main thing was wanting

yet in your sins.' We see, that notwithstanding the apostle had planted pure Christianity among the Corinthians, and had confirmed it by the most extraordinary miracles and supernatural operations, yet such was the contagion of evil example and corrupt communication, that the members of the Corinthian Church, in a very short time, departed from the fundamental article of the truth as it is in Jesus Christ; and hence we may learn the importance, nay, the necessity, of being on our guard in this respect, and of avoiding such confidence in ourselves as might induce us to neglect the caution here so forcibly expressed—' Be not deceived; evil communications corrupt good manners.' "—*R. Hall's Works*, (Lond. 1846,) vol. vi. pp. 273, 274.—*Ed.*

[1] The original word ἐκνήψατε, properly signifies to *awake sober out of a drunken sleep.* It is used in this sense in some instances in the *Septuagint.* Thus in Joel i. 5, Εκνηψατε, οἱ μεθυοντες, Awake, ye drunkards. See also Gen. ix. 24, and 1 Sam. xxv. 37. It is used in the same sense by classical writers. " ' Awake to righteousness and sin not, for some have not the knowledge of God. I speak this to your shame ;' that is, shake off the mental delusion and stupor in which the *intoxication* of error has involved you, that, with clear and exerted faculties, you may attend to the most important subject."—*Brown's Expository Discourses on Peter*, vol. iii. p. 8. The expression ἐκνήψατε δικαίως, (*awake righteously*,) is rendered by *Luther* wachet recht auf—" Wake right up." It is, however, generally considered to be elliptical. Some supply ζησοντες—" Awake, *that ye may live* righteously. Others understand δικαίως, as equivalent to ὡς δικαίως δεῖ—" as it is fit you should." " Arrian and Menander," says *Parkhurst*, " use δικαίως in this sense, as may be seen in Alberti on the text." To the two authorities quoted by Alberti, Alexander in his Paraphrase on 1 Cor. xv., adds one from Ocellus Lucanus—'Ο δε διαμαχομενος δικαιως—" but the man who stands up for his own authority *as he ought to do.*"—*Apud Gale*, p. 533, l. 20. Ed. 1688.—*Ed.*

in them. A useful admonition to those who lay out all their agility in flying through the air, while in the mean time they do not see what is before their feet, and are stupid where they ought, most of all, to have been clear-sighted.

To your shame. Just as fathers, when reproving their children for their faults, put them to shame, in order that they may by that shame cover their shame. When, however, he declared previously that he did not wish to shame them, (1 Cor. iv. 14,) his meaning was that he did not wish to hold them up to disgrace, by bringing forward their faults to public view in a spirit of enmity and hatred.[1] In the mean time, however, it was of advantage for them to be sharply reproved, as they were still indulging themselves in evils of such magnitude. Now Paul in reproaching them with *ignorance of God,* strips them entirely of all honour.

35. But some *man* will say, How are the dead raised up? and with what body do they come?

36. *Thou* fool, that which thou sowest is not quickened, except it die.

37. And that which thou sowest, thou sowest not that body that shall be, but bare grain, it may chance of wheat, or of some other *grain :*

38. But God giveth it a body as it hath pleased him, and to every seed his own body.

39. All flesh *is* not the same flesh : but *there is* one *kind of* flesh of men, another flesh of beasts, another of fishes, *and* another of birds.

40. *There are* also celestial bodies, and bodies terrestrial : but the glory of the celestial *is* one, and the *glory* of the terrestrial *is* another.

41. *There is* one glory of the sun, and another glory of the moon, and another glory of the stars : for *one* star differeth from *another* star in glory.

42. So also *is* the resurrection of the dead ; it is sown in corruption ; it is raised in incorruption :

43. It is sown in dishonour, it is

35. Sed dicet quispiam : Quomodo suscitabuntur mortui ? quali autem corpore venient ?

36. Demens, tu quod seminas, non vivificatur nisi mortuum fuerit.

37. Et quod seminas, non corpus quod nascetur, seminas, sed nudum granum : exempli gratia, tritici, aut alterius cujusvis generis :

38. Deus autem illi dat corpus, quemadmodum voluerit, et unicuique seminum proprium corpus.

39. Non omnis caro, eadem caro : sed alia caro hominum, alia vero caro pecudum, alia volucrum, alia piscium.

40. Sunt et corpora cœlestia, sunt corpora terrestria : quin etiam alia cœlestium gloria, alia terrestrium.

41. Alia gloria solis, alia gloria lunae, alia gloria stellarum : stella a stella differt in gloria :

42. Sic et resurrectio mortuorum.

43. Seminatur in corruptione, re-

---

[1] See CALVIN on the Corinthians, vol. i. p. 167.

raised in glory: it is sown in weakness, it is raised in power:

44. It is sown a natural body, it is raised a spiritual body. There is a natural body, and there is a spiritual body.

45. And so it is written, The first man Adam was made a living soul; the last Adam *was made* a quickening spirit.

46. Howbeit that *was* not first which is spiritual, but that which is natural; and afterward that which is spiritual.

47. The first man *is* of the earth, earthy; the second man *is* the Lord from heaven.

48. As *is* the earthy, such *are* they also that are earthy: and as *is* the heavenly, such *are* they also that are heavenly.

49. And as we have borne the image of the earthy, we shall also bear the image of the heavenly.

50. Now this I say, brethren, that flesh and blood cannot inherit the kingdom of God; neither doth corruption inherit incorruption.

surgit in incorruptione: seminatur in ignominia, resurgit in gloria: seminatur in infirmitate, resurgit in potentia:

44. Seminatur corpus animale, resurgit corpus spirituale: est corpus animale, est et corpus spirituale.

45. Quemadmodum et scriptum est, (*Gen.* ii. 7,) Factus est primus homo Adam in animam viventem, ultimus Adam in spiritum vivificantem.

46. Sed non primum quod spirituale est: sed animale, deinde spirituale.

47. Primus homo ex terra terrenus, secundus homo, Dominus e cœlo.

48. Qualis terrenus, tales et terreni, et qualis cœlestis, tales et cœlestes.

49. Et quemadmodum portavimus imaginem terreni, portabimus et imaginem cœlestis.

50. Hoc autem dico, fratres, quod caro et sanguis regnum Dei hereditate possidere non possunt, neque corruptio incorruptionem hereditate possidebit.

35. *How will they be raised up?* There is nothing that is more at variance with human reason than this article of faith. For who but God alone could persuade us that bodies, which are now liable to corruption, will, after having rotted away, or after they have been consumed by fire, or torn in pieces by wild beasts, will not merely be restored entire, but in a greatly better condition. Do not all our apprehensions of things straightway reject this as a thing fabulous, nay, most absurd?[1] Paul, with the view of removing entirely this appearance of absurdity, makes use of an *anthypophora,*[2] that is, he brings forward by way of objection, in the person of another, what appears at first view to be at variance with

---

[1] " Comme la plus grande absurdite du monde ;"—" As the greatest absurdity in the world."

[2] See CALVIN on the Corinthians, vol. i. p. 281, *n.* 1.

the doctrine of a resurrection. For this question is not that of one who inquires doubtingly as to the mode, but of one who argues from impossibility—that is, what is said as to the resurrection is a thing incredible. Hence in his reply he repels such an objection with severity. Let us observe, then, that the persons who are here introduced as speaking, are those who endeavour to disparage, in a way of scoffing, a belief in the resurrection, on the ground of its being a thing that is impossible.

36. *Thou fool, that which thou sowest.* The Apostle might have replied, that the mode, which is to us incomprehensible, is nevertheless easy with God. Hence, we must not here form our judgment according to our own understanding, but must assign to the stupendous and secret power of God the honour of believing, that it will accomplish what we cannot comprehend. He goes to work, however, in another way. For he shows, that the resurrection is so far from being against nature, that we have every day a clear illustration of it in the course of nature itself—in the growth of the fruits of the earth. For from what but from rottenness spring the fruits that we gather out of the earth ? For when the seed has been sown, unless the grains *die,* there will be no increase. Corruption, then, being the commencement and cause of production, we have in this a sort of picture of the resurrection. Hence it follows, that we are beyond measure spiteful and ungrateful in estimating the power of God, if we take from him what is already manifest before our eyes.

37. *Thou sowest not that body that will spring up.* This comparison consists of two parts—*first,* that it is not to be wondered that bodies rise from rottenness, inasmuch as the same thing takes place as to seed ; and *secondly,* that it is not at variance with reason, that our bodies should be restored in another condition, since, from bare grain, God brings forth so many ears of corn, clothed with admirable contrivance, and stored with grains of superior quality. As, however, he might seem to intimate, by speaking in this way, that many bodies will therefore rise out of one, he modifies his discourse in another way, by saying that God *forms the body as it*

pleases him, meaning that in that also there is a difference in respect of quality.

He adds, *to every seed its own body.* By this clause he restricts what he had said respecting another body; for he says that, while the body is different, it is in such a way as to retain, nevertheless, its particular kind.

39. *All flesh is not,* &c. Here we have another comparison leading to the same conclusion, though there are some that explain it otherwise. For when he says, that under the name of *flesh* is comprehended the body of a man as well as of a beast, and yet the *flesh* in those two cases is different, he means by this that the substance indeed is the same, but there is a difference as to quality. The sum is this—that whatever diversity we see in any particular kind is a sort of prelude of the resurrection, because God clearly shows, that it is no difficult thing with him to renew our bodies by changing the present condition of things.[1]

41. *There is one glory of the sun, and another glory of the moon.* Not only is there a difference betweeen heavenly

---

[1] " Nearly allied to these are the examples of peculiar transformations undergone by various insects, and the state of rest and insensibility which precede those transformations; such as the chrysalis or aurelia state of butterflies, moths, and silkworms. The myrmeleon formicaleo, of whose larva, and its extraordinary history, Reaumur and Roesel have given accurate descriptions, continues in its insensible or chrysalis state about four weeks. The libellula, or dragon-fly, continues still longer in its state of inaction. Naturalists tell us that the worm repairs to the margin of its pond, in quest of a convenient place of abode, during its insensible state. It attaches itself to a plant, or piece of dry wood, and the skin, which gradually becomes parched and brittle, at last splits opposite to the upper part of the thorax: through this aperture the insect, now become winged, quickly pushes its way, and being thus extricated from confinement, begins to expand its wings, to flutter, and, finally, to launch into the air with that gracefulness and ease which are peculiar to this majestic tribe. Now who that saw, for the first time, the little pendant coffin in which the insect lay entombed, and was ignorant of the transformation of which we are now speaking, would ever predict that, in a few weeks, perhaps in a few days or hours, it would become one of the most elegant and active of *winged* insects? And who that contemplates, with the mind of a philosopher, this current transformation, and knows that two years before the insect mounts into the air, even while it is living in water, it has the rudiments of wings, can deny that the body of a dead man may, at some future period, be again invested with vigour and activity, and soar to regions for which some latent organization may have peculiarly fitted it?"—*Olynthus Gregory's* Letters on the Evidences of the Christian Religion, p. 225.—*Ed.*

bodies and earthly, but even the heavenly bodies have not all the same glory ; for the sun surpasses the moon, and the other stars differ from each other. This dissimilarity, accordingly, appears[1] in the resurrection of the dead. A mistake, however, is commonly fallen into in the application ;[2] for it is supposed that Paul meant to say, that, after the resurrection, the saints will have different degrees of honour and glory. This, indeed, is perfectly true, and is proved by other declarations of Scripture ; but it has nothing to do with Paul's object. For he is not arguing as to what difference of condition there will be among the saints after the resurrection, but in what respect our bodies at present differ from those that we will one day receive.[3]

He removes, then, every idea of absurdity, by instituting this comparison : The substance of the sun and moon is the same, but there is a great difference between them in point of dignity and excellence. Is it to be wondered, then, if our body puts on a more excellent quality ?[4] " I do not teach that anything will take place at the resurrection but what is already presented before the eyes of all." That such is the meaning of the words is clear from the context. For whence and for what purpose would Paul make such a transition, were he now comparing them with one another in respect of the difference of their condition, while up to this point he has been comparing the present condition of all with their future condition, and immediately proceeds with that comparison ?

43. *It is sown in corruption.* That there may be no doubt remaining, Paul explains himself, by unfolding the difference between their present condition, and that which will be after the resurrection. What connection, then, would there be in his discourse, if he had intended in the first instance[5] to

---

[1] " Ceste diuersite de qualite se monstre ;"—" This difference of quality shows itself."

[2] " En l'application de ceste similitude ;"—" In the application of this similitude."

[3] " Comment different nos corps que nous auons maintenant de ceux que nous aurons apres ;"—" In what respect our bodies, which we have now, will differ from those that we shall have afterwards."

[4] " Qu'il n'ha maintenant ;"—" Than it has now."

[5] " Au propos precedent ;"—" In the foregoing statement."

distinguish between the different degrees of future glory among the saints? There can, therefore, be no doubt, that he has been, up to this point, following out one subject. He now returns to the first similitude that he had made use of, but applies it more closely to his design. Or, if you prefer it, keeping up that similitude, he figuratively compares the time of the present life to the seed-time, and the resurrection to the harvest; and he says, that our body is now, indeed, subject to mortality and ignominy, but will then be glorious and incorruptible. He says the same thing in other words in Phil. iii. 21. *Christ will change our vile body, that he may make it like to his own glorious body.*

44. *It is sown an animal body.* As he could not express each particular by enumerating one by one, he sums up all comprehensively in one word, by saying that the body is now *animal*,[1] but it will then be *spiritual.* Now that is called *animal* which is quickened by (*anima*) the soul: that is *spiritual* which is quickened by the *Spirit.*[2] Now it is the soul that quickens the body, so as to keep it from being a dead carcase. Hence it takes its title very properly from it. After the resurrection, on the other hand, that quickening influence, which it will receive from the Spirit, will be more excellent.[3] Let us, however, always bear in mind, what we have seen previously—that the substance of

[1] " It is generally agreed on by the best expositors, that ψυχικὸς here, as being opposed to πνευματικὸς, (*spiritual*,) especially as the expression is used with a reference to the words of Moses respecting the body of Adam, ἐγένετο εἰς ψυχὴν ζῶσαν, (*became a living soul*,) must signify *animal*, (literally that which draws in the breath of life, necessary to the existence of all animal bodies,) that which is endowed with faculties of sense, and has need of food, drink, and sleep for its support."—*Bloomfield.* " Ψυχικὸν, not φυσικὸν, (says *Granville Penn*,) and therefore not '*naturale*' but '*animale*,' as rendered in the Latin. Wiclif," (he adds,) " strangely rendered, from the Vulg., ' *a beastli bodi*,' in correcting whom, our revisers would have done well to prefer '*animal*' to '*natural*."—*Ed.*

[2] " Au reste là où nous traduisons, Sensuel, il y auroit à le tourner au plus pres du Grec, Animal: c'est à dire, gouuerné et viuifié de l'ame. Voyla donc que signifie Le corps sensuel. Le corps spirituel est celuy qui est viuifié de l'Esprit;"—" But what we translate *sensual*, might be rendered, more closely to the Greek, *animal*: that is to say, governed and quickened by the soul. Mark then what is meant by *the sensual body.* The spiritual body is that which is quickened by the Spirit."

[3] " Sera vne chose beaucoup plus excellente;"—" Will be a thing much more excellent."

the body is the same,[1] and that it is the quality only that is here treated of. Let the present quality of the body be called, for the sake of greater plainness, *animation;*[2] let the future receive the name of *inspiration.* For as to the soul's now *quickening* the body, that is effected through the intervention of many helps; for we stand in need of drink, food, clothing, sleep, and other things of a similar nature. Hence the weakness of *animation* is clearly manifested. The energy of the Spirit, on the other hand, for *quickening,* will be much more complete, and, consequently, exempted from necessities of that nature. This is the simple and genuine meaning of the Apostle; that no one may, by philosophizing farther, indulge in airy speculations, as those do, who suppose that the substance of the body will be spiritual, while there is no mention made here of substance, and no change will be made upon it.

45. As it is written, *The first Adam was made.* Lest it should seem to be some new contrivance as to the *animal body,*[3] he quotes Scripture, which declares that Adam *became a living soul,* (Gen. ii. 7)—meaning, that his body was quickened by the soul, so that he became a living man. It is asked, what is the meaning of the word *soul* here? It is well known, that the Hebrew word נֶפֶשׁ, (*nephesh,*) which Moses makes use of, is taken in a variety of senses; but in this passage it is taken to mean either vital motion, or the very essence of life itself. The second of these I rather prefer. I observe that the same thing is affirmed as to beasts —that they were made *a living soul,* (Gen. i. 20, 24 ;) but as the soul of every animal must be judged of according to its kind, there is nothing to hinder that a *soul,* that is to say, vital motion, may be common to all; and yet at the same time the *soul* of man may have something peculiar and distinguishing, namely, immortal essence, as the light of intelligence and reason.

---

[1] " La substance du corps sera tousiours vne ;"—" The substance of the body will always be the same."

[2] "*Animation,* qui est nom descendant de ce mot *Ame;*"—"*Animation,* which is a name derived from this word *Soul.*"

[3] " Vne nouuelle imagination qu'il ait forgee ;"—" A new fancy that he had contrived."

The last Adam. This expression we do not find anywhere *written.*[1] Hence the phrase, *It is written,* must be understood as referring exclusively to the first clause; but after bringing forward this testimony of Scripture, the Apostle now begins in his own person to draw a contrast between Christ and Adam. "Moses relates that Adam was furnished with a *living soul:* Christ, on the other hand, is endowed with a *life-giving Spirit.* Now it is a much greater thing to be *life,* or the *source of life,* than simply to *live.*"[2] It must be observed, however, that Christ did also, like us, become a *living soul;* but, besides the *soul,* the Spirit of the Lord was also poured out upon him, that by his power he might rise again from the dead, and raise up others. This, therefore, must be observed, in order that no one may imagine, (as Apollinaris[3] did of old,) that the Spirit was in Christ in place

---

[1] "Ceci n'est point trouué en lieu quelconque de l'Escriture;"—"This is not found in any passage of Scripture."

[2] "As it is said, Adam was at first *a living soul,* ('So God breathed into him the breath of life,'—that pure, divine, and heavenly breath,) 'and he became a living soul;' so, *then* to have asked the question, 'What is man?' must have been to receive the answer, 'He is a *living soul:* he is all soul, and that soul all life.' But *now* is this living soul buried in flesh, a lost thing to all the true, and great, and noble ends and purposes of that life which was at first given it. It is true, indeed, that this is a thing much less than what is said of the second Adam, in 1 Cor. xv. 45. 'The first man Adam was made a living soul; the second Adam was a quickening Spirit.' This latter is a great deal more. A *living soul* signified him to live himself; but a quickening spirit signifies a power to make others live. *That* the first Adam could not do; the more excellent kind of life which he had (for there was a complication of lives in the first creation of this man) he could not *lose:* but he could not *give.* He could not *lose* it from himself; but he could never have *given* it, by any power or immediate efficiency of his own, to another. Here the second Adam—the constitution of the second Adam—was far above that of the first, in that he could quicken others—a *quickening spirit,* not only quickened passively, but quickened actively, such a spirit as could give spirit, and diffuse life." —Howe's Works, (Lond. 1834,) p. 1209.—*Ed.*

[3] The views held by Apollinaris were as follows: "Christum corpus assumpsisse sine anima, quod pro animâ ei fuerit deitas illudque corpus consubstantiale fuisse deitati, nec ex substantia Mariæ efformatum;"— "That Christ assumed a body without a soul, because Deity was to him in place of a soul, and that body was co-essential with Deity, and was not formed from the substance of Mary."—See Mastricht's Theology, (1698,) vol. ii. p. 975. "Apollinaris, or Apollinarius, taught that the Son of God assumed manhood *without a soul,* (ψυχης ανευ,) as Socrates relates; but afterwards, changing his mind, he said that he assumed a soul, but that it *did not possess the intelligent or rational principle,* (νουν δε ουκ

of a soul.   And independently of this, the interpretation of this passage may be taken from the eighth chapter of the Romans, where the Apostle declares, that *the body, indeed, is dead, on account of sin,* and we carry in us the elements of death ; but that *the Spirit of Christ, who raised him up from the dead, dwelleth also in us,* and that he is life, to raise up us also one day from the dead. (Rom. viii. 10, 11.) From this you see, that we have *living souls,* inasmuch as we are men, but that we have the *life-giving Spirit* of Christ poured out upon us by the grace of regeneration.   In short, Paul's meaning is, that the condition that we obtain through Christ is greatly superior to the lot of the *first man,* because a *living soul* was conferred upon Adam in his own name, and in that of his posterity, but Christ has procured for us the Spirit, who is *life.*

Now as to his calling Christ *the last Adam,* the reason is this, that as the human race was created in the *first man,* so it is renewed in Christ.   I shall express it again, and more distinctly : All men were created in the *first man,* because, whatever God designed to give to all, he conferred upon that one man, so that the condition of mankind was settled in his person.   He by his fall[1] ruined himself and those that were his, because he drew them all, along with himself, into the same ruin : Christ came to restore our nature from ruin, and raise it up to a better condition than ever.   They[2] are then, as it were, two sources, or two roots of the human race. Hence it is not without good reason, that the one is called the *first man,* and the other the *last.*   This, however, gives no support to those madmen, who make Christ to be one of ourselves, as though there were and always had been only two men, and that this multitude which we behold, were a mere phantom !   A similar comparison occurs in Rom. v. 12.

46. *But this is not first, which is spiritual.*   " It is necessary," says he, " that before we are restored in Christ, we

---

εχειν αυτην,) and that the λογος (*word*) was *instead of that principle,* (αντι νου.)"—*Dick's* Lectures on Theology vol. iii. p. 22.—*Ed.*

[1] " Le poure mal-heureux par sa transgression ;"—' The poor miserable creature by his transgression."

[2] " Adam donc et Christ ;"—" Adam and Christ, therefore."

derive our origin from Adam, and resemble him. Let us, therefore, not wonder, if we begin with the *living soul*, for as *being born* precedes in order *being born again*, so *living* precedes *rising again.*"

47. *The first Adam was from the earth.* The *animal* life comes first, because the *earthy man* is first.[1] The spiritual life will come afterwards, as Christ, the *heavenly man*, came after Adam. Now the Manichees perverted this passage, with the view of proving that Christ brought a body from heaven into the womb of the Virgin. They mistakingly imagined, however, that Paul speaks here of the substance of the body, while he is discoursing rather as to its condition, or quality. Hence, although the *first man* had an immortal soul, and that too, not taken from the earth, yet he, nevertheless, savoured of the earth, from which his body had sprung, and on which he had been appointed to live. Christ, on the other hand, brought us from heaven a *life-giving Spirit*, that he might regenerate us into a better life, and elevated above the earth.[2] In fine, we have it from Adam —that we live in this world, as branches from the root : Christ, on the other hand, is the beginning and author of the heavenly life.

But some one will say in reply, Adam is said to be *from the earth*—Christ *from heaven ;* the nature of the comparison[3] requires this much, that Christ have his body *from heaven*, as the body of Adam was formed *from the earth ;* or, at least, that the origin of man's soul should be *from the earth*, but that Christ's soul had come forth from heaven. I answer, that Paul had not contrasted the two departments of the subject with such refinement and minuteness, (for this was not necessary ;) but when treating of the nature of Christ and Adam, he made a passing allusion to the creation of Adam, that he had been formed *from the earth*, and at the

---

[1] " La vie sensuelle, ou animale, c'est à dire, que nous auons par le moyen de l'ame, precede :"—" The sensual or animal life, that is to say, what we have by means of the soul, comes first."

[2] " Plus haute et excellente que la terre ;"—" Higher and more excellent than the earth."

[3] " La nature de l'antithese et comparison :"—" The nature of the contrast and comparison."

same time, for the purpose of commending Christ's excellence, he states, that he is the Son of God, who came down to us from heaven, and brings with him, therefore, a heavenly nature and influence. This is the simple meaning, while the refinement of the Manichees is a mere calumny.

We must, however, reply to another objection still. For Christ, so long as he lived in the world, lived a life similar to ours, and therefore earthly : hence it is not a proper contrast. The solution of this question will serve farther to refute the contrivance[1] of the Manichees. For we know, that the body of Christ was liable to death, and that it was exempted from corruption, not by its essential property, (as they speak,)[2] but solely by the providence of God. Hence Christ was not merely *earthy* as to the essence of his body, but was also for a time in an earthly condition ; for before Christ's power could show itself in conferring the heavenly life, it was necessary that he should die in the *weakness of the flesh,* (2 Cor. xiii. 4.)   Now this heavenly life appeared first in the resurrection, that he might quicken us also.

49. *As we have borne.*   Some have thought, that there is here an exhortation to a pious and holy life, into which Paul was led by way of digression ; and on that account they have changed the verb from the future tense into the hortative mood.   Nay more, in some Greek manuscripts the reading is φορέσωμεν (*let us bear,*)[3] but as that does not suit so well in respect of connection, let us adopt in preference what corresponds better with the object in view and the context.[4]   Let us observe, in the first place, that this is not an exhortation, but pure doctrine, and that he is not treating here of newness of life, but pursues, without any

[1] " La meschante imagination ;"—" The wicked fancy."
[2] " Afin que i'use du terme commun ;"—" To use the common phrase."
[3] " Pourtant en lieu de *Nous porterons,* aucuns ont traduit *Portons.* Et mesme aucuns liures Grecs le lisent ainsi ;"—" Hence instead of *We shall bear,* some have rendered it, *Let us bear.*   And even some Greek manuscripts read it thus."
[4] The Alexandrine manuscript, with some others, reads φορέσωμεν, *let us bear.*   The rendering of the Vulgate is *portemus—(let us bear.)*   Wiclif (1380) following the Vulgate, as he is wont, renders as follows : *bere we also the ymage of the heuenli.—Ed.*

interruption, the thread of his discourse respecting the resurrection of the flesh. The meaning accordingly will be this : " As the *animal nature*, which has the precedency in us, is the image of Adam, so we shall be conformed to Christ in the *heavenly nature ;* and this will be the completion of our restoration. For we *now* begin to bear the image of Christ, and are every day more and more transformed into it ;[1] but that image consists in spiritual regeneration. But *then* it will be fully restored both in body and in soul, and what is now begun will be perfected, and accordingly we will obtain in reality what we as yet only hope for." If, however, any one prefers a different reading, this statement will serve to spur forward the Corinthians ; and if there had been a lively meditation of sincere piety and a new life, it might have been the means of kindling up in them at the same time the hope of heavenly glory.

50. *Now this I say.* This clause intimates, that what follows is explanatory of the foregoing statement. " What I have said as to *bearing the image of the heavenly Adam* means this—that we must be renewed in respect of our bodies, inasmuch as our bodies, being liable to corruption, cannot inherit God's incorruptible kingdom. Hence there will be no admission for us into the kingdom of Christ, otherwise than by Christ's renewing us after his own image." *Flesh* and *blood,* however, we must understand, *according to the condition in which they at present are,* for our flesh will be a participant in the glory of God, but it will be—as renewed and quickened by the Spirit of Christ.

51. Behold, I shew you a mystery; We shall not all sleep, but we shall all be changed,

52. In a moment, in the twinkling of an eye, at the last trump : for the trumpet shall sound, and the dead shall be raised incorruptible, and we shall be changed.

53. For this corruptible must put on incorruption, and this mortal *must* put on immortality.

51. Ecce, mysterium vobis dico : Non omnes quidem dormiemus, omnes tamen immutabimur.

52. In puncto temporis, in nictu oculi, cum extrema tuba, (canet enim tuba,) et mortui resurgent incorruptibiles, et nos immutabimur.

53. Oportet enim corruptibile hoc induere immortalitatem.

---

[1] " Car nous ne faisons encore que commencer à porter l'image de Jesus Christ ;"—" For as yet we do but begin to bear the image of Jesus Christ."

54. So when this corruptible shall have put on incorruption, and this mortal shall have put on immortality, then shall be brought to pass the saying that is written, Death is swallowed up in victory.

55. O death, where *is* thy sting? O grave, where *is* thy victory?

56. The sting of death *is* sin; and the strength of sin *is* the law.

57. But thanks *be* to God, which giveth us the victory, through our Lord Jesus Christ.

58. Therefore, my beloved brethren, be ye stedfast, unmoveable, always abounding in the work of the Lord, forasmuch as ye know that your labour is not in vain in the Lord.

54. Quum autem corruptibile hoc induerit incorruptibilitatem, et mortale hoc induerit immortalitatem: tunc fiet sermo qui scriptus est: (*Hos.* 13, 14, *vel Ies.* 25, 8.) Absorpta est mors in victoriam.

55. Ubi, mors, tuus aculeus? Ubi tua, inferne, victoria?

56. Aculeus autem mortis, peccatum est: virtus autem peccati, Lex.

57. Sed Deo gratia, qui dedit nobis victoriam per Dominum nostrum Iesum Christum.

58. Itaque, fratres mei dilecti, stabiles sitis, immobiles, abundantes in opere Domini semper, hoc cognito, quod labor vester non sit inanis in Domino.

Hitherto he has included two things in his reasoning. In the *first* place, he shows that there will be a resurrection from the dead: *secondly*, he shows of what nature it will be. Now, however, he enters more thoroughly into a description of the manner of it. This he calls a *mystery*, because it had not been as yet so clearly unfolded in any statement of revelation; but he does this to make them more attentive. For that wicked doctrine had derived strength from the circumstance, that they disputed as to this matter carelessly and at their ease,[1] as if it were a matter in which they felt no difficulty. Hence by the term *mystery*, he admonishes them to learn a matter, which was not only as yet unknown to them, but ought to be reckoned among God's heavenly secrets.

51. *We shall not indeed all sleep.* Here there is no difference in the Greek manuscripts, but in the Latin versions there are three different readings. The *first* is, *We shall indeed all die, but we shall not all be changed.* The *second* is, *We shall indeed all rise again, but we shall not all be changed.*[2] The *third* is, *We shall not indeed all sleep, but we*

---

[1] " Par maniere de passe-temps, et tout à leur aise;"—" By way of pastime, and quite at their ease."

[2] This is the reading of the Vulgate. Wiclif (1380) translates the verse as follows: *Lo, I seie to you pryuyte (secret) of holi things, and alle we schulen rise agen, but not alle we schulen be chaungid.—Ed.*

shall all be changed. This diversity, I conjecture, had arisen from this—that some readers, who were not the most discerning, dissatisfied with the true reading, ventured to conjecture a reading which was more approved by them.[1] For it appeared to them, at first view, to be absurd to say, that *all would not die,* while we read elsewhere, that *it is appointed unto all men once to die.* (Heb. ix. 27.) Hence they altered the meaning in this way—*All will not be changed, though all will rise again, or will die ;* and the *change* they interpret to mean—the glory that the sons of God alone will obtain. The true reading, however, may be judged of from the context.

Paul's intention is to explain what he had said—that we will be conformed to Christ, because *flesh and blood cannot inherit the kingdom of God.* A question presented itself,[2] what then will become of those who will be still living at the day of the Lord ? His answer is, that although *all will not die,* yet they will be renewed, that mortality and corruption may be done away. It is to be observed, however, that he speaks exclusively of believers ; for although the resurrection of the wicked will also involve *change,* yet as there is no mention made of them here, we must consider everything that is said, as referring exclusively to the elect. We now see, how well this statement corresponds with the preceding one, for as he had said, that *we shall bear the image of Christ,* he now declares, that this will take place when we shall be *changed,* so that *mortality may be swallowed up of life,* (2 Cor. v. 4,) and that this renovation is not inconsistent with the fact, that Christ's advent will find some still alive.

We must, however, unravel the difficulty—that *it is appointed unto all men once to die ;* and certainly, it is not difficult to unravel it in this way—that as a *change* cannot take place without doing away with the previous system, that *change* is reckoned, with good reason, a kind of *death ;* but, as it is not a separation of the soul from the body, it is

---

[1] " Qui leur estoit plus probable ;"—" Which appeared to them more probable."

[2] " Il y auoit sur ceci vne question qu'on pouuoit faire ;"—" There was a question as to this, which might be proposed "

not looked upon as an ordinary death. It will then be *death*, inasmuch as it will be the destruction of corruptible nature : it will not be a *sleep*, inasmuch as the soul will not quit the body ; but there will be a sudden transition from corruptible nature into a blessed immortality.

52. *In a moment.* This is still of a general nature ; that is, it includes all. For in all the change will be sudden and instantaneous, because Christ's advent will be sudden. And to convey the idea of *a moment*, he afterwards makes use of the phrase *twinkling* (or *jerk*) of the eye, for in the Greek manuscripts there is a twofold. reading—*ῥοπῇ* (*jerk,*) or *ῥιπῇ* (*twinkling.*)[1] It matters nothing, however, as to the sense. Paul has selected a movement of the body, that surpasses all others in quickness ; for nothing is more rapid than a movement of the eye, though at the same time he has made an allusion to *sleep*, with which *twinkling of the eye* is contrasted.[2]

With the last trump. Though the repetition of the term might seem to place it beyond a doubt, that the word *trumpet* is here taken in its proper acceptation, yet I prefer to understand the expression as metaphorical. In 1 Thess. iv. 16, he connects together the *voice of the archangel* and the *trump of God.* As therefore a commander, with the sound of a trumpet, summons his army to battle, so Christ, by his far sounding proclamation, which will be heard throughout the whole world, will summon all the dead. Moses tells us, (Exod. xix. 16,) what loud and terrible sounds were uttered on occasion of the promulgation of the law. Far different will be the commotion *then*, when not one people merely, but the whole world will be summoned to the tribunal of God. Nor will the living only be convoked, but

---

[1] It is stated by *Semler*, that some in the times of Jerome preferred *ῥοπη*, but Jerome himself preferred *ῥιπη*. 'Ροπη is derived from *ῥεπω*, to tend or incline to. It means *force* or *impetus*. It is used by Thucydides (v. 103) to mean the preponderance of *a scale*. In connection with *ὀφθαλμοῦ*, (*the eye*,) it would probably mean, a *cast* or *inclination* of the eye. 'Ριπη, (the common reading,) is derived from *ῥιπτω*, to *throw*. 'Ριπη ὀφθαλμοῦ is explained by *Nyssenus*, (as stated by *Parkhurst*,) to mean—*επιμύσις βλέφαρων*—the *shutting* or *twinkling of the eyelids*.

[2] " Pour ce que quand on se resueille, on cleigne ainsi des yeux ;"— " Because, when persons awake, they twinkle in this way with their eyes."

even the dead will be called forth from their graves.[1]   Nay more, a commandment must be given to dry bones and dust that, resuming their former appearance and reunited to the spirit, they come forth straightway as living men into the presence of Christ.

The dead shall rise.   What he had declared generally as to all, he now explains particularly as to the living and the dead.   This distinction, therefore, is simply an exposition of the foregoing statement—that *all will not die, but all will be changed.*   " Those who have already died," says he, " will rise again incorruptible."   See what a change there will be upon the *dead !*   " Those," says he, " who will be still alive will themselves also be *changed.*"   You see then as to both.[2] You now then perceive how it is, that *change* will be common to all, but not *sleep.*[3]

When he says, *We shall be changed,* he includes himself in the number of those, who are to live till the advent of Christ.   As it was now the *last times,* (1 John ii. 18,) *that day* (2 Tim. i. 18) was to be looked for by the saints every hour.   At the same time, in writing to the Thessalonians, he utters that memorable prediction respecting the scattering[4] that would take place in the Church before Christ's coming.   (2 Thess. ii. 3.)   This, however, does not hinder that he might, by bringing the Corinthians, as it were, into immediate contact with the event, associate himself and them with those who would at that time be alive.

---

[1] " *The trumpet shall sound,* (1 Cor. xv. 52,) says the prophetic teacher. And how startling, how stupendous the summons!   Nothing equal to it, nothing like it, was ever heard through all the regions of the universe, or all the revolutions of time.   When conflicting armies have discharged the bellowing artillery of war, or when victorious armies have shouted for joy of the conquest, the seas and shores have rung, the mountains and plains have echoed.   But the shout of the archangel, and the trump of God, will resound from pole to pole—will pierce the centre and shake the pillars of heaven.   Stronger—stronger still—it will penetrate even the deepest recesses of the tomb!   It will pour its amazing thunder into all those abodes of silence.   The dead, the very dead, shall hear."—*Hervey's* Theron and Aspasio, vol. ii. p. 66.—*Ed.*

[2] " Voyla donc ques les viuans et les morts ;"—" Mark then how it will be as to the living and the dead."

[3] " Non pas le dormir, c'est à dire la mort ;"—" Not sleep, that is to say, death."

[4] " La dissipation horrible ;"—" The dreadful scattering."

53. *For this corruptible must.* Mark, how we shall live in the kingdom of God both in body and in soul, while at the same time *flesh and blood cannot inherit the kingdom of God*—for they shall previously be delivered from corruption. Our nature then, as being now corruptible and mortal, is not admissible into the kingdom of God, but when it shall have put off corruption, and shall have been beautified with incorruption, it will then make its way into it. This passage, too, distinctly proves, that we shall rise again in that same flesh that we now carry about with us, as the Apostle assigns a new quality to it which will serve as a garment. If he had said, *This corruptible must be renewed,* the error of those fanatics, who imagine that mankind will be furnished with new bodies, would not have been so plainly or forcibly overthrown. Now, however, when he declares that *this corruptible shall be invested with glory,* there is no room left for cavil.

54. *Then shall be brought to pass the saying.* This is not merely an amplification, ($\epsilon\pi\epsilon\xi\epsilon\rho\gamma\alpha\sigma\iota\alpha$,)[1] but a confirmation, too, of the preceding statement. For what was foretold by the Prophets must be fulfilled. Now this prediction will not be fulfilled, until our bodies, laying aside corruption, will *put on incorruption.* Hence this last result, also, is necessary. To *come to pass,* is used here in the sense of being *fully accomplished,* for what Paul quotes is now begun in us, and is daily, too, receiving further accomplishment; but it will not have its complete fulfilment until the last day.

It does not, however, appear quite manifest, from what passage he has taken this quotation, for many statements occur in the Prophets to this effect. Only the probability is, that the first clause is taken either from Isaiah xxv. 8, where it is said that *death will be for ever destroyed* by the Lord,[2] or, (as almost all are rather inclined to think,) from

---

[1] " Vne declaration ou amplification;"—" A declaration or amplification."

[2] " The words, as alleged by Paul," (from Isaiah xxv. 8,) " are found in the version of Theodotion, with which the Targum and Syriac agree, in reading the verb as a passive. בלע in Piel, as here, commonly signifies to destroy, *destroy utterly ;* in Kal., the more usual signification is that of *swallowing,* which most of the versions have unhappily adopted. לנצח the Greek translators render by ἰσχύσας, εἰς τέλος, εἰς νἶκος ; attaching to

Hosea xiii. 14, where the Prophet, bewailing the obstinate wickedness of Israel, complains that he was like an untimely child, that struggles against the efforts of his mother in travail, that he may not come forth from the womb, and from this he concludes, that it was owing entirely to himself, that he was not delivered from death. *I will ransom them,* says he, *from the power of the grave : I will rescue them from death.* It matters not, whether you read these words in the future of the indicative, or in the subjunctive,[1] for in either way the meaning amounts to this—that God was prepared to confer upon them salvation, if they would have allowed the favour to be conferred upon them, and that, therefore, if they perished, it was their own fault.

He afterwards adds, *I will be thy destruction, O death ! thy ruin, O grave !* In these words God intimates, that he accomplishes the salvation of his people[2] only when death and the grave are reduced to nothing. For no one will deny, that in that passage there is a description of completed salvation. As, therefore, we do not see such a destruction of death, it follows, that we do not yet enjoy that complete salvation, which God promises to his people, and that, consequently, it is delayed until *that day.* Then, accordingly, *will death be swallowed up,* that is, it will be reduced to nothing,[3] that we may have manifestly, in every particular,

the term the idea of what is *overpowering, durable, complete.* The significations of the Hebrew root נצח, used only in Niphal and Piel, are—to *shine, lead, lead on, be complete;* in Chald. to *surpass, excel, vanquish;* hence the idea of *victory, eternity,* &c., attaching to נצח, and of *completely, entirely, for ever,* &c., to לנצח, נצח נצח. The words are therefore equivalent to ὁ θάνατος οὐκ ἔσται ἔτι,—(*Death shall be no longer,*) Rev. xxi. 4, where there seems to be an evident allusion to our text ; and where the subject is, as here, not the millennial state of the Church, but the state of glory after the resurrection of the body. It will be then only, that a period shall be put to the reproachful persecutions of the righteous, which Isaiah likewise predicts."—*Henderson* on Isaiah.—*Ed.*

[1] " Ie les eusse rachetez—ie les eusse deliurez ;"—" I could have ransomed them—I could have rescued them."

[2] " Lors vrayement et à bon escient il sauue les fideles ;"—" He then truly and effectually saves believers."

[3] " This victory will not be gradual only, but total and entire. Every thing of mortality, that was hanging about these glorious victors, shall be *swallowed up* in perfect and endless life. Death is unstung first—disarmed—and then easily overcome. Its sting is said to be sin—the deadliest thing in death. A plain farther proof, by the way, the Apostle in-

and in every respect, (as they say,) a complete victory over it.[1]

As to the second clause, in which he triumphs over death and the grave, it is not certain whether he speaks of himself, or whether he meant there also to quote the words of the Prophet. For where we render it, "I will be thy destruction, O death!—thy ruin, O grave!" the Greeks have translated it, "*Where, O death, is thy suit?*[2] *where, O grave, thy sting?*" Now although this mistake of the Greeks is excusable from the near resemblance of the words,[3] yet if any one will attentively examine the context, he will see that they have gone quite away from the Prophet's intention. The true meaning, then, will be this—that the Lord will put an end to death, and destroy the grave. It is possible, however, that, as the Greek translation was in common use, Paul alluded to it, and in that there is nothing inconsistent, though he has not quoted literally, for instead of *victory* he has used the term *action*, or *law-suit*.[4] I am certainly of opinion, that

tended death also in the moral sense. And the insulting inquiry, 'where is it?' implies 'tis not any where to be found; and signifies a total abolition of it, and, by consequence, must infer that every thing of death besides must, as to them, for ever cease and be no more. Which also the phrase of *swallowing up* doth with great emphasis express."—*Howe's* Works, (Lond. 1834,) p. 1035.—*Ed.*

[1] "En sorte que nous aurons plene et parfaite victoire à l'encontre d'elle ;"—"So that we shall have a full and complete victory over it."

[2] "Où est ton plaid, c'est à dire, le proces que tu intentes contre nous, ô mort ?"—"O death, where is thy suit—that is to say, the process that thou carriest on against us?"

[3] "The passage (says Dr. Bloomfield) is from Hosea xiii. 14, and the Apostle's words differ only by the transposition of νῖκος (*victory*) and κέντρον, (*sting*,) from the ancient versions; except that for νῖκος the Sept. has δίκη, (*law-suit*.)" It is noticed, however, by *Granville Penn*, that "in the *most ancient* of all the existing MSS. (*Vat.* and *Ephr.*) there is *no transposition* of θάνατος (*death*) and κέντρον (*sting*;) and the Apostle's sentence preserves the same order as in the Greek of Hosea; so that the transposition lies wholly at the door of those MSS. which are *more recent than those ancient copies.*" The *Vat.* version has νεῖκος instead of νικος, but from the circumstance that in that version νεῖκος is used in the 54th verse manifestly instead of νικος. it abundantly appears that it is a mere difference of spelling. The words to which CALVIN refers, as having been mistaken for each other from their *near resemblance*, are, δίκη (*law-suit*) and νικος, (or νικη,) *victory.*—*Ed.*

[4] "Car en lieu du mot *diki*, qui signifie *plaid* ou *proces*, il a mis *nicos*, qui signifie *victoire* ;"—"For in place of the word δίκη, which signifies an *action* or *law-suit*, they have used νῖκος, which signifies *victory.*"

the Apostle did not deliberately intend to call in the Prophet as a witness, with the view of making a wrong use of his authority, but simply accommodated, in passing, to his own use a sentiment that had come into common use, as being, independently of this, of a pious nature.[1] The main thing is this—that Paul, by an exclamation of a spirited nature, designed to rouse up the minds of the Corinthians, and lead them on, as it were, to a near view of the resurrection. Now, although we do not as yet behold the victory with our eyes, and the day of triumph has not yet arrived, (nay more, the dangers of war must every day be encountered,) yet the assurance of faith, as we shall have occasion to observe ere long, is not at all thereby diminished.

56. *The sting of death is sin.* In other words, " Death has no dart with which to wound us except *sin*, since *death* proceeds from the anger of God. Now it is only with our sins that God is angry. Take away sin, therefore, and death will no more be able to harm us." This agrees with what he said in Rom. vi. 23, that *the wages of sin is death.* Here, however, he makes use of another metaphor, for he compared sin to a *sting*, with which alone death is armed for inflicting upon us a deadly wound. Let *that* be taken away, and death is disarmed, so as to be no longer hurtful. Now with what view Paul says this, will be explained by him ere long.

The strength of sin is the law. It is the law of God that imparts to that sting its deadly power, because it does not merely discover our guilt, but even increases it. A clearer exposition of this statement may be found in Rom. vii. 9, where Paul teaches us that we *are alive,* so long as we are *without the law,* because in our own opinion it is well with us, and we do not feel our own misery, until the law summons us to the judgment of God, and wounds our conscience with an apprehension of eternal death. Farther, he teaches us that sin has been in a manner lulled asleep, but is kindled up by the law, so as to rage furiously. Meanwhile, however, he vindicates the law from calumnies, on the ground that it is *holy, and good, and just,* and is not of itself the parent of sin or

---

[1] " Bonne et saincte ;"—" Good and holy."

the cause of death.   Hence he concludes, that whatever there is of evil is to be reckoned to our own account, inasmuch as it manifestly proceeds from the depravity of our nature. Hence the law is but the *occasion* of injury.   The true *cause* of ruin is in ourselves.   Hence he speaks of the law here as the *strength* or *power* of sin, because it executes upon us the judgment of God.   In the mean time he does not deny, that sin inflicts death even upon those that know not the law ; but he speaks in this manner, because it exercises its tyranny upon them with less violence.   For the *law came that sin might abound*, (Rom. v. 20,) or that it *might become beyond measure sinful.*   (Rom. vii. 13.)

57. *But thanks be to God.*   From this it appears, why it it was that he made mention both of sin and of the law, when treating of death.   Death has no *sting* with which to wound except *sin,* and the law imparts to this *sting* a deadly power.   But Christ has conquered sin, and by conquering it has procured victory for us, and has *redeemed us from the curse of the law.*   (Gal. iii. 13.)   Hence it follows, that we are no longer lying under the power of death.   Hence, although we have not as yet a full discovery of those benefits, yet we may already with confidence glory in them, because it is necessary that what has been accomplished in the Head should be accomplished, also, in the members.   We may, therefore, triumph over death as subdued, because Christ's victory is ours.

When, therefore, he says, that *victory has been given to us,* you are to understand by this in the *first* place, that it is inasmuch as Christ has in his own person abolished sin, has satisfied the law, has endured the curse, has appeased the anger of God, and has procured life ; and farther, because he has already begun to make us partakers of all those benefits. For though we still carry about with us the remains of sin, it, nevertheless, does not reign in us : though it still *stings* us, it does not do so fatally, because its edge is blunted, so that it does not penetrate into the vitals of the soul.   Though the law still threatens, yet there is presented to us on the other hand, the liberty that was procured for us by Christ, which is an antidote to its terrors.   Though the remains of sin still dwell in us, yet the Spirit who raised up Christ from the dead is *life, because of righteousness.* (Rom. viii. 10.) Now follows the conclusion.

58. *Wherefore, my brethren.* Having satisfied himself that he had sufficiently proved the doctrine of the resurrection, he now closes his discussion with an exhortation ; and this has much more force, than if he had made use of a simple conclusion with an affirmation. *Since your labour,* says he, *is not in vain in the Lord, be steadfast, and abound in good works.* Now he says that *their labour is not in vain,* for this reason, that there is a reward laid up for them with God. This is that exclusive hope which, in the first instance, encourages believers, and afterwards sustains them, so that they do not stop short in the race. Hence he exhorts them to remain *steadfast,* because they rest on a firm foundation, as they know that a better life is prepared for them in heaven.

He adds—*abounding in the work of the Lord ;* for the hope of a resurrection makes us not be weary in well-doing, as he teaches in Col. i. 10. For amidst so many occasions of offence as constantly present themselves to us, who is there that would not despond, or turn aside from the way, were it not that, by thinking of a better life he is by this means kept in the fear of God ? Now, on the other hand, he intimates, that if the hope of a resurrection is taken away, then, the foundation (as it were) being rooted up, the whole structure of piety falls to the ground.[1] Unquestionably, if the hope of reward is taken away and extinguished, alacrity in running will not merely grow cold, but will be altogether destroyed.

CHAPTER XVI.

1. Now concerning the collection for the saints, as I have given order to the Churches of Galatia, even so do ye.

2. Upon the first *day* of the week let every one of you lay by him in store, as *God* hath prospered him, that there be no gatherings when I come.

1. Cæterum de collecta quæ fit in sanctos, quemadmodum ordinavi Ecclesiis Galatiæ, ita et vos facite.

2. In una sabbatorum unusquisque vestrum apud se seponat, thesaurizans quod successerit, ne, quum venero, tunc collectæ fiant.[2]

[1] " D'autant que ceste esperance en est le fondement ;"—" Inasmuch as that hope is the foundation of it."
[2] " C'est qu'en vn des Sabbaths (ou, que chacun premier iour de la sep-

3. And when I come, whomsoever ye shall approve by *your* letters, them will I send to bring your liberality unto Jerusalem.

4. And if it be meet that I go also, they shall go with me.

5. Now I will come unto you, when I shall pass through Macedonia; for I do pass through Macedonia.

6. And it may be that I will abide, yea, and winter with you, that ye may bring me on my journey whithersoever I go.

7. For I will not see you now by the way; but I trust to tarry a while with you, if the Lord permit.

3. Ubi autem affuero, quos probaveritis per epistolas, eos mittam, ut perferant beneficentiam vestram in Ierusalem.

4. Quodsi fuerit operæ pretium me quoque proficisci, mecum proficiscentur.

5. Veniam autem ad vos, quum Macedoniam transiero: Macedoniam enim pertransiturus sum.

6. Apud vos autem forte permanebo, aut etiam hibernabo, ut vos me deducatis quocunque proficiscar.

7. Nolo enim vos nunc in transcursu videre: sed spero me ad aliquod tempus mansurum apud vos, si Dominus permiserit.

1. *But concerning the collection.* Luke relates (Acts xi. 28) that the prediction of Agabus, foretelling that there would be a famine under Claudius Cæsar, gave occasion for alms being collected by the saints, with the view of affording help to the brethren in Jerusalem. For though the Prophet had foretold, that this calamity would be generally prevalent almost throughout the world, yet as they were more heavily oppressed with penury at Jerusalem, and as all the Gentile Churches were bound, if they would not be held guilty of very great ingratitude, to afford aid to that place from which they had received the gospel, every one, consequently, forgetful of self, resolved to afford relief to Jerusalem. That the pressure of want was felt heavily at Jerusalem, appears from the Epistle to the Galatians, (ii. 10,) where Paul relates, that he had been charged by the Apostles to stir up the Gentiles to afford help.[1] Now the Apostles would never have given such a charge, had they not been

maine) chacun de vous mette à part par deuers soy, thesaurizant de ce qu'il aura prosperé, afin que (ou, serrant ce qu'il pourra par la benignite *de Dieu*, afin) lors que ie viendray, les collectes ne se facent point ;"—"It is, that on one of the Sabbaths (or, that every first day of the week) every one of you lay apart by himself, treasuring up according as he has prospered, (or, laying up what he shall be able to do through the kindness of God,) that there may be no collections made when I come."

[1] " D'inciter les Gentiles à subuenir à la pourete qui y estoit ;"—" To stir up the Gentiles to relieve the poverty that existed there."

constrained by necessity. Farther, this passage is an evidence of the truth of what Paul states there also—that he had been careful to exhort the Gentiles to afford help in such a case of necessity. Now, however, he prescribes the method of relief; and that the Corinthians may accede to it the more readily, he mentions that he had already prescribed it to the Churches of Galatia; for they would necessarily be the more influenced by example, as we are wont to feel a natural backwardness to anything that is not ordinarily practised. Now follows the method—by which he designed to cut off all hinderances and impediments.

2. *On one of the Sabbaths.* The end is this—that they may have their alms ready in time. He therefore exhorts them not to wait till he came, as anything that is done suddenly, and in a bustle, is not done well, but to contribute on the Sabbath what might seem good, and according as every one's ability might enable—that is, on the day on which they held their sacred assemblies. The clause rendered *on one of the Sabbaths,* (κατὰ μίαν σαββάτων,) Chrysostom explains to mean—*the first Sabbath.* In this I do not agree with him; for Paul means rather that they should contribute, one on one Sabbath and another on another; or even each of them every Sabbath, if they chose. For he has an eye, first of all, to convenience, and farther, that the sacred assembly, in which the communion of saints is celebrated, might be an additional spur to them. Nor am I more inclined to admit the view taken by Chrysostom—that the term *Sabbath* is employed here to mean the *Lord's day,* (Rev. i. 10,) for the probability is, that the Apostles, at the beginning, retained the day that was already in use, but that afterwards, constrained by the superstition of the Jews, they set aside that day, and substituted another. Now the *Lord's day* was made choice of, chiefly because our Lord's resurrection put an end to the shadows of the law. Hence the day itself puts us in mind of our Christian liberty. We may, however, very readily infer from this passage, that believers have always had a certain day of rest from labour—not as if the worship of God consisted in idleness, but because it is of importance for the common harmony, that a certain day

should be appointed for holding sacred assemblies, as they cannot be held every day.   For as to Paul's forbidding else-where (Gal. iv. 10) that any distinction should be made be-tween one day and another, *that* must be understood to be with a view to religion,[1] and not with a view to polity or external order.[2]

Treasuring up.   I have preferred to retain the Greek participle, as it appeared to me to be more emphatic.[3]   For although ϑησαυρίζειν means to *lay up*, yet in my opinion, he designed to admonish the Corinthians, that whatever they might contribute for the saints would be their best and safest *treasure*.   For if a heathen poet could say—" What riches you give away, those alone you shall always have,"[4] how much more ought that consideration to have influence among us, who are not dependent on the gratitude of men, but have God to look to, who makes himself a debtor in the room of the poor man, to restore to us one day, with large interest, whatever we give away? (Prov. xix. 17.) Hence this statement of Paul corresponds with that saying of Christ— *Lay up for yourselves treasure in heaven, where it will not be exposed either to thieves, or to moths.*   (Matt. vi. 20.)

According as he has prospered.   Instead of this the old translation has rendered it, *What may seem good to him,* mis-led, no doubt, by the resemblance between the word made use of, and another.[5]   Erasmus renders it, *What will be conve-*

---

[1] See CALVIN's Institutes, vol. i. p. 464.

[2] " Quand on le fait pour deuotion, comme cela estant vn seruice de Dieu, et non pas pour la police externe ;"—" When it is done for the sake of devotion, as though it were a service done to God, and not with a view to external polity."

[3] " On a par ci deuant traduit, *amassant ;* mais i'ay mieux aimé retenir la propriete du mot Grec ;"—" The word before us has been rendered *laying up ;* but I have preferred to retain the peculiar force of the Greek word."

[4] " Quas dederis, solas semper habebis opes." (Martial. Ep. v. 42.) A si-milar sentiment occurs in the writings of the poet *Rabirius.*   " Hoc habeo, quodcunque dedi ;"—" I have whatever I have given away." (See *Seneca,* lib. vi. de Benef.) Alexander the Great, (as stated by *Plutarch,*) when asked where he had laid up his *treasures,* answered, " Apud amicos ;"—" Among my friends."—*Ed.*

[5] " S'abusant a l'affinite des deux mots Grecs ;"—" Misled by the re-semblance between two Greek words." CALVIN's meaning seems to be that the verb εὐοδόομαι, (*to be prospered,*) made use of here by Paul, had

nient.[1] Neither the one nor the other pleased me, for this reason—that the proper signification of the word brings out a meaning that is much more suitable; for it means—to *go on prosperously.* Hence he calls every one to consider his ability—"Let every one, according as God hath blessed him, lay out upon the poor from his increase."

3. *And when I come.* As we are cheerful in giving, when we know for certain, that what we give is well laid out, he points out to the Corinthians a method, by which they may be assured of a good and faithful administration—by selecting approved persons, to whom they may intrust the matter. Nay more, he offers his own services, if desired, which is an evidence that he has the matter at heart.

5. *When I shall pass through Macedonia.* The common opinion is, that this epistle was sent from Philippi. Persons coming thence to Corinth by land, required to pass through Macedonia; for that colony is situated in the farthest extremity, towards the Emathian mountains. Paul, it is true, might, instead of going by land, have gone thither by sea, but he was desirous to visit the Macedonian Churches, that he might confirm them in passing. So much for the common opinion. To me, however, it appears more probable, that the epistle was written at Ephesus; for he says a little afterwards, that *he will remain there until Pentecost,* (verse 8)[2]; and he salutes the Corinthians, not in the name of the Philippians, but of the *Asiatics.* (verse 19.)[3] Besides, in the second epistle he explicitly states, that, after he had sent

been confounded with εὐδοκέω. (*to seem good.*) Wiclif (1380) in accordance with the Vulgate, renders as follows—*Kepynge that that plesith to hym.*— Ed.

[1] " C'est a dire, selon sa commodite;"—" That is to say, according to his convenience."

[2] " St. Paul was now at *Ephesus;* for almost all allow, in opposition to the *subscription* at the end of this epistle, that states it to have been written from *Philippi,* that it was written from *Ephesus;* and this is supported by many strong arguments; and the 8th verse here seems to put it past all question: *I will tarry at Ephesus; i.e.,* I am in Ephesus, and here I purpose to remain until Pentecost."—*Dr. Adam Clarke.*—*Ed.*

[3] " *The Churches of Asia salute you, i.e.,* the Churches in *Asia Minor.* Ephesus was in this Asia, and it is clear from this that the Apostle was not at *Philippi.* Had he been at Philippi, as the subscription states, he would have said, The *Churches of* MACEDONIA, not the Churches of ASIA, *salute you.*"—*Dr. Adam Clarke.*—*Ed.*

away this epistle, he passed over into Macedonia. (2 Cor. ii. 13.) Now after passing through Macedonia, he would be at a distance from Ephesus, and in the neighbourhood of Achaia. Hence I have no doubt that he was at Ephesus at that time: thence he could sail by a straight course to Achaia. For visiting Macedonia, a long circuit was needed, and a more disagreeable route. Accordingly he lets them know that he will not come to them by a direct course, as he required to *go through Macedonia.*

To the Corinthians, however, he promises something farther—that he would *make a longer stay with them.* By this he shows his affection towards them. For what reason had he for delay, except that he was concerned as to their welfare? On the other hand, he lets them know how fully assured he is of their affection towards him in return, by taking it, as it were, for granted that he would be conducted forward by them in the way of kindness ; for he says this from confidence in their friendship.[1]

After saying everything, however, he subjoins this limitation —*if the Lord permit.* With this reservation, saints ought to follow up all their plans and deliberations; for it is an instance of great rashness to undertake and determine many things for the future, while we have not even a moment in our power. The main thing indeed is, that, in the inward affection of the mind, we submit to God and his providence, whatever we resolve upon ;[2] but at the same time, it is becoming that we should accustom ourselves to such forms of expression, that whenever we have to do with what is future we may make everything depend on the divine will.[3]

8. But I will tarry at Ephesus until Pentecost.	8. Commorabor autem Ephesi usque ad Pentecosten.
9. For a great door and effectual	9. Nam ostium mihi apertum

[1] " Ils le conduiront par tout où il ira ;"—" They will conduct him forward wherever he may go."

[2] " Tout ce que nous entreprenons et consultons ;"—" Everything that we undertake and resolve upon."

[3] " De remettre à la volonte de Dieu tout ce que nous entreprendrons pour le temps aduenir ;"—" So as to give up to the will of God everything that we shall undertake for the time to come."

is opened unto me, and *there are* many adversaries.

10. Now if Timotheus come, see that he may be with you without fear: for he worketh the work of the Lord, as I also *do*.

11. Let no man therefore despise him; but conduct him forth in peace, that he may come unto me: for I look for him with the brethren.

12. As touching *our* brother Apollos, I greatly desired him to come unto you with the brethren: but his will was not at all to come at this time; but he will come when he shall have convenient time.

est magnum et efficax, et[1] adversarii multi.

10. Quodsi venerit Timotheus, videte, ut absque metu sit apud vos: opus enim Domini operatur, quemadmodum et ego.

11. Ne quis igitur eum spernat: sed prosequamini eum cum pace,[2] ut veniat ad me: exspecto enim eum cum fratribus.

12. Porro de Apollo fratre, multum hortatus sum illum, ut veniret ad vos cum fratribus, at omnino non fuit voluntas nunc eundi: veniet autem, quum opportunitatem nactus erit.

8. *I will remain.* From this statement I have argued above,[3] that this epistle was sent from Ephesus, rather than from Philippi. For the probability is, that the Apostle speaks of the place in which he was at the time, and not of a place, in going to which he would require to make a long circuit; and farther, in passing through Macedonia,[4] it would have been necessary to leave Corinth when already in the neighbourhood of it, and cross the sea in order to reach Ephesus. He accordingly tells them beforehand that he will *remain at Ephesus until Pentecost,* adding the reason —in order that they may wait for him the more patiently. Erasmus has preferred to render it—*until the fiftieth day,* influenced by frivolous conjectures rather than by any solid argument. He objects, that there was as yet no day of Pentecost appointed among Christians, as it is now celebrated; and this I grant. He says, that it ought not to be understood as referring to the Jewish solemnity, because in various instances he annuls and condemns the superstitious observance of days. (Gal. iv. 10; Rom. xiv. 5; Col. ii. 16, 17.) I do not concede to him, however, that Paul celebrated that day at Ephesus from being influenced by a superstitious regard to the day, but because there would be a larger assembly at that time, and he hoped that, in that

---

[1] " Et, ou mais, il y a;"—" And, or but, there are."

[2] " En paix (ou, seurete);"—" In peace (or, safety.)"

[3] See p. 70.

[4] " En passant de Philippes par Macedone;"—" In passing from Philippi through Macedonia."

way, an opportunity would be presented to him of propagat-
ing the gospel.   Thus, when he was hastening forward to
Jerusalem, he assigned as the reason of his haste, *that he
might arrive there at Pentecost,* (Acts xx. 16 ;) but while
others presented themselves there for the purpose of sacri-
ficing according to the ritual of the law, he himself had another object in view—that his ministry might be the more
useful in proportion to the largeness of the attendance.   It
were, however, an excessively poor meaning to understand
Paul here as simply specifying fifty days.   Besides, when
he expressly says τὴν πεντηκοστήν (*the Pentecost,*) he cannot
but be understood as speaking of a particular day.   As to
this festival, see Lev. xxiii. 16.

9. *For a great and effectual door is opened to me.*   He
assigns two reasons for remaining for a longer time at
Ephesus—1st, Because an opportunity is afforded him there
of furthering the gospel ; and 2dly, Because, in consequence
of the great number of *adversaries* that were there, his presence was particularly required.   " I shall do much good by
prolonging my stay here for a little while, and were I absent,
Satan would do much injury."   In the first clause, he makes
use of a metaphor that is quite in common use, when he
employs the term *door* as meaning *an opportunity.*   For the
Lord opened up a way for him for the furtherance of the
gospel.   He calls this a *great* door, because he could gain
many.   He calls it *effectual,* inasmuch as the Lord blessed
his labour, and rendered his doctrine *effectual* by the power
of His Spirit.   We see, then, how this holy man[1] sought
everywhere Christ's glory, and did not select a place with a
view to his own convenience or his own pleasure ; but simply
looked to this—*where* he might do most good, and serve his
Lord with most abundant fruit ; and in addition to this, he
did not merely not shrink back from hardships, but presented himself, of his own accord, where he saw that he
would have to contend more keenly, and with greater difficulty.   For the reason why he *remained*[2] was, that *many
adversaries* were at hand ; and the better equipped he was

[1] " Ce sainct Apostre ;"—" This holy Apostle."
[2] " En Ephese ;"—" In Ephesus."

for enduring their assault, he required to be so much the better prepared, and the more resolute.

10. *But if Timothy come.* He speaks as if he were not as yet certain as to his coming. Now he charges them as to Timothy, so that he may be with them in safety—not as though he were in danger of his life among them, but because he would have enemies of Christ[1] to oppose him. He wishes, therefore, that they should carefully take heed that no injury be done to him.

He adds the reason—*for he worketh the work of the Lord.* Hence we infer, that the Church of Christ ought to be concerned for the preservation of the lives of ministers. And assuredly, it is reasonable, that, in proportion as an individual is endowed with superior gifts for the edification of believers, and applies himself to it the more strenuously, his life ought to be so much dearer to us.

The clause—*as I also do,* is made use of, either to express his excellence, or simply to point out the similarity as to office, inasmuch as both laboured in the word.

11. *Let no man, therefore, despise him.* Here we have a *second* charge, *that they may not despise him*—perhaps because he was as yet of a youthful age, which usually draws forth less respect. He wishes them, therefore, to take care, that there be no hinderance in the way of this faithful minister of Christ being held in due esteem—unless, perhaps, it be that Paul reckoned this very thing to be an evidence of contempt, if they were not concerned, as it became them to be, in reference to his life. This injunction, however, appears to include something farther, that they should not undervalue Timothy, from ignorance of his worth.

In the *third* place, he charges them to *conduct him forward in peace,* or, in other words, *safe from all harm,* for *peace* here means safety.

12. *As to our brother Apollos.* He had succeeded Paul in the work of building up the Corinthians ; and hence he has in previous passages ascribed to him the office of *watering.* (1 Cor. iii. 6, and Acts xix. 1.) He now states a reason why he does not come with the others, and he states the

---

[1] " Beaucoup d'ennemis de Christ ;"—" Many enemies of Christ."

reason of this, in order that the Corinthians may not suspect that he had been hindered by him. For the better he was known by them, they were so much the more favourably disposed towards him, and they would be the more ready to conjecture, that matters had been designedly contrived, that he should not go to them, in consequence of offence having been taken.[1] They might, at least, be prepared to inquire among themselves : " Why has he sent these persons to us rather than Apollos ?" He answers, that it was not owing to him, inasmuch as he *entreated him ;* but he promises that he *will come as soon as he has opportunity.*

13. Watch ye, stand fast in the faith, quit you like men, be strong.

14. Let all your things be done with charity.

15. I beseech you, brethren, (ye know the house of Stephanas, that it is the first-fruits of Achaia, and *that* they have addicted themselves to the ministry of the saints,)

16. That ye submit yourselves unto such, and to every one that helpeth with *us*, and laboureth.

17. I am glad of the coming of Stephanas and Fortunatus and A-chaicus : for that which was lacking on your part they have supplied.

18. For they have refreshed my spirit and yours : therefore acknowledge ye them that are such.

19. The churches of Asia salute you. Aquila and Priscilla salute you much in the Lord, with the church that is in their house.

20. All the brethren greet you. Greet ye one another with an holy kiss.

21. The salutation of *me* Paul with mine own hand.

22. If any man love not the Lord Jesus Christ, let him be Anathema Maran-atha.

23. The grace of our Lord Jesus Christ *be* with you.

13. Vigilate, state in fide, viriliter agite, robusti estote.

14. Omnia vestra in caritate fiant.

15. Hortor autem vos, fratres, nôstis domum Stephanæ, primitias esse Achaiæ, atque ut se in ministerium sanctorum ordinaverint :

16. Ut etiam subiecti sitis talibus, et omnibus qui cooperantur et laborant.

17. Gaudeo autem de præsentia Stephanæ, et Fortunati, et Achaici : quia quod deerat a vobis, ipsi suppleverunt.

18. Refocillârunt enim spiritum meum et vestrum : agnoscite ergo tales.

19. Salutant vos Ecclesiæ Asiæ : salutant vos multum in Domino Aquila et Priscilla cum domestica eorum Ecclesia.

20. Salutant vos fratres omnes : salutate vos invicem in osculo sancto.

21. Salutatio mea manu Pauli.

22. Si quis non amat Dominum Iesum Christum, sit anathema maranatha.

23. Gratia Domini Iesu Christi sit vobiscum.

---

[1] " Que sainct Paul se sentant offensé par les Corinthiens, auoit attitré cela tout exprés, qu' Apollos n'allast point vers eux ;"—" That St. Paul feeling offended with the Corinthians, had intentionally brought it about, that Apollos should not go to them."

24. My love *be* with you all in Christ Jesus. Amen.

¶ The first *epistle* to the Corinthians was written from Philippi by Stephanas, and Fortunatus, and Achaicus, and Timotheus.

24. Dilectio mea cum vobis omnibus in Christo Iesu. Amen.

Ad Corinthios prior missa fuit e Philippis per Stephanam, et Fortunatum, et Andronicum, et Timotheum.[1]

13. *Watch ye.* A short exhortation, but of great weight. He exhorts them to *watch,* in order that Satan may not oppress them, finding them off their guard. For as the warfare is incessant, the *watching* requires to be incessant too. Now watchfulness of spirit is this—when, free and disentangled from earthly cares, we meditate on the things of God. For as the body is weighed down by *surfeiting and drunkenness,* (Luke xxi. 34,) so as to be fit for nothing, so the cares and lusts of the world, idleness or carelessness, are like a spiritual surfeiting that overpowers the mind.[2]

The *second* thing is that they *persevere in the faith,* or that they hold fast the faith, so as to *stand firm;* because that is the foundation on which we rest. It is certain, however, that he points out the means of perseverance—by resting upon God with a firm faith.

In the *third* exhortation, which is much of the same nature, he stirs them up to manly fortitude. And, as we are naturally weak, he exhorts them *fourthly* to strengthen themselves, or gather strength. For where we render it *be strong,* Paul makes use of only one word, which is equivalent to *strengthen yourselves.*

14. *Let all your things be done in love.* Again he repeats what is the rule in all those transactions, in which we have dealings with one another. He wishes, then, that *love* shall be the directress; because the Corinthians erred chiefly in this respect—that every one looked to himself without caring for others.

15. *Ye know the house of Stephanas.* We know, from daily

---

[1] It appears from *Hug* (in his treatise on the antiquity of the Vatican version) that the subscription to this epistle in that version is as follows—προς Κορινθιους ά ενραφη απο Εφισου—*The first to the Corinthians was written from Ephesus.* This, it will be observed, favours the view taken by CALVIN of the statement made by Paul in 1 Cor. xvi. 8. (See pp. 70-72.)—*Ed.*

[2] " Sont comme vne yurongnerie spirituelle, qui assopit et estourdit l'entendement ;"—" Are like a spiritual drunkenness, which makes the mind drowsy and stupid."

experience, of what advantage it is, that those should have the highest authority, whom God has adorned with the most distinguished gifts. Accordingly, if we wish to secure the welfare of the Church, let us always take care that honour be conferred upon the good: let their counsels have the greatest weight; let others give way to them, and allow themselves to be governed by their prudence. This Paul does in this instance, when admonishing the Corinthians to show respect to the *house of Stephanas.* Some manuscripts add, *and Fortunatus.*[1] For God manifests himself to us when he shows us the gifts of his Spirit. Hence, if we would not appear to be despisers of God, let us voluntarily *submit ourselves* to those, on whom God has conferred superior gifts.

Now, that they may be the more inclined to put honour upon *that house,* (for as to the other, it appears to me to be, in this place at least, a spurious addition,) he reminds them that they were the *first-fruits of Achaia,* that is, that the household of Stephanas were the first that had embraced the gospel. Not indeed as though the first in order of time were in every case superior to the others, but where there is perseverance along with this, it is with good reason, that honour is conferred upon those, who have in a manner paved the way for the gospel by promptitude of faith. It must be observed, however, that he dignifies with this honourable title those, who had consecrated to believers their services and resources. For the same reason, he bestows commendation a little afterwards upon Fortunatus and Achaicus, that, in proportion to a man's superiority of excellence,[2] he might be held so much the more in esteem, that he might be able to do the more good. Farther, in order that the Corinthians may be the more disposed to love them, he says, that what *had been wanting* on the part of their entire Church *had been compensated for* by their vicarious services.

19. *With the Church that is in their house.* A magnificent

---

[1] The Alex. and Copt. MSS. read—*and Fortunatus.* The Vulgate reads—*Fortunatum et Achaicum;* in accordance with which the rendering in Wiclif (1380) is, Ye *knowen the hous of stephan and of fortunati, and acacie.* The Rheims version (1582) reads—You know *the house of Stephanas and of Fortunatus.*—*Ed.*

[2] " Selon que chacun estoit plus homme de bien et vertueux;"—" In proportion as an individual was an honourable and virtuous man."

eulogium, inasmuch as the name of the Church is applied to
a single family! At the same time it is befitting, that all
the families of the pious should be regulated in such a manner as to be so many little Churches. As to the term *Congregation*, which Erasmus has used in preference, it is foreign
to Paul's design; for it was not his intention to designate a
crowd of persons by a mere common term, but to speak in
honourable terms of the management of a Christian household. His saluting them in the name of Aquila and Priscilla, confirms what I have noticed above[1]—that the Epistle
was written at Ephesus, not at Philippi. For Luke informs
us, that they remained at Ephesus, when Paul went elsewhere. (Acts xviii. 19.)

20. *Salute one another with a holy kiss.* The practice of
kissing was very common among the Jews, as is manifest
from the Scriptures. In Greece, though it was not so common and customary, it was by no means unknown; but the
probability is, that Paul speaks here of a solemn kiss, with
which they saluted each other in the sacred assembly. For
I could easily believe, that from the times of the Apostles
a kiss was used in connection with the administration of the
Supper;[2] in place of which, among nations that were some-

---

[1] See p. 70.

[2] "That the Apostle," says Dr. Brown in his Commentary on 1st Peter,
"meant the members of the Churches, on receiving this Epistle, to salute
one another is certain; that he meant, that at all their religious meetings
they should do so, is not improbable. That he meant to make this an
everlasting ordinance in all Christian Churches, though it has sometimes
been asserted, has never been proved, and is by no means likely. That
the practice prevailed extensively, perhaps universally, in the earlier ages,
is established on satisfactory evidence. 'After the prayers,' says Justin
Martyr, who lived in the earlier part of the second century, giving an account in his Apology of the religious customs of the Christians—'after the
prayers, we embrace each other with a kiss.' Tertullian speaks of it as
an ordinary part of the religious services of the Lord's day; and in the
Apostolical Constitutions, as they are termed, the manner in which it was
performed is particularly described. 'Then let the men apart, and the
women apart, salute each other with a kiss in the Lord.' Origen's Note
on Romans xvi. 16, is: 'From this passage the custom was delivered to
the Churches, that, after prayer, the brethren should salute one another
with a kiss.' This token of love was generally given at the Holy Supper.
It was likely, from the prevalence of this custom, that the calumny of
Christians indulging in licentiousness at their religious meetings originated;
and it is not improbable that, in order to remove everything like an occasion to calumniators, the practice which, though in itself innocent, had

what averse to the practice of kissing, there crept in the custom of kissing the patine.[1] However this may be, as it was a token of mutual love. I have no doubt, that Paul meant to exhort them to the cultivation of good-will among them-

become not for the use of edifying, was discontinued."—*Brown's* Expository Discourses on 1st Peter, vol. iii. pp. 309, 310. " It is remarkable that, by the testimony of Suetonius, an edict was published by one of the Roman Emperors, for the abolition of this practice among his subjects,—perhaps in order to check abuses, for the prevention of which our Apostle enjoins that it shall be a *holy salutation.*"—*Chalmers* on the Romans, vol. iii. p. 428.—*Ed.*

[1] By the *patine* or *paten*, is meant the *plate* or *salver* on which the wafer or bread was placed in the observance of the mass. The term is made use of by *Dr. Stillingfleet* in his " Preservative from Popery," (title vii. chap. v.,) in speaking of the practice of the Church of Rome in the adoration of the host : " The priest in every mass, as soon as he has consecrated the bread and wine, with bended knees, he adores the sacrament ; that which he has consecrated, that very thing which is before him, upon the *patine*, and in the chalice ; and gives the same worship and subjection, both of body and mind, to it as he could to God or Christ himself." In *Young's* Lectures on Popery, (Lond. 1836,) p. 140, the following account is given of the sacrifice of the mass : " Upon the altar is the chalice, or cup, which is to contain the wine, mixed with a little water ; and covering the cup is the *paten*, or *plate*, intended to hold the cake or wafer. After an almost endless variety of movements, and forms, and prayers, and readings, the priest goes to the altar, and, taking the cup containing wine and water, with the wafer upon the *cover*,—these having been before consecrated and transubstantiated into the body and blood of Christ,—he raises his eyes and says, ' Take, O Holy Trinity, this oblation, which I, unworthy sinner, offer in honour of thee, of the blessed Virgin Mary, and of all the saints, for the salvation of the living, and for the rest and quiet of all the faithful that are dead.' Then, setting down the chalice, he says, ' Let this sacrifice be acceptable to Almighty God.'" The name *paten* is preserved in the English Liturgy to this day. In the prayer of consecration, in the communion service—in connection with the words, " who, in the same night that he was betrayed, took bread," it is said, " here the priest is to take the *paten* into his hands." CALVIN, when commenting upon Rom. xvi. 16, after having stated that it was customary among the primitive Christians, before partaking of the Lord's Supper, to kiss each other in token of sacred friendship, and afterwards to give alms, says, " Hinc fluxit ritus ille, qui hodie est apud Papistas, *osculandæ patenæ*, et conferendæ oblationis. Quorum alterum meræ est superstitionis, sine ullo fructu : alterum non alio facit, nisi ad explendam sacerdotum avaritiam, si tamen expleri posset ;"—" From this has sprung that ceremony which is at this day among Papists, of *kissing the patine*, and making an offering. The former is mere superstition without any advantage : the latter serves no purpose, except to *satisfy* the greed of the priests, if *satisfied* it can be." *Poole*, in his Annotations on Rom. xvi. 16, says, " The primitive Christians did use it" (the *holy kiss*) " in their assemblies ; so *Tertullian* testifieth, (Lib. Dec.,) and they did it especially in receiving the Eucharist. So Chrysostom witnesseth, (Hom. 77 in Joh. xvi.,) ' we do well,' saith he, ' to kiss *in the mysteries*, that we may become *one*.'

selves—not merely in their minds[1] and in needful services, but also by that token, provided only it was *holy,* that is, neither unchaste nor deceitful,[2]—though, at the same time, *holy* may be taken to mean *sacred.*

22. *If any man love not the Lord Jesus.* The close of the Epistle consists of *three* parts. He entreats the grace of Christ in behalf of the Corinthians: he makes a declaration of his love towards them, and, with the severest threatening, he inveighs against those that falsely took upon themselves the Lord's name, while not loving him from the heart. For he is not speaking of strangers, who avowedly hated the Christian name, but of pretenders and hypocrites, who troubled the Churches for the sake of their own belly, or from empty boasting.[3] On such persons he denounces an anathema, and he also pronounces a curse upon them. It is not certain, however, whether he desires their destruction in the presence of God, or whether he wishes to render them odious—nay, even execrable, in the view of believers. Thus in Gal. i. 8, when pronouncing one who corrupts the Gospel to be *accursed,*[4] he does not mean that he was rejected or condemned by God, but he declares that he is to be abhorred by us. I expound it in a simple way as follows: "Let them perish and be cut off, as being the pests of the Church." And truly, there is nothing that is more pernicious, than that class of persons, who prostitute a profession of piety to their own depraved affections. Now he points out the origin of this evil, when he says, that they do not love Christ, for a sincere and earnest love to Christ will not suffer us to give occasion of offence to brethren.[5]

This custom for good reasons is laid down, and the *Romanists* in room of it, keep up a foolish and superstitious ceremony, which is to *kiss the pax* in the mass."—*Ed.*

[1] " Par affection interieure ;"—" By inward affection."

[2] " Ou consistast en mine seulement ;"—" Or consisted in mere appearance."

[3] " Ne cherchans que le proufit de leurs ventres, et leur propre gloire ;" —" Seeking only the profit of their bellies, and their own glory."

[4] CALVIN, when commenting on Gal. i. 8, remarks that the original term there employed, *anathema,* denotes *cursing,* and answers to the Hebrew word חֵרֶם; and he explains the expression—" let him be accursed," as meaning, " Let him be held by you as accursed."

[5] " Car si nous aimons Christ purement, et à bon escient, ce nous sera

What he immediately adds — *Maranatha,* is somewhat more difficult. Almost all of the ancients are agreed, that they are Syriac terms.[1] Jerome, however, explains it: *The Lord cometh;* while others render it, *At the coming of the Lord,* or, *Until the Lord comes.* Every one, however, I think, must see how silly and puerile is the idea, that the Apostle spoke to Greeks in the Syriac tongue, when meaning to say — *The Lord has come.* Those who translate it, *at the coming of the Lord,* do so on mere conjecture; and besides, there is not much plausibility in that interpretation. How much more likely it is, that this was a customary form of expression among the Hebrews, when they wished to excommunicate any one. For the Apostles never speak in foreign tongues, except when they repeat anything in the person of another, as for example, *Eli, Eli, lammah sabathani,* (Matt. xxvii. 46,) *Talitha cumi,* (Mark v. 41,) and *Ephphata,* (Mark vii. 34,) or when they make use of a word that has come into common use, as *Amen — Hosanna.* Let us see, then, whether *Maranatha* suits with excommunication. Now Bullinger,[2] on the authority of Theodore Bibliander, has affirmed, that,

vne bride qui nous retiendra de donner scandale à nos freres;"—"For if we love Christ sincerely and in good earnest, this will be a bridle to restrain us from giving offence to our brethren."

[1] " Que ce sont mots empruntez de la langue Syrienne;"—" That they are words borrowed from the Syriac language."

[2] Beza, in his poems, has recorded the following tribute to the memory of this distinguished man—

" HENRICI BULLINGERI, Ecclesiastæ Tigurini, spectatiss. doctrinæ, pietatis, et eximii candoris viri, memoriae;"—(To the memory of HENRY BULLINGER, ecclesiastick of Tigurum, a man most distinguished for learning and piety, and extraordinary candour.)

" Doctrina si interire, si Pietas mori,
    Occidere si Candor potest :
Doctrina, Pietas, Candor, hoc tumulo iacent,
    Henrice, tecum condita.
Mori sed absit illa posse dixerim;
    Quae viuere jubent mortuos,
Immo interire forsan illa si queant
    Subireque tumuli specum,
Tu tu, illa doctis, tu piis, tu candidis,
    Et non mori certissimis,
Edaci ab ipsa morte chartis asseras,
    Ipso approbante Numine.
Fœdus beatum! mortuum illa te excitant,
    Et tu mori illa non sinis :

in the Chaldee dialect, *Maharamata* has the same meaning as the Hebrew term הרם, *cherem*, (*accursed*,)[1] and I was myself at one time assured of the same thing by Wolfgang Capito,[2] a man of blessed memory. It is nothing unusual, however, for the Apostles to write such terms differently from the way in which they are pronounced in the language from which they are derived; as may be seen even from the instances brought forward above. Paul, then, after pronouncing an anathema on those who *do not love Christ*,[3] deeply affected with the seriousness of the matter, as if he reckoned that he had not said enough, added a term that was in common use among the Jews, and which they made use of in pronouncing a sentence of anathema—just as if, speaking in

> At hunc, amici, cur fleamus mortuum,
>   Qui viuat aliis et sibi ?"
>
> "If Learning could expire, if Piety could die,
>   If Candour could sink down,
> Learning, Piety, Candour, are laid in this mound,
>   O Henry, buried along with thee !
> But forbid that I should say that those things could die,
>   Which command the dead to live.
> Nay, if they could possibly expire,
>   And be entombed,
> Thou, by thy writings learned, pious, candid,
>   And perfectly secured against death,
> Wouldst shield them from devouring death,
>   The Deity himself approving.
> Blessed agreement !   *They* raise *thee* up from death,
>   And *thou* dost not suffer *them* to die !
> But, my friends, why should we weep for him, as *dead*,
>   Who *lives* to others and himself?"
>   *Beza's* " Poemata Varia," p. 59.—*Ed.*

[1] Thus in 1 Kings xx. 42, we have the expression, איש־חרמי, (*ish cheremi,*) *the man of my curse,* or *the man whom I anathematize.*   See also Is. xxxiv. 5; Zech. xiv. 11.—*Ed.*

[2] CALVIN, when commenting on Phil. iii. 5, having occasion to speak of the etymology of the term *Pharisees*, says that he considered it to be derived—not as was commonly supposed, from a word signifying to *separate* —but from a term denoting *interpretation*, this having been the view given of it by *Capito*—" sanctae memoriae viro,"—" a man of sacred memory." It is stated by Beza in his life of CALVIN, that when at Basle, CALVIN lived on intimate terms with those two distinguished men, Simon Grynæus and Wolfgang Capito, and devoted himself to the study of Hebrew.—CALVIN's Tracts, vol. i. p. xxvii.—*Ed.*

[3] " Ayant excommunié, et declaré execrables ceux-la qui n'aiment point Iesus Christ;"—" Having excommunicated, and pronounced execrable those who do not love Jesus Christ."

Latin, I should say, " I excommunicate thee," but if I add
—" and pronounce thee an anathema," this would be an expression of more intense feeling.[1]

---

[1] " Μαρὰν ἀθὰ (Maran atha) is a Syro-Chaldee expression, signifying ' the
Lord is to come,' i.e., will come, to take vengeance on the disobedient
and vicious. Hence with the words Anathema Maranatha the Jews began their papers of excomunication."—*Bloomfield*.

END OF THE COMMENTARIES ON THE FIRST EPISTLE.

THE

COMMENTARIES OF JOHN CALVIN

ON

THE SECOND EPISTLE OF PAUL THE APOSTLE

TO THE

CORINTHIANS.

TRANSLATOR'S PREFACE.

THE EPISTLES OF PAUL TO THE CORINTHIANS contain more of admonition and reproof than most of his other Epistles. While THE CHURCH OF CORINTH was more than ordinarily distinguished in respect of spiritual gifts, it had fallen into corruptions and abuses, from which the other Churches appear to have been, to a great extent, free. There is, accordingly—as might be expected—in these Epistles, more frequent reference to local evils, than in most of the other Epistles of the New Testament. They are not, however, on that account the less adapted for general utility. While the reproofs which they contain were occasioned by the corrupt state of a particular Church, they will be found to involve general principles of the highest importance to the Church of Christ under all circumstances. The Epistles to the Corinthians " have," says Dr. Guyse, in his Preface to the *Second* Epistle, " some advantages that are not to be met with in any other part of the word of God, as they may be deemed the seat of divine directions, relating to the spiritual privileges, rights, and powers, worship and discipline of the Churches of Christ; to the purity of doctrines, manners, and celebrations of Gospel ordinances ; and to the unity, peace, and order, mutual watch and care, and religious respect to faithful pastors, that ought to be preserved among them."

As, in the perusal of the four Gospels, the attentive reader can scarcely fail to observe, that many of the instructive sayings of our blessed Lord, which are placed on record by the Evangelists, arose naturally out of occurrences of an accidental nature,—though taking place under the watchful superintendence of him *without whom not even a sparrow falleth on the ground,* (Matt. x. 29,)—so we find a large portion of the invaluable directions furnished in the Epistles of the New Testament for the regulation of the Church in every subsequent age, presented *incidentally*—as if suggested to the mind of the sacred writer by corruptions of doctrine and practice, into which some particular Church in the primitive age had been left to fall. While the unhappily corrupt state of the Church of Corinth, as indicated in the two Epistles addressed to it, tended to mar, in no inconsiderable degree, the prosperity of the cause of Christ in that city, and was an occasion of poignant grief to the mind of Paul, who felt the more solicitous for their welfare from his sustaining to them the relationship—not simply of an *instructor*, but of a *father*, (1 Cor. iv. 15,) the flagrant abuses which had crept in among them were, in the providence of God, overruled for good to the Church of Christ generally, by giving occasion for a fuller development than might otherwise have been necessary, of some of the most important principles of practical Christianity.

The Epistles to the Church of Corinth are a portion of Paul's writings, which, as is justly observed by DR. ALEXANDER, in his Preface to BILLROTH on the Corinthians, " occupies a very important place in the sacred canon. Besides containing some *loca classica* upon several of the most essential positions in doctrinal theology, such, for instance, as the deity of Christ, the personality and agency of the Holy Spirit, the resurrection of the body, &c., the two Epistles to the Corinthians may be regarded as constituting the great code of practical ethics for the Christian Church. In this respect they stand to the science of practical theology in a relation analogous to that occupied by the Epistles to the Romans, the Galatians, and the Hebrews, to the science of systematic divinity ; they contain the fullest development of those principles on which that science must rest, and the practices which its rules are to authorize or inculcate."[1]

What increases not a little the utility of Paul's Epistles

---

[1] *Biblical Cabinet,* vol. xxi. pp. v. vi.

to the Corinthian Church is the circumstance that the *latter* Epistle was written by him a considerable time (about a year, it is generally supposed) subsequently to the *former*, when opportunity had been given for the Apostle's receiving accounts as to the effect produced upon the minds of the Corinthians by the faithful, though at the same time affectionate counsels and admonitions, which he had addressed to them in his *first* Epistle. The Apostle had been intensely anxious as to the effect, which his former Epistle might produce on the minds of the Corinthians. While his authority as an Apostle, and that too in a Church which he had himself planted, was at stake, he was, we may believe, chiefly concerned for the purity of doctrine and discipline, as in danger of being seriously impaired by the corrupt state of the Church of Corinth. With feelings of deep solicitude he left Ephesus, where it is generally believed he wrote his *first* Epistle to the Corinthian Church,[1] and proceeded to Troas, a sea-port town on the coast of the Ægean Sea, hoping to meet with Titus there on his return from Corinth. Disappointed in this expectation, he went forward to Macedonia, where he at length met with Titus, and received most gratifying accounts as to the favourable reception, which his former Epistle had met with from the Corinthians, and the salutary effect which it had produced in remedying, to a great extent, the evils that he had found occasion to censure.

It must have afforded to the mind of the Apostle no ordinary satisfaction to learn, that his admonitions and reproofs had awakened in the minds of the Corinthians the most poignant grief in reflecting on the unworthy part which they had acted—that they had manifested unabated esteem and affection toward him as their spiritual father—that they had, in accordance with his instructions, excluded from their society a gross offender, whose unnatural crime they had too long connived at; and farther, that the exercise of discipline in that painful case had been most salutary in its effects upon the offender himself, so that the Apostle, from what he had learned as to the evidences of repentance, was now prepared to in-

[1] See p. 70.

struct the Corinthian Christians to receive him back, without hesitation or delay, into their fellowship. He had, also, the satisfaction of learning, that his exhortations, in the close of his former Epistle, to liberality in contributing for the relief of the "poor saints at Jerusalem," had been promptly and cheerfully responded to. While Paul's *second* Epistle to the Corinthians furnishes in these and other respects, express proofs of the beneficial effects of his *former* Epistle, his entire silence in the *latter* Epistle in reference to various evils unsparingly censured by him in the *former*, gives reason to believe that, in connection with these also, a more hopeful state of matters had begun to appear. Among these we may notice their party contendings, their vexatious lawsuits, their corrupt administration of the Sacred Supper, their disorderly exercise of spiritual gifts, and, in fine, their erroneous views on the important subject of the resurrection.

Thus "the success" of the first Epistle to the Corinthians, as is justly observed by BARNES, in the Introduction to his Notes on that Epistle, "was all that Paul could desire. It had the effect to repress their growing strifes, to restrain their disorders, to produce true repentance, and to remove the person who had been guilty of incest in the Church. The whole Church was deeply affected with his reproofs, and engaged in hearty zeal in the work of reform. (2 Cor. vii. 9-11.) The authority of the Apostle was recognised, and his Epistle read with fear and trembling. (2 Cor. vii. 15.) The act of discipline which he had required on the incestuous person was inflicted by the whole Church. (2 Cor. ii. 6.) The collection which he had desired, (1 Cor. xvi. 1-4,) and in regard to which he had boasted of their liberality to others, and expressed the utmost confidence that it would be liberal, (2 Cor. ix. 2, 3,) was taken up agreeably to his wishes, and their disposition on the subject was such as to furnish the highest satisfaction to his mind. (2 Cor. vii. 13, 14.) Of the success of his letter, however, and of their disposition to take up the collection, Paul was not apprised until he had gone into Macedonia, where Titus came to him, and gave him information of the happy state of things in the Church at Corinth. (2 Cor. vii. 4-7, 13.) Never was a letter more effectual than this was, and never was authority in discipline exercised in a more happy and successful way."

At the same time, Paul's *second* Epistle to the Corinthian Church is of a mixed character, being designed in part to rectify evils still existing among them, and to vindicate the Apostle from injurious aspersions, thrown out against him by the false teachers. In various parts of the Epistle, but more particularly toward the close, he establishes his claims to apostolical authority.

A succinct view of the general tenor and design of this Epistle is given by POOLE, in his Annotations, in the following terms :—" The occasion of his" (Paul's) " writing this second Epistle seemeth to be partly the false teachers aspersing him: 1. As an *inconstant man*, because he had promised to come in person to Corinth, and was not yet come ; the reason of which he showeth, chap. i., was not levity, but the troubles he met with in Asia, and his desire to hear that they had first reformed the abuses he had taxed them for. 2. As an *imperious man*, because of the incestuous person against whom he had wrote ; which charge he avoids, by showing the necessity of his writing in that manner, and giving new orders for the restoring him, upon the repentance he had showed. 3. As a *proud* and *vain-glorious man*. 4. As a *contemptible person—base in his person*, as he expresseth it. The further occasions of his writing were—to commend them for their kind reception of, and compliance with, the precepts and admonitions of his former Epistle, and their kind reception of Titus—as also to exhort them to a liberal contribution to the necessities of the saints in Judea, to which they had showed their forwardness a year before ; and his hearing that there was yet a party amongst them bad enough, that went on vilifying him and his authority, as well as in other sinful courses ; against whom he vindicateth himself, magnifying his office, assuring them that he was about to come to Corinth, when they should find him present, such as being absent he had by his letters declared himself, if they were not reformed.

" The substance, therefore, of this Epistle, is partly *apologetical*, or *excusatory*, where he excuseth himself for his not

coming to Corinth so soon as he thought, and for his so
severe writing as to the incestuous person—partly *hortatory*,
where he persuadeth them *more generally* to walk worthy
of the gospel; *more specially* (chap. viii. 9) to a liberal
contribution to the saints—partly *minatory* or *threatening*,
where he threateneth severity against those whom, when he
came amongst them, he should find contumacious and im-
penitent offenders. He concludes the Epistle (as usually)
with a salutation of them, pious exhortations to them, and
a prayer for them."

CALVIN, it will be observed, dedicates his Commentary on
the *second* Epistle to the Corinthians to MELCHIOR WOLMAR,
a man of great celebrity, under whom CALVIN acquired a
knowledge of the Greek language. "The academy of Bourges," says BEZA, in his Life of Calvin, "had . . . acquired
great celebrity through ANDREW ALCIAT, (undoubtedly the
first lawyer of his age,) who had been invited to it from
Italy. CALVIN thought right to study under him also. He
accordingly went thither, and on grounds both religious and
literary, formed a friendship with MELCHIOR WOLMAR, a
German from Rothweil, and professor of Greek. I have the
greater pleasure in mentioning his name, because he was
my own teacher, and the only one I had from boyhood up
to youth. His learning, piety, and other virtues, together
with his admirable abilities as a teacher of youth, cannot be
sufficiently praised. On his suggestion, and with his assistance, CALVIN learned Greek. The recollection of the benefit
which he thus received from WOLMAR he afterwards publicly
testified, by dedicating to him his Commentary on the First"
(*Second*) "Epistle to the Corinthians."[1]

The circumstances connected with his attendance on the
instructions of that distinguished teacher are interesting, as
giving occasion to mark the leadings of providence in preparing CALVIN for the important work, which was afterwards
assigned him in the Church of Christ. His father had originally intended him for the ministry, and procured for him
a benefice in the cathedral church of Noyon, and afterwards
the rectory of Pont-Eveque, the birthplace of his father.

---

[1] CALVIN's *Tracts*, vol. i. pp. xxiii. xxiv.

Not long afterwards, however, his father resolved to send him to study civil law, as a more likely means of worldly preferment, while in the mean time CALVIN, having been made acquainted with the doctrines of the reformed faith by one of his own relations, PETER ROBERT OLIVET, had begun to feel dissatisfied with the Romish Church, and had left off attendance on the public services of the Church. With the view of devoting himself to the study of law, he removed to Orleans, and placed himself under the tuition of PETER DE L'ETOILE, a French lawyer of great celebrity, and made in a short time surprising progress, so that very frequently, in the absence of the professors, he supplied their place, and was regarded as a teacher rather than a pupil. He afterwards went to Bourges, with the view of prosecuting the study of law under the celebrated ANDREW ALCIAT. While there he formed, as is stated in the foregoing extract from BEZA's Life of Calvin, an intimate friendship with MELCHIOR WOLMAR, his instructor in the Greek tongue. Having received intimation of the sudden death of his father, he broke off abruptly the studies in which he was engaged, and having returned to Noyon, his native town, he soon afterwards devoted himself to other and higher pursuits. The study of civil law, to which he had devoted himself for a time, in compliance with his father's wishes, though ultimately abandoned, was not without its use, in connection with those sacred pursuits to which his subsequent life was devoted. It may be interesting to the reader to observe unequivocal evidences of this, as furnished in the following encomiums pronounced upon CALVIN by two eminent writers of sound and unbiassed judgment:—

" A founder," says Hooker, "it" (the Presbyterian polity) "had, whom, for mine own part, I think incomparably the wisest man that ever the French Church did enjoy, since the hour it enjoyed him. *His bringing up was in the study of the civil law.* Divine knowledge he gathered, not by hearing and reading, so much as by teaching others. For, though thousands were debtors to him as touching knowledge in that kind, yet he to none but only to God, the Author of that most blessed fountain, the Book of Life, and of the admirable dexterity of wit, together with the helps of other learning, which were his guide."[1] "CALVIN," says M. D'ALEMBERT, "who with justice enjoyed a high reputation, was a scholar of the first order. He wrote in Latin as well as is possible in a dead language, and in French with a purity that was extraordinary for his time. This purity, which is to the present day admired by our critics, renders his writings greatly superior to almost all of the same age; as the works of MM. de Port Royal are still distinguished on the same account, from the barbarous rhapsodies of their opponents and contemporaries. CALVIN *being a skilful lawyer*, and as enlightened a divine as a heretic can be, *drew up, in concert with the magistrates, a code of laws*," &c.[2]

While CALVIN's large acquirements in the study of civil law were thus eminently serviceable in other and higher departments of labour, the other branch of study cultivated by him while at Bourges—the knowledge of the Greek tongue—was more directly fitted to prepare him, though he little thought of it at the time, for the sacred pursuits in which Providence called him to engage, with devotedness and success, in after years. Under the tuition of WOLMAR, he appears to have applied himself to the study of the Greek language with the greatest diligence and ardour. "He did not indeed," says THOLUCK, "learn Greek before his residence in Bourges, but he could not have been then, at most, more than twenty-two years old; and it is not therefore strange, that, with his resolute spirit, he made himself complete master of it."[3] His instructor in this department, MELCHIOR WOLMAR, was a man of distinguished talent, and of high moral worth. BEZA, who, as we have seen, expresses in his Life of CALVIN, in the strongest terms, his esteem for WOLMAR, his sole instructor, has furnished in his *Icones*, (French edition,) entitled, "Les vrais Pourtraits des Hommes illustres," (à Génève 1581, pp. 148-51,) the following interesting sketch of the leading particulars of the life of this distinguished man.

---

[1] *Hooker's* Ecclesiastical Polity, pref., p. 44. Folio. Lond. 1676.
[2] *Encyclopédie*, Art. *Génève*.
[3] Merits of CALVIN, p. 26.

" MELIOR WOLMAR of Rotweil, Professor of Civil Law, and of the Greek Language, in the University of Tübingen, (originally called MELCHIOR, but latterly JOACHIM CAMERARIUS, a very learned personage, and also Professor of Literature in Tübingen, admiring the probity of Wolmar, softened the name and changed it thus,) was born at Rotweil, which is an allied town of the Cantons, was brought up at Berne, and studied at Paris, where he immediately became well known for his admirable expertness in the Greek and Latin languages, as also in the town of Orleans, and more particularly at Bourges, where, being in the pay of MARGARET OF VALOIS, QUEEN OF NAVARRE, and Duchess of Berry, he read in Greek and in Latin, was admitted as teacher by the advice of ANDREW ALCIAT, the prince of lawyers in our times. Farther, his house was frequented by men that were learned and fearers of God, among whom must be numbered JOHN CALVIN, who had no hesitation in placing himself under Wolmar, to learn from him the Greek language, he having opened a school expressly for certain young men of good family and of great hope, in which he succeeded so admirably, that there could not have been found a man better qualified for the successful training of youth, and there was no one who had educated in a proper manner so large a number as he had done.

" France would have reaped more fruits of Melior's industry, had not the persecutions that arose against the Church of God, and respect for ULRICH, DUKE OF WITTEMBERG, by whom he was invited, drawn him away to Tübingen in the year 1535, when, having read in law, and having interpreted Greek authors during upwards of twenty years with great honour, he was at length permitted to resign. Having retired, with his wife, named Margaret, to Isne, a town belonging to that lady, he was attacked with paralysis, and at the end of some months, he and his wife (overcome as she was with grief) died on the same day—it being the will of God, that those whom a sacred friendship had held bound during the space of twenty-seven years complete, should be inclosed in the same tomb.

" He was an accomplished personage in all the gifts that are requisite for making a man accomplished. Above all he was amazingly charitable to the poor, and at the same time so remote from ambition, that, while he had the Greek and Latin languages at his command, he put to the press nothing but an elegant preface,[1] introductory to the Grammar of Demetrius Chalcondyles.

"Having had in my childhood, as my preceptor, so distinguished a personage, (revered by me, while he lived, as my own father), I have bewailed his death, and that of his wife, in three Latin Epigrams, now rendered into French. He died at Isne in the year 1561, at the age of 64 years.

I.

Vous, que le sainct lien de mariage assemble,
En ces deux contemplez d'vn mariage heureux,
L'exemplaire certain et rare tout ensemble,
MELIOR, Marguerite, en mesme iour es cieux,
Se virent esleuez. Ainsi ceux que la vie
Auoit apariez eurent par mesme mort,
La vie en mesme tombe à la mort asseruie,
Attendant ce iour plaisant et lumineux,
Que de l'heur eternel ils iouiront tous deux.

II.

MELIOR, le meilleur, et le plus docte aussi
     Qu'ait bienheuré ce temps ci,
Es tu donques couché, muet, dessous la charge
     D'vn tombeau pesant et large ?
Et ton disciple parle et demeure debout ?
     Las ! oui, mais iusques au bout
Le viure et le parler desormais le martyre :
     Car son cœur rien ne desire,

---

[1] It is stated by *Lemprière*, in his Universal Dictionary, (Art. *Wolmar Melchior*,) that Wolmar " wrote Commentaries on the two first Books of the Iliad." Beza's meaning evidently is, that he did not publish any *original work.—Ed.*

Sinon en mesme creux estre pres toy couché
   Puis qu'auec toy gist caché
Le beau chœur des neuf sœurs, du ciel de fauorites,
   La douceur, les Charites.

III.

Mausolee superbe, et vous, tant rechantees,
En l'Egypte iadis Pyramides plantees,
A iust occasion vous pouuez d'vn faux œil
Regarder maintenant de ces deux le cercueil.
Il n'y a rien meilleur que nostre Melior,[1]
La perle ou Marguerite[2] est d'Inde le Thresor.

---

[1] There is here, obviously, a play upon words, (common in that age,) founded on the coincidence between the names of *Melior* and *Margaret* with *melior* (*Fr. meilleur*) *better*, and *margarita* (*Fr. marguerite*) a *pearl.* —*Ed.*

[2] The original versions of the *first* and *third* Epigrams are given in Beza's " Poemata Varia," (Genevæ, 1614,) p. 47, as follows :—

" MELIORIS VOLMARII, patria Rotvillensis, viri spectatiss. tum pietatis, tum doctrinæ, praeceptoris perpetua memoria colendi, et Margaritæ ipsius coniugis : uno eodemque die fato functorum, et eodem tumulo conditorum, Memoriæ ;"—" To the memory of MELCHIOR WOLMAR, a native of Rotweil, a man most highly esteemed at once for piety and learning, an instructor to be ever kept in remembrance, and Margaret, his spouse, who died on one and the same day, and were buried in the same tomb "

" Coniugii exemplum rarum, certumque beati
   Spectate cuncti coniuges :
Una dies nobis Meliorem sustulit, una
   Et Margaritam sustulit :
Sic uno quos vita thoro coniunxerat, uno
   Mors una tumulo condidit :
Una ambos donec reddat lux unius olim
   Beatitatis compotes."

" Quum tumulo lateat Melior Volmarius isto,
   Cui Margarita adest comes,
Est illi cur inuideas Mausole, diuque
   Celebrata Pyramidum strues,
Namque nihil melius Meliore, nec India quidquam
   Fert Margarita carius."

In addition to the above, two Latin Epigrams by Beza, in honour of Wolmar, are to be found in his " Poemata Varia : "—

" In MELIOREM VOLMARUM praeceptorem summe observandum, doctissime Homerum in Academia Bituricensi interpretantem, anno Domini cIɔIɔxxxiv, quum ageret annum Beza xv.

CALVIN'S COMMENTARY ON THE SECOND EPISTLE TO THE
CORINTHIANS appears to have been published by him only a
few months after his Commentary on the *First* Epistle, his
dedication to his Commentary on the *Second* Epistle bearing
date 1st August 1546, while his *first* dedication to the Commentary on the *First* Epistle bears date 24th January 1546.

In SENEBIER'S Literary History of Geneva, quoted in CAL-
VIN on Genesis, (vol. i. p. xviii.) a list of CALVIN'S Commentaries is given in the order in which they are supposed to have
been published. In that list the Commentary on the Epistle
to the Romans is placed first in order, and is stated to have
been published in 1540. Next in order is the "Commentary
on all the Epistles of Paul," which is stated to have been
published in 1548. It will be observed, however, that while
the Commentary on the Epistle to the Romans is supposed
to have been published in 1540, the *first* dedication to the
Commentary on the *First* Epistle to the Corinthians, and the
dedication to the Commentary on the *Second* Epistle, both
of them bear date 1546. It is stated by BEZA in his Life of
Calvin, that during the contentions which prevailed in the
Church in 1548, and some preceding years, CALVIN was "not
only not idle, but, as if he had been living in retirement,

> " Flacce, tibi quandoque bonus dormitat Homerus,
>   Sed num propterea caecus Homerus erat ?
> Immo oculis captus quinam credatur Homerus,
>   Quem sequitur vatum caetera turba ducem ?
> Illius sed enim splendorem longa vetustas
>   Obruerat densis, heu, nimium tenebris.
> Tu Melior, donec fato meliora renato
>   Dux ipsi fieres, Volmare magne, duci."
>   BEZA'S " *Poemata Varia,*" p. 77.

> " MELIORI VOLMARO praeceptori, summe observando.
> Ergo placet nostros iterum vulgare furores ?
>   Ergo semel non est desipuisse satis ?
> Sic, Volmare, iubes : et ego tibi (quaeso) iubenti
>   Quid tandem iusta cum ratione negem ?
> Quid facerem ? quæ nos tibi consecrauimus olim,
>   Eripere haec eadem quo tibi iure queam ?
> Adde, quod ipse tuus quum sit quoque muneris auctor
>   Haec quum dona petis, tu tua dona petis.
> Fama igitur valeat, nos iam nil fama moratur
>   Fas, tibi quo placeam, displicuisse mihi."
>   BEZA'S " *Poemata Varia,*" p. 87.

wrote most learned commentaries on six of Paul's Epistles."[1] The six Epistles referred to appear to have been the two Epistles to the Corinthians, and the Epistles to the Galatians, Ephesians, Philippians, and Colossians, CALVIN's Commentary on the last four of these having been published, as appears from the dedication prefixed to it, in 1548.

What is chiefly of importance to be observed, in connection with the respective dates of the Epistles above referred to, is the circumstance noticed by BEZA—that CALVIN wrote his "most learned Commentaries" on those Epistles "*as if he had been living in retirement,*" while in reality amidst scenes, which would have incapacitated any ordinary mind for such pursuits. In the careful study of these interesting portions of the Volume of Inspiration, CALVIN's devout mind found refreshment amidst scenes of turmoil; and we cannot doubt, that while preparing, under circumstances like these, his Commentaries on the Epistles to the Corinthians, and most of Paul's other Epistles, he had ample experience of what he himself so beautifully expresses, when commenting on Psalm cxix. 50, *This is my comfort in my affliction, for thy word hath quickened me :* "The Prophet ...... had good reason for stating, that in the time of affliction the faithful experience animation and vigour solely from the *word of God inspiring them with life.* Hence, if we meditate carefully on his word, we shall live even in the midst of death, nor will we meet with any sorrow so heavy for which it will not furnish us with a remedy. And if we are bereft of consolation and succour in our adversities, the blame must rest with ourselves; because, despising or overlooking the word of God, we purposely deceive ourselves with vain consolation."[2]

J. P.

ELGIN, *June* 1849.

---

[1] CALVIN's *Tracts,* vol. i. p. liii.
[2] CALVIN on the Psalms, vol. iv. p. 437

THE AUTHOR'S DEDICATORY EPISTLE.

TO THAT MOST ACCOMPLISHED MAN,

MELCHIOR WOLMAR RUFUS, LAWYER.

JOHN CALVIN,

HEALTH.

SHOULD you be disposed to charge me, not merely with neglect, but even with incivility, for not having written to you
for so long a time, I confess I have scarcely any apology to
offer.   For if I were to allege that the distance between us
is so great, and that, during fully five years, I have met with
no one that was going in your direction, this indeed were
true, but it would be, I readily acknowledge, but a lame excuse.   It appeared to me, accordingly, that I could not do
better than offer to you some compensation, that might make
up for the errors of the past, and might at once set me clear
from all blame.   Here, then, you have a commentary on the
Second Epistle of Paul to the Corinthians, prepared by me
with as much care as was in my power.[1]   For I have no
doubt that you will, in your kindness, accept of this as a
sufficient compensation.   At the same time there are other
and weightier considerations, that have induced me to dedicate this to you.

First of all, I remember with what fidelity[2] you cherished
and strengthened the friendship, which had begun, (now long
since,) in some small degree, to subsist between us—how

---

[1] " Composé et dressé par moy, auec le plus grand soin et dexterite qu'il
m'a este possible;"—" Composed and prepared by me with the utmost
care and skill in my power."
[2] " De quelle affection;"—" With what affection."

generously you were prepared to lay out yourself and your services on my account, when you thought that you had an opportunity presented to you of testifying your affection towards me; how carefully you made offer to me of your assistance[1] for my advancement, had not the calling in which I was at that time engaged prevented me from availing myself of it. Nothing, however, has had greater weight with me than the recollection of the first time I was sent by my father to learn civil law. Under your direction and tuition, I conjoined with the study of law Greek literature, of which you were at that time a most celebrated professor.[2] And certainly it was not owing to you that I did not make greater proficiency; for, with your wonted kindness of disposition, you would have had no hesitation in lending me a helping hand for the completion of my course, had I not been called away by my father's death, when I had little more than started. I am, however, under no small obligations to you in this respect, that I was initiated by you in the rudiments, at least, which were afterwards of great advantage to me. Hence I could not satisfy myself without leaving to posterity some memorial of my gratitude, and at the same time rendering to you some fruit, such as it is, of your labour.[3] Farewell.

GENEVA, 1st *August* 1546.

---

[1] " Votre credit ;"—" Your influence."   [2] See p. 94.
[3] " De vostre labeur ancien, duquel ie sens encore auiourd'huy le proufit ;"—" Of your ancient labour, of which I feel even at this day the advantage."

THE ARGUMENT

ON THE

SECOND EPISTLE TO THE CORINTHIANS.

So far as we can judge from the connection of this Epistle, it appears that the *first* Epistle was not without some good effect among the Corinthians,[1] but at the same time was not productive of so much benefit as it ought to have been ; and farther, that some wicked persons, despising Paul's authority, persisted in their obstinacy. For the fact of his being so much occupied, at one time in declaring his fidelity, and at another in maintaining the dignity of his office, is itself a token that they had not as yet been thoroughly confirmed. He himself, too, complains in express terms, that there were some that made sport of his former Epistle, instead of deriving benefit from it. Understanding, then, the condition of the Church among them to be such, and being detained by other matters, so as to be prevented from coming to them so soon as he had at that time contemplated, he wrote this Epistle from Macedonia. We are now in possession of the purpose which he had in view in writing this Epistle—that he might perfect what he had already begun, in order that he might, when he came, find every thing in proper order.

He begins, as he is wont, with thanksgiving, rendering thanks to God, that he had been marvellously rescued from the most imminent dangers, and at the same time he calls them to notice, that all his afflictions and distresses tended to their benefit and welfare, that he may the better secure

---

[1] " N'auoit point este du tout inutile et sans fruit;"—" Was not altogether useless and without fruit."

their favour by this farther pledge of union,[1] while the wicked perversely took occasion from this to lessen his influence. Farther, when wishing to apologize for delaying to come to them, he declares that he had not changed his purpose from lightness or unsteadiness, and that he had not, for the purpose of deceiving, professed anything that he had not really had in view ;[2] for there was the same consistency to be seen by them in all his sayings, that they had had experience of in his doctrine. Here, too, he briefly notices, how stable and sure was the truth of his preaching, as being founded on Christ, by whom all the promises of God are fixed and ratified—which is a high recommendation of the gospel.

After this he declares, that the reason why he had not come was this, that he could not appear among them cheerful and agreeable. In this statement, he reproves those, who, from his change of purpose, took occasion to calumniate him. He accordingly throws the blame upon the Corinthians, as being not yet well prepared for receiving him. He shows, at the same time, with what fatherly forbearance he was actuated, inasmuch as he kept himself back from visiting their city for this reason—that he might not be under the necessity of exercising severity upon them.

Farther, lest any one should object, that he had in the mean time not at all refrained from handling the Corinthians severely in his writings, he apologizes for the vehemence that he made use of in his first Epistle, by saying that it was owing to others—they having shut him up to the necessity of this against his will. That this keenness had proceeded from a friendly disposition he satisfactorily shows, by ordering that the incestuous person himself, on whose account he had been much exasperated, should be received back into favour, having since that time given some evidence of repentance. Farther, he brings forward this additional

[1] " Afin que cela luy serue d'vn gage et nouueau lien pour entrer en leur bonne grace ;"—" That this may serve as a pledge and new tie to establish them in their good graces."

[2] " Qu'il n'a point pretendu de les tromper, leur donnant à entendre d'vn, et pensant d'autre ;"—" That he had not intended to deceive them, by giving them to understand one thing while he was thinking of another."

evidence of his affection towards them, that he *had no rest
in his mind* (2 Cor. ii. 13) until he had learned through
means of Titus the state of their affairs, for an anxiety of
this kind originates in affection.

Having had occasion, however, to make mention here of
his journey to Macedonia, he begins to speak of the glory
of his ministry. As, however, those darling Apostles, who
endeavoured to detract from him, had obtained an easy
victory over him by trumpeting their own praises, that he
may have nothing in common with them, and that he may
at the same time beat down their foolish boasting, he declares that he derives commendation from the work itself,[1]
and does not borrow it from men. In the same passage, he
extols in magnificent terms the efficacy of his preaching,
and sets off to advantage the dignity of his Apostleship by
comparing the gospel with the law, declaring, however, first
of all, that he claimed nothing as his own, but acknowledged
everything, whatever it might be, to have come forth from
God.

After this he relates again, with what fidelity and integrity he had discharged the office intrusted to him, and in
this he reproves those who malignantly reproached him.
Nay more, rising still higher in holy confidence, he declares,
that all are blinded by the devil, who do not perceive the
lustre of his gospel. Perceiving, however, that the meanness of his person (as being contemptible)[2] detracted much
from the respect due to his Apostleship, embracing this favourable opportunity, he does not merely remove this occasion
of offence, but turns it into an opposite direction, by saying,
that the excellence of God's grace shines forth so much the
more brightly, from the circumstance that so valuable a *treasure was presented in earthen vessels.* (2 Cor. iv. 7.) Thus
he turns to his own commendation those things which the
malevolent were wont to cast up to him by way of reproach,
because on his being weighed down with so many distresses,

---

[1] " De l'auancement de l'œuure ;"—" From the advancement of the
work."
[2] " Comme de faict il estoit contemptible au monde ;"—" As in fact he
was contemptible in the view of the world."

he always, nevertheless, after the manner of the palm tree,[1] rises superior to them. He treats of this subject up to the middle of the *fourth* chapter. As, however, the true glory of Christians lies beyond this world, he teaches that we must, by contempt of this present life and mortification of the *outward man,* set ourselves with the whole bent of our mind to meditation on a blessed immortality.

Farther, near the beginning of the *fifth* chapter, he glories in this—that being actuated by such a disposition, he has nothing else as the object of his desire, than to have his services approved unto the Lord, and he entertains a hope, that he will have the Corinthians as witnesses of his sincerity. As, however, there was a danger of his being suspected of vanity, or arrogance, he again repeats, that he is constrained to this by the unreasonableness of wicked persons, and that it was not for his own sake, as though he were eager to retain their good opinion, but for the benefit of the Corinthians, to whom it was of advantage to have this opinion and persuasion ; and he declares that he is concerned for nothing but their welfare. With the view of confirming this, he subjoins a universal statement, showing what ought to be the object aimed at by the servants of Christ— that, losing sight of themselves, they should live to the honour of their Lord ; and at length he concludes, that everything except newness of life ought to be reckoned of no importance, so that he alone, who has denied himself, is to be held in esteem. From this he passes on to unfold the sum of the Gospel message, that by the magnitude and excellence of it he may stir up both ministers and people to a pious solicitude. This he does in the beginning of the *sixth* chapter.

Here again, after having noticed how faithfully he dis-

---

[1] The palm is one of the most beautiful trees in the vegetable kingdom; it is upright, lofty, verdant, and embowering. It grows by the brook or well of living water ; and, *resisting every attempt to press or bend it downwards,* shoots directly towards heaven. For this reason, perhaps, it was regarded by the ancients as peculiarly sacred, and, therefore, most frequently used in adorning their temples. The chosen symbol of constancy, fruitfulness, patience, and victory ; *the more it is oppressed the more it flourishes, the higher it grows, and the stronger and broader the top expands.*"—*Paxton's* Illustrations, (Edin. 1842,) vol. ii. p. 51.—*Ed.*

charged his office, he gently reproves the Corinthians, as
being hinderances to themselves in the way of their reaping
advantage. To this expostulation he immediately subjoins
an exhortation, to *flee from idolatry*—from which it appears,
that the Corinthians had not yet been brought so far as he
wished. Hence it is not without good reason that he complains, that they had themselves to blame, inasmuch as they
had not had their ears open to doctrine so plain. But lest
he should, by pressing too severely their tender minds, dis-
hearten or alienate them, he again assures them of his kind
disposition towards them, and resuming his apology for
severity, which he had left off in a manner abruptly, he
brings it to a conclusion, though in a different way. For
assuming greater confidence, he acknowledges that he is not
dissatisfied with himself for having grieved them, inasmuch
as he had done it for their good;[1] while at the same time,
by congratulating them on the happy issue, he shows them
how cordially he desires their best interests. These things
he treats of to the end of the *seventh* chapter.

From the beginning of the *eighth* chapter to the end of
the *ninth*, he stirs them up to cheerfulness in giving alms,
of which he had made mention in the last chapter of the
first Epistle. He commends them, it is true, for having
begun well, but lest the ardour of their zeal should cool in
process of time, as often happens, he encourages them by a
variety of arguments to go on perseveringly in the course on
which they had entered.

In the *tenth* chapter he begins to defend himself, and his
office as an Apostle, from the calumnies with which the
wicked assailed him. And in the first place, he shows that
he is admirably equipped with the armour that is requisite
for maintaining Christ's warfare.[2] Farther, he declares, that
the authority which he had exercised in the former Epistle
was grounded on the assurance of a good conscience, and he
shows them that he had no less power in his actions, when

---

[1] " Pour ce que ce qu'il en auoit fait, estoit tourné à leur grand proufit ;"—" Because, what he had done had turned out to their great advantage."

[2] " Pour bataillier sous l'enseigne de Iesu Christ :"—" For fighting under
the banners of Jesus Christ."

present, than authority in his words when absent. Lastly, by instituting a comparison between himself and them, he shows how vain their boasting is.[1]

In the *eleventh* chapter he calls upon the Corinthians to renounce those depraved inclinations, by which they had been corrupted, showing them that nothing is more dangerous than to allow themselves to be drawn aside from the simplicity of the Gospel. The fact of his having begun to be somewhat disesteemed among them, while others had been more favourably received by them, had arisen, as he shows, not from any fault on his part, but from their being haughty or nice to please ; inasmuch as those others had brought them nothing better or more excellent, while he was contemptible in their view because he did not set himself off to advantage by elegance of speech,[2] or because he had, by voluntary subjection, by way of humouring their weakness, given up his just claim. This irony[3] contains in it an indirect reproach for their ingratitude, for where was the reasonableness of esteeming him the less, because he had accommodated himself to them ? He declares, however, that the reason why he had refrained from taking the wages to which he was entitled, was not that he had less affection to the Corinthians,[4] but in order that no advantage might be gained over him in any respect by the false apostles, who, he saw, laid snares for him by this stratagem.

Having reproved the unreasonable and malignant judgment of the Corinthians, he magnifies himself in a strain of pious glorying, letting them know in what magnificent terms he could boast, were he so inclined, premising how-

---

[1] " Finalement, faisant comparaison de sa personne auec telles gens, il monstre que c'est folie à eux de s'esleuer et vanter ainsi, sans auoir dequoy ;"—" Lastly, by drawing a comparison between himself and such persons, he shows that it is folly in them to exalt themselves and vaunt, as they did, without having any ground for doing so."

[2] " Par vne eloquence de paroles ornees et magnifiques ;"—" By an eloquence of elegant and magnificent words."

[3] " Qui est vne façon de parler par ironie (c'est à dire par maniere de mocquerie) ;"—" Which is an instance of irony, that is to say, by way of mockery."

[4] " Qu'enuers les autres Eglises ;"—" Than to the other Churches."

ever, that it is for their sakes that he acts the fool[1] in
heralding his own praises.   At length, checking himself, as
it were, in the middle of the course, he says that his chief
ground of glorying is that abasement which was despised by
the proud, for he had been admonished by the Lord, not to
glory in anything but in his infirmities.

Towards the close of the *twelfth* chapter he again expos-
tulates with them for shutting him up to the necessity of
thus playing the fool, while they give themselves up to ambitious men,[2] by whom they are estranged from Christ.
Farther, he inveighs keenly against those who wantonly
raged against him, adding to their previous crimes this impudence of opposition.[3]

In the *thirteenth* chapter, by forewarning such persons,
that he will treat them with peculiar severity, he exhorts all
in general to recognise his apostleship, as it will be for their
advantage to do so ; while it is a dangerous thing for them
to despise one, whom they had found by experience to be a
trusty and faithful ambassador from the Lord.

---

[1] " Que pour l'amour d'eux il est contraint de faire du sot ;"—" That it
is from love to them, that he is constrained to act the fool."

[2] " Ils se laissoyent manier et gouuerner à un tas d'ambitieux ;"—
" They allowed themselves to be directed and governed by a band of ambitious men."

[3] " Ne se contentans point de leurs fautes passees, sinon qu'ils pour-
suyuissent de luy resister impudemment ;"—" Not contented with their
previous faults, without persisting in impudently opposing him."

COMMENTARY

SECOND EPISTLE TO THE CORINTHIANS.

CHAPTER I.

1. Paul, an apostle of Jesus Christ by the will of God, and Timothy *our* brother, unto the Church of God which is at Corinth, with all the saints which are in all Achaia:

2. Grace *be* to you, and peace, from God our Father, and *from* the Lord Jesus Christ.

3. Blessed *be* God, even the Father of our Lord Jesus Christ, the Father of mercies, and the God of all comfort;

4. Who comforteth us in all our tribulation, that we may be able to comfort them which are in any trouble, by the comfort wherewith we ourselves are comforted of God.

5. For as the sufferings of Christ abound in us, so our consolation also aboundeth by Christ.

1. Paulus Apostolus Iesu Christi per voluntatem Dei, et Timotheus frater, Ecclesiæ Dei quæ est Corinthi, cum sanctis omnibus qui sunt in tota Achaia:

2. Gratia vobis et pax a Deo Patre nostro, et Domino Iesu Christo.

3. Benedictus Deus, et Pater Domini nostri Iesu Christi, Pater misericordiarum, et Deus omnis consolationis,

4. Qui consolatur nos in omni tribulatione nostra, ut possimus consolari eos qui in omni tribulatione sunt, per consolationem qua consolatur nos Deus.

5. Quia sicuti abundant passiones Christi in nos: ita per Christum abundat etiam consolatio nostra.

1. *Paul an Apostle.* As to the reasons why he designates himself an *Apostle of Christ,* and adds that he has obtained this honour *by the will of God,* see the foregoing Epistle, where it has been observed that none are to be listened to but those, who have been sent by God, and speak from his mouth, and that, consequently, to secure authority for any one, two things are required—a call, and fidelity on the part of the person who is called, in the execution of his

office.[1] Both of these Paul claims for himself. The false apostles, it is true, do the same; but then, by usurping a title that does not belong to them, they gain nothing among the sons of God, who can with the utmost ease convict them of impertinence. Hence the mere name is not enough, if there be not the reality along with it, so that he who gives himself out as an Apostle must also show himself to be such by his work.

To the Church of God. We must always keep it in view, his recognising a Church to exist, where there was such a conflux of evils. For the faults of individuals do not prevent a society that has genuine marks of religion[2] from being recognised as a Church.[3] But what does he mean by the expression—*with all saints?* Were those *saints* unconnected with the Church? I answer, that this phrase refers to believers, who were dispersed hither and thither, throughout various corners of the province—it being likely, that in that greatly disturbed period, when the enemies of Christ were everywhere venting their rage, many were scattered abroad, who could not conveniently hold sacred assemblies.

3. *Blessed be God.* He begins (as has been observed) with this thanksgiving—partly for the purpose of extolling the goodness of God—partly, with the view of animating the Corinthians by his example to the resolute endurance of persecutions; and partly, that he may magnify himself in a strain of pious glorying, in opposition to the malignant slanderings of the false apostles. For such is the depravity of the world, that it treats with derision martyrdoms,[4] which it ought to have held in admiration, and endeavours to find matter of reproach in the splendid trophies of the pious.[5]

---

[1] See CALVIN on the Corinthians, vol. i. p. 48.

[2] See CALVIN on the Corinthians, vol. i. pp. 51, 52.

[3] " A true child of God may have sad falls, as we see in Peter and David, yet for all this not be quite excluded out of the covenant of grace: they did not lose their sonship, even in those sad transgressions, and will God be more severe to a whole Church than to one person?"—*Burgesse* on 2 Cor. i. p. 76. (Lond. 1661.)—*Ed.*

[4] " Des martyres et afflictions des fideles;"—" The martyrdoms and afflictions of believers."

[5] " Cherche matiere de mespris et diffamation aux enseignes magnifiques de victoire, lesquelles Dieu dresse à ses enfans;"—" Seeks matter

Blessed be God, says he.   On what account ? *who comforteth us*[1]—the relative being used instead of the causal particle.[2] He had endured his tribulations with fortitude and alacrity : this fortitude he ascribes to God, because it was owing to support derived from his consolation that he had not fainted.

He calls him the *Father of our Lord Jesus Christ,* and not without good reason, where blessings are treated of ; for where Christ is not, *there* the beneficence of God is not.   On the other hand, where Christ intervenes, *by whom the whole family in heaven and earth is named,* (Eph. iii. 15,) *there* are all mercies and all consolations of God—nay, more, *there* is fatherly love, the fountain from which everything else flows.

4. *That we may be able to comfort.*   There can be no doubt, that, as he had a little before cleared his afflictions from reproach and unfavourable reports, so now he instructs the Corinthians, that his having come off victorious through heavenly consolation was for their sake and with a view to their advantage, that they may stir themselves up to fellowship in suffering, instead of haughtily despising his conflicts.   As, however, the Apostle lived not for himself but for the Church, so he reckoned, that whatever favours God conferred upon him, were not given for his own sake merely,[3] but in order that he might have more in his power for helping others.   And, unquestionably, when the Lord confers upon us any favour, he in a manner invites us by his example to be generous to our neighbours.   The riches of the Spirit, therefore, are not to be kept by us to ourselves, but every one must communicate to others what he has received. This, it is true, must be considered as being applicable chiefly to ministers of the Word.[4]   It is, however, common to all,

---

of contempt and defamation in those splendid tokens of victory, which God furnishes to his children."

[1] " *Who is comforting* (ὁ παρακαλῶν)—that doth never cease to do it, that never withdraweth his consolations.   It is his nature to be *always comforting*—as the devil is called ὁ πειράζων, because he is *always tempting.*"—*Burgesse* on 2 Cor. p. 157.—*Ed.*

[2] " Ce mot, *Qui,* est mis pour *Car,* ou, *Pource que ;*"—" This word, *Who,* being used instead of *For,* or, *Because.*"

[3] " Pour son proufit particulier ;"—" For his own private advantage."

[4] " It is not enough for the ministers of the gospel to have devoured

according to the measure of each.   Thus Paul here acknowledges, that he had been sustained by the *consolation of God,
that he might be able himself to comfort others.*

5. *For as the sufferings of Christ abound.*—This statement
may be explained in two ways—actively and passively.   If
you take it *actively,* the meaning will be this : "The more I
am tried with various afflictions, so much the more resources
have I for comforting others." I am, however, more inclined to take it in a *passive* sense, as meaning that God
multiplied his consolations according to the measure of his
tribulations.   David also acknowledges that it had been
thus with him : *According to the multitude,* says he, *of my
anxieties within me, thy consolations have delighted my soul.*
(Ps. xciv. 19.)   In Paul's words, however, there is a fuller
statement of doctrine ; for the afflictions of the pious he calls
the *sufferings of Christ,* as he says elsewhere, that *he fills up
in his body what is wanting in the sufferings of Christ.*   (Col.
i. 24.)

The miseries and vexations, it is true, of the present life
are common to good and bad alike, but when they befall the
wicked, they are tokens of the curse of God, because they
arise from sin, and nothing appears in them except the anger
of God and participation with Adam, which cannot but
depress the mind.   But in the mean time believers are conformed to Christ, and *bear about with them in their body
his dying, that the life of Christ may one day be manifested
in them.*   (2 Cor. iv. 10.)   I speak of the afflictions which
they endure *for the testimony of Christ,* (Rev. i. 9,) for although the Lord's chastisements, with which he chastises
their sins, are beneficial to them, they are, nevertheless, not
partakers, properly speaking, of Christ's sufferings, except in
those cases in which they *suffer on his account,* as we find
in 1 Peter iv. 13.   Paul's meaning then is, that God is al-

many books of learning, to be able to decide polemical questions in divinity,
to convince gainsayers, to be doctors angelical, subtle or profound ; to be
mallei hereticorum—the *hammers of heretics.*   Unless also they have the
experimental works of God's Spirit upon their own souls, they are not
able to apply themselves to the hearts of others.   Paul had not been able
to *comfort others,* if the Lord had not practically acquainted him with
heavenly consolations."—*Burgesse* on 2 Cor. i. p. 178.—*Ed.*

ways present with him in his tribulations, and that his infirmity is sustained by the consolations of Christ, so as to prevent him from being overwhelmed with calamities.

6. And whether we be afflicted, *it is* for your consolation and salvation, which is effectual in the enduring of the same sufferings which we also suffer : or whether we be comforted, *it is* for your consolation and salvation.

7. And our hope of you *is* stedfast, knowing, that as ye are partakers of the sufferings, so *shall ye be* also of the consolation.

8. For we would not, brethren, have you ignorant of our trouble which came to us in Asia, that we were pressed out of measure, above strength, insomuch that we despaired even of life :

9. But we had the sentence of death in ourselves, that we should not trust in ourselves, but in God which raiseth the dead :

10. Who delivered us from so great a death, and doth deliver ; in whom we trust that he will yet deliver *us :*

11. Ye also helping together by prayer for us, that, for the gift *bestowed* upon us by the means of many persons, thanks may be given by many on our behalf.

6. Sive autem affligimur pro vestra consolatione et salute,[1] quæ efficitur in tolerantia ipsarum passionum, quas et nos patimur : sive consolationem accipimus pro vestra consolatione et salute :

7. Spes nostra firma est de vobis,[2] scientes, quod quemadmodum socii estis passionum, ita et consolationis.

8. Nolo enim vos nescire, fratres, de tribulatione nostra, quæ accidit nobis in Asia : nempe quod praeter modum gravati fuerimus supra vires, ita ut de vita quoque anxii essemus.

9. Quin etiam[3] ipsi in nobis ipsis sententiam mortis acceperamus : ne confideremus in nobis, sed in Deo, qui ad vitam suscitat mortuos :

10. Qui ex tanta morte eripuit nos, et eripit, in quo spem fixam habemus, quod etiam posthæc eripiet ;

11. Simul adiuvantibus et vobis per deprecationem pro nobis : ut donum, ex multis personis erga nos collatum, gratiarum actione per multos[4] celebretur pro nobis.

6. *Whether we are afflicted.* From the circumstance that before the clause *our hope of you is steadfast,* there is introduced the connecting particle *and,* Erasmus has conceived the idea, that some word must be understood to correspond with those words—*for your consolation and salvation*—in this way, *whether we are afflicted,* IT IS *for your consolation.* I think it, however, more probable, that the connecting par-

---

[1] " *Pour vostre consolation et salut, ou, C'est pour vostre ;*"—" *For your consolation and salvation,* or, *It is for your,*" &c.

[2] " *Nostre esperance est ferme de vous, ou, Et l'esperance que nous auons de vous est ferme, scachans ;*"—" *Our hope is firm respecting you,* or, *And the hope which we have respecting you is firm. Knowing.*"

[3] " *Mesme, ou, Mais ;*"—" *Nay more,* or, *But.*"

[4] " *Pour l'esgard de plusieurs personnes, ou, Par le moyen de plusieurs personnes ;*"—" *For the sake of many persons,* or, *By means of many persons.*"

ticle *and* is used here as meaning: *Thus also,* or *in both
cases.* He had already stated, that he received consolation
in order that he might communicate it to others. Now he
goes a step farther, and says, that he has a *steadfast hope,*
that they *would be partakers of the consolation.* Besides,
some of the most ancient Greek manuscripts introduce
immediately after the first clause this statement—*and our
hope of you is steadfast.*[1] This reading removes all ambiguity. For when it is introduced in the middle, we must
necessarily refer it to the latter clause, equally as to the
former. At the same time, if any one wishes to have a
complete sentence in each clause, by supplying some verb,
there will be no great harm in this, and there will be no
great difference as to the meaning. For if you read it as
one continued statement, you must, at the same time, explain the different parts in this manner—that the Apostle
is afflicted, and is refreshed with consolation for the advantage of the Corinthians; and that he entertains, therefore,
the hope,[2] that they will be at length partakers of the same
consolation, with what is in reserve for himself. For my
own part, I have adopted the way that I have judged the
more suitable.

It is, however, to be observed, that the word *afflicted* here
refers not merely to outward misery, but also to that of the
mind, so as to correspond with the opposite term *comforted.*
(παρακαλεῖσθαι.) Thus the meaning is, that the person's
mind is pressed down with anxiety from a feeling of misery.[3]
What we render *consolation,* is in the Greek παράκλησις—a
term which signifies also *exhortation.* If, however, you understand that kind of consolation, by which a person's mind
is lightened of grief, and is raised above it, you will be in
possession of Paul's meaning. For example, Paul himself
would well-nigh have fallen down dead under the pressure

---

[1] Dr. Bloomfield, who gives to this reading of the passage his decided
preference, says of it: " The evidence in its favour is exceedingly strong;
while that for the common reading is exceedingly weak."—*Ed.*

[2] " Qu'il ha certain espoir;"—" That he has a sure hope."

[3] Θλίψις, says Dr. Bloomfield, in his Notes on Matt. xxiv. 9, " properly
signifies *compression,* and figuratively constraint, oppression, affliction, and
persecution."—*Ed.*

of so many afflictions, had not God encouraged him, by raising him up by means of his consolation. Thus, too, the Corinthians derive strength and fortitude of mind from his sufferings,[1] while they take comfort from his example. Let us now sum up the whole matter briefly. As he saw that his afflictions were made by some an occasion of holding him in contempt, with the view of calling back the Corinthians from an error of this nature,[2] he shows in the first place that he ought to be in high esteem among them, in consideration of advantage redounding to themselves ; and then afterwards he associates them with himself, that they may reckon his afflictions to be in a manner their own. " Whether I suffer afflictions, or experience consolation, it is all for your benefit, and I cherish an assured hope, that you will continue to enjoy this advantage."[3]

For such were Paul's afflictions, and his consolations also, that they would have contributed to the edification of the Corinthians, had not the Corinthians of their own accord deprived themselves of the advantage redounding from it. He, accordingly, declares his confidence in the Corinthians to be such, that he entertains the assured hope that it will not be vain, that he has been afflicted, and has received consolation for their advantage. The false apostles made every effort to turn to Paul's reproach everything that befell him. Had they obtained their wish, the afflictions which he endured for their salvation, had been vain and fruitless ; they would have derived no advantage from the consolations with which the Lord refreshed him. To contrivances of this nature he opposes his present confidence. His afflictions tended to promote the comfort of believers, as furnishing them with occasion of confirmation, on their perceiving that he suffered willingly, and endured with fortitude so many hardships for the sake of the gospel. For however we may acknowledge that afflictions ought to be endured by us for the sake of the gospel, we, nevertheless, tremble through a

---

[1] " Voyans les passions du sainct Apostre ;"—" Beholding the sufferings of the holy Apostle."

[2] " Afin d'oster aux Corinthiens ceste mauuaise fantasie ;"—" With the view of ridding the Corinthians of this wicked fancy."

[3] " Iusques en la fin ;"—" Until the end."

consciousness of our weakness, and think ourselves not prepared for it.[1] In that case, we should call to mind the examples
of the saints, which should make us more courageous.

On the other hand, his personal consolation flowed out to
the whole Church, inasmuch as they concluded,[2] that God
who had sustained and refreshed him in his emergency,
would, in like manner, not be wanting to them. Thus their
welfare was promoted in both ways, and this is what he introduces as it were by way of parenthesis, when he says—
which is made effectual in the endurance, &c. For he wished
to add this clause, by way of explanation, that they might
not think that they had nothing to do with the afflictions
which he alone endured. Erasmus takes the participle ἐνερ-
γουμένης in an active sense,[3] but a passive signification is
more suitable,[4] as Paul designed simply to explain in what
respect everything that befell him was for their *salvation*.
He says, accordingly, that he suffers, indeed, alone, but that
his sufferings are of use for promoting their *salvation*—not
as though they were expiations or sacrifices for sins, but as
edifying them by confirming them. Hence he conjoins consolation and salvation, with the view of pointing out the
way in which their salvation was to be accomplished.

7. *Knowing, that as.* However there might be some of
the Corinthians that were drawn away for the time by the
calumnies of the false Apostles, so as to entertain less
honourable views of Paul, on seeing him shamefully handled
before the world, he, nevertheless, associates them with himself both in fellowship of afflictions, and in hope of consola-

---

[1] " Et ne pensons point estre assez forts ;"—" And do not think that we
are sufficiently strong."

[2] " Les fideles recueilloyent de là, et s'asseuroyent ;"—" Believers inferred from this, and assured themselves."

[3] " Traduisant, Qui œuure ou besongne ;"—" Rendering it, Which works
or labours."

[4] Dr. Bloomfield, in his Notes on 1 Thess. ii. 13, explains ἐνεργεῖται
to mean—" *is made effectual*," or " shews itself in its effects," and
adds : " This view I find supported by the opinion of Schott, who maintains
that ἐνεργεῖσθαι is never in the New Testament used as a *middle* form,
with an active sense ; but always (especially in St. Paul's writings) as a
passive. Indeed, BP. BULL, Exam. p. 9, goes yet farther, and asserts,
that it is scarcely ever so used, even in the *Classical* writers (I believe he
might have said *never*) but always in a passive sense."—*Ed.*

tion.[1] Thus he corrects their perverse and malignant view, without subjecting them to an open rebuke.

8. *For I would not have you ignorant.* He makes mention of the greatness and difficulty of his conflicts, that the glory of victory may thereby the more abundantly appear. Since the time of his sending them the former epistle, he had been exposed to great dangers, and had endured violent assaults. The probability, however, is that he refers here to the history, which Luke relates in Acts xix. 23, though in that passage he does not so distinctly intimate the extent of the danger. As, however, he states that *the whole city was in a tumult*, (Acts xix. 29,) it is easy from this to infer the rest. For we know what is the usual effect of a popular tumult, when it has been once kindled. By this persecution Paul declares he had been oppressed *beyond measure*, nay more, *above strength*, that is, so as not to be able to endure the burden. For it is a metaphor taken from persons who give way under the pressure of a heavy load, or from ships that sink from being overladen—not that he had actually fainted, but that he felt that his strength would have failed him, if the Lord had not imparted fresh strength.[2]

---

[1] " The Corinthians . . . . were *κοινωνοί partakers of*, or *in communion with him in his afflictions.* What is more humble and lowly (τὶ ταπεινοφρωνέστερον) than Paul in this expression? saith Chrysostom—they who had not in the least measure shared with him in sufferings, yet he maketh them copartners with him. They are, as Salmeron expresseth it, *Copartners in the gain and in the loss with Paul.* They venture (as it were) in the ship together."—*Burgesse.*—*Ed.*

[2] " *Pressed above measure.* (κὰθ᾽ ὑπερβολὴν ἐβαρήθημεν.) The words βάρος and βάρουμαι, are applied sometimes to the *enduring of a burden*, (Matt. xx. 12; Gal. vi. 2,) whether it be a temporal burden or spiritual . . . In this place it seemeth to be taken from porters, who have a burden imposed upon them, more than they are able to stand under; or as Chrysostom, from ships which are over much burdened, and so are in danger of being lost. And as if there were not emphasis enough in the word *pressed*, he addeth another to aggravate it—(κὰθ᾽ ὑπερβολὴν)—*above measure.* . . . *Above strength.* (ὑπὲρ δύναμιν.) Chrysostom observeth this differeth from the other. For a burden may be exceeding heavy, yet to some mighty man it may not be above his strength. When *Samson* (Judg. xvi. 3) carried away the gates of the city Gaza, with the posts and barre upon his shoulders, here was a burden out of measure heavy; no ordinary man could do so; but yet to *Samson* it was not above his strength. Thus it was with Paul, who may be called a *spiritual Samson*, for that heavenly might and power which God had endowed him with; he is assaulted with a trouble that was not only *hyperbolically weighty*, but also *above his strength.* Paul

So that we were in anxiety even as to life itself—that is,
"So that I thought life was gone, or at least I had very
little hope of it remaining, as those are wont to feel who are
shut up so as to see no way of escape." Was then so valiant
a soldier of Christ, so brave a wrestler, left without strength,
so as to look for nothing but death ?[1] For he mentions it as
the reason of what he had stated—that he *despaired of life.*
I have already observed, that Paul does not measure his
strength in connection with help from God, but according to
his own personal feeling of his ability. Now there can be
no doubt, that all human strength must give way before the
fear of death. Farther, it is necessary that even saints
themselves should be in danger of an entire failure of
strength, that, being put in mind of their own weakness,
they may learn, agreeably to what follows, to place their
entire dependence on God alone. At the same time I have
preferred to explain the word ἐξαπορεῖσθαι,, which is made
use of by Paul, as denoting a *trembling anxiety*, rather than
render it, as Erasmus has done by the word *despair;* because
he simply means, that he was hemmed in by the greatest
difficulties, so that no means of preserving life seemed to
remain.[2]

9. *Nay more, we had the sentence of death.* This is as
though we should say—" I had already laid my account
with dying, or had regarded it as a thing fixed." He borrows, however, a similitude from those who are under sentence of death, and look for nothing but the hour when they
are to die. At the same time he says, that this sentence
had been pronounced by him upon himself, by which he
intimates, that it was in his own view that he had been
sentenced to death—that he might not seem to have had it

had no more power to stand under it."—*Burgesse* on 2 Cor. i. pp. 269,
270, 278.—*Ed.*

[1] " Vn champion si preux et magnanime, perdoit-il courage attendant
la mort ?"—" Did a champion so valiant and magnanimous lose heart,
looking for nothing but death ?"

[2] Ἐξαπορεῖσθαι properly signifies to be utterly at a stand, not knowing how
to proceed.— In Psalms lxxxviii. 8, where David, says—*I am shut up, and
I cannot come forth,* the Hebrew words אֵצֵא אֹלוְ, (*velo etse,*) are rendered
in the Septuagint—καὶ οὐκ ἐξεπορευόμην—*and I could not come forth.* It
is worthy of notice that, in the metre version, the idea expressed by CALVIN,

from any revelation from God. In this *sentence*,[1] there-fore, there is something more implied than in the feeling of *anxiety* (ἐξαπορεῖσθαι) that he had made mention of, be-cause in the former case there was despair of life, but in this case there is certain death. We must, however, take notice, chiefly, of what he adds as to the design—that he had been reduced to this extremity, *that he might not trust in himself.* For I do not agree with what Chrysostom says—that the Apostle did not stand in need of such a remedy, but set himself forth to others as a pattern merely in ap-pearance.[2] For he was a man that was *subject,* in other respects, *to like passions* as other men—(James v. 17)—not merely to cold and heat, but also to misdirected confidence, rashness, and the like. I do not say that he was addicted to these vices, but this I say, that he was capable of being tempted to them, and that this was the remedy that God seasonably interposed, that they might not make their way into his mind.[3]

There are, accordingly, two things to be observed here. In the *first* place—that the fleshly confidence with which we are puffed up, is so obstinate, that it cannot be overthrown in any other way than by our falling into utter despair.[4] For as the flesh is proud, it does not willingly give way, and

as implied in the verb ἐξαπορεῖσθαι, is fully brought out—"find no *evasion* for me."—*Ed.*

[1] " The Greek word is ἀπόκριμα, used here in this place onely in the New Testament. . . . The most genuine translation is *sentence;* for so Hesychius expounds the word κατακρίμα—ψῆφος, whom *Favorinus* follow-eth *verbatim* in this, as in many other particulars. . . . The word then doth signifie a *sentence* passing upon him, *that he must die.* This he had received, but from whom? Not from God, for God delivered him; nor from the magistrate; there was no such decree that we read of against him. Therefore it was onely from his own feares, his own thoughts, which maketh him say—he *had received it in himself.* . . . God's thoughts were other than Paul's. Paul absolutely concluded he should die, but God had purposed the contrary."—*Burgesse.—Ed.*

[2] " Il se propose aux autres comme pour exemple, non pas qu'il en fust ainsi quant à luy ;"—"He sets himself forth, as it were by way of example —not that it had been so as to himself."

[3] " De peur qu'ils ne saisissent plenement son esprit et son cœur ;"— " That they might not take full possession of his mind and his heart."

[4] " Sinon que nous tombions en telle extremite que nous ne voyons aucune esperance en nous ;"—" Except by our falling into such an ex-tremity, that we see no hope in ourselves."

never ceases to be insolent until it has been constrained; nor are we brought to true submission, until we have been brought down by the *mighty hand of God.* (1 Peter v. 6.) *Secondly,* it is to be observed, that the saints themselves have some remains of this disease adhering to them, and that for this reason they are often reduced to an extremity, that, stript of all self-confidence, they may learn humility: nay more, that this malady is so deeply rooted in the minds of men, that even the most advanced are not thoroughly purged from it, until God sets death before their eyes. And hence we may infer, how displeasing to God confidence in ourselves must be, when for the purpose of correcting it, it is necessary that we should be condemned to death.

But in God that raiseth the dead. As we must first die,[1] in order that, renouncing confidence in ourselves, and conscious of our own weakness, we may claim no honour to ourselves, so even that were not sufficient, if we did not proceed a step farther. Let us begin, therefore, with despairing of ourselves, but with the view of placing our hope in God. Let us be brought low in ourselves, but in order that we may be raised up by his power. Paul, accordingly, having brought to nothing the pride of the flesh, immediately substitutes in its place a confidence that rests upon God. *Not in ourselves,* says he, *but in God.*

The epithet that follows, Paul has adapted to the connection of the subject, as he does in Rom. iv. 17, where he speaks of Abraham. For to *believe in God, who calleth those things that are not, as though they were,* and to *hope in God who raiseth the dead,* are equivalent to his setting before him as an object of contemplation, the power of God in creating his elect out of nothing, and raising up the dead. Hence Paul says, that death had been set before his eyes, that he might, in consequence of this, recognise the more distinctly the power of God, by which he had been raised up from the dead. The first thing in order, it is true, is this— that, by means of the strength with which God furnishes us, we should acknowledge him as the Author of life; but as

---

[1] " Comme il nous est necessaire premierement de venir comme à mourir;"—" As we need first to come as it were to die "

in consequence of our dulness the light of life often dazzles our eyes, it is necessary that we should be brought to God by having death presented to our view.[1]

10. *Who hath delivered us from so great a death.* Here he applies to himself personally, what he had stated in a general way, and by way of proclaiming the grace of God, he declares that he had not been disappointed in his expectation, inasmuch as he had been *delivered from death,* and that too, in no common form. As to his manner of expression, the hyperbole, which he makes use of, is not unusual in the Scriptures, for it frequently occurs, both in the Prophets and in the Psalms, and it is made use of even in common conversation. What Paul acknowledges as to himself personally, let every one now take home as applicable to himself.

In whom we have an assured hope. He promises himself as to the future, also, that beneficence of God, which he had often experienced in the past. Nor is it without good reason; for the Lord, by accomplishing in part what he has promised, bids us hope well as to what remains. Nay more, in proportion to the number of favours that we receive from him, does he by so many pledges, or earnests, as it were, confirm his promises.[2] Now, although Paul had no doubt that God would of his own accord be present with him, yet he exhorts the Corinthians to commend to God in their prayers his safety. For when he assumes it as certain, that he will be aided by them, this declaration has the force of an exhortation, and he means that they would not merely do it as a matter of duty, but also with advantage.[3]

---

[1] " Il nous est necessaire pour estre amenez à Dieu, d'estre reduits à telle extremite que nous voyons la mort presente deuant nos yeux;"—" It is necessary, in order that we may be brought back to God, that we should be brought to such an extremity, that we see death presented before our eyes."

[2] *Granville Penn* reads the passage as follows: "Who hath delivered us from so great a death; and *will deliver* us: in whom we hope that he will deliver us."—" The *Vat.* and *Ephrem* MSS." he observes, "read ῥύσεται, not ῥύεται, as in the *rec.* text. The latter reading seems to have been substituted, because ῥύεται occurs again in the following sentence; but the Apostle repeats the word, that he may qualify it by ἠλπίκαμεν, (we hope.")—*Ed.*

[3] " Mais aussi auec bonne issue, d'autant qu'ils seront exaucez;"—" But also with good success, inasmuch as they will be heard."

"Your prayers, also," he says, "will help me."[1] For God wills not that the duty of mutual intercession, which he enjoins upon us, should be without advantage. This ought to be a stimulus to us, on the one hand, to solicit the intercession of our brethren, when we are weighed down by any necessity, and, on the other, to render similar assistance in return, since we are informed, that it is not only a duty that is well pleasing to God, but also profitable to ourselves. Nor is it owing to distrust that the Apostle implores the friendly aid of his brethren,[2] for, while he felt assured, that his safety would be the object of God's care,[3] though he were destitute of all human help, yet he knew that it was well pleasing to God, that he should be aided by the prayers of the saints. He had respect, also, to the promises that were given, that assistance of this kind would not be in vain. Hence, in order that he might not overlook any assistance that was appointed to him by God, he desired that the brethren should pray for his preservation.

The sum is this—that we follow the word of God, that is, that we obey his commandments and cleave to his promises. This is not the part of those who have recourse to the assist-

---

[1] "L'aide, dit il, que vous me feriez par vos prieres, ne sera point sans fruit;"—"The aid, he says, that you will afford me by your prayers, will not be without advantage."

[2] "*You also helping together by prayer for us,* (Συνυπουργούντων καὶ ὑμῶν ὑπὲρ ἡμῶν τῇ δεήσει.) The particle καὶ is emphatical, *You also*—implying, that neither God's promise, nor his power, would procure this mercy alone without their prayer. Besides the goodness of God on his part, there must be prayer on their part. The word in the original for *helping* is emphatical, being twice compounded. Ὑπουργούντων doth denote the *service* and *ministry* of those who are *under* us; and so it doth imply, that the Church doth owe as a debt unto their spiritual guides earnest prayer for them. . . Then there is the preposition σὺν added, which doth denote not only their effectual prayers, but their *concord* and *agreement* therein, and that in their public and solemn assemblies. Again, the word signifying—to *work*, and *labour*, doth denote what the nature of prayer is—that the soul *labours* therein, is fervent, full of agonies; which showeth that the customary formal prayers of most people are not worthy of the name: there is no *labour*, or fervency of the soul therein.—They laboured by *prayer*. They did not labour by using friends to solicit the magistrate in Paul's behalf, for there was no hope from them, but they made their addresses to God."—*Burgesse.—Ed.*

[3] "Que Dieu auroit soin de son salut et proufit;"—"That God would take care of his safety and advantage."

ance of the dead ;[1] for not contented with the sources of help appointed by God, they call in to their aid a new one, that has no countenance from any declaration of Scripture. For whatever we find mentioned there as to mutual intercession, has no reference to the dead, but is expressly restricted to the living. Hence Papists act childishly in perverting those passages, so as to give some colour to their superstition.[2]

11. *That the gift bestowed upon us through means of many persons.* As there is some difficulty in Paul's words, interpreters differ as to the meaning. I shall not spend time in setting aside the interpretations of others, nor indeed is there any need for this, provided only we are satisfied as to the true and proper meaning. He had said, that the prayers of the Corinthians would be an assistance to him. He now adds a second advantage that would accrue from it—a higher manifestation of God's glory. "For whatever God will confer upon me," says he, "being as it were *obtained through means of many persons,* will, also, by *many* be celebrated with praises :" or in this way—"Many will give thanks to God in my behalf, because, in affording help to me, he has favourably regarded the prayers, not merely of one but of many." In the first place, while it is our duty to allow no favour from God to pass without rendering praise, it becomes us, nevertheless, more especially when our prayers have been favourably regarded by him, to acknowledge his mercy with thanksgiving, as he commands us to do in Psalm l. 15. Nor ought this to be merely where our own personal interest is concerned, but also where the welfare of the Church in general, or that of any one of our brethren is involved. Hence when we mutually pray one for another, and obtain our desire, the glory of God is so much the more set forth, inasmuch as we all acknowledge, with thanksgiving, God's benefits—both those that are conferred publicly upon the whole Church, and also those that are bestowed privately upon individuals.

---

[1] " Qui out leurs recours aux prieres des saincts trespassez ;"—" Who have recourse to the prayers of departed saints."

[2] " Pour desguiser et farder leur superstition ;"—" To disguise and colour over their superstition."

In this interpretation there is nothing forced ; for as to
the circumstance that in the Greek the article being introduced between the two clauses *by many persons*, and the *gift
conferred upon me* appears to disjoin them,[1] *that* has no force,
as it is frequently found introduced between clauses that are
connected with each other. Here, however, it is with propriety introduced in place of an adversative particle ;[2] for
although it had come forth from many persons, it was nevertheless peculiar to Paul. To take the phrase διὰ πολλῶν
(*by means of many*) in the neuter gender,[3] as some do, is at
variance with the connection of the passage.

It may, however, be asked, why he says *From many persons*, rather than *From many men*, and what is the meaning
of the term *person* here ? I answer, it is as though he had
said—*With respect to many*. For the favour was conferred
upon Paul in such a way, that it might be given to many.
Hence, as God had respect to many, he says on that account,
that many persons were the cause of it. Some Greek manuscripts have ὑπὲρ ὑμῶν—*on your account ;* and although
this appears to be at variance with Paul's design, and the
connection of the words, it may, nevertheless, be explained
with propriety in this manner : " When God shall have
heard you in behalf of my welfare, and that too for your own
welfare, thanks will be given by many on your account."

12. For our rejoicing is this, the
testimony of our conscience, that in
simplicity and godly sincerity, not
with fleshly wisdom, but by the grace
of God, we have had our conversation in the world, and more abundantly to you-ward.

12. Nam gloriatio nostra hæc
est : testimonium conscientiæ nostræ, quod in simplicitate et puritate[4]
Dei, non in sapientia carnali, sed in
gratia Dei versati sumus in mundo;
abundantius autem erga vos.

[1] " Car à suyure l'ordre du texte Grec il y auroit ainsi mot à mot, Afin
que de plusieurs personnes, à nous le don conferé, par plusieurs soit recognu
en action de graces pour nous ;"—" For, following the order of the Greek
text, it would be literally thus : In order that from many persons the gift
conferred upon us, may by many be acknowledged with thanksgiving on
our account."
[2] " En lieu de quelque particle aduersative qu'on appelle, comme Toutesfois ou Neantmoins ;"—" In place of some adversative particle, as it is
called, as for example, Notwithstanding or Nevertheless."
[3] " De rapporter ce mot *Par plusieurs*, aux choses ;"—" To take this
phrase, *By means of many*, as referring to *things*."
[4] " Purete, ou, integrite ;"—" Purity, or integrity."

13. For we write none other things unto you than what ye read or acknowledge, and I trust ye shall acknowledge even to the end ;

14. As also ye have acknowledged us in part, that we are your rejoicing, even as ye also *are* ours in the day of the Lord Jesus.

13. Non enim alia scribimus vobis quam quæ recognoscitis vel etiam agnoscitis : spero autem, quod usque in finem agnoscetis :

14. Quemadmodum et agnovistis nos ex parte : siquidem gloriatio vestra sumus : sicuti et vos nostra in die Domini Iesu.

12. *For our glorying is this.* He assigns a reason why his preservation should be a subject of interest to all—that he had conducted himself[1] among them all in *simplicity and sincerity.* He deserved, therefore, to be dear to them, and it would have been very unfeeling not to be concerned in reference to such a servant of the Lord, that he might be long preserved for the benefit of the Church. " I have conducted myself before all in such a manner, that it is no wonder if I have the approbation and love of all good men." He takes occasion from this, however, for the sake of those to whom he was writing, to make a digression for the purpose of declaring his own integrity. As, however, it is not enough to be approved of by man's judgment, and as Paul himself was harassed by the unjust and malignant judgments of some, or rather by corrupt and blind attachments,[2] he adduces his own conscience as his witness—which is all one as though he had cited God as a witness, or had made what he says matter of appeal to his tribunal.

But how does Paul's glorying in his integrity comport with that statement, *He that glorieth, let him glory in the Lord ?* (2 Cor. x. 17.) Besides, who is so upright[3] as to dare

---

[1] " *We have had our conversation* (ἀνεστράφημεν.) The verb ἀναστρέφω, is compounded of ἀνὰ, *again,* and στρέφω, to *turn*—a continual coming back again to the point from which he set out—a circulation—beginning, continuing, and ending everything to the glory of God ; setting out with divine views, and still maintaining them ; beginning in the Spirit, and ending in the Spirit ; acting in reference to God, as the *planets* do in reference to the *sun,* deriving all their light, heat, and motion from him ; and incessantly and regularly revolving round him. Thus acted Paul : thus acted the primitive Christians ; and thus must every Christian act who expects to see God in his glory."—*Dr. Adam Clarke.—Ed.*

[2] " Par les affections qu'ils portoyent à d'autres pour des raisons friuoles, et quasi sans scauoir pourquoy ;"—" By attachments that they cherished towards others on trivial grounds, and in a manner without knowing why."

[3] " Qui est celuy, tant pur et entier soit il?"—" Where is the man, be he ever so pure and perfect ?"

to boast in the presence of God ? In the first place, Paul does not oppose himself to God, as though he had anything that was his own, or that was from himself. Farther, he does not place the foundation of his salvation in that integrity to which he lays claim, nor does he make confidence in *that* the ground of his dependence. Lastly, he does not glory in God's gifts in such a way as not at the same time to render all the glory to him as their sole Author, and ascribe everything to him.[1] These three exceptions lay a foundation for every godly person glorying on good grounds in all God's benefits ; while the wicked, on the other hand, cannot glory even in God, except on false and improper grounds. Let us therefore, first of all, acknowledge ourselves to be indebted to God for everything good that we possess, claiming no merit to ourselves. Secondly, let us hold fast this foundation—that our dependence for salvation be grounded exclusively on the mercy of God. Lastly, let us repose ourselves[2] in the sole author of every blessing. Then in that there will be a pious[3] glorying in every kind of blessing.

That in the simplicity[4] *of God.* He employs the expression *simplicity of God* here, in the same way as in Rom. iii. 23, *the glory of God;* and in John xii. 43, *the glory of God and of men.* Those who love the *glory of men,* wish to appear something before men, or to stand well in the opinion of men. The *glory of God* is what a man has in the sight of God. Hence Paul does not reckon it enough to declare that his sincerity was perceived by men, but adds, that he was such in the sight of God. Εἰλικρινεία (which I have rendered *purity*) is closely connected with *simplicity;* for it is an open and upright way of acting, such as makes a man's heart as it were transparent.[5] Both terms stand opposed to craft, deception, and all underhand schemes.

---

[1] " Et rapporte toutes choses a sa bonte ;"—" And ascribes everything to his goodness."

[2] " Arrestons nous et reposons du tout ;"—" Let us stay ourselves, and wholly repose."

[3] " Bonne et saincte ;"—" Good and holy."

[4] " The most ancient MSS. read ἁγιοτητι, (*holiness*)—not ἁπλοτητι, (*simplicity.*)"—*Penn.*

[5] " The word used here—εἰλικρινείᾳ, and rendered *sincerity,* denotes properly—*clearness,* such as is judged of or discerned in sunshine, (from εἵλη,

Not in fleshly wisdom. There is here a sort of anticipation ; for what might be felt to be wanting in him he readily acknowledges, nay more, he openly proclaims, that he is destitute of, but adds, that he is endowed with what is incomparably more excellent—the *grace of God.* "I acknowledge," says he, "that I am destitute of *fleshly wisdom,* but I have been furnished with divine influence, and if any one is not satisfied with *that,* he is at liberty to depreciate my Apostleship. If, on the other hand, *fleshly wisdom* is of no value, then I want nothing that is not fitted to secure well-grounded praise." He gives the name of *fleshly wisdom* to everything apart from Christ, that procures for us the reputation of *wisdom.* See the *first* and *second* chapters of the former epistle. Hence, by the grace of God, which is contrasted with it, we must understand everything that transcends man's nature and capacity, and the gifts of the Holy Spirit, which openly manifested the power of God in the weakness of the flesh.

More abundantly towards you. Not that he had been less upright elsewhere, but that he had remained longer at Corinth, in order that he might (not to mention other purposes) afford a fuller and clearer proof of his integrity. He has, however, expressed himself intentionally in such a way as to intimate that he did not require evidences that were far-fetched, inasmuch as they were themselves the best witnesses of all that he had said.

13. *For we write no other things.* Here he indirectly reproves the false apostles, who recommended themselves by immoderate boastings, while they had little or no ground for it; and at the same time he obviates calumnies, in order that no one may object, that he claims for himself more than

sunshine, and κρίνω, to *judge,*) and thence pureness, integrity. It is most probable that the *phrase* here denotes that sincerity which God produces and approves; and the sentiment is, that pure religion, the religion of God, produces entire sincerity in the heart. Its purposes and aims are open and manifest, *as if seen in the sunshine.* The plans of the world are obscure, deceitful, and dark, *as if in the night."—Barnes.* The same term is made use of by Paul in 1 Cor. v. 8, and in 2 Cor. ii. 17. On comparing the various instances in which this term is employed by the Apostle, we have occasion to observe the admirable harmony between his exhortations and practice.—*Ed.*

is his due. He says, therefore, that he does not in words boast of anything that he is not prepared to make good by deeds, and that, too, from the testimony of the Corinthians.

The ambiguity, however, of the words, has given occasion for this passage being misinterpreted. Ἀναγινώσκειν, among the Greeks, signifies sometimes to *read*, and at other times to *recognise*. Ἐπιγινώσκειν sometimes signifies to *discover*, while at other times it means what the Latins properly express by the verb *agnoscere*, to *own*, as among lawyers the phrase is used to *own a child*,[1] as Budaeus also has observed. In this way ἐπιγινώσκειν means more than ἀναγινώσκειν. For we say that a person *recognises* a thing, that is, that being silently convinced of it in his judgment, he perceives it to be true, while at the same time he does not *acknowledge* it, or, in other words, cordially intimate his assent to it.

Let us now examine Paul's words. Some read thus— *We write no other things than what ye read and acknowledge*, which it is very manifest is exceedingly lifeless, not to say senseless. For as to Ambrose's qualifying the statement in this way—*You not only read, but also acknowledge*, there is no one that does not perceive that it is quite foreign to the import of the words. And the meaning that I have stated is plain, and hangs together naturally, and, up to this point, there is nothing to prevent readers from understanding it, were it not that they have had their eyes shut, from being misled by the different meanings of the word. The sum is this—that Paul declares, that he brings forward no other things than what were known and perceived by the Corinthians—nay more, things as to which they would bear him witness. The first term employed is *recognoscere*, (to *recognise*,) which is applicable, when persons are convinced from experience that matters are so. The second is *agnos-cere*, (to *acknowledge*,) meaning that they give their assent to the truth.[2]

---

[1] " Ce que disons *Auouer*: comme on dira *Auouer vn enfant;*"—" What we express by the verb to *own*, as when you speak of *owning a child*."

[2] The word ἀναγινώσκετε " properly means to *know accurately*, to *distinguish*. It is probably used here in the sense of knowing accurately or surely, of *recognising* from their former acquaintance with him." Ἐπιγιν-ώσκειν " here means that they would *fully recognise*, or know entirely to

And, I hope, will acknowledge even to the end.   As the Corinthians had not yet perfectly returned to a sound mind, so as to be prepared to weigh his fidelity in a just and even balance,[1] but at the same time had begun to abate somewhat of their perverse and malignant judgment respecting him, he intimates, that he hopes better as to the future. " You have already," says he, " to some extent acknowledged me.   I hope that you will acknowledge more and more what I have been among you, and in what manner I have conducted myself."[2]   From this it appears more clearly what he meant by the word ἐπιγινώσκειν. (*acknowledge.*[3])   Now this relates to a season of repentance, for they had at the beginning acknowledged him fully and thoroughly ; afterwards their right judgment had been beclouded[4] by unfair statements, but they had at length begun to return in part to a sound mind.

14. *For we are your glorying.*   We have briefly adverted to the manner in which it is allowable for saints to glory in God's benefits—when they repose themselves in God alone, and have no other object of aim.[5]   Thus it was a ground of pious glorying on the part of Paul, that he had, by his ministry, brought the Corinthians under obedience to Christ ; and of the Corinthians, on the other hand, that they had been trained up so faithfully and so virtuously by such an Apostle—a privilege that had not been allotted to all.   This

their satisfaction, that the sentiments which he here expressed were such as accorded with his general manner of life."—*Barnes.*   Dr. Bloomfield, who approves of the view taken by CALVIN of the meaning of the verb ἀναγινώσκετε, remarks, that the word is employed in the same sense by Xenophon.   Anab., v. 8, 6, as well as elsewhere in the Classical writers.—*Ed.*

[1] " C'est à dire, pour en iuger droitement ;"—" That is to say, to judge of it aright."

[2] " Que vous cognoistrez de plus en plus comme i'ay conversé entre vous, et comme ie m'y suis gouuerné, et ainsi auouërez ce que maintenant i'en di ;"—" That you will acknowledge more and more how I have conducted myself among you, and how I have regulated myself, and thus you will assent to what I now say."

[3] " Que c'est qu'il a entendu par le dernier des deux mots desquels nous auons parler, lequel nous auons traduit *Auouer ;*"—" What it was that he meant by the last of the two words of which we have spoken, which we have rendered—*Acknowledge.*"

[4] " Obscurci et abbastardi en eux par les propos obliques des faux-Apostres et autres malins ;"—" Obscured and corrupted by the unfair statements of the false Apostles, and other malicious persons."   [5] See p. 127.

way of glorying in men does not stand in the way of our glorying in God alone. Now he instructs the Corinthians, that it is of the greatest importance for themselves that they should acknowledge him to be a faithful, and not a merely pretended, servant of Christ; because, in the event of their withdrawing from him, they would deprive themselves of the highest glory. In these words he reproves their fickleness, inasmuch as they voluntarily deprived themselves of the highest glory, by listening too readily to the spiteful and envious.

In the day of the Lord. By this I understand the last day, which will put an end to all the fleeting[1] glories of this world. He means, then, that the glorying of which he is now speaking is not evanescent, as those things are that glitter in the eyes of men, but is abiding and stable, inasmuch as it will remain until the day of Christ. For *then* will Paul enjoy the triumph of the many victories that he had obtained under Christ's auspices, and will lead forth in splendour all the nations that have, by means of his ministry, been brought under Christ's glorious yoke; and the Church of the Corinthians will glory in having been founded and trained up by the services of so distinguished an Apostle.

15. And in this confidence I was minded to come unto you before, that ye might have a second benefit;

15. Et hac fiducia volui primum ad vos venire, ut secundam[2] gratiam haberetis, et per vos transire in Macedoniam:

16. And to pass by you into Macedonia, and to come again out of Macedonia unto you, and of you to be brought on my way toward Judea.

16. Et rursum e Macedonia venire ad vos, et a vobis deduci in Iudæam.

17. When I therefore was thus minded, did I use lightness? or the things that I purpose, do I purpose according to the flesh, that with me there should be yea, yea, and nay, nay?

17. Hoc igitur quum animo propositum haberem, nuncubi levitate usus sum? aut quæ cogito, secundum carnem cogito? ut sit apud me Etiam, etiam: et Non, non.

18. But *as* God *is* true, our word toward you was not yea and nay.

18. Fidelis Deus, quod sermo noster apud vos non fuit Etiam et non.

19. For the Son of God, Jesus Christ, who was preached among

19. Dei enim Filius Iesus Christus in vobis per nos praedicatus, per

---

[1] " Vaines et caduques ;"—" Empty and fading."

[2] " Seconde, *ou double* ;"—" Second, *or double.*"

| you by us, *even* by me, and Silvanus, and Timotheus, was not yea and nay, but in him was yea. | me, et Silvanum, et Timotheum, non fuit Etiam et non : sed Etiam fuit in ipso. |
| 20. For all the promises of God in him *are* yea, and in him Amen, unto the glory of God by us. | 20. Quæcunque enim sunt Dei promissiones, in illo sunt Etiam : quare et per ipsum sit Amen Deo ad gloriam per nos. |

15. *In this confidence.* After having given them reason to expect that he would come, he had subsequently changed his intention. This was made an occasion of calumny against him, as appears from the excuse that he brings forward. When he says that it was from relying on *this confidence* that he formed the purpose of coming to them, he indirectly throws the blame upon the Corinthians, inasmuch as they had, by their ingratitude, hindered, to some extent, his coming to them, by depriving him of *that confidence.*

That ye might have a second benefit. The *first* benefit had been this—that he had devoted himself for the entire period of *a year and six months* (Acts xviii. 11) to the work of gaining them to the Lord ; the *second* was their being confirmed, by means of his coming to them, in the faith which they had once received, and being stirred up by his sacred admonitions to make farther progress. Of this latter benefit the Corinthians had deprived themselves, inasmuch as they had not allowed the apostle to come to them. They were paying, therefore, the penalty of their own fault, and they had no ground for imputing any blame to Paul. If any one, however, prefers, with Chrysostom, to take χάριν (*benefit*) as used instead of χαράν, (*joy*,) I do not much object to it.[1] The former interpretation, however, is more simple.

17. *Did I use fickleness ?* There are two things, more especially, that prevent the purposes of men from being carried into effect, or their promises from being faithfully performed.

---

[1] " Most modern Commentators explain the χάριν *gift* or *benefit ;* but the ancient Commentators, and some modern ones, as Wolf and Schleus, *gratification* for χαράν. It should seem to mean *benefit* generally, every spiritual advantage, or gratification from his society, imparted by his presence."—*Bloomfield. One* MS. reads χαράν. *Kypke,* who renders χάριν *joy,* adduces instances in support of this meaning of χάρις, though acknowledged to be unusual, from *Plutarch, Polybius,* and *Euripides.* The phrase is rendered in Tyndale's version, (1534,) and also in Cranmer's, (1539,) and Geneva, (1557,) versions—*one pleasure moare.*—*Ed.*

The one is that they make changes upon them almost every hour, and the other is that they are too rash in forming their plans. It is a sign of changeableness to purpose or promise what you almost immediately afterwards regret. With that fault Paul declares he had not been chargeable. "I have not," says he, "through *fickleness* drawn back from the promise that I made." He declares also that he had been on his guard against rashness and misdirected confidence ; for such is the way in which I explain the expression—*purpose according to the flesh.* For it is, as I have stated, the common practice of men, as though they were not dependent on God's providence, and were not subject to his will, to determine rashly and presumptuously what they will do. Now God, with the view of punishing this presumption, defeats their plans, so as to prevent them from having a prosperous issue, and in many instances holds up themselves to ridicule.

The expression, it is true, *according to the flesh*, might be extended farther, so as to include all wicked schemes, and such as are not directed to a right end, as for example such as are dictated by ambition, avarice, or any other depraved affection. Paul, however, in my opinion, did not intend here to refer to any thing of that nature, but merely to reprove that rashness which is but too customary on the part of man, and in daily use in the forming of plans. To *purpose*, therefore, *according to the flesh*, is not owning God as our ruler, but, instead of this, being impelled by a rash presumption, which is afterwards justly derided by God, and punished. The apostle, with the view of clearing himself from these faults, proposes a question, as if in the person of his opponents. Hence it is probable, as I have already said,[1] that some unfavourable report had been put in circulation by wicked persons.

That with me there should be yea, yea. Some connect this statement with what goes before, and explain it thus: "As if it were in my power to perform whatever I purpose, as men determine that they will do whatever comes into their mind, and *order their ways*, as Solomon speaks, (Prov. xvi. 1,) while they cannot so much as govern their tongue." And,

[1] See p. 131.

undoubtedly, the words seem to imply this much—that what
has been once affirmed must remain fixed, and what has
been once denied must never be done.   So James in his
Epistle (v. 12) says, *Let your yea be yea, and your nay nay,
lest ye fall into dissimulation.*   Farther, the context would
in this way suit exceedingly well as to what goes before.
For to *purpose according to the flesh* is this—when we wish
that, without any exception, our determinations shall be
like oracles.[1]   This interpretation, however, does not accord
with what immediately follows—*God is faithful,* &c., where
Paul makes use of the same form of expression, when he
has it in view to intimate, that he had not been unfaithful
in his preaching.   Now it were absurd, if almost in the same
verse he reckoned it as a fault that his yea should be yea,
and his nay nay, and yet at the same time laid claim to it
as his highest praise.   I am aware of what could be said in
reply, if any one were disposed to sport himself with sub-
tleties, but I have no relish for anything that is not solid.

I have, therefore, no doubt, that in these words Paul designed to reprove fickleness, although they may seem to be
susceptible of another meaning, for the purpose of clearing
himself from that calumny—that he was accustomed to promise in words what he failed to perform in deeds.[2]   Thus
the reiterating of the affirmation and negation will not have
the same meaning as in Matt. v. 37 and in James, but will
bear this meaning—"that *yea* should with me be in this
instance *yea,* and on the other hand, when it pleases me,
nay, nay."   At the same time it is possible that it may
have crept in through the ignorance of transcribers, as the
old translation does not redouble the words.[3]   However

---

[1] " Que nos deliberations et conseils soyent comme oracles et reuelations
Diuines ;"—" That our purposes and plans shall be like oracles and Divine
revelations."

[2] " He (the apostle) anticipates and repels a reproach of ἐλαφρία, or
' *lightness of purpose,*' in that change of mind, as if he was ' *a yea and nay
man,*' (SHAKSP.), on whose word no secure reliance could be placed.   In
the next verse he calls God to witness that his word to them was not
' *both yea and nay* ;' and in the beginning of the following chapter, he explains to them, that it was for their sakes that he abstained from executing
his first intention."—*Penn.*—*Ed.*

[3] The rendering of the Vulgate is as follows: " Ut sit apud me *est* et

this may be, we ought not to be very solicitous as to the words, provided we are in possession of the apostle's intention, which, as I have said, clearly appears from what follows.[1]

18. *God is faithful.* By the term *word* he means doctrine, as is manifest from the reason that he adds, when he says, that the *Son of God, who is preached by him,* is not variable, &c. As to his being always consistent with himself in point of doctrine, and not differing from himself,[2] he intends that by this they shall form a judgment as to his integrity, and in this way he removes every unfavourable suspicion of fickleness or unfaithfulness. It does not, however, necessarily follow, that the man who is faithful in doctrine, is also observant of truth in all his *words.* But as Paul did not reckon it of much importance in what estimation he was held, provided only the majesty of his doctrine remained safe and sound, he, on that account, calls the attention of the Corinthians chiefly to that matter. He intimates, it is true, that he observed in his whole life the same course of fidelity, as the Corinthians had seen in his ministry. He seems, however, as if intentionally, in repelling the calumny, to transfer it from his person to his doctrine, because he was unwilling that his apostleship should be indirectly defamed,

non ;"—" That with me there should be *yea* and *nay.*" This reading—τὸ ναὶ καὶ τὸ οὔ, (yea and nay,) is found in one Greek MS., as stated by *Semler.* *Wiclif,* (1380,) following the Vulgate, reads—" that at me, be *it is* and *it is not.*"—*Ed.*

[1] " It was a proverbial manner among the Jews (see Wet.) of characterizing a man of strict probity and good faith, by saying, ' his *yes* is *yes,* and his *no* is *no*'—that is, you may depend upon his word ; as he declares, so it is; and as he promises, so he will do. Our Lord is therefore to be considered here (Matt. v. 37) not as prescribing the precise terms wherein we are to affirm or deny ; in which case it would have suited better the simplicity of his style to say barely ναὶ καὶ οὔ (*yea and nay,*) without doubling the words; but as enjoining such an habitual and inflexible regard to truth, as would render swearing unnecessary. That this manner οι converting these adverbs into nouns, is in the idiom of the sacred penmen, we have another instance, (2 Cor. i. 20,) ' For all the promises of God in him are *yea,* and in him *Amen.*' (ἐν αὐτῷ τὸ ναὶ καὶ ἐν αὐτῷ τὸ ἀμὴν)—that is, *certain and infallible truths.* It is indeed a common idiom of the Greek tongue, to turn by means of the article any of the parts of speech into a noun."—*Campbell on the Gospels,* vol. ii. p. 278.—*Ed.*

[2] " N'a point dit l'vn, puis l'autre ;"—" Does not say one thing and then another."

while he was not greatly concerned as to himself in other respects.

But observe, with what zeal he applies himself to this. For he calls God to witness, how simple and pure his preaching was—not ambiguous, not variable, not temporizing. In his oath, too, he connects the truth of God with the truth of his doctrine. " The truth of my preaching is as sure and stable as God is faithful and true." Nor is this to be wondered at, for the word of God, which Isaiah says *endureth for ever*, (Isaiah xl. 8,) is no other than what prophets and apostles published to the world, as Peter explains it. (1 Peter i. 25.) Hence, too, his confidence[1] in denouncing a curse upon angels, if they dared to bring another gospel, one that was at variance with his. (Gal. i. 8.) Who would dare to make the angels of heaven subject to his doctrine, if he had not God as his authority and defence? With such an assurance of a good conscience does it become ministers[2] to be endowed, who mount the pulpit to speak the word in Christ's name— so as to feel assured that their doctrine can no more bè over- thrown than God himself.

19. *For the Son of God.* Here we have the proof—be- cause his preaching[3] contained nothing but Christ alone, who is the eternal and immutable truth of God. The clause *preached by us* is emphatic. For, as it may be, and often does happen, that Christ is disfigured by the inventions[4] of men, and is adulterated, as it were, by their disguises, he declares that it had not been so as to himself or his associates, but that he had sincerely and with an integrity that was befitting, held forth Christ pure and undisguised. Why it is that he makes no mention of Apollos, while he mentions by name Timotheus and Silvanus, does not exactly appear;

---

[1] " De là vient aussi que S. Paul est bien si. hardi;"—" Hence, too, it comes that St. Paul is so very bold."

[2] " Et annonciateurs de la parolle de Dieu;"—" And heralds of the word of God."

[3] " Il dit donc que sa parolle n'a point este oui et non, c'est à dire va- riable; pource que sa predication," &c.;—" He says, then, that his word had not been yea and nay, that is to say, variable; because his preach- ing," &c.

[4] " Et mensonges;"—" And fallacies."

unless the reason be, as is probable, that the more that individuals were assailed by the calumnies of the wicked,[1] he
was so much the more careful to defend them.

In these words, however, he intimates that his whole doctrine was summed up in a simple acquaintance with Christ
alone, as in reality the whole of the gospel is included in it.
Hence those go beyond due limits, who teach anything else
than Christ alone, with whatever show of wisdom they may
otherwise be puffed up. For as he is the *end of the law*,
(Rom. x. 4,) so he is the head—the sum—in fine, the consummation—of all spiritual doctrine.

In the *second* place, he intimates that his doctrine respecting Christ had not been variable, or ambiguous, so as to present him from time to time in a new shape after the manner
of Proteus ;[2] as some persons make it their sport to make
changes upon him,[3] just as if they were tossing a ball to
and fro with their hand, simply for the purpose of display-
ing their dexterity. Others, with a view to procure the
favour of men, present him under various forms, while there
is still another class, that inculcate one day what on the
next they retract through fear. Such was not Paul's Christ,
nor can that of any true apostle[4] be such. Those, accordingly, have no ground to boast that they are ministers of
Christ, who paint him in various colours with a view to their
own advantage. For he alone is the true Christ, in whom
there appears that uniform and unvarying *yea*, which Paul
declares to be characteristic of him.

20. *For all the promises of God.*—Here again he shows
how firm and unvarying the preaching of Christ ought to be,

---

[1] " Des calomniateurs et mesdisans;"—" By calumniators and slanderers."

[2] " En sorte qu'il l'ait transfiguré, maintenant en vne sorte, tantost en
vne autre, comme les Poëtes disent que Proteus se transformoit en diuerses
sortes ;"—" So as to present him in different shapes, now in one form, then
in another, as the poets say that Proteus transformed himself into different
shapes." The following poets (among others) make mention of the
" shape-changing " Proteus:—*Virgil*, (Georg. iv. 387); *Ovid*, (Met. viii.
730); *Horace*, (Sat. ii. 3, 71, Ep. I. i. 90.) See CALVIN on John, vol.
ii. p. 256, *n*. 1.—*Ed.*

[3] " En toutes manieres;"—" In every way."

[4] " Celui de tous vrais et fideles ministres ;"—" That of all true and faithful ministers."

inasmuch as he is the groundwork[1] of *all the promises of God.* For it were worse than absurd to entertain the idea that he, in whom *all the promises of God* are established, is like one that wavers.[2] Now though the statement is general, as we shall see ere long, it is, notwithstanding, accommodated to the circumstances of the case in hand, with the view of confirming the certainty of Paul's doctrine. For it is not simply of the gospel in general that he treats, but he honours more especially his own gospel with this distinction. "If the promises of God are sure and well-founded, my preaching also must of necessity be sure, inasmuch as it contains nothing but Christ, in whom they are all established." As, however, in these words he means simply that he preached a gospel that was genuine, and not adulterated by any foreign additions,[3] let us keep in view this general doctrine, that all the promises of God rest upon Christ alone as their support—a sentiment that is worthy of being kept in remembrance, and is one of the main articles of our faith. It depends, however, on another principle—that it is only in Christ that God the Father is propitious to us. Now the promises are testimonies of his fatherly kindness towards us. Hence it follows, that it is in him alone that they are fulfilled.

The promises, I say, are testimonies of Divine grace : for although God shows kindness even to the unworthy, (Luke vi. 35,) yet when promises are given in addition to his acts of kindness, there is a special reason—that in them he declares himself to be a Father. *Secondly,* we are not qualified for enjoying the promises of God, unless we have received the remission of our sins, which we obtain through Christ. *Thirdly,* the promise, by which God adopts us to himself as his sons, holds the first place among them all. Now the

---

[1] "Le fondement et la fermete ;"—"The foundation and security."

[2] "Que celuy en qui toutes les promesses de Dieu sont establies et ratifices, fust comme vn homme chancelant et inconstant ;"—"That he, in whom all the promises of God are established and ratified, should be like a man that is wavering and unsteady."

[3] "Il a presché le vray et pur Evangile, et sans y auoir rien adiousté qu'il ait corrompu ou falsifié ;"—"He preached the true and pure gospel, and without having added to it anything that had corrupted or adulterated it."

cause and root of adoption is Christ ; because God is not a Father to any that are not members and brethren of his only-begotten Son. Everything, however, flows out from this source—that, while we are without Christ, we are hated by God rather than favourably regarded, while at the same time God promises us everything that he does promise, because he loves us. Hence it is not to be wondered if Paul here teaches, that all the promises of God are ratified and confirmed in Christ.

It is asked, however, whether they were feeble or powerless, previously to Christ's advent; for Paul seems to speak here of Christ as *manifested in the flesh.* (1 Tim. iii. 16.) I answer, that all the promises that were given to believers from the beginning of the world were founded upon Christ. Hence Moses and the Prophets, in every instance in which they treat of reconciliation with God, of the hope of salvation, or of any other favour, make mention of him, and discourse at the same time respecting his coming and his kingdom. I say again, that the promises under the Old Testament were fulfilled to the pious, in so far as was advantageous for their welfare; and yet it is not less true, that they were in a manner suspended until the advent of Christ, through whom they obtained their true accomplishment. And in truth, believers themselves rested upon the promises in such a way, as at the same time to refer the true accomplishment of them to the appearing of the Mediator, and suspended their hope until that time. In fine, if any one considers what is the fruit of Christ's death and resurrection, he will easily gather from this, in what respect the promises of God have been sealed and ratified in him, which would otherwise have had no sure accomplishment.

Wherefore, also, through him let there be Amen. Here also the Greek manuscripts do not agree, for some of them have it in one continued statement—*As many promises of God as there are, are in him Yea, and in him Amen to the glory of God through us.*[1] The different reading, however,

---

[1] " The most ancient MSS. and versions read the verse thus:—ὅσαι γὰρ ἐπαγγελίαι Θεοῦ, ἐν αὐτῷ τὸ ναί· διὸ καὶ δι' αὐτοῦ, τοῦ 'Αμὴν, τῷ Θεῷ πρὸς

which I have followed, is easier, and contains a fuller meaning.   For as he had said, that, in Christ, God has confirmed
the truth of all his promises, so now he teaches us, that it is
our duty to acquiesce in this ratification.   This we do, when,
resting upon Christ by a sure faith, we subscribe and *set our
seal that God is true,* as we read in John iii. 33, and that
with a view to his glory, as this is the end to which everything should be referred.   (Eph. i. 13, and Rom. iii. 4.)

The other reading, I confess, is the more common one,
but as it is somewhat meagre, I have not hesitated to prefer
the one that contains the fuller meaning, and, besides, is
much better suited to the context.   For Paul reminds the
Corinthians of their duty—to utter their *Amen* in return,
after having been instructed in the simple truth of God.   If,
however, any one is reluctant to depart from the other reading, there must, in any case, be an exhortation deduced from
it[1] to a mutual agreement in doctrine and faith.

21. Now he which stablisheth us with you in Christ, and hath anointed us, *is* God ;	21. Qui autem confirmat nos vobiscum in Christo, et qui unxit nos, Deus est :
22. Who hath also sealed us, and given the earnest of the Spirit in our hearts.	22. Qui et obsignavit nos, et dedit arrhabonem Spiritus in cordibus nostris.

God, indeed, is always true and steadfast in his promises,
and has always his *Amen,* as often as he speaks.   But as for
us, such is our vanity, that we do not utter our Amen in
return, except when he gives a sure testimony in our hearts
by his word.   This he does by his Spirit.   That is what
Paul means here.   He had previously taught, that this is
a befitting harmony—when, on the one hand, *the calling of
God is without repentance,* (Rom. xi. 29,) and we, in our turn,
with an unwavering faith, accept of the blessing of adoption
that is held out to us.   That God remains steadfast to his
promise is not surprising ; but to keep pace with God in

δοξαν δι' ἡμῶν ;"—" For all the promises of God are in him yea ; because they
are, through him, who is the AMEN, to the glory of God by us."—*Penn.*

[1] " Qu'il scache tousiours qu'il en faut tirer vne exhortation ;"—" Let
him always know this—that we must deduce from it an exhortation."

the steadfastness of our faith in return—*that* truly is not in man's power.[1]   He teaches us, also, that God cures our weakness or defect, (as they term it,) when, by correcting our belief, he confirms us by his Spirit.   Thus it comes, that we glorify him by a firm steadfastness of faith.   He associates himself, however, with the Corinthians, expressly for the purpose of conciliating their affections the better, with a view to the cultivation of unity.[2]

21. *Who hath anointed us.* He employs different terms to express one and the same thing.   For along with *confirmation*, he employs the terms *anointing* and *sealing*, or, by this twofold metaphor,[3] he explains more distinctly what he had previously stated without a figure.   For God, by pouring down upon us the heavenly grace of the Spirit, does, in this manner, *seal* upon our hearts the certainty of his own word. He then introduces a *fourth* idea—that the Spirit has been given to us as an *earnest*—a similitude which he frequently makes use of, and is also exceedingly appropriate.[4]   For as the Spirit, in bearing witness of our adoption, is our security, and, by confirming the faith of the promises, is the *seal* ($\sigma\phi\rho\alpha\gamma\grave{\iota}s$), so it is on good grounds that he is called an *earnest*,[5] because it is owing to him, that the covenant of God is ratified on both sides, which would, but for this, have hung in suspense.[6]

---

[1] " D'apporter de nostre costé vne correspondance mutuelle à la vocation de Dieu en perseuerant constamment en la foy ;"—" To maintain on our part a mutual correspondence to the call of God by persevering steadfastly in the faith."

[2] " Expressement afin de les gaigner et attirer a vraye vnite ;"—" Expressly for the purpose of gaining them over and drawing to a true unity."

[3] " Par les deux mots qui sont dits par metaphore et similitude ;"— " By these two words which are employed by way of metaphor and similitude."

[4] " Aῤῥαβών and the Latin *arrhabo* are derived from the Hebrew ערבן, (*gnarabon*)—a pledge or earnest; *i.e.*, a part of any price agreed on, and *paid down* to ratify the engagement; German, *Hand-gift*."—*Bloomfield.* " The word appears to have passed, probably as a commercial term, out of the Hebrew or Phenician into the western languages."—*Gesenius.—Ed.*

[5] " If God having once given this *earnest*, should not also give the rest of the inheritance, he should undergoe the losse of his earnest, as Chrysostome most elegantly and soundly argueth."—*Leigh's* Annotations.—*Ed.*

[6] " A *seal* was used for different purposes: to mark a person's property, to secure his treasures, or to authenticate a deed.   In the *first* sense, the

Here we must notice, in the *first* place, the relation[1] which
Paul requires between the gospel of God and our faith; for
as every thing that God says is more than merely certain,
so he wishes that this should be established in our minds
by a firm and sure assent.   *Secondly,* we must observe that,
as an assurance of this nature is a thing that is above the
capacity of the human mind, it is the part of the Holy Spirit
to confirm within us what God promises in his word.   Hence
it is that he has those titles of distinction—the *Anointing*,
the *Earnest*, the *Comforter*, and the *Seal*.   In the *third*
place we must observe, that all that have not the Holy Spirit
as a witness, so as to return their *Amen* to God, when calling them to an assured hope of salvation, do on false grounds
assume the name of Christians.

23. Moreover, I call God for a record upon my soul, that to spare you I came not as yet unto Corinth.	23. Ego autem testem invoco Deum in animam meam, quod parcens vobis nondum venerim Corinthum.
24. Not for that we have dominion over your faith, but are helpers of your joy: for by faith ye stand.	24. Non quod dominemur fidei vestrae, sed adiutores sumus[2] gaudii vestri: fide enim statis.

CHAPTER II.	CAPUT II.
1. But I determined this with myself, that I would not come again to you in heaviness.	1. Decreveram autem hoc in me ipso, non amplius venire in tristitia ad vos.[3]
2. For if I make you sorry, who is he then that maketh me glad, but the same which is made sorry by me?	2. Si enim ego contristo vos: et quis est qui me exhilaret, nisi is qui erit tristitia affectus ex me?

23. *I call God for a witness.*   He now begins to assign

Spirit distinguishes believers as the peculiar people of God; in the *second*,
he guards them as his precious jewels; in the *third*, he confirms or ratifies
their title to salvation. . . . An *earnest* is a part given as a security for
the future possession of the whole.   The Holy Ghost is the *earnest* of the
heavenly inheritance, because he begins that holiness in the soul which
will be perfected in heaven, and imparts those joys which are foretastes of
its blessedness."—*Dick's Theology*, vol. iii. pp. 524, 525.—*Ed.*

[1] " La correspondance mutuelle;"—" The mutual correspondence."

[2] " Nous sommes adiuteurs de vostre ioye; ou, *nous aidons à;*"—" We
are helpers of your joy, or, *we aid.*"

[3] " De ne venir à vous derechef auec tristesse, ou, *pour vous apporter
fascherie;*"—" Not to come again to you in sorrow, or, *to cause you distress.*"

a reason for his change of purpose ; for hitherto he has merely repelled calumny. When, however, he says that *he spared them,* he indirectly throws back the blame upon them, and thus shows them that it would be unfair if he were put to grief through their fault, but that it would be much more unfair if they should permit this ; but most of all unfair if they should give their assent to so base a calumny, as in that case they would be substituting in their place an innocent person, as if he had been guilty of their sin. Now he *spared* them in this respect, that if he had come he would have been constrained to reprove them more severely, while he wished rather that they should of their own accord repent previously to his arrival, that there might be no occasion for a harsher remedy,[1] which is a signal evidence of more than paternal lenity. For how much forbearance there was in shunning this necessity, when he had just ground of provocation !

He makes use, also, of an oath, that he may not seem to have contrived something to serve a particular purpose. For the matter in itself was of no small importance, and it was of great consequence that he should be entirely free from all suspicion of falsehood and pretence. Now there are two things that make an oath lawful and pious—the occasion and the disposition. The *occasion* I refer to is, where an oath is not employed rashly, that is, in mere trifles, or even in matters of small importance, but only where there is a call for it. The *disposition* I refer to is, where there is not so much regard had to private advantage, as concern felt for the glory of God, and the advantage of the brethren. For this end must always be kept in view, that our oaths may promote the honour of God, and promote also the advantage of our neighbours in a matter that is befitting.[2]

The form of the oath must also be observed—*first,* that he calls God to witness ; and, *secondly,* that he says *upon my soul.* For in matters that are doubtful and obscure, where

---

[1] " Remede plus aspre et rigoureux ;"—" A harsher and more rigorous remedy."

[2] " Moyennant que ce soit en chose iuste et raisonable ;"—" Provided it is in a matter that is just and reasonable."

man's knowledge fails, we have recourse to God, that he, who alone is truth, may bear testimony to the truth. But the man that appeals to God as his witness, calls upon him at the same time to be an avenger of perjury, in the event of his declaring what is false. This is what is meant by the phrase *upon my soul.* " I do not object to his inflicting punishment upon me, if I am guilty of falsehood." Although, however, this is not always expressed in so many words, it is, notwithstanding, to be understood. For *if we are unfaithful, God remaineth faithful and will not deny himself.* (2 Tim. ii. 13.) He will not suffer, therefore, the profanation of his name to go unpunished.

24. *Not that we exercise dominion.* He anticipates an objection that might be brought forward. " What! Do you then act so tyrannically[1] as to be formidable in your very look ? Such were not the gravity of a Christian pastor, but the cruelty of a savage tyrant." He answers this objection first *indirectly,* by declaring that matters are not so ; and afterwards *directly,* by showing that the very circumstance, that he had been constrained to treat them more harshly, was owing to his fatherly affection. When he says that he does not *exercise dominion over their faith,* he intimates, that such a power is unjust and intolerable—nay more, is tyranny in the Church. For faith ought to be altogether exempt, and to the utmost extent free, from the yoke of men. We must, however, observe, who it is that speaks, for if ever there was a single individual of mortals, that had authority to claim for himself such a *dominion,* Paul assuredly was worthy of such a privilege. Yet he acknowledges,[2] that it does not belong to him. Hence we infer, that faith owns no subjection except to the word of God, and that it is not at all in subjection to human control.[3]

[1] " Es-tu si insupportable, et si orgueilleux ?"—" Are you so insufferable and so proud ?"

[2] " Il confesse franchement ;"—" He frankly confesses."

[3] The views here expressed by CALVIN are severely animadverted upon in the following terms by the Romanists, in the Annotations appended to the Rheims version of the New Testament : " CALVIN and his seditious sectaries with other like which *despise dominion,* as St. Jude describeth such, would by this place deliver themselves from all yoke of spiritual Magistrates and Rulers : namely, that they be subject to no man touching

Erasmus has observed in his Annotations, that by supplying the Greek particle ἕνεκα, it may be understood in this way— *Not that we exercise dominion over you—with respect to your faith*—a rendering which amounts almost to the same thing. For he intimates, that there is no spiritual dominion, except that of God only. This always remains a settled point— pastors have no peculiar *dominion* over men's consciences,[1] inasmuch as they are ministers, *not lords.* (1 Pet. v. 3.)

What then does he leave to himself and others? He calls them *helpers of their joy*—by which term I understand *happiness.* At the same time he employs the term *joy* as opposed to the terror which tyrants awaken through means of their cruelty, and also false prophets,[2] resembling tyrants, that *rule with rigour and authority*, as we read in Ezekiel xxxiv. 4. He argues from contraries, that he did by no means usurp dominion over the Corinthians, inasmuch as he endeavoured rather to maintain them in the possession of a peace that was free, and full of joy.

their faith, or for the examination and trial of their doctrine, but to God and his word only. And no marvel that the malefactors and rebels of the Church would come to no tribunal but God's, that so they may remain unpunished at least during this life. For though the Scriptures plainely condemne their heresies, yet they could writhe themselves out by false glosses, constructions, corruptions, and denials of the bookes to be canonical, if there were no lawes or judicial sentences of men to rule and represse them." To these statements Dr. Fulke in his elaborate work in refutation of the errors of Popery, (Lond. 1601.) p. 559, appropriately replies as follows: " This is nothing els but a lewd and senselesse slander of CALVIN and vs, that we despise lordship, because we will not be subiect to the tyranny of Antichrist, that would be Lord of our faith, and arrogateth vnto himselfe auctoritie to make new articles of fayth, which have no ground or warrant in the word of God. But CALVIN did willingly acknowledge all auctoritie of the ministers of the Church, which the Scripture doth allow unto them, and both practised, and submitted himselfe to the discipline of the Church, and the lawful gouernours thereof, although he would not yield unto the tyrannicall yoke of the Pope, who is neither soueraigne of the Church, nor any true member of the same. Yea, CALVIN and we submit ourselves, not only to the auctoritie of the Church, but also of the Ciuile Magistrates to be punished, if we shall be found to teach or doe any thing contrary to the doctrine of faith, receyued and approved by the Church, whereas the Popish clergy, in causes of religion, will not be subject to the temporal gouernors, judgement, and correction."—*Ed.*

[1] " Que les Pasteurs et Evesques n'ont point de iurisdiction propre sur les consciences;"—" That Pastors and Bishops have no peculiar jurisdiction over consciences."

[2] " Et les faux-apostres aussi;"—" And false Apostles also."

For by faith ye stand. As to the reason why he adds this, others either pass it over altogether in silence, or they do not explain it with sufficient distinctness. For my part, I am of opinion that he here again argues from contraries. For if the nature and effect of faith be such that we lean, in order that we may *stand*,[1] it is absurd to speak of faith as being subject to men. Thus he removes that unjust domi-nion, with which, he had a little before declared, he was not chargeable.

CHAPTER II.

1. *But I had determined.* Whoever it was that divided the chapters, made here a foolish division. For now at length the Apostle explains, in what manner he had *spared* them. " I had determined," says he, " not to come to you any more in sorrow," or in other words, to occasion you sor-row by my coming. For he had come once by an Epistle, by means of which he had severely pained them. Hence, so long as they had not repented, he was unwilling to come to them, lest he should be constrained to grieve them again, when present with them, for he chose rather to give them longer time for repentance.[2] The word ἔκρινα (*I determined*) must be rendered in the pluperfect tense,[3] for, when assign-ing a reason for the delay that had occurred, he explains what had been his intention previously.

2. *For if I make you sorry.* Here we have the proof of the foregoing statement. No one willingly occasions sorrow to himself. Now Paul says, that he has such a fellow-feeling with the Corinthians,[4] that he cannot feel joyful, unless he sees them happy. Nay more, he declares that they were

---

[1] " Afin que nous demeurions fermes ;"—" In order that we may remain secure."

[2] " De se repentir et amender ;"—" For repentance and amendment."

[3] " Et de faict il faut necessairement traduire, *l'auoye deliberé* : non pas, *l'ay deliberé ;*"—" And indeed we must necessarily render it—*I had deter-mined* : not *I have determined.*"

[4] " C'est à dire vne telle conuenance et conionction de nature et d'affec-tions, entre luy et les Corinthiens ;"—" That is to say, such an agreement and connection of nature and affections between him and the Corinthians."

the source and the authors of his joy—which they could not be, if they were themselves sorrowful. If this disposition prevail in pastors, it will be the best restraint, to keep them back from alarming with terrors those minds, which they ought rather to have encouraged by means of a cheerful affability. For from this arises an excessively morose harshness[1]—so that we do not rejoice in the welfare of the Church, as were becoming.

3. And I wrote this same unto you, lest, when I came, I should have sorrow from them of whom I ought to rejoice; having confidence in you all, that my joy is *the joy* of you all.

4. For out of much affliction and anguish of heart I wrote unto you with many tears; not that ye should be grieved, but that ye might know the love which I have more abundantly unto you.

5. But if any have caused grief, he hath not grieved me, but in part; that I may not overcharge you all.

3. Et scripseram vobis hoc, ne veniens tristitiam super tristitiam haberem, a quibus oportebat me gaudere: fiduciam habens de vobis omnibus, quod meum gaudium vestrum omnium sit.

4. Ex multa enim afflictione et angustia cordis scripsi vobis per multas lacrimas: non ut contristaremini, sed ut caritatem cognosceretis, quam habeo abundantius erga vos.

5. Si quis autem contristavit, non me contristavit, sed ex parte: ut ne vos omnes gravem.

3. *I had written to you.* As he had said a little before, that he delayed coming to them, in order that he *might not come a second time in sorrow* and with severity, (ver. 1,) so now also he lets them know, that he came the first time in sadness by an Epistle, that they might not have occasion to feel this severity when he was present with them. Hence they have no ground to complain of that former sadness, in which he was desirous to consult their welfare. He goes even a step farther, by stating that, when writing, he did not wish to occasion them grief, or to give any expression of displeasure, but, on the contrary, to give proof of his attachment and affection towards them. In this way, if there was any degree of keenness in the Epistle, he does not merely soften it, but even shows amiableness and suavity. When, however, he confesses afterwards, what he here denies, he appears to contradict himself. I answer, that there is no inconsistency, for he does not come afterwards to confess, that it

[1] " La seuerite trop grande et chagrin ;"—" An excessive severity and chagrin."

was his ultimate object to *grieve* the Corinthians, but that this was the means, by which he endeavoured to conduct them to true joy.   Previously, however, to his stating this, he speaks here simply as to his design.   He passes over in silence, or delays mentioning for a little the means, which were not so agreeable.

Having confidence.   This confidence he exercises towards the Corinthians, that they may thus in their turn be persuaded of his friendly disposition.   For he that hates, is envious; but where joy is felt in common, there must in that case be perfect love.[1]   If, however, the Corinthians are not in accordance with Paul's opinion and judgment as to them, they shamefully disappoint him.

4. *For out of much affliction.*   Here he brings forward another reason with the view of softening the harshness which he had employed.   For those who smilingly take delight in seeing others weep, inasmuch as they discover thereby their cruelty, cannot and ought not to be borne with.   Paul, however, declares that his feeling was very different.   "Intensity of grief," says he, "has extorted from me every thing that I have written."   Who would not excuse, and take in good part what springs from such a temper of mind, more especially as it was not on his own account or through his own fault, that he suffered grief, and farther, he does not give vent to his grief, with the view of lightning himself by burdening them, but rather, for the purpose of shewing his affection for them?   On these accounts, it did not become the Corinthians to be offended at this somewhat severe reproof.

He adds, *tears*—which, in a man that is brave and magnanimous are a token of intense grief.   Hence we see, from what emotions of mind pious and holy admonitions and reproofs must of necessity proceed.   For there are many noisy reprovers, who, by declaiming, or rather, fulminating against vices, display a surprising ardour of zeal, while in the mean time they are at ease in their mind,[2] so that it might seem

[1] " Il faut bien dire que l'amitie y est entiere;"—" We cannot but say that there is entire friendship."

[2] " Ils ne s'en soucient point, et n'en sont nullement touchez;"—" They feel no concern as to it, and are in no degree affected by it."

as if they exercised their throat and sides[1] by way of sport.
It is, however, the part of a pious pastor, to weep within
himself, before he calls upon others to weep :[2] to feel tortured
in silent musings, before he shows any token of displeasure ;
and to keep within his own breast more grief, than he causes
to others. We must, also, take notice of Paul's tears, which,
by their abundance, shew tenderness of heart, but it is of a
more heroical character than was the iron-hearted hardness
of the Stoics.[3] For the more tender the affections of love
are, they are so much the more praiseworthy.

The adverb *more abundantly* may be explained in a comparative sense ; and, in that case, it would be a tacit complaint—that the Corinthians do not make an equal return
in respect of affection, inasmuch as they love but coldly one
by whom they are ardently loved. I take it, however, in a
more simple way, as meaning that Paul commends his affection towards them, in order that this assurance may soften
down every thing of harshness that might be in his words.

5. *But if any one.* Here is a *third* reason with the view
of alleviating the offence—that he had grief in common with
them, and that the occasion of it came from another quarter.
" We have," says he, " been alike grieved, and another is to
blame for it." At the same time he speaks of that person,
too, somewhat mildly, when he says, *if any one*—not affirming the thing, but rather leaving it in suspense. This passage, however, is understood by some, as if Paul meant to
say : " He that has given me occasion of grief, has given
offence to you also ; for you ought to have felt grieved along
with me, and yet I have been left almost to grieve alone
For I do not wish to say so absolutely—*that I may not put
the blame upon you all.*" In this way the second clause would
contain a correction of the first. Chrysostom's exposition,
however, is much more suitable ; for he reads it as one con-

---

[1] " En criant ;"—" In crying."
[2] There can be little doubt that our author had here in his eye the
celebrated sentiment of *Horace*, in his " Ars Poetica," l. 102—" Si vis me
flere, dolendum primum ipsi tibi ;"—" If you would have me weep, weep
first yourself."—*Ed.*
[3] " Qui vouloyent apparoistre comme insensibles ;"—" Who wished to
seem as if they were devoid of feeling."

tinued sentence—" *He hath not grieved me alone, but almost all of you.* And as to my saying *in part,* I do so in order that I may not *bear too hard upon him.*"[1] I differ from Chrysostom merely in the clause *in part,* for I understand it as meaning *in some measure.* I am aware, that Ambrose understands it as meaning—part of the saints, inasmuch as the Church of the Corinthians was divided ; but that is more ingenious than solid.

6. Sufficient to such a man *is* this punishment, which *was inflicted* of many.

7. So that contrariwise ye *ought* rather to forgive *him,* and comfort *him,* lest perhaps such an one should be swallowed up with overmuch sorrow.

8. Wherefore I beseech you, that ye would confirm *your* love toward him.

9. For to this end also did I write, that I might know the proof of you, whether ye be obedient in all things.

10. To whom ye forgive any thing, I *forgive* also : for if I forgave any thing, to whom I forgave *it,* for your sakes *forgave I it* in the person of Christ ;

11. Lest Satan should get an advantage of us : for we are not ignorant of his devices.

6. Sufficit ei, qui talis est, correctio, quæ illi contigit a pluribus.

7. Ut potius e diverso debeatis condonare, et consolari : ne forte abundantiori tristitia absorbeatur, qui eiusmodi est.

8. Quamobrem obsecro vos, ut confirmetis erga eum caritatem.

9. Nam in hoc etiam scripseram vobis, ut probationem vestri cognoscerem : an ad omnia obedientes sitis.

10. Cui autem condonatis, etiam ego : etenim cui condonavi, si quid condonavi, propter vos condonavi in conspectu Christi.

11. Ut ne occupemur a Satana : non enim cogitationes eius ignoramus.

6. *Sufficient.* He now extends kindness even to the man who had sinned more grievously than the others, and on whose account his anger had been kindled against them all, inasmuch as they had connived at his crime. In his showing indulgence even to one who was deserving of severer punishment, the Corinthians have a striking instance to convince them, how much he disliked excessive harshness. It is true, that he does not act this part merely for the sake of the Corinthians, but because he was naturally of a for-

[1] " The words may be rendered : ' But if any one (meaning the incestuous person) have occasioned sorrow, he hath not so much grieved *me,* as, in some measure (that I may not bear too hard upon him) all of *you.*' . . . 'Επιβαρῶ must, with the Syr. version and Emmerling, be taken intransitively, in the sense—' ne quid gravius dicam,' (that I may not say anything too severe,) *i.e.,* ' ne dicam nos solos,' (that I may not say—us alone.) Of this sense of ἐπιβαρεῖν τινι, to *bear hard upon,* two examples are adduced by Wetstein from Appian."—*Bloomfield.—Ed.*

giving temper; but still, in this instance of mildness, the Corinthians could not but perceive his remarkable kindness of disposition. In addition to this, he does not merely show himself to be indulgent, but exhorts others to receive him into favour, in the exercise of the same mildness.

Let us, however, consider these things a little more minutely. He refers to the man who had defiled himself by an incestuous marriage with his mother-in-law. As the iniquity was not to be tolerated, Paul had given orders, that the man should be excommunicated. He had, also, severely reproved the Corinthians, because they had so long given encouragement to that enormity[1] by their dissimulation and patient endurance. It appears from this passage, that he had been brought to repentance, after having been admonished by the Church. Hence Paul gives orders, that he be forgiven, and that he be also supported by consolation.

This passage ought to be carefully observed, as it shows us, with what equity and clemency the discipline of the Church ought to be regulated, in order that there may not be undue severity. There is need of strictness, in order that the wicked may not be rendered more daring by impunity, which is justly pronounced an allurement to vice. But on the other hand, as there is a danger of the person, who is chastised, becoming dispirited, moderation must be used as to this—so that the Church shall be prepared to extend forgiveness, so soon as she is fully satisfied as to his penitence. In this department, I find a lack of wisdom on the part of the ancient bishops; and indeed they ought not to be excused, but on the contrary, we ought rather to mark their error, that we may learn to avoid it. Paul is satisfied with the repentance of the offender, that a reconciliation may take place with the Church. They, on the other hand, by making no account of his repentance, have issued out canons as to repentance during three years, during seven years, and in some cases during life. By these they exclude poor unhappy men from the fellowship of the Church. And, in this

---

[1] " De ce qu'ils auoyent si longuement nourri ce mal-heureux en son peche;"—" Because they had so long encouraged that unhappy man in his sin."

way, the offender is either alienated the more from the Church, or[1] is induced to practise hypocrisy. But even if the enactment were more plausible in itself, this consideration would, in my view, be enough to condemn it—that it is at variance with the rule of the Holy Spirit, which the Apostle here prescribes.

7. *Lest such an one should be swallowed up by overmuch sorrow.* The end of excommunication, so far as concerns the power of the offender, is this: that, overpowered with a sense of his sin, he may be humbled in the sight of God and the Church, and may solicit pardon with sincere dislike and confession of guilt. The man who has been brought to this, is now more in need of consolation, than of severe reproof. Hence, if you continue to deal with him harshly, it will be— not discipline, but cruel domineering. Hence we must carefully guard against pressing them beyond this limit.[2] For nothing is more dangerous, than to give Satan a handle, to tempt an offender to despair. Now we furnish Satan with arms in every instance, in which we leave without consolation those, who are in good earnest affected with a view of their sin.

9. *For I had written to you also for this purpose.* He anticipates an objection, that they might bring forward. " What then did you mean, when you were so very indignant, because we had not inflicted punishment upon him ? From being so stern a judge, to become all at once a defender—is not this indicative of a man, that wavers between conflicting dispositions ?"[3] This idea might detract greatly from Paul's authority ; but he answers, that he has obtained what he asked, and that he was therefore satisfied, so that he must now give way to compassion. For, their carelessness having been corrected, there was nothing to hinder their lifting up the man by their clemency, when now prostrate and downcast.[4]

---

[1] " Ou pour le moins ;"—" Or at least."

[2] " Plus qu'il est yci demonstré ;"—" Beyond what is here pointed out."

[3] " D'vn homme inconstant, et qui est mené de contraires affections ;"— " Of a man that is unsteady, and is influenced by conflicting dispositions."

[4] " Ce poure homme le voyans bien confus et abbatu ;"—" This poor man, on seeing him much abashed and overcome."

10. *To whom ye forgive.* That he might the more readily appease them, he added his vote in support of the pardon extended by them.[1] " Do not hesitate to forgive: I promise that I shall confirm whatever you may have done, and I already subscribe your sentence of forgiveness." *Secondly,* he says that he does this *for their sake ;* and that too, sincerely and cordially. He had already shown how desirous he was, that the man's welfare should be consulted: he now declares, that he grants this willingly to the Corinthians.

Instead of the expression *in the sight of Christ,* some prefer *person,*[2] because Paul in that reconciliation was in the room of Christ,[3] and did in a manner represent his person.[4] I am, however, more inclined to understand him as declaring, that he forgives sincerely and without any pretence. For he is accustomed to employ this phrase to express pure and undisguised rectitude. If, however, any one prefers the former interpretation, it is to be observed that the *person of Christ* is interposed, because there is nothing that ought to incline us more to the exercise of mercy.

11. *That we may not be taken advantage of by Satan.* This may be viewed as referring to what he had said previously respecting excessive sorrow. For it is a most wicked[5] fraud of Satan, when depriving us of all consolation, he swallows us up, as it were, in a gulf of despair ; and such is the explanation that is given of it by Chrysostom. I prefer, however, to view it as referring to Paul and the Corinthians. For there was a twofold danger, that beset them from the stratagems of Satan—in the event of their being excessively harsh and rigorous, or, on the other hand, in case of dissension arising among them. For it very frequently happens,

---

[1] " A ce pecheur ;"—" To this offender."

[2] " Aucuns aiment mieux dire, En la personne de Christ;"—" Some prefer to say, In the person of Christ."

[3] " Estoit comme lieutenant de Christ ;"—" Was as it were Christ's lieutenant."

[4] Raphelius, in his Semicent. Annot., quotes a passage from Eusebius, (Hist. Eccl. lib. iii. cap. 38,) in which he makes mention of the Epistle of Clement, ἣν ἐκ προσώπου τῆς Ῥωμαίων Ἐκκλησίας τῇ Κορινθίων διετυπώσατο— " which he wrote in the *name* of the Church of the Romans to that of the Corinthians."—*Ed.*

[5] " Tres dangereuse ;"—" Very dangerous."

that, under colour of zeal for discipline, a Pharisaical rigour creeps in, which hurries on the miserable offender to ruin, instead of curing him.   It is rather, however, in my opinion, of the *second* danger that he speaks ; for if Paul had not to some extent favoured the wishes of the Corinthians, Satan would have prevailed by kindling strife among them.

For we are not ignorant of his devices.   That is, " We know, from being warned of it by the Lord, that one strata- gem to which he carefully has recourse is, that when he can- not ruin us by open means, he surprises us when off our guard by making a secret attack.[1]   As, then, we are aware that he makes an attack upon us by indirect artifices, and that he assails us by secret machinations, we must look well before us, and carefully take heed that he may not, from some quarter, do us injury.   He employs the word *devices* in the sense in which the Hebrews make use of the term זִמָּה, (*zimmah,*) but in a bad sense,[2] as meaning artful schemes and machinations, which ought not to be unknown to be- lievers, and will not be so, provided they give themselves up to the guidance of God's Spirit.   In short, as God warns us, that Satan employs every means to impose upon us, and, in addition to this, shows us by what methods he may practise imposture upon us, it is our part to be on the alert, that he may have not a single chink to creep through.

12. Furthermore, when I came to Troas to *preach* Christ's gospel, and a door was opened unto me of the Lord,

13. I had no rest in my spirit, be- cause I found not Titus my brother; but taking my leave of them, I went from thence into Macedonia.

14. Now thanks *be* unto God, which always causeth us to triumph in Christ, and maketh manifest the savour of his knowledge by us in every place.

12. Porro quum venissem Troa- dem in Evangelium Christi ; etiam ostio mihi aperto in Domino,

13. Non habui relaxationem spi- ritui meo, eo quod non inveneram Titum fratrem meum ; sed illis vale- dicens profectus sum in Macedoniam.

14. Deo autem gratia, qui semper triumphare nos facit in Christo ; et odorem cognitionis eius manifestat per nos in omni loco.

---

[1] The reader will find the same sentiment expressed more fully by CALVIN, in the Argument on the First Epistle to the Corinthians, vol. i. p. 38.—*Ed.*

[2] The Hebrew term זִמָּה, (*zimmah,*) is used in a bad sense, (as meaning *a wicked device,*) in Prov. xxi. 27, and xxiv. 9.   The word employed by the apostle—νοήματα—is made use of by Homer, (Iliad x. 104, xviii. 328,) as meaning *schemes* or *devices.*—*Ed.*

15. For we are unto God a sweet savour of Christ, in them that are saved, and in them that perish.

16. To the one *we are* the savour of death unto death; and to the other the savour of life unto life. And who *is* sufficient for these things?

17. For we are not as many, which corrupt the word of God : but as of sincerity, but as of God, in the sight of God speak we in Christ.

15. Quia Christi suavis odor sumus Deo, in iis qui salvi fiunt, et in iis qui pereunt.

16. His quidem odor mortis in mortem, illis vero odor vitae in vitam; et ad haec quis idoneus?

17. Non enim sumus quemadmodum multi, adulterantes sermonem Dei: sed tanquam ex sinceritate, tanquam ex Deo, in conspectu Dei in Christo loquimur.[1]

12. *When I had come to Troas.* By now mentioning what he had been doing in the mean time, in what places he had been, and what route he had pursued in his journeyings, he more and more confirms what he had said previously as to his coming to the Corinthians. He says that he had come to Troas from Ephesus for the sake of the gospel, for he would not have proceeded in that direction, when going into Achaia, had he not been desirous to pass through Macedonia. As, however, he did not find Titus there, whom he had sent to Corinth, and by whom he ought to have been informed respecting the state of that Church, though he might have done much good there, and though he had an opportunity presented to him, yet, he says, setting everything aside, he came to Macedonia, desirous to see Titus. Here is an evidence of a singular degree of attachment to the Corinthians, that he was so anxious respecting them, that he *had no rest* anywhere, even when a large prospect of usefulness presented itself, until he had learned the state of their affairs. Hence it appears why it was that he delayed his coming. He did not wish to come to them until he had learned the state of their affairs. Hence it appears, why it was that he delayed his coming. He did not wish to come to them, until he had

[1] " Car nous ne sommes point comme plusieurs, corrompans la parolle de Dieu: ains nous parlons comme en purete, et comme de par Dieu, deuant Dieu en Christ, *ou,* Car nous ne faisons pas traffique de la parolle de Dieu, comme *font* plusieurs, ains nous parlons touchant Christ, *ou selon Christ,* comme en integrite, et comme de par Dieu, deuant Dieu;"—" For we are not as many, corrupting the word of God; but we speak, as in purity, and as from God, before God in Christ; *or,* For we do not make traffic of the word of God, as many *do;* but we speak concerning Christ, *or according to Christ,* as in integrity, and as from God, before God."

first had a conversation with Titus.   He afterwards learned
from the report brought him by Titus, that matters were at
that time not yet ripe for his coming to them.   Hence it is
evident, that Paul loved the Corinthians so much, that he
accommodated all his journeyings and long circuits to their
welfare, and that he had accordingly come to them later than
he had promised—not from having, in forgetfulness of his
promise, rashly changed his plan, or from having been carried away by some degree of *fickleness*, (2 Cor. i. 17,) but
because delay was more profitable for them.

A door also having been opened to me.   We have spoken
of this metaphor when commenting on the last chapter of
the First Epistle.   (1 Cor. xvi. 9.)   Its meaning is, that an
opportunity of promoting the gospel had presented itself.[1]
For as an opportunity of entering is furnished when the *door
is opened*, so the servants of the Lord make advances when
an opportunity is presented.   The *door is shut*, when no
prospect of usefulness is held out.   Now as, on the door being
shut, it becomes us to enter upon a new course, rather than
by farther efforts to weary ourselves to no purpose by useless
labour, so where an opportunity presents itself of edifying,
let us consider that by the hand of God a door is opened to
us for introducing Christ there, and let us not withhold compliance with so kind an indication from God.[2]

It may seem, however, as if Paul had erred in this—that
disregarding, or at least leaving unimproved, an opportunity
that was placed within his reach, he betook himself to Macedonia.   " Ought he not rather to have applied himself to
the work that he had in hand, than, after making little more

---

[1] Elsner, when commenting on 1 Cor. xvi. 9, " *a great door and effectual is opened*," after quoting a variety of passages from Latin and Greek
authors, in which a corresponding metaphor is employed, observes that
Rabbinical writers employ in the same sense the term פֶתַח, (*phethach*,) a
gate.   Thus Raschi, when speaking of the question proposed to Hagar by
the angel, (*Whence camest thou?* Gen. xvi. 8,) remarks : " Noverat id
(angelus) sed (interrogavit) ut פֶתַח, *januam*, ei daret colloquendi ;"—" He
(the angel) knew this, but (he proposed the question) that he might afford
her an *opportunity* of speaking to him."—*Ed.*

[2] " Ne refusons point de nous employer en ce que nous pourrons seruir,
quand nous voyons que Dieu nous y inuite si liberalement ;"—" Let us not
refuse to employ ourselves in rendering what service we can, when we see
that God invites us so kindly."

than a commencement, break away all on a sudden in another direction?" We have also observed already, that the *opening of a door* is an evidence of a divine call, and this is undoubtedly true. I answer, that, as Paul was not by any means restricted to one Church, but was bound to many at the same time, it was not his duty, in consequence of the present aspect of one of them, to leave off concern as to the others. Farther, the more connection he had with the Corinthian Church, it was his duty to be so much the more inclined to aid it; for we must consider it to be reasonable, that a Church, which he had founded by his ministry, should be regarded by him with a singular affection[1]—just as at this day it is our duty, indeed, to promote the welfare of the whole Church, and to be concerned for the entire body of it; and yet, every one has, nevertheless, a closer and holier connection with his own Church, to whose interests he is more particularly devoted. Matters were in an unhappy state at Corinth, so that Paul was in no ordinary degree anxious as to the issue. It is not, therefore, to be wondered, if, under the influence of this motive, he left unimproved an opportunity that in other circumstances was not to be neglected; as it was not in his power to occupy every post of duty at one and the same time. It is not, however, at all likely that he left Troas, till he had first introduced some one in his place to improve the opening that had occurred.[2]

14. *But thanks be to God.* Here he again glories in the success of his ministry, and shows that he had been far from idle in the various places he had visited; but that he may do this in no invidious way, he sets out with a thanksgiving, which we shall find him afterwards repeating. Now he does not, in a spirit of ambition, extol his own actions, that his name may be held in renown, nor does he, in mere pretence, give thanks to God in the manner of the Pharisee, while lifted up, in the mean time, with pride and arrogance. (Luke xviii. 11.) Instead of this, he desires from his heart,

---

[1] " Fust aimee de luy d'vne affection singuliere et speciale;"—" Should be loved by him with a singular and special affection."

[2] " L'ouuerture que Dieu auoit faite;"—" The opening that God had made."

that whatever is worthy of praise, be recognised as the work of God alone, that his power alone may be extolled.   Farther, he recounts his own praises with a view to the advantage of the Corinthians, that, on hearing that he had served the Lord with so much fruit in other places, they may not allow his labour to be unproductive among themselves, and may learn to respect his ministry, which God everywhere rendered so glorious and fruitful.   For what God so illustriously honours, it is criminal to despise, or lightly esteem.   Nothing was more injurious to the Corinthians, than to have an unfavourable view of Paul's Apostleship and doctrine : nothing, on the other hand, was more advantageous, than to hold both in esteem.   Now he had begun to be held in contempt by many, and hence, it was not his duty to be silent.   In addition to this, he sets this holy boasting in opposition to the revilings of the wicked.

Who causeth us to triumph.   If you render the word literally, it will be, *Qui nos triumphat—Who triumpheth over us.*[1]   Paul, however, means something different from what this form of expression denotes among the Latins.[2]   For captives are said to be *triumphed over,* when, by way of disgrace, they are bound with chains and dragged before the chariot of the conqueror.   Paul's meaning, on the other hand, is, that he was also a sharer in the triumph enjoyed by God, because it had been gained by his instrumentality, just as the lieutenants accompanied on horseback the chariot of the chief general, as sharers in the honour.[3]   As, accordingly, all the ministers of the gospel fight under God's auspices, so they also procure for him the victory and the honour of the *triumph ;*[4] but, at the same time, he honours each of them

[1] " Qui triomphe tousiours de nous ;"—" Who always triumpheth over us."

[2] " Θριαμβεύειν with the accusative is used here like the hiphil of the Hebrew in the same way as μαθητεύειν (to make a disciple) (Matt. xiii. 52.) βασιλεύειν (to make a king) (1 Sam. viii. 22) and others."—*Billroth* on the Corinthians.—Bib. Cab. No. xxiii. p. 181.   The meaning is—" maketh us to triumph."—*Ed.*

[3] On such occasions the *legati* (lieutenants) of the general, and military tribunes, commonly rode by his side.   (See Cic. Pis. 25.)—*Ed.*

[4] " A *triumph* among the Romans, to which the Apostle here alludes, was a public and solemn honour conferred by them on a victorious general,

with a share of the *triumph*, according to the station assigned him in the army, and proportioned to the exertions made by him. Thus they enjoy, as it were, a *triumph*, but it is God's rather than theirs.[1]

He adds, *in Christ*, in whose person God himself *triumphs*, inasmuch as he has conferred upon him all the glory of empire. Should any one prefer to render it thus: " Who triumphs by means of us," even in that way a sufficiently consistent meaning will be made out.

The odour of his knowledge. The *triumph* consisted in this, that God, through his instrumentality, wrought powerfully and gloriously, perfuming the world with the health-giving *odour* of his grace, while, by means of his doctrine, he brought some to the knowledge of Christ. He carries out, however, the metaphor of *odour*, by which he expresses both the delectable sweetness of the gospel, and its power and efficacy for inspiring life. In the mean time, Paul instructs them, that his preaching is so far from being savourless, that it quickens souls by its very *odour*. Let us, however, learn from this, that those alone make right proficiency in the gospel, who, by the sweet fragrance of Christ, are stirred up to desire him, so as to bid farewell to the allurements of the world.

He says *in every place*, intimating by these words, that he went to no place in which he did not gain some fruit, and that, wherever he went, there was to be seen some reward of his labour. The Corinthians were aware, in how many places he had previously sowed the seed of Christ's gospel. He now says, that the last corresponded with the first.[2]

---

by allowing him a magnificent procession through the city. This was not granted by the senate unless the general had gained a *very signal and decisive victory;* conquered a *province,* &c.........The people at Corinth were sufficiently acquainted with the nature of a *triumph:* about two hundred years before this, *Lucius Mummius,* the Roman consul, had conquered all *Achaia,* destroyed *Corinth, Thebes,* and *Chalcis;* and, by order of the senate, had a grand triumph, and was surnamed *Achaicus."—Dr. A. Clarke.—Ed.*

[1] " C'est plustot au nom de Dieu, que en leur propre nom ;"—" It is in God's name, rather than in their own."

[2] " La benediction de Dieu continue sur son ministere comme on l'y

15. *A sweet odour of Christ.* The metaphor which he had applied to the knowledge of Christ, he now transfers to the persons of the Apostles, but it is for the same reason. For as they are called the *light of the world,* (Matt. v. 14,) because they enlighten men by holding forth the torch of the gospel, and not as if they shone forth upon them with their own lustre ; so they have the name of *odour,* not as if they emitted any fragrance of themselves, but because the doctrine which they bring is odoriferous, so that it can imbue the whole world with its delectable fragrance.[1] It is certain, however, that this commendation is applicable to all the ministers of the gospel, because wherever there is a pure and unvarnished proclamation of the gospel, there will be found *there* the influence of that *odour,* of which Paul here speaks. At the same time, there is no doubt, that he speaks particularly of himself, and those that were like him, turning to his own commendation what slanderers imputed to him as a fault. For his being opposed by many, and exposed to the hatred of many, was the reason why they despised him. He, accordingly, replies, that faithful and upright ministers of the gospel have a sweet odour before God, not merely when they quicken souls by a wholesome savour, but also, when they bring destruction to unbelievers. Hence the gospel ought not to be less esteemed on that account. " Both odours," says he, " are grateful to God—that by which the elect are refreshed unto salvation, and that from which the wicked receive a deadly shock."

auoit apperceue au commencement ;"—" The blessing of God continues upon his ministry, as they had seen it do at the beginning."

[1] " Elsner and many other commentators think, with sufficient reason, that there is here an allusion to the perfumes that were usually censed during the triumphal processions of Roman conquerors. Plutarch, on an occasion of this kind, describes the streets and temples as being Συμιαματων πληρεις—' full of incense,' which might not improperly be called an odour of death to the vanquished, and of life to the conquerors. It is possible that in the following verses the Apostle further alludes to the different effects of strong perfumes, to cheer some, and to throw others into various disorders, according to the different dispositions they may be in to receive them. There is, perhaps, not equal foundation for another conjecture which has been offered, that the expression, *causeth us to triumph in Christ,* contains an allusion to the custom of victorious generals, who, in their triumphal processions, were wont to carry some of their relations with them in their chariot."—*Illustrated Commentary.—Ed.*

Here we have a remarkable passage, by which we are taught, that, whatever may be the issue of our preaching, it is, notwithstanding, well-pleasing to God, if the Gospel is preached, and our service will be acceptable to him ; and also, that it does not detract in any degree from the dignity of the Gospel, that it does not do good to all ; for God is glorified even in this, that the Gospel becomes an occasion of ruin to the wicked, nay, it must turn out so. If, however, this is a *sweet odour* to God, it ought to be so to us also, or in other words, it does not become us to be offended, if the preaching of the Gospel is not salutary to all ; but on the contrary, let us reckon, that it is quite enough, if it advance the glory of God by bringing just condemnation upon the wicked. If, however, the heralds of the Gospel are in bad odour in the world, because their success does not in all respects come up to their desires, they have this choice consolation, that they waft to God the perfume of a sweet fragrance, and what is to the world an offensive smell, is a *sweet odour* to God and angels.[1]

The term *odour* is very emphatic. " Such is the influence of the Gospel in both respects, that it either quickens or kills, not merely by its taste, but by its very smell. Whatever it may be, it is never preached in vain, but has invariably an effect, either for life, or for death."[2] But it is asked,

[1] " ' We are unto God a sweet *savour* (or *odour*, rather, as the word ὀσμὴ more properly signifies) of Christ in them that are saved and in them that perish. To the one we are the odour of death unto death ; to the other, the odour of life unto life.' And this lay with a mighty weight upon his spirit. O that ever we should be the savour of death unto death to any ! Who is sufficient for these things ! But whether of life or death, we are a sweet odour to God in Christ, as to both ; when he sees the sincerity of our hearts, and how fain we would fetch souls out of the state of death into this life. So grateful and pleasant to him is the work effected of saving souls, that the attempt and desire of it is not ungrateful."— *Howe's Works*, (Lond. 1834,) p. 999.

[2] " *We are the savour of death unto death.* It is probable that the language here used is borrowed from similar expressions which were common among the Jews. Thus in Debarim Rabba, sect. i. fol. 248, it is said, ' As the bee brings some honey to the owner, but stings others ; so it is with the words of the law.' ' They (the words of the law) are a *savour of life* to Israel, but a *savour of death* to the people of this world.' Thus in Taarieth, fol. vii. 1, ' Whoever gives attention to the law on account of the law itself, to him it becomes an *aromatic of life*, םייח םס, (*sam chiim*); but to him who does not attend to the law on account of the law itself, to

how this accords with the nature of the Gospel, which we shall find him, a little afterwards, calling the *ministry* of life? (2 Cor. iii. 6.) The answer is easy: The Gospel is preached for salvation : this is what properly belongs to it ; but believers alone are partakers of that salvation. In the mean time, its being an occasion of condemnation to unbelievers—that arises from their own fault. Thus *Christ came not into the world to condemn the world,* (John iii. 17,) for what need was there of this, inasmuch as without him we are all condemned ? Yet he sends his apostles to *bind,* as well as to *loose,* and to *retain* sins, as well as *remit* them. (Matt. xviii. 18 ; John xx. 23.) He is the *light of the world,* (John viii. 12,) but he blinds unbelievers. (John ix. 39.) He is a Rock, for a foundation, but he is also to many a stone of stumbling.[1] (Isaiah viii. 14.) We must always, therefore, distinguish between the proper office of the Gospel,[2] and the accidental one (so to speak) which must be imputed to the depravity of mankind, to which it is owing, that life to them is turned into death.

16. *And who is sufficient for these things?* This exclamation is thought by some[3] to be introduced by way of guard-

him it becomes an *aromatic of death,* מות סם, (*sam maveth*)'—the idea of which is, that as medicines skilfully applied will heal, but if unskilfully applied will aggravate a disease, so it is with the words of the law. Again, ' The word of the law which proceeds out of the mouth of God is an *odour of life* to the Israelites, but an *odour of death* to the Gentiles.' "—*Barnes.* —*Ed.*

[1] " De scandale et achoppement ;"—" Of offence and stumbling."

[2] " Le propre et naturel office de l'Euangile ;"—" The proper and natural office of the Gospel."

[3] Among these is Chrysostom, who, when commenting upon this passage, says : Ἐπειδὴ μεγάλα ἐφθέγξατο, ὅτι θυσία ἐσμὲν τοῦ Χριστοῦ καὶ εὐωδία, καὶ θριαμβευόμεθα πανταχοῦ, πάλιν μετριάζει τῷ θεῷ πάντα ἀνατίθεις· διὸ καὶ φησὶ, καὶ πρὸς ταῦτα τίς ἱκανός; τὸ γὰρ πᾶν τοῦ Χριστοῦ, φησιν, εστιν· οὐδὲν ἡμέτερον· ὁρᾷς ἐπεναντίας ψευδαποστόλοις φθεγγόμενον· οἱ μὲν γὰρ καυχῶνται ὡς παρ' ἑαυτῶν εἰσφέροντές τι εἰς τὸ κήρυγμα. οὗτος δὲ διὰ τοῦτό φησι καυχᾶσθαι, ἐπειδὴ οὐδὲν αὐτοῦ φησιν εἶναι.—" Having uttered great things—that we are an offering, and a sweet savour of Christ, and that we are made to triumph everywhere, he again qualifies this by ascribing everything to God. Accordingly he says : *And who is sufficient for these things?* For everything, says he, is Christ's—nothing is ours: you see that he expresses himself in a manner directly opposite to that of the false apostles. For these, indeed, boast, as if they of themselves contributed something towards their preaching, while he, on the other hand, says, that he boasts on this ground—because nothing, he says, is his."—*Ed.*

ing against arrogance, for he confesses, that to discharge the office of a good Apostle[1] to Christ is a thing that exceeds all human power, and thus he ascribes the praise to God. Others think, that he takes notice of the small number of good ministers. I am of opinion, that there is an implied contrast that is shortly afterwards expressed. " Profession, it is true, is common, and many confidently boast ; but to have the reality, is indicative of a rare and distinguished excellence.[2] I claim nothing for myself, but what will be discovered to be in me, if trial is made." Accordingly, as those, who hold in common the office of instructor, claim to themselves indiscriminately the title, Paul, by claiming to himself a peculiar excellence, separates himself from the herd of those, who had little or no experience of the influence of the Spirit.

17. *For we are not.* He now contrasts himself more openly with the false apostles, and that by way of amplifying, and at the same time, with the view of excluding them from the praise that he had claimed to himself. " It is on good grounds," says he, " that I speak in honourable terms of my apostleship, for I am not afraid of being convicted of vanity, if proof is demanded. But many on false grounds arrogate the same thing to themselves, who will be found to have nothing in common with me. For they *adulterate the word of the Lord,* which I dispense with the greatest faithfulness and sincerity for the edification of the Church." I do not think it likely, however, that those, who are here reproved, preached openly wicked or false doctrines ; but am rather of opinion, that they corrupted the right use of doctrine, for the sake either of gain or of ambition, so as utterly to deprive it of energy. This he terms *adulterating.* Erasmus prefers to render it—*cauponari*—*huckstering.*[3] The Greek word καπηλεύειν is taken from retailers, or tavern-

---

[1] " Loyale et fidele Apostre ;"—" A loyal and faithful Apostle."

[2] " C'est vne vertu excellente, et bien clair semee ;"—" It is a distinguished excellence, and very thin sown."

[3] " Erasme l'a traduit par vn autre mot Latin que moy, qui vient d'vn mot qui signifie tauernier ;"—" Erasmus has rendered it by a Latin word different from what I have used—derived from a word that signifies a tavern-keeper."

keepers, who are accustomed to adulterate their commodities, that they may fetch a higher price. I do not know whether the word *cauponari* is used in that sense among the Latins.[1]

It is, indeed, certain from the corresponding clause, that Paul intended to express here—corruption of doctrine—not as though they had revolted from the truth, but because they presented it under disguise, and not in its genuine purity. For the doctrine of God is corrupted in two ways. It is corrupted in a *direct* way, when it is mixed up with falsehood and lies, so as to be no longer the pure and genuine doctrine of God, but is falsely commended under that title. It is corrupted *indirectly*, when, although retaining its purity, it is turned hither and thither to please men, and is disfigured by unseemly disguises, by way of hunting after favour. Thus there will be found some, in whose doctrine there will be no impiety detected, but as they hunt after the applauses of the world by making a display of their acuteness and eloquence, or are ambitious of some place, or gape for *filthy lucre*, (1 Tim. iii. 8,) or are desirous by some means or other to rise, they, nevertheless, corrupt the doctrine itself by wrongfully abusing it, or making it subservient to their depraved inclinations. I am, therefore, inclined to retain the word *adulterate*, as it expresses better what ordinarily happens in the case of all that play with the sacred word of God, as with a ball, and transform it according to their own convenience.[2] For it must necessarily be, that

[1] *Raphelius* adduces a passage from Herodotus, (lib. iii. page 225,) in which, when speaking of Darius Hystaspes, who first exacted tribute from the Persians, he says that the Persians said, " ὡς Δαρειος μέν ἦν κάπηλος, ὅτι εκαπηλευε παντα τὰ πράγματα,"—"that Darius was a huckster, for he *made gain* of everything." Herodian (lib. vi. cap. 11) uses the expression, 'Ειρήνην χρυσιου καπηλευοντες,"—" Making peace *for money*." The phrase, *Cauponari bellum*, is employed in a similar sense by Cicero (Off. i. 12) as meaning, " to make war *for money*." In Isaiah i. 22, the Septuagint version reads as follows: " Οἱ κάπηλοί σου μισγοῦσι τον οἰνον ὕδατι;"—" Thy vintners mix the wine with water." Καπηλος, as Dr. Bloomfield shows by two passages from Plato, properly means a *retail-dealer*, one who deals at second hand. " The κάπηλοι," he observes, " were *petty chapmen*, (and that chiefly in eatables or drinkables,) exactly corresponding to our hucksters."—*Ed.*

[2] The reader will find this class of persons referred to at greater length by CALVIN, when commenting on 2 Cor. i. 19. (See p. 135.)—*Ed.*

they degenerate from the truth, and preach a sort of artificial and spurious Gospel.

But as of sincerity. The word *as* here is superfluous, as in many other places.[1] In contrast with the corruption that he had made mention of, he makes use, first of all, of the term *sincerity,* which may be taken as referring to the manner of preaching, as well as to the disposition of the mind. I approve rather of the latter. *Secondly,* he places in contrast with it a faithful and conscientious dispensation of it, inasmuch as he faithfully delivers to the Church from hand to hand,[2] as they say, the Gospel which God had committed to him, and had given him in charge. *Thirdly,* he subjoins to this a regard to the Divine presence. For whoever has the three following things, is in no danger of forming the purpose of corrupting the word of God. The *first* is—that we be actuated by a true zeal for God. The *second* is—that we bear in mind that it is his business that we are transacting, and bring forward nothing but what has come from him. The *third* is—that we consider, that we do nothing of which he is not the witness and spectator, and thus learn to refer every thing to his judgment.

In Christ means *according to Christ.* For the rendering of Erasmus, *By Christ,* is foreign to Paul's intention.[3]

CHAPTER III.

1. Do we begin again to commend ourselves? or need we, as some *others,* epistles of commendation to you, or *letters* of commendation from you?	1. Incipimus rursum nos ipsos commendare? numquid, sicuti quidam, commendaticiis epistolis opus habemus ad vos? aut commendaticiis a vobis?
2. Ye are our epistle written in our hearts, known and read of all men :	2. Epistola nostra vos estis, scripta in cordibus nostris, quæ cognoscitur et legitur ab omnibus hominibus.

[1] Thus in Acts xvii. 14, we read that the brethren sent away Paul to go (ὡς ἐπὶ τὴν θαλασσαν) *as* to the sea, where ὡς (*as*) is redundant, in accordance with various instances cited by *Wetstein* from *Pausanias* and *Arrian* of the very same expression.—*Ed.*

[2] See CALVIN on the Corinthians, vol. i. pp. 150, 373, and vol. ii. p. 9.

[3] The expression is rendered by Dr. Bloomfield, " In the name of Christ, as his legates."—*Ed.*

3. *Forasmuch as ye are* manifestly declared to be the epistle of
Christ ministered by us, written not
with ink, but with the Spirit of the
living God; not in tables of stone,
but in fleshly tables of the heart.

3. Dum palam fit, vos esse Epis-
tolam Christi, subministratam a
nobis, scriptam non atramento, sed
Spiritu Dei vivi: non in tabulis la-
pideis, sed in tabulis cordis carneis.[1]

1. *Do we begin.* It appears that this objection also was
brought forward against him—that he was excessively fond
of publishing his own exploits, and brought against him, too,
by those who were grieved to find that the fame, which they
were eagerly desirous to obtain, was effectually obstructed
in consequence of his superior excellence.   They had already,
in my opinion, found fault with the former Epistle, on this
ground, that he indulged immoderately in commendations
of himself.   To *commend* here means to boast foolishly and
beyond measure, or at least to recount one's own praises in a
spirit of ambition.   Paul's calumniators had a plausible
pretext—that it is a disgusting[2] and odious thing in itself
for one to be the trumpeter of his own praises.   Paul, however, had an excuse on the ground of necessity, inasmuch as
he gloried, only because he was shut up to it.   His design
also raised him above all calumny, as he had nothing in view
but that the honour of his apostleship might remain unimpaired for the edification of the Church; for had not Christ's
honour been infringed upon, he would readily have allowed
to pass unnoticed what tended to detract from his own reputation.   Besides, he saw that it was very much against
the Corinthians, that his authority was lessened among
them.   In the first place, therefore, he brings forward their
calumny, letting them know that he is not altogether ignorant as to the kind of talk, that was current among them.

Have we need?   The answer is suited (to use a common
expression) to the person rather than to the thing, though
we shall find him afterwards saying as much as was required
in reference to the thing itself.   At present, however, he
reproves their malignity, inasmuch as they were displeased,

---

[1] " Tables de cœur de chair; *ou*, tables charnelles du cœur; *ou*, tables
du cœur *qui sont* de chair ;"—" Tables of heart of flesh; *or*, fleshly tables
of the heart ; *or*, tables of the heart *which are* of flesh."

[2] " Mal sonnante aux aureilles ;"—" Sounding offensively to the ears."

if he at any time reluctantly, nay even when they themselves constrained him, made mention of the grace that God had bestowed upon him, while they were themselves begging in all quarters for epistles, that were stuffed entirely with flattering commendations. He says that he has no need of commendation in words, while he is abundantly commended by his deeds. On the other hand, he convicts them of a greedy desire for glory, inasmuch as they endeavoured to acquire favour through the suffrages of men.[1] In this manner, he gracefully and appropriately repels their calumny. We must not, however, infer from this, that it is absolutely and in itself wrong to receive recommendations,[2] provided you make use of them for a good purpose. For Paul himself recommends many ; and this he would not have done had it been unlawful. Two things, however, are required here—*first*, that it be not a recommendation that is elicited by flattery, but an altogether unbiassed testimony ;[3] and *secondly*, that it be not given for the purpose of procuring advancement for the individual, but simply that it may be the means of promoting the advancement of Christ's kingdom. For this reason, I have observed, that Paul has an eye to those who had assailed him with calumnies.

2. *Ye are our Epistle.* There is no little ingenuity in his making his own glory hinge upon the welfare of the Corinthians. " So long as you shall remain Christians, I shall have recommendation enough. For your faith speaks my praise, as being *the seal of my apostleship.*" (1 Cor. ix. 2.)

When he says—*written in our hearts*, this may be understood in reference to Silvanus and Timotheus, and in that case the meaning will be : " We are not contented with this praise, that we derive from the thing itself. The recommendations, that others have, fly about before the eyes of

---

[1] " Par la faueur et recommandation des hommes ;"—" By the favour and recommendation of men."

[2] " Letres recommandatoires ;"—" Recommendatory letters."

[3] " Enucleatum testimonium ;"—" Vn vray tesmoignage rendu d'vn iugement entier auec prudence et en verite ;"—" A true testimony, given with solid judgment, with prudence, and with truth." Cicero makes use of a similar expression, which CALVIN very probably had in his eye—" Enucleata suffragia ;"—" Votes given judiciously, and with an unbiassed judgment."—(Cic. Planc. 4.)—*Ed.*

men, but this, that *we* have, has its seat in men's consciences."
It may also be viewed as referring in part to the Corinthians,
in this sense : "Those that obtain recommendations by dint
of entreaty, have not in the conscience what they carry about
written upon paper, and those that recommend others often
do so rather by way of favour than from judgment. We, on
the other hand, have the testimony of our apostleship, on
this side and on that, engraven on men's hearts."

Which is known and read. It might also be read—" Which
is known and *acknowledged*," owing to the ambiguity of the
word ἀναγινωσκεσθαι, and I do not know but that the latter
might be more suitable. I was unwilling, however, to depart
from the common rendering, when not constrained to do so.
Only let the reader have this brought before his view, that
he may consider which of the two renderings is the preferable one. If we render it *acknowledged*, there will be an
implied contrast between an epistle that is sure and of unquestionable authority, and such as are counterfeit.[2] And,
unquestionably, what immediately follows, is rather on the
side of the latter rendering, for he brings forward the *Epistle of Christ*, in contrast with those that are forged and pretended.

3. *Ye are the Epistle of Christ.* Pursuing the metaphor,
he says that the Epistle of which he speaks was written by
Christ, inasmuch as the faith of the Corinthians was his
work. He says that it was *ministered* by him, as if meaning by this, that he had been in the place of ink and pen.
In fine, he makes Christ the author and himself the instrument, that calumniators may understand, that it is with
Christ that they have to do, if they continue to speak against

---

[1] CALVIN has had occasion to notice the double signification of this
word when commenting on 2 Cor. i. 13. See p. 128. An instance of the
ambiguity of the word occurs in Matt. xxiv. 15, where the words ὁ ἀναγιν-
ώσκων νοείτω are understood by *Kypke* as the words, not of the evangelist,
but of Christ, and as meaning—"He who *recognises* this, (that is, the
completion of Daniel's prophecy by the 'abomination of desolation standing where it ought not,') let him take notice and reflect," while most other
interpreters consider the words in question as an admonition of the evangelist to the reader—" Let him that readeth *understand* or *take notice*."—
Ed.

[2] " Celles qui sont attitrees et faites à plaisir ;"—" Such as are procured
by unfair means, and are made to suit convenience."

him[1] with malignity.   What follows is intended to increase the authority of that *Epistle*.   The second clause,[2] however, has already a reference to the comparison that is afterwards drawn between the law and the gospel.   For he takes occasion from this shortly afterwards, as we shall see, to enter upon a comparison of this nature.   The antitheses here employed—*ink* and *Spirit, stones* and *heart*—give no small degree of weight to his statements, by way of amplification. For in drawing a contrast between *ink* and the *Spirit* of God, and between *stones* and *heart,* he expresses more than if he had simply made mention of the *Spirit* and the *heart,* without drawing any comparison.

Not on tables of stone.   He alludes to the promise that is recorded in Jer. xxxi. 31, and Ezek. xxxvii. 26, concerning the grace of the New Testament.   *I will make,* says he, *a new covenant with them, not such as I had made with their fathers; but I will write my laws upon their hearts, and engrave them on their inward parts.*   Farther, *I will take away the stony heart from the midst of thee, and I will give thee a heart of flesh, that thou mayest walk in my precepts.* (Ezek. xxxvi. 26, 27.)   Paul says, that this blessing was accomplished through means of his preaching.   Hence it abundantly appears, that he is a faithful minister of the New Covenant—which is a legitimate testimony in favour of his apostleship.   The epithet *fleshly* is not taken here in a bad sense, but means soft and flexible,[3] as it is contrasted with *stony,* that is, hard and stubborn, as is the heart of man by nature, until it has been subdued by the Spirit of God.[4]

4. And such trust have we through Christ to God-ward :

5. Not that we are sufficient of ourselves to think any thing as of ourselves ; but our sufficiency *is* of God.

4. Fiduciam autem eiusmodi per Christum habemus erga Deum :

5. Non quod idonei simus ex nobis ad cogitandum quicquam, tanquam ex nobis : sed facultas nostra ex Deo est.

[1] " De son apostre ;"—" Against his apostle."
[2] " Le dernier membre de la sentence ;"—" The last clause of the sentence."
[3] " Vn cœur docile et ployable, ou aisé à ranger ;"—" A heart that is teachable and flexible, or easy to manage."
[4] " Jusques à ce qu'il soit donté et amolli par le sainct Esprit ;"—" Until it has been tamed and softened by the Holy Spirit."

6. Who also hath made us able ministers of the new testament; not of the letter, but of the spirit: for the letter killeth, but the spirit giveth life.

7. But if the ministration of death, written *and* engraven in stones, was glorious, so that the children of Israel could not stedfastly behold the face of Moses for the glory of his countenance ; which *glory* was to be done away :

8. How shall not the ministration of the Spirit be rather glorious ?

9. For if the ministration of condemnation *be* glory, much more doth the ministration of righteousness exceed in glory.

10. For even that which was made glorious, had no glory in this respect, by reason of the glory that excelleth.

11. For if that which is done away *was* glorious, much more that which remaineth *is* glorious.

6. Qui nos fecit idoneos ministros Novi testamenti,[1] non literae, sed Spiritus: nam litera quidem occidit : Spiritus autem vivificat.

7. Quodsi ministerium mortis in literis insculptum in lapidibus fuit in gloria, ita ut non possent intueri filii Israel in faciem Mosis propter gloriam vultus eius, quæ aboletur :

8. Quomodo non magis ministerium Spiritus erit in gloria?

9. Si enim ministerium damnationis, gloria : quomodo non magis abundet (*vel, excellat*) ministerium iustitiæ in gloria ?

10. Etenim quod glorificatum fuit, in hac parte, non fuit glorificatum propter antecellentem gloriam.

11. Si enim quod aboletur, per gloriam : multo magis quod manet, erit in gloria.

4. *And such confidence.* As it was a magnificent commendation, that Paul had pronounced to the honour of himself and his Apostleship, lest he should seem to speak of himself more confidently than was befitting, he transfers the entire glory to God, from whom he acknowledges that he has received everything that he has. " By this boasting," says he, " I extol God rather than myself, *by whose grace I am what I am.*" (1 Cor. xv. 10.) He adds, as he is accustomed to do *by Christ,* because he is, as it were, the channel, through which all God's benefits flow forth to us.

5. *Not that we are competent.*[2] When he thus disclaims all merit, it is not as if he abased himself in merely pretended modesty, but instead of this, he speaks what he truly thinks. Now we see, that he leaves man nothing. For the smallest part, in a manner, of a good work is *thought*. In other words,[3] it has neither the *first* part of the praise, nor

---

[1] " Du nouueau Testament, *ou, de la nouuelle alliance ;*"—" Of the New Testament, *or, of the new covenant.*"

[2] " Non point que soyons suffisans ;"—" Not that we are sufficient."

[3] " Pour le moins ;"—" At least."

the *second ;* and yet he does not allow us even *this.* As it
is less to *think* than to *will,* how foolish a part do those act,
who arrogate to themselves a right *will,* when Paul does not
leave them so much as the power of *thinking* aught![1] Papists
have been misled by the term *sufficiency,* that is made use
of by the Old Interpreter.[2] For they think to get off by
acknowledging that man is not qualified to form good purposes, while in the mean time they ascribe to him a right
apprehension of the mind, which, with some assistance from
God, may effect something of itself. Paul, on the other
hand, declares that man is in want, not merely of *sufficiency
of himself,* (αὐτάρκειαν,) but also of *competency* (ἱκανότητα,)[3]
which would be equivalent to *idoneitas* (fitness), if such a
term were in use among the Latins. He could not, therefore, more effectually strip man bare of every thing good.[4]

6. *Who hath made us competent.*[5] He had acknowledged
himself to be altogether useless. Now he declares, that, by
the grace of God, he has been qualified[6] for an office, for

[1] See *Institutes,* vol. i. pp. 328, 332.—*Ed.*

[2] Wiclif (1380) following, as he is wont, the *Vulgate,* renders the
verse as follows : " Not that we ben sufficiente to thenke ony thing of us
as of us : but oure sufficience is of God."—*Ed.*

[3] " La disposition, preparation, et inclination ;"—" Disposition, preparation, and inclination."

[4] *Charnock,* in his " Discourse on the Efficient of Regeneration,"
makes an interesting allusion to CALVIN'S exposition of this verse.
" *Thinking,*" says he, " is the lowest step in the ladder of preparation;
'tis the first act of the creature in any rational production ; yet this
the Apostle doth remove from man, as in every part of it his own act, (2
Cor. iii. 5.) *Not that we are sufficient of ourselves to think any thing as of
ourselves, but our sufficiency is of God.* The word signifies—reasoning :
no rational act can be done without reasoning ; this is not purely our own.
We have no sufficiency of ourselves, *as of ourselves,* originally and radi-
cally of ourselves, as if we were the author of that sufficiency, either
naturally or meritoriously. And CALVIN observes, that the word is not
αὐτάρκεια, but ἱκανότης—not a *self-ability,* but an *aptitude* or *fitness* to any
gracious thought. How can we oblige him by any act, since, in every part
of it, it is from him, not from ourselves? For as *thinking* is the first requisite, so it is perpetually requisite to the progress of any rational act, so
that every thought in any act, and the whole progress, wherein there must
be a whole flood of thoughts, is from the sufficiency of God."—*Charnock's
Works,* vol. ii. p. 149.—*Ed.*

[5] " Lequel aussi nous a rendus suffisans ministres ;"—" Who also hath
made us sufficient ministers."

[6] It is justly observed by *Barnes,* that the rendering in our authorized
version—" Who hath made us *able* ministers"—" does not *quite* meet the

which he was previously unqualified. From this we infer its magnitude and difficulty, as it can be undertaken by no one, that has not been previously prepared and fashioned for it by God. It is the Apostle's intention, also, to extol the dignity of the gospel. There is, at the same time, no doubt, that he indirectly exposes the poverty of those, who boasted in lofty terms of their endowments, while they were not furnished with so much as a single drop of heavenly grace.

Not of the letter but of the spirit. He now follows out the comparison between the law and the gospel, which he had previously touched upon. It is uncertain, however, whether he was led into this discussion, from seeing, that there were at Corinth certain perverse[1] devotees of the law, or whether he took occasion from something else to enter upon it. For my part, as I see no evidence, that the false apostles had there confounded the law and the gospel, I am rather of opinion, that, as he had to do with lifeless declaimers, who endeavoured to obtain applause through mere prating,[2] and as he saw, that the ears of the Corinthians were captivated with such glitter, he was desirous to show

---

force of the original," as it " would seem to imply that Paul regarded himself and his fellow-labourers as men of talents, and of signal ability ; and that he was inclined to boast of it," while instead of this " he did not esteem himself *sufficient* for this work in his own strength, (ch. ii. 16 ; iii. 5) ; and he here says, that God had made him *sufficient* : not able, talented, learned, but *sufficient,* (ἱκάνωσεν ἡμᾶς) ; he has supplied our deficiency ; he has rendered us competent or fit ;—if a word may be coined after the manner of the Greek here, ' he has *sufficienced* us for this work.' " The unhappy rendering referred to had originated (as is shown by *Granville Penn*) in the circumstance, that the Vulgate having rendered the expression—*qui idoneos nos fecit ministros,* Wiclif translated it as follows : *which made us also able mynystris,* and that, while Erasmus suggested that it should be rendered—*qui idoneos nos fecit ut essemus ministri,* quasi dicas, *idoneavit*—who *fitted* or *qualified* us to be ministers—and while, besides, in the first translation from the original Greek, in 1526, Tyndale rendered — made us able to minister, Wiclif's original version from the Latin was *recalled,* and is now the reading of our authorized version.— *Ed.*

¹ " Mauuais et inconsiderez ;"—" Wicked and reckless."

² " Il auoit affaire auec des gens qui sans zele preschoyent l'Euangile, comme qui prononceroit vne harangue pour son plaisir, et n'ayans que le babil, pourchassoyent par cela la faueur des hommes ;"—" He had to do with persons, who without zeal preached the gospel, like one that makes a harangue according to his own liking, and while they had nothing but mere talk, endeavoured by this means to procure the applause of men."

them what was the chief excellence of the gospel, and what was the chief praise of its ministers. Now this he makes to consist in the efficacy of the Spirit. A comparison between the law and the gospel was fitted in no ordinary degree to show this. This appears to me to be the reason why he came to enter upon it.

There is, however, no doubt, that by the term *letter*, he means the Old Testament, as by the term *spirit* he means the gospel; for, after having called himself a *minister of the New Testament*, he immediately adds, by way of exposition, that he is a *minister of the spirit*, and contrasts the *letter* with the *spirit*. We must now enquire into the reason of this designation. The exposition contrived by Origen has got into general circulation—that by the *letter* we ought to understand the grammatical and genuine meaning of Scripture, or the *literal* sense, (as they call it,) and that by the *spirit* is meant the allegorical meaning, which is commonly reckoned to be the *spiritual* meaning. Accordingly, during several centuries, nothing was more commonly said, or more generally received, than this—that Paul here furnishes us with a key for expounding Scripture by allegories, while nothing is farther from his intention. For by the term *letter* he means outward preaching, of such a kind as does not reach the heart; and, on the other hand, by *spirit* he means living doctrine, of such a nature as *worketh effectually* (1 Thess. ii. 13) on the minds of men,[1] through the grace of the Spirit. By the term *letter*, therefore, is meant *literal* preaching—that is, *dead* and *ineffectual*, perceived only by the ear. By the term *spirit*, on the other hand, is meant *spiritual* doctrine, that is, what is not merely uttered with the mouth, but effectually makes its way to the souls of men with a lively feeling. For Paul had an eye to the passage in Jeremiah, that I quoted a little ago, (Jer. xxxi. 31,)[2] where the Lord says, that his law had been proclaimed merely with the mouth, and that it had, therefore, been of short duration, because the people did not embrace it in their heart, and he

---

[1] " Es cœurs des auditeurs ;"—" In the hearts of the hearers."
[2] See p. 168.

promises the Spirit of regeneration under the reign of Christ, to write his gospel, that is, the new covenant, upon their hearts.   Paul now makes it his boast, that the accomplishment of that prophecy is to be seen in his preaching, that the Corinthians may perceive, how worthless is the loquacity of those vain boasters, who make incessant noise[1] while devoid of the efficacy of the Spirit.

It is asked, however, whether God, under the Old Testament, merely sounded forth in the way of an external voice, and did not also speak inwardly to the hearts of the pious by his Spirit.   I answer in the *first* place, that Paul here takes into view what belonged peculiarly to the law ; for although God then wrought by his Spirit, yet that did not take its rise from the ministry of Moses, but from the grace of Christ, as it is said in John i. 17—*The law was given by Moses; but grace and truth came by Jesus Christ.*   True, indeed, the grace of God did not, during all that time, lie dormant, but it is enough that it was not a benefit that belonged to the law.[2]   For Moses had discharged his office, when he had delivered to the people the doctrine of life, adding threatenings and promises.   For this reason he gives to the law the name of the *letter*, because it is in itself a dead preaching ; but the gospel he calls *spirit*, because the ministry of the gospel is *living*, nay, *lifegiving*.

I answer *secondly*, that these things are not affirmed absolutely in reference either to the law or to the gospel, but in respect of the contrast between the one and the other ; for even the gospel is not always *spirit*.   When, however, we come to compare the two, it is truly and properly affirmed, that the nature of the law is to teach men *literally*, in such a way that it does not reach farther than the ear ; and that, on the other hand, the nature of the gospel is to teach *spiritually*, because it is the instrument of Christ's grace.   This depends on the appointment of God, who has seen it meet to manifest the efficacy of his Spirit more clearly in the

---

[1]   " Crient et gazouillent :"—" Cry and chirp."

[2]   " Il suffit, que ce n'estoit point par le moyen de la loy : car elle n'auoit point cela de propre ;"—" It is enough that it was not by means of the law ; for it did not belong peculiarly to it."

gospel than in the law, for it is his work exclusively to teach effectually the minds of men.

When Paul, however, calls himself a *Minister of the Spirit*, he does not mean by this, that the grace of the Holy Spirit and his influence, were tied to his preaching, so that he could, whenever he pleased, breathe forth the Spirit along with the utterance of the voice. He simply means, that Christ blessed his ministry, and thus accomplished what was predicted respecting the gospel. It is one thing for Christ to connect his influence with a man's doctrine,[1] and quite another for the man's doctrine[2] to have such efficacy of itself. We are, then, *Ministers of the Spirit*, not as if we held him inclosed within us, or as it were captive—not as if we could at our pleasure confer his grace upon all, or upon whom we pleased—but because Christ, through our instrumentality, illuminates the minds of men, renews their hearts, and, in short, regenerates them wholly.[3] It is in consequence of there being such a connection and bond of union between Christ's grace and man's effort, that in many cases *that* is ascribed to the minister which belongs exclusively to the Lord. For in that case it is not the mere individual that is looked to, but the entire dispensation of the gospel, which consists, on the one hand, in the secret influence of Christ, and, on the other, in man's outward efforts.

For the letter killeth. This passage was mistakingly perverted, first by Origen, and afterwards by others, to a spurious signification. From this arose a very pernicious error —that of imagining that the perusal of Scripture would be not merely useless, but even injurious,[4] unless it were drawn out into allegories. This error was the source of many evils. For there was not merely a liberty allowed of adulterating the genuine meaning of Scripture,[5] but the more of

---

[1] " Au ministere de l'homme qui enseigne ;"—" To the ministry of the man that teaches."

[2] " La doctrine de l'homme, c'est à dire, son ministere ;"—" The doctrine of the man, that is to say, his ministry."

[3] The reader will find the same subject largely treated of by CALVIN, when commenting on 1 Cor. iii. 6. See CALVIN on the Corinthians, vol. i. pp. 128-9.—*Ed.*

[4] " Dangereuse ;"—" Dangerous."

[5] " De corrompre et desguiser le vray et naturel sens de l' Escriture :"

audacity any one had in this manner of acting, so much the more eminent an interpreter of Scripture was he accounted. Thus many of the ancients recklessly played with the sacred word of God,[1] as if it had been a ball to be tossed to and fro. In consequence of this, too, heretics had it more in their power to trouble the Church ; for as it had become a general practice to make any passage whatever[2] mean anything that one might choose, there was no frenzy so absurd or monstrous, as not to admit of being brought forward under some pretext of allegory. Even good men themselves were carried headlong, so as to contrive very many mistaken opinions, led astray through a fondness for allegory.

The meaning of this passage, however, is as follows—that, if the word of God is simply uttered with the mouth, it is an occasion of death, and that it is *lifegiving*, only when it is received with the heart. The terms *letter* and *spirit*, therefore, do not refer to the exposition of the word, but to its influence and fruit. Why it is that the doctrine merely strikes upon the ear, without reaching the heart, we shall see presently.

7. *But if the ministry of death.* He now sets forth the dignity of the gospel by this argument—that God conferred distinguished honour upon the law, which, nevertheless, is nothing in comparison with the gospel. The law was rendered illustrious by many miracles. Paul, however, touches here upon *one* of them merely—that the face of Moses shone with such splendour as dazzled the eyes of all. That splendour was a token of the glory of the law. He now draws an

---

—" Of corrupting and disguising the true and natural meaning of Scripture."

[1] " Can you seriously think the Scriptures," says Rev. Andrew Fuller, in his Thoughts on Preaching, " to be a book of riddles and conundrums, and that a Christian minister is properly employed in giving scope to his fancy in order to discover their solution ? . . . . All Scripture is profitable in some way, some for doctrine, some for reproof, some for correction, and some for instruction in righteousness, but all is not to be turned into allegory. If we must *play*, let it be with things of less consequence than the word of the eternal God."—*Fuller's Works*, vol. iv. p. 694. The attentive reader cannot fail to observe, how very frequently our author exposes, in the strongest terms, the exercise of mere fancy in the interpretation of the Holy Scriptures. See CALVIN on the Corinthians, vol. i. p. 294.—*Ed.*

[2] " Vn propos et vn mot ;"—" A passage and a word."

argument from the less to the greater—that it is befitting, that the glory of the gospel should shine forth with greater lustre, inasmuch as it is greatly superior to the law.

In the *first* place, he calls the law the *ministry of death*. *Secondly,* he says, that the doctrine of it was written in letters, and with ink. *Thirdly,* that it was *engraven on stones*. *Fourthly,* that it was not of perpetual duration ; but, instead of this, its condition was temporary and fading. And, *fifthly,* he calls it the ministry of *condemnation.* To render the antitheses complete, it would have been necessary for him to employ as many corresponding clauses in reference to the gospel; but he has merely spoken of it as being the *ministry of the Spirit,* and of *righteousness,* and as enduring for ever. If you examine the *words,* the correspondence is not complete, but so far as the matter itself is concerned, what is expressed is sufficient.[1] For he had said that the *Spirit giveth life,* and farther, that men's *hearts* served instead of *stones,* and *disposition* in the place of *ink.*

Let us now briefly examine those attributes of the law and the gospel. Let us, however, bear in mind, that he is not speaking of the whole of the doctrine that is contained in the law and the Prophets ; and farther, that he is not treating of what happened to the fathers under the Old Testament, but merely notices what belongs peculiarly to the ministry of Moses. The law was *engraven on stones,* and hence it was a literal doctrine. This defect of the law required to be corrected by the gospel, because it could not

---

[1] *Piscator* brings out the comparison here drawn by the Apostle between the law and the gospel, as presenting *eight* points of contrast, as follows :—

1. Novi Testamenti. (New Testament.)	1. Veteris Testamenti. (Old Testament.)
2. Spiritus. (Spirit.)	2. Literæ. (Letter.)
3. Vitæ. (Life.)	3. Mortis. (Death.)
4. Inscriptum cordibus. (Written on men's hearts.)	4. Inscriptum lapidibus. (Written on stones.)
5. Semper durans. (Everlasting.)	5. Abolendum. (To be done away.)
6. Justitiæ. (Righteousness.)	6. Damnationis. (Condemnation.)
7. Excellenter gloriosum. (Eminently glorious.)	7. Illius Respectu ἄδοξον. (Comparatively devoid of glory.)
8. Perspicuum. (Clear.)	8. Obscurum. (Obscure.)

Piscatoris Scholia in Epist. ii. *ad Corinth.—Ed.*

but be brittle, so long as it was merely engraven on tables of stone. The gospel, therefore, is a holy and inviolable covenant, because it was contracted by the Spirit of God, acting as security. From this, too, it follows, that the law was the *ministry of condemnation* and of *death;* for when men are instructed as to their duty, and hear it declared, that all who do not render satisfaction to the justice of God are cursed, (Deut. xxvii. 26,) they are convicted, as under sentence of sin and death. From the law, therefore, they derive nothing but a condemnation of this nature, because God there demands what is due to him, and at the same time confers no power to perform it. The gospel, on the other hand, by which men are regenerated, and are reconciled to God, through the free remission of their sins, is the ministry of righteousness, and, consequently, of life also.

Here, however, a question arises: As the gospel is the *odour of death unto death* to some, (2 Cor. ii. 16,) and as Christ is a *rock of offence,* and a *stone of stumbling set for the ruin of many,*[1] (Luke ii. 34 ; 1 Peter ii. 8,) why does he represent, as belonging exclusively to the law, what is common to both ? Should you reply, that it happens accidentally that the gospel is the source of death, and, accordingly, is the occasion of it rather than the cause, inasmuch as it is in its own nature salutary to all, the difficulty will still remain unsolved; for the same answer might be returned with truth in reference to the law. For we hear what Moses called the people to bear witness to—that he had set before them life and death. (Deut. xxx. 15.) We hear what Paul himself says in Rom. vii. 10—that the law has turned out to our ruin, not through any fault attaching to it, but in consequence of our wickedness. Hence, as the entailing of condemnation upon men is a thing that *happens* alike to the law and the gospel, the difficulty still remains.

My answer is this—that there is, notwithstanding of this, a great difference between them ; for although the gospel is an occasion of condemnation to many, it is nevertheless, on

---

[1] The occasion of the *ruin* of unbelievers is explained by CALVIN at considerable length in the Harmony, vol. i. pp. 148, 149.—*Ed.*

good grounds, reckoned the doctrine of life, because it is
the instrument of regeneration, and offers to us a free reconciliation with God. The law, on the other hand, as it simply
prescribes the rule of a good life, does not renew men's
hearts to the obedience of righteousness, and denounces
everlasting death upon transgressors, can do nothing but
condemn.[1] Or if you prefer it in another way, the office of
the law is to show us the disease, in such a way as to show
us, at the same time, no hope of cure : the office of the gospel
is, to bring a remedy to those that were past hope. For as
the law leaves man to himself, it condemns him, of necessity, to death ; while the gospel, bringing him to Christ,
opens the gate of life. Thus, in one word, we find that it
is an accidental property of the law, that is perpetual and
inseparable, that it *killeth ;* for as the Apostle says elsewhere,
(Gal. iii. 10,) *All that remain under the law are subject to
the curse.* It does, not, on the other hand, invariably happen
to the gospel, that it *kills,* for in it is *revealed the righteousness of God from faith to faith,* and therefore it is the *power
of God unto salvation to every one that believeth.* (Rom i.
17, 18.)[2]

It remains, that we consider the last of the properties that
are ascribed. The Apostle says, that the law was but for
a time, and required to be abolished, but that the gospel, on
the other hand, remains for ever. There are various reasons
why the ministry of Moses is pronounced transient, for it
was necessary that the shadows should vanish at the coming
of Christ, and that statement—*The law and the Prophets*

[1] " Elle ne nous peut apporter autre chose que condemnation ;"—" It
can bring us nothing but condemnation."

[2] *Turretine,* in his Institutes of Controversial Theology, (vol. ii. p. 159,)
gives a much similar view of the matter, of which CALVIN here treats.
" Quando lex vocatur litera occidens, et ministerium mortis et condemna-
tionis, (2 Cor. iii. 6, 7, 8, 9.) intelligenda est non per se et naturâ suâ, sed
per accidens, ob corruptionem hominis, non absolute et simpliciter, sed
secundum, quid quando spectatur ut fœdus operum, opposite ad fœdus
gratiæ ;"—" When the law is called a *killing letter,* and the *ministry of
death and condemnation,* (2 Cor. iii. 6, 7, 8, 9,) it must be understood to
be so, not in itself and in its own nature, but accidentally, in consequence
of man's corruption—not absolutely and expressly, but relatively, when
viewed as a covenant of works, as contrasted with the covenant of grace."
—*Ed.*

were until John—(Matt. xi. 13)—applies to more than the mere shadows. For it intimates, that Christ has put an end to the ministry of Moses, which was peculiar to him, and is distinguished from the gospel. Finally, the Lord declares by Jeremiah, that the weakness of the Old Testament arose from this—that it was not engraven on men's hearts. (Jer. xxxi. 32, 33.) For my part, I understand that abolition of the law, of which mention is here made, as referring to the whole of the Old Testament, in so far as it is opposed to the gospel, so that it corresponds with the statement—*The law and the Prophets were until John.* For the context requires this. For Paul is not reasoning here as to mere ceremonies, but shows how much more powerfully the Spirit of God exercises his power in the gospel, than of old under the law.

So that they could not look. He seems to have had it in view to reprove, indirectly, the arrogance of those, who despised the gospel as a thing that was excessively mean,[1] so that they could scarcely deign to give it a direct look. "So great," says he, "was the splendour of the law, that the Jews could not endure it. What, then, must we think of the gospel, the dignity of which is as much superior to that of the law, as Christ is more excellent than Moses?"

10. *What was rendered glorious.* This is not a correction of what goes before, but rather a confirmation; for he means that the glory of the law is extinguished when the gospel comes forth. As the moon and stars, though in themselves they are not merely luminous, but diffuse their light over the whole earth, do, nevertheless, disappear before the brightness of the sun; so, however glorious the law was in itself, it has, nevertheless, no glory in comparison with the excellence of the gospel. Hence it follows, that we cannot sufficiently prize, or hold in sufficient esteem the glory of Christ, which shines forth in the gospel, like the splendour of the sun when beaming forth; and that the gospel is foolishly handled, nay more, is shamefully profaned, where the power and majesty of the Spirit do not come forth to view, so as to draw up men's minds and hearts heavenward.

[1] " 'Trop abiecte et contemptible :'"—" Excessively mean and contemptible."

12. Seeing then that we have such hope, we use great plainness of speech :

13. And not as Moses, *which* put a vail over his face, that the children of Israel could not steadfastly look to the end of that which is abolished:

14. But their minds were blinded: for until this day remaineth the same vail untaken away in the reading of the old testament ; which *vail* is done away in Christ.

15. But even unto this day, when Moses is read, the vail is upon their heart.

16. Nevertheless, when it shall turn to the Lord, the vail shall be taken away.

17. Now the Lord is that Spirit : and where the Spirit of the Lord *is*, there *is* liberty.

18. But we all, with open face beholding as in a glass the glory of the Lord, are changed into the same image, from glory to glory, *even* as by the Spirit of the Lord.

12. Habentes igitur hanc spem, multa fiducia (*vel, libertate*) utimur.

13. Et non quemadmodum Moses (Exod. xxxiv. 33-35) ponebat velamen ante faciem suam, ut non intuerentur filii Israel in finem eius quod aboletur.[1]

14. Sed excœcati sunt[2] sensus eorum : nam usque in hunc diem velamen illud in lectione Veteris Testamenti[3] manet : nec tollitur, eo quod aboletur per Christum.[4]

15. Sed usque in hodiernum diem, quum legitur Moses, velamen eorum cordibus impositum est.

16. At ubi conversus fuerit ad Dominum, auferetur velamen.

17. Dominus Spiritus est : ubi autem Spiritus Domini, illic libertas.

18. Nos autem omnes retecta facie gloriam Domini in speculo conspicientes, in eandem imaginem transformamur a gloria in gloriam, tanquam a Domini Spiritu.

---

[1] " Ne regardassent à la fin de ce qui deuoit prendre fin ;" ou, " ne veissent de bout de ce," &c. ; ou, " ne veissent iusqu'au fons de ce qui," &c. ; —" Could not look to the end of what required to be abolished ;" or, " could not see to the close of what," &c. ; or, " could not see to the bottom of what," &c.

[2] " Aueuglez ou endurcis ;"—" Blinded or hardened."

[3] " The Apostle says, (2 Cor. iii. 14,) speaking of his countrymen— ' Until this day remaineth the veil untaken away in the reading of the Old Testament.' (ἐπὶ τῇ ἀναγνώσει τῆς παλαιᾶς διαθήκης.) The word in this application is always rendered in our language *Testament*. We have in this followed the Vulgate, as most modern translators also have done. In the Geneva French, the word is rendered both ways in the title, that the one may serve in explaining the other. 'Le Nouveau Testament, c'est à dire, La Nouvelle Alliance ;'—(' The New Testament, that is to say, The New Covenant,') in which they copied Beza, who says—' Testamentum Novum, sive Fœdus Novum ;'—(' The New Testament, or the New Covenant.') That the second rendering of the word is the better version, is unquestionable ; but the title appropriated by custom to a particular book is on the same footing with a proper name, which is hardly considered as a subject for criticism. Thus we call Cæsar's Diary Cæsar's Commentaries, from their Latin name, though very different in meaning from the English word."—*Campbell on the Gospels*, Dissertation v. p. iii. sect. 3. —*Ed.*

[4] " Pource qu'elle est abolie. ou, *laquelle est ;*"—" Because it is abolished. or, *which is.*"

12. *Having therefore this hope.*   Here he advances still farther, for he does not treat merely of the nature of the law, or of that enduring quality of which we have spoken, but also of its abuse.   True, indeed, this also belonged to its nature, that, being covered with a veil, it was not so manifest to the eye, and that by its brightness it inspired terror, and accordingly Paul says elsewhere, what amounts to the same thing—that the people of Israel had *received* from it the *spirit of bondage unto fear.* (Rom. viii. 15.)   Here, however, he speaks rather of an abuse that was foreign and adventitious.[1]   There was at that time in all quarters a grievous stumbling-block arising from the wantonness of the Jews, inasmuch as they obstinately rejected Christ.[2]   In consequence of this, weak consciences were shaken, being in doubt, whether they should embrace Christ, inasmuch as he was not acknowledged by the chosen people.[3]   This kind of scruple the Apostle removes, by instructing them, that their blindness had been prefigured even from the beginning, inasmuch as they could not behold the face of Moses, except through the medium of a *veil.*   As, therefore, he had stated previously, that the law was rendered glorious by the lustre of Moses' countenance, so now he teaches, that the *veil* was an emblem of the blindness that was to come upon the people of Israel, for the person of Moses represents the law.   The Jews, therefore, acknowledged by this, that they had not eyes to behold the law, except when veiled.

This *veil*, he adds, is not taken away, except by Christ. From this he concludes, that none are susceptible of a right apprehension, but those who direct their minds to Christ.[4]   In the *first* place, he draws this distinction between the law and the Gospel—that the brightness of the former rather dazzled men's eyes, than enlightened them, while in the lat-

---

[1] " D'vn abus accidental, et qui estoit venu d'ailleurs;"—" Of an abuse that was accidental, and that had come from another quarter."

[2] " De ce qu'ils reiettoyent Iesus Christ d'vne malice endurcie;"—" Inasmuch as they rejected Christ with a hardened malice."

[3] " Veu que le peuple esleu ne le recognoissoit point pour Sauueur;"— " Inasmuch as the chosen people did not acknowledge him as a Saviour."

[4] " Ceux qui appliquent leur entendement à cognoistre Christ;"— " Those who apply their understandings to the knowledge of Christ."

ter, Christ's glorious face is clearly beheld. He now trium-
phantly exults, on the ground that the majesty of the Gospel
is not terrific, but amiable[1]—is not hid, but is manifested
familiarly to all. The term παῤῥησία, *confidence*, he employs
here, either as meaning an elevated magnanimity of spirit,
with which all ministers of the Gospel ought to be endowed,
or as denoting an open and full manifestation of Christ ; and
this second view is the more probable, for he contrasts this
confidence with the obscurity of the law.[2]

13. *Not as Moses.* Paul is not reasoning as to the intention of Moses. For as it was his office, to publish the law to
his people, so, there can be no doubt that he was desirous,
that its true meaning should be apprehended by all, and
that he did not intentionally involve his doctrine in obscurity,
but that the fault was on the part of the people. As, therefore, he could not renew the minds of the hearers, he was
contented with faithfully discharging the duty assigned to
him. Nay more, the Lord having commanded him to put a
veil between his face and the eyes of the beholders, he
obeyed. Nothing, therefore, is said here to the dishonour of
Moses, for he was not required to do more than the commission, that was assigned to him, called for. In addition to
this, that bluntness, or that weak and obtuse vision, of which
Paul is now speaking, is confined to unbelievers exclusively,
because the law though wrapt up in figures,[3] did nevertheless *impart wisdom to babes*, Ps. xix. 7.[4]

14. *Their understandings were blinded.* He lays the
whole blame upon them, inasmuch as it was owing to their

---

[1] " Aimable, et attrayante ;"—" Amiable, and attractive."

[2] " We speak not only with all *confidence*, but with all imaginable *plainness;* keeping back nothing ; disguising nothing ; concealing nothing ; and
here we differ greatly from Jewish doctors, and from the Gentile philosophers, who affect *obscurity*, and endeavour, by figures, metaphors, and
allegories, to hide everything from the vulgar. But we wish that all may
hear; and we speak so that all may *understand.*"—*Dr. Adam Clarke.*—
Ed.

[3] " Figures et ombres ;"—" Figures and shadows."

[4] " The clause rendered in our authorized version—*making wise the
simple*, is rendered by CALVIN, instructing the *babe* in wisdom. In Tyndale's Bible the reading is, ' And giveth wisdom even unto *babes.*' *Babes*
is the word used in most of the versions."—CALVIN on the Psalms, vol. i.
p. 317, n. 2.—*Ed.*

blindness, that they did not make any proficiency in the doctrine of the law.   He afterwards adds, *That veil remaineth even until this day.*   By this he means, that that dulness of vision was not for a single hour merely, but prefigured what the condition of the nation would be in time to come. " That *veil* with which Moses covered his face, when publishing the law, was the emblem of a stupidity, that would come upon that people, and would continue upon them for a long period.   Thus at this day, when the law is preached to them, in *hearing they hear not, and in seeing they see not.* (Matt. xiii. 13.)   There is no reason, however, why we should be troubled, *as though some new thing had happened.* (1 Peter iv. 12.)   God has shown long ago under the type of the *veil,* that it would be so.   Lest, however, any blame should attach to the law, he again repeats it, that *their hearts were covered with a veil.*

And it is not removed, because it is done away through Christ.   He assigns a reason, why they are so long in blindness in the midst of light.   For the law is in itself bright, but it is only when Christ appears to us in it, that we enjoy its splendour.   The Jews turn away their eyes as much as they can from Christ.   It is not therefore to be wondered, if they see nothing, refusing as they do to behold the sun. This blindness on the part of the chosen people, especially as it is so long continued, admonishes us not to be lifted up with pride, relying on the benefits that God has conferred upon us.   This point is treated of in Rom. xi. 20.   Let, however, the reason of this blindness deter us from contempt of Christ, which God so grievously punishes.   In the mean time, let us learn, that without Christ, the *Sun of righteousness,* (Mal. iv. 2,) there is no light even in the law, or in the whole word of God.

16. *But when he shall have turned to the Lord.*   This passage has hitherto been badly rendered, for both Greek and Latin writers have thought that the word *Israel* was to be understood, whereas Paul is speaking of Moses.   He had said, that a *veil is upon the hearts* of the Jews, *when Moses is read.*   He immediately adds, *As soon as he will have turned to the Lord, the veil will be taken away.*   Who does

not see, that this is said of *Moses,* that is, of the law ? For as Christ is the *end*[1] of it, (Rom. x. 4,) to which it ought to be referred, it was turned away in another direction, when the Jews shut out Christ from it. Hence, as in the law[2] they wander into by-paths, so the law, too, becomes to them involved like a labyrinth, until it is brought to refer to its *end,* that is, Christ. If, accordingly, the Jews seek Christ in the law, the truth of God will be distinctly seen by them,[3] but so long as they think to be wise without Christ, they will wander in darkness, and will never arrive at a right understanding of the law. Now what is said of the law applies to all Scripture—that where it is not taken as referring to Christ as its one aim, it is mistakingly twisted and perverted.[4]

17. *The Lord is the Spirit.* This passage, also, has been misinterpreted, as if Paul had meant to say, that Christ is of a spiritual essence, for they connect it with that statement in John iv. 24, *God is a Spirit.* The statement before us, however, has nothing to do with Christ's essence, but simply points out his office, for it is connected with what goes before, where we found it stated, that the doctrine of the law is literal, and not merely dead, but even an occasion of death. He now, on the other hand, calls Christ its spirit,[5] meaning by this, that it will be living and life-giving, only if it is breathed into by Christ. Let the soul be connected with the body, and then there is a living man, endowed with intelligence and perception, fit for all vital functions.[6] Let the soul be removed from the body, and there will remain nothing but a useless carcase, totally devoid of feeling.

---

[1] " La fin et l'accomplissement d'icelle ;"—" The end and accomplishment of it."

[2] " En lisant la Loy ;"—" In reading the Law."

[3] " Ils y trouuerout clairement la pure verité de Dieu ;"—" They will clearly discover in it the pure truth of God."

[4] " C'est la destourner hors de son droit sens et du tout la peruertir;"— " This is to turn it away from its right meaning, and altogether to pervert it."

[5] " L'esprit de la Loy ;"—" The spirit of the law."

[6] " Tous mouuemens et operations de la vie ;"—" All the movements and operations of life."

The passage is deserving of particular notice,[1] as teaching us, in what way we are to reconcile those encomiums which David pronounces upon the law—(Psalm xix. 7, 8)—" the law of the Lord *converteth souls, enlighteneth the eyes, imparteth wisdom to babes,*" and passages of a like nature, with those statements of Paul, which at first view are at variance with them—that it is the *ministry of sin and death*—the *letter* that does nothing but *kill.* (2 Cor. iii. 6, 7.) For when it is animated by Christ,[2] those things that David makes mention of are justly applicable to it. If Christ is taken away, it is altogether such as Paul describes. Hence Christ is the life of the law.[3]

Where the Spirit of the Lord. He now describes the manner, in which Christ gives life to the law—by giving us his Spirit. The term *Spirit* here has a different signification from what it had in the preceding verse. *There,* it denoted the soul, and was ascribed metaphorically to Christ. *Here,* on the other hand, it means the Holy Spirit, that Christ himself confers upon his people. Christ, however, by regenerating us, gives life to the law, and shows himself to be the fountain of life, as all vital functions proceed from man's soul. Christ, then, is to all (so to speak) the universal soul, not in respect of essence, but in respect of grace. Or, if you prefer it, Christ is *the Spirit,* because he quickens us by the life-giving influence of his Spirit.[4]

He makes mention, also, of the blessing that we obtain from that source. " *There,*" says he, " is *liberty.*" By the term *liberty* I do not understand merely emancipation from the servitude of sin, and of the flesh, but also that confidence, which we acquire from His bearing witness as to our adoption. For it is in accordance with that statement—*We have not again received the spirit of bondage, to fear,* &c. (Rom. viii. 15.) In that passage, the Apostle makes mention of

[1] " Voici vn beau passage, et bien digne d'estre noté ;"—"Here is a beautiful passage, and well deserving to be carefully noticed."

[2] " Quand l'ame luy est inspiree par Christ ;"—" When a soul is breathed into by Christ."

[3] " La vie et l'esprit de la Loy ;"—" The life and spirit of the Law."

[4] " Par l'efficace et viue vertu de son Sainct Esprit ;"—" By the efficacy and living influence of his Holy Spirit."

two things—*bondage,* and *fear.* The opposites of these are *liberty* and *confidence.* Thus I acknowledge, that the inference drawn from this passage by Augustine is correct—that we are by nature the slaves of sin, and are made free by the grace of regeneration. For, where there is nothing but the bare letter of the law, *there* will be only the dominion of sin, but the term *Liberty,* as I have said, I take in a more extensive sense. The grace of the Spirit might, also, be restricted more particularly to ministers, so as to make this statement correspond with the commencement of the chapter, for ministers require to have another grace of the Spirit, and another liberty from what others have. The former signification, however, pleases me better, though at the same time I have no objection, that this should be applied to every one according to the measure of his gift. It is enough, if we observe, that Paul here points out the efficacy of the Spirit, which we experience for our salvation—as many of us, as have been regenerated by his grace.

18. *But we all, with unveiled face.* I know not how it had come into the mind of Erasmus, to apply to ministers exclusively, what is evidently common to all believers. The word κατοπτρίζεσθαι, it is true, has a double signification among the Greeks, for it sometimes means to hold out a mirror to be looked into, and at other times to look into a mirror when presented.[1] The old interpreter, however, has correctly judged, that the *second* of these is the more suitable to the passage before us. I have accordingly followed his rendering.[2] Nor is it without good reason, that Paul has added a term of universality—" *We all,*" says he ; for he takes in the whole body of the Church. It is a conclusion that suits well with the doctrine stated previously—that we

[1] " It is made use of in the *former* sense by *Plutarch,* (2. 894. D.) It is more frequently employed in the *latter* signification. Thus *Plato* says, Τοις μεθυουσι συνεβουλευε κατοπτριζεσθαι—" He advised drunken persons to *look at themselves in a mirror.*" So also Diogenes Laert. (in Socrate) Ηξιου δε τους νεους συνεχως κατοπτριζεσθαι. He thought that young men should frequently *look at themselves in a mirror.—Ed.*

[2] Wiclif (1380) following, as he is wont to do, the Vulgate, renders as follows : " And alle we that with open face seen the glorie of the Lord." CALVIN'S rendering, it will be observed, is—" In speculo conspicientes;" —" beholding in a mirror."*—Ed.*

have in the gospel a clear revelation from God.   As to this, we shall see something farther in the *fourth* chapter.

He points out, however, at the same time, both the strength of the revelation, and our daily progress.[1]   For he has employed such a similitude to denote *three* things : *first*, That we have no occasion to fear obscurity, when we approach the gospel, for God *there* clearly discovers to us His face ;[2] *secondly*, That it is not befitting, that it should be a dead contemplation, but that we should be transformed by means of it into the image of God ; and, *thirdly*, that the one and the other are not accomplished in us in one moment, but we must be constantly making progress both in the knowledge of God, and in conformity to His image, for this is the meaning of the expression—*from glory to glory.*

When he adds,—*as by the Spirit of the Lord*, he again reminds of what he had said—that the whole excellence of the gospel depends on this, that it is made life-giving to us by the grace of the Holy Spirit.   For the particle of comparison—*as*, is not employed to convey the idea of something not strictly applicable, but to point out the manner.   Observe, that the design of the gospel is this—that the image of God, which had been effaced by sin, may be stamped anew upon us, and that the advancement of this restoration may be continually going forward in us during our whole life, because God makes his glory shine forth in us by little and little.

There is one question that may be proposed here.   " Paul says, that we behold God's face with an unveiled face,[3] while in the former Epistle we find it stated, that we do not, for the present, know God otherwise than through a mirror, and

---

[1] " Le proufit ou auancement que nous sentons en cela tous les iours ;"— " The profit or advancement, which we experience in it every day."

[2] " Car là Dieu se descouure à nous face à face ;"—" For God there discovers Himself to us face to face."

[3] *Granville Penn* renders the verse as follows: " And we all, looking, as in a glass, at the glory of the Lord with *his* face unveiled," and adds the following note : " St. Paul contrasts the condition of the Jews, when they could not fix their eyes on the glory of the unveiled face of Moses, with the privilege of Christians, who are empowered to look, as in a mirror, on the open and unveiled face of Christ ; and in that gazing, to be transformed into the same glorious image : The ' unveiled face,' therefore, is that of *our Lord*, not that of the beholder."—*Ed.*

in an obscure manner." In these statements there is an appearance of contrariety. They are, however, by no means at variance. The knowledge that we have of God for the present is obscure and slender, in comparison with the glorious view that we shall have on occasion of Christ's last coming. At the same time, He presents Himself to us at present, so as to be seen by us, and openly beheld, in so far as is for our advantage, and in so far as our capacity admits of.[1] Hence Paul makes mention of progress being made, inasmuch as there will *then* only be perfection.

CHAPTER IV.

1. Therefore, seeing we have this ministry, as we have received mercy, we faint not ;

2. But have renounced the hidden things of dishonesty, not walking in craftiness, nor handling the word of God deceitfully; but by manifestation of the truth, commending ourselves to every man's conscience in the sight of God.

3. But if our gospel be hid, it is hid to them that are lost :

4. In whom the god of this world hath blinded the minds of them which believe not, lest the light of the glorious gospel of Christ, who is the image of God, should shine unto them.

5. For we preach not ourselves, but Christ Jesus the Lord ; and ourselves your servants for Jesus' sake.

6. For God, who commanded the light to shine out of darkness, hath shined in our hearts, to *give* the light of the knowledge of the glory of God in the face of Jesus Christ.

1. Quamobrem habentes ministerium hoc, sicuti misericordiam sumus consequuti, non deficimus,

2. Sed reiicimus latebras dedecoris, non ambulantes in astutia, neque dolo tractantes sermonem Dei : sed manifestatione veritatis commendantes nos apud omnem conscientiam hominum coram Deo.

3. Si autem velatum est Evangelium nostrum : in iis qui pereunt velatum est.

4. Quibus deus sæculi hujus excœcavit sensus : nempe infidelibus, ut ne illis resplendeat claritas Evangelii gloriæ Christi, qui est imago Dei invisibilis.

5. Non enim nosmetipsos prædicamus, sed Iesum Christum Dominum : nos vero servos vestros propter Iesum.

6. Quoniam Deus qui iussit e tenebris lumen splendescere, idem illuxit in cordibus nostris ad illuminationem cognitionis gloriæ Dei in facie Iesu Christi.

---

[1] " 'Tis not a change only into the image of God with slight colours, an image drawn as with charcoal; but a glorious image even in the rough draught, which grows up into greater beauty by the addition of brighter colours : *Changed* (saith the Apostle, 2 Cor. iii. 18) *into the same image from glory to glory :* glory in the first lineaments as well as glory in the last lines."—*Charnock's* Works, vol. ii. p. 209.—*Ed.*

1. *Having this ministry.* He now returns to a commendation of himself personally, from which he had digressed
into a general discussion, in reference to the dignity of the
gospel. As, therefore, he has been treating of the nature of
the gospel, so he now shows how faithful and upright a
minister of it he is. He has previously shown, what is the
true gospel of Christ. He now shows what he preaches to
be such. "*Having,*" says he, "*this ministry*"—that *ministry,* the excellence of which he had extolled in terms so
magnificent, and the power and usefulness of which he had
so abundantly shown forth. Hence, in order that he may
not seem to extol himself too much, he premises that it was
not by his own efforts, or by his own merits, that he had
reached such a pinnacle of honour, but had been led forward
by the mercy of God exclusively. Now there was more implied in making the *mercy* of God the reason of his Apostleship, than if he had attributed it to the *grace* of God. *We
faint not,*[1] that is, we are not deficient in our duty,[2] so as
not to discharge it with fidelity.

2. *But renounce the hidden things.* While he commends
his own sincerity,[3] he, on the other hand, indirectly reproves
the false Apostles, who, while they corrupted by their ambition the genuine excellence of the gospel, were, nevertheless, desirous of exclusive distinction. Hence the faults,
from which he declares himself to be exempt, he indirectly
imputes to them. By the *hidden things of disgrace,* or *concealments,* some understand the shadows of the Mosaic law.
Chrysostom understands the expression to mean the vain
show, by which they endeavoured to recommend themselves.
I understand by it—all the disguises, with which they
adulterated the pure and native beauty of the gospel. For as

---

[1] " Instead of οὐκ ἐκκακοῦμεν, *we faint not,* οὐκ ἐγκακοῦμεν, *we act not
wickedly,* is the reading of ADFG, and some others. Wakefield thinks
it the genuine reading; it certainly makes a very good sense with what
goes before and what follows. If we follow this reading, the whole verse
may be read thus—' Wherefore, as we have obtained mercy, or been graciously intrusted, ἐλεήθημεν, with this ministry, we do not act wickedly, but
have renounced the hidden things of dishonesty."—*Dr. A. Clarke.—Ed.*
[2] " Nous n'omettons rien de ce qui est de nostre office;"—" We do not
omit any thing of what belongs to our office."
[3] " Sa droiture et syncerite:"—" His own uprightness and sincerity."

chaste and virtuous women, satisfied with the gracefulness of natural beauty, do not resort to artificial adornings, while harlots never think themselves sufficiently adorned, unless they have corrupted nature, so Paul glories in having set forth the pure gospel, while others set forth one that was disguised, and covered over with unseemly additions. For as they were ashamed of the simplicity of Christ, or at least could not have distinction[1] from true excellencies of Apostles, they framed a new gospel, not unlike a profane philosophy, swelled up with empty bombast, while altogether devoid of the efficacy of the Spirit. Spurious ornaments of this nature,[2] by which the gospel is disfigured, he calls the *concealments of disgrace,* because the nakedness of those, who have recourse to concealments and disguises, must of necessity be dishonourable and disgraceful.

As to himself, he says that he rejects or disdains disguises, because Christ's face, the more that it is seen opened up to view in his preaching, shines forth so much the more gloriously. I do not, however, deny, that he alludes at the same time to the veil of Moses, (Exod. xxxiv. 33,) of which he had made mention, but he ascribes a quite different veil to the false Apostles. For Moses covered his face, because the excessive brightness of the glory of the law could not be endured by tender and blear eyes. They,[3] on the other hand, put on a veil by way of ornament. Besides, as they would be despicable, nay, infamous, if the simplicity of the gospel shone forth, they, on this account, hide their shame under ever so many cloaks and masks.

Not walking in craftiness. There can be no doubt, that the false Apostles delighted themselves greatly in the *craftiness* that Paul reproves, as though it had been a distinguished excellence, as we see even at this day some, even of those who profess the gospel, who would rather be esteemed subtile than sincere, and sublime rather than solid, while in the mean time all their refinement is mere childishness. But

---

[1] " Ne pouuoyent pas estre excellens et en estime;"—" Could not be eminent, and be held in estimation."

[2] " Ces couleurs fausses, et ces desguisemens;"—" Those false colours, and those disguises."

[2] " Les faux apostres;"—" The false apostles."

what would you do? It delights them to have a name for
acuteness, and they have, under that pretext, applause
among the ignorant.[1] We learn, however, in what estimation Paul holds this appearance of excellence. *Craftiness* he
declares to be unworthy of Christ's servants.

As to what follows—*nor handling deceitfully*—I am not
sure that this sufficiently brings out Paul's meaning; for
the verb δολοῦν does not so properly mean *acting fraudulently,* as what is called *falsifying,*[2] as horse-jockeys[3] are
wont to do. In this passage, at least, it is placed in contrast
with upright preaching, agreeably to what follows.

But by manifestation of the truth. He claims to himself
this praise—that he had proclaimed the pure doctrine of the
gospel in simplicity and without disguise, and has the *consciences of all* as witnesses of this *in the sight of God.* As he
has placed the *manifestation of the truth* in contrast with
the disguised[4] doctrine of the sophists, so he appeals the
decision to their consciences, and to the judgment-seat of
God, whereas they abused the mistaken judgment of men,
or their corrupt affection, and were not so desirous to be in
reality worthy of praise as they were eager to appear so.
Hence we infer, that there is a contrast here between the
consciences of men and their *ears.* Let the servants of Christ,
therefore, reckon it enough to have approved their integrity
to the *consciences* of men *in the sight of God,* and pay no
regard to the corrupt inclinations of men, or to popular
applause.

3. *But if our gospel is hid.* It might have been an easy
thing to pour calumny upon what he had said as to the
clearness of his preaching, because he had many adversaries.

---

[1] " Enuers les gens simples, et qui ne scauent pas iuger des choses ;"—
" Among simple people, and those that do not know how to judge of things."

[2] The verb δολοῦν is applied by *Lucian* (in Hermot. 59) to vintners adulterating wine, in which sense it is synonymous with καπηλεύειν, made use of
by Paul in 2 Cor. ii. 17. (See p. 163, *n.* 1.) Beza's rendering of the clause
exactly corresponds with the one to which CALVIN gives the preference—
" Neque falsantes sermonem Dei ;"—" Nor falsifying the word of God."
Tyndale (1534) renders the clause thus—" Nether corrupte we the worde
of God." The rendering in the Rheims version (1582) is—" Nor adulterating the word of God."—*Ed.*

[3] " Et frippiers ;"—" And brokers."

[4] " Fardee et desguisee ;"—" Painted and disguised "

That calumny he repels with stern authority, for he threatens all who do not acknowledge the power of his gospel, and warns them that this is a token of reprobation and ruin. " Should any one affirm that he does not perceive that manifestation of Christ of which I boast, he clearly shows himself, by this very token, to be a reprobate,[1] for my sincerity in the work of instructing[2] is clearly and distinctly perceived by all that have eyes. Those, therefore, from whom it is hid, must be blind, and destitute of all rational understanding." The sum is this—that the blindness of unbelievers detracts nothing from the clearness of his gospel; for the sun is not less resplendent, that the blind do not perceive his light.[3]

But some one will say that this applies equally to the law, for in itself it is a *lamp*[4] *to guide our feet,* (Ps. cxix. 105,) *enlightens the eyes,* (Ps. xix. 8,) &c., and is hid only from those that perish. I answer that, when Christ is included in the law, the sun shines forth through the midst of the clouds, so that men have light enough for their use; but when Christ is disjoined from it, there is nothing left but darkness, or a false appearance of light, that dazzles men's eyes instead of assisting them. It is, however, a token of great confidence, that he ventures to regard as reprobates all that reject his doctrine. It is befitting, however, that all that would be looked upon as ministers of God's word should be endued with the like confidence, that with a fearless confidence they may unhesitatingly summon all the adversaries of their doctrine to the judgment-seat of God, that they may bring thence a sure condemnation.

4. *Whose minds the god of this world.* He intimates, that no account should be made of their perverse obstinacy. " They do not see," says he, " the sun at mid-day, because *the devil has blinded their understandings."* No one that judges rightly can have any doubt, that it is of Satan that the Apostle speaks. Hilary, as he had to do with Arians,

---

[1] " Il ne pourra mieux monstrer signe de sa reprobation, que par là :" — " He could not give a clearer evidence of his reprobation than this."
[2] " La syncerite et droiture que ie tien à enseigner ;"—" The sincerity and uprightness that I maintain in teaching."
[3] See CALVIN on Corinthians, vol. i. p. 116.—*Ed.*
[4] " Vne lanterne ardente :"—" A lantern burning."

who abused this passage, so as to make it a pretext for de-
nying Christ's true divinity, while they at the same time
confessed him to be God, twists the text in this way—"God
hath blinded the understandings of this world." In this he
was afterwards followed by Chrysostom, with the view of
not conceding to the Manicheans their *two first principles*.[1]
What influenced Ambrose does not appear. Augustine had
the same reason as Chrysostom, having to contend with the
Manicheans.

We see what the heat of controversy does in carrying on
disputes. Had all those men calmly read Paul's words, it
would never have occurred to any one of them to twist them
in this way into a forced meaning ; but as they were harassed
by their opponents, they were more concerned to refute
them, than to investigate Paul's meaning. But what occasion
was there for this ? For the subterfuge of the Arians was
childish—that if the devil is called the *god of this world*,
the name of God, as applied to Christ, does not express a
true, eternal, and exclusive divinity. For Paul says elsewhere, *many are called gods*, (1 Cor. viii. 5 ;) but David, on
the other hand, sings forth—*the gods of the nations are demons*.[2] (Ps. xcvi. 5.) When, therefore, the devil is called the
god of the wicked, on the ground of his having dominion over
them, and being worshipped by them in the place of God,
what tendency has this to detract from the honour of Christ ?
And as to the Manicheans, this appellation gives no more
countenance to the Manicheans, than when he is called the
prince of this world. (John xiv. 30.)[3]

[1] The Manicheans, so called from Manes their founder, held the doctrine
of *two first principles*, a *good* and an *evil*, thinking to account in this way
for the origin of evil. See CALVIN's Institutes, vol. i. p. 147.—*Ed*.

[2] " Les dieux des Gentils sont diables;"—" The gods of the Gentiles
are devils. CALVIN here, as in many other instances, quotes according to
the *sense*, not according to the *words*. The passage referred to is rendered
by CALVIN—" All the gods of the nations are vanities," (" *ou, idoles*," " *or
idols*,") the Hebrew word being, as he notices, אלילים, (*elilim*,) *mere no-
things*, (1 Cor. viii. 4,) instead of אלהים, (*elohim*,) *gods*. (See CALVIN on
the Psalms, vol. iv. pp. 50, 51.) There can be no doubt that CALVIN, in
quoting this passage here, has an eye to what is stated by Paul in 1 Cor.
x. 20.—*Ed*.

[3] CALVIN, when commenting on the passage referred to, remarks, that
" the devil is called *the prince of this world*, not because he has a kingdom

There is, therefore, no reason for being afraid to interpret this passage as referring to the devil, there being no danger in doing so. For should the Arians come forward and contend,[1] that Christ's divine essence is no more proved from his having the appellation *God* applied to him, than Satan's is proved from its being applied to *him*, a cavil of this nature is easily refuted; for Christ is called God without any addition,[2] nay, he is called *God blessed for ever*. (Rom. ix. 5.) He is said to be that God who was *in the beginning, before the creation of the world*. (John i. 1-3.) The devil, on the other hand, is called the *god of this world*, in no other way than as Baal is called the god of those that worship him, or as the dog is called the god of Egypt.[3] The Manicheans, as I have said, for maintaining their delusion, have recourse to other declarations of Scripture, as well as this, but there is no difficulty in refuting those also. They contend not so much respecting the *term*, as respecting the *power*. As the *power* of *blinding* is ascribed to Satan, and dominion over unbelievers, they conclude from this that he is, from his own resources, the author of all evil, so as not to be subject to God's control—as if Scripture did not in various instances declare, that devils, no less than the angels of heaven, are servants of God, each of them severally in his own manner. For, as the latter dispense to us God's benefits for our salvation, so the former execute his wrath. Hence good angels are called *powers* and *principalities*, (Eph. iii. 10,) but it is simply because they exercise the power given them by God. For the same reason Satan is *the prince of*

separated from God, (as the Manicheans imagined,) but because, by God's permission, he exercises his tyranny over the world."—CALVIN on John, vol. ii. p. 104.—*Ed.*

[1] " Tant qu'ils voudront ;"—" As much as they please."

[2] CALVIN obviously means by this clause—without anything being added having a tendency to qualify or limit the appellation. In accordance with this he says in the *Institutes*, (vol. i. p. 156,) that the " title," God, " is not conferred on any man *without some addition*, as when it is said that Moses would be a god to Pharaoh." (Exod. vii. 1.)—*Ed.*

[3] A variety of animals, besides the dog, were worshipped by the Egyptians, and even some vegetable substances, growing in their gardens, were adored by them as deities! CALVIN, when commenting on 1 Cor. viii. 5, speaks of the Egyptians as having rendered divine homage to "the ox, the serpent, the cat, the onion, the garlic."—CALVIN *on Corinthians*, vol. i. p. 277.—*Ed.*

this world, not as if he conferred dominion upon himself, or obtained it by his own right, or, in fine, exercised it at his own pleasure.   On the contrary, he has only so much as the Lord allows him.   Hence Scripture does not merely make mention of the good spirit of God, and good angels, but he also speaks of evil spirits of God.   *An evil spirit from God came upon Saul.* (1 Sam. xvi. 14.)   Again, chastisements through means of *evil angels.*   (Ps. lxxviii. 49.)

With respect to the passage before us, the *blinding* is a work common to God and to Satan, for it is in many instances ascribed to God; but the *power* is not alike, nor is the *manner* the same.   I shall not speak at present as to the manner.   Scripture, however, teaches that Satan *blinds* men,[1] not merely with God's permission, but even by his command, that he may execute his vengeance.   Thus Ahab was deceived by Satan, (1 Kings xxii. 21,) but could Satan have done this of himself? By no means ; but having offered to God his services for inflicting injury, he was sent to be a *lying spirit in the mouth of all his prophets.* (1 Kings xxii. 22.)   Nay more, the reason why God is said to *blind* men is, that after having deprived us of the right exercise of the understanding, and the light of his Spirit, he delivers us over to the devil, to be hurried forward by him to a *reprobate mind,* (Rom. i. 28,) gives him the power of deception, and by this means inflicts just vengeance upon us by the minister of his wrath.   Paul's meaning, therefore, is, that all are possessed by the devil, who do not acknowledge his doctrine to be the sure truth of God.   For it is more severe to call them slaves of the devil,[2] than to ascribe their blind-

---

[1] " Les reprouuez ;"—" The reprobate."

[2] " ' *The god of this world.*'   O that we could consider this, according to what it doth import and carry in it of horror and detestableness! It is a thing that we do not yet believe, that a world inhabited by reasonable creatures, God's own offspring, is universally fallen into a confederacy and combination with another god, with an enemy-god, an adversary-god, against the living and true God! Men have changed their God.   And what a fearful choice have they made! Fallen into a league with those wicked creatures that were weary of his government before, and that were, thereupon, thrown down into an abyss of darkness, and bound up in the chains thereof, unto the judgment of the great day.   But doth the Scripture say this in vain? or hath it not a meaning when it calls the devil *the god of this world ?* O with what amazement should it strike our hearts,

196   COMMENTARY ON THE   CHAP. IV. 4.

ness to the judgment of God. As, however, he had a little
before adjudged such persons to destruction, (verse 3,) he
now adds that they perish, for no other reason than that
they have drawn down ruin upon themselves, as the effect
of their own unbelief.

*Lest the light of the glorious gospel of Christ should shine
upon them.* This serves to confirm what he had said—that
if any one rejected his gospel, it was his own blindness that
prevented him from receiving it. " For nothing," says he,
" appears in it but Christ, and that not obscurely, but so as
to shine forth clearly." He adds, that Christ is the *image
of God,* by which he intimates that they were utterly devoid
of the knowledge of God, in accordance with that statement
—*He that knoweth not me knoweth not my Father.* (John
xiv. 7.) This then is the reason, why he pronounced so severe
a sentence upon those that had doubts as to his Apostleship
—because they did not behold Christ, who might there be
distinctly beheld. It is doubtful whether he employed the
expression, *the gospel of the glory of Christ,* as meaning the
glorious gospel, agreeably to the Hebrew idiom ; or whether
he means by it—the gospel, in which Christ's glory shone
forth. The *second* of these meanings I rather prefer, as
having in it more completeness.

When, however, Christ is called the *image of the invisible
God,* this is not meant merely of his essence, as being the
" co-essential of the Father," as they speak,[1] but rather has

to think that so it is, that the whole order of creatures is gone off from
God, and fallen into a confederacy with the devil and his angels, against
their rightful sovereign Lord."—*Howe's Works.* (London, 1834.) p. 1206.
—*Ed.*

[1] CALVIN manifestly refers to an expression made use of by the Council
of Nice, A.D. 325, to express unity of essence in the first and second persons of the Trinity, the Son having been declared to be ὁμοούσιος τῷ Πατρὶ
—*co-essential with the Father.* " It had been used in the same sense by
some writers before the meeting of the Council. It is remarkable, however, that it had been rejected by the Council of Antioch, A.D. 263, on
account of the inference which Paul of Samosata pretended to draw from
it, namely, that if Christ and the Spirit were consubstantial with the
Father, it followed that there were three substances—one prior and two
posterior—derived from it. To guard against this inference, the Council
declared that the Son was *not* ὁμοούσιος τῷ Πατρὶ. (*consubstantial with the
Father.*) " Paul " (*of Samosata*) " seems to have explained the term as
signifying *specific,* or *of the same species ;* and it is certain that this sense

a reference to us, because he represents the Father to us.
The Father himself is represented as *invisible,* because he is
in himself not apprehended by the human understanding.
He exhibits himself, however, to us by his Son, and makes
himself in a manner visible.[1]   I state this, because the
ancients, having been greatly incensed against the Arians,
insisted more than was befitting on this point—how it is
that the Son is inwardly the *image of the Father* by a secret
unity of essence, while they passed over what is mainly for
edification—in what respects he is the *image of God* to us,
when he manifests to us what had otherwise been hid in
him.   Hence the term *image* has a reference to us, as we
shall see again presently.[2]   The epithet *invisible,* though
omitted in some Greek manuscripts, I have preferred to retain, as it is not superfluous.[3]

5. *For we preach not ourselves.*   Some make this to be an
instance of *Zeugma,*[4] in this manner: We preach not ourselves to be lords, but God's only Son, whom the Father has
set over all things, to be the one Lord.[5]   I do not, indeed,

had sometimes been given to it.   Thus Aristotle calls the stars ὁμοούσια,
meaning that they were all of the same nature.   But in the creed of Nice
it is expressive of unity of essence, and was adopted, after considerable
discussion, as proper to be opposed to the Arians, who affirmed that the
essence of the Son was different and separate from the Father."—*Dick's
Theology,* vol. ii. pp. 62, 63.   The reader will also find the same expression largely treated of by CALVIN in the *Institutes,* vol. i. pp. 150-1.   See
also *Institutes,* vol. ii. p. 33, and CALVIN on John, vol. i. p. 417.—*Ed.*

   [1] " Christ is the *image of God,* as a child is the image of his father; not
in regard of the individual property which the Father hath distinct from
the child, and the child from the father, but in respect of the same substance and nature, derived from the father by generation.   Christ is here
called the *image of God,* (2 Cor. iv. 4,) 'not so much,' saith CALVIN, 'in
relation to God, as the *Father* is the exemplar of his beauty and excellency,
as in relation to *us,* as he represents the Father to us in the perfections of
his nature, as they respect us and our welfare, and renders him visible to
the eyes of our minds."—*Charnock's Works,* (Lond. 1684,) vol. ii. p.
476.—*Ed.*

   [2] See on verse 6.

   [3] Three manuscripts (as stated by Poole in his Synopsis) have ἀοράτου,
(*invisible,*) but it is generally believed to have been an interpolation from
Col. i. 15.—*Ed.*

   [4] *Zeugma* is a figure of speech, in which two subjects are *used jointly*
(the term being derived from ξεύγνυμι, *to join*) with the same predicate,
which strictly belongs only to one.—*Ed.*

   [5] " Auquel le Pere a baillé superintendance sur toutes choses;"—" To
whom the Father has given superintendence over all things."

find fault with that interpretation, but as the expression is more emphatic (ἐμφατικωτέρα) and has a more extensive signification,[1] when it is said, that one *preaches himself*. I am more inclined to retain this interpretation, especially as it is almost unanimously approved of. For there are other ways in which men *preach themselves*, than by arrogating to themselves dominion, as for example, when they aim at show, rather than at edification—when they are desirous in any way to have distinction—when, farther, they make gain of the gospel. Ambition, therefore, and avarice, and similar vices in a minister, taint the purity of his doctrine, so that Christ has not there the exclusive distinction. Hence, he that would preach Christ alone, must of necessity forget himself.

And ourselves your servants. Lest any one should mutter out the objection—" But in the mean time you say many things respecting yourself," he answers, that he desires nothing farther, than that he should be their *servant*. " Whatever things I declare respecting myself (so loftily, and boastfully, in your opinion) have this object in view— that I may in Christ *serve* you advantageously." It follows, that the Corinthians are excessively proud and ungrateful, if they reject this condition. Nay more, it follows, that they had been previously of a corrupt judgment, inasmuch as they had not perceived his holy affection.

Here, however, all pastors of the Church are admonished as to their state and condition, for by whatever title of honour they may be distinguished, they are nothing more than the *servants* of believers, and unquestionably, they cannot serve Christ, without serving his Church at the same time. An honourable servitude, it is true, this is, and superior to any principality,[2] but still it is a *servitude*, so that Christ alone may be elevated to distinction—not encumbered by the shadow of a single rival.[3] Hence it is the part of a good

---

[1] " Comme ainsi soit que la façon de parler est de plus grand poids, et s'estend plus loin ;"—" As it is a form of expression that has greater weight, and is more extensive."

[2] " Plus heureuse que toutes les principautez du monde ;"—" Happier than all the principalities of the world."

[3] " N'estant nullement empesché par l'ombre de quelque autre qui luy seroit donne pour compagnon ;"—" In no degree hindered by the shadow of any other, that might be given him as a companion."

pastor, not merely to keep aloof from all desire of domineering, but to regard it as the highest pitch of honour, at which
he aspires—that he may *serve* the people of God.   It is the
duty of the people, on the other hand, to esteem the servants
of Christ first of all on the ground of the dignity of their
Master, and then farther on account of the dignity and excellence of their office, that they may not despise those,
whom the Lord has placed in so illustrious a station.

    6. *God who commanded light to shine out of darkness.*   I
see that this passage may be explained in four different
ways.   In the *first* place thus: " God has *commanded light
to shine forth out of darkness:* that is, by the ministry of
men, who are in their own nature *darkness,* He has brought
forward the *light* of His gospel into the world." *Secondly,*
thus: " God has made the *light* of the gospel to take the
place of the law, which was wrapt up in *dark* shadows, and
thus, He has brought *light* out of *darkness.*" Those that are
fond of subtilties, would be prepared readily to receive ex-
positions of that sort, but any one, who will examine the
matter more closely, will perceive, that they do not correspond with the Apostle's intention.   The *third* exposition is
that of Ambrose: " When all things were involved in darkness, God kindled up the light of His gospel.   For mankind
were sunk in the darkness of ignorance, when God on a sudden shone forth upon them by his gospel."   The *fourth* is
that of Chrysostom, who is of opinion, that Paul alluded to
the creation of the world, in this way: " God, who by his
word created light, drawing it, as it were, out of the darkness[1]—that same Being has now enlightened us in a spiritual manner, when we were buried in darkness."   This
transition,[2] from light that is visible and corporeal to what
is spiritual, has more of elegance, and there is nothing forced

---

[1] " Du profond des tenebres ;"—" Out of the depth of darkness."

[2] *Anagoge.*   The Reader will find in the *Harmony* (vol. i. p. 436. *n.*
1,) a lucid view of the import of the word *anagoge,* or rather ἀναγωγὴ as
employed, on the one hand, by " divines of the allegorizing school," and on
the other by CALVIN, whose reverence for the inspired oracles would not
permit him to give way to mere fancy in the interpretation of them, even
in a single instance.—*Ed.*

in it. The preceding one,[1] however, is not unsuitable. Let every one follow his own judgment.

Hath shined in our hearts. He speaks of a twofold illumination, which must be carefully observed—the one is that of the gospel, the other is secret, taking place in our hearts.[2] For as God, the Creator of the world, pours forth upon us the brightness of the sun, and gives us eyes to receive it, so, as the Redeemer, in the person of his Son, He shines forth, indeed, upon us by His gospel, but, as we are blind, that would be in vain, if He did not at the same time enlighten our understandings by His Spirit. His meaning, therefore, is, that God has, by His Spirit, opened the eyes of our understandings, so as to make them capable of receiving the light of the gospel.

In the face of Jesus Christ. In the same sense in which he had previously said that Christ is the *image of the Father*, (verse 4th) he now says, that the glory of God is manifested to us *in his face.* Here we have a remarkable passage, from which we learn that God is not to be *sought out* (Job xi. 7) in His unsearchable height, (*for He dwells in light that is inaccessible*, 1 Tim. vi. 16,) but is to be known by us, in so far as He manifests himself in Christ. Hence, whatever men desire to know respecting God, apart from Christ, is evanescent, for they wander out of the way. True, indeed, God in Christ appears in the first instance to be mean, but He appears at length to be glorious in the view of those, who hold on, so as to come from the cross to the resurrection.[3] Again we see, that in the word *person*[4] there is a reference made to us,[5] because it is more advantageous for us to behold God, as He appears in His only-begotten Son, than to search out His secret essence.

---

[1] " La troisieme exposition ;"—" The third exposition."

[2] " Interieurement en nos cœurs ;"—" Inwardly in our hearts."

[3] " Ceux, qui ont la patience de venir de la croix à la resurrection ;"— " Those, who have the patience to come from the cross to the resurrection."

[4] The original expression is ἐν προσώπῳ Ἰησοῦ Χριστοῦ—in the *person* of Jesus Christ.—*Ed.*

[5] " Ce qui est dit de Dieu, c'est pour le regard de nous ;"—" What is said respecting God, is in relation to us."—See p. 197.

7. But we have this treasure in earthen vessels, that the excellency of the power may be of God, and not of us.

8. *We are* troubled on every side, yet not distressed; *we are* perplexed, but not in despair;

9. Persecuted, but not forsaken; cast down, but not destroyed;

10. Always bearing about in the body the dying of the Lord Jesus, that the life also of Jesus might be made manifest in our body.

11. For we which live are alway delivered unto death for Jesus' sake, that the life also of Jesus might be made manifest in our mortal flesh.

12. So then death worketh in us, but life in you.

7. Habemus autem thesaurum hunc in vasis testaceis: ut exsuperantia potentiæ sit Dei, et non ex nobis:

8. Quando in omnibus premimur, at non anxii reddimur: laboramus inopia, at non destituimur:

9. Persequutionem patimur, at non deserimur: deiicimur, at non perimus:

10. Semper mortificationem Iesu Christi circumferentes in corpore nostro, ut vita Iesu manifestetur in corpore nostro.

11. Semper enim nos, dum vivimus,[1] in mortem tradimur propter Iesum, ut vita Iesu manifestetur[2] in mortali carne nostra.

12. Itaque mors quidem in nobis operatur, vita autem in vobis.[3]

7. *But we have this treasure.* Those that heard Paul glorying in such a magnificent strain as to the excellence of his ministry, and beheld, on the other hand, his person, contemptible and abject in the eyes of the world, might be apt to think that he was a silly and ridiculous person, and might look upon his boasting as childish, while forming their estimate of him from the meanness of his person.[4] The wicked, more particularly, caught hold of this pretext, when they wished to bring into contempt every thing that was in him. What, however, he saw to be most of all unfavourable to the honour of his Apostleship among the ignorant, he turns by an admirable contrivance into a means of advancing it. First of all, he employs the similitude of a *treasure,* which is not usually laid up in a splendid and elegantly adorned chest, but rather in some *vessel* that is mean and worthless;[5] and then farther, he subjoins, that the

[1] " Nous en viuant, or, *nous qui viuons ;*"—" We, while living, or, *we who live.*"

[2] " Soit aussi manifestee ;"—" May also be manifested."

[3] " La vie en vous, ou, vous en reuient ;"—" Life in you, or, comes from it to you."

[4] " Ils le iugeoyent selon l'apparence de sa personne, qui estoit petite et contemptible ;"—" They judged of him according to the appearance of his person, which was small and contemptible."

[5] " The term σκεῦος (vessel), from σχίω to hold, has an allusion to the body's being the *depository* of the soul. "Οστρακον properly signifies a *shell.*

power of God is, by that means, the more illustrated, and is the better seen. "Those, who allege the contemptible appearance of my person, with the view of detracting from the dignity of my ministry, are unfair and unreasonable judges, for a *treasure* is not the less valuable, that the vessel, in which it is deposited, is not a precious one. Nay more, it is usual for great *treasures* to be laid up in earthen pots. Farther, they do not consider, that it is ordered by the special Providence of God, that there should be in ministers no appearance of excellence, lest any thing of distinction should throw the *power of God* into the shade. As, therefore, the abasement of ministers, and the outward contempt of their persons give occasion for glory accruing to God, that man acts a wicked part, who measures the dignity of the gospel by the person of the minister."

Paul, however, does not speak merely of the universal condition of mankind, but of his own condition in particular. It is true, indeed, that all mortal men are *earthen vessels.* Hence, let the most eminent of them all be selected, and let him be one that is adorned to admiration with all ornaments of birth, intellect, and fortune,[1] still, if he be a minister of the gospel, he will be a mean and merely *earthen* depository of an inestimable *treasure.* Paul, however, has in view himself, and others like himself, his associates, who were held in contempt, because they had nothing of show.

8. *While we are pressed on every side.* This is added by way of explanation, for he shows, that his abject condition is so far from detracting from the glory of God, that it is the occasion of advancing it. "We are reduced," says he, "to straits, but the Lord at length opens up for us an outlet ;[2]

(of which material, probably, the primitive *vessels* were formed,) and, 2*dly,* a *vessel,* of baked earth. And as that is proverbially brittle, ὀστράκινος denoted *weak, fragile,* both in a natural and a metaphorical sense ; and therefore was very applicable to the human body, both as *frail,* and as *mean."*—*Bloomfield.*—*Ed.*

[1] " De tous ornamens, de race, d'esprit, de richesses, et toutes autres choses semblables';"—" With all ornaments of birth, intellect, riches, and all other things of a like nature."

[2] " *We are troubled on every side.* In respect of the nature of it, (the trouble,) it is plain it was external trouble. The very word there used, Θλιβόμενοι, signifies dashing a thing from without. As the beating and allision of the waves *against* a rock make no trouble *in* the rock, no commo-

we are oppressed with poverty, but the Lord affords us help. Many enemies are in arms against us, but under God's protection we are safe. In fine, though we are brought low, so that it might seem as if all were over with us,[1] still we do not perish." The last is the severest of all. You see, how he turns to his own advantage every charge that the wicked bring against him.[2]

10. *The mortification of Jesus.*[3] He says more than he

---

tion *there*, but a great deal of noise, clamour, and tumult *round about it.* That is the sort of trouble which that word in its primary signification holds forth to us, and which the circumstances of the text declare to be the signification of the thing here meant. . . . . . The word στενοχωρούμενοι expresseth such a kind of straitening as doth infer a difficulty of drawing breath; that a man is so compressed, that he cannot tell how to breathe. That is the native import of the word. As if he had said, 'We are not reduced to that extremity by all the troubles that surround us, but we can breathe well enough for all that.' Probably there are meant by this thing desired, two degrees or steps of inward trouble. . . . Either it is a trouble that reacheth not the heart, or if it doth, it does not *oppress* or *overwhelm* it."—*Howe's Works,* (London, 1834,) p. 706.—*Ed.*

[1] " There is an allusion," says Dr. Bloomfield, " to an army so entirely surrounded and hemmed in ἐν στενοῖς, (*in straits,*) as the Roman army at the Caudinae Furcæ, that there is left no hope of escape."—*Ed.*

[2] " Pour le rendre contemptible;"—" To render him contemptible."

[3] " *Mortificationem.*"—Such is CALVIN's rendering of the original term νέκρωσιν, and it is evidently employed to convey the idea of *putting to death,* the main idea intended to be expressed being, as our author shows, that the apostles were, for the sake of Christ, subjected to humiliating and painful sufferings, which gave them, in a manner, an outward conformity to their Divine Master in the *violent death* inflicted upon him. The term *mortification,* when taken in strict accordance with its etymology, in the sense of *putting to death,* appears to bring out more fully the apostle's meaning, than the word " dying," made use of in our authorized version. Beza, who gives the same rendering as CALVIN, subjoins the following valuable observations :—" *Mortificationem.* (τὴν νέκρωσιν.) — Sic vocat Paulus miseram illam conditionem fidelium, ac præsertim ministrorum (de his enim proprie agitur) qui *quotidie* (ut ait David) *occiduntur,* quasi *destinationem ad cœdem* dicas: additurque *Domini Iesu,* vel, (ut legit vetus interpres) *Iesu Christi,* tum ut declaretur causa propter quam mundus illos ita persequitur ; tum etiam quia hac quoque in parte Christo capiti sunt conformes, Christusque adeo ipse quodammodo in iis morte afficitur. Ambrosius maluit *mortem* interpretari, nempe quia in altero membro sit mentio *vitæ* Christi. At ego, si libuisset a Pauli verbis discedere, *cœdem* potius exposuissem : quia non temere Paulus νέκρωσιν maluit scribere quam Θάνατον, quoniam etiam Christus hic considerandus nobis est non ut simpliciter mortuus, sed ut interemptus. Verum ut modo dixi νέκρωσις nec *mortem* nec *cœdem* hic significat, sed conditionem illam *quotidianis mortibus* obnoxiam, qualis etiam fuit Christi ad tempus ;"—" *Mortification.* (τὴν νέκρωσιν.) This term Paul makes use of to denote that miserable condition of believers, and more especially of ministers, (for it is of them pro-

had done previously, for he shows, that the very thing that the false apostles used as a pretext for despising the gospel, was so far from bringing any degree of contempt upon the gospel, that it tended even to render it glorious.   For he employs the expression—*the mortification of Jesus Christ*—to denote everything that rendered him contemptible in the eyes of the world, with the view of preparing him for participating in a blessed resurrection.   In the first place, the sufferings of Christ,[1] however ignominious they may be in the eyes of men, have, nevertheless, more of honour in the sight of God, than all the triumphs of emperors, and all the pomp of kings. The end, however, must also be kept in view, that we *suffer with him,* that we may be *glorified together with him.* (Rom. viii. 17.)   Hence he elegantly reproves the madness of those, who made his peculiar fellowship with Christ a matter of reproach.   At the same time, the Corinthians are admonished to take heed, lest they should, while haughtily despising Paul's mean and abject appearance, do an injury to Christ himself, by seeking an occasion of reproach[2] in his sufferings, which it becomes us to hold in the highest honour.

The word rendered *mortification,*[3] is taken here in a different sense from what it bears in many passages of Scripture.

perly that he speaks,) who are, as David says, *killed every day*—as though you should say a *setting apart for slaughter ;* and it is added—*of the Lord Jesus,* or (as the old interpreter renders it) *of Jesus Christ,* partly with the view of explaining the reason why the world thus persecutes them, and partly because in this respect also they are conformed to Christ, the Head, and even Christ himself is, in them, in a manner put to death.   Ambrose has preferred to render it *death,* for this reason, that in the other clause mention is made of the *life* of Christ.   For my own part, however, were I to depart from Paul's words, I would rather render it *slaughter,* inasmuch as Paul did not rashly make use of νίκρωσιν rather than θάνατον, since Christ also is to be viewed by us here, not simply as *having died,* but as *having been put to death.*   But, as I said a little ago, νίκρωσις here does not mean *death* nor *slaughter,* but a condition which exposed *every day to deaths,* such as Christ's, also, was for a time."—*Ed.*

[1] By the " sufferings of Christ," here, CALVIN obviously means—not the sufferings of our Redeemer *personally,* but *sufferings endured for Christ in the persons of his members,* as in Col. i. 24.—*Ed.*

[2] " Matiere d'opprobre et deshonneur ;"— " Matter of reproach and dishonour."

[3] Wiclif (1380) renders the expression as follows : " euermore we beren aboute the sleyng of Ihesus in oure bodi."—*Ed.*

For it often means self-denial, when we renounce the lusts of the flesh, and are renewed unto obedience to God.   Here, however, it means the afflictions by which we are stirred up to meditate on the termination of the present life.   To make the matter more plain, let us call the former the *inward* mortification, and the latter the *outward*.   Both make us conformed to Christ, the one directly, the other indirectly, so to speak.   Paul speaks of the former in Col. iii. 5, and in Rom. vi. 6, where he teaches that *our old man is crucified, that we may walk in newness of life.*   He treats of the second in Rom. viii. 29, where he teaches, that we were *predestinated* by God to this end—that we might be *conformed to the image of his Son.*   It is called, however, a *mortification* of Christ only in the case of believers, because the wicked, in the endurance of the afflictions of this present life, share with Adam, but the elect have participation with the Son of God, so that all those miseries that are in their own nature accursed, are helpful to their salvation.   All the sons of God, it is true, have this in common, that they *bear about the mortification of Christ ;*[1] but, according as any one is distinguished by a larger measure of gifts, he, in that proportion, comes so much the nearer to conformity with Christ in this respect.

That the life of Jesus.   Here is the best antidote to adversity—that as Christ's death is the gate of life, so we know that a blessed resurrection will be to us the termination of all miseries,[2] inasmuch as Christ has associated us with himself on this condition, that we shall be partakers of his life, if in this world we submit to die with him.

The sentence that immediately follows may be explained in two ways.   If you understand the expression *delivered*

[1] " Here we have a strong mode of expressing the *mortal* peril to which he was continually exposed; (as in 1 Cor. xv. 31, καθ' ἡμέραν ἀποθνήσκω, *I die daily,*) together with an indirect comparison of the sufferings endured by himself and the other apostles, with those endured by the Lord Jesus even *unto death.*   The genitive τοῦ Κυρίου, (*of the Lord,*) is, as Grotius remarks, a genitive of *likeness.*   The sense is—'*bearing about*—continually sustaining, perils and sufferings, like those of the Lord Jesus.'"—*Bloomfield.—Ed.*

[2] " La fin et l'issue de toutes miseres et calamitez ;"—" The end and issue of all miseries and calamities."

unto death as meaning to be incessantly harassed with persecutions and exposed to dangers, this would be more particularly applicable to Paul, and those like him, who were
openly assailed by the fury of the wicked. And thus the
expression, for Jesus' sake, will be equivalent to *for the testimony of Christ.* (Rev. i. 9.) As, however, the expression
to be daily delivered unto death, means otherwise—to have
death constantly before our eyes, and to live in such a manner, that our life is rather a shadow of death,[1] I have no objection, that this passage, also, should be expounded in such
a way as to be applicable to all believers, and that, too, to
every one in his order. Paul himself, in Rom. viii. 36, explains in this manner Psalm xliv. 22. In this way *for
Christ's sake* would mean—because this condition is imposed
upon all his members. Erasmus, however, has rendered it,
with not so much propriety, *we who live.* The rendering that
I have given is more suitable—*while we live.* For Paul means
that, so long as we are in the world, we resemble the dead
rather than the living.

12. *Hence death indeed.* This is said ironically, because
it was unseemly that the Corinthians should live happily, and
in accordance with their desire, and that they should, free
from anxiety, take their ease, while in the mean time Paul
was struggling with incessant hardships.[2] Such an allotment
would certainly have been exceedingly unreasonable. It was
also necessary that the folly of the Corinthians should be reproved, inasmuch as they contrived to themselves a Christianity without the cross, and, not content with this, held in
contempt the servants of Christ, because they were not so
effeminate.[3] Now as *death* denotes all afflictions, or a life
full of vexations, so also *life* denotes a condition that is
prosperous and agreeable; agreeably to the maxim : " Life
is—not *to live,* but *to be well.*"[4]

---

[1] CALVIN manifestly alludes to the expression which occurs in Psalms
xxiii. 4, *the valley of the shadow of death,* which he explains in a metaphorical sense, as denoting deep affliction.—*See* CALVIN *on the Psalms,*
vol. i. pp. 394-396.—*Ed.*

[2] " Eust à combatre contre tant de miseres et calamitez ;"—" Had to
struggle against so many miseries and calamities."

[3] " Comme eux ;"—" As they."

[4] " Non est *vivere,* sed *valere,* vita."—Martial. Ep. vi. 70.—*Ed.*

13. We having the same spirit of faith, according as it is written, I believed, and therefore have I spoken; we also believe, and therefore speak;

14. Knowing that he which raised up the Lord Jesus, shall raise up us also by Jesus, and shall present *us* with you.

15. For all things *are* for your sakes, that the abundant grace might, through the thanksgiving of many, redound to the glory of God.

16. For which cause we faint not; but though our outward man perish, yet the inward *man* is renewed day by day.

17. For our light affliction, which is but for a moment, worketh for us a far more exceeding *and* eternal weight of glory;

18. While we look not at the things which are seen, but at the things which are not seen: for the things which are seen *are* temporal; but the things which are not seen *are* eternal.

13. Habentes autem eundem Spiritum fidei, quemadmodum scriptum est (Ps. cxvi. 10) Credidi, propterea loquutus sum : nos quoque credimus, ideo et loquimur :

14. Scientes, quod qui suscitavit Dominum Iesum, nos etiam cum Iesu suscitabit, et constituet vobiscum.

15. Nam omnia propter vos, ut gratia quæ abundaverit propter gratiarum actionem, quæ a multis proficiscetur, abundet in gloriam Dei.

16. Quamobrem non deficimus: verum etsi externus homo noster corrumpitur, noster internus renovatur de die in diem.

17. Levitas enim afflictionis nostrae supramodum momentanea,[1] æternum supramodum pondus gloriæ operatur in nobis (*vel, momentanea levitas operatur in excellentia excellenter.*)

18. Dum non spectamus ea quæ videntur, sed quæ non videntur : nam quæ videntur, temporaria sunt : quæ autem non videntur, æterna.

13. *Having the same spirit.* This is a correction of the foregoing irony. He had represented the condition of the Corinthians as widely different from his own, (not according to his own judgment, but according to *their* erroneous view,) inasmuch as they were desirous of a gospel that was pleasant and free from all molestation of the cross, and entertained less honourable views of him, because his condition was less renowned. Now, however, he associates himself with them in the hope of the same blessedness. "Though God spares you, and deals with you more indulgently, while he treats me with somewhat more severity, this diversity, nevertheless, will be no hinderance in the way of the like glorious resurrection awaiting both of us. For where there is oneness of faith, there will, also, *there* be one inherit-

---

[1] " Car nostre legere affliction qui est de peu de duree à merueille, ou, *qui ne fait que passer ;*"—" For our light affliction, which is of marvellously short duration, or, *which does but pass away.*"

ance." It has been thought, that the Apostle speaks here of the holy fathers, who lived under the Old Testament, and represents them as partakers with us, in the same faith. This, indeed, is true, but it does not accord with the subject in hand. For it is not Abraham, or the rest of the fathers, that he associates with himself in a fellowship of faith, but rather the Corinthians, whereas they separated themselves from him by a perverse ambition. "However my condition," says he, "may appear to be the worse for the present, we shall, nevertheless, one day be alike participants in the same glory, for we are connected together by one faith." Whoever will examine the connection attentively, will perceive, that this is the true and proper interpretation. By metonymy, he gives the name of the *spirit of faith*[1] to faith itself, because it is a gift of the Holy Spirit.

As it is written. What has given occasion for the mistake[2] is, that he quotes the testimony of David. It ought, however, to be taken in connection with the confession—not with the oneness of faith, or if you prefer it, it agrees with what follows—not with what goes before, in this way: "Because we have an assured hope of a blessed resurrection, we are bold to speak and preach what we believe, as it is written, *I believed, therefore have I spoken.*" Now, this is the commencement of Psalm cxvi.,[3] where David acknowledges, that, when he had been reduced to the last extremity, he was so overpowered that he almost gave way, but, having soon afterwards regained confidence, he had overcome that temptation. Accordingly, he opens the Psalm thus: *I believed, therefore will I speak.* For faith is the mother[4] of confes-

---

[1] CALVIN adverts to this form of expression in the *Institutes*, (vol. ii. p. 138,) as an evidence that faith is implanted by the Divine Spirit.—*Ed.*

[2] "Que i'ay dit;"—"That I have mentioned." CALVIN refers to the mistake of supposing that Paul alludes to the Old Testament believers.—*Ed.*

[3] "The Septuagint, and some other ancient versions, make the latter part of the 116th Psalm" (commencing with the 10th verse—*I believed, therefore have I spoken*) "a distinct Psalm, separate from the former, and some have called it the *Martyr's Psalm*, I suppose for the sake of ver. 15."—*Henry's* Commentary.—*Ed.*

[4] "Comme la mere;"—"As it were, the mother."

sion. Paul, it is true, stirring himself up to imitate him,[1] exhorts the Corinthians to do the same, and, in accordance with the common Greek translation, has used the preterite instead of the future, but this is of no consequence.[2] For he simply means to say, that believers ought to be magnanimous, and undaunted, in *confessing*[3] *what they have believed with their heart.* (Rom. x. 9, 10.) Let now our pretended followers of Nicodemus[4] mark, what sort of fiction they contrive for themselves in the place of faith, when they would have faith remain inwardly buried, and altogether silent, and glory in this wisdom—that they utter, during their whole life, not a single word of right confession.

15. *For all things are for your sakes.* He now associates himself with the Corinthians, not merely in the hope of future blessedness, but also in these very afflictions, in which they might seem to differ from him most widely, for he lets them know, that, if he is afflicted, it is for their benefit. Hence it follows, that there was good reason why they should transfer part of them to themselves. What Paul states, depends *first* of all on that secret fellowship, which the mem-

---

[1] " S'accourageant à imiter cest exemple de Dauid ;"—" Stirring himself up to imitate this example of David."

[2] " *1 believed, for I did speak,* (Ps. cxvi. 10)—which is a sure proof of the presence of faith. Confession and faith are inseparably connected. Compare 2 Cor. iv. 13. The Apostle places, after the example of the Septuagint, *therefore* instead of *for :* ' I believed, *therefore* I spake,' without any material alteration of the sense."—*Hengstenberg* on the Psalms, (Edin. 1848,) vol. iii. p. 372.—*Ed.*

[3] " A faire confession de bouche ;"—" In making confession with the mouth.

[4] " There were also at this time" (about the year 1540) " certain persons who, having renounced the Protestant faith through dread of persecution, flattered themselves, that there was no harm in remaining in the external communion of the Church of Rome, provided they embraced the true religion in their hearts. And because CALVIN who condemned so pernicious a sentiment was considered by them as carrying his severity to an extreme, he showed clearly that his opinion was in unison, not only with those of the fathers of the Church, but also with the doctrine of the most learned theologians of the age, such as Melancthon, Bucer, and Martyr, as well as the ministers of Zurich ; and so completely extinguished that error, that all pious persons censured the *Nicodemites*—a name given to those who defended their dissimulation by the example of Nicodemus."—*Mackenzie's* Life of CALVIN, p. 59. See also CALVIN on John, vol. i. p. 317, CALVIN on the Psalms, vol. v. p. 481 ; and CALVIN'S Tracts, vol. i. p. xlix.— *Ed.*

bers of Christ have with one another, but *chiefly* on that mutual connection and relationship, which required more especially to be manifested among them. Now this admonition was fraught with great utility to the Corinthians, and brought with it choice consolation. For what consolation there is in this—that while God, sparing our weakness, deals with us more gently, those that are endowed with more distinguished excellence, are afflicted for the common advantage of all! They were also admonished, that, since they could not aid Paul otherwise, they should, at least, help him by their prayers and sympathy.

That the grace which hath abounded. That agreement[1] between the members of Christ he now commends on the ground of the fruit that springs from it—its tendency to advance the glory of God. By a metonymy, according to his usual manner, he means, by the term *grace*, that blessing of deliverance, of which he had made mention previously—that, *while he was weighed down, he was, nevertheless, not in anxiety: while oppressed with poverty, he was not left destitute*, &c., (verses 8, 9,) and in fine, that he had a deliverance continually afforded him from every kind of evil.[2] *This grace*, he says, *overflows.* By this he means, that it was not confined to himself personally, so that he alone enjoys it, but it extends itself farther—namely, to the Corinthians, to whom it was of great advantage. When he makes the overflowing of God's gift consist in gratitude, tending to the glory of its Author, he admonishes us, that every blessing that God confers upon us perishes through our carelessness, if we are not prompt and active in rendering thanks.

16. *For which cause we faint not.*[3] He now, as having

---

[1] " Ceste vnite et consentemente mutuel ;"—" That unity and mutual agreement."

[2] " De toutes sortes de maux desquels il estoit assailli ;"—" From all sorts of evils with which he was assailed."

[3] " *For which cause we faint not.* (οὐκ ἐκκακοῦμιν.) Here we have the same various reading," (as in verse 1, see p. 189, *n.* 1,) " οὐκ ἐγκακοῦμιν— *we do no wickedness;* and it is supported by BDEFG, and some others; but it is remarkable that Mr. Wakefield follows the common reading *here*, though the various reading is at least as well supported in this verse as in verse first. The common reading, *faint not*, appears to agree best with the Apostle's meaning."—*Dr. A. Clarke.—Ed.*

carried his point, rises to a higher confidence than before.
" There is no cause," says he, " why we should lose heart,
or sink down under the burden of the cross, the issue of
which is not merely so desirable to myself, but is also salutary
to others." Thus he exhorts the Corinthians to fortitude
by his own example, should they happen at any time to be
similarly afflicted. Farther, he beats down that insolence,
in which they in no ordinary degree erred, inasmuch as
under the influence of ambition, they held a man in higher
estimation, the farther he was from the cross of Christ.

Though our outward man. The *outward man,* some improperly and ignorantly confound with the *old man,* for
widely different from this is the *old man,* of which we have
spoken in Romans vi. 6. Chrysostom, too, and others restrict it entirely to the body ; but it is a mistake, for the
Apostle intended to comprehend, under this term, everything that relates to the present life. As he here sets before us *two men,* so you must place before your view *two
kinds of life*—the *earthly* and the *heavenly.* The *outward
man* is the maintenance of the *earthly* life, which consists
not merely in the *flower of one's age,* (1 Cor. vii. 36,) and in
good health, but also in riches, honours, friendships, and
other resources.[1] Hence, according as we suffer a dimi-
nution or loss of these blessings, which are requisite for
keeping up the condition of the present life, is our *outward
man* in that proportion corrupted. For as we are too much
taken up with the present life, so long as everything goes
on to our mind, the Lord, on that account, by taking away
from us, by little and little, the things that we are engrossed with, calls us back to meditate on a better life.
Thus, therefore, it is necessary, that the condition of the
present life should decay,[2] in order that the inward man
may be in a flourishing state ; because, in proportion as the
earthly life declines, does the *heavenly* life advance, at least
in believers. For in the reprobate, too, the *outward man*
decays,[3] but without anything to compensate for it. In the

[1] " Autres aides et commoditez ;"—" Other helps and conveniences."
[2] " De iour en iour ;"—" From day to day."
[3] " Il est vray que l'homme exterieur tend à decadence aussi bien es

sons of God, on the other hand, a decay of this nature is the beginning, and, as it were, the cause of production. He says that this takes place *daily*, because God continually stirs us up to such meditation. Would that this were deeply seated in our minds, that we might uninterruptedly make progress amidst the decay of the *outward man* !

17. *Momentary lightness.* As our flesh always shrinks back from its own destruction, whatever reward may be presented to our view, and as we are influenced much more by present feeling than by the hope of heavenly blessings, Paul on that account admonishes us, that the afflictions and vexations of the pious have little or nothing of bitterness, if compared with the boundless blessings of everlasting glory. He had said, that the decay of the *outward man* ought to occasion us no grief, inasmuch as the renovation of the *inward man* springs out of it. As, however, the *decay* is visible, and the *renovation* is invisible, Paul, with the view of shaking us off from a carnal attachment to the present life, draws a comparison between present miseries and future felicity. Now this comparison is of itself abundantly sufficient for imbuing the minds of the pious with patience and moderation, that they may not give way, borne down by the burden of the cross. For whence comes it, that patience is so difficult a matter but from this,—that we are confounded on having experience of evils for a brief period,[1] and do not raise our thoughts higher ? Paul, therefore, prescribes the best antidote against your sinking down under the pressure of afflictions, when he places in opposition to them that future blessedness which is *laid up for thee in heaven.* (Col. i. 5.) For this comparison makes that *light* which previously seemed *heavy*, and makes that *brief* and *momentary* which seemed of boundless duration.

There is some degree of obscurity in Paul's words, for as he says, *With hyperbole unto hyperbole*,[2] so the Old Inter-

reprouuez et infideles;"—" It is true that the outward man tends to decay quite as much in reprobates and unbelievers."
[1] " En ce sentiment des maux qui passent tontesfois auec le temps ;"— " In this feeling of evils, which nevertheless pass away with the occasion."
[2] " A outrance par outrance;"—" From extreme to extreme." " It is not merely eminent, but it is eminent *unto* eminence ; excess *unto*

preter, and Erasmus,[1] have thought that in both terms the magnitude of the heavenly glory, that awaits believers is extolled ; or, at least, they have connected them with the verb *worketh out.* To this I have no objection, but as the distinction that I have made is also not unsuitable, I leave it to my readers to make their choice.

Worketh out an eternal weight. Paul does not mean, that this is the invariable effect of afflictions ; for the great majority are most miserably weighed down here with evils of every kind, and yet that very circumstance is an occasion of their heavier destruction, rather than a help to their salvation.   As, however, he is speaking of believers, we must restrict exclusively to them what is here stated ; for this is a blessing from God that is peculiar to them—that they are prepared for a blessed resurrection by the common miseries of mankind.

As to the circumstance, however, that Papists abuse this passage, to prove that afflictions are the causes of our salvation, it is exceedingly silly ;[2] unless, perhaps, you choose to take *causes* in the sense of *means,* (as they commonly speak.) We, at least, cheerfully acknowledge, that *we must through many tribulations*[3] *enter into the kingdom of heaven,* (Acts

excess; a hyperbole *unto* hyperbole—one hyperbole heaped on another; and the expression means, that it is *exceeding exceedingly* glorious ; glorious in the highest possible degree.   The expression is the Hebrew form of denoting the highest superlative, and it means, that all hyperboles fail of expressing that external glory which remains for the just.   It is infinite and boundless.   You may pass from one degree to another; from one sublime height to another; but still an infinity remains beyond.   Nothing can describe the uppermost height of that glory, nothing can express its infinitude."—*Barnes.*   Chrysostom explains the words καθ᾽ ὑπερβολὴν εἰς ὑπερβολὴν to be equivalent to μέγεθος ὑπερβολικῶς ὑπερβολικόν—a greatness *exceedingly exceeding.*   " The repetition having an intensitive force, (like the Hebrew מאד מאד,) it may be rendered *infinitely exceeding.*"—*Bloomfield.*—*Ed.*

[1] The words of the Vulgate are, " Supra modum in sublimitate ;"— " Above measure in elevation."   The rendering of Erasmus is, " Mire supra modum ;"—" Wonderfully above measure."—*Ed.*

[2] " C'est vn argument trop debile ;"—" It is an exceedingly weak argument."

[3] " Per multas tribulationes ;"—" Par beaucoup de tribulations ;"— " By many tribulations."   This is the literal rendering of the original words made use of, διὰ πολλῶν θλίψεων.   Wiclif (1380) renders as follows, " bi many tribulaciouns."   Rheims (1582) " by many tribulations."—*Ed.*

xiv. 22,) and as to this there is no controversy. While, however, our doctrine is, that the momentary lightness of afflictions worketh out in us an *eternal weight*[1] *of life*, for this reason, that all the sons of God are *predestinated to be conformed to Christ*, (Rom. viii. 29,) in the endurance of the cross, and in this manner are prepared for the enjoyment of the heavenly inheritance, which they have through means of God's gracious adoption ; Papists, on the other hand, imagine that they are meritorious works,[2] by which the heavenly kingdom is acquired.

I shall repeat it again in a few words. We do not deny that afflictions are the path by which the heavenly kingdom is arrived at, but we deny that by afflictions we merit the inheritance,[3] which comes to us in no other way than through means of God's gracious adoption. Papists, without consideration, seize hold of one little word, with the view of building upon it a tower of Babel, (Gen. xi. 9,)—that the kingdom of God is not an inheritance procured for us by Christ, but a reward that is due to our works. For a fuller solution, however, of this question, consult my Institutes.[4]

While we look not. Mark what it is, that will make all the miseries of this world easy to be endured,—if we carry forward our thoughts to the eternity of the heavenly kingdom. For a moment is long, if we look around us on this side and on that ; but, when we have once raised our minds heavenward, a thousand years begin to appear to us to be like a moment. Farther, the Apostle's words intimate, that we are imposed upon by the view of present things, because there is nothing there that is not *temporal ;* and that, consequently, there is nothing for us to rest upon but confidence in a future life. Observe the expression, *looking at the things which are unseen*,[5] for the eye of faith penetrates beyond all

---

[1] " St. Paul in this expression—βάρος δόξης—*weight of glory*, elegantly joins together the two senses of the Heb. כבוד, which denotes both *weight* and *glory*, i.e., shining or being irradiated with light."—*Parkhurst.—Ed.*

[2] " Que les afflictions sont œuures meritoires ;"—" That afflictions are meritorious works."

[3] " L'heritage eternel ;"—" The everlasting inheritance."

[4] See *Institutes*, vol. ii. pp. 285-289, 417-419.—*Ed.*

[5] " The word which is here rendered *look* signifies to *take aim at*, (σκο-πούντων ἡμῶν.) This is a very steady intuition, which a man hath of the

our natural senses, and faith is also on that account represented as a *looking at things that are invisible.* (Heb. xi. 1.)

CHAPTER V.

1. For we know, that, if our earthly house of *this* tabernacle were dissolved, we have a building of God, an house not made with hands, eternal in the heavens.

2. For in this we groan, earnestly desiring to be clothed upon with our house which is from heaven:

3. If so be that being clothed, we shall not be found naked.

4. For we that are in *this* tabernacle do groan, being burdened: not for that we would be unclothed, but clothed upon, that mortality might be swallowed up of life.

5. Now he that hath wrought us for the selfsame thing *is* God, who also hath given unto us the earnest of the Spirit.

6. Therefore *we are* always confident, knowing that, whilst we are at home in the body, we are absent from the Lord:

7. (For we walk by faith, not by sight:)

8. We are confident, *I say,* and willing rather to be absent from the body, and to be present with the Lord.

1. Scimus enim, quod, si terrenum nostrum domicilium destruatur, ædificationem ex Deo habemus, domum non manufactam, æternam in cœlis.

2. Etenim in hoc gemimus, domicilium nostrum quod est e cœlo, superinduere desiderantes:

3. Siquidem etiam vestiti, non nudi reperiamur.[1]

4. Etenim dum sumus in tabernaculo, gemimus gravati: eo quod non exui volumus,[2] sed superindui, ut destruatur, quod mortale est, a vita.

5. Qui autem aptavit nos ad hoc ipsum, Deus est: qui etiam dedit nobis arrhabonem Spiritus.

6. Confidimus ergo semper, et scimus, quod habitantes in corpore, peregrinamur a Domino.

7. Per fidem enim ambulamus, et non per aspectum.

8. Confidimus, inquam, et libentius optamus peregrinari a corpore, et habitare apud Dominum.

mark which he is aiming at, or the end which he designs; he must always have it in his eye.   And by this *looking,* saith the Apostle, we find that, notwithstanding all the decays of the *outward man,* the *inward man is renewed day by day*—life, and vigour, and spirit continually entering in at our eyes from that glorious aim which we have before us.   This will need a very steady determination of mind unto such objects by a commanding light and glory that they carry with them, so that the soul feels not a disposition in itself to direct or look off."—*Howe's Works,* (Lond. 1834,) p. 543.—*Ed.*

[1] " Si toutesfois nous sommes trouuez aussi vestus, et non point nuds, *ou,* Si toutesfois nous sommes trouuez vestus, *ou,* Veu qu' aussi nous serons trouuez, &c., *ou,* Veu que mesmes apres auoir este despouillez, nous ne serons trouuez nuds;"—" If, nevertheless, we are found also clothed, and not naked—*or,* If, nevertheless, we are found clothed—*or,* Since we shall also be found, &c., *or,* Since even after having been stript, we shall not be found naked."

[2] " Pource que nous desirons, *ou,* en laquelle nous desirons;"—" Because we desire, *or,* in which we desire."

1. *For we know.* Here follows an amplification (ἐπεξερ-γασία) or embellishment of the foregoing statement.[1] For Paul has it in view, to correct in us impatience, dread, and dislike of the cross, contempt for what is mean, and in fine, pride, and effeminacy ; and this can only be accomplished by raising up our minds as high as heaven, through contempt of the world. Now he has recourse to two arguments. On the one hand, he shows the miserable condition of mankind in this life, and on the other hand, the supreme and perfect blessedness, which awaits believers in heaven after death. For what is it that keeps men so firmly bound in a misplaced attachment to this life, but their deceiving themselves with a false imagination—thinking themselves happy in living here? On the other hand, it is not enough to be aware of the mise-ries of this life, if we have not at the same time in view the felicity and glory of the future life. This is common to good and bad alike—that both are desirous to live. This, also, is common to both—that, when they consider, how many and how great miseries they are here exposed to, (with this difference, however, that unbelievers know of no adversities but those of the body merely, while the pious are more deeply affected[2] by spiritual distresses,) they often groan, often deplore their condition, and desire a remedy for their evils. As, however, all naturally view death with horror, unbelievers never wil-lingly quit this life, except when they throw it off in disgust or despair. Believers, on the other hand, depart willingly, because they have a better hope set before them beyond this world. This is the sum of the argument. Let us now ex-amine the words one by one.

We know, says he. This knowledge does not spring from the human intellect, but takes its rise from the revelation of the Holy Spirit. Hence it is peculiar to believers. Even the heathens had some idea of the immortality of the soul, but there was not one of them, that had assurance of it— not one of them could boast that he spoke of a thing that

---

[1] " S' ensuit vne declaration de la sentence precedente, plus ample et comme enrichie ;"—" There follows an explanation of the foregoing state-ment, more ample, and as it were enriched."

[2] " Sont touchez plus au vif;"—" Are more touched to the quick."

was *known* to him.[1] Believers alone can *affirm* this,[2] to whom it has been testified of by the word and Spirit of God. Besides, it is to be observed, that this knowledge is not merely of a general kind, as though believers were merely in a general way persuaded, that the children of God will be in a better condition after death, and had no assurance as to themselves individually,[3] for of how very little service this would be for affording a consolation, so difficult of attainment ! On the contrary, every one must have a knowledge peculiar to himself, for this, and this only, can animate me to meet death with cheerfulness—if I am fully persuaded, that I am departing to a better life.

The body, such as we now have it, he calls a *house of tabernacle*. For as *tabernacles*[4] are constructed, for a temporary purpose, of slight materials, and without any firm foundation, and then shortly afterwards are thrown down, or fall of their own accord, so the mortal body is given to men as a frail hut,[5] to be inhabited by them for a few days. The same metaphor is made use of, also, by Peter in his Second Epistle, (2 Pet. i. 13, 14,) and by Job, (iv. 19,) when he calls it a *house of clay*. He places in contrast with this a *building of perpetual duration*. It is not certain, whether he means by this term a state of blessed immortality, which awaits believers after death, or the incorruptible and glorious body, such as it will be after the resurrection. In whichever of these senses it is taken, it will not be unsuitable ; though I prefer to understand it as meaning, that the blessed

---

[1] Cicero, who argues at considerable length, and as it might seem most convincingly, for the immortality of the soul, introduces one as complaining that while, on reading the arguments in favour of this tenet, he thought himself convinced, as soon as he laid aside the book and began to reason with himself, his conviction was gone. " I know not," says he, " how it happens, that when I read, I assent, but when I have laid down the book, all that assent vanishes."   Hence Seneca, (Ep. 102,) when speaking of the reasonings of the ancient heathen philosophers on this important point, justly observes, that " immortality, however desirable, was rather *promised* than *proved* by those great men."—*Ed.*

[2] " Puissent parler ainsi ;"—" Can speak thus"—that is, *with confidence.*

[3] " Et que cependant chacun d'eux ne fust point asseuré de sa propre felicité ;"—" And as if each of them were not in the mean time assured as to his own felicity."

[4] " Tabernacles ou loges ;"—" Tabernacles or huts."

[5] " Comme vne logette caduque ;"—" As a frail little hut."

condition of the soul after death is the commencement of this *building*, and the glory of the final resurrection is the consummation of it.[1] This exposition will correspond better with the Apostle's context. The epithets, which he applies to this building, tend to confirm more fully its perpetuity.

3. *Since clothed.* He restricts to believers, what he had stated respecting the certainty of a future life, as it is a thing peculiar to them. For the wicked, too, are stript of the body, but as they bring nothing within the view of God, but a disgraceful nakedness, they are, consequently, not clothed with a glorious body. Believers, on the other hand, who appear in the view of God, clothed with Christ, and adorned with His image, receive the glorious robe of immortality. For I am inclined to take this view, rather than that of Chrysostom and others, who think that nothing new is here stated, but that Paul simply repeats here, what he had previously said as to putting on an eternal habitation. The Apostle, therefore, makes mention here of a twofold clothing, with which God invests us—the righteousness of Christ, and sanctification of the Spirit in this life ; and, after death, immortality and glory. The *first* is the cause of the *second*, because *those whom God has determined to glorify, he first justifies.* (Rom. viii. 30.) This meaning, too, is elicited from the particle *also*, which is without doubt introduced for the purpose of amplifying—as if Paul had said, that a new robe will be prepared for believers after death, since they have been clothed in this life *also*.

4. *We groan, being burdened, because we desire not to be unclothed.* The wicked, too, *groan*, because they are not contented with their present condition ; but afterwards an opposite disposition prevails, that is, a clinging to life, so that they view death with horror, and do not feel the long continuance of this mortal life to be a burden. The *groaning* of believers, on the other hand, arises from this—that they know, that they are here in a state of exile from their native land, and that they know, that they are here shut up in the body as in a prison. Hence they feel this life to be

---

[1] " La consommation et accomplissement ;"—" The consummation and accomplishment."

a *burden*, because in it they cannot enjoy true and perfect blessedness, because they cannot escape from the bondage of sin otherwise than by death, and hence they aspire to be elsewhere.

As, however, it is natural for all animals to desire existence, how can it be, that believers are willing to cease to exist ? The Apostle solves this question, when he says, that believers do not desire death for the sake of losing any thing, but as having regard to a better life. At the same time, the words express more than this. For he admits, that we have naturally an aversion to the quitting of this life, considered in itself, as no one willingly allows himself to be stript of his garments. Afterwards, however, he adds, that the natural horror of death is overcome by confidence ;[1] as an individual will, without any reluctance, throw away a coarse, dirty, threadbare, and, in one word, tattered garment, with the view of his being arrayed in an elegant, handsome, new, and durable one.

Farther, he explains the metaphor by saying—*that what is mortal may be destroyed*[2] *by life.* For as *flesh and blood cannot inherit the kingdom of God,* (1 Cor. xv. 50,) it is necessary, that what is corruptible in our nature should perish, in order that we may be thoroughly renewed, and restored to a state of perfection. On this account, our body is called a prison, in which we are confined.

5. *Now he that hath fitted us.* This is added in order that we may know, that this disposition is supernatural. For mere natural feeling will not lead us forward to this, for it does not comprehend that hundredfold recompense which springs from the *dying* of a single *grain.* (John xii. 24.) We must, therefore, be *fitted* for it by God. The manner of it is at the same time subjoined—that he confirms us by his Spirit, who is as it were an *earnest.* At the same time the particle *also* seems to be added for the sake of amplification. " It is God who forms in us this desire, and, lest our courage should give way or waver, the Holy Spirit is given us as an

---

[1] " Par la fiance qu'ont les fideles ;"—" By the confidence which believers have."

[2] " Soit englouti par la vie ;"—" May be swallowed up by life."

earnest, because by his testimony he confirms, and ratifies the truth of the promise." For these are *two* offices of the Holy Spirit—*first*, to show to believers what they ought to desire, and *secondly*, to influence their hearts efficaciously, and remove all their doubt, that they may steadfastly persevere in choosing what is good. There would, however, be nothing unsuitable in extending the word *fitted*, so as to denote that renovation of life, with which God adorns his people even in this life, for in this way he already separates them from others, and shows that they are, by means of his grace, marked out for a peculiar condition.

6. *Therefore we are always confident.* That is, as exercising dependence on the *earnest of the Spirit;* for, otherwise, we always tremble, or, at least, are courageous or alarmed by turns, and do not retain a uniform and even tenor of mind. Hence, that good courage of which Paul speaks has no place in us, unless it is maintained by the Spirit of God. The connecting particle *and*, which immediately follows, ought to be understood as meaning *because*, in this way : We are of good courage, BECAUSE *we know that we are absent*, &c. For this knowledge is the cause of our calmness and confidence ; for the reason, why unbelievers are constantly in a ferment of anxiety, or obstinately murmur against God, is, that they think they will ere long cease to exist, and they place in this life the highest and uppermost summit of their felicity.[1] We, on the other hand, live in the exercise of contentment,[2] and go forward to death with alacrity,[3] because a better hope is laid up for us.

We are absent from the Lord. Scripture everywhere proclaims, that God is *present* with us : Paul here teaches, that we are *absent* from him. This is seemingly a contradiction ; but this difficulty is easily solved, when we take into view the different respects, in which he is said to be *present* or *absent*. He is, then, *present* with all men, inasmuch as he upholds them by his power. He dwells in them, because *in him*

---

[1] See CALVIN's observations on the same point, when commenting on 1 Cor. xv. 32, pp. 41, 42.—*Ed.*

[2] "Nous viuons en paix, prenans tout en gre ;"—"We live in peace, taking everything favourably."

[3] "Ioyeusement ;"—"Joyfully."

they live and move and have their being. (Acts xvii. 28.)
He is *present* with his believing people by the energy of his
Spirit ; he lives in them, resides in the midst of them, nay
more, *within* them.   But in the mean time he is *absent* from
us, inasmuch as he does not present himself to be seen face
to face, because we are as yet in a state of exile from his
kingdom, and have not as yet attained that blessed immortality, which the angels that are *with* him enjoy.   At the
same time, to be *absent*, in this passage, refers merely to
knowledge, as is manifest from the reason that is afterwards
added.

    7. *For we walk by faith. Εἶδος* I have here rendered
aspectum, (sight,) because few understood the meaning of
the word *species, (appearance.)*[1]   He states the reason, why
it is that we are now *absent from the Lord*—because we do
not as yet see him *face to face.* (1 Cor. xiii. 12.)   The
manner of that absence is this—that God is not openly beheld by us.   The reason why he is not seen by us is, that
we *walk by faith.*   Now it is on good grounds that *faith* is
opposed to *sight*, because it perceives those things that are
hid from the view of men—because it reaches forth to future
things, which do not as yet appear.   For such is the condition of believers, that they resemble the dead rather than
the living—that they often seem as if they were forsaken by
God—that they always have the elements of death shut up
within them.   Hence they must necessarily *hope against
hope.* (Rom. iv. 18.)   Now the things that are hoped for
are hid, as we read in Rom. viii. 24, and faith is the *manifestation of things which do not appear.* (Heb. xi. 1.)[2]   It

---

    [1] " *Espece,* ainsi qu'on a accoustumé de traduire en Latin ce mot Grec ;"
—" *Species,* as they have been accustomed to render in Latin this Greek
word." Those interpreters who have rendered εἶδος, *species,* (appearance,)
employ the word *species* to mean what is *seen,* as distinguished from what is
invisible—*what has a visible form.*   The term, however, (as CALVIN hints,)
is ambiguous, being frequently employed to denote *appearance, as distinguished from reality.—Ed.*
    [2] " Concerning the import of the original term ὑπόστασις, translated *sub-
stance,* (Heb. xi. 1,) there has been a good deal of discussion, and it has
been understood to signify *confidence* or *subsistence.*   Faith is the *confidence* of things hoped for ; because it assures us, not only that there are
such things, but that, through the power and faithfulness of God, we shall
enjoy them.   It is the *subsistence* of things hoped for ; because it gives

is not to be wondered, then, if the apostle says, that we have not as yet the privilege of *sight*, so long as we *walk by faith*. For we *see*, indeed, but it is *through a glass, darkly ;* (1 Cor. xiii. 12,) that is, in place of the reality we rest upon the word.

8. *We are confident, I say.* He again repeats, what he had said respecting the confidence of the pious—that they are so far from breaking down under the severity of the cross, and from being disheartened by afflictions, that they are made thereby more courageous. For the worst of evils is death, yet believers long to attain it, as being the commencement of perfect blessedness. Hence *and* may be regarded as equivalent to *because*, in this way : " Nothing can befall us, that can shake our confidence and courage, since death (which others so much dread) is to us *great gain*. (Phil. i. 21.) For nothing is better than to quit the body, that we may attain near intercourse with God, and may truly and openly enjoy his presence. Hence by the decay of the body we lose nothing that belongs to us."

Observe here—what has been once stated already—that true faith begets not merely a contempt of death, but even a desire for it,[1] and that it is, accordingly, on the other hand, a token of unbelief, when dread of death predominates in us above the joy and consolation of hope. Believers, however, desire death—not as if they would, by an importunate desire,

them, although future, a present *subsistence* in the minds of believers, so that they are influenced by them as if they were actually present. Thus the word was understood by some of the Greek commentators, who were the most competent judges of its meaning. ' Since things which we hope for,' says Chrysostom, ' seem not to subsist, faith gives them subsistence, or rather it does not *give* it, but is itself their substance. Thus the resurrection of the dead is not past, nor does it subsist, but faith gives it subsistence in our souls.' 'Faith,' says another, 'gives subsistence to the resurrection of the dead, and places it before our eyes. . . . . The objects of faith are not only future good, but invisible things, both good and evil, which are made known by divine revelation ; and of these it is the evidence, (ἔλεγχος,) the *demonstration* or *conviction*. . . . . Being past, and future, and invisible on account of their distance from us, or the spirituality of their nature, they cannot be discovered by our senses, but the conviction of their reality is as strong in the mind of a believer, as if they were placed before his eyes."—*Dick's Theology*, vol. iii. pp. 314, 315. —*Ed.*

[1] See p. 216.

anticipate their Lord's day, for they willingly retain their footing in their earthly station, so long as their Lord may see good, for they would rather live to the glory of Christ than *die to themselves,* (Rom. xiv. 7,) and for their own advantage.[1] For the desire, of which Paul speaks, springs from faith. Hence it is not at all at variance with the will of God. We may, also, gather from these words of Paul, that souls, when released from the body, live in the presence of God, for if, on being *absent from the body,* they have God *present,*[2] they assuredly live with him.

Here it is asked by some—" How then did it happen that the holy fathers dreaded death so much, as for example David, Hezekiah, and the whole of the Israelitish Church, as appears from Psalm vi., from Isaiah xxxviii. 3, and from Psalm cxv. 17 ?" I am aware of the answer, that is usually returned—that the reason, why death was so much dreaded by them was, that the revelation of the future life was as yet obscure, and the consolation, consequently, was but small. Now I acknowledge, that this, in part, accounts for it, but not entirely, for the holy fathers of the ancient Church did not in every case tremble, on being forewarned of their death. Nay more, they embraced death with alacrity, and with joyful hearts. For Abraham departed without regret, *full of*

---

[1] " C'est à dire pour leur propre proufit et vtilite ;"—" That is to say, for their own profit and advantage."

[2] " In this world," says *Howe*, in a discourse on 2 Cor. v. 8, " we find ourselves encompassed with objects that are suitable, grateful, and entertaining to our bodily senses, and the several principles, perceptions, and appetites that belong to the bodily life ; and these things familiarize and habituate us to this world, and make us, as it were, one with it. There is particularly a *bodily* people, as is intimated in the text, that we are associated with, by our being *in the body.* The words ἐνδημῆσαι and ἐκδημῆσαι in this verse, (and the same are used in verses 6th and 9th,) signify there is such a people of which we are, and from which we would be disassociated ; ἐνδημος is *civis*, *incola*, or *indigena*—an *inhabitant* or *native* among this or that people ; an ἐκδημος is *peregrinus*, one that *lives abroad*, and is *severed* from the *people* he belonged unto. The apostle considers himself, while in the body, as living among such a sort of people as dwell in bodies, a like sort of people to himself, and would be no longer a *home-dweller* with them, but travel away from them, to join and be a dweller with another people. For also, on the other hand, he considers, ' with the Lord,' an invisible world where he resides, and an incorporeal people he presides over."—*Howe's Works*, (Lond. 1834,) p. 1023.—*Ed.*

days.[1] (Gen. xxv. 8.) We do not read that Isaac was reluctant to die. (Gen. xxxv. 29.) Jacob, with his last breath, declares that he is *waiting for the salvation of the Lord.* (Gen. xlix. 18.) David himself, too, dies peacefully, without any regrets, (1 Kings ii. 10,) and in like manner Hezekiah. As to the circumstance, that David and Hezekiah did, each of them, on one occasion deprecate death with tears, the reason was, that they were punished by the Lord for certain sins, and, in consequence of this, they felt the anger of the Lord in death. Such was the cause of their alarm, and this believers might feel even at this day, under the reign of Christ. The *desire,* however, of which Paul speaks, is the disposition of a well-regulated mind.[2]

9. Wherefore we labour, that, whether present or absent, we may be accepted of him.

10. For we must all appear before the judgment-seat of Christ; that every one may receive the things *done* in *his* body, according to that he hath done, whether *it be* good or bad.

11. Knowing therefore the terror of the Lord, we persuade men; but we are made manifest unto God;

9. Quapropter contendimus, sive domi agentes, sive foris peregrinantes, ut illi placeamus.

10. Omnes enim nos manifestari[3] oportet coram tribunali Christi, ut reportet unusquisque, quæ per corpus facta fuerint, prout fecerit, sive bonum, sive malum.[4]

11. Scientes igitur terrorem illum Domini, suademus hominibus,[5] Deo autem manifesti sumus; confido au-

---

[1] "Rassassié de iours, et sans regret;"—"Satisfied with days and without regret." "In the Hebrew," says *Poole* in his Annotations, "it is only *full* or *satisfied;* but you must understand *with days* or *years,* as the phrase is fully expressed in Gen. xxxv. 29; 1 Chron. xxiii. 1; 1 Chron. xxix. 28; Job xlii. 17; Jer. vi. 11. When he (Abraham) had lived as long as he desired, being in some sort weary of life, and desirous to be dissolved, or *full of all good,* as the Chaldee renders it—*satisfied,* as it is said of Naphtali, (Deut. xxxiii. 23,) *with favour,* and full with the *blessing of the Lord* upon himself and upon his children."—*Ed.*

[2] "Vn esprit bien posé, et deliuré de trouble;"—"A mind well regulated, and free from alarm."

[3] "Estre manifestez, *ou* comparoir;"—"Be manifested or appear."

[4] "Afin qu'vn chacun reporte les choses faites par son corps, selon qu'il a fait, soit bien, soit mal," *ou,* "reporte en son corps selon qu'il aura fait, ou bien ou mal;"—"That every one may give an account of the things, done in his body, according as he has done, whether it be good, or whether it be evil," *or,* "may give an account in his body, according as he shall have done, whether good or evil."

[5] "Nous induisons les hommes, ascauoir à la foy, *ou,* nous persuadons les hommes;"—"We induce men, that is, to the faith, *or,* we persuade men."

and I trust also are made manifest in your consciences.

12. For we commend not ourselves again unto you, but give you occasion to glory on our behalf, that ye may have somewhat to *answer* them which glory in appearance, and not in heart.

tem nos et in conscientiis vestris, manifestos esse.

12. Non enim nosmetipsos iterum commendamus vobis, sed occasionem vobis damus gloriandi de nobis, ut aliquid habeatis adversus eos,[1] qui in facie gloriantur, et non in corde.

9. *Wherefore we strive.* Having shown how magnanimous Christians ought to be in the endurance of afflictions,[2] so that even in dying they may be conquerors over death, and that too, because by afflictions and death they attain to a blessed life, he now from the same source draws also another conclusion—that they must, by all means, make it their main desire to please God. And indeed it cannot but be, that the hope of a resurrection, and thoughtfulness as to the judgment, will awaken in us this desire ; as, on the other hand, the true reason why we are so indolent and remiss in duty is, that we seldom, if ever, think of what ought to be constantly kept in remembrance,[3] that we are here but lodgers[4] for a short time, that we may, after finishing our course, return to Christ. Observe, however, what he says—that this is the desire both of the *living* and of the *dead*, by which statement the immortality of the soul is again confirmed.

10. *We must be manifested.* Though this is common to all, yet all without distinction do not raise their views in such a way as to consider every moment, that they must appear before the judgment-seat of Christ. But while Paul, from a holy desire of acting aright, constantly sisted himself before the bar of Christ, he had it in view to reprove indirectly those ambitious teachers, who reckoned it enough to have the plaudits of their fellow-men.[5] For when he says,

[1] "Afin qu'ayez *de quoy respondre* a ceux ;"—" That ye may have *wherewith to answer* those."

[2] " Quelle constance et magnanimite doyuent auoir les Chrestiens en leurs afflictions ;"—" What constancy and magnanimity Christians ought to have in their afflictions."

[3] " Nous deurions auoir incessamment deuant les yeux et en memoire ;"—" We ought to have unceasingly before our eyes and in our remembrance."

[4] " Nous sommes yci estrangers ;"—" We are strangers here."

[5] " Se contentoyent d'auoir l'applaudissement des hommes, comme fe-

that no one can escape, he seems in a manner to summon them to that heavenly tribunal. Farther, though the word translated *to be manifested* might be rendered *to appear*, yet Paul had, in my opinion, something farther in view—that we shall then come forth to the light, while for the present many are concealed, as it were, in the darkness. For then *the books*, which are now shut, *will be opened.* (Dan. vii. 10.)

That every one may give account. As the passage relates to the recompensing of deeds, we must notice briefly, that, as evil deeds are punished by God, so also good deeds are rewarded, but for a different reason ; for evil deeds are requited with the punishment that they deserve, but God in rewarding good deeds does not look to merit or worthiness. For no work is so full and complete in all its parts as to be deservedly well-pleasing to him, and farther, there is no one whose works are in themselves well-pleasing to God, unless he render satisfaction to the whole law. Now no one is found to be thus perfect. Hence the only resource is in his accepting us through unmerited goodness, and justifying us, by not imputing to us our sins. After he has received us into favour, he receives our works also by a gracious acceptance. It is on this that the reward hinges. There is, therefore, no inconsistency in saying, that he rewards good works, provided we understand that mankind, nevertheless, obtain eternal life gratuitously. On this point I have expressed myself more fully in the preceding Epistle, and my Institutes will furnish a full discussion of it.[1] When he says *in the body*, I understand him to mean, not merely outward actions, but all the deeds that are done in this corporeal life.

11. *Knowing therefore.* He now returns to speak of himself, or he again applies the general doctrine to himself personally. " I am not ignorant," says he, " nor devoid of the fear of God, which ought to reign in the hearts of all the pious." To *know the terror of the Lord*, then, is to be influenced by this consideration—that an account must one

royent ceux qui ioueroyent quelque rolle en vn theatre ;"—" Reckoned it enough to have the applause of men, like persons who act some part in a theatre."

[1] See CALVIN on the Corinthians, vol. i. pp. 303, 304; and CALVIN'S *Institutes*, vol. ii. pp. 413-427.

day be rendered before the judgment-seat of Christ ; for the
man who seriously considers this must of necessity be touched
with fear, and shake off all negligence.[1]   He declares, therefore, that he discharges his apostleship faithfully and with a
pure conscience, (2 Tim. i. 3,) as one that *walks in the fear
of the Lord*, (Acts ix. 31,) thinking of the account to be
rendered by him.   As, however, his enemies might object :
" You extol yourself, it is true, in magnificent terms, but
who is there that sees what you affirm ?"   He says, in reply
to this, that he discharges indeed the work of a teacher in
the sight of men, but that it is known to God with what
sincerity of mind he acts.   " As my mouth speaks to men,
so does my heart to God."

And I trust. This is a kind of correction of what he had
said, for he now boasts that he has not merely God as the
witness of his integrity, but also the Corinthians themselves,
to whom he had given proof of himself.   Two things, therefore, are to be observed here : in the *first* place, that it is
not enough that an individual conducts himself honourably
and assiduously[2] among men, if his *heart is not right in the
sight of God*, (Acts viii. 21;) and *secondly*, that boasting is
vain, where evidence of the reality itself is wanting.   For
none are more bold in arrogating everything to themselves,
than those that have nothing.   Let, therefore, the man who
would have credit given him, bring forward such works as
may afford confirmation to his statements.   To be *made manifest in their consciences* is more than to be known by proofs ;
for conscience reaches farther than carnal judgment.

12. *For we commend not ourselves.* He confirms what he
had said immediately before, and at the same time anticipates a calumny that might be brought against him.   For
it might seem as if he were too careful as to his own praise,
inasmuch as he spoke so frequently respecting himself.   Nay,
it is probable that this reproach had been cast upon him by
the wicked.   For when he says—*We commend not ourselves
again*, he says this as if speaking in his own person.   To

---

[1] " Tout mespris et toute nonchalance ;"—" All contempt and all carelessness."

[2] " Vertueusement ;"—" Virtuously."

commend is taken in a bad sense, as meaning to *boast*, or to *brag.*

When he adds—that he *gives them occasion of glorying,* he intimates in the *first* place, that he pleads *their* cause rather than his own, inasmuch as he gives up all with a view to their glory, and he again indirectly reproves their ingratitude, because they had not perceived it to be their duty to magnify, of their own accord, his Apostleship, so as not to impose upon him this necessity ; and farther, because they had not perceived, that it was *their* interest rather than that of Paul himself, that his Apostleship should be accounted honourable. We are here taught, that Christ's servants ought to be concerned as to their own reputation, only in so far as is for the advantage of the Church. Paul affirms with truth, that he is actuated by this disposition.[1] Let others see that they do not on false grounds pretend to follow his example.[2] We are taught farther, that *that* alone is a minister's true praise, that is common to him with the whole Church, rather than peculiar to himself exclusively—in other words, that redounds to the advantage of all.

That ye may have something in opposition to those. He intimates, in passing, that it is necessary to repress the vanity of those that make empty boasts, and that it is the duty of the Church to do so. For as ambition of this nature is a peculiarly destructive pestilence, it is dangerous to encourage it by dissimulation. As the Corinthians had not taken care to do this, Paul instructs them how they should act for the future.

To *glory in appearance, not in heart,* is to disguise one's self by outward show, and to regard sincerity of heart as of no value ; for those that will be truly wise *will never glory but in God.* (1 Cor. i. 31.) But wherever there is empty show, *there* is no sincerity, and no integrity of heart.

---

[1] " Sainct Paul afferme qu'il a eu vne telle affection, et en cela dit verite ;"—" Saint Paul affirms, that he has exercised such a disposition, and in this he says truth."

[2] " Que les autres aduisent, quand à son exemple ils voudront parler ainsi, que ce ne soit point à fausses enseignes ;"—" Let others take care, when they would wish to speak of themselves in this manner, after his example, that it be not under false colours."

13. For whether we be beside ourselves, *it is* to God; or whether we be sober, *it is* for your cause.

14. For the love of Christ constraineth us; because we thus judge, that if one died for all, then were all dead:

15. And *that* he died for all, that they which live should not henceforth live unto themselves, but unto him which died for them, and rose again.

16. Wherefore, henceforth know we no man after the flesh; yea, though we have known Christ after the flesh, yet now henceforth know we *him* no more.

17. Therefore if any man *be* in Christ, *he is* a new creature: old things are passed away; behold, all things are become new.

13. Nam sive insanimus, Deo insanimus: sive sani sumus, vobis sani sumus.

14. Caritas enim Christi constringit nos: iudicantes illud, quodsi unus pro omnibus mortuus fuit, ergo omnes sunt mortui.[1]

15. Et quidem pro omnibus mortuus est: ut qui vivunt, posthac non sibi vivant, sed ei qui pro omnibus mortuus est, et resurrexit.

16. Itaque nos posthac neminem novimus secundum carnem: quin etiam si secundum carnem novimus Christum, iam non amplius novimus.

17. Proinde si quis in Christo, nova sit creatura,[2] vetera præterierunt: ecce, nova facta sunt omnia.

13. *Whether we are beside ourselves.* This is said by way of concession; for Paul's glorying was sane, or it was, if we may so term it, a sober and most judicious madness;[3] but as he appeared foolish in the eyes of many, he speaks according to their views. Now he declares two things: in the *first* place, that he makes no account of himself, but has this one object in view—that he may serve God and the Church; and, *secondly,* that he fears not the opinion of men, so that he is prepared for being reckoned either sane or insane, provided only he transacts faithfully the affairs of God and the Church. The meaning, therefore, is this: " As to my making mention so frequently of my integrity, persons will take this as they choose. It is not, however, for my own sake that I do it, but, on the contrary, I have God and the Church exclusively in view. Hence I am prepared to be silent and to speak, according as the glory of God and the advantage of the Church will require, and I shall be quite contented that the world reckon me *beside myself,* provided only it is

---

[1] " Sont morts, ou ont este morts;"—" Are dead, or have been dead."

[2] " Si aucun donc est en Christ, *qu'il soit* nouuelle creature, *ou,* Il est;" —" If any one, therefore, is in Christ, *let him be* a new creature, *or,* He is."

[3] " Estoit bonne, et procedoit d'vn esprit prudent: ou si ainsi faut parler, sa folie estoit d'vn sens rassis, et pleine de sagesse;"—" Was good, or proceeded from a prudent mind; or, if we may speak so, his folly was from a settled judgment, and full of wisdom."

not to myself, but to God, that I am *beside myself*."[1]   This is a passage that is deserving not merely of notice, but also of constant meditation ; for unless we shall have our minds thus regulated, the smallest occasions of offence will from time to time draw us off from our duty.

14. *For the love of Christ.*   The term *love* may be taken either in a *passive* signification, or in an *active*.   I prefer the latter.   For if we be not harder than iron, we cannot refrain from devoting ourselves entirely to Christ, when we consider what great love he exercised towards us, when he endured death in our stead.   Paul, too, explains himself when he adds, that it is reasonable that we should *live to him*, being dead to ourselves.   Hence, as he had previously stated, (verse 11,) that he was stirred up to duty by fear, inasmuch as an account was one day to be rendered by him, so he now brings forward another motive—that measureless love of Christ towards us, of which he had furnished us with an evidence in his death.   "The knowledge," I say, "of this love, ought to *constrain* our affections, that they may go in no other direction than that of loving him in return.

There is a metaphor[2] implied in the word *constrain*, denoting that it is impossible but that every one that truly considers and ponders that wonderful love, which Christ has manifested towards us by his death, becomes, as it were, bound to him, and *constrained* by the closest tie, and devotes himself wholly to his service.

If one died for all.   This design is to be carefully kept in

---

view—that *Christ died for us, that we might die to ourselves.*
The exposition is also to be carefully noticed—that to *die to
ourselves* is to *live to Christ;* or if you would have it at
greater length, it is to renounce ourselves, that we may *live
to Christ;* for Christ redeemed us with this view—that he
might have us under his authority, as his peculiar possession.   Hence it follows that we are no longer our own masters.   There is a similar passage in Rom. xiv. 7-9.   At the
same time, there are *two* things that are here brought forward separately—that we are dead in Christ, in order that
all ambition and eagerness for distinction may be laid aside,
and that it may be felt by us no hardship to be made as
nothing; and farther, that we owe to Christ our life and
death, because he has wholly bound us to himself.[1]

16. *Therefore we henceforth know no man.*   To *know,* here,
is taken as meaning to *reckon.*   " We do not judge according to external appearance, so as to reckon that man to be
the most illustrious who seems so in appearance." Under
the term *flesh,* he includes all external endowments which
mankind are accustomed to hold in estimation ; and, in
short, every thing which, apart from regeneration, is reckoned worthy of praise.   At the same time, he speaks more
particularly of outward disguise, or *appearance,* as it is
termed.   He alludes, also, without doubt, to the death of
which he had made mention.   " Since we ought, all of us,
to be dead to the present life, nay more, to be nothing in
ourselves, no one must be reckoned a servant of Christ on
the ground of carnal excellence."

Nay, though we have known Christ.   The meaning is—
" Though Christ lived for a time in this world, and was
known by mankind in those things that have to do with the
condition of the present life, he must now be known in another way—*spiritually,* so that we may have no worldly
thoughts respecting him."   This passage is perverted by
some fanatics, such as Servetus,[2] for the purpose of proving,

---

[1] " Pource qu'il a tant pour nous, que nous sommes du tout à luy ;"
—" Because he has done so much for us, that we are wholly his."

[2] The views held by Servetus respecting the Supreme Being, and a
Trinity of persons in the Godhead, " were obscure and chimerical beyond
all measure, and amounted, in general, to the following propositions :—

that Christ's human nature is now absorbed by the Divinity. But how very far removed such a frenzy is from the Apostle's intention, it is not difficult to perceive ; for he speaks here, not of the substance of his body, but of external appearance, nor does he affirm that the flesh is no longer perceived by us in Christ, but says, that Christ is not *judged* of from that.[1]

Scripture proclaims throughout, that Christ does now as certainly lead a glorious life in our flesh, as he once suffered in it.[2]   Nay more, take away this foundation, and our whole faith falls to the ground ; for whence comes the hope of immortality, except from this, that we have already a pattern[3] of it in the person of Christ ?   For as righteousness is restored to us on this ground, that Christ, by fulfilling the law in our nature, has abolished Adam's disobedience, so also life has been restored to us by this means, that he has opened up for our nature the kingdom of God, from which it had been banished, and has given it a place in the heavenly dwelling.   Hence, if we do not now recognise Christ's flesh,[4] we lose the whole of that confidence and consolation that we

That the Deity, before the creation of the world, had produced within himself two personal representations, or manners of existence, which were to be the medium of intercourse between him and mortals, and by whom, consequently, he was to reveal his will, and to display his mercy and beneficence to the children of men ; . . . . and that these two representations were to cease after the destruction of this terrestrial globe, and to be *absorbed into the substance of the Deity*, from whence they had been formed."—*Mosheim's Ecclesiastical History*, vol. iv. pp. 475, 476.—*Ed.*

[1] " He (Paul) remembered the words of his Divine Master—' Whosoever shall do the will of God, the same is my brother, and sister, and mother ;' and he was taught by them, that though Christianity does not burst asunder the ties of kindred, it requires of all its followers that they be guided by higher considerations in advancing its interests.   This may throw light on the bold expression which we find him elsewhere using, when he is speaking of the obligations which believers are under, ' not to live to themselves, but unto him which died for them, and rose again.' ' Henceforth know we no man after the flesh ; yea, though we have known Christ after the flesh, yet now henceforth know we him no more.' "— *M'Crie's Sermons*, p. 21.—*Ed.*

[2] " Comme il a souffert mort vne fois en icelle ;"—" As he has once suffered death in it."

[3] " Comme vne image et gage certain en la personne de Christ ;"—" As it were an image and sure pledge in the person of Christ."

[4] Calvin's meaning plainly is—" If we do not recognise the fact, that Christ is still a partaker of our nature."—*Ed.*

ought to have in him.   But we acknowledge Christ as man, and as our brother in his flesh—not in a fleshly manner; because we rest solely in the consideration of his spiritual gifts.   Hence he is spiritual to us, not as if he laid aside the body, and became a spirit, but because he regenerates and governs his own people by the influence of his Spirit.

17. *Therefore if any man is in Christ.*   As there is something wanting in this expression, it must be supplied in this way—"*If any one* is desirous to hold some place *in Christ,* that is, in the kingdom of Christ, or in the Church,[1] let him be a *new creature.*"   By this expression he condemns every kind of excellence that is wont to be in much esteem among men, if renovation of heart is wanting.   " Learning, it is true, and eloquence, and other endowments, are valuable, and worthy to be honoured ; but, where the fear of the Lord and an upright conscience are wanting, all the honour of them goes for nothing.   Let no one, therefore, glory in any distinction, inasmuch as the chief praise of Christians is self-renunciation."

Nor is this said merely for the purpose of repressing the vanity of the false apostles, but also with the view of correcting the ambitious judgments of the Corinthians, in which outward disguises were of more value than real sincerity— though this is a fault that is common to almost all ages. For where shall we find the man that does not attach much more importance to show, than to true holiness ?   Let us, therefore, keep in view this admonition—that all that are not renewed by the Spirit of God, should be looked upon as nothing in the Church, by whatever ornaments they may in other respects be distinguished.

Old things are passed away.   When the Prophets speak of the kingdom of Christ, they foretell that there will be *new heavens and a new earth,* (Isaiah lxv. 17,) meaning thereby, that all things will be changed for the better, until the happiness of the pious is completed.   As, however, Christ's kingdom is spiritual, this change must take place chiefly in the Spirit, and hence it is with propriety that he begins

[1] " Et estre tenu pour membre de ceste saincte compagnie ;"—" And to be regarded as a member of that holy society."

with this. There is, therefore, an elegant and appropriate allusion, when Paul makes use of a commendation of this kind, for the purpose of setting forth the value of regeneration. Now by *old things* he means, the things that are not formed anew by the Spirit of God. Hence this term is placed in contrast with renewing grace. The expression *passed away*, he uses in the sense of *fading away*, as things that are of short duration are wont to fall off, when they have passed their proper season. Hence it is only the *new man*, that flourishes and is vigorous[1] in the kingdom of Christ.

18. And all things *are* of God, who hath reconciled us to himself by Jesus Christ, and hath given to us the ministry of reconciliation ;	18. Porro omnia ex Deo, qui nos reconciliavit sibi Iesum Christum : et dedit nobis ministerium reconciliationis.
19. To wit, that God was in Christ, reconciling the world unto himself, not imputing their trespasses unto them ; and hath committed unto us the word of reconciliation.	19. Quoniam erat Deus in Christo mundum reconcilians sibi, non imputando illis sua ipsorum peccata : et deposuit in nobis sermonem reconciliationis.
20. Now then we are ambassadors for Christ, as though God did beseech *you* by us : we pray *you* in Christ's stead, be ye reconciled to God.	20. Itaque pro Christo legatione fungimur, tanquam Deo exhortante per nos : rogamus pro Christo, reconciliemini Deo.
21. For he hath made him *to be* sin for us, who knew no sin ; that we might be made the righteousness of God in him.	21. Eum qui peccatum non noverat, pro nobis peccatum fecit, ut nos efficeremur iustitia Dei in ipso.

18. *All things are of God.* He means, all things that belong to Christ's kingdom. " If we would be Christ's, we must be regenerated by God. Now that is no ordinary gift." He does not, therefore, speak here of creation generally, but of the grace of regeneration, which God confers peculiarly upon his elect, and he affirms that it is *of God*—not on the ground of his being the Creator and Artificer of heaven and earth, but inasmuch as he is the new Creator of the Church, by fashioning his people anew, according to his own image. Thus all flesh is abased, and believers are admonished that they must now live to God, inasmuch as they

---

[1] " C'est à dire, dont il falle faire cas ;"—" That is to say, that we must esteem."

are a *new creature.* (verse 17.) This they cannot do, unless
they forget the world, as they are also no longer *of the world,*
(John xvii. 16,) because they are *of God.*

Who hath reconciled us. Here there are *two* leading
points—the *one* relating to the reconciliation of men with
God; and the *other*, to the way in which we may enjoy the
benefit of this reconciliation. Now these things correspond
admirably with what goes before, for as the Apostle had
given the preference to a good conscience above every kind
of distinction, (verse 11,) he now shows that the whole of the
gospel tends to this. He shows, however, at the same time,
the dignity of the Apostolical office, that the Corinthians
may be instructed as to what they ought to seek in him,
whereas they could not distinguish between true and false
ministers, for this reason, that nothing but show delighted
them. Accordingly, by making mention of this, he stirs
them up to make greater proficiency in the doctrine of the
gospel. For an absurd admiration of profane persons, who
serve their own ambition rather than Christ, originates in
our not knowing, what the office of the preaching of the
gospel includes, or imports.

I now return to those *two leading points* that are here
touched upon. The first is—that God *hath reconciled us to
himself by Christ.* This is immediately followed by the declaration—*Because God was in Christ,* and has in his person
accomplished reconciliation. The manner is subjoined—*By
not imputing unto men their trespasses.* Again, there is
annexed a *second* declaration—*Because Christ having been
made a sin-offering for our sins, has procured righteousness
for us.* The *second* part of the statement is—that the grace
of reconciliation is applied to us by the gospel, that we may
become partakers of it. Here we have a remarkable passage,
if there be any such in any part of Paul's writings. Hence
it is proper, that we should carefully examine the words one
by one.

The ministry of reconciliation. Here we have an illustrious designation of the gospel, as being an embassy for
reconciling men to God. It is also a singular dignity of
ministers—that they are sent to us by God with this com-

mission, so as to be messengers, and in a manner sureties.[1]
This, however, is not said so much for the purpose of commending ministers, as with a view to the consolation of the
pious, that as often as they hear the gospel, they may know
that God treats with them, and, as it were, stipulates with
them as to a return to his grace. Than this blessing what
could be more desirable? Let us therefore bear in mind,
that this is the main design of the gospel—that whereas we
are *by nature children of wrath,* (Eph. ii. 3,) we may, by the
breaking up of the quarrel between God and us, be received
by him into favour. Ministers are furnished with this commission, that they may bring us intelligence of so great a
benefit, nay more, may assure us of God's fatherly love towards us. Any other person, it is true, might also be a
witness to us of the grace of God, but Paul teaches, that this
office is specially intrusted to ministers. When, therefore,
a duly ordained minister proclaims in the gospel, that God
has been made propitious to us, he is to be listened to just
as an ambassador of God, and sustaining, as they speak, a
public character, and furnished with rightful authority for
assuring us of this.

19. *God was in Christ.* Some take this as meaning simply
—*God reconciled the world to himself in Christ;* but the
meaning is fuller and more comprehensive—*first,* that God
was in Christ; and, *secondly,* that he reconciled the world
to himself by his intercession. It is also of the Father that
this is affirmed; for it were an improper expression, were
you to understand it as meaning, that the divine nature of
Christ was in him.[2] The Father, therefore, was in the Son,
in accordance with that statement—*I am in the Father, and
the Father in me.* (John x. 38.) Therefore he that hath the
Son, hath the Father also. For Paul has made use of this
expression with this view—that we may learn to be satisfied
with Christ alone, because in him we find also God the Father, as he truly communicates himself to us by him. Hence

---

[1] " Et comme pleges de sa bonne volonte enuers nous;"—" And as it
were pledges of his good will toward us."

[2] " Car ce seroit improprement, de dire que la nature Diuine de Christ
estoit en Christ;"—" For it were to speak improperly, to say that the
Divine nature of Christ was in Christ."

the expression is equivalent to this—" Whereas God had withdrawn to a distance from us, he has drawn near to us in Christ, and thus Christ has become to us the true Emmanuel, and his coming is God's drawing near to men."

The *second* part of the statement points out the office of Christ—his being *our propitiation*, (1 John ii. 2,) because *out of Him*, God is displeased with us all, inasmuch as we have revolted from righteousness.[1]   For what purpose, then, has God appeared to men in Christ ?   For the purpose of *reconciliation*—that, hostilities being removed, those who were aliens, might be adopted as sons.   Now, although Christ's coming as our Redeemer originated in the fountain of Divine love towards us, yet until men perceive that God has been propitiated by the Mediator, there must of necessity be a variance remaining, with respect to them, which shuts them out from access to God.   On this point we shall speak more fully ere long.

Not imputing to them.   Mark, in what way men return into favour with God—when they are regarded as righteous, by obtaining the remission of their sins.   For so long as God imputes to us our sins, He must of necessity regard us with abhorrence ; for he cannot be friendly or propitious to sinners.   But this statement may seem to be at variance with what is said elsewhere—that we were loved by Him before the creation of the world, (Eph. i. 4,) and still more with what he says, (John iii. 16,) that the love, which he exercised towards us was the reason, why He expiated our sins by Christ, for the cause always goes before its effect.   I answer, that we were loved before the creation of the world, but it was only *in Christ*.   In the mean time, however, I confess, that the love of God was first in point of time, and of order, too, as to God, but with respect to us, the commencement of his love has its foundation in the sacrifice of Christ.   For when we contemplate God without a Mediator, we cannot conceive of Him otherwise than as angry with us: a Mediator interposed between us, makes us feel, that He is pacified towards us.   As, however, this also is necessary to be known by us—that Christ came forth to us from the

---

[1] " De iustice et obeissance ;"—" From righteousness and obedience."

fountain of God's free mercy, the Scripture explicitly teaches both—that the anger of the Father has been appeased by the sacrifice of the Son, and that the Son has been offered up for the expiation of the sins of men on this ground—because God, exercising compassion towards them, receives them, on the ground of such a pledge, into favour.[1]

The whole may be summed up thus: " Where sin is, *there* the anger of God is, and therefore God is not propitious to us without, or before, his blotting out our sins, by not imputing them. As our consciences cannot apprehend this benefit,[2] otherwise than through the intervention of Christ's sacrifice, it is not without good reason, that Paul makes *that* the commencement and cause of reconciliation, with regard to us.

And hath committed to us. Again he repeats, that a commission has been given to the ministers of the gospel to communicate to us this grace. For it might be objected, " Where is Christ now, the peacemaker between God and us? At what a distance he resides from us!" He says, therefore, that as he has *once suffered*,[3] (1 Pet. iii. 18,) so he daily presents to us the fruit of his suffering through means of the Gospel, which he designed, should be in the world,[4] as a sure and authentic register of the reconciliation, that has once been effected. It is the part of ministers, therefore, to apply to us, so to speak, the fruit of Christ's death.

Lest, however, any one should dream of a magical application, such as Papists contrive,[5] we must carefully observe what he immediately subjoins—that it consists wholly in the preaching of the Gospel. For the Pope, along with his priests, makes use of this pretext for giving a colour of war-

---

[1] " C'est d' autant que Dieu ayant compassion d'eux, a voulu que ceste mort fust le gage et le moyen par lequel il les receuroit en grace ;"—" It is, because God, having compassion upon them, determined that this death should be the pledge and means, by which he would receive them into favour."

[2] " Et en estre participantes ;"—" And be partakers of it."

[3] " Comme il a souffert la mort vne fois ;"—" As he has suffered death once."

[4] " Lequel il a voulu estre gardé et publié au monde ;"—" Which he designed, should be maintained and published in the world."

[5] See CALVIN on John, vol. ii. p. 272.—*Ed.*

rant for the whole of that wicked and execrable system of merchandise, which they carry on, in connection with the salvation of souls. " The Lord," say they, " has furnished us with a commission and authority to forgive sins." This I acknowledge, provided they discharge that embassy, of which Paul here makes mention. The absolution, however, which they make use of in the Papacy, is entirely magical; and besides, they inclose pardon of sins in lead and parchment, or they connect it with fictitious and frivolous superstitions. What resemblance do all these things bear to the appointment of Christ? Hence the ministers of the Gospel restore us to the favour of God in a right and orderly manner, when they bear testimony to us by means of the Gospel as to the favour of God having been procured for us. Let this *testimony* be removed, and nothing remains but mere imposture. Beware, then, of placing even the smallest drop of your confidence on any thing apart from the Gospel.

I do not, indeed, deny, that the grace of Christ is applied to us in the sacraments, and that our reconciliation with God is then confirmed in our consciences; but, as the testimony of the Gospel is engraven upon the sacraments, they are not to be judged of separately by themselves, but must be taken in connection with the Gospel, of which they are appendages. In fine, the ministers of the Church are *ambassadors*, for testifying and proclaiming the benefit of *reconciliation*, only on this condition—that they speak from the Gospel, as from an authentic register.

20. *As if God did beseech you.* This is of no small importance for giving authority to the embassy: nay more, it is absolutely necessary, for who would rest upon the testimony of men, in reference to his eternal salvation? It is a matter of too much importance, to allow of our resting contented with the promise of men, without feeling assured that they are ordained by God, and that God speaks to us by them. This is the design of those commendations, with which Christ himself signalizes his Apostles: *He that heareth you, heareth me*, &c. (Luke x. 16.) *Whatsoever you shall loose on earth, shall be loosed in heaven*, (Matt. xviii. 18,) and the like.

We entreat you, in Christ's stead. Hence we infer, with

what propriety Isaiah exclaims, *How blessed are the feet of them that preach the Gospel!* (Isaiah lii. 7.) For that one thing, that is of itself sufficient for completing our felicity, and without which we are most miserable, is conferred upon us, only through means of the Gospel. If, however, this duty is enjoined upon all the ministers of the Church, in such a way, that he who does not discharge this embassy is not to be regarded either as an Apostle, or as a Pastor, we may very readily judge from this, as to the nature of the Pope's entire hierarchy. They are desirous, indeed, to be looked upon as Apostles and Pastors ; but as they are dumb idols, how will their boasting[1] correspond with this passage of Paul's writings. The word *entreat* is expressive of an unparalleled[2] commendation of the grace of Christ, inasmuch as He stoops so low, that he does not disdain to *entreat* us. So much the less excusable is our depravity, if we do not, on meeting with such kindness, show ourselves teachable and compliant.

Be reconciled. It is to be observed, that Paul is here addressing himself to believers. He declares, that he brings to them every day this embassy. Christ therefore, did not suffer, merely that he might once expiate our sins, nor was the gospel appointed merely with a view to the pardon of those sins which we committed previously to baptism, but that, as we daily sin, so we might, also, by a daily remission, be received by God into his favour. For this is a continued embassy,[3] which must be assiduously sounded forth in the Church, till the end of the world ; and the gospel cannot be preached, unless remission of sins is promised.

We have here an express and suitable declaration for refuting the impious tenet of Papists, which calls upon us to seek the remission of sins after Baptism from some other source, than from the expiation that was effected through the death of Christ. Now this doctrine is commonly held in all the schools of Popery—that, after baptism, we merit

---

[1] " Leur vanterie orgueilleuse ;"—" Their haughty boasting."

[2] " Vne singuliere et inestimable louange ;"—" A singular and inestimable commendation."

[3] " Vne ambassade et commission perpetuelle ;"—" A perpetual embassy and commission."

the remission of sins by penitence, through means of the aid of the *keys*,[1] (Matt. xvi. 19,)—as if baptism itself could confer this[2] upon us without penitence.   By the term *penitence*, however, they mean *satisfactions*.   But what does Paul say here ?   He calls us to go, not less *after* baptism, than *before* it, to the one expiation made by Christ, that we may know that we always obtain it gratuitously.   Farther, all their prating as to the administration of the *keys* is to no purpose, inasmuch as they conceive of *keys* apart from the Gospel, while they are nothing else than that testimony of a gratuitous reconciliation, which is made to us in the Gospel.

21. *Him who knew no sin.*   Do you observe, that, according to Paul, there is no return to favour with God, except what is founded on the sacrifice of Christ alone ?   Let us learn, therefore, to turn our views in that direction, whenever we desire to be absolved from guilt.   He now teaches more clearly, what we adverted to above—that God is propitious to us, when he acknowledges us as righteous.   For these two things are equivalent—that we are acceptable to God, and that we are regarded by him as righteous.

To *know no sin* is to be free from sin.   He says, then, that Christ, while he was entirely exempt from sin, was *made sin for us*.   It is commonly remarked, that *sin* here denotes an expiatory sacrifice for sin, and in the same way the Latins term it, *piaculum*.[3]   Paul, too, has in this, and other passages, borrowed this phrase from the Hebrews, among whom אשם (*asham*) denotes an *expiatory sacrifice*, as well as an *offence* or *crime*.[4]   But the signification of this word, as well as the entire statement, will be better understood from a comparison of both parts of the antithesis.   *Sin* is here contrasted with *righteousness*, when Paul teaches us, that *we were made the righteousness of God*, on the ground of *Christ's*

---

[1] The reader will find this tenet of Popery adverted to by CALVIN at considerable length in the *Institutes*, vol. iii. pp. 330, 331.—*Ed.*

[2] " La remission de nos pechez ;"—" The remission of our sins."

[3] The Latin term *piaculum* is sometimes employed to denote a *crime requiring expiation*, and at other times, an *expiatory victim*.—*Ed.*

[4] Thus in Lev. v. 6, אשם, (*asham*,) denotes a trespass-offering ; and in the verse immediately following, it means an offence or trespass.   See CALVIN's *Institutes*, vol. ii. pp. 54, 55.—*Ed.*

having been made sin. Righteousness, here, is not taken to denote a quality or habit, but by way of imputation, on the ground of Christ's righteousness being reckoned to have been received by us. What, on the other hand, is denoted by *sin?* It is the guilt, on account of which we are arraigned at the bar of God. As, however, the curse of the individual was of old cast upon the victim, so Christ's condemnation was our absolution, and *with his stripes we are healed.* (Isaiah liii. 5.)

The righteousness of God in him. In the first place, the *righteousness of God* is taken here to denote—not that which is given us by God, but that which is approved of by him, as in John xii. 43, the *glory of God* means—that which is in estimation with him: the *glory of men* denotes the vain applause of the world. Farther, in Romans iii. 23, when he says, that we have *come short of the glory of God*, he means, that there is nothing that we can glory in before God, for it is no very difficult matter to appear righteous before men, but it is a mere delusive appearance of righteousness, which becomes at last the ground of perdition. Hence, *that* is the only true righteousness, which is acceptable to God.

Let us now return to the contrast between *righteousness* and *sin*. How are we righteous in the sight of God? It is assuredly in the same respect in which Christ was a sinner. For he assumed in a manner our place, that he might be a criminal in our room, and might be dealt with as a sinner, not for his own offences, but for those of others, inasmuch as he was pure and exempt from every fault, and might endure the punishment that was due to us—not to himself. It is in the same manner, assuredly, that we are now *righteous in him*—not in respect of our rendering satisfaction to the justice of God by our own works, but because we are judged of in connection with Christ's righteousness, which we have put on by faith, that it might become ours. On this account I have preferred to retain the particle ἐν, (*in*,) rather than substitute in its place *per*, (*through*,) for that signification corresponds better with Paul's intention.[1]

[1] The force of the preposition ἐν, (*in*,) as made use of by the Apostle in this passage, is more fully brought out by *Beza* in the following terms:

CHAPTER VI.

1. We then, *as* workers together with him, beseech *you* also that ye receive not the grace of God in vain.

2. (For he saith, I have heard thee in a time accepted, and in the day of salvation have I succoured thee : behold, now *is* the accepted time ; behold, now *is* the day of salvation.)

3. Giving no offence in any thing, that the ministry be not blamed :

4. But in all *things* approving ourselves as the ministers of God, in much patience, in afflictions, in necessities, in distresses,

5. In stripes, in imprisonments, in tumults, in labours, in watchings, in fastings ;

6. By pureness, by knowledge, by longsuffering, by kindness, by the Holy Ghost, by love unfeigned,

7. By the word of truth, by the power of God, by the armour of righteousness on the right hand and on the left,

1. Nos vero adiuvantes (*vel, collaborantes*)[1] etiam obsecramus, ne frustra gratiam Dei receperitis.

2. Dicit enim (*Ies.* 49, 8) Tempore accepto exaudivi te, et in die salutis auxiliatus sum tibi : ecce, nunc tempus acceptum : ecce, nunc dies salutis.

3. Nullum dantes[2] ulla in re offensionem, ut ne vituperetur ministerium :

4. Sed in omnibus commendantes nos[3] tanquam Dei ministri, in patientia multa, in afflictionibus, in necessitatibus, in angustiis,

5. In plagis, in carceribus, in seditionibus, in laboribus, in vigiliis, in ieiuniis ;

6. In sinceritate, in scientia, in tolerantia, in mansuetudine, in Spiritu Sancto, in caritate non ficta,

7. In sermone veritatis, in potentia Dei, per arma iustitiæ dextra et sinistra :

" Justi apud Deum, et quidem justitia non nobis inhærente, sed quæ, quum in Christo sit, nobis per fidem a Deo imputatur.   Ideo enim additum est : ἐν αὐτῷ.   Sic ergo sumus justitia Dei in ipso, ut ille est peccatum in nobis, nempe ex imputatione.   Libet autem hic ex Augustino locum insignem exscribere, velut istius commentarium plenissimum.   Sic igitur ille Serm. 5. de verbis Apostoli : *Deus Pater eum, qui non noverat peccatum* (nempe Iesum Christum) *peccatum effecit, ut nos simus justitia Dei* (non nostra) *in ipso* (non in nobis.)   His adde Phil. iii. 9 ;"— " Righteous before God, and that by a righteousness which is not inherent in us, but which, being in Christ, is imputed to us by God through faith. For it is on this account that it is added : ἐν αὐτῷ (*in him.*)   We are, therefore, the righteousness of God *in him* in the same way as he is sin in us—by imputation.   I may here quote a remarkable passage from Augustine, as a most complete commentary upon it.   In Serm. 5 on the words of the Apostle he expresses himself thus : *God the Father made him sin who had not known sin,* (Jesus Christ,) *that we might be the righteousness of God* (not our own) *in him* (not in ourselves.)   To these add Phil. iii. 9."—*Ed.*

[1] " Ainsi donc en ouurant auec luy, *ou*, estans ses ouuriers ;"—" Thus then in working with him, *or*, being his workmen."

[2] " Ne donnans aucun scandale, *ou*, donnons ;"—" Giving no offence, *or*, we give."

[3] " Mais nous rendans louables en toutes choses, *ou*, Mais rendons nous louables ;"—" But rendering ourselves approvable in all things, *or*, We render ourselves approvable."

8. By honour and dishonour, by evil report and good report : as deceivers, and *yet* true ;	8. Per gloriam et ignominiam, per infamiam, et bonam famam: tanquam impostores, tamen veraces :
9. As unknown, and *yet* well known ; as dying, and, behold, we live ; as chastened, and not killed ;	9. Tanquam ignoti, tamen celebres : tanquam morientes, et ecce, vivimus : tanquam castigati, tamen morte non affecti :
10. As sorrowful, yet alway rejoicing ; as poor, yet making many rich ; as having nothing, and *yet* possessing all things.	10. Tanquam mœrore affecti, semper tamen gaudentes : tanquam inopes, multos tamen ditantes : tanquam nihil habentes, et omnia possidentes.

1. *Assisting.* He has repeated the instructions of embassy with which the ministers of the gospel have been furnished by God. After they have faithfully communicated these instructions, they must also use their endeavour, that they may be carried into effect,[1] in order that their labour may not be in vain. They must, I say, add continual exhortations,[2] that their embassy may be efficacious. This is what he means by συνεργοῦντες, (*fellow-workers,*) that is, devoted to the advancement of the work ; for it is not enough to *teach,* if you do not also *urge.* In this way, the particle σύν would have a relation to God, or to the embassy, which he assigns to his servants. For the doctrine of the gospel is helped by exhortations, so as not to be without effect, and ministers connect their endeavours with God's commission ;[3] as it is the part of an ambassador to enforce by arguments, what he brings forward in the name of his prince.

The particle σύν may also be taken as referring to the endeavours of ministers in common ; for if they do the Lord's work in good earnest, they must mutually lend a helping hand to each other, so as to give assistance to each other. I rather prefer, however, the former exposition. Chrysostom interprets it as referring to the hearers, with whom ministers are *fellow-workers,* when they rouse them up from slothfulness and indolence.

---

[1] " Qu'ils ayent lieu, et proufitent ;"—" That they may have place, and may be profitable."

[2] " Les exhortations par chacun iour ;"—" Exhortations daily."

[3] " Les ministres auec leur mandement qu'ils ont en charge, de declarer de par Dieu, conioignent aussi leur diligence, et affection ardente ;"— " Ministers, along with their commission which they have in charge to declare, as from God, conjoin also their diligence, and ardent desire."

Ministers are here taught, that it is not enough simply to advance doctrine. They must also labour that it may be received by the hearers, and that not once merely, but continually. For as they are messengers between God and men, the *first* duty devolving upon them is, to make offer of *the grace of God*,[1] and the *second* is, to strive with all their might, that it may not be offered in vain.

2. *For he saith, In an acceptable time.* He quotes a prediction of Isaiah, exceedingly appropriate to the exhortation of which he speaks. It is without doubt of the kingdom of Christ that he there speaks,[2] as is manifest from the context. The Father, then, appointing his Son a leader, for the purpose of gathering together a Church, addresses him in these words: " *I have heard thee in an acceptable time.*" (Isaiah xlix. 8.) We know, however, what a degree of cor-

---

[1] " *The grace of God*," says Dr. Brown, when commenting on 1 Peter v. 12, " properly signifies—the kindness, the free favour of God, as a principle in the Divine mind; but is often employed to signify the deeds of kindness, the gifts and benefits, in which the principle finds expression. It has been common to interpret the phrase here as equivalent to the gospel, the revelation of God's grace; and the Apostle has been considered as affirming that the doctrine which those he was writing to had embraced, and to which they had adhered—to use the Apostle Paul's phrase, 'which they had received, and in which they stood,' was the true gospel. But I doubt if the gospel is ever called *the grace of God* in the New Testament; and I equally doubt whether the words, thus understood, are an accurate statement of what this Epistle actually contains. There are just two other passages in the New Testament in which *the grace of God* has been supposed to be a designation of the gospel. After stating the message of mercy, which the ministers of reconciliation are called to deliver, the Apostle, in his Second Epistle to the Corinthians, says—' We beseech you that ye receive not *the grace*, or *this grace of God* in vain,' (2 Cor. vi. 1.) The reference here is, no doubt, to the gospel, but the meaning of the phrase, *the grace of God*, is plainly just this divine favour, this benefit which so expresses, and, as it were, embodies, the divine grace. And in the Epistle to Titus, the same Apostle states, that ' the grace of God bringing salvation' has been manifested, or has ' appeared, teaching' those who apprehend it, ' to deny ungodliness, and worldly lusts, and to live soberly, righteously, and godly in the present world.' (Titus ii. 11, 12.) The grace of God is often said to mean here the gospel, but the gospel is the manifestation, the revelation of this grace; and the truth, taught in the passage is, that the free, sovereign mercy of God, when it is apprehended by the sinner, is the true principle of holiness in the heart and life."—*Brown's* Expository Discourses on First Peter, vol. iii. pp. 295, 296.—*Ed.*

[2] " Il ne faut point douter, que le Prophete ne parle du regne de Christ;"—" There is no room to doubt, that the Prophet speaks of the kingdom of Christ."

respondence[1] there is between the Head and the members.
For Christ was heard in our name, as the salvation of all of
us is entrusted into his hand, and nothing else has he taken
under his charge. Hence we are all admonished in the person
of Christ—not to slight the opportunity that is afforded for
obtaining salvation. While the rendering of the Greek interpreter is, εὐπρόσδεκτον, (acceptable,)[2] the word made use
of by the Prophet is, רצון, (ratson,) that is, benevolence, or
free favour.[3]

The quotation must be applied to the subject in hand in
this way: "As God specifies a particular time for the exhibition of his grace, it follows that all times are not suitable
for that. As a particular *day of salvation* is named, it follows that a free offer of salvation is not made every day."
Now this altogether depends on the providence of God, for
the *acceptable time* is no other than what is called in Gal.
iv. 4, *the fulness of the time.*[4] The order of arrangement also
must be observed. First, he makes mention of a *time of benevolence*, and then afterwards of a *day of salvation*. By
this it is intimated, that salvation flows to us from the
mercy of God exclusively, as from a fountainhead. Hence
we must not seek the cause in ourselves, as if we by means

---

[1] "Quelle similitude et proportion ou conuenance ;"—"What a resemblance, and proportion, or correspondence."

[2] The precise word in the Septuagint version (with which the Apostle's
quotation exactly corresponds) is δεκτῷ, (acceptable.) CALVIN had probably been led to make use of the word εὐπρόσδεκτον from the circumstance,
that that adjective is employed by the Apostle in the latter part of the
verse, when commenting upon the passage quoted.—*Ed.*

[3] The Hebrew term referred to is employed in this sense in the following (among other) instances: Ps. v. 13 ; xxx. 7 ; Prov. xvi. 15 ; xix. 12.—
Ed.

[4] CALVIN makes a similar observation when commenting on the expression here referred to, in Gal. iv. 4. "Pergit in similitudine adducta, et
suo instituto definitum a Patre tempus accommodat : simul tamen ostendit,
tempus illud, quod Dei providentia ordinatum erat, maturum fuisse et op-
portunum. Ea igitur demum iusta est opportunitas ac recta agendi dispensatio, quæ providentia Dei regitur ;"—"He proceeds with the comparison which he had brought forward, and applies to his purpose the
expression which had been made use of—the *time appointed by the Father*,
but still showing that that time, which had been ordained by the providence of God, was proper and suitable. *That* alone is the fit season, and
that the right system of acting, which is directed by the providence of God."
—*Ed.*

of our own works moved God to assign to us his favour, for whence comes the *day of salvation ?* It is because it is the *acceptable time,* that is, the time which God has in his free favour appointed.   In the mean time, we must keep in view what Paul designs to teach—that there is need of prompt expedition, that we may not allow the opportunity to pass unimproved, inasmuch as it displeases God, that the grace that he offers to us should be received by us with coolness and indifference.

Behold now is the time.   The Prophet had spoken of the time, when Christ was to be manifested in the flesh for the redemption of men.   Paul transfers the prophecy to the time when Christ is revealed by the continued preaching of the gospel, and it is with good reason that he does so, for as *salvation* was once sent to the whole world, when Christ appeared, so now it is sent to us every day, when we are made partakers of the gospel.   Here we have a beautiful passage, and affording no ordinary consolation, because, while the gospel is preached to us, we know assuredly that the way is opened up for us into the kingdom of God, and that there is a signal of divine benevolence raised aloft, to invite us to receive *salvation,* for the opportunity of obtaining it must be judged of by the call.   Unless, however, we embrace the opportunity, we must fear the threatening that Paul brings forward—that, in a short time, the door will be shut against all that have not entered in, while opportunity was afforded. For this retribution always follows contempt of the word.

3. *Giving no offence.*   We have already on several occasions remarked,[1] that Paul sometimes commends the ministry of the gospel generally, and at other times his own integrity.[2] In the present instance, then, he speaks of himself, and sets before us in his own person a living picture of a good and faithful apostle, that the Corinthians may be led to see how unfair they were in their judgment, in preferring before him empty blusterers.[3]   For as they assigned the praise to mere

---

[1] See pp. 189, 226.

[2] " Tantost met en auant la rondeur de sa conscience en la predication d'iceluy ;"—" Sometimes he brings into view the uprightness of his conscience in the preaching of it."

[3] " Thrasones."   See CALVIN on the Corinthians, vol. i. p. 98, *n.* 1.

pretences,[1] they held in the highest esteem persons that were effeminate and devoid of zeal, while, on the other hand, as to the best ministers, they cherished no views but such as were mean and abject. Nor is there any reason to doubt, that those very things that Paul makes mention of to his own commendation, had been brought forward by them in part as a ground of contempt; and they were so much the more deserving of reproof, inasmuch as they converted into matter of reproach, what was ground of just praise.

Paul, therefore, treats here of *three* things: In the *first* place, he shows what are the excellences, on the ground of which preachers of the gospel ought to be esteemed; *secondly,* he shows that he is himself endowed with those excellences; *thirdly,* he admonishes the Corinthians not to acknowledge as Christ's servants those who conduct themselves otherwise than he prescribes here by his example. His design is, that he may procure authority for himself and those that were like him, with a view to the glory of God and the good of the Church, or may restore it where it has fallen into decay; and *secondly,* that he may call back the Corinthians from an unreasonable attachment to the false apostles, which was a hinderance in the way of their making so much proficiency in the gospel as was necessary. Ministers give occasion of stumbling, when by their own misconduct they hinder the progress of the gospel on the part of their hearers. *That* Paul says he does not do; for he declares that he carefully takes heed not to stain his apostleship by any spot of disgrace.

For this is the artifice of Satan—to seek some misconduct on the part of ministers, that may tend to the dishonour of the gospel. For when he has been successful in bringing the ministry into contempt, all hope of profit is at an end. Hence the man who would usefully serve Christ, must strive with his whole might to maintain the credit of his ministry. The method is—to take care that he be deserving of honour,

---

[1] " Ne faisans cas que de masques, c'est à dire, de l'apparence externelle;"—" Setting no value on anything but masks; that is to say, outward appearance."

for nothing is more ridiculous than striving to maintain your reputation before others, while you call forth upon yourself reproach by a wicked and base life. That man, therefore, will alone be honourable, who will allow himself in nothing that is unworthy of a minister of Christ.

4. *In much patience.* The whole of the enumeration that follows is intended to show, that all the tests by which the Lord is accustomed to try his servants were to be found in Paul, and that there was no kind of test to which he had not been subjected, in order that the faithfulness of his ministry might be more fully established.[1] Among other things that he enumerates, there are some that are under all circumstances required for all the servants of Christ. Of this nature are *labours, sincerity, knowledge, watchings, gentleness, love, the word of truth, the Spirit, the power of God, the armour of righteousness.* There are other things that are not necessary in all cases; for in order that any one may be a servant of Christ, it is not absolutely necessary, that he be put to the test by means of *stripes* and *imprisonments.* Hence these things will in some cases be wanting in the experience of the best. It becomes all, however, to be of such a disposition as to present themselves to be tried, as Paul was, with *stripes* and *imprisonments,* if the Lord shall see meet.

Patience is the regulation of the mind in adversity, which is an excellence that ought invariably to distinguish a good minister.[2] *Afflictions* include more than *necessities ;* for by the term *necessity* here I understand *poverty.* Now this is common to many ministers, there being few of them that are not in poor circumstances ; but at the same time not to all. For why should a moderate amount of riches prevent a

---

[1] " Afin que sa fidelite fust tant plus notoire, et la certitude de son ministere tant mieux approuvee ;"—" In order that his faithfulness might be so much the better known, and the stability of his ministry so much the better approved."

[2] " The words ἐν ὑπομονῇ πολλῇ, (*in much patience,*) must be connected with the following clauses up to ἐν νηστείαις, (*in watchings,*) and denote patient endurance of the various afflictions specified in the words following, which are not to be treated (with Rosenm.) as merely *synonymes* denoting evils *in general,* but considered *specially,* and (as I conceive the Apostle meant) in *groups.*"—*Bloomfield.—Ed.*

man from being reckoned a servant of Christ, who, in other respects, is pious, is of upright mind and honourable deportment, and is distinguished by other excellences. As the man that is poor is not on that account to be straightway accounted a good minister, so the man that is rich is not on that account to be rejected. Nay more, Paul in another passage glories not less in his *knowing how to abound,* than in *knowing how to be in want.* (Phil. iv. 12.)   Hence we must observe the distinction that I have mentioned, between *occasional* and *invariable* grounds of commendation.[1]

5. *In tumults.*   In proportion to the calmness and gentleness of Paul's disposition was there the greater excellence displayed in his standing undaunted in the face of *tumults ;* and he takes praise to himself on this account—that while he regarded tumults with abhorrence, he nevertheless encountered them with bravery.[2]   Nor does the praise simply consist in his being unmoved by *tumults,* (this being commonly found among all riotous persons,[3]) but in his being thrown into no alarm by tumults that had been stirred up through the fault of others.   And, unquestionably, two things are required on the part of ministers of the Gospel—that they should endeavour to the utmost of their power to maintain peace, and yet on the other hand go forward, undaunted, through the midst of commotions, so as not to turn aside from the right course, though heaven and earth should be mingled.[4]   Chrysostom, however, prefers to understand ἀκα-ταστασίαις to mean—frequent expulsions,[5] inasmuch as there

---

[1] " Entre les louanges temporelles et perpetuelles, c'est à dire qui doyuent tousiours estre es vrais ministres ;"—" Between occasional grounds of commendation and perpetual, that is to say, what ought to be found invariably in true ministers."

[2] " D'vne courage magnanime ;"—" With magnanimous heroism."

[3] " Veu que cela est coustumier à tous mutins de ne s'estonner point quand seditions s'esmeuuent ;"—" As it is customary for all riotous persons to be thrown into no alarm when tumults break out."

[4] A proverbial expression made use of by Virgil.   Æn. I. 133, 134.—*Ed.*

[5] "L' incommodite de ce qu'il estoit souuent contraint de changer de pays, pource qu' on ne le laissoit en paix en quelque lieu qu' il fust ;"—" The inconvenience of being frequently under the necessity of changing his country, because they did not allow him to be in peace in any place in which he might be."

was nowhere afforded him a place of rest.[1] *In fastings.* He does not mean—hunger arising from destitution, but a voluntary exercise of abstinence.

Knowledge may be taken in two senses—either as meaning doctrine itself, or skill in acting properly and *knowingly.* The latter appears to me the more likely, as he immediately adds—*the word of truth.* The *Spirit* is taken by *metonymy,* to denote spiritual graces. Frivolous, however, is the cavil of Chrysostom, who infers from this, that the other excellences are peculiar to the Apostle, because he makes mention of the *Spirit* separately, as if *kindness, knowledge, pureness, armour of righteousness,* were from any other source, than from the Holy Spirit. He makes mention, however, of the Spirit separately, as a general term in the midst of particular instances.[2] The *power of God* showed itself in many things—in magnanimity, in efficacy in the maintaining of the truth, in the propagation of the Gospel, in victory over enemies, and the like.

7. *By the armour of righteousness.* By *righteousness* you must understand—rectitude of conscience, and holiness of

---

[1] *Semler* understands the term in the same sense—" Quod non licet diu manere et quiescere quasi uno in loco, sed semper periculorum vitandorum causa locum et solum mutare. Iudæi autem faciunt jam infensi et infesti hostes Pauli, ut vel ex actibus Lucæ satis patet; Paulus ἀκατάστατος, (Jacobi i. 8) dici potest, licet sine animi sui vitio;"—(" As not being allowed to remain long at rest, as it were, in one place, but always changing his place and soil.* The Jews were enemies to Paul, so exasperated and deadly, as appears even from Luke's narrative in the Acts, that Paul may be said to have been *unstable,* (James i. 8,) though without any fault on his part."—" I agree," says *Dr. Bloomfield,* " with Theophyl., Schleus., and Leun., that the term refers to that *unsettled and wandering kind of life,* which, that the Apostle thought very miserable, is plain from his connecting it at 1 Cor. iv. 11, with the endurance of hunger, thirst, and nakedness, (Πεινῶμεν, καὶ διψῶμεν, καὶ γυμνητεύομεν, καὶ ἀστατοῦμεν,) which passage, indeed, is the best comment on the present, and shows that κόποις (*labours*) must be chiefly understood of his labours at his trade, and νηστείαις, (*fastings,*) of that insufficient support, which labours so interrupted by his ministerial duties, could alone be expected to supply. Ἀγρυπνίαις (*watchings*) seems to refer to the abridgment of his rest by night, to make up for the time expended by day on his ministerial labours."—*Ed.*

[2] " Ἐν πνεύματι ἁγίω—' In demonstration of the *Holy Spirit*—so that I showed that the Holy Spirit wrought by me.' It is possible, that in these words, Paul makes an allusion to the χαρίσματα, (*gifts,*) but it seems better, nevertheless, to suppose with CALVIN, that he sets *genus* and *species* over against each other."—*Billroth.*—*Ed.*

---

* for the sake of avoiding dangers.

life. He employs the metaphor of *armour,* because all that
serve God require to fight, inasmuch as the devil is always
on the alert, to molest them. Now they must be completely
armed, because, if he does not succeed in one onset, he thereupon makes a new attempt, and attacks them at one time
from before, at another from behind—now on this side, and
then on that.[1]

8. *By honour and dishonour.* This is no slight test for
subjecting a man to trial, for to a man of a noble spirit
nothing is more unpleasant, than to incur disgrace. Hence
we may observe in all histories, that there have been few
men of heroism that have not fallen back, on being irritated
by insults.[2] Hence it is indicative of a mind well established
in virtue, not to be moved away from one's course by any
disgrace that may be incurred—a rare virtue, but one without which you cannot show, that you are a servant of God.
We must, it is true, have a regard to good character, but it
must be only in so far as the edification of our brethren requires it, and in such a way as not to be dependent on reports[3]—nay more, so as to maintain the same even course
in *honour* and in *dishonour.* For God allows us to be tried
even by the slander of wicked men, with the view of trying
us,[4] whether we act uprightly from disinterested motives;[5]
for if one is drawn aside from duty by the ingratitude of
men, that man shows that he had not his eye directed to

[1] " Here the spiritual arms are not *particularized;* yet the terms τῶν
δεξιῶν καὶ ἀριστερῶν, (*on the right hand and the left,*) are very *comprehensive,*
referring to the complete armour and arms, on both sides, with which the
ὁπλίτης, or *completely armed* soldier was furnished, who was thus said to
be ἀμφιδέξιος (*ambidexter.*) Thus the general sense is: ' We employ no
other arms than the *panoply of righteousness.*'"—*Bloomfield.—Ed.*

[2] " Il y en a eu bien peu, qui estans irritez des iniures et mauuais traitte-
mens que on leur faisoit, ne se soyent descouragez, et n'ayent laissez leur
train de vertu;"—" There have been very few of them, who have not, on
being irritated by injuries and bad treatment shown them, felt discouraged,
and left off their virtuous career."

[3] " Du bruit qu'on fera courir de nous;"—" On reports that may be
circulated against us."

[4] " Voulant essayer si nous cheminons droit seulement pour l'amour de
luy, sans cercher autre recompense;"—" Wishing to try whether we walk
aright, purely from love to Him, without seeking any other reward."

[5] " *Gratuito;*"—" *gratuitously.*"—There can be no doubt, that CALVIN
has here in his eye Job i. 9. " Doth Job fear God *for nought?*" The

God alone.   As then we see that Paul was exposed to infamy and insults, and yet did not on that account stop short, but held forward with undaunted courage, and broke through every impediment so as to reach the goal,[1] let us not give way, if the same thing should befall us.

As deceivers.   Here he relates, not simply in what estimation he was held by the wicked and those that were *without*, (1 Cor. v. 12,) but also what views were entertained of him by those that were *within.*   Now let every one consider with himself, how unseemly was the ingratitude of the Corinthians, and how great was his magnanimity in struggling forward, in spite of such formidable obstacles.   By indirect representations, however, he sharply reproves their perverse judgment, when he says that he *lives* and is *joyful,* while they despised him as one that was dead and overwhelmed with grief.   He reproaches them, also, with ingratitude, when he says, that he *made many rich,* while he was contemned on account of his poverty.   For they were of the number of those whom he enriched by his wealth: nay more, all of them to a man were under obligations to him on many accounts.   Thus he said previously, by way of irony, that he was *unknown,* while at the same time the fruit of his labour was everywhere known and celebrated. But how cruel to despise the poverty of the man who supplies you[2] from his abundance !   He means *spiritual* riches, which ought to be much more esteemed than *earthly.*

11. O *ye* Corinthians, our mouth is open unto you, our heart is enlarged.

12. Ye are not straitened in us, but ye are straitened in your own bowels.

13. Now, for a recompence in the

11. Os nostrum apertum est ad vos, O Corinthii, cor nostrum dilatatum est.

12. Non estis angusti in nobis, sed angusti estis in visceribus vestris.[3]

13. Eandem vero remuneratio-

Hebrew word הַחִנָּם, (*hachinnam,*) is rendered in the Septuagint δωρεὰν— *gratuitously.*

[1] " Mesme faisant violence à tous empeschemens, est venu, comme par force, jusques au bout ;"—" Even breaking violently through all impediments, came, as it were, by force to the goal."

[2] " Qui te fournit et enrichit par son abundance ;"—" Who furnishes and enriches thee by his abundance."

[3] " En vos entrailles, *ou,* affections ;"—" In your bowels, *or,* affections."

same, (I speak as unto *my* children,) be ye also enlarged.[1]

14. Be ye not unequally yoked together with unbelievers: for what fellowship hath righteousness with unrighteousness? and what communion hath light with darkness?

15. And what concord hath Christ with Belial? or what part hath he that believeth with an infidel?

16. And what agreement hath the temple of God with idols? for ye are the temple of the living God; as God hath said, I will dwell in them, and walk in *them;* and I will be their God, and they shall be my people.

17. Wherefore, come out from among them, and be ye separate, saith the Lord, and touch not the unclean *thing;* and I will receive you,

18. And will be a Father unto you, and ye shall be my sons and daughters, saith the Lord Almighty.

nem, ut a filiis, exigo: dilatamini et vos.

14. Ne ducatis iugum cum infidelibus: quæ enim participatio iustitiæ cum iniquitate: quæ communicatio luci cum tenebris?

15. Quis consensus Christo cum Belial: aut quæ portio fideli cum infideli?

16. Quæ autem conventio templo Dei cum idolis? vos enim estis templum Dei viventis: quemadmodum dicit Deus (*Lev.* xxvi. 12,) Habitabo in ipsis, et in medio eorum ambulabo: et ero Deus illorum, et erunt mihi populus.

17. Quamobrem exite de medio eorum et separamini, dicit Dominus (*Ies.* lii. 11,) et immundum ne tetigeritis:

18. Et ego suscipiam vos, et ero vobis in patrem, et eritis mihi in filios et filias, dicit Dominus omnipotens, (*Jer.* xxxi. 9.)

CHAPTER VII.

1. Having therefore these promises, dearly beloved, let us cleanse ourselves from all filthiness of the flesh and spirit, perfecting holiness in the fear of God.

CAPUT VII.

1. Has igitur promissiones quum habeamus, dilecti, mundemus nos ab omni inquinamento carnis et spiritus, sanctificationem perficientes in timore Dei.

11. *Our mouth is opened.* As the *opening of the mouth* is a sign of boldness,[2] if you are inclined to connect this with what goes before, the meaning will be this,—"I have ample ground of glorying, and an upright conscience *opens my mouth.* Your entertaining unfavourable views of us, is not owing to any fault on our part, but arises from your being

---

[1] " Or ie requier de vous la pareille, comme de mes enfans, *ou,* Or pour nous recompenser de mesmes (ie parle comme à mes enfans;)"—" But I require the like from you—as from my children, *or,* But for a recompense to us of the same, I speak as to my children."

[2] God promised to Ezekiel that he would give him " the *opening of the mouth* in the midst of the house of Israel," (Ezek. xxix. 21,) which is explained by *Gill* to mean, " *boldness* and *courage* of speech when he should see his prophecies fulfilled." Paul himself makes use of a similar expression in Eph. vi. 19, " that utterance may be given unto me, that I may *open my mouth boldly.*"—*Ed.*

unfair judges. For you ought to have entertained more favourable views of my ministry, which God has rendered honourable to you in so many ways." I explain it, however, otherwise ; for he says that the reason why his *mouth was opened* was, that his *heart was enlarged.* Now what is meant by *enlargement of heart ?* Undoubtedly it means the cheerfulness that springs from benevolence.[1] It is quite a common figure, to speak of a *narrow and contracted heart* as denoting either *grief,* or *disgust,* while, on the other hand, an *enlarged heart* is employed to denote dispositions of an opposite kind. Hence Paul here says nothing but what we every day experience, for when we have to do with friends, our *heart is enlarged,* all our feelings are laid open, there is nothing there that is hid, nothing shut,—nay more, the whole mind leaps and exults to unfold itself openly to view.[2] Hence it is, that the tongue, also, is free and unfettered, does not faulter, does not with difficulty draw up from the bottom of the throat broken syllables, as usually happens when the mind is influenced by a less joyful affection.

12. *Ye are not straitened in us.* That is, " It is owing to your own fault that you are not able to share in this feeling

---

[1] The same view, in substance, is taken by *Chrysostom*—Καθάπερ γὰρ τὸ θερμαῖνον εὐρύνειν εἴωθεν, οὔτω καὶ τῆς ἀγάπης ἔργον τὸ πλατύνειν ἐστί· θερμὴ γάρ ἐστιν ἡ ἀρετὴ καὶ ζέουσα αὕτη· καὶ τὸ στόμα ἀνεπέτασε Παύλου καὶ τὴν καρδίαν ἐπλάτυνεν—" For as heat is wont to expand, so it is the part of love to *enlarge.* For virtue is warm and fervent. It was this that *opened* Paul's *mouth,* and *enlarged* his *heart.*"—*Ed.*

[2] " From a tender and considerate regard to the good of the Christians at Corinth, he" (Paul) " had determined not to revisit them, until their unseemly heats and factions were allayed. How was he affected while he waited at Ephesus to receive the tidings of this longed-for but protracted issue? ' O ye Corinthians ! our mouth is opened unto you ; our heart is enlarged !' What a picture of a heart ! We see him standing on the shore of the Ægean Sea, over against Corinth, with his arms extended towards that city, and in the attitude of speaking. We hear the words by which he seeks to relieve his overcharged breast, heaving and ready to burst with the fulness of those desires which he had long felt to come among them, satisfy them of the sincerity of his affection, and replenish their souls with the consolation with which he himself had been comforted. ' O ye Corinthians, our mouth is open to you, our heart is enlarged ! Ye are not straitened in us, but ye are straitened in your own bowels. Now, for a recompense in the same, (I speak as unto my children,) be ye also enlarged.' "—*M'Crie's Sermons,* p. 29.—*Ed.*

of cheerfulness, which I entertain towards you. My *mouth is opened,* so that I deal familiarly with you, my very heart would willingly pour itself forth,[1] but you shut up your bowels." He means to say, that it is owing to their corrupt judgment, that the things that he utters are not relished by them.

13. *Now the same requital.* He softens his reproof by addressing them kindly as his sons, and also by this exhortation, by which he intimates that he still entertains good hopes of them. By the *same requital* he means—mutual duty, for there is a mutual return of duty between a father and his sons. For as it is the duty of parents to nourish their children, to instruct them, to direct them by their counsel, and to defend them, so it is the dictate of equity, that children should *requite their parents.* (1 Tim. v. 4.) In fine, he means what the Greeks call ἀντιπελαργίαν—*affection exercised in return.*[2] " I cherish," says he, " towards you paternal affection : show yourselves then to be my sons by affection and respect in return." At the same time there is a particular circumstance that must be noticed. That the Corinthians, having found so indulgent a father, may also show gentleness in their turn, and may requite his kind condescension by their docility, he exhorts them with this view

---

[1] " Mon cœur mesme s'ouuriroit volontiers pour vous mettre deuant les yeux l'affection que i' ay enuers vous ;"—" My very heart would willingly open itself up, so as to place before your eyes the affection which I entertain towards you."

[2] The term ἀντιπελαργία is compounded of αντι, over against, and πέλαργος, a stork. It is employed to denote *reciprocal affection,* from an interesting peculiarity in the disposition of the *stork.* " This bird," says *Paxton,* in his Illustrations of Scripture, (Edin. 1842,) vol. ii. p. 432, " has long been celebrated for her amiable and pious dispositions, in which she has no rival among the feathered race. . . . Her kind benevolent temper she discovers in feeding her parents in the time of incubation, when they have not leisure to seek their food, or when they have become old, and unable to provide for themselves." The English word *stork* is derived from στοργὴ, affection, while the Hebrew name for this animal, חסידה, (*chasidah,*) is derived from חסד, (*chesed,*) *beneficence,* because, says *Bythner,* " the stork nourishes, supports, and carries on its back, when weary, its aged parents." See CALVIN on the Psalms, vol. iv. p. 158, *n.* 2. CALVIN, when commenting on 1 Tim. v. 4, says, " Ipsæ quoque ciconiæ gratitudinem suo exemplo nos docent. Unde et nomen ἀντιπελαργία ;" —" The very storks, too, teach us gratitude by their example. Hence the term ἀντιπελαργία—*affection in return.*"—*Ed.*

to be *enlarged in their own bowels.* The Old Interpreter, not having caught Paul's meaning, has added the participle *having*, and has thus expressed his own view rather than Paul's. In our exposition, on the other hand, (which is Chrysostom's, also,) there is nothing forced.[1]

14. *Be not yoked.* As if regaining his authority, he now reproves them more freely, because they associated with unbelievers, as partakers with them in outward idolatry. For he has exhorted them to show themselves docile to him as to a father : he now, in accordance with the rights that belong to him,[2] reproves the fault into which they had fallen. Now we mentioned in the former epistle[3] what this fault was; for, as they imagined that there was nothing that was unlawful for them in outward things, they defiled themselves with wicked superstitions without any reserve. For in frequenting the banquets of unbelievers, they participated along with them in profane and impure rites, and while they sinned grievously, they nevertheless thought themselves innocent. On this account Paul inveighs here against outward idolatry, and exhorts Christians to stand aloof from it, and have no connection with it. He begins, however, with a general statement, with the view of coming down from that to a particular instance, for to be *yoked with unbelievers* means nothing less than to *have fellowship with the unfruitful works of darkness,* (Eph. v. 11,) and to hold out the hand to them[4] in token of agreement.

Many are of opinion that he speaks of marriage, but the context clearly shows that they are mistaken. The word that Paul makes use of means—to be connected together in drawing the same yoke. It is a metaphor taken from oxen or horses, which require to walk at the same pace, and to act together in the same work, when fastened under one

---

[1] The rendering of the Vulgate—" Eandem remunerationem *habentes ;*" —" *Having* the same reward,"—is followed by Wiclif, (1380,) *ye that haw the same reward,* and also in the Rheims version, (1582,) *hauing the same reward.—Ed.*

[2] " Parlant comme en puissance et aùthorite de pere ;"—" Speaking as with the power and authority of a father."

[3] See vol. i. p. 282.

[4] " Aux infideles ;"—" To unbelievers."

yoke.[1] When, therefore, he prohibits us from having part-nership with unbelievers in drawing the same yoke, he means simply this, that we should have no fellowship with them in their pollutions. For *one* sun shines upon us, we eat of the same bread, we breathe the same air, and we can-not altogether refrain from intercourse with them; but Paul speaks of the yoke of impiety, that is, of participation in works, in which Christians cannot lawfully have fellowship. On this principle marriage will also be prohibited, inasmuch as it is a snare, by which both men and women are entangled into an agreement with impiety; but what I mean is simply this, that Paul's doctrine is of too general a nature to be restricted to marriage exclusively, for he is discoursing here as to the shunning of idolatry, on which account, also, we are prohibited from contracting marriages with the wicked.

For what fellowship. He confirms his exhortation on the ground of its being an absurd, and, as it were, monstrous connecting together of things in themselves much at vari-ance; for these things can no more coalesce than fire and water. In short it comes to this, that unless they would have everything thrown into confusion, they must refrain from the pollutions of the wicked. Hence, too, we infer, that even those that do not in their hearts approve of super-stitions are, nevertheless, polluted by dissimulation if they do not openly and ingenuously stand aloof from them.

15. *What concord has Christ with Belial?* As to the etymology of the word *Belial,* even the Hebrews themselves are not agreed.[2] The meaning, however, is not doubt-

---

[1] " *Joachim Camerarius,* in his Commentary on the New Testament, (Cambridge 1642,) suggests, that ἑτεροζυγοῦντες, may have a reference to a *balance,* and that Paul—would not have the Corinthians *unequally balanced* with unbelievers. The verb ζυγοστατεῖν, as he observes, is employed to denote the *adjusting of scales in a balance.* It seems more natural, how-ever, to understand the word, as CALVIN and most other interpreters do, as derived from ἕτερος, (another,) and ζυγὸς, as meaning a *yoke,* and as employed by Paul to mean, drawing on the other side of a yoke with another; or, as *Beza* explains it, " Qui cum sint diversæ conditionis, tamen in eodem opere mutuam operam præstant;"—" Those who, while in a different condition from each other, do nevertheless take their corre-sponding part in the same work."—*Ed.*

[2] *Beza,* when mentioning the different views which have been taken of the etymology of the term *Belial,* remarks, that some derive it from

ful.[1] For Moses takes a word or thought of *Belial*[2] to mean
a wicked and base thought,[3] and in various instances[4] those
who are wicked and abandoned to iniquity, are called *men*,
or *sons of Belial.* (Deut. xiii. 13; Judges xix. 22; 1 Sam.
ii. 12.)   Hence it is, that Paul has employed the word here
to mean the devil, the head of all wicked persons.   For from
what holds good as to the two heads, he comes down without delay to the members: " As there is an irreconcilable
variance between Christ and Satan, so we also must keep
aloof from partnership with the wicked." When, however,
Paul says that a Christian has no participation with an unbeliever, he does not mean as to food, clothing, estates, the
sun, the air, as I have mentioned above,[5] but as to those
things that are peculiar to unbelievers, from which the Lord
has separated us.

16. *What agreement hath the temple of God with idols ?*
Hitherto he has in general terms prohibited believers from
associating with the wicked.   He now lets them know what
was the chief reason, why he had prohibited them from such

בלי יעל, *beli jahal, (not profitable,)* or from בלי מועיל, *beli mohil, (worthless,)*
and that the term, viewed as having this derivation, is peculiarly appropriate to Satan, as being diametrically opposed to Christ, the Greatest and
Best ; while Jerome derives it from בלי, *beli, (not,)* and עול, *hol, (a yoke,)*
as though you should say—*without a yoke, not subject to the yoke.*   Beza
gives the preference to the *former* etymology, while he observes that the
latter is also most appropriate to Satan as an *apostate* spirit.—The original
term *Belial* is rendered in various instances in the Septuagint παράνομος,
lawless.—" There is here a slight variation in reading.   The Edit. Princ.
and the Textus Receptus have Βελίαλ.   The Erasmian, Stephanic, and
other early editions have Βελίαρ, which has been restored by Bengelius,
Matthias, Griesbach, and Tittmann ; and justly, for both external and
internal evidence are in its favour ; it being found in the majority of the
MSS., in many early ecclesiastical writers, and Greek Fathers."—*Bloomfield.—Ed.*

[1] " Et assez notoire ;"—" And is sufficiently well known."

[2] Thus in Deut. xv. 9, " Beware that there be not a *thought in thy wicked heart.*"   The expression made use of is פן־יהיה דבר עם־לבבך בליעל,
" Lest there be in thine heart a *thing of Belial.*"   The same expression occurs in Psalm xli. 9, where David's enemies represent him as suffering the punishment of *detestable wickedness,* דבר בליעל, " *a thing of
Belial.*"—See CALVIN *on the Psalms,* vol. ii. p. 120.—*Ed.*

[3] " Vne meschante et abominable parolle ou pensee ;"—" A wicked and
abominable word or thought."

[4] " Souvent en l'Escriture ;"—" Frequently in Scripture."

[5] See p. 258.

an association—because they had ceased to reckon the profession of idolatry to be a sin. He had censured that liberty, and had exposed it at great length in the former Epistle. It is probable, however, that all had not yet been gained over, so as to receive the counsel which he had given. Hence it was that he complained of their being *straitened in their own bowels*—the only thing that hindered their proficiency.[1] He does not, however, resume that subject anew, but contents himself with a short admonition, as we are accustomed to do, when we treat of things that are well known. At the same time his brevity does not prevent his giving sharp cuts. For how much emphasis there is in that single word, where he teaches that there is no agreement between the *temple of God* and *idols !* " It is a sacrilegious profanation,[2] when an *idol* or any *idolatrous* service is introduced into the *temple of God.* Now we are the true *temples of God.* Hence it is sacrilege to defile ourselves with any contamination of idols. This one consideration, I say, should be to you as good as a thousand. If you are a Christian, *what have you to do with idols,* (Hosea xiv. 8,) for you are the *temple of God ?*" Paul, however, as I have already in part noticed, contends rather by way of exhortation than of doctrine, inasmuch as it would have been superfluous to be still treating of it, as if it were a thing doubtful or obscure.

As God saith, I will walk. He proves that we are the *temples of God* from this, that God of old promised to the people of Israel that he would dwell in the midst of them. In the first place, God cannot dwell *among* us, without dwelling *in* each one of us, for he promises this as a singular privilege—*I will dwell in the midst of you.* Nor does this *dwelling* or presence consist merely in earthly blessings, but must be understood chiefly of spiritual grace. Hence it does not mean simply that God is near us, as though he were in the air, flying round about us, but it means rather that he has his abode in our hearts. If, then, any one objects, that

[1] " Ce qui seul empeschoit que son enseignement ne proufitast enuers eux ;"—" What alone hindered his teaching from being of advantage to them."

[2] " C'est vn profanation horrible, et vn sacrilege detestable ;"—" It is a horrible profanation, and a detestable sacrilege."

the particle *in* simply means *among*, I grant it ; but I affirm
that, from the circumstance that God promises that he will
dwell *among* us, we may infer that he also remains *in* us.[1]
And such was the type of the ark, of which mention is made
by Moses in that passage, from which Paul appears to have
borrowed this quotation.   (Lev. xxvi. 12.)   If, however, any
one thinks that Paul had rather in his eye Ezek. xxxvii. 27,
the argument will be the same.   For the Prophet, when describing the restoration of the Church, mentions as the chief
good, the presence of God, which he had himself in the beginning promised by Moses.   Now what was prefigured by
the ark, was manifested to us more fully in Christ, when he
became to us Immanuel.[2]   (Matt. i. 23.)   On this account,
I am of opinion that it is Ezekiel, rather than Moses, that
is here quoted, because Ezekiel alludes at the same time
to the type of the ark, and declares that it will have its
fulfilment under the reign of Christ.   Now the Apostle
takes it for granted, that God dwells nowhere but in a sacred
place.   If we say of a man, " he dwells here," that will not
make the place a *temple;* but as to God there is this peculiarity, that whatever place he honours with his presence,
he at the same time sanctifies.

17. *Wherefore come out from the midst of them.*   This
exhortation is taken from Isaiah lii. 11, where the Prophet,
when foretelling the deliverance, at length addresses the
priests in these terms.   For he makes use of a circumlocution to describe the priests, when he says, *Ye that bear the
vessels of the Lord,* inasmuch as they had the charge of the
vessels, by means of which the sacrifices, and other parts of
divine worship, were performed.   There can be no doubt that
his design is to admonish them, that, while eagerly desirous
to come forth,[3] they should be on their guard against any con-

---

[1] " *I will dwell in them.*   The words are very significant in the original,
ἐνοικήσω ἐν αὐτοῖς, ' *I will indwell in them,*' so the words are.   There are
two *ins* in the original, as if God could have never enough communion
with them."—*Leigh's Annotations.*—*Ed.*

[2] " C'est à-dire Dieu auec nous ;"—" That is to say, God with us."

[3] " Cependant qu'ils sont attendans auec ardent desir le iour de deli-
uerance ;"—" While they are waiting with eager desire for the day of deliverance."

tamination from the many pollutions with which the country[1] was overrun. Now this is no less applicable to us, than to the ancient Levites, for if so much purity is required on the part of the *keepers of the vessels*, how much more in the *vessels* themselves![2] Now all our members are *vessels*, set apart for the spiritual worship of God; we are also a *royal priesthood.* (1 Peter ii. 9.) Hence, as we are redeemed by the grace of God, it is befitting that we keep ourselves undefiled in respect of all uncleanness, that we may not pollute the sanctuary of God. As, however, while remaining in this world, we are nevertheless redeemed, and rescued, from the pollutions of the world, so we are not to quit life with the view of departing from all uncleanness, but must simply avoid all participation. The sum is this: "If with a true affection of the heart, we aim at the benefit of redemption, we must beware of defiling ourselves by any contamination from its pollutions."

18. *I will be a Father unto you.* This promise does not occur in one passage merely, but is repeated in various instances. Paul has added it with this view, that a recognition of the great honour to which God has exalted us, might be a motive to stir us up to a more ardent desire for holiness. For when God has restored his Church which he has gathered from profane nations, their redemption is attended with this fruit, that believers are seen to be his *sons and daughters.* It is no common honour that we are reckoned among the sons of God: it belongs to us in our turn to take care, that we do not show ourselves to be degenerate children to him. For what injury we do to God, if while we call him father, we defile ourselves with abominations of idols! Hence, the thought of the high distinction to which he has elevated us, ought to whet our desire for holiness and purity.

---

[1] " Où ils estoyent ;"—" Where they were."

[2] *Diodati*, in his Annotations, explains the expression *ye that bear the vessels of the Lord*, (Isaiah lii. 11,) to mean—" You sacred officers, to whom only it belongeth to carry the vessels and ornaments of the temple; and thereby are spiritually meant all believers, whereof every one beareth a vessel sacred to the Lord, viz., himself."—*Ed.*

CHAPTER VII.

1. *These promises, therefore.* God, it is true, anticipates us in his promises by his pure favour; but when he has, of his own accord, conferred upon us his favour, he immediately afterwards requires from us gratitude in return. Thus what he said to Abraham, *I am thy God,* (Gen. xvii. 7,) was an offer of his undeserved goodness, yet he at the same time added what he required from him—*Walk before me, and be thou perfect.* As, however, this second clause is not always expressed, Paul instructs us that in all the promises this condition is implied,[1] that they must be incitements to us to promote the glory of God. For from what does he deduce an argument to stimulate us? It is from this, that God confers upon us such a distinguished honour. Such, then, is the nature of the promises, that they call us to sanctification, as if God had interposed by an implied agreement. We know, too, what the Scripture teaches in various passages in reference to the design of redemption, and the same thing must be viewed as applying to every token of his favour.

From all filthiness of flesh and spirit. Having already shown, that we are called to purity,[2] he now adds, that it ought to be seen in the body, as well as in the soul ; for that the term *flesh* is taken here to mean the *body,* and the term *spirit* to mean the *soul,* is manifest from this, that if the term *spirit* meant the grace of regeneration, Paul's statement in reference to the pollution of the spirit would be absurd. He would have us, therefore, pure from defilements, not merely *inward,* such as have God alone as their witness ; but also *outward,* such as fall under the observation of men. " Let us not merely have chaste consciences in the sight of God. We must also consecrate to him our whole body and all its members, that no impurity may be seen in any part of us."[3]

---

[1] " Ceste condition est tacitement attachee a toutes les promesses ;"— " This condition is tacitly appended to all the promises."

[2] " Appelez à purete et sainctete ;"—" Called to purity and holiness."

[3] " Afin qu'il n'apparoisse en nul endroit de nous ancune macule ou

Now if we consider what is the point that he handles, we shall readily perceive, that those act with excessive impudence,[1] who excuse outward idolatry on I know not what pretexts.[2] For as inward impiety, and superstition, of whatever kind, is a defilement of the spirit, what will they understand by defilement of the flesh, but an outward profession of impiety, whether it be pretended, or uttered from the heart? They boast of a pure conscience; that, indeed, is on false grounds, but granting them what they falsely boast of, they have only the half of what Paul requires from believers. Hence they have no ground to think, that they have given satisfaction to God by that half; for let a person show any appearance of idolatry at all, or any indication of it, or take part in wicked or superstitious rites, even though he were— what he cannot be—perfectly upright in his own mind, he would, nevertheless, not be exempt from the guilt of polluting his body.

Perfecting holiness. As the verb ἐπιτελεῖν in Greek sometimes means, to perfect, and sometimes to perform sacred rites,[3] it is elegantly made use of here by Paul in the former signification, which is the more frequent one—in such a way, however, as to allude to sanctification, of which he is now treating. For while it denotes perfection, it seems to have been intentionally transferred to sacred offices, because there ought to be nothing defective in the service of God, but everything complete. Hence, in order that you may sanctify yourself to God aright, you must dedicate both body and soul entirely to him.

In the fear of God. For if the *fear of God* influences us, we will not be so much disposed to indulge ourselves, nor

souillure;"—" That there may not appear in any part of us any spot or filth."

[1] " Combien sont impudens et deshontez;"—" How impudent they are and unabashed."

[2] CALVIN manifestly refers here, as in a variety of other instances, to the temporizing conduct of the *Nicodemites.* See CALVIN on the Corinthians, vol. i. pp. 286, 384.—*Ed.*

[3] It is employed by Herodotus in the sense of *perfecting* or *completing,* (see Herod. I. 51,) while in various instances it is made use of by him to mean—discharging a religious service—in connection with θρησκείας, (ceremonies,) εὐχωλὰς, (vows,) and θυσίας, (sacrifices.) See Herod. II. 37, 63, iv. 26.—*Ed.*

will there be a bursting forth of that audacity of wantonness, which showed itself among the Corinthians. For how does it happen, that many delight themselves so much in outward idolatry, and haughtily defend so gross a vice, unless it be, that they think that they mock God with impunity ? If the fear of God had dominion over them, they would immediately, on the first moment, leave off all cavils, without requiring to be constrained to it by any disputations.

2. Receive us : we have wronged no man, we have corrupted no man, we have defrauded no man.

3. I speak not *this* to condemn *you :* for I have said before, that ye are in our hearts to die and live with *you.*

4. Great *is* my boldness of speech toward you, great *is* my glorying of you : I am filled with comfort, I am exceeding joyful in all our tribulation.

5. For, when we were come into Macedonia, our flesh had no rest, but we were troubled on every side ; without *were* fightings, within *were* fears.

6. Nevertheless God, that comforteth those that are cast down, comforted us by the coming of Titus;

7. And not by his coming only, but by the consolation wherewith he was comforted in you, when he told us your earnest desire, your mourning, your fervent mind toward me ; so that I rejoiced the more.

2. Capaces estote nostri : nemini fecimus iniuriam, neminem corrupimus, neminem fraudavimus.

3. Non [hoc] ad condemnationem vestri dico : siquidem iam ante dixi vobis, quod in cordibus nostris sitis ad commoriendum et convivendum.

4. Multa mihi fiducia erga vos, multa mihi gloriatio de vobis : impletus sum consolatione supra modum, exundo gaudio in omni tribulatione nostra.

5. Etenim quum venissemus in Macedoniam, nullam relaxationem habuit caro nostra, sed in omnibus fuimus afflicti : foris pugnæ, intus timores.

6. Sed qui consolatur humiles, consolatus est nos Deus in adventu Titi.

7. Neque solum in adventu eius, sed in consolatione quam acceperat de vobis, annuntians nobis vestrum desiderium, vestras lacrimas, vestrum studium pro me : ita ut magis gauderem.

2. *Make room for us.* Again he returns from a statement of doctrine to treat of what more especially concerns himself, but simply with this intention—that he may not lose his pains in admonishing the Corinthians. Nay more, he closes the preceding admonition with the same statement, which he had made use of by way of preface. For what is meant by the expression—*Receive us,* or *Make room for us ?* It is equivalent to, *Be ye enlarged,* (2 Cor. vi. 13 ;) that is, " Do not allow corrupt affections, or unfavourable apprehensions, to prevent this doctrine from making its way into

your minds, and obtaining a place within you. For as I lay myself out for your salvation with a fatherly zeal, it were unseemly that you should turn a deaf ear[1] upon me."[2]

We have done injury to no man. He declares that there is no reason why they should have their minds alienated,[3] inasmuch as he had not given them occasion of offence in any thing. Now he mentions *three* kinds of offences, as to which he declares himself to be guiltless. The *first* is, manifest hurt or injury. The *second* is, the corruption that springs from false doctrine. The *third* is, defrauding or cheating in worldly goods. These are *three* things by which, for the most part, pastors[4] are wont to alienate the minds of the people from them—when they conduct themselves in an overbearing manner, and, making their authority their pretext, break forth into tyrannical cruelty or unreasonableness,—or when they draw aside from the right path those to whom they ought to have been guides, and infect them with the corruption of false doctrine,—or when they manifest an insatiable covetousness, by eagerly desiring what belongs to another. Should any one wish to have it in shorter compass—the *first* is, fierceness and an abuse of power by excessive insolence:[5] the *second*, unfaithfulness in teaching: the *third*, avarice.

3. *I say not this to condemn you.* As the foregoing apology was a sort of expostulation, and we can scarcely avoid reproaching when we expostulate, he softens on this account what he had said. "I clear myself," says he, "in such a way as to be desirous to avoid, what would tend to your dishonour." The Corinthians, it is true, were unkind, and they

---

[1] " Indignum esset me surdis fabulam canere ;"—" It were unseemly that I should be like one that tells a story to the deaf." A similar expression is made use of by Horace, (Ep. 2, 1, 200,)—" Scriptores autem narrare putaret asello fabellam surdo ;"—" But he would think that the writers were telling a story to a deaf ass."—*Ed.*

[2] " Que ie perdisse mon temps en vous admonestant ;"—" That I should lose my time in admonishing you."

[3] " De luy ou de sa doctrine ;"—" From him or from his doctrine."

[4] " Les ministres et pasteurs ;"—" Ministers and pastors."

[5] " Quand on est arrogant, et on abuse de la puissance en se desbordant et vsurpant plus qu'il ne faut ;"—" When one is presumptuous, and abuses his power by going beyond bounds and assuming more than he ought."

deserved that, on Paul's being acquitted from blame, *they* should be substituted in his place as the guilty party; nay more, that they should be held guilty in two respects—in respect of ingratitude, and on the ground of their having calumniated the innocent. Such, however, is the Apostle's moderation, that he refrains from recrimination, contenting himself with standing simply on the defensive.

For I have before said. Those that love do not assail;[1] nay more, if any fault has been committed, they either cover it over by taking no notice of it, or soften it by kindness. For a disposition to reproach is a sign of hatred. Hence Paul, with the view of showing that he has no inclination to distress the Corinthians, declares his affection towards them. At the same time, he undoubtedly in a manner *condemns* them, while he says that he does not do so. As, however, there is a great difference between gall and vinegar, so there is also between that condemnation, by which we harass a man in a spirit of hatred, with the view of blasting him with infamy, and, on the other hand, that, by which we endeavour to bring back an offender into the right way, that, along with safety, he may in addition to this regain his honours unimpaired.

Ye are in our hearts—that is, " I carry you about with me inclosed in my heart." *To die and live with you*—that is, " So that no change can loosen our attachment, for I am prepared not merely to *live with you*, but also to be associated with you in death, if necessary, and to endure anything rather than renounce your friendship." Mark well, in what manner all pastors[2] ought to be affected.

4. *Great is my boldness.* Now, as if he had obtained the enlargement of heart that he had desired on the part of the Corinthians, he leaves off complaining, and pours out his heart with cheerfulness. " What need is there that I should expend so much labour upon a matter already accomplished? For I think I have already what I asked. For the things

---

[1] " Ceux qui aiment vn autre, ne prenent point plaisir a le poursuyure et picquer;"—" Those who love another take no pleasure in pursuing and stinging him."

[2] " Pasteurs et ministres;"—" Pastors and ministers."

that Titus has reported to me respecting you are not merely sufficient for quieting my mind, but afford me also ground of glorying confidently on your account.[1] Nay more, they have effectually dispelled the grief, which many great and heavy afflictions had occasioned me." He goes on step by step, by way of climax ; for *glorying* is more than being of an easy and quiet mind ; and *being freed from grief occasioned by many afflictions*, is greater than either of those. Chrysostom explains this *boldness* somewhat differently, in this manner—" If I deal with you the more freely, it is on this account, that, relying on the assurance of your good will towards me, I think I may take so much liberty with you." I have stated, however, what appeared to me to be the more probable meaning—that the report given by Titus had removed the unfavourable impression, which had previously racked his mind.[2]

5. *For when we had come into Macedonia.* The heaviness of his grief tends to show, how efficacious the consolation was. " I was pressed on every side," says he, " by afflictions both internal and external. All this, however, has not prevented the joy that you have afforded me from prevailing over it,

---

[1] " Timothy is despatched " (by Paul) " to Corinth, and after him Titus is sent. In the mean time, ' a door is opened of the Lord ' to the Apostles to preach Christ's gospel at Troas; but, strange to relate ! he who panted so earnestly for such opportunities, had neither heart nor tongue to improve the present. The expected messenger from Corinth had not arrived —he had ' no rest in his spirit,' and abandoning the rich harvest which invited his labours, he wandered into Macedonia. Nor yet did he find ease : ' For when we were come into Macedonia, our flesh had no rest, but we were troubled on every side—without were fightings ; within were fears.' At last Titus arrives with tidings from Corinth. The Apostle's letter had been well received ; it had produced the intended effects ; a spirit of repentance had fallen upon the Church ; they had applied themselves vigorously to the correction of abuses ; the love which they bore to their spiritual father had revived with additional strength. ' Now ! thanks be unto God, who always causeth us to triumph in Christ, and maketh manifest the savour of his knowledge by us in every place !' ' Great is my boldness of speech towards you, great is my glorying of you; I am filled with comfort, I am exceeding joyful in all our tribulation.' (2 Cor. ii. 14 ; vii. 4.) What a sudden change ! what a wonderful transformation ! Formerly we saw him like a soldier, wounded, weak, disabled, dispirited, fallen to the ground ; now he is lifted up, victorious, and borne on the triumphant car."—*M'Crie's Sermons*, p. 39.—*Ed.*

[2] " La mauuaise opinion ou le souspeçon qu'il auoit d'eux, et dont il estoit tourmenté en son cœur ;"—" The bad opinion or suspicion that he had of them, and with which he had been tormented in his heart."

and even overflowing."[1]   When he says that he *had no rest
in his flesh*, it is as if he had said—" As a man, I had no
relief."[2]   For he excepts spiritual consolations, by which he
was in the mean time sustained.   He was afflicted, therefore,
not merely in body, but also in mind, so that, as a man, he
experienced nothing but great bitterness of afflictions.

Without were fightings.   By *fightings* he means outward
assaults, with which his enemies molested him : by *fears* he
means the anxieties, that he endured on account of the internal maladies of the Church, for it was not so much by
personal as by public evils, that he was disquieted.   What
he means, then, to say is this—that there were not merely
avowed enemies that were hostile to him, but that he endured, nevertheless, much distress in consequence of domestic evils.   For he saw how great was the infirmity of many,
nay of almost all, and in the mean time what, and how diversified, were the machinations, by which Satan attempted to
throw every thing into confusion—how few were wise, how
few were sincere, how few were steadfast, and how many, on
the other hand, were either mere pretenders, and worthless,
or ambitious, or turbulent.   Amidst these difficulties, the servants of God must of necessity feel alarmed, and be racked
with anxieties ; and so much the more on this account—that
they are constrained to bear many things silently, that they
may consult the peace of the Churches.   Hence he expressed
himself with propriety when he said—*Without were fightings ; within were fears.*   For faithful pastors openly set
themselves in opposition to those enemies that avowedly
attack Christ's kingdom, but they are inwardly tormented,
and endure secret tortures, when they see the Church afflicted

---

[1] CALVIN here has manifestly in his eye the singularly emphatic word
made use of by Paul in the preceding verse—ὑπερπερισσεύομαι, *I am exceeding joyful.*   " The word here used occurs nowhere else in the New Testament except in Rom. v. 20.   It is not found in the classic writers, and is
a word which Paul evidently compounded, (from ὑπὲρ and περισσεύω,) and
means to *superabound over*, to superabound greatly, or exceedingly.   It is
a word which would be used only when the heart was full, and when it
would be difficult to find words to express its conceptions.   Paul's heart
was full of joy, and he pours forth his feelings in the most fervid and glow-
ing language—' I have joy which cannot be expressed.' "—*Barnes.—Ed.*

[2] " Je n'ay point eu de relasche ou soulagement ;"—" I had no relief or
alleviation."

with internal evils, for the exterminating of which they dare not openly sound the trumpet.[1] But although he had almost incessant conflicts, it is probable that he was at that time more severely pressed than usual. The servants of Christ, undoubtedly, have scarcely at any time exemption from *fears*, and Paul was seldom free from outward *fightings ;* but as he was at that time more violently oppressed, he makes use of the plural number—*fightings* and *fears*, meaning that he required to fight in many ways, and against various enemies, and that he had at the same time many kinds of fear.

6. *Who comforteth the lowly.* This is mentioned as a reason ; for he means that consolation had been offered to him, because he was borne down with evils, and almost overwhelmed, inasmuch as God is wont to *comfort the lowly*, that is, those that are cast down. Hence a most profitable doctrine may be inferred—that the more we have been afflicted, so much the greater consolation has been prepared for us by God. Hence, in the epithet here applied to God, there is a choice promise contained, as though he had said, that it is peculiarly the part of God to comfort those that are miserable and are abased to the dust.

7. *And not by his coming only.* Lest the Corinthians should object in these terms—" What is it to us if Titus has cheered you by his coming? No doubt, as you loved him, you would feel delighted to see him ;" he declares, that the occasion of his joy was, that Titus had, on returning from them, communicated the most joyful intelligence. Accordingly he declares, that it was not so much the presence of one individual, as the prosperous condition of the Corinthians, that had cheered him.

Your desire. Mark, what joyful tidings were communicated to Paul respecting the Corinthians. Their *desire* originated in the circumstance, that they held Paul's doctrine in high estimation. Their *tears* were a token of respect ; because, being affected with his reproof, they mourned over

---

[1] " Pour les quelles chasser et y remedier, ils n'osent pas sonner la trompette tout haut, comme on dit :"—" For putting down which evils, and remedying them, they dare not sound the trumpet aloud, as they say."

their sins. Their *zeal* was an evidence of good will. From these *three* things he inferred that they were penitent. This afforded him full satisfaction, because he had no other intention or anxiety, than the consulting of their welfare.

So that I rejoiced the more—that is, " So that all my griefs and distresses gave way to joy." Hence we see, not merely with what fervour of mind he desired the public good of the Church, but also how mild and gentle a disposition he possessed, as being one that could suddenly bury in oblivion offences of so serious a nature. At the same time, this may rather be taken in another way, so as to be viewed in connection with what follows, and I am not sure but that this meaning would correspond better with Paul's intention. As, however, it is a matter of no great moment, I pass over it slightly.

8. For though I made you sorry with a letter, I do not repent, though I did repent: for I perceive that the same epistle hath made you sorry, though *it were* but for a season.

9. Now I rejoice, not that ye were made sorry, but that ye sorrowed to repentance: for ye were made sorry after a godly manner, that ye might receive damage by us in nothing.

10. For godly sorrow worketh repentance to salvation not to be repented of: but the sorrow of the world worketh death.

11. For, behold, this selfsame thing, that ye sorrowed after a godly sort, what carefulness it wrought in you, yea, *what* clearing of yourselves, yea, *what* indignation, yea, *what* fear, yea, *what* vehement desire, yea, *what* zeal, yea, *what* revenge!

8. Quoniam etsi contristavi vos in epistola, non me pœnitet: etiamsi pœnituerit. Video enim, quod epistola illa, etsi ad tempus, vos contristavit.

9. Nunc gaudeo: non quod sitis contristati, sed quod sitis contristati in pœnitentiam, contristati enim estis secundum Deum, ita ut nulla in re damno affecti sitis ex nobis.

10. Nam quæ secundum Deum est tristitia, pœnitentiam ad salutem non pœnitendam efficit: mundi autem tristitia mortem efficit.

11. Ecce enim hoc ipsum, quod secundum Deum, contristati estis quantum produxit in vobis studium! imo defensionem, imo indignationem, imo timorem, imo desiderium, imo zelum, imo vindictam!

8. *For though I grieved you.* He now begins to apologize to the Corinthians for having handled them somewhat roughly in the former Epistle. Now we must observe, in what a variety of ways he deals with them, so that it might appear as though he sustained different characters. The reason is—that his discourse was directed to the whole of the Church. There were some there, that entertained an unfavourable view of him—there were others that held him, as he de-

served, in the highest esteem—some were doubtful: others were confident—some were docile: others were obstinate.[1] In consequence of this diversity, he required to direct his discourse now in one way, then in another, in order to suit himself to all. Now he lessens, or rather he takes away altogether any occasion of offence, on account of the severity that he had employed, on the ground of its having turned out to the promotion of their welfare. " Your welfare," says he, " is so much an object of desire to me, that I am delighted to see that I have done you good." This softening-down is admissible only when the teacher[2] has done good so far as was needed, by means of his reproofs; for if he had found, that the minds of the Corinthians still remained obstinate, and had he perceived an advantage arising from the discipline that he had attempted, he would, undoubtedly, have abated nothing from his former severity. It is to be observed, however, that he rejoices to have been an occasion of grief to those whom he loved ; for he was more desirous to profit, than to please them.

But what does he mean when he adds—*though I did repent ?* For if we admit, that Paul had felt dissatisfied with what he had written, there would follow an inconsistency of no slight character—that the former Epistle had been written under a rash impulse, rather than under the guidance of the Spirit. I answer, that the word *repent* is used here in a loose sense for being *grieved.* For while he made the Corinthians sad, he himself also participated in the grief, and in a manner inflicted grief at the same time upon himself. " Though I gave you pain against my inclination, and it grieved me to be under the necessity of being harsh to you, I am grieved no longer on that account, when I see that it has been of advantage to you." Let us take an instance from the case of a father ; for a father feels grief in connection with his severity, when at any time he chastises his son, but approves of it, notwithstanding, because he sees that it is conducive to his son's advantage. In like manner Paul could feel no pleasure in irritating the minds of the

---

[1] " Obstinez et endurcis ;"—" Obstinate and obdurate."
[2] " Le Docteur et Ministre ;"—" The Teacher and Minister."

Corinthians; but, being conscious of the motive that influenced his conduct, he preferred duty to inclination.

For I see. The transition is abrupt; but that does not at all impair the distinctness of the sense. In the *first* place, he says, that he had fully ascertained by the effect, that the former Epistle, though for a time unwelcome, had nevertheless at length been of advantage, and *secondly,* that he rejoiced on account of that *advantage.*

9. *Not because you have been made sorry.* He means, that he feels no pleasure whatever in their sorrow—nay more, had he his choice, he would endeavour to promote equally their welfare and their joy, by the same means; but that as he could not do otherwise, their welfare was of so much importance in his view, that he rejoiced that they had been made *sorry unto repentance.* For there are instances of physicians, who are, indeed, in other respects good and faithful, but are at the same time harsh, and do not spare their patients. Paul declares, that he is not of such a disposition as to employ harsh cures, when not constrained by necessity. As, however, it had turned out well, that he had made trial of that kind of cure, he congratulates himself on his success. He makes use of a similar form of expression in chap. v. 4, *We in this tabernacle groan, being burdened, because we are desirous not to be unclothed, but clothed upon.*

10. *Sorrow according to God.*[1] In the *first* place, in order to understand what is meant by this clause—*according to God,* we must observe the contrast, for the *sorrow that is according to God* he contrasts with the *sorrow of the world.* Let us now take, also, the contrast between two kinds of joy. The *joy of the world* is, when men foolishly, and without the fear of the Lord, exult in vanity, that is, in the world, and, intoxicated with a transient felicity, look no higher than the earth. The *joy that is according to God* is, when men place all their happiness in God, and take satisfaction in His grace, and show this by contempt of the world, using earthly prosperity

---

[1] " Tristitia secundum Deum;"—" La tristesse qui est selon Dieu;"—" The sorrow which is according to God." " Κατὰ Θεὸν, *in such a way as God requires—with reference to his will and glory, i.e.,* as Rosenm. explains, ' arising from causes out of which he would have it arise, and producing effects such as he would approve.' "—*Bloomfield.—Ed.*

as if they used it not, and joyful in the midst of adversity. Accordingly, the *sorrow of the world* is, when men despond in consequence of earthly afflictions, and are overwhelmed with grief; while *sorrow according to God* is that which has an eye to God, while they reckon it the *one* misery—to have lost the favour of God; when, impressed with fear of His judgment, they mourn over their sins. This sorrow Paul makes the cause and origin of repentance. This is carefully to be observed, for unless the sinner be dissatisfied with himself, detest his manner of life, and be thoroughly grieved from an apprehension of sin, he will never betake himself to the Lord.[1] On the other hand, it is impossible for a man to experience a sorrow of this kind, without its giving birth to a new heart. Hence repentance takes its rise in grief, for the reason that I have mentioned—because no one can return to the right way, but the man who hates sin; but where hatred of sin is, *there* is self-dissatisfaction and grief.

There is, however, a beautiful allusion here to the term *repentance*, when he says—*not to be repented of;* for however unpleasant the thing is at first taste, it renders itself desirable by its usefulness. The epithet, it is true, might apply to the term *salvation*, equally as to that of *repentance;* but it appears to me to suit better with the term *repentance.* "We are taught by the result itself, that grief ought not to be painful to us, or distressing. In like manner, although repentance contains in it some degree of bitterness, it is spoken of as *not to be repented of*, on account of the precious and pleasant fruit which it produces."

To salvation. Paul seems to make repentance the ground of salvation. Were it so, it would follow, that we are justified by works. I answer, that we must observe what Paul here treats of, for he is not inquiring as to the ground of salvation, but simply commending repentance from the fruit which it produces, he says that it is like a way by which we arrive at salvation. Nor is it without good reason; for Christ *calls us* by way of free favour, but it is *to repentance.* (Matt. ix. 13.) God by way of free favour pardons our sins,

---

[1] " Ne pensons pas que jamais il se convertisse au Seigneur;"—" Let us not think that ever he will turn to the Lord."

but only when we renounce them.   Nay more, God accomplishes in us at one and the same time two things : being renewed by repentance, we are delivered from the *bondage* of our sins ; and, being justified by faith, we are delivered also from the *curse* of our sins.   They are, therefore, inseparable fruits of grace, and, in consequence of their invariable connection, repentance may with fitness and propriety be represented as an introduction to salvation, but in this way of speaking of it, it is represented as an *effect* rather than as a *cause.*   These are not refinements for the purpose of evasion, but a true and simple solution, for, while Scripture teaches us that we never obtain forgiveness of sins without repentance, it represents at the same time, in a variety of passages, the mercy of God alone as the ground of our obtaining it.

11. *What earnest desire it produced in you.*   I shall not enter into any dispute as to whether the things that Paul enumerates are effects of repentance, or belong to it, or are preparatory to it, as all this is unnecessary for understanding Paul's design, for he simply proves the repentance of the Corinthians from its signs, or accompaniments.   At the same time he makes *sorrow according to God* to be the source of all these things, inasmuch as they spring from it— which is assuredly the case ; for when we have begun to feel self-dissatisfaction, we are afterwards stirred up to seek after the other things.

What is meant by *earnest desire,* we may understand from what is opposed to it ; for so long as there is no apprehension of sin, we lie drowsy and inactive.   Hence drowsiness or carelessness, or unconcern,[1] stands opposed to that *earnest desire,* that he makes mention of.   Accordingly, *earnest desire* means simply an eager and active assiduity in the correcting of what is amiss, and in the amendment of life.

Yea, what clearing of yourselves.   Erasmus having rendered it *satisfaction,* ignorant persons, misled by the ambiguity of the term, have applied it to popish *satisfactions,* whereas Paul employs the term ἀπολογίαν, *(defence.)*   It is on this account that I have preferred to retain the word

---

[1] " Nonchalance, ou paresse, ou asseurance qui procede de stupidite ;"— " Carelessness or indolence, or confidence arising from stupidity."

defensionem, which the Old Interpreter had made use of.[1]
It is, however, to be observed, that it is a kind of *defence*
that consists rather in supplication for pardon, than in ex-
tenuation of sin. As a son, who is desirous to clear himself
to his father, does not enter upon a regular pleading of his
cause, but by acknowledging his fault excuses himself, rather
in the spirit of a suppliant, than in a tone of confidence,
hypocrites, also, excuse themselves—nay more, they haughtily defend themselves, but it is rather in the way of disputing with God, than of returning to favour with him ; and
should any one prefer the word *excusationem,* (*excuse,*) I do
not object to it ; because the meaning will amount to the
same thing,—that the Corinthians were prompted to clear
themselves, whereas previously they cared not what Paul
thought of them.

Yea, what indignation.[2] This disposition, also, is attendant on sacred sorrow—that the sinner is indignant against
his vices, and even against himself, as also all that are actuated by a right zeal[3] are indignant, as often as they see
that God is offended. This disposition, however, is more
intense than sorrow. For the *first* step is, that evil be displeasing to us. The *second* is, that, being inflamed with
anger, we press hard upon ourselves, so that our consciences
may be touched to the quick. It may, however, be taken
here to mean the *indignation,* with which the Corinthians
had been inflamed against the sins of one or a few, whom
they had previously spared. Thus they repented of their
concurrence or connivance.

Fear is what arises from an apprehension of divine judgment, while the offender thinks—" Mark it well, an account
must be rendered by thee, and what wilt thou advance in
the presence of so great a judge ?" For, alarmed by such a
consideration, he begins to tremble.

As, however, the wicked themselves are sometimes touched

---

[1] Wiclif, (1380,) following the Vulgate, reads, *defendynge.—Ed.*

[2] " *Voire marrissement.* Il y a proprement au Grec, Indignation ou
courroux ;"—" *Yea what concern.* It is properly in the Greek, Indignation or wrath."

[3] " Qui ont vn bon et sainct zele ;"—" Who have a good and holy
zeal."

with an alarm of this nature, he adds *desire*.   This disposition we know to be more of a voluntary nature than *fear*,
for we are often afraid against our will, but we never desire
but from inclination.   Hence, as they had dreaded punishment on receiving Paul's admonition, so they eagerly aimed
at amendment.

But what are we to understand by *zeal ?*   There can be no
doubt that he intended a climax.   Hence it means more
than *desire*.   Now we may understand by it, that they
stirred up each other in a spirit of mutual rivalry.   It is
simpler, however, to understand it as meaning, that every
one, with great fervour of zeal, aimed to give evidence of
his repentance.   Thus zeal is intensity of desire.

Yea, what revenge.   What we have said as to *indignation*,
must be applied also to *revenge ;* for the wickedness which
they had countenanced by their connivance and indulgence,
they had afterwards shown themselves rigorous in aveng-
ing.   They had for some time tolerated incest ; but, on being
admonished by Paul, they had not merely ceased to countenance him, but had been strict reprovers in chastening him,
—this was the *revenge* that was meant.   As, however, we
ought to punish sins wherever they are,[1] and not only so,
but should begin more especially with ourselves, there is
something farther meant in what the Apostle says here, for
he speaks of the signs of repentance.   There is, among others,
this more particularly—that, by punishing sins, we anticipate, in a manner, the judgment of God, as he teaches elsewhere, If we would judge ourselves, we would not be judged
by the Lord.   (1 Cor. xi. 31.)   We are not, however, to infer from this, that mankind, by taking vengeance upon
themselves, compensate to God for the punishment due to
him,[2] so that they redeem themselves from his hand.   The
case stands thus—that, as it is the design of God by chastising us, to arouse us from our carelessness, that, being re-
minded of his displeasure, we may be on our guard for the
future, when the sinner himself is beforehand in inflicting

[1] " En quelque personne qu'ils soyent trouuez ;"—" In any person in
whom they are found."

[2] " La peine qu'il leur pourroit iustement imposer ;"—" The punishment
which he could justly have inflicted upon them."

punishment of his own accord, the effect is, that he no longer stands in need of such an admonition from God.

But it is asked, whether the Corinthians had an eye to Paul, or to God, in this *revenge,* as well as in the *zeal,* and *desire,* and the rest.[1] I answer, that all these things are, under all circumstances, attendant upon repentance, but there is a difference in the case of an individual sinning secretly before God, or openly before the world. If a person's sin is secret, it is enough if he has this disposition in the sight of God. On the other hand, where the sin is open, there is required besides an open manifestation of repentance. Thus the Corinthians, who had sinned openly and to the great offence of the good, required to give evidence of their repentance by these tokens.

In all *things* ye have approved yourselves to be clear in this matter.

Modis omnibus comprobastis vos puros esse in negotio.

12. Wherefore, though I wrote unto you, *I did it* not for his cause that had done the wrong, nor for his cause that suffered wrong, but that our care for you in the sight of God might appear unto you.

12. Itaque si scripsi vobis, non eius causa qui læserat, neque eius causa qui læsus fuerat, scripsi: sed ut palam fieret studium vestrum pro nobis apud vos, (*vel, studium nostrum in nobis erga vos,*) in conspectu Dei.

13. Therefore we were comforted in your comfort: yea, and exceedingly the more joyed we for the joy of Titus, because his spirit was refreshed by you all.

13. Idcirco consolationem accepimus ex consolatione vestri: quin uberius etiam gavisi sumus ob gaudium Titi, quod refocillatus sit eius spiritus ab omnibus vobis.

14. For if I have boasted any thing to him of you, I am not ashamed; but as we spake all things to you in truth, even so our boasting, which *I made* before Titus, is found a truth.

14. Quodsi quid apud illum de vobis gloriatus sum, non fuerim pudefactus: sed ut omnia in veritate loquuti sumus vobis, ita et gloriatio nostra apud Titum veritas facta est.

15. And his inward affection is more abundant toward you, whilst he remembereth the obedience of you all, how with fear and trembling ye received him.

15. Et viscera eius maiorem in modum erga vos affecta sunt: dum memoria repetit vestram omnium obedientiam, quemadmodum cum timore et tremore exceperitis eam.

16. I rejoice therefore that I have confidence in you in all *things.*

16. Gaudeo, quod vobis in omnibus confidam.

Ye have approved yourselves to be clear. The Old Interpreter reads, " Ye have shown yourselves." Erasmus renders it, " Ye have commended yourselves." I have preferred a *third* rendering, which appeared to me to suit better—that

[1] " Et autres affections yci nommees ;"—" And other dispositions here mentioned."

the Corinthians showed by clear evidences, that they were in no degree participants in the crime, with which they had appeared, from their connivance, to have had some connection. What those evidences were, we have already seen. At the same time, Paul does not altogether clear them, but palliates their offence. For the undue forbearance, which they had exercised, was not altogether free from blame. He acquits them, however, from the charge of concurrence.[1] We must farther observe, that he does not acquit all of them without exception, but merely the body of the Church. For it may readily be believed, that some were concerned in it, and countenanced it ; but, while all of them together were involved in disgrace, it afterwards appeared that only a few were in fault.

12. *Wherefore if I wrote.* He acts as persons are wont to do, that are desirous of a reconciliation. He wishes all past things to be buried, he does not any more reproach them, he does not reprove them for any thing, he does not expostulate as to any thing ; in fine, he forgets every thing, inasmuch as he was satisfied with their simply repenting. And, certainly, this is the right way—not to press offenders farther, when they have been brought to repentance. For if we still *call their sins to remembrance*, (1 Kings xvii. 18,) it is certain that we are actuated by malevolence, rather than by pious affection, or a desire for their welfare. These things, however, are said by Paul by way of concession, for, unquestionably, he had followed up the offence that he had taken, and had felt desirous that the author of this offence should be chastised, but now he puts his foot upon what had been in some degree offensive. " I am now desirous, that whatever I have written may be looked upon as having been written with no other view, than that you might perceive your affection towards me. As to all other things, let us now leave them as they are." Others explain it in this way,—that he had not regard to one individual in particular, but consulted the common advantage of all. The former interpretation, however, is the more natural one.

---

[1] " Il les absout quant à ce qu'on leur pouuoit obiecter qu'ils auoyent consenti a ce mesfait ;"—" He acquits them in so far as it might be alleged that they had concurred in that crime."

Your concern for us. As this reading occurs very generally in the Greek versions, I have not ventured to go so far as to erase it, though at the same time in one ancient manuscript the reading is ἡμῶν, *(of us,)*[1] and it appears from Chrysostom's Commentaries, that the Latin rendering[2] was more commonly received in his times even among the Greeks—*that our concern for you might become manifest to you,* that is, that it might be manifest to the Corinthians, how much concerned Paul was in regard to them. The other rendering, however, in which the greater part of the Greek manuscripts concur, is, notwithstanding, a probable one. For Paul congratulates the Corinthians on their having learned at length, through means of this test, how they stood affected towards him. "You were not yourselves aware of the attachment that you felt towards me, until you had trial of it in this matter." Others explain it as referring to the particular disposition of an individual, in this way : "That it might be manifest among you, how much respect each of you entertained for me, and that, through the occurrence of this opportunity, each of you might discover what had previously been concealed in his heart." As this is not of great moment, my readers are at liberty, so far as I am concerned, to make choice of either ; but, as he adds at the same time, *in the sight of God,* I rather think that he meant this—that each of them, having made a thorough search, as if he had come into the presence of God,[3] had come to know himself better than before.

13. *We received consolation.* Paul was wholly intent upon

---

[1] " Some (as *Newcome* and *Wakefield*) would read, from several MSS., and Versions, Fathers, and early editions, including that of *R. Stephens,* τὴν σπονδὴν ὑπὲρ ἡμῶν, (*your care for us.*) But though that produces *a sense,* yet it is one far-fetched and jejune, which does not arise naturally from the subject, and is not so agreeable to the context. The *external* authority for the reading in question is but slender ; the Ed. Princ., and the great bulk of the MSS., having ἡμῶν ὑπὲρ ὑμῶν,—*our* (care) *for you.*" —*Bloomfield.—Ed.*

[2] The rendering of the Vulgate is as follows : "Solicitudinem nostram quam habemus pro vobis ;"—" Our anxiety which we have for you." Wiclif, (1380,) following, as usual, the Vulgate, renders it thus : " Our busynesse which we haw for you bifor God."—*Ed.*

[3] " Ne plus ne moins que s'il eust este deuant Dieu ;"—" Neither more nor less than if he had been in the presence of God."

persuading the Corinthians, that nothing was more eagerly desired by him than their advantage. Hence he says, that he had shared with them in their consolation. Now their consolation had been this—that, acknowledging their fault, they did not merely take the reproof in good part, but had received it joyfully. For the bitterness of a reproof is easily sweetened, so soon as we begin to taste the profitableness of it to us.

What he adds—that he *rejoiced more abundantly on account of the consolation of Titus*, is by way of congratulation. Titus had been overjoyed in finding them more obedient and compliant than could have been expected—nay more, in his finding a sudden change for the better. Hence we may infer, that Paul's gentleness was anything but flattery, inasmuch as he rejoiced in their joy, so as to be, at the same time, chiefly taken up with their repentance.

14. *But if I have boasted any thing to him.* He shows indirectly, how friendly a disposition he had always exercised towards the Corinthians, and with what sincerity and kindness he had judged of them ; for at the very time that they seemed to be unworthy of commendation, he still promised much that was honourable on their behalf. Here truly we have a signal evidence of a rightly constituted and candid mind,—reproving to their face those that you love, and yet hoping well, and giving others good hopes respecting them. Such sincerity ought to have induced them not to take amiss any thing that proceeded from him. In the mean time, he takes this opportunity of setting before them again, in passing, his fidelity in all other matters. "You have hitherto had opportunity of knowing my candour, so that I have shown myself to be truthful, and not by any means fickle. I rejoice, therefore, that I have now also been found truthful, when boasting of you before others."

15. *His bowels more abundantly.* As the *bowels* are the seat of the affections, the term is on that account employed to denote compassion, love, and every pious affection.[1] He

---

[1] "The word σπλάγχνα," as is observed by *Barnes* in his Notes on 2 Cor. vi. 12, "commonly means in the Bible the tender affections. The Greek word properly denotes the *upper* viscera—the heart, the lungs, the

wished, however, to express emphatically the idea, that
while Titus had loved the Corinthians previously, he had
been, at that time, more vehemently stirred up to love them ;
and that, from the innermost affections of his heart. Now,
by these words he insinuates Titus into the affections of the
Corinthians, as it is of advantage that the servants of Christ
should be loved, that they may have it in their power to do
the more good. He at the same time encourages them to go
on well, that they may render themselves beloved by all the
good.

With fear and trembling. By these two words he sometimes
expresses simply *respect,* (Eph. vi. 5,) and this perhaps would
not suit ill with this passage, though I should have no objection to view the *trembling* as mentioned particularly to mean,
that, being conscious of having acted amiss, they were afraid
to face him. It is true that even those, that are resolute in
their iniquities, tremble at the sight of the judge, but voluntary trembling, that proceeds from ingenuous shame, is a sign
of repentance. Whichever exposition you may choose, this
passage teaches, what is a right reception for the ministers of
Christ. Assuredly, it is not sumptuous banquets, it is not
splendid apparel, it is not courteous and honourable salutations, it is not the plaudits of the multitude, that gratify the
upright and faithful pastor. He experiences, on the other
hand, an overflowing of delight, when the doctrine of salvation
is received with reverence from his mouth, when he retains
the authority that belongs to him for the edification of the
Church, when the people give themselves up to his direction,
to be regulated by his ministry under Christ's banners.
An example of this we see here in Titus. He at length, in
the close, confirms again, what he had previously stated—
that he had never been offended to such a degree, as altogether to distrust the Corinthians.

liver. It is applied by Greek writers to denote those parts of victims
which were eaten during or after the sacrifice. Hence it is applied to the
heart, as the seat of the emotions and passions ; and especially the tender
affections—compassion, pity, love, &c. Our word *bowels* is applied usually
to the *lower* viscera, and by no means expresses the idea of the word which
is used in Greek."—*Ed.*

CHAPTER VIII.

1. Moreover, brethren, we do you to wit of the grace of God bestowed on the churches of Macedonia ;

2. How that in a great trial of affliction, the abundance of their joy, and their deep poverty, abounded unto the riches of their liberality.

3. For to *their* power, (I bear record,) yea, and beyond *their* power, *they were* willing of themselves ;

4. Praying us with much entreaty that we would receive the gift, and *take upon us* the fellowship of the ministering to the saints.

5. And *this they did,* not as we hoped, but first gave their own selves to the Lord, and unto us by the will of God :

6. Insomuch that we desired Titus, that as he had begun, so he would also finish in you the same grace also.

7. Therefore, as ye abound in every *thing, in* faith, and utterance, and knowledge, and *in* all diligence, and *in* your love to us; *see* that ye abound in this grace also.

1. Certiores autem vos facio, fratres, de gratia Dei, quæ data est in Ecclesiis Macedoniæ ;

2. Quoniam in multa probatione afflictionis exsuperavit gaudium ipsorum, et profunda illorum paupertas exundavit in divitias simplicitatis[1] eorum.

3. Nam pro viribus (testor) atque etiam supra vires fuerunt voluntarii ;

4. Multa cum obtestatione rogantes nos, ut gratiam et societatem ministerii susciperemus in sanctos.

5. Ac non quatenus sperabamus: sed se ipsos dediderunt, primum Domino, deinde et nobis per voluntatem Dei :

6. Ut adhortaremur Titum, ut quemadmodum ante cœpisset, ita et consummaret erga vos hanc quoque gratiam.

7. Verum quemadmodum ubique abundatis fide, et scientia, et omni diligentia, et ea, quæ ex vobis erga nos est, caritate: facite, ut in hac quoque beneficentia abundetis.

As, in the event of the Corinthians retaining any feeling of offence, occasioned by the severity of the preceding Epistle, *that* might stand in the way of Paul's authority having influence over them, he has hitherto made it his endeavour to conciliate their affections. Now, after clearing away all occasion of offence, and regaining favour for his ministry, he recommends to them the brethren at Jerusalem, that they may furnish help to their necessities. He could not, with any great advantage, have attempted this in the commencement of the Epistle. Hence, he has prudently deferred it, until he has prepared their minds for it. Accordingly, he takes up the whole of this chapter, and the next, in exhorting the Corinthians to be active and diligent in collecting alms to be taken to Jerusalem for relieving the in-

[1] " Simplicite ou promptitude ;".—" Simplicity or promptitude."

digence of the brethren.　For they were afflicted with a great famine, so that they could scarcely support life, without being aided by other churches.　The Apostles had intrusted Paul with this matter, (Gal. ii. 10,) and he had promised to concern himself in reference to it, and he had already done so in part, as we have seen in the former Epistle.[1]　Now, however, he presses them still farther.

1. *I make known to you.*　He commends the Macedonians, but it is with the design of stimulating the Corinthians by their example, although he does not expressly say so ; for the former had no need of commendation, but the latter had need of a stimulus.　And that he may stir up the Corinthians the more to emulation, he ascribes it to the *grace of God* that the Macedonians had been so forward to give help to their brethren.　For although it is acknowledged by all, that it is a commendable virtue to give help to the needy, they, nevertheless, do not reckon it to be a gain, nor do they look upon it as the *grace of God.*　Nay rather, they reckon, that it is so much of what was theirs taken from them, and lost. Paul, on the other hand, declares, that we ought to ascribe it to the grace of God, when we afford aid to our brethren, and that it ought to be desired by us as a privilege of no ordinary kind.

He makes mention, however, of a twofold favour, that had been conferred upon the Macedonians.　The *first* is, that they had endured afflictions with composure and cheerfulness.　The *second* is, that from their slender means, equally as though they had possessed abundance,[2] they had taken something—to be laid out upon their brethren.　Each of these things, Paul affirms with good reason, is a work of the Lord, for all quickly fail, that are not upheld by the Spirit of God, who is the Author of all consolation, and distrust clings to us, deeply rooted, which keeps us back from all offices of love, until it is subdued by the grace of the same Spirit.

2. *In much trial*—In other words, while they were tried with adversity, they, nevertheless, did not cease to rejoice

---

[1] See CALVIN on the Corinthians, vol. i. pp. 67-70.

[2] " D'aussi bon cœur qu'ils eussent este bien riches ;"—" As heartily as if they had been very rich."

in the Lord : nay, this disposition rose so high, as to swallow up sorrow ; for the minds of the Macedonians, which must otherwise have been straitened, required to be set free from their restraints, that they might liberally[1] furnish aid to the brethren.

By the term *joy* he means that spiritual consolation by which believers are sustained under their afflictions ; for the wicked either delude themselves with empty consolations, by avoiding a perception of the evil, and drawing off the mind to rambling thoughts, or else they wholly give way to grief, and allow themselves to be overwhelmed with it.   Believers, on the other hand, seek occasions of *joy* in the affliction itself, as we see in the 8th chapter of the Romans.[2]

And their deep poverty.   Here we have a metaphor taken from exhausted vessels, as though he had said, that the Macedonians had been emptied, so that they had now reached the bottom.   He says, that even in such straits they had abounded in liberality, and had been rich, so as to have enough—not merely for their own use, but also for giving assistance to others.   Mark the way, in which we shall always be liberal even in the most straitened poverty— if by liberality of mind we make up for what is deficient in our coffers.

Liberality is opposed to niggardliness, as in Rom. xii. 8, where Paul requires this on the part of deacons.   For what makes us more close-handed than we ought to be is—when we look too carefully, and too far forward, in contemplating the dangers that may occur—when we are excessively cautious and careful—when we calculate too narrowly what we will require during our whole life, or, in fine, how much we lose when the smallest portion is taken away.   The man,

---

[1] " Franchement et d'vne affection liberale ;"—" Cheerfully, and with a liberal spirit."

[2] CALVIN refers, it is probable, more particularly to Paul's statement in Rom. viii. 28, *And we know that all things shall work together for good,* &c. ; in commenting upon which passage, our author observes : " Ex supradictis nunc concludit, tantum abesse, quin salutem nostram remorentur hujus vitæ ærumnæ, ut sint potius eius adminicula ;"—" From what has been said previously, he now draws this conclusion, that the distresses of this life are so far from being hinderances to our salvation, that they are rather helps to it."—*Ed.*

that depends upon the blessing of the Lord, has his mind set free from these trammels, and has, at the same time, his hands opened for beneficence. Let us now draw an argument from the less to the greater. " Slender means, nay poverty, did not prevent the Macedonians from doing good to their brethren : What excuse, then, will the Corinthians have, if they keep back, while opulent and affluent in comparison of them ?"

3. *To their power, and even beyond their power.* When he says that they were *willing of themselves,* he means that they were, of their own accord, so well prepared for the duty, that they needed no exhortation. It was a great thing— to strive up to the measure of their ability ; and hence, to exert themselves *beyond* their ability, showed a rare, and truly admirable excellence.[1] Now he speaks according to the common custom of men, for the common rule of doing good is that which Solomon prescribes, (Prov. v. 15)—to *drink water out of our own fountains, and let the rivulets go past, that they may flow onwards to others.*[2] The Macedonians, on the other hand, making no account of themselves, and almost losing sight of themselves, concerned themselves rather as to providing for others.[3] In fine, those that are in straitened circumstances are willing beyond their ability, if they lay out any thing upon others from their slender means.

4. *Beseeching us with much entreaty.* He enlarges upon their promptitude, inasmuch as they did not only not wait for any one to admonish them, but even *besought* those, by whom they would have been admonished, had they not anticipated the desires of all by their activity.[4] We must again repeat the

[1] " *To their power, yea, and beyond their power.* This is a noble hyperbole, like that of Demosthenes, ' I have performed all, even with an industry beyond my power.' "—*Doddridge.—Ed.*

[2] *Poole,* in his Annotations, observes that the " metaphor" made use of in the passage referred to, (Prov. v. 15,) " is to be understood either 1, of the free and lawful use of a man's estate, both for his own comfort and for the good of others, or 2, of the honest use of matrimony." " The latter meaning," he remarks, " better suits with the whole context, both foregoing and following, and thus it is explained in the end of verse 18."—*Ed.*

[3] " Ont employé leur soin a secourir les autres plustost qu'a subuenir a leur propre necessite ;"—" Made it their care rather to assist others, than to relieve their own necessities."

[4] " Le desir et la solicitation de tous par leur diligence et prompti-

comparison formerly made between the less and the greater.[1]
" If the Macedonians, without needing to be besought, press
forward of their own accord, nay more, anticipate others by
using entreaties, how shameful a thing is it for the Corinthians to be inactive, more especially after being admonished !   If the Macedonians lead the way before all, how
shameful a thing is it for the Corinthians not, at least, to
imitate their example !   But what are we to think, when, not
satisfied with *beseeching,* they added to their requests *earnest entreaty,* and much of it too ?"   Now from this it appears, that they had *besought,* not as a mere form, but in
good earnest.

That the favour and the fellowship. The term *favour* he has
made use of, for the purpose of recommending alms, though
at the same time the word may be explained in different
ways. This interpretation, however, appears to me to be
the more simple one ; because, as our heavenly Father freely
bestows upon us all things, so we ought to be imitators of
his unmerited kindness in doing good, (Matt. v. 45) ; or at
least, because, in laying out our resources, we are simply the
dispensers of his *favour.* The *fellowship of this ministry*
consisted in his being a helper to the Macedonians in this
ministry. They contributed of their own, that it might be
administered to the saints. They wished, that Paul would
take the charge of collecting it.

5. *And not as.* He expected from them an ordinary degree of willingness, such as any Christian should manifest ;
but they went beyond his expectation, inasmuch as they not
only had their worldly substance in readiness, but were prepared to devote even *themselves.* *They gave themselves,* says
he, *first to God, then to us.*

It may be asked, whether their giving themselves to God,
and to Paul, were two different things. It is quite a common thing, that when God charges or commands through
means of any one, he associates the person whom he
employs as his minister, both in authority to enjoin, and

tude ;"—" The desire and solicitation of all by their diligence and promp--
titude."

[1] See p. 286.

in the obedience that is rendered. *It seemed good to the Holy Spirit, and to us;* say the Apostles, (Acts xv. 28,) while at the same time they merely, as instruments, declared what had been revealed and enjoined by the Spirit. Again, *The people believed the Lord and his servant Moses,* (Exod. xiv. 31,) while at the same time Moses had nothing apart from God. This, too, is what is meant by the clause that follows—*by the will of God.* For, as they were obedient to God, who had committed themselves to his ministry, to be regulated by his counsel, they were influenced by this consideration in listening to Paul, as speaking from God's mouth.

6. *That we should exhort Titus.* Now this is an exhortation that is of greater force, when they learn that they are expressly summoned to duty.[1] Nor was it offensive to the Macedonians, that he was desirous to have the Corinthians as partners in beneficence. In the mean time an apology is made for Titus, that the Corinthians may not think that he pressed too hard upon them, as if he had not confidence in their good disposition. For he did that, from having been entreated, and it was rather in the name of the Macedonians, than in his own.

7. *But as.* He had already been very careful to avoid giving offence, inasmuch as he said, that Titus had entreated them, not so much from his own inclination, as in consideration of the charge given him by the Macedonians. Now, however, he goes a step farther, by admonishing them, that they must not even wait for the message of the Macedonians being communicated to them; and that too, by commending their other virtues. "You ought not merely to associate yourselves as partners with the Macedonians, who require that; but surpass them in this respect, too, as you do in others."

He makes a distinction between *utterance* and *faith,* because it is impossible that any one should have *faith,* and that, too, in an eminent degree, without being at the same time much exercised in the word of God. *Knowledge* I un-

---

[1] " Quand ils oyent qu'on les somme nommeement et presentement de faire leur droit ;"—" When they hear that they summon them expressly and presently to do their duty."

derstand to mean, *practice* and *skill*, or *prudence*.   He makes mention of their *love* to himself, that he may encourage them also from regard to himself personally, and in the mean time he 'gives up, with a view to the public advantage of the brethren, the personal affection with which they regarded him.[1]   Now in this way he lays a restraint upon himself in everything, that he may not seem to accuse them when exhorting them.

8. I speak not by commandment, but by occasion of the forwardness of others, and to prove the sincerity of your love.	8. Non secundum imperium loquor, sed per aliorum sollicitudinem, et vestræ dilectionis sinceritatem approbans.
9. For ye know the grace of our Lord Jesus Christ, that, though he was rich, yet for your sakes he became poor, that ye through his poverty might be rich.	9. Nostis enim gratiam Domini nostri Iesu Christi, quod propter vos pauper factus sit, quum esset dives: ut vos illius paupertate ditesceretis.
10. And herein I give *my* advice: for this is expedient for you, who have begun before, not only to do, but also to be forward a year ago.	10. Et consilium in hoc do: nam hoc vobis conducit: qui quidem non solum facere, verum etiam velle cœpistis anno superiore.
11. Now therefore perform the doing *of it;* that as *there was* a readiness to will, so *there may be* a performance also out of that which ye have.	11. Nunc autem etiam *illud quod* facere cœpistis, perficite: ut quemadmodum voluntas prompta fuit, ita et perficiatis ex eo quod suppetit.
12. For if there be first a willing mind, *it is* accepted according to that a man hath, *and* not according to that he hath not.	12. Etenim si iam adest animi promptitudo, ea iuxta id quod quisque possidet, accepta est: non iuxta id quod non possidet.

8. *I speak not according to commandment.*   Again he qualifies his exhortation, by declaring that he did not at all intend to compel them, as if he were imposing any necessity upon them, for that is to *speak according to commandment,* when we enjoin any thing definite, and peremptorily require that it shall be done.   Should any one ask—" Was it not lawful for him to prescribe what he had by commandment of the Lord?"   The answer is easy—that God, it is true, everywhere charges us to help the necessities of our brethren, but he nowhere specifies the sum;[2] that, after making a calculation, we might divide between ourselves and the poor.

---

[1] " De laquelle les Corinthiens l'aimoyent et ses compagnons;"—" With which the Corinthians loved him and his associates."

[2] " Combien nous leur deuons donner;"—" How much we ought to give them."

He nowhere binds us to circumstances of times, or persons, but calls us to take the rule of love as our guide.

At the same time, Paul does not here look to what is lawful for him, or unlawful, but says, that he does not *command* as if he reckoned that they required to be constrained by *command* and requirement, as though they refused to do their duty, unless shut up to it by necessity. He assigns, on the other hand, two reasons why he, notwithstanding, stirs them up to duty. *1st*, Because the concern felt by him for the saints compels him to do so; and, *2dly*, Because he is desirous, that the love of the Corinthians should be made known to all. For I do not understand Paul to have been desirous to be assured of their love, (as to which he had already declared himself to be perfectly persuaded,)[1] but he rather wished that all should have evidence of it. At the same time, the first clause in reference to the anxiety of others, admits of two meanings—either that he felt an anxiety as to the individuals, which did not allow him to be inactive, or that, yielding to the entreaties of others, who had the matter at heart, he spoke not so much from his own feeling, as at the suggestion of others.

9. *For ye know the grace.* Having made mention of love, he adduces Christ as an all perfect and singular pattern of it. "Though he was rich," says he, "he resigned the possession of all blessings, that he might enrich us by his poverty." He does not afterwards state for what purpose he makes mention of this, but leaves it to be considered by them; for no one can but perceive, that we are by this example stirred up to beneficence, that we may not spare ourselves, when help is to be afforded to our brethren.

Christ *was rich*, because he was God, under whose power and authority all things are; and farther, even in our human nature, which he put on, as the Apostle bears witness, (Heb. i. 2 ; ii. 8,) he was the *heir of all things*, inasmuch as he was placed by his Father over all creatures, and all things were placed under his feet. He nevertheless *became poor*, because he refrained from possessing, and thus he gave up his right for a time. We see, what destitution and penury as to all

---

[1] " Bien persuadé et asseuré;"—" Well persuaded and assured."

things awaited him immediately on his coming from his mother's womb. We hear what he says himself, (Luke ix. 58,) *The foxes have holes, and the birds of the air have nests: the Son of man hath not where to lay his head.* Hence he has consecrated poverty in his own person, that believers may no longer regard it with horror. By his *poverty* he has *enriched* us all for this purpose—that we may not feel it hard to take from our abundance what we may lay out upon our brethren.

10. *And in this I give my advice.* The *advice* he places in contrast with the *commandment* of which he had spoken a little before. (verse 8.) "I merely point out what is expedient in the way of *advising* or *admonishing.*" Now this *advantage* is not perceived by the judgment of the flesh; for where is the man to be found, who is persuaded that it is of *advantage* to deprive himself of something with the view of helping others? It is, indeed, the saying of a heathen— "What you have given away is the only riches that you will always have;"[1] but the reason is, that "whatever is given to friends is placed beyond all risk." The Lord, on the other hand, would not have us influenced by the hope of a reward, or of any remuneration in return, but, on the contrary, though men should be ungrateful, so that we may seem to have lost what we have given away, he would have us, notwithstanding, persevere in doing good. The advantage, however, arises from this—that "*He that giveth to the poor* (as Solomon says in Prov. xix. 17) *lendeth to the Lord,*" whose

---

[1] CALVIN, it is to be observed, quotes the same sentiment, when commenting on 1 Cor. xvi. 2, (see p. 69,) but in the present instance he takes occasion, most appropriately to his particular purpose, to notice the connection in which the poet introduces it, which is as follows:—
> " Callidus effracta nummos fur auferet arca ;
>   Prosternet patrios impia flamma Lares.
>   Extra fortunam est, quicquid donatur amicis ;
>   Quas dederis, solas semper habebis opes."

" The dexterous thief will break open your chest, and carry off your money ; a fire, raised by a base incendiary, will lay in the dust your paternal mansion ; but whatever has been given to friends is placed beyond all risk. What you have given away is the only wealth that you will always retain."—MARTIAL, *Ep.* 5. 39-42.

It is mentioned by *Dr. Bennett,* in his Lectures on Christ's Preaching, (p. 104,) that on the tomb of Robert of Doncaster, there was the following inscription—" What I gave, I have ; what I kept, I lost."—*Ed.*

blessing, of itself, is to be regarded as a hundredfold more precious than all the treasures of the world.   The word *useful*, however, is taken here to mean *honourable*, or at least Paul measures what is *useful* by what is *honourable*, because it would have been disgraceful to the Corinthians to draw back, or to stop short in the middle of the course, when they had already advanced so far.   At the same time it would also have been *useless*, inasmuch as everything that they had attempted to do would have come short of acceptance in the sight of God.

Who had begun not only to do.   As *doing* is more than *willing*, the expression may seem an improper one ; but *willing* here is not taken simply, (as we commonly say,) but conveys the idea of spontaneous alacrity, that waits for no monitor.   For there are *three* gradations, so to speak, as to acting.   *First*, we sometimes act unwillingly, but it is from shame or fear.   *Secondly*, we act willingly, but at the same time it is from being either impelled, or induced from influence, apart from our own minds.   *Thirdly*, we act from the promptings of our own minds, when we of our own accord set ourselves to do what is becoming.   Such cheerfulness of anticipation is better than the actual performance of the deed.[1]

11. *Now what ye have begun to do.*   It is probable, that the ardour of the Corinthians had quickly cooled down : otherwise they would, without any delay, have prosecuted their purpose.   The Apostle, however, as though no fault had as yet been committed, gently admonishes them to complete, what had been well begun.

When he adds—*from what you have,* he anticipates an objection ; for the flesh is always ingenious in finding out subterfuges.   Some plead that they have families, which it were inhuman to neglect ; others, on the ground that they cannot give much, make use of this as a pretext for entire exemption.   Could I give so small a sum ?   All excuses of

---

[1] " Vne telle promptitude de s'auancer a faire sans estre incité ou aduerti d'ailleurs, est plus que le faict mesme ;"—" Such promptitude in being forward to act, without requiring to be stirred up or admonished by any one, is more than the deed itself."

this nature Paul removes, when he commands every one to
contribute according to the measure of his ability.   He adds,
also, the reason : that God looks to the heart—not to what
is given, for when he says, that readiness of mind is acceptable to God, according to the individual's ability, his meaning is this—" If from slender resources you present some
small sum, your disposition is not less esteemed in the sight
of God, than in the case of a rich man's giving a large sum
from his abundance. (Mark xii. 44.)   For the disposition
is not estimated according to what you have not, that is,
God does by no means require of thee, that thou shouldst
contribute more than thy resources allow."   In this way
none are excused ; for the rich, on the one hand, owe to God
a larger offering, and the poor, on the other hand, ought not
to be ashamed of their slender resources.

13. For *I mean* not that other
men be eased, and you burdened ;

14. But by an equality, *that* now at
this time your abundance *may be a
supply* for their want, that their abundance also may be *a supply* for your
want ; that there may be equality :

15. As it is written, He that *had
gathered* much had nothing over ;
and he that *had gathered* little had
no lack.

16. But thanks *be* to God, which
put the same earnest care into the
heart of Titus for you.

17. For indeed he accepted the exhortation ; but, being more forward,
of his own accord he went unto you.

13. Non enim ut aliis relaxatio
sit, vobis autem angustia : sed ut ex
æquabilitate.

14. In præsenti tempore vestra
copia illorum succurrat inopiæ : et
illorum copia vestræ succurrat inopiæ, quo fiat æquabilitas.

15. Quemadmodum scriptum est
(*Exod.* xvi. 18.) Qui multum habebat, huic nihil superfluit : et qui paulum habebat, is nihilominus habuit.

16. Gratia autem Deo, qui dedit
eandem sollicitudinem pro vobis in
corde Titi,

17. Qui exhortationem acceperit :
quin potius, quum esset diligentior,
suapte sponte ad vos venerit.

13. *Not that others.* This is a confirmation of the preceding statement—that a readiness of will is well-pleasing
to God alike in poverty and in wealth, inasmuch as God does
not mean that we should be reduced to straits, in order that
others may be at ease through our liberality.   True, indeed,
it is certain, that we owe to God, not merely a part, but all
that we are, and all that we have, but in His kindness He
spares us thus far, that He is satisfied with that participation of which the Apostle here speaks.   What he teaches

here you must understand to mean an abatement from the rigour of law.[1] In the mean time, it is our part to stir ourselves up from time to time to liberality, because we must not be so much afraid of going to excess in this department. The danger is on the side of excessive niggardliness.

This doctrine, however, is needful in opposition to fanatics, who think that you have done nothing, unless you have stript yourself of every thing, so as to make every thing common;[2] and, certainly, they gain this much by their frenzy, that no one can give alms with a quiet conscience. Hence we must carefully observe Paul's (ἐπιείκεια) *mildness*,[3] and moderation, in stating that our alms are well-pleasing to God, when we relieve the necessity of our brethren from our abundance—not in such a way that they are at ease, and we are in want, but so that we may, from what belongs to us, distribute, so far as our resources allow, and that with a cheerful mind.[4]

By an equality. *Equality* may be taken in two senses, either as meaning a mutual compensation, when like is given for like, or as meaning a proper adjustment. I understand ἰσότητα simply as meaning—an *equality of proportional right*,[5] as Aristotle terms it.[6] In this signification it is made

---

[1] " Est vn relaschement de ce a quoy nous sommes tenus en rigueur de droict comme on dit ;"—" Is an abatement from what we are bound to by strictness of right, as they say."

[2] CALVIN alludes to the same class of persons, when commenting on Acts ii. 44—*had all things common.* " Verum sana expositione indiget hic locus propter spiritus fanaticos, qui bonorum κοινωνίαν fingunt, qua omnis politia evertatur ;"—" This passage, however, requires to be soundly interpreted—for the sake of those fanatical spirits, who pretend (κοινωνίαν)—a *community* of goods, by which all civil government is overturned."—*Ed.*

[3] *Beza,* when commenting on 2 Cor. x. 1, observes, that ἐπιεικείας means " an inclination to clemency and mercy, as opposed to a disposition to follow out to the utmost one's just right." " Aristotle," he remarks, " contrasts τὸ ἐπιεικὲς, (*mildness*,) with τῷ ἀκριβοδικαίῳ, (*rigorous justice,*) and Hermogenes contrasts it with τῷ βιαίῳ (*violence.*)"—*Ed.*

[4] " Et ce d'vne gayete de cœur et franc courage ;"—" And that with cheerfulness of heart and frank courage."

[5] " C'est a dire qui est compassee par proportion selon des qualitez des personnes et autres circonstances ;"—" That is to say, which is regulated proportionally according to the stations of individuals, and other circumstances."

[6] " Quærenda omnino ἰσότης est, sed *analogica* qualis est membrorum in corpore humano, qua quidem non omnia in eodem pretio et dignitate ha-

use of, also, in Colossians iv. 1, where he exhorts " masters to give to their servants what is *equal.*" He certainly does not mean, that they should be equal in condition and station, but by this term he expresses that humanity and clemency, and kind treatment, which masters, in their turn, owe to their servants. Thus the Lord recommends to us a proportion of this nature, that we may, in so far as every one's resources admit, afford help to the indigent, that there may not be some in affluence, and others in indigence. Hence he adds—*at the present time.* At that time, indeed, necessity pressed upon them. Hence we are admonished that, in exercising beneficence, we must provide for the present necessity, if we would observe the true rule of equity.

14. *And their abundance.* It is uncertain, what sort of *abundance* he means. Some interpret it as meaning, that this had been the case, inasmuch as the Gospel had flowed out to them from the Church at Jerusalem, from which source they had, in their penury, been assisted by their spiritual riches. This, I think, is foreign to Paul's intention. It ought rather, in my opinion, to be applied to the communion of saints, which means, that whatever duty is discharged to one member, redounds to the advantage of the entire body. " If it is irksome to you to help your brethren with riches that are of no value, consider how many blessings you are destitute of, and these too, far more precious, with which you may be enriched by those who are poor as to worldly substance. This participation, which Christ has established among the members of his body, should animate you to be more forward, and more active in doing good." The meaning may, also, be this : " You now relieve them according to the necessity of the occasion, but they will have an opportunity given them at another time of requiting you."[1] I approve rather of the other sentiment, which is of

bentur, sed omnia tamen, quæ ornamento vel integumento indigent, ornantur et teguntur ;"—" *Equality* must by all means be aimed at, but *proportional*, such as subsists among the members of the human body, according to which they are not, indeed, all held in the same estimation and dignity, but all of them notwithstanding, that require ornament or clothing, are adorned and clothed."—*Heideggerus.*—*Ed.*

[1] " Quelque iour Dieu leur donnera moyen de vous recompenser ;"— " God will one day give them the means of requiting you."

a more general nature, and with this accords what he again repeats in reference to equality. For the system of proportional right in the Church is this—that while they communicate to each other mutually according to the measure of gifts and of necessity, this mutual contribution produces a befitting symmetry, though some have more, and some less, and gifts are distributed unequally.[1]

15. *As it is written.* The passage, that Paul quotes, refers to the manna, but let us hear what the Lord says by Moses. He would have this to serve as a never-failing proof, that men do not live by bread alone, but are Divinely supported, by the secret influence of *His* will, who maintains and preserves all things that he has created. Again, in another passage, (Deut. viii. 3,) Moses admonishes them, that they had been nourished for a time with such food, that they might learn that men are supported—not by their own industry or labour, but by the blessing of God. Hence it appears, that in the manna, as in a mirror, there is presented to us an emblem of the ordinary food that we partake of. Let us now come to the passage that Paul quotes. When the manna had fallen, they were commanded to gather it in heaps, so far as every one could, though at the same time, as some are more active than others, there was more gathered by some than was necessary for daily use,[2] yet no one took for his own private use more than an homer,[3] for that was the measure that was prescribed by the Lord. This being the case, all had as much as was sufficient, and no one was in want. This we have in Exodus xvi. 18.

---

[1] " Fait vne proportion fort conuenable, et comme vne belle harmonie ;"—" Makes a very suitable proportion, and as it were a beautiful harmony."

[2] " Combien qu'aucuns en amassassent plus qu'il ne leur estoit de besoin pour la nourriture d'vn iour, et les autres moins (comme les vns sont plus habiles que les autres ;)"—" Though some gathered more of it than was needed by them as the food of a day, and others less (as some are more expert than others)."

[3] " An omer was about three quarts English measure. . . . . It is inferred by some that, when any one had gathered more than his due share, he gave the overplus to those who had gathered less. Others, however, suppose that the whole quantity gathered by any one family was first put into a common mass, and then measured out to the several individuals composing the household."—*Bush's Notes on Exodus.—Ed.*

Let us now apply the history to Paul's object. The Lord has not prescribed to us an homer, or any other measure, according to which the food of each day is to be regulated, but he has enjoined upon us frugality and temperance, and has forbidden, that any one should go to excess, taking advantage of his abundance. Let those, then, that have riches, whether they have been left by inheritance, or procured by industry and efforts, consider that their abundance was not intended to be laid out in intemperance or excess, but in relieving the necessities of the brethren. For whatever we have is *manna*, from whatever quarter it comes, provided it be really *ours*, inasmuch as riches acquired by fraud, and unlawful artifices, are unworthy to be called so, but are rather *quails* sent forth by the anger of God. (Num. xi. 31.) And as in the case of one hoarding the manna, either from excessive greed or from distrust, what was laid up immediately putrified, so we need not doubt that the riches, that are heaped up at the expense of our brethren, are accursed, and will soon perish, and that too, in connection with the ruin of the owner ; so that we are not to think that it is the way to increase, if, consulting our own advantage for a long while to come, we defraud our poor brethren of the beneficence that we owe them.[1] I acknowledge, indeed, that there is not enjoined upon us an equality of such a kind, as to make it unlawful for the rich to live in any degree of greater elegance than the poor ; but an equality is to be observed thus far—that no one is to be allowed to starve, and no one is to hoard his abundance at the expense of defrauding others. The poor man's *homer*[2] will be coarse food and a spare diet ; the rich man's *homer* will be a more abundant portion, it is true, according to his circumstances, but at the same time in such a way that they live temperately, and are not wanting to others.

16. *But thanks be to God who hath put.* That he may leave the Corinthians without excuse, he now at length adds, that there had been provided for them active prompters,

---

[1] " Le secours et assistance ;"—" The help and assistance."
[2] " L'homer, c'est a dire la mesure des poures ;"—" The homer, that is to say, the measure of the poor."

who would attend to the matter.   And, in the first place, he
names Titus, who, he says, had been divinely raised up.   This
was of great importance in the case.   For his embassy would
be so much the more successful, if the Corinthians recognised
him as having come to them, from having been stirred up to
it by God.   From this passage, however, as from innumerable others, we infer that there are no pious affections that
do not proceed from the Spirit of God ;[1] and farther, that
this is an evidence of God's concern for his people, that he
raises up ministers and guardians, to make it their endeavour
to relieve their necessities.   But if the providence of God
shows itself in this manner, in providing the means of
nourishment for the body, how much greater care will he
exercise as to the means of spiritual nourishment, that his
people may not be in want of them !   Hence it is His special
and peculiar work to raise up pastors.[2]

His receiving the exhortation means that he had undertaken this business,[3] from being exhorted to it by Paul.
He afterwards corrects this by saying, that Titus had not
been so much influenced by the advice of others, as he had
felt stirred up of his own accord, in accordance with his
active disposition.

18. And we have sent with him the brother, whose praise *is* in the gospel throughout all the churches;
19. And not *that* only, but who was also chosen of the churches to travel with us with this grace, which is administered by us to the glory of the same Lord, and *declaration of* your ready mind :
20. Avoiding this, that no man should blame us in this abundance which is administered by us :
21. Providing for honest things, not only in the sight of the Lord, but also in the sight of men.
22. And we have sent with them

18. Misimus autem una cum illo fratrem, cuius laus est in Evangelio per omnes Ecclesias.
19. Nec id solum, verum etiam delectus ab Ecclesiis est comes pere-grinationis nostræ, cum hac benefi-centia[4] quæ administratur a nobis, ad eiusdem Domini gloriam, et animi vestri promptitudinem :
20. Declinantes hoc, ne quis nos carpat in hac exsuperantia, quæ ad-ministratur a nobis.
21. Procurantes honesta, non tantum coram Deo, sed etiam coram hominibus.
22. Misimus autem una cum illis

[1] See CALVIN's Institutes, vol. i. p. 378.
[2] " Les pasteurs et ministres ;"—" Pastors and ministers."
[3] " Que Tite auoit receu ceste charge ;"—" That Titus had received this charge."
[4] " Cestes aumone ou grace ;"—" This alms or grace."

our brother, whom we have oftentimes proved diligent in many things,
but now much more diligent, upon
the great confidence which *I have*
in you.

23. Whether *any do enquire* of
Titus, *he is* my partner and fellow-
helper concerning you ; or our
brethren *be enquired of, they are* the
messengers of the churches, *and* the
glory of Christ.

24. Wherefore shew ye to them,
and before the churches, the proof
of your love, and of our boasting on
your behalf.

fratrem nostrum, quem probavera-
mus in multis sæpenumero diligen-
tem ; nunc autem multo diligenti-
orem, ob multam fiduciam quam
habeo ergo vos :

23. Sive Titi nomine, qui socius
meus est, et erga vos adiutor, sive
aliorum, qui fratres nostri sunt, et
Apostoli Ecclesiarum, gloria Christi.[1]

24. Proinde documentum caritatis vestræ et nostræ de vobis gloriationis erga eos ostendit et in conspectu Ecclesiarum.

18. *We have sent with him the brother.* The circumstance
that *three* persons are sent, is an evidence, that great expectations were entertained respecting the Corinthians, and it
became them to be so much the more attentive to duty,
that they might not disappoint the hopes of the Churches.
It is uncertain, however, who this *second* person was ; only
that some conjecture that it was Luke, others that it was
Barnabas. Chrysostom prefers to consider it to have been
Barnabas. I agree with him, because it appears that, by
the suffrages of the Churches,[2] he was associated with Paul
as a companion. As, however, it is almost universally agreed,
that Luke was one of those who were the bearers of this
Epistle, I have no objection that he be reckoned to be the
third that is made mention of.

Now the second person, whoever he may be, he honours
with a signal commendation, that he had conducted himself
as to the gospel in a praiseworthy manner, that is, he had
earned applause by promoting the gospel. For, although

[1] " Soit a cause de Tite qui est mon compagnon, et coadiuteur enuers
vous : soit aussi a cause des autres, qui sont nos freres Apostres des Eglises,
la gloire de Christ ; *ou,* Ainsi donc quant a Tite, il est mon compagnon et
coadiuteur enuers vous ; et quant a nos freres, ils sont ambassadeurs des
Eglises, et la gloire de Christ ;"—" Be it on account of Titus, who is my
companion and fellow-helper towards you : be it also on account of the
others, who are our brethren, Apostles of the Churches, the glory of Christ ;
or, Thus then, as to Titus, he is my companion and fellow-helper towards
you ; and as to our brethren, they are the ambassadors of the Churches,
and the glory of Christ."

[2] " Par le commun accord des Eglises :"—" By the common agreement
of the Churches."

Barnabas gave place to Paul in the department of *speaking*, yet in *acting* they both concurred. He adds farther, that he had received praise, not from one individual, or even from one Church merely, but from all the Churches. To this general testimony he subjoins a particular one, that is suitable to the subject in hand—that he had been chosen for this department by the concurrence of the Churches. Now it was likely, that this honour would not have been conferred upon him, had he not been long before known to be qualified for it. We must observe, however, the mode of election— that which was customary among the Greeks—χειροτονία, (*a show of hands*,)[1] in which the leaders[2] took the precedence by authority and counsel, and regulated the whole proceeding, while the common people intimated their approval.[3]

19. *Which is administered by us.* By commending his ministry, he still farther encourages the Corinthians. He says, that it tends to promote the glory of God, and their kindness of disposition. Hence it comes, that these two things are conjoined—the glory of God and their liberality, and that the *latter* cannot be given up without the *former* being proportionally diminished. There is, in addition to this, the labour of those distinguished men, which it were very inconsistent to reject, or allow to pass unimproved.

20. *Avoiding this,*[4] *that no one.* Lest any one should

---

[1] " Laquelle les Grecs appellent d'vn nom qui signifie Eleuation des mains ;"—" Which the Greeks express by a term that signifies a show of hands."

[2] " Les principaux ou gouerneurs ;"—" The leaders or governors."

[3] *Beza*, in his Annotations on Acts xiv. 23, when commenting on the word χειροτονήσαντες, made use of in that passage in connection with the *ordaining* of elders in every Church, remarks, that the word in this application took its rise from the practice of the Greeks—" qui porrectis manibus suffragia ferebant : unde illud Ciceronis pro L. Flacco, *Porrexerunt manus : psephisma natum est ;*"—" Who gave their votes by holding up their hands : hence that statement made by Cicero in his Oration in behalf of L. Flaccus —*They held up their hands—a decree was passed.*" Allusion is made to the same custom among the Greeks in the writings of *Xenophon*, Καὶ ὅτῳ δοκεῖ, ἔφη, ταῦτα, αἱρέτω τὴν χεῖρα, ἀνέτειναν πάντες—" Whoever is of this mind," says he, " let him lift up his hand—they all lifted up their hands." (Xen. de Exped. Cyri. lib. v. p. 283.) "Ἔνδοξε δ'ἀναβαλέσθαι ἐς ἑτέραν ἐκκλησίαν· τότε γὰρ ὀψὲ ἦν, καὶ τὰς χεῖρας οὐκ ἂν καθεώρων—" But it seemed good to postpone the matter till another assembly, for it was then late, and they could not see the hands."—(Xen. Hist. Graec. lib. i. p. 350.)—*Ed.*

[4] The original word, στελλόμενοι, " sometimes signifies the furling or

think, that the Churches had an unfavourable opinion of
Paul, as if it had been from distrusting his integrity that
they had associated partners with him, as persons that are
suspected are wont to have guards set over them, he declares
that he had been the adviser of this measure, with the view
of providing against calumnies.   Here some one will ask,
" Would any one have been so impudent, as to venture to
defame with even the slightest suspicion the man, whose
fidelity must have been, in all quarters, beyond every
surmise ?"   I answer, Who is there that will be exempt
from Satan's bite, when even Christ himself was not
spared by them ?   Behold, Christ is exposed to the reproaches[1] of the wicked, and shall his servants be in
safety ? (Matt. x. 25.)   Nay rather, the more upright a
person is, in that proportion does Satan assail him by
every kind of contrivance, if he can by any means shake
his credit, for there would arise from this a much greater
occasion of stumbling.[2]   Hence the higher the station in
which we are placed, we must so much the more carefully imitate Paul's circumspection and modesty.   He
was not so lifted up, as not to be under control equally
with any individual of the flock.[3]   He was not so self-
complacent, as to think it beneath his station to provide
against calumnies.   Hence he prudently shunned dangers,
and used great care not to furnish any wicked person
with a handle against him.   And, certainly, nothing is

altering of the sails of a ship, to change her course, that she may avoid
rocks, or other dangers lying in her way.   Here it is used in a metaphorical sense for *taking care*, that no one should find fault with the Apostle,
as unfaithful in the management of the collections."—*M‘Knight.*   The
verb is employed in substantially the same sense by Plutarch : οἱ κατὰ
ψυχὴν χειμῶνες βαρύτεροι, στείλασθαι τὸν ἄνθρωπον οὐκ ἐῶντες οὐδὲ ἐπιστῆσαι τετα-
ραγμένον τὸν λογισμὸν—" The tempests of the mind are more severe—not
allowing a man to shift his course, or to calm down troubled reason."—
(Plut. tom. ii. p. 501.)—*Ed.*

    [1] " Aux reproches et calomnies ;"—" To the reproaches and calumnies."
    [2] " Car le scandale qui procederoit de là, seroit beaucoup plus grand que
si cela estoit aduenu a vn autre ;"—" For the offence that would arise from
that would be much greater than if this had happened to another."
    [3] " Il n'estoit point si arrogant, qu'il ne voulust bien estre admonesté
et censuré aussi bien que le plus petit de la bande ;"—" He was not so
arrogant, as not to be quite willing to be admonished and censured equally
with the humblest of the band."

more apt to give rise to unfavourable surmises, than the management of public money.

21. *Providing things honest.* I am of opinion, that there were not wanting, even among the Corinthians, some who would have proceeded so far as to revile, if occasion had been allowed them. Hence he wished them to know the state of matters, that he might shut the mouths of all everywhere. Accordingly he declares, that he is not merely concerned to have a good conscience in the sight of God, but also to have a good character among men. At the same time, there can be no doubt, that he designed to instruct the Corinthians, as well as all others, by his example, that, in doing what is right, the opinion of men is not to be disregarded. The first thing,[1] it is true, is that the person take care, that he be a good man. This is secured, not by mere outward actions, but by an upright conscience. The next thing is, that the persons, with whom you are conversant, recognise you as such.

Here, however, the object in view must be looked to. Nothing, assuredly, is worse than ambition, which vitiates the best things in the world, disfigures, I say, the most graceful, and makes sacrifices of the sweetest smell have an offensive odour before the Lord. Hence this passage is slippery, so that care must be taken,[2] lest one should pretend to be desirous, in common with Paul, of a good reputation, and yet be very far from having Paul's disposition, for he *provided things honest in the sight of men*, that no one might be stumbled by his example, but that, on the contrary, all might be edified. Hence we must, if we would desire to be like him, take care that we be not on our own account desirous of a good name. " He that is regardless of fame," says Augustine, " is cruel, because it is not less necessary before our neighbour, than a good conscience is before God." This is true, provided you consult the welfare of your brethren with a view to the glory of God, and in the mean time are prepared to bear reproaches

---

[1] " Le premier et le principal ;"—" The first and the chief thing."

[2] " Ainsi c'est yci vn passage glissant ; et pourtant il faut que chacun aduise a soy ;"—" Thus there is here a slippery passage ; and hence every one must take heed to himself."

and ignominy in place of commendation, if the Lord should see it meet. Let a Christian man, however, always take care to frame his life with a view to the edification of his neighbours, and diligently take heed, that the ministers of Satan shall have no pretext for reviling, to the dishonour of God and the offence of the good.

22. *On account of the great confidence.* The meaning is, " I am not afraid of their coming to you proving vain and fruitless ; for I have felt beforehand an assured confidence, that their embassy will have a happy issue ; I am so well aware of their fidelity and diligence." He says that the brother, whose name he does not mention, had felt more eagerly inclined ; partly because he saw that he[1] had a good opinion of the Corinthians, partly because he had been encouraged by Titus, and partly because he saw many distinguished men apply themselves to the same business with united efforts. Hence one thing only remained—that the Corinthians themselves should not be wanting on their part.[2]

In calling them the *Apostles of the Churches,* he might be understood in *two* senses—either as meaning that they had been set apart by God as *Apostles to the Churches,* or that they had been appointed by the Churches to undertake that office. The *second* of these is the more suitable. They are called also the *glory of Christ,* for this reason, that as he alone is the glory of believers, so he ought also to be glorified by them in return. Hence, all that excel in piety and holiness are the *glory of Christ,* because they have nothing but by Christ's gift.

He mentions two things in the close : " See that our brethren behold your love," and secondly, " Take care, that it be not in vain that I have boasted of you." For εἰς αὐτούς, (*to them,*) appears to me to be equivalent to *coram ipsis,* (*before them,*) for this clause does not refer to the poor, but to the messengers of whom mention had been made.[3]

---

[1] " Sainct Paul ;"—" St. Paul. "

[2] " Que les Corinthiens auisassent a ne defailler point de faire leur deuoir de leur costé ;"—" That the Corinthians should take care not to fail of doing their duty on their part."

[3] " Qui estoyent enuoyez comme ambassadeurs vers les Corinthiens ;" —" Who had been sent as ambassadors to the Corinthians."

For he immediately afterwards subjoins, that they would not be alone witnesses, but in consequence of the report given by them, a report would go out even to distant Churches.

CHAPTER IX.

1. For as touching the ministering to the saints, it is superfluous for me to write to you:

2. For I know the forwardness of your mind, for which I boast of you to them of Macedonia, that Achaia was ready a year ago; and your zeal hath provoked very many.

3. Yet have I sent the brethren, lest our boasting of you should be in vain in this behalf; that, as I said, ye may be ready:

4. Lest haply if they of Macedonia come with me, and find you unprepared, we (that we say not, you) should be ashamed in this same confident boasting.

5. Therefore I thought it necessary to exhort the brethren, that they would go before unto you, and make up beforehand your bounty, whereof ye had notice before, that the same might be ready, as *a matter of* bounty, and not as *of* covetousness.

1. Nam de subministratione quæ fit in sanctos, supervacuum mihi est scribere vobis.

2. Novi enim promptitudinem animi vestri, de qua pro vobis gloriatus sum apud Macedones: quod Achaia parata sit ab anno superiori: et aemulatio vestri excitavit complures.

3. Misi autem fratres, ut ne gloriatio nostra de vobis inanis fiat in hac parte: ut, quemadmodum dixi, parati sitis.

4. Ne si forte mecum venerint Macedones, et vos deprehenderint imparatos, nos pudore suffundamur (ne dicam vos) in hac fiducia gloriationis.

5. Necessarium ergo existimavi, exhortari fratres, ut ante venirent ad vos: ut præpararent ante promissam benedictionem vestram, quo in promptu sit, atque ita ut benedictio,[1] non tenacitas.

This statement may seem at first view to suit ill, or not sufficiently well, with what goes before ; for he seems to speak of a new matter, that he had not previously touched upon, while in reality he is following out the same subject. Let the reader, however, observe, that Paul treats of the very same matter that he had been treating of before—that it was from no want of confidence that he exhorted the Corinthians, and that his admonition is not coupled with any reproof as to the past, but that he has particular reasons that

---

[1] " Comme benediction, c'est a dire, don liberal, ou beneficence;"— " As a blessing, that is to say, a liberal gift or kindness."

influence him.   The meaning, then, of what he says now is
this: " I do not teach you that it is a duty to afford relief
to the saints, for what need were there of this ?   For that
is sufficiently well known to you, and you have given practical evidence that you are not prepared to be wanting to
them ;[1] but as I have, from boasting everywhere of your
liberality, pledged my credit along with yours, this consideration will not allow me to refrain from speaking."   But
for this, such anxious concern might have been somewhat
offensive to the Corinthians, because they would have
thought, either that they were reproached for their indolence, or that they were suspected by Paul.   By bringing forward, however, a most suitable apology, he secures
for himself the liberty of not merely exhorting them, without giving offence, but even from time to time urging
them.

Some one, however, may possibly suspect, that Paul here
pretends what he does not really think.   This were exceedingly absurd ; for if he reckons them to be sufficiently prepared for doing their duty, why does he set himself so vigorously to admonish them ? and, on the other hand, if he is in
doubt as to their willingness, why does he declare it to be unnecessary to admonish them ?   Love carries with it these two
things,—good hope, and anxious concern.   Never would he
have borne such a testimony in favour of the Corinthians, had
he not been fully of the mind that he expresses.   He had seen
a happy commencement: he had hoped, that the farther
progress of the matter would be corresponding ; but as he
was well aware of the unsteadiness of the human mind, he
could not provide too carefully against their turning aside
from their pious design.

1. *Ministering.* This term seems not very applicable to
those that give of their substance to the poor, inasmuch as
liberality is deserving of a more splendid designation.[2]   Paul,
however, had in view, what believers owe to their fellow-

---

[1] " Ou vous espargner en leur endroit ;"—" Or to spare yourselves as to
what you owe them."
[2] " Vn titre plus magnifique et honorable ;"—" A more magnificent and
honourable designation."

members.[1] For the members of Christ ought mutually to minister to each other. In this way, when we relieve the brethren, we do nothing more than discharge a ministry that is due to them. On the other hand, to neglect the saints, when they stand in need of our aid, is worse than inhuman, inasmuch as we defraud them of what is their due.

2. *For which I have boasted.* He shows the good opinion that he had of them from this, that he had, in a manner, stood forward as their surety by asserting their readiness. But what if he rashly asserted more than the case warranted? For there is some appearance of this, inasmuch as he boasted, that they had been *ready a year before* with it, while he is still urging them to have it in readiness. I answer, that his words are not to be understood as though Paul had declared, that what they were to give was already laid aside in the chest, but he simply mentioned what had been resolved upon among them. This involves no blame in respect of fickleness or mistake. It was, then, of this promise that Paul spoke.[2]

3. *But I have sent the brethren.* He now brings forward the reason—why it is that, while entertaining a favourable opinion as to their willingness, he, nevertheless, sets himself carefully to exhort them. " I consult," says he, " my own good name and yours ; for while I promised in your name, we would, both of us in common, incur disgrace, if words and deeds did not correspond. Hence you ought to take my fears in good part.

4. *In this confidence.* The Greek term being ὑπόστασις, the Old Interpreter has rendered it *substantiam, (substance.)*[3] Erasmus renders it *argumentum, (subject-matter,)* but neither is suitable. Budaeus, however, observes, that this term is sometimes taken to mean *boldness,* or *confidence,* as it is used by Polybius when he says, οὐχ οὕτω τὴν δύναμιν ὡς τὴν ὑπόστασιν καὶ τόλμαν αὐτοῦ καταπεπληγμένον τῶν

---

[1] " Ceux qui sont membres d'vn mesme corps auec eux ;"—" Those that are members of the same body with themselves."

[2] " Le Sainct Apostre donc parloit de ceste promesse des Corinthiens ;" —" The holy Apostle, therefore, spoke of this promise of the Corinthians."

[3] In Wiclif's version, (1380,) the rendering is, " in this substaunce ;" Rheims (1582) has, " in this substance."

ἐναντίων—" It was not so much his bodily strength, as his *boldness* and intrepidity, that proved confounding to the enemy."[1]   Hence ὑποστατικός sometimes means one that is *bold* and *confident*.[2]   Now every one must see, how well this meaning accords with Paul's thread of discourse.   Hence it appears, that other interpreters have, through inadvertency, fallen into a mistake.

5. *As a blessing, not in the way of niggardliness.*   In place of *blessing*, some render it *collection*.   I have preferred, however, to render it literally, as the Greeks employed the term εὐλογίας to express the Hebrew word ברכה, (*beracah*,) which is used in the sense of *a blessing*, that is, an invoking of prosperity, as well as in the sense of *beneficence*.[3]   The reason I reckon to be this, that it is in the first instance ascribed to God.[4]   Now we know how God blesses us efficiently by his simple nod.[5]   When it is from this transferred to men, it retains the same meaning,—improperly, indeed, inasmuch

[1] The expression here quoted from Polybius, (lib. vi. cap. 53, p. 691,) is made use of by the historian in relating a heroic exploit of Publius Horatius Cocles, who, on occasion of a sudden attempt being made upon the city of Rome by Porsena, king of Clusium, the most powerful prince at that time in Italy, having stationed himself, with singular intrepidity, on the Sublician bridge, along with two others, withstood the attack of the enemy, and effectually obstructed their progress, until the bridge was cut down from behind, after which he leaped into the river, and swam across to his friends in safety, amidst the darts of the enemy.   In honour of this daring adventure, a statue of Cocles, as is stated by Livy, (ii. 10,) was placed in the *Comitium*, and a grant of land was made to him, as much as he could plow round in one day.   *Raphelius* adduces another instance in which Polybius employs ὑπόστασις in the same sense—" When the Rhodians," says he, " perceive τὴν τῶν Βυζαντιῶν ὑπόστασιν—the *intrepidity* of the Byzantians."   (Pol. lib. vi. p. 440.)—*Ed.*

[2] The adjective ὑποστατικός is used in this sense by Aristotle, Eth. End. ii. 5, 5, and the adverb derived from it, ὑποστατικῶς, has a corresponding signification in Polybius, (lib. v. cap. 16, p. 508, line 1,) Τοῦ δὲ βασιλέως ὑποστατικῶς φήσαντος—" the king having spoken *with firmness*."—*Ed.*

[3] " Qui signifie tant benediction, c'est a dire vn souhait ou priere pour la prosperite d'autruy, que beneficence ou liberalite ;"—" Which denotes blessing—that is to say, a desire or prayer for the prosperity of another, as well as beneficence, or liberality."

[4] " Ie pense que la raison de ceste derniere signification est, pource que ce mot est en premier lieu et proprement attribue a Dieu ;"—" I think that the reason of this last signification is—because it is in the first place and properly ascribed to God."

[5] " Par la seule et simple volonte ;"—" By a mere simple exercise of the will."

as men have not the same efficacy in blessing,[1] but yet not
unsuitably by transference.[2]

To *blessing* Paul opposes πλεονεξίαν, (*grudging*,) which
term the Greeks employ to denote excessive greediness, as
well as fraud and niggardliness.[3] I have rather preferred
the term *niggardliness* in this contrast; for Paul would have
them give, not grudgingly, but with a liberal spirit, as will
appear still more clearly from what follows.

6. But this *I say*, He which soweth sparingly shall reap also sparingly; and he which soweth bountifully shall reap also bountifully.

7. Every man according as he purposeth in his heart, *so let him give;* not grudgingly, or of necessity: for God loveth a cheerful giver.

8. And God *is* able to make all grace abound toward you; that ye, always having all-sufficiency in all *things*, may abound to every good work:

9. (As it is written, He hath dispersed abroad; he hath given to the poor: his righteousness remaineth for ever.

6. Hoc autem (*est*): Qui sementem facit parce, is parce messurus est: et qui sementem facit in benedictionibus,[4] in benedictionibus[5] etiam metet.

7. Unusquisque secundum propositum cordis, non ex molestia aut necessitate: nam hilarem datorem diligit Deus.

8. Potens est autem Deus efficere, ut tota gratia in vos exuberet: ut in omnibus omnem sufficientiam habentes, exuberetis in omne opus bonum.

9. Quemadmodum scriptum est (*Ps.* cxii. 9): Dispersit, dedit pauperibus, iustitia eius manet in sæculum.

6. Now the case is this.[6] He now commends alms-giving
by a beautiful similitude, comparing it to sowing. For in
sowing, the seed is cast forth by the hand, is scattered upon
the ground on this side and on that, is harrowed, and at

[1] " Que Dieu ha ;"—" That God has."

[2] " God's blessing of us, and our blessing of God, differ exceedingly. For God blesseth us efficiently, by exhibiting his mercies to us. We bless God, not by adding any good to him, but declaratively only. God's *benedicere* is *benefacere*—his *words* are *works*, but our blessing (as Aquinas says) is only *recognoscitium*, and *expressivum*—an *acknowledgment only and celebration of that goodness which God hath.*"—*Burgesse* on 2 Cor. i. p. 127.—*Ed.*

[3] " Qui signifie tant couuoitise excessiue, ou auarice, que chichete, et quand on rogne quelque chose de ce qu'il faudroit donner;"—" Which denotes excessive covetousness or avarice, as well as niggardliness, and when one pares off something from what he should give."

[4] " En benedictions, c'est a dire, a foison et abondamment, ou liberalement;"—" In blessings, that is to say, in plenty and abundantly, or liberally."

[5] " En benedictions, ou liberalement;"—" In blessings, or liberally."

[6] " Or ie di ceci;"—" Now this I say."

length rots; and thus it seems as good as lost. The case is similar as to alms-giving. What goes from you to some other quarter seems as if it were a diminishing of what you have, but the season of harvest will come, when the fruit will be gathered. For as the Lord reckons every thing that is laid out upon the poor as given to himself, so he afterwards requites it with large interest. (Prov. xix. 17.)

Now for Paul's similitude. He that *sows sparingly* will have a poor harvest, corresponding to the sowing : he that *sows bountifully* and with a full hand, will reap a correspondingly bountiful harvest. Let this doctrine be deeply rooted in our minds, that, whenever carnal reason keeps us back from doing good through fear of loss, we may immediately defend ourselves with this shield—" But the Lord declares that we are *sowing.*" The *harvest,* however, should be explained as referring to the spiritual recompense of eternal life, as well as to earthly blessings, which God confers upon the beneficent. For God requites, not only in heaven, but also in this world, the beneficence of believers. Hence it is as though he had said, " The more beneficent you are to your neighbours, you will find the blessing of God so much the more abundantly poured out upon you." He again contrasts here *blessing* with *sparing,* as he had previously done with *niggardliness.* Hence it appears, that it is taken to mean—a large and bountiful liberality.

7. *Every one according to the purpose of his heart.* As he had enjoined it upon them to give liberally, this, also, required to be added—that liberality is estimated by God, not so much from the sum, as from the disposition. He was desirous, it is true, to induce them to give largely, in order that the brethren might be the more abundantly aided; but he had no wish to extort any thing from them against their will. Hence he exhorts them to give willingly, whatever they might be prepared to give. He places *purpose of heart* in contrast with *regret* and *constraint.* For what we do, when compelled by necessity, is not done by us with *purpose of heart,* but with reluctance.[1] Now the *necessity* meant you must understand to be what is extrinsic, as it is called—

---

[1] " Auec regret et tristesse ;"—" With regret and sadness."

that is, what springs from the influence of others. For we obey God, because it is necessary, and yet we do it willingly. We ourselves, accordingly, in that case impose a necessity of our own accord, and because the flesh is reluctant, we often even constrain ourselves to perform a duty that is necessary for us. But, when we are constrained from the influence of others, having in the mean time an inclination to avoid it, if by any means we could, we do nothing in that case with alacrity—nothing with cheerfulness, but every thing with reluctance or constraint of mind.

For God loveth a cheerful giver. He calls us back to God, as I said in the outset,[1] for alms are a sacrifice. Now no sacrifice is pleasing to God, if it is not voluntary. For when he teaches us, that *God loveth a cheerful giver,* he intimates that, on the other hand, the niggardly and reluctant are loathed by Him. For He does not wish to lord it over us, in the manner of a tyrant, but, as He acts towards us as a Father, so he requires from us the cheerful obedience of children.[2]

8. *And God is able.* Again he provides against the base thought, which our infidelity constantly suggests to us. " What ! will you not rather have a regard to your own interest ? Do you not consider, that when this is taken away, there will be so much the less left for yourself ?" With the view of driving away this, Paul arms us with a choice promise—that whatever we give away will turn out to our advantage. I have said already,[3] that we are by nature excessively niggardly—because we are prone to distrust, which tempts every one to retain with eager grasp what belongs to him. For correcting this fault, we must lay hold of this promise—that those that do good to the poor do no less provide for their own interests than if they were watering their lands. For by alms-givings, like so many canals, they make the blessing of God flow forth towards themselves, so as to be enriched by it. What Paul means is this: "Such liberality will deprive you of nothing, but God will make it return to you

---

[1] See p. 307.
[2] " Vne obeissance filiale, qui soit prompte et franche ;"—" A filial obedience, which is prompt and cheerful."
[3] See p. 294,

in much greater abundance." For he speaks of the power of God, not as the Poets do, but after the manner of Scripture, which ascribes to him a power put forth in action, the present efficacy of which we ourselves feel—not any inactive power that we merely imagine.

That having all sufficiency in all things. He mentions a twofold advantage arising from that grace, which he had promised to the Corinthians—that they should have what is enough for themselves, and would have something over and above for doing good. By the term *sufficiency* he points out the measure which the Lord knows to be useful for us, for it is not always profitable for us, to be filled to satiety. The Lord therefore, ministers to us according to the measure of our advantage, sometimes more, sometimes less, but in such a way that we are satisfied—which is much more, than if one had the whole world to luxuriate upon. In this *sufficiency* we must abound, for the purpose of doing good to others, for the reason why God does us good is—not that every one may keep to himself what he has received, but that there may be a mutual participation among us, according as necessity may require.

9. *As it is written, He hath dispersed.* He brings forward a proof from Psalms cxii. 9, where, along with other excellencies of the pious man, the Prophet mentions this, too,—that he will not be wanting in doing good, but as water flows forth incessantly from a perennial fountain, so the gushing forth of his liberality will be unceasing. Paul has an eye to this—that we be not *weary in well doing*, (Gal. vi. 9,) and this is also what the Prophet's words mean.[1]

10. Now he that ministereth seed to the sower, both minister bread for *your* food, and multiply your seed sown, and increase the fruits of your righteousness;)	10. Porro qui suppeditat semen seminanti, is et panem in cibum suppeditet, et multiplicet sementem vestram, et augeat proventus iustitiæ vestræ.

[1] Our author, when commenting on the passage here referred to, remarks: "This passage is quoted by Paul, (2 Cor. ix. 9,) in which he informs us, that it is an easy matter for God to bless us with plenty, so that we may exercise our bounty freely, deliberately, and impartially, and this accords best with the design of the Prophet."—CALVIN on the Psalms, vol. iv. p. 329.—*Ed.*

11. Being enriched in every thing to all bountifulness, which causeth through us thanksgiving to God.

11. Ut in omnibus locupletemini in omnem simplicitatem, quæ per vos producit gratiarum actionem Deo.

12. For the administration of this service not only supplieth the want of the saints, but is abundant also by many thanksgivings unto God;

12. Nam ministerium huius functionis[1] non solum supplet ea quæ desunt sanctis: verum etiam exuberat in hoc, quod per multos agantur gratiæ Deo:

13. (Whiles by the experiment of this ministration, they glorify God for your professed subjection unto the gospel of Christ, and for *your* liberal distribution unto them, and unto all *men;*)

13. Quod per probationem ministerii huius glorificant Deum super obedientia consensus vestri in Evangelium Christi: et de simplicitate communicationis in ipsos, et in omnes:

14. And by their prayer for you, which long after you for the exceeding grace of God in you.

14. Et precatione eorum pro vobis: qui desiderant vos propter eminentem Dei gratiam in vobis.

15. Thanks *be* unto God for his unspeakable gift.

15. Gratia autem Deo super inenarrabili suo munere.

10. *He that supplieth.* A beautiful circumlocution, in place of the term *God,* and full of consolation.[2] For the person that sows seed in the proper season, appears when reaping to gather the fruit of his labour and industry, and sowing appears as though it were the fountainhead from which food flows forth to us. Paul opposes this idea, by maintaining that the seed is afforded and the food is furnished by the favour of God even to the husbandmen that sow, and who are looked upon as supporting themselves and others by their efforts. There is a similar statement in Deut. viii. 16, 18—*God fed thee with manna—food which thy fathers knew not: lest perhaps when thou hast come into the land which he shall give thee, thou shouldst say, My hand and my strength have gotten me this wealth; for it is the Lord that giveth power to get wealth, &c.*

Supply. Here there are two different readings, even in the Greek versions. For some manuscripts render the three verbs in the future—*will supply, will multiply, will increase.* In this way, there would be a confirmation of the foregoing

[1] " De ceste oblation ;"—" Of this offering."

[2] " The words ὁ ἐπιχορηγῶν—βρῶσιν are a periphrasis of GOD (*i.e.,* the Good Being) ' who giveth us all things richly to enjoy.' It is formed on Isaiah lv. 10."—*Bloomfield.—Ed.*

[3] " The Vatican MS. reads with the futures—χορηγήσει, (*will supply,*) πληθύνει, (*will multiply,*) and αὐξήσει, (*will increase*)."—*Penn.—Ed.*

statement, for it is no rare thing with Paul to repeat the same promise in different words, that it may be the better impressed upon men's minds. In other manuscripts these words occur in the infinitive mood, and it is well known that the infinitive is sometimes used in place of the optative. I rather prefer this reading, both because it is the more generally received one, and because Paul is accustomed to follow up his exhortations with prayers, entreating from God what he had previously comprised in his doctrine ; though at the same time the former reading would not be unsuitable.

Bread for food. He mentions a two-fold fruit of the blessing of God upon us—*first*, that we have a sufficiency for ourselves for the support of life ; and, *secondly*, that we have something to lay up for relieving the necessities of others. For as we are not born for ourselves merely,[1] so a Christian man ought neither to live to himself, nor lay out what he has, merely for his own use.

Under the terms *seed,* and *fruits of righteousness,* he refers to *alms.* The *fruits of righteousness* he indirectly contrasts with those returns that the greater number lay up in cellars, barns, and keeping-places, that they may, every one of them, cram in whatever they can gather, nay, scrape together, so as to enrich themselves. By the *former* term he expresses the means of doing good ; by the *latter* the work itself, or office of love ;[2] for *righteousness* is taken here, by *synecdoche,* to mean *beneficence.* " May God not only supply you with what may be sufficient for every one's private use, but also to such an extent, that the fountain of your liberality, ever flowing forth, may never be exhausted !" If, however, it is one department of *righteousness*—as assuredly it is not the least[3]—to relieve the necessities of neighbours, those must be unrighteous who neglect this department of duty.

---

[1] Our Author has here very probably in his eye a celebrated passage in Horace—" Nos numerus sumus, et fruges consumere nati ;"—" We do but add to the numbers of mankind, and seem born only to consume the fruits of the earth." (Hor. Ep. i. 2, 27.)—*Ed.*

[2] " L'assistance laquelle on fait par charite ;"—" The assistance which one gives in love."

[3] " Comme a la verite s'en est vne des principales ;"— " As in truth it is one of the chief."

11. *May be enriched unto all bountifulness.* Again he makes use of the term *bountifulness,* to express the nature of true liberality—when, *casting all our care upon God,* (1 Peter v. 7,) we cheerfully lay out what belongs to us for whatever purposes he directs. He teaches us[1] that these are the true riches of believers, when, relying upon the providence of God for the sufficiency of their support, they are not by distrust kept back from doing good. Nor is it without good reason, that he dignifies with the title of affluence the satisfying abundance of a mind that is simple, and contented with its moderate share ; for nothing is more famished and starved than the distrustful, who are tormented with an anxious desire of having.

Which produces through you. He commends, in consideration of another result, the alms which they were about to bestow—that they would tend to promote the glory of God. He afterwards, too, expresses this more distinctly, with amplification, in this way : "Besides the ordinary advantage of love, they will also produce thanksgiving." Now he amplifies by saying, that *thanks will be given to God by many,* and that, not merely for the liberality itself, by which they have been helped, but also for the entire measure of piety among the Corinthians.

By the term *administration,* he means what he had undertaken at the request of the Churches. Now what we render *functionem (service),* is in the Greek λειτουργία—a term that sometimes denotes a sacrifice, sometimes any office that is publicly assigned.[2] Either of them will suit this passage

---

[1] " Or yci il nous remonstre et donne a entendre ;"—" Now here he shows us and gives us to understand."

[2] The term λειτουργία is very frequently made use of in the Septuagint, in connection with the sacrifices and other services of the priests and Levites. (See Exod. xxxviii. 21; Numb. iv. 24, and viii. 22.) It is commonly employed by the Greek writers to denote a public service, more especially at Athens, discharged by the richer citizens at their own expense, and usually in rotation. The λειτουργοὶ, says *Potter,* in his Grecian Antiquities, (vol. i. pp. 99, 100,) were " persons of considerable estates, who, by their own tribe, or the whole people, were ordered to perform some public duty, or supply the commonwealth with necessaries at their own expenses. Of these there were diverse sorts, all of which were elected out of twelve hundred of the richest citizens, who were appointed by the people to undergo, when they should be required, all the burdensome and chargeable

well.   For on the one hand, it is no unusual thing for alms
to be termed sacrifices ; and, on the other hand, as on occasion of offices being distributed among citizens,[1] no one
grudges to undertake the duty that has been assigned him,
so in the Church, imparting to others ought to be looked
upon as a necessary duty.[2]   The Corinthians, therefore, and
others, by assisting the brethren at Jerusalem, presented a
sacrifice to God, or they discharged a service that was proper, and one which they were bound to fulfil.   Paul was the
minister of that sacrifice, but the term *ministry*, or *service*,
may also be viewed as referring to the Corinthians.   It is,
however, of no particular importance.

13. *By the experiment of that administration.*   The term
experiment here, as in a variety of other places, means *proof*
or *trial*.[3]   For it was a sufficient token for bringing the love
of the Corinthians to the test—that they were so liberal to
brethren that were at a great distance from them.   Paul,
however, extends it farther—to their concurrent obedience
in the gospel.[4]   For by such proofs we truly manifest, that
we are obedient to the doctrine of the gospel.   Now their
concurrence appears from this—that alms are conferred
with the common consent of all.

14. *And their prayer.*   He omits no advantage which
may be of any use for stirring up the Corinthians.[5]   In the

offices in the commonwealth, every tribe electing an hundred and twenty
out of their own body, though this was contrary to Solon's constitution, by
which every man, of what quality soever, was obliged to serve the public
according to his ability, with this exception only, that two offices should
not be imposed on the same person at once, as we are informed by Demosthenes, in his oration against Leptines, where he likewise mentions an
ancient law, requiring every man to undergo some λειτουργία every second
year."—*Ed.*

[1] " Les charges estans distribuees, en vne ville entre les citoyens d'icelle ;"
" Offices being distributed in a town among the citizens of it."

[2] " Ainsi en l'Eglise la communication consiste en ce que chacun s'ac-
quitte enuers ses prochains de ce qu'il leur doit en charite ;"—" So in the
Church, imparting to others consists in every one's discharging to his neighbours, what he owes them, in love."

[3] " Tesmoignage, enseignement, ou experience ;"—" Proof, voucher, or
trial."

[4] " Leur obeissance qu'ils rendoyent tous d'vn accord a l'euangile ;"—
" Their obedience which they rendered, all with one accord, to the gospel."

[5] " Qui puisse seruir a esmouuoir et encourager les Corinthiens ;"—
" That may serve to stir up and encourage the Corinthians."

first place, he has made mention of the comfort that believers would experience ; *secondly*, the thanksgiving, by means of which God was to be glorified. Nay more, he has said that this would be a confession, which would manifest to all their unanimous concurrence in faith, and in pious obedience. He now adds the reward that the Corinthians would receive from the saints—good-will springing from gratitude,[1] and earnest prayers. " They will have," says he, " the means of requiting you in return ; for they will regard you with the love with which they ought, and they will be careful to commend you to God in their prayers." At length, as though he had obtained his desire, he prepares himself[2] to celebrate the praises of God, by which he was desirous to testify the confidence felt by him, as though the matter were already accomplished.

CHAPTER X.

1. Now I Paul myself beseech you by the meekness and gentleness of Christ, who in presence *am* base among you, but being absent am bold toward you :

2. But I beseech *you*, that I may not be bold when I am present with that confidence wherewith I think to be bold against some, which think of us as if we walked according to the flesh.

3. For though we walk in the flesh, we do not war after the flesh :

4. (For the weapons of our warfare *are* not carnal, but mighty through God to the pulling down of strong holds ;)

5. Casting down imaginations, and every high thing that exalteth itself against the knowledge of God, and bringing into captivity every thought to the obedience of Christ ;

1. Porro ipse ego Paulus exhortor vos[3] per lenitatem et mansuetudinem Christi, qui secundum faciem humilis quidem sum inter vos, absens autem audax sum in vos.

2. Rogo autem, ne præsens audeam ea fiducia, qua cogito audax esse in quosdam, qui nos æstimant, acsi secundum carnem ambularemus.

3. Nam in carne ambulantes, non secundum carnem militamus.

4. Siquidem arma militiæ nostræ non carnalia sunt, sed potentia Deo ad destructionem munitionum, quibus consilia destruimus.

5. Et omnem celsitudinem, quæ extollitur adversus cognitionem Dei : et captivam ducimus omnem cogitationem ad obediendum Christo :[4]

[1] " Procedante de la recognoissance du benefice qu'ils auoyent receu des Corinthiens ;"—" Proceeding from an acknowledgment of the kindness that they had received from the Corinthians."
[2] " D'vne grande affection ;"—" With great ardour."
[3] " Je vous exhorte, ou prie ;"—" I exhort or entreat you."
[4] " Et reduisons en captiuite toute intelligence, ou, amenans comme pri-

6. And having in a readiness to revenge all disobedience, when your obedience is fulfilled.	6. Et in promptu habemus vindictam adversus omnem inobedientiam, quum impleta fuerit vestra obedientia.

Having finished his exhortation, he now proceeds partly to refute the calumnies with which he had been defamed by the false apostles, and partly to repress the insolence[1] of certain wicked persons, who could not bear to be under restraint. Both parties, with the view of destroying Paul's authority, construed the vehemence with which he thundered in his Epistles to be θρασοδειλίαν—(*mere bravado*,)[2] because when present he was not equally prepared to show himself off in respect of appearance, and address, but was mean and contemptible. " See," said they, " here is a man, that, under a consciousness of his inferiority, is so very modest and timid, but now, when at a distance, makes a fierce attack! Why is he less bold in speech than in letters? Will *he* terrify us, when he is at a distance, who, when present, is the object of contempt? How comes he to have such confidence as to imagine, that he is at liberty to do anything with us?"[3] They put speeches of this kind into circulation, with the view of disparaging his strictness, and even rendering it odious. Paul replies, that he is not *bold* except in so far as he is constrained by necessity, and that the meanness of his bodily presence, for which he was held in contempt, detracted nothing from his authority, inasmuch as he was distinguished by spiritual excellence, not by carnal show. Hence those would not pass with impunity, who derided either his exhortations, or his reproaches, or his threatenings. The words *I myself* are emphatic; as though he had said, that however the malevolent might blame him for inconstancy, he was in reality not changeable, but remained uniformly the same.

sonnier, toute," &c. ;—" And we bring into captivity every thought, or, leading forth as a prisoner every," &c.

[1] " L'insolence et audace ;"—" The insolence and audacity."

[2] " Vne hardiesse d'vn vanterau ;"—" The boldness of a braggadocio." Θρασοδειλία is a compound of θράσος (*boldness*) and δείλια (*timidity*.)

[3] " Qu'il pense auoir toute authorite sur nous ;"—" That he thinks he has entire authority over us."

1. *I exhort you.* The speech is abrupt, as is frequently the case with speeches uttered under the influence of strong feeling. The meaning is this: " I beseech you, nay more, I earnestly entreat you by the *gentleness of Christ,* not to compel me, through your obstinacy, to be more severe than I would desire to be, and than I will be, towards those who despise me, on the ground of my having nothing excellent in external appearance, and do not recognise that spiritual excellence, with which the Lord has distinguished me, and by which I ought rather to be judged of."

The form of entreaty, which he makes use of, is taken from the subject in hand, when he says—*by the meekness and gentleness of Christ.* Calumniators took occasion to find fault with him, because his bodily presence was deficient in dignity,[1] and because, on the other hand, when at a distance, he thundered forth in his Epistles. Both calumnies he befittingly refutes, as has been said, but he declares here, that nothing delights him more than *gentleness,* which becomes a minister of Christ, and of which the Master himself furnished an example. *Learn of me,* says he, *for I am meek and lowly. My yoke is easy and my burden is light.* (Matt. xi. 29, 30.) The Prophet also says of him, *His voice will not be heard in the streets : a bruised reed he shall not break,* &c. (Isaiah xlii. 2, 3.) That gentleness, therefore, which Christ showed, he requires also from his servants. Paul, in making mention of it, intimates that he is no stranger to it.[2] " I earnestly beseech you not to despise that *gentleness,* which Christ showed us in his own person, and shows us every day in his servants, nay more, which ye see in me."

Who in presence. He repeats this, as if in the person of his adversaries, by way of imitating them.[3] Now he confesses, so far as words go, what they upbraided him with, yet, as we shall see, in such a way as to concede nothing to them in reality.

---

[1] " Auoit bien peu de dignite et maieste en apparence ;"—" Had very little dignity and majesty in appearance."

[2] " Il n'est pas nouueau a la pratiquer ;"—" He is no stranger to the practice of it."

[3] " En contrefaisant les propos qu'ils tenoyent de luy ;"—" By imitating the speeches that they uttered respecting him."—See vol. i. p. 65.

2. *I beseech you, that I may not be bold, when I am present.*
Some think, that the discourse is incomplete, and that he
does not express the matter of his request.[1] I am rather of
opinion, however, that what was wanting in the former
clause is here completed, so that it is a general exhortation :
" Show yourselves docile and tractable towards me, that I
may not be constrained to be more severe." It is the duty
of a good pastor to allure his sheep peacefully and kindly,
that they may allow themselves to be governed, rather than
to constrain them by violence. Severity, it is true, is, I acknowledge, sometimes necessary, but we must always set out
with *gentleness*, and persevere in it, so long as the hearer shews
himself tractable.[2] Severity must be the last resource. " We
must," says he, " try all methods, before having recourse to
rigour ; nay more, let us never be rigorous, unless we are
constrained to it." In the mean time, as to their reckoning
themselves pusillanimous and timid, when he had to come
to close quarters, he intimates that they were mistaken as
to this, when he declares that he will stoutly resist face to
face the contumacious.[3] " They despise me," says he, " as
if I were a pusillanimous person, but they will find that I
am braver and more courageous than they could have wished,
when they come to contend in good earnest." From this
we see, *when* it is time to act with severity—after we have
found, on trial being made, that allurements and mildness
have no good effect. " I shall do it with reluctance," says
Paul, " but still I have determined to do it." Here is an admirable medium ; for as we must, in so far as is in our power,
draw men rather than *drive* them, so, when mildness has no
effect, in dealing with those that are stern and refractory,
rigour must of necessity be resorted to : otherwise it will not
be moderation, nor equableness of temper, but criminal
cowardice.[4]

Who account of us. Erasmus renders it—" Those who

---

[1] " Et le sens seroit, Ie vous prie, afin qu'il ne faille point vser de
hardiesse ;"—" And the meaning would be, I beseech you, in order that I
may not have occasion to use boldness."

[2] " Docile et traittable ;"—" Teachable and tractable."

[3] " Aux rebelles et obstinez ;"—" The rebellious and obstinate."

[4] " Couardice ou nonchalance ;"—" Cowardice or indifference."

think that we walk, as it were, according to the flesh." The Old Interpreter came nearer, in my opinion, to Paul's true meaning—" Qui nos arbitrantur, tanquam secundum carnem ambulemus ;"—(" Those who think of us as though we walked according to the flesh ;"[1]) though, at the same time, the phrase is not exactly in accordance with the Latin idiom, nor does it altogether bring out the Apostle's full meaning. For λογιζεσθαι is taken here to mean—*reckoning* or *esteeming*.[2] " They think of us," says Paul, " or they take this view of us, as though we walked according to the flesh."

To walk according to the flesh, Chrysostom explains to mean—acting unfaithfully, or conducting one's self improperly in his office;[3] and, certainly, it is taken in this sense in various instances in Paul's writings. The term *flesh,* however, I rather understand to mean—outward pomp or show, by which alone the false Apostles are accustomed to recommend themselves. Paul, therefore, complains of the unreasonableness of those who looked for nothing in him except the *flesh,* that is, visible appearance, as they speak, or in the usual manner of persons who devote all their efforts to ambition. For as Paul did not by any means excel in such endowments, as ordinarily procure praise or reputation among the *children of this world,* (Luke xvi. 8,) he was despised as though he had been one of the common herd. But by whom ?[4]

---

[1] Wiclif (1380) renders it : " that demen" (*i.e., judge*) " us as if we wandren aftir the fleisch." Tyndale (1534,) Cranmer (1539,) and Geneva (1557,) read as follows : " which repute us as though we walked carnally." Rheims (1582)—" which thinke us as though we walke according to the flesh."—*Ed.*

[2] " The sense is, ' I entreat, I say, that I may not have to be bold when I am *present,* with that confidence, wherewith I intend to be bold against certain, who regard me as *walking after the flesh,*' i.e., guided by worldly principles. There seems to be a *paranomasia* in λογίζομαι and λογιζομένους, which, if introduced into English, may perhaps be best expressed by *reckon.*"—*Bloomfield.—Ed.*

[3] " Nec satis recte (ut opinor) Chrysostomus κατὰ σάρκα perinde exposuit, acsi accusaretur Apostolus eo nomine quod Spiritu Dei non duceretur, sed pravis carnis affectibus ;"—" Nor is it altogether with propriety, in my opinion, that Chrysostom has explained κατὰ σάρκα, as if the Apostle were accused on this ground—that he was not led by the Spirit of God, but by the depraved affections of the flesh."—*Beza —Ed.*

[4] " Mais qui estoyent ceux qui le mesprisoyent ainsi ?"—" But who are those that despised him thus ?"

Certainly, by the ambitious, who estimated him from mere appearance, while they paid no regard to what lay concealed within.

3. *For though we walk in the flesh.* *Walking in the flesh* means here—*living in the world ;* or, as he expresses it elsewhere, *being at home in the body.* (2 Cor. v. 6.) For he was shut up in the prison of his body. This, however, did not prevent the influence of the Holy Spirit from showing itself marvellously in his weakness. There is here again a kind of concession, which, at the same time, is of no service to his adversaries.

Those *war according to the flesh,* who attempt nothing but in dependence upon worldly resources, in which alone, too, they glory. They have not their confidence placed in the government and guidance of the Holy Spirit. Paul declares that he is not one of this class, inasmuch as he is furnished with other weapons than those of the flesh and the world. Now, what he affirms respecting himself is applicable, also, to all true ministers of Christ.[1] For they *carry an inestimable treasure in earthen vessels,* as he had previously said. (2 Cor. iv. 7.) Hence, however they may be surrounded with the infirmities of the flesh, the spiritual power of God, nevertheless, shines forth resplendently in them.

4. *For the weapons of our warfare.* The warfare corresponds with the kind of weapons. He glories in being furnished with *spiritual* weapons. The warfare, accordingly, is *spiritual.* Hence it follows by way of contraries,[2] that it is not *according to the flesh.* In comparing the ministry of the gospel to a *warfare,* he uses a most apt similitude. The life of a Christian, it is true, is a perpetual warfare, for whoever gives himself to the service of God will have no truce from Satan at any time, but will be harassed with incessant disquietude. It becomes, however, ministers of the word and pastors to be standard-bearers, going before the others ; and, certainly, there are none that Satan harasses more,

---

[1] " Tous vrais seruiteurs et ministres de Jesus Christ ;"—" All true servants and ministers of Jesus Christ."

[2] " Par vn argument prins (comme on appelle) des choses contraires ;" —" By an argument taken (as the expression is) from things contrary."

that are more severely assaulted, or that sustain more numerous or more dreadful onsets. That man, therefore, is mistaken, who girds himself for the discharge of this office, and is not at the same time furnished with courage and bravery for contending; for he is not exercised otherwise than in fighting. For we must take this into account, that the gospel is like a fire, by which the fury of Satan is enkindled. Hence it cannot but be that he will arm himself for a contest, whenever he sees that it is advanced.

But by what weapons is he to be repelled? It is only by spiritual weapons that he can be repelled. Whoever, therefore, is unarmed with the influence of the Holy Spirit, however he may boast that he is a minister of Christ, will nevertheless, not prove himself to be such. At the same time, if you would have a full enumeration of spiritual weapons, doctrine must be conjoined with zeal, and a good conscience with the efficacy of the Spirit, and with other necessary graces. Let now the Pope go, and assume to himself the apostolic dignity.[1] What could be more ridiculous, if our judgment is to be formed in accordance with the rule here laid down by Paul!

Mighty through God. Either *according to God*, or *from God*. I am of opinion, that there is here an implied antithesis, so that this *strength* is placed in contrast with the *weakness* which appears outwardly before the world, and thus, paying no regard to the judgments of men, he would seek from God approbation of his fortitude.[2] At the same time, the *antithesis* will hold good in another sense—that the power of his arms depends upon God, not upon the world.

In the demolishing of fortresses. He makes use of the term *fortresses* to denote contrivances, and every high thing that is exalted against God,[3] as to which we shall find him

---

[1] " Qu'il s'attribue tant qu'il voudra le titre de dignite Apostolique ;"— " Let him assume to himself, as much as he pleases, the title of Apostolic dignity."

[2] " Ainsi le sens seroit, que laissant là tous les jugemens des hommes, il se retireroit vers Dieu pour auoir approbation de sa force ;"—" Thus the meaning would be, that, disregarding all the judgments of men, he would direct his view God-ward to have approbation of his fortitude."

[3] " The word here rendered *strongholds* ($\delta\chi\upsilon\rho\dot\omega\mu\alpha\tau\alpha$) means properly— fastnesses, fortresses, or strong fortifications. It is here beautifully used

speaking afterwards. It is, however, with propriety and expressiveness that he so designates them ; for his design is to
boast, that there is nothing in the world so strongly fortified
as to be beyond his power to overthrow. I am well aware
how carnal men glory in their empty shows, and how disdainfully and recklessly they despise me, as though there
were nothing in me but what is mean and base, while they,
in the mean time, were standing on a lofty eminence. But
their confidence is foolish, for that armour of the Lord, with
which I fight, will prevail in opposition to all the bulwarks,
in reliance upon which they believe themselves to be invincible. Now, as the world is accustomed to fortify itself in a
twofold respect for waging war with Christ—on the one
hand, by cunning, by wicked artifices, by subtilty, and other
secret machinations ; and, on the other hand, by cruelty and
oppression, he touches upon both these methods. For by
contrivances he means, whatever pertains to carnal wisdom.

The term *high thing* denotes any kind of glory and power
in this world. There is no reason, therefore, why a servant
of Christ should dread anything, however formidable, that
may stand up in opposition to his doctrine. Let him, in
spite of it, persevere, and he will scatter to the winds every
machination of whatever sort. Nay more, the kingdom of
Christ cannot be set up or established, otherwise than by
throwing down everything in the world that is exalted.
For nothing is more opposed to the spiritual wisdom of God
than the wisdom of the flesh ; nothing is more at variance
with the grace of God than man's natural ability, and so as
to other things. Hence the only foundation of Christ's
kingdom is the abasement of men. And to this effect are

to denote the various obstacles, resembling a *fortress*, which exist, and
which are designed and adapted to oppose the truth and the triumph of
the Christian's cause.   All these obstacles are strongly *fortified*. . . . . .
The whole world is *fortified* against Christianity ; and the nations of the
earth have been engaged in little else, than in raising and strengthening
such strongholds for the space of six thousand years.   The Christian religion goes forth against all the combined and concentrated powers of
resistance of the whole world ; and the warfare is to be waged against
every strongly *fortified* place of error and of sin.   These strong *fortifications* of error and of sin are to be battered down and laid in ruins by our
spiritual weapons."—*Barnes.—Ed.*

those expressions in the Prophets: *The moon shall be ashamed, and the sun shall be confounded, when the Lord shall begin to reign in that day :* Again, *The loftiness of man shall be bowed down, and the high looks of mortals shall be abased, and the Lord alone shall be exalted in that day.* (Isaiah v. 15, and ii. 17.) Because, in order that God alone may shine forth, it is necessary that the glory of the world should vanish away.

5. *And bring into captivity.* I am of opinion, that, having previously spoken more particularly of the conflict of spiritual armour, along with the hinderances that rise up in opposition to the gospel of Christ, he now, on the other hand, speaks of the ordinary preparation, by which men must be brought into subjection to him. For so long as we rest in our own judgment, and are wise in our own estimation, we are far from having made any approach to the doctrine of Christ. Hence we must set out with this, that *he who is wise must become a fool,* (1 Cor. iii. 18,) that is, we must give up our own understanding, and renounce the wisdom of the flesh, and thus we must present our minds to Christ empty that he may fill them. Now the form of expression must be observed, when he says, that he *brings every thought into captivity,* for it is as though he had said, that the liberty of the human mind must be restrained and bridled, that it may not be wise, apart from the doctrine of Christ ; and farther, that its audacity cannot be restrained by any other means, than by its being carried away, as it were, *captive.* Now it is by the guidance of the Spirit, that it is brought to allow itself to be placed under control, and remain in a voluntary captivity.

6. *And are in readiness to avenge.* This he adds, lest insolent men should presumptuously lift themselves up in opposition to his ministry, as if they could do so with impunity. Hence he says, that power had been given him—not merely for constraining voluntary disciples to subjection to Christ, but also for inflicting *vengeance* upon the rebellious,[1] and that his threats were not empty bugbears,[2] but had the

---

[1] " Des-rebelles et obstinez ;"—" Upon the rebellious and obstinate."

[2] " Pour faire peur (comme on dit) aux petits enfans ;"—" To frighten (as they say) little children."

execution quite in readiness—to use the customary expression. Now this vengeance is founded on Christ's word—*whatsoever ye shall bind on earth shall be bound also in heaven.* (Matt. xviii. 18.) For although God does not thunder forth immediately on the minister's pronouncing the sentence, yet the decision is ratified,[1] and will be accomplished in its own time. Let it, however, be always understood, that it is when the minister fights with spiritual armour. Some understand it as referring to bodily punishments, by means of which the Apostles inflicted vengeance upon contumacious and impious persons ; as for example, Peter struck Ananias and Sapphira dead, and Paul struck Elymas the sorcerer blind. (Acts v. 1-10, and xiii. 6-11.) But the other meaning suits better, for the Apostles did not make use of that power invariably or indiscriminately. Paul, however, speaks in general terms—that he has *vengeance* ready at hand against all the disobedient.

When your obedience shall be fulfilled. How prudently he guards against alienating any by excessive severity ! For as he had threatened to inflict punishment upon the rebellious, that he may not seem to provoke them, he declares that another duty had been enjoined upon him with regard to them—simply that of making them obedient to Christ. And, unquestionably, this is the proper intention of the gospel, as he teaches both in the commencement and in the close of the Epistle to the Romans. (Rom. i. 5, and xvi. 26.) Hence all Christian teachers ought carefully to observe this order, that they should first endeavour with gentleness to bring their hearers to obedience, so as to invite them kindly before proceeding to inflict punishment upon rebellion.[2] Hence, too, Christ[3] has given the commandment as to *loosing* before that of *binding.*[4]

---

[1] " Ferme et stable ;"—" Firm and stable."

[2] " Auant qu'entrer à les menacer, et leur denoncer la peine de rebellion ;"—" Before proceeding to threaten them, and denounce upon them the punishment of rebellion."

[3] " Et pour ceste cause Jesus Christ luy-mesme ;"—" And for this reason Jesus Christ himself."

[4] CALVIN manifestly alludes here to John xx. 23, in commenting on which he says, " As the embassy of salvation and of eternal life has been committed to the Apostles, so, on the other hand, they have been armed

7. Do ye look on things after the outward appearance? If any man trust to himself that he is Christ's, let him of himself think this again, that, as he *is* Christ's, even so *are* we Christ's.

8. For though I should boast somewhat more of our authority, which the Lord hath given us for edification, and not for your destruction, I should not be ashamed:

9. That I may not seem as if I would terrify you by letters.

10. For *his* letters, say they, *are* weighty and powerful; but *his* bodily presence *is* weak, and *his* speech contemptible.

11. Let such an one think this, that such as we are in word by letters when we are absent, such *will we be* also in deed when we are present.

7. Quæ secundum faciem sunt videtis: si quis sibi confidit, quia sit Christi, hoc reputet etiam ex se ipso rursum, quod sicuti ipse Christi, ita et nos Christi.

8. Nam etsi abundantius glorier de potestate nostra, quam dedit nobis Dominus in ædificationem, et non in destructionem vestram, non pudefiam;

9. Ne autem videar terrere vos per Epistolas.

10. (Siquidem Epistolæ, inquiunt, graves sunt ac robustæ; præsentia autem corporis infirma, et sermo contemptus.)

11. Hoc cogitet qui talis est, quod quales sumus absentes, sermone per Epistolas, tales sumus etiam præsentes, opere.

7. *That are according to appearance.* In the first place, the clause *according to appearance,* may be taken in two ways: either as meaning the reality itself, visible and manifest, or an outward mask,[1] that deceives us. The sentence, too, may be read either interrogatively or affirmatively: nay more, the verb βλέπετε may be taken either in the imperative mood, or in the subjunctive. I am rather of opinion, however, that it is expressive of chiding, and that the Corinthians are reproved, because they suffered their eyes to be dazzled with empty show. "You greatly esteem others who swell out with mighty airs of importance, while you look down upon me, because I have nothing of show and boast-

with *vengeance* against all the ungodly, who reject the salvation offered to them, as Paul teaches. (2 Cor. x. 6.) But this is placed last in order, because it was proper that the true and real design of preaching the gospel should be first exhibited. That we are reconciled to God belongs to the nature of the gospel; that believers are adjudged to eternal life may be said to be accidentally connected with it. For this reason, Paul, in the passage which I lately quoted, when he threatens vengeance against unbelievers, immediately adds—*after that your obedience shall have been fulfilled;* (2 Cor. x. 6;) for he means, that it belongs peculiarly to the gospel to invite all to salvation, but that it is accidental to it that it brings destruction to any."—CALVIN on John, vol. ii. p. 273.—*Ed.*

[1] "La masque et apparence exterieure;"—"An outward mask and appearance."

ing." For Christ himself contrasts the *judgment that is according to appearance* with *righteous judgment.* (John vii. 24, and viii. 15.) Hence he reproves the Corinthians, because, contenting themselves with show, or appearance, they did not seriously consider, what kind of persons ought to be looked upon as the servants of Christ.

If any one trusteth in himself—an expression that is full of great confidence, for he takes it, as it were, for granted, that he is so certainly a minister of Christ, that this distinction cannot be taken from him. " Whoever," says he, " is desirous to be looked upon as a minister of Christ, must necessarily count me in along with himself." For what reason ? " *Let him,*" says he, " *think for himself,* for whatever things he may have in himself, that make him worthy of such an honour, the same will he find in me." By this he hinted to them, that, whoever they might be that reviled him, ought not to be looked upon as the servants of Christ. It would not become all to speak thus confidently, for it might certainly happen—nay, it happens every day, that the same claim is haughtily advanced by persons, that are of no reputation, and are nothing else than a dishonour to Christ.[1] Paul, however, affirmed nothing respecting himself but what he had openly given proof of by clear and sure evidences among the Corinthians. Now should any one, while destitute of all proof of the reality, recommend himself in a similar manner, what would he do but expose himself to ridicule ? To *trust in one's self* is equivalent to assuming to one's self power and authority on the pretext that he serves Christ, while he is desirous to be held in estimation.

8. *For though I should boast more largely of my authority.* It was a sign of modesty, that he put himself into the number of those, whom he greatly excelled. At the same time, he was not disposed to show such modesty, as not to retain his authority unimpaired. He accordingly adds, that he had said less than his authority entitled him to say ; for he was not one of the ordinary class of ministers, but was

---

[1] " Vn tas de garnement ;"—" A band of profligates."

even distinguished among the Apostles. Hence he says: " Though I should boast more, *I should not be ashamed,* for there will be good ground for it." He anticipates an objection, because he does not fail to speak of his own glory, while at the same time he refrains from making farther mention of it, that the Corinthians may understand, that, if he boasts, it is against his will, as in truth the false Apostles constrained him to it ; otherwise he would not have done so.

By the term *power* he means—the authority of his Apostleship, which he had among the Corinthians, for, though all the ministers of the word have the same office in common, there are, nevertheless, degrees of honour. Now God had placed Paul on a higher eminence than others, inasmuch as he had made use of his endeavours for founding[1] that Church, and had in many ways put honour upon his Apostleship. Lest, however, malevolent persons should stir up odium against him, on the ground of his making use of the term *power,* he adds the purpose for which it was given him —the salvation of the Corinthians. Hence it follows, that it ought not to be irksome to them, or grievous, for who would not bear patiently, nay more, who would not love what he knows to be of advantage to him ? In the mean time, there is an implied contrast between *his* power, and that in which the false Apostles gloried—which was of such a nature, that the Corinthians received no advantage from it, and experienced no edification. There can, however, be no doubt, that all the ministers of the word are, also, furnished with *power ;* for of what sort were a preaching of the word, that was without *power ?* Hence it is said to all— *He that heareth you, heareth me ; he that rejecteth you, rejecteth me.* (Luke x. 16.)

As, however, many, on false grounds, claim for themselves what they have not, we must carefully observe, how far Paul extends his *power*—so as to be to the edification of believers. Those, then, who exercise *power* in the way of destroying the Church, prove themselves to be tyrants, and robbers—not pastors. In the *second* place, we must observe,

---

[1] " Pour fonder et batir ;"—" For founding and building up."

that he declares, that it was given to him by God. He, therefore, that is desirous to have any thing in his power to do, must have God as the Author of his power. Others, it is true, will boast of this also, as the Pope with full mouth thunders forth, that he is Christ's vicar. But what evidence does he give of this?[1] For Christ has not conferred *power* of this kind upon dumb persons, but upon the Apostles, and his other ministers, that the doctrine of his Gospel might not be without defence. Hence the whole *power* of ministers is included in the word—but in such a way, nevertheless, that Christ may always remain Lord and Master. Let us, therefore, bear in mind, that in lawful authority these two things are required—that it be given by God, and that it be exercised for the welfare of the Church. It is well known, who they are, on whom God has conferred this *power*, and in what way he has limited the power he has given. Those exercise it in a proper manner, who faithfully obey his commandment.

Here, however, a question may be proposed. " God says to Jeremiah, Behold, I set thee over the nations, and kingdoms, *to plant, and to pluck up, to build and to destroy.* (Jer. i. 10.) We have, also, found it stated a little before, (verse 5,) that the Apostles were set apart on the same footing— that they might destroy every thing that exalted itself against Christ. Nay more, the teachers of the gospel cannot build up in any other way, than by destroying the old man. Besides, they preach the gospel to the condemnation and destruction of the wicked." I answer that, what Paul says here, has nothing to do with the wicked, for he addresses the Corinthians, to whom he wished his Apostleship to be beneficial. With regard to them, I say, he could do nothing but with a view to edification. We have already observed, also, that this was expressly stated, that the Corinthians might know, that the authority of this holy man was not assailed by any one but Satan, the enemy of their salvation, while the design of that authority was their edification.

---

[1] " Mais que fait-il? quel tesmoignage en rend-il, pour luy adiouster foy ;"—" But what does he do? what proof does he give of it, that credit may be given him ?"

At the same time, it is in other respects true in a general way, that the doctrine of the gospel has in its own nature a tendency to *edification*—not to *destruction*. For as to its destroying, that comes from something apart from itself— from the fault of mankind, while they stumble at the stone that was appointed for them as a *foundation*. (1 Peter ii. 8.) As to the fact, that we are renewed after the image of God by the destruction of the old man—that is not at all at variance with Paul's words, for in that case destruction is taken in a good sense, but here in a bad sense, as meaning the ruin of what is God's, or as meaning the destruction of the soul—as if he had said, that his *power* was not injurious to them, for instead of this the advantage of it for their sal- vation was manifest.

9. *That I may not seem to terrify.* Again he touches on the calumny which he had formerly refuted, (verse 1,) that he was bold in his writings, while in their presence his courage failed him. On this pretext they disparaged his writings.[1] "What!" said they, "will he terrify us by letters when at a distance, while, if present with us, he would scarcely venture to mutter a word!" Lest, therefore, his letters should have less weight, he answers, that no objection is advanced against him, that should either destroy or weaken his credit, and that of his doctrine, for *deeds* were not to be less valued than *words*. He was not less powerful in actions when present, than he was by words when absent. Hence it was unfair, that his bodily presence should be looked upon as contemptible. By *deed*, here, he means, in my opinion, the efficacy and success of his preaching, as well as the excellences that were worthy of an Apostle, and his whole manner of life. *Speech*, on the other hand, denotes—not the very substance of doctrine, but simply the form of it, and the bark, so to speak : for he would have contended for doctrine with greater keenness. The contempt, however, proceeded from this—that he was deficient in that ornament and splendour of eloquence, which secures favour.[2]

---

[1] " Ils rendoyent ses ecrits contemptibles ;"—" They made his writings contemptible."

[2] " Par laquelle on acquiert grace enuers les hommes ;"—" By which they acquire favour among men."

12. For we dare not make ourselves of the number, or compare ourselves with some that commend themselves: but they, measuring themselves by themselves, and comparing themselves among themselves, are not wise.

13. But we will not boast of things without *our* measure, but according to the measure of the rule which God hath distributed to us, a measure to reach even unto you.

14. For we stretch out ourselves beyond *our measure*, as though we reached not unto you; for we are come as far as to you also in *preaching* the gospel of Christ:

15. Not boasting of things without *our* measure, *that is*, of other men's labours ; but having hope, when your faith is increased, that we shall be enlarged by you according to our rule abundantly,

16. To preach the gospel in the *regions* beyond you, *and* not to boast in another man's line of things made ready to our hand.

17. But he that glorieth, let him glory in the Lord.

18. For not he that commendeth himself is approved, but whom the Lord commendeth.

12. Non enim audemus nos quibusdam inserere aut comparare, qui se ipsos commendant: verum ipsi in se ipsis se metientes, et se ipsos comparantes sibi, non sapiunt.

13. Nos autem non sine modo gloriabimur, sed pro mensura regulæ, quam nobis distribuit Deus: mensura, inquam, perveniendi etiam usque ad vos.

14. Non enim quasi ad vos non perveniremus, supra modum extendimus nos ipsos : siquidem usque ad vos pertigimus in Evangelio Christi.

15. Non gloriantes sine modo in alienis laboribus,[1] spem autem habentes, crescente fide vestra in vobis, nos magnificatum iri secundum nostram regulam in exuberantiam.

16. Ut etiam ultra vos evangelizem, non in aliena regula, ut de iis, quæ parata sunt, glorier.

17. Cæterum qui gloriatur in Domino glorietur.

18. Non enim qui se ipsum commendat, ille probatus est : sed quem Dominus commendat.

12. *For we dare not.*   He says this by way of *irony*, for afterwards he does not merely compare himself boldly with them, but, deriding their vanity, he leaves them far behind him.   Now by this *irony* he gives a stroke, not merely to those foolish boasters,[2] but also to the Corinthians, who encouraged them in their folly by their misdirected approbation.   " I am satisfied," says he, " with my moderate way ; for I would not dare to put myself on a footing with your Apostles, who are the heralds of their own excellence.   In the mean time, when he intimates that their glory consists of mere speaking and boasting, he shows, how silly and worth-

---

[1] " Ne nous glorifians point outre mesure es labeurs d'autres, *ou*, Ne nous glorifians point en ce qui n'est point de *nostre* mesure, *c'est à dire*," &c. ;—" Not boasting beyond measure in the labours of others, *or*, not boasting in what is not within *our* measure, *that is to say*," &c.

[2] *Thrasones.*—See vol. i. p. 98, *n*. 1.

less they are, while he claims for himself deeds instead of
words, that is, true and solid ground of glorying. He may
seem, however, to err in the very thing for which he reproves
others, for he immediately afterwards commends himself. I
answer, that his design must be taken into view, for those
do not aim at their own commendation, who, entirely free
from ambition, have no desire but to serve the Lord usefully.[1]
As to this passage, however, there is no need of any other
explanation than what may be gathered from the words
themselves, for those are said to *commend themselves*, who,
while in poverty and starvation as to true praise, exalt
themselves in vain-glorious boasting, and falsely give out,
that they are what they are not. This, also, appears from
what follows.

But they measure themselves by themselves. Here he points
out, as with his finger, their folly. The man that has but
one eye sees well enough among the blind : the man that
is dull of hearing hears distinctly enough among the totally
deaf. Such were those that were satisfied with themselves,
and showed themselves off among others, simply because
they did not look to any that were superior to themselves,
for if they had compared themselves with Paul, or any one
like him, they would have felt constrained to lay aside immediately that foolish impression which they entertained,
and would have exchanged boasting for shame.

For an explanation of this passage we need look no farther than to the monks ; for as they are almost all of them
the most ignorant asses, and at the same time are looked
upon as learned persons, on account of their long robe and
hood, if any one has merely a slight smattering of elegant
literature, he proudly spreads out his feathers like a pea-
cock—a marvellous fame goes abroad respecting him—
among his companions he is adored.[2] Were, however, the

---

[1] " Car ceux qui estans vuides de toute ambition, desirent seulement de
seruir a Dieu auec fruit et proufit, ne regardent point a se priser eux-
mesmes;"—" For those who being void of all ambition, simply desire to
serve God with advantage and profit, have no view to exalt themselves."

[2] " The principal places in the public schools of learning were filled very
frequently by monks of the mendicant orders. This unhappy circumstance prevented their emerging from that ignorance and darkness which

mask of the hood laid aside,[1] and a thorough examination
entered upon, their vanity would at once be discovered.
Why so ? The old proverb holds good: " Ignorance is pert."[2]
But the excessively insolent arrogance of the monks[3] proceeds chiefly from this—that they *measure themselves by
themselves;* for, as in their cloisters there is nothing but
barbarism,[4] it is not to be wondered, if the man that has
but one eye is a king among the blind. Such were Paul's
rivals, for inwardly they flattered themselves, not considering what virtues entitled a person to true praise, and how
far short they came of the excellence of Paul, and those like
him.   And, certainly, this single consideration might justly
have covered them with shame, but it is the just punishment of the ambitious, that by their silliness they expose
themselves to ridicule, (than which there is nothing that they
are more desirous to avoid,) and in place of glory, which
they are immoderately desirous of,[5] they incur disgrace.

13. *But we will not boast beyond our measure.* He now
contrasts his own moderation with the folly of the false
Apostles,[6] and, at the same time, he shows what is the true
measure of glorying—when we keep within the limits that

had so long enveloped them ; and it also rendered them inaccessible to
that auspicious light of improved science, whose salutary beams had
already been felt in several of the European provinces.   The instructors
of youth, dignified with the venerable titles of Artists, Grammarians,
Physicians, and Dialecticians, loaded the memories of their laborious
pupils with a certain quantity of barbarous terms, arid and senseless distinctions, and scholastic precepts delivered in the most inelegant style, and
all such that could repeat this jargon with a certain readiness and rapidity
were considered as men of uncommon eloquence and erudition.   The whole
body of the philosophers extolled Aristotle beyond all measure, while
scarcely any studied him, and none understood him."—*Mosheim's* Ecclesiastical History, (Lond. 1825,) vol. iv. p. 22.—*Ed.*

[1] " Laisser derriere ceste masque de frocs et coqueluches ;"—" To
leave behind that mask of frocks and cowls."

[2] Our author quotes the same proverb in vol. i. p. 460 ; and also when
commenting on 1 Tim. i. 7.—*Ed.*

[3] " Ceste arrogance intolerable des moines ;"—" This intolerable arrogance of the monks."

[4] " Pure barbarie et bestise ;"—" Mere barbarism and stupidity."

[5] " Laquelle ils appetent par moyens mal propres ;"—" Which they aim
at by improper means."

[6] " Il oppose maintenant sa modestie a la sotte outrecuidance des faux-
apostres ;"—" He now contrasts his modesty with the foolish presumption
of the false Apostles."

have been marked out for us by the Lord. " Has the Lord given me such a thing? I shall be satisfied with this measure. I shall not either desire or claim to myself any thing more." This he calls the *measure of his rule.*[1] For every one's rule, according to which he ought to regulate himself is this—God's gift and calling. At the same time, it is not lawful for us to glory in God's gift and calling on our own account, but merely in so far as it is expedient for the glory of him, who is so liberal to us with this view—that we may acknowledge ourselves indebted to him for everything.[2]

A measure to reach. By this clause he intimates, that he stands in no need of commendations expressed in words among the Corinthians, who were a portion of his glory, as he says elsewhere, (Phil. iv. 1,) *ye are my crown.* He carries out, however, the form of expression, which he had previously entered upon. " I have," says he, " a most ample field for glorying, so as not to go beyond my own limits, and you are one department of that field." He modestly reproves, how-

---

[1] " Within the measured and determinate limits of the stadium, the athletæ were bound to contend for the prize, which they forfeited without hope of recovery, if they deviated even a little from the appointed course. In allusion to this inviolable arrangement, the Apostle tells the Corinthians: *We will not boast of things without our measure,* &c. It may help very much to understand this and the following verses, if, with Hammond, we consider the terms used in them as *agonistical.* In this view of them, the ' measure of the rule' (τὸ μέτρον τοῦ κανόνος) alludes to the path marked out, and bounded by a white line, for racers in the Isthmian games, celebrated among the Corinthians; and so the Apostle represents his work in preaching the gospel as his spiritual race, and the province to which he was appointed as the compass or stage of ground, which God had distributed or measured out (ἐμέρισεν αὐτῳ) for him to run in. Accordingly, ' to boast without his measure,' (ver. 14, εἰς τὰ ἄμετρα,) and to ' stretch himself beyond his measure,' (ὑπερεκτείνεσθαι,) refer to one that ran beyond or out of his line. ' We are come as far as to you' (ver. 14, ἄχρι ὑμῶν ἐφθάσαμεν) alludes to him that came foremost to the goal; and ' in another man's line' (ver. 16, ἐν ἀλλοτρίῳ κανόνι) signifies—' in the province that was marked out for somebody else,' in allusion to the line by which the race was bounded, each of the racers having the path which he ought to run chalked out to him, and if one stepped over into the other's path he extended himself over his line."—*Paxton's* Illustrations (" Manners and Customs," vol. ii. pp. 218, 219.)—*Ed.*

[2] " Afin que nous luy facions hommage de tout ce que nous avons, confessans le tenir de luy;"—" That we may make acknowledgment to him as to every thing that we have, confessing that we hold it from him."

ever, their ingratitude,[1] in overlooking, in a manner, his
apostleship, which ought to have been especially in estimation among them, on the ground of God's commendation of
it.   In each clause, too, we must understand as implied, a
contrast between him and the false Apostles, who had no
such approbation to show.

14. *For we do not overstretch.*   He alludes to persons who
either forcibly stretch out their arms, or raise themselves up
on their feet, when wishing to catch hold of what is not at
their hand,[2] for of this nature is a greedy thirst for glory, nay
more, it is often more disgusting.   For ambitious persons do
not merely stretch out their arms and lift up their feet, but
are even carried headlong with the view of obtaining some
pretext for glorying.[3]   He tacitly intimates that his rivals
were of this stamp.   He afterwards declares on what ground
he had come to the Corinthians—because he had founded
their Church by his ministry.   Hence he says, *in the gospel
of Christ;* for he had not come to them empty,[4] but had
been the first to bring the gospel to them.   The preposition
in is taken by some in another way; for they render it, *by*
the gospel, and this meaning does not suit ill.   At the same
time, Paul seems to set off to advantage his coming to the
Corinthians, on the ground of his having been furnished
with so precious a gift.

15. *In the labours of others.*   He now reproves more freely
the false Apostles, who, while they had put forth their hand
in the reaping of another man's harvest, had the audacity at
the same time to revile those, who had prepared a place for
them at the expense of sweat and toil.   Paul had built up
the Church of the Corinthians—not without the greatest

---

[1] " Or en parlant ainsi, il taxe (modestement toutesfois) leur ingratitude ;"—" But by speaking thus he reproves, (modestly, however,) their
ingratitude."

[2] " 'Εκτείνω is to extend, to stretch himselfe to the full of his measure :
ὑπερεκτείνω, to stretch himselfe beyond it,—to tenter himself far beyond his
scantling."—*Leigh's* Critica Sacra.—*Ed.*

[3] " Courent a bride auallee, et sont comme transportez a pour chasser
quelque couleur de se glorifier ;"—" They run with a loose bridle, and are,
as it were, hurried forward with the view of obtaining some pretext for
glorying."

[4] " Vuide ne despourueu ;"—" Empty nor unprovided."

struggle, and innumerable difficulties. Those persons afterwards come forward, and find the road made and the gate
open. That they may appear persons of consequence, they
impudently claim for themselves what did not of right belong to them, and disparage Paul's labours.

But having hope. He again indirectly reproves the Corinthians, because they had stood in the way of his making
greater progress in advancing the gospel. For when he says
that he hopes that, when *their faith is increased* the boundaries of his glorying will be enlarged, he intimates, that the
weakness of faith under which they laboured was the reason,
why his career had been somewhat retarded. "I ought now
to have been employed in gaining over new Churches, and
that too with your assistance, if you had made as much proficiency as you ought to have done ; but now you retard me
by your infirmity. I hope, however, that the Lord will grant,
that greater progress will be made by you in future, and that
in this way the glory of my ministry will be increased according to the rule of the divine calling."[1] To *glory in
things that have been prepared* is equivalent to *glorying in the
labours of others ;* for, while Paul had fought the battle, *they*
enjoyed the triumph.[2]

17. *But he that glorieth.* This statement is made by way
of correction, as his glorying might be looked upon as having
the appearance of empty boasting. Hence he cites himself
and others before the judgment-seat of God, saying, that those
glory on good grounds, who are approved by God. To *glory
in the Lord,* however, is used here in a different sense from
what it bears in the first chapter of the former Epistle, (1
Cor. i. 31,) and in Jeremiah ix. 24. For in those passages it
means—to recognise God as the author of all blessings, in
such a way that every blessing is ascribed to his grace,
while men do not extol themselves, but glorify him alone.

---

[1] " Selon la regle et mesure de la vocation Diuine ;"—" According to
the rule and measure of the Divine calling."

[2] " Car combien que S. Paul eust guerroyé, toutesfois les autres tri-
omphoyent ; c'est à dire, combien qu'il eust soustenu tout le fais et la
peine, les autres en raportoyent la gloire :"—" For although Paul had
fought the battle, yet others enjoyed the triumph : that is to say, though
he had borne all the burden and trouble, others carried off the glory."

Here, however, it means—to place our glory at the disposal of God alone,[1] and reckon every thing else as of no value. For while some are dependent on the estimation of men, and weigh themselves in the false balance of public opinion, and others are deceived by their own arrogance, Paul exhorts us to be emulous of this glory—that we may please the Lord, by whose judgment we all stand or fall.

Even heathens say, that true glory consists in an upright conscience.[2] Now that is so much, but it is not all ; for, as almost all are blind through excessive self-love, we cannot safely place confidence in the estimate that we form of our-selves. For we must keep in mind what he says elsewhere, (1 Cor. iv. 4,) that he is not conscious to himself of anything wrong, and yet is *not thereby justified*. What then ? Let us know, that to God alone must be reserved the right of passing judgment upon us ; for we are not competent judges in our own cause. This meaning is confirmed by what follows— *for not he that commendeth himself is approved*. " For it is easy to impose upon men by a false impression, and this is matter of every day occurrence. Let us, therefore, leaving off all other things, aim exclusively at this—that we may be approved by God, and may be satisfied to have his approba-tion alone, as it justly ought to be regarded by us as of more value than all the applauses of the whole world. There was one that said, that to have Plato's favourable judgment was to him worth a thousand.[3] The question here is not as to the judgment of mankind, in respect of the superiority of one to another, but as to the sentence of God himself, who

---

[1] " Et a ce qu'il en iugera ;"—" And according as he will judge of it."

[2] " The heathens, though they could never attain to a true, spiritually sanctified, conscience, yet to live according to the natural dictates thereof, they accounted the only happiness, *Nil conscire sibi*. (*To be conscious to one's self of no crime*, Hor. Ep. i. 1, 61,) was the only thing that made happy. . . . . Pindar called it, *the good nurse in our old age*. So great a matter is it to have the testimony of a good conscience, void of offence, for that is *mille testes*—more than all the testimonies in the world."—*Burgesse* on 2 Cor. i. p. 385.—*Ed.*

[3] The expression referred to occurs in the writings of Cicero. " Plato mihi unus est instar omnium ;"—" Plato, even singly, is to me equal to all."—(Cic. Brut. 51.)   Cicero says elsewhere, that " he would rather err with Plato than think rightly with others."—(Cic. Tusc. i. 17.)—*Ed.*

has it in his power to overturn all the decisions that men have pronounced.

CHAPTER XI.

1. Would to God ye could bear with me a little in *my* folly : and indeed bear with me.

2. For I am jealous over you with godly jealousy : for I have espoused you to one husband, that I may present *you as* a chaste virgin to Christ.

3. But I fear, lest by any means, as the serpent beguiled Eve through his subtilty, so your minds should be corrupted from the simplicity that is in Christ.

4. For if he that cometh preacheth another Jesus, whom we have not preached, or *if* ye receive another spirit, which ye have not received, or another gospel, which ye have not accepted, ye might well bear with *him*.

5. For I suppose I was not a whit behind the very chiefest apostles.

6. But though *I be* rude in speech, yet not in knowledge ; but we have been throughly made manifest among you in all things.

1. Utinam tolerassetis me paulisper in insipientia mea : imo etiam sufferte me.[1]

2. Nam zelotypus sum erga vos Dei zelo : adiunxi enim vos uni viro, ad exhibendam virginem castam Christo.

3. Sed metuo, ne qua fiat, ut quemadmodum serpens Evam decepit versutia sua : ita corrumpantur sensus vestri a simplicitate, quæ est in Christo.

4. Nam si is qui venit, (*vel, si quis veniens,*) alium Iesum prædicat, quem non prædicavimus ; aut si alium Spiritum accipitis, quem non accepistis : aut Evangelium aliud, quod non accepistis, recte sustinuissetis.

5. Arbitror enim me nihilo inferiorem fuisse eximiis Apostolis.

6. Cæterum licet imperitus sim sermone, non tamen scientia : verum ubique manifesti fuimus in omnibus erga vos.

1. *Would that ye did bear with me.* As he saw that the ears of the Corinthians were still in part pre-engaged,[2] he has recourse to another contrivance, for he turns to express a wish, as persons do when they do not venture openly to entreat.[3] Immediately afterwards, however, as if gathering confidence, he nevertheless entreats the Corinthians to bear with his *folly.* He gives the name of *folly* to that splendid proclamation of his praises, which afterwards follows. Not as if he were a fool in glorying ; for he was constrained to it by necessity, and besides, he restrained himself in such a

---

[1] " Mesme aussi supportez moy, *ou,* et certes vous me supportez ;"— " Even so bear with me, *or,* and certainly you do bear with me."

[2] " Des propos des faux apostres ;"—" By the speeches of the false apostles."

[3] " Ceux ausquels ils ont affaire ;"—" Those with whom they have to do."

manner, that no one could justly regard him as going beyond bounds ; but as it is an unseemly thing to herald one's
own praises, and a thing that is foreign to the inclinations
of a modest man, he speaks by way of concession.

What I have rendered in the imperative—*bear with me*,
Chrysostom interprets as an affirmation, and certainly the
Greek word is ambiguous, and either sense suits sufficiently
well. As, however, the reasons that the Apostle subjoins
are designed to induce the Corinthians to *bear with him*,
and as we will find him afterwards expostulating with them
again on the ground of their not conceding anything to him,
I have followed the Old Interpreter.[1] By saying, *Would that*,
&c., he had seemed to be distrustful ; *now*, as if correcting
that hesitation, he openly and freely commands.

2. *For I am jealous.* Mark why it is that he acts the fool,
for *jealousy* hurries a man as it were headlong. " Do not
demand that I should show the equable temper[2] of a man
that is at ease, and not excited by any emotion, for that
vehemence of jealousy, with which I am inflamed towards
you, does not suffer me to be at ease." As, however, there
are two kinds of jealousy—the one springing from self-love,
and of a wicked and perverse nature, while the other is
cherished by us on God's account,[3] he intimates of what sort
his zeal is. For many are zealous—for themselves, not for
God. *That*, on the other hand, is the only pious and right
zeal, that has an eye to God, that he may not be defrauded
of the honours that of right belong to him.

For I have united you to one man. That his zeal was of
such a nature, he proves from the design of his preaching,
for its tendency was to join them to Christ in marriage, and
retain them in connection with him.[4] Here, however, he
gives us in his own person a lively picture of a good minister ;

---

[1] The rendering of the Vulgate is as follows: " Sed supportate me."
(" But bear with me.") Wiclif (1380) reads: " But also supporte ye me."
Tyndale (1534) also renders in the imperative, as follows: " Yee, and I
pray you forbeare me."—*Ed.*

[2] " Vne equalite et moderation ;"—" An evenness and moderation."

[3] " De laquelle nous sommes esmeus pour l'amour de nostre Dieu ;"—
" By which we are influenced out of love to our God."

[4] " Et les faire perseuerer en saincte conionction auec luy ;"—" And to
lead them to persevere in a holy connection with him."

for One alone is the Bridegroom of the Church—the Son of God. All ministers are the *friends of the Bridegroom,* as the Baptist declares respecting himself. (John iii. 29.) Hence all ought to be concerned, that the fidelity of this sacred marriage remain unimpaired and inviolable. This they cannot do, unless they are actuated by the dispositions of the Bridegroom, so that every one of them may be as much concerned for the purity of the Church, as a husband is for the chastity of his wife. Away then with coldness and indolence in this matter, for one that is cold[1] will never be qualified for this office. Let them, however, in the mean time, take care, not to pursue their own interest rather than that of Christ, that they may not intrude themselves into his place, lest while they give themselves out as his *paranymphs,*[2] they turn out to be in reality adulterers, by alluring the bride to love themselves.

To present you as a chaste virgin. We are married to Christ, on no other condition than that we bring virginity as our dowry, and preserve it entire, so as to be free from all corruption. Hence it is the duty of ministers of the gospel to purify our souls, that they may be *chaste virgins to Christ;* otherwise they accomplish nothing. Now we may understand it as meaning, that they individually present themselves as *chaste virgins to Christ,* or that the minister presents the whole of the people, and brings them forward into Christ's presence. I approve rather of the second interpretation. Hence I have given a different rendering from Erasmus.[3]

3. *But I fear.* He begins to explain, what is the nature of that *virginity* of which he has made mention—our cleaving to Christ alone, sincerely, with our whole heart. God, indeed, everywhere requires from us, that we be joined with him in body and in spirit, and he warns us that he is a *jealous God,* (Exod. xx. 5,) to avenge with the utmost severity the wrong done to him, in the event of any one's

---

[1] " Quiconque est froid et lasche ;"—" Whoever is cold and indolent."

[2] " Paranymphos ;"—" Friends of the bridegroom." The reader will find the office and duties of *paranymph* detailed at considerable length by *Dr. Adam Clarke,* when commenting on John iii. 29.—*Ed.*

[3] The rendering of Erasmus, as stated by Beza, (who, like CALVIN, disapproves of it,) is " ut exhiberetis ;"—" that *ye* may present."—*Ed.*

drawing back from him.   This connection, however, is accomplished in Christ, as Paul teaches in Ephesians, (v. 25, 27.)   He points out, however, at present the means of it—when we remain in the pure simplicity of the gospel, for, as in contracting marriages among men, there are written contracts[1] drawn out, so the spiritual connection between us and the Son of God is confirmed by the gospel, as a kind of written contract.[2]   Let us maintain the fidelity, love, and obedience, that have been there promised by us ; he will be faithful to us on his part.

Now Paul says that he is concerned, that the minds of the Corinthians may not be *corrupted from the simplicity that is in Christ*.   Paul, it is true, says in Greek εἰς Χριστόν, which Erasmus renders *towards Christ*,[3] but the Old Interpreter has come nearer, in my opinion, to Paul's intention,[4] because by the *simplicity that is in Christ* is meant, that which keeps us in the unadulterated and pure doctrine of the gospel, and admits of no foreign admixtures.[5]   By this he intimates that men's minds are *adulterated*,[6] whenever they turn aside, even in the least degree, to the one side or to the other, from the pure doctrine of Christ.   Nor is it without good reason, for who would not condemn a matron as guilty of unchastity, so soon as she lends an ear to a seducer ?   So in like manner we, when we admit wicked and false teachers, who are

[1] *Tabulæ.*—Juvenal makes use of this term in the same sense : " Signatæ *tabulæ ;*"—" The *marriage contract* is signed."—(Juv. ii. 119.)   See also Juv. ix. 75.—*Ed.*

[2] " Est confermé et establi par l'Euangile, comme par vn instrument authentique ;"—" Is confirmed and established by the gospel, as by an authentic instrument."

[3] Beza, while, like CALVIN, he views the expression εἰς τὸν Χριστόν as meaning " *in* Christ," makes mention of the rendering of Erasmus, adding a note of explanation, " *Quæ erat erga Christum*, nempe quia pure ac simpliciter illi obtemperabatis ;"—" Which was *towards Christ ;* that is, inasmuch as you obeyed him in purity and simplicity."   Cranmer (1539) renders as follows : " Euen so youre wyttes shuld be corrupte from the singlenes that ye had toward Christ."—*Ed.*

[4] The rendering of the Vulgate is the same as that adopted by CALVIN, " A simplicitate quæ est in Christo ;"—" From the simplicity which is in Christ."—*Ed.*

[5] " Corruptions et desguisemens venans d'ailleurs :"—" Corruptions and disguises springing from some other sources."

[6] " S'abbastardissent, corrompent, et debauchent ;"—" Are adulterated, corrupted, and debauched."

Satan's vile agents, show but too clearly, that we do not maintain conjugal fidelity towards Christ. We must also take notice of the term *simplicity*, for Paul's fear was not, lest the Corinthians should all at once openly draw back altogether from Christ, but lest, by turning aside, by little and little, from the simplicity which they had learned, so as to go after profane and foreign contrivances, they should at length become adulterated.

He brings forward a comparison—*as the serpent beguiled Eve through his subtilty.* For if false teachers have a show of wisdom, if they have any power of eloquence for persuading, if they plausibly insinuate themselves into the minds of their hearers, and instil their poison by fawning artifices, it was in a similar way that Satan also *beguiled Eve*, as he did not openly declare himself to be an enemy, but crept in privily under a specious pretext.

4. *For if he that cometh.* He now reproves the Corinthians for the excessive readiness, which they showed to receive the false apostles. For while they were towards Paul himself excessively morose and irritable,[1] so that on any, even the least occasion, they were offended if he gave them even the slightest reproof, there was, on the other hand, nothing that they did not bear with, on the part of the false Apostles. They willingly endured their pride, haughtiness, and unreasonableness. An absurd reverence of this nature he condemns, because in the mean time they showed no discrimination or judgment. "How is it that they take[2] so much liberty with you, and you submit patiently to their control? Had they brought you another Christ, or another gospel, or another Spirit, different from what you received through my hands, I would assuredly approve of your regard for them, for they would be deserving of such honour. But as they have conferred upon you nothing, that I had not given you previously, what sort of gratitude do you show in all but adoring those, to whom you are indebted for nothing, while

---

[1] "Trop chagrins, difficiles, mal-aises a contenter, et faciles a estre irritez;"—"Excessively fretful, hard to please, not easily satisfied, and very readily provoked."

[2] "Entreprenent et vsurpent;"—"Assume and usurp."

you despise me, through whom God has bestowed upon you so many and so distinguished benefits?" Such is the reverence that is shown even at this day by Papists towards their pretended Bishops. For while they are oppressed by their excessively harsh tyranny,[1] they submit to it without difficulty; but, at the same time, do not hesitate to treat Christ himself with contempt.[2]

The expressions—*another Christ*, and *another gospel*, are made use of here in a different sense from what they bear in Gal. i. 8. For *another* is used there in opposition to what is true and genuine, and hence it means *false* and *counterfeit*. Here, on the other hand, he means to say—"If the gospel had come to you through their ministry, and not through mine."

5. *For I reckon that I am.* He now convicts them of ingratitude, by removing the only thing that could serve as an excuse for them, for he shows that he is on a level, even with the chief of the Apostles. The Corinthians, therefore, were ungrateful[3] in not esteeming him more highly, after having found him, by experience, to be such; while, on the other hand, the authority that was justly due to him, they transferred to persons of no value. For the sake of modesty, however, he says that he *reckons* so, while the thing was known and manifest to all. His meaning, however, is, that God had honoured his Apostleship with no less distinguished marks of favour, than that of John or Peter. Now the man that despises the gifts of God, which he himself recognises, cannot clear himself from the charge of being spiteful and ungrateful. Hence, wherever you see the gifts of God, you must there reverence God himself:[4] I mean,

[1] "Leur dure et insupportable tyrannie;"—"Their harsh and intolerable tyranny."

[2] "Mais de Christ, il ne leur en chaut, et ne font point de conscience de l'auoir en mespris;"—"But as for Christ, they do not care for him, and they make no scruple to hold him in contempt."

[3] "Monstroyent bien en cela leur ingratitude;"—"Showed clearly in this their ingratitude."

[4] "En quelque lieu que nous apperceuerons les dons de Dieu, il faut que là il soit honore de nous, et que nous luy portions reuerence;"—"Wherever we recognise the gifts of God, he must there be honoured by us, and we must give him reverence."

that every one is worthy of honour, in so far as he is distinguished by graces received from God, and especially if any advantage has redounded to thee from them.

6. *But though I am rude.* There was one thing,[1] in which he might appear, at first view, to be inferior—that he was devoid of eloquence. This judgment,[2] therefore, he anticipates and corrects, while he acknowledges himself, indeed, to be *rude* and unpolished *in speech,* while at the same time he maintains that he has *knowledge.* By *speech* here he means, elegance of expression; and by *knowledge* he means, the very substance of doctrine. For as man has both a soul and a body, so also in doctrine, there is the thing itself that is taught, and the ornament of expression with which it is clothed. Paul, therefore, maintains that he understands, what should be taught, and what is necessary to be known, though he is not an eloquent orator, so as to know how to set off his doctrine by a polished and eloquent manner of expression.

It is asked, however, whether elegance of speech[3] is not also necessary for Apostles; for how will they otherwise be prepared for teaching? *Knowledge* might perhaps suffice for others, but how could a teacher be dumb? I answer, that, while Paul acknowledges himself to be *rude in speech,* it is not as though he were a mere infant, but as meaning, that he was not distinguished by such splendid eloquence as others, to whom he yields the palm as to this, retaining for himself what was the principal thing—the reality itself,[4] while he leaves them talkativeness without gravity. If, however, any one should inquire, why it is that the Lord, who *made men's tongues,* (Exod. iv. 11,) did not also endow so eminent an apostle with eloquence, that nothing might be wanting to him, I answer, that he was furnished with a sufficiency for supplying the want of eloquence. For we see and feel, what majesty there is in his writings, what elevation appears in them, what a weight of meaning is couched

[1] " Il n'y auoit que ceci seul;"—" There was only this one thing."
[2] " Ce fol iugement;"—" This foolish judgment."
[3] " La faculte de bien parler et auec grace;"—" The power of speaking well and gracefully."
[4] " La substance de la chose;"—" The substance of the thing."

under them, what power is discovered in them. In fine, they are thunderbolts, not mere words. Does not the efficacy of the Spirit appear more clearly in a naked rusticity of words, (so to speak,) than under the disguise of elegance and ornament? Of this matter, however, we have treated more largely in the former Epistle.[1] In short, he admits, as far as words are concerned, what his adversaries allege by way of objection, while he denies in reality what they hold forth. Let us also learn, from his example, to prefer deeds to words, and, to use a barbarous but common proverb— " Teneant alii quid *nominis,* nos autem quid *rei ;"*—" Let others know something of the *name,* but let us know something of the *reality.*"[2] If eloquence is superadded, let it be regarded by us as something over and above; and farther, let it not be made use of for disguising doctrine, or adulterating it, but for unfolding it in its genuine simplicity.

But everywhere. As there was something magnificent in placing himself on a level with the chief Apostles, that this may not be ascribed to arrogance, he makes the Corinthians judges, provided they judge from what they have themselves experienced ; for they had known sufficiently well, from many proofs, that he did not boast needlessly, or without good reason. He means, therefore, that he needs not make use of words, inasmuch as reality and experience afford clear evidence of every thing that he was about to say.[3]

7. Have I committed an offence in abasing myself, that ye might be exalted, because I have preached to you the gospel of God freely?

7. Num illud peccavi, quod me ipsum humiliaverim,[4] ut vos exaltaremini: quod gratuito Evangelium Dei prædicaverim vobis ?

[1] See CALVIN on the Corinthians, vol. i. pp. 75-77.

[2] " Et afin que i'vse d'vn prouerbe des Latins barbare, commun toutesfois —' Que les autres scachent les mots, mais que nous ayons bonne cognoissance de la chose ;' "—" And to use a proverb of the Latins, barbarous, indeed, but common—' Let others know the words, but let us have a good acquaintance with the reality.' " Tymme, in his translation of CALVIN on the Corinthians, (1573,) renders this proverb as follows: " Let other haue the shell, so we may haue the kernell."—*Ed.*

[3] " Monstrent au doigt tout ce qu'il en pourroit dire ;"—" Show with the finger every thing that he might be prepared to say as to it."

[4] " En ce que ie me suis humilié moy mesme, ou, abbaissé ;"—" Because I have humbled or abased myself."

8. I robbed other churches, taking wages *of them*, to do you service.

9. And when I was present with you, and wanted, I was chargeable to no man: for that which was lacking to me the brethren which came from Macedonia supplied; and in all *things* I have kept myself from being burdensome unto you, and *so* will I keep *myself*.

10. As the truth of Christ is in me, no man shall stop me of this boasting in the regions of Achaia.

11. Wherefore? because I love you not? God knoweth.

12. But what I do, that I will do, that I may cut off occasion from them which desire occasion; that wherein they glory, they may be found even as we.

8. Cæteras Ecclesias deprædatus sum accepto ab illis stipendio, quo vobis inservirem.

9. Et quum apud vos essem et egerem, non onerosus fui cuiquam;[1] nam quod mihi deerat, suppleverunt fratres, qui venerant ex Macedonia; et in omnibus sic me servavi, ne cui essem onerosus, atque ita servabo.

10. Est veritas Christi in me, quod hæc gloriatio non interrumpetur contra me in regionibus Achaiæ.

11. Quapropter? an quod non diligam vos? Deus novit.

12. Verum quod facio, idem et faciam: ut amputem occasionem iis qui cupiunt occasionem, ut in quo gloriantur, reperiantur, quemadmodum et nos.

7. *Have I committed an offence?* His humility was cast up to him by way of reproach, while it was an excellence that was deserving of no ordinary commendation. *Humility* here means—voluntary abasement; for in conducting himself modestly, as if he had nothing in him that was particularly excellent, so that many looked upon him as one of the common people, he had done that for the advantage of the Corinthians. For the man was inflamed with so great a desire,[2] and so great an anxiety for their salvation, that he made a regard to himself a secondary consideration. Hence he says, that he had of his own accord made a surrender of his own greatness, that they might become great through his abasement. For his design was, that he might promote their salvation. He now indirectly charges them with ingratitude, in imputing to him as a fault so pious a disposition—not indeed for the purpose of reproaching him, but with the view of restoring them so much the better to a sound mind. And certainly, he wounded them more

---

[1] " Je n'ay foullé personne, ou, ne suis point deuenu lasche en besongne au dommage de quelqu'vn;"—" I was not burdensome to any one, or, I did not become remiss in labour to the hurt of any one."

[2] " Car ce sainct Apostre estoit tellement embrassé du desir;"—" For this holy Apostle was to such a degree inflamed with desire."

severely by speaking *ironically*, than if he had spoken in a
simple way, and without a figure. He might have said:
" What is this? Am I despised by you, because I have
lowered myself for your advantage ?" The questioning, however, which he makes use of, was more forcible for putting
them to shame.

Because I preached freely. This is a part of his abasement. For he had given up his own right, as though his
condition had been inferior to that of others ; but such was
the unreasonableness of some of them, that they esteemed
him the less on that account, as if he had been undeserving
of remuneration. The reason, why he had given his services
to the Corinthians gratuitously, is immediately subjoined—
for he did not act in this manner everywhere, but, as we
have seen in the former Epistle,[1] there was a danger of his
furnishing the false Apostles with a handle against him.

8. *I robbed other churches.* He has intentionally, in my
opinion, made use of an offensive term, that he might the
more forcibly express the unreasonableness of the matter—
in respect of his being despised by the Corinthians. " I
have," says he, " procured pay for myself from the *spoils* of
others, that I might serve you. While I have thus spared
you, how unreasonable it is to make me so poor a return !"
It is, however, a metaphor, that is taken from what is customary among soldiers ; for as conquerors take *spoils* from
the nations that they have conquered, so every thing that
Paul took from the Churches that he had gained to Christ
was, in a manner, the *spoils* of his victories, though, at the
same time, he never would have taken it from persons against
their will, but what they contributed gratuitously was, in a
manner, due by right of spiritual warfare.[2]

---

[1] See CALVIN on the Corinthians, vol. i. p. 288.

[2] The word ἐσύλησα, rendered in our authorized version *robbed*, is derived from σύλη, spoils, and comes originally from the Hebrew verb שָׁלַל
(*shalal*), which is frequently employed to denote *spoiling*, or *making booty*.
(See Isaiah x. 6; Ezek. xxix. 19.)—" The word ἐσύλησα," says *Barnes*,
" means properly, ' I spoiled, plundered, robbed,' but the idea of Paul here
is, that he, *as it were*, robbed them, because he did not render an equivalent
for what they gave him. They supported him, when he was labouring for
another people. A conqueror who plunders a country gives *no equivalent*
for what he takes. In this sense only could Paul say, that he had plun-

Observe, however, that he says that he *had been in want,* for he would never have been a burden to them, had he not been constrained by necessity. . He, nevertheless, in the mean time, *laboured with his hands,* as we have seen before, (1 Cor. iv. 12,) but as the *labour of his hands* was not sufficient for sustaining life, something additional was contributed by the Macedonians. Accordingly he does not say, that his living had been furnished to him by the Macedonians,[1] but merely that they had supplied what was wanting. We have spoken elsewhere of the Apostle's holy prudence and diligence in providing against dangers.[2] Here we must take notice of the pious zeal of the Macedonians, who did not hesitate to contribute of their substance for his pay, that the gospel might be proclaimed to others, and those, too, that were wealthier than themselves. Ah! how few *Macedonians* are there in the present day, and on the other hand how many *Corinthians* you may find everywhere!

10. *The truth of Christ is in me.* Lest any one should suspect, that Paul's words were designed to induce the Corinthians to be more liberal to him in future, and endeavour to make amends for their error in the past, he affirms with an oath, that he would take nothing from them, or from others in Achaia, though it were offered to him. For this manner of expression—*the truth of Christ is in me,* is in the form of oath. Let me not be thought to have the *truth of Christ* in me if I do not retain this glorying among the inhabitants of Achaia. Now Corinth was in Achaia.[3]

11. *Is it because I love you not?* Those that we love, we treat with greater familiarity. Lest the Corinthians, therefore, should take it amiss, that he refused their liberality, while he allowed himself to be assisted by the Macedonians, and even declared with an oath that he would do so still,

dered the Church at Philippi. His general principle was, that 'the labourer was worthy of his hire;' and that a man was to receive his support from the people for whom he laboured, (See 1 Cor. ix. 7-14,) but this rule he had not observed in this case."—*Ed*.

[1] " Il ne dit pas que les Macedoniens luy eussent donné tout ce qui luy estoit necessaire ;"—" He does not say that the Macedonians had given him every thing that was necessary."

[2] " See p. 300.

[3] " See CALVIN on the Corinthians, vol. i. p. 37.

he anticipates that suspicion also.   And by the figure termed *anthypophora*,[1] he asks, as it were in their name, whether
this is a token of a malevolent mind?   He does not return
a direct answer to the question, but the indirect answer that
he returns has much more weight, inasmuch as he calls God
to be a witness of his good disposition towards them.   You
see here, that in the course of three verses[2] there are two
oaths, but they are lawful and holy, because they have a good
design in view, and a legitimate reason is involved.   Hence
to condemn indiscriminately all oaths is to act the part of
fanatics, who make no distinction between white and black.[3]

12. *But what I do.* He again explains the reason of his
intention.[4] The false Apostles, with the view of alluring to
themselves ignorant persons, took no pay.   Their serving
gratuitously was a show of uncommon zeal.[5] If Paul had
availed himself of his right, he would have given them occasion to raise their crest, as if they had been greatly superior
to him.   Paul, accordingly, that he might give them no occasion of doing injury, did himself, also, preach the Gospel,
free of charge, and this is what he adds—that he is desirous
to *cut off occasion from those that desire occasion.* For the
false Apostles were desirous to insinuate themselves by this
artifice, and to detract, in proportion to this, from Paul's
credit, if they were superior to him in any respect.   He says,
that he will not give them this advantage.   " They will be
found," says he, " on a level with us in that glorying which

[1] " Pour repoudre à l'objection ;"—" With the view of replying to the
objection."—See CALVIN on the Corinthians, vol. i. p. 281, *n*. 1.

[2] " Ces trois lignes ;"—" These three lines."

[3] " An oath is to be used, when other means are deficient ; and more
particularly, we are then only to swear, when the honour of God is concerned, or Religion and Christianity is falsely accused ; and these are
public grounds.   To which we may add the good of the Commonwealth :
or we are to swear upon a particular occasion to clear ourselves from false
accusations and crimes charged upon us, if otherwise our innocency cannot
appear ; or in the behalf of others, when they shall suffer either in name,
life, or estate, and we are required thereunto by the Magistrate, that so
justice may proceed."—Burgesse on 2 Cor. i. p. 681.—See CALVIN's *Harmony*, vol. i. p. 294.—*Ed.*

[4] " C'estoit vne fausse monstre de quelque zele excellent, de seruir sans
rien prendre ;"—" It was a false show of eminent zeal, to serve without
taking any thing."

[5] " De la resolution qu'il a prinse en cest endroit ;"—" Of the resolution
that he had taken as to this matter."

they would wish to have for themselves exclusively." This, however, is a useful admonition in connection with cutting off occasion from the wicked, as often as they desire one. For this is the only way to overcome them—not in the way of furnishing them with arms through our imprudence.[1]

13. For such *are* false apostles, deceitful workers, transforming themselves into the apostles of Christ.	13. Siquidem istiusmodi pseudo-apostoli; operarii dolosi sunt, qui transformant se in Apostolos Christi.
14. And no marvel; for Satan himself is transformed into an angel of light.	14. Neque id mirum: quandoquidem ipse Satanas transfiguratur in Angelum lucis.
15. Therefore *it is* no great thing if his ministers also be transformed as the ministers of righteousness: whose end shall be according to their works.	15. Non magnum igitur, si et ministri illius transformant se, perinde acsi essent ministri iustitiæ: quorum finis erit secundum opera ipsorum.

13. *For such are false Apostles.* While he has already taken away from them what they chiefly desired, yet, not contented with having put himself on a level with them with respect to that in which they were desirous to excel, he leaves them nothing for which they deserve any commendation. It was apparently a laudable thing to despise money, but he says, that they make use of a pretence for the purpose of deceiving, exactly as if a harlot were to borrow the apparel of a decent matron. For it was necessary to pull off the mask, which obscured the glory of God.

They are *deceitful workers*, says he, that is—they do not discover their wickedness at first view, but artfully insinuate themselves under some fair pretext.[2] Hence they require to be carefully and thoroughly sifted, lest we should receive persons as servants of Christ, as soon as any appearance of excellence is discovered. Nor does Paul in malice and envy put an unfavourable construction upon what might be looked upon as an excellence, but, constrained by their dishonesty, he unfolds to view the evil that lay hid, because there was a dangerous profanation of virtue in pretending to burn with greater zeal than all the servants of Christ.

[1] " Par nostre imprudence et inconsideration ;"—" By our imprudence and inconsideration."
[2] " S'insinuent finement sans qu'on y prene garde ;"—" They artfully insinuate themselves, unless one be on his guard against them."

14. *And no marvel.* It is an argument from the greater
to the less. "If Satan, who is the basest of all beings, nay,
the head and chief of all wicked persons, transforms himself, what will his ministers do?" We have experience of
both every day, for when Satan tempts us to evil, he does
not profess to be what he really is. For he would lose his
object, if we were made aware of his being a mortal enemy,
and opposer of our salvation. Hence he always makes use
of some cloak for the purpose of insnaring us, and does not
immediately *show his horns*, (as the common expression is,)
but rather makes it his endeavour to appear as an *angel*.
Even when he tempts us to gross crimes, he makes use,
nevertheless, of some pretext that he may draw us, when we
are off our guard, into his nets. What then, if he attacks
us under the appearance of good, nay, under the very title
of God? His life-guards imitate, as I have said, the same
artifice. These are golden preambles—" Vicar of Christ"—
" Successor of Peter"—" Servant of God's servants," but let
the masks be pulled off, and who and what will the Pope be
discovered to be? Scarcely will Satan himself, his master,
surpass so accomplished a scholar in any kind of abomination. It is a well known saying as to Babylon, that she
gives poison to drink in a golden cup. (Jer. li. 7.) Hence
we must be on our guard against masks.

Should any one now ask, " Shall we then regard all with
suspicion?" I answer, that the Apostle did not by any means
intend this; for there are marks of discrimination, which it
were the part of stupidity, not of prudence, to overlook. He
was simply desirous to arouse our attention, that we may
not straightway judge of the lion from the skin.[1] For if we
are not hasty in forming a judgment, the Lord will order it
so that the ears of the animal will be discovered ere long.
Farther, he was desirous in like manner to admonish us, in
forming an estimate of Christ's servants, not to regard masks,
but to seek after what is of more importance. *Ministers of
righteousness* is a Hebraism for *faithful and upright persons.*[2]

[1] " Comme porte le prouerbe des Latins;"—" As the proverb in use
among the Latins runs."
[2] *Beza* takes the same view of this expression: " Nec enim illi dicuntur

15. *Whose end shall be.* He adds this for the consolation of the pious. For it is the statement of a courageous man, who despises the foolish judgments of men, and patiently waits for the day of the Lord. In the mean time, he shows a singular boldness of conscience, which does not dread the judgment of God.

16. I say again, Let no man think me a fool: if otherwise, yet as a fool receive me, that I may boast myself a little.

16. Iterum dico, ne quis me putet insipientem esse: alioqui iam etiam ut insipientem accipite me, ut paululum quiddam et ego glorier.

17. That which I speak, I speak *it* not after the Lord, but as it were foolishly, in this confidence of boasting.

17. Quod dico, non dico secundum Dominum, sed velut per insipientiam: in hac audacia gloriationis.

18. Seeing that many glory after the flesh, I will glory also.

18. Quandoquidem multi gloriantur secundum carnem, et ego gloriabor.

19. For ye suffer fools gladly, seeing ye *yourselves* are wise.

19. Libenter enim suffertis insipientes: quum sitis ipsi sapientes.

20. For ye suffer, if a man bring you into bondage, if a man devour *you,* if a man take *of you,* if a man exalt himself, if a man smite you on the face.

20. Suffertis enim, si quis vos in servitutem adigit, si quis exedit, si quis accipit, si quis attollit sese, si quis vos in faciem cædit.

21. I speak as concerning reproach, as though we had been weak. Howbeit, whereinsoever any is bold, (I speak foolishly,) I am bold also.

21. Iuxta contumeliam loquor, perinde quasi nos infirmi fuerimus: imo in quocunque audet aliquis, per insipientiam loquor, ego quoque audeo.

16. *I say again.* The Apostle has a twofold design. He has it partly in view to expose the disgusting vanity of the false Apostles, inasmuch as they were such extravagant trumpeters of their own praises; and farther, to expostulate with the Corinthians, because they shut him up to the necessity of glorying, contrary to the inclinations of his own mind. " *I say again,*" says he. For he had abundantly shown previously, that there was no reason, why he should

sese transfigurare in Satanam, sed in ministros probos et integros, quibus opponuntur δόλιοι. Hoc enim declarat epitheton *justitiæ* ex Hebræorum idiotismo;"—" For they are not said to transform themselves into Satan, but into ministers, who are honest and upright, as contrasted with those who are (δόλιοι) *deceitful.* For this is the import of the epithet, *of righteousness,* according to the Hebrew idiom." Another instance of the same Hebrew idiom is noticed by CALVIN in p. 196.—*Ed.*

be despised. He had also shown at the same time, that he
was very unlike others, and therefore ought not to have his
grounds of glorying estimated according to the rule of their
measure. Thus he again shows, for what purpose he had
hitherto gloried—that he might clear his apostleship from
contempt; for if the Corinthians had done their duty, he
would not have said one word as to this matter.

Otherwise now as a fool. " If I am reckoned by you a
fool, allow me at least to make use of my right and liberty
—that is, to speak foolishly after the manner of fools." Thus
he reproves the false Apostles, who, while they were exceedingly silly in this respect, were not merely borne with by
the Corinthians, but were received with great applause. He
afterwards explains what kind of folly it is—the publishing
of his own praises. While they did so without end and
without measure, he intimates that it was a thing to which
he was unaccustomed; for he says, *for a little while.* For I
take this clause as referring to time, so that the meaning is,
that Paul did not wish to continue it long, but assumed, as
it were, for the moment, the person of another, and immediately thereafter laid it aside, as we are accustomed to pass
over lightly those things that are foreign to our object, while
fools occupy themselves constantly ($\dot{\epsilon}\nu$ $\pi\alpha\rho\acute{\epsilon}\rho\gamma o\iota\varsigma$)[1] *in matters
of inferior moment.*

17. *What I speak, I speak not after the Lord.* His disposition, it is true, had an eye to God, but the outward appearance[2] might seem unsuitable to a servant of the Lord.
At the same time, the things that Paul confesses respecting
himself, he, on the other hand, condemns in the false Apostles.[3] For it was not his intention to praise himself, but
simply to contrast himself with them, with the view of humbling them.[4] Hence he transfers to his own person what

---

[1] The term $\pi\alpha\rho\acute{\epsilon}\rho\gamma o\nu$ denotes—a matter of mere secondary importance.
Thus Thucydides (vi. 58) says, $\dot{o}\varsigma$ $o\dot{v}x$ $\dot{\epsilon}x$ $\pi\alpha\rho\acute{\epsilon}\rho\gamma o\upsilon$ $\tau\dot{o}\nu$ $\pi\dot{o}\lambda\epsilon\mu o\nu$ $\dot{\epsilon}\pi o\iota\epsilon\tilde{\iota}\tau o$—who
did not make the war a secondary consideration.—*Ed.*

[2] " La façon exterieure en laquelle il procede;"—" The outward manner
in which he goes to work."

[3] " C'est plustos afin de les condamner es faux-Apostres;"—" It is rather
with the view of condemning them in the false Apostles."

[4] " Afin de leur abbaisser le caquet;"—" With the view of bringing
down their talk."

belonged to them, that he may thus open the eyes of the Corinthians. What I have rendered *boldness*, is in the Greek ὑπόστασις, as to the meaning of which term we have spoken in the ninth chapter. (2 Cor. ix. 4.) *Subject-matter*[1] or *substance*, unquestionably, would not be at all suitable here.[2]

18. *Since many glory.* The meaning is—" Should any one say to me, by way of objection, that what I do is faulty, what then as to others? Are not they my leaders? Am I alone, or am I the first, in *glorying according to the flesh?* Why should that be reckoned praiseworthy in *them*, that is imputed to *me* as a fault?" So far then is Paul from ambition in recounting his own praises, that he is contented to be blamed on that account, provided he exposes the vanity of the false apostles.

To glory after the flesh, is to boast one's self, rather in what has a tendency towards show, than in a good conscience. For the term *flesh*, here, has a reference to the world—when we seek after praise from outward masks, which have a showy appearance before the world, and are regarded as excellent. In place of this term he had a little before made use of the expression—*in appearance*. (2 Cor. x. 7.)

19. *For ye bear with fools willingly.* He calls them *wise*— in my opinion, *ironically*. He was despised by them, which could not have been, had they not been puffed up with the greatest arrogance.[3] He says, therefore: " Since you are so wise, act the part of wise men in bearing with me, whom you treat with contempt, as you would a *fool.*" Hence I infer, that this discourse is not addressed to all indiscriminately, but some particular persons are reproved, who conducted themselves in an unkind manner.[4]

[1] CALVIN refers here to the rendering of Erasmus, and of the Vulgate. The term employed by Erasmus is *argumentum* (*subject-matter*.) In accordance with this, Cranmer's version (1539) reads, " in this *matter* of boastinge." The Vulgate makes use of the term *substantia*, (*substance*.) Wiclif (1380) reads, " in this substaunce of glorie." The Rheims version (1582), " in this substance of glorying."—*Ed.*

[2] " Certes il ne conueniendroit pas bien yci de traduire *matiere* ou *substance*, combien que le mot signifie quelque fois cela ;"—" Certainly it would not be suitable here to render it *subject-matter* or *substance*, though the word sometimes bears that meaning."

[3] " D'vne merueilleuse arrogance ;"—" With an amazing arrogance."

[4] " Enuers luy ;"—" Towards him."

20. *For ye bear with it, if any one.* There are *three* ways in which this may be understood. He may be understood as reproving the Corinthians in *irony*, because they could not endure any thing, as is usually the case with effeminate persons ; or he charges them with indolence, because they had given themselves up to the false Apostles in a disgraceful bondage ; or he repeats, as it were, in the person of another, what was spitefully affirmed respecting himself,[1] as if he claimed for himself a tyrannical authority over them. The *second* meaning is approved by Chrysostom, Ambrose, and Augustine, and hence it is commonly received ; and, indeed, it corresponds best with the context, although the *third* is not less in accordance with my views. For we see, how he was calumniated from time to time by the malevolent, as if he domineered tyrannically, while he was very far from doing so. As, however, the other meaning is more generally received, I have no objection, that it should be held as the true one.

Now this statement will correspond with the preceding one in this way : " You bear with every thing from others, if they oppress you, if they demand what belongs to you, if they treat you disdainfully. Why then will you not bear with me, as they are in no respect superior to me ?" For as to his saying that he is not *weak*, he means that he had been endowed by God with such excellent graces, that he ought not to be looked upon as of the common order. For the word *weak* has a more extensive signification, as we shall see again ere long.

It has been the invariable custom, and will be so to the end, to resist contumaciously[2] the servants of God, to get enraged on the least occasion,[3] to grumble and murmur incessantly, to complain of even a moderate strictness,[4] to hold all discipline in abhorrence ; while, on the other hand, they

---

[1] " Ce que malicieusement on disoit de luy pour le rendre odieux ;"— " What they said of him maliciously, with the view of making him odious."

[2] " De resister et contredire opiniastrement ;"—" To resist and contradict obstinately."

[3] " Se corroucer aigrement contr' eux a la moindre occasion ;"—" To be fiercely enraged against them on the least occasion."

[4] " Se plaindre de leur seuerite, en disant qu'elle est excessiue ;"—" To complain of their strictness, by saying that it is excessive."

put themselves under servile subjection to false apostles, impostors, or mere worthless pretenders, give them liberty to do any thing whatever, and patiently submit to and endure, whatever burden they may choose to impose upon them. Thus, at the present day, you will scarcely find one in thirty, who will put his neck willingly under Christ's yoke, while all have endured with patience a tyranny so severe as that of the Pope. Those very persons are all at once in an uproar,[1] in opposition to the fatherly and truly salutary reproofs of their pastors, who, on the other hand, had formerly swallowed down quietly every kind of insult, even the most atrocious, from the monks.[2] Are not those worthy of Antichrist's torturing rack, rather than of Christ's mild sway, who have ears so tender and backward to listen to the truth? But thus it has been from the beginning.

21. *Nay, in whatsoever.* Paul had asked, why the Corinthians showed more respect to others than to him, while he had not been by any means *weak*, that is, contemptible. He now confirms this, because, if a comparison had been entered upon, he would not have been inferior to any one in any department of honour.

22. Are they Hebrews? so *am* I. Are they Israelites? so *am* I. Are they the seed of Abraham? so *am* I.

23. Are they ministers of Christ? (I speak as a fool,) I *am* more: in labours more abundant, in stripes above measure, in prisons more frequent, in deaths oft.

24. Of the Jews five times received I forty *stripes* save one.

25. Thrice was I beaten with rods, once was I stoned, thrice I suffered shipwreck, a night and a day I have been in the deep;

26. *In* journeyings often, *in* perils of waters, *in* perils of robbers, *in* perils by *mine own* countrymen, *in* perils by the heathen, *in* perils in

22. Hebræi sunt? ego quoque. Israelitæ sunt? ego quoque: semen Abrahæ sunt? ego quoque.

23. Ministri Christi sunt? desipiens loquor, plus ego; in laboribus abundantius, in plagis supra modum, in carceribus copiosius, in mortibus sæpe.

24. A Iudæis quinquies quadraginta plagas accepi una minus.

25. Ter virgis cæsus sum, semel lapidatus sum, ter naufragium feci, noctes et dies egi in profundo.

26. In itineribus saepe, periculis fluminum, periculis latronum, periculis ex genere, periculis ex Gentibus, periculis in urbe, periculis in deserto,

---

[1] " Ils tempestent et grincent les dents ;"—" They storm and gnash their teeth."

[2] " Toutes sortes d'iniures et outrages horribles que les moines leur faisoyent ;"—" All sorts of horrible injuries and insults that the monks could inflict upon them."

the city, *in* perils in the wilderness, *in* perils in the sea, *in* perils among false brethren;

27. In weariness and painfulness, in watchings often, in hunger and thirst, in fastings often, in cold and nakedness.

28. Besides those things that are without, that which cometh upon me daily, the care of all the Churches.

29. Who is weak, and I am not weak? who is offended, and I burn not?

periculis in mari, periculis in falsis fratribus:

27. In labore et molestia, in vigiliis sæpe, in fame et siti, in ieiuniis sæpe, in frigore et nuditate:

28. Præter ea quæ extrinsecus accidunt, quotidiana mea moles,[1] sollicitudo omnium Ecclesiarum.

29. Quis infirmatur, et ego non infirmor? quis offenditur, et ego non uror?

22. He now, by enumerating particular instances, lets them see more distinctly, that he would not by any means be found inferior, if matters came to a contest. And in the first place, he makes mention of the glory of his *descent,* of which his rivals chiefly vaunted. "If," says he, "they boast of illustrious *descent,* I shall be on a level with them, for I also am an *Israelite,* of the *seed of Abraham."* This is a silly and empty boast, and yet Paul makes use of *three* terms to express it; nay more, he specifies, as it were, *three* different marks of excellence. By this repetition, in my opinion, he indirectly reproves their folly, inasmuch as they placed the sum-total[2] of their excellence in a thing that was so trivial,[3] and this boasting was incessantly in their mouth, so as to be absolutely disgusting, as vain men are accustomed to pour forth empty bravadoes as to a mere nothing.

As to the term *Hebrews,* it appears from Gen. xi. 14, that it denotes descent, and is derived from *Heber;* and farther, it is probable, that Abraham himself is so called in Gen. xiv. 13, in no other sense than this—that he was descended from that ancestor.[4] Not altogether without some appearance of truth is the conjecture of those, who explain the term to mean *those dwelling beyond the river.*[5] We do not read, it

---

[1] " La pesanteur ordinaire des affaires que i'ay; *ou,* il y a ce qui m'assiege de iour en iour;"—" The ordinary burden of affairs which I have; *or,* there is that which besieges me from day to day."

[2] " Proram et puppim;"—" The prow and stern."

[3] " Vne chose si vaine, et de si petite consequence;"—" A thing so empty, and of so small importance."

[4] " Qu'il estoit descendu d'Heber de pere en fils;"—" That he was descended from Heber, from father to son."

[5] " Vray est que la coniecture de ceux qui disent qu'ils sont ainsi appelez comme *habitans outre la riuiere,* n'est pas du tout sans couleur;"—" It is

is true, that any one was called so before Abraham, who had *passed over the river*, when he quitted his native country, and afterwards the appellation came to be a customary one among his posterity, as appears from the history of Joseph. The termination, however, shows that it is expressive of descent, and the passage, that I have quoted, abundantly confirms it.[1]

23. *Are they ministers of Christ?* Now when he is treating of matters truly praiseworthy, he is no longer satisfied with being on an equality with them, but exalts himself above them. For their carnal glories he has previously been scattering like smoke by a breath of wind,[2] by placing in opposition to them those which he had of a similar kind ; but as they had nothing of solid worth, he on good grounds separates himself from their society, when he has occasion to glory in good earnest. For to be a *servant of Christ* is a thing that is much more honourable and illustrious, than to be the first-born among all the first-born of Abraham's posterity. Again, however, with the view of providing against calumnies, he premises that he *speaks as a fool.* "Imagine this," says he, "to be foolish boasting : it is, nevertheless, true."

In labours. By these things he proves that he is a more eminent servant of Christ, and *then* truly we have a proof that may be relied upon, when *deeds* instead of *words* are brought forward. He uses the term *labours* here in the plural number, and afterwards *labour.* What difference there

---

true, that the conjecture of those who say that they are so called, as *dwelling beyond the river*, is not without some appearance of truth."

[1] "The word 'Hebrew' signified properly *one who was from beyond*, (עברי from עבר to *pass*, to *pass over*,) hence applied to Abraham, because he had come from a foreign land ; and the word denoted properly *a foreigner*—a man from the land or country *beyond* (עבר) the Euphrates. The name Israelite denoted properly one descended from Israel or Jacob, and the difference between them was, that the name *Israelite*, being a patronymic derived from one of the founders of their nation, was in use among themselves ; the name *Hebrew* was applied by the Canaanite to them, as having come from *beyond* the river, and was the current name among foreign tribes and nations."—*Barnes.—Ed.*

[2] " Car quant a leurs gloires charnelles, qui n'estoyent que choses vaines, iusques yci il les a fait esuanoir comme en soufflant dessus ;"—" For as to their carnal glories, which were but vain things, he has hitherto made them vanish by, as it were, blowing upon them."

is between the former and the latter I do not see, unless perhaps it be, that he speaks here in a more general way, including those things that he afterwards enumerates in detail. In the same way we may also understand the term *deaths* to mean any kind of *perils* that in a manner threatened present death, instances of which he afterwards specifies. "I have given proof of myself in *deaths often*, in *labours* oftener still." He had made use of the term *deaths* in the same sense in the first chapter. (2 Cor. i. 10.)

24. *From the Jews.* It is certain that the Jews had at that time been deprived of jurisdiction, but as this was a kind of moderate punishment (as they termed it) it is probable that it was allowed them. Now the law of God was to this effect, that those who did not deserve capital punishment should be beaten in the presence of a judge, (Deut. xxv. 2, 3,) provided not more than *forty stripes* were inflicted, lest the body should be disfigured or mutilated by cruelty. Now it is probable, that in process of time it became customary to stop at the thirty-ninth lash,[1] lest perhaps they should on any occasion, from undue warmth, exceed the number prescribed by God. Many such precautions,[2] prescribed by the Rabbins,[3] are to be found among the Jews, which make some restriction upon the permission that the Lord had given. Hence, perhaps, in process of time, (as

---

[1] The custom of excepting *one* stripe from the *forty* is made mention of by Josephus : πληγὰς μίας λειπούσης τεσσαράκοντα, "forty stripes save one." (Joseph. Antiq. lib. iv. cap. viii. sect. 21.) It is noticed by *Wolfius*, that the Jews in modern times make use of the same number of stripes— thirty-nine—in punishing offenders, there being evidence of this from what is stated by Uriel Acosta, who, in his Life, subjoined by Limborch to his Conversation with a learned Jew, declares that he had in punishment of his departure from the Jews, received stripes up to that number.—*Ed*.

[2] "Plusieurs semblables pouruoyances et remedes inuentez par les Rabbins :"—"Many similar provisions and remedies, invented by the Rabbins."

[3] "The *Mishna* gives this as a rule, (MISH. Maccoth. fol. xxii. 10,) 'How often shall he, the culprit, be smitten? Ans. אלכעים חסר אחד, forty stripes, wanting one, *i.e.*, with the number which is nighest to forty.' . . . 'They also thought it right to stop under *forty*, lest the person who counted should make a mistake, and the criminal get more than *forty* stripes, which would be injustice, as the law required only *forty*.'"—*Dr. A. Clarke.* "As the whip was formed of three cords, and every stroke was allowed to count for three stripes, the number of strokes never exceeded thirteen, which made thirty-nine stripes."—*Bloomfield.*—*Ed.*

things generally deteriorate,) they came to think, that all criminals should be beaten with stripes to that number, though the Lord did not prescribe, how far severity should go, but where it was to stop ; unless perhaps you prefer to receive what is stated by others, that they exercised greater cruelty upon Paul. This is not at all improbable, for if they had been accustomed ordinarily to practise this severity upon all, he might have said that he was beaten according to custom. Hence the statement of the number is expressive of extreme severity.

25. *Thrice was I beaten with rods.* Hence it appears, that the Apostle suffered many things, of which no mention is made by Luke ;[1] for he makes mention of only *one* stoning,[2] *one* scourging, and *one* shipwreck. We have not, however, a complete narrative, nor is there mention made in it of every particular that occurred, but only of the principal things.

By *perils from the nation* he means those that befell him from his own nation, in consequence of the hatred, that was kindled against him among all the Jews. On the other hand, he had the Gentiles as his adversaries ; and in the *third* place snares were laid for him by *false brethren.* Thus it happened, that *for Christ's name's sake he was hated by all.* (Matt. x. 22.) By *fastings* I understand those that are voluntary, as he has spoken previously of *hunger* and *want.*

[1] See p. 41.

[2] " *Once* was I stoned." Paley remarks in his " Horæ Paulinæ," that this clause, " when confronted with the history," (contained in the Acts of the Apostles,) " furnishes the nearest approach to a contradiction, without a contradiction being actually incurred, of any that he remembers to have met with." While the narrative contained in the Acts of the Apostles gives an account of only *one* instance in which Paul was actually stoned, (Acts xiv. 19,) there was, previously to that, "an assault" made upon Paul and Barnabas at Iconium, "both of the Gentiles, and also of the Jews, with their rulers, to use them despitefully, and to stone them, but they were ware of it, and fled unto Lystra and Derbe." (Acts xiv. 5, 6.) " Now had the ' assault,'" says Paley, " been completed ; had the history related that a stone was thrown, as it relates that preparations were made both by Jews and Gentiles to stone Paul and his companions ; or even had the account of this transaction stopped, without going on to inform us that Paul and his companions were *aware of their danger and fled,* a contradiction between the history and the Apostle would have ensued. Truth is necessarily consistent ; but it is scarcely possible that independent accounts, not having truth to guide them, should thus advance to the very brink of contradiction without falling into it."—*Ed.*

Such were the tokens by which he showed himself, and on good grounds, to be an eminent servant of Christ. For how may we better distinguish Christ's servants than by proofs so numerous, so various, and so important ? On the other hand, while those effeminate boasters[1] had done nothing for Christ, and had suffered nothing for him, they, nevertheless, impudently vaunted.

It is asked, however, whether any one can be a servant of Christ, that has not been tried with so many evils, perils, and vexations? I answer, that all these things are not indispensably requisite on the part of all;[2] but where these things are seen, there is, undoubtedly, a greater and more illustrious testimony afforded. That man, therefore, who will be signalized by so many marks of distinction, will not despise those that are less illustrious, and less thoroughly tried, nor will he on that account be elated with pride ; but still, whenever there is occasion for it, he will be prepared, after Paul's example, to exult with a holy triumph, in opposition to pretenders[3] and worthless persons, provided he has an eye to Christ, not to himself—for nothing but pride or ambition could corrupt and tarnish all these praises. For the main thing is—that we serve Christ with a pure conscience. All other things are, as it were, additional.

28. *Besides those things that are without.* " *Besides those things,*" says he, " which come upon me from all sides, and are as it were extraordinary, what estimate must be formed of that ordinary burden that constantly presses upon me— the care that I have of all the Churches." *The care of all the Churches* he appropriately calls his *ordinary burden.* For I have taken the liberty of rendering ἐπισύστασιν in this way, as it sometimes means—whatever *presses upon* us.[4]

---

[1] " Thrasones."—See CALVIN on the Corinthians, vol. i. p. 98, *n.* 1.

[2] " Il n'est pas necessairement requis que tous vniversellement endurent toutes telles fascheries ;"—" It is not indispensably requisite that all universally endure all such vexations."

[3] " Des mercenaires ;"—" Hirelings."

[4] The word (ἐπισύστασις) is *translated* or rather *paraphrased* by Beza as follows : " Agmen illud in me consurgens ;"—" That troop which rises up together against me." He adds by way of explanation : " Certum est enim ἐπισύστασιν dici multitudinem quæ adversus aliquem coierit, idque non

Whoever is concerned in good earnest as to the Church of
God, stirs up himself and bears a heavy burden, which
presses upon his shoulders. What a picture we have here
of a complete minister, embracing in his anxieties and aims
not one Church merely, or ten, or thirty, but all of them
together, so that he instructs some, confirms others, exhorts
others, gives counsel to some, and applies a remedy to the
diseases of others ! Now from Paul's words we may infer,
that no one can have a heartfelt concern for the Churches,
without being harassed with many difficulties; for the
government of the Church is no pleasant occupation, in which
we may exercise ourselves agreeably and with delight of
heart,[1] but a hard and severe warfare, as has been previously mentioned, (2 Cor. x. 4,)—Satan from time to time
giving us as much trouble as he can, and leaving no stone
unturned to annoy us.

29. *Who is weak.* How many there are that allow all
offences to pass by unheeded—who either despise the infirmities of brethren, or trample them under foot ! This, however, arises from their having no concern for the Church.
For concern, undoubtedly, produces συμπάθειαν, (*sympathy*,)[2]
which leads the Minister of Christ to participate in the feelings of all,[3] and put himself in the place of all, that he may
suit himself to all.

---

semel, sed repetitis vicibus. Quia igitur multiplices erant curæ, quarum
tanquam agmine magis ac magis veluti obruebatur, Apostolus usus est
translatitie hoc vocabulo, admodum significanter ;"—" For it is certain that
ἐπισύστασιν denotes a multitude that has come together against any one,
and that not once merely, but in repeated instances. As, therefore, there
were manifold cares, by which rushing upon him like a troop, more and
more, he was in a manner overwhelmed, the Apostle, by way of metaphor,
made use of this term very significantly." *Raphelius* considers the term
to be synonymous with an expression made use of by Cicero : " concursus
occupationum ;"—" a crowding together of engagements."—(Cic. Fam. vii.
33.)—*Ed.*

[1] " Car le gouvernement de l'Eglise n'est pas vne occupation ioyeuse pour
nous exercer tout doucement, et par maniere de passe-temps et exercice
gracieux pour recreer nos esprits ;"—" For the government of the Church
is not a pleasant occupation for exercising ourselves quite agreeably, and
by way of pass-time, and an agreeable exercise for refreshing our minds."

[2] See CALVIN'S *Harmony*, vol. ii. p. 232.

[3] " Prend en soy les afflictions de tous ;"—" Take upon himself the afflictions of all."

30. If I must needs glory, I will glory of the things which concern mine infirmities.

30. Si gloriari oportet, in iis quæ infirmitatis meæ sunt gloriabor.

31. The God and Father of our Lord Jesus Christ, which is blessed for evermore, knoweth that I lie not.

31. Deus et Pater Domini nostri Iesu Christi novit, qui est benedictus in sæcula, quod non mentiar.

32. In Damascus the governor under Aretas the king kept the city of the Damascenes with a garrison, desirous to apprehend me;

32. Damasci Aretas, regius gentis præfectus, custodiebat urbem Damascenorum, volens me apprehendere. (Act. ix. 24, 25.)

33. And through a window in a basket was I let down by the wall, and escaped his hands.

33. Et per fenestram demissus fui in sporta per muros, atque effugi manus eius.

30. *If he must glory.* Here we have the conclusion, drawn from all that has gone before—that Paul is more inclined to boast of those things that are connected with his *infirmity,* that is, those things which might, in the view of the world, bring him contempt, rather than glory, as, for example, hunger, thirst, imprisonments, stonings, stripes, and the like—those things, in truth, that we are usually as much ashamed of, as of things that incur great dishonour.[1]

31. *The God and Father.* As he was about to relate a singular feat,[2] which, at the same time, was not well known, he confirms it by making use of an oath. Observe, however, what is the form of a pious oath,[3]—when, for the purpose of declaring the truth, we reverently call God as our witness. Now this persecution was, as it were, Paul's first apprenticeship,[4] as appears from Luke, (Acts ix. 23-25) ; but if, while yet a raw recruit, he was exercised in such beginnings, what shall we think of him, when a veteran soldier ? As, however, flight gives no evidence of a valiant spirit, it may be asked, why it is that he makes mention of his flight ? I answer, that the gates of the royal city having been closed, clearly showed with what rage the wicked were

---

[1] " De toutes lesquelles nous n'avons point de honte coustumierement, que si nous estions vileinement diffamez ;"—" Of all which we feel ordinarily as much ashamed, as if we had been shockingly defamed."

[2] " Vn acte singulier de vray champion de guerre ;"—" A singular feat of a true champion of war."

[3] " De iurement saincte et licite ;"—" Of a holy and lawful oath."

[4] CALVIN, when commenting on the passage referred to, (Acts ix. 23-25,) makes use of a similar expression : " Hoc tirocinio ad crucem ferendam mature assuefactus fuit ;"—" By this apprenticeship he was early inured to the endurance of the cross."—*Ed.*

inflamed against him ; and it was on no light grounds that they had been led to entertain such a feeling,[1] for if Paul had not fought for Christ with a new and unusual activity, the wicked would never have been thrown into such a commotion. His singular perseverance, however, shone forth chiefly in this—that, after escaping from so severe a persecution, he did not cease to stir up the whole world against him, by prosecuting fearlessly the Lord's work.

It may be, however, that he proceeds to mock those ambitious men, who, while they had never had experience of any thing but applauses, favours, honourable salutations, and agreeable lodgings, wished to be held in the highest esteem. For, in opposition to this, he relates, that he was shut in, so that he could with difficulty save his life by a miserable and ignominious flight.

Some, however, ask, whether it was lawful for Paul to leap over the walls, inasmuch as it was a capital crime to do so ? I answer, in the first place, that it is not certain, whether that punishment was sanctioned by law in the East ; and farther, that even if it was so, Paul, nevertheless, was guilty of no crime, because he did not do this as an enemy, or for sport, but from necessity. For the law would not punish a man, that would throw himself down from the walls to save his life from the flames ; and what difference is there between a fire, and a fierce attack from robbers ? We must always, in connection with laws, have an eye to reason and equity.[2] This consideration will exempt Paul entirely from blame.

---

[1] " Et qu'ils n'auoyent point conceu telle fureur pour vne chose leger et de petite consequence ;"—" And that they had not conceived such a rage for a slight matter, and one of small consequence."

[2] CALVIN seems to have here in his eye a passage expressly alluded to by him, when commenting on Acts ix. 23-25, from the writings of Cicero, to the following effect : " Etiamsi peregrinum lex arceat a muri accessu, minime tamen peccat, qui murum conscendit servandæ urbis causa, quia leges semper ad æquitatem flectendæ sunt ;"—" Although the law forbids a foreigner to approach the wall, no offence is committed by the man, who scales the wall with a view to the defence of the city ; for the laws must always be made to bend towards equity."—Ed.

CHAPTER XII.

1. It is not expedient for me doubtless to glory: I will come to visions and revelations of the Lord.

2. I knew a man in Christ above fourteen years ago, (whether in the body, I cannot tell; or whether out of the body, I cannot tell: God knoweth,) such an one caught up to the third heaven.

3. And I knew such a man, (whether in the body, or out of the body, I cannot tell: God knoweth,)

4. How that he was caught up into paradise, and heard unspeakable words, which it is not lawful for a man to utter.

5. Of such an one will I glory: yet of myself I will not glory, but in mine infirmities.

1. Gloriari sane non expedit mihi: veniam enim ad visiones et revelationes Domini.

2. Novi hominem in Christo ante annos quatuordecim (sive in corpore, nescio: sive extra corpus, nescio, Deus novit) eiusmodi, inquam, hominem raptum fuisse usque in tertium coelum:

3. Scio de eiusmodi homine (sive in corpore, nescio: sive extra corpus, nescio, Deus scit.)

4. Quod raptus sit in Paradisum, et audierit verba ineffabilia,[1] quae non licet[2] homini loqui.

5. De eiusmodi homine gloriabor: de me ipso non gloriabor, nisi in infirmitatibus meis.

1. *It is not expedient for me to glory.* Now, when as it were in the middle of the course, he restrains himself from proceeding farther, and in this way he most appropriately reproves the impudence of his rivals, and declares that it is with reluctance, that he engages in this sort of contest with them. For what a shame it was to scrape together from every quarter commendations, or rather to go a-begging for them, that they might be on a level with so distinguished a man! As to the latter, he admonishes them by his own example, that the more numerous and the more excellent the graces by which any one of us is distinguished, so much the less ought he to think of his own excellence. For such a thought is exceedingly dangerous, because, like one entering into a labyrinth, the person is immediately dazzled, so as to be too quick-sighted in discerning his gifts,[3] while in the mean time he is ignorant of himself. Paul is afraid, lest this should befall him. The graces conferred by God are, indeed,

---

[1] " Parolles inenarrables, *ou*, qui ne se doyuent dire;"—" Words unutterable, *or*, that ought not to be spoken."

[2] " Il n'est possible, ou loisible;"—" It is not possible, or lawful."

[3] " Ses dons et graces;"—" His gifts and graces."

to be acknowledged, that we may be aroused,—*first,* to gratitude for them, and *secondly,* to the right improvement of them ; but to take occasion from them to boast—*that* is what cannot be done without great danger.

For I will come[1] *to visions.* " I shall not creep on the ground, but will be constrained to mount aloft. Hence I am afraid, lest the height of my gifts should hurry me on, so as to lead me to forget myself." And certainly, if Paul had gloried ambitiously, he would have fallen headlong from a lofty eminence; for it is humility alone, that can give stability to our greatness in the sight of God.

Between *visions* and *revelations* there is this distinction— that a *revelation* is often made either in a dream, or by an oracle, without any thing being presented to the eye, while a *vision* is scarcely ever afforded without a *revelation,* or in other words, without the Lord's discovering what is meant by it.[2]

2. *I knew a man in Christ.* As he was desirous to restrain himself within bounds, he merely singles out *one* instance, and that, too, he handles in such a way as to show, that it is not from inclination that he brings it forward ; for why does he speak in the person of another rather than in his

---

[1] " *I will come.* Marg. '*For* I will.' Our Translators have omitted (γὰρ), *for,* in the text, evidently supposing that it is a mere expletive. Doddridge renders it ' nevertheless.' But it seems to me that it contains an important sense, and that it should be rendered by *then.* ' Since it is not fit that I should glory, *then* I will refer to visions, &c. I will turn away, *then,* from that subject, and come to another.' Thus the word (γὰρ), *for,* is used in John vii. 41, ' Shall *then* (μὴ γὰρ) Christ come out of Galilee ?' Acts viii. 31, ' How can I *then* (πῶς γὰρ) except some man should guide me ?' "—*Barnes.* *Granville Penn* renders the passage as follows: " Must I needs boast ? it is not good indeed, yet I will come to visions and revelations of the Lord." This rendering he adopts, as corresponding with the reading of the *Vat.* and most ancient MS. Καυχᾶσθαι δεῖ; οὐ συμφέρον μὲν, ἐλεύσομαι δὲ εἰς ὀπτασίας καὶ ἀποκαλύψεις Κυρίου.—*Ed.*

[2] " C'est qu'il signifie en ce qui s'est presenté a nous ;"—" What he intends in what is presented to our view."

" *Visions*" (ὀπτασίας)—symbolical representations of spiritual and celestial things, in which matters of the deepest importance are exhibited to the eye of the mind by a variety of emblems, the nature and properties of which serve to illustrate those spiritual things.—*Revelations* (ἀποκαλύψεις)—a manifestation of things not before known, and such as God alone can make known, because they are a part of his own inscrutable counsels."—*Dr. A. Clarke.*—*Ed.*

own ? It is as though he had said, " I should have preferred to be silent, I should have preferred to keep the
whole matter suppressed within my own mind, but those
persons[1] will not allow me. I shall mention it, therefore, as
it were in a stammering way, that it may be seen that I
speak through constraint." Some think that the clause *in
Christ* is introduced for the purpose of confirming what he
says. I view it rather as referring to the disposition, so as to
intimate that Paul has not here an eye to himself, but looks
to Christ exclusively.

When he confesses, that he does not know whether he
was *in the body*, or *out of the body*, he expresses thereby the
more distinctly the greatness of the revelation. For he
means, that God dealt with him in such a way,[2] that he did
not himself understand the manner of it. Nor should this
appear to us incredible, inasmuch as he sometimes manifests himself to us in such a way, that the manner of his
doing so is, nevertheless, hid from our view.[3] At the same
time, this does not, in any degree, detract from the assurance of faith, which rests simply on this single point—that
we are aware that God speaks to us. Nay more, let us learn
from this, that we must seek the knowledge of those things
only that are necessary to be known, and leave other things
to God. (Deut. xxix. 29.) He says, then, that he does not
know, whether he was wholly taken up—soul and body—into
heaven, or whether it was his soul only, that was *caught up*.

Fourteen years ago. Some[4] enquire, also, as to the place,
but it does not belong to us to satisfy their curiosity.[5] The
Lord manifested himself to Paul in the beginning by a
vision, when he designed to convert him from Judaism to
the faith of the gospel, but he was not then admitted as

---

[1] " Ces opiniastres ambitieux ;"—" Those ambitious, obstinate persons."

[2] " Que Dieu a tellement besongné et procedé enuers luy ;"—" That
God had in such a manner wrought and acted towards him."

[3] " Est incomprehensible à nostre sens ;"—" Is incomprehensible to our
mind."

[4] " Ne se contentans point de ceci ;"—" Not contenting themselves with
this."

[5] " Mais nous n'auons point deliberé, et aussi il n'est pas en nous de
satisfaire a leur curiosite ;"—" But we have not determined as to this, and
it does not belong to us to satisfy their curiosity."

yet into those secrets, as he needed even to be instructed by Ananias in the first rudiments.[1] (Acts ix. 12.) That vision, therefore, was nothing but a preparation, with the view of rendering him teachable. It may be, that, in this instance, he refers to that vision, of which he makes mention also, according to Luke's narrative. (Acts xxii. 17.) There is no occasion, however, for our giving ourselves much trouble as to these conjectures, as we see that Paul himself kept silence respecting it for fourteen years,[2] and would not have said one word in reference to it, had not the unreasonableness of malignant persons constrained him.

Even to the third heaven. He does not here distinguish between the different heavens in the manner of the philosophers, so as to assign to each planet its own heaven. On the other hand, the number *three* is made use of (κατ᾽ ἐξοχὴν) *by way of eminence,* to denote what is highest and most complete. Nay more, the term *heaven,* taken by itself, denotes here the blessed and glorious kingdom of God, which is above all the spheres,[3] and the firmament itself, and even the entire frame-work of the world. Paul, however, not contenting himself with the simple term,[4] adds, that he had reached even the greatest height, and the innermost recesses. For our faith scales heaven and enters it, and those that are superior to others in knowledge get higher in degree and elevation, but to reach the *third heavens* has been granted to very few.

4. *In paradise.*[5] As every region that is peculiarly

---

[1] " Es premiers commencemens de la religion ;"—" In the first elements of religion."

[2] " This vision Paul had kept secret for fourteen years. He had doubtless *often* thought of it ; and the remembrance of that glorious hour was doubtless one of the reasons why he bore trials so patiently, and was willing to endure so much. But before this he had had no occasion to mention it. He had other proofs in abundance that he was called to the work of an Apostle ; and to mention this would savour of pride and ostentation. It was only when he was *compelled* to refer to the evidences of his apostolic mission that he refers to it here."—*Barnes.—Ed.*

[3] " Par dessus tous les cieux ;"—" Above all the heavens."

[4] " Non content de nommer simplement le ciel ;"—" Not contented with simply employing the term *heaven.*"

[5] " The word *paradise* (παράδεισος) occurs but three times in the New Testament, (Luke xxiii. 43, 2 Cor. xii. 4, and Rev. ii. 7.) It occurs often in the Septuagint, as the translation of the word garden, (גן) *gan ;* and of

agreeable and delightful[1] is called in the Scriptures the
garden of God, it came from this to be customary among the
Greeks to employ the term *paradise* to denote the heavenly
glory, even previously to Christ's advent, as appears from
Ecclesiasticus. (Sirach, 40, 17, 27.) It is also used in this
sense in Luke xxiii. 43, in Christ's answer to the robber—
" To-day shalt thou be with me in *paradise,*" that is, " Thou
shalt enjoy the presence of God, in the condition and life
of the blessed."

Heard unspeakable words. By *words* here I do not understand *things,* as the term is wont to be made use of after
the manner of the Hebrews ;[2] for the word *heard* would not
correspond with this. Now if any one inquires, what they
were, the answer is easy—that it is not without good reason
that they are called *unspeakable*[3] *words,* and such as it is
unlawful to utter. Some one, however, will reply, that what
Paul heard was, consequently, needless and useless, for what
purpose did it serve to hear, what was to be buried in perpetual silence ? I answer, that this took place for the sake of
Paul himself, for one who had such arduous difficulties await-

the word (פרדס) *pardes,* in Neh. ii. 8, Eccl. ii. 5, Cant. ii. 13. It is a
word which had its origin in the language of Eastern Asia, and which
has been adopted in the Greek, the Roman, and other western languages.
In Sanscrit, the word *paradésha* means a land elevated and cultivated ; in
Armenian, *pardes* denotes a garden around the house, planted with trees,
shrubs, grass for use and ornament. In Persia, the word denotes the
pleasure-gardens, and *parks* with wild animals, around the country resi-
dences of the monarchs and princes. Hence it denotes, in general, a
garden of pleasure ; and in the New Testament is applied to the abodes
of the blessed after death, the dwelling-place of God, and of happy spirits ;
or to heaven as a place of blessedness."—*Barnes.—Ed.*

[1] " Toute region delectable et excellente en fertilite et abondance de
biens de la terre ;"—" Every region that is delightful and distinguished by
fertility and abundance of the good things of the earth."

[2] Calvin's meaning evidently is, that ῥήματα, here rendered *words,* is
often made use of, like the corresponding Hebrew word, דברים (*dabarim,*)
to mean *things.* Accordingly דבר, (*dabar,*) when employed to denote
thing, is very frequently rendered in the Septuagint by ῥῆμα, as, for example, in Gen. xviii. 14, Exod. xviii. 17, Deut. xvii. 1. Calvin, when
commenting on the expression—*with God nothing shall be impossible,*
(Luke i. 37,) remarks that " a *word* often means a *thing* in the idiom of
the Hebrew language, which the Evangelists followed, though they wrote
in Greek."—Calvin's Harmony, vol. i. p. 45.—*Ed.*

[3] " Secretes, ou impossibles à dire ;"—" Secret, or such as it is impossible
to utter."

ing him, enough to break a thousand hearts, required to be strengthened by special means, that he might not give way, but might persevere undaunted.[1] Let us consider for a little, how many adversaries his doctrine had, and of what sort they were ; and farther, with what a variety of artifices it was assailed, and then we shall wonder no longer, why he heard more than it was *lawful for him to utter.*

From this, too, we may gather a most useful admonition as to setting bounds to knowledge. We are naturally prone to curiosity. Hence, neglecting altogether, or tasting but slightly, and carelessly, doctrine that tends to edification, we are hurried on to frivolous questions. Then there follow upon this—boldness and rashness, so that we do not hesitate to decide on matters unknown, and concealed.

From these two sources has sprung up a great part[2] of scholastic theology, and every thing, which that trifler Dionysius[3]

---

[1] " Mais qu'il perseuerast constamment, sans se laisser vaincre ;"—" But might persevere steadfastly, without allowing himself to be overcome."

[2] " La plus grande partie ;"—" The greatest part."

[3] CALVIN refers here to one Dionysius, whose writings appear to have been looked upon by many in CALVIN'S times, as having been composed by Dionysius the Areopagite, who was converted by Paul at Athens. (Acts xvii. 34.) A copy of the work referred to, printed at Paris in 1555, bears the following title : " S. Dionysii Areopagitæ, Martyris Inclyti, Athenarum Episcopi, et Galliarum Apostoli, opera—Translatio Noua Ambrosii Florentini," &c. ;—" The works of St. Dionysius the Areopagite, the renowned Martyr, Bishop of Athens, and Apostle of the Gauls—a New Translation by Ambrosius Florentine," &c.—CALVIN, in his Institutes, (vol. i. p. 194,) when treating of angels, adverts to the writings of Dionysius, in the following terms : " None can deny that Dionysius (whoever he may have been) has many shrewd and subtle disquisitions in his Celestial Hierarchy, but on looking at them more closely, every one must see that they are merely idle talk. The duty of a theologian, however, is not to tickle the ear, but confirm the conscience, by teaching what is true, certain, and useful. When you read the work of Dionysius, you would think that the man had come down from heaven, and was relating, not what he had learned, but what he had actually seen. Paul, however, though he was carried to the third heaven, so far from delivering any thing of the kind positively, declares, that it was not lawful for man to speak the secrets which he had seen. Bidding adieu, therefore, to that nugatory wisdom, let us endeavour to ascertain from the simple doctrine of Scripture, what it is the Lord's pleasure that we should know concerning angels."—*Beza,* in his Annotations on 1 Cor. iii. 15, when expounding the expression—" he himself shall be saved, yet so as by fire," makes mention of Dionysius, as having been, in his opinion, Bishop of Corinth, and speaks of him as having devoted himself to unprofitable speculations, and as harassing himself, for the most part in vain, in describing the Celestial Hierarchy.—The

has been so daring as to contrive in reference to the Heavenly
Hierarchies.   It becomes us so much the more to keep within
bounds,[1] so as not to seek to know any thing, but what the
Lord has seen it good to reveal to his Church.   Let this be
the limit of our knowledge.

5. *Of such a man.*   It is as though he had said : " I have
just ground for glorying, but I do not willingly avail myself
of it.   For it is more in accordance with my design, to *glory
in my infirmities.*   If, however, those malicious persons
harass me any farther, and constrain me to boast more than
I am inclined to do, they shall feel that they have to do with
a man, whom God has illustriously honoured, and raised up
on high, with a view to his exposing their follies.

6. For though I would desire to glory, I shall not be a fool; for I will say the truth: but *now* I forbear, lest any man should think of me above that which he seeth me *to be,* or *that* he heareth of me.

6. Nam si voluero gloriari, non ero insipiens: veritatem enim dicam: sed supersedeo: ne quis de me cogitet supra id quod videt esse me, aut quod audit ex me.

Rhemish Translators, when commenting on Acts xvii. 34, contend for the
genuineness of the writings referred to.   " *Dionysius Areopagita.*   This
is that famous Denys that first converted France, and wrote those notable
and divine works—' De Ecclesiastica et Cœlesti Hierarchia, de diuinis no-
minibus,' and others ; in which he confirmeth, and proveth plainely, almost
all things that the Church now useth in the ministration of the Holy Sacrament, and affirmeth that he learned them of the Apostles, giving also
testimony for the Catholike faith in most things now controuersed, so
plainely that our adversaries have no shift but to deny this Denys to have
been the author of them, faining that they be another's of later age."   To
these statements Dr. Fulke, in his elaborate work in refutation of the
errors of the Rhemish Translators, (p. 403,) replies as follows : " That
Dionysius Areopagita was author of those bookes which now beare his
name, you bring no proofe at all.   We alleage that Eusebius, Hierome,
Gennadius, neuer heard of his writings, for if they had heard, Dionysius
Areopagita should have been registered by them among ecclesiasticall
writers."—It is stated by *Mosheim* in his Ecclesiastical History, (London
1825,) vol. ii. p. 330, *n.* (*u*), that " the spuriousness of these works is now
universally granted by the most learned and impartial of the Roman
Catholic writers, as they contain accounts of many events that happened
several ages after the time of Dionysius, and were not at all mentioned
until after the fifth century."   *Turretine* in his Theology brings forward,
at considerable length, evidence to show, that the work referred to was not,
as pretended, the production of Dionysius the Areopagite, who was "σύγχρονος
Apostolis," (" a contemporary of the Apostles,") but was written by an
author of much later date—born in the fifth century.—*Turretini* Theo-
logia, (Genevæ, 1690,) tom. iii. pp. 233, 234.—*Ed.*

[1] " Il faut que nous soyons d'autant plus sobres et modestes ;"—" It is
necessary, that we should be so much the more sober and modest."

7. And lest I should be exalted above measure through the abundance of the revelations, there was given to me a thorn in the flesh, the messenger of Satan to buffet me, lest I should be exalted above measure.

7. Et ne excellentia revelationum supra modum efferrer, datus mihi fuit stimulus carni, nuntius Satanæ, qui me colaphis cæderet, ne supra modum efferrer.

8. For this thing I besought the Lord thrice, that it might depart from me.

8. Supra hoc ter Dominum rogavi, ut discederet a me :

9. And he said unto me, My grace is sufficient for thee; for my strength is made perfect in weakness. Most gladly therefore will I rather glory in my infirmities, that the power of Christ may rest upon me.

9. Et dixit mihi : Sufficit tibi gratia mea : nam virtus mea in infirmitate perficitur : libentissime igitur gloriabor super infirmitatibus meis, ut inhabitet in me virtus Christi.

10. Therefore I take pleasure in infirmities, in reproaches, in necessities, in persecutions, in distresses, for Christ's sake : for when I am weak, then am I strong.

10. Quamobrem placeo mihi in infirmitatibus, in contumeliis, in necessitatibus, in persequutionibus, in anxietatibus pro Christo: quum enim infirmus sum, tunc robustus sum.

6. *For if I should desire.* Lest what he had said, as to his having no inclination to glory, should be turned into an occasion of calumny, and malevolent persons should reply— "You are not inclined for it, because it is not in your power," he anticipates such a reply. " I would have it quite in my power," says he, "on good grounds ; nor would I be justly accused of vanity, for I have ground to go upon, but I refrain from it." He employs the term *folly* here in a different sense from what he had done previously, for even those that boast on good grounds act a silly and disgusting part, if there appears any thing of boasting or ambition. The folly, however, is more offensive and insufferable, if any one boasts groundlessly, or, in other words, pretends to be what he is not ; for in that case there is impudence in addition to silliness. The Apostle here proceeded upon it as a settled matter, that his glorying was as humble as it was well founded. Erasmus has rendered it—" I spare you,"[1]

[1] The same rendering is given in Cranmer's version, (1539,) "Neuerthelesse I spare you." The Vulgate reads : "Parco autem;"—(" But I spare.") This rendering is followed in Wiclif's version, (1380,) Tyndale's (1534,) and the Rheims version, (1582.) The Geneva version (1557) has : "but I refraine."—*Joachim Camerarius* remarks, that φείδομαι is elliptical, as being used instead of φείδομαι τοῦ ἐρεῖν, or, τοῦ μεγαλαυχεῖν;— " I refrain from speaking, or from boasting."—*Ed.*

but I prefer to understand it as meaning—" I refrain," or, as I have rendered it, " I forbear."

Lest any one should think of me.   He adds the reason— because he is contented to occupy the station, which God has assigned him. " My appearance," says he, " and speech do not give promise of any thing illustrious in me : I have no objection, therefore, to be lightly esteemed." Here we perceive what great modesty there was in this man, inasmuch as he was not at all concerned on account of his meanness, which he discovered in his appearance and speech, while he was replenished with such a superiority of gifts. There would, however, be no inconsistency in explaining it in this way, that satisfied with the reality itself, he says nothing respecting himself, that he may thus reprove indirectly the false Apostles, who gloried in themselves as to many things, none of which were to be seen. What I mentioned first, however, is what I rather approve of.

7. *And lest through the superiority of revelations.*   Here we have a *second* reason—that God, designing to repress in him every approach to insolence, subdued him with a rod. That rod he calls a *goad,* by a metaphor taken from oxen. The word *flesh* is, in the Greek, in the dative.[1] Hence Erasmus has rendered it " *by* the flesh." I prefer, however, to understand him as meaning, that the prickings of this *goad* were *in* his flesh.

Now it is asked, what this *goad* was. Those act a ridiculous part, who think that Paul was tempted to lust. We must therefore repudiate that fancy.[2] Some have supposed, that he was harassed with frequent pains in the head. Chrysostom is rather inclined to think, that the reference is to Hymeneus and Alexander, and the like, because, instigated by the devil, they occasioned Paul very much annoyance. My opinion is, that under this term is comprehended every kind of temptation, with which Paul was exercised. For *flesh* here, in my opinion, denotes—not the body, but that

---

[1] " Selon le Grec il faudroit dire *A la chair ;*"—"According to the Greek, we would require to say, TO *the flesh.*"

[2] " Il faut reietter loin ce songe ;"—"We must put far away from us that dream."

part of the soul which has not yet been regenerated. "There was given to me a *goad* that my flesh might be spurred up by it, for I am not yet so spiritual, as not to be exposed to temptations according to the flesh."

He calls it farther the *messenger of Satan* on this ground, that as all temptations are sent by Satan, so, whenever they assail us, they warn us that Satan is at hand. Hence, at every apprehension of temptation, it becomes us to arouse ourselves, and arm ourselves with promptitude for repelling Satan's assaults. It was most profitable for Paul to think of this, because this consideration did not allow him to exult like a man that was off his guard.[1] For the man, who is as yet beset with dangers, and dreads the enemy, is not prepared to celebrate a triumph. "The Lord, says he, has provided me with an admirable remedy, against being unduly elated ; for, while I am employed in taking care that Satan may not take advantage of me, I am kept back from pride."

At the same time, God did not cure him by this means exclusively, but also by humbling him. For he adds, *to buffet me ;* by which expression he elegantly expresses this idea—that he has been brought under control.[2] For to be *buffeted* is a severe kind of indignity. Accordingly, if any one has had his face made black and blue,[3] he does not, from a feeling of shame, venture to expose himself openly in the view of men. In like manner, whatever be the infirmity under which we labour, let us bear in mind, that we are, as it were, *buffeted by the Lord,* with the view of making us ashamed, that we may learn humility. Let this be carefully reflected upon by those, especially, who are otherwise distinguished by illustrious virtues, if they have any mixture of defects, if they are persecuted by any with hatred, if they are assailed by any revilings—that these things are not

---

[1] " Ceste consideration ne luy donnoit point le loisir de s'egayer, comme vn homme sans souci, mais l'admonestoit de se tenir sur ses gardes ;"— " This consideration did not allow him leisure to sport himself, like a man that is devoid of care, but warned him to be upon his guard."

[2] " Qu'il a este reprimé et rangé a humilite ;"—" That he has been restrained and brought down to subjection."

[3] " Si quelq'vn a este tellement frappé au visage, que les taches noires y demeurent ;"—" If any one has been struck on the face, in such a way, as to leave black marks upon it."

merely *rods* of the Heavenly Master, but *buffetings*, to fill them with shame, and beat down all forwardness.[1] Now let all the pious take notice as to this, that they may see[2] how dangerous a thing the "poison of pride" is, as Augustine speaks in his third sermon "On the words of the Apostle," inasmuch as it "cannot be cured except by poison."[3] And unquestionably, as it was the cause of man's ruin, so it is the last vice with which we have to contend, for other vices have a connection with evil deeds, but *this* is to be dreaded in connection with the best actions ; and farther, it naturally clings to us so obstinately, and is so deeply rooted, that it is extremely difficult to extirpate it.

Let us carefully consider, who it is that here speaks—He had overcome so many dangers, tortures, and other evils— had triumphed over all the enemies of Christ—had driven away the fear of death—had, in fine, renounced the world ; and yet he had not altogether subdued pride. Nay more, there awaited him a conflict so doubtful, that he could not overcome without being *buffeted*. Instructed by his example, let us wage war with other vices in such a way, as to lay out our main efforts for the subduing of this one.

But what does this mean—that Satan, who was a *man-slayer*[4] *from the beginning*, (John viii. 44,) was a physician to

---

[1] "Toute orgueil et insolence ;"—"All pride and insolence."

[2] "Or ie prie maintenant sur cepassage tous fideles, qu'ils auisent ;"— "But I entreat now in connection with this passage all believers to take notice."

[3] "Veu qu'il ne peut estre guari que par d'autre poison ;"—"Inasmuch as it cannot be cured except by another poison."

[4] Dr. Campbell, in his Translation of the Gospels, makes use of the term *manslayer*, as CALVIN does here, and makes the following observations in support of this rendering: "The common term for *murderer* in the New Testament is φονεὺς. I have here made choice of a less usual name, not from any disposition to trace etymologies, but because I think it is not without intention, that the devil, as being not of earthly extraction, is rather called ἀνθρωποκτόνος than φονεὺς, as marking, with greater precision, his ancient enmity to the human race. When the name *murderer* is applied to a rational being of a species different from ours, it naturally suggests, that the being so denominated is a destroyer of others of his own species. As this is not meant here, the Evangelist's term is peculiarly apposite. At the same time, I am sensible, that our word *manslaughter* means, in the language of the law, such killing as is, indeed, criminal, though not so atrocious as murder. But, in common use, it is not so limited. Heylyn says, to the same purpose—*a slayer of men.*"— *Campbell* on the Gospels, (Edin. 1807,) vol. ii. p. 539.—*Ed.*

Paul, and that too, not merely in the cure of the body, but —what is of greater importance—in the cure of the soul? I answer, that Satan, in accordance with his disposition and custom, had nothing else in view than to *kill and to destroy,* (John x. 10,) and that the *goad,* that Paul makes mention of, was dipt in deadly poison; but that it was a special kindness from the Lord, to render medicinal what was in its own nature deadly.

8. *For this thing I besought the Lord thrice.* Here, also,[1] the number *three* is employed to denote frequent repetition.[2] He means, however, to intimate, that this annoyance had been felt by him distressing, inasmuch as he had so frequently prayed to be exempted from it. For if it had been slight, or easy to be endured, he would not have been so desirous to be freed from it; and yet he says that he had not obtained this: hence it appears, how much need he had of being humbled. He confirms, therefore, what he had said previously—that he had, by means of this bridle, been held back from being haughty; for if relief from it had been for his advantage, he would never have met with a refusal.

It may seem, however, to follow from this, that Paul had not by any means prayed in faith, if we would not make void all the promises of God.[3] " We read everywhere in Scripture, that we shall obtain whatever we ask in faith: Paul prays, and does not obtain." I answer, that as there are different ways of asking, so there are different ways of obtaining. We ask in simple terms those things as to which we have an express promise—as, for example, the perfecting of God's kingdom, and the *hallowing of his name,* (Matt. vi. 9,) the remission of our sins, and every thing that is advantageous to us; but, when we think that the kingdom of God

---

[1] CALVIN alludes to what he had said as to the number *three,* when commenting on an expression, which occurs in verse 2—*third heavens.* See p. 368.—*Ed.*

[2] " Τρὶς is considered by the commentators as a certain for an uncertain, but large number, (i.e., *oftentimes.*) To the passages cited by them I add Eurip. Hippol. 46; and Job xxxiii. 29, which I would render—' So all these things doth God work with man unto three times,' namely, by divinely sent disorders, by nocturnal visions, and by divine messengers."— *Bloomfield.*—*Ed.*

[3] " Si nous ne voulons faire toutes les promesses de Dieu vaines et inutiles;"—" If we would not make all the promises of God vain and useless."

can, nay *must* be advanced, in this particular manner, or in that, and that this thing, or that, is necessary for the *hallowing of his name,* we are often mistaken in our opinion. In like manner, we often fall into a serious mistake as to what tends to promote our own welfare. Hence we ask those former things confidently, and without any reservation, while it does not belong to us to prescribe the means. If, however, we specify the means, there is always a condition implied, though not expressed. Now Paul was not so ignorant as not to know this. Hence, as to the *object* of his prayer, there can be no doubt that he was heard, although he met with a refusal as to the express *form.* By this we are admonished not to give way to despondency, as if our prayers had been lost labour, when God does not gratify or comply with our wishes, but that we must be *satisfied with his grace,* that is, in respect of our not being forsaken by him. For the reason, why he sometimes mercifully refuses to his own people, what, in his wrath, he grants to the wicked, is this—that he foresees better what is expedient for us, than our understanding is able to apprehend.

9. *He said to me.* It is not certain, whether he had this answer by a special revelation, and it is not of great importance.[1] For God answers us, when he strengthens us inwardly by his Spirit, and sustains us by his consolation, so that we do not give up hope and patience. He bids Paul be *satisfied with his grace,* and, in the mean time, not refuse chastisement. Hence we must bear up under evil of ever so long continuance, because we are admirably well dealt with, when we have the grace of God to be our support.[2] The term *grace,* here, does not mean here, as it does elsewhere, the favour of God, but by *metonymy,* the aid of the Holy Spirit, which comes to us from the unmerited favour of God ; and it ought to be *sufficient* for the pious, inasmuch as it is a sure and invincible support against their ever giving way.

For my strength. Our weakness may seem, as if it were an obstacle in the way of God's perfecting his strength in

---

[1] " Et aussi il n'est pas fort requis de la scauoir ;"—" And besides, it is not greatly requisite to know it."

[2] " Et c'est assez ;"—" And that is enough."

us. Paul does not merely deny this, but maintains, on the other hand, that it is only when our weakness becomes apparent, that God's *strength* is duly *perfected*. To understand this more distinctly, we must distinguish between God's strength and ours; for the word *my* is emphatic. "*My* strength," says the Lord, (meaning that which helps man's need—which raises them up when they have fallen down, and refreshes them when they are faint,) "is perfected in the weakness of men;" that is, it has occasion to exert itself, when the weakness of men becomes manifest; and not only so, but it is more distinctly recognised as it ought to be. For the word *perfected* has a reference to the perception and apprehension of mankind, because it is not *perfected* unless it openly shines forth, so as to receive its due praise. For mankind have no taste of it, unless they are first convinced of the need of it, and they quickly lose sight of its value, if they are not constantly exercised with a feeling of their own weakness.

Most gladly, therefore. This latter statement confirms the exposition that I have given. *I will glory*, says he, *in my infirmities, that the power of Christ may dwell in me.*[1] Hence, the man that is ashamed of this glorying, shuts the door upon Christ's grace, and, in a manner, puts it away from him. For *then* do we make room for Christ's grace, when in true humility of mind, we feel and confess our own weakness. The *valleys* are watered with rain to make them fruitful, while in the mean time, the high summits of the lofty mountains re-

[1] The original word, ἐπισκηνώσῃ, properly means, to *pitch a tent*, or *tabernacle, upon*. Raphelius quotes two passages from Polybius, in which the verb is used as meaning—to *enter into, and dwell in*. Τὸ δὲ τελευταῖον, ἐπισκηνώσαντες ἐπὶ τὰς οἰκίας—" and at last, having *entered in*, and taken *possession of* the houses." Μετὰ δὲ ταῦτα ταῖς οἰκίαις ἐπισκηνώσαντες, κατεῖχον τὴν πόλιν—" And after these things, having *entered into* the houses, they took possession of the city."—Œcumenius, cited by Parkhurst, considers ἐπισκηνώσῃ, as employed by the Apostle here, to be equivalent to ὅλη ἐν ὅλῳ κατοικήσῃ—" may *entirely take possession of me, and dwell in me.*"—It is admirably well observed by Dr. Adam Clarke, that " the same *Eternal* WORD," (of whom it is said in John i. 14, that he " was made flesh, and *made his tabernacle among us*, (ἐσκήνωσιν ἐν ἡμῖν,) full of grace and truth,") " promised to make his *tabernacle* with the Apostle, and gives him a proof that he was still the same—*full of grace and truth*, by assuring him that his *grace should be sufficient for him.*"—Ed.

main dry.[1] Let that man, therefore, become a *valley*, who is desirous to receive the heavenly rain of God's spiritual grace.[2]

He adds *most gladly*, to show that he is influenced by such an eager desire for the grace of Christ, that he refuses nothing for the sake of obtaining it. For we see very many yielding, indeed, submission to God, as being afraid of incurring sacrilege in coveting his glory, but, at the same time, not without reluctance, or at least, less cheerfully than were becoming.[3]

10. *I take pleasure in infirmities.* There can be no doubt, that he employs the term *weakness* in different senses; for he formerly applied this name to the punctures that he experienced in the flesh. He now employs it to denote those external qualities, which occasion contempt in the view of the world. Having spoken, however, in a general way, of *infirmities* of every kind, he now returns to that particular description of them, that had given occasion for his turning aside into this general discourse. Let us take notice, then, that *infirmity* is a general term, and that under it is comprehended the weakness of our nature, as well as all tokens of abasement. Now the point in question was Paul's outward abasement. He proceeded farther, for the purpose of showing, that the Lord humbled him in every way, that, in his defects, the glory of God might shine forth the more resplendently, which is, in a manner, concealed and buried, when a man is in an elevated position. He now again

---

[1] " Secs et steriles;"—" Dry and barren."

[2] Much in accordance with this beautiful sentiment is Bunyan's description of the " Valley of Humiliation," in the *second* part of his " Pilgrim's Progress." " It is the best and most fruitful piece of ground in all these parts. It is fat ground, and, as you see, consisteth much in meadows; and if a man was to come here in the summer-time, as we do now, if he knew not any thing before thereof, and if he also delighted himself in the sight of his eyes, he might see that which would be delightful to him. 'Behold how green this valley is! also how beautiful with lilies!' (Song ii. 1.) I have known many labouring men that have got good estates in this Valley of Humiliation. (1 Pet. v. 5.) 'For God resisteth the proud, but giveth grace unto the humble.' (James iv. 6.) For indeed it is a very fruitful soil, and doth bring forth by handfuls."—*Bunyan's Allegorical Works,* (Glasgow, 1843,) p. 164.—*Ed.*

[3] " Ce n'est point si nayfuement et franchement qu'il faloit;"—" It is not so ingenuously and frankly, as it ought to be."

returns to speak of his excellences, which, at the same time, made him contemptible in public view, instead of procuring for him esteem and commendation.

For when I am weak, that is—"The more deficiency there is in me, so much the more liberally does the Lord, from his strength, supply me with whatever he sees to be needful for me." For the fortitude of philosophers is nothing else than contumacy, or rather a mad enthusiasm, such as fanatics are accustomed to have. "If a man is desirous to be truly *strong,* let him not refuse to be at the same time *weak.* Let him," I say, "be *weak* in himself, that he may be *strong in the Lord."* (Eph. vi. 10.) Should any one object, that Paul speaks here, not of a failure of strength, but of poverty, and other afflictions, I answer, that all these things are exercises for discovering to us our own weakness; for if God had not exercised Paul with such trials, he would never have perceived so clearly his weakness. Hence, he has in view not merely poverty, and hardships of every kind, but also those effects that arise from them, as, for example, a feeling of our own weakness, self-distrust, and humility.

11. I am become a fool in glorying; ye have compelled me: for I ought to have been commended of you; for in nothing am I behind the very chiefest apostles, though I be nothing.

12. Truly the signs of an apostle were wrought among you in all patience, in signs, and wonders, and mighty deeds.

13. For what is it wherein you were inferior to other churches, except *it be* that I myself was not burdensome to you? forgive me this wrong.

14. Behold, the third time I am ready to come to you; and I will not be burdensome to you: for I seek not yours, but you : for the children ought not to lay up for the parents, but the parents for the children.

15. And I will very gladly spend and be spent for you; though the more abundantly I love you, the less I be loved.

11. Factus sum insipiens gloriando: vos me coegistis : nam ego debueram a vobis commendari : nulla enim in re inferior fui summis Apostolis, tametsi nihil sum.

12. Signa quidem Apostoli peracta fuerunt inter vos, in omni patientia, et signis, et prodigiis, et virtutibus.

13. Nam quid est, in quo fueritis inferiores cæteris Ecclesiis, nisi quod ego ipse non fui vobis onerosus? Condonate mihi hanc iniuriam.

14. Ecce, tertio propensus animo sum, ut veniam ad vos, neque vobis ero oneri: non enim quæro quæ vestra sunt, sed vos: etenim non debent filii parentibus, recondere, sed parentes filiis.

15. Ego vero libentissime impendam et expendar pro animabus vestris : licet uberius vos diligens, minus diligar.

11. *I have become a fool.*   Hitherto he had, by various apologies, solicited their forgiveness for what was contrary to his own custom and manner of acting, and contrary, also, to propriety, and what was due to his office as an Apostle—the publishing of his own praises.   *Now,* instead of soliciting, he upbraids, throwing the blame upon the Corinthians, who ought to have been beforehand in this.[1]   For when the false Apostles calumniated Paul, they should have set themselves vigorously in opposition to them, and should have faithfully borne the testimony that was due to his excellences.   He chides them, however, thus early, lest those, who were unfavourably disposed towards them, should put a wrong construction upon the defence which he brought forward, in consequence of his being constrained to it by their ingratitude,[2] or should persist in calumniating him.

For in nothing.   We are ungrateful to God, if we allow his gifts, of which we are witnesses, to be disparaged, or contemned.   He charges the Corinthians with this fault, for they knew him to be equal to the *chiefest Apostles,* and yet they lent an ear to calumniators, when they slandered him.

By the *chiefest Apostles* some understand his rivals, who arrogated to themselves the precedence.[3]   I understand it, however, as meaning—those that were chief among the twelve.   " Let me be compared with any one of the Apostles,[4] I have no fear, that I shall be found inferior."   For,

---

[1] " Qui deuoyent les premiers faire cet office—ascauoir de le loyer ;"—" Who ought to have been the first to discharge that office—that of praising him."

[2] " The Apostle, in defending himself, was aware how near he approached the *language* of a *fool,* that is, a man desirous of vain glory, and how liable what he had written was to be attributed to that motive.   It is on this account that he obviates the charge which he knew his adversaries would allege.   ' Yes,' says he, ' I speak as a fool .   .   but ye have *compelled* me."   This was owning that, as to his *words,* they might, indeed, be considered as vain glorying, if the *occasion* were overlooked : but, if that were justly considered, it would be found that *they* ought rather to be ashamed than *he,* for having reduced him to the disagreeable necessity of speaking in his own behalf."—*Fuller's Works,* vol. iii. p. 632.—*Ed.*

[3] " Qui s'attribuoyent le premier lieu et souuerain degre ;"—" Who claimed for themselves the first place and highest rank."

[4] " Qu'on m'accompare auec lequel qu'on voudra des Apostres ;"—" Let them compare me with whom they choose among the Apostles."

although Paul was on the best of terms with all the Apostles, so that he was prepared to extol them above himself, he, nevertheless, contended against their names when falsely assumed.[1] For the false Apostles abused this pretext, that they had been in the company of the twelve—that they were in possession of all their views[2]—that they were fully acquainted with all their institutions, and the like. Hence Paul, perceiving that they falsely gloried in these masks and counterfeit titles, and were successful, to some extent, among unlearned persons,[3] reckoned it necessary to enter upon a comparison of that nature.[4]

The correction that he adds—*though I am nothing*, means, that Paul was not disposed to claim any thing as his own, but simply *gloried in the Lord*, (2 Cor. x. 17,) unless, perhaps, you prefer to consider this as a concession, in which he makes mention of what is thrown out against him by adversaries and slanderers.[5]

12. *The signs of an Apostle.* By the *signs of an Apostle* he means—the seals, that tend to confirm the evidence of his Apostleship, or, at least, for the proofs and evidences of it. " God has confirmed my Apostleship among you to such a degree, that it stands in no need of proof being adduced." The *first sign* he makes mention of is *patience*—either because he had remained invincible,[6] by nobly withstanding all the assaults of Satan and his enemies, and on no occasion giving way ; or because, regardless of his own distinction, he suffered all injuries patiently, endured in silence countless

---

[1] " Faussement vsurpez et controuuez ;"—" When falsely claimed and counterfeited."

[2] " Qu'ils entendoyent bien toute leur intention ;"—" That they understood well their entire design."

[3] " Et par ce moyen ils acqueroyent credit enuers les simples et idiots ;"—" And by this means they gained credit among the simple and unlearned."

[4] " Ne pouuoit faire autrement qu'il ne veinst a faire ceste comparaison de soy et des plus excellens Apostres ;"—" Could not do otherwise than enter upon this comparison between himself and the most eminent of the Apostles."

[5] " Ce que les malueillans et detracteurs gazouilloyent de luy ;"— " What malevolent persons and slanderers chirped respecting him."

[6] " Il a tousiours demeuré inuincible, et ferme sans se reculer ;"—" He has always remained invincible and firm, without shrinking back."

grievances,[1] and, by patience, overcame indignities.[2] For a virtue so heroic is, as it were, a heavenly seal, by which the Lord marks out his Apostles.

He assigns the *second* place to *miracles*, for while he makes mention of *signs* and *wonders* and *mighty deeds*, he makes use of *three* terms, as he does elsewhere, (2 Thess. ii. 9,) for expressing one and the same thing. Now he calls them *signs*, because they are not empty shows, but are appointed for the instruction of mankind—*wonders*, because they ought, by their novelty, to arouse men, and strike them with astonishment—and *powers* or *mighty deeds*, because they are more signal tokens of Divine power,[3] than what we behold in the ordinary course of nature. Farther, we know that this was the main design of miracles, when the gospel began to be preached—that its doctrine might have greater authority given to it. Hence, the more that any one was endowed with the power of working miracles, so much the more was his ministry confirmed, as has been stated in the fifteenth chapter of the Epistle to the Romans.[4]

13. *What is there in which.* Here is an aggravation of their ingratitude—that he had been distinguished, that they might receive benefit—that they had derived advantage from the attestation furnished of his Apostleship, and had, notwithstanding, given their concurrence to the slanders[5] of

---

[1] " Il a laissé passer beaucoup de fascheries sans en faire semblant de rien ;"—" He has allowed many grievances to pass, without seeming to take any notice of them."

[2] " Beaucoup de lasches tours ;"—" Many base tricks."

[3] " Ce sont exemples et tesmoignages plus excellent et euidens de la vertu Diuine ;"—" Those are signal and manifest instances and evidences of Divine power."

[4] CALVIN seems to refer here more particularly to the observations made by him, when commenting on Rom. xv. 18. " Hic nobilis est locus de miraculorum usu : nempe ut reverentiam obedientiamque Deo apud homines comparent. Sic apud Marcum (xvi. 20,) legis, Dominum *confirmasse doctrinam subsequentibus signis.* Sic Lucas in Actis (xiv. 3,) narrat, Dominum *per miracula testimonium reddidisse sermoni gratiæ suæ ;*"—" This is an admirable passage in reference to the use of miracles—that they may secure among men reverence and obedience towards God. Thus you read in Mark xvi. 20, that the Lord *confirmed their doctrine by signs following.* So also Luke, in Acts xiv. 3, relates that the Lord *by miracles gave testimony to the word of his grace.*"—*Ed.*

[5] " Aux iniures et detractions ;"—" The insults and slanders."

the false Apostles. He subjoins one exception—that he *had not been burdensome to them ;* and this, by way of *irony*, for in reality this was over and above so many acts of kindness, which he had conferred upon them—that he had served them gratuitously. To busy themselves after this, as they did, in pouring contempt upon him, what was this but to insult his modesty ? Nay, what cruelty there was in it ! Hence, it is not without good reason, that he sharply reproves pride so frantic. *Forgive me this wrong,* says he. For they were doubly ungrateful, inasmuch as they not only contemned the man, by whose acts of kindness they had been brought under obligation, but even turned his kind disposition into an occasion of reproach. Chrysostom is of opinion, that there is no *irony* implied, and that, instead of this, there is an expression of apology ; but, if any one examines the entire context more narrowly, he will easily perceive, that this gloss is quite foreign to Paul's intention.

14. *Behold, this third time.* He commends his own deed, for which he had received a very poor requital from the Corinthians. For he says, that he refrained from taking their worldly substance for two reasons : *first,* because he sought *them,* not their wealth ; and *secondly,* because he was desirous to act the part of a father towards them. From this it appears, what commendation was due to his modesty, which occasioned him contempt among the Corinthians.

I seek not yours. It is the part of a genuine and upright pastor, not to seek to derive gain from his sheep, but to endeavour to promote their welfare ; though, at the same time, it is to be observed, that men are not to be sought with the view of having[1] every one his own particular followers. It is a bad thing, to be devoted to gain, or to undertake the office of a pastor with the view of making a trade of it ; but for a person to *draw away disciples after him,* (Acts xx. 30,) for purposes of ambition, is greatly worse. Paul, however, means, that he is not greedy of hire, but is concerned only for the welfare of souls. There is, however, still more of

---

[1] " Que les Ministres ne doyuent pas cercher les hommes a ceste intention d'auoir, chacun des disciples a soy en particulier ;"—" That Ministers ought not to seek men with the intention of having, each one, disciples to himself peculiarly."

elegance in what he says, for it is as though he had said:
" I am in quest of a larger hire than you think of. I am
not contented with your wealth, but I seek to have you
wholly, that I may present a sacrifice to the Lord of the
fruits of my ministry." But, what if one is supported by
his labours ? Will he in that case seek the worldly substance
of the people ?[1] Unquestionably, if he is a faithful Pastor,
he will always seek the welfare of the sheep—nothing else.
His pay will, it is true, be an additional thing ; but he
ought to have no other aim, than what we have mentioned.
Woe to those, that have an eye to any thing else !

Parents for their children. Was he then no *father* to the
Philippians, who supported him even when absent from
them ? (Phil. iv. 15, 16.) Was there no one of the other
Apostles that was a *father*, inasmuch as the Churches ministered to their support ? He did not by any means intend
this ; for it is no new thing for even parents to be supported
by their children in their old age. Hence, those are not
necessarily unworthy of the honour due to *fathers*, who
live at the expense of the Church ; but Paul simply wished
to show from the common law of nature, that what he
had done proceeded from fatherly affection. This argument, therefore, ought not to be turned in a contrary
direction. For he did this as a *father;* but, though he had
acted otherwise, he would, notwithstanding, have been a
father still.

15. *And I will most gladly spend.* This, certainly, was
an evidence of a more than fatherly affection—that he was
prepared to lay out in their behalf not merely his endeavours, and every thing in his power to do, but even life itself.
Nay more, while he is regarded by them with coldness, he
continues, nevertheless, to cherish this affection. What
heart, though even as hard as iron, would such ardour of
love not soften or break, especially in connection with
such constancy ? Paul, however, does not here speak of
himself, merely that we may admire him, but that we may,

___

[1] " Est-ce pourtant a dire que vn tel cerche la substance du peuple ?"—
" Must we then say, that such a man seeks the worldly substance of the
people ?"

also, imitate him.   Let all Pastors, therefore, learn from this, what they owe to their Churches.

16. But be it so, I did not burden you: nevertheless, being crafty, I caught you with guile.

17. Did I make a gain of you by any of them whom I sent unto you?

18. I desired Titus, and with *him* I sent a brother: did Titus make a gain of you? walked we not in the same spirit? *walked we* not in the same steps?

19. Again, think ye that we excuse ourselves unto you? we speak before God in Christ: but *we do* all things, dearly beloved, for your edifying.

20. For I fear, lest, when I come, I shall not find you such as I would, and *that* I shall be found unto you such as ye would not; lest *there be* debates, envyings, wraths, strifes, backbitings, whisperings, swellings, tumults:

21. *And* lest, when I come again, my God will humble me among you, and *that* I shall bewail many which have sinned already, and have not repented of the uncleanness, and fornication, and lasciviousness, which they have committed.

16. Sed esto: ipse non gravavi vos: verum quum essem astutus, dolo vos cepi.

17. Num per quenquam eorum, quos misi ad vos, expilavi vos?[1]

18. Rogavi Titum, et una cum illo misi fratrem: num quid a vobis extorsit Titus? an non eodem spiritu ambulavimus? an non iisdem vestigiis?

19. Rursum arbitramini, quod nos vobis excusemus? in conspectu Dei in Christo loquimur: sed omnia, carissimi, pro vestra ædificatione.

20. Nam metuo, ne qua fiat, ut, si venero, non quales velim reperiam vos: et ego reperiar a vobis, qualem nolitis: ne quo modo sint contentiones, æmulationes, iræ, concertationes, obtrectationes, susurri, tumores, seditiones.

21. Ne iterum, ubi venero, humiliet me Deus meus apud vos, et lugeam multos eorum qui ante peccaverunt, nec pœnitentiam egerunt immunditiæ, libidinis et impudicitiæ, quam patrarunt.

16. *But be it so.* These words intimate, that Paul had been blamed by malevolent persons, as though he had in a clandestine way procured, through means of hired persons, what he had refused to receive with his own hands[2]—not that he had done any such thing, but they "measure others," as they

[1] " Vous ay-ie affrontez, ou, pillez ?"—" Did I take advantage of you, or plunder you?"

[2] " This passage is so far from being friendly to the exercise of guile, that it is a manifest disavowal of it.   It is an *irony*.   The Apostle does not describe what had actually been his conduct, but that of which he stood accused by the Corinthian teachers.   They insinuated, that he was a sly, crafty man, going about preaching, persuading, and catching people with guile.   Paul acknowledges, that he and his colleagues did, indeed, ' persuade men,' and could not do otherwise, for ' the love of Christ constrained them.' (Chap. v. 11, 14.)   But he indignantly repels the insinuation of its being from mercenary motives.   ' We have wronged no man,' says he, ' we have corrupted no man ; we have defrauded no man.' (Chap. vii. 2.) Having denied the charge, he shows the *absurdity* of it.   Mercenary men,

say, " by their own ell."[1]   For it is customary for the wicked
impudently to impute to the servants of God, whatever they
would themselves do, if they had it in their power.   Hence,
Paul is constrained, with the view of clearing himself of a
charge impudently fabricated,[2] to defend the integrity of
those whom he sent, for if they had committed any error, it
would have been reckoned to his account.   Now, who would
be surprised at his being so cautious as to alms, when he had
been harassed by such unfair judgments as to his conduct,
after having made use of every precaution ?[3]   Let his case,
however, be a warning to us, not to look upon it as a thing
that is new and intolerable, if at any time we find occasion
to answer similar calumnies; but, more especially, let this be
an admonition to us to use strict caution, not to furnish any
handle to revilers.   For we see, that it is not enough to give
evidence of being ourselves upright, if those, whose assistance we have made use of, are not, also, found to be so.
Hence, our choice of them must not be made lightly, or as
a matter of mere form, but with the utmost possible care.

19. *Do you again think.*   As those that are conscious to
themselves of something wrong are sometimes more anxious
than others to clear themselves, it is probable, that this, also,
was turned into a ground of calumny—that Paul had in the
former Epistle applied himself to a defence of his ministry.
Farther, it is a fault in the servants of Christ, to be too much

who wish to draw people after them, have an *end* to answer: and ' what
end, says Paul, could I have in view, in *persuading* you to embrace the
gospel?   Have I gained any thing by you?   When I was with you, was I
burdensome to you?   No: nor, as things are, will I be burdensome.   *Yet
being crafty,* forsooth, *I caught you with guile.'"*—*Fuller's Works,* vol. iii.
pp. 579, 580.—*Ed.*

[1] The reader will find the same proverb made use of by CALVIN, when
commenting on 1 Cor. vii. 36.   (See vol. i. p. 265.)   He probably alludes,
in both instances, to a sentiment of Horace: " Metiri se quenquam suo
modulo ac pede verum est ;"—" It is proper, that every one should measure himself by his own measure and foot."   (Hor. Epist. i. 7. 98.)—*Ed.*

[2] " Pour refuter et repousser loin de soy le blasme qu'on auoit controuué
impudemment ;"—" With the view of repelling, and putting far away from
himself the blame which they had inpudently contrived."

[3] " Veu qu'on semoit de luy des souspeçons et iugemens si iniques, apres
qu'il auoit si diligemment poureu a toutes choses ?"—" Inasmuch as they
propagated such unfair surmises and judgments respecting him, after he
had so carefully used precaution as to every thing ?"

concerned as to their own reputation. With the view, therefore, of repelling those calumnies, he declares in the *first*
place, that he speaks in the presence of God, whom evil consciences always dread. In the *second* place, he maintains,
that he has not so much a view to himself, as to them. He
was prepared to go through *good report and bad report*,
(2 Cor. vi. 8,) nay, even to be reduced to nothing; but it
was of advantage to the Corinthians, that he should retain
the reputation that he deserved, that his ministry might not
be brought into contempt.

20. *For I fear.* He declares, in what way it tends to
their edification, that his integrity should be vindicated, for,
on the ground that he had come into contempt, many grew
wanton, as it were, with loosened reins. Now respect for
him would have been a means of leading them to repentance,
for they would have listened to his admonitions.

I fear, says he. This *fear* proceeded from love, for, unless he had been concerned as to their welfare, he would very
readily have overlooked all this, from which he sought to
obtain no personal advantage. For otherwise we are afraid
to give occasion of offence, when we foresee that it will be
hurtful to ourselves.

And I shall be found by you. Here is a *second* ground
of fear—lest he should be constrained to act with greater
severity. Now it is a token not merely of love, but even of
indulgence, to shun severity, and have recourse to milder
measures. "As to my striving at present to maintain my
authority, and endeavouring to bring you back to obedience,
I do this, lest I should find occasion to punish your obstinacy more severely, if I come, and find among you nothing
of amendment." He teaches, accordingly, by his example,
that mild remedies must always be resorted to by Pastors,
for the correction of faults, before they have recourse to extreme severity; and, at the same time, that we must, by
admonitions and reproofs, prevent the necessity of having
recourse to the utmost rigour.

Lest, by any means, there be contentions. He enumerates
the vices, which chiefly prevailed among the Corinthians;
almost all of which proceeded from the same source. For

had not every one been devoted to self, they would never
have contended with each other—they would never have
envied one another—there would have been no slandering
among them.[1] Thus the sum and substance of the first
catalogue[2] is want of love, because (φιλαυτία) self-love,[3] and
ambition prevailed.

21. *Lest, when I come, my God should humble me.*   His
abasement was reckoned to him as a fault.[4] The blame of
it he throws back upon the Corinthians, who, when they
should have honoured his Apostleship, loaded it, on the
contrary, with disgrace ; for their proficiency[5] would have
been the glory and honour of Paul's Apostleship. When,
therefore, they were, instead of this, overrun with many vices,
they heaped disgrace upon him to the utmost of their power.
He does not, indeed, charge them all with this crime, but
only a few, who had impudently despised all his admonitions.
The meaning, then, is this : " They think contemptuously of
me, because I appear contemptible. Let them, then, give
me no occasion of abasement : nay more, let them, on the
contrary, laying aside their forwardness, begin to feel shame ;
and let them, confounded at their iniquities, prostrate themselves on the ground, instead of looking down upon others
with disdain."

In the mean time, he lets us know the disposition of a true
and genuine Pastor, when he says that he will look upon
the sins of others with grief. And, undoubtedly, the right
way of acting is this—that every Christian shall have his
Church inclosed within his heart, and be affected with its
maladies, as if they were his own,—sympathize with its sor-

---

[1] " Ils n'eussent iamais mesdit l'vn de l'autre ;"—" They would never
have slandered one another."

[2] " Du premier denombrement de leur vices qu'il fait yci ;"—" Of the
first enumeration that he makes here of their vices."

[3] CALVIN has here very probably in his eye 2 Tim. iii. 2, in commenting on which, he calls his readers to remark, that the vice first noticed by
the Apostle in that passage—self-love (φιλαυτία), may be considered to be
the *fountain*, as it were, of all the other vices there enumerated by him—
avarice, boasting, pride, &c.—See CALVIN's *Harmony*, vol. ii. p. 69, and
vol. iii. p. 60 ; also CALVIN's *Institutes*, vol. i. p. 313.

[4] See p. 346.

[5] " Qu'ils eussent proufité en sainctete de vie ;"—" That they had made
progress in holiness of life."

rows, and bewail its sins. We see, how Jeremiah entreats, that there may be given him a *fountain of tears*, (Jer. ix. 1,) that he may bewail the calamity of his people. We see, how pious kings and prophets, to whom the government of the people was committed, were touched with similar feelings. It is, indeed, a thing that is common to all the pious, to be grieved in every case in which God is offended, and to bewail the ruin of brethren, and present themselves before God in their room as in a manner guilty, but it is more particularly requisite on the part of Pastors.[1] Farther, Paul here brings forward a second catalogue of vices, which, however, belong to one general head—unchastity.

CHAPTER XIII.

1. This *is* the third *time* I am coming to you. In the mouth of two or three witnesses shall every word be established.

2. I told you before, and foretell you, as if I were present, the second time; and being absent, now I write to them which heretofore have sinned, and to all other, that, if I come again, I will not spare:

3. Since ye seek a proof of Christ speaking in me, which to you-ward is not weak, but is mighty in you.

4. For though he was crucified through weakness, yet he liveth by the power of God: for we also are weak in him, but we shall live with him by the power of God toward you.

1. Hic tertius erit adventus meus ad vos. In ore duorum aut trium testium stabilietur omne verbum.— (*Deut.* xix. 15 ; *Matt.* xviii. 16 ; *Jo.* viii. 17 ; *Heb.* x. 28.)

2. Prædixi et prædico, ut præsens quum essem iterum, ita et absens nunc scribo iis, qui ante peccaverunt, et reliquis omnibus: quod, si venero denuo, non parcam.

3. Quandoquidem experimentum quæritis in me loquentis Christi : qui erga vos non est infirmus, sed potens est in vobis.

4. Nam quamvis crucifixus fuit ex infirmitate, vivit tamen ex virtute Dei : siquidem et nos infirmi sumus in illo, sed vivimus cum illo ex virtute Dei erga vos.

1. *This will be the third.* He goes on to reprove still farther the insolence of those of whom he had been speaking, some of whom living in profligacy and licentiousness, and others, carrying on contentions and strifes among themselves, cared nothing for his reproof. For his discourse did not apply to the entire body of the Church, but to certain diseased and half-rotten members of it. Hence he now, with

---

[1] " Des Pasteurs et Ministres ;"—" Of Pastors and Ministers."

greater freedom, uses sharpness, because he has to do with particular individuals, not with the whole body of the people, and besides this, it was with persons of such a stamp, that he perceived, that he would do them no good by kindness, and mild remedies.   After having spent a year and a half among them, (Acts xviii. 11,) he had visited them a *second* time.   Now he forewarns them, that he will come to them a *third* time, and he says, that his three comings to them will be in the place of three witnesses.   He quotes the law as to the authority of witnesses ; not in the natural and literal sense, as it is termed, but by accommodation,[1] or similitude, applying it to his particular purpose.   "The declaration of the law," says he, "is, that we must rest on the testimony of *two or three witnesses* for putting an end to disputes."[2] (Deut. xix. 15.)   For the word *established* means that a decision is pronounced respecting a matter, that the strife may cease.   "I, indeed, am but one individual, but coming a *third* time I shall have the authority of *three* witnesses, or, my three comings will be in the place of three testimonies." For the threefold effort that was made for their welfare, and perseverance, as made trial of on three different occasions, might, with good reason, be held equivalent to three persons.

2. *I told you before, and foretell you.*   The friendly and agreeable admonitions, that he had addressed to them so frequently, had been of no advantage.   He, accordingly, betakes himself to a more severe remedy, with which he had previously threatened them in words when present with them. When we see him act with so much strictness, we need have no doubt, that they were surprisingly ungovernable and obstinate ; for it appears from his writings, what mildness, and what unwearied patience he was otherwise prepared to manifest.   As, however, it is the part of a good parent to forgive and bear with many things, so it is the part of a

---

[1] " *Anagogen.*"   See p. 199, *n.* 2.

[2] " This is only an allusion : it is taken, with a trifling abridgement, from the Alexandrine copy of the Septuagint, which is an exact translation of the Hebrew."—*Horne's* Introduction, (Lond. 1823,) vol. ii. p. 384, *n.* 4.—*Ed.*

foolish parent, and one that has no proper regard for the
welfare of his children, to neglect to use severity, when there
is occasion for it, and to mingle strictness with mildness.
We are well aware, that nothing is more hurtful than excessive indulgence.[1]   Let us, therefore, use mildness, when we
can safely do so, and that too, dignified and properly regulated : let us act with greater severity, when necessity requires.

It is asked, however, why it was, that the Apostle allowed
himself to expose the particular faults of individuals in so
open a manner, as in a manner to point his finger at the
very persons?   I answer, that he would never have done so,
if the sins had been hid, but as they were manifest to all,
and matter of notoriety, so as to furnish a pernicious example, it was necessary that he should not spare the authors
of a public scandal.[2]

It is asked, *secondly*, what kind of chastisement he threatens to inflict upon them, as he could scarcely chastise them
more severely in words.   I have no doubt that he means,
that he will inflict punishment upon them by excommunication.   For what is more to be dreaded, than being cut off
from the body of Christ, expelled from the kingdom of God,
and *delivered over to Satan for destruction*, (1 Cor. v. 5,)
unless you repent ?

3. *Since ye seek a proof.*   A twofold meaning may be
drawn from these words.   The *first* is, "Since you wish to
try me, whether I speak of myself, or whether Christ speaks
by me ;" and in this way Chrysostom, and Ambrose, explain

---

[1] " Vn abandon desmesuré, et douceur trop grande ;"—" Excessive indulgence, and too great sweetness."

[2] It might almost seem as if Baxter must have had this passage of
CALVIN in his eye, when penning his celebrated apology for animadverting
so freely on the faults of the ministers of religion in his times.   " If it
should be objected, that I should not have spoken so plainly and sharply
against the sins of the ministry, or that I should not have published it to
the view of the world, or, at least, that I should have done it in another
tongue, and not in the ears of the vulgar   .   .   .   when the sin is open
in the sight of the world, it is in vain to attempt to hide it ; and when the
sin is public, the confession should also be public.   If the ministers of
England had sinned only in Latin, I would have made shift to have admonished them in Latin, or else should have said nothing to them.   But
if they will sin in English, they must hear of it in English."—*Baxter's*
Reformed Pastor, (Glasgow, 1829,) pp. 60, 61.—*Ed.*

it. I am rather inclined, however, to understand him as
declaring, that it does not so much concern himself as Christ,
when his authority is detracted from—that when his admonitions are despised, Christ's patience is tried. "It is Christ
that speaks by me ; when therefore, you bring my doctrine
under your lash, it is not so much to me as to him that you
do injury."

Some one, however, will object thus : "What ! Will a
man's doctrine, then, be exempted from all investigation, so
soon as he makes it his boast, that he has Christ as his
authority ? And what false prophet will not make this his
boast ? What distinction, then, will there be between truth
and falsehood, and what will, in that case, become of that
injunction : *Try the spirits, whether they are of God.*" (1
John iv. 1.) Every objection of this nature Paul anticipates,
when he says that Christ has wrought efficaciously in them
by his ministry. For these two clauses, *Christ speaking in
me*, and, *who is mighty in you, not weak*, must be read in
connection, in this sense : " Christ, by exercising his power
towards you in my doctrine, has declared that he spoke by
my mouth, so that you have no excuse on the ground of
ignorance."

We see, that he does not merely boast in words, but proves
in reality that Christ speaks in him, and he convinces the
Corinthians, before requiring them to give him credit.
Whoever, then, will speak in the Church, whatever be the
title that he claims for himself, it will be allowable to inquire
as to his doctrine, until Christ has manifested himself in
him, and thus it will not be of Christ that judgment will be
formed, but of the man. When, however, it is apparent, that
it is the word of God that is advanced, what Paul says holds
good—that it is God himself who is not believed.[1] Moses
spake with the same confidence. (Num. xvi. 11.) *What are
we—I and Aaron ? You are tempting God.* In like manner,
Isaiah : *Is it too small a thing that you grieve men, unless
you grieve my God also ?* (Isaiah vii. 13.) For there is no

---

[1] " Que si on ne la reçoit, c'est oster a Dieu son authorite ;"—" That if
this is not received, that is to take from God the authority, which belongs
to him."

more room for shuffling, when it has been made apparent,
that it is a minister of God that speaks, and that he discharges his office faithfully. I return to Paul. As the confirmation of his ministry had been so decided among the
Corinthians, inasmuch as the Lord had shown himself openly,
it is not to be wondered, if he takes it so much amiss, that
he meets with resistance. On good grounds, truly,[1] might
he throw back upon them, as he does, the reproach, that
they were rebels against Christ.

4. *For though he was crucified.* He speaks, with particular
intention, of Christ's abasement, with the view of intimating
indirectly,[2] that nothing was despised in him, but what they
would have been prepared to despise, also, in Christ himself,
inasmuch as he *emptied himself, even to the death of the cross.*
(Phil. ii. 8.) He shows, however, at the same time, how absurd
it is to despise in Christ[3] the abasement of the cross, inasmuch
as it is conjoined with the incomparable glory of his resurrection. " Shall Christ be esteemed by you the less, because
he showed signs of weakness in his death, as if his heavenly
life, that he leads subsequently to his resurrection, were not
a clear token of his Divine power!" For as the term *flesh*
here means Christ's human nature,[4] so the word *God* is
taken here to denote his Divinity.

Here, however, a question arises—whether Christ laboured
under such infirmity as to be subjected to necessity against
his will ; for, what we suffer *through weakness,* we suffer from
constraint, and not from our own choice. As the Arians of
old abused this pretext for effectually opposing the divinity
of Christ, the orthodox Fathers gave this explanation of it
—that it was effected by appointment, inasmuch as Christ
so desired, and not from his being constrained by any necessity. This answer is true, provided it be properly understood. There are some, however, that mistakingly extend

---

[1] " Tant y a qu'il auoit bonne occasion et droict ;"—" To such an extent
had he good occasion and right."
[2] " Afin de donner tacitement à entendre ;"—" That he may tacitly give
them to understand."
[3] " En nostre Seigneur Iesus ;"—" In our Lord Jesus."
[4] " Car comme que par *infirmite*, est yci signifiee l'humanite de Christ ;"
—" For as by *weakness* is here meant the humanity of Christ."

the appointment to Christ's human will—as if this were not the condition of his nature, but a permission contrary to his nature. For example: "His dying," they say, "did not happen because his humanity was, properly speaking, liable to death, but by appointment, because he chose to die." I grant, indeed, that he died, because he chose to do so ; but, whence came this choice, but from this—that he had, of his own accord, clothed himself with a mortal nature.[1] If, however, we make Christ's human nature so unlike ours, the main support of our faith is overturned. Let us, therefore, understand it in this way—that Christ suffered by appointment, not by constraint, because, *being in the form of God* he could have exempted himself from this necessity, but, nevertheless, he suffered *through weakness*, because he *emptied himself.* (Phil. ii. 6.)

We are weak in him. To be *weak in Christ* means here to be a partaker of Christ's weakness. Thus he makes his own weakness glorious, because in it he is conformed to Christ, and he no longer shrinks back from the disgrace, that he has in common with the Son of God ; but, in the mean time, he says that he will *live towards them* after Christ's example. "I also," says he, "will be a partaker of Christ's life, after I shall have been exempted from weakness."[2] To *weakness* he opposes *life*, and, accordingly, he understands by this term a condition that is flourishing, and full of honour.[3] The clause *towards you* may also be taken in connection with the *power of God*, but it is of no importance, as the meaning always remains the same—that the Corinthians, when they began to judge aright, would have respectful and honourable views of the power of God, which was in Paul, and would no longer despise outward infirmity.

5. Examine yourselves, whether ye be in the faith ; prove your own selves : know ye not your own

5. Vosmet ipsos tentate, num sitis in fide : vos ipsos probate. Annon cognoscitis vosmet ipsos, quod

---

[1] " Nostre nature mortelle ;"—" Our mortal nature."

[2] " Apres que mon infirmite aura comme fait son temps ;"—" After my weakness shall have, as it were, served its time."

[3] " Ascauoir quand vn homme est en estime et reputation ;"—" That is, when a man is held in esteem and reputation."

selves, how that Jesus Christ is in you, except ye be reprobates?

6. But I trust that ye shall know that we are not reprobates.

7. Now I pray to God that ye do no evil; not that we should appear approved, but that ye should do that which is honest, though we be as reprobates.

8. For we can do nothing against the truth, but for the truth.

9. For we are glad, when we are weak, and ye are strong: and this also we wish, *even* your perfection.

Iesus Christus in vobis est, nisi sicubi reprobi estis?

6. At spero vos cognituros, quod nos non simus reprobi.

7. Opto autem apud Deum, ne quid mali faciatis; non quo nos probati appareamus, sed ut vos quod honestum est faciatis, nos vero veluti reprobi simus.

8. Non enim possumus quicquam adversus veritatem, sed pro veritate.

9. Gaudemus enim, quum nos infirmi fuerimus, vos autem validi fueritis: hoc vero etiam optamus, vestram integritatem.

5. *Try yourselves.* He confirms, what he had stated previously—that Christ's power showed itself openly in his ministry. For he makes them the judges of this matter, provided they descend, as it were, into themselves, and acknowledge what they had received from him. In the first place, as there is but one Christ, it must be of necessity, that the same Christ must dwell alike in minister and people. Now, dwelling in the people, how will he deny himself in the minister.[1] Farther, he had shown his power in Paul's preaching, in such a manner that it could be no longer doubtful or obscure to the Corinthians, if they were not altogether stupid.[2] For, whence had they faith? whence had they Christ? whence, in fine, had they every thing? It is with good reason, therefore, that they are called to look into themselves, that they may discover there, what they despise as a thing unknown. *Then* only has a minister a true and well grounded assurance for the approbation of his doctrine, when he can appeal to the consciences of those whom he has taught, that, if they have any thing of Christ, and of sincere piety, they may be constrained to acknowledge his fidelity. We are now in possession of Paul's object.

This passage, however, is deserving of particular observation on two accounts. For, in the *first* place, it shows the relation,[3] which subsists between the faith of the people, and

1 "En la personne du Ministre;"—"In the person of the Minister."

2 "Du tout stupides et abbrutis;"—"Altogether stupid and besotted."

3 "La relation et correspondance mutuelle;"—"The relation and mutual correspondence."

the preaching of the minister—that the one is the mother, that produces and brings forth, and the other is the daughter, that ought not to forget her origin.[1]   In the *second* place, it serves to prove the assurance of faith, as to which the Sorbonnic sophists have made us stagger, nay more, have altogether rooted out from the minds of men.   They charge with rashness all that are persuaded that they are the members of Christ, and have Him remaining in them, for they bid us be satisfied with a " moral conjecture,"[2] as they call it—that is, with a mere opinion,[3] so that our consciences remain constantly in suspense, and in a state of perplexity. But what does Paul say here ?   He declares, that all are *reprobates*, who doubt whether they profess Christ and are a part of His body.   Let us, therefore, reckon *that* alone to be right faith, which leads us to repose in safety in the favour of God, with no wavering opinion, but with a firm and steadfast assurance.

Unless by any means you are reprobates.   He gives them in a manner their choice, whether they would rather be *reprobates*, than give due testimony to his ministry ; for he leaves them no alternative, but either to show respect to his Apostleship, or to allow that they are *reprobates*.   For, unquestionably, their faith had been founded upon his doctrine, and they had no other Christ, than they had received

---

[1] " Que ne doit point oublier le lieu d'où elle a prins la naissance ;"— " Which ought not to forget the place, from which she has taken her birth."
[2] See CALVIN on the Corinthians, vol. i. p. 112.
[3] " D'vne opinion et vn cuider ;"—" With an opinion and an imagination." —The Rhemish Translators, when commenting on this very passage, take occasion to oppose the idea of the attainableness of assurance of faith. " The Heretiques," say they, " argue hereupon, that every one may know himself certainly to be in grace ; where the Apostle speaketh expressly and onely of faith, the act whereof a man may know and feele to be in himself, because it is an act of understanding, though he cannot be assured that he hath his sinnes remitted, and that he is in all pointes in a state of grace and salvation ; because euery man that is of the Catholike faith is not alwaies of good life and agreeable thereunto, nor the acts of our will so subiect to understanding, that we can knowe certainely whether we be good or euill."   Dr. Fulke, in his Refutation of the errors of the Rhemish Doctors, (Lond. 1601,) p. 584, after furnishing suitable replies to the arguments thus advanced, concludes by remarking, that " our certeintie dependeth not upon our will or workes, but upon the promise of God through faith, that Christ is in us, and we in him, therefore we shall not misse of the performance of his promises."—*Ed.*

from him, and no other gospel than what they had embraced, as delivered to them by him, so that it were vain for them to attempt to separate any part of their salvation from his praise.

6. *I hope that you shall know.* He presses them still more urgently, while indulging this confident persuasion—that he will not be rejected by the Corinthians. One of two things was necessary—that they should either assign to Paul the honour due to an Apostle, or condemn themselves for unbelief, and acknowledge that they have no Church. He softens, however, the severity of the statement, by making use of the expression—*I hope;* but in such a manner as to remind them the better of their duty; for to disappoint the hopes that have been entertained as to our integrity, is excessively cruel. " I hope," says he, " that you shall know—when you have been restored to a sound mind." He prudently, however, says nothing as to himself in this second clause, calling them to consider God's benefits, by which they had been distinguished; nay more, he puts their salvation in the place of his authority.

7. *I desire before God.* Again he declares, that he cares nothing for his own honour, but is simply desirous of promoting their advantage. For nothing was so undesirable for them, as to deprive themselves of advantage from his doctrine—as they had begun to do, through their pride and contempt. " As to myself," says he, " or my reputation among men, I am not concerned. My only fear is, lest you should offend God. Nay more, I am prepared to be as a *reprobate,* provided you are free from all blame." " I am a *reprobate,*" says he, " in the judgment of mankind, who very frequently reject those who are deserving of the highest honour."[1] At the same time, the particle *as* is not superfluous. For it corresponds with what he says elsewhere— AS *deceivers and yet true.* (2 Cor. vi. 8.) And this, certainly, is the true rule—that the Pastor, having no regard to himself, should be devoted exclusively to the edification of the Church. Let him be concerned as to his own reputation,

---

[1] " Qui estoyent dignes d'honneur sur tous autres;"—" Who were worthy of honour above all others."

in so far as he sees it to be conducive to the public advantage. Let him be prepared to feel indifferent to it, whenever he may do so, without public disadvantage.

8. *For we can do nothing :* That is—" I do not seek, or desire any other power, than what the Lord has conferred upon me, that I may promote the truth. To false Apostles it is all one, provided they have power; and they feel no concern to make use of their power for the promotion of what is good." In short, he defends and maintains the honour of his ministry, in so far as it is connected with the truth of God. " What does it matter to me? For unless I have in view to promote the truth, all the power that I shall claim will be false and groundless. If, however, I lay out, whatever I have, for the promotion of the truth, I, in that case, do not consult my own interest. Now, when the authority of doctrine is safe, and truth is uninjured, I have what I desire. In contending, therefore, so keenly, I am not influenced by any exclusive regard for myself personally." By this consideration, however, he intimates, that the man, who fights and labours for the truth alone will not take it amiss, should occasion require it, to be regarded in the judgment of men as a *reprobate*, provided this does not interfere with the glory of God, the edification of the Church, and the authority of sound doctrine.

This passage must be carefully observed, because it limits the power, which the Pastors of the Church should have, and fixes its proper bounds—that they be ministers of the truth. Papists loudly tell us, that it is said, *He that heareth you, heareth me ; he that despiseth you, despiseth me,* (Luke x. 16); and likewise : *Obey them that are set over you,* (Heb. xiii. 17); and under this pretext they take to themselves the utmost liberty, so as to usurp unbounded dominion, while they are, at the same time, the avowed and sworn enemies of the truth, and aim at its destruction by every means in their power. For exposing such impudence, this one statement of Paul will suffice—which declares, that they must themselves be in subjection to the truth.[1]

---

[1] " Qu'il faut que ceux qui ont le gouvernement en l'Eglise, seruent la verite ;"—" That it is necessary that those, who have the government of the Church, be subject to the truth."

9. *For we rejoice.* Either the causal particle γὰρ, (*for,*) must be taken as meaning—*therefore;* or it is a second reason, why he does not refuse to be regarded as a *reprobate*— for their sake, and with a view to their advantage. Let the reader select whichever he may choose, for it is of no consequence.[1] When he says, *Provided you are strong, I shall willingly submit to be reckoned weak,* there is an antithesis in the words—not in the meaning; for *weakness* means here, as formerly, (ver. 4,) *contempt.* On the other hand, he means that the Corinthians will be *strong,* if they are full of the power and grace of God.

And this also. He now again repeats, what he had already stated several times, that he was from necessity—not from his own inclination, more severe than they would have wished; and farther, that by this means, too,[2] he *spared* them, that he might not be constrained to resort to severer measures, when he was present with them.

The *perfection,* of which he speaks, consists in a fit proportion, and sound condition, of all the members. Now[3] he alludes to good physicians, who cure particular diseases in such a way as not in any part to mutilate the body;[4] and, as he is concerned to secure a perfection of this nature, he says, that, for that reason, he provides against the necessity of having recourse to severer measures.[5] For we see, that those, who

---

[1] " Car c'est tout vn ;"—" For it is all one."

[2] " Mesme en ce faisant ;"—" Even in doing this."

[3] " Or en parlant ainsi ;"—" Now in speaking thus."

[4] The same view, in substance, is taken by Beza, of the meaning of the term καταϱτισιν, which he renders—*integram concinnationem* (*complete adjustment.*) " Varia enim est et multiplex verbi καταϱτίζειν significatio. Mihi vero proximum versiculum cum isto comparanti videtur Apostolus nihil aliud hoc nomine significare, quam suum hoc esse consilium ut Corinthiacæ Ecclesiæ membris, quæ luxata fuerant, rursus in locum suum veluti repositis, totum illud corpus mutuo connexis membris instauretur, Gal. vi. 1. Itaque licebat etiam *reconcinnationem* interpretari ;"—" For the meaning of the word καταϱτίζειν is various and manifold. On comparing, however, this verse with a subsequent one, I am of opinion that Paul by this term simply means, that it was his design, that those members of the Corinthian Church which had been dislocated, as it were, having been restored to their proper place, the entire body should be renovated by the members being mutually connected together, (as in Gal. vi. 1.) Hence we might even render the term—*readjustment.*" See CALVIN on the Corinthians, vol. i. p. 63, *n.* 2.—*Ed.*

[5] " Plus facheux et aspres ;"—" More irksome and severe."

at first shrink back from the slight pain, or uneasy feeling of a plaster, are at length constrained to endure the torture of burning, or amputating, and that, too, where the issue is extremely doubtful.[1]

10. Therefore I write these things being absent, lest being present I should use sharpness, according to the power which the Lord hath given me to edification, and not to destruction.

10. Propterea hæc absens scribo : ne quum præsens fuero, rigidus sim iuxta potestatem, quam dedit mihi Dominus in aedificationem, et non in destructionem.

11. Finally, brethren, farewell. Be perfect, be of good comfort, be of one mind, live in peace ; and the God of love and peace shall be with you.

11. Quod superest, fratres, valete, integri estote,[2] consolationem habete, unanimes sitis, in pace agite : et Deus caritatis ac pacis erit vobiscum.

12. Greet one another with an holy kiss.

12. Salutate vos mutuo in osculo sancto.

13. All the saints salute you.

13. Salutant vos sancti omnes.

14. The grace of the Lord Jesus Christ, and the love of God, and the communion of the Holy Ghost, *be* with you all. Amen.

14. Gratia Domini Iesu Christi, et caritas Dei, et communicatio Spiritus sancti sit cum omnibus vobis. Amen.

The second *epistle* to the Corinthians was written from Philippi, *a city* of Macedonia, by Titus and Lucas.

Ad Corinthios secunda missa fuit a Philippis Macedoniæ—per Titum et Lucam.

10. *According to the power.*   In the *first* place, he arms the strictness of which he speaks, with the authority of God, that it may not appear to be thunder without lightning, or a rashly excited onset.[3]   Farther, he lets them know, that he would rather employ his power to another purpose, for which it was peculiarly designed—the promoting of their edification.   " I shall not rashly have recourse to cruel remedies, nor will I give indulgence to my passion, but will simply execute the commission that the Lord has given me."

When he speaks of *power given him for edification, and not for destruction,* he employs these terms for a somewhat

---

[1] " Voire sans asseurance de guarir pour cela ;"—" Even where there is no confidence as to effecting a cure by that means."

[2] " Soyez entiers, ou, Auancez-vous à vous parfaire ;"—" Be perfect, or Go on to perfect yourselves."

[3] " Vne escarmouche d'vn homme qui se soit enflambé sans raison ;"— " A skirmishing on the part of a man who has kindled himself up without any just cause."

different purpose from what he had done previously in chapter x. 8. For in that passage there was a commendation of the Gospel from the advantage it yields—because what is for our advantage is wont to be agreeable, and is willingly received by us. Here, however, he simply means to declare, that although he might justly inflict upon the Corinthians a severe blow, yet it was much more his inclination to exercise his power for their *advantage*, than for their *destruction* —the former being its proper design. For as the Gospel, in its own nature, is the *power of God unto salvation*, (Rom. i. 16,) and an *odour of life unto life*, (2 Cor. ii. 15, 16,) but, in a way of contingency, is an *odour of death ;* so the authority, which is conferred upon the Ministers of it, ought to be salutary to the hearers. If, on the other hand, it turns out to their condemnation, that is contrary to its nature. The meaning, therefore, is this : " Do not, through your own fault, allow *that* to turn to your destruction, which God has appointed for salvation." In the mean time, the Apostle admonishes all pastors by his example, in what manner they should limit the use of their power.

11. *Finally, brethren.* He qualifies whatever there has been of sharpness throughout the whole of the epistle, as he did not wish to leave their minds in an exasperated state,[1] but rather to soothe them. For *then* only are reproofs beneficial, when they are in a manner seasoned with honey, that the hearer may, if possible, receive them in an agreeable spirit. At the same time, he appears to turn from a few diseased persons[2] to the entire Church. Hence he declares, that he aims at promoting its *perfection*, and desires its consolation.

To *be of one mind*, and to *live in peace*, are expressions which mean two different things ; for the one takes its rise

[1] " Il ne vouloit point laisser leurs cœurs offenses ou saisis d'amertume ;" —" He did not wish to leave their minds exasperated, or under the influence of bitterness."

[2] " Combien qu'il semble que d'vn propos qu'il addressoit a aucuns qui estoyent comme brebis rogneuses en la compagnie il reuient maintenant à toute l'Eglise ;"—" At the same time, it appears as if, from a discourse which he addressed to some who were like diseased sheep in the herd, he now turns to the entire Church."

from the other.   The *former* relates to agreement of sentiment ; the *latter* denotes benevolence, and union of hearts.

And the God of peace.   This he adds, that his exhortation
may have more weight with them, but, at the same time, he
intimates that God will be with us, if we cultivate peace
among ourselves ; but that those that are at variance with
each other are at a distance from him.[1]   For where there
are strifes and contentions, *there,* it is certain, the devil
reigns.   Now *what agreement is there between light and
darkness?*   (2 Cor. vi. 14.)   He calls him the *God of peace
and love,* because he has recommended to us peace and love,
because he loves them, and is the author of them.   Of the
kiss here mentioned we have spoken in the two preceding
Epistles.[2]

14. *The grace of the Lord Jesus.*   He closes the Epistle
with a prayer, which contains three clauses, in which the
sum of our salvation consists.   In the *first* place, he desires
for them the *grace of Christ ; secondly,* the *love of God ;* and,
thirdly, the *communion of the Spirit.*   The term *grace* does
not here mean unmerited favour, but is taken by metonymy,
to denote the whole benefit of redemption.   The order, however, may appear to be here inverted, because the *love of
God* is placed *second,* while it is the source of that grace,
and hence it is *first* in order.   I answer, that the arrangement of terms in the Scriptures is not always so very exact ;
but, at the same time, this order, too, corresponds with the
common form of doctrine, which is contained in the Scriptures—that *when we were enemies to God, we were reconciled
by the death of his Son,* (Rom. v. 10,) though the Scripture is
wont to speak of this in two ways.   For it sometimes declares what I have quoted from Paul—that there was enmity
between us and God, before we were reconciled through
Christ.   On the other hand, we hear what John says—that
God so loved the world, that he gave his only-begotten Son,
&c. (John iii. 16.)   The statements are apparently opposite ;

---

[1] " Que tous ceux qui ont debats en sont eslongnez, et n'ont point d'ac-
cointance auec luy ;"—" That all those who have contentions are at a distance from him, and have no acquaintance with him."

[2] See pp. 78-80.

but it is easy to reconcile them ; because in the one case we look to God, and in the other to ourselves. For God, viewed in himself, loved us before the creation of the world, and redeemed us for no other reason than this—because he loved us. As for us, on the other hand, as we see in ourselves nothing but occasion of wrath, that is, sin, we cannot apprehend any love of God towards us without a Mediator. Hence it is that, with respect to us, the beginning of love is from the grace of Christ. According to the former view of the matter, Paul would have expressed himself improperly, had he put the love of God before the grace of Christ, or, in other words, the cause before the effect ; but according to the latter, it were a suitable arrangement to begin with the grace of Christ, which was the procuring cause of God's adopting us into the number of his sons, and honouring us with his love, whom previously he regarded with hatred and abhorrence on account of sin.

The *fellowship of the Holy Spirit* is added, because it is only under his guidance, that we come to possess Christ, and all his benefits. He seems, however, at the same time, to allude to the diversity of gifts, of which he had made mention elsewhere, (2 Cor. xii. 11 ;) because God does not give the Spirit to every one in a detached way, but distributes to each according to the measure of grace, that the members of the Church, by mutually participating, one with another, may cherish unity.

TABLES AND INDEX

TO THE

COMMENTARY

ON

THE EPISTLES OF PAUL THE APOSTLE

TO

THE CORINTHIANS.

TABLE I.

OF PASSAGES FROM THE HOLY SCRIPTURES, AND FROM THE APOCRYPHA,
WHICH ARE QUOTED, OR INCIDENTALLY ILLUSTRATED, IN THE
COMMENTARY ON THE EPISTLES TO THE CORINTHIANS.

GENESIS.

Chap.	Ver.	Vol.	Page	Chap.	Ver.	Vol.	Page	Chap.	Ver.	Vol.	Page
i.	20, 24	ii.	51	iii.	17	ii.	80	xvii.	7	ii.	263
	27	i.	360	v.	2	i.	360	xviii.	14	ii.	369, *n.* 2
ii.	7	ii.	46, 51	ix.	24	ii.	44, *n.* 1		25	i.	217, *n.* 3
	18	i.	223, 358,	xi.	4	i.	341	xxiv.	38	i.	245, *n.* 3
			361		9	ii.	214	xxv.	8	ii.	224
	19	ii.	30		14	ii.	357		27	i.	102, *n.* 1
	21	i.	252	xiv.	13	ii.	357	xxxv.	22	i.	179
	21, 22	i.	358	xv.	16	i.	393		29	ii.	224, *n.* 1
	24	i.	238	xvi.	8	ii.	155, *n.* 1	xlix.	18	ii.	224

EXODUS.

Chap.	Ver.	Vol.	Page	Chap.	Ver.	Vol.	Page	Chap.	Ver.	Vol.	Page
iv.	11	ii.	344	xviii.	17	ii.	369, *n.* 2	xxxii.	6	i.	321
vii.	1	ii.	194, *n.* 2	xix.	16	ii.	59		7	i.	322
xii.	5	i.	102, *n.* 1		21	i.	83	xxxiv.	33	ii.	190
	46	i.	381	xx.	5	ii.	340		33-35	ii.	180
xiv.	31	ii.	288	xxx.	14	ii.	11, *n.* 4	xxxviii.	21	ii.	314, *n.* 2
xvi.	18	ii.	293, 296								

LEVITICUS.

Chap.	Ver.	Vol.	Page	Chap.	Ver.	Vol.	Page	Chap.	Ver.	Vol.	Page
i.	3	i.	102, *n.* 1	xxiii.	16	ii.	73	xxvii.	7	ii.	11, *n.* 4
v.	6	ii.	241, *n.* 4	xxvi.	12	ii.	254, 261				

NUMBERS.

Chap.	Ver.	Vol.	Page	Chap.	Ver.	Vol.	Page	Chap.	Ver.	Vol.	Page
iv.	24	ii.	314, *n.* 2	xi.	31	ii.	297	xvi.	31-50	i.	326
viii.	22	ii.	314, *n.* 2		34	i.	322	xxi.	6	i.	325
x.	1, 2, 9	i.	440, *n.* 1	xii.	8	i.	429, *n.* 1	xxv.	9	i.	824
xi.	4	i.	322	xiv.	29	i.	321	xxvi.	64	i.	322
	28	i.	463	xvi.	11	ii.	393				

PHILIPPIANS.

COLOSSIANS.

I. THESSALONIANS.

II. THESSALONIANS.

I. TIMOTHY

II. TIMOTHY.

TITUS.

PHILEMON.

Chap.	Ver.	Vol.	Page
	25	i.	445, *n.* 2

HEBREWS.

Chap.	Ver.	Vol.	Page		Chap.	Ver.	Vol.	Page		Chap.	Ver.	Vol.	Page
i.	2	ii.	30, 290		v.	13, 14	i.	122		xi.	3	i.	429, *n.* 2
ii.	8	ii.	290		vi.	5	i.	471			7	i.	199
'	14	ii.	20			11	i.	310			37	i.	57, *n.* 2
iii.	1	i.	49, *n.* 3		ix.	27	ii.	58		xii.	6	ii.	22
	14	i.	61		x.	23	i.	59, *n.* 1			9	i.	172
iv.	1	i.	57, *n.* 2			28	ii.	390			15	i.	57, *n.* 2
	12	i.	456			32	i.	60		xiii.	4	i.	235
v.	7	i.	185		xi.	1	ii.	215, 221			17	ii.	399

JAMES.

Chap.	Ver.	Vol.	Page		Chap.	Ver.	Vol.	Page		Chap.	Ver.	Vol.	Page
i.	8	ii.	251, *n.* 1		iv.	15	i.	175		v.	13	i.	447, *n.* 4
iv.	6	ii.	379, *n.* 2		v.	12	ii.	133			17	ii.	119

I. PETER.

Chap.	Ver.	Vol.	Page		Chap.	Ver.	Vol.	Page		Chap.	Ver.	Vol.	Page
i.	18, 19	i.	221		ii.	8	ii.	177, 330		iv.	17	ii.	22
	23	ii.	29		iii.	1	i.	245		v.	3	ii.	144
	24	ii.	29			18	ii.	238			5	ii.	379, *n.* 2
	24, 25	i.	170		iv.	3	i.	211			6	ii.	120
	25	ii.	135			12	ii.	183			7	ii.	314
ii.	2	i.	121			13	ii.	112			12	ii.	245, *n.* 1
	5	i.	142										

II. PETER.

Chap.	Ver.	Vol.	Page		Chap.	Ver.	Vol.	Page		Chap.	Ver.	Vol.	Page
i.	8	ii.	19		i.	11	ii.	31		i.	13, 14	ii.	217
	9	i.	59										

I. JOHN.

Chap.	Ver.	Vol.	Page		Chap.	Ver.	Vol.	Page		Chap.	Ver.	Vol.	Page
ii.	2	ii.	237		iv.	1	i.	147		v.	4	i.	432
	18	ii.	60				ii.	393			19	i.	192
iii.	1, 2	i.	431										

JUDE.

Ver.	Vol.	Page
5	i.	313

REVELATIONS.

Chap.	Ver.	Vol.	Page		Chap.	Ver.	Vol.	Page		Chap.	Ver.	Vol.	Page
i.	9	ii.	112, 206		ii.	7	ii.	368, *n.* 5		xxi.	4	ii.	61, *n.* 2
	10	ii.	68		xiv.	4	i.	267					

APOCRYPHA.

ECCLESIASTICUS.

xl. 17, 27 ii. 369

BARUCH.

iv. 7 i. 339

TABLE II.

OF GREEK WORDS EXPLAINED.

	Vol. Page		Vol. Page
ἀγάπη	i. 418, n. 2	ἀποκαλύψεις	ii. 366, n. 3
ἀγαπῶν	i. 369	ἀπόκριμα	ii. 119, n. 1
ἀγαπῶσιν	i. 108, n. 1	ἀπολογίαν	ii. 275
ἁγιοτητι	ii. 126, n. 4	ἀπόστολος	i. 49, n. 3
ἀγνοεῖται	i. 472, n. 1	ἀριστερῶν	ii. 252, n. 1
ἄγνωστη	i. 435, n. 1	ἅρπαγες	i. 209, n. 1
ἀγρυπνίαις	ii. 251, n. 1	ἅρπυίαι	i. 209, n. 1
ἀγωνοθέται	i. 157, n. 1	ἀρραβων	ii. 140, n. 4
ἀθετεῖν	i. 79	ἀσχημονεῖν	i. 265, 423, n. 3
αἴνιγμα	i. 429, n. 1	ἀταξία	i. 231, n. 2, 261
ἄκαρπος	i. 445, n. 2	ἀταξίαν	i. 365
ἄκαρπον	i. 446	αὐτάρκειαν	ii. 170
ἀκαταστασίαις	ii. 250	αὐτόπτας	ii. 10
ἀκατάστατος	ii. 251, n. 1	αὔξησιν	i. 97, 366
ἀκοινώνητοι	i. 362	ἄφωνων	i. 440, n. 4
ἀλλοτρίῳ	ii. 334, n. 1	βάρβαρος	i. 442, n. 1
ἄμετρα	ii. 334, n. 1	βάρος	{ ii. 117, n. 2,
ἀμφιδέξιος	ii. 252, n. 1		214, n. 1
ἀναγινώσκειν	ii. 128	βάρουμαι	ii. 117, n. 2
ἀναγινώσκεσθαι	ii. 167	βασιλεύειν	ii. 157, n. 2
ἀναγωγή	ii. 199, n. 2	βλασφημία	i. 165
ἀνακρίνειν	i. 291	βλασφημούμενοι	i. 165
ἀνακρίνεσθαι	i. 343	βλέπετε	{ i. 89,
ἀνθρώπινος	i. 331, n. 3		ii. 326
ἀνθρωποκτόνος	ii. 375, n. 4	γὰρ	ii. 366, n. 1, 400
ἀνθυποφορα	{ i. 281, n. 1, 337, n. 5	γενέσθαι	i. 249
ἀνθυποφοράν	i. 214	γνώμη	i. 252
ἀνοικοδομοῦνται	i. 283, n. 2	γνώμην	i. 63
ἀντὶ	i. 97	γραμματεῖς	i. 81
ἀντιλήψεις	i. 416, n. 1	Δαίδαλος	i. 74, n. 1
ἀντιπελαργία	ii. 256, n. 2	δαιμόνια	i. 339
ἀοράτου	ii. 197, n. 3	δεκτῳ	ii. 246, n. 2
ἁπλοτητι	ii. 126, n. 4	δεξιῶν	ii. 252, n. 1
ἀπάγεσθαι	i. 396, n. 2	δήλόω	i. 64, n. 3
ἀπό	ii. 20	διαθηκης	ii. 180, n. 3
ἀποδείξεως	i. 100	διακρίνων	i. 389, n. 3
		δια πολλῶν	ii. 124

418   TABLE OF GREEK WORDS EXPLAINED.

	Vol. Page		Vol. Page
ὑπομονῇ	ii. 249, n. 2	χαρᾶν	ii. 131, n. 1
ὑπομένουσιν	i. 108, n. 1	χάριν	ii. 131, n. 1
ὑπουργούντων	ii. 122, n. 2	χαρίσματα	{ i. 58, 403, n. 4
ὑπόστασις	ii. 221, n. 2, 306		ii. 251, n. 2
ὑποστατικός	ii. 307, n. 2	χειροτονήσαντες	ii. 300, n. 3
ὑποστατικῶς	ii. 307, n. 2	χειροτονία	ii. 300
ὑπωπιάζειν	i. 310	Χλόης	i. 64, n. 4
ὑστερεῖσθαι	i. 57	χρηστεύεσθαι	i. 422
φείδομαι	ii. 372, n. 1	χρώμενοι	i. 258
φιλαυτία	ii. 389, n. 3	ψαλῶ	i. 447, n. 4
φονεὺς	ii. 375, n. 4	ψηλαφήσειαν	i. 87, n. 1
φορέσωμεν	ii. 55	ψυχή	i. 115, n. 4
φυσικὸν	ii. 50, n. 1	ψυχικὸν	i. 50, n. 1
φύσις	i. 361, n. 1	ὡς.	{ ii. 126
φωνὴ	i. 440, n. 4		ii. 164, n. 1

TABLE III.

OF HEBREW WORDS EXPLAINED.

GENERAL INDEX.

A

ACHAIA, Corinth was a city of, i. 37 ; the household of Stephanas were the *first-fruits* of, ii. 77.

Achilles Tatius quoted, i. 262, *n.* 1.

Adam, why Christ is called *the last*, ii. 52, 53 ; Christ's superiority to, 52, 53; entailed ruin upon himself and his posterity, 53; his body was formed from the earth, 54.

Adam's Roman Antiquities, quoted, ii. 41, *n.* 2.

Adoption, effectual calling is an evidence of, i. 60; is the source of the choicest blessings, 109 ; the grace of Christ was the procuring cause of it, ii. 404.

Æschylus quoted, i. 429, *n.* 1.

Afflictions are the means of purifying the people of God, i. 140; are evidences of fatherly love, 393; are in various ways useful to believers, 394; reasons why Christians have a more than ordinary share of, ii. 22, 23 ; are to the wicked tokens of the curse of God, ii. 112.

Afrania, Caia, the wife of a Roman Senator, her effrontery, i. 468.

Alciat, Andrew, CALVIN studied law under him, ii. 92, 93.

Alembert quoted, ii. 94.

Alexander's Paraphrase on 1 Cor. xv. quoted, ii. 8, *n.* 2, 44, *n.* 1.

Allegorical interpretation of Scripture, absurdities connected with, i. 294 ; injurious effects of, ii. 174, 175.

Almsgiving resembles sowing, ii. 308, 309; liberality in, estimated by God from the disposition, rather than from the sum, 309 ; is a sacrifice, 310; liberality in, draws down the Divine blessing, 310; the neglect of it involves unrighteousness, 313.

Ambition must be carefully guarded

against, i. 124, 274 ; is injurious to the interests of the Church, 436, 470.

Ambrose quoted, i. 140, 191, 202, 444; ii. 34, 128, 149, 193, 199, 355, 392.

Anacharsis, a Scythian philosopher, quoted, i. 441, *n.* 2.

Anastrophe, a figure of speech, i. 126, *n.* 1.

Anathema, meaning of the term, ii. 80.

Angels, in what sense they will be judged by the saints, i. 201 ; are sometimes employed in executing Divine judgments, 327; ministers of religion are sometimes in Scripture called, 359 ; are spectators of what is transacted in the house of God, 359; have Christ as their head, 359; what is meant by the *tongues of*, 419 ; have a near view of God's glory, 430.

Antigenides, a musician of Thebes, a saying of, i. 435, *n.* 2.

Antiquity, unduly exalted by Papists, i. 369.

Anthypophora, a figure of speech, i. 281, 337; ii. 349.

Apollinaris, his erroneous views as to Christ's person, ii. 52.

Apollos was Paul's successor at Corinth, i. 65; ii. 74.

Apostles, import of the term, i. 49; Paul's title to be reckoned among the, 49, 50 ; Popish Bishops have no claim to be reckoned successors of, 171, 301 ; were not at liberty to bring forward any thing that they had not *received from the Lord*, 373; ii. 9 ; the dignity of the office, 235 ; Paul was not inferior to the most eminent of them, 381.

Arians, their erroneous views in reference to the Trinity, i. 399 ; their endeavours to subvert the doctrine

115; the *spiritual*, what is meant by, 117-119; how far it is lawful to follow, 173 ; what is meant by *speaking as a man*, 294 ; faith must not be in subjection to, ii. 143.

Manichees, The, their erroneous views respecting Christ's body, ii. 54, 55; held the doctrine of *two first principles*, 193.

Manna, The, had a spiritual significancy, i. 315, 316 ; is instructive to us as to our daily dependence upon God, ii. 296; is instructive, also, as to the duty of beneficence, 297.

Maranatha, import of the term, ii. 81-83.

Marriage, is necessary for those who have not the gift of continence, i. 222; Jerome's views as to, 222; has been corrupted by sin, 224 ; is a remedy for unchastity, 230 ; appalling effects of prohibiting the ministers of the Church from it, 233; is honourable, 235; is not to be dissolved on light grounds, 239 ; is the closest earthly tie, 241 ; its anxieties and distresses are to be traced to the entrance of sin, 255; must in a short time be dissolved by death, 257 ; inconveniences attendant upon, 259; anxieties connected with, 261 ; is not a sacrament, 268 ; a second, was branded by the ancients with reproach, 269; should be entered into in the fear of the Lord, 270 ; is not unsuitable to the ministers of the Church, 291; was entered into by Peter, and some others of the Apostles, 291; ought not to be entered into by Christians with unbelievers, ii. 258.

Martial quoted, ii. 69, *n.* 4, 206, *n.* 4, 291, *n.* 1.

Martyr, Justin, quoted, i. 448, *n.* 2.

Martyr, Peter, (Vermilius,) was instrumental in the conversion of Galeacius Caracciolus, i. xvi; extract from a discourse of, xvi, xvii.

Martyrs, The, their blood, along with that of Christ, conceived by Papists to be the treasure of the Church, i. 68; their devotement of themselves truly noble, 420.

Mass, The Popish, involves sacrilege, i. 190; a fearful corruption of the Lord's Supper, 372 ; is an unmeaning show, 375 ; is regarded by Papists as a sacrifice, 376; is full of abominable superstitions, 384 ;

its abominations largely exposed, 390, 391 ; Paul's authority alleged in support of it, 394.

Mastricht's Theology quoted, ii. 52, *n.* 3.

M‘Crie, Rev. Dr., quoted, i. xv, xvii, xviii, xxi, xxii; ii. 232, *n.* 1, 255, *n.* 2, 268, *n.* 1.

M‘Knight quoted, i. 441, *n.* 2; ii. 11, *n.* 1, 12, *n.* 4, 300, *n.* 4.

Menander quoted, i. 96, *n.* 2; ii. 42.

Menenius Agrippa, a Roman Consul, his celebrated apologue, i. 405, 408.

Mercantile cities, the vices usually prevalent in them, i. 38, 208.

Merit, no man can justly claim for himself, i. 94 ; the erroneous views of Pelagians in reference to, 159; false views of Papists in reference to, 432 ; faith does not justify on the ground of, 433; good deeds are not rewarded on the ground of, ii. 226.

" Merits of CALVIN" quoted, ii. 94.

Metonymy, a figure of speech, i. 56, 299, 358, 377, 399, 411, *n.* 1; ii. 208, 210, 251.

Michaelis quoted, ii. 34, *n.* 1.

Milner's Church History quoted, ii. 37, *n.* 1.

Ministers of the Gospel, two qualifications necessary for, i. 48; what ought to be their chief aim, 66, 67 ; what they ought to teach, 97 ; should enter on the discharge of their work with *fear* and *trembling*, 99; should accommodate themselves to the capacities of their hearers, 122; should lead on their hearers towards perfection, 123; must endeavour to gain disciples to Christ, not to themselves, 125 ; are merely instruments, 126; must diligently employ means, 127 ; spoken of by Paul in two different ways, 128; their success depends on the Divine blessing, 130; should maintain among themselves a spirit of harmony, 130; must be careful to build upon Christ as the foundation, 135; should have an eye to the day of accounts, 139; must not exercise dominion over men's consciences, 147; are *stewards* of the word and sacraments, 150 ; must reprove in a friendly spirit, 168; should be careful to act in a uniform and consistent manner, 174; the excellences to be cultivated by them, 176; should be inclined to

cultivate, i. 244; the servants of
Christ ought to make it their aim,
466 ; the ministers of the gospel
must bear many things silently,
with a view to the maintaining of,
ii. 269; Paul exhorts the Corinthians
to live in, 402.

Pearce, Bishop, quoted, i. 424, n. 2.

Pedagogue, Paul's attachment to the
Corinthians was higher than that
of a, 169; import of the term, 169, n.
1; etymology of the term, 169, n. 3.

Pelagians, their erroneous views as to
merit, i. 159.

Penn, Granville, quoted, i. 252, n. 3,
286, n. 2, 358, n. 5, 418, n. 2, 424,
n. 1, 435, n. 1; ii. 11, n. 1, 50, n. 1,
63, n. 3, 121, n. 2, 126, n. 4, 133,
n. 2, 138, n. 1, 170, n. 6, 187, n. 3,
312, n. 3, 366, n. 1.

Pentecost, feast of, ii. 72, 73.

Perfect, who are so termed by Paul,
i. 102.

Perseverance, final, Christians have an
assured hope of, i. 61; the doctrine
of Papists tends to shake the assurance of, 112 ; believers are assured
of it by the Spirit, 112; are, nevertheless, exhorted to it, 308, 309 ;
the means of it, ii. 76.

Phalaris, a tyrant of Sicily, noted for
cruelty, i. 352.

Philetus, along with Hymeneus, held
erroneous views as to the resurrection, ii. 7.

Pindar quoted, i. 187, n. 3, 429, n. 1;
ii. 337, n. 2.

Piscator quoted, ii. 176, n. 1.

Plato quoted, i. 87, n. 1, 329, n. 1, 339,
n. 2, 340, n. 2, 362, n. 3, 440; ii.
163, n. 1, 186, n. 1.

Plautus quoted, i. 239, n. 2.

Pleonasm, a figure of speech, i. 435.

Pliny quoted, i. 276, 369, n. 5, 447 ;
ii. 21, n. 2, 41, n. 2.

Plutarch quoted, ii. 8, n. 2, 69, n. 4,
131, n. 1, 159, n. 1, 186, n. 1, 300,
n. 4.

Polybius quoted, i. 412, n. 1; ii. 131,
n. 1, 306, 307, n. 1, 307, n. 2, 378,
n. 1.

Polygamy condemned by Paul, i. 225,
226.

Poole quoted, i. 108, n. 1; ii. 91, 92,
197, n. 3, 224, n. 1, 286, n. 2.

Pope, The, his claims to authority in-
valid, i. 151; his tyrannical law, in
connection with excommunication,
195 ; daringly sets aside the authority of parents over their children

in connection with marriage, 267;
reckons it unbecoming his station
to teach, 301; keeps those under
him in ignorance, 453; his edicts
are tyrannical, 474 ; claims to be
regarded as Christ's vicar, ii. 329;
his high-sounding titles, 351 ; his
cruel tyranny slavishly submitted
to, 356.

Potter's Grecian Antiquities, quoted,
i. 81, n. 2, 440, n. 3, 463, n. 4; ii.
314, n. 2.

Prayer ought not to be offered up to
departed saints, i. 425, 426 ; the
mind ought to be occupied in the
exercise, 446, 447; public, should
be offered up in the vernacular
tongue, 449; Christians ought to
afford help to each other by mutual,
ii. 122 ; the duty, however, of
mutual intercession is restricted to
the living, 123; even that of faith,
not always answered in the express
form, 377.

Presbyters were appointed in the
primitive Church, i. 183; there
were two kinds of, 417.

Pride is the cause of all contentions,
i. 158; affliction is intended to sub-
due, ii. 374; not easily rooted out,
375; even Paul himself required
special means to be used for the
subduing of it, 375.

Priests, Popish, have no claim to be
regarded as successors of the
Apostles, i. 48, 49, 171; all of them
are guilty of sacrilege, 299.

Princes of this world, import of the
expression, i. 103.

Promises of God, The, are testimonies
of God's grace, ii. 137; are ratified
in Christ, 138; were in part fulfilled to the pious under the Old
Testament dispensation, 138; call
us to holiness, 263.

Prophets, a class of office-bearers in
the primitive church, i. 414; their
peculiar duties, 415, 416.

Prophecy, The gift of, was comparatively neglected among the Corinthians, i. 417; its inferiority to
Christian love, 419; its great utility, 436, 455; is commended by
Paul above all other gifts, 473.

Proteus, his fabled transformations,
ii. 136.

Proverbial sayings quoted, i. 234, 249,
265, 274, 280, 347, 343, n. 3, 353,
435, 460, 460, n. 5; ii. 42, 206, 250,
333, 345, 351, 386.

Providence, The, of God, overrules evil for the promotion of good to his people, i. 368; supplies our daily necessities, ii. 298; should be confided in by us, 314.

Psalms, The early Christians were accustomed to sing them to Christ before day-break, i. 447.

Purgatory, The doctrine of, i. 141.

Q

Questions, not tending to edify, ought to be avoided, i. 427; ii. 45; danger of indulging a taste for unprofitable, 370.

Quinctilian quoted, i. 218, *n.* 4, 407, *n.* 1; ii. 39, *n.* 5, 39, *n.* 6.

R

Rabirius, a Latin poet, a saying of, ii. 69, *n.* 4.

Ranke's "History of the Popes of Rome," quoted, i. xx, *n.* 2.

Raphelius quoted, i. 411, *n.* 1; ii. 20, *n.* 1, 152, *n.* 4, 163, *n.* 1, 307, *n.* 1, 361, *n.* 4.

Regeneration, The gospel the means of, i. 170; God is the Author of it, 172; the efficacy of the ministry in producing it, 289; the necessity of it, ii. 233, 234.

Repentance, the discipline of the Church is intended to produce, ii. 151; the term sometimes employed to denote grief, apart from any feeling of having done wrong, 272; takes its rise in self-dissatisfaction, 274; its accompaniments, 275.

Reputation, Paul was comparatively regardless of it, i. 152; to purchase it by death is a diabolical madness, ii. 38; how far it ought to be an object of desire, 228, 302, 398.

Resurrection of Christ, a fundamental doctrine of the gospel, ii. 9; righteousness was procured to us through means of it, 10; there were many who were eye-witnesses of it, 10, 11; our resurrection is the fruit of it, 17; if it were taken away, faith were useless, 20.

Resurrection, The final, some of the Corinthians had begun to have doubts respecting it, ii. 6; was unknown to the ancient heathens, 6; some have attempted to explain it away as merely allegorical, 7; a doctrine essential to salvation, 8; is the completion of our salvation,

21; is at variance with unenlightened reason, 46; is nevertheless consonant with sound reason, 47; corresponds with the analogy of nature, 47,48; identity of the body in connection with, 48; qualities of the glorified body on occasion of, 49-51; will afford a complete victory over death, 62; the hope of it stimulates Christians, 66.

Revelations, how distinguished from visions, ii. 366.

Revenge, law-suits are usually prosecuted in a spirit of, i. 205; Christians are altogether prohibited from, 206; the term sometimes employed in a good sense, ii. 277.

Reward, what ministers of the gospel ought chiefly to seek as their, i. 131; the works performed by Christians do not in themselves merit a, 303, 304; will be conferred on believers through a gracious acceptance, ii. 226.

Rheims version of the Scriptures, quoted, i. 114, *n.* 1, 137, *n.* 2, 153, *n.* 3, 307, *n.* 1, 364, *n.* 2, 444, *n.* 1; ii. 77, *n.* 1, 191, *n.* 2, 213, *n.* 3, 257, *n.* 1, 306, *n.* 3, 320, *n.* 1, 354, *n.* 1, 372, *n.* 1.

Riches, Christians ought to abound in spiritual, i. 56; do not necessarily exclude from the kingdom of God, 91; spiritual, ought to be much more esteemed than earthly, ii. 253; ought not to be hoarded, 297.

Righteousness, comes to us through the resurrection of Christ, ii. 10; of Christ, reckoned to our account, 242; the term sometimes employed to denote beneficence, 313.

Robertson's History of Greece, quoted, ii. 42, *n.* 1.

Rosenmüller quoted, ii. 249, *n.* 2, 273, *n.* 1.

S

Sacraments, The, are spoken of by Paul in two different ways, i. 128, 129, *n.* 2; ministers of the gospel have authority to administer, 150; those of the Law had the same virtue as ours, 316; dogma of the schoolmen respecting, 317; unbelievers do not receive the reality represented in them, 320; those of the Old Testament were real, though typical, 328; tend to promote piety, 364; are an important

U